TAX FORMULA FOR CORPORATE TAXPAYERS

Income (*from whatever source*)	$xxx,xxx
Less: Exclusions from gross income	− xx,xxx
Gross Income	$xxx,xxx
Less: Deductions	− xx,xxx
Taxable Income	$xxx,xxx
Applicable tax rates	× xx%
Gross Tax	$ xx,xxx
Less: Tax credits and prepayments	− x,xxx
Tax Due (*or refund*)	$ xx,xxx

STUDY GUIDE AVAILABLE

For more practice problems that help you to expand your understanding of corporations, partnerships, estates, and trusts, we recommend the *Study Guide* that accompanies *West's Federal Taxation: Corporations, Partnerships, Estates, and Trusts*. The *Study Guide* uses a workbook approach and includes chapter outlines and summaries highlighting major points in the text, self-evaluation tests, problems, and drills using furnished tax forms.

If you cannot locate copies of the *Study Guide* in your bookstore, ask your bookstore manager to order a copy for you.

WEST'S FEDERAL TAXATION AVAILABLE ON CD-ROM

Considering a career in tax accounting? Do you have access to a CD-ROM player? You should check out the CD-ROM Edition of *West's Federal Taxation*. The CD includes this complete text as well as all the relevant cases, Code, Regulations, revenue procedures and rulings, and tax forms, tables, and schedules. Hypertext links let you jump directly from the text to any of these references or tables in a matter of seconds—great for research and reference. The CD also includes other helpful features such as notebook capabilities and an electronic bookmark feature, and it's fully supported by West's CD-ROM customer service representatives so you can call for **any technical assistance your projects require**.

See the preface of this text for more information about how this exciting learning tool can enhance your study of federal taxation. To order, contact your campus bookstore for more information or call the Academic Resource Center at 1-800-423-0563.

WEST'S FEDERAL TAXATION:
CORPORATIONS, PARTNERSHIPS, ESTATES, AND TRUSTS

1998 ANNUAL EDITION

WEST'S FEDERAL TAXATION:

CORPORATIONS, PARTNERSHIPS, ESTATES, AND TRUSTS

GENERAL EDITORS

William H. Hoffman, Jr., J.D., Ph.D., C.P.A. **William A. Raabe,** Ph.D., C.P.A.

James E. Smith, Ph.D., C.P.A. **David M. Maloney,** Ph.D., C.P.A.

CONTRIBUTING AUTHORS

James H. Boyd,
Ph.D., C.P.A.
Arizona State University

D. Larry Crumbley,
Ph.D., C.P.A.
Louisiana State University

Steven C. Dilley,
J.D., Ph.D., C.P.A.
Michigan State University

Mary Sue Gately,
Ph.D., C.P.A.
Texas Tech University

William H. Hoffman, Jr.,
J.D., Ph.D., C.P.A.
University of Houston

David M. Maloney,
Ph.D., C.P.A.
University of Virginia

William A. Raabe,
Ph.D., C.P.A.
Samford University

Boyd C. Randall,
J.D., Ph.D.
Brigham Young University

W. Eugene Seago,
J.D., Ph.D., C.P.A.
*Virginia Polytechnic Institute
and State University*

James E. Smith,
Ph.D., C.P.A.
College of William and Mary

Eugene Willis,
Ph.D., C.P.A.
University of Illinois at Urbana

WEST

SOUTH-WESTERN College Publishing

An International Thomson Publishing Company

Accounting Team Director: Richard Lindgren
Acquisitions Editor: Alex von Rosenberg
Developmental Editor: Esther Craig
Production Editor: Peggy A. Williams
Copyediting: Patricia A. Lewis
Composition: Carlisle Communications, Ltd.
Index: Catalyst Communication Arts
Cover Design: David J. Farr, *ImageSmythe*
Internal Design: LightSource Images
Marketing Manager: Matthew Filimonov

MacinTax® and *TurboTax®* are registered trademarks of Intuit,® Inc.

ISBN: 0–314–20551–9

1 2 3 4 5 6 7 8 9 WST 5 4 3 2 1 0 9 8 7

Printed in the United States of America

Library of Congress Cataloging-in-Publication Data

Main entry under title:
  West's Federal Taxation.
  Includes index.
  1. Income tax—United States—Law
I. Hoffman, William H.   III.   Willis, Eugene

ISBN 0–314–20551–9, 0–314–20955–7
KF6335.H63   343'.73'04   77–54355

ISSN 0270–5265
1998 ANNUAL EDITION

International Thomson Publishing
WEST/South-Western College Publishing is an ITP Company.
The ITP trademark is used under license.

PREFACE

The publication of the 1998 Edition marks the twenty-first year of West's Federal Taxation (WFT). From a single text on Corporations, Partnerships, Estates and Trusts with accompanying solutions manual, the WFT series has grown to four major texts and a package of more than 50 ancillaries. During this period, WFT has made every effort to improve the quality of the materials and has consistently added attractive innovations. With sales well in excess of the one million mark, WFT looks forward to continued success in the future. This work was originally inspired by and designed to relieve the absence of suitable textual material for a second course in Federal taxation—the follow-up to a course outlining the Federal income taxation of individuals. It is especially valuable (a) for a second course offered at either the undergraduate or graduate level, (b) in the context of continuing professional education as a means to broaden one's professional capabilities, (c) as a reference for practitioners needing a refresher or review of seldom-encountered tax provisions, and (d) as a tool for self-study.

Throughout the text, the authors stress the practical application of the materials through a liberal use of examples, most of which have been classroom tested and found to be effective learning devices. At the same time, the evolution of specific statutory provisions through the interaction of case law, political compromise, and economic considerations is discussed to offer the user a broad base for understanding and applying the tax law. Our text does not purport to be a treatise on historical and fiscal policy considerations; its primary concern is tax practice. For this reason, such discussions of the law's development are minimized. In our opinion, this minimization does not compromise the subject matter's presentation.

ENHANCED PEDAGOGICAL PLAN

The pedagogy has been enhanced to assist the user in the learning process and to address the recommendations of the Accounting Education Change Commission (AECC).

- *Learning Objectives.* Each chapter begins with learning objectives for the material. These behavioral objectives provide the users with guidance in learning the key concepts and principles.
- *Chapter Outline.* The learning objectives are followed by a topical outline of the material in the chapter. Page references appear in the outline to provide ready access to each topic.
- *Chapter Introductions.* The introductions link the material in the current chapter to previous chapters and demonstrate its relevance. Frequently, the chapter introduction includes a "real world" illustration to help show the utility of the material.

- *Margin Notes.* Each of the learning objectives appears in the margin where the related material is introduced and helps guide the user through the chapter.
- *Tax in the News.* Tax in the News items appear in each chapter as a boxed feature to enliven the text discussion. The items are drawn from today's business press and present current issues that are relevant to the chapter material.
- *Ethical Considerations.* Ethical Considerations features appear in each chapter presenting thought-provoking issues related to the chapter topics. In response to the recommendation of the AECC, they also demonstrate that many issues do not have a single correct answer. The questions raised in the Ethical Considerations are selected to provoke discussion and offer opportunities for debate based on the student's value system.
- *Key Terms.* Before the Problem Materials in each chapter is a list of key terms to assist student learning. When the key term is introduced in the chapter, it appears in bold print. The list of key terms includes page references to the chapter discussion. In addition, each key term is defined in the Glossary (Appendix C).

- *Communication Assignments.* In recognition of the increasing emphasis in accounting and tax education on communication skills, identified items in the Problem Materials include a written communication component. Selected Problems and certain Research Problems are identified as communication assignments with a "scroll" icon.

- *Decision-Making Problems.* The Problem Materials include decision-making problems that are designed to enhance the user's analytical skills. These problems are identified with a "scales" icon.

- *Issue Recognition* situations. These involve factual patterns where the tax issue is not readily apparent. In coping with the tax system, the starting point is what, if any, tax problems exist. These questions and problems are identified with a "light bulb" icon.

- *Internet exercises.* Included as part of the Research Problems for each chapter are questions which require the use of the tax resources of the internet. These exercises are identified with a globe and computer mouse icon.

- *CD-ROM Capabilities.* West's Federal Taxation on CD-ROM can be used in preparing the solutions to most of the Research Problems appearing at the end of every chapter.

WEST'S FEDERAL TAXATION ON CD-ROM

West continues to offer this text on CD-ROM. It includes the entire text of the printed version of **WEST'S FEDERAL TAXATION: Corporations, Partnerships, Estates & Trusts, 1998 Edition** as well as the full text of all referenced cases, code sections, regulations, revenue procedures, and revenue rulings, and all tax forms, tables and schedules from the Appendixes. Users can shift directly from the text they are reading to the full text of any of the references included on the disc.

Other features include "notebook" capabilities allowing users to cut and paste from the text, type in their own comments, and convert the text and notes into other word processing packages. Records are kept of all queries which allows viewing and editing of past queries. Each disc has an electronic "bookmark" feature which indicates the spot where the user left off and returns to the last page that was viewed when the project is resumed. WFT on CD-ROM is fully supported by West's CD-ROM Customer Service Technicians and Research Attorneys. Users can request technical or research assistance if required.

System requirements include an IBM or compatible PC with a 486 processor or higher; Windows version 3.1 or higher (includes Windows 95); DOS version 3.3 or higher; 4 MB of available RAM, 8 MB recommended (after loading all memory-resident software including device drivers and MSCDEX); minimum of 16 MB of available hard disk space; VGA monitor or better; CD-ROM drive using Microsoft CD-ROM Extensions (MSCDEX) version 2.1 or higher (compatible CD-ROM drives must meet the ISO 9660 standard). To print images off the CD, 1.5 MG RAM on a printer is required.

OTHER SPECIAL FEATURES

Some of the other pedagogical features, and reasons behind the organization include:

- At the center of the practical application of tax law is tax planning—the legal minimization of the tax burden. The authors are sensitive to this facet of tax law education; therefore, all chapters conclude with a special section—*Tax Planning Considerations.*
- Most chapters contain one or more *Concept Summaries* that synthesize important concepts in chart or tabular form.
- Any advanced Federal tax course should offer the user the opportunity to learn and utilize the methodology of tax research; therefore, Chapter 1 is devoted in part to this topic, and each chapter contains several research projects. The effectiveness of the text does not, however, depend upon the use of these research materials. They may be omitted without diminishing the presentation of all other topics.
- The text is divided into parts to facilitate a compartmentalization of the subjects covered. Thus, Part 2, which includes Chapters 2 through 9, largely deals with C corporations. Part 3, which is designated Flow-through Entities, contains the material on partnerships (Chapters 10 and 11) and S corporations (Chapter 12). Further groupings are made to help the user work through the text.
- The material on C corporations is arranged to flow logically, to parallel the life-cycle of the entity.
- Chapter 9 covers international transactions in a comprehensive manner. Increased foreign trade has generated new interest in the tax aspects of this area.
- Part 4 (Advanced Tax Practice Considerations) contains material of critical interest to the serious tax practitioner. Chapter 13 presents a detailed analysis of the various considerations that enter into the decision-making process in choosing the form of doing business. As such, the material is the capstone of what has been previously discussed and furnishes the foundation for choosing the appropriate business form. Chapter 14 deals with tax-exempt organizations, a controversial area that is receiving considerable media attention and Congressional inquiry, and one that plays an important role in the CPA exam. Chapter 15 explores the problems encountered when business is (or could be) conducted in more than one state. Many of the multistate taxation issues are of vital interest in today's climate of competitive economic development.
- The purpose of Part 4 is to illustrate *some* of the specialized areas that tax practice involves. Furthermore, the subjects are arranged so as to maximize selectivity. For example, the user may wish to omit tax-exempt organizations (Chapter 14) and emphasize the material on multistate taxation (Chapter 15). Since these modules are not interdependent, selective omission does not detract from the effectiveness of what the user chooses to cover.

- There is a great deal of useful material contained in the appendixes to the text. In addition to the usual Subject Index, the following items are included: Tax Rates and Tables (Appendix A); Tax Forms (Appendix B); Glossary of Tax Terms (Appendix C); Table of Code Sections Cited (Appendix D–1); Table of Regulations Cited (Appendix D–2); Table of Revenue Procedures and Revenue Rulings Cited (Appendix D–3); and Table of Cases Cited (Appendix E).

FOR THE INSTRUCTOR

Accompanying the text is a comprehensive package of instructional aids.

- INSTRUCTOR'S GUIDE with Lecture Notes that contains the following materials:

  - Instructor's Summaries that can be used as lecture outlines and provide the instructor with teaching aids and information not contained in the text.
    - Incorporated as part of the Instructor's Summaries are selected queries that facilitate the use of WESTLAW, a computerized compilation of legal sources (judicial, legislative, and administrative) pertinent to the area of taxation. WESTLAW, a service available from West Publishing Co., provides a sophisticated short cut for carrying out in-depth analysis of various tax issues. Limited free use of WESTLAW is available to qualified adopters.
    - The solutions to the Research Problems contained in the text.
    - The solutions to the Comprehensive Tax Return Problems contained in the text.
    - The lecture notes are also available on disk in ASCII files.

- SOLUTIONS MANUAL contains answers to the Discussion Questions and Problems. These solutions have been carefully checked to insure accuracy and are referenced to pages in the text. To assist in selecting problems, a matrix is included indicating topic coverage for each problem, which problems are new, modified, or unchanged in the new edition, and the problem number for the unchanged and modified problems in the prior edition. The solutions manual is also available on disk in ASCII files.
- TEST BANK contains examination questions and their solutions, page-referenced to the text. The questions are arranged in accordance with the sequence of the material in the chapter. To assist in selecting questions for an examination, all questions are labeled by topical coverage in a matrix which also includes which questions are new, modified, or unchanged in the new edition, and the question for the unchanged and modified questions in the prior edition.
- WESTEST, a microcomputer test generation program for IBM PC's and compatibles and the Macintosh family of computers.
- INSTRUCTOR'S RESOURCE NOTEBOOK is a three-ring binder that can be used to house all or portions of the supplements and text. The 1998 edition will continue to offer the text in looseleaf form so the instructor can reorganize the book and incorporate supplemental materials to fit course lectures.
- PowerPoint PRESENTATION SOFTWARE allows qualified adopters to create interactive lectures and manipulative graphs, charts, and figures during in-class lectures. The package contains numerous transparency masters per chapter consisting of alternate figures, outlines, and key points.

- TEACHING TRANSPARENCY ACETATES contain the key charts and tables from the PowerPoint package for instructors who wish to use traditional overheads.
- WFT ON-LINE puts the most current information in the user's hands as soon as it is available. Adopters can log onto WFT On-line via West Publishing's Internet home page (http://www.westpub.com/Educate/) and gain access to recent taxation information, including newsworthy tax developments designed for classroom use, extra problem material and quizzes, topical news items (including graphics), the latest news on West supplements and publication dates, and more.
- TAX LEGISLATION UPDATE covering new tax laws enacted since the publication of this edition are sent to adopters in January. If a major new law is passed, West will provide a separate tax update pertaining to that tax legislation.
- WEST'S CD-ROM FEDERAL TAX LIBRARY (Compact Disk with Read-Only Memory) provides a complete tax research library on a desktop. The Federal Tax Library is a set of compact disks with a software package that reads the disks through a PC. Each of these disks has a remarkable storage capacity—roughly 1,000 times more than a single-sided floppy disk. A brief list of the library contents includes: complete Code and Regulations, Federal Court Cases on tax topics, Tax Court Cases, Revenue Rulings, and Revenue Procedures. This vital resource is available to qualified adopters.

FOR THE STUDENT

- A STUDENT STUDY GUIDE, prepared by Paul R. O'Brien, Governors State University, includes key concepts, self-evaluation tests, return problems and flowcharts of various sections of the Internal Revenue Code.
- A STUDENT NOTE-TAKING GUIDE includes selected screens from the PowerPoint package consisting of chapter outlines and key points. This unique guide provides students with the core chapter information, so they can concentrate in class on learning key concepts instead of copying basic lecture outlines and transparencies. In addition, the charts and graphs in the PowerPoint package are printed and bound in a manner similar to accounting working papers. The pages include all the information from the PowerPoint screens while still leaving room for student notes.
- WEST'S INTERNAL REVENUE CODE OF 1987 AND TREASURY REGULATIONS: ANNOTATED AND SELECTED: 1998 EDITION by James E. Smith, College of William and Mary. This provides the opportunity for the student to be exposed to the Code and the Regulations in single volume form and also contains useful annotations.
- CORPORATION, S CORPORATION, AND PARTNERSHIP PRACTICE SETS by Donald Trippeer, Lehigh University.
- WFT: CORPORATION AND PARTNERSHIP TAX RETURN PREPARATION WITH TURBOTAX Pro Series 1120/1120S/1065 is a commercial tax preparation package that includes disks bound with a workbook containing exercises and problems. The manual is prepared by Debra L. Sanders, Washington State University and Intuit.

ACKNOWLEDGMENTS

We are extremely grateful to the users of our text who have been kind enough to provide us with constructive comments concerning its effectiveness both as a teaching and as a learning device. Many of these comments and suggestions have been incorporated in past editions and in the 1998 edition.

We also thank the people who have painstakingly worked through all the problems and test questions and generally acted as problem checkers to ensure accuracy of the book and ancillary package. They are Tracey Anderson, Indiana University at South Bend; Caroline K. Craig, Illinois State University; Frank Linton, University of Scranton; Mark B. Persellin, St. Mary's University; Debra L. Sanders, Washington State University; Randall K. Serrett, Fort Lewis College; Donald Trippeer, Lehigh University; and Raymond Wacker, Southern Illinois University at Carbondale.

Lastly, we appreciate the invaluable assistance provided to us by Bonnie S. Hoffman, M.S.A., CPA.

William H. Hoffman, Jr.
William A. Raabe
James E. Smith
David M. Maloney

April 1, 1997

ABOUT THE EDITORS

William H. Hoffman, Jr., earned B.A. and J.D. degrees from the University of Michigan and M.B.A. and Ph.D. degrees from The University of Texas. He is a licensed CPA and attorney in Texas. His teaching experience includes: The University of Texas (1957–1961), Louisiana State University (1961–1967), and the University of Houston (1967 to present). Professor Hoffman has addressed many tax institutes and conferences and has published extensively in academic and professional journals. His articles appear in *The Journal of Taxation, The Tax Adviser, Taxes—The Tax Magazine, The Journal of Accountancy, The Accounting Review,* and *Taxation for Accountants.*

William A. Raabe is a Professor in the Samford University School of Business. A graduate of Carroll College and the University of Illinois, Dr. Raabe's teaching and research interests include international and multistate taxation, technology in tax education, personal financial planning, and the economic impact of sports teams and fine arts groups. Dr. Raabe also is the author of *West's Federal Tax Research* and the *Multistate Corporate Tax Guide.* He coordinates the *West's Federal Taxation* material on West Publishing's Internet page, and he has written estate planning software used widely by tax professionals. Dr. Raabe has been a visiting tax faculty member for a number of public accounting firms, bar associations, and CPA societies. He has received numerous teaching awards, including the Accounting Educator of the Year from the Wisconsin Institute of CPAs.

James E. Smith is the John S. Quinn Professor of Accounting at the College of William and Mary. He has been a member of the Accounting Faculty for twenty-seven years. He received his Ph.D. degree from the University of Arizona.

Jim has served as a discussion leader for Continuing Professional Education programs for the AICPA, Federal Tax Workshops, and various state CPA societies. He has conducted programs in over 40 states for approximately 25,000 CPAs. He has been the recipient of the AICPAs' Outstanding Discussion Leader Award.

Other awards received by Jim include the Virginia Society of CPAs' Outstanding Accounting Educator Award and the James Madison University's Outstanding Accounting Educator Award. He was the President of the Administrators of Accounting Programs Group (AAPG) in 1991–1992. He was the faculty adviser for the William and Mary teams that received first place in the Arthur Andersen Tax Challenge in 1994 and 1995.

David M. Maloney, Ph.D., CPA, completed his graduate work at the University of Illinois at Urbana-Champaign. He teaches courses in Federal taxation in the graduate and undergraduate programs at the University of Virginia's McIntire School of Commerce. Since joining the Virginia faculty in January 1984, Professor Maloney has been a recipient of major research grants from the Ernst & Young and Peat Marwick Foundations. In addition, his work has been published in numerous professional journals, including *The Tax Adviser, Tax Notes, The Journal of Corporate Taxation, Accounting Horizons,* and *The Journal of Accountancy.* He is a member of several professional organizations, including the AICPA, the American Accounting Association, and the American Taxation Association.

CONTENTS IN BRIEF

CONTENTS

APPENDIXES

I

INTRODUCTION

The Federal law is an unbelievably complex set of rules. In working with these rules, however, it is helpful to understand *why* they came about. Also necessary is the ability to locate the sources of these rules. Part I, therefore, is devoted to the "whys" of the tax law and the applications of the tax research process.

Chapter 1

Understanding and Working with the Federal Tax Law

UNDERSTANDING AND WORKING WITH THE FEDERAL TAX LAW

LEARNING OBJECTIVES

After completing Chapter 1, you should be able to:

1. Realize the importance of revenue needs as an objective of Federal tax law.

2. Appreciate the influence of economic, social, equity, and political considerations on the development of the tax law.

3. Understand how the IRS, as the protector of the revenue, has affected tax law.

4. Recognize the role of the courts in interpreting and shaping tax law.

5. Identify tax law sources—statutory, administrative, and judicial.

6. Locate tax law sources.

7. Assess the validity and weight of tax law sources.

8. Make use of various tax planning procedures.

9. Have an awareness of computer-assisted tax research.

▼ THE WHYS OF THE TAX LAW

The Federal tax law is a mixture of statutory provisions, administrative pronouncements, and court decisions. Anyone who has attempted to work with this body of knowledge is familiar with its complexity. Commenting on his 48-page tax return, the author James Michener said, "it is unimaginable in that I graduated from one of America's better colleges, yet I am totally incapable of understanding tax returns." For the person who has to wade through rule upon rule to find the solution to a tax problem, it may be of some consolation to know that the law's complexity can be explained. There is a reason for the formulation of every rule. Knowing these reasons, therefore, is a considerable step toward understanding the Federal tax law.

The major objective of the Federal tax law is the raising of revenue. Despite the importance of the fiscal needs of the government, however, other considerations explain certain portions of the law. In particular, economic, social, equity, and political factors play a significant role. Added to these factors is the marked impact the Internal Revenue Service (IRS) and the courts have had and will continue to have on the evolution of Federal tax law. These matters are treated in the first part of this chapter. Wherever appropriate, the discussion is related to subjects covered later in the text.

REVENUE NEEDS

1 ▼ LEARNING OBJECTIVE
Realize the importance of revenue needs as an objective of Federal tax law.

The foundation of any tax system has to be the raising of revenue to absorb the cost of government operations. Ideally, annual outlays should not exceed anticipated revenues. This situation leads to a balanced budget with no deficit. Many states have achieved this objective by passing laws or constitutional amendments precluding deficit spending. Unfortunately, the Federal government has no such prohibition, and mounting annual deficits have become an increasing concern for many. Aware of this concern, Congress itself has been more deficit-conscious when enacting tax legislation in the past decade.

In most of the recent tax legislation, Congress was guided by the concept of **revenue neutrality.** This concept means that the changes made neither increased nor decreased the net revenues raised under the prior rules. Revenue neutrality does not mean that any one taxpayer's tax liability will remain the same. Since this liability depends upon the circumstances involved, one taxpayer's increased tax liability could be another's tax saving. Revenue-neutral tax reform does not reduce deficits, but at least it does not aggravate the problem.

Given the ongoing budget deficits, such considerations are likely to play an ever-increasing role in shaping tax policy.

ECONOMIC CONSIDERATIONS

2   **LEARNING OBJECTIVE**
Appreciate the influence of economic, social, equity, and political considerations on the development of the tax law.

Using the tax system in an effort to accomplish economic objectives has become increasingly popular in recent years. Generally, this process involves amending the Internal Revenue Code[1] through tax legislation and emphasizes measures designed to help control the economy or encourage certain activities and businesses.

Control of the Economy.   Congress has made use of depreciation write-offs as a means of controlling the economy. Theoretically, shorter asset lives and accelerated methods should encourage additional investment in depreciable property acquired for business use. Conversely, longer class lives and the required use of the straight-line method of depreciation dampen the tax incentive for capital outlays.

A change in the tax rate structure has a more immediate impact on the economy. When tax rates are lowered, taxpayers are able to obtain additional spendable funds. In the interest of revenue neutrality, however, rate decreases may be accompanied by a reduction or elimination of deductions or credits. Thus, lower rates do not always mean lower taxes.

Encouragement of Certain Activities.   Without passing judgment on the wisdom of any such choices, it is quite clear that the tax law does encourage certain types of economic activity or segments of the economy. For example, the desire to foster technological progress helps explain the favorable treatment accorded to research and development expenditures. Under the tax law, such expenditures can be deducted in the year incurred or, alternatively, capitalized and amortized over a period of 60 months or more. In terms of timing the tax saving, such options usually are preferable to a capitalization of the cost with a write-off over the estimated useful life of the asset created.[2]

The encouragement of technological progress can also explain why the tax law places the inventor in a special position. Not only can patents qualify as capital assets, but under certain conditions their disposition automatically carries long-term capital gain treatment.[3]

Are ecological considerations a desirable objective? If they are, it explains why the tax law permits a 60-month amortization period for costs incurred in the installation of pollution control facilities.

---

[1] The Internal Revenue Code is a compilation of Federal tax legislation that appears in Title 26 of the U.S. Code.

[2] If the asset developed has no estimated useful life, no write-off would be available without the two options allowed by the tax law.

[3] At this point, a long-term capital gain has a favorable tax advantage for individuals.

Does stimulating the development and rehabilitation of low-income rental housing benefit the economy? The tax law definitely favors these activities by allowing generous tax credits to taxpayers incurring such costs.

Is saving desirable for the economy? Saving leads to capital formation and thus makes funds available to finance home construction and industrial expansion. The tax law provides incentives to encourage saving by giving private retirement plans preferential treatment. Not only are contributions to Keogh (H.R. 10) plans and certain Individual Retirement Accounts (IRAs) deductible, but income from such contributions accumulates on a tax-free basis. As noted in a following section, the encouragement of private-sector pension plans can be justified under social considerations as well.

Is it wise to stimulate U.S. exports of goods and services? Considering the pressing and continuing problem of a deficit in the U.S. balance of payments, the answer should be clear. Along this line, Congress has created foreign sales corporations (FSCs), a unique type of organization designed to encourage exports. A portion of the export income from eligible FSCs is exempt from Federal income taxes. Further, a domestic corporation is allowed a 100 percent dividends received deduction for distributions from an FSC out of earnings attributable to certain foreign trade income. Congress has also deemed it advisable to establish incentives for U.S. citizens who accept employment overseas. Such persons receive generous tax breaks through special treatment of their foreign-source income and certain housing costs.

Encouragement of Certain Industries. Who can question the proposition that a sound agricultural base is necessary for a well-balanced national economy? Undoubtedly, this belief can explain why farmers are accorded special treatment under the Federal tax system. Among the benefits are the election to expense rather than capitalize certain expenditures for soil and water conservation and fertilizers and the election to defer the recognition of gain on the receipt of crop insurance proceeds.

The tax law also favors the development of natural resources by permitting the use of percentage depletion on the extraction and sale of oil and gas and specified mineral deposits and a write-off (rather than a capitalization) of certain exploration costs. The railroad and banking industries also receive special tax treatment. All of these provisions can be explained, in whole or in part, by economic considerations.

Encouragement of Small Business. At least in the United States, a consensus exists that what is good for small business is good for the economy as a whole. This assumption has led to a definite bias in the tax law favoring small business.

In the corporate tax area, several provisions can be explained by the desire to benefit small business. One provision enables a shareholder in a small business corporation to obtain an ordinary deduction for any loss recognized on a stock investment. Normally, such a loss would receive the less attractive capital loss treatment. The point of this favoritism is to encourage additional equity investments in small business corporations.[4] Another provision permits the shareholders of a small business corporation to make a special election that generally will avoid the imposition of the corporate income tax.[5] Furthermore, such an election

---

[4] Known as Section 1244 stock, this subject is covered in Chapter 3.
[5] Known as the S corporation election, the subject is discussed extensively in Chapter 12. The rules applicable to S corporations were recently made more tenable by the enactment of the Small Business Job Protection Act of 1996.

enables the corporation to pass through to its shareholders any of its operating losses.[6]

The tax rates applicable to corporations tend to favor small business in that size is relative to the amount of taxable income generated in any one year. Since a corporate tax rate of 34 percent applies only to taxable income in excess of $75,000, corporations that stay within this limit are subject to lower average tax rates.

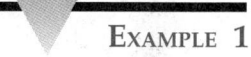

EXAMPLE 1   For calendar year 1997, Brown Corporation has taxable income of $75,000, and Red Corporation has taxable income of $100,000. Based on this information, the corporate income tax is $13,750 for Brown Corporation and $22,250 for Red Corporation (see Chapter 2). Brown Corporation is subject to an average tax rate of 18.33% ($13,750/$75,000), while Red Corporation is subject to an average rate of 22.25% ($22,250/$100,000). ▼

If a corporation has taxable income in excess of $100,000, the benefits of the lower brackets are phased out until all income is taxed at the maximum rate of 34 percent. Once taxable income reaches $10 million, the rate becomes 35 percent.

One of the justifications for the enactment of the tax law governing corporate reorganizations (see Chapter 7) was the economic benefit it would provide for small businesses. By allowing corporations to combine without adverse tax consequences, small corporations would be in a position to compete more effectively with larger concerns.

SOCIAL CONSIDERATIONS

Some of the tax laws, especially those related to the Federal income tax of individuals, can be explained by social considerations. The following are some notable examples:

- The nontaxability of certain benefits provided to employees through accident and health plans financed by employers. It is socially desirable to encourage such plans, since they provide medical benefits in the event of an employee's illness or injury.
- The nontaxability to the employee of some of the premiums paid by an employer for group term insurance covering the life of the employee. These arrangements can be justified in that they provide funds to help the family unit adjust to the loss of wages caused by the employee's death.
- The tax treatment to the employee of contributions made by an employer to qualified pension or profit sharing plans. The contribution and any income it earns are not taxed to the employee until the funds are distributed. Private retirement plans are encouraged because they supplement the subsistence income level the employee would otherwise have under the Social Security system.[7]
- The deduction allowed for contributions to qualified charitable organizations. The deduction attempts to shift some of the financial and administrative burden of socially desirable programs from the public (the government) to the private (the citizens) sector.
- The credit allowed for amounts spent to furnish care for certain minor or disabled dependents to enable the taxpayer to seek or maintain gainful

---

[6]In general, an operating loss can benefit only the corporation incurring the loss through a carryback or carryover to profitable years. Consequently, the shareholders of the corporation usually cannot take advantage of any such loss.

[7]The same rationale explains the availability of similar arrangements for self-employed persons (the H.R. 10 or Keogh plan).

employment. Who could deny the social desirability of encouraging taxpayers to provide care for their children while they work?

- The disallowance of a tax deduction for certain expenditures that are deemed to be contrary to public policy. This disallowance extends to such items as fines, penalties, illegal kickbacks, and bribes to government officials. Public policy considerations also have been used to disallow gambling losses in excess of gambling gains and political campaign expenditures in excess of campaign contributions. Social considerations dictate that the tax law should not encourage these activities by permitting a deduction.
- The imposition of the Federal estate tax on large estates. From one viewpoint, permitting large accumulations of wealth to pass by death from generation to generation without being subject to some type of transfer tax would be socially undesirable.[8]

Many other examples could be included, but the conclusion would be unchanged: Social considerations do explain a significant part of the Federal tax law.

EQUITY CONSIDERATIONS

The concept of equity is relative. Reasonable persons can, and often do, disagree about what is fair or unfair. In the tax area, moreover, equity is generally tied to a particular taxpayer's personal situation. To illustrate, Ms. Jones may have difficulty understanding why none of the rent she pays on her apartment is deductible, while, her brother, Mr. Jones, is able to deduct a large portion of the monthly payments he makes on his personal residence in the form of interest and taxes.[9]

In the same vein, compare the tax treatment of a corporation with that of a partnership. Two businesses may be of equal size, similarly situated, and competitors in the production of goods or services, but they are not comparably treated under the tax law. The corporation is subject to a separate Federal income tax; the partnership is not. Whether the differences in tax treatment can be logically justified in terms of equity is beside the point. The tax law can and does make a distinction between these business forms.

Equity, then, is not what appears fair or unfair to any one taxpayer or group of taxpayers. It is, instead, what the tax law recognizes. Some recognition of equity does exist, however, and explains part of the law. The concept of equity appears in tax provisions that alleviate the effect of multiple taxation and postpone the recognition of gain when the taxpayer lacks the ability or wherewithal to pay the tax. Equity also helps mitigate the effect of the application of the annual accounting period concept and helps taxpayers cope with the eroding result of inflation.

Alleviating the Effect of Multiple Taxation.   The same income earned by a taxpayer may be subject to taxes imposed by different taxing authorities. If, for example, the taxpayer is a resident of New York City, income might generate Federal, State of New York, and City of New York income taxes. To compensate for this inequity, the Federal tax law allows a taxpayer to claim a deduction for state and local income taxes. The deduction, however, does not neutralize the effect of

---

[8] Portions of Chapter 18 are devoted to procedures that permit taxpayers to pass wealth from one generation to another with minimal tax consequences.

[9] The encouragement of home ownership can be justified on both economic and social grounds. In this regard, it is interesting to note that some state income tax laws allow a form of relief (e.g., tax credit) to the taxpayer who rents his or her personal residence.

multiple taxation since the benefit derived depends on the taxpayer's Federal income tax rate.[10]

Equity considerations can explain the Federal tax treatment of certain income from foreign sources. Since double taxation results when the same income is subject to both foreign and U.S. income taxes, the tax law permits the taxpayer to choose either a credit or a deduction for the foreign taxes paid.

The imposition of a separate income tax on corporations leads to multiple taxation of the same income.

EXAMPLE 2   During the current year, Gray Corporation has net income of $100,000, of which $5,000 was received as dividends from stock it owns in Xerox Corporation. Assume Gray Corporation distributes the after-tax income to its shareholders (all individuals). At a minimum, the distribution received by the shareholders will be subject to two income taxes: the corporate income tax when the income is earned by Gray Corporation and the individual income tax when the balance is distributed to the shareholders as a dividend. The $5,000 Gray receives from Xerox Corporation fares even worse. Because it is paid from income earned by Xerox, it has been subjected to a third income tax (the corporate income tax imposed on Xerox).[11] ▼

For corporate shareholders, for whom triple taxation is possible, the law provides a deduction for dividends received from certain domestic corporations. The deduction, usually 70 percent of the dividends, would be allowed to Gray Corporation for the $5,000 it received from Xerox Corporation. (See the discussion in Chapter 2.)

In the area of the Federal estate tax, several provisions reflect attempts to mitigate the effect of multiple taxation. Some degree of equity is achieved, for example, by allowing a limited credit against the estate tax for foreign death taxes imposed on the same transfer. Other estate tax credits are available and can be explained on the same grounds.[12]

The Wherewithal to Pay Concept. The **wherewithal to pay** concept recognizes the inequity of taxing a transaction when the taxpayer lacks the means with which to pay the tax. It is particularly suited to situations when the taxpayer's economic position has not changed significantly as a result of a transaction.

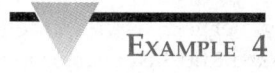

EXAMPLE 3   White Corporation holds unimproved land as an investment. The land has a basis to White of $60,000 and a fair market value of $100,000. The land is exchanged for a building (worth $100,000) that White will use in its business.[13] ▼

EXAMPLE 4   White Corporation owns a warehouse that it uses in its business. At a time when the warehouse has an adjusted basis of $60,000, it is destroyed by fire. White collects the insurance proceeds of $100,000 and, within two years of the end of the year in which the fire occurred, uses all of the proceeds to purchase a new warehouse.[14] ▼

---

[10] A tax credit, rather than a deduction, would eliminate the effects of multiple taxation on the same income.

[11] This result materializes because under the tax law a corporation is not allowed a deduction for the dividend distributions it makes.

[12] See Chapter 17.

[13] The nontaxability of like-kind exchanges applies to the exchange of property held for investment or used in a trade or business for property to be similarly held or used.

[14] The nontaxability of gains realized from involuntary conversions applies when the proceeds received by the taxpayer are reinvested within a prescribed period of time in property similar or related in service or use to that converted. Involuntary conversions take place as a result of casualty losses, theft losses, and condemnations by a public authority.

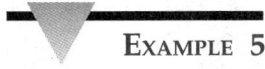

EXAMPLE 5　Tom, a sole proprietor, decides to incorporate his business. In exchange for the business's assets (adjusted basis of $60,000 and a fair market value of $100,000), Tom receives all of the stock of Azure Corporation, a newly created corporation.[15] The Azure stock is worth $100,000. ▼

EXAMPLE 6　Rose, Sam, and Tom want to develop unimproved land owned by Tom. The land has a basis to Tom of $60,000 and a fair market value of $100,000. The RST Partnership is formed with the following investment: land worth $100,000 transferred by Tom, $100,000 cash by Rose, and $100,000 cash by Sam. Each party receives a one-third interest in the RST Partnership.[16] ▼

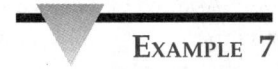

EXAMPLE 7　Amber Corporation and Crimson Corporation decide to consolidate to form Aqua Corporation.[17] Pursuant to the plan of reorganization, Tera exchanges her stock in Amber Corporation (basis of $60,000 and fair market value of $100,000) for stock in Aqua Corporation worth $100,000. ▼

In all of the preceding examples, White Corporation, Tom, or Tera had a realized gain of $40,000 [$100,000 (fair market value of the property received) – $60,000 (basis of the property given up)].[18] It seems inequitable to force the taxpayer to recognize any of this gain for two reasons. First, without disposing of the property or interest acquired, the taxpayer would be hard-pressed to pay the tax.[19] Second, the taxpayer's economic situation has not changed significantly. To illustrate by referring to Example 5, can it be said that Tom's position as sole shareholder of Azure Corporation is much different from his prior status as owner of a sole proprietorship?

Several warnings are in order concerning the application of the wherewithal to pay concept. Recognized gain is merely postponed and not necessarily avoided. Because of the basis carryover to the new property or interest acquired in these nontaxable transactions, the gain element is still present and might be recognized upon a subsequent taxable disposition. Referring to Example 5, suppose Tom later sold the stock in Azure Corporation for $100,000. Tom's basis in the stock is $60,000 (the same basis as in the assets transferred), and the sale results in a recognized gain of $40,000. Also, many of the provisions previously illustrated prevent the recognition of realized losses. Since such provisions are automatic in application (not elective with the taxpayer), they could operate to the detriment of a taxpayer who wishes to obtain a deduction for a loss. The notable exception involves involuntary conversions (Example 4). Here, nonrecognition treatment is elective with the taxpayer and will not apply to a realized loss if it is otherwise deductible.

The wherewithal to pay concept has definitely served as a guideline in shaping part of the tax law. Nevertheless, it is not a hard and fast principle that is followed in every case. Only when the tax law specifically provides for no tax consequences will this result materialize.

---

[15] Transfers of property to controlled corporations are discussed in Chapter 3.

[16] The formation of a partnership is discussed in Chapter 10.

[17] Corporate reorganizations are discussed in Chapter 7.

[18] Realized gain can be likened to economic gain. However, the Federal income tax is imposed only on that portion of realized gain considered to be recognized under the law. Generally, recognized (or taxable) gain can never exceed realized gain.

[19] If the taxpayer ends up with other property (boot) as part of the transfer, gain may be recognized to this extent. The presence of boot, however, helps solve the wherewithal to pay problem, since it provides property (other than the property or interest central to the transaction) with which to pay the tax.

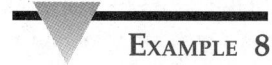

EXAMPLE 8   Mary Jo exchanges stock in Green Corporation (basis of $60,000 and fair market value of $100,000) for stock in Purple Corporation (fair market value of $100,000). The exchange is not pursuant to a reorganization. Under these circumstances, Mary Jo's realized gain of $40,000 is recognized for Federal income tax purposes.[20] ▼

The result reached in Example 8 seems harsh in that the exchange does not place Mary Jo in a position to pay the tax on the $40,000 gain. How can this result be reconciled with that reached in Example 7 when the exchange was nontaxable? In other words, why does the tax law apply the wherewithal to pay concept to the exchange of stock pursuant to a corporate reorganization (Example 7) but not to certain other stock exchanges (Example 8)?

Recall that the wherewithal to pay concept is particularly suited to situations in which the taxpayer's economic position has not changed significantly as a result of a transaction. In Example 7, Tera's stock investment in Amber Corporation really continues in the form of the Aqua Corporation stock since Aqua was formed through a consolidation of Amber and Crimson Corporations.[21] In Example 8, however, the investment has not continued. Here Mary Jo's ownership in Green Corporation has ceased, and an investment in an entirely different corporation has been substituted.

Mitigating the Effect of the Annual Accounting Period Concept. For purposes of effective administration of the tax law, all taxpayers must report to and settle with the Federal government at periodic intervals. Otherwise, taxpayers would remain uncertain as to their tax liabilities, and the government would have difficulty judging revenues and budgeting expenditures. The period selected for final settlement of most tax liabilities is one year. At the close of each year, a taxpayer's position becomes complete for that particular year. Referred to as the annual accounting period concept, the effect is to divide each taxpayer's life into equal annual intervals for tax purposes.

The finality of the annual accounting period concept can lead to dissimilar tax treatment for taxpayers who are, from a long-range standpoint, in the same economic position.

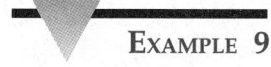

EXAMPLE 9   Rena and Samuel are both sole proprietors and have experienced the following results during the past four years:

| | Profit (or Loss) | |
Year	Rena	Samuel
1994	$50,000	$150,000
1995	60,000	60,000
1996	70,000	70,000
1997	50,000	(50,000)

Although Rena and Samuel have the same profit of $230,000 over the period 1994–1997, the finality of the annual accounting period concept places Samuel at a definite disadvantage for tax purposes. The net operating loss procedure offers Samuel some relief by allowing

---

[20] The exchange of stock does not qualify for nontaxable treatment as a like-kind exchange (refer to Example 3).

[21] This continuation is known as the continuity of interest concept, which forms the foundation for all nontaxable corporate reorganizations. The concept is discussed at length in Chapter 7.

him to apply some or all of his 1997 loss to the earliest profitable years (in this case 1994). Thus, Samuel, with a net operating loss carryback, would be in a position to obtain a refund for some of the taxes he paid on the $150,000 profit reported for 1994. ▼

ETHICAL CONSIDERATIONS

From Rags to Riches

Although the net operating loss procedure does a great deal to provide relief from the "riches to rags" situation (see Example 9), what about the reverse result? Consider, for example, Victor's quandary.

Year	Profit (or Loss)
1994	$ 20,000
1995	20,000
1996	20,000
1997	170,000

Is there any doubt that Victor will have a horrific tax liability for 1997? Yet, with his overall total of $230,000 for 1994–1997, is he in any less sympathetic position than Samuel in Example 9?

At one time the tax law provided relief (called the income-averaging procedure) for the "rags to riches" situation. However, when maximum income tax rates were lowered to 31 percent a few years ago, the income-averaging procedure was rescinded. Income tax rates have since been raised, but income averaging has not been reinstated as a means of alleviating one possible effect of the annual accounting period concept.

The same reasoning used to support the deduction of net operating losses can be applied to explain the special treatment excess capital losses and excess charitable contributions receive. Carryback and carryover procedures help mitigate the effect of limiting a loss or a deduction to the accounting period in which it is realized. With such procedures, a taxpayer may be able to salvage a loss or a deduction that might otherwise be wasted.

The installment method of recognizing gain on the sale of property allows a taxpayer to spread tax consequences over the payout period.[22] The harsh effect of taxing all the gain in the year of sale is avoided. The installment method can also be explained by the wherewithal to pay concept since recognition of gain is tied to the collection of the installment notes received from the sale of the property. Tax consequences tend to correspond to the seller's ability to pay the tax.

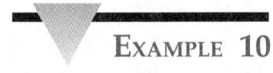

EXAMPLE 10

In 1995, Tim sold unimproved real estate (cost of $40,000) for $100,000. Under the terms of the sale, Tim receives two notes from the purchaser, each for $50,000 (plus interest). One note is payable in 1996 and the other note in 1997. Without the installment method, Tim would have to recognize and pay a tax on the gain of $60,000 for the year of the sale (1995).

---

[22] Under the installment method, each payment received by the seller represents a return of basis (the nontaxable portion) and profit from the sale (the taxable portion).

This result is harsh, since none of the sale proceeds will be received until 1996 and 1997. With the installment method, and presuming the notes are paid when each comes due, Tim recognizes half of the gain ($30,000) in 1996 and the remaining half in 1997. ▼

The annual accounting period concept has been modified to apply to situations in which taxpayers may have difficulty accurately assessing their tax positions by year-end. In many such cases, the law permits taxpayers to treat transactions taking place in the next year as having occurred in the prior year.

▼
EXAMPLE 11

Monica, a calendar year taxpayer, is a participant in an H.R. 10 (Keogh) retirement plan. (See Appendix C for a definition of a Keogh plan.) Under the plan, Monica contributes 20% of her net self-employment income, such amount being deductible for Federal income tax purposes. On April 10, 1997, Monica determines that her net self-employment income for calendar year 1996 was $80,000. Consequently, she contributes $16,000 (20% × $80,000) to the plan. Even though the $16,000 contribution was made in 1997, the law permits Monica to claim it as a deduction for tax year 1996. Requiring Monica to make the contribution by December 31, 1996, in order to obtain the deduction for that year would force her to arrive at an accurate determination of net self-employment income long before her income tax return must be prepared and filed. ▼

Similar exceptions to the annual accounting period concept cover certain charitable contributions by accrual basis corporations (Chapter 2), dividend distributions by S corporations (Chapter 12), and the dividend deduction allowed in applying the tax on unreasonable accumulation of corporate earnings and the tax on personal holding companies (Chapter 6).

Coping with Inflation.   During periods of inflation, bracket creep has plagued the working person. Because of the progressive nature of the income tax, any wage adjustment to compensate for inflation can increase the income tax bracket of the recipient. The overall impact is an erosion of purchasing power. Congress recognized this problem and began to adjust various income tax components (the **indexation** procedure) in 1985, based upon the rise in the consumer price index over the prior year. For example, due to the inflation factor, the amount of a personal and dependency exemption has been increased over the years. Indexation also applies to dollar amounts of other components, including the tax brackets and the standard deduction.

POLITICAL CONSIDERATIONS

A large segment of the Federal tax law is made up of statutory provisions. Since these statutes are enacted by Congress, is it any surprise that political considerations influence tax law? For purposes of discussion, the effect of political considerations on the tax law is divided into the following topics: special interest legislation, political expediency, and state and local influences.

Special Interest Legislation.   Unquestionably, certain provisions of the tax law can be explained largely by looking to the political influence some pressure groups have exerted on Congress. For example, is there any other reason why prepaid subscription and dues income is not taxed until earned while prepaid rents are taxed to the landlord in the year received? These exceptions came about because certain organizations (e.g., the American Automobile Association) convinced Congress that special tax treatment was needed to cover income received from multiyear dues and subscriptions.

Special interest legislation is not necessarily to be condemned if it can be justified on economic or social grounds. At any rate, it is an inevitable product of our political system.

Political Expediency.   Various tax reform proposals rise and fall in favor, depending upon the shifting moods of the American public. That Congress is sensitive to popular feeling is an accepted fact. Therefore, certain provisions of the tax law can be explained on the basis of the political climate at the time of enactment. Once the general public became aware that certain large and profitable corporations were able to avoid the corporate income tax, Congress responded with an alternative minimum tax. Since a portion of a corporation's adjusted current earnings has been made a tax preference item, many corporations no longer escape taxation (see Chapter 6).

Measures that deter more affluent taxpayers from obtaining so-called preferential tax treatment have always had popular appeal and, consequently, the support of Congress. Provisions such as the alternative minimum tax, the imputed interest rules, and the limitation on the deductibility of interest on investment indebtedness can be explained on this basis. In the same vein are the provisions imposing penalty taxes on corporations that unreasonably accumulate earnings or are classified as personal holding companies (see Chapter 6).

The provisions raising income tax rates on more affluent taxpayers and increasing the amount of the earned income credit are also at least partially attributable to political expediency.

State and Local Influences.   Political considerations have played a major role in the exclusion from gross income of interest received on state and local obligations. In view of the furor that has been raised by state and local political figures every time repeal of this tax provision has been proposed, one might well regard it as sacred.

Somewhat less apparent has been the influence state law has had in shaping our present Federal tax law. Of prime importance in this regard has been the effect of the community property system employed in nine states.[23] At one time, the tax position of the residents of these states was so advantageous that many common law states actually adopted community property systems.[24] The political pressure placed on Congress to correct the disparity in tax treatment was considerable. To a large extent, this was accomplished in the Revenue Act of 1948, which extended many of the community property tax advantages to residents of common law jurisdictions.[25] Thus, common law states avoided the trauma of discarding the time-honored legal system familiar to everyone. The impact of community property law on the Federal estate and gift taxes is further explored in Chapters 17 and 18.

---

[23] The states with community property systems are Louisiana, Texas, New Mexico, Arizona, California, Washington, Idaho, Nevada, and Wisconsin. The rest of the states are classified as common law jurisdictions. The difference between common law and community property systems centers around the property rights possessed by married persons. In a common law system, each spouse owns whatever he or she earns. Under a community property system, one-half of the earnings of each spouse is considered owned by the other spouse. Assume, for example, Harold and Ruth are husband and wife, and their only income is the $40,000 annual salary Harold receives. If they live in New York (a common law state), the $40,000 salary belongs to Harold.

If, however, they live in Texas (a community property state), the $40,000 salary is divided equally, in terms of ownership, between Harold and Ruth.

[24] Such states included Michigan, Oklahoma, and Pennsylvania.

[25] The major advantage extended was the provision allowing married taxpayers to file joint returns and compute the tax liability as if the income had been earned one-half by each spouse. This result is automatic in a community property state since half of the income earned by one spouse belongs to the other spouse. The income-splitting benefits of a joint return are now incorporated as part of the tax rates applicable to married taxpayers.

INFLUENCE OF THE INTERNAL REVENUE SERVICE

The IRS has been influential in many areas beyond its role in issuing administrative pronouncements. In its capacity as the protector of the national revenue, the IRS has been instrumental in securing the passage of much legislation designed to curtail the most flagrant tax avoidance practices (closing tax loopholes). In its capacity as the administrator of the tax laws, the IRS has sought and obtained legislation to make its job easier (administrative feasibility).

The IRS as Protector of the Revenue.   Innumerable examples can be given of provisions in the tax law that have stemmed from the direct efforts of the IRS to prevent taxpayers from exploiting a loophole. Working within the letter of existing law, ingenious taxpayers and their advisers devise techniques that accomplish indirectly what cannot be accomplished directly. As a consequence, legislation is enacted to close the loophole that taxpayers have located and exploited. The following examples can be explained in this fashion and are discussed in more detail in the chapters to follow:

- The use of a fiscal year by personal service corporations, partnerships, S corporations, and trusts to defer income recognition to the owners (see Chapters 2, 10, 12, and 19).
- The use of the cash basis method of accounting by certain large corporations (see Chapter 2).
- The deduction of passive investment losses and expenses against other income (see Chapter 11).
- The shifting of income to lower-bracket taxpayers through the use of reversionary trusts (see Chapter 19).

In addition, the IRS has secured from Congress legislation of a more general nature that enables it to make adjustments based upon the substance, rather than the formal construction, of what a taxpayer has done. One provision, for example, authorizes the IRS to establish guidelines on the thin capitalization issue. This question involves when corporate debt will be recognized as debt for tax purposes and when it will be reclassified as equity or stock (see the discussion of thin capitalization in Chapter 3). Another provision permits the IRS to make adjustments to a taxpayer's method of accounting when the method used by the taxpayer does not clearly reflect income. The IRS also has been granted the authority to allocate income and deductions among businesses owned or controlled by the same interests when the allocation is necessary to prevent the evasion of taxes or to reflect the income of each business clearly.

EXAMPLE 12

Gold Corporation and Silver Corporation are brother-sister corporations (the stock of each is owned by the same shareholders), and both use the calendar year for tax purposes. For the current tax year, each has taxable income as follows: $335,000 for Gold Corporation and $50,000 for Silver Corporation. Not included in Gold Corporation's taxable income, however, is $10,000 of rent income usually charged Silver Corporation for the use of some property owned by Gold. Since the parties have not clearly reflected the taxable income of each business, the IRS can allocate $10,000 of rent income to Gold Corporation. After the allocation, Gold Corporation has taxable income of $345,000, and Silver Corporation has taxable income of $40,000.[26] ▼

---

[26]By shifting $10,000 of income to Gold Corporation (which is in the 34% bracket), the IRS gains $3,400 in taxes. Allowing the $10,000 deduction to Silver Corporation (which is in the 15% bracket) costs the IRS only $1,500. See Chapter 2 for a further discussion of the income tax rates applicable to corporations.

Also of a general nature is the authority Congress has given the IRS to prevent taxpayers from acquiring corporations to obtain a tax advantage when the principal purpose of the acquisition is the evasion or avoidance of the Federal income tax. The provision of the tax law that provides this authority is discussed briefly in Chapter 7.

Administrative Feasibility.   Some of the tax law is justified on the grounds that it simplifies the task of the IRS in collecting the revenue and administering the law. With regard to collecting the revenue, the IRS long ago realized the importance of placing taxpayers on a pay-as-you-go basis. Elaborate withholding procedures apply to wages, while the tax on other types of income may have to be paid at periodic intervals throughout the year. The IRS has been instrumental in convincing the courts that accrual basis taxpayers should pay taxes on prepaid income in the year received and not when earned. This approach may be contrary to generally accepted accounting principles, but it is consistent with the wherewithal to pay concept.

Of considerable aid to the IRS in collecting revenue are the numerous provisions that impose interest and penalties on taxpayers for noncompliance with the tax law. These provisions include penalties for failure to pay a tax or to file a return that is due and the negligence penalty for intentional disregard of rules and regulations. Various penalties for civil and criminal fraud also serve as deterrents to taxpayer noncompliance. This aspect of the tax law is discussed in Chapter 16.

One of the keys to the effective administration of our tax system is the audit process conducted by the IRS. To carry out this function, the IRS is aided by provisions that reduce the chance of taxpayer error or manipulation and therefore simplify the audit effort that is necessary. An increase in the amount of the standard deduction reduces the number of individual taxpayers who will be in a position to claim itemized deductions. With fewer deductions to check, the audit function is simplified.[27] The same objective can be used to explain the $192,800 unified estate and gift tax credit and the $10,000 annual gift tax exclusion (see Chapter 17). These provisions decrease the number of tax returns that must be filed (as well as reduce the taxes paid) and thereby save audit effort.[28]

The audit function of the IRS has also been simplified by provisions of the tax law dealing with the burden of proof. Suppose, for example, the IRS audits a taxpayer and questions a particular deduction. Who has the burden of proving the propriety of the deduction? Except in the case of fraud (see Chapter 16), the burden is always on the taxpayer.

4 LEARNING OBJECTIVE
Recognize the role of the courts in interpreting and shaping tax law.

INFLUENCE OF THE COURTS

In addition to interpreting statutory provisions and the administrative pronouncements issued by the IRS, the Federal courts have influenced tax law in two other respects.[29] First, the courts have formulated certain judicial concepts that serve as guides in the application of various tax provisions. Second, certain key decisions have led to changes in the Internal Revenue Code. Understanding this influence helps explain some of our tax law.

---

[27] The IRS gave the same justification when it proposed to Congress the $100 per event limitation on personal casualty and theft losses. Imposition of the limitation eliminated many casualty and theft loss deductions and, as a consequence, saved the IRS considerable audit time. Also, an additional limitation equal to 10% of adjusted gross income applies to the total of nonbusiness losses after reduction by the floor of $100 for each loss.

[28] Particularly in the case of nominal gifts among family members, taxpayer compliance in reporting and paying a tax on such transfers would be questionable. The absence of the $10,000 gift tax exclusion would create a serious enforcement problem for the IRS.

[29] A great deal of case law is devoted to ascertaining congressional intent. The courts, in effect, ask: What did Congress have in mind when it enacted a particular tax provision?

Judicial Concepts Relating to Tax Law.   Although ranking the tax concepts developed by the courts in order of importance is difficult, the concept of substance over form would almost certainly be near the top of any list. Variously described as the "telescoping" or "collapsing" process or the "step transaction approach," it involves determining the true substance of what occurred. In a transaction involving many steps, any one step may be collapsed (or disregarded) to arrive directly at the result reached.

EXAMPLE 13

In the current year, Mrs. Greer, a widow, wants to give $20,000 to Jean without incurring any gift tax liability.[30] She knows that the law permits her to give up to $10,000 each year per person without any tax consequences (the annual exclusion). With this in mind, the following steps are taken: a gift by Mrs. Greer to Jean of $10,000 (nontaxable because of the $10,000 annual exclusion), a gift by Mrs. Greer to Ben of $10,000 (also nontaxable), and a gift by Ben to Jean of $10,000 (nontaxable because of Ben's annual exclusion). Considering only the form of what Mrs. Greer and Ben have done, all appears well from a tax standpoint. In substance, however, what has happened? By collapsing the steps involving Ben, it is apparent that Mrs. Greer has made a gift of $20,000 to Jean and therefore has not avoided the Federal gift tax. ▼

The substance over form concept plays an important role in transactions involving corporations.

Another leading tax concept developed by the courts deals with the interpretation of statutory tax provisions that operate to benefit taxpayers. The courts have established the rule that these relief provisions are to be narrowly construed against taxpayers if there is any doubt about their application. Suppose, for example, Beige Corporation wants to be treated as an S corporation (see Chapter 12) but has not satisfied the statutory requirements for making the required election. Because S corporation status is a relief provision favoring taxpayers, chances are the courts will deny Beige Corporation this treatment.

Important in the area of corporate-shareholder dealings (see the discussion of constructive dividends in Chapter 4) and in the resolution of valuation problems for estate and gift tax purposes (see Chapters 17 and 18) is the **arm's length concept.** Particularly in dealings between related parties, transactions can be tested by questioning whether the taxpayers acted in an "arm's length" manner. The question to be asked is: Would unrelated parties have handled the transaction in the same way?

EXAMPLE 14

The sole shareholder of a corporation leases property to the corporation for a monthly rental of $50,000. To test whether the corporation should be allowed a rent deduction for this amount, the IRS and the courts will apply the arm's length concept. Would the corporation have paid $50,000 a month in rent if the same property had been leased from an unrelated party (rather than from the sole shareholder)? ▼

The **continuity of interest concept** originated with the courts but has, in many situations, been incorporated into statutory provisions of the tax law. Primarily concerned with business readjustments, the concept permits tax-free treatment only if the taxpayer retains a substantial continuing interest in the property transferred to the new business. Due to the continuing interest retained, the transfer should not have tax consequences because the position of the taxpayer has not changed. This concept applies to transfers to controlled corporations (Chapter 3), corporate reorganizations (Chapter 7), and transfers to partnerships (Chapter 10).

---

[30] The example assumes that Mrs. Greer has exhausted her unified tax credit. See Chapter 17.

The continuity of interest concept helps explain the results reached in Examples 5 through 7 of this chapter. This concept is further discussed in Chapter 7.

Also developed by the courts, the **business purpose concept** principally applies to transactions involving corporations. Under this concept, some sound business reason that motivates the transaction must be present in order for the prescribed tax treatment to result. The avoidance of taxation is not considered to be a sound business purpose.

EXAMPLE 15

Beth and Charles are equal shareholders in Brown Corporation. They have recently disagreed about the company's operations and are at an impasse about the future of Brown Corporation. This shareholder disagreement on corporate policy constitutes a sound business purpose and would justify a division of Brown Corporation that will permit Beth and Charles to go their separate ways. Whether the division of Brown would be nontaxable to the parties depends on their compliance with the statutory provisions dealing with corporate reorganizations. The point is, however, that compliance with statutory provisions would not be enough to ensure nontaxability without a business purpose for the transaction. ▼

The business purpose concept is discussed further in Chapter 7.

Judicial Influence on Statutory Provisions.   Some court decisions have been of such consequence that Congress has incorporated them into statutory tax law. An illustration of this influence appears in Example 16.

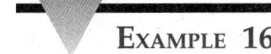
EXAMPLE 16

In 1983, Brad claimed a capital loss of $100,000 for Tan Corporation stock that had become worthless during the year. In the absence of any offsetting gains, the capital loss deduction produced no income tax savings for Brad either in 1983 or in future years. In 1986, Brad institutes a lawsuit against the former officers of Tan Corporation for their misconduct that resulted in the corporation's failure and thereby led to Brad's $100,000 loss. In settlement of the suit, the officers pay $50,000 to Brad. The IRS argued that the full $50,000 should be taxed as gain to Brad. The Tan stock was written off in 1983 and had a zero basis for tax purposes. The $50,000 recovery Brad received on the stock was, therefore, all gain. The IRS's position was logical, but not equitable. The court stated that Brad should not be taxed on the recovery of an amount previously deducted unless the deduction produced a tax savings. Since the $100,000 capital loss deduction in 1983 produced no tax benefit, none of the $50,000 received in 1986 results in gain. ▼

The decision reached by the courts in Example 16, known as the **tax benefit rule,** is part of the statutory tax law. The tax benefit rule is discussed later in connection with transfers to controlled corporations (Chapter 3).

Court decisions sometimes create uncertainty about the tax law. Such decisions may reach the right result but do not produce the guidelines necessary to enable taxpayers to comply. In many situations, Congress may be compelled to add certainty to the law by enacting statutory provisions specifying when a particular tax consequence will or will not materialize. The following are examples of this type of judicial "cause" and the statutory "effect":

- When a stock redemption will be treated as an exchange or as a dividend (see Chapter 5).
- What basis a parent corporation will have in the assets received from a subsidiary that is liquidated shortly after its acquisition (see Chapter 5).

Some of the statutory provisions can be explained by a negative reaction by Congress to a particular court decision. One decision, for example, held that the transfer of a liability to a controlled corporation should be treated as boot received by the transferor (see Chapter 3). Congress apparently disagreed with this treatment and promptly enacted legislation to change the result.

SUMMARY

In addition to its revenue-raising objective, the Federal tax law has developed in response to several other factors:

- *Economic considerations.* Here, the emphasis is on tax provisions that help regulate the economy and encourage certain activities and types of businesses.
- *Social considerations.* Some tax provisions are designed to encourage or discourage certain socially desirable or undesirable practices.
- *Equity considerations.* Of principal concern in this area are tax provisions that alleviate the effect of multiple taxation, recognize the wherewithal to pay concept, mitigate the effect of the annual accounting period concept, and recognize the eroding effect of inflation.
- *Political considerations.* Of significance in this regard are tax provisions that represent special interest legislation, reflect political expediency, and illustrate the effect of state law.
- *Influence of the IRS.* Many tax provisions are intended to aid the IRS in collecting revenue and administering the tax law.
- *Influence of the courts.* Court decisions have established a body of judicial concepts relating to tax law and have, on occasion, led Congress to enact statutory provisions that either clarify or negate their effect.

These factors explain various tax provisions and thereby help in understanding why the tax law developed to its present state. The next step involves learning to work with the tax law.

WORKING WITH THE TAX LAW—
TAX SOURCES

Understanding taxation requires a mastery of the sources of tax law. These sources include not only the legislative provisions in the Internal Revenue Code, but also congressional Committee Reports, Regulations, Treasury Department pronouncements, and court decisions. Thus, the primary sources of tax information are the pronouncements of the three branches of government: legislative, executive, and judicial.

The law is of little significance, however, until it is applied to a set of facts and circumstances. A tax researcher must not only be able to read and interpret the sources of the law but must also understand the relative weight of authority within the rules of law. Learning to work with the tax law involves three basic steps:

1. Familiarity with the sources of the law.
2. Application of research techniques.
3. Effective use of planning procedures.

The remainder of this chapter introduces the sources of tax law and explains how the law is applied to problems and conditions of individual and business transactions. Statutory, administrative, and judicial sources of the tax law are considered first.

STATUTARY SOURCES OF THE TAX LAW

5 **LEARNING OBJECTIVE**
Identify tax law sources—
statutory, administrative, and
judicial.

Origin of the Internal Revenue Code.   Before 1939, the statutory provisions relating to taxation were contained in the individual revenue acts enacted by Congress. The inconvenience and confusion that resulted from dealing with many separate acts led Congress to codify all of the Federal tax laws. Known as the Internal

> ### TAX IN THE NEWS
>
> #### COMPLEXITY AS A PRODUCT OF GROWTH
>
> In 32 of the 42 years since the passage of the Internal Revenue Code of 1954, Congress has enacted significant tax legislation. As a result of this legislation, the number of sections in the Code has risen from 103 to 698, an increase of 578 percent.
>
> This type of growth not only produces uncertainty but leads to complexity. It is the complexity that has stimulated the development of a highly specialized tax industry.
>
> SOURCE: Adapted from A. P. Hall, "Growth of Federal Government Tax 'Industry' Parallels Growth of Tax Code," *Tax Notes,* November 28, 1994, pp. 1133–38.

Revenue Code of 1939, the codification arranged all Federal tax provisions in a logical sequence and placed them in a separate part of the Federal statutes. A further rearrangement took place in 1954 and resulted in the Internal Revenue Code of 1954.

Perhaps to emphasize the magnitude of the changes made by the Tax Reform Act (TRA) of 1986, Congress redesignated the Internal Revenue Code of 1954 as the Internal Revenue Code of 1986. This change is somewhat deceiving since the tax law was not recodified in 1986, as it had been in 1954. TRA of 1986 merely amended, deleted, or added provisions to the Internal Revenue Code of 1954. For example, before TRA of 1986, § 336 provided the general rule that no gain or loss would be recognized by a corporation when it distributed assets in kind to its shareholders in complete liquidation (see Chapter 5). After the effective date of TRA of 1986, § 336 provides that gain or loss will be recognized upon the same distributions.

The following observations will help clarify the significance of the three Codes:

- Neither the 1939, the 1954, nor the 1986 Code changed all of the tax law existing on the date of enactment. Much of the 1939 Code, for example, was incorporated into the 1954 Code. The same can be said for the transition from the 1954 to the 1986 Code. This point is important in assessing judicial and administrative decisions interpreting provisions under prior Codes. For example, a decision interpreting § 121 of the Internal Revenue Code of 1954 will have continuing validity since this provision carried over unchanged to the Internal Revenue Code of 1986.
- Statutory amendments to the tax law are integrated into the existing Code. Thus, the Small Business Job Protection Act of 1996 became part of the Internal Revenue Code of 1986.

Do not conclude, however, that the codification and recodification process has made the Internal Revenue Code a simplistic body of laws. As the comments in the Tax in the News indicate, the complexity of our current Code is largely attributable to its growth.

The Legislative Process.   Federal tax legislation generally originates in the House of Representatives, where it is first considered by the House Ways and Means Committee. Tax bills originate in the Senate when they are attached as riders to other legislative proposals.[31] If acceptable to the House Ways and Means

---

[31] The Tax Equity and Fiscal Responsibility Act of 1982 originated in the Senate; its constitutionality was unsuccessfully challenged in the courts. The Senate version of the Deficit Reduction Act of 1984 was attached as an amendment to the Federal Boat Safety Act.

Committee, the proposed bill is referred to the entire House of Representatives for approval or disapproval. Approved bills are sent to the Senate, where they are referred to the Senate Finance Committee for further consideration.

In the next step, the bill is referred from the Senate Finance Committee to the whole Senate. Assuming no disagreement between the House and the Senate, passage by the Senate means referral to the President for approval or veto. If the bill is approved or if the President's veto is overridden, the bill becomes law and part of the Internal Revenue Code.

When the Senate version of the bill differs from that passed by the House, the Joint Conference Committee resolves these differences. The Joint Conference Committee includes members of the House Ways and Means Committee and the Senate Finance Committee.

Referrals from the House Ways and Means Committee, the Senate Finance Committee, and the Joint Conference Committee are usually accompanied by Committee Reports. These Committee Reports often explain the provisions of the proposed legislation and are therefore a valuable source in ascertaining the intent of Congress. What Congress has in mind when it considers and enacts tax legislation is, of course, the key to interpreting that legislation. Since Regulations normally are not issued immediately after a statute is enacted, taxpayers often look to legislative history materials to ascertain congressional intent.

The typical legislative process dealing with tax bills can be summarized as follows:

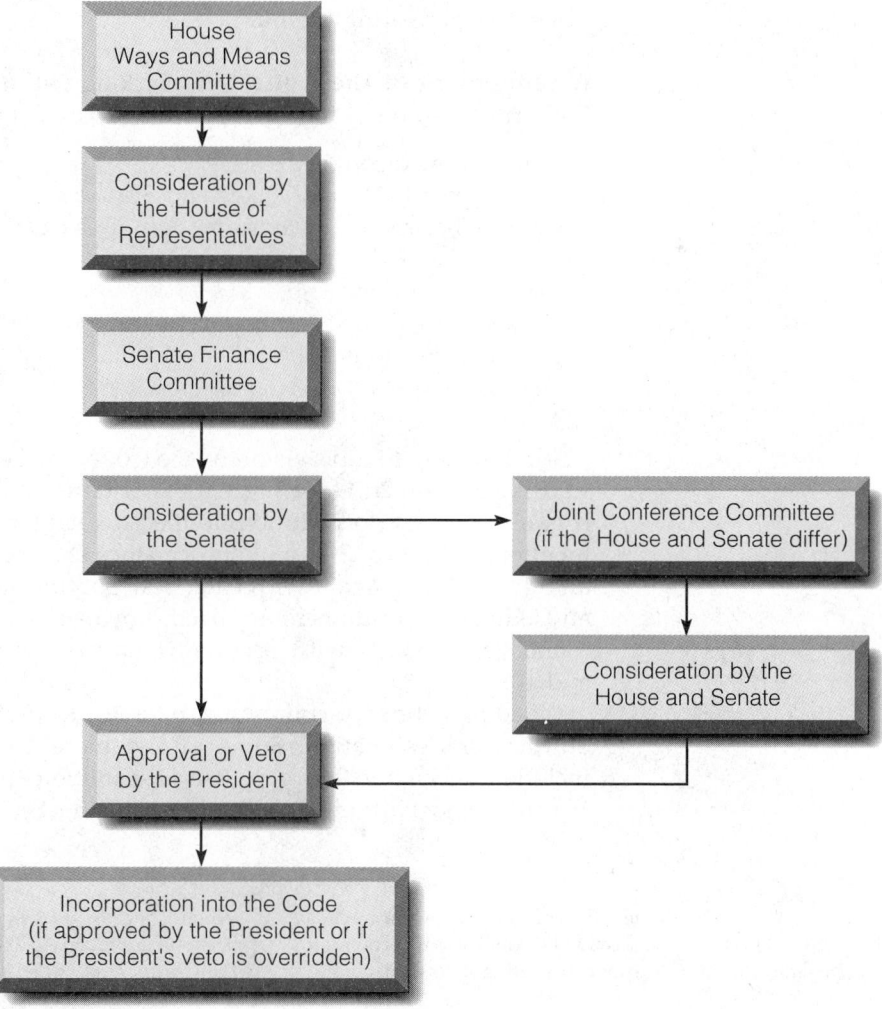

The role of the Joint Conference Committee indicates the importance of compromise in the legislative process. The practical effect of the compromise process can be illustrated by reviewing what happened in the Revenue Reconciliation Act (RRA) of 1993 (H.R. 2264) with respect to the amortization of acquired goodwill:

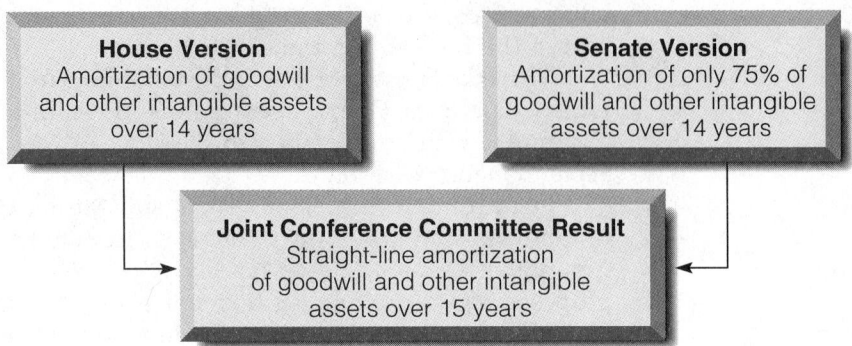

Some tax provisions are commonly referred to by the number the bill received in the House when first proposed or by the name of the member of Congress sponsoring the legislation. For example, the Self-Employed Individuals Tax Retirement Act of 1962 is popularly known as H.R. 10 (the House of Representatives Bill No. 10) or as the Keogh Act (Keogh being one of the members of Congress sponsoring the bill).

Arrangement of the Code.   In working with the Code, it helps to understand the format. Note the following partial table of contents:

Subtitle A. Income Taxes
    Chapter 1. Normal Taxes and Surtaxes
        Subchapter A. Determination of Tax Liability
            Part I. Tax on Individuals
                Sections 1–5
            Part II. Tax on Corporations
                Sections 11–12

* * *

In referring to a provision of the Code, the key is usually the Section number. In citing Section 2(a) (dealing with the status of a surviving spouse), for example, it is unnecessary to include Subtitle A, Chapter 1, Subchapter A, Part I. Merely mentioning Section 2(a) will suffice since the Section numbers run consecutively and do not begin again with each new Subtitle, Chapter, Subchapter, or Part. Not all Code Section numbers are used, however. Note that Part I ends with Section 5 and Part II starts with Section 11 (at present there are no Sections 6, 7, 8, 9, and 10).[32]

Tax practitioners commonly refer to a specific area of income taxation by Subchapter designation. Some of the more common Subchapter designations include Subchapter C (Corporate Distributions and Adjustments), Subchapter K (Partners and Partnerships), and Subchapter S (Tax Treatment of S Corporations

---

[32] When the 1954 Code was drafted, Section numbers were intentionally omitted. This omission provided flexibility to incorporate later changes into the Code without disrupting its organization. When Congress does not leave enough space, subsequent Code Sections are given A, B, C, etc., designations. A good example is the treatment of §§ 280A through 280H.

and Their Shareholders). Particularly in the last situation, it is much more convenient to describe the subject of the applicable Code provisions (Sections 1361 through 1379) as S corporation status rather than as the "Tax Treatment of S Corporations and Their Shareholders."

Citing the Code.   Code Sections often are broken down into subparts.[33] Section 2(a)(1)(A) serves as an example.

Broken down as to content, § 2 (a)(1)(A) becomes:

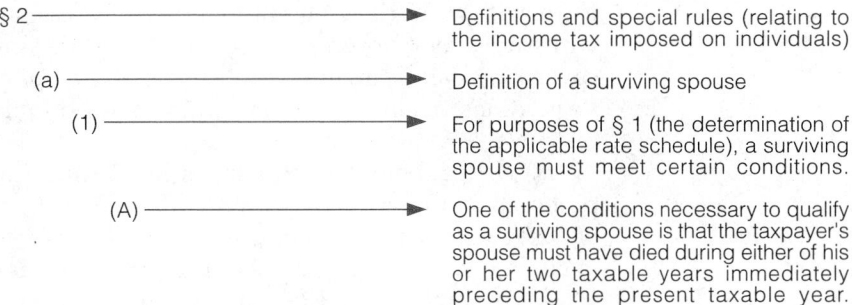

§ 2 → Definitions and special rules (relating to the income tax imposed on individuals)

(a) → Definition of a surviving spouse

(1) → For purposes of § 1 (the determination of the applicable rate schedule), a surviving spouse must meet certain conditions.

(A) → One of the conditions necessary to qualify as a surviving spouse is that the taxpayer's spouse must have died during either of his or her two taxable years immediately preceding the present taxable year.

Throughout the remainder of the text, references to Code Sections are in the form just given. The symbols "§" and "§§" are used in place of "Section" and "Sections." Unless otherwise stated, all Code references are to the Internal Revenue Code of 1986. The format followed in the remainder of the text is summarized as follows:

Complete Reference	Text Reference
Section 2(a)(1)(A) of the Internal Revenue Code of 1986	§ 2(a)(1)(A)
Sections 1 and 2 of the Internal Revenue Code of 1986	§§ 1 and 2
Section 2 of the Internal Revenue Code of 1954	§ 2 of the Internal Revenue Code of 1954
Section 12(d) of the Internal Revenue Code of 1939[35]	§ 12(d) of the Internal Revenue Code of 1939

---

[33]Some Code Sections do not have subparts. See, for example, § 482.

[34]Some Code Sections omit the subsection designation and use, instead, the paragraph designation as the first subpart. See, for example, §§ 212(1) and 1221(1).

[35]Section 12(d) of the Internal Revenue Code of 1939 is the predecessor to § 2 of the Internal Revenue Code of 1954. Keep in mind that the 1954 Code superseded the 1939 Code.

ADMINISTRATIVE SOURCES OF THE TAX LAW

The administrative sources of the Federal tax law can be grouped as follows: Treasury Department Regulations, Revenue Rulings and Procedures, and other administrative pronouncements. All are issued either by the U.S. Treasury Department or by one of its instrumentalities (e.g., the IRS or a District Director). The role played by the IRS in this process is considered in greater depth in Chapter 16.

Treasury Department Regulations. Regulations are issued by the U.S. Treasury Department under authority granted by Congress. Interpretative by nature, they provide taxpayers with considerable guidance on the meaning and application of the Code. Although not issued by Congress, Regulations do carry considerable weight. They are an important factor to consider in complying with the tax law. Anyone taking a position contrary to a finalized Regulation must disclose that fact on Form 8275 or Form 8275–R in order to avoid costly penalties.

Since Regulations interpret the Code, they are arranged in the same sequence. Regulations are, however, prefixed by a number that indicates the type of tax or administrative, procedural, or definitional matter to which they relate. For example, the prefix 1 designates the Regulations under the income tax law. Thus, the Regulations under Code § 2 would be cited as Reg. § 1.2, with subparts added for further identification. The numbering of these subparts often has no correlation with the Code subsections. The prefix 20 designates estate tax Regulations; 25 covers gift tax Regulations; 31 relates to employment taxes; and 301 refers to Regulations dealing with procedure and administration. This listing is not all-inclusive.

New Regulations and changes in existing Regulations usually are issued in proposed form before they are finalized. The time interval between the proposal of a Regulation and its finalization permits taxpayers and other interested parties to comment on the propriety of the proposal. **Proposed Regulations** under Code § 2, for example, would be cited as Prop.Reg. § 1.2.

Sometimes the Treasury Department issues **Temporary Regulations** relating to elections and other matters where speed is critical. Temporary Regulations often are needed for recent legislation that takes effect immediately. Temporary Regulations have the same authoritative value as final Regulations and may be cited as precedent for three years. Temporary Regulations also are issued as Proposed Regulations and automatically expire within three years after the date of issuance. Temporary Regulations and the simultaneously issued Proposed Regulations carry more weight than traditional Proposed Regulations.

Proposed, final, and Temporary Regulations are published in the *Federal Register* and are reproduced in major tax services. Final Regulations are issued as Treasury Decisions (TDs).

Revenue Rulings and Revenue Procedures. **Revenue Rulings** are official pronouncements of the National Office of the IRS. Like Regulations, they are designed to provide interpretation of the tax law. However, they do not carry the same legal force and effect as Regulations and usually deal with more restricted problems. Both Revenue Rulings and Revenue Procedures serve an important function in that they provide guidance to both IRS personnel and taxpayers in handling routine tax matters.

A Revenue Ruling often results from a specific taxpayer's request for a letter ruling. If the IRS believes that a taxpayer's request for a letter ruling deserves official publication due to its widespread impact, the holding will be converted into a Revenue Ruling. In making this conversion, names, identifying facts, and money amounts will be changed to disguise the identity of the requesting taxpayer. The IRS then will issue what would have been a letter ruling as a Revenue Ruling.

Revenue Procedures are issued in the same manner as Revenue Rulings, but deal with the internal management practices and procedures of the IRS. Familiarity with these procedures increases taxpayer compliance and helps make the administration of the tax laws more efficient.

Both Revenue Rulings and Revenue Procedures are published weekly by the U.S. Government in the *Internal Revenue Bulletin* (I.R.B.). Semiannually, the bulletins for a six-month period are gathered together, reorganized by Code Section classification, and published in a bound volume called the *Cumulative Bulletin* (C.B.).[36] The proper form for citing Rulings and Procedures depends on whether the item has been published in the *Cumulative Bulletin* or is available in I.R.B. form. Consider, for example, the following transition:

Temporary Citation	Rev.Rul. 95–69, I.R.B. No. 42, 4. *Explanation:* Revenue Ruling Number 69, appearing on page 4 of the 42d weekly issue of the *Internal Revenue Bulletin* for 1995.
Permanent Citation	Rev.Rul. 95–69, 1995–2 C.B. 38. *Explanation:* Revenue Ruling Number 69, appearing on page 38 of volume 2 of the *Cumulative Bulletin* for 1995.

Since the second volume of the 1995 *Cumulative Bulletin* was not published until summer of 1996, the I.R.B. citation had to be used until that time. After the publication of the *Cumulative Bulletin*, the C.B. citation became proper. The basic portion of both citations (Rev.Rul. 95–69) indicates that this was the 69th Revenue Ruling issued by the IRS during 1995.

Revenue Procedures are cited in the same manner, except that "Rev.Proc." is substituted for "Rev.Rul." Procedures, like Rulings, are published in the *Internal Revenue Bulletin* (the temporary source) and later transferred to the *Cumulative Bulletin* (the permanent source).

Other Administrative Pronouncements.   Treasury Decisions (TDs) are issued by the Treasury Department to promulgate new Regulations, to amend or otherwise change existing Regulations, or to announce the position of the Government on selected court decisions. Like Revenue Rulings and Revenue Procedures, TDs are published in the *Internal Revenue Bulletin* and subsequently transferred to the *Cumulative Bulletin*.

Technical Information Releases (TIRs) are usually issued to announce the publication of various IRS pronouncements (e.g., Revenue Rulings, Revenue Procedures).

Letter rulings are issued (for a fee) by the National Office of the IRS upon a taxpayer's request and describe how the IRS will treat a proposed transaction for tax purposes. In general, they apply only to the taxpayer who asks for and obtains the ruling, but post-1984 rulings may be substantial authority for purposes of avoiding the accuracy-related penalties.[37] This procedure may sound like the only real way to carry out effective tax planning. However, the IRS limits the issuance of letter rulings to restricted, preannounced areas of taxation. Thus, a ruling may not be obtained on many of the problems that are particularly troublesome for

---

[36] Usually, only two volumes of the *Cumulative Bulletin* are published each year. However, when major tax legislation has been enacted by Congress, other volumes may be published containing the congressional Committee Reports supporting the Revenue Act. See, for example, the two extra volumes for 1984 dealing with the Deficit Reduction Act of 1984. The 1984–3 *Cumulative Bulletin*, Volume 1, contains the text of the law itself; 1984–3, Volume 2, contains the Committee Reports. There are a total of four volumes of the *Cumulative Bulletin* for 1984: 1984–1; 1984–2; 1984–3, Volume 1; and 1984–3, Volume 2.

[37] Notice 90–20, 1990–1 C.B. 328, part V (A).

taxpayers.[38] For example, the IRS will not issue a ruling as to whether compensation paid to shareholder-employees is reasonable (see Chapter 4) or whether § 269 applies (the acquisition of a corporation to evade or avoid income tax [see Chapter 7]). The main reason the IRS will not rule on such matters is that they involve fact-oriented situations.

The IRS must make letter rulings available for public inspection after identifying details are deleted. Published digests of private letter rulings can be found in *Private Letter Rulings* (published by Research Institute of America), *BNA Daily Tax Reports,* and Tax Analysts & Advocates *TAX NOTES. IRS Letter Rulings Reports* (published by Commerce Clearing House) contains both digests and full texts of all letter rulings. *Letter Ruling Review* (Tax Analysts), a monthly publication, selects and discusses the more important of the approximately 300 letter rulings per month.

The National Office of the IRS releases technical advice memoranda (TAMs) weekly. TAMs resemble letter rulings in that they give the IRS's determination of an issue. Letter rulings, however, are responses to requests by taxpayers, whereas TAMs are issued by the National Office of the IRS in response to questions raised by IRS field personnel during audits. TAMs deal with completed rather than proposed transactions and are often requested for questions relating to exempt organizations and employee plans. Although TAMs are not officially published and may not be cited or used as precedent, post-1984 TAMs may be substantial authority for purposes of the accuracy-related penalties. See Chapter 16 for a discussion of these penalties.

Both letter rulings and TAMs are issued with multidigit file numbers. Consider, for example, the following ruling dealing with the tax on unrelated business income of schools leasing land: Ltr.Rul. 9631025. Broken down by digits, the file number reveals the following information:

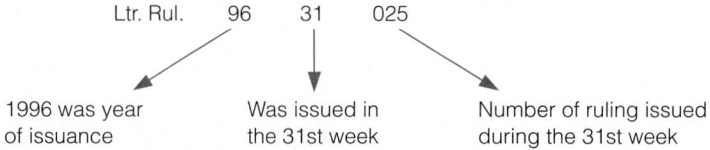

Ltr. Rul.	96	31	025
	1996 was year of issuance	Was issued in the 31st week	Number of ruling issued during the 31st week

Like letter rulings, **determination letters** are issued at the request of taxpayers and provide guidance concerning the application of the tax law. They differ from individual rulings in that the issuing source is the District Director rather than the National Office of the IRS. Also, determination letters usually involve completed (as opposed to proposed) transactions. Determination letters are not published but are made known only to the party making the request.

The following examples illustrate the distinction between individual rulings and determination letters:

EXAMPLE 17

The shareholders of Black Corporation and White Corporation want assurance that the consolidation of the corporations into Gray Corporation will be a nontaxable reorganization (see Chapter 7). The proper approach would be to request from the National Office of the IRS an individual ruling concerning the income tax effect of the proposed transaction. ▼

---

[38] Rev.Proc. 97–3, I.R.B. No. 1, 84, contains a listing of areas in which the IRS will not issue advance rulings. From time to time, subsequent Revenue Procedures are issued that modify or amplify Rev.Proc. 97–3.

▼ FIGURE 1–1
Federal Judicial Tax Process

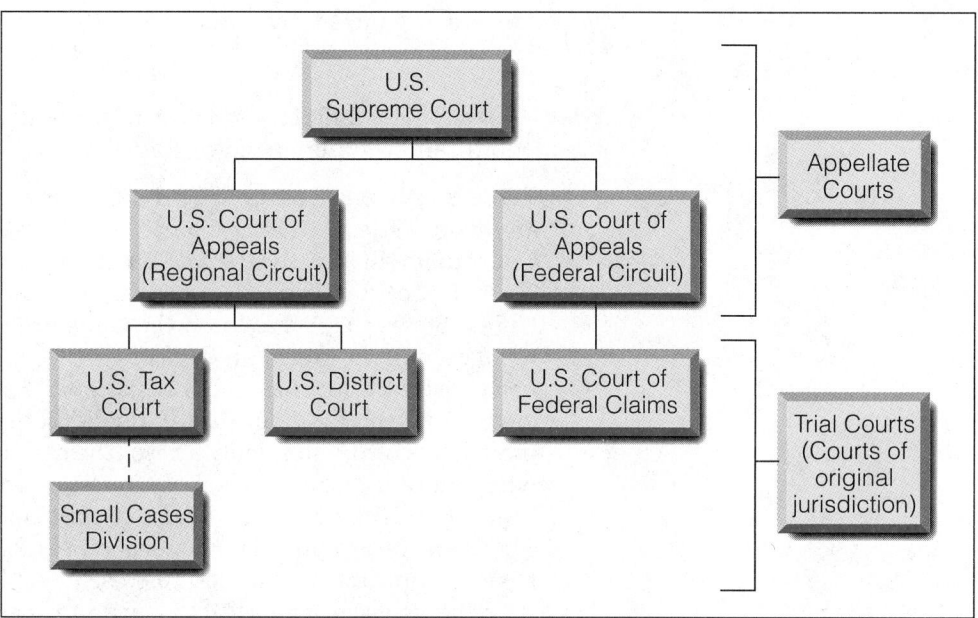

EXAMPLE 18

Gilbert operates a barber shop in which he employs eight barbers. To comply with the rules governing income tax and payroll tax withholdings, Gilbert wants to know whether the barbers working for him are employees or independent contractors. The proper procedure would be to request a determination letter on the status of the barbers from the appropriate District Director. ▼

JUDICIAL SOURCES OF THE TAX LAW

The Judicial Process in General. After a taxpayer has exhausted some or all of the remedies available within the IRS (no satisfactory settlement has been reached at the agent or at the conference level discussed in Chapter 16), the dispute can be taken to the Federal courts. The dispute is first considered by a court of original jurisdiction (known as a trial court) with any appeal (either by the taxpayer or the IRS) taken to the appropriate appellate court. In most situations, the taxpayer has a choice of any of four trial courts: a Federal District Court, the U.S. Court of Federal Claims, the Tax Court, or the Small Cases Division of the Tax Court. The trial and appellate court system for Federal tax litigation is illustrated in Figure 1–1.

The broken line between the Tax Court and the Small Cases Division indicates that there is no appeal from the Small Cases Division. Currently, the jurisdiction of the Small Cases Division of the Tax Court is limited to $10,000 or less. The proceedings of the Small Cases Division are informal, and its decisions are not precedents for any other court decision and are not reviewable by any higher court. Proceedings can be more timely and less expensive in the Small Cases Division.

American law, following English law, is frequently "made" by judicial decisions. Under the doctrine of *stare decisis*, each case (except in the Small Cases Division) has precedential value for future cases with the same controlling set of facts. Most Federal and state appellate court decisions and some decisions of trial courts are published. More than 4 million judicial opinions have been published in the United States; over 130,000 cases are published each year.[39] Published court

---

[39] Jacobstein, Mersky, and Dunn, *Fundamentals of Legal Research*, 6th edition (Westbury, N.Y.: The Foundation Press, 1994).

decisions are organized by jurisdiction (Federal or state) and level of court (appellate or trial).

Trial Courts.   The differences between the various trial courts (courts of original jurisdiction) can be summarized as follows:

- There is only one Court of Federal Claims and only one Tax Court, but there are many Federal District Courts. The taxpayer does not select the District Court that will hear the dispute but must sue in the one that has jurisdiction.
- The U.S. Court of Federal Claims has jurisdiction over any claim against the United States that is based on the Constitution, any Act of Congress, or any regulation of an executive department.
- Each District Court has only one judge, the Court of Federal Claims has 16 judges, and the Tax Court has 19 regular judges. In the case of the Tax Court, the whole court will review a case (the case is sent to court conference) only when more important or novel tax issues are involved. Many cases will be heard and decided by one of the 19 regular judges.
- The Court of Federal Claims meets most often in Washington, D.C., while a District Court meets at a prescribed seat for the particular district. Since each state has at least one District Court and many of the populous states have more, the inconvenience and expense of traveling for the taxpayer and counsel (present with many suits in the Court of Federal Claims) are largely eliminated. The Tax Court is officially based in Washington, D.C., but the various judges travel to different parts of the country and hear cases at predetermined locations and dates. This procedure eases the distance problem for the taxpayer, but it can mean a delay before the case comes to trial and is decided.
- The Tax Court hears only tax cases; the Court of Federal Claims and District Courts hear nontax litigation as well. This difference, as well as the fact that many Tax Court justices have been appointed from IRS or Treasury Department positions, has led some to conclude that the Tax Court has more expertise in tax matters.
- The only court in which a taxpayer can obtain a jury trial is a District Court. Juries can decide only questions of fact and not questions of law, however. Therefore taxpayers who choose the District Court route often do not request a jury trial. In this event, the judge will decide all issues. Note that a District Court decision is controlling only in the district in which the court has jurisdiction.
- Before the Court of Federal Claims or a District Court can have jurisdiction, the taxpayer must pay the tax deficiency assessed by the IRS and then sue for a refund. If the taxpayer wins (assuming no successful appeal by the Government), the tax paid plus appropriate interest will be recovered. Jurisdiction in the Tax Court, however, is usually obtained without first paying the assessed tax deficiency. In the event the taxpayer loses in the Tax Court (and no appeal is taken or any appeal is unsuccessful), the deficiency must be paid with accrued interest.
- Appeals from a District Court or a Tax Court decision are to the appropriate U.S. Court of Appeals. Appeals from the Court of Federal Claims go to the Court of Appeals for the Federal Circuit.

Some of the characteristics of the judicial system described above are summarized in Concept Summary 1–1.

Appellate Courts.   An appeal from a trial court goes to the Court of Appeals of appropriate jurisdiction. Generally, a three-judge panel hears a Court of Appeals

CONCEPT SUMMARY 1–1

Federal Judicial System

Issue	U.S. Tax Court	U.S. District Court	U.S. Court of Federal Claims
Number of judges per court	19*	1	16
Payment of deficiency before trial	No	Yes	Yes
Jury trial available	No	Yes	No
Types of disputes	Tax cases only	Most criminal/civil decisions	Claims against the United States
Jurisdiction	Nationwide	Location of taxpayer	Nationwide
Appeal route	U.S. Court of Appeals	U.S. Court of Appeals	U.S. Court of Appeals for the Federal Circuit

*There are also 14 special trial judges and 9 senior judges.

case, but occasionally the *full* court will decide more controversial conflicts. A jury trial is not available.

Figure 1–2 shows the geographical area within the jurisdiction of each Federal Court of Appeals.

If the Government loses at the trial court level (District Court, Tax Court, or Court of Federal Claims), it need not (and frequently does not) appeal. The fact that an appeal is not made, however, does not indicate that the IRS agrees with the result and will not litigate similar issues in the future.

The IRS may decide not to appeal for a number of reasons. First, the current litigation load may be heavy. As a consequence, the IRS may decide that available personnel should be assigned to other, more important cases. Second, the IRS may determine that this is not a good case to appeal. For example, the taxpayer may be in a sympathetic position, or the facts may be particularly strong in his or her favor. In such event, the IRS may wait to test the legal issues involved with a taxpayer who has a much weaker case. Third, if the appeal is from a District Court or the Tax Court, the Court of Appeals of jurisdiction could have some bearing on whether the IRS decides to pursue an appeal. Based on past experience and precedent, the IRS may conclude that the chance for success on a particular issue might be more promising in another Court of Appeals. The IRS will wait for a similar case to arise in a different jurisdiction.

District Courts, the Tax Court, and the Court of Federal Claims must abide by the precedents set by the Court of Appeals of jurisdiction. A particular Court of Appeals need not follow the decisions of another Court of Appeals. All courts, however, must follow the decisions of the U.S. Supreme Court.

The Tax Court is a national court, meaning that it hears and decides cases from all parts of the country. For many years, the Tax Court followed a policy of deciding cases based on what it thought the result should be, even when its decision might be appealed to a Court of Appeals that had previously decided a similar case differently.

Some years ago, this policy was changed. Now the Tax Court will still decide a case as it feels the law should be applied *only* if the Court of Appeals of

▼ FIGURE 1–2
The Federal Courts of Appeals

LEGEND
━━━ Circuit Boundaries
─── State Boundaries
∙∙∙∙ District Boundaries

ADMINISTRATIVE OFFICE OF THE UNITED STATES SUPREME COURTS
APRIL 1988

appropriate jurisdiction has not yet passed on the issue or has previously decided a similar case in accordance with the Tax Court's decision. If the Court of Appeals of appropriate jurisdiction has previously held squarely in point otherwise, the Tax Court will conform even though it disagrees with the holding.[40] This policy is known as the *Golsen* rule.

EXAMPLE 19

Gene lives in Texas and sues in the Tax Court on Issue A. The Fifth Court of Appeals, the appellate court of appropriate jurisdiction, has already decided, in a case involving similar facts but a different taxpayer, that Issue A should be resolved against the Government. Although the Tax Court feels that the Fifth Court of Appeals is wrong, under the *Golsen* rule, it will render judgment for Gene. Shortly thereafter, Beth, a resident of New York, in a comparable case, sues in the Tax Court on Issue A. Assume that the Second Court of Appeals, the appellate court of appropriate jurisdiction, has never expressed itself on Issue A. Presuming the Tax Court has not reconsidered its position on Issue A, it will decide against Beth. Thus, it is entirely possible for two taxpayers suing in the same court to end up with opposite results merely because they live in different parts of the country. ▼

Appeal to the U.S. Supreme Court is by Writ of **Certiorari.** If the Court accepts jurisdiction, it will grant the Writ (*Cert. Granted*). Most often, it will deny jurisdiction (*Cert. Denied*). For whatever reason or reasons, the Supreme Court rarely hears tax cases. The Court usually grants certiorari to resolve a conflict among the Courts of Appeals (e.g., two or more appellate courts have assumed

[40] *Jack E. Golsen*, 54 T.C. 742 (1970); see also *John A. Lardas*, 99 T.C. 490 (1992).

opposing positions on a particular issue) or when the tax issue is extremely important. The granting of a Writ of Certiorari indicates that at least four members of the Supreme Court believe that the issue is of sufficient importance to be heard by the full Court.

The role of appellate courts is limited to a review of the trial record compiled by the trial courts. Thus, the appellate process usually involves a determination of whether the trial court applied the proper law in arriving at its decision. Usually, an appellate court will not dispute a lower court's fact-finding determination.

An appeal can have any of a number of possible outcomes. The appellate court may approve (affirm) or disapprove (reverse) the lower court's finding, and it may also send the case back for further consideration (remand). When many issues are involved, it is not unusual to encounter a mixed result. Thus, the lower court may be affirmed (*aff'd.*) on Issue A and reversed (*rev'd.*) on Issue B, while Issue C is remanded (*rem'd.*) for additional fact finding.

When more than one judge is involved in the decision-making process, disagreement is not uncommon. In addition to the majority view, one or more judges may concur (agree with the result reached but not with some or all of the reasoning) or dissent (disagree with the result). In any one case, the majority view controls. But concurring and dissenting views can have influence on other courts or, at some subsequent date when the composition of the court has changed, even on the same court.

Judicial Citations—General. Having briefly described the judicial process, it is appropriate to consider the more practical problem of the relationship of case law to tax research. As previously noted, court decisions are an important source of tax law. The ability to cite a case and to locate it is therefore a must in working with the tax law. The usual pattern for a judicial citation is as follows: case name, volume number, reporter series, page or paragraph number, and court (where necessary).

Judicial Citations—The U.S. Tax Court. A good starting point is the U.S. Tax Court. The Tax Court issues two types of decisions: Regular and Memorandum. The distinction between the two involves both substance and form. In terms of substance, Memorandum decisions deal with situations necessitating only the application of already established principles of law. Regular decisions involve novel issues not previously resolved by the Court. In actual practice, this distinction is not always preserved. Not infrequently, Memorandum decisions will be encountered that appear to warrant Regular status and vice versa. At any rate, do not conclude that Memorandum decisions possess no value as precedents. Both represent the position of the Tax Court and, as such, can be relied upon.

The Regular and Memorandum decisions issued by the Tax Court also differ in form. The Memorandum decisions are published officially in mimeograph form only, but Regular decisions are published by the U.S. Government in a series called *Tax Court of the United States Reports*. Each volume of these reports covers a six-month period (January 1 through June 30 and July 1 through December 31) and is given a succeeding volume number. But, as was true of the *Cumulative Bulletin,* there is usually a time lag between the date a decision is rendered and the date it appears in bound form. A temporary citation may be necessary to help the researcher locate a recent Regular decision. Consider, for example, the temporary and permanent citations for *John D. Beatty,* a decision filed on April 17, 1996:

Temporary Citation	*John D. Beatty,* 106 T.C. —, No. 14 (1996). *Explanation:* Page number left blank because not yet known.
Permanent Citation	*John D. Beatty,* 106 T.C. 268 (1996). *Explanation:* Page number now available.

Both citations tell us that the case ultimately will appear in Volume 106 of the *Tax Court of the United States Reports*. But until this volume is bound and made available to the general public, the page number must be left blank. Instead, the temporary citation identifies the case as being the 14th Regular decision issued by the Tax Court since Volume 105 ended. With this information, the decision can be easily located in either of the special Tax Court services published by Commerce Clearing House (CCH) and by Research Institute of America (RIA—formerly by Prentice-Hall [P-H]). Once Volume 106 is released, the permanent citation can be substituted and the number of the case dropped.

Before 1943, the Tax Court was called the Board of Tax Appeals, and its decisions were published as the *United States Board of Tax Appeals Reports* (B.T.A.). These 47 volumes cover the period from 1924 to 1942. For example, the citation *Karl Pauli*, 11 B.T.A. 784 (1928) refers to the 11th volume of the *Board of Tax Appeals Reports*, page 784, issued in 1928.

Although Memorandum decisions are not published by the U.S. Government, they are published by CCH and by RIA (formerly by P-H). Consider, for example, the three different ways that *Walter H. Johnson* can be cited:

Walter H. Johnson, T.C.Memo. 1975–245
The 245th Memorandum decision issued by the Tax Court in 1975.

Walter H. Johnson, 34 TCM 1056
Page 1056 of Vol. 34 of the CCH *Tax Court Memorandum Decisions*.

Walter H. Johnson, P-H T.C.Mem.Dec. ¶75,245
Paragraph 75,245 of the P-H *T.C. Memorandum Decisions*.

Note that the third citation contains the same information as the first. Thus, ¶75,245 indicates the following information about the case: year 1975, 245th T.C.Memo. decision.[41]

Judicial Citations—The U.S. District Courts, Claims Court, and Courts of Appeals.
District Court, Claims Court (now Court of Federal Claims), Court of Appeals, and Supreme Court decisions dealing with Federal tax matters are reported in both the CCH *U.S. Tax Cases* (USTC) and the RIA (formerly P-H) *American Federal Tax Reports* (AFTR) series.

Federal District Court decisions, dealing with *both* tax and nontax issues, are also published by West Publishing Company in its Federal Supplement Series. The following examples illustrate how a District Court case can be cited in three different forms:

Simons-Eastern Co. v. U.S., 73–1 USTC ¶9279 (D.Ct.Ga., 1972). *Explanation:* Reported in the first volume of the *U.S. Tax Cases* (USTC) published by Commerce Clearing House for calendar year 1973 (73–1) and located at paragraph 9279 (¶9279).

Simons-Eastern Co. v. U.S., 31 AFTR2d 73–640 (D.Ct.Ga., 1972). *Explanation:* Reported in the 31st volume of the second series of the *American Federal Tax Reports* (AFTR2d) published by Prentice-Hall (now RIA) and beginning on page 640. The "73" preceding the page number indicates the year the case was published but is a designation used only in recent decisions.

---

[41] In this text, the Research Institute of America (RIA) citation for Memorandum decisions of the U.S. Tax Court is omitted. Thus, *Walter H. Johnson* would be cited as: 34 TCM 1056, T.C.Memo. 1975–245. Prentice-Hall is now owned by RIA. This edition continues to use the Prentice-Hall name in some instances of older volumes.

Simons-Eastern Co. v. U.S., 354 F.Supp. 1003 (D.Ct.Ga., 1972). *Explanation:* Reported in the 354th volume of the *Federal Supplement Series* (F.Supp.) published by West Publishing Company and beginning on page 1003.

In all of the preceding citations, note that the name of the case is the same (Simons-Eastern Co. being the taxpayer), as is the reference to the Federal District Court of Georgia (D.Ct.Ga.,) and the year the decision was rendered (1972).[42]

Beginning in October of 1982, decisions of the Claims Court are reported by West Publishing Company in a series designated *Federal Claims Reporter*. Thus, the Claims Court decision in *Recchie v. U.S.* appears as follows:

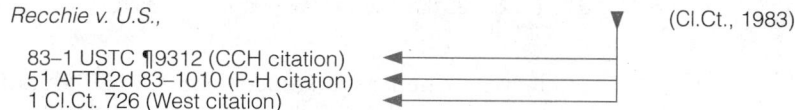

Recchie v. U.S.,   (Cl.Ct., 1983)

83–1 USTC ¶9312 (CCH citation)
51 AFTR2d 83–1010 (P-H citation)
1 Cl.Ct. 726 (West citation)

Beginning October 30, 1992, the Claims Court underwent a further name change. The new designation, U.S. Court of Federal Claims, began with Volume 27 of the former *Cl.Ct.* (West citation), now abbreviated as *Fed.Cl.*

Decisions of the Courts of Appeals are published in a West Publishing Company reporter designated as the Federal Second Series (F.2d). Beginning in October of 1993, the West Publishing Company reporter went to a Federal Third Series (F.3d). Illustrations of the different forms follow:

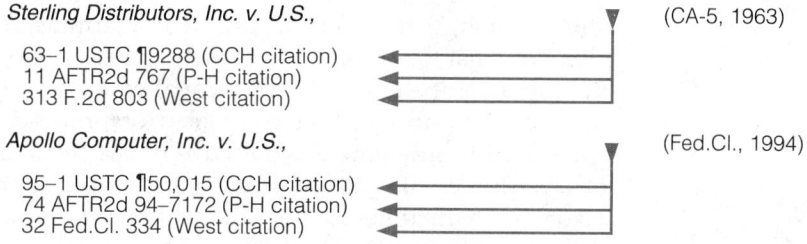

Sterling Distributors, Inc. v. U.S.,   (CA-5, 1963)

63–1 USTC ¶9288 (CCH citation)
11 AFTR2d 767 (P-H citation)
313 F.2d 803 (West citation)

Apollo Computer, Inc. v. U.S.,   (Fed.Cl., 1994)

95–1 USTC ¶50,015 (CCH citation)
74 AFTR2d 94–7172 (P-H citation)
32 Fed.Cl. 334 (West citation)

Note that *Sterling Distributors, Inc.* is a decision rendered by the Fifth Court of Appeals in 1963 (CA–5, 1963) while *Apollo Computer, Inc. v. U.S.* was rendered in 1994 by the U.S. Court of Federal Claims.

If the IRS loses in a decision, it may indicate whether it agrees or disagrees with the results reached by the Court by publishing an **acquiescence** ("A" or "Acq.") or **nonacquiescence** ("NA" or "Nonacq."), respectively. The acquiescence or nonacquiescence is published in the *Internal Revenue Bulletin* and the *Cumulative Bulletin* as an *Action on Decision*. The IRS can retroactively revoke an acquiescence or nonacquiescence. Originally, acquiescences and nonacquiescences were published only for Regular U.S. Tax Court decisions, but since 1991 the IRS has expanded its acquiescence program to include other civil tax cases where guidance is helpful.

Judicial Citations—The U.S. Supreme Court.   Like all other Federal tax cases (except those rendered by the U.S. Tax Court), Supreme Court decisions are published by Commerce Clearing House in the USTCs and by Research Institute of America (formerly P-H) in the AFTRs. The U.S. Government Printing Office

---

[42] In this text, the case will be cited in the following form: *Simons-Eastern Co. v. U.S.*, 73–1 USTC ¶9279, 31 AFTR2d 73–640, 354 F.Supp. 1003 (D.Ct.Ga., 1972).

also publishes these decisions in the *United States Supreme Court Reports* (U.S.) as does West Publishing Company in its *Supreme Court Reporter* (S.Ct.) and the Lawyer's Co-operative Publishing Company in its *United States Reports, Lawyer's Edition* (L.Ed.). The following illustrates the different ways the same decision can be cited:

U.S. v. The Donruss Co.,   (USSC, 1969)

    69–1 USTC ¶9167 (CCH citation)
    23 AFTR2d 69–418 (P-H citation)
    89 S.Ct. 501 (West citation)
    393 U.S. 297 (U.S. Government Printing Office citation)
    21 L.Ed.2d 495 (Lawyer's Co-operative Publishing Co. citation)

The parenthetical reference (USSC, 1969) identifies the decision as having been rendered by the U.S. Supreme Court in 1969. The citations given in this text for Supreme Court decisions will be limited to the CCH (USTC), the RIA or P-H for older volumes (AFTR), and the West (S.Ct.) versions.

WORKING WITH THE TAX LAW— TAX RESEARCH

Tax research is the method used to determine the best available solution to a situation that possesses tax consequences. In other words, it is the process of finding a competent and professional conclusion to a tax problem. The problem may originate from either completed or proposed transactions. In the case of a completed transaction, the objective of the research is to determine the tax result of what has already taken place. For example, is the expenditure incurred by the taxpayer deductible or not deductible for tax purposes? When dealing with proposed transactions, the tax research process is concerned with the determination of possible tax consequences. To the extent that tax research leads to a choice of alternatives or otherwise influences the future actions of the taxpayer, it becomes the key to effective tax planning.

Tax research involves the following procedures:

- Identifying and refining the problem.
- Locating the appropriate tax law sources.
- Assessing the validity of the tax law sources.
- Arriving at the solution or at alternative solutions while giving due consideration to nontax factors.
- Effectively communicating the solution to the taxpayer or the taxpayer's representative.
- Following up on the solution (where appropriate) in light of new developments.

This process is depicted schematically in Figure 1–3. The broken lines indicate steps of particular interest when tax research is directed toward proposed, rather than completed, transactions.

IDENTIFYING THE PROBLEM

Problem identification starts with a compilation of the relevant facts involved. In this regard, *all* of the facts that might have a bearing on the problem must be

▼ FIGURE 1–3
Tax Research Process

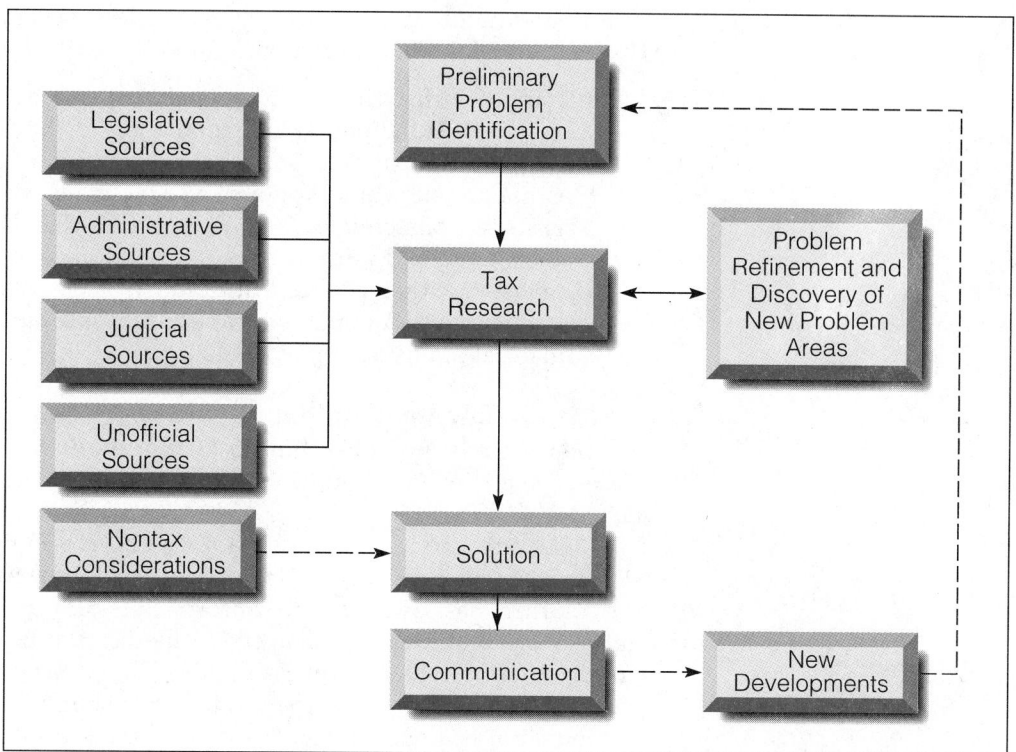

gathered as any omission could modify the solution reached. To illustrate, consider what appears to be a very simple problem.

EXAMPLE 20

A widowed mother advances $52,000 to her son in 1990 to enable him to attend a private college. Seven years later, the mother claims a bad debt deduction for $42,000 that the son has not repaid. The problem: Is the mother entitled to a bad debt deduction? ▼

Refining the Problem.   Before a bad debt deduction can arise, it must be established that a debt really existed. In a related-party setting (e.g., mother and son), the IRS may contend that the original advance was not a loan but, in reality, a gift. Of key significance in this regard would be whether the lender (the mother) had an honest and real expectation of payment by the borrower (the son).[43] Indicative of this repayment expectation is whether the parties preserved the formalities of a loan, including the following:

- The borrower issued a written instrument evidencing the obligation.
- Interest was provided for as part of the loan arrangement.
- The note specified a set due date.
- Collateral was available to the lender in the event of default by the borrower.[44]

The presence of some or all of these formalities does not, however, guarantee that a bona fide loan will be found. By the same token, the absence of some or all of the formalities does not make the advance a gift. Applying the formalities criteria to Example 20 is not possible since key facts (e.g., the presence or absence

---

[43] *William F. Mercil,* 24 T.C. 1150 (1955), and *Evans Clark,* 18 T.C. 780 (1952), *aff'd.* 53–2 USTC ¶9452, 44 AFTR 70, 205 F.2d 353 (CA–2, 1953).

[44] *Arthur T. Davidson,* 37 TCM 725, T.C.Memo. 1978–167.

of a written note) are not given. Nevertheless, several inferences might be made that lead to a loan interpretation:

- It appears that the son has repaid at least $10,000 of the $52,000 that he borrowed. If the parties intended a gift of the full amount of the loan, why was partial repayment made?
- Although one would not expect a son on his way to college to have assets to serve as collateral for a loan, the fact that he was obtaining additional education could reinforce any expectation of repayment. In most situations, a person with a college education will possess a higher earning potential than one without such education. This education would improve the son's financial ability to repay the loan.

Further Refinement of the Problem.   It may be impossible to determine whether the advance constitutes a loan or a gift with any degree of certainty. In either event, however, the tax consequences of each possibility must be ascertained.

If the advance is determined to be a gift, it is subject to the Federal gift tax.[45] Whether or not a gift tax results depends upon how much of the unified tax credit the mother has available to absorb the gift tax on $42,000 [$52,000 (total gift) – $10,000 (annual exclusion)].[46] Whether the transfer results in a gift tax or not, it must be reported on Form 709 (United States Gift Tax Return) since the amount of the gift exceeds the annual exclusion.

Even if it is assumed that the mother made a gift to the son in 1990, does not the intervention of seven years preclude the IRS from assessing any gift tax that might be due as a result of the transfer?[47] Further research indicates that the statute of limitations on assessments does not begin to run when a tax return is not filed.[48]

To complete the picture, what are the tax consequences if the advance is treated as a loan? Aside from the bad debt deduction aspects (covered later in the chapter), the tax law provides more immediate tax ramifications:[49]

- If interest is not provided for, it is imputed with the following effect:
  a. The lender (the mother) must recognize interest income as to the imputed value.
  b. Since the lender has not received the interest, she is deemed to have made a gift of the interest to the borrower.
  c. The borrower (son) may be entitled to deduct (as an itemized expense) in some tax years a portion of the amount of interest deemed paid to the lender (mother).

- If interest is provided for but the rate is lower than market (as determined by the yield on certain U.S. government securities), the differential is treated as noted above.
- For gift loans of $100,000 or less, the imputed element cannot exceed the net investment income of the borrower.

---

[45] The transfer does not come within the unlimited gift tax exclusion of § 2503(e)(2)(A) since the mother did not pay the amount directly to an educational institution. Besides, the exclusion covers only tuition payments and not other costs attendant on going to college (e.g., room and board).

[46] The tax, in turn, depends upon the amount of taxable gifts the mother has made in the past. For a discussion of the mechanics of the Federal gift tax, see Chapter 17.

[47] Throughout the discussion of Example 20, the assumption has been made that if a gift occurred, it took place in 1990. That assumption need not be the case. Depending upon the mother's intent, she could have decided to make a gift of the unpaid balance anytime after the loan was made (e.g., 1991, 1992, etc.).

[48] See § 6501(c)(3) and the discussion of the statute of limitations in Chapter 16.

[49] § 7872.

LOCATING THE APPROPRIATE TAX LAW SOURCES

6 LEARNING OBJECTIVE
Locate tax law sources.

Once the problem is clearly defined, what is the next step? Although the next step is a matter of individual judgment, most tax research begins with the index volume of the tax service or a key word search on an on-line tax service (see the subsequent discussion of Electronic Tax Research). If the problem is not complex, the researcher may bypass the tax service and turn directly to the Internal Revenue Code and the Treasury Regulations. For the beginner, this latter procedure saves time and will solve many of the more basic problems. If the researcher does not have a personal copy of the Code or Regulations, resorting to the appropriate volume(s) of a tax service is necessary. Several of the major tax services publish paperback editions of the Code and Treasury Regulations that can be purchased at modest prices. These editions are usually revised twice each year. The following major services are available:

> *Standard Federal Tax Reporter*, Commerce Clearing House.
>
> *United States Tax Reporter*, Research Institute of America (entitled *Federal Taxes* prior to July 1992).
>
> *Mertens Law of Federal Income Taxation*, Callaghan and Co.
>
> *Federal Tax Coordinator 2d*, Research Institute of America.
>
> *Tax Management Portfolios*, Bureau of National Affairs.
>
> Rabkin and Johnson, *Federal Income, Gift and Estate Taxation*, Matthew Bender, Inc.
>
> CCH's *Federal Tax Service*, Commerce Clearing House.

Working with the Tax Services.   In this text, it is not feasible to teach the use of any particular tax service because this knowledge can be obtained only by practice. The representatives of the various tax services provide users with printed booklets and individual instruction on the use of the services. However, several important observations about the use of tax services cannot be overemphasized. First, never forget to check for current developments. The main text of any service is revised too infrequently to permit reliance on that portion as the *latest* word on any subject. Where such current developments can be found depends on which service is being used. The CCH service contains a special volume devoted to current matters. Second, when dealing with a tax service synopsis of a Treasury Department pronouncement or a judicial decision, remember there is no substitute for the original source.

To illustrate, do not base a conclusion solely on a tax service's commentary on *Simons-Eastern Co. v. U.S.*[50] If the case is vital to the research, look it up. The facts of the decision may be distinguishable from those in the problem being researched. This is not to say that the case synopsis contained in the tax service is wrong; it might just be misleading or incomplete.

Tax Periodicals.   Additional sources of tax information are the various tax periodicals. The easiest way to locate a journal article on a particular tax problem is through CCH's *Federal Tax Articles*. This six-volume service includes a subject index, a Code Section number index, and an author's index. In addition, the RIA tax service has a topical "Index to Tax Articles" section that is organized using that service's paragraph index system. Also, beginning in 1992, *The Accounting & Tax Index* is available in three quarterly issues plus a cumulative year-end volume

---

[50] Cited in Footnote 42.

covering all four quarters. The original *Accountant's Index* started in 1921 and ended in 1991.

The following are some of the more useful tax periodicals:

The Journal of Taxation
Tax Law Review
Taxation for Accountants
Journal of Corporate Taxation
Estate Planning
Journal of Partnership Taxation
Warren, Gorham and Lamont
31 St. James Avenue
Boston, MA 02116–4112

The Tax Executive
1300 North 17th Street
Arlington, VA 22209

The Practical Accountant
11 Penn Plaza
New York, NY 10001

Trusts and Estates
6151 Powers Ferry Rd. NW
Atlanta, GA 30339–2941

TAXES—The Tax Magazine
CCH, Inc.
2700 Lake Cook Road
Riverwood, IL 60015

National Tax Journal
5310 East Main Street
Columbus, OH 43215

The Tax Adviser
A.I.C.P.A.
1211 Avenue of the Americas
New York, NY 10036

The Tax Lawyer
American Bar Association
750 N. Lake Shore Drive
Chicago, IL 60611

Journal of the American Taxation Association
American Accounting Association
5717 Bessie Drive
Sarasota, FL 33583

Oil and Gas Tax Quarterly
Matthew Bender & Co.
2 Park Avenue
New York, NY 10016

The International Tax Journal
Panel Publishers
14 Plaza Road
Greenvale, NY 11548

Tax Notes
6830 Fairfax Drive
Arlington, VA 22213

ASSESSING THE VALIDITY OF TAX LAW SOURCES

7　Learning Objective
Assess the validity and weight of tax law sources.

After a source has been located, the next step is to assess the source in light of the problem at hand. Proper assessment involves careful interpretation of the tax law and consideration of the law's relevance and validity.

Interpreting the Internal Revenue Code. The language of the Code can be extremely difficult to comprehend. For example, a subsection [§ 341(e)] relating to collapsible corporations contains *one* sentence of more than 450 words (twice as many as in the Gettysburg Address). Within this same subsection is another sentence of 300 words.

The Code must be read carefully for restrictive language such as *"at least* 80 percent" and *"more* than 80 percent", or *"less* than 50 percent" and *"exceeds* 50 percent." It also makes a great deal of difference, for example, whether two or more clauses are connected by *"or"* or by *"and."*

If an answer is not in the Code, it may be necessary to resort to the Regulations and judicial decisions. In 1969, Congress directed the Treasury Department to promulgate Regulations under § 385 to distinguish corporate debt from corporate equity. As of yet, there are no Regulations under § 385. The researcher, therefore, must resort to past judicial decisions for a definition of debt.

Sometimes the Code directs the researcher elsewhere for the answer. For example, § 162(c) refers to the Foreign Corrupt Practices Act for purposes of determining when payments to foreign officials are deductible.

Cross-referencing between Code Sections is often poor or nonexistent. Code Sections are enacted at different times by Congresses that are operating under stringent deadlines. Consequently, a certain lack of integration within the Code is frequently apparent.

Definitions vary from one Code Section to another. For example, § 267 disallows losses between related parties and includes brothers and sisters in the definition of related parties. Not so with § 318, which deals with the definition of related parties as to certain stock redemptions.

Assessing the Validity of a Treasury Regulation.   Treasury Regulations are often said to have the force and effect of law. This statement is certainly true for most Regulations, but some judicial decisions have held a Regulation or a portion thereof invalid. Usually, this is done on the grounds that the Regulation is contrary to the intent of Congress.

Keep the following observations in mind when assessing the validity of a Regulation:

- In a challenge, the burden of proof is on the taxpayer to show that the Regulation is wrong. However, a court may invalidate a Regulation that varies from the language of the statute and has no support in the Committee Reports.
- If the taxpayer loses the challenge, the negligence penalty may be imposed. This accuracy-related provision deals with the "intentional disregard of rules and regulations" on the part of the taxpayer and is explained further in Chapter 16.
- Some Regulations merely reprint or rephrase what Congress has stated in its Committee Reports issued in connection with the enactment of tax legislation. Such Regulations are "hard and solid" and almost impossible to overturn because they clearly reflect the intent of Congress.
- In some Code Sections, Congress has given to the "Secretary or his delegate" the authority to prescribe Regulations to carry out the details of administration or to otherwise complete the operating rules. Under such circumstances, it could almost be said that Congress is delegating its legislative powers to the Treasury Department. Regulations issued pursuant to this type of authority truly possess the force and effect of law and are often called "legislative" Regulations. They are to be distinguished from "interpretative" Regulations, which purport to explain the meaning of a particular Code Section. Examples of legislative Regulations are those dealing with consolidated returns issued under §§ 1501 through 1505. As a further example, note the authority granted to the Treasury Department by § 385 to issue Regulations setting forth guidelines on when corporate debt can be reclassified as equity (see Chapter 3).

Assessing the Validity of Other Administrative Sources of the Tax Law. Revenue Rulings issued by the IRS carry less weight than Treasury Department Regulations. Rulings are important, however, in that they reflect the position of the IRS on tax matters. In any dispute with the IRS on the interpretation of tax law, taxpayers should expect agents to follow the results reached in any applicable rulings.

Actions on Decisions further tell the taxpayer the IRS's reaction to certain court decisions. Recall that the IRS follows a practice of either acquiescing (agreeing) or nonacquiescing (not agreeing) with court decisions where guidance may be helpful. This practice does not mean that a particular decision has no value if the IRS has nonacquiesced in the result. It does, however, indicate that the IRS will continue to litigate the issue involved.

The validity of individual letter rulings issued by the IRS is discussed in Chapter 16.

Assessing the Validity of Judicial Sources of the Tax Law.   The judicial process as it relates to the formulation of tax law has been described. How much reliance can be placed on a particular decision depends upon the following variables:

- The level of the court. A decision rendered by a trial court (e.g., a Federal District Court) carries less weight than one issued by an appellate court (e.g., the Fifth Court of Appeals). Unless Congress changes the Code, decisions by the U.S. Supreme Court represent the last word on any tax issue.
- The legal residence of the taxpayer. If, for example, a taxpayer lives in Texas, a decision of the Fifth Court of Appeals means more than one rendered by the Second Court of Appeals. This is true because any appeal from a U.S. District Court or the U.S. Tax Court would be to the Fifth Court of Appeals and not to the Second Court of Appeals.
- Whether the decision represents the weight of authority on the issue. In other words, is it supported by the results reached by other courts?
- The outcome or status of the decision on appeal. For example, was the decision appealed and, if so, with what result?

In connection with the last two variables, the use of a manual citator or a computer search is invaluable to tax research.[51] The use of a manual citator is described in the last section of this chapter.

Assessing the Validity of Other Sources.   Primary sources of tax law include the Constitution, legislative history materials, statutes, treaties, Treasury Regulations, IRS pronouncements, and judicial decisions. The IRS regards only primary sources as substantial authority. However, reference to secondary materials such as legal periodicals, treatises, legal opinions, general counsel memoranda, technical advice memoranda, and written determinations can be useful. In general, secondary sources are not authority.

Although the statement that the IRS regards only primary sources as substantial authority is generally true, there is one exception. The IRS has expanded the list of substantial authority for purposes of the accuracy-related penalty in § 6662 to include a number of secondary materials (e.g., letter rulings, general counsel and technical advice memoranda, and the "Blue Book").[52] The "Blue Book" is the general explanation of tax legislation prepared by the Joint Committee on Taxation of the U.S. Congress.

As under former § 6661, "authority" does not include conclusions reached in treatises, legal periodicals, and opinions rendered by tax professionals.

---

[51] The major manual citators are published by Commerce Clearing House, RIA, and Shepard's Citations, Inc.

[52] Notice 90–20, 1990–1 C.B. 328, part V (A).

ARRIVING AT THE SOLUTION OR AT ALTERNATIVE SOLUTIONS

Returning to Example 20, assume the parties decide that the loan approach can be justified from the factual situation involved. Does this assumption lead to a bad debt deduction for the mother? Before this question can be resolved, the loan needs to be classified as either a business or a nonbusiness debt. One of the reasons the classification is important is that a nonbusiness bad debt cannot be deducted until it becomes entirely worthless. Unlike a business debt, no deduction for partial worthlessness is allowed.[53]

It is very likely that the loan the mother made in 1990 falls into the nonbusiness category. Unless exceptional circumstances exist (e.g., the lender was in the trade or business of lending money), loans in a related-party setting are treated as nonbusiness. The probability is high that the mother would be relegated to nonbusiness bad debt status.

The mother has the burden of proving that the remaining unpaid balance of $42,000 is *entirely* worthless.[54] In this connection, what collection effort, if any, has the mother made? But would any such collection effort be fruitless? Perhaps the son is insolvent, ill, unemployed, or has disappeared for parts unknown.

Even if the debt is entirely worthless, one further issue remains to be resolved. In what year did the worthlessness occur? It could be, for example, that worthlessness took place in a year before it was claimed.[55]

A clear-cut answer may not be possible as to a bad debt deduction for the mother in year 1997 (seven years after the advance was made). This uncertainty does not detract from the value of the research. Often a guarded judgment is the best possible solution to a tax problem.

COMMUNICATING TAX RESEARCH

Once the problem has been researched adequately, a memo setting forth the result may need to be prepared. The form such a memo takes could depend on a number of considerations. For example, is any particular procedure or format recommended for tax research memos by either an employer or an instructor? Is the memo to be given directly to the client, or will it first pass to the preparer's employer? Whatever form it takes, a good research memo should contain the following elements:

- A clear statement of the issue.
- In more complex situations, a short review of the factual pattern that raises the issue.
- A review of the tax law sources (e.g., Code, Regulations, Rulings, judicial authority).
- Any assumptions made in arriving at the solution.
- The solution recommended and the logic or reasoning in its support.
- The references consulted in the research process.

In short, a good tax memo should tell the reader what was researched, the results of that research, and the justification for the recommendation made.

Figures 1–4, 1–5, and 1–6 present a sample client letter and memoranda for the tax files.

---

[53] See § 166 and the discussion on "Investor Losses" in Chapter 3.
[54] Compare *John K. Sexton*, 48 TCM 512, T.C.Memo. 1984–360, with *Stewart T. Oatman*, 45 TCM 214, T.C.Memo. 1982–684.

[55] *Ruth Wertheim Smith*, 34 TCM 1474, T.C.Memo. 1975–339.

▼ **FIGURE 1–4**
Client Letter

Hoffman, Raabe, Smith, & Maloney, CPAs
50 Kellogg Blvd.
St. Paul, MN 55164

August 30, 1997

Homer Lynch
111 Avenue G
Lakeway, MN 55164

Dear Mr. Lynch:

This letter is in response to your request that we review the tax result of a gift made in 1976 and determine the unified tax credit available upon Sonya's death in 1997. Our conclusions are based upon the facts as outlined in your letter of August 14.

The gift of $66,000 made to your son on October 1, 1976, did not result in any Federal gift tax for several reasons. First, your wife, Sonya, elected to split the gift with you. Second, both of you chose to use the $30,000 specific exemption that was in effect at that time. As a consequence, the transfer was treated as follows:

	Homer	Sonya
Amount of gift made	$33,000	$33,000
Annual exclusion available in 1976	(3,000)	(3,000)
Specific exemption used	(30,000)	(30,000)
Taxable gift	$–0–	$–0–

When the specific exemption is used after September 8, 1976, an adjustment must be made to the unified transfer tax credit. The adjustment requires that the credit be reduced by 20 percent of the exemption used.

When Sonya died in 1997, the credit available to her estate was not the standard $192,800. Because of the adjustment required, the credit must be reduced by $6,000 (20% × $30,000 specific exemption previously used). Her credit, then, is $186,800 ($192,800 – $6,000).

Should you desire more information or a further clarification of our conclusions, do not hesitate to contact me.

Sincerely,

James Randolph, CPA
Partner

▼ **FIGURE 1–5**
Tax File Memorandum

August 16, 1997
TAX FILE MEMORANDUM
FROM: James Randolph
SUBJECT: Homer Lynch
          Engagement Issues
Today, I talked to Homer Lynch with regard to his letter of August 14, 1997.

On October 1, 1976, Homer made a gift of $66,000 to his son. Homer's wife, Sonya, elected to split the gift, and each elected to use the full $30,000 specific exemption. Sonya died this year, and Homer is the executor of her estate.
ISSUE: Was any gift tax due on the 1976 transfer? How much unified transfer tax credit can Homer claim when he files a Form 706 for Sonya's estate? I told Homer that we would have the answers to these questions within a month.

▼ **FIGURE 1–6**
Tax File Memorandum

August 30, 1997
TAX FILE MEMORANDUM
FROM: James Randolph
SUBJECT: Homer Lynch
           Engagement Issues
Homer made a gift of $66,000 to his son on October 1, 1976. No gift tax resulted because Homer's wife, Sonya, elected (under § 2513) to split the gift. This election made two annual exclusions available ($3,000 each) and allowed the use of the specific exemptions ($30,000 each). As neither spouse had a taxable gift ($33,000 – $3,000 – $30,000 = $0), no gift tax resulted.

    What is the unified tax credit available to Sonya's estate when she dies in 1997? Section 2010(b) requires that the credit be reduced by 20 percent of the specific exemption used after September 8, 1976. Does this adjustment apply to a nonowner donor spouse such as Sonya? *Estate of James O. Gawne*, 80 T.C. 478 (1983), makes clear that it does.

WORKING WITH THE TAX LAW— TAX PLANNING

8   **LEARNING OBJECTIVE**
Make use of various tax planning procedures.

Tax research and tax planning are inseparable. The primary purpose of effective tax planning is to reduce the taxpayer's total tax bill. This reduction does not mean that the course of action selected must produce the lowest possible tax under the circumstances. The minimization of tax payments must be considered in the context of the legitimate business goals of the taxpayer.

A secondary objective of effective tax planning is to reduce, defer, or eliminate the tax. Specifically, this objective aims to accomplish one or more results. Some possibilities are eradicating the tax entirely, eliminating the tax in the current year, deferring the receipt of income, and proliferating taxpayers (i.e., forming partnerships and corporations or making lifetime gifts to family members). Further examples include eluding double taxation, avoiding ordinary income, or creating, increasing, or accelerating deductions. However, this second objective should be pursued with considerable reservation. Although the maxim "A bird in the hand is worth two in the bush" has general validity, the rule frequently breaks down. For example, a tax election in one year may accomplish a current reduction in taxes, but it could saddle future years with a disadvantageous tax position.

NONTAX CONSIDERATIONS

There is a danger that tax motivations may take on a significance that does not conform to the true values involved. In other words, tax considerations can operate to impair the exercise of sound business judgment. Thus, the tax planning process can lead to ends that are socially and economically objectionable. Unfortunately, a tendency exists for planning to move toward the opposing extremes of either not enough or too much emphasis on tax considerations. The happy medium is a balance that recognizes the significance of taxes, but not beyond the point at which planning detracts from the exercise of good business judgment.

The remark is often made that a good rule to follow is to refrain from pursuing any course of action that would not be followed were it not for certain tax considerations. This statement is not entirely correct, but it does illustrate the desirability of preventing business logic from being "sacrificed at the altar of tax planning."

TAX AVOIDANCE AND TAX EVASION

A fine line exists between legal tax planning and illegal tax planning—tax avoidance versus tax evasion. Tax avoidance is merely tax minimization through legal techniques. In this sense, tax avoidance becomes the proper objective of all tax planning. Though eliminating or reducing taxes is also a goal of tax evasion, the term implies the use of subterfuge and fraud as a means to this end. Perhaps because common goals are involved, popular usage has blurred the distinction between the two concepts. Consequently, the association of tax avoidance with tax evasion has kept some taxpayers from properly taking advantage of planning possibilities. The now-classic words of Judge Learned Hand in *Commissioner v. Newman* reflect the true values a taxpayer should have:

> Over and over again courts have said that there is nothing sinister in so arranging one's affairs as to keep taxes as low as possible. Everybody does so, rich or poor; and all do right, for nobody owes any public duty to pay more than the law demands: taxes are enforced extractions, not voluntary contributions. To demand more in the name of morals is mere cant.[56]

FOLLOW-UP PROCEDURES

Tax planning usually involves a proposed (as opposed to a completed) transaction and is based upon the continuing validity of the advice resulting from tax research. A change in the tax law (either legislative, administrative, or judicial) could alter the original conclusion. Additional research may be necessary to test the solution in light of current developments.

Under what circumstances does a tax practitioner have an obligation to inform a client as to changes in the tax law? The legal and ethical aspects of this question are discussed in Chapter 16.

TAX PLANNING—A PRACTICAL APPLICATION

Returning to the facts in Example 20, what should be done to help protect the mother's bad debt deduction?

- All formalities of a loan should be present (e.g., written instrument, definite and realistic due date).
- Upon default, the lender (mother) should make a reasonable effort to collect from the borrower (son). If not, the mother should be in a position to explain why any such effort would be to no avail.
- If interest is provided for, it should be paid.
- Any interest paid (or imputed under § 7872) should be recognized as income by the mother.
- Because of the annual exclusion of $10,000, it appears doubtful that actual (or imputed) interest would necessitate the filing of a Federal gift tax return by the mother. But should one be due, it should be filed.
- If § 7872 applies (not enough or no interest is provided for), the son should keep track of his net investment income. This record keeping is important since the income the mother must recognize may be limited by this amount.

Throughout this text, each chapter concludes with observations on Tax Planning Considerations. Such observations are not all-inclusive but are intended

---

[56] 47–1 USTC ¶9175, 35 AFTR 857, 159 F.2d 848 (CA–2, 1947).

to illustrate some of the ways in which the material in the chapter can be effectively used to minimize taxes.

ELECTRONIC TAX RESEARCH

9 LEARNING OBJECTIVE
Have an awareness of computer-assisted tax research.

The computer is being used more frequently in the day-to-day practice of tax professionals, students, and educators. Many software vendors offer tax return software programs for individual, corporate, partnership, and fiduciary returns. The use of computers, however, is not limited to batch-processed tax returns. Computer timesharing for quantitative tax and problem-solving planning and calculations has added a new dimension to tax research.

Computer-based tax research tools now have a prominent position in the tax practice. Electronic tax resources allow the tax library to reflect the tax law with its dynamic and daily changes. Using electronic means to locate tax law sources is not a substitute, however, for developing and maintaining a thorough knowledge of the tax law and applying logical and analytical review in addressing open tax research issues.

Accessing tax documents through electronic sources offers several important advantages over a strictly paper-based approach to the task:

- Materials are available to the practitioner more quickly through an electronic system, which eliminates delays by streamlining the composition and proofreading, production, and distribution of the new materials.
- Some tax documents, such as so-called slip opinions of trial-level courts and interviews with policymakers, are available only through electronic sources.
- Commercial subscriptions to electronic tax services are likely to provide, at little or no cost, additional tax law sources to which the researcher would not have access through stand-alone purchases of traditional material. For example, the full texts of private letter rulings are quite costly to acquire in a paper-based format, but electronic publishers may bundle the rulings with other materials for a reasonable cost.

Comparing the cost of paper and electronic tax research materials is difficult, especially when the practitioner uses hardware, including workstations and communications equipment, that is already in place and employed elsewhere in the practice. Over time, though, it is clear that the convenience, cost, and reliability of electronic research tools will make them the dominant means of finding and analyzing tax law.

Using Electronic Services.   Tax researchers often use electronic sources to find the tax law. Usually, the law is found using one of the following approaches:

- *Search* various databases using key words that are likely to be found in the underlying documents, as written by Congress, the judiciary, or administrative sources.
- *Link* to tax documents for which all or part of the proper citation is known.
- *Browse* the tax databases, examining various tables of contents and indexes in a traditional manner, or using cross-references in the documents to jump from one tax law source to another.

Virtually all of the major commercial tax publishers, and some of the primary sources of the law itself (e.g., the Supreme Court and some of the Courts of Appeals), now provide tax materials in electronic formats. Competitive pressures are forcing tax practitioners to become computer literate. Thus, the user-friendliness of the best of the tax search software is of great benefit to both the daily and the occasional user.

Service	Description
CCH ACCESS	Includes the CCH tax service, primary sources including treaties, and other subscription materials. 10–20 disks.
RIA OnPoint	Includes the RIA topical *Coordinator* and the annotated tax service formerly provided by Prentice-Hall. The citator has elaborate document-linking features, and major tax treatises also are provided. 1–10 disks.
WESTLAW	Code, Regulations, *Cumulative Bulletins*, cases, citators, and editorial material. About 12 disks.
Kleinrock's	A single disk with all tax statute, administrative, and judicial law. Another single disk provides tax forms and instructions for Federal and state jurisdictions.

CD-ROM Services.   The CD has been a major source of electronic tax data for about a decade. Every year data compression techniques continue to allow more tax materials to fit on a single disk. CCH, RIA, WESTLAW, and others offer vast tax libraries to the practitioner. Often these resources are available in conjunction with a subscription to traditional paper-based resources and are accompanied by newsletters, training seminars, and ongoing technical support.

At its best, a CD-based tax library forms the archival data that make up the permanent, core library of tax documents. For about $200 a year, the tax CDs are updated quarterly and provide more comprehensive tax resources than the researcher is ever likely to need. In contrast, a paper-based library of a decade ago cost perhaps $20,000 to establish, and $10,000 per year in perpetuity to maintain. If the library is contained on a small number of disks, portability (through use on notebook computers) can be an additional feature of the service. Exhibit 1–1 summarizes the most popular of the CD tax services on the market today.

On-Line Systems.   An on-line research system allows a practitioner to access the computer of the service provider, giving virtually instantaneous use of tax law sources. On-line services employ price-per-search cost structures that average more than $100 per hour, making them significantly more expensive than paper or CD-ROM services. Thus, unless a practitioner can pass along related costs to clients or others, on-line searching is limited to the most important issues and to the researchers with the most experience and training in search techniques.

Perhaps the best combination of electronic tax resources is to use a CD system for day-to-day work where the budget is known in advance and augment the CD with on-line access where it is deemed to be critical. Exhibit 1–2 lists the most commonly used commercial on-line tax services.

The Internet.   The Internet provides a wealth of tax information in several popular forms, sometimes at no direct cost to the researcher. Using so-called browser software, which is often distributed with new computer systems and their communication devices, a tax professional can access worldwide information in several popular forms, that can aid the research process:

- *Home pages on the World Wide Web (WWW)* are provided by accounting firms, consulting firms, publishers, tax academics, libraries, and governmental bodies as a means of making information widely available or soliciting subscriptions or consulting engagements. Links to other sites and direct contact to the site providers are found in the best pages. One of the most

▼ **EXHIBIT 1–2**
On-Line Services

Provider Service	Description
LEXIS/NEXIS	Federal and state statutory, administrative, and judicial material. Extensive libraries of newspapers, magazines, patent records, and medical and economic databases, both U.S.- and foreign-based.
WESTLAW	Federal and state statutes, administrative documents, and court opinions. Extensive citator access, editorial material, and gateways to third-party publications. Extensive government document databases.
CCH ACCESS	Includes the CCH tax service, primary sources including treaties, and other subscription materials. Tax and economic news sources, extensive editorial material, and practitioner support tools.

▼ **EXHIBIT 1–3**
IRS Digital Daily

useful sites available to the tax practitioner is the Internal Revenue Service's *Digital Daily*, illustrated in Exhibit 1–3. This site offers downloadable forms and instructions, "plain English" versions of Regulations, and news update items. Exhibit 1–4 lists some of the other web sites that may be most useful to tax researchers along with their Internet addresses as of press date.

▼ **EXHIBIT 1–4**
Web Sites for the Tax
Practitioner

Web Site	WWW Address at Press Date (Usually preceded by http://www.)	Description
Internal Revenue Service	**irs.ustreas.gov/**	News releases, downloadable forms and instructions, tables, and E-mail
Court opinions	The official site of the Fifth Court of Appeals is **law.utexas.edu/us5th/us5th.html** and the site at **law.emory.edu/FEDCTS** allows the researcher to link to the site of the jurisdiction that is the subject of the query (see Exhibit 1–5).	
Discussion groups moderated by Tax Analysts	**tax.org/notes**	Policy-oriented discussions of the tax law and proposals to change it, links to student tax clinics, excerpts from the *Tax Notes* newsletter, and a tax calendar
Tax Sites Directory	**uni.edu/schmidt/tax.html**	References and links to tax sites on the Internet, including state and Federal tax sites, academic and professional pages, tax forms and software
Tax laws on-line	Regulations are at **http://law.house.gov/cfr.htm** and the Code is at **fourmilab.ch/ustax/ustax.html**	
Tax World	**http://omer.actg.uic.edu**	References and links to tax sites on the Internet, including property tax and international tax links
Commercial tax publishers	For instance, **riatax.com** and **cch-.com**	Information about products and services available for subscription, newsletter excerpts
Large accounting firms and professional organizations	For instance, the AICPA's page is at **aicpa.org** and an Ernst and Young Tax Services site is at **ey.com/tax/default.stm**	Tax planning newsletters, descriptions of services offered and career opportunities, exchange of data with clients and subscribers
West Publishing	**westpub.com**	Informational updates, newsletters, support materials for subscribers and adopters, and continuing education

- *Newsgroups* provide a means by which information related to the tax law can be exchanged among taxpayers, tax professionals, and others who subscribe to the group's services. Newsgroup members can read the exchanges among other members and offer replies and suggestions to inquiries as desired. Discussions address the interpretation and application of existing law, analysis of proposals and new pronouncements, and reviews of tax software.
- *E-mail capabilities* are available to most tax professionals through an employer's equipment or by a subscription providing Internet access at a low and usually fixed cost for the period. E-mail allows for a virtually instantaneous sending and receiving of messages, letters, tax returns and supporting data, spreadsheets, and other documents necessary to solve tax problems.

▼ **EXHIBIT 1–5**
The Emory *Federal Courts Finder*

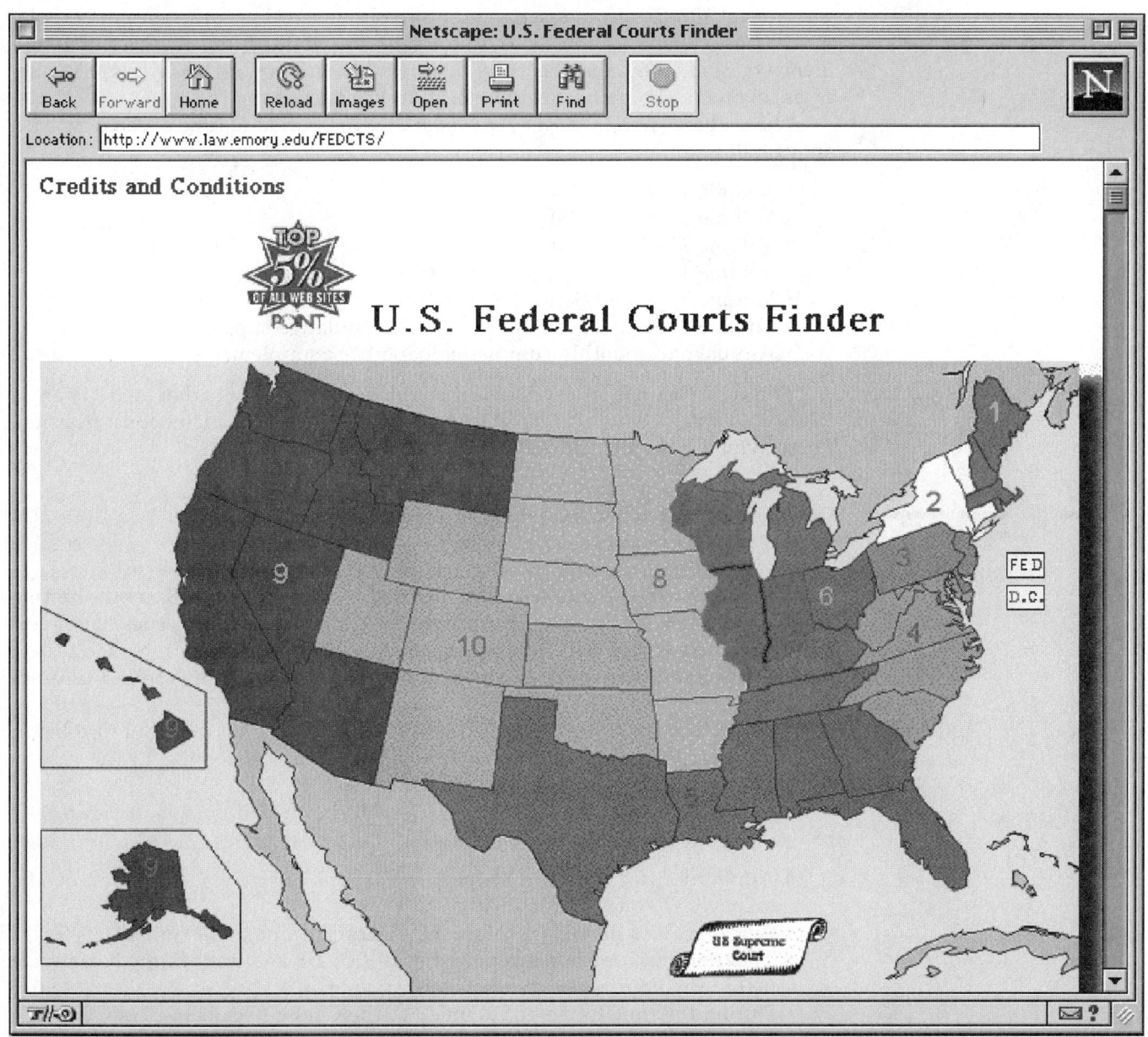

Throughout this text, solutions to research problems will benefit from, or require, the use of various electronic tax research tools. The competent tax professional must become familiar and proficient with the various means of using electronic tax resources to meet the expectations of clients and the necessities of work in the modern world.[57]

---

[57] For more detail, see W. A. Raabe, G. E. Whittenburg, and J. C. Bost, *West's Federal Tax Research,* 4th edition (St. Paul: West Publishing Co., 1997).

USE OF THE RIA CITATOR

The *Federal Tax Citator* is a separate multivolume service with monthly supplements. Cases that are reported by the *Citator* are divided into the various issues involved. Since the researcher may be interested in only one or two issues, only cases involving the particular issue need to be checked.

The volumes of the *Federal Tax Citator* and the period of time covered by each are as follows:

- Volume 1 (1863–1941)
- Volume 2 (1942–1948)
- Volume 3 (1948–1954)
- Volume 1, Second Series (1954–1977)
- Volume 2, Second Series (1978–1989)
- Volume 3, Second Series (1990–1995) cumulative supplement
- Annual and monthly cumulative paperback supplements

Through the use of symbols, the *Citator* indicates whether a decision is followed, explained, criticized, questioned, or overruled by a later court decision. These symbols are reproduced in Figure 1–7.

EXAMPLE 21

Determine the background and validity of *Adda v. Comm.*, 49 USTC ¶9109, 37 AFTR 654, 171 F.2d 457 (CA–4, 1948). ▼

Turning directly to the case itself (reproduced as Figure 1–8), note the two issues involved ("1" and "2"). For purposes of emphasis, these issues have been bracketed and identified by a marginal notation added to Figure 1–8. The reason for the division of the issues becomes apparent when the case is traced through the *Citator.*

Refer to Volume 3 for the AFTR Series (covering the period from October 7, 1948, through July 29, 1954) of the *Federal Tax Citator.* Reference to the case is located on page 5505 (reproduced in Figure 1–9).

Correlating the symbols in Figure 1–7 with the shaded portion of Figure 1–9 reveals the following information about *Adda v. Comm.*:

- Application for certiorari (appeal to the U.S. Supreme Court) filed by the taxpayer (T) on March 1, 1949.
- Certiorari was denied (x) by the U.S. Supreme Court on April 18, 1949.
- The trial court decision is reported in 10 T.C. 273 and was affirmed on appeal (sa) to the Fourth Court of Appeals.
- During the time frame of Volume 3 of the *Citator* (October 7, 1948, through July 29, 1954), one decision (*Milner Hotels, Inc.*) has agreed "on all fours with the cited case" (iv). One decision (*Comm. v. Nubar*) has limited the cited case to its facts (l), and two decisions (*The Scottish American Investment Co., Ltd.* and *Zareh Nubar*) have distinguished the cited case on issue 1 (g–1).

Reference to Volume 1 of the *Citator* Second Series (covering the period from 1954 through 1977) shows the *Adda v. Comm.* case on page 25. This page is reproduced in Figure 1–10.

Correlating the symbols in Figure 1–7 with the shaded portion of Figure 1–10 reveals the following additional information about *Adda v. Comm.*:

- The case was cited without comment in two rulings and two decisions: Rev.Rul. 56–145 and Rev.Rul. 56–392, *Balanovski* and *Liang.*
- It was followed in *Asthmanefrin Co.* (f–1).

▼ **FIGURE 1–7**
RIA Citator Symbols

Citator Symbols*
COURT DECISIONS
Judicial History of the Case

a	affirmed (by decision of a higher court)
d	dismissed (appeal to a higher court dismissed)
m	modified (decision modified by a higher court, or on rehearing)
r	reversed (by a decision of a higher court)
s	same case (e.g., on rehearing)
rc	related case (companion cases and other cases arising out of the same subject matter are so designated)
x	certiorari denied (by the Supreme Court of the United States)
(C or G)	The Commissioner or Solicitor General has made the appeal
(T)	Taxpayer has made the appeal
(A)	Tax Court's decision acquiesced in by Commissioner
(NA)	Tax Court's decision nonacquiesced in by Commissioner
sa	same case affirmed (by the cited case)
sd	same case dismissed (by the cited case)
sm	same case modified (by the cited case)
sr	same case reversed (by the cited case)
sx	same case—certiorari denied

Syllabus of the Cited Case

iv	four (on all fours with the cited case)
f	followed (the cited case followed)
e	explained (comment generally favorable, but not to a degree that indicates the cited case is followed)
k	reconciled (the cited case reconciled)
n	dissenting opinion (cited in a dissenting opinion)
g	distinguished (the cited case distinguished either in law or on the facts)
l	limited (the cited case limited to its facts. Used when an appellate court so limits a prior decision, or a lower court states that in its opinion the cited case should be so limited)
c	criticized (adverse comment on the cited case)
q	questioned (the cited case not only criticized, but its correctness questioned)
o	overruled

*Reproduced from the *Federal Taxes 2nd Citator* with the permission of the publisher, Research Institute of America, Englewood Cliffs, N.J. 07632.

- It was distinguished in *de Vegvar* and *Purvis* (g–1).
- It was reconciled in *deKrause* (k–1).

Reference to the "Court Decisions" section of Volume 2, Second Series of the *Citator* covering the period from 1978 through 1989 shows that *Adda v. Comm.* was cited in *Robert E. Cleveland* and *Judith C. Connelly*, each case limited to its facts (l).

The *Citator* includes a cumulative supplement (i.e., 1990–1996), and each month there is a cumulative paperback supplement. Be sure to refer to these monthly supplements, or very recent citations might be overlooked.

Except as otherwise noted, it would appear that *Adda v. Comm.* has withstood the test of time.

▼ **FIGURE 1–8**
Actual Court Case

ADDA v. COMMISSIONER OF INTERNAL REVENUE   457
Cite as 171 F.2d 457

ADDA v. COMMISSIONER OF INTERNAL REVENUE.
No. 5796.

United States Court of Appeals
Fourth Circuit.

Dec. 3, 1948.

ISSUE 1

1. Internal revenue ⊕792

Where nonresident alien's brother residing in United States traded for alien's benefit on commodity exchanges in United States at authorization of alien, who vested full discretion in brother with regard thereto, and many transactions were effected through different brokers, several accounts were maintained, and substantial gains and losses realized, transactions constituted a "trade or business," profits of which were "capital gains" taxable as income to the alien. 26 U.S.C.A. § 211(b).

See Words and Phrases, Permanent Edition, for other judicial constructions and definitions of "Capital Gains" and "Trade or Business".

ISSUE 2

2. Internal revenue ⊕792

The exemption of a nonresident alien's commodity transactions in the United States provided for by the Internal Revenue Code does not apply where alien has agent in United States using his own discretion in effecting transactions for alien's account. 26 U.S.C.A. § 211(b).

On Petition to Review the Decision of The Tax Court of the United States.

Petition by Fernand C. A. Adda to review a decision of the Tax Court redetermining a deficiency in income tax imposed by the Commissioner of Internal Revenue.

Decision affirmed.

Rollin Browne and Mitchell B. Carroll, both of New York City, for petitioner.

Irving I. Axelrad, Sp. Asst. to Atty. Gen. (Theron Lamar Caudle, Asst. Atty. Gen., and Ellis N. Slack and A. F. Prescott, Sp. Assts. to Atty. Gen., on the brief), for respondent.

Before PARKER, Chief Judge, and SOPER and DOBIE, Circuit Judges.

PER CURIAM.

[1, 2] This is a petition by a non-resident alien to review a decision of the Tax Court. Petitioner is a national of Egypt, who in the year 1941 was residing in France. He had a brother who at that time was residing in the United States and who traded for petitioner's benefit on commodity exchanges in the United States in cotton, wool, grains, silk, hides and copper. This trading was authorized by petitioner who vested full discretion in his brother with regard thereto, and it resulted in profits in the sum of $193,857.14. The Tax Court said: "While the number of transactions or the total amount of money involved in them has not been stated, it is apparent that many transactions were effected through different brokers, several accounts were maintained, and gains and losses in substantial amounts were realized. This evidence shows that the trading was extensive enough to amount to a trade or business, and the petitioner does not contend, nor has he shown, that the transactions were so infrequent or inconsequential as not to amount to a trade or business." We agree with the Tax Court that, for reasons adequately set forth in its opinion, this income was subject to taxation, and that the exemption of a non-resident alien's commodity transactions in the United States, provided by section 211(b) of the Internal Revenue Code, 26 U.S.C.A. § 211(b), does not apply to a case where the alien has an agent in the United States using his own discretion in effecting the transactions for the alien's account. As said by the Tax Court, "Through such transactions the alien is engaging in trade or business within the United States, and the profits on these transactions are capital gains taxable to him." Nothing need be added to the reasoning of the Tax Court in this connection, and the decision will be affirmed on its opinion.

Affirmed.

▼ FIGURE 1–9
From Volume 3

» Adamson — Adler «   5505

ADAMSON, JAMES H. & MARION C. v U. S., — F Supp —, 36 AFTR 1529, 1946 P.-H. ¶ 72,418 (DC Calif) (See Adamson v U. S.)
ADAMSON, R. R., MRS. — BTA —, 1934 (P.-H.) BTA Memo. Dec. ¶ 34,370
ADAMSON v U. S., 26 AFTR 1188 (DC Calif, Sept 8, 1939)
iv—Coggan, Linus C., 1939 (P.-H.) BTA Memo. Dec. page 39—806
ADAMSON; U. S. v, 161 F(2d) 942, 35 AFTR 1404 (CCA 9)
1—Lazier v U. S., 170 F(2d) 524, 37 AFTR 545, 1948 P.-H. page 73,174 (CCA 8)
1—Grace Bros., Inc. v Comm., 173 F(2d) 178, 37 AFTR 1014, 1949 P.-H. page 72,433 (CCA 9)
1—Briggs; Hofferbert v, 178 F(2d) 744, 38 AFTR 1219, 1950 P.-H. page 72,267 (CCA 4)
1—Rogers v Comm., 180 F(2d) 722, 39 AFTR 115, 1950 P.-H. page 72,531 (CCA 4)
1—Lamar v Granger, 99 F Supp 41, 40 AFTR 270, 1951 P.-H. page 72,945 (DC Pa)
1—Herbert v Riddell, 103 F Supp 383, 41 AFTR 975, 1952 P.-H. page 72,383 (DC Calif)
1—Hudson, Galvin, 20 TC 737, 20-1953 P.-H. TC 418
ADAMSON v U. S., — F Supp —, 36 AFTR 1529, 1946 P.-H. ¶ 72,418 (DC Calif, Jan 28, 1946)
ADAMS-ROTH BAKING CO., 8 BTA 458
1—Gunderson Bros. Engineering Corp., 16 TC 129, 16-1951 P.-H. TC 72
ADAMSTON FLAT GLASS CO. v COMM., 162 F(2d) 875, 35 AFTR 1579 (CCA 6)
4—Forrest Hotel Corp. v Fly, 112 F Supp 789, 43 AFTR 1080, 1953 P.-H. page 72,856 (DC Miss)
ADDA v COMM., 171 F(2d) 457, 37 AFTR 654, 1948 P.-H. ¶ 72,655 (CCA 4, Dec 3, 1948)
Cert. filed, March 1, 1949 (T)
No cert. (G) 1949 P-H ¶ 71,050
x—Adda v Comm., 336 US 952, 69 S Ct 883, 93 L Ed 1107, April 18, 1949 (T)
sa—Adda, Fernand C. A., 10 TC 273 (No. 33), ¶ 10.33 P.-H. TC 1948
iv—Milner Hotels, Inc., N. Y., 173 F (2d) 567, 37 AFTR 1170, 1949 P.-H. page 72,528 (CCA 6)
1—Nubar; Comm. v, 185 F(2d) 588, 39 AFTR 1315, 1950 P.-H. page 73,423 (CCA 4)
g-1—Scottish Amer. Invest. Co., Ltd., The, 12 TC 59, 12-1949 P.-H. TC 32
g-1—Nubar, Zareh, 13 TC 579, 13-1949 P.-H. TC 318
ADDA, FERNAND C. A., 10 TC 273 (No. 33), ¶ 10.33 P.-H. TC 1948 (A) 1948-2 CB 1
a—Adda v Comm., 171 F(2d) 457, 37 AFTR 654, 1948 P.-H. ¶ 72,655 (CCA 4)
1—Nubar; Comm. v, 185 F(2d) 588, 39 AFTR 1315, 1950 P.-H. page 73,423 (CCA 4)
g-1—Scottish Amer. Invest. Co., Ltd., The, 12 TC 59, 12-1949 P.-H. TC 32
g-1—Nubar, Zareh, 13 TC 579, 13-1949 P.-H. TC 318
ADDA, FERNAND C. A., 10 TC 1291 (No. 168), ¶ 10.168 P.-H. TC 1948 (A) 1953-1 CB 3, 1953 P.-H. ¶ 76,453 (NA) 1948-2 CB 5, 1948 P.-H. ¶ 76,434 withdrawn
1—Scottish Amer. Invest. Co., Ltd., The, 12 TC 59, 12-1949 P.-H. TC 32
ADDA INC., 9 TC 199 (A) 1949-1 CB 1, 1949 P.-H. ¶ 76,260 (NA) 1947-2 CB 6 withdrawn
a—Adda, Inc.; Comm. v, 171 F(2d) 367, 37 AFTR 641, 1948 P.-H. ¶ 72,654 (CCA 2)
a—Adda, Inc.; Comm. v, 171 F(2d) 367, 37 AFTR 641, 1949 P.-H. ¶ 72,303 (CCA 2)
e-1—G.C.M. 26069, 1949-2 CB 38, 1949 P.-H. page 76,226
3—Koshland, Execx.; U.S. v, 208 F(2d) 640, — AFTR —, 1953 P.-H. page 73,597 (CCA 9)
4—Kent, Otis Beall, 1954 (P. H.) TC Memo. Dec. page 54—47

ADDA, INC.; COMM. v, 171 F(2d) 367, 37 AFTR 641, 1948 P.-H. ¶ 72,654 (CCA 2, Dec 6, 1948)
sa—Adda, Inc., 9 TC 199
s—Adda, Inc.; Comm. v, 171 F(2d) 367, 37 AFTR 641, 1949 P.-H. ¶ 72,303 (CCA 2) reh. den.
e-1—G.C.M. 26069, 1949-2 CB 39, 1949 P.-H. page 76,227
e-2—G.C.M. 26069, 1949-2 CB 39, 1949 P.-H. page 76,227
ADDA, INC.; COMM. v, 171 F(2d) 367, 37 AFTR 641, 1949 P.-H. ¶ 72,303 (CCA 2, Dec 6, 1948) reh. den.
sa—Adda, Inc., 9 TC 199
s—Adda, Inc.; Comm. v, 171 F(2d) 367, 37 AFTR 641, 1948 P.-H. ¶ 72,654 (CCA 2)
ADDISON-CHEVROLET SALES, INC. v CHAMBERLAIN, L. A. & NAT. BANK OF WASH., THE, — F Supp —, — AFTR —, 1954 P.-H. ¶ 72,550 (DC DC) (See Campbell v Chamberlain)
ADDISON v COMM., 177 F(2d) 521, 38 AFTR 821, 1949 P.-H. ¶ 72,637 (CCA 8, Nov 3, 1949)
sa—Addison, Irene D., — TC —, 1948 (P.-H.) TC Memo. Dec. ¶ 48,177
1—Roberts, Supt. v U. S., 115 Ct Cl 439, 87 F Supp 937, 38 AFTR 1314, 1950 P.-H. page 72,292
1—Cold Metal Process Co., The, 17 TC 934, 17-1951 P.-H. TC 512
1—Berger, Samuel & Lillian, 1954 (P.-H.) TC Memo. Dec. page 54—232
2—Urquhart, George Gordon & Mary F., 20 TC 948, 20-1953 P.-H. TC 536
ADDISON, IRENE D., — TC —, 1948 (P.-H.) TC Memo. Dec. ¶ 48,177
App (T) Jan 14, 1949 (CCA 8)
a—Addison v Comm., 177 F(2d) 521, 38 AFTR 821, 1949 P.-H. ¶ 72,637 (CCA 8)
1—Urquhart, George Gordon & Mary F., 20 TC 948, 20-1953 P.-H. TC 536
ADDITON, HARRY L. & ANNIE S., 3 TC 427
1—Lum, Ralph E., 12 TC 379, 12-1949 P.-H. TC 204
1—Christie, John A. & Elizabeth H., — TC —, 1949 (P.-H.) TC Memo. Dec. page 49—795
ADDRESSOGRAPH - MULTIGRAPH CORP., 1945 (P.-H.) TC Memo. Dec. ¶ 45,058
f-10—Rev. Rul. 54-71, 1954 P.-H. page 76.453
ADDRESSOGRAPH-MULTIGRAPH CORP. v U. S., 112 Ct Cl 201, 78 F Supp 111, 37 AFTR 53, 1948 P.-H. ¶ 72,504 (June 1, 1948)
No cert (G) 1949 P.-H. ¶ 71,041
1—New Oakmont Corp., The v U. S., 114 Ct Cl 686, 86 F Supp 901, 38 AFTR 924, 1949 P.-H. page 73,181
ADELAIDE PARK LAND, 25 BTA 211
g—Amer. Security & Fidelity Corp., — BTA —, 1940 (P.-H.) BTA Memo. Dec. page 40—571
ADELPHI PAINT & COLOR WORKS, INC., 18 BTA 436
1—Neracher, William A., — BTA —, 1939 (P.-H.) BTA Memo. Dec. page 39—69
1—Lyman-Hawkins Lumber Co., — BTA —, 1939 (P.-H.) BTA Memo. Dec. page 39—350
ADEMAN v U. S., 174 F(2d) 283, 37 AFTR 1406 (CCA 9, April 25, 1949)
ADICONIS, NOELLA L. (PATNAUDE), 1953 (P.-H.) TC Memo. Dec. ¶ 53,305
ADJUSTMENT BUREAU OF ST. LOUIS ASSN., OF CREDIT MEN, 21 BTA 232
1—Cook County Loss Adjustment Bureau, — BTA —, 1940 (P.-H.) BTA Memo. Dec. page 40—331
ADKINS, CHARLES I., — BTA —, 1933 (P.-H.) BTA Memo. Dec. ¶ 33,457
ADLER v COMM., 77 F(2d) 733, 16 AFTR 162 (CCA 5)
g-2—McEuen v Comm., 196 F(2d) 130, 41 AFTR 1172, 1952 P.-H. page 72,604 (CCA 5)

▼ **FIGURE 1–10**
From Volume 1, Second Series

ADASKAVICH—ADELSON

25

ADASKAVICH, STEPHEN A. v U.S., 39 AFTR2d 77-517, 422 F Supp 276 (DC Mont) (See Wiegand, Charles J., Jr v U.S.)
AD. AURIEMA, INC., 1943 P-H TC Memo ¶ 43,422
  e-1—Miller v U S , 13 AFTR2d 1515, 166 Ct Cl 257, 331 F2d 859
ADAY v SUPERIOR CT. OF ALAMEDA COUNTY, 8 AFTR2d 5367, 13 Cal Reptr 415, 362 P2d 47 (Calif, 5-11-61)
ADCO SERVICE, INC., ASSIGNEE v CYBERMATICS, INC., 36 AFTR2d 75-6342 (NJ) (See Adco Service, Inc., Assignee v Graphic Color Plate)
ADCO SERVICE, INC., ASSIGNEE v GRAPHIC COLOR PLATE, 36 AFTR2d 75-6342 (NJ, Supr Ct, 11-10-75)
ADCO SERVICE, INC., ASSIGNEE v GRAPHIC COLOR PLATE, INC., 36 AFTR2d 75-6342 (NJ) (See Adco Service, Inc., Assignee v Graphic Color Plate)
ADDA v COMM., 171 F2d 457, 37 AFTR 654 (USCA 4)
· Rev. Rul. 56-145, 1956-1 CB 613
  1—Balanovski, U.S. v., 236 F2d 304, 49 AFTR 2013 (USCA 2)
  1—Liang, Chang Hsiao, 23 TC 1045, 23-1955 P-H TC 624
  f-1—Asthmanefrin Co. Inc., 25 TC 1141, 25-1956 P-H TC 639
  g-1—de Vegvar, Edward A. Neuman, 28 TC 1061, 28-1957 P-H TC 599
  g-1—Purvis, Ralph E. & Patricia Lee, 1974 P-H TC Memo 74-669
  k-1—deKrause, Piedad Alvarado, 1974 P-H TC Memo 74-1291
  1—Rev. Rul. 56-392, 1956-2 CB 971
ADDA, FERNAND C.A., 10 TC 273, ¶ 10,133 P-H TC 1948
  1—Balanovski, U.S. v. 236 F2d 303, 49 AFTR 2012 (USCA 2)
  1—Liang, Chang Hsiao, 23 TC 1045, 23-1955 P-H TC 624
  g-1—de Vegvar, Edward A. Neuman, 28 TC 1061, 28-1957 P-H TC 599
  g-1—Purvis, Ralph E. & Patricia Lee, 1974 P-H TC Memo 74-669
  k-1—deKrause, Piedad Alvarado, 1974 P-H TC Memo 74-1291
ADDA, INC., 9 TC 199
  Pardee, Marvin L., Est. of, 49 TC 152, 49 P-H TC 107 [See 9 TC 206-208]
  f-1—Asthmanefrin Co., Inc., 25 TC 1141, 25-1956 P-H TC 639
  1—Keil Properties, Inc. (Dela), 24 TC 1117, 24-1955 P-H TC 615
  1—Saffan, Samuel, 1957 P-H TC Memo 57—701
  1—Rev. Rul. 56-145, 1956-1 CB 613
  1—Rev. Rul. 56-392, 1956-2 CB 971
  4—Midler Court Realty, Inc., 61 TC 597, 61 P-H TC 368
ADDA, INC.; COMM. v, 171 F2d 367, 37 AFTR 641 (USCA 2)
  1—Pardee, Marvin L., Est. of, 49 TC 152, 49 P-H TC 107
  1—Saffan, Samuel, 1957 P-H TC Memo 57-701
  2—Midler Court Realty, Inc., 61 TC 597, 61 P-H TC 368
ADDELSTON, ALBERT A. & SARAH M., 1965 P-H TC Memo ¶ 65,215
ADDISON v COMM., 177 F2d 521, 38 AFTR 821 (USCA 8)
  g-1—Industrial Aggregate Co. v U.S., 6 AFTR2d 5963, 284 F2d 645 (USCA 8)
  1—Sturgeon v McMahon, 155 F Supp 630, 52 AFTR 789 (DC NY)
  1—Gilmore v U.S., 16 AFTR2d 5211, 5213, 245 F Supp 384, 386 (DC Calif)
  1—Waldheim & Co., Inc., 25 TC 599, 25-1955 P-H TC 332
  g-1—Galewitz, Samuel & Marian, 50 TC 113, 50 P-H TC 79
  1—Buder, G. A., Est. of, 1963 P-H TC Memo 63-345
  e-1—Rhodes, Lynn E. & Martha E., 1963 P-H TC Memo 63-1374
  2—Shipp v Comm., 217 F2d 402, 46 AFTR 1170 (USCA 9)

ADDISON—Contd.
  g-2—Industrial Aggregate Co. v U.S., 6 AFTR2d 5964, 284 F2d 645 (USCA 8)
  e-2—Buder, Est. of v Comm., 13 AFTR2d 1238, 330 F2d 443 (USCA 8)
  2—Iowa Southern Utilities Co. v Comm., 14 AFTR2d 5063, 333 F2d 385 (USCA 8)
  2—Kelly, Daniel, S.W., 23 TC 687, 23-1955 P-H TC 422
  f-2—Morgan, Joseph P., Est. of, 37 TC 36, 37, 37-1961 P-H TC 26, 27
  n-2—Woodward, Fred W. & Elsie M., 49 TC 385, 49 P-H TC 270
ADDISON, IRENE D., 1948 P-H TC Memo ¶ 48,177
  1—Waldheim & Co., Inc., 25 TC 599, 25-1955 P-H TC 332
  f-1—Morgan, Joseph P., Est. of, 37 TC 36, 37, 37-1961 P-H TC 26, 27
  1—Buder, G. A., Est. of, 1963 P-H TC Memo 63-345
  e-1—Rhodes, Lynn E. & Martha E., 1963 P-H TC Memo 63-1374
ADDISON, JOHN MILTON, BKPT; U.S. v, 20 AFTR2d 5630, 384 F2d 748 (USCA 5) (See Rochelle Jr., Trtee; U.S. v)
ADDRESSOGRAPH - MULTIGRAPH CORP., 1945 P-H TC Memo ¶ 45,058
  Conn. L. & P. Co., The v U.S., 9 AFTR2d 679, 156 Ct Cl 312, 314, 299 F2d 264
  Copperhead Coal Co., Inc., 1958 P-H TC Memo 58-33
  1—Seas Shipping Co. Inc. v Comm., 19 AFTR2d 596, 371 F2d 529 (USCA 2)
  e-1—Hitchcock, E. R., Co., The v U.S., 35 AFTR2d 75-1207, 514 F2d 487 (USCA 2)
  f-2—Vulcan Materials Co. v U.S., 25 AFTR2d 70-446, 308 F Supp 57 (DC Ala)
  f-3—Marlo Coil Co. v U.S., 1969 P-H 58,133 (Ct Cl Comr Rep)
  4—United Gas Improvement Co. v Comm., 240 F2d 318, 50 AFTR 1354 (USCA 3)
  10—St. Louis Co. (Del) (in Dissolution) v U.S., 237 F2d 156, 50 AFTR 257 (USCA 3)
ADDRESSOGRAPH - MULTIGRAPH CORP. v U.S., 112 Ct Cl 201, 78 F Supp 111, 37 AFTR 53
  f-1—St. Joseph Lead Co. v U.S., 9 AFTR2d 712, 299 F2d 350 (USCA 2)
  e-1—Central & South West Corp. v U.S., 1968 P-H 58,175 (Ct Cl Comr Rep)
  1—Smale & Robinson, Inc. v U.S., 123 F Supp 469, 46 AFTR 375 (DC Calif)
  1—St. Joseph Lead Co. v U.S., 7 AFTR2d 401, 190 F Supp 640 (DC NY)
  1—Eisenstadt Mfg. Co., 28 TC 230, 28-1957 P-H TC 132
  f-2—St. Joseph Lead Co. v U.S., 9 AFTR2d 712, 299 F2d 350 (USCA 2)
  f-3—Consol, Coppermines Corp. v U.S., 8 AFTR2d 5873, 155 Ct Cl 736, 296 F2d 745
ADELAIDE PARK LAND, 25 BTA 211
  g—Custom Component Switches, Inc. v U.S., 19 AFTR2d 560 (DC Calif) [See 25 BTA 215]
  O'Connor, John C., 1957 P-H TC Memo 57-190
ADELBERG, MARVIN & HELEN, 1971 P-H TC Memo ¶ 71,015
ADELMAN v U.S., 27 AFTR2d 71-1464, 440 F2d 991 (USCA 9, 5-3-71)
  sa—Adelman v U.S., 24 AFTR2d 69-5769, 304 F Supp 599 (DC Calif)
ADELMAN v U.S., 24 AFTR2d 69-5769, 304 F Supp 599 (DC Calif, 9-30-69)
  a—Adelman v U.S., 27 AFTR2d 71-1464, 440 F2d 991 (USCA 9)
ADELSON, SAMUEL; U.S. v, 52 AFTR 1798 (DC RI) (See Sullivan Co., Inc.; U.S. v)
ADELSON v U.S., 15 AFTR2d 246, 342 F2d 332 (USCA 9, 1-13-65)
  sa—Adelson v U.S., 12 AFTR2d 5010, 221 F Supp 31 (DC Calif)
  g-1—Greenlee, L. C. & Gladys M., 1966 P-H TC Memo 66-985
  f-1—Cochran, Carol J., 1973 P-H TC Memo 73-459
  f-1—Marchionni, Siro L., 1976 P-H TC Memo 76-1321
  f-2—Krist, Edwin F. v Comm., 32 AFTR2d 73-5663, 483 F2d 1351 (USCA 2)
  f-2—Fugate v U.S., 18 AFTR2d 5607, 259 F Supp 401 (DC Tex) [See 15 AFTR2d 249, 342 F2d 335]

KEY TERMS

PROBLEM MATERIALS

DISCUSSION QUESTIONS

1. What is meant by revenue-neutral tax reform?

2. How does the tax law encourage technological progress?

3. Does the tax law provide any stimulus for the development of international trade? Explain.

4. Do the tax laws provide any stimulus for farmers and natural resources?

5. TRA of 1986 eliminated many low-income persons from being subject to the Federal income tax. On what grounds can this be justified?

6. Explain how the following tax provisions encourage small business:
   a. The nature of a shareholder's loss on a stock investment.
   b. The tax rates applicable to corporations.
   c. Nontaxable corporate divisive reorganizations.

7. Although death taxes imposed on large estates can be justified on the grounds of social desirability, can such taxes carry economic implications? Explain.

8. What purpose is served by the credit allowed for certain child or disabled dependent care expenses?

9. Why should the deductibility of excess political campaign expenditures be contrary to public policy?

10. In the past, Congress has considered proposals that would allow a taxpayer to claim a tax credit for tuition paid to send a dependent to a private school. Is there any justification for such a proposal?

11. What purpose is served by allowing a deduction for home mortgage interest and property taxes?

12. Some states that impose a state income tax allow the taxpayer a deduction for any Federal income taxes paid. What is the justification for such an approach?

13. A provision of the Code allows a taxpayer a deduction for Federal income tax purposes for state and local income taxes paid. Does this provision eliminate the effect of multiple taxation of the same income? Why or why not? In this connection, consider the following:
   a. Taxpayer, an individual, has itemized deductions that are less than the standard deduction.

    b. Taxpayer is in the 15% tax bracket for Federal income tax purposes. The 31% tax bracket.

14. Yvonne operates a profitable sole proprietorship. Because the business is expanding, she would like to transfer it to a newly created corporation. Yvonne is concerned, however, over the possible tax consequences that would result from incorporating. Please comment.

15. Assume the same facts as in Question 14. Yvonne is also worried that once she incorporates, the business will be subject to the Federal corporate income tax. Any suggestions?

16. In situations in which the tax law recognizes the wherewithal to pay concept, discuss the effect of the following:
    a. The basis to the transferor of property received in an exchange.
    b. The recognition by the transferor of any realized loss on the transfer.
    c. The receipt of boot or other property by the transferor.

17. Can it be said that the application of the wherewithal to pay concept permanently avoids the recognition of any gain or loss by a transferor? Explain.

18. Ralph exchanges 200 shares of Azure Corporation stock for 200 shares of Aqua Corporation stock. The exchange is not pursuant to a nontaxable reorganization. Does the wherewithal to pay concept shield Ralph from the recognition of gain or loss? Why?

19. Mel, a calendar year cash basis taxpayer, is a participant in an H.R. 10 (Keogh) retirement plan for self-employed persons. To get the deduction for 1997, Mel makes his contribution on December 30, 1997.
    a. Why was there an element of urgency in Mel's action?
    b. Was Mel misinformed about the tax law? Explain.

20. Explain why prepaid subscription and dues income is not taxed until earned while prepaid rents are taxed to the landlord in the year received.

21. Indexation causes complexity throughout the tax laws. What is the purpose of the indexation procedure?

22. Gina operates a service business as a sole proprietor. For tax purposes, she recognizes income using the cash method but deducts expenses as they accrue.
    a. What is Gina trying to accomplish?
    b. Is this procedure proper?
    c. Does the IRS have any recourse?

23. In what way does the wherewithal to pay concept aid the IRS in the collection of tax revenue?

24. Describe how the IRS achieves administrative feasibility through each of the following tax provisions:
    a. The standard deduction allowed to individual taxpayers.
    b. The $192,800 unified tax credit allowed for estate tax purposes.
    c. The $10,000 annual exclusion allowed for gift tax purposes.

25. What is meant by the concept of substance over form? Why is it variously described as the "telescoping," "collapsing," or "step transaction" approach?

26. What is meant by the concept that statutory relief provisions of the tax law are to be narrowly construed? Where did the concept originate?

27. When does the tax benefit rule apply? With what effect?

28. White Corporation loans $20,000 to Tan Corporation with no provision for interest. White Corporation and Tan Corporation are owned by the same shareholders. How might the IRS restructure this transaction with adverse tax consequences?

29. Under what circumstances can court decisions lead to changes in the Code?

30. Judicial decisions interpreting a provision of the Internal Revenue Code of 1939 are no longer of any value in view of the enactment of the Internal Revenue Code of 1986. Assess the validity of this statement.

31. What happens when differing tax bills emerge from the House and the Senate?

32. Before a tax provision becomes law, the President must sign the bill. Discuss the validity of this statement.

33. Why are Committee Reports of Congress important as a source of tax laws?

34. Why are certain Code Section numbers missing from the Internal Revenue Code (e.g., §§ 6, 7, 8, 9, 10)?

35. Explain how Regulations are arranged. How would a Proposed Regulation under § 385 be cited?

36. Do Temporary Regulations carry more weight than traditional Proposed Regulations?

37. Explain the publication process for Revenue Rulings and Revenue Procedures.

38. Does the government publish letter rulings?

39. Cy Young calls you requesting an explanation of the fact-finding determination of a Federal Court of Appeals. Prepare a letter dated October 15, 1997, to be sent to Cy answering this query. His address is 1072 Richmond Lane, Keene, NH 01720.

40. Milt Pappas calls you with respect to a tax issue. He has found a tax case in the U.S. District Court of North Carolina that is in favor of his position. The IRS lost and did not appeal the case. Over the phone, you explain to Milt the significance of the failure to appeal. Prepare a tax file memorandum dated September 13, 1997, outlining your remarks to Milt.

41. Explain the following abbreviations:
    a. CA–2   i. USTC
    b. Cls.Ct.   j. AFTR
    c. *aff'd.*   k. F.2d
    d. *rev'd.*   l. F.Supp.
    e. *rem'd.*   m. USSC
    f. *Cert. denied*   n. S.Ct.
    g. *acq.*   o. D.Ct.
    h. B.T.A.   p. Fed.Cl.

42. Where can a researcher locate a 1994 Tax Court Memorandum decision?

43. In assessing the validity of a court decision, discuss the significance of the following:
    a. The decision was rendered by the U.S. District Court of Wyoming. Taxpayer lives in Wyoming.
    b. The decision was rendered by the U.S. Court of Federal Claims. Taxpayer lives in Wyoming.
    c. The decision was rendered by the Second Court of Appeals. Taxpayer lives in California.
    d. The decision was rendered by the U.S. Supreme Court.
    e. The decision was rendered by the U.S. Tax Court. The IRS has acquiesced in the result.
    f. Same as (e) except that the IRS has issued a nonacquiescence as to the result.

44. Refer to Figures 1–10 and 1–7 illustrating the use of the RIA *Citator.* Locate *Addressograph-Multigraph Corp. v. U.S.,* 112 Ct.Cl. 201. What did *Consol. Coppermines Corp. v. U.S.* hold with respect to issue 3 in *Addressograph-Multigraph Corp.?* What did *Central & South West Corp. v. U.S.* hold with respect to *Addressograph?*

45. Kenny Rogers needs to learn quickly about the tax consequences of a collapsible corporation. How should Kenny approach his research?

PROBLEMS

46. Thelma owns some real estate (basis of $105,000 and fair market value of $65,000) that she would like to sell to her son, Sandy, for $60,000. Thelma is aware, however, that losses on sales between certain related parties are disallowed for Federal income tax

purposes [§ 267(a)(1)]. Thelma therefore sells the property to Paul (an unrelated party) for $65,000. On the next day, Paul sells the property to Sandy for the same amount. Is Thelma's realized loss of $40,000 deductible? Explain.

47. Bart exchanges some real estate (basis of $800,000 and fair market value of $1,000,000) for other real estate owned by Roland (basis of $1,200,000 and fair market value of $900,000) and $100,000 in cash. The real estate involved is unimproved and is held by Bart and Roland, before and after the exchange, as investment property.
    a. What is Bart's realized gain on the exchange? Recognized gain?
    b. What is Roland's realized loss? Recognized loss?
    c. Support your results to (a) and (b) under the wherewithal to pay concept as applied to like-kind exchanges (§ 1031).

48. Using the legend provided, classify the overall objective of the particular tax provision:

Legend

CE = Control of the economy	W = Wherewithal to pay concept
EA = Encouragement of certain activities	AF = Administrative feasibility
EI = Encouragement of certain industries	ESB = Encouragement of small business
SC = Social considerations	

---

    a. Involuntary conversion of a business building.
    b. A decrease in the individual tax rate.
    c. The S corporation election.
    d. Write-off of research and development expenditures.
    e. Percentage depletion.
    f. Unified estate tax credit.
    g. Charitable contribution deduction.

49. Ivy exchanges common stock in Crimson Corporation (adjusted basis of $40,000 and fair market value of $95,000) for common stock in Amber Corporation (fair market value of $95,000). The exchange is not pursuant to any reorganization. Calculate the realized gain and any recognized gain to Ivy.

50. Troy sells property (basis of $20,000) to Beige Corporation for $35,000. Based on the following conditions, how could the IRS challenge this transaction?
    a. Troy is the sole shareholder of Beige Corporation.
    b. Troy is the son of the sole shareholder of Beige Corporation.
    c. Troy is neither a shareholder in Beige Corporation nor related to any of Beige's shareholders.

51. Using the legend provided, classify each of the following statements (Note that more than one answer per statement may be appropriate):

Legend

D = Applies to the U.S. District Court	A = Applies to the U.S. Court of Appeals
T = Applies to the U.S. Tax Court	U = Applies to the U.S. Supreme Court
C = Applies to the U.S. Court of Federal Claims	N = Applies to none of the above

---

    a. Decides only Federal tax matters.
    b. Decisions are reported in the F.2d Series.
    c. Decisions are reported in the USTCs.
    d. Decisions are reported in the AFTRs.
    e. Appeal is by Writ of Certiorari.
    f. Court meets generally in Washington, D.C.

    g. A jury trial is available.

    h. Trial court.

    i. Appellate court.

    j. Appeal is to the U.S. Court of Appeals for the Federal Circuit.

    k. Has a Small Cases Division.

    l. The only trial court where the taxpayer does not have to first pay the tax assessed by the IRS.

52. Identify the governmental unit that produces the following tax sources:

    a. Proposed Regulations.

    b. Revenue Procedures.

    c. Letter rulings.

    d. Determination letters.

    e. Technical advice memoranda.

53. Locate the following Internal Revenue Code citations and give a brief description of each:

    a. § 127(b)(3).

    b. § 197(d)(1)(C)(iv).

    c. § 346(a).

54. Locate the following Regulation citations and give a brief description of each:

    a. Reg. § 1.274–2(b)(2).

    b. Reg. § 1.355–2(b)(4).

    c. Reg. § 1.706–1(b)(3).

55. Using the legend provided, classify each of the following tax sources:

Legend			
P =	Primary tax source	B =	Both
S =	Secondary tax source	N =	Neither

    a. Sixteenth Amendment to the Constitution.

    b. Tax treaty between the United States and France.

    c. Proposed Regulations.

    d. Revenue Rulings.

    e. General Counsel Memoranda (1988).

    f. Tax Court Memorandum decision.

    g. *Yale Law Review* article.

    h. Temporary Regulations.

    i. Letter ruling (before 1985).

    j. District Court decision.

    k. Small Cases Division of U.S. Tax Court decision.

    l. Senate Finance Committee Report.

    m. Technical advice memorandum (1991).

56. What group or company publishes the following tax periodicals?

    a. *Taxation for Accountants.*

    b. *Journal of the American Taxation Association.*

    c. *TAXES—The Tax Magazine.*

    d. *The Tax Adviser.*

    e. *The Tax Lawyer.*

57. Locate the following tax services in your library and indicate the name of the publisher and whether the service is organized by topic or by Code Section:

    a. *United States Tax Reporter.*

    b. *Standard Federal Tax Reporter.*

    c. *Federal Tax Coordinator 2d.*

    d. *Mertens Law of Federal Income Taxation.*

   e. *Tax Management Portfolios.*
   f. Rabkin & Johnson, *Federal Income, Gift and Estate Taxation.*
   g. CCH's *Federal Tax Service.*

58. What is the meaning of a citation in this form: Rev.Proc. 95–3, I.R.B. No. 1, 85?

59. Determine the acquiescence/nonacquiescence position of the IRS with respect to the following:
   a. *Sidney Merians,* 60 T.C. 187 (1973).
   b. *Charles Crowther,* 28 T.C. 1293 (1957).
   c. *Ray Durden,* 3 T.C. 1 (1944).
   d. *John P. White,* 48 T.C. 430 (1967).

60. Using the legend provided, classify each of the following decisions or statements in regard to the RIA *Federal Tax Citator:*

Legend			
a	= affirmed	q	= questioned
d	= dismissed	c	= criticized
r	= reversed	f	= followed
o	= overruled	x	= certiorari denied

   a. *Frank v. Comm.,* 83 T.C. 162 (1984), *aff'd.* 784 F.2d 119 (CA–2, 1986), *cert. den.*
   b. *Anderson v. Comm.,* 67 T.C. 522 (1977), *aff'd.* 583 F.2d 953 (CA–7, 1978).
   c. *Tilford v. Comm.,* 75 T.C. 134 (1980), *rev'd.* 705 F.2d 828 (CA–6, 1983), *cert. den.*
   d. q–2 *McEuen v. Comm.,* 196 F.2d 127 (CA–5, 1952).
   e. f–2 *Joseph P. Morgan,* 37 T.C. 31 (1961).

RESEARCH PROBLEMS

Note: **West's Federal Taxation on CD-ROM** *can be used in preparing solutions to the Research Problems. Alternatively, tax research materials contained in a standard tax library can be used.*

Research Problem 1.   Determine the validity of the following items:
   a. Rev.Proc. 77–37, 1977–2 C.B. 568.
   b. Rev.Rul. 56–116, 1956–1 C.B. 164.
   c. *Esmark Inc.,* 90 T.C. 171 (1988).
   d. *J. A. Martin,* 56 T.C. 1255 (1971).

Research Problem 2.   Go to pages 43,554 to 43,563 of the *Federal Register* for August 22, 1995, and determine the action taken by the IRS and the subject matter.

Research Problem 3.   Determine the disposition of the following decisions at the appellate level:
   a. *Gary A. Sargent,* 93 T.C. 572 (1989).
   b. *Charles Johnson,* 78 T.C. 882 (1982).
   c. *Smith & Wiggins Gin, Inc.,* 37 T.C. 861 (1962).
   d. *George W. Wiesbusch,* 59 T.C. 777 (1973).
   e. *Zanesville Inv. Co.,* 38 T.C. 406 (1962).

Research Problem 4.   Determine the disposition of the following decisions at the Supreme Court level or on rehearing.
   a. *Union Pacific R.R. Co. v. U.S.,* 524 F.2d 1343 (Ct.Cl., 1975).
   b. *Gordon v. Comm.,* 424 F.2d 378 (CA–2, 1970).
   c. *Rafferty v. Comm.,* 452 F.2d 767 (CA–1, 1971).
   d. *Davant v. Comm.,* 366 F.2d 874 (CA–5, 1966).

Research Problem 5.   If a taxpayer is engaged in litigation on a complex issue under a long-standing Code Section that has not obtained the benefit of Regulations, might a court use a letter ruling as legal authority to help the taxpayer?

Research Problem 6.   In December of last year, Dean Powell, a cash basis and calendar year taxpayer, embezzles $200,000 from a bank where he is employed as an assistant cashier. Dean disappears for parts unknown and goes on a three-month spending spree. In the current year, Dean is apprehended by law enforcement authorities and forced to make restitution of the $150,000 still unspent. In a tax file memorandum, dated February 12, 1997, comment on Dean's income tax position, with special reference to the mitigation of the annual accounting period concept.

Partial list of research aids:
Code §§ 61, 172, and 1341.
Bernard A. Yerkie, 67 T.C. 388 (1976).

Research Problem 7.   Complete the following citations to the extent the research materials are available to you:
  a. *Junior Miss Co.,* 14 T.C. ___ (1950).
  b. Rev.Rul. 68–344, 1968–1 C.B. ___.
  c. *U.S. v. Kintner,* 216 F.2d ___ (CA–9, 1954).
  d. Rev.Proc. 89–12, ___ C.B. 798.
  e. *Hagy v. U.S.,* 91–2 USTC ___ (D.Ct. Va., 1991).
  f. _____ , 335 U.S. 595 (1949).

Research Problem 8.   Find *Estate of Shelfer,* 103 T.C. 10 (1994) and answer these questions:
  a. Who is the petitioner (plaintiff)?
  b. Who is the respondent (defendant)?
  c. What is the holding of the court?
  d. What is Rule 122(a)?
  e. Was this a reviewed decision?
  f. How many judges agreed with the majority opinion?
  g. Was this decision entered under Rule 155?

Use the tax resources of the internet to address the following questions. Do not restrict your search to the World Wide Web, but include a review of newsgroups and general reference materials, practitioner sites and resources, primary sources of the tax law, chat rooms and discussion groups, and other opportunities.

Research Problem 9.   Go to each of the following internet locations.
  a. Several primary sources of the tax law, including the U.S. Supreme Court, a circuit Court of Appeal, the Internal Revenue Service, and final Regulations.
  b. Sources of proposed Federal tax legislation.
  c. A collection of tax rules for your state.

Research Problem 10.   Go to each of the following internet locations.
  a. Several newspapers and magazines, such as *USA Today,* the *New York Times,* the *Washington Post, Newsweek* magazine, your local newspaper, and a local television station.
  b. Other news sources such as *CNN Interactive,* Newspapers OnLine, and a collection of on-line versions of magazines.

Research Problem 11.   Go to each of the following internet locations.
  a. The American Institute of CPAs, the American Taxation Association, several tax-related newsgroups, and tax information provided by enrolled agents.
  b. Tax World, the Tax Prophet, Taxing Times, and Dennis Schmidt's internet tax index.
  c. Home pages for the professor of your course, Price Waterhouse, Ernst & Young, Deloitte & Touche, a local tax consulting firm, and a local tax law firm.

CORPORATIONS

Corporations are separate entities for Federal income tax purposes. Subchapter C of the Code is devoted to the tax treatment of regular corporations. Part II deals mainly with the operating rules contained in Subchapter C that apply to regular corporations and with the effects of various capital transactions on the C corporation and its shareholders.

2

CORPORATIONS: INTRODUCTION, OPERATING RULES, AND RELATED CORPORATIONS

LEARNING OBJECTIVES

After completing Chapter 2, you should be able to:

1. Summarize the various forms of conducting a business.

2. Determine when an entity will be treated as a corporation.

3. Compare the taxation of individuals and corporations.

4. Discuss the tax rules unique to corporations.

5. Compute the corporate income tax.

6. Explain the tax rules unique to multiple corporations.

7. Describe the reporting process for corporations.

8. Evaluate corporations for conducting a business.

TAX TREATMENT OF VARIOUS BUSINESS FORMS

1 LEARNING OBJECTIVE
Summarize the various forms of conducting a business.

Business operations can be conducted in a number of different forms. Among the various possibilities are the following:

- Sole proprietorships.
- Partnerships.
- Trusts and estates.
- S corporations (also known as Subchapter S corporations).
- Regular corporations (also called Subchapter C or C corporations).

For Federal income tax purposes, the distinctions between these forms of business organization are very important. The following discussion of the tax treatment of sole proprietorships, partnerships, and regular corporations highlights these distinctions. Trusts and estates are covered in Chapter 19, and S corporations are discussed in Chapter 12.

SOLE PROPRIETORSHIPS

A sole proprietorship is not a taxable entity separate from the individual who owns the proprietorship. The owner of a sole proprietorship reports all business transactions of the proprietorship on Schedule C of Form 1040. The net profit or loss from the proprietorship is then transferred from Schedule C to Form 1040, which is used by the taxpayer to report taxable income. The proprietor reports all of the net profit from the business, regardless of the amount actually withdrawn during the year.

Income and expenses of the proprietorship retain their character when reported by the proprietor. For example, ordinary income of the proprietorship is treated as ordinary income when reported by the proprietor, and capital gain is treated as capital gain.

TAX IN THE NEWS

THE COST OF COMPLYING WITH THE TAX LAW

Which is more costly for many corporations—their Federal income tax liability or the steps they must take to comply with the tax law? According to a Tax Foundation study conducted by Professors Joel Slemrod and Marsha Blumenthal, complying with the 1990 tax law was almost four times more costly than the actual tax owed. Slemrod and Blumenthal studied 365 corporations with assets of less than $1 million (90 percent of U.S. corporations fall into this category) and found that for every $1,000 paid in taxes, the compliance cost was $3,900. Larger corporations also had significant compliance costs. Slemrod and Blumenthal estimated that Fortune 500 companies spent an average of $2.11 million in compliance costs for 1992.

EXAMPLE 1

George is the sole proprietor of George's Record Shop. Gross income of the business in 1997 is $200,000, and operating expenses are $110,000. George also sells a capital asset held by the business for a $10,000 long-term capital gain. During 1997, he withdraws $60,000 from the business for living expenses. George reports the income and expenses of the business on Schedule C, resulting in net profit (ordinary income) of $90,000. Even though he withdrew only $60,000, George reports all of the $90,000 net profit from the business on Form 1040, where he computes taxable income for the year. He also reports a $10,000 long-term capital gain. ▼

PARTNERSHIPS

Partnerships are not subject to the income tax. However, a partnership is required to file Form 1065, which reports the results of the partnership's business activities. Most income and expense items are aggregated in computing the net profit of the partnership on Form 1065. Any income and expense items that are not aggregated in computing the partnership's net income are reported separately to the partners. Some examples of separately reported income items are interest income, dividend income, and long-term capital gain. Examples of separately reported expenses include charitable contributions and expenses related to interest and dividend income. Partnership reporting is discussed in detail in Chapter 10.

The partnership net profit (loss) and the separately reported items are allocated to each partner according to the partnership's profit sharing agreement, and the partners receive separate K–1 schedules from the partnership. Schedule K–1 reports each partner's share of the partnership net profit and separately reported income and expense items. Each partner reports these items on his or her own tax return.

EXAMPLE 2

Jim and Bob are equal partners in Canary Enterprises, a calendar year partnership. During 1997, Canary Enterprises had $500,000 gross income and $350,000 operating expenses. In addition, the partnership sold land that had been held for investment purposes for a long-term capital gain of $60,000. During the year, Jim withdrew $40,000 from the partnership, and Bob withdrew $45,000. The partnership's Form 1065 reports net profit of $150,000 ($500,000 income − $350,000 expenses). The partnership also reports the $60,000 long-term capital gain as a separately stated item on Form 1065. Jim and Bob both receive a Schedule K–1 reporting net profit of $75,000 and separately stated long-term capital gain of $30,000. Each partner reports net profit of $75,000 and long-term capital gain of $30,000 on his own return. ▼

REGULAR CORPORATIONS

Corporations are governed by Subchapter C or Subchapter S of the Internal Revenue Code. Those governed by Subchapter C are referred to as **C corporations** or **regular corporations.** Corporations governed by Subchapter S are referred to as **S corporations.**

S corporations, which do not pay Federal income tax, are similar to partnerships in that net profit or loss flows through to the shareholders to be reported on their separate returns. Also like partnerships, S corporations do not aggregate all income and expense items in computing net profit or loss. Certain items flow through to the shareholders and retain their separate character when reported on the shareholders' returns. See Chapter 12 for detailed coverage of S corporations.

Unlike proprietorships, partnerships, and S corporations, C corporations are taxpaying entities. This results in what is known as a *double tax* effect. A C corporation reports its income and expenses on Form 1120 (or Form 1120–A, the corporate short form). The corporation computes tax on the net income reported on the corporate tax return using the rate schedule applicable to corporations (refer to the rate schedule inside the front cover of this text). When a corporation distributes its income, the corporation's shareholders report dividend income on their own tax returns. Thus, income that has already been taxed at the corporate level is also taxed at the shareholder level.

EXAMPLE 3

Tan Corporation files Form 1120, which reports net profit of $100,000. The corporation pays tax of $22,250. This leaves $77,750, all of which is distributed as a dividend to Carla, the sole shareholder of the corporation. Carla, who has income from other sources and is in the 39.6% tax bracket, pays income tax of $30,789 on the distribution. The combined tax on the corporation's net profit is $53,039. ▼

EXAMPLE 4

Assume the same facts as in Example 3, except that the business is organized as a sole proprietorship. Carla reports the $100,000 net profit from the business on her tax return and pays tax of $39,600 ($100,000 net profit × 39.6% marginal rate). Therefore, operating the business as a sole proprietorship results in a tax saving of $13,439 ($53,039 tax from Example 3 – $39,600). ▼

Shareholders in closely held corporations frequently attempt to avoid double taxation by paying out all the profit of the corporation as salary to themselves.

EXAMPLE 5

Orange Corporation has net income of $180,000 during the year ($300,000 revenue – $120,000 operating expenses). Emilio is the sole shareholder of Orange Corporation. In an effort to avoid tax at the corporate level, Emilio has Orange pay him a salary of $180,000, which results in zero taxable income for the corporation. ▼

Will the strategy described in Example 5 effectively avoid double taxation? The answer depends on whether the compensation paid to the shareholder is *reasonable.* Section 162 provides that compensation is deductible only to the extent that it is reasonable in amount. The IRS is aware that many taxpayers use this strategy to bail out corporate profits and, in an audit, looks closely at compensation expense. If the IRS believes that compensation is too high based on the amount and quality of services performed by the shareholder, the compensation deduction of the corporation is reduced to a reasonable amount. Compensation that is determined to be unreasonable is usually treated as a constructive dividend to the shareholder and is not deductible by the corporation.

EXAMPLE 6

Assume the same facts as in Example 5, and that the IRS determines that $80,000 of the amount paid to Emilio is unreasonable compensation. As a result, $80,000 of the corporation's compensation deduction is disallowed and treated as a constructive dividend to Emilio. Orange has taxable income of $80,000. Emilio would report salary of $100,000 and a taxable dividend of $80,000. The net effect is that $80,000 is subject to double taxation. ▼

The unreasonable compensation issue is discussed in more detail in Chapter 4.

Comparison of Corporations and Other Forms of Doing Business. Comparison of the tax results in Examples 3 and 4 might lead to the conclusion that incorporation is not a wise tax strategy. In some cases that would be a correct conclusion, but in others it would not. In many situations, tax and nontax factors combine to make the corporate form of doing business the only reasonable choice.

Chapter 13 presents a detailed comparison of sole proprietorships, partnerships, S corporations, and C corporations as forms of doing business. However, it is appropriate at this point to consider some of the tax and nontax factors that favor corporations over proprietorships.

Consideration of tax factors requires an examination of the corporate rate structure. The income tax rate schedule applicable to corporations is reproduced below.

Taxable Income		Tax Is:	Of the Amount Over—
Over—	But Not Over—		
$ 0	$ 50,000	15%	$ 0
50,000	75,000	$ 7,500 + 25%	50,000
75,000	100,000	13,750 + 34%	75,000
100,000	335,000	22,250 + 39%	100,000
335,000	10,000,000	113,900 + 34%	335,000
10,000,000	15,000,000	3,400,000 + 35%	10,000,000
15,000,000	18,333,333	5,150,000 + 38%	15,000,000
18,333,333	—	35%	–0–

As this schedule shows, corporate rates on taxable income up to $75,000 are lower than individual rates for persons in the 28 percent and higher brackets. Therefore, corporate tax will be lower than individual tax. Furthermore, there is no corporate marginal rate that is higher than the 39.6 percent top bracket for individuals. When dividends are paid, however, the double taxation problem occurs. This leads to an important question: Will incorporation ever result in Federal income tax savings? The following example illustrates a situation where this occurs.

EXAMPLE 7

Ned, an individual in the 39.6% tax bracket, owns a business that produces net profit of $50,000 each year. Ned has significant income from other sources, so he does not withdraw any of the profit from the business. If the business is operated as a proprietorship, Ned's

Federal income tax on the net profit of the business is $19,800 ($50,000 × 39.6%). However, if the business is operated as a corporation and pays no dividends, the tax will be $7,500 ($50,000 × 15%). Operating as a corporation saves $12,300 of Federal income tax each year. If Ned invests his $12,300 tax saving each year for several years, it is possible that a positive cash flow will result, even though Ned will be required to pay tax on dividends distributed by the corporation some time in the future. ▼

The preceding example deals with a specific set of facts. The conclusions reached in this situation cannot be extended to all decisions about a form of business organization. Each specific set of facts and circumstances requires a thorough analysis of the tax factors.

Another tax consideration involves the nature of dividend income. All income and expense items of a proprietorship retain their character when reported on the proprietor's tax return. In the case of a partnership, several separately reported items (e.g., charitable contributions and long-term capital gains) retain their character when passed through to the partners. However, the tax attributes of income and expense items of a corporation are lost as they pass through the corporate entity to the shareholders.

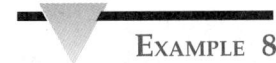

EXAMPLE 8

During the current year, Waxwing Company receives tax-exempt interest, which is distributed to its owners. If Waxwing Company is a regular corporation, the distribution to the shareholders constitutes a dividend. The fact that it originated from tax-exempt interest is of no consequence.[1] On the other hand, if Waxwing is a partnership or an S corporation, the tax-exempt interest retains its identity and passes through to the individual owners. ▼

Losses of a C corporation are treated differently than losses of a proprietorship, partnership, or S corporation. A loss incurred by a proprietorship may be deductible by the owner, because all income and expense items are reported by the proprietor. Partnership losses are passed through the partnership entity and may be deductible by the partners, and S corporation losses are passed through to the shareholders. C corporation losses, however, have no effect on the taxable income of the shareholders. Income from a C corporation is reported when the shareholders receive dividends. C corporation losses are not reported by the shareholders.

Nontax Considerations.   Nontax considerations will sometimes override tax considerations and lead to the conclusion that a business should be operated as a corporation. The following are some of the more important nontax considerations:

- Sole proprietors and *general* partners in partnerships face the danger of *unlimited liability.* That is, creditors of the business may file claims not only against the assets of the business but also against the personal assets of proprietors or general partners. Shareholders are protected from claims against their personal assets by state corporate law.
- The corporate form of business organization can provide a vehicle for raising large amounts of capital through widespread stock ownership. Most major businesses in the United States are operated as corporations.
- Shares of stock in a corporation are freely transferable, whereas a partner's sale of his or her partnership interest is subject to approval by the other partners.

---

[1] As noted in Chapter 4, such items will, however, affect the distributing corporation's earnings and profits.

- Shareholders may come and go, but a corporation can continue to exist. Death or withdrawal of a partner, on the other hand, may terminate the existing partnership and cause financial difficulties that result in dissolution of the entity. This *continuity of life* is a distinct advantage of the corporate form of doing business.
- Corporations have *centralized management*. All management responsibility is assigned to a board of directors, who appoint officers to carry out the corporation's business. Partnerships, by contrast, may have decentralized management, in which every owner has a right to participate in the organization's business decisions; **limited partnerships,** though, may have centralized management. Centralized management is essential for the smooth operation of a widely held business.

A more in-depth discussion of the different forms of business organizations is presented in Chapter 13. See especially the Concept Summary in Chapter 13 that provides a detailed comparison of the tax attributes of the sole proprietorship, partnership, S corporation, and regular C corporation.

The tax consequences of operating a business in the regular corporate form fall within Subchapter C of the Code and are the subject of this chapter and Chapters 3, 4, 5, and 7. Corporations that either unreasonably accumulate earnings or meet the definition of a personal holding company may be subject to further taxation. These so-called penalty taxes are imposed in addition to the corporate income tax and are discussed in Chapter 6.

Clearly, the form of organization chosen to carry on a trade or business has significant Federal income tax consequences. Though tax considerations may not control the choice, it could be unfortunate if they are not taken into account.

WHAT IS A CORPORATION?

2 LEARNING OBJECTIVE
Determine when an entity will be treated as a corporation.

The first step in any discussion of the Federal income tax treatment of corporations must be definitional. Specifically, what is a corporation? At first glance, the answer to this question appears to be quite simple. Merely look to the appropriate state law to determine whether the entity has satisfied the requirements for corporate status. Have articles of incorporation been drawn up and filed with the state regulatory agency? Has a charter been granted? Has stock been issued to shareholders? These are all points to consider.

Compliance with state law, although important, may not tell the full story as to whether an entity will be recognized as a corporation for Federal income tax purposes. On the one hand, a corporation qualifying under state law may be disregarded as a taxable entity if it is a mere sham. On the other hand, an organization not qualifying as a regular corporation under state law may be taxed as a corporation under the *association* approach. These two possibilities are discussed in the following sections.

DISREGARD OF CORPORATE ENTITY

In most cases, the IRS and the courts will recognize a corporation legally constituted under state law. In exceptional situations, however, the corporate entity may be disregarded because it lacks substance. The key to such treatment is the degree of business activity conducted at the corporate level. The more the corporation is involved in trade or business activities, the less likely it will be treated as a sham and disregarded as a separate entity.

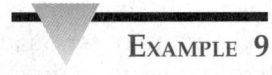

EXAMPLE 9

Don and Jane are joint owners of a tract of unimproved real estate that they wish to protect from future creditors. Consequently, Don and Jane form Condor Corporation, to which they transfer the land in return for all of the latter's stock. The corporation merely holds title to the land and conducts no other activities. In all respects, Condor meets the requirements of a corporation under applicable state law. ▼

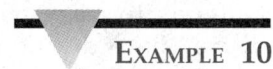

EXAMPLE 10

Assume the same facts as in Example 9. In addition to holding title to the land, Condor Corporation leases the property, collects rents, and pays the property taxes. ▼

Condor Corporation may not be recognized as a separate entity under the facts set forth in Example 9. In Example 10, however, the opposite should prove true. It appears that enough activity has taken place at the corporate level to warrant the conclusion that Condor Corporation should be treated as a real corporation for Federal income tax purposes.[2]

Depending on the circumstances, either the IRS or the taxpayers may attempt to disregard the corporate entity. More often than not, the IRS may try to disregard (or "collapse") a corporation to make its income taxable directly to the shareholders. In other situations, a corporation may try to avoid the corporate income tax or permit its shareholders to take advantage of excess corporate deductions and losses.[3]

Theoretically speaking, the disregard-of-corporate-entity approach should be equally available to both the IRS and the taxpayers. From a practical standpoint, however, taxpayers have enjoyed considerably less success than has the IRS. Courts generally conclude that since the taxpayers created the corporation in the first place, they should not be permitted to disregard it later in order to avoid taxes.

The preceding discussion relates to the classification of an entity for *Federal* income tax purposes. State corporate income taxes or other corporate taxes (e.g., franchise taxes) may still be imposed. An entity may possibly be treated as a corporation for state tax purposes and not for Federal and vice versa. This will become even more apparent when dealing with S corporations (Chapter 12) because some states do not recognize S corporation status.

ASSOCIATIONS TAXED AS CORPORATIONS

The definition of a corporation includes "associations, joint stock companies, and insurance companies." What Congress intended by including associations in the definition has never been entirely clear. To some extent, judicial decisions have clarified the status of associations and the relationship between associations and corporations.

The designation given to the entity under state law is not controlling. In one case, an entity that was a business trust under state law was deemed to be an **association** (and therefore taxable as a corporation) for Federal income tax purposes.[4] In another case, a partnership of physicians was held to be an association even though state law applicable to the tax year in question prohibited

---

[2] A classic case in this area is *Paymer v. Comm.*, 45–2 USTC ¶9353, 33 AFTR 1536, 150 F.2d 334 (CA–2, 1945). Here, two corporations were involved. The Court chose to disregard one corporate entity but to recognize the other.

[3] An election under Subchapter S would generally accomplish this if the parties qualify and the election is made on a timely basis. See Chapter 12.

[4] *Morrissey v. Comm.*, 36–1 USTC ¶9020, 16 AFTR 1274, 56 S.Ct. 289 (USSC, 1935).

the practice of medicine in the corporate form.[5] As an association, the partnership was taxed as a corporation.

Whether an entity will be considered an association for Federal income tax purposes depends upon the number of corporate characteristics it possesses. Corporate characteristics include the following:[6]

1. Associates.
2. An objective to carry on a business and divide the gains.
3. Continuity of life.
4. Centralized management.
5. Limited liability.
6. Free transferability of interests.

An unincorporated organization is not classified as an association unless it possesses more corporate than noncorporate characteristics. In making the determination, the characteristics common to both corporate and noncorporate business organizations are disregarded.

Both corporations and partnerships generally have associates (shareholders and partners) and an objective to carry on a business and divide the gains. In testing whether a particular partnership is an association, these criteria would be disregarded.

It then becomes a matter of determining whether the partnership possesses a majority of the remaining corporate characteristics (items 3 through 6). Does the partnership terminate upon the withdrawal or death of a partner (no continuity of life)? Is the management of the partnership centralized, or do all partners participate? Are all partners individually liable for the debts of the partnership, or is the liability of some limited to their actual investment in the partnership (limited partnership)? May a partner freely transfer his or her interest without the consent of the other partners?

Courts have ruled that any partnership lacking two or more of these characteristics will not be classified as an association. Conversely, any partnership having three or more of these characteristics will be classified as an association.[7]

For trusts, the first two characteristics are considered in testing for association status. The conventional type of trust often does not have associates and usually restricts its activities to investing rather than carrying on a trade or business. These characteristics, however, are common to corporations. Consequently, whether a trust qualifies as an association depends upon the satisfaction of the first two corporate characteristics.

From a taxpayer's standpoint, the desirability of association status turns on the tax implications involved. In some cases, the parties may find it advantageous to have the entity taxed as a corporation while in others they may not. These possibilities are explored at length under Tax Planning Considerations in this chapter.

LIMITED LIABILITY COMPANIES

The **limited liability company (LLC)** has proliferated greatly in recent years, particularly since 1988 when the IRS first ruled that it would treat qualifying LLCs as partnerships for tax purposes. All 50 states and the District of Columbia have

---

[5] *U.S. v. Kinter*, 54–2 USTC ¶9626, 46 AFTR 995, 216 F.2d 418 (CA–9, 1954).

[6] Reg. § 301.7701.

[7] See *Zuckman v. U.S.*, 75–2 USTC ¶9778, 36 AFTR2d 6193, 524 F.2d 729 (Ct.Cls., 1975), and *P. G. Larson*, 66 T.C. 159 (1976).

passed laws that allow LLCs, and more than 20,000 companies have chosen LLC status.[8] As with a corporation, operating as an LLC allows an entity to avoid unlimited liability, which is a primary *nontax* consideration in choosing the form of business organization. The tax advantage of LLCs is that qualifying businesses are treated as partnerships for tax purposes, thereby avoiding the problem of double taxation associated with regular corporations.

Some states allow an LLC to have centralized management, but not continuity of life or free transferability of interests. Other states allow LLCs to adopt any or all of the corporate characteristics of centralized management, continuity of life, and free transferability of interests. The IRS has issued Revenue Rulings dealing with the tax treatment of LLCs in 18 different states. All rulings issued to date make it *possible* for LLCs to be treated as partnerships. As a general rule, LLCs must avoid the corporate characteristics of continuity of life and free transferability of interests in order to qualify to be taxed as partnerships.

A SIMPLE WAY TO SELECT ENTITY STATUS

The advent of new types of entities due to the enactment of state laws (see the previous discussion of LLCs) created administrative problems for the IRS and compliance costs for taxpayers. Upon the request of concerned taxpayers, each state statute had to be tested under the association criteria. The testing was necessary to ascertain whether the entity was to be treated as a corporation or as a partnership.

To curtail this time-consuming and costly evaluation process, the IRS amended existing Regulations.[9] These Regulations, referred to as *check-the-box rules,* permit an entity to elect to be taxed either as a partnership or as a corporation, regardless of its corporate or noncorporate characteristics. The status of existing entities will not be changed by the new rules. Further, the elective option is only available to *domestic* entities. The check-the-box Regulations became effective January 1, 1997. The election is made by filing Form 8832, Entity Classification Election, and cannot be changed within 60 months unless there is a more-than-50 percent ownership change *and* IRS consents to the new election.[10]

The new rules will provide a simple and desirable solution for what has been a troublesome entity classification problem. They should prove particularly attractive to small businesses that want limited liability and pass-through treatment for tax purposes.

An Introduction to the Income Taxation of Corporations

AN OVERVIEW OF CORPORATE VERSUS INDIVIDUAL INCOME TAX TREATMENT

3   **LEARNING OBJECTIVE**
Compare the taxation of individuals and corporations.

In a discussion of how corporations are treated under the Federal income tax, a useful approach is to compare their treatment with that applicable to individual taxpayers.

Similarities. Gross income of a corporation is determined in much the same manner as it is for individuals. Thus, gross income includes compensation for

---

[8] H. W. Cecil, C. S. Ciccotello, and C. T. Grant, "The Choice of Organizational Form," *Journal of Accountancy,* December 1995.

[9] See Reg. §§ 301.7701–1 to –6. TD 8697, I.R.B. 1997, No. 2, 11.

[10] Reg. §§ 301.7701–3(c)(iii) and (iv).

services rendered, income derived from a business, gains from dealings in property, interest, rents, royalties, dividends—to name only a few items. Both individuals and corporations are entitled to exclusions from gross income. However, corporate taxpayers are allowed fewer exclusions. Interest on municipal bonds is excluded from gross income whether the bondholder is an individual or a corporate taxpayer.

Gains and losses from property transactions are handled similarly. For example, whether a gain or loss is capital or ordinary depends upon the nature of the asset in the hands of the taxpayer making the taxable disposition. In defining what is not a capital asset, § 1221, makes no distinction between corporate and noncorporate taxpayers.

In the area of nontaxable exchanges, corporations are like individuals in that they do not recognize gain or loss on a like-kind exchange and may defer recognized gain on an involuntary conversion of property. The nonrecognition of gain provisions dealing with the sale of a personal residence do not apply to corporations. Both corporations and individuals are vulnerable to the disallowance of losses on sales of property to related parties or on wash sales of securities. The wash sales rules do not apply to individuals who are traders or dealers in securities or to corporations that are dealers if the securities are sold in the ordinary course of the corporation's business.

Upon the sale or other taxable disposition of depreciable property, the recapture rules generally make no distinction between corporate and noncorporate taxpayers.[11] However, § 291(a) does cause a corporation to have more recapture on § 1250 property. This difference is discussed later in the chapter.

The business deductions of corporations also parallel those available to individuals. Deductions are allowed for all ordinary and necessary expenses paid or incurred in carrying on a trade or business.[12] Specific provision is made for the deductibility of interest, certain taxes, losses, bad debts, accelerated cost recovery, charitable contributions, net operating losses, research and experimental expenditures, and other less common deductions. A corporation does not distinguish between business and nonbusiness interest or business and nonbusiness bad debts. Thus, these amounts are deductible in full as ordinary deductions by corporations. No deduction is permitted for interest paid or incurred on amounts borrowed to purchase or carry tax-exempt securities. The same holds true for expenses contrary to public policy and certain unpaid expenses and interest between related parties.

Some of the tax credits available to individuals can also be claimed by corporations. This is the case with the foreign tax credit. Not available to corporations are certain credits that are personal in nature, such as the child care credit, the credit for elderly or disabled taxpayers, and the earned income credit.

Dissimilarities. The income taxation of corporations and individuals also differs significantly. As noted earlier, different tax rates apply to corporations and to individuals. Corporate tax rates are discussed in more detail later in the chapter (see Examples 30 and 31).

All allowable corporate deductions are treated as business deductions. Thus, the determination of adjusted gross income (AGI), so essential for individual taxpayers, has no relevance to corporations. Taxable income is computed simply by subtracting from gross income all allowable deductions and losses. Corporations need not be concerned with itemized deductions or the standard deduction. The deduction for personal and dependency exemptions is not available to corporations.

---

[11] §§ 1245 and 1250.

[12] § 162.

The $100 floor on the deductible portion of personal casualty and theft losses applicable to individuals does not apply to corporations. Also inapplicable is the provision limiting the deductibility of nonbusiness casualty losses to the amount in excess of 10 percent of AGI.

SPECIFIC PROVISIONS COMPARED

In comparing the tax treatment of individuals and corporations, the following areas warrant special discussion:

- Accounting periods and methods.
- Capital gains and losses.
- Recapture of depreciation.
- Passive losses.
- Charitable contributions.
- Net operating losses.
- Special deductions available only to corporations.

ACCOUNTING PERIODS AND METHODS

Accounting Periods. Corporations generally have the same choices of accounting periods as do individual taxpayers. Like an individual, a corporation may choose a calendar year or a fiscal year for reporting purposes. Corporations, however, enjoy greater flexibility in the selection of a tax year. For example, corporations usually can have different tax years from those of their shareholders. Also, newly formed corporations (as new taxpayers) usually have a choice of any approved accounting period without having to obtain the consent of the IRS. **Personal service corporations (PSCs)** and S corporations, however, are subject to severe restrictions in the use of a fiscal year. The rules applicable to S corporations are discussed in Chapter 12.

A PSC has as its principal activity the performance of personal services. Such services are substantially performed by owner-employees. The performance of services must be in the fields of health, law, engineering, architecture, accounting, actuarial science, performing arts, or consulting.[13] Because placing a PSC on a fiscal year and retaining a calendar year for the employee-owner can result in a significant deferral of income, a PSC must generally use a calendar year.[14] However, a PSC can *elect* a fiscal year under any of the following conditions:

- A business purpose for the year can be demonstrated.
- The PSC year results in a deferral of not more than three months' income. The corporation must pay the shareholder-employee's salary during the portion of the calendar year after the close of the fiscal year. Furthermore, the salary for that period must be at least proportionate to the employee's salary received for the fiscal year.
- The PSC retains the same year that was used for its fiscal year ending 1987, provided the latter two requirements applicable to the preceding condition are satisfied.

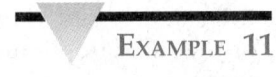

EXAMPLE 11   Valdez & Vance is a professional association of public accountants. Because it receives over 40% of its gross receipts in March and April of each year from the preparation of tax returns, Valdez & Vance has a May 1 to April 30 fiscal year. Under these circumstances, the IRS

---

[13] § 448(d)(2)(A).   [14] § 441(i).

might permit Valdez & Vance to continue to use the fiscal year chosen since it reflects a natural business cycle (the end of the tax season). Valdez & Vance has a business purpose in using a fiscal year. ▼

EXAMPLE **12**

Beige Corporation, a PSC, paid Burke $120,000 in salary during its fiscal year ending September 30, 1997. The corporation cannot satisfy the business purpose test for a fiscal year. However, the corporation can continue to use its fiscal year without any negative tax effects, provided Burke receives at least $30,000 [(3 months/12 months) × $120,000] as salary during the period October 1 through December 31, 1997. ▼

Accounting Methods.   As a general rule, the cash method of accounting is unavailable to *regular* corporations.[15] Exceptions apply to the following types of corporations:

- S corporations.
- Corporations engaged in the trade or business of farming and timber.
- Qualified PSCs.
- Corporations with average annual gross receipts of $5 million or less.
  (In applying the $5 million-or-less test, the corporation uses the average of the three prior taxable years.)

Both individuals and corporations that maintain inventory for sale to customers are required to use the accrual method of accounting for determining sales and cost of goods sold.

A corporation that uses the accrual method of accounting must observe a special rule in dealing with related parties. If the corporation has an accrual outstanding at the end of any taxable year, it cannot claim a deduction until the recipient reports the amount as income.[16] This rule is most often encountered when a corporation deals with a person who owns more than 50 percent of the corporation's stock.

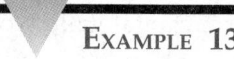

EXAMPLE **13**

Teal, an accrual method corporation, uses the calendar year for tax purposes. Bob, a cash method taxpayer, owns more than 50% of the corporation's stock at the end of 1997. On December 31, 1997, Teal has accrued $25,000 of salary to Bob. Bob receives the salary in 1998 and reports it on his 1998 tax return. Teal cannot claim a deduction for the $25,000 until 1998. ▼

ETHICAL CONSIDERATIONS

Knowledge of a Client's Error

In early 1998, you are engaged by a new client, Grebe Corporation, to prepare its 1997 Federal income tax return. Grebe has one shareholder, Bill Jones. Bill has an excellent reputation in the community, and you hope to gain more work from him in the future. You have never had a social relationship with Bill and are not acquainted with anyone in his family.

Bill has told you that he was dissatisfied with his prior accountant, because he thought that Grebe's taxes were too high. Bill brings in a copy of Grebe's 1996 tax return. You review the 1996 return and conclude that the prior accountant's work was thorough and accurate. The corporation has properly used the accrual method of accounting and accrues

---

[15]§ 448.   [16]§ 267(a)(2).

substantial bonuses to several of its employees at the end of each year. One of the employees is Susan Smith, the office manager. You are not acquainted with Susan Smith.

You prepare the 1997 tax return for Grebe and deduct the accrued bonuses in accordance with the corporation's past practices. Before you deliver the return to Bill Jones for filing, you attend a charitable fund-raising dinner and are seated next to Susan Smith. She mentions to you that she works as the office manager for Grebe, a corporation that is owned by her brother, Bill Jones, and she has noticed that you have been appointed as the corporation's tax adviser. You and Susan do not discuss any of the corporation's business or tax problems during the evening.

When you return to your office the next day, you realize that Grebe cannot deduct any accrued salary to Susan Smith, since she constructively owns all of the stock of the corporation due to the attribution rules of § 267(b) and the disallowance rule of § 267(a)(2). You would have no way of knowing that Susan was Bill's sister if you had not attended the dinner the night before. You must decide whether you will sign a return for Grebe if the accrued salary to Susan Smith is deducted as an expense.

CAPITAL GAINS AND LOSSES

Capital gains and losses result from the taxable sales or exchanges of capital assets. Whether these gains and losses are long term or short term depends upon the holding period of the assets sold or exchanged. Each year, a taxpayer's long-term capital gains and losses are combined, and the result is either a *net* long-term capital gain or a *net* long-term capital loss. A similar aggregation is made with short-term capital gains and losses, the result being a *net* short-term capital gain or a *net* short-term capital loss. The following combinations and results are possible:

1. A net long-term capital gain and a net short-term capital loss. These are combined, and the result is either a net capital gain or a net capital loss.
2. A net long-term capital gain and a net short-term capital gain. No further combination is made.
3. A net long-term capital loss and a net short-term capital gain. These are combined, and the result is either capital gain net income or a net capital loss.
4. A net long-term capital loss and a net short-term capital loss. No further combination is made.

Capital Gains.   Individuals generally pay tax on net (long-term) capital gains at a maximum rate of 28 percent. Corporations, by contrast, receive no favorable rate on capital gains and must include the net capital gain, in full, as part of taxable income.

Capital Losses.   Net capital losses (refer to combinations 3 and 4 and, possibly, to combination 1) of corporate and noncorporate taxpayers receive different income tax treatment. Generally, noncorporate taxpayers can deduct up to $3,000 of such net losses against other income.[17] Any remaining capital losses can be carried forward to future years until absorbed by capital gains or by the $3,000

---

[17] The limitations on capital losses for both corporate and noncorporate taxpayers are contained in § 1211.

deduction.[18] Carryovers do not lose their identity but remain either long term or short term.

EXAMPLE 14

Robin, an individual, incurs a net long-term capital loss of $7,500 for calendar year 1997. Assuming adequate taxable income, Robin may deduct $3,000 of this loss on his 1997 return. The remaining $4,500 ($7,500 – $3,000) of the loss is carried to 1998 and years thereafter until completely deducted. The $4,500 will be carried forward as a long-term capital loss. ▼

Unlike individuals, corporate taxpayers are not permitted to claim any net capital losses as a deduction against ordinary income. Capital losses, therefore, can be used only as an offset against capital gains. Corporations may, however, carry back net capital losses to three preceding years, applying them first to the earliest year in point of time. Carryforwards are allowed for a period of five years from the year of the loss. When carried back or forward, a long-term capital loss is treated as a short-term capital loss.

EXAMPLE 15

Assume the same facts as in Example 14, except that Robin is a corporation. None of the $7,500 long-term capital loss incurred in 1997 can be deducted in that year. Robin Corporation may, however, carry back the loss to years 1994, 1995, and 1996 (in this order) and offset it against any capital gains recognized in these years. If the carryback does not exhaust the loss, it may be carried forward to calendar years 1998, 1999, 2000, 2001, and 2002 (in this order). Either a carryback or a carryforward of the long-term capital loss converts the loss to a short-term capital loss. ▼

RECAPTURE OF DEPRECIATION

Depreciation recapture for § 1245 property is computed in the same manner for individuals and for corporations. However, corporations have more recapture of depreciation under § 1250 than do individuals. Corporations that sell depreciable real estate that is § 1250 property are subject to additional recapture of depreciation under § 291(a)(1). This provision requires recapture of 20 percent of the excess of any amount that would be treated as ordinary income under § 1245 over the amount treated as ordinary income under § 1250. The amount of ordinary income under § 291 is computed as shown in Figure 2–1.

EXAMPLE 16

Amber Corporation purchased an office building on January 3, 1984, for $300,000. Accelerated depreciation was taken in the amount of $270,000 before the building was sold on January 5, 1997, for $350,000. Straight-line depreciation would have been $260,000 (using a 15-year recovery period under ACRS). The corporation's depreciation recapture and § 1231 gain are computed as follows:

Determine realized gain:	
Sales price	$350,000
Less: Adjusted basis [$300,000 (cost of building) – $270,000 (ACRS depreciation)]	30,000
Realized gain	$320,000

Because the building is 15-year real estate, it is § 1245 recovery property. The gain of $320,000 is recaptured to the extent of all depreciation taken. Thus, $270,000 of the gain is ordinary income under § 1245, and there is $50,000 of § 1231 gain. ▼

---

[18]Carryback and carryover rules for both corporate and noncorporate taxpayers can be found in § 1212.

▼ **FIGURE 2–1**
Computation of Depreciation
Recapture under § 291

Ordinary income under § 1245	$ xx,xxx
Less: Ordinary income under § 1250	(x,xxx)
Equals: Excess ordinary income under § 1245 as compared to ordinary income under § 1250	$ x,xxx
Apply § 291 percentage	× 20%
Equals: Amount of ordinary income under § 291	$ xxx

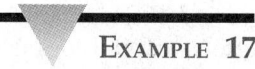

EXAMPLE 17

Assume the building in Example 16 is residential rental property, making it § 1250 property. Gain recaptured under § 1250 would be $10,000 [$270,000 (depreciation taken) – $260,000 (straight-line depreciation)]. However, for a corporate taxpayer, § 291(a) causes additional § 1250 ordinary income of $52,000, computed as follows:

Ordinary income under § 1245	$270,000
Less: Ordinary income under § 1250	10,000
Excess ordinary income under § 1245	$260,000
Apply § 291 percentage	20%
Additional § 1250 income (ordinary income under § 291)	$ 52,000

Thus, of the total gain of $320,000, $62,000 [$10,000 (§ 1250 recapture) + $52,000 (§ 291 recapture)] would be ordinary income, and $258,000 would be § 1231 gain. ▼

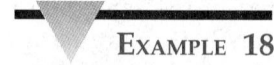

EXAMPLE 18

Assume the building in Example 17 is commercial property and straight-line depreciation was used. An individual would report all gain as § 1231 gain. However, a corporate taxpayer would recapture as ordinary income (under § 291) 20% of the depreciation that would be ordinary income if the property were § 1245 property.

First, determine realized gain:	
Sales price	$350,000
Less: Adjusted basis [$300,000 (cost of building) – $260,000 (straight-line depreciation)]	40,000
Realized gain	$310,000
Second, determine § 291 gain:	
Ordinary income if property were § 1245 property	$260,000
Less: Ordinary income under § 1250	–0–
Excess ordinary income under § 1245	$260,000
Apply § 291 percentage	20%
Ordinary income under § 291	$ 52,000

For a corporate taxpayer, $52,000 of the $310,000 gain would be ordinary, and $258,000 would be § 1231 gain. ▼

PASSIVE LOSSES

The **passive loss** rules apply to noncorporate taxpayers and to closely held C corporations and personal service corporations (PSCs).[19] For S corporations and

---

[19] § 469(a).

partnerships, passive income or loss flows through to the owners, and the passive loss rules are applied at the owner level. The passive loss rules are applied to closely held corporations and to PSCs to prevent taxpayers from incorporating to avoid the passive loss limitation.

A corporation is closely held if, at any time during the taxable year, more than 50 percent of the value of the corporation's outstanding stock is owned, directly or indirectly, by or for not more than five individuals. The definition used for a closely held corporation is the same as that used in determining the ownership requirement for personal holding companies (see Chapter 6). A corporation is classified as a PSC if it meets the following requirements:

- The principal activity of the corporation is the performance of personal services.
- Such services are substantially performed by owner-employees.
- More than 10 percent of the stock (in value) is held by owner-employees. *Any* stock held by an employee on *any* one day causes the employee to be an owner-employee.

The general passive activity loss rules apply to PSCs. Passive activity losses cannot be offset against either active income or portfolio income. The application of the passive activity rules is not as harsh for closely held corporations. They may offset passive losses against active income, but not against portfolio income.

EXAMPLE 19

Brown, a closely held corporation, has $300,000 of passive losses from a rental activity, $200,000 of active business income, and $100,000 of portfolio income. The corporation may offset $200,000 of the $300,000 passive loss against the $200,000 active business income, but may not offset the remainder against the $100,000 of portfolio income. ▼

Individual taxpayers are not allowed to offset passive losses against *either* active or portfolio income.

CHARITABLE CONTRIBUTIONS

Both corporate and noncorporate taxpayers may deduct charitable contributions if the recipient is a qualified charitable organization. Generally, a deduction will be allowed only for the year in which the payment is made. However, an important exception is made for *accrual basis corporations*. They may claim the deduction in the year preceding payment if two requirements are met. First, the contribution must be authorized by the board of directors by the end of that year. Second, it must be paid on or before the fifteenth day of the third month of the next year.

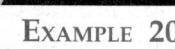

EXAMPLE 20

On December 28, 1997, Blue Company, a calendar year, accrual basis taxpayer, authorizes a $5,000 donation to the Atlanta Symphony Association (a qualified charitable organization). The donation is made on March 14, 1998. If Blue Company is a partnership, the contribution can be deducted only in 1998.[20] However, if Blue Company is a corporation and the December 28, 1997 authorization was made by its board of directors, Blue may claim the $5,000 donation as a deduction for calendar year 1997. ▼

Property Contributions.   The amount that can be deducted for a noncash charitable contribution depends on the type of property contributed. Property

---

[20] Each calendar year partner will report an allocable portion of the charitable contribution deduction as of December 31, 1998 (the end of the partnership's tax year). See Chapter 10.

must be identified as long-term capital gain property or ordinary income property. *Long-term capital gain property* is property that, if sold, would result in long-term capital gain for the taxpayer. Such property generally must be a capital asset and must be held for the long-term holding period (more than one year). *Ordinary income property* is property that, if sold, would result in ordinary income for the taxpayer.

The deduction for a charitable contribution of long-term capital gain property is generally measured by fair market value.

EXAMPLE 21

In 1997, Mallard Corporation donated a parcel of land (a capital asset) to Oakland Community College. Mallard acquired the land in 1987 for $60,000, and the fair market value on the date of the contribution was $100,000. The corporation's charitable contribution deduction (subject to a percentage limitation discussed later) is measured by the asset's fair market value of $100,000, even though the $40,000 appreciation on the land has never been included in income. ▼

In two situations, a charitable contribution of long-term capital gain property is measured by the basis of the property, rather than fair market value. If the corporation contributes *tangible personal property* and the charitable organization puts the property to an unrelated use, the appreciation on the property is not deductible. Unrelated use is defined as use that is not related to the purpose or function that qualifies the organization for exempt status.

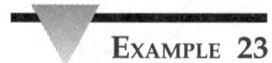

EXAMPLE 22

White Corporation donates a painting worth $200,000 to Western States Art Museum (a qualified organization), which exhibits the painting. White had acquired the painting in 1980 for $90,000. Because the museum put the painting to a related use, White is allowed to deduct $200,000, the fair market value of the painting. ▼

EXAMPLE 23

Assume the same facts as in the previous example, except that White Corporation donates the painting to the American Cancer Society, which sells the painting and deposits the $200,000 proceeds in the organization's general fund. White's deduction is limited to the $90,000 basis because it contributed tangible personal property that was put to an unrelated use by the charitable organization. ▼

The deduction for charitable contributions of long-term capital gain property to certain private nonoperating foundations is also limited to the basis of the property.

Ordinary income property is property that, if sold, would result in ordinary income. Examples of ordinary income property include inventory and capital assets that have not been held long term. In addition, § 1231 property (depreciable property used in a trade or business) is treated as ordinary income property to the extent of any ordinary income recaptured under § 1245 or § 1250. As a general rule, the deduction for a contribution of ordinary income property is limited to the basis of the property. However, corporations enjoy two special exceptions where 50 percent of the appreciation (but not to exceed twice the basis) on property is allowed on certain contributions. The first exception concerns inventory if the property is used in a manner related to the exempt purpose of the charity. Also, the charity must use the property solely for the care of the ill, the needy, or infants.

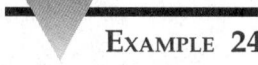

EXAMPLE 24

Lark Corporation, a grocery chain, donates canned goods to the Salvation Army to be used to feed the needy. Lark's basis in the canned goods was $2,000, and the fair market value was $3,000. Lark's deduction is $2,500 [$2,000 basis + 50%($3,000 − $2,000)]. ▼

The second exception involves gifts of scientific property to colleges and certain scientific research organizations for use in research, provided certain conditions are met.[21] As was true of the inventory exception, 50 percent of the appreciation on such property is allowed as an additional deduction.

Limitations Imposed on Charitable Contribution Deductions. Like individuals, corporations are subject to percentage limits on the charitable contribution deduction.[22] For any one year, a corporate taxpayer's contribution deduction is limited to 10 percent of taxable income. For this purpose, taxable income is computed without regard to the charitable contribution deduction, any net operating loss carryback or capital loss carryback, and the dividends received deduction. Any contributions in excess of the 10 percent limitation may be carried forward to the five succeeding tax years. Any carryforward must be added to subsequent contributions and will be subject to the 10 percent limitation. In applying this limitation, the current year's contributions must be deducted first, with excess deductions from previous years deducted in order of time.[23]

EXAMPLE 25

During 1997, Orange Corporation (a calendar year taxpayer) had the following income and expenses:

Income from operations	$140,000
Expenses from operations	110,000
Dividends received	10,000
Charitable contributions made in May 1997	5,000

For purposes of the 10% limitation *only*, Orange Corporation's taxable income is $40,000 ($140,000 − $110,000 + $10,000). Consequently, the allowable charitable deduction for 1997 is $4,000 (10% × $40,000). The $1,000 unused portion of the contribution can be carried forward to 1998, 1999, 2000, 2001, and 2002 (in that order) until exhausted. ▼

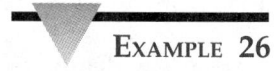

EXAMPLE 26

Assume the same facts as in Example 25. In 1998, Orange Corporation has taxable income (for purposes of the 10% limitation) of $50,000 and makes a charitable contribution of $4,500. The maximum deduction allowed for 1998 would be $5,000 (10% × $50,000). The first $4,500 of the allowed deduction must be allocated to the contribution made in 1998, and $500 of the balance is carried over from 1997. The remaining $500 of the 1997 contribution may be carried over to 1999, etc. ▼

NET OPERATING LOSSES

Like the net operating loss (NOL) of an individual, the NOL of a corporation may be carried back 3 years and forward 15 to offset taxable income for those years. A corporation does not adjust its tax loss for the year for capital losses as do individual taxpayers, because a corporation is not permitted a deduction for net capital losses. Nor does a corporation make adjustments for any nonbusiness deductions as do individual taxpayers. Further, a corporation is allowed to include the dividends received deduction (discussed below) in computing its NOL.[24]

---

[21] These conditions are set forth in § 170(e)(4). For the inventory exception, see § 170(e)(3).

[22] The percentage limitations applicable to individuals and corporations are set forth in § 170(b).

[23] The carryover rules relating to all taxpayers are in § 170(d).

[24] The modifications required to arrive at the amount of NOL that can be carried back or forward are in § 172(d).

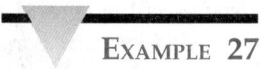

EXAMPLE 27

In 1997, Green Corporation has gross income (including dividends) of $200,000 and deductions of $300,000 excluding the dividends received deduction. Green Corporation had received taxable dividends of $100,000 from Exxon stock. Green has an NOL computed as follows:

Gross income (including dividends)		$ 200,000
Less:		
Business deductions	$300,000	
Dividends received deduction (70% of $100,000)	70,000	(370,000)
Taxable income (or loss)		($ 170,000)

The NOL is carried back three years to 1994. (Green Corporation may forgo the carryback option and elect instead to carry forward the loss.) Assume Green had taxable income of $40,000 in 1994. The carryover to 1995 is computed as follows:

Taxable income for 1994	$ 40,000
Less NOL carryback	(170,000)
Taxable income for 1994 after NOL carryback (carryover to 1995)	($ 130,000)

DEDUCTIONS AVAILABLE ONLY TO CORPORATIONS

Dividends Received Deduction. The purpose of the **dividends received deduction** is to mitigate triple taxation. Without the deduction, income paid to a corporation in the form of a dividend would be taxed to the recipient corporation with no corresponding deduction to the distributing corporation. Later, when the recipient corporation paid the income to its individual shareholders, the income would again be subject to taxation with no corresponding deduction to the corporation. The dividends received deduction alleviates this inequity by causing only some or none of the dividend income to be taxable to the recipient corporation.

As the following table illustrates, the amount of the dividends received deduction depends upon the percentage of ownership the recipient corporate shareholder holds in a domestic corporation making the dividend distribution.[25]

Percentage of Ownership by Corporate Shareholder	Deduction Percentage
Less than 20%	70%
20% or more (but less than 80%)	80%
80% or more*	100%

*The payor corporation must be a member of an affiliated group with the recipient corporation.

The dividends received deduction is limited to a percentage of the taxable income of a corporation. For this purpose, taxable income is computed without regard to the NOL, the dividends received deduction, and any capital loss carryback to the current tax year. The percentage of taxable income limitation

---

[25] § 243(a).

4 LEARNING OBJECTIVE
Discuss the tax rules unique to corporations.

corresponds to the deduction percentage. Thus, if a corporate shareholder owns less than 20 percent of the stock in the distributing corporation, the dividends received deduction is limited to 70 percent of taxable income. However, the taxable income limitation does not apply if the corporation has an NOL for the current taxable year.[26]

In working with this myriad of rules, the following steps are useful:

1. Multiply the dividends received by the deduction percentage.
2. Multiply the taxable income by the deduction percentage.
3. The deduction is limited to the lesser of Step 1 or Step 2, unless subtracting the amount derived in Step 1 from 100 percent of taxable income *generates* an NOL. If so, the amount derived in Step 1 should be used. This is referred to as the NOL rule.

EXAMPLE 28

Red, White, and Blue Corporations, three unrelated calendar year corporations, have the following transactions for the year:

	Red Corporation	White Corporation	Blue Corporation
Gross income from operations	$ 400,000	$ 320,000	$ 260,000
Expenses from operations	(340,000)	(340,000)	(340,000)
Dividends received from domestic corporations (less than 20% ownership)	200,000	200,000	200,000
Taxable income before the dividends received deduction	$ 260,000	$ 180,000	$ 120,000

In determining the dividends received deduction, use the three-step procedure described above:

	Red	White	Blue
Step 1 (70% × $200,000)	$140,000	$140,000	$140,000
Step 2			
70% × $260,000 (taxable income)	$182,000		
70% × $180,000 (taxable income)		$126,000	
70% × $120,000 (taxable income)			$ 84,000
Step 3			
Lesser of Step 1 or Step 2	$140,000	$126,000	
Deduction generates an NOL			$140,000

White Corporation is subject to the 70 percent of taxable income limitation. It does not qualify for NOL rule treatment since subtracting $140,000 (Step 1) from $180,000 (100 percent of taxable income) does not yield a negative figure. Blue Corporation does qualify for NOL rule treatment because subtracting $140,000 (Step 1) from $120,000 (100 percent of taxable income) yields a negative figure. In summary, each corporation has a dividends received deduction for the year as follows: $140,000 for Red Corporation, $126,000 for White Corporation, and $140,000 for Blue Corporation.

[26] § 246(b).

Deduction of Organizational Expenditures.   Expenses incurred in connection with the organization of a corporation normally are chargeable to a capital account. That they benefit the corporation during its existence seems clear. But how can they be amortized when most corporations possess unlimited life? The lack of a determinable and limited estimated useful life would therefore preclude any tax write-off. Code § 248 was enacted to solve this problem.

Under § 248, a corporation may elect to amortize **organizational expenditures** over a period of 60 months or more. The period begins with the month in which the corporation begins business.[27] Organizational expenditures *subject to the election* include the following:

- Legal services incident to organization (e.g., drafting the corporate charter, bylaws, minutes of organizational meetings, terms of original stock certificates).
- Necessary accounting services.
- Expenses of temporary directors and of organizational meetings of directors or shareholders.
- Fees paid to the state of incorporation.

Expenditures that *do not qualify* include those connected with issuing or selling shares of stock or other securities (e.g., commissions, professional fees, and printing costs) or with the transfer of assets to a corporation. Such expenditures reduce the amount of capital raised and are not deductible at all.

To qualify for the election, the expenditure must be *incurred* before the end of the taxable year in which the corporation begins business. In this regard, the corporation's method of accounting is of no consequence. Thus, an expense incurred by a cash basis corporation in its first tax year qualifies even though not paid until a subsequent year.

The election is made in a statement attached to the corporation's return for its first taxable year. The return and statement must be filed no later than the due date of the return (including any extensions).

If the election is not made on a timely basis, organizational expenditures cannot be deducted until the corporation ceases to do business and liquidates. These expenditures will be deductible if the corporate charter limits the life of the corporation.

EXAMPLE 29

Black Corporation, an accrual basis taxpayer, was formed and began operations on May 1, 1997. The following expenses were incurred during its first year of operations (May 1–December 31, 1997):

Expenses of temporary directors and of organizational meetings	$500
Fee paid to the state of incorporation	100
Accounting services incident to organization	200
Legal services for drafting the corporate charter and bylaws	400
Expenses incident to the printing and sale of stock certificates	300

Assume Black Corporation makes a timely election under § 248 to amortize qualifying organizational expenses over a period of 60 months. The monthly amortization is $20 [($500 + $100 + $200 + $400) ÷ 60 months], and $160 ($20 × 8 months) is deductible for tax year

---

[27] The month in which a corporation begins business may not be immediately apparent. See Reg. § 1.248–1(a)(3). For a similar problem in the Subchapter S area, see Chapter 12.

1997. Note that the $300 of expenses incident to the printing and sale of stock certificates does not qualify for the election. These expenses cannot be deducted at all but reduce the amount of the capital realized from the sale of stock. ▼

Organizational expenditures are distinguished from start-up expenditures covered by § 195. Start-up expenditures include various investigation expenses involved in entering a new business, whether incurred by a corporate or a noncorporate taxpayer. Start-up expenses also include operating expenses, such as rent and payroll, that are incurred by a corporation before it actually begins to produce any gross income. At the election of the taxpayer, such expenditures (e.g., travel, market surveys, financial audits, legal fees) can be amortized over a period of 60 months or longer rather than capitalized as part of the cost of the business.

DETERMINING THE CORPORATE INCOME TAX LIABILITY

CORPORATE INCOME TAX RATES

5 **LEARNING OBJECTIVE**
Compute the corporate income tax.

Corporate income tax rates have fluctuated widely over past years. Refer to the inside front cover of the text for a schedule of current corporate income tax rates.

EXAMPLE 30

Gold Corporation, a calendar year taxpayer, has taxable income of $90,000 for 1997. Its income tax liability is $18,850, determined as follows:

Tax on $75,000	$13,750
Tax on $15,000 × 34%	5,100
Tax liability	$18,850

▼

For a corporation that has taxable income in excess of $100,000 for any tax year, the amount of the tax is increased by the lesser of (1) 5 percent of the excess or (2) $11,750. In effect, the additional tax means a 39 percent rate for every dollar of taxable income from $100,000 to $335,000.[28]

EXAMPLE 31

Silver Corporation, a calendar year taxpayer, has taxable income of $335,000 for 1997. Its income tax liability is $113,900, determined as follows:

Tax on $100,000	$ 22,250
Tax on $235,000 × 39%	91,650
Tax liability	$113,900

Note that the tax liability of $113,900 is 34% of $335,000. Thus, due to the 39% rate (34% normal rate + 5% additional tax on taxable income between $100,000 and $335,000), the benefit of the lower rates on the first $75,000 of taxable income completely phases out at $335,000. Note that the normal rate drops back to 34% on taxable income between $335,000 and $10 million. ▼

Qualified PSCs are taxed at a flat 35 percent rate on all taxable income. Thus, PSCs do not enjoy the tax savings of being in the 15 percent to 34 percent brackets

---

[28]§ 11(b).

applicable to other corporations. For this purpose, a PSC is a corporation that is substantially employee owned. Also, it must engage in one of the following activities: health, law, engineering, architecture, accounting, actuarial science, performing arts, or consulting.

ALTERNATIVE MINIMUM TAX

Corporations are subject to an alternative minimum tax (AMT) that is similar to the AMT applicable to individuals. The AMT for corporations, as for individuals, involves a broader tax base than does the regular tax. Like an individual, a corporation is required to apply a minimum tax rate to the expanded base and pay the difference between the AMT tax liability and the regular tax. Many of the adjustments and tax preference items necessary to arrive at alternative minimum taxable income (AMTI) are the same for individuals and corporations.

   Although the objective of the AMT is the same for individual and corporate taxpayers, the rate and exemptions are different. Computation of the AMT for corporations is discussed in Chapter 6.

TAX LIABILITY OF RELATED CORPORATIONS

6   **LEARNING OBJECTIVE**
Explain the tax rules unique to multiple corporations.

Related corporations are subject to special rules for computing the income tax, the accumulated earnings credit, the AMT exemption, and the prior environmental tax exemption.[29] If these restrictions did not exist, the shareholders of a corporation could gain significant tax advantages by splitting a single corporation into *multiple* corporations. The next two examples illustrate the potential *income tax* advantage of multiple corporations.

EXAMPLE 32

Gray Corporation annually yields taxable income of $300,000. The corporate tax on $300,000 is $100,250, computed as follows:

Tax on $100,000	$ 22,250
Tax on $200,000 × 39%	78,000
Tax liability	$100,250

▼

EXAMPLE 33

Assume that Gray Corporation in the previous example is divided equally into four corporations. Each corporation would have taxable income of $75,000, and the tax for each (absent the special provisions for related corporations) would be computed as follows:

Tax on $50,000	$ 7,500
Tax on $25,000 × 25%	6,250
Tax liability	$13,750

The total liability for the four corporations would be $55,000 ($13,750 × 4). The savings would be $45,250 ($100,250 − $55,000). ▼

   To preclude the advantages that could be gained by using multiple corporations, the tax law requires special treatment for *controlled groups* of corporations. A comparison of Examples 32 and 33 reveals that the income tax savings that could be achieved by using multiple corporations result from having more of the total income taxed at lower rates. To close this potential loophole, the law limits a

---

[29] § 1561(a).

controlled group's taxable income in the tax brackets below 35 percent to the amount the corporations in the group would have if they were one corporation. Thus, in Example 33, under the controlled corporation rules, only $12,500 (one-fourth of the first $50,000 of taxable income) for each of the four related corporations would be taxed at the 15 percent rate. The 25 percent rate would apply to the next $6,250 (one-fourth of the next $25,000) of taxable income of each corporation. This equal allocation of the $50,000 and $25,000 amounts is required unless all members of the controlled group consent to an apportionment plan providing for an unequal allocation.

Similar limitations apply to the $250,000 accumulated earnings credit for controlled groups and to the $40,000 exemption amount for purposes of computing the AMT. Both the accumulated earnings tax and the AMT are discussed in Chapter 6.

CONTROLLED GROUPS

A **controlled group** of corporations includes parent-subsidiary groups, brother-sister groups, combined groups, and certain insurance companies. Groups of the first three types are discussed in the following sections. Insurance groups are not discussed in this text.

Parent-Subsidiary Controlled Group. A **parent-subsidiary controlled group** consists of one or more *chains* of corporations connected through stock ownership with a common parent corporation. The ownership connection can be established through either a *voting power test* or a *value test*. The voting power test requires ownership of stock possessing at least 80 percent of the total voting power of all classes of stock entitled to vote.[30]

EXAMPLE 34
Aqua Corporation owns 80% of White Corporation. Aqua and White Corporations are members of a parent-subsidiary controlled group. Aqua is the parent corporation, and White is the subsidiary. ▼

The parent-subsidiary relationship illustrated in Example 34 is easy to recognize because Aqua Corporation is the direct owner of White Corporation. Real-world business organizations are often much more complex, sometimes including numerous corporations with chains of ownership connecting them. In these complex corporate structures, determining whether the controlled group classification is appropriate becomes more difficult. The ownership requirements can be met through direct ownership (refer to Example 34) or through indirect ownership, as illustrated in the two following examples.

EXAMPLE 35
Red Corporation owns 80% of the voting stock of White Corporation, and White Corporation owns 80% of the voting stock of Blue Corporation. Red, White, and Blue Corporations constitute a controlled group in which Red is the common parent and White and Blue are subsidiaries. The same result would occur if Red Corporation, rather than White Corporation, owned the Blue Corporation stock. This parent-subsidiary relationship is diagrammed in Figure 2–2. ▼

EXAMPLE 36
Brown Corporation owns 80% of the stock of Green Corporation, which owns 30% of Blue Corporation. Brown also owns 80% of White Corporation, which owns 50% of Blue

[30]§ 1563(a)(1).

▼ **FIGURE 2–2**
Controlled Groups—Parent-
Subsidiary Corporations

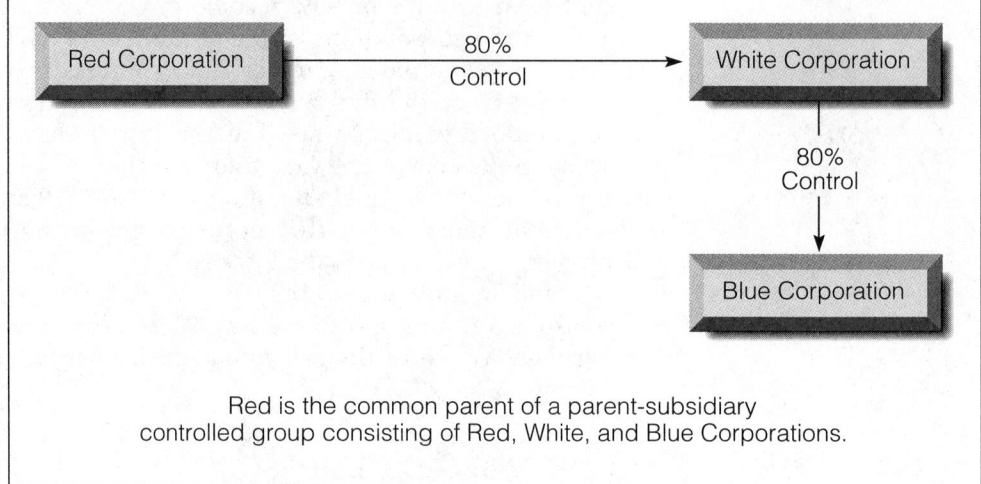

Red is the common parent of a parent-subsidiary
controlled group consisting of Red, White, and Blue Corporations.

▼ **FIGURE 2–3**
Controlled Groups—Parent-
Subsidiary Corporations

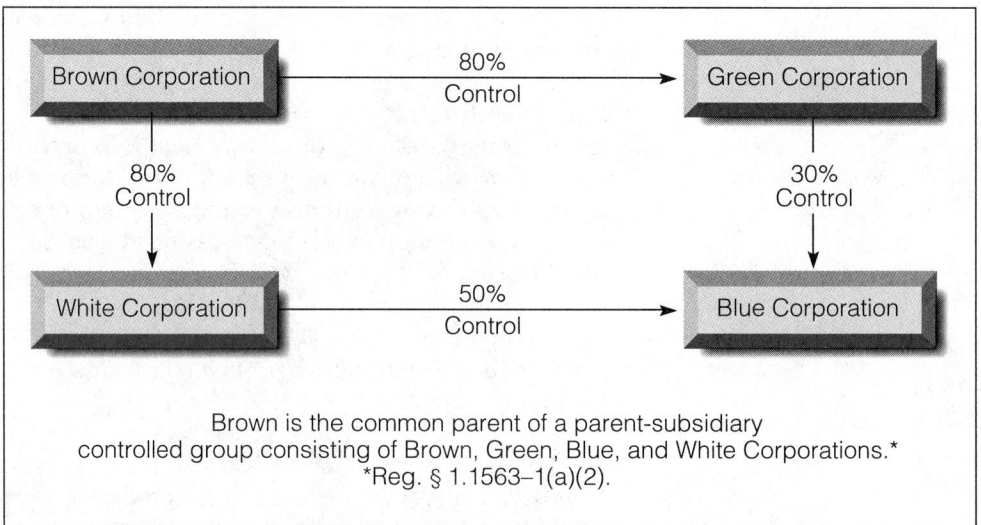

Brown is the common parent of a parent-subsidiary
controlled group consisting of Brown, Green, Blue, and White Corporations.*
*Reg. § 1.1563–1(a)(2).

Corporation. Brown, Green, Blue and White Corporations constitute a parent-subsidiary controlled group in which Brown is the common parent and Green, Blue and White are subsidiaries. This parent-subsidiary relationship is diagrammed in Figure 2–3. ▼

The value test requires ownership of at least 80 percent of the total value of all shares of all classes of stock of each of the corporations, except the parent corporation, by one or more of the other corporations.

Brother-Sister Corporations. A **brother-sister controlled group** *may* exist if two or more corporations are owned by five or fewer *persons* (individuals, estates, or trusts). Brother-sister status will apply if such a shareholder group meets an 80 percent total ownership test *and* a 50 percent common ownership test.[31]

---

[31] § 1563(a)(2).

- The *total* ownership test is met if the shareholder group possesses stock representing at least 80 percent of the total combined voting power of all classes of stock entitled to vote, *or* at least 80 percent of the total value of shares of all classes of stock of each corporation.
- The *common* ownership test is met if the shareholder group owns more than 50 percent of the total combined voting power of all classes of stock entitled to vote, *or* more than 50 percent of the total value of shares of all classes of stock of each corporation.

In applying the common ownership test, the stock held by each person is considered only to the extent that the stock ownership is *identical* for each corporation. That is, if a shareholder owns 30 percent of Silver Corporation and 20 percent of Gold Corporation, such shareholder has identical ownership of 20 percent of each corporation.

▼ **EXAMPLE 37**

The outstanding stock of Hawk, Eagle, Crane, and Dove Corporations, each of which has only one class of stock outstanding, is owned by the following unrelated individuals:

	Corporations				Identical Ownership
Individuals	**Hawk**	**Eagle**	**Crane**	**Dove**	
Allen	40%	30%	60%	60%	30%
Barton	50%	20%	30%	20%	20%
Carter	10%	30%	10%	10%	10%
Dixon		20%		10%	
Total	100%	100%	100%	100%	60%

Five or fewer individuals (Allen, Barton, and Carter) with more than a 50% common ownership own at least 80% of all classes of stock in Hawk, Eagle, Crane, and Dove. They own 100% of Hawk, 80% of Eagle, 100% of Crane, and 90% of Dove. Consequently, Hawk, Eagle, Crane, and Dove are regarded as members of a brother-sister controlled group. ▼

▼ **EXAMPLE 38**

Changing the facts in Example 37, assume the ownership is as follows:

	Corporations				Identical Ownership
Individuals	**Hawk**	**Eagle**	**Crane**	**Dove**	
Allen	20%	10%	5%	60%	5%
Barton	10%	20%	60%	5%	5%
Carter	10%	70%	35%	25%	10%
Dixon	60%			10%	
Total	100%	100%	100%	100%	20%

In this situation, the identical ownership is only 20%. Consequently, the four corporations are not members of a brother-sister controlled group. However, Eagle and Crane would be brother-sister corporations because both the total ownership and the common ownership tests are met. Allen, Barton, and Carter own 100% of each corporation, and common ownership exceeds 50% (5% by Allen, 20% by Barton, and 35% by Carter). ▼

▼ **EXAMPLE 39**

The outstanding stock of Black Corporation and Brown Corporation, each of which has only one class of stock outstanding, is owned as follows:

Individuals	Corporations		Identical Ownership
	Black	Brown	
Rossi	55%	100%	55%
Smith	45%		
Total	100%	100%	55%

Although the 50% common ownership test is met, the 80% test is not since there is no common ownership in Brown Corporation. Are Black and Brown brother-sister corporations? No, according to the U.S. Supreme Court.[32] ▼

ETHICAL CONSIDERATIONS

Must Voting Rights Reflect Ownership?

Andrews, Barnes, and Clark are shareholders in Gull, Plover, and Kite Corporations—each has shares in all three corporations. Their tax adviser points out that if the shareholders would trade some shares among themselves, the three corporations would no longer be classified as affiliated corporations, and substantial tax savings would result. The three shareholders would like to complete the trades, but are concerned because the new ownership percentages will give Andrews voting control in Kite Corporation. To solve this problem, Andrews proposes that all three shareholders continue voting based on the ownership percentages that existed prior to the trades. Evaluate Andrews's proposal.

Combined Groups. A combined controlled group exists if all of the following conditions are met:

- Each corporation is a member of either a parent-subsidiary controlled group or a brother-sister controlled group.
- At least one of the corporations is a parent of a parent-subsidiary controlled group.
- The parent corporation is also a member of a brother-sister controlled group.

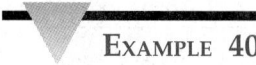

EXAMPLE 40

Robert owns 80% of all classes of stock of Red and Orange Corporations. Red Corporation, in turn, owns 80% of all classes of stock of Blue Corporation. Orange owns all the stock of Green Corporation. Red, Blue, Orange, and Green are members of the same combined group. As a result, Red, Blue, Orange, and Green are limited to taxable income in the tax brackets below 35% and the $250,000 accumulated earnings credit as though they were one corporation. This is also the case for the election to expense certain depreciable business assets under § 179 and the $40,000 exemption for purposes of computing the AMT. ▼

Application of § 482. Congress has recognized that a parent corporation has the power to shift income among its subsidiaries. Likewise, shareholders who control brother-sister groups can shift income and deductions among the related corporations.

---

[32] *U.S. v. Vogel Fertilizer Co.,* 82-1 USTC ¶9134, 49 AFTR2d 82-491, 102 S.Ct. 821 (USSC, 1982). See also Reg. § 1.1563–1(a)(3), which was amended to comply with the conclusions reached in *Vogel.*

When the true taxable income of a subsidiary or other related corporation has been understated or overstated, the IRS can reallocate the income and deductions of the related corporations under § 482. Section 482 permits the IRS to allocate gross income, deductions, and credits between any two or more organizations, trades, or businesses that are owned or controlled by the same interests. This is appropriate when the allocation is necessary to prevent avoidance of taxes or to reflect income correctly. Controlled groups of corporations are particularly vulnerable to § 482.

▼ PROCEDURAL MATTERS

FILING REQUIREMENTS FOR CORPORATIONS

7 ▼ **LEARNING OBJECTIVE**
Describe the reporting process for corporations.

A corporation must file a Federal income tax return whether or not it has taxable income.[33] A corporation that was not in existence throughout an entire annual accounting period is required to file a return for the fraction of the year during which it was in existence. In addition, a corporation must file a return even though it has ceased to do business if it has valuable claims for which it will bring suit. A corporation is relieved of filing income tax returns only when it ceases to do business and retains no assets.

The corporate return is filed on Form 1120 unless the corporation is a small corporation entitled to file the shorter Form 1120–A. A corporation may file Form 1120–A if it meets *all* the following requirements:

- Gross receipts or sales are under $500,000.
- Total income (gross profit plus other income including gains on sales of property) is under $500,000.
- Total assets are under $500,000.
- The corporation is not involved in a dissolution or liquidation.
- The corporation is not a member of a controlled group under §§ 1561 and 1563.
- The corporation does not file a consolidated return.
- The corporation does not have ownership in a foreign corporation.
- The corporation does not have foreign shareholders who directly or indirectly own 50 percent or more of its stock.

Corporations electing under Subchapter S (see Chapter 12) file on Form 1120S. Forms 1120, 1120–A, and 1120S are reproduced in Appendix B.

The return must be filed on or before the fifteenth day of the third month following the close of a corporation's tax year. As noted previously, a regular corporation, other than a PSC, can use either a calendar or a fiscal year to report its taxable income. The tax year of the shareholders has no effect on the corporation's tax year.

Corporations can receive an automatic extension of six months for filing the corporate return by filing Form 7004 by the due date for the return.[34] However, the IRS may terminate the extension by mailing a 10-day notice to the taxpayer corporation. A Form 7004 must be accompanied by the corporation's estimated tax liability.

---

[33] § 6012(a)(2).

[34] § 6081.

ESTIMATED TAX PAYMENTS

A corporation must make payments of estimated tax unless its tax liability can reasonably be expected to be less than $500. The required annual payment (which includes any estimated AMT liability) is the lesser of (1) 100 percent of the corporation's final tax or (2) 100 percent of the tax for the preceding year (if that was a 12-month tax year and the return filed showed a tax liability).[35] Estimated payments can be made in four installments due on or before the fifteenth day of the fourth month, the sixth month, the ninth month, and the twelfth month of the corporate taxable year. The full amount of the unpaid tax is due on the due date of the return. For a calendar year corporation, the payment dates are as follows:

April 15

June 15

September 15

December 15

A corporation failing to pay its required estimated tax payments will be subjected to a nondeductible penalty on the amount by which the installments are less than the tax due. However, the underpayment penalty will not be imposed if the estimated payments are timely and are equal to the tax liability of the corporation for the prior year or equal to the tax due computed on an annualized basis. If the annualized method is used for one installment and the corporation does not use this method for a subsequent installment, any shortfall from using the annualized method for a prior payment(s) must be made up in the subsequent installment payment. The penalty is imposed on each installment; that is, a corporation must pay one-fourth of its required annual payment by the due date of each installment.

A *large* corporation cannot base its installment payments on its previous year's tax liability except for its first installment payment. A corporation is considered large if it had taxable income in excess of $1 million in any of its three preceding years.

RECONCILIATION OF TAXABLE INCOME AND FINANCIAL NET INCOME

Schedule M–1 on the last page of Form 1120 is used to reconcile net income as computed for financial accounting purposes with taxable income reported on the corporation's income tax return. The starting point on Schedule M–1 is net income per books (financial accounting net income). Additions and subtractions are entered for items that affect net income per books and taxable income differently. The following items are entered as additions (see lines 2 through 5 of Schedule M–1):

* Federal income tax liability (deducted in computing net income per books but not deductible in computing taxable income).
* The excess of capital losses over capital gains (deducted for financial accounting purposes but not deductible by corporations for income tax purposes).
* Income that is reported in the current year for tax purposes that is not reported in computing net income per books (e.g., prepaid income).
* Various expenses that are deducted in computing net income per books but are not allowed in computing taxable income (e.g., charitable contributions in excess of the 10 percent ceiling applicable to corporations).

The following subtractions are entered on lines 7 and 8 of Schedule M–1:

---

[35] §§ 6655(d) and (e).

- Income reported for financial accounting purposes but not included in taxable income (e.g., tax-exempt interest).
- Expenses deducted on the tax return but not deducted in computing net income per books (e.g., a charitable contributions carryover deducted in a prior year for financial accounting purposes but deductible in the current year for tax purposes).

The result is taxable income (before the NOL deduction and the dividends received deduction).

EXAMPLE 41

During the current year, Tern Corporation had the following transactions:

Net income per books (after tax)	$92,400
Taxable income	50,000
Federal income tax liability (15% × $50,000)	7,500
Interest income from tax-exempt bonds	5,000
Interest paid on loan, the proceeds of which were used to purchase the tax-exempt bonds	500
Life insurance proceeds received as a result of the death of a key employee	50,000
Premiums paid on key employee life insurance policy	2,600
Excess of capital losses over capital gains	2,000

For book and tax purposes, Tern Corporation determines depreciation under the straight-line method. Tern's Schedule M–1 for the current year is as follows:

Schedule M-1	Reconciliation of Income (Loss) per Books With Income per Return (See page 16 of instructions.)			
1	Net income (loss) per books	92,400	7 Income recorded on books this year not included on this return (itemize): Tax-exempt interest $ 5,000, Life insurance proceeds on key employee $50,000	
2	Federal income tax	7,500		
3	Excess of capital losses over capital gains	2,000		
4	Income subject to tax not recorded on books this year (itemize):			55,000
5	Expenses recorded on books this year not deducted on this return (itemize):		8 Deductions on this return not charged against book income this year (itemize):	
a	Depreciation . . . . $		a Depreciation . . . . $	
b	Contributions carryover $		b Contributions carryover $	
c	Travel and entertainment $ Int. on tax-exempt bonds $500, Prem. on key employee ins. $2,600	3,100	9 Add lines 7 and 8	55,000
6	Add lines 1 through 5	105,000	10 Income (line 28, page 1)—line 6 less line 9	50,000

Schedule M–2 reconciles unappropriated retained earnings at the beginning of the year with unappropriated retained earnings at year-end. Beginning balance plus net income per books, as entered on line 1 of Schedule M–1, less dividend distributions during the year equals ending retained earnings. Other sources of increases or decreases in retained earnings are also listed on Schedule M–2.

EXAMPLE 42

Assume the same facts as in Example 41. Tern Corporation's beginning balance in unappropriated retained earnings is $125,000. During the year, Tern distributed a cash dividend of $30,000 to its shareholders. Based on these further assumptions, Tern's Schedule M–2 for the current year is as follows:

Schedule M-2	Analysis of Unappropriated Retained Earnings per Books (Line 25, Schedule L)			
1	Balance at beginning of year	125,000	5 Distributions: a Cash	30,000
2	Net income (loss) per books	92,400	b Stock	
3	Other increases (itemize):		c Property	
			6 Other decreases (itemize):	
			7 Add lines 5 and 6	30,000
4	Add lines 1, 2, and 3	217,400	8 Balance at end of year (line 4 less line 7)	187,400

FORM 1120 ILLUSTRATED

Swift Corporation was formed on January 10, 1985, by James Brown and Martha Swift to sell men's clothing. Pertinent information regarding Swift is summarized as follows:

- The business address is 6210 Norman Street, Buffalo, TX 79330.
- The employer identification number is 75–3284680; the principal business activity code is 5600.
- James Brown and Martha Swift each own one-half of the outstanding common stock; no other class of stock is authorized. James Brown is president of the company, and Martha Swift is secretary-treasurer. Both are full-time employees of the corporation, and each receives a salary of $70,000. James's Social Security number is 299–50–2593; Martha's Social Security number is 400–40–6680.
- The corporation uses the accrual method of accounting and reports on a calendar basis. The specific chargeoff method is used in handling bad debt losses, and inventories are determined using the lower of cost or market method. For book and tax purposes, the straight-line method of depreciation is used.
- During 1996, the corporation distributed a cash dividend of $35,000. Selected portions of Swift's profit and loss statement reflect the following debits and credits:

Account	Debit	Credit
Gross sales		$1,040,000
Sales returns and allowances	$ 50,000	
Purchases	506,000	
Dividends received from stock investments in less-than-20%-owned U.S. corporations		60,000
Interest income		
State bonds	$ 9,000	
Certificates of deposit	11,000	20,000
Premiums on term life insurance policies on the lives of James Brown and Martha Swift; Swift Corporation is the designated beneficiary	8,000	
Salaries—officers	140,000	
Salaries—clerical and sales	100,000	
Taxes (state, local, and payroll)	35,000	
Repairs	20,000	
Interest expense		
Loan to purchase state bonds	$ 4,000	
Other business loans	10,000	14,000
Advertising	8,000	
Rental expense	24,000	
Depreciation	16,000	
Other deductions	21,000	

A comparative balance sheet for Swift Corporation reveals the following information:

Assets	January 1, 1996	December 31, 1996
Cash	$ 240,000	$ 163,850
Trade notes and accounts receivable	404,200	542,300
Inventories	300,000	356,000
Federal and state bonds	150,000	150,000
Prepaid Federal tax	—	1,700
Buildings and other depreciable assets	120,000	120,000
Accumulated depreciation	(44,400)	(60,400)
Land	10,000	10,000
Other assets	1,800	1,000
Total assets	$1,181,600	$1,284,450

Liabilities and Equity	January 1, 1996	December 31, 1996
Accounts payable	$ 150,000	$ 125,000
Other current liabilities	40,150	33,300
Mortgages	105,000	100,000
Capital stock	250,000	250,000
Retained earnings	636,450	776,150
Total liabilities and equity	$1,181,600	$1,284,450

Net income per books (before any income tax accrual) is $234,000. During 1996, Swift Corporation made estimated tax payments to the IRS of $61,000. Swift Corporation's Form 1120 for 1996 is reproduced on the following pages.

Although most of the entries on Form 1120 for Swift Corporation are self-explanatory, the following comments may be helpful:

- In order to arrive at the cost of goods sold amount (line 2 on page 1), Schedule A (page 2) must be completed.
- Reporting of dividends requires the completion of Schedule C (page 2). Gross dividends are shown on line 4 (page 1), and the dividends received deduction appears on line 29b (page 1). Separating the dividend from the deduction facilitates the application of the 80 percent and 70 percent of taxable income exception (which did not apply in Swift's case).
- Income tax liability is $59,300, computed as follows:

Tax on $100,000	$22,250
Tax on $95,000 at 39%	37,050
	$59,300

The result is transferred to line 3 of Schedule J and ultimately is listed on line 31 (page 1). Because the estimated tax payment of $61,000 is more than the tax liability of $59,300, Swift will receive a tax refund of $1,700.

- In completing Schedule M–1 (page 4), the net income per books (line 1) is net of the Federal income tax ($234,000 – $59,300). The left-hand side of Schedule M–1 (lines 2–5) represents positive adjustments to net income per books. After the negative adjustments are made (line 9), the result is taxable income before NOLs and special deductions (line 28, page 1).

- In completing Schedule M–2 (page 4) the beginning retained earnings figure of $636,450 is added to the net income per books as entered on Schedule M–1 (line 1). The dividends distributed in the amount of $35,000 are entered on line 5 and subtracted to arrive at the ending balance in unappropriated retained earnings of $776,150.
- Because this example lacks certain details, supporting schedules that would be attached to Form 1120 have not been included. For example, a Form 4562 would be included to verify the depreciation deduction (line 20, page 1), and other deductions (line 26, page 1) would be supported by a schedule.

CONSOLIDATED RETURNS

Corporations that are members of a parent-subsidiary affiliated group may be able to file a consolidated income tax return for a taxable year. Consolidated returns are discussed in Chapter 8.

TAX PLANNING
CONSIDERATIONS

8 **LEARNING OBJECTIVE**
Evaluate corporations for
conducting a business.

CORPORATE VERSUS NONCORPORATE FORMS OF BUSINESS ORGANIZATION

The decision to use the corporate form in conducting a trade or business must be weighed carefully. Besides the nontax considerations attendant on the corporate form (limited liability, continuity of life, free transferability of interests, and centralized management), tax ramifications will play an important role in any such decision. Close attention should be paid to the following:

1. Operating as a regular corporate entity (C corporation) results in the imposition of the corporate income tax. Corporate taxable income will be taxed twice—once as earned by the corporation and again when distributed to the shareholders. Since dividends are not deductible, a closely held corporation has a strong incentive to structure corporate distributions in a deductible form. Thus, profits can be bailed out by the shareholders in the form of salaries, interest, or rents. Such procedures lead to a multitude of problems, one of which, the reclassification of debt as equity, is discussed in Chapter 3. The problems of unreasonable salaries and rents are covered in Chapter 4 in the discussion of constructive dividends.
2. The current tax rates appear to favor corporations over individuals, since corporations have a maximum tax rate of 35 percent and individuals may be subject to a 39.6 percent top rate. Relatively few individuals or corporations are in the top rate brackets, however. For moderate-income taxpayers, the differences in Federal tax brackets between an individual and a corporation may not be substantial. Several state and local governments impose higher taxes on corporations than on individuals. In these jurisdictions, the combined Federal, state, and local tax rates on the two types of taxpayers are practically identical. If a corporation's taxable income does not exceed $100,000, a substantial tax savings may be achieved by accumulating income inside the corporation. Refer to Example 7.
3. Corporate-source income loses its identity as it passes through the corporation to the shareholders. Thus, items that normally receive preferential tax treatment (e.g., interest on municipal bonds) are not taxed as such to the shareholders.
4. As noted in Chapter 4, it may be difficult for shareholders to recover some or all of their investment in the corporation without an ordinary income result. Most corporate distributions are treated as dividends to the extent of the corporation's earnings and profits.

Form **1120**	**U.S. Corporation Income Tax Return**	OMB No. 1545-0123
Department of the Treasury Internal Revenue Service	For calendar year 1996 or tax year beginning ...., 1996, ending ...., 19 ... ▶ Instructions are separate. See page 1 for Paperwork Reduction Act Notice.	19**96**

A Check if a:
1 Consolidated return (attach Form 851) ☐
2 Personal holding co. (attach Sch. PH) ☐
3 Personal service corp. (as defined in Temporary Regs. sec. 1.441-4T— see instructions) ☐

Use IRS label. Otherwise, print or type.

Name — *Swift Corporation*
Number, street, and room or suite no. (If a P.O. box, see page 6 of instructions.) — *6210 Norman Street*
City or town, state, and ZIP code — *Buffalo, TX 79330*

B Employer identification number — 75 : 3284680
C Date incorporated — *1-10-85*
D Total assets (see page 6 of instructions) — $ 1,284,450 | 00

E Check applicable boxes: (1) ☐ Initial return (2) ☐ Final return (3) ☐ Change of address

Income	**1a** Gross receipts or sales 1,040,000 00 **b** Less returns and allowances 50,000 00 **c** Bal ▶	**1c**	990,000 00
	2 Cost of goods sold (Schedule A, line 8)	**2**	450,000 00
	3 Gross profit. Subtract line 2 from line 1c	**3**	540,000 00
	4 Dividends (Schedule C, line 19)	**4**	60,000 00
	5 Interest	**5**	11,000 00
	6 Gross rents	**6**	
	7 Gross royalties	**7**	
	8 Capital gain net income (attach Schedule D (Form 1120))	**8**	
	9 Net gain or (loss) from Form 4797, Part II, line 20 (attach Form 4797)	**9**	
	10 Other income (see page 7 of instructions—attach schedule)	**10**	
	11 **Total income.** Add lines 3 through 10 ▶	**11**	611,000 00
Deductions (See instructions for limitations on deductions.)	**12** Compensation of officers (Schedule E, line 4)	**12**	140,000 00
	13 Salaries and wages (less employment credits)	**13**	100,000 00
	14 Repairs and maintenance	**14**	20,000 00
	15 Bad debts	**15**	
	16 Rents	**16**	24,000 00
	17 Taxes and licenses	**17**	35,000 00
	18 Interest	**18**	10,000 00
	19 Charitable contributions (see page 8 of instructions for 10% limitation)	**19**	
	20 Depreciation (attach Form 4562) **20** 16,000 00		
	21 Less depreciation claimed on Schedule A and elsewhere on return **21a**	**21b**	16,000 00
	22 Depletion	**22**	
	23 Advertising	**23**	8,000 00
	24 Pension, profit-sharing, etc., plans	**24**	
	25 Employee benefit programs	**25**	
	26 Other deductions (attach schedule)	**26**	21,000 00
	27 **Total deductions.** Add lines 12 through 26 ▶	**27**	374,000 00
	28 Taxable income before net operating loss deduction and special deductions. Subtract line 27 from line 11	**28**	237,000 00
	29 **Less:** **a** Net operating loss deduction (see page 10 of instructions) **29a**		
	b Special deductions (Schedule C, line 20) **29b** 42,000 00	**29c**	42,000 00
Tax and Payments	**30** **Taxable income.** Subtract line 29c from line 28	**30**	195,000 00
	31 **Total tax** (Schedule J, line 10)	**31**	59,300 00
	32 **Payments: a** 1995 overpayment credited to 1996 **32a**		
	b 1996 estimated tax payments **32b**		
	c Less 1996 refund applied for on Form 4466 **32c** ( ) **d** Bal ▶ **32d** 61,000 00		
	e Tax deposited with Form 7004 **32e**		
	f Credit from regulated investment companies (attach Form 2439) **32f**		
	g Credit for Federal tax on fuels (attach Form 4136). See instructions **32g**	**32h**	61,000 00
	33 Estimated tax penalty (see page 11 of instructions). Check if Form 2220 is attached ▶ ☐	**33**	
	34 **Tax due.** If line 32h is smaller than the total of lines 31 and 33, enter amount owed	**34**	
	35 **Overpayment.** If line 32h is larger than the total of lines 31 and 33, enter amount overpaid	**35**	1,700 00
	36 Enter amount of line 35 you want: **Credited to 1997 estimated tax** ▶ **Refunded** ▶	**36**	1,700 00

Sign Here
Under penalties of perjury, I declare that I have examined this return, including accompanying schedules and statements, and to the best of my knowledge and belief, it is true, correct, and complete. Declaration of preparer (other than taxpayer) is based on all information of which preparer has any knowledge.

▶ Signature of officer   Date   ▶ Title

Paid Preparer's Use Only

Preparer's signature ▶	Date	Check if self-employed ☐	Preparer's social security number
Firm's name (or yours if self-employed) and address ▶		EIN ▶	
		ZIP code ▶	

Cat. No. 11450Q

5. Corporate losses cannot be passed through to the shareholders.[36]
6. The liquidation of a corporation will normally generate tax consequences to both the corporation and its shareholders (see Chapter 5).

[36] Points 1, 2, and 5 could be resolved through a Subchapter S election (see Chapter 12), assuming the corporation qualifies for such an election. In part, the same can be said for point 3.

Form 1120 (1996)   Page **2**

Schedule A   Cost of Goods Sold (See page 11 of instructions.)

1	Inventory at beginning of year	**1** 30,000 00
2	Purchases	**2** 506,000 00
3	Cost of labor	**3**
4	Additional section 263A costs (attach schedule)	**4**
5	Other costs (attach schedule)	**5**
6	**Total.** Add lines 1 through 5	**6** 806,000 00
7	Inventory at end of year	**7** 356,000 00
8	**Cost of goods sold.** Subtract line 7 from line 6. Enter here and on page 1, line 2	**8** 450,000 00

9a   Check all methods used for valuing closing inventory:
- (i) ☐ Cost as described in Regulations section 1.471-3
- (ii) ☒ Lower of cost or market as described in Regulations section 1.471-4
- (iii) ☐ Other (Specify method used and attach explanation.) ▶ ....

b   Check if there was a writedown of subnormal goods as described in Regulations section 1.471-2(c) . . . . ▶ ☐

c   Check if the LIFO inventory method was adopted this tax year for any goods (if checked, attach Form 970) . . . . . ▶ ☐

d   If the LIFO inventory method was used for this tax year, enter percentage (or amounts) of closing
inventory computed under LIFO   **9d**

e   If property is produced or acquired for resale, do the rules of section 263A apply to the corporation? . . . . . ☐ Yes ☒ No

f   Was there any change in determining quantities, cost, or valuations between opening and closing inventory? If "Yes,"
attach explanation . . . . ☐ Yes ☒ No

Schedule C   Dividends and Special Deductions (See page 12 of instructions.)

		(a) Dividends received	(b) %	(c) Special deductions (a) × (b)
1	Dividends from less-than-20%-owned domestic corporations that are subject to the 70% deduction (other than debt-financed stock)	60,000	70	42,000
2	Dividends from 20%-or-more-owned domestic corporations that are subject to the 80% deduction (other than debt-financed stock)		80	
3	Dividends on debt-financed stock of domestic and foreign corporations (section 246A)		see instructions	
4	Dividends on certain preferred stock of less-than-20%-owned public utilities		42	
5	Dividends on certain preferred stock of 20%-or-more-owned public utilities		48	
6	Dividends from less-than-20%-owned foreign corporations and certain FSCs that are subject to the 70% deduction		70	
7	Dividends from 20%-or-more-owned foreign corporations and certain FSCs that are subject to the 80% deduction		80	
8	Dividends from wholly owned foreign subsidiaries subject to the 100% deduction (section 245(b))		100	
9	**Total.** Add lines 1 through 8. See page 12 of instructions for limitation			42,000
10	Dividends from domestic corporations received by a small business investment company operating under the Small Business Investment Act of 1958		100	
11	Dividends from certain FSCs that are subject to the 100% deduction (section 245(c)(1))		100	
12	Dividends from affiliated group members subject to the 100% deduction (section 243(a)(3))		100	
13	Other dividends from foreign corporations not included on lines 3, 6, 7, 8, or 11			
14	Income from controlled foreign corporations under subpart F (attach Form(s) 5471)			
15	Foreign dividend gross-up (section 78)			
16	IC-DISC and former DISC dividends not included on lines 1, 2, or 3 (section 246(d))			
17	Other dividends			
18	Deduction for dividends paid on certain preferred stock of public utilities			
19	**Total dividends.** Add lines 1 through 17. Enter here and on line 4, page 1 ▶	60,000		
20	**Total special deductions.** Add lines 9, 10, 11, 12, and 18. Enter here and on line 29b, page 1 . . . ▶			42,000

Schedule E   Compensation of Officers (See instructions for line 12, page 1.)

Complete Schedule E only if total receipts (line 1a plus lines 4 through 10 on page 1, Form 1120) are $500,000 or more.

	(a) Name of officer	(b) Social security number	(c) Percent of time devoted to business	(d) Common	(e) Preferred	(f) Amount of compensation
1	James Brown	299-50-2593	100 %	50 %	%	70,000
	Martha Swift	400-40-6680	100 %	50 %	%	70,000
			%	%	%	
			%	%	%	
			%	%	%	

2	Total compensation of officers	140,000
3	Compensation of officers claimed on Schedule A and elsewhere on return	
4	Subtract line 3 from line 2. Enter the result here and on line 12, page 1	140,000

7. The corporate form provides shareholders with the opportunity to be treated as employees for tax purposes if the shareholders render services to the corporation. Such status makes a number of attractive tax-sheltered fringe benefits available. They include, but are not limited to, group term life insurance and excludible meals and lodging. One of the most attractive benefits of incorporation is the ability of the business to provide accident and health insurance to its employees, including shareholders. Such ben-

Form 1120 (1996) Page **3**

Schedule J — Tax Computation (See page 13 of instructions.)

1	Check if the corporation is a member of a controlled group (see sections 1561 and 1563) . . . . ▶ ☐			

Important: Members of a controlled group, see instructions on page 13.

2a If the box on line 1 is checked, enter the corporation's share of the $50,000, $25,000, and $9,925,000 taxable income brackets (in that order):

(1) $ _____ (2) $ _____ (3) $ _____

b Enter the corporation's share of:

(1) Additional 5% tax (not more than $11,750) $ _____

(2) Additional 3% tax (not more than $100,000) $ _____

3	Income tax. Check this box if the corporation is a qualified personal service corporation as defined in section 448(d)(2) (see instructions on page 13) . . . . ▶ ☐	**3**	59,300	00
4a	Foreign tax credit (attach Form 1118)	**4a**		
b	Possessions tax credit (attach Form 5735)	**4b**		
c	Check: ☐ Nonconventional source fuel credit ☐ QEV credit (attach Form 8834)	**4c**		
d	General business credit. Enter here and check which forms are attached: ☐ 3800 ☐ 3468 ☐ 5884 ☐ 6478 ☐ 6765 ☐ 8586 ☐ 8830 ☐ 8826 ☐ 8835 ☐ 8844 ☐ 8845 ☐ 8846 ☐ 8820 ☐ 8847	**4d**		
e	Credit for prior year minimum tax (attach Form 8827)	**4e**		
5	**Total credits.** Add lines 4a through 4e	**5**		
6	Subtract line 5 from line 3	**6**	59,300	00
7	Personal holding company tax (attach Schedule PH (Form 1120))	**7**		
8	Recapture taxes. Check if from: ☐ Form 4255 ☐ Form 8611	**8**		
9	Alternative minimum tax (attach Form 4626)	**9**		
10	**Total tax.** Add lines 6 through 9. Enter here and on line 31, page 1	**10**	59,300	00

Schedule K — Other Information (See page 15 of instructions.)

		Yes	No
1	Check method of accounting: **a** ☐ Cash **b** ☐ Accrual **c** ☐ Other (specify) ▶		
2	See page 17 of the instructions and state the principal:		
a	Business activity code no. ▶ *5600*		
b	Business activity ▶ *Sales*		
c	Product or service ▶ *Men's Clothing*		
3	Did the corporation at the end of the tax year own, directly or indirectly, 50% or more of the voting stock of a domestic corporation? (For rules of attribution, see section 267(c).)		X
	If "Yes," attach a schedule showing: (a) name and identifying number, (b) percentage owned, and (c) taxable income or (loss) before NOL and special deductions of such corporation for the tax year ending with or within your tax year.		
4	Is the corporation a subsidiary in an affiliated group or a parent-subsidiary controlled group?		X
	If "Yes," enter employer identification number and name of the parent corporation ▶		
5	Did any individual, partnership, corporation, estate or trust at the end of the tax year own, directly or indirectly, 50% or more of the corporation's voting stock? (For rules of attribution, see section 267(c).)	X	
	If "Yes," attach a schedule showing name and identifying number. (Do not include any information already entered in **4** above.) Enter percentage owned ▶ *100*		
6	During this tax year, did the corporation pay dividends (other than stock dividends and distributions in exchange for stock) in excess of the corporation's current and accumulated earnings and profits? (See secs. 301 and 316.) . . .		X
	If "Yes," file Form 5452. If this is a consolidated return, answer here for the parent corporation and on **Form 851,** Affiliations Schedule, for each subsidiary.		

		Yes	No
7	Was the corporation a U.S. shareholder of any controlled foreign corporation? (See sections 951 and 957.) . . . If "Yes," attach Form 5471 for each such corporation. Enter number of Forms 5471 attached ▶		
8	At any time during the 1996 calendar year, did the corporation have an interest in or a signature or other authority over a financial account (such as a bank account, securities account, or other financial account) in a foreign country? If "Yes," the corporation may have to file Form TD F 90-22.1. If "Yes," enter name of foreign country ▶		X
9	During the tax year, did the corporation receive a distribution from, or was it the grantor of, or transferor to, a foreign trust? If "Yes," see page 16 of the instructions for other forms the corporation may have to file		X
10	Did one foreign person at any time during the tax year own, directly or indirectly, at least 25% of: **(a)** the total voting power of all classes of stock of the corporation entitled to vote, or **(b)** the total value of all classes of stock of the corporation? If "Yes,"		X
a	Enter percentage owned ▶		
b	Enter owner's country ▶		
c	The corporation may have to file Form 5472. Enter number of Forms 5472 attached ▶		
11	Check this box if the corporation issued publicly offered debt instruments with original issue discount . ▶ ☐ If so, the corporation may have to file Form 8281.		
12	Enter the amount of tax-exempt interest received or accrued during the tax year ▶ $ *9,000*		
13	If there were 35 or fewer shareholders at the end of the tax year, enter the number ▶ *2*		
14	If the corporation has an NOL for the tax year and is electing to forego the carryback period, check here ▶ ☐		
15	Enter the available NOL carryover from prior tax years (Do not reduce it by any deduction on line 29a.) ▶ $		

efits are not included in the employee's gross income. Similar rules apply to other medical costs paid by the employer. These benefits are not available to partners and sole proprietors.

OPERATING THE CORPORATION

Tax planning to reduce corporate income taxes should occur before the end of the tax year. Effective planning can cause income to be shifted to the next tax year and

Form 1120 (1996)   Page **4**

Schedule L — Balance Sheets per Books

	Assets	Beginning of tax year (a)	Beginning of tax year (b)	End of tax year (c)	End of tax year (d)
1	Cash		240,000		163,850
2a	Trade notes and accounts receivable	404,200		542,300	
b	Less allowance for bad debts	( )	404,200	( )	542,300
3	Inventories		300,000		356,000
4	U.S. government obligations		150,000		150,000
5	Tax-exempt securities (see instructions)				
6	Other current assets (attach schedule)				1,700
7	Loans to stockholders				
8	Mortgage and real estate loans				
9	Other investments (attach schedule)				
10a	Buildings and other depreciable assets	120,000		120,000	
b	Less accumulated depreciation	(44,400)	75,600	(60,400)	59,600
11a	Depletable assets				
b	Less accumulated depletion	( )		( )	
12	Land (net of any amortization)		10,000		10,000
13a	Intangible assets (amortizable only)				
b	Less accumulated amortization	( )		( )	
14	Other assets (attach schedule)		1,800		1,000
15	Total assets		1,181,500		1,284,450
	Liabilities and Stockholders' Equity				
16	Accounts payable		150,000		125,000
17	Mortgages, notes, bonds payable in less than 1 year				
18	Other current liabilities (attach schedule)		40,150		33,300
19	Loans from stockholders				
20	Mortgages, notes, bonds payable in 1 year or more		105,000		100,000
21	Other liabilities (attach schedule)				
22	Capital stock: a Preferred stock				
	b Common stock	250,000	250,000	250,000	
23	Paid-in or capital surplus				
24	Retained earnings—Appropriated (attach schedule)				
25	Retained earnings—Unappropriated		636,450		776,150
26	Less cost of treasury stock		( )		( )
27	Total liabilities and stockholders' equity		1,181,600		1,284,450

Note: *You are not required to complete Schedules M-1 and M-2 below if the total assets on line 15, column (d) of Schedule L are less than $25,000.*

Schedule M-1 — Reconciliation of Income (Loss) per Books With Income per Return (See page 16 of instructions.)

1	Net income (loss) per books	174,700	7	Income recorded on books this year not included on this return (itemize):	
2	Federal income tax	59,300		Tax-exempt interest $ 9,000	
3	Excess of capital losses over capital gains				
4	Income subject to tax not recorded on books this year (itemize):				9,000
5	Expenses recorded on books this year not deducted on this return (itemize):		8	Deductions on this return not charged against book income this year (itemize):	
a	Depreciation . . . $		a	Depreciation . . . $	
b	Contributions carryover $		b	Contributions carryover $	
c	Travel and entertainment $				
	Prem. — life ins. $8,000				
	Int. — state bonds $4,000	12,000	9	Add lines 7 and 8	9,000
6	Add lines 1 through 5	246,000	10	Income (line 28, page 1)—line 6 less line 9	237,000

Schedule M-2 — Analysis of Unappropriated Retained Earnings per Books (Line 25, Schedule L)

1	Balance at beginning of year	636,450	5	Distributions: a Cash	35,000
2	Net income (loss) per books	174,700		b Stock	
3	Other increases (itemize):			c Property	
			6	Other decreases (itemize):	
			7	Add lines 5 and 6	35,000
4	Add lines 1, 2, and 3	811,150	8	Balance at end of year (line 4 less line 7)	776,150

can produce large deductions by incurring expenses before year-end. Particular attention should be focused on the following.

Charitable Contributions.   Recall that accrual basis corporations may claim a deduction for charitable contributions in the year preceding payment. The contribution must be authorized by the board of directors by the end of the tax year and paid on or before the fifteenth day of the third month of the following year. Even though the contribution may not ultimately be made, it might well be authorized. A deduction cannot be thrown back to the previous year (even if paid within the two and one-half months) if it has not been authorized.

Timing of Capital Gains and Losses.   A corporation should consider offsetting profits on the sale of capital assets by selling some of the depreciated securities in the corporate portfolio. In addition, any already realized capital losses should be carefully monitored. Recall that corporate taxpayers are not permitted to claim any net capital losses as deductions against ordinary income. Capital losses can be used only as an offset against capital gains. Further, net capital losses can only be carried back three years and forward five. Gains from the sales of capital assets should be timed to offset any capital losses. The expiration of the carryover period for any net capital losses should be watched carefully so that sales of appreciated capital assets occur before that date.

Net Operating Losses.   In some situations, electing to forgo an NOL carryback and utilizing the carryforward option may generate greater tax savings.

EXAMPLE 43   Ruby Corporation incurred a $50,000 NOL in 1997. Ruby, which was in the 15% bracket from 1994 through 1996, has developed a new product that management predicts will push the corporation into the 34% bracket in 1998. If Ruby carries the NOL back, the tax savings will be $7,500 ($50,000 × 15%). However, if Ruby elects to carry the NOL forward, assuming management's prediction is accurate, the tax savings will be $17,000 ($50,000 × 34%). ▼

When deciding whether to forgo the carryback option, take into account three considerations. First, the time value of the tax refund that is lost by not using the carryback procedure should be calculated. Second, the election to forgo an NOL carryback is irrevocable. Thus, one cannot later choose to change if the predicted high profits do not materialize. Third, consider the future increases (or decreases) in corporate income tax rates that can reasonably be anticipated. This last consideration is the most difficult to work with. Although corporate tax rates have remained relatively stable in past years, projected budget deficits do little to assure taxpayers that future rates will remain constant.

Dividends Received Deduction.   The dividends received deduction normally is limited to the lesser of 70 percent of the qualifying dividends or 70 percent of taxable income. The deduction limits are raised to 80 percent for a dividend received from a corporation in which the recipient owns 20 percent or more of the stock. An exception is made when the full deduction yields an NOL. In close situations, therefore, the proper timing of income or deductions to generate an NOL may yield a larger dividends received deduction.

Organizational Expenditures.   To qualify for the 60-month amortization procedure of § 248, only organizational expenditures incurred in the first taxable year of the corporation can be considered. This rule could prove to be an unfortunate trap for corporations formed late in the year.

EXAMPLE 44   Thrush Corporation is formed in December 1997. Qualified organizational expenditures are incurred as follows: $2,000 in December 1997 and $3,000 in January 1998. If Thrush uses the calendar year for tax purposes, only $2,000 of the organizational expenditures can be written off over a period of 60 months. ▼

CONCEPT SUMMARY 2–1

Income Taxation of Individuals and Corporations Compared

	Individuals	**Corporations**
Computation of gross income	§ 61.	§ 61.
Computation of taxable income	§§ 62, 63(b) through (h).	§ 63(a). Concept of AGI has no relevance.
Deductions	Trade or business (§ 162); nonbusiness (§ 212); some personal and employee expenses (generally deductible as itemized deductions).	Trade or business (§ 162).
Charitable contributions	Limited in any tax year to 50% of AGI; 30% for long-term capital gain property unless election is made to reduce fair market value of gift.	Limited in any tax year to 10% of taxable income computed without regard to the charitable contribution deduction, net operating loss, and dividends received deduction.
	Excess charitable contributions carried over for five years.	Same as for individuals.
	Amount of contribution is the fair market value of long-term capital gain property; ordinary income property is limited to adjusted basis; capital gain property is treated as ordinary income property if certain tangible personalty is donated to a nonuse charity or a private nonoperating foundation is the donee.	Same as individuals, but exceptions allowed for certain inventory and for scientific property where one-half of the appreciation is allowed as a deduction.
	Time of deduction—year in which payment is made.	Time of deduction—year in which payment is made unless accrual basis taxpayer. Accrual basis corporation can take deduction in year preceding payment if contribution was authorized by board of directors by end of year and contribution is paid by fifteenth day of third month of following year.
Casualty losses	$100 floor on personal casualty and theft losses; personal casualty losses deductible only to extent losses exceed 10% of AGI.	Deductible in full.
Depreciation recapture under § 1250	Recaptured to extent accelerated depreciation exceeds straight-line.	20% of excess of amount that would be recaptured under § 1245 over amount recaptured under § 1250 is additional ordinary income.

	Individuals	Corporations
Net operating loss	Adjusted for several items, including nonbusiness deductions over nonbusiness income and personal exemptions.	Generally no adjustments.
	Carryback period is 3 years while carryforward period is 15 years.	Same as for individuals.
Dividends received deduction	None.	70%, 80%, or 100% of dividends received depending on percentage of ownership by corporate shareholder.
Net capital gains	Taxed in full. Tax rate cannot exceed 28%.	Taxed in full.
Capital losses	Only $3,000 of capital loss per year can offset ordinary income; loss is carried forward indefinitely to offset capital gains or ordinary income up to $3,000; carryovers retain their character as long term or short term.	Can offset only capital gains; carried back three years and forward five; carryovers and carrybacks are short-term losses.
Passive losses	Passive activity losses cannot offset either active income or portfolio income.	Passive loss rules apply to closely held C corporations and personal service corporations.
		For personal service corporations, the rule is the same as for individuals.
		For closely held C corporations, passive losses may offset active income but not portfolio income.
Tax rates	Progressive with five rates (15%, 28%, 31%, 36%, 39.6%).	Progressive with four rates (15%, 25%, 34%, 35%). Two lowest brackets phased out between $100,000 and $335,000 of taxable income, and additional tax imposed between $15,000,000 and $18,333,333 of taxable income.
Alternative minimum tax	Applied at a graduated rate schedule of 26% and 28%. Exemption allowed depending on filing status (e.g., $45,000 for married filing jointly); phase-out begins when AMTI reaches a certain amount (e.g., $150,000 for married filing jointly).	Applied at a 20% rate on AMTI less exemption; $40,000 exemption allowed but phase-out begins when AMTI reaches $150,000; adjustments and tax preference items are similar to those applicable to individuals but also include 75% adjusted current earnings.

The solution to the problem posed by Example 44 is for Thrush Corporation to adopt a fiscal year that ends on or beyond January 31. All organizational expenditures will then have been incurred before the close of the first taxable year.

Shareholder-Employee Payment of Corporate Expenses.   In a closely held corporate setting, shareholder-employees often pay corporate expenses (e.g., travel and entertainment) for which they are not reimbursed by the corporation. The IRS often disallows the deduction of these expenses by the shareholder-employee, since the payments are voluntary on his or her part. If the deduction is more beneficial at the shareholder-employee level, a corporate policy against reimbursement of such expenses should be established. Proper planning in this regard would be to decide before the beginning of each tax year where the deduction would do the most good. Corporate policy on reimbursement of such expenses could be modified on a year-to-year basis depending upon the circumstances.

In deciding whether corporate expenses should be kept at the corporate level or shifted to the shareholder-employee, the treatment of unreimbursed employee expenses must be considered. First, since employee expenses are itemized deductions, they will be of no benefit to the taxpayer who chooses the standard deduction option. Second, these expenses will be subject to the 2 percent-of-AGI floor. No such limitation will be imposed if the corporation claims the expenses.

RELATED CORPORATIONS

Controlled Groups.   Recall that § 1561 was designed to prevent shareholders from operating a business as multiple corporations to obtain lower tax brackets and multiple accumulated earnings tax credits or AMT exemptions. Corporations in which substantially all the stock is held by five or fewer persons are subject to the provisions of § 1561. Dividing ownership so that control of each corporation does not lie with individuals having common control of all corporations avoids the prohibitions of § 1561.

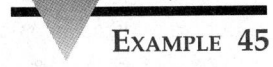
EXAMPLE 45

Arthur, Baker, and Collins have voting stock in Red, White, and Blue Corporations as follows:

Shareholder	Red	White	Blue	Common Ownership
Arthur	40%	30%	30%	30%
Baker	40%	20%	30%	20%
Collins	20%	50%	40%	20%
Total	100%	100%	100%	70%

Because the total combined ownership is more than 50% and the three individuals own at least 80% of the combined voting power, Red, White, and Blue are treated as a controlled group and are subject to § 1561. Thus, Red, White, and Blue are limited to taxable income in the first two tax brackets and to the $250,000 accumulated earnings tax credit as though they were one corporation. ▼

Assume, however, that the voting stock is divided differently so that each of the individuals—Arthur, Baker, and Collins—controls one of the corporations rather than having common control of all the corporations.

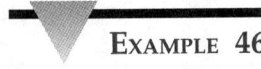
EXAMPLE 46

Arthur, Baker, and Collins hold voting stock in Red, White, and Blue Corporations in the following percentages:

Shareholder	Red	White	Blue	Common Ownership
Arthur	80%	10%	10%	10%
Baker	10%	80%	10%	10%
Collins	10%	10%	80%	10%
Total	100%	100%	100%	30%

Now the total combined ownership is less than 50%. Consequently, the corporations are not treated as a controlled group, since the prohibitions of § 1561 are not applicable. ▼

The differences in ownership in the corporations can be alleviated somewhat by issuing nonvoting preferred stock to the shareholders with the 10 percent ownership. (Nonvoting stock is not considered to be stock for purposes of § 1563.)

KEY TERMS

Association, 2–8

Brother-sister controlled group, 2–26

C corporation, 2–4

Controlled group, 2–25

Dividends received deduction, 2–20

Limited liability company (LLC), 2–9

Limited partnership, 2–7

Organizational expenditures, 2–22

Parent-subsidiary controlled group, 2–25

Passive loss, 2–16

Personal service corporation (PSC), 2–12

Regular corporation, 2–4

Related corporations, 2–24

S corporation, 2–4

Schedule M–1, 2–30

PROBLEM MATERIALS

DISCUSSION QUESTIONS

1. Robin, who owns and operates a sole proprietorship, is considering incorporating her business as a regular corporation. She has asked you to explain how a corporate tax return differs from the return for a sole proprietorship.

2. Edgar owns a sole proprietorship, and Frank is the sole shareholder of a corporation. Both businesses make a profit of $50,000 in 1997. Neither owner withdraws any funds from his business during the year. Discuss the tax treatment of each owner.

3. Art, an executive with Azure Corporation, plans to start a part-time business selling products on the Internet. He will devote about 15 hours each week to running the business. Art's salary from Azure places him in the 39.6% tax bracket. He projects substantial losses from the new business in each of the first three years and expects sizable profits thereafter. Art plans to leave the profits in the business for several years, sell the business, and retire. Would you advise Art to incorporate the business or operate it as a sole proprietorship?

4. Abdul owns 25% of the stock in a C corporation, which earned $100,000 during 1997. He also owns a 25% interest in a partnership, which earned $100,000 during the year. The corporation did not pay any dividends, and the partnership did not make any distributions. Contrast Abdul's tax treatment as a shareholder with his tax treatment as a partner.

5. Rosita, who owns a proprietorship, has scheduled an appointment to talk with you about the advisability of incorporating. At this time, you know nothing about Rosita's business or her existing tax situation. List the questions you will need to ask during the appointment so you can help her make an informed decision.

6. Yolanda is the president and sole shareholder of Canary Corporation. She also lends money and rents a building to the corporation. Discuss how these business relationships between Yolanda and the corporation can help her avoid double taxation.

7. List and explain at least five nontax factors that should be considered when deciding whether to incorporate a business.

8. In some circumstances, an unincorporated business may be classified as an association. What are the circumstances? Why would the IRS take this action? Why would taxpayers try to avoid this outcome?

9. Ann and Fran, who are sisters, own adjacent parcels of land they inherited from their parents. They form Twin Properties, Inc., and transfer the land to the corporation. At the date of transfer, each parcel of land is worth $25,000. Ann wants to have the corporation hold the land until it appreciates to $100,000 and then sell it. Fran wants to have the corporation subdivide the property, put in streets and a sewer system, and then sell the lots. What are the Federal income tax implications of the two different plans?

10. Why might the IRS attempt to disregard a legally constituted corporate entity? Why might the shareholders attempt to disregard such an entity?

11. Ray and Kay plan to start a new business. They expect the business to generate substantial profits and do not want to incorporate because of the problem of double taxation. Compare the partnership and LLC forms of business entities as options that Ray and Kay should consider for the new business.

12. Explain the possible tax classifications for a limited liability company. In what situations might such an organization be treated as a partnership? As a corporation?

13. C corporations can elect fiscal years that are different from those of their shareholders, but personal service corporations (PSCs) are subject to substantial restrictions in the choice of a fiscal year. Why are the fiscal year choices for PSCs limited?

14. Karen is the sole shareholder of Blue Corporation, a newly formed C corporation. Linda is the sole shareholder of Mauve Corporation, a newly formed C corporation that is classified as a PSC. Both Karen and Linda plan to have their corporations elect a March 31 fiscal year. Will the IRS treat both corporations alike with respect to the fiscal year election? Explain.

15. Which of the following corporations will be allowed to use the cash method of accounting? Explain your answers.
    a. Lark Corporation, which had net profits of $24 million in 1996, $35 million in 1997, and $44 million in 1998.
    b. Dove Corporation, a PSC, which had gross receipts of $3 million in 1996, $4 million in 1997, and $7 million in 1998.

16. Wren Corporation, a calendar year, cash basis taxpayer, accrues a performance bonus of $50,000 to Brad, a cash basis taxpayer who is the sole shareholder of the corporation. When can Wren deduct the bonus?

17. A taxpayer realized a net long-term capital gain of $10,000 during the year. How is the gain treated if the taxpayer is a corporation? An individual?

18. A taxpayer incurred a net long-term capital loss of $5,000 during the year. How is the loss treated if the taxpayer is a corporation? An individual?

19. John, a sole proprietor, incurs a $5,000 capital loss from the sale of an asset used in his business. Fox Corporation incurs a $5,000 capital loss on the sale of an asset used in its business. How do John and Fox Corporation treat these losses in computing taxable income?

20. A taxpayer sells a warehouse for a gain of $50,000. The warehouse has been depreciated as 15-year property under ACRS. If the straight-line method was used, depreciation recapture will be higher if the taxpayer is a corporation than if the taxpayer is an individual. Explain.

21. Crimson Corporation had $135,000 of active income, $180,000 of portfolio income, and a $150,000 passive loss during the year. How much of the passive loss is deductible if Crimson is a closely held corporation? A PSC?

22. On December 30, 1997, Bonnie, a sole proprietor, pledged to make a $10,000 charitable contribution on or before January 15, 1998. Hunter Corporation made a similar pledge on the same date, and the contribution was authorized by Hunter's board of directors. Assuming both Bonnie and Hunter Corporation are calendar year taxpayers, discuss when these contributions will be deductible.

23. Red Corporation owns 78% of the stock of Blue Corporation, which pays Red a substantial dividend each year. Red Corporation plans to acquire an additional 2% of Blue's stock. After acquiring this additional stock, Red Corporation will qualify as Blue Corporation's parent. How will this stock acquisition affect the amount of dividend income that Red Corporation will report for the year?

24. In connection with organizational expenditures, comment on the following:
    a. Those that qualify for amortization.
    b. Those that do not qualify for amortization.
    c. The period over which amortization can take place.
    d. Expenses incurred but not paid by a cash basis corporation.
    e. Expenses incurred by a corporation in its second year of operation.
    f. The alternative if no election to amortize is made.
    g. The timing of the election to amortize.

25. Silver Corporation, which owns stock in Gold Corporation, had net operating income of $150,000 for the year. Gold pays Silver a dividend of $30,000. Under what circumstances can Silver take a dividends received deduction of $21,000? A dividends received deduction of $30,000?

26. At what level of taxable income does a corporation reach a marginal income tax rate of 35% if it is a PSC? If it is not a PSC? At what level of taxable income does a corporation reach an average income tax rate of 35% if it is not a PSC?

27. Ted, an individual, owns 80% of all classes of stock of Brown Corporation and Green Corporation. Brown Corporation, in turn, owns all the stock of White Corporation, and Green Corporation owns 80% of the stock of Orange Corporation. Would Brown, Green, Orange, and White Corporations be members of a combined group? Explain.

28. Taxable income and financial accounting income for a corporation are seldom the same amount. Discuss some common reasons for differences and how these differences affect the reconciliation of taxable income and financial accounting income on Schedule M–1 of Form 1120.

29. Mallard Corporation incorporated in January 1998 and incurred $12,000 of rent and payroll expense before it opened its store for business in March. How much, if any, of the $12,000 is deductible in 1998?

30. Martin Corporation was organized in 1995 and had profits in 1995, 1996, and 1997. The corporation had an NOL in 1998. Under what circumstances should the corporation elect to forgo carrying the NOL back to the three prior years?

PROBLEMS

31. Eagle Company, which was formed in 1997, had operating income of $120,000 and operating expenses of $100,000 in 1997. In addition, Eagle had a long-term capital loss of $3,000. Based on this information, how does Andy, the owner of Eagle Company, report this information on his individual tax return under the following assumptions?
    a. Eagle Company is a corporation and pays no dividends during the year.
    b. Eagle Company is a proprietorship, and Andy does not withdraw any funds from Eagle during the year.

32. Osprey Company had a net loss of $80,000 from merchandising operations in 1997. Mary owns Osprey and works 20 hours a week in the business. She has a large amount of income from other sources and is in the 39.6% marginal tax bracket. Would Mary's tax situation be better if Osprey Company were a proprietorship or a C corporation?

33. Indigo Company has approximately $200,000 in net income in 1997 before deducting any compensation or other payment to its sole owner, Kim. Kim is single. Her income aside from the company's profits is low and would offset her personal exemption and standard deduction. Discuss the tax aspects of each of the following arrangements:
    a. Kim operates Indigo Company as a proprietorship.
    b. Kim incorporates Indigo Company and pays herself a salary of $50,000 and no dividend.
    c. Kim incorporates the company and pays herself a $50,000 salary and a dividend of $108,250 ($150,000 − $41,750 corporate income tax).
    d. Kim incorporates the company and pays herself a salary of $200,000.

34. Mike owns 100% of White Company, which had net operating income of $60,000 in 1997 ($100,000 operating income − $40,000 operating expenses). In addition, White Company had a long-term capital gain of $10,000. Mike has sufficient income from other activities to place him in the 39.6% marginal tax bracket before considering results from White Company. Using this information, explain the tax treatment under the following circumstances:
    a. White Company is a corporation and pays no dividends during the year.
    b. White Company is a corporation and pays Mike $70,000 of dividends during the year.
    c. White Company is a corporation and pays Mike a $70,000 salary during the year.
    d. White Company is a proprietorship, and Mike withdraws $0 during the year.
    e. White Company is a proprietorship, and Mike withdraws $70,000 during the year.

35. Jane owns 100% of Green Company, which had an NOL of $50,000 in 1997 ($100,000 operating income − $150,000 operating expenses). Jane was a material participant in the activities of the business during the year. Green Company also had a long-term capital loss of $10,000. Jane has sufficient income from other activities to place her in the 31% marginal tax bracket before considering results from Green Company. Explain the tax treatment under the following circumstances:
    a. Green Company is a corporation.
    b. Green Company is a proprietorship.

36. Jones Company had revenue of $100,000 and incurred business expenses of $20,000 in 1997. Ken Jones, owner of the company, is single, has no dependents, and uses the $4,150 standard deduction in computing taxable income for 1997. The personal exemption amount for 1997 is $2,650. Jones Company is Ken's only source of income.
    a. Compute Ken's after-tax income if Jones Company is a sole proprietorship and Ken withdrew $60,000 for living expenses during the year.
    b. Compute Ken's after-tax income if Jones Company is a corporation, Ken is the sole shareholder, and the corporation pays out all of its after-tax income as a dividend to Ken.
    c. Compute Ken's after-tax income if Jones Company is a corporation, Ken is the sole shareholder, and the corporation pays Ken a salary of $80,000. This will increase the corporation's business expenses to $100,000.
    d. Assume the same facts as in (c). What will Ken's after-tax income be if the IRS disallows $20,000 of the salary as unreasonable compensation?

37. Rust Corporation and Al and Bob form a limited partnership on January 1 to construct office buildings. Rust Corporation is the general partner, and Al and Bob are both limited partners. The partnership agreement provides that Rust will have sole management of the business. Al's and Bob's liabilities for debts of the partnership will be limited to their investments. The partnership agreement provides that the partnership will not end upon the death of any of the partners. The agreement also provides that both Al and Bob may sell their interests without the consent of the other parties. Al and Bob each invest $50,000 in the partnership. Rust Corporation, which has a net worth of only $20,000, invests $10,000. The partnership secures a loan from the bank to help finance the initial cost of construction. How will the partnership be classified for tax purposes? Explain.

38. A limited liability company is formed in a state with a flexible statute. Under the state law, no member of the LLC has personal liability for the debts of the business. The company may decide which of the other corporate characteristics it may have. Indicate the most likely classification (corporation or partnership) by the IRS in each of the following situations:
    a. The LLC has centralized management, but does not have transferability of interests or continuity of life.
    b. The LLC does not have centralized management, but does have transferability of interests and continuity of life.
    c. The LLC does not have centralized management or transferability of interests, but does have continuity of life.
    d. The LLC has centralized management and transferability of interests, but does not have continuity of life.

39. Bluebird Company, a calendar year taxpayer, suffered a casualty loss of $27,000 during the current year. How much of the casualty loss can Bluebird deduct assuming the entity is a corporation? How much can be deducted if Bluebird Company is a sole proprietorship and Charles Hughes, its owner, has adjusted gross income of $250,000?

40. Benton Company has one owner, who is in the 39.6% Federal income tax bracket. Benton's gross income is $180,000, and its ordinary trade or business deductions are $65,000. It also pays accident and health insurance premiums for the benefit of its owner, in the amount of $3,000 for the current year. Compute the tax liability on Benton's income for 1997 under the following assumptions:
    a. Benton Company is operated as a proprietorship, and the owner withdraws $75,000 for personal use.
    b. Benton is operated as a corporation, pays out $75,000 as salary, and pays no dividends.
    c. Benton is operated as a corporation and pays out no salary or dividends.
    d. Benton is operated as a corporation, pays out $75,000 as salary, and pays out the remainder of its earnings as dividends.
    e. Assume Robert Benton of 1121 Monroe Street, Ironton, OH 45638 is the owner of Benton Company, which was operated as a proprietorship in 1997. Robert is thinking about incorporating the business in 1998 and asks your advice. He expects about the same amounts of income and expenses in 1998 and plans to take $75,000 per year out of the company whether he incorporates or not. Write a letter to Robert (based on your analysis in [a] and [b] above) containing your recommendations.

41. Sarita, an attorney, is the sole shareholder of Pelican Corporation, a professional association. The corporation paid Sarita a salary of $180,000 during its fiscal year ending October 31, 1997. How much salary must Pelican pay Sarita during the period November 1 through December 31, 1997, to permit the corporation to continue to use its fiscal year without negative tax effects?

42. Seagull Corporation had $200,000 operating income and $175,000 operating expenses during the year. In addition, Seagull had a $15,000 long-term capital gain and a $26,000 short-term capital loss.
    a. Compute Seagull's taxable income for the year.
    b. Assume the same facts as above except that Seagull's long-term capital gain was $32,000. Compute Seagull's taxable income for the year.

43. Flamingo has two shareholders, who are unrelated to each other. Carl owns 51% of the stock, and Owen owns the remaining 49%. During the current year, Flamingo pays $50,000 of salary to each shareholder. At the beginning of the year, it had accrued $10,000 salary to each shareholder, and at the end of the year, had accrued $15,000 to each shareholder.

    a. Compute Flamingo's deduction for the above amounts if it uses the cash method of accounting.

    b. Compute Flamingo's deduction for the above amounts if it uses the accrual method of accounting.

44. In 1997, a business sells a capital asset, which it had held for two years, at a loss of $15,000. How much of the capital loss may be deducted in 1997 and how much is carried back or forward under the following circumstances?

    a. The business was a sole proprietorship owned by Kim. Kim had a short-term capital gain of $3,000 in 1997 and a long-term capital gain of $2,000. Kim had ordinary net income from the proprietorship of $60,000.

    b. The business is incorporated. The corporation had a short-term capital gain of $3,000 and a long-term capital gain of $2,000. Its ordinary net income from the business was $60,000.

45. Stork Corporation realized a net long-term capital loss of $130,000 and a net short-term capital gain of $10,000 during 1997. Taxable income from other sources was $650,000. Other years' transactions included the following:

1993	Net long-term capital gain (NLTCG)	$20,000
1994	Net short-term capital gain (NSTCG)	48,000
1995	Net long-term capital gain (NLTCG)	17,000
1996	Net long-term capital gain (NLTCG)	30,000
1998	Net short-term capital gain (NSTCG)	23,000

    a. How are the capital gains and losses treated on the 1997 tax return?

    b. Compute the capital loss carryback to the carryback years.

    c. Compute the amount of capital loss carryforward to 1998, and indicate how it should be used.

46. Peregrine Corporation acquired residential rental property on January 18, 1986, for $100,000. The property was depreciated using the accelerated method and a 19-year recovery period under ACRS. Depreciation in the amount of $66,375 was claimed. Straight-line depreciation for the period would have been $58,221. Peregrine sold the property on January 1, 1997, for $110,000. What is the gain on the sale, and how is it taxed?

47. Assume the property in Problem 46 was a commercial building and Peregrine Corporation used the straight-line method of depreciation with a 19-year recovery period under ACRS. What would be the gain on the sale, and how would it be taxed?

48. Jansen, a calendar year taxpayer engaged in the catering business, makes the following donations to qualified charitable organizations during the current year:

	Adjusted Basis	Fair Market Value
Painting to half-way house, which sold it immediately	$3,200	$3,900
Common stock held two years as an investment to Goodwill, which sold it immediately	8,000	6,500
Canned groceries to Catholic Meals for the Poor	4,000	5,100

Ignoring percentage limitations, what is the amount of the charitable contribution deduction if Jansen is an individual? A corporation?

49. Joseph Thompson is president and sole shareholder of Jay Corporation . In December 1997, Joe asks your advice regarding a charitable contribution he plans to have the corporation make to the University of Maine, a qualified public charity. Joe is considering the following alternatives as charitable contributions in December 1997:

	Fair Market Value
(1) Cash donation	$120,000
(2) Unimproved land held for six years ($20,000 basis)	120,000
(3) Maize Corporation stock held for eight months ($20,000 basis)	120,000
(4) Brown Corporation stock held for two years ($170,000 basis)	120,000

Joe has asked you to help him decide which of these potential contributions will be most advantageous taxwise. Jay's taxable income is $3,500,000 before considering the contribution. Rank the four alternatives and write a letter to Joe communicating your advice. The corporation's address is 1442 Main Street, Freeport, ME 04032.

50. During the current year, Heron Corporation (a calendar year taxpayer) had the following income and expenses:

Income from operations	$270,000
Expenses from operations	198,000
Qualifying dividends from domestic corporation in which Heron owns a 40% interest	18,000
NOL carryover from prior year	5,400

On October 1, Heron Corporation made a contribution to a qualified charitable organization of $12,600 in cash (not included in any of the above items).
a. Determine Heron Corporation's charitable contribution deduction for the current year.
b. What happens to any excess charitable contribution deduction not allowable for the current year?

51. Dan Simms is the president and sole shareholder of Simms Corporation, 1121 Madison Street, Seattle, WA 98121. Dan plans for the corporation to make a charitable contribution to the University of Washington, a qualified public charity. He will have the corporation donate Jaybird Corporation stock with a basis of $8,000 and a fair market value of $20,000. Dan projects a $200,000 net profit for Simms Corporation in 1997 and a $100,000 net profit in 1998. Dan calls you on December 5, 1997, and asks whether he should make the contribution in 1997 or 1998. Write a letter advising Dan about the timing of the contribution.

52. During 1997, Bobolink Corporation has $320,000 of gross income and $400,000 in allowable business deductions. Included in gross income is $96,000 in qualifying dividends from less-than-20%-owned domestic corporations.
a. Determine the corporation's NOL for 1997.
b. What happens to the loss if the corporation was newly created in 1997? In 1994?

53. In each of the following independent situations, determine the dividends received deduction. Assume that none of the corporate shareholders owns 20% or more of the stock in the corporations paying the dividends.

	Red Corporation	White Corporation	Blue Corporation
Income from operations	$ 700,000	$ 800,000	$ 700,000
Expenses from operations	(600,000)	(900,000)	(740,000)
Qualifying dividends	100,000	200,000	200,000

54. Snipe Corporation was formed on December 1, 1997. Qualifying organizational expenses were incurred and paid as follows:

Incurred and paid in December 1997	$12,000
Incurred in December 1997 but paid in January 1998	6,000
Incurred and paid in February 1998	3,600

Assume Snipe Corporation makes a timely election under § 248 to amortize organizational expenditures over a period of 60 months. What amount may be amortized in the corporation's first tax year under each of the following assumptions?
a. Snipe Corporation adopts a calendar year and the cash basis of accounting for tax purposes.
b. Same as (a), except that Snipe Corporation chooses a fiscal year of December 1–November 30.
c. Snipe Corporation adopts a calendar year and the accrual basis of accounting for tax purposes.
d. Same as (c), except that Snipe Corporation chooses a fiscal year of December 1–November 30.

55. Topaz Corporation, an accrual basis taxpayer, was formed and began operations on July 1, 1997. The following expenses were incurred during the first tax year (July 1 to December 31, 1997) of operations:

Expenses of temporary directors and of organizational meetings	$ 5,000
Fee paid to the state of incorporation	600
Accounting services incident to organization	1,200
Legal services for drafting the corporate charter and bylaws	2,800
Expenses incident to the printing and sale of stock certificates	1,000
	$10,600

Assume Topaz Corporation makes an appropriate and timely election under § 248(c) and the related Regulations.
a. What is the maximum organizational expense Topaz may write off for tax year 1997?
b. What would be the result if a proper election had not been made?

56. In each of the following independent situations, determine the corporation's income tax liability. Assume that all corporations use a calendar year for tax purposes and that the tax year involved is 1997.

	Taxable Income
Wren Corporation	$ 47,000
Thrush Corporation	240,000
Gull Corporation	1,200,000
Oriole Corporation	19,000,000

57. Red Corporation owns 80% of the total combined voting power of all classes of stock entitled to vote in White Corporation. White owns 20% of the stock in Blue Corporation. Red owns 90% of Green Corporation, while the latter owns 60% of Blue Corporation. Which corporations are part of a controlled group?

58. The outstanding stock of Starling, Robin, Crow, Grouse, and Swallow Corporations is owned by the following unrelated individual and corporate shareholders:

	Corporations				
Shareholders	**Starling**	**Robin**	**Crow**	**Grouse**	**Swallow**
Albert	20%		5%	10%	
Burke	30%		40%	50%	
Clark	20%		15%	10%	
Dave	10%		20%	10%	
Starling Corporation		90%			
Grouse Corporation					85%

Which, if any, of the above corporations are members of a controlled group?

59. Eagle and Cardinal Corporations both have 100 shares of stock outstanding. Each shareholder paid $500 for his stock in each corporation, and the fair market value of the stock of each corporation is $800 per share. The stock is owned by the following unrelated individuals:

Shareholders	**Eagle Shares**	**Cardinal Shares**
George	30	15
Sam	5	50
Tom	65	35
Total	100	100

a. Does a brother-sister controlled group exist?
b. Will a brother-sister controlled group exist if Tom sells 10 of his shares in Cardinal Corporation to Sam?
c. Discuss any tax advantages that will result if Tom sells 10 of his Cardinal shares to Sam.
d. Sam has suggested to Tom that they complete the transaction in (c). Tom asks your advice and says that he is in the 31% marginal bracket. Write a letter to Tom Roland at 3435 Grand Avenue, South Point, OH 45680, explaining the tax advantages that will result if he sells 10 of his Cardinal shares to Sam. Also, identify any problems, both tax and nontax, that the sale could cause for Tom.

60. The outstanding stock in corporations Amber, Sand, Tan, Beige, and Purple, which have only one class of stock outstanding, is owned by the following unrelated individuals:

	Corporations				
Individuals	**Amber**	**Sand**	**Tan**	**Beige**	**Purple**
Anna	55%	51%	55%	55%	55%
Bill	45%	49%	–0–	–0–	–0–
Carol	–0–	–0–	45%	–0–	–0–
Don	–0–	–0–	–0–	45%	–0–
Eve	–0–	–0–	–0–	–0–	45%
Total	100%	100%	100%	100%	100%

Determine if a brother-sister controlled group exists.

61. Indicate in each of the following independent situations whether the corporation may file Form 1120–A:

	Jay Corporation	Shrike Corporation	Martin Corporation
Sales of merchandise	$600,000	$400,000	$300,000
Total assets	200,000	360,000	400,000
Total income (gross profit plus other income, including gains)	480,000	490,000	380,000
Member of controlled group	no	yes	no
Ownership in foreign corporation	no	no	no
Entitled to file Form 1120–A (Circle Y for yes or N for no)	Y N	Y N	Y N

62. Heron Corporation, a calendar year, accrual method taxpayer, provides the following information for 1996 and asks you to prepare Schedules M–1 and M–2:

Net income per books (after-tax)	$257,950
Taxable income	150,000
Federal income tax liability	41,750
Interest income from tax-exempt bonds	15,000
Interest paid on loan incurred to purchase tax-exempt bonds	1,500
Life insurance proceeds received as a result of death of Heron's president	150,000
Premiums paid on policy on life of Heron's president	7,800
Excess of capital losses over capital gains	6,000
Retained earnings at beginning of year	375,000
Cash dividends paid	90,000

63. For 1996, Rose Corporation, an accrual basis, calendar year taxpayer, had net income per books of $172,750 and the following special transactions:

Life insurance proceeds received through the death of the corporation president	$100,000
Premiums paid on the life insurance policy on the president	10,000
Prepaid rent received and properly taxed in 1995 but credited as rent income in 1996	15,000
Rent income received in 1996 ($10,000 is prepaid and relates to 1997)	25,000
Interest income on tax-exempt bonds	5,000
Interest on loan to carry tax-exempt bonds	3,000
MACRS depreciation in excess of straight-line (straight-line was used for book purposes)	4,000
Capital loss in excess of capital gains	6,000
Federal income tax liability and accrued tax provision for 1996	22,250

Using Schedule M–1 of Form 1120 (the most recent version available), compute Rose Corporation's taxable income for 1996.

64. In January, Don and Steve each invested $100,000 cash to form a corporation to conduct business as a retail golf equipment store. On January 5, they paid Bill, an attorney, to

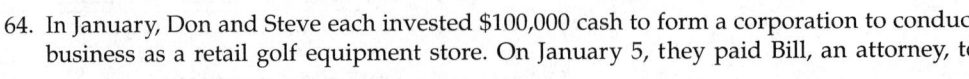

draft the corporate charter, file the necessary forms with the state, and write the bylaws. They leased a store building and began to acquire inventory, furniture, display equipment, and office equipment in February. They hired a sales staff and clerical personnel in March and conducted training sessions during the month. They had a successful opening on April 1, and sales increased steadily throughout the summer. The weather turned cold in October, and all local golf courses closed by October 15, which resulted in a drastic decline in sales. Don and Steve expect business to be very good during the Christmas season and then to taper off significantly from January 1 through February 28. The corporation accrued bonuses to Don and Steve on December 31, payable on April 15 of the following year. The corporation made timely estimated tax payments throughout the year. The corporation hired a bookkeeper in February, but he does not know much about taxation. Don and Steve have hired you as a tax consultant and have asked you to identify the tax issues that they should consider.

COMPREHENSIVE TAX RETURN PROBLEM

On April 20, 1988, Tim Potten and Brandon Kuhl formed GolfPro Corporation to sell golf equipment. Pertinent information regarding GolfPro is summarized as follows:

- The business address is 1820 Sagvaro Street, Green Valley, AZ 85622.

- The employer identification number is 75–3392543; the principal business activity code is 5600.

- Tim and Brandon each own one-half of the outstanding common stock; no other class of stock is authorized. Tim is president of the company, and Brandon is secretary-treasurer. Both are full-time employees of the corporation, and each receives a salary of $144,000. Tim's Social Security number is 399–50–2953; Brandon's Social Security number is 400–30–4495.

- The corporation uses the accrual method of accounting and reports on a calendar basis. Inventories are determined using the lower of cost or market method. For book and tax purposes, the straight-line method of depreciation is used.

- During 1996, the corporation distributed a cash dividend of $72,000.

Selected portions of GolfPro's profit and loss statement for 1996 reflect the following debits and credits:

Account	Debit	Credit
Gross sales		$2,070,000
Sales returns and allowances	$ 72,000	
Cost of goods sold	828,000	
Dividends received from stock investments in less-than-20%-owned U.S. corporations		108,000
Interest income		
State bonds	$12,600	
Certificates of deposit	9,000	21,600
Premiums on term life insurance policies on the lives of Tim and Brandon; GolfPro Corporation is the designated beneficiary	14,000	
Salaries—officers	288,000	
Salaries—clerical and sales	261,000	
Taxes (state, local, and payroll)	94,500	
Repairs	54,000	

Account	Debit	Credit
Interest expense		
Loan to purchase state bonds	$ 7,200	
Other business loans	10,800	18,000
Advertising		5,400
Rental expense		74,700
Depreciation		36,000

A comparative balance sheet for GolfPro Corporation reveals the following information:

Assets	January 1, 1996	December 31, 1996
Cash	$ 432,000	$ 301,194
Trade notes and accounts receivable	727,560	976,140
Inventories	540,000	640,800
Federal bonds	126,000	126,000
State bonds	144,000	144,000
Prepaid Federal tax	—	1,620
Buildings and other depreciable assets	216,000	216,000
Accumulated depreciation	(79,920)	(115,920)
Land	18,000	18,000
Other assets	3,240	1,800
Total assets	$2,126,880	$2,309,634

Liabilities and Equity		
Accounts payable	$ 270,000	$ 248,004
Other current liabilities	72,270	35,600
Mortgages	189,000	180,000
Capital stock	450,000	450,000
Retained earnings	1,145,610	1,396,030
Total liabilities and equity	$2,126,880	$2,309,634

Net income per books (before any income tax accrual) is $454,000. During 1996, GolfPro Corporation made estimated tax payments of $133,200 to the IRS. Prepare a Form 1120 for GolfPro Corporation for tax year 1996.

RESEARCH PROBLEMS

Note: ***West's Federal Taxation on CD-ROM*** *can be used in preparing solutions to the Research Problems. Alternatively, tax research materials contained in a standard tax library can be used.*

Research Problem 1.   John Lamkin and Eric Williams are partners in a business that has been in operation for five years. Because of several lawsuits that have been filed against the business this year, John and Eric are considering converting the partnership to a limited liability company (LLC), but they want to continue to be taxed as a partnership. They have asked what they need to do to continue being taxed as a partnership if they convert to LLC status. Write a letter to Eric at 1205 South Fifth Street, St. Paul, MN 55164 and explain what actions are necessary to ensure that the business will continue to be taxed as a partnership.

Partial list of research aids:
§ 7701 and Regulations or Proposed Regulations under § 7701.

Research Problem 2.   Joe and Tom Moore are brothers and equal shareholders in Black Corporation, a calendar year taxpayer. In 1996, they incurred certain travel and entertainment expenditures, as employees, on behalf of Black Corporation. Because Black was in a precarious financial condition, Joe and Tom decided not to seek reimbursement for these expenditures. Instead, each brother deducted what he spent on his own individual return (Form 1040). Upon audit of the returns filed by Joe and Tom for 1996, the IRS disallowed these expenditures. Write a letter to Joe at 568 Inwood Avenue, Waynesburg, PA 15370, and indicate whether he should challenge the IRS action. Explain your conclusion to Joe using nontechnical language.

Research Problem 3.   Soon-Yi owns all the stock of White Corporation and 90% of the stock of Red Corporation. Red Corporation has had profitable years whereas White Corporation has suffered losses for several years. Red loaned White Corporation $90,000 in 1996 and did not charge White any interest on the loan. Upon audit of its 1996 return, the IRS determined that Red Corporation had interest income for 1996 in the amount of $9,900, causing Red to have a tax deficiency of $3,366 for 1996. Red is challenging the tax deficiency. It contends that White Corporation produced no taxable income from the use of the $90,000. Is the IRS correct in increasing the taxable income of Red Corporation?

Partial list of research aids:
Reg. §§ 1.482–2(a)(1) and 1.482–1(d)(4).
§ 7872.

Use the tax resources of the internet to address the following questions. Do not restrict your search to the World Wide Web, but include a review of newsgroups and general reference materials, practitioner sites and resources, primary sources of the tax law, chat rooms and discussion groups, and other opportunities.

Research Problem 4.   The Code subsidizes charitable contributions by corporations through the income tax deduction for such gifts. How have corporations responded? Find the dollar amount of charitable gifts by corporations for the last two years.

Research Problem 5.   What is the current status of the check-the-box provisions of the Regulations? Does the tax community embrace these opportunities?

Research Problem 6.   Download the forms used to compute a corporation's estimated tax payments and to transmit the payment to an approved bank. Complete the forms for a corporation that must make quarterly estimated payments of $11,000 this year.

3

CORPORATIONS: ORGANIZATION AND CAPITAL STRUCTURE

LEARNING OBJECTIVES

After completing Chapter 3, you should be able to:

1. Identify the tax consequences of incorporating a business.

2. Appreciate the tax problems involved when making later property transfers to a controlled corporation.

3. Understand the tax aspects of the capital structure of a corporation.

4. Recognize the tax differences between debt and equity investments.

5. Handle the tax treatment of shareholder debt and stock losses.

Chapter 2 dealt with three principal areas fundamental to working with corporations: (1) the recognition of an entity as a corporation for Federal income tax purposes, (2) the tax rules applicable to the day-to-day operation of a corporation, and (3) the filing and reporting procedures governing corporations.

Chapter 3 addresses more sophisticated problems in dealing with corporations:

- The tax consequences to the shareholders and the corporation upon the organization of the corporation.
- Once the corporation has been formed, the tax result that ensues when shareholders make later transfers of property.
- The capital structure of a corporation, including the treatment of capital contributions by nonshareholders and shareholders and the handling of investor losses suffered by shareholders.

ORGANIZATION OF AND TRANSFERS TO CONTROLLED CORPORATIONS

IN GENERAL

1 LEARNING OBJECTIVE
Identify the tax consequences of incorporating a business.

Generally, property transfers have tax consequences. This is because gain or loss is normally realized on a property transfer. As a result, unless special provisions in the Code apply, a transfer of property to a corporation in exchange for stock is a sale or exchange of property that constitutes a taxable transaction. Gain or loss is measured by the difference between the tax basis of the property transferred and the value of the stock received.

The Code, however, does provide for special exceptions. Exceptions from the recognition of gain or loss are appropriate where a taxpayer's economic status has not changed and the wherewithal to pay is lacking.

One such exception is a like-kind exchange. When a taxpayer exchanges some of his or her property for other property of a like kind, § 1031 of the Code provides that gain (or loss) on the exchange is postponed because there has not been a substantive change in the taxpayer's investment. Section 1031 is a deferral mechanism, not an avoidance provision. The deferral mechanism is accomplished by a carryover of basis. Due to this carryover of basis, the potential gain or loss on the property given up is recognized when the property received in the exchange is sold.

Another exception to the general rule that a property transfer results in tax consequences is § 351. Section 351 provides for the nonrecognition of gain or loss upon the transfer of property to a corporation when certain conditions are met.

The nonrecognition of gain or loss under § 351 also reflects the principle that gain should not be recognized when a taxpayer's investment has not substantively changed. When a business is incorporated, the owner's economic status has not really changed. The investment in the business assets carries over to the investment in corporate stock. Since only stock in the new corporation is received, the taxpayer is hardly in a position to pay a tax on any realized gain. As noted later, when the taxpayer receives property other than stock (i.e., boot) from the corporation, realized gain may be recognized.

The same principles govern the nonrecognition of gain or loss under § 1031 and § 351. The concept of nonrecognition of gain or loss, present in both Code provisions, causes gain or loss to be postponed until a substantive change in the taxpayer's investment occurs (a sale to or a taxable exchange with outsiders). This approach is justified under the wherewithal to pay concept discussed in Chapter 1.

A further justification for the nonrecognition of gain or loss provisions under § 351 is that tax rules should not impede the exercise of sound business judgment (e.g., choice of corporate form of doing business).

EXAMPLE 1

Ron is considering incorporating his donut shop. He is concerned about potential liability for the shop's obligations in case he encounters financial difficulties in the future. Ron realizes that if he incorporates the shop, he will be liable only for the debts of the business that he has personally guaranteed. If Ron incorporates, the following assets will be transferred to the corporation:

	Tax Basis	Fair Market Value
Cash	$10,000	$ 10,000
Furniture and fixtures	20,000	60,000
Land and building	40,000	100,000
	$70,000	$170,000

Ron will receive stock in the newly formed corporation worth $170,000 in exchange for the assets. Without the nonrecognition provisions of § 351, Ron would recognize a taxable gain of $100,000 on the transfer. Under § 351, however, Ron does not recognize any gain because his economic status has not really changed. Ron's investment in the assets of his unincorporated donut shop carries over to his investment in the incorporated donut shop. Thus, § 351 provides for tax neutrality on the initial incorporation of Ron's donut shop. ▼

When a taxpayer exchanges property in a like-kind exchange, gain is not recognized only to the extent that the taxpayer receives like-kind property. The taxpayer must recognize gain on any "boot" (i.e., property of an unlike kind). For example, if a taxpayer exchanges a truck used in a business for another truck to be used in the business and also receives cash, the taxpayer has the wherewithal to pay an income tax on the cash involved. Further, the taxpayer's economic status has changed to the extent of the cash (not like-kind property) received. Thus, any "realized" gain on the exchange is recognized to the extent of the cash received. In like manner, if a taxpayer transfers property to a corporation and receives property or money other than stock, § 351(b) provides that gain is recognized to the extent of the lesser of the gain realized or the boot received (the amount of money and the fair market value of other property received). The gain is characterized according to the type of asset transferred.[1] Loss is never recognized. The nonrecognition of gain or loss is accompanied by a carryover of basis.[2]

---

[1] Rev.Rul. 68–55, 1968–1 C.B. 140.

[2] §§ 358(a) and 362(a). See the discussion preceding Example 18.

EXAMPLE 2

Abby and Bill form White Corporation. Abby transfers property with an adjusted basis of $30,000, fair market value of $60,000, for 50% of the stock. Bill transfers property with an adjusted basis of $70,000, fair market value of $60,000, for the remaining 50% of the stock. The transfer qualifies under § 351. Abby has an unrecognized gain of $30,000, and Bill has an unrecognized loss of $10,000. Both have a carryover basis in the stock in White Corporation. Abby has a basis of $30,000 in her stock, and Bill has a basis of $70,000 in his stock. Assume instead that Abby receives stock and cash of $10,000. Abby would recognize a gain of $10,000. ▼

Section 351 is mandatory. If a transaction falls within its provisions, neither gain nor loss is recognized on the transfer (except that realized gain is recognized to the extent of boot received), and there is a carryover of basis.

There are three requirements for nonrecognition of gain or loss: (1) *property* is transferred for (2) *stock* and (3) the transferors must be in *control* of the transferee corporation.

TRANSFER OF PROPERTY

Questions have arisen concerning what constitutes **property** for purposes of § 351. The Code specifically excludes services rendered from the definition of property. With this exception, the definition of property is comprehensive. Unrealized receivables for a cash basis taxpayer and installment obligations are considered property, for example.[3] The transfer of an installment obligation in a transaction qualifying under § 351 is not a disposition of the installment obligation. Thus, gain is not recognized to the transferor. Secret processes and formulas, as well as secret information in the general nature of a patentable inventory, also qualify as property under § 351.[4]

Services are not considered to be property under § 351 for a critical reason. A taxpayer must report as income the fair market value of property received as compensation for services rendered.[5] Thus, if a taxpayer receives stock in a corporation as consideration for rendering services to the corporation, the taxpayer has taxable income. The amount of income is the fair market value of the stock received. The taxpayer's basis in the stock then is the fair market value of the stock.

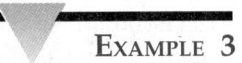

EXAMPLE 3

Ann and Bob form Brown Corporation and transfer the following property to it:

	Property Transferred		
	Basis to Transferor	Fair Market Value	Number of Shares Issued
From Ann:			
Personal services rendered to Brown Corporation	$ –0–	$20,000	200
From Bob:			
Installment obligation	5,000	40,000	
Inventory	10,000	30,000	800
Secret process	–0–	10,000	

---

[3] *Hempt Brothers, Inc. v. U.S.*, 74–1 USTC ¶9188, 33 AFTR2d 74–570, 490 F.2d 1172 (CA–3, 1974), and Reg. § 1.453–9(c)(2).

[4] Rev.Rul. 64–56, 1964–1 C.B. 133.
[5] §§ 61 and 83.

The value of each share in Brown Corporation is $100.[6] Ann has income of $20,000 on the transfer because services do not qualify as "property." She has a basis of $20,000 in her 200 shares of stock in Brown. Bob has no gain on the transfer because all of the consideration he transferred to Brown qualifies as "property" under § 351 (and he has "control" of Brown). (See discussion below.) Bob has a basis of $15,000 in his stock in Brown. ▼

If property is transferred to a corporation in exchange for any property other than stock, the property constitutes boot. The boot is taxable to the transferor shareholder to the extent of any realized gain.

STOCK

The Regulations state that the term "stock" does not include stock rights and stock warrants.[7] Generally, however, the term "stock" needs no clarification. It includes both common stock and preferred stock.

All debt constitutes boot. Included in debt are **securities** (e.g., long-term debt such as bonds). Thus, the receipt of debt in exchange for the transfer of appreciated property to a controlled corporation causes recognition of gain.

CONTROL OF THE TRANSFEREE CORPORATION

To qualify as a nontaxable transaction under § 351, the transferor must be in **control** of the transferee corporation immediately after the exchange. Control means that the person or persons transferring the property must have an 80

---

[6]The value of closely held stock normally is presumed to be equal to the value of the property transferred.

[7]Reg. § 1.351–1(a)(1)(ii).

percent stock ownership in the transferee corporation. The transferor shareholders must own stock possessing at least 80 percent of the total combined voting power of all classes of stock entitled to vote and at least 80 percent of the total *number* of shares of all other classes of stock.[8]

Control Immediately after the Transfer.   Control can apply to a single person or to several individuals if they are all parties to an integrated transaction. Section 351 requires control "immediately after the exchange." The Regulations provide that when more than one person is involved, the exchange does not necessarily require simultaneous exchanges by two or more persons. The Regulations do, however, require that the rights of the parties (e.g., those transferring property to the corporation) be previously set out and determined. Also, the agreement to transfer property should be executed "... with an expedition consistent with orderly procedure."[9]

If two or more persons transfer property to a corporation for stock, the transfers should occur close together in time and should be made in accordance with an agreement among the parties.

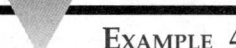

EXAMPLE 4   Jack exchanges property, basis of $60,000 and fair market value of $100,000, for 70% of the stock of Gray Corporation. The other 30% is owned by Jane, who acquired it several years ago. The fair market value of Jack's stock is $100,000. Jack recognizes a taxable gain of $40,000 on the transfer. ▼

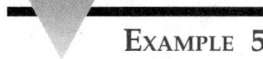

EXAMPLE 5   Lana, Leo, and Lori incorporate their respective businesses by forming Green Corporation. Lana exchanges her property for 300 shares in Green on January 5, 1997. Leo exchanges his property for 400 shares of Green Corporation stock on January 10, 1997, and Lori exchanges her property for 300 shares in Green on March 5, 1997. The three exchanges are part of a prearranged plan. The nonrecognition provisions of § 351 apply to all of the exchanges. ▼

Control is not lost if stock received by shareholders in a § 351 exchange is sold or given to persons who are not parties to the exchange shortly after the transaction. A different result might materialize if a *plan* for the ultimate disposition of the stock existed *before* the exchange.[10]

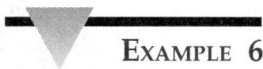

EXAMPLE 6   Lee and Pat form Black Corporation. They transfer appreciated property to the corporation with each receiving 50 shares of the stock. Shortly after the formation, Lee gives 25 shares to his son. Because Lee was not committed to make the gift, he is considered to own his original shares of the Black Corporation stock "immediately after the exchange." The requirements of § 351 are met, and neither Lee nor Pat is taxed on the exchange. ▼

ETHICAL CONSIDERATIONS

A Gift of Shares

Lee, in Example 6, intended to give half his shares to his son when he incorporated. His attorney, who was not well versed in the tax law, initially prepared stock certificates evidencing 50 shares to Pat, 25 shares to Lee, and 25 shares to Lee's son. Prior to the transfer of property in exchange for the shares certificates, the attorney

---

[8] § 368(c).
[9] Reg. § 1.351–1.

[10] *Wilgard Realty Co. v. Comm.*, 42–1 USTC ¶9452, 29 AFTR 325, 127 F.2d 514 (CA–2, 1942).

realized that the transfer of appreciated property to the corporation would result in recognized gain to both Pat and Lee, because they would have only 75 percent control. Accordingly, the attorney tore up the original certificates and prepared new ones. Fifty of the shares were then issued to Pat and 50 to Lee. Six months later, Lee gave 25 shares to his son. Did Lee and his attorney act correctly?

Transfers for Property and Services.   Section 351 treatment is lost if stock is transferred to persons who did not contribute property, causing those who did to lack control immediately after the exchange.

EXAMPLE 7

Kate transfers property with a value of $60,000 and a basis of $5,000 for 600 shares of stock in newly formed Wren Corporation. Kevin receives 400 shares in Wren for services rendered to the corporation. Each share of stock is worth $100. Both Kate and Kevin have taxable gain on the transaction. Kevin is not part of the control group because he did not transfer "property" for stock. He has taxable income of $40,000 (400 shares × $100). Kate has a taxable gain of $55,000 [$60,000 (fair market value of the stock in Wren Corporation) – $5,000 (basis in the transferred property)]. Kate is taxed on the exchange because she received only 60% of the stock in Wren Corporation. ▼

A person who performs services for the corporation in exchange for stock and also transfers some property is treated as a member of the transferring group. That person is taxed on the value of the stock issued for services but not on the stock issued for property. In this case, all the stock received by the person transferring both property and services is counted in determining whether the transferors acquired control of the corporation.[11]

EXAMPLE 8

Assume the same facts as in Example 7 except that Kevin transfers property worth $30,000 (basis of $3,000) in addition to services rendered to the corporation (valued at $10,000). Now Kevin becomes a part of the control group. Kate and Kevin together received 100% of the stock in Wren Corporation. Consequently, § 351 is applicable to the exchanges. Kate has no recognized gain. Kevin does not recognize gain on the transfer of the property but has taxable income to the extent of the value of the shares issued for services rendered. Thus, Kevin has income of $10,000. ▼

Transfers for Services and Nominal Property.   To be a member of the group and aid in qualifying all transferors under the 80 percent test, the person contributing services must transfer property having more than a relatively small value compared to the services performed. Stock issued for property whose value is relatively small compared to the value of the stock already owned (or to be received for services rendered) will not be treated as issued in return for property. This will be the result when the primary purpose of the transfer is to qualify the transaction under § 351 for concurrent transferors.[12]

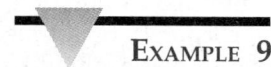

EXAMPLE 9

Olga and Otis transfer property to Redbird Corporation, each in exchange for one-third of the stock. Olaf receives the other one-third of the stock for services rendered. The transaction will not qualify under § 351 because Olaf is not a member of the group

---

[11] Reg. § 1.351–1(a)(2), Ex. 3.   [12] Reg. § 1.351–1(a)(1)(ii).

transferring property and Olga and Otis together received only 66⅔% of the stock. The post-transfer control requirement is not met.

Assume instead that Olaf also transfers property. Then he is a member of the group, and the transaction qualifies under § 351. Olaf is taxed on the value of the stock issued for services, but the remainder of the transaction is tax-free. However, if the property transferred by Olaf is of a relatively small value in comparison to the stock he receives for his services, and the primary purpose for including the property is to cause the transaction to be tax-free for Olga and Otis, the exchange does not qualify under § 351. Gain or loss is recognized by all parties. ▼

The IRS generally requires that before a transferor who receives stock for both property and services can be included in the control group, the value of the property transferred must be at least 10 percent of the value of the services provided.[13] If the value of the property transferred is less than this amount, the IRS will not issue an advance ruling that the exchange meets the requirements of § 351.

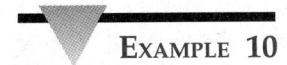

EXAMPLE 10

Sara and Rick form White Corporation. Sara transfers land (worth $100,000, basis of $20,000) for 50% of the stock in White. Rick transfers equipment (worth $50,000, adjusted basis of $10,000) and provides services worth $50,000 for 50% of the stock. Rick's stock in White Corporation is counted in determining control for purposes of § 351; thus, the transferors own 100% of the stock in White. All of Rick's stock, not just the shares received for the equipment, is counted in determining control because property he transferred has more than a nominal value in comparison to the value of the services rendered. Sara does not recognize gain on the transfer of the land. She has a basis of $20,000 in her White stock. Rick, however, must recognize income of $50,000 on the transfer. Even though the transfer of the equipment qualifies under § 351, his transfer of services for stock does not. Rick has a $60,000 basis in his White stock, computed as follows: $10,000 (adjusted basis of equipment Rick transferred to White) + $50,000 (income recognized by Rick on the transfer). ▼

2 ▸ LEARNING OBJECTIVE
Appreciate the tax problems involved when making later property transfers to a controlled corporation.

Transfers to Existing Corporations.   Once a corporation is in operation, § 351 also applies to any later transfers of property for stock by either new or former shareholders.

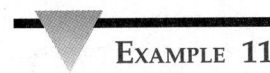

EXAMPLE 11

Sam and Seth formed Blue Corporation three years ago. Both Sam and Seth transferred appreciated property to Blue in exchange for 50 shares each in the corporation. The original transfers qualified under § 351, and neither Sam nor Seth was taxed on the exchange. In the current year, Sam transfers property (worth $90,000, adjusted basis of $5,000) for 50 additional Blue shares. Sam has a taxable gain of $85,000 on the transfer. The exchange does not qualify under § 351 because Sam does not have 80% control of Blue Corporation. (Sam has 100 shares of the 150 shares outstanding, or a 66⅔% ownership.) ▼

See the Tax Planning Considerations portion of this chapter for a further discussion of this problem.

ASSUMPTION OF LIABILITIES—§ 357

Without § 357, the transfer of mortgaged property to a controlled corporation could trigger gain to the extent of the mortgage whether the corporation assumed the mortgage or took property subject to it. This is the rule in nontaxable like-kind exchanges under § 1031. Liabilities assumed by the other party are considered the

---

[13] Rev.Proc. 77–37, 1977–2 C.B. 568; § 3.07.

equivalent of cash and treated as boot. Section 357(a) provides, however, that when the acquiring corporation **assumes a liability** or takes property subject to a liability in a § 351 transaction, the transfer does not result in boot to the transferor shareholder. Nevertheless, liabilities assumed by the transferee corporation are treated as boot in determining the basis of the stock received. The basis of the stock received is reduced by the amount of the liabilities assumed by the corporation.

EXAMPLE 12

Vera transfers property with an adjusted basis of $60,000, fair market value of $100,000, to Gray Corporation for 100% of the stock in Gray. The property is subject to a liability of $25,000 that Gray Corporation assumes. The exchange is tax-free under §§ 351 and 357. However, the basis to Vera of the Gray stock is $35,000 [$60,000 (basis of property transferred) – $25,000 (amount of mortgage)]. ▼

The rule of § 357(a) has two exceptions. Section 357(b) provides that if the principal purpose of the assumption of the liabilities is to avoid tax *or* if there is no bona fide business purpose behind the exchange, the liabilities are treated as boot. Further, § 357(c) provides that if the sum of the liabilities exceeds the adjusted basis of the properties transferred, the excess is taxable gain.

Tax Avoidance or No Bona Fide Business Purpose Exception. Unless liabilities are incurred shortly before incorporation, § 357(b) generally poses few problems. A tax avoidance purpose for transferring liabilities to a controlled corporation seems unlikely in view of the basis adjustment as noted above. Since the liabilities transferred reduce the basis of the stock received, any realized gain is deferred and not avoided. The gain materializes when and if the stock is disposed of in a taxable sale or exchange.

Satisfying the bona fide business purpose is not difficult if the liabilities were incurred in connection with the transferor's normal course of conducting a trade or business. But the bona fide business purpose requirement can cause difficulty if the liability is taken out shortly before the property is transferred and the proceeds are utilized for personal purposes.[14] This type of situation is analogous to a cash distribution by the corporation, which is taxed as boot.

EXAMPLE 13

Dan transfers real estate (basis of $40,000 and fair market value of $90,000) to a controlled corporation in return for stock in the corporation. Shortly before the transfer, Dan mortgages the real estate and uses the $20,000 proceeds to meet personal obligations. Along with the real estate, the mortgage is transferred to the corporation. In this case, the assumption of the mortgage appears to lack a bona fide business purpose. The amount of the liability is boot, and Dan has a taxable gain on the transfer of $20,000.[15] ▼

The effect of the application of § 357(b) is to taint *all* liabilities transferred even if some are supported by a bona fide business purpose.

EXAMPLE 14

Tim, an accrual basis taxpayer, incorporates his sole proprietorship. Among the liabilities transferred to the new corporation are trade accounts payable of $100,000 and a MasterCard bill of $5,000. Tim had used the MasterCard to purchase a wedding anniversary gift for his wife. Under these circumstances, all of the $105,000 liabilities are boot. ▼

---

[14]See, for example, *Campbell, Jr. v. Wheeler*, 65–1 USTC ¶9294, 15 AFTR2d 578, 342 F.2d 837 (CA–5, 1965).

[15]§ 351(b).

ETHICAL CONSIDERATIONS

Rectifying a Mistake?

Jean incorporates her sole proprietorship. Inadvertently, she transfers to the new corporation a credit charge for a family dinner she hosted. After the corporation pays the bill, she realizes her mistake and issues a note payable to the corporation in the amount of the charge. Has Jean avoided § 357(b)?

Liabilities in Excess of Basis Exception.   Section 357(c) states that if the sum of **liabilities** assumed and the liabilities to which transferred property is subject **exceeds** the total of the adjusted **bases** of the properties transferred, the excess is taxable gain. Without this provision, if liabilities exceed basis in property exchanged, a taxpayer would have a negative basis in the stock received in the controlled corporation.[16] Section 357(c) precludes the negative basis possibility by treating the excess over basis as gain to the transferor.

EXAMPLE 15

Andre transfers assets with an adjusted tax basis of $40,000 to a newly formed corporation in exchange for 100% of the stock. The corporation assumes liabilities on the transferred properties in the amount of $50,000. Without § 357(c), Andre's basis in the stock of the new corporation would be a negative $10,000 [$40,000 (basis of property transferred) + $0 (gain recognized) – $0 (boot received) – $50,000 (liabilities assumed)]. Section 357(c) causes Andre to recognize a gain of $10,000. As a result, the stock has a zero basis in Andre's hands, determined as follows:

Basis in the property transferred	$40,000
Add: Gain recognized	10,000
Less: Boot received	–0–
Less: Liabilities assumed	50,000
Basis in the stock received	$ –0–

Thus, no negative basis results. ▼

Accounts payable of a cash basis taxpayer that give rise to a deduction are not considered to be liabilities for purposes of § 357(c).

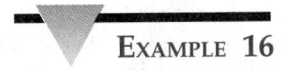

EXAMPLE 16

Tina, a cash basis taxpayer, incorporates her sole proprietorship. In return for all of the stock of the new corporation, she transfers the following items:

	Adjusted Basis	Fair Market Value
Cash	$10,000	$10,000
Unrealized accounts receivable (amounts due to Tina but not yet paid to her)	–0–	40,000
Trade accounts payable	–0–	30,000
Note payable	5,000	5,000

[16] *Easson v. Comm.*, 33 T.C. 963 (1960), *rev'd.* in 61–2 USTC ¶9654, 8 AFTR2d 5448, 294 F.2d 653 (CA–9, 1961).

Unrealized accounts receivable and trade accounts payable have a zero basis. Under the cash method of accounting, no income is recognized until the receivables are collected, and no deduction materializes until the payables are satisfied. The note payable has a basis because it was issued for consideration received.

The accounts receivable and the trade accounts payable are disregarded for gain recognition purposes. Thus, Tina transfers only cash ($10,000) and a note payable ($5,000) and does not have a problem of liabilities in excess of basis. ▼

The definition of liabilities under § 357(c) excludes obligations that would have been deductible to the transferor had those obligations been paid before the transfer. Consequently, Tina, in Example 16, has no gain.

ETHICAL CONSIDERATIONS

Structuring to Avoid Liabilities in Excess of Basis?

Ann has operated a sole proprietorship for three years. On January 1 she formed Green Corporation. She transfers all of the assets of the proprietorship, subject to all of the liabilities, to Green Corporation in exchange for all of its shares. At the time of the transfer, the sole proprietorship's balance sheet showed the basis of its assets as $15,000 and its liabilities (a note payable to the bank) as $25,000. The fair market value of the assets is $45,000. Thus, the fair market value of the Green stock is $20,000 [$45,000 (value of the assets) – $25,000 (note payable)]. To avoid $10,000 gain under § 357(c), measured by the excess of the liabilities ($25,000) over the basis of the assets ($15,000), Ann contributes to Green Corporation, in the same transaction, a personal note in the amount of $10,000. The note bears interest at two points above the prime rate and is payable in five equal annual installments (principal plus interest). Has Ann successfully avoided the application of § 357(c)?

If §§ 357(b) and (c) both apply to the same transfer, § 357(b) predominates.[17] This could be significant because § 357(b) does not create gain on the transfer, as does § 357(c), but merely converts the liability to boot. Thus, the realized gain limitation continues to apply to § 357(b) transactions.

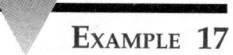

EXAMPLE 17

Chris forms Robin Corporation by transferring land with a basis of $100,000, fair market value of $1,000,000. The land is subject to a mortgage of $300,000. One month prior to incorporating Robin, Chris borrows $200,000 for personal purposes and gives the lender a second mortgage on the land. Robin Corporation issues stock worth $500,000 to Chris and assumes the mortgages on the land. Section 357(c) applies to the transfer. The mortgages on the property ($500,000) exceed the basis of the property ($100,000). Thus, Chris has a gain of $400,000 under § 357(c). Section 357(b) also applies to the transfer. Chris borrowed $200,000 just prior to the transfer and used the $200,000 for personal purposes. Under § 357(b), Chris has boot of $500,000 in the amount of the liabilities (*all* of which are treated as boot). He has realized gain of $900,000 [$1,000,000 (fair market value of the land) – $100,000 (basis in the land)]. Gain is recognized to the extent of the boot of $500,000. Note that § 357(b) predominates over § 357(c). ▼

---

[17] § 357(c)(2)(A).

▼ **FIGURE 3–1**
Shareholder's Basis in Stock Received

Adjusted basis of property transferred	$xx,xxx
Plus: Gain recognized	x,xxx
Minus: Boot received (including any liabilities transferred)	(x,xxx)
Equals: Basis of stock received	$xx,xxx

▼ **FIGURE 3–2**
Corporation's Basis in Properties
Received

Adjusted basis of property transferred	$xx,xxx
Plus: Gain recognized by transferor shareholder	xxx
Equals: Basis of property to corporation	$xx,xxx

BASIS DETERMINATION

Recall that § 351(a) postpones gain or loss until the taxpayer's investment changes substantially. Postponement of the realized gain or loss is accomplished through a carryover of basis.

Basis of Stock to Shareholder.   For a taxpayer transferring property to a corporation in a § 351 transaction, the basis of stock received in the transfer is the same as the basis the taxpayer had in the property transferred, increased by any gain recognized on the exchange and decreased by boot received. For basis purposes, boot received includes any liabilities transferred by the shareholder to the corporation.[18]

Basis of Property to Corporation.   The basis of properties received by the corporation is determined under § 362(a). The basis to the corporation is the basis in the hands of the transferor increased by the amount of any gain recognized to the transferor shareholder.[19]

The basis rules are summarized in Figures 3–1 and 3–2 and illustrated in Examples 18 and 19.

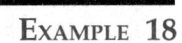

EXAMPLE 18

Maria and Ned form Brown Corporation. Maria transfers land (basis of $30,000 and fair market value of $70,000); Ned invests cash ($60,000). They each receive 50 shares in Brown Corporation, worth $1,200 per share, but Maria also receives $10,000 cash from Brown. The transfers of property, the realized and recognized gain on the transfers, and the basis of the stock in Brown Corporation to Maria and Ned are as follows:

	A	B	C	D	E	F
	Basis of Property Transferred	**FMV of Stock Received**	**Boot Received**	**Realized Gain (B + C − A)**	**Recognized Gain (Lesser of C or D)**	**Basis of Stock in Brown (A − C + E)**
From Maria:						
Land	$30,000	$60,000	$10,000	$40,000	$10,000	$30,000
From Ned:						
Cash	60,000	60,000	–0–	–0–	–0–	60,000

---

[18] § 358(a).   [19] § 362(a).

Brown Corporation has a basis of $40,000 in the land. The basis to Brown is Maria's basis of $30,000 plus her recognized gain of $10,000. ▼

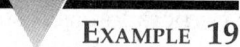

EXAMPLE 19

Assume the same facts as in Example 18 except that Maria's basis in the land is $68,000 (instead of $30,000). Because recognized gain cannot exceed realized gain, the transfer generates only $2,000 of gain to Maria. The realized and recognized gain and the basis of the stock in Brown Corporation to Maria are as follows:

	A	B	C	D	E	F
	Basis of Property Transferred	FMV of Stock Received	Boot Received	Realized Gain (B + C − A)	Recognized Gain (Lesser of C or D)	Basis of Stock in Brown (A − C + E)
Land	$68,000	$60,000	$10,000	$2,000	$2,000	$60,000 ▼

Stock Issued for Services Rendered. A corporation's disposition of stock for property is not a taxable exchange.[20] A transfer of shares for services is also not a taxable transaction to a corporation.[21] Can a corporation deduct the fair market value of the stock it issues in consideration of services as a business expense? Yes, unless the services are such that the payment is characterized as a capital expenditure.[22]

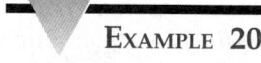

EXAMPLE 20

Carol and Carl form White Corporation. Carol transfers cash of $500,000 for 100 shares of White Corporation stock. Carl transfers property worth $480,000 (basis of $90,000) and agrees to serve as manager of the corporation for one year; in return, Carl receives 100 shares of stock in White. The value of Carl's services to White Corporation is $20,000. The transfers qualify under § 351. Carl is not taxed on the transfer of the appreciated property. However, Carl has income of $20,000, the value of the services he will render to White Corporation. White has a basis of $90,000 in the property it acquired from Carl. It has a business deduction under § 162 of $20,000 for the value of services Carl will render. ▼

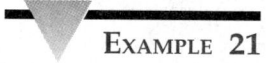

EXAMPLE 21

Assume, in Example 20, that Carl receives the 100 shares of White Corporation stock in consideration for the appreciated property and for providing legal services in organizing the corporation. The value of Carl's legal services is $20,000. Carl has no gain on the transfer of the property but has income of $20,000 for the value of the services rendered. White Corporation has a basis of $90,000 in the property it acquired from Carl and must capitalize the $20,000 as organizational expenses. ▼

Holding Period for Shareholder and Transferee Corporation. The shareholder's holding period for stock received for a capital asset or for § 1231 property includes the holding period of the property transferred to the corporation. The holding period of the property is "tacked on" to the holding period of the stock. The holding period for stock received for any other property (e.g., inventory or property held primarily for sale) begins on the day after the exchange.[23] The transferee corporation's holding period for property acquired in a § 351 transfer is the holding period of the transferor shareholder regardless of the character of the property to the transferor.

---

[20] § 1032.
[21] Reg. § 1.1032–1(a).
[22] Rev.Rul. 62–217, 1962–2 C.B. 59, modified by Rev.Rul. 74–503, 1974–2 C.B. 117.

[23] §§ 1223(1) and (2).

RECAPTURE CONSIDERATIONS

In a pure § 351(a) nontaxable transfer (no boot involved) to a controlled corporation, the recapture of accelerated cost recovery rules do not apply.[24] Moreover, any recapture potential of the property carries over to the corporation as it steps into the shoes of the transferor-shareholder for purposes of basis determination.

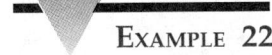

EXAMPLE 22

Paul transfers equipment (basis of $30,000 and fair market value of $100,000) to a controlled corporation in return for additional stock. If Paul had sold the equipment, it would have yielded a gain of $70,000, all of which would be recaptured as ordinary income under § 1245. If the transfer comes within § 351(a), Paul has no recognized gain and no accelerated cost recovery to recapture. If the corporation later disposes of the equipment in a taxable transaction, it must take into account the § 1245 recapture potential originating with Paul. ▼

CAPITAL STRUCTURE OF A CORPORATION

CAPITAL CONTRIBUTIONS

3   LEARNING OBJECTIVE
Understand the tax aspects of the capital structure of a corporation.

The receipt of money or property in exchange for capital stock (including treasury stock) produces neither gain nor loss to the recipient corporation. Nor does a corporation's gross income include shareholders' contributions of money or property to the capital of the corporation. Additional funds received from shareholders through voluntary pro rata payments are not income to the corporation. This is the case even though there is no increase in the outstanding shares of stock of the corporation. The payments represent an additional price paid for the shares held by the shareholders and are treated as additions to the operating capital of the corporation.[25]

     Contributions by nonshareholders, such as land contributed to a corporation by a civic group or a governmental group to induce the corporation to locate in a particular community, are also excluded from the gross income of a corporation.[26] Property that is transferred to a corporation by a nonshareholder for services rendered or for merchandise is taxable income to the corporation.[27]

EXAMPLE 23

A television company charges its customers an initial fee to hook up to a new television system installed in the area. These payments are used to finance the total cost of constructing the television facilities. The customers will make monthly payments for the television service. The initial payments are used for capital expenditures, but they represent payments for services to be rendered by the television company. As such, they are taxable income and not contributions to capital by nonshareholders. ▼

     The basis of property received by a corporation from a shareholder as a **capital contribution** is the basis of the property in the hands of the shareholder increased by any gain recognized to the shareholder. The basis of property transferred to a corporation by a nonshareholder as a contribution to capital is zero.

     If a corporation receives money as a contribution to capital from a nonshareholder, a special rule applies. The basis of any property acquired with the money during a 12-month period beginning on the day the contribution was received is

---

[24] §§ 1245(b)(3) and 1250(d)(3).

[25] § 118 and Reg. § 1.118–1.

[26] See *Edwards v. Cuba Railroad Co.*, 1 USTC ¶139, 5 AFTR 5398, 45 S.Ct. 614 (USSC, 1925).

[27] Reg. § 1.118–1. See also *Teleservice Co. of Wyoming Valley v. Comm.*, 27 T.C. 722 (1957), *aff'd.* in 58–1 USTC ¶9383, 1 AFTR2d 1249, 254 F.2d 105 (CA–3, 1958), *cert. den.* 78 S.Ct. 1360 (USSC, 1958).

reduced by the amount of the contribution. The excess of money received over the cost of new property is used to reduce the basis of other property held by the corporation and is applied in the following order:

- Depreciable property.
- Property subject to amortization.
- Property subject to depletion.
- All other remaining properties.

The basis of property within each category is reduced in proportion to the relative bases of the properties.[28]

EXAMPLE 24

A city donates land to Brown Corporation as an inducement for Brown to locate in the city. The receipt of the land does not produce taxable income. However, the land's basis to the corporation is zero. Assume the city also pays the corporation $10,000 in cash. The money is not taxable income to the corporation. However, if the corporation purchases property with the $10,000 within the next 12 months, the basis of the property is reduced by $10,000. ▼

DEBT IN THE CAPITAL STRUCTURE

4   **LEARNING OBJECTIVE**
Recognize the tax differences between debt and equity investments.

Advantages of Debt.   Shareholders must be aware of the differences between debt and equity in the capital structure. The advantages of issuing long-term debt are numerous. Interest on debt is deductible by the corporation, while dividend payments are not. Further, the shareholders are not taxed on loan repayments unless the repayments exceed basis. As long as a corporation has earnings and profits (see Chapter 4), an investment in stock cannot be withdrawn tax-free. Withdrawals will be deemed to be taxable dividends to the extent of earnings and profits of the distributing corporation.

EXAMPLE 25

Wade transfers cash of $100,000 to a newly formed corporation for 100% of the stock. In the first year of operations, the corporation has net income of $40,000. The income is credited to the earnings and profits account of the corporation. If the corporation distributes $9,500 to Wade, the distribution is a taxable dividend with no corresponding deduction to the corporation. Assume, instead, that Wade transfers cash of $50,000 for stock. In addition, he loans the corporation $50,000, transferring cash of $50,000 to the corporation for a note in the amount of $50,000. The note is payable in equal annual installments of $5,000 and bears interest at the rate of 9%. At the end of the year, the corporation pays Wade $4,500 interest, which is tax deductible to the corporation. The $5,000 principal repayment on the loan is not taxed to Wade. ▼

Reclassification of Debt as Equity (Thin Capitalization Problem).   In certain instances, known as **thin capitalization** situations, the IRS contends that debt is really an equity interest and denies the shareholders the tax advantages of debt financing. If the debt instrument has too many features of stock, it may be treated as a form of stock. In that case, the principal and interest payments are considered dividends. Under § 385, the IRS has the authority to characterize corporate debt wholly as equity or as part debt and part equity.

Section 385 lists several factors that *may* be used to determine whether a debtor-creditor relationship or a shareholder-corporation relationship exists. The thrust of § 385 is to authorize the Treasury to prescribe Regulations that provide more definite guidelines for determining when debt should be reclassified as

---

[28]§ 362 and Reg. § 1.362-2(b).

equity. To date, the Treasury has not drafted acceptable Regulations. Consequently, taxpayers must rely on judicial decisions to determine whether a true debtor-creditor relationship exists.

Together, Congress, through § 385, and the courts have identified the following factors to be considered in resolving the thin capitalization problem:

- Whether the debt instrument is in proper form. An open account advance is more easily characterized as a contribution to capital than a loan evidenced by a properly written note executed by the shareholder.[29]
- Whether the debt instrument bears a reasonable rate of interest and has a definite maturity date. When a shareholder advance does not provide for interest, the return expected is that inherent in an equity interest (e.g., a share of the profits or an increase in the value of the shares).[30] Likewise, a lender unrelated to the corporation will usually be unwilling to commit funds to the corporation for an indefinite period of time (i.e., no definite due date).
- Whether the debt is paid on a timely basis. A lender's failure to insist upon timely repayment (or satisfactory renegotiation) indicates that the return sought does not depend upon interest income and the repayment of principal.
- Whether payment is contingent upon earnings. A lender ordinarily will not advance funds that are likely to be repaid only if the venture is successful.
- Whether the debt is subordinated to other liabilities. Subordination tends to eliminate a significant characteristic of the creditor-debtor relationship. Creditors should have the right to share with other general creditors in the event of the corporation's dissolution or liquidation. Subordination also destroys another basic attribute of creditor status—the power to demand payment at a fixed maturity date.[31]
- Whether holdings of debt and stock are proportionate. When debt and equity obligations are held in the same proportion, shareholders are, apart from tax considerations, indifferent as to whether corporate distributions are in the form of interest or dividends.
- Whether funds loaned to the corporation are used to finance initial operations or capital asset acquisitions. Funds used to finance initial operations or to acquire capital assets the corporation needs to operate are generally obtained through equity investments.
- Whether the corporation has a high ratio of shareholder debt to shareholder equity. Thin capitalization occurs when shareholder debt is high relative to shareholder equity. This indicates the corporation lacks reserves to pay interest and principal on debt when corporate income is insufficient to meet current needs.[32] In determining a corporation's debt-equity ratio, courts look at the relation of the debt both to the book value of the corporation's assets and to their actual fair market value.[33]

For the most part, the principles used to classify debt as equity developed in connection with closely held corporations. Here, the holders of the debt are also shareholders. The rules have often proved inadequate for dealing with such problems in large, publicly traded corporations.

---

[29] *Estate of Mixon v. U.S.*, 72–2 USTC ¶9537, 30 AFTR2d 72–5094, 464 F.2d 394 (CA–5, 1972).

[30] *Slappey Drive Industrial Park v. U.S.*, 77–2 USTC ¶9696, 40 AFTR2d 77–5941, 561 F.2d 572 (CA–5, 1977).

[31] *Fin Hay Realty Co. v. U.S.*, 68–2 USTC ¶9438, 22 AFTR2d 5004, 398 F.2d 694 (CA–3, 1968).

[32] A court held that a debt-equity ratio of approximately 4:1 was not excessive. See *Tomlinson v. 1661 Corp.*, 67–1 USTC ¶9438, 19 AFTR2d 1413, 377 F.2d 291 (CA–5, 1967).

[33] In *Bauer v. Comm.*, 84–2 USTC ¶9996, 55 AFTR2d 84–433, 748 F.2d 1365 (CA–9, 1984), a debt-equity ratio of 92:1 resulted when book value was used. But the ratio ranged from 2:1 to 8:1 when equity included both paid-in capital and accumulated earnings.

Section 385 authorizes the Treasury to issue Regulations classifying an instrument either as *wholly* debt or equity or as *part* debt and *part* equity. This flexible approach is important because some instruments cannot readily be classified either wholly as stock or wholly as debt. It may also provide an avenue for the IRS to address problems in publicly traded corporations.

INVESTOR LOSSES

5 **LEARNING OBJECTIVE**
Handle the tax treatment of shareholder debt and stock losses.

The choice between debt and equity financing leads to a consideration of the tax treatment of worthless stock and securities versus the treatment of bad debts.

Stock and Security Losses. If stocks and bonds are capital assets in the hands of the holder, losses from their worthlessness are governed by § 165(g)(1). Under this provision, a capital loss materializes as of the last day of the taxable year in which the stocks or bonds become worthless. No deduction is allowed for a mere decline in value. The burden of proving complete worthlessness is on the taxpayer claiming the loss. One way to recognize partial worthlessness is to dispose of the stocks or bonds in a taxable sale or exchange.[34] But even then, the **investor loss** is disallowed if the sale or exchange is to a related party.

When the stocks or bonds are not capital assets, worthlessness yields an ordinary loss.[35] For example, if the stocks or bonds are held by a broker for resale to customers in the normal course of business, they are not capital assets. Usually, however, stocks and bonds are held as investments and are capital assets.

Under certain circumstances involving stocks and bonds of affiliated corporations, an ordinary loss is allowed upon worthlessness.[36] A corporation is an affiliate of another corporation if the corporate shareholder owns at least 80 percent of the voting power of all classes of stock entitled to vote and 80 percent of each class of nonvoting stock. An ordinary loss is allowed upon worthlessness of the stock if the affiliated corporation derived 90 percent of its aggregate gross receipts for all taxable years from sources other than passive income. Passive income includes such items as rents, royalties, dividends, and interest.

The possibility of an ordinary loss on the stock of small business corporations (§ 1244) is discussed later in the chapter.

Business versus Nonbusiness Bad Debts. In addition to the possible worthlessness of stocks and bonds, the financial end of a corporation can lead to bad debt deductions. These deductions can be either business bad debts or **nonbusiness bad debts.** The distinction between the two types of deductions is important for tax purposes in the following respects:

- Business bad debts are deducted as ordinary losses while nonbusiness bad debts are treated as short-term capital losses.[37] A business bad debt can generate a net operating loss while a nonbusiness bad debt cannot.[38]
- A deduction is allowed for the partial worthlessness of a business debt. Nonbusiness debts can be written off only when they become entirely worthless.[39]
- Nonbusiness bad debt treatment is limited to noncorporate taxpayers. All of the bad debts of a corporation qualify as business bad debts.[40]

---

[34] Reg. § 1.165–4(a).
[35] § 165(a) and Reg. § 1.165–5(b).
[36] § 165(g)(3).
[37] Compare § 166(a) with § 166(d)(1)(B).

[38] Note the adjustments necessitated by § 172(d)(2).
[39] Compare § 166(a)(2) with § 166(d)(1)(A).
[40] § 166(d)(1).

TAX IN THE NEWS

INVESTMENTS THAT CANNOT LOSE

Some brokerage firms, banks, and mutual-fund companies have recently decided to pay irate investors who have suffered substantial losses rather than to risk investor lawsuits. Although statistics are scarce on such "guilt money," securities lawyers suggest that brokerage firms have been "ponying up more cash more quickly than ever when faced with protests over questionable investments." In most cases, the investors are reimbursed for derivatives losses in money-market and bond funds. Derivatives—financial arrangements whose value is linked to, or derived from, the performance of some underlying asset, such as bonds—plunged in value, pummeling the funds that held them, when interest rates rose sharply in the latter part of 1994. Many funds had been aggressively using derivatives to reap big returns in early 1994 when interest rates were declining and were caught unawares when rates began to rise.

When is a debt business or nonbusiness? Unfortunately, since the Code sheds little light on the matter, the distinction has been left to the courts.[41] In a leading decision, the Supreme Court somewhat clarified the picture when it held that if individual shareholders loan money to a corporation in their capacity as investors, any resulting bad debt is classified as nonbusiness.[42] Nevertheless, the Court did not preclude the possibility of a shareholder-creditor's incurring a business bad debt.

If a loan is made in some capacity that qualifies as a trade or business, nonbusiness bad debt treatment is avoided. For example, has the loan been made to protect the shareholder's employment with the corporation? Employee status is a trade or business, and a loss on a loan made for this purpose qualifies for business bad debt treatment.[43] Shareholders also receive business bad debt treatment if they are in the trade or business of loaning money or of buying, promoting, and selling corporations.

Suppose the shareholder has multiple motives for making the loan. According to the Supreme Court, the "dominant" or "primary" motive for making the loan controls the classification of the loss.[44]

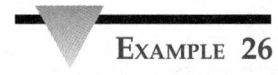

EXAMPLE 26

Norman owns 48% of the stock of Plover Corporation, which he acquired several years ago at a cost of $200,000. Norman is also employed by the corporation at an annual salary of $80,000. At a time when Plover Corporation is experiencing financial problems, Norman loans it $100,000. Subsequently, the corporation becomes bankrupt, and both Norman's stock investment and his loans become worthless. ▼

Granted that Norman's stock investment is treated as a long-term capital loss (assuming § 1244 does not apply, as discussed below), how is the bad debt classified? If Norman can prove that his dominant or primary reason for making

---

[41] For definitional purposes, § 166(d)(2) is almost as worthless as the debt it purports to describe.

[42] *Whipple v. Comm.*, 63–1 USTC ¶9466, 11 AFTR2d 1454, 83 S.Ct. 1168 (USSC, 1963).

[43] *Trent v. Comm.*, 61–2 USTC ¶9506, 7 AFTR2d 1599, 291 F.2d 669 (CA–2, 1961).

[44] *U.S. v. Generes*, 72–1 USTC ¶9259, 29 AFTR2d 72–609, 92 S.Ct. 827 (USSC, 1972).

the loan was to protect his salary, a business bad debt deduction results. If not, it is assumed that Norman was trying to protect his stock investment, and nonbusiness bad debt treatment results. Factors to be considered in resolving this matter include the following:

- A comparison of the amount of the stock investment with the trade or business benefit derived. In Example 26, the stock investment of $200,000 is compared with the annual salary of $80,000. In this regard, the salary should be considered as a recurring item and not viewed in isolation. A salary of $80,000 each year means a great deal to a person who has no other means of support and who may have difficulty obtaining similar employment elsewhere.
- A comparison of the amount of the loan with the stock investment and the trade or business benefit derived.
- The percentage of ownership held by the shareholder. A minority shareholder, for example, is under more compulsion to loan the corporation money to protect his or her job than one who is in control of corporate policy.

In summary, it is impossible to conclude whether Norman in Example 26 suffered a business or nonbusiness bad debt without additional facts. Even with such facts, the guidelines are vague. Recall that a taxpayer's intent or motivation is at issue. For this reason, the problem is the subject of frequent litigation.[45]

Section 1244 Stock. Section 1244 permits ordinary loss treatment for losses on the sale or worthlessness of stock of so-called small business corporations. By placing shareholders on a more nearly equal basis with proprietors and partners in terms of the tax treatment of losses, the provision encourages investment of capital in small corporations. Gain on the sale of § 1244 stock remains capital. Consequently, the shareholder has nothing to lose and everything to gain by complying with § 1244.

Only a small business corporation can issue qualifying **§ 1244 stock.** The total amount of stock that can be offered under the plan to issue § 1244 stock cannot exceed $1 million. For these purposes, property received in exchange for stock is valued at its adjusted basis, reduced by any liabilities assumed by the corporation or to which the property is subject. The fair market value of the property is not considered. The $1 million limitation is determined by property and money received for the stock as a contribution to capital and as paid-in capital on the date the stock is issued. Consequently, even though a corporation fails to meet these requirements when the stock later is disposed of by the shareholder, the stock can still qualify as § 1244 stock if the requirements were met on the date the stock was issued.

For § 1244 to apply to a loss, the corporation issuing the stock must also be an *operating company*. To be distinguished from an investment or holding company, an operating company must derive more than 50 percent of its aggregate gross receipts from sources other than royalties, rents, dividends, interest, annuities, and sales and exchanges of stock or securities (only the gains are considered). The test applies for the corporation's most recent five tax years. The gross receipts requirement applies only if the corporation's receipts equal or exceed its deductions other than a net operating loss deduction or the dividends received deduction.

---

[45]See, for example, *Kelson v. U.S.,* 74–2 USTC ¶9714, 34 AFTR2d 74–6007, 503 F.2d 1291 (CA–10, 1974).

The amount of ordinary loss deductible in any one year on § 1244 stock is limited to $50,000 (or $100,000 for husband and wife filing a joint return). If the amount of the loss sustained in the taxable year exceeds these amounts, the remainder is considered a capital loss.

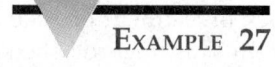

EXAMPLE 27   Harvey acquires § 1244 stock at a cost of $100,000. He sells the stock for $10,000 in one tax year. He has an ordinary loss of $50,000 and a capital loss of $40,000. On a joint return, the entire $90,000 loss is ordinary. ▼

Only the original holder of § 1244 stock, whether an individual or a partnership, qualifies for ordinary loss treatment. If the stock is sold or donated, it loses its § 1244 status.

Recall the advantages of issuing some debt to shareholders in exchange for cash contributions to a corporation. A disadvantage of issuing debt is that it does not qualify under § 1244. Should the debt become worthless, the taxpayer generally has a short-term capital loss rather than the ordinary loss for § 1244 stock.

The basis of § 1244 stock issued by a corporation in exchange for property that has an adjusted basis above its fair market value immediately before the exchange is reduced to the fair market value of the property on the date of the exchange. The basis is reduced for the purpose of determining ordinary loss upon a subsequent sale.

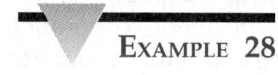

EXAMPLE 28   Dana transfers property with a basis of $10,000 and a fair market value of $5,000 to a corporation in exchange for shares of § 1244 stock. Assuming the transfer qualifies under § 351, the basis of the stock is $10,000, the same as Dana's basis in the property. For purposes of § 1244, the basis is only $5,000. If the stock is later sold for $3,000, the total loss sustained is $7,000 ($10,000 – $3,000); however, only $2,000 is ordinary loss ($5,000 – $3,000). The remaining portion, $5,000, is capital loss. ▼

If a shareholder contributes additional property or money to a corporation after acquiring § 1244 stock, the amount of ordinary loss upon a sale of the § 1244 stock is limited to the original contribution.

GAIN FROM QUALIFIED SMALL BUSINESS STOCK

Shareholders are given some tax relief for gains recognized on the sale or exchange of stock acquired in a **qualified small business corporation.**[46] The holder of **qualified small business stock** may exclude 50 percent of any gain from the sale or exchange of such stock. To qualify for the 50 percent exclusion, the taxpayer must have held the stock for more than five years and must have acquired the stock as part of an original issue.[47] Only noncorporate shareholders qualify for the exclusion.

A qualified small business corporation is a C corporation whose aggregate gross assets did not exceed $50 million on the date the stock was issued.[48] The corporation must be actively involved in a trade or business. This means that at least 80 percent of the corporation's assets must be used in the active conduct of one or more qualified trades or businesses.

---

[46] § 1202.

[47] The stock must have been issued after August 10, 1993, which is the effective date of § 1202.

[48] § 1202(d). Its aggregate assets may not exceed this amount at any time between August 10, 1993, and the date the stock was issued.

A shareholder can apply the 50 percent exclusion to the greater of (1) $10 million or (2) 10 times the shareholder's aggregate adjusted basis in the qualified stock disposed of during a taxable year.[49]

TAX PLANNING CONSIDERATIONS

WORKING WITH § 351

Effective tax planning with transfers of property to corporations requires a clear understanding of § 351 and its related Code provisions. The most important question in planning is simply: Does compliance with the requirements of § 351 yield the desired tax result?

Utilizing § 351.   In using § 351(a), ensure that all parties transferring property (which includes cash) receive control of the corporation. Simultaneous transfers are not necessary, but a long period of time between transfers is vulnerable if the transfers are not properly documented as part of a single plan. To do this, the parties should document and preserve evidence of their intentions. Also, it is helpful to have some reasonable explanation for any delay in the transfers.

To meet the requirements of § 351, mere momentary control on the part of the transferor may not suffice if loss of control is compelled by a prearranged agreement.[50]

EXAMPLE 29

For many years, Zelda operated a business as a sole proprietor employing Zina as manager. To dissuade Zina from quitting and going out on her own, Zelda promised her a 30% interest in the business. To fulfill this promise, Zelda transfers the business to newly formed

---

[49] § 1202(b). The amount is $5 million for married filing separately.   [50] Rev.Rul. 54–96, 1954–1 C.B. 111.

Green Corporation in return for all its stock. Immediately thereafter, Zelda transfers 30% of the stock to Zina. Section 351 probably does not apply to Zelda's transfer to Green Corporation. It appears that Zelda was under an obligation to relinquish control. If this is not the case and the loss of control was voluntary on Zelda's part, momentary control would suffice.[51] ▼

Be sure that later transfers of property to an existing corporation satisfy the control requirement if recognition of gain is to be avoided. In this connection, a transferor's interest cannot be counted if the value of stock received is relatively small compared with the value of stock already owned. Further, the primary purpose of the transfer may not be to qualify other transferors for § 351 treatment.[52]

Avoiding § 351. Section 351(a) provides for the nonrecognition of gain on transfers to controlled corporations. As such, it is often regarded as a relief provision favoring taxpayers. In some situations, however, avoiding § 351(a) may produce a more advantageous tax result. The transferors might prefer to recognize gain on the transfer of property if they cannot be particularly harmed by the gain. For example, they may be in low tax brackets, or the gain may be a capital gain from which substantial capital losses can be offset. The corporation will then have a stepped-up basis in the transferred property.

Another reason a particular transferor might wish to avoid § 351 concerns possible loss recognition. Recall that § 351 refers to the nonrecognition of both gains and losses. Section 351(b)(2) specifically states: "No loss to such recipient shall be recognized." A transferor who wishes to recognize loss has several alternatives:

- Sell the property to the corporation for its stock. The IRS could attempt to collapse the "sale," however, by taking the approach that the transfer really falls under § 351(a).[53] If the sale is disregarded, the transferor ends up with a realized, but unrecognized, loss.
- Sell the property to the corporation for other property or boot. Because the transferor receives no stock, § 351 is inapplicable.
- Transfer the property to the corporation in return for securities. Recall that § 351 does not apply to a transferor who receives securities. In both this and the previous alternatives, watch for the possible disallowance of the loss under the related-party rules.

ETHICAL CONSIDERATIONS

Will the Sale Be Recognized?

Early in the year, Quinn, Ross, and Fran form the Harrier Corporation for the express purpose of developing a shopping center. All parties are experienced contractors, and they transfer various business assets (e.g., building materials, land) to Harrier in exchange for all of its stock. Three months after it is formed, Harrier purchases two cranes

---

[51] Compare *Fahs v. Florida Machine and Foundry Co.*, 48–2 USTC ¶9329, 36 AFTR 1161, 168 F.2d 957 (CA–5, 1948), with *John C. O'Connor*, 16 TCM 213, T.C.Memo. 1957–50, *aff'd.* in 58–2 USTC ¶9913, 2 AFTR2d 6011, 260 F.2d 358 (CA–6, 1958).

[52] Reg. § 1.351–1(a)(1)(ii).

[53] *U.S. v. Hertwig*, 68–2 USTC ¶9495, 22 AFTR2d 5249, 398 F.2d 452 (CA–5, 1968).

from Ross for their fair market value of $400,000 by issuing four annual installment notes of $100,000 each. Since the adjusted basis of the cranes is $550,000, Ross plans to recognize a § 1231 loss of $150,000 in the year of the sale. Does Ross have any potential income tax problem with this plan?

Suppose the loss property is to be transferred to the corporation and no loss is recognized by the transferor due to § 351(a). This could present an interesting problem in terms of assessing the economic realities involved.

EXAMPLE 30

Iris and Ivan form Wren Corporation with the following investment: property by Iris (basis of $40,000 and fair market value of $50,000) and property by Ivan (basis of $60,000 and fair market value of $50,000). Each receives 50% of the Wren stock. Has Ivan acted wisely in settling for only 50% of the stock? At first, it would appear so, since Iris and Ivan each invested property of the same value ($50,000). But what about tax considerations? Due to basis carryover, the corporation now has a basis of $40,000 in Iris's property and $60,000 in Ivan's property. In essence, Iris has shifted a possible $10,000 gain to the corporation while Ivan has transferred a $10,000 potential loss. With this in mind, an equitable allocation of the Wren stock would call for Ivan to receive a greater percentage interest than Iris. ▼

OTHER CONSIDERATIONS IN INCORPORATING A BUSINESS

When a business is incorporated, the organizers must determine which assets and liabilities should be transferred to the corporation. A transfer of assets that produce passive income (rents, royalties, dividends, and interest) can cause the corporation to be a personal holding company in a tax year when operating income is low. Thus, the corporation could be subject to the personal holding company penalty tax (see the discussion in Chapter 6).

A transfer of the accounts payable of a cash basis taxpayer may prevent the taxpayer from taking a tax deduction when the accounts are paid. These payables should generally be retained.

Leasing some property to the corporation may be a more attractive alternative than transferring ownership. Leasing provides the taxpayer with the opportunity of withdrawing money from the corporation without the payment being characterized as a dividend. If the property is donated to a family member in a lower tax bracket, the lease income can be shifted as well. If the depreciation and other deductions available in connection with the property are larger than the lease income, the taxpayer would retain the property until the income exceeds the deductions.

Shareholder debt in a corporation can be given to family members in a lower tax bracket. This technique also causes income to be shifted without a loss of control of the corporation.

DEBT IN THE CAPITAL STRUCTURE

The advantages of debt as opposed to equity have previously been emphasized. The main hurdle to overstressing debt is the thin capitalization problem. In avoiding the problem, consider the following:

- Preserve the formalities of the debt. This includes providing for written instruments, realistic interest rates, and specified due dates.
- If possible, have the corporation repay the debt when it becomes due. If this is not possible, have the parties renegotiate the arrangement. Try to proceed

as a third-party (i.e., nonshareholder) creditor would. It is not unusual, for example, for bondholders of publicly held corporations to extend due dates when default occurs. The alternative is to foreclose and perhaps seriously impair the amount the creditors will recover.

• Avoid provisions in the debt instrument that make the debt convertible to equity in the event of default. These provisions are standard practice when nonshareholder creditors are involved. They make no sense if the shareholders are also the creditors.

EXAMPLE 31

Gail, Gary, and Grace are equal shareholders in White Corporation. Each transfers cash of $100,000 to White in return for its bonds. The bond agreement provides that the holders will receive additional voting rights in the event White Corporation defaults on its bonds. The voting rights provision is worthless and merely raises the issue of thin capitalization. Gail, Gary, and Grace already control White Corporation, so what purpose is served by increasing their voting rights? The parties probably used a "boiler plate" bond agreement that was designed for third-party lenders (e.g., banks and financial institutions). ▼

• Pro rata holding of debt is difficult to avoid. For example, if each of the shareholders owns one-third of the stock, then each will want one-third of the debt. Nevertheless, some variation is possible.

EXAMPLE 32

Assume the same facts as Example 31 except that only Gail and Gary acquire the bonds. Grace leases property to White Corporation at an annual rent that approximates the yield on the bonds. Presuming the rent passes the arm's length test (i.e., what unrelated parties would charge), all parties reach the desired result. Gail and Gary withdraw corporate profits in the form of interest income, and Grace is provided for with rent income. White Corporation can deduct both the interest and the rent payments. ▼

• Try to keep the debt-equity ratio within reasonable proportions. A problem frequently arises when the parties first form the corporation. Often the amount invested in capital stock is the minimum required by state law. For example, if the state of incorporation permits a minimum of $1,000, limiting the investment to this amount does not provide much safety for later debt financing by the shareholders.

• Stressing the fair market value of the assets rather than their tax basis to the corporation can be helpful in preparing to defend debt-equity ratios.

EXAMPLE 33

Emily, Earl, and Ed form Black Corporation with the following capital investments: cash of $200,000 from Emily; land worth $200,000 (basis of $20,000) from Earl; and a patent worth $200,000 (basis of $0) from Ed. To state that the equity of Black Corporation is $220,000 (the tax basis to the corporation) does not reflect reality. The equity account is more properly stated at $600,000 ($200,000 + $200,000 + $200,000). ▼

• The nature of the business can have an effect on what is an acceptable debt-equity ratio. Capital-intensive industries (e.g., manufacturing, transportation) characteristically rely heavily on debt financing. Consequently, larger debt should be tolerated.

INVESTOR LOSSES

In connection with § 1244, be aware that there is a danger of losing § 1244 attributes. Recall that only the original holder of § 1244 stock is entitled to ordinary loss treatment. If a corporation is formed to shift income within the family group by transferring shares of stock to family members, the benefits of § 1244 are lost.

EXAMPLE 34

Norm incorporates his business by transferring property with a basis of $100,000 for 100 shares of stock. The stock qualifies as § 1244 stock. Norm later gives 50 shares each to his children, Susan and Paul. Eventually, the business fails, and the corporation becomes bankrupt. The shares of stock become worthless. If Norm had retained the stock, he would have had an ordinary loss deduction of $100,000 (assuming he filed a joint return). Susan and Paul, however, have a capital loss of $50,000 each because the § 1244 attributes were lost. ▼

KEY TERMS

Assumption of liabilities, 3–9

Capital contribution, 3–14

Control, 3–5

Investor losses, 3–17

Liabilities in excess of basis, 3–10

Nonbusiness bad debt, 3–17

Property, 3–4

Qualified small business corporation, 3–20

Qualified small business stock, 3–20

Section 1244 stock, 3–19

Securities, 3–5

Thin capitalization, 3–15

PROBLEM
MATERIALS

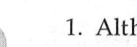

DISCUSSION QUESTIONS

1. Although the tax consequences of § 351 and § 1031 (like-kind exchange) generally parallel each other, they differ in one major respect. What is this difference?

2. Both § 351 and § 1031 (like-kind exchange) illustrate the application of the wherewithal to pay concept. Explain.

3. Why are services not treated as property under § 351?

4. Can boot ever be taxable in a § 351 transfer in the absence of realized gain? Explain.

5. Does stock include stock rights and stock warrants under § 351? Does it include preferred stock?

6. Several entrepreneurs plan to form a corporation to construct a housing project. Travis, the party who will be contributing the land for the project, wants more security than shareholder status provides. He is contemplating two possibilities: receive corporate bonds for his land, or take out a mortgage on the land before transferring it to the corporation for stock. Comment on the choices Travis is considering. What other alternatives can you suggest?

7. What is the control requirement of § 351? Describe the effect of the following in satisfying this requirement:
   a. A shareholder renders services to the corporation for stock.
   b. A shareholder both renders services and transfers property to the corporation for stock.
   c. A shareholder has only momentary control after the transfer.
   d. A long period of time elapses between the transfers of property by different shareholders.

8. Marvin and June form Warbler Corporation. They transfer appreciated property to the corporation with each receiving 50 shares of the Warbler stock. If Marvin gives his shares to his daughter immediately after the exchange, is the exchange taxable?

9. Paul and Mary transfer property to Falcon Corporation, each in exchange for one-third of Falcon's stock. Matt receives the other one-third of Falcon's stock for services rendered. Will the exchange be taxable?

10. May a transferor who receives stock for both property and services be included in the control group in determining whether an exchange meets the requirements of § 351? Explain.

11. At a point when Robin Corporation has been in existence for six years, shareholder Ted transfers real estate (adjusted basis of $20,000 and fair market value of $100,000) to the corporation for additional stock. At the same time, Peggy, the other shareholder, purchases one share of stock for cash. After the two transfers, the percentage of stock ownership is as follows: 79% by Ted and 21% by Peggy.
    a. What were the parties trying to accomplish?
    b. Will it work? Explain.

12. How does the transfer of mortgaged property to a controlled corporation affect the transferor shareholder's basis in stock received in the corporation when gain is recognized on the transfer?

13. Does the transfer of mortgaged property to a controlled corporation trigger gain to the extent of the mortgage? Explain.

14. Before incorporating her apartment rental business, Beth takes out second mortgages on several of the units. She uses the mortgage funds to make capital improvements to the rental units. Along with all of the rental units, Beth transfers the mortgages to the newly formed corporation in return for all of its stock. Discuss the tax consequences to Beth of these procedures.

15. Why does the application of § 357(c) cause gain to be recognized? Why is this not the case with § 357(b)?

16. When, if ever, can a corporation deduct the value of the stock it issues for the rendition of services?

17. Pursuant to a § 351 transfer, Mallard Corporation receives property in exchange for stock. Will Mallard's holding period for the property be the same as the shareholder's holding period for the stock? Explain.

18. A corporation acquires property as a contribution to capital from a shareholder and from a nonshareholder. Are the basis rules the same? Explain.

19. In structuring the capitalization of a corporation, what are the advantages of utilizing debt rather than equity?

20. In determining whether the debt of a corporation should be reclassified as stock, comment on the relevance of the following:
    a. The loan is on open account.
    b. The loan is a demand loan.
    c. Although the loan has a definite maturity date, the corporation has not made payments on a timely basis.
    d. Payments on the loan are contingent upon corporate earnings.
    e. The corporation's shareholders loaned funds to the corporation in the same proportion as their shareholdings, and the debt was used to purchase a new building.
    f. The corporation has a debt-equity ratio of 5:1.

21. In determining a corporation's debt-equity ratio, should book value or fair market value of the assets be used?

22. Assuming § 1244 does not apply, what is the tax treatment of stock that has become worthless?

23. Under what circumstances, if any, may a shareholder deduct a business bad debt on a loan he or she has made to the corporation?

24. Emily incorporates her sole proprietorship, but does not transfer the building the business uses to the corporation. Subsequently, the building is leased to the corporation for an annual rental. What tax reasons might Emily have for not transferring the building to the corporation when the business was incorporated?

PROBLEMS

25. Cecil and Edie form Heron Corporation with the following investment:

| | Property Transferred | | |
	Basis to Transferor	Fair Market Value	Number of Shares Issued
From Cecil—			
Cash	$ 80,000	$ 80,000	
Installment obligation	280,000	720,000	80
From Edie—			
Cash	280,000	280,000	
Equipment	240,000	360,000	120
Patent	8,000	560,000	

The installment obligation has a face amount of $720,000 and was acquired last year from the sale of land held for investment purposes (adjusted basis of $280,000).
a. How much gain, if any, must Cecil recognize?
b. What will be Cecil's basis in the Heron Corporation stock?
c. What will be Heron Corporation's basis in the installment obligation?
d. How much gain, if any, must Edie recognize?
e. What will be Edie's basis in the Heron Corporation stock?
f. What will be Heron Corporation's basis in the equipment and the patent?
g. How would your answer change if Cecil received common stock and Edie received preferred stock?
h. How would your answer change if Edie were a partnership?

26. Brad, Otis, Wade, and Andrea form Teal Corporation with the following investment:

| | Property Transferred | | |
	Basis to Transferor	Fair Market Value	Number of Shares Issued
From Brad—			
Personal services rendered to Teal Corporation	$ –0–	$ 30,000	30
From Otis—			
Equipment	345,000	300,000	270*
From Wade—			
Cash	60,000	60,000	
Unrealized accounts			150
receivable	–0–	90,000	
From Andrea—			
Land & building	210,000	450,000	
Mortgage on land			150
& building	300,000	300,000	

*Otis receives $30,000 in cash in addition to the 270 shares.

The mortgage transferred by Andrea is assumed by Teal Corporation. The value of each share of Teal Corporation stock is $3,000.

a. What, if any, is Brad's recognized gain or loss?
b. What basis will Brad have in the Teal Corporation stock?
c. How much gain or loss must Otis recognize?
d. What basis will Otis have in the Teal Corporation stock?
e. What basis will Teal Corporation have in the equipment?
f. What, if any, is Wade's recognized gain or loss?
g. What basis will Wade have in the Teal Corporation stock?
h. What basis will Teal have in the unrealized accounts receivable?
i. How much gain or loss must Andrea recognize?
j. What basis will Andrea have in the Teal stock?
k. What basis will Teal Corporation have in the land and building?

27. Sam, Seth, Pat, and Kelly form Lark Corporation with the following investment:

| | **Property Transferred** | | |
	Basis to Transferor	Fair Market Value	Number of Shares Issued
From Sam—			
Inventory	$30,000	$96,000	30*
From Seth—			
Equipment ($30,000 of depreciation taken by Seth in prior years)	45,000	99,000	30**
From Pat—			
Secret process	15,000	90,000	30
From Kelly—			
Cash	30,000	30,000	10

*Sam receives $6,000 in cash in addition to the 30 shares.
**Seth receives $9,000 in cash in addition to the 30 shares.

Assume the value of each share of Lark Corporation stock is $3,000.

a. What, if any, is Sam's recognized gain or loss? How is any such gain or loss treated?
b. What basis will Sam have in the Lark Corporation stock?
c. What basis will Lark Corporation have in the inventory?
d. How much gain or loss must Seth recognize? How is the gain or loss treated?
e. What basis will Seth have in the Lark Corporation stock?
f. What basis will Lark Corporation have in the equipment?
g. What, if any, is Pat's recognized gain or loss?
h. What basis will Pat have in the Lark Corporation stock?
i. What basis will Lark Corporation have in the secret process?
j. How much income, if any, must Kelly recognize?
k. What basis will Kelly have in the Lark Corporation stock?

28. Ron Smith exchanges property, basis of $40,000 and fair market value of $150,000, for 60% of the stock of Dove Corporation. The other 40% is owned by Mary, who acquired it several years ago. You represent Ron, who asks whether he must report gain on the transfer. Prepare a letter to your client Ron and a memo for the file. Ron's address is 320 Ferris Avenue, Big Rapids, MI 49307.

29. Lee exchanges property, basis of $20,000 and fair market value of $500,000, for 65% of the stock of Pelican Corporation. The other 35% is owned by Abby, Lee's daughter, who acquired her stock last year. What are the tax issues?

30. Kate transfers property worth $400,000 (basis of $50,000) to Crow Corporation in exchange for 50% of Crow's stock. Kevin transfers a secret process worth $300,000 (zero basis) and services he rendered in obtaining the process and a letter of credit, which states that the newly formed Crow Corporation could obtain a loan to develop the process (worth $100,000 according to Kevin), for 50% of Crow's stock. What are the tax issues?

31. Dan and Vera form Crane Corporation. Dan transfers land (worth $200,000, basis of $60,000) for 50% of the stock in Crane. Vera transfers machinery (worth $150,000, adjusted basis of $30,000) and provides services worth $50,000 for 50% of the stock.
    a. Will the transfer qualify under § 351?
    b. What are the tax consequences to Dan and Vera?
    c. What basis will Crane Corporation have in the land and the machinery?

32. Perry organized Cardinal Corporation 10 years ago by contributing property worth $1 million, basis of $200,000, for 2,000 shares of stock in Cardinal, representing 100% of the stock in the corporation. Perry later gave each of his children, Brittany and Julie, 500 shares of stock in Cardinal Corporation. In the current year, Perry transfers property worth $320,000, basis of $100,000, to Cardinal for 500 shares in the corporation. What gain, if any, will Perry recognize on this transfer?

33. Ann and Bob form Robin Corporation. Ann transfers property worth $420,000 (basis of $150,000) for 70 shares in Robin Corporation. Bob receives 30 shares for property worth $165,000 (basis of $30,000) and for legal services in organizing the corporation; the services are worth $15,000.
    a. What gain, if any, will the parties recognize on the transfer?
    b. What basis will Ann and Bob have in the stock in Robin Corporation?
    c. What basis will Robin Corporation have in the property and services it received from Ann and Bob?

34. Assume in Problem 33 that the property Bob transfers to Robin Corporation is worth $15,000 (basis of $3,000) and his services in organizing the corporation are worth $165,000. What are the tax consequences to Ann, Bob, and Robin Corporation?

35. Kim is an employee of Azure Corporation. In the current year, she receives a salary of $50,000 and is also given 20 shares of Azure stock for services she renders to the corporation. The shares in Azure Corporation are worth $1,000 each. How will the transfer of the 20 shares to Kim be handled for tax purposes by Kim and by Azure Corporation?

36. Brady transfers property with an adjusted basis of $150,000, fair market value of $1,200,000, to Swift Corporation for 100% of the stock. The property is subject to a liability of $180,000, which Swift assumes. What is the basis of the Swift stock to Brady? What is the basis of the property to Swift Corporation?

37. Three years ago, Chris exchanged an apartment worth $1,500,000 (basis of $300,000), which was subject to a mortgage of $200,000, for land worth $1,150,000, subject to a mortgage of $150,000, and cash of $300,000. In the current year, Chris transfers the land that he received in the exchange to newly formed Amber Corporation for all the stock in Amber. Amber Corporation assumes the original mortgage on the land, currently in the amount of $100,000, and another mortgage in the amount of $20,000 that Chris later places on the land to secure his purchase of some equipment that he uses in his business. What are the tax issues?

38. Lori, a sole proprietor, was engaged in a service business and reported her income on a cash basis. On February 1, 1997, she incorporated her business and transferred the assets of the business to the corporation in return for all the stock in the corporation plus the corporation's assumption of the liabilities of her proprietorship. All the receivables and the unpaid trade payables were transferred to the newly formed corporation. The balance sheet of the corporation immediately following the incorporation was as follows:

GREEN CORPORATION
BALANCE SHEET
February 1, 1997

Assets

	Basis to Green	Fair Market Value
Cash	$ 80,000	$ 80,000
Accounts receivable	–0–	240,000
Equipment (cost $180,000; depreciation $60,000)	120,000	320,000
Building (straight-line depreciation)	160,000	400,000
Land	40,000	160,000
	$400,000	$1,200,000

Liabilities and Stockholders' Equity

Liabilities:		
Accounts payable—trade		$ 120,000
Notes payable—bank		360,000
Stockholders' equity:		
Common stock		720,000
		$1,200,000

Discuss the tax consequences of the incorporation of the business to Lori and to Green Corporation.

39. Cliff organized Crimson Corporation and transferred land with a basis of $400,000, fair market value of $1,200,000, and subject to a mortgage of $300,000. A month before incorporation, Cliff borrowed $200,000 for personal purposes and gave the bank a lien on the land. Crimson Corporation issued stock worth $700,000 to Cliff and assumed the loans in the amount of $300,000 and $200,000. Discuss the tax consequences of the incorporation to Cliff and to Crimson Corporation.

40. Sara and Jane form Wren Corporation. Sara transfers property, basis of $25,000 and value of $200,000, for 50 shares in Wren Corporation. Jane transfers property, basis of $10,000 and value of $185,000, and agrees to serve as manager of Wren for one year; in return Jane receives 50 shares in Wren. The value of Jane's services to Wren is $15,000.
   a. What gain will Sara and Jane recognize on the exchange?
   b. What basis will Wren Corporation have in the property transferred by Sara and Jane? How will Wren treat the value of the services Jane renders?

41. Assume in Problem 40, that Jane receives the 50 shares of Wren Corporation stock in consideration for the appreciated property and for providing legal services in organizing the corporation. The value of Jane's services is $15,000.
   a. What gain does Jane recognize?
   b. What basis will Wren Corporation have in the property transferred by Jane? How will Wren treat the value of the services Jane renders?

42. On January 10, 1997, Carol transferred machinery worth $100,000 (basis of $20,000) to a controlled corporation, Kite, in a transfer that qualified under § 351. Carol had deducted depreciation on the machinery in the amount of $85,000 when she held the machinery for use in her proprietorship. On November 15, 1997, Kite Corporation sells the machinery for $95,000. What are the tax consequences to Carol and to Kite Corporation on the sale of the machinery?

43. Tan Corporation desires to set up a manufacturing facility in the south. After considerable negotiation with Alexandria, Louisiana, Tan accepts the following offer: land (fair market value of $3 million) and cash of $1 million.
    a. How much gain, if any, must Tan Corporation recognize?
    b. What basis will Tan Corporation have in the land?
    c. Within one year of the donation, Tan constructs a building for $800,000 and purchases inventory for $300,000. What basis will Tan Corporation have in each of these assets?

44. Stock in Jaybird Corporation is held equally by Vera, Wade, and Wes. Jaybird seeks additional capital to construct a building in the amount of $900,000. Vera, Wade, and Wes each propose to loan Jaybird Corporation $300,000, taking from Jaybird a $300,000 four-year note with interest payable annually at two points below the prime rate. Jaybird Corporation has current taxable income of $2 million. You represent Jaybird Corporation. It asks you how the payments on the notes might be treated for tax purposes. Prepare a letter to your client and a memo for your file. Jaybird's address is 420 Magnolia St., Birmingham, AL 35229.

45. Sam, a single taxpayer, acquired stock in a corporation that qualified as a small business corporation under § 1244, at a cost of $100,000 three years ago. He sells the stock for $10,000 in the current tax year. How will the loss be treated for tax purposes?

46. Assume that Sam in Problem 45 gave the stock to his sister, Kara, a few months after he acquired it. The stock was worth $100,000 on the date of the gift. Kara sells the stock for $10,000 in the current tax year. How will Kara treat the loss for tax purposes?

47. Ann formed Dove Corporation four years ago with an investment of $200,000 for which she received 100% of the stock in Dove. Two years later when Dove was experiencing financial difficulty, Ann loaned Dove $50,000 and received in exchange bonds bearing 9% interest and maturing in five years. Last year she loaned Dove an additional $20,000 on open account. In the current year, Dove is insolvent and is adjudged bankrupt. As president of Dove Corporation, Ann has received an annual salary of $40,000. What are the tax issues in determining the tax treatment of Ann's loss in her investment in Dove and in the amounts she has loaned to Dove?

48. Sam Sanders, a married taxpayer who files a joint return with his wife, acquired stock in a corporation that qualified as a small business corporation under § 1244. The stock cost $100,000 and was acquired three years ago. A few months after he acquired the stock he gave it to his brother, Mike Sanders. The stock was worth $100,000 on the date of the gift. Mike, who is married and files a joint return with his wife, sells the stock for $10,000 in the current tax year. You represent Mike who asks you whether he can take a loss deduction on the sale of the stock. If so, how will the loss be treated for tax purposes? Prepare a letter to your client and a memo to the file. Mike's address is 2600 Riverview Drive, Plank, MO 63701.

49. Troy transfers property with a basis of $40,000 and a fair market value of $20,000 to Thrush Corporation in exchange for shares of § 1244 stock. (Assume the transfer qualifies under § 351.)
    a. What is the basis of the stock to Troy?
    b. What is the basis of the stock for purposes of § 1244 to Troy?
    c. If Troy sells the stock for $10,000 two years later, how will the loss be treated for tax purposes?

50. Frank, Cora, and Mitch are equal shareholders in Blue Corporation. The corporation's assets have a tax basis of $50,000 and a fair market value of $600,000. In the current year, Frank and Cora each loan Blue Corporation $150,000. The notes to Frank and Cora bear interest of 8% per annum. Mitch leases equipment to Blue Corporation for an annual rental of $12,000. Discuss whether the shareholder loans from Frank and Cora might be reclassified as equity. Consider in your discussion whether Blue Corporation has an acceptable debt-equity ratio.

RESEARCH PROBLEMS

Note: **West's Federal Taxation on CD-ROM** *can be used in preparing solutions to the Research Problems. Alternatively, tax research materials contained in a standard tax library can be used.*

Research Problem 1. A cash basis partnership is incorporated. The newly formed corporation elects the cash method of accounting. The partnership transfers $30,000 of accounts receivable along with equipment, land, and cash. The corporation also agrees to pay accounts payable of the partnership in the amount of $40,000. The corporation files its return for its first year of operation and does not report the $30,000 received on accounts receivable of the partnership as income. It does deduct the $40,000 it paid on the partnership's accounts payable. The IRS disallows the deductions totaling $40,000 and increases the corporation's taxable income by $30,000, which represents the collection of partnership accounts receivable. What is the result?

Partial list of research aids:
Arthur Kniffen, 39 T.C. 553 (1962).
Rev.Rul. 80–198, 1980–2 C.B. 122.

Research Problem 2. Lynn Jones, Shawn, Walt, and Donna want to organize a corporation and transfer their shares of stock in several corporations to the newly formed corporation. All their shares are listed on the New York Stock Exchange and are readily marketable. Lynn will transfer shares in Brown Corporation; Shawn will transfer stock in Black Corporation; Walt will transfer stock in White Corporation; and Donna will transfer stock in several corporations. The stock will be held by the newly formed corporation for investment purposes. Lynn asks you, her tax adviser, if she will have gain on the transfer of her substantially appreciated shares in Brown Corporation if she transfers the shares to a newly formed corporation. She also asks whether there will be tax consequences if she, Shawn, Walt, and Donna form a partnership, rather than a corporation, to which they will transfer their readily marketable stock. Prepare a written memo to the client, Lynn Jones, and a memo for the firm's files. Lynn's address is 1540 Maxwell Avenue, Highland, KY 41099.

Research Problem 3. Wyatt has enjoyed considerable financial success as a broker of commercial real estate. A few years ago, he became convinced that considerable profits could be made through the manufacture and sale of "video lottery" machines, which allow a person to play games of chance such as poker and blackjack against the machine. With many states legalizing various forms of gambling, video lottery machines could be a highly marketable product.

Wyatt was aware of a concern called Tern Corporation, which manufactured and sold video machines to amusement parks and game parlors. Tern Corporation was closely held, and its owners were willing to sell their stock for $2 million.

Upon the advice of his attorneys, Wyatt formed Vireo Corporation with a cash investment of $40,000 in return for all of its stock. After borrowing the funds from Union Bank, Vireo purchased all of the stock of Tern Corporation. As part of the loan arrangement, Union required Wyatt to guarantee the note and also to put up collateral worth $500,000. For collateral, Wyatt used stock he owns in Willet Corporation. The Willet stock has an adjusted basis to Wyatt of $60,000 and a fair market value of $500,000.

During its four years of existence, Vireo Corporation experienced consecutive losses and had gross receipts in only one year. It did, however, hire a marketing director, rent a warehouse, and maintain some inventory. It also acquired the rights to use certain technology and negotiated permission to operate in certain western states that had enacted gaming laws. However, all of the manufacturing of video lottery machines was handled by Vireo's subsidiary, Tern Corporation.

Four years after its creation, Vireo Corporation ceases business and declares bankruptcy. Unable to collect from Vireo, Union Bank forces Wyatt to make good on his guarantee of the loan. As part of the bankruptcy proceeding, Tern Corporation is liquidated. The proceeds from the liquidation of Tern are used to help pay off some of the creditors of both corporations.

On a joint income tax return for the year in which Vireo Corporation declares bankruptcy, Wyatt claims an *ordinary loss* under § 1244 of $540,000 and a *business* bad debt for the additional amount he had to pay Union Bank on his guarantee. Needless to say, Wyatt recovered nothing from the bankruptcy of Vireo Corporation or the liquidation of Tern Corporation.

   a. How does Wyatt arrive at the amount of the § 1244 loss? Would the IRS be justified in questioning the amount claimed as a § 1244 loss?
   b. On what basis could the IRS argue that there is no § 1244 loss at all?
   c. Is Wyatt correct in claiming a *business* bad debt? Explain.

Research Problem 4. In 1987, Pat and Maria formed Robin Corporation by transferring assets in exchange for stock. Pat and Maria each received 100 shares in Robin Corporation. Robin Corporation filed a proper election to qualify as an S corporation. In 1990, Pat and Maria obtained a $100,000 loan from a bank and transferred the cash to Robin Corporation as a contribution to its capital. Robin used the $100,000 to purchase stock in Bluebird Corporation. Bluebird met the requirements of a small business corporation under § 1244.

Bluebird Corporation ultimately encountered financial problems and filed for bankruptcy in 1995. Robin Corporation sold its Bluebird stock in 1996 for $20,000. On their 1996 tax returns, Pat and Maria each deducted an ordinary loss of $40,000.

Upon audit of Pat's return in 1997, the IRS disallowed the deduction of the entire $40,000 loss as an ordinary loss. The IRS contends the Bluebird stock does not qualify for ordinary loss treatment under § 1244 because the stock was held by an S corporation. According to the IRS, § 1244 treatment is available only where § 1244 stock is issued to an individual or to a partnership and then is sold by that individual or partnership. Pat insists she is entitled to ordinary loss treatment because income of an S corporation flows through to the shareholders of the corporation in the same manner as partnership income. How would you advise Pat?

Partial list of research aids:
Virgil Rath, 101 T.C. 196 (1993).

Research Problem 5. Bob Martin purchased all of the stock of White Corporation in 1990. On the date of the purchase, he executed a continuing guaranty agreement obligating himself to pay all of the future indebtedness of the corporation to a bank on a standing line of credit. By the end of 1993, the corporation was indebted to the bank in the amount of $500,000.

In addition to executing the guaranty, Bob loaned $30,000 to the corporation in 1992 and 1993. He had substantial income from other sources so he drew no salary from White Corporation in 1992 and 1993. For 1994 and 1995, however, Bob was paid a salary of $40,000.

White Corporation began to suffer severe financial reversals in 1993 as a result of several construction jobs that were seriously underbid. In addition, Bob became ill about this time, and this contributed to the corporation's problems.

In late 1994, the bank called upon Bob to pay under the guaranty. Consequently, Bob paid the bank $200,000 in 1994 and $300,000 in 1995. On his tax returns, Bob claimed business bad debts. The deductions resulted in net operating losses that Bob carried back with favorable tax effect.

In 1997, the IRS audited Bob's tax returns and disallowed the net operating loss carrybacks. It determined that Bob was entitled only to nonbusiness bad debt deductions. Bob retains your firm for advice.

   a. Write a letter to Bob regarding your advice. Bob's address is 1120 Pear Avenue, Corvallis, OR 97331.
   b. Prepare a memo for your firm's files.

Use the tax resources of the internet to address the following questions. Do not restrict your search to the World Wide Web, but include a review of newsgroups and general reference materials, practitioner sites and resources, primary sources of the tax law, chat rooms and discussion groups, and other opportunities.

Research Problem 6.   The U.S. stock market has seen a record number of initial public offerings (IPOs) in the last few years. How should the tax professional advise companies considering an IPO and the investors who might purchase the shares?

Research Problem 7.   Trace developments in the tax law during the last twelve months with respect to the rules of § 357.

Research Problem 8.   Does it seem that the provisions of § 1202 relating to qualified small business stock have become popular since they became effective in 1993? What leads you to that conclusion?

CORPORATIONS: EARNINGS & PROFITS AND DIVIDEND DISTRIBUTIONS

LEARNING OBJECTIVES

After completing Chapter 4, you should be able to:

1. Identify and understand the concept of earnings and profits.

2. Recognize the importance of earnings and profits in measuring dividend income.

3. Master the tax treatment of dividends, including property dividends, to both the recipient shareholder and the corporation making the distribution.

4. Understand the nature and treatment of constructive dividends.

5. Distinguish between taxable and nontaxable stock dividends and stock rights.

Afters a corporation begins operations, one of the most important tax considerations is the tax treatment of corporate distributions to the shareholders. The tax results to the shareholders and to the corporation vary, depending on the form of the distributions. Dividends are taxed as ordinary income to the recipient shareholder unless stock dividends are distributed. In this case, the distribution may or may not be taxed to the shareholder. Distributions that qualify as stock redemptions, or that are made in partial or complete liquidation of the shareholder's interest in the corporation, are treated as a return of the shareholder's capital. They are tax-free to the extent of the shareholder's investment in the corporation, with any excess being a capital gain.

For tax purposes, corporate distributions are classified as follows:

1. Regular distributions of a corporation's earnings. These are taxed as dividend income to the extent of the earnings and profits of the corporation.
2. Distributions of stock and stock rights.
3. Distributions to a shareholder in exchange for the shareholder's stock that qualify as stock redemptions or as partial liquidations for tax purposes.
4. Distributions in complete liquidation of the corporation.
5. Distributions of stock of a subsidiary of the parent corporation.

Regular distributions of a corporation's earnings and distributions of stock and stock rights are covered in this chapter. The other types of corporate distributions are discussed in Chapter 5.

TAXABLE DIVIDENDS—IN GENERAL

Distributions by a corporation to its shareholders are presumed to be dividends unless the parties can prove otherwise. Dividend income results to the extent of the distribution's pro rata share of earnings and profits (E & P) of the distributing corporation accumulated since February 28, 1913, or to the extent of corporate E & P for the current year.[1]

The portion of a corporate distribution that is not taxed as a dividend (because of insufficient E & P) is nontaxable to the extent of the shareholder's basis in the

---

[1] § 316.

stock. The stock basis is reduced accordingly. The excess of the distribution over the shareholder's basis is treated as a capital gain if the stock is a capital asset.[2]

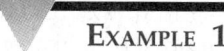

EXAMPLE 1

At the beginning of the year, Amber Corporation (a calendar year taxpayer) has accumulated E & P of $30,000. The corporation has no current E & P. During the year, the corporation distributes $40,000 to its *equal* shareholders, Bob and Bonnie. Only $30,000 of the $40,000 distribution is a taxable dividend. Suppose Bob's basis in his stock is $8,000, while Bonnie's basis is $4,000. Under these conditions, Bob recognizes a taxable dividend of $15,000 and reduces the basis of the stock from $8,000 to $3,000. The $20,000 Bonnie receives from Amber Corporation is accounted for as follows: a taxable dividend of $15,000, a reduction in stock basis from $4,000 to zero, and a capital gain of $1,000. ▼

EARNINGS AND PROFITS (E & P)—§ 312

1 LEARNING OBJECTIVE
Identify and understand the concept of earnings and profits.

The Code does not define the term **earnings and profits.** Although E & P is similar in some respects to the accounting concept of retained earnings (earnings retained in the business), E & P and retained earnings are often not the same.

Several observations are helpful in understanding the concept of E & P. E & P can be described as the factor that fixes the upper limit on the amount of dividend income shareholders must recognize as a result of a distribution by the corporation. In this sense, E & P represents the corporation's economic ability to pay a dividend without impairing its capital. The effect of a specific transaction on the E & P account can be determined simply by considering whether or not the transaction increases or decreases the corporation's capacity to pay a dividend.

COMPUTATION OF E & P

A corporation's taxable income for the year is the starting point in computing its E & P for the year. Taxable income is converted into E & P through certain adjustments that cause E & P to conform more closely to economic income. If the corporation uses the cash method of accounting in computing taxable income, it must also use this method to determine the changes in E & P.[3]

Additions to Taxable Income in Determining E & P. E & P is increased for all items of income. Interest on municipal bonds, for example, though not taxed to the corporation, increases the corporation's E & P. The dividends received deduction is added back to compute E & P. A corporation's E & P for the year in which it sells property on the installment basis is increased by the amount of any deferred gain. This is accomplished by treating all principal payments as having been received in the year of sale.[4]

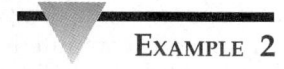

EXAMPLE 2

A corporation collects $100,000 on a key employee life insurance policy (the corporation is the owner and beneficiary of the policy). At the time the policy matured on the death of the insured employee, it possessed a cash surrender value of $30,000. None of the $100,000 is included in the corporation's taxable income, but $70,000 is added to the current E & P account. ▼

---

[2] § 301(c).

[3] Code § 312 contains most of the adjustments necessary to determine E & P. It accomplishes this by setting out the effect of a number of transactions on E & P. Regulations relating to E & P begin at Reg. § 1.312–6.

[4] § 312(n)(5).

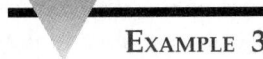

EXAMPLE 3

During 1997, a corporation makes charitable contributions, $12,000 of which cannot be deducted in arriving at the taxable income for the year because of the 10% limitation. However, the $12,000 is carried over to 1998 and fully deducted in that year. The excess charitable contribution reduces the corporation's current E & P for 1997 by $12,000 and increases its current E & P for 1998, when the deduction is allowed, by a like amount. The increase in E & P in 1998 is necessary because the charitable contribution carryover reduces the taxable income for that year (the starting point for computing E & P) and already has been taken into account in determining the E & P for 1997. ▼

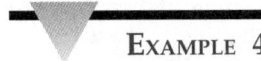

EXAMPLE 4

In 1997, Cardinal Corporation, a calendar year taxpayer, sells unimproved real estate (basis of $20,000) for $100,000. Under the terms of the sale, beginning in 1998, Cardinal will receive two annual payments of $50,000 each with interest of 9%. Cardinal Corporation does not elect out of the installment method. Although Cardinal's taxable income for 1997 will not reflect any of the gain from the sale, the corporation must increase E & P for 1997 by $80,000 (the deferred profit component). ▼

Subtractions from Taxable Income in Determining E & P. The E & P account is affected by both deductible and nondeductible items. Consequently, excess capital losses, expenses incurred to produce tax-exempt income, and Federal income taxes all reduce E & P. Such items do not enter into the calculation of taxable income.

The E & P account is reduced only by cost depletion, even though the corporation is using percentage (statutory) depletion for income tax purposes. E & P cannot be reduced by accelerated depreciation.[5] However, if a depreciation method such as units-of-production or machine hours is used, the adjustment to E & P is determined on this basis.[6]

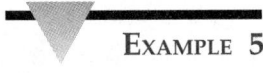

EXAMPLE 5

A corporation sells property (basis of $10,000) to its sole shareholder for $8,000. Because of § 267 (disallowance of losses on sales between related parties), the $2,000 loss cannot be deducted in arriving at the corporation's taxable income. But since the overall economic effect of the transaction is a decrease in the corporation's assets by $2,000, the loss reduces the current E & P for the year of sale. ▼

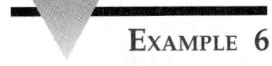

EXAMPLE 6

A corporation pays a $10,000 premium on a key employee life insurance policy covering the life of its president. As a result of the payment, the cash surrender value of the policy is increased by $7,000. Although none of the $10,000 premium is deductible for tax purposes, current E & P is reduced by $3,000. ▼

Other Adjustments. Gains and losses from property transactions generally affect the determination of E & P only to the extent they are recognized for tax purposes. Thus, a gain on an involuntary conversion not recognized by the corporation because the insurance proceeds are suitably reinvested does not affect E & P.

The alternative depreciation system must be used for purposes of computing E & P.[7] If cost recovery is figured under MACRS, E & P must be computed using the straight-line recovery method over a recovery period equal to the asset's Asset Depreciation Range (ADR) midpoint life.[8] Later, when the asset is sold, the

---

[5] § 312(k).

[6] Reg. § 1.312–15(a)(2).

[7] § 312(k)(3)(A).

[8] See § 168(g)(2). The ADR midpoint life for most assets is set out in Rev.Proc. 87–56, 1987–2 C.B. 674. The recovery period is 5 years

for automobiles and light-duty trucks and 40 years for real property. For assets with no class life, the recovery period is 12 years. Any amount expensed under § 179 is deducted over a period of 5 years in computing E & P. See § 312(k)(3)(B).

increase or decrease in E & P is determined by using the adjusted basis of the asset for E & P purposes.[9]

Intangible drilling costs and mine exploration and development costs are required to be capitalized for purposes of computing E & P. Once capitalized, these expenditures can be charged to E & P over a specified period: 60 months for intangible drilling costs and 120 months for mine exploration and development costs.[10]

EXAMPLE 7

On January 2, 1995, White Corporation purchased equipment with an alternative recovery period of 10 years for $30,000. The equipment was then depreciated under MACRS. The asset was sold on July 2, 1997, for $27,000. For purposes of determining taxable income and E & P, cost recovery claimed on the equipment and the equipment's adjusted basis are summarized as follows:

		Taxable Income	E & P	Difference
Amount realized		$27,000	$27,000	–0–
Original cost		$30,000	$30,000	–0–
Cost recovery:				
1995:	$30,000 × 14.29%	$ 4,287		
	$30,000 ÷ 10-year recovery period × ½ (half-year for first year of service)		$ 1,500	$2,787
1996:	$30,000 × 24.49%	7,347		
	$30,000 ÷ 10-year recovery period		3,000	4,347
1997:	$30,000 × 17.49% × ½ (half-year for year of disposal)	2,624		
	$30,000 ÷ 10-year recovery period × ½ (half-year for year of disposal)		1,500	1,124
Total cost recovery		$14,258	$ 6,000	$8,258
Adjusted basis		$15,742	$24,000	$8,258
Gain		$11,258	$ 3,000	$8,258

SUMMARY OF E & P ADJUSTMENTS

2 **LEARNING OBJECTIVE**
Recognize the importance of earnings and profits in measuring dividend income.

E & P serves as a measure of the earnings of the corporation that are available for distribution as taxable dividends to the shareholders. Initially, E & P is increased by the corporation's taxable income. However, various transactions for taxable income must be adjusted in determining the corporation's current E & P. These adjustments are reviewed in Concept Summary 4–1. Other items that affect E & P, such as property dividends, are covered later in the chapter and are not incorporated in the concept summary. The effect of stock redemptions on E & P is covered in Chapter 5.

THE SOURCE OF THE DISTRIBUTION

In determining the source of a dividend distribution, the dividend is deemed to have been made first from **current E & P** and then from **accumulated E & P** (since February 28, 1913).[11]

---

[9]§ 312(f)(1).
[10]§ 312(n)(2).

[11]Regulations relating to the source of a distribution are at Reg. § 1.316–2.

CONCEPT SUMMARY 4–1

E & P Adjustments

Nature of the Transaction	Effect on Taxable Income in Arriving at Current E & P	
	Addition	Subtraction
Tax-exempt income	X	
Collection of proceeds on insurance policy on life of corporate officer	X	
Deferred gain on installment sale (all gain is added to E & P in year of sale)	X	
Future recognition of installment sale gross profit		X
Excess charitable contribution (over 10% limitation)		X
Deduction of excess charitable contribution in succeeding taxable year (increase E & P because deduction reduces taxable income while E & P was reduced in a prior year)	X	
Federal income taxes		X
Loss on sale between related parties		X
Payment of premiums on insurance policy on life of corporate officer (in excess of increase in cash surrender value of policy)		X
Realized gain (not recognized) on an involuntary conversion	No effect	
Percentage depletion (only cost depletion can reduce E & P)	X	
Accelerated depreciation (E & P is reduced only by straight-line, units-of-production, or machine hours depreciation)	X	
Intangible drilling costs deducted currently (reduce E & P in future years by amortizing costs over 60 months)	X	
Mine exploration and development costs (reduce in future years by amortizing costs over 120 months)	X	

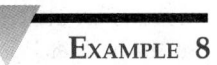

EXAMPLE 8

At the beginning of the current year, Brown Corporation has a deficit of $30,000 in accumulated E & P. For the year, it has current E & P of $10,000 and distributes $5,000 to its shareholders. The $5,000 distribution is treated as a taxable dividend since it is deemed to have been made from current E & P. This is the case even though Brown Corporation still has a deficit in accumulated E & P at the end of the current year. ▼

Distributions made during the year may exceed the current year's E & P. In this case, the portion of each distribution considered to have been made from current E & P is the percentage that the total E & P for the year bears to the total distributions for that year. This allocation is important if any of the shareholders sell their stock during the year and current distributions exceed current E & P.

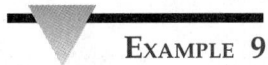

EXAMPLE 9

As of January 1, 1997, Black Corporation has two *equal* shareholders, Megan and Matt, and accumulated E & P of $10,000. Current E & P for 1997 amounts to $30,000. On August 1, 1997, Megan sells all of her stock to Helen. During 1997, $40,000 is distributed to Megan and

Matt ($20,000 to each) on July 1 and $40,000 to Matt and Helen ($20,000 to each) on December 1. The distributions are allocated as follows:

| | Source of Distribution | | |
	Current E & P	Accumulated E & P	Return of Capital
July 1 distribution ($40,000)	$15,000	$10,000	$15,000
December 1 distribution ($40,000)	15,000	—	25,000

The tax consequences to the shareholders are as follows:

| | Shareholder | | |
	Megan	Matt	Helen
July distribution ($40,000)			
Dividend income—			
From current E & P ($15,000)	$ 7,500	$ 7,500	$ –0–
From accumulated E & P ($10,000)	5,000	5,000	–0–
Return of capital ($15,000)	7,500	7,500	–0–
December distribution ($40,000)			
Dividend income—			
From current E & P ($15,000)	–0–	7,500	7,500
From accumulated E & P ($0)	–0–	–0–	–0–
Return of capital ($25,000)	–0–	12,500	12,500
Total dividend income	$12,500	$20,000	$ 7,500
Nontaxable return of capital (presuming sufficient basis in the stock investment)	$ 7,500	$20,000	$12,500

Note that the current E & P is allocated between both distributions, while the accumulated E & P is applied to and exhausted by the first distribution. ▼

DISTINGUISHING BETWEEN CURRENT AND ACCUMULATED E & P

Accumulated E & P is the total of all previous years' current E & P as computed on the first day of each taxable year. The computation is made in accordance with the tax law in effect during that year. The factors that affect the computation of the current E & P for any one year have been discussed previously. Why must current and accumulated E & P be distinguished when it is clear that distributions are taxable if and to the extent that current *and* accumulated E & P exist?

1. When a deficit exists in accumulated E & P and a positive balance exists in current E & P, distributions are regarded as dividends to the extent of the current E & P. Refer to Example 8.
2. Current E & P is allocated on a pro rata basis to the distributions made during the year; accumulated E & P is applied (to the extent necessary) in chronological order beginning with the earliest distributions. Refer to Example 9.
3. Unless and until the parties can show otherwise, it is presumed that any distribution is covered by current E & P.

4. When a deficit exists in current E & P (a current loss develops) and a positive balance exists in accumulated E & P, the accounts are netted at the date of distribution. If the resulting balance is zero or a deficit, the distribution is a return of capital. If a positive balance results, the distribution is a dividend to the extent of the balance. Any loss is allocated ratably during the year unless the parties can show otherwise.

The following examples illustrate distinctions 3 and 4.

EXAMPLE 10

Green Corporation uses a fiscal year of July 1 through June 30 for tax purposes. Carol, Green's only shareholder, uses a calendar year. As of July 1, 1997, Green Corporation has a zero balance in its accumulated E & P account. For fiscal year 1997–1998, the corporation suffers a $5,000 operating loss. On August 1, 1997, Green distributes $10,000 to Carol. The distribution is dividend income to Carol and is reported as such when she files her income tax return for calendar year 1997 on or before April 15, 1998. Because Carol cannot prove until June 30, 1998, that the corporation has a deficit for fiscal 1997–1998, she must assume the $10,000 distribution is fully covered by current E & P. When Carol learns of the deficit, she can file an amended return for 1997 showing the $10,000 as a return of capital. ▼

EXAMPLE 11

At the beginning of the current year, Gray Corporation (a calendar year taxpayer) has accumulated E & P of $10,000. During the year, the corporation incurs a $15,000 net loss from operations that accrues ratably. On July 1, Gray Corporation distributes $6,000 in cash to Hal, its sole shareholder. To determine how much of the $6,000 cash distribution represents dividend income to Hal, the balance of both accumulated and current E & P as of July 1 is determined and netted. This is necessary because of the deficit in current E & P.

| | Source of Distribution | |
	Current E & P	Accumulated E & P
January 1		$10,000
July 1 (½ of $15,000 net loss)	($7,500)	2,500
July 1 distribution—($6,000):		
Dividend income: ($2,500)		
Return of capital: ($3,500)		

The balance in E & P on July 1 is $2,500. Thus, of the $6,000 distribution, $2,500 is taxed as a dividend, and $3,500 represents a return of capital. ▼

PROPERTY DIVIDENDS—IN GENERAL

3   LEARNING OBJECTIVE
Master the tax treatment of dividends, including property dividends, to both the recipient shareholder and the corporation making the distribution.

The previous discussion assumed that all distributions by a corporation to its shareholders are in the form of cash. Although most corporate distributions are cash, a corporation may distribute a **property dividend** for various reasons. The shareholders could want a particular property that is held by the corporation. Or the corporation may be strapped for cash, but does not want to forgo distributing a dividend to its shareholders.

Generally, the distribution of a property dividend is treated in the same manner as a cash distribution. However, the value of the property distributed and the basis of that property to the corporation are seldom the same. Consequently, the distribution of a property dividend involves additional tax considerations. The following questions must be asked when property is distributed as a dividend:

DIVIDEND PAYOUT RATES ARE AT A HISTORIC LOW

Dividend payouts are at a new low because of the gap between income tax rates on ordinary income and capital gains. Many corporations are buying back stock to generate capital gains for their shareholders rather than paying the shareholders dividends, which are taxed as ordinary income. The result, as financial analysts have noted, is that more corporate stocks are being retired through stock redemptions than are being issued. This excess of retired stock over new issues is called "equity liquidation."

- What is the amount of the dividend distributed to the shareholder?
- What is the basis of the property received by the shareholder?
- Does the corporation recognize gain or loss upon the distribution?
- What is the effect of the property distribution on the E & P of the corporation?

PROPERTY DIVIDENDS—EFFECT ON THE SHAREHOLDER

When a corporation distributes property rather than cash to a shareholder, the amount distributed is measured by the fair market value of the property on the date of distribution.[12] The portion of the distribution covered by existing E & P is a dividend, and any excess is treated as a return of capital. If the fair market value of the property distributed exceeds the corporation's E & P and the shareholder's basis in the stock investment, a capital gain results.

The amount distributed is reduced by any liabilities to which the distributed property is subject immediately before and immediately after the distribution and by any liabilities of the corporation assumed by the shareholder. The basis in the distributed property is the fair market value of the property on the date of the distribution.

EXAMPLE 12

Robin Corporation has E & P of $60,000. It distributes land with a fair market value of $50,000 (adjusted basis of $30,000) to its sole shareholder, Charles. The land is subject to a liability of $10,000, which Charles assumes. Charles has a taxable dividend of $40,000 [$50,000 (fair market value) – $10,000 (liability)]. The basis of the land to Charles is $50,000. ▼

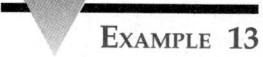

EXAMPLE 13

Ten percent of Tan Corporation is owned by Red Corporation. Tan Corporation has ample E & P to cover any distributions made during the year. One distribution made to Red Corporation consists of a vacant lot with adjusted basis of $5,000 and a fair market value of $3,000. Red has a taxable dividend of $3,000, and its basis in the lot becomes $3,000. ▼

Property that has depreciated in value is usually not suited for distribution as a property dividend. Note what happens in Example 13. The loss of $2,000 (adjusted basis $5,000, fair market value $3,000) disappears. Tan Corporation can

---

[12]Section 301 deals with the tax treatment to the shareholder of a distribution by the corporation.

preserve the loss for itself if it sells the lot and then distributes the $3,000 proceeds.

PROPERTY DIVIDENDS—EFFECT ON THE CORPORATION

A property distribution by a corporation to its shareholders poses two questions. Does the distribution result in recognized gain or loss to the corporation making the distribution? What effect does the distribution have on the corporation's E & P?

Recognition of Gain or Loss.   All distributions of appreciated property cause gain to the distributing corporation.[13] In effect, the corporation that makes a property dividend is treated as if it had sold the property to the shareholder for its fair market value. However, the distributing corporation does not recognize loss on distributions of property with a tax basis in excess of fair market value.

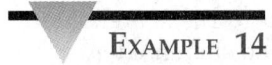

EXAMPLE 14   A corporation distributes land (basis of $10,000 and fair market value of $30,000) to a shareholder. The corporation recognizes a gain of $20,000. ▼

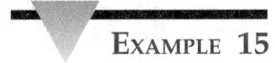

EXAMPLE 15   Assume the property in Example 14 has a fair market value of $10,000 and a basis of $30,000. The corporation does not recognize a loss on the distribution. ▼

If the distributed property is subject to a liability in excess of basis or the shareholder assumes such a liability, a special rule applies. The fair market value of the property for purposes of determining gain on the distribution is treated as not being less than the amount of the liability.[14]

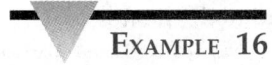

EXAMPLE 16   Assume the land in Example 14 is subject to a liability of $35,000. The corporation recognizes gain of $25,000 on the distribution. ▼

Effect of Corporate Distributions on E & P.   In the event of a corporate distribution, the E & P account is reduced by the amount of money distributed or by the greater of the fair market value or the adjusted basis of property distributed, less the amount of any liability on the property.[15] E & P is increased by gain recognized on appreciated property distributed as a property dividend.

EXAMPLE 17   Crimson Corporation distributes property (basis of $10,000 and fair market value of $20,000) to Brenda, its shareholder. Crimson Corporation recognizes a gain of $10,000, which is added to its E & P. E & P is then reduced by $20,000, the fair market value of the property. Brenda has dividend income of $20,000. ▼

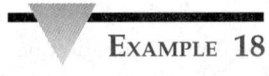

EXAMPLE 18   Assume the same facts as in Example 17, except that the fair market value of the property is $15,000 and the adjusted basis in the hands of Crimson Corporation is $20,000. Because loss is not recognized and the adjusted basis is greater than fair market value, E & P is reduced by $20,000. Brenda reports dividend income of $15,000. ▼

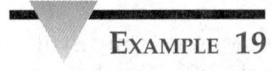

EXAMPLE 19   Assume the same facts as in Example 18, except that the property is subject to a liability of $6,000. E & P is now reduced by $14,000 [$20,000 (adjusted basis) – $6,000 (liability)]. Brenda has a dividend of $9,000 [$15,000 (amount of the distribution) – $6,000 (liability)], and her basis in the property is $15,000. ▼

---

[13] Section 311 covers the taxability of a corporation on distributions.
[14] § 311(b)(2).

[15] §§ 312(a), (b), and (c).

Under no circumstances can a distribution, whether cash or property, either generate a deficit in E & P or add to a deficit in E & P. Deficits can arise only through corporate losses.

EXAMPLE 20

Teal Corporation has accumulated E & P of $10,000 at the beginning of the current tax year. During the year, it has current E & P of $15,000. At the end of the year, it distributes cash of $30,000 to its sole shareholder, Walter. Teal's E & P at the end of the year is zero. The beginning E & P of $10,000 is increased by current E & P of $15,000 and reduced $25,000 by the dividend distribution. The remaining $5,000 of the distribution to Walter does not reduce E & P because a distribution cannot generate a deficit in E & P. ▼

CONSTRUCTIVE DIVIDENDS

4 **LEARNING OBJECTIVE**
Understand the nature and treatment of constructive dividends.

A distribution by a corporation to its shareholders can be treated as a dividend for Federal income tax purposes even though it is not formally declared or designated as a dividend. Also, it need not be issued pro rata to all shareholders.[16] Nor must the distribution satisfy the legal requirements of a dividend as set forth by applicable state law. The key factor determining dividend status is a measurable economic benefit conveyed to the shareholder. This benefit, often described as a **constructive dividend,** is distinguishable from actual corporate distributions of cash and property in form only.

Constructive dividend situations usually arise in the context of closely held corporations. Here, the dealings between the parties are less structured, and frequently, formalities are not preserved. The constructive dividend serves as a substitute for actual distributions. Usually, it is intended to accomplish some tax objective not available through the use of direct dividends. The shareholders may be attempting to bail out corporate profits in a form deductible to the corporation. (Dividend distributions do not provide the distributing corporation with an income tax deduction, although they do reduce E & P.) Alternatively, the shareholders may be seeking benefits for themselves while avoiding the recognition of income. Constructive dividends are, in reality, disguised dividends.

Do not conclude that all constructive dividends are deliberate attempts to avoid actual and formal dividends. Often, constructive dividends are inadvertent. Consequently, a dividend result may come as a surprise to the parties. For this reason, if for none other, an awareness of the various constructive dividend situations is essential to protect the parties from unanticipated tax consequences.

TYPES OF CONSTRUCTIVE DIVIDENDS

The most frequently encountered types of constructive dividends are summarized below.

Shareholder Use of Corporate-Owned Property. A constructive dividend can occur when a shareholder uses corporation property for personal purposes at no cost. Personal use of corporate-owned automobiles, airplanes, yachts, fishing camps, hunting lodges, and other entertainment facilities is commonplace in some closely held corporations. The shareholder has dividend income to the extent of the fair rental value of the property for the period of its personal use.

---

[16]See *Lengsfield v. Comm.*, 57–1 USTC ¶9437, 50 AFTR 1683, 241 F.2d 508 (CA–5, 1957).

Bargain Sale of Corporate Property to a Shareholder.   Shareholders often purchase property from a corporation at a cost below the fair market value of the property. These bargain sales produce dividend income to the extent of the difference between the property's fair market value on the date of sale and the amount the shareholder paid for the property.[17] These situations might be avoided by appraising the property on or about the date of the sale. The appraised value should become the price to be paid by the shareholder.

Bargain Rental of Corporate Property.   A bargain rental of corporate property by a shareholder also produces dividend income. Here the measure of the constructive dividend is the excess of the property's fair rental value over the rent actually paid. Again, appraisal data should be used to avoid any questionable situations.

Payments for the Benefit of a Shareholder.   If a corporation pays an obligation of a shareholder, the payment is treated as a constructive dividend. The obligation involved need not be legally binding on the shareholder; it may, in fact, be a moral obligation.[18] Forgiveness of shareholder indebtedness by the corporation creates an identical problem.[19] Excessive rentals paid by a corporation for the use of shareholder property are treated as constructive dividends.

Unreasonable Compensation.   A salary payment of a shareholder-employee that is deemed to be **unreasonable compensation** is frequently treated as a constructive dividend. As a consequence, it is not deductible by the corporation. In determining the reasonableness of salary payments, the following factors are considered:

- The employee's qualifications.
- A comparison of salaries with dividend distributions.
- The prevailing rates of compensation for comparable positions in comparable business concerns.
- The nature and scope of the employee's work.
- The size and complexity of the business.
- A comparison of salaries paid with both gross and net income.
- The taxpayer's salary policy toward all employees.
- For small corporations with a limited number of officers, the amount of compensation paid the employee in question in previous years.[20]

Loans to Shareholders.   Advances to shareholders that are not bona fide loans are constructive dividends. Whether an advance qualifies as a bona fide loan is a question of fact to be determined in light of the particular circumstances. Factors considered in determining whether the advance is a bona fide loan include the following:

- Whether the advance is on open account or is evidenced by a written instrument.
- Whether the shareholder furnished collateral or other security for the advance.
- How long the advance has been outstanding.

---

[17] Reg. § 1.301–1(j).

[18] *Montgomery Engineering Co. v. U.S.*, 64–2 USTC ¶9618, 13 AFTR2d 1747, 230 F.Supp. 838 (D.Ct.N.J., 1964); *aff'd.* in 65–1 USTC ¶9368, 15 AFTR2d 746, 344 F.2d 996 (CA–3, 1965).

[19] Reg. § 1.301–1(m).

[20] *Mayson Manufacturing Co. v. Comm.*, 49–2 USTC ¶9467, 38 AFTR 1028, 178 F.2d 115 (CA–6, 1949).

TAX IN THE NEWS

WHEN IS COMPENSATION UNREASONABLE?

What is reasonable compensation for the head of the Chicago Stadium Corporation, which manages the arena where the Chicago Blackhawks hockey team and the Chicago Bulls basketball team play? For the fiscal year ending on July 31, 1977, the corporation paid its chairman and CEO, Arthur Wirtz, $335,750, but the IRS insisted reasonable compensation would be only $138,000 and disallowed the company's deduction for the remainder.

A long legal battle ensued, but the Federal District Court in Chicago finally upheld the IRS [*Chicago Stadium Corporation v. U.S.*, 91–2 USTC ¶50,352 (D.Ct.Ill., 1991)]. Among other things, the court said that Wirtz was paid considerably more than the executives of similar arenas, yet he did not even work full-time for the corporation. Besides, much of his pay consisted of "commissions" for arranging to lease the arena to the Bulls, which he also controlled. Under the circumstances, said the court, the $138,000 allowed by the IRS was generous.

- Whether any payments have been made.
- The shareholder's financial capability to repay the advance.
- The shareholder's use of the funds (e.g., payment of routine bills versus nonrecurring, extraordinary expenses).
- The regularity of the advances.
- The dividend-paying history of the corporation.

If a corporation succeeds in proving that an advance to a shareholder is a bona fide loan, the advance is not a constructive dividend. But getting past this hurdle does not necessarily eliminate all constructive dividend treatment. The shareholder still has a constructive dividend in the amount of any forgone interest. Interest-free or below-market loans by a corporation to a shareholder cause the shareholder to have a constructive dividend to the extent of "imputed interest." This is the difference between the rate the Federal government pays on new borrowings, compounded semiannually, and the interest charged on the loan.[21] The corporation is deemed to have made a dividend distribution to the shareholder to the extent of the forgone interest. The shareholder is then deemed to have made an interest payment to the corporation for the same amount. Although the shareholder may be permitted to deduct the deemed interest payment, the corporation has interest income. No corresponding deduction is allowed since the imputed interest element is a constructive dividend.

EXAMPLE 21

Mallard Corporation loans its principal shareholder, Henry, $100,000 on January 2, 1997. The loan is interest-free. On December 31, 1997, Mallard is deemed to have made a dividend distribution to Henry in the amount of the imputed interest on the loan, determined by using the Federal rate and compounded semiannually. Assume the Federal rate is 6%. Mallard is deemed to have paid a dividend to Henry in the amount of $6,180.

Although Henry has dividend income of $6,180, he may be permitted to offset the income with a $6,180 deemed interest payment to Mallard. The corporation has deemed

---

[21] See § 7872.

interest income of $6,180, but has no corresponding deduction. The deemed payment from Mallard to Henry is a nondeductible dividend. ▼

Loans to a Corporation by Shareholders.   Shareholder loans to a corporation may be reclassified as equity because the debt has too many features of stock. Any interest and principal payments made by the corporation to the shareholder are then treated as constructive dividends.

TAX TREATMENT OF CONSTRUCTIVE DIVIDENDS

Constructive distributions possess the same tax attributes as actual distributions.[22] Thus, a corporate shareholder is entitled to the dividends received deduction (see Chapter 2). The constructive distribution is taxable as a dividend only to the extent of the corporation's current and accumulated E & P. The burden of proving that the distribution constitutes a return of capital because of inadequate E & P rests with the taxpayer.[23]

▼ STOCK DIVIDENDS AND STOCK RIGHTS

STOCK DIVIDENDS—§ 305

5   ▼   **LEARNING OBJECTIVE**
Distinguish between taxable and nontaxable stock dividends and stock rights.

A shareholder's proportionate interest in a corporation generally does not change upon receipt of a **stock dividend.** Accordingly, such distributions were initially accorded tax-free treatment.[24] Subsequently, the test for taxability of a stock dividend was based on whether the proportionate interest of a shareholder changed following the distribution. The 1954 Code simply stated that stock dividends would not be taxable unless (1) the shareholder could elect to receive either stock or property or (2) the stock dividends were in discharge of preference dividends. In response, corporations devised various methods to distribute stock dividends that would change the shareholder's interest and still qualify as tax-free.[25]

The provisions of § 305 that currently govern the taxability of stock dividends are based on the proportionate interest concept. Stock dividends are not taxable if they are pro rata distributions of stock, or stock rights, on common stock. The general rule that stock dividends are nontaxable has five exceptions, summarized as follows:

1. Distributions payable either in stock or property.
2. Distributions resulting in the receipt of property by some shareholders and an increase in the proportionate interest of other shareholders in the assets or E & P of the distributing corporation.
3. Distributions that result in the receipt of preferred stock by some common stock shareholders and the receipt of common stock by other shareholders.
4. Distributions on preferred stock other than an increase in the conversion ratio of convertible preferred stock made solely to take account of a stock dividend or stock split with respect to stock into which the preferred is convertible.
5. Distributions of convertible preferred stock, unless it can be shown that the distribution will not result in a disproportionate distribution.

---

[22] *Simon v. Comm.,* 57–2 USTC ¶9989, 52 AFTR 698, 248 F.2d 869 (CA–8, 1957).

[23] *DiZenzo v. Comm.,* 65–2 USTC ¶9518, 16 AFTR2d 5107, 348 F.2d 122 (CA–2, 1965).

[24] See *Eisner v. Macomber,* 1 USTC ¶32, 3 AFTR 3020, 40 S.Ct. 189 (USSC, 1920).

[25] See "Stock Dividends," Senate Report 91–552, 1969–3 C.B. 519.

Note that the exceptions to nontaxability of stock dividends deal with various disproportionate distribution situations.

Holders of convertible securities are considered shareholders. As a result, payment of interest on convertible debentures causes stock dividends paid on common stock to be taxable. This result is avoided if the conversion ratio or conversion price is adjusted to reflect the stock dividend.[26]

If stock dividends are not taxable, the corporation's E & P is not reduced.[27] If the stock dividends are taxable, the distributing corporation treats the distribution in the same manner as any other taxable property dividend.

If a stock dividend is taxable, basis to the shareholder-distributee is fair market value, and the holding period starts on the date of receipt. If a stock dividend is not taxable, the basis of the stock on which the dividend is distributed is reallocated.[28] If the dividend shares are identical to these formerly held shares, basis in the old stock is reallocated by dividing the taxpayer's cost in the old stock by the total number of shares. If the dividend stock is not identical to the underlying shares (e.g., a stock dividend of preferred on common), basis is determined by allocating the basis of the formerly held shares between the old and new stock according to the fair market value of each. The holding period includes the holding period of the formerly held stock.[29]

EXAMPLE 22

Gail bought 1,000 shares of stock two years ago for $10,000. In the current tax year, Gail receives 10 shares of common stock as a nontaxable stock dividend. Gail's basis of $10,000 is divided by 1,010. Each share of stock has a basis of $9.90 instead of the pre-dividend $10 basis. ▼

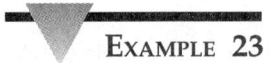

EXAMPLE 23

Assume Gail received, instead, a nontaxable preferred stock dividend of 100 shares. The preferred stock has a fair market value of $1,000, and the common stock, on which the preferred is distributed, has a fair market value of $19,000. After the receipt of the stock dividend, the basis of the common stock is $9,500, and the basis of the preferred is $500, computed as follows:

Fair market value of common	$19,000
Fair market value of preferred	1,000
	$20,000
Basis of common: $^{19}/_{20} \times \$10,000$	$ 9,500
Basis of preferred: $^1/_{20} \times \$10,000$	$ 500

▼

STOCK RIGHTS

The rules for determining taxability of **stock rights** are identical to those for determining taxability of stock dividends. If the rights are taxable, the recipient has income to the extent of the fair market value of the rights. The fair market value then becomes the shareholder-distributee's basis in the rights.[30] If the rights are exercised, the holding period for the new stock is the date the rights (whether taxable or nontaxable) are exercised. The basis of the new stock is the basis of the rights plus the amount of any other consideration given.

If stock rights are not taxable and the value of the rights is less than 15 percent of the value of the old stock, the basis of the rights is zero. However, the

---

[26] See Reg. § 1.305–3(d) for illustrations on how to compute required adjustments on conversion ratios or prices.
[27] § 312(d)(1).

[28] § 307(a).
[29] § 1223(5).
[30] Reg. § 1.305–1(b).

shareholder may elect to have some of the basis in the formerly held stock allocated to the rights.[31] If the fair market value of the rights is 15 percent or more of the value of the old stock and the rights are exercised or sold, the shareholder must allocate some of the basis in the formerly held stock to the rights.

Assume the value of the stock rights is less than 15 percent of the value of the stock and the shareholder makes an election to allocate basis to the rights. The election is made by attaching a statement to the shareholder's return for the year in which the rights are received.[32]

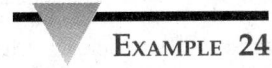

EXAMPLE 24

A corporation with common stock outstanding declares a nontaxable dividend payable in rights to subscribe to common stock. Each right entitles the holder to purchase one share of stock for $90. One right is issued for every two shares of stock owned. Fred owns 400 shares of stock purchased two years ago for $15,000. At the time of the distribution of the rights, the market value of the common stock is $100 per share, and the market value of the rights is $8 per right. Fred receives 200 rights. He exercises 100 rights and sells the remaining 100 rights three months later for $9 per right. Fred need not allocate the cost of the original stock to the rights because the value of the rights is less than 15% of the value of the stock ($1,600 ÷ $40,000 = 4%).

If Fred does not allocate his original stock basis to the rights, the tax consequences are as follows:

- Basis in the new stock is $9,000 ($90 × 100). The holding period of the new stock begins on the date the stock was purchased.
- Sale of the rights would produce long-term capital gain of $900 ($9 × 100). The holding period of the rights starts with the date the original 400 shares of stock were acquired.

If Fred elects to allocate basis to the rights, the tax consequences are as follows:

- Basis in the stock is $14,423 [$40,000 ÷ $41,600 (value of rights and stock) × $15,000 (cost of stock)].
- Basis in the rights is $577 [$1,600 (value of rights) ÷ $41,600 (value of rights and stock) × $15,000 (cost of stock)].
- When Fred exercises the rights, his basis in the new stock will be $9,288.50 [$9,000 (cost) + $288.50 (basis in 100 rights)].
- Sale of the rights would produce a long-term capital gain of $611.50 [$900 (selling price) – $288.50 (basis in the remaining 100 rights)]. ▼

TAX PLANNING CONSIDERATIONS

CORPORATE DISTRIBUTIONS

In connection with the discussion of corporate distributions, the following points need reinforcement:

- Because E & P is the measure of dividend income, its periodic determination is essential to corporate planning. Thus, an E & P account should be established and maintained, particularly if the possibility exists that a corporate distribution might be a return of capital.
- Accumulated E & P is the sum of all past years' current E & P. There is no statute of limitations on the computation of E & P. The IRS can, for example, redetermine a corporation's current E & P for a tax year long since passed. Such a change affects accumulated E & P and has a direct impact on the taxability of current distributions to shareholders.
- Distributions can be manipulated to avoid or minimize dividend exposure.

---

[31] § 307(b)(1).

[32] Reg. § 1.307–2.

EXAMPLE 25

Flicker Corporation has accumulated E & P of $100,000 as of January 1, 1997. During 1997, it expects to have earnings from operations of $80,000 and to make a cash distribution of $60,000. Flicker Corporation also expects to sell an asset for a loss of $100,000. Thus, it anticipates incurring a deficit of $20,000 for the year. The best approach is to recognize the loss as soon as possible and immediately thereafter make the cash distribution to the shareholders. Suppose these two steps take place on January 1, 1997. Because the current E & P for 1997 has a deficit, the accumulated E & P account must be brought up to date (refer to Example 11 in this chapter). Thus, at the time of the distribution, the combined E & P balance is zero [$100,000 (beginning balance in accumulated E & P) – $100,000 (existing deficit in current E & P)], and the $60,000 distribution to the shareholders constitutes a return of capital. Current deficits are allocated pro rata throughout the year unless the parties can prove otherwise. Here they can. ▼

EXAMPLE 26

After several unprofitable years, Darter Corporation has a deficit in accumulated E & P of $100,000 as of January 1, 1997. Starting in 1997, Darter expects to generate annual E & P of $50,000 for the next four years and would like to distribute this amount to its shareholders. The corporation's cash position (for dividend purposes) will correspond to the current E & P generated. Compare the following possibilities:

1. On December 31 of 1997, 1998, 1999, and 2000, Darter Corporation distributes a cash dividend of $50,000.
2. On December 31 of 1998 and 2000, Darter Corporation distributes a cash dividend of $100,000.

The two alternatives are illustrated as follows:

Year	Accumulated E & P (First of Year)	Current E & P	Distribution	Amount of Dividend
		Alternative 1		
1997	($100,000)	$50,000	$50,000	$50,000
1998	(100,000)	50,000	50,000	50,000
1999	(100,000)	50,000	50,000	50,000
2000	(100,000)	50,000	50,000	50,000
		Alternative 2		
1997	($100,000)	$50,000	$ –0–	$ –0–
1998	(50,000)	50,000	100,000	50,000
1999	(50,000)	50,000	–0–	–0–
2000	–0–	50,000	100,000	50,000

Alternative 1 leads to an overall result of $200,000 in dividend income, since each $50,000 distribution is fully covered by current E & P. Alternative 2, however, results in only $100,000 of dividend income to the shareholders. The remaining $100,000 is a return of capital. Why? At the time Darter Corporation made its first distribution of $100,000 on December 31, 1998, it had a deficit of $50,000 in accumulated E & P (the original deficit of $100,000 is reduced by the $50,000 of current E & P from 1997). Consequently, the $100,000 distribution yields a $50,000 dividend (the current E & P for 1998) and $50,000 as a return of capital. As of January 1, 1999, Darter's accumulated E & P now has a deficit balance of $50,000 (a distribution cannot increase a deficit in E & P). Add in $50,000 of current E & P from 1999, and the balance as of January 1, 2000, is zero. Thus, the second distribution of $100,000 made on December 31, 2000, also yields $50,000 of dividends (the current E & P for 2000) and $50,000 as a return of capital. ▼

ETHICAL
CONSIDERATIONS

Playing Games with the Statute of Limitations

In 1990, Beige Corporation made a cash distribution to its shareholders, one of whom was Steve Jordan. At that time, the parties involved honestly believed that the distribution was a return of capital because Beige had no E & P. Accordingly, none of the shareholders reported dividend income. In Steve's case, he reduced the $200,000 original basis of his stock investment by $40,000 (his share of the distribution). In 1997, it is discovered that E & P had been incorrectly computed. Instead, the 1990 distribution was fully covered by E & P and *should not have been treated as a return of capital.*

In 1998, Steve sells his stock in Beige Corporation for $350,000. He plans to report a gain of $150,000 [$350,000 (selling price) – $200,000 (original basis)] on the sale. Although Steve realizes that he should have recognized dividend income of $40,000 for 1990, the statute of limitations has made this a closed year.

Comment on Steve's situation.

CONSTRUCTIVE DIVIDENDS

Tax planning can be particularly effective in avoiding constructive dividend situations. Shareholders should try to structure their dealings with the corporation on an arm's length basis. For example, reasonable rent should be paid for the use of corporate property, and a fair price should be paid for its purchase. The parties should make every effort to support the amount involved with appraisal data or market information obtained from reliable sources at or close to the time of the transaction. Dealings between shareholders and a closely held corporation should be as formal as possible. In the case of loans to shareholders, for example, the parties should provide for an adequate rate of interest, written evidence of the debt, and a realistic repayment schedule that is both arranged and followed.

If shareholders wish to bail out corporate profits in a form deductible to the corporation, a balanced mix of the possible alternatives lessens the risk of disallowance by the IRS. Rent for the use of shareholder property, interest on amounts borrowed from shareholders, or salaries for services rendered by shareholders are all feasible substitutes for dividend distributions. But overdoing any one approach may attract the attention of the IRS. Too much interest, for example, may mean the corporation is thinly capitalized, and some of the debt may be equity investment.

Much can be done to protect against the disallowance of corporate deductions for compensation that is determined to be unreasonable in amount. Example 27 is an illustration, all too common in a family corporation, of what *not* to do.

EXAMPLE 27

Crow Corporation is wholly owned by Cole. Corporate employees and annual salaries include Mrs. Cole ($15,000), Cole, Jr. ($10,000), Cole ($80,000), and Ed ($40,000). The operation of Crow Corporation is shared about equally between Cole and Ed (an unrelated party). Mrs. Cole (Cole's wife) performed significant services for the corporation during the corporation's formative years but now merely attends the annual meeting of the board of directors. Cole, Jr. (Cole's son), is a full-time student and occasionally signs papers for the corporation in his capacity as treasurer. Crow Corporation has not distributed a dividend for 10 years, although it has accumulated substantial E & P. What is wrong with this situation?

- Mrs. Cole's salary seems vulnerable unless proof is available that some or all of her $15,000 annual salary is payment for services rendered to the corporation in prior years (she was underpaid for those years).[33]
- Cole, Jr.'s, salary is also vulnerable; he does not appear to earn the $10,000 paid to him by the corporation. It is true that neither Cole, Jr., nor Mrs. Cole is a shareholder, but each one's relationship to Cole is enough of a tie-in to raise the unreasonable compensation issue.
- Cole's salary appears susceptible to challenge. Why is he receiving $40,000 more than Ed when it appears they share equally in the operation of the corporation?
- Crow Corporation has not distributed dividends for 10 years, although it is capable of doing so. ▼

What could have been done to improve the tax position of the parties in Example 27? Mrs. Cole and Cole, Jr., are not entitled to a salary as neither seems to be performing any services for the corporation. Paying them a salary simply aggravates the problem. The IRS is more apt to consider *all* the salaries to members of the family as being excessive under the circumstances. Mr. Cole should probably reduce his compensation to correspond to that paid Ed. He can then attempt to distribute corporate earnings to himself in some other form.

ETHICAL CONSIDERATIONS

Disallowed Deductions

Upon audit of Eagle Corporation's income tax return for tax year 1996, the IRS disallowed as a deduction $250,000 of the $600,000 salary paid to Ron, Eagle's president and principal shareholder. The disallowed salary was deemed to be unreasonable. In 1997, Eagle Corporation again pays Ron a salary of $600,000. Can Eagle Corporation deduct this salary on its 1997 tax return or is it bound by the audit conducted by the IRS for the prior year?

Paying some dividends to Mr. Cole also helps alleviate the problem raised in Example 27. The IRS has been successful in denying a deduction for salary paid to a shareholder-employee, even when the payment was reasonable, in a situation where the corporation had not distributed any dividends.[34] Most courts, however, have not denied deductions for compensation solely because a dividend was not paid. A better approach is to compare an employee's compensation with the level of compensation prevalent in the particular industry.

The corporation can substitute *indirect* compensation for Mr. Cole by paying expenses that benefit him personally but are nevertheless deductible to the corporation. For example, premiums paid by the corporation for sickness, accident, and hospitalization insurance for Mr. Cole are deductible to the corporation and nontaxable to Mr. Cole.[35] The payments under the policy are not taxable to Mr. Cole unless they exceed his medical expenses.[36] The corporation can also pay for travel and entertainment expenses incurred by Mr. Cole on behalf of the

---

[33] See, for example, *R. J. Nicoll Co.*, 59 T.C. 37 (1972).

[34] *McCandless Tile Service v. U.S.*, 70–1 USTC ¶9284, 25 AFTR2d 70–870, 422 F.2d 1336 (Ct.Cls., 1970). The court in *McCandless* concluded that a return on equity of 15% of net profits was reasonable.

[35] Reg. § 1.162–10.

[36] The medical reimbursement plan must meet certain nondiscrimination requirements of § 105(h)(2).

corporation. Such expenditures must be primarily for the benefit of the corporation to be deductible. Mr. Cole will not have taxable income in the amount of the expenditures.[37]

In making indirect compensation payments to a shareholder-employee, be aware that the IRS looks to the total compensation package when testing for reasonableness. Indirect payments must not be overlooked.

EXAMPLE 28

Cora, the president and sole shareholder of Willet Corporation, is paid an annual salary of $100,000 by the corporation. Cora would like to draw funds from the corporation but is concerned that additional salary payments might cause the IRS to contend her salary is unreasonable. Cora does not want Willet to pay any dividends. She also wishes to donate $50,000 to her alma mater to establish scholarships for needy students. Willet Corporation could make the contribution on behalf of Cora. The payment clearly benefits Cora, but the amount of the contribution will not be taxed to her.[38] Willet can take a charitable contribution deduction for the payment. ▼

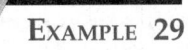

EXAMPLE 29

Assume in Example 28 that Cora has made an individual pledge to the university to provide $50,000 for scholarships for needy students. Willet Corporation satisfies Cora's pledge by paying the $50,000 to the university. The $50,000 will be taxed to Cora.[39] In this context, the $50,000 payment to the university may be treated as *indirect* compensation to Cora. In determining whether Cora's salary is unreasonable, both the *direct* payment of $100,000 and the *indirect* $50,000 payment will be considered. Cora's total compensation package is $150,000. ▼

---

[37] Reg. § 1.62–2(c)(4).

[38] *Henry J. Knott*, 67 T.C. 681 (1977).

[39] *Schalk Chemical Co. v. Comm.*, 62–1 USTC ¶9496, 9 AFTR2d 1579, 304 F.2d 48 (CA–9, 1962).

KEY TERMS

Accumulated earnings and profits, 4–5

Constructive dividend, 4–11

Current earnings and profits, 4–5

Earnings and profits (E & P), 4–3

Property dividend, 4–8

Stock dividend, 4–14

Stock rights, 4–15

Unreasonable compensation, 4–12

PROBLEM MATERIALS

DISCUSSION QUESTIONS

1. How are regular distributions of a corporation's earnings taxed to a shareholder?

2. What is meant by the term *earnings and profits?*

3. In determining Wren Corporation's current E & P for 1997, how should the following transactions be handled in adjusting taxable income?
   a. Collection of an installment note receivable resulting from a 1996 sale. (Wren Corporation did not elect out of the installment method.)
   b. An NOL carryover from 1996 fully used in 1997.
   c. An excess capital loss for 1997 that is not carried back.
   d. Collection on a key employee life insurance policy upon the death of an executive.
   e. Excess charitable contribution deduction on a donation made in 1997.

4. Describe the effect of a distribution in a year when the distributing corporation has
   a. A deficit in accumulated E & P and a positive amount in current E & P.
   b. A positive amount in accumulated E & P and a deficit in current E & P.
   c. A deficit in both current and accumulated E & P.
   d. A positive amount in both current and accumulated E & P.

5. How do gains and losses from property transactions affect the determination of E & P?

6. Five years ago, a corporation determined its current E & P to be $100,000. In the current year, it makes a distribution of $200,000 to its shareholders. The IRS contends that the current E & P of the corporation five years ago really was $150,000.
   a. Can the IRS successfully make this contention?
   b. What difference would the additional $50,000 in E & P make?

7. A calendar year corporation has no accumulated E & P but expects to earn current E & P for the year. A cash distribution to its shareholders on January 1 should result in a return of capital. Comment on the validity of this assumption.

8. Why would a corporation distribute a property dividend?

9. Warbler Corporation has an excess of unimproved real estate. It desires to distribute $200,000 in value to its shareholders as a property dividend. Available choices are as follows: parcel A (basis of $150,000); parcel B (basis of $200,000); and parcel C (basis of $250,000). If all parcels have a value of $200,000, what do you suggest?

10. A corporation is considering making a property distribution to its shareholders. If appreciated property is to be used, does its classification (e.g., depreciable property subject to recapture versus long-term capital asset) matter to the distributing corporation?

11. Discuss the effects of the following in generating or adding to a deficit in E & P:
    a. A dividend distribution by the corporation.
    b. An operating loss of the corporation.

12. Yellow Corporation distributes $50,000 to each of its three shareholders, Ted, Tiffany, and Maize Corporation. Discuss the issues involved in determining how the distribution is treated tax-wise both to the shareholders and to Yellow Corporation.

13. Must a corporation's distribution to its shareholders meet the legal requirements of a dividend as set forth by applicable state law, be formally declared, or be issued pro rata to all shareholders to be treated as a dividend for tax purposes? Discuss.

14. Tina is the president and sole shareholder of Buff Corporation. She is paid a salary of $250,000 in the current year. Buff Corporation also advances her $50,000 as an interest-free loan. What are the tax issues?

15. Crow Corporation declares a dividend permitting its shareholders to elect to receive $20 per share or 4 additional shares of Crow stock for every 10 shares currently held. Crow has only common stock outstanding. Crow stock has a fair market value of $50 per share. All shareholders elect to receive stock. Your client, Crow Corporation, asks whether the shareholders have any taxable gain on the receipt of the stock. Prepare a letter to your client and a memo for the file. Crow's address is 1400 Boone Street, Baton Rouge, LA 70803.

16. Flamingo Corporation has two classes of common stock outstanding, Class A and Class B. During the current year, Flamingo distributes a preferred stock dividend to the Class A shareholders and a common stock dividend to the Class B shareholders. Is either of these distributions a taxable dividend to the shareholders? Explain.

17. When are stock dividends taxable?

18. How are nontaxable stock rights handled for tax purposes? Taxable stock rights?

19. Whether compensation paid to a corporate employee is reasonable is a question of fact to be determined from the surrounding circumstances. How would the resolution of this problem be affected by each of the following factors?
    a. The employee is not a shareholder but is related to the sole owner of the corporate employer.
    b. The shareholder-employee never completed high school.
    c. The shareholder-employee is a full-time college student.
    d. The shareholder-employee was underpaid for her services during the formative period of the corporate employer.
    e. The corporate employer pays a nominal dividend each year.
    f. Year-end bonuses are paid to all shareholder-employees.

20. Aqua Corporation has both individual and corporate shareholders. The individual shareholders want profits paid out in a form deductible to Aqua Corporation (e.g., interest, rents) and not as dividends. Would the corporate shareholders be similarly motivated? Why or why not?

21. Falcon Corporation is wholly owned by Sharon. Corporation employees and their annual salaries include Sharon, $150,000; Dawn, Sharon's daughter, $60,000; Rick, Sharon's son, $50,000; and Troy, $30,000. Falcon's operation is shared about equally between Sharon and Troy (an unrelated party). Dawn and Rick are full-time college students at a university about 200 miles away. Falcon Corporation has substantial E & P but has not distributed a dividend in the past six years. Discuss problems related to Falcon's salary arrangement.

22. Leroy, the president and sole shareholder of Azure Corporation, is paid an annual salary of $250,000 by the corporation. Leroy would like to draw funds from the corporation but is concerned that additional salary payments might cause the IRS to contend his salary is unreasonable. Leroy does not want the corporation to distribute any dividends to him. He wants to contribute $100,000 to his alma mater to establish

scholarships for needy students. If Leroy makes a pledge to the university to provide $100,000 for scholarships, would he have a problem if Azure Corporation paid the pledge on his behalf? Explain.

PROBLEMS

23. At the beginning of the year, Crane Corporation (a calendar year taxpayer) has accumulated E & P of $75,000. Its current E & P is $45,000. During the year, Crane Corporation distributes $135,000 ($67,500 each) to its equal shareholders, Pat and Chris. Pat has a basis of $12,000 in her stock, and Chris has a basis of $3,000 in his stock. How will the $135,000 distribution be treated for tax purposes?

24. In 1997, Gull Corporation received dividend income of $200,000 from a corporation in which it holds a 10% interest. Gull also received interest income of $40,000 from municipal bonds. The municipality used the proceeds from the sale of the bonds to construct a needed facility to house city documents and to provide office space for several city officials. Gull borrowed funds to purchase the municipal bonds and paid $20,000 in interest on the loan in 1997. Gull's taxable income exclusive of the items noted above was $150,000.
    a. What is Gull Corporation's taxable income for 1997 after considering the dividend income, the interest from the municipal bonds, and the interest paid on the indebtedness to purchase the municipals?
    b. What is Gull Corporation's E & P as of December 31, 1997, if its E & P account balance was $90,000 as of January 1, 1997?

25. Orange Corporation has a deficit in E & P of $90,000 on January 1, 1997. Without considering a land sale in 1997, Orange has a tax loss of $180,000 that increases the deficit in E & P by that amount. On November 15, 1997, the corporation sold a tract of land in consideration of a $1,800,000 note to be paid in five equal installments; the first installment is due and payable on December 15, 1998. The land had a tax basis to Orange of $450,000. Because Orange did not elect out of the installment method, it did not include any of the $1,350,000 gain on the sale of the land in its taxable income for 1997. If Orange distributes $200,000 to its shareholder, Nick, on December 31, 1997, how must Nick report the $200,000 for tax purposes? Nick has a basis of $150,000 in his Orange stock.

26. At the beginning of the current year, Stork Corporation (a calendar year taxpayer) has accumulated E & P of $120,000. During the year, the corporation incurs an $160,000 net loss from operations that accrued ratably. On July 1, Stork distributes $80,000 to its sole individual shareholder. How much of the $80,000 is dividend income?

27. Complete the following schedule for each case. Assume the shareholder has ample basis in the stock investment.

	Accumulated E & P Beginning of Year	Current E & P	Cash Distributions (All on Last Day of Year)	Amount Taxable	Return of Capital
a.	$ 80,000	($ 20,000)	$100,000	$	$
b.	(100,000)	60,000	80,000		
c.	60,000	100,000	140,000		
d.	120,000	(40,000)	90,000		

e. Same as (d), except the distribution of $90,000 is made on June 30 and the corporation uses the calendar year for tax purposes.

28. Complete the following schedule for each case. Assume the shareholder has ample basis in the stock investment.

	Accumulated E & P Beginning of Year	Current E & P	Cash Distributions (All on Last Day of Year)	Amount Taxable	Return of Capital
a.	($ 70,000)	$ 80,000	$120,000	$ _____	$ _____
b.	40,000	50,000	100,000	_____	_____
c.	(180,000)	100,000	60,000	_____	_____
d.	120,000	(110,000)	80,000	_____	_____
e.	Same as (d), except the distribution of $80,000 is made on June 30 and the corporation uses the calendar year for tax purposes.			_____	_____

29. Dana, the sole shareholder of Tern Corporation, had a basis of $30,000 in Tern stock that he sold to Eli on July 30, 1997, for $180,000. Tern had accumulated E & P of $75,000 on January 1, 1997, and current E & P (for 1997) of $60,000. During 1997, Tern made the following distributions: $120,000 cash to Dana on July 1, 1997, and $120,000 cash to Eli on December 30, 1997. How will the distributions be taxed to Dana and to Eli? What gain will Dana recognize on the sale of his stock to Eli?

30. Indicate in each of the following independent situations the effect on taxable income and E & P, stating the amount of any increase (or decrease) as a result of the transaction. (In determining the effect on E & P, assume E & P has already been increased by current taxable income.)

Transaction	Taxable Income Increase (Decrease)	E & P Increase (Decrease)
a. Receipt of $15,000 tax-exempt income	_____	_____
b. Payment of $15,150 Federal income taxes	_____	_____
c. Collection of $100,000 on life insurance policy on corporate president (assume no cash surrender value)	_____	_____
d. Charitable contribution, $30,000, $20,000 allowable as a deduction in the current tax year	_____	_____
e. Deduction of remaining $10,000 charitable contribution in succeeding year	_____	_____
f. Realized gain on involuntary conversion of $200,000 ($30,000 of gain is recognized)	_____	_____

31. Indicate in each of the following independent situations the effect on taxable income and E & P, stating the amount of any increase (or decrease) as a result of the transaction.

(In determining the effect on E & P, assume E & P has already been increased by current taxable income.)

Transaction	Taxable Income Increase (Decrease)	E & P Increase (Decrease)
a. Intangible drilling costs incurred on January 1 of the current tax year and deductible from current taxable income in the amount of $50,000		
b. Sale of unimproved real estate, basis of $200,000, fair market value of $800,000 (no election out of installment method; payments in year of sale total $40,000)		
c. Accelerated depreciation of $70,000 (straight-line would have been $40,000)		
d. Sale of equipment to 100%-owned corporation (adjusted basis was $120,000 and selling price was $50,000)		

32. Swift Corporation distributes a vacant lot (basis of $120,000, fair market value of $360,000) to its sole shareholder, Walt. The lot is subject to a liability of $368,000, which Walt assumes. Swift has E & P of $150,000 prior to the distribution.
    a. What gain, if any, does Swift recognize on the distribution?
    b. What is the amount of Walt's dividend income on the distribution?

33. Starling Corporation, with E & P of $300,000, distributes property worth $70,000, adjusted basis of $100,000, to Raven, a corporate shareholder. The property is subject to a liability of $15,000, which Raven assumes.
    a. What is the amount of dividend income to Raven?
    b. What is Raven's basis in the property it received?
    c. How does the distribution affect Starling Corporation's E & P account?

34. At the beginning of the current year, Dove Corporation (a calendar year taxpayer) has accumulated E & P of $40,000. During the year, Dove incurs a $30,000 loss from operations that accrued ratably. On July 1, Dove distributes $35,000 in cash to Marv, its sole shareholder. How will the $35,000 be taxed to Marv?

35. Snipe Corporation has E & P of $100,000. It distributes equipment with a fair market value of $90,000 (adjusted basis of $20,000) to its sole shareholder, Mary. The land is subject to a liability of $15,000, which Mary assumes. What are the tax consequences to Snipe Corporation and to Mary?

36. Gold Corporation distributes land with an adjusted basis of $100,000 and a fair market value of $60,000 to its shareholder, Homer. What are the tax consequences to Gold Corporation and to Homer?

37. Silver Corporation has two equal shareholders, Bonnie and Ann. Bonnie acquired her Silver stock three years ago by transferring property worth $500,000, basis of $100,000, for 50 shares of the stock. Ann acquired 50 shares in Silver Corporation two years ago by transferring property worth $520,000, basis of $50,000. Silver Corporation's accumulated E & P as of January 1 of the current year is $210,000. On March 1 of the current year, the corporation distributed to Bonnie property worth $100,000, basis to Silver of

$20,000. It distributed cash of $100,000 to Ann. On July 1 of the current year, Ann sold her stock to Bob for $700,000. On December 1 of the current year, Silver distributed cash of $50,000 each to Bob and to Bonnie. What are the tax issues?

38. A corporation sells property (adjusted basis of $200,000, fair market value of $180,000) to its sole shareholder for $160,000. How much loss can the corporation deduct as a result of this transaction? What is the effect on the corporation's E & P for the year of sale?

39. Shrike Corporation has beginning E & P of $300,000. Its current taxable income is $150,000. During the year, it distributed land worth $500,000, adjusted basis of $150,000, to Paul, its shareholder. Paul assumes a liability on the property in the amount of $50,000. The corporation had tax-exempt interest income of $10,000 and received $200,000 on a term life insurance policy on the death of a corporate officer. Premiums on the policy for the year were $5,000.
    a. What is the amount of taxable income to Paul?
    b. What is the E & P of Shrike Corporation after the property distribution?
    c. What is Paul's tax basis in the property received?

    (Note: Disregard the effect of the corporate income tax.)

40. Peregrine Corporation owns 15% of the stock of Gray Corporation. Gray Corporation, with E & P of $80,000 on December 20, 1997, distributes land with a fair market value of $30,000 and a basis of $60,000 to Peregrine Corporation. The land is subject to a liability of $20,000, which Peregrine assumes.
    a. How is Peregrine Corporation taxed on the distribution?
    b. What is Gray Corporation's E & P after the distribution?

41. Bluebird Corporation, a cash basis, calendar year taxpayer, had the following income and expenses in the current year: income from services rendered, $80,000; salaries paid to employees, $40,000; tax-exempt interest, $10,000; dividends from a corporation in which Bluebird holds a 5% interest, $16,000; STCL on the sale of stock, $12,000; estimated Federal income taxes paid, $4,600. Bluebird Corporation purchased five-year MACRS property in the current year for $56,000; no § 179 election was made. The property has a seven-year class life. Determine taxable income and E & P for Bluebird Corporation.

42. At the beginning of its taxable year 1997, Green Corporation had E & P of $200,000. Green Corporation sold an asset at a loss of $200,000 on June 30, 1997. Green incurred a total deficit of $220,000, which includes the $200,000 loss on the sale of the asset, for the calendar year 1997. Assume Green made a distribution of $60,000 to its sole individual shareholder on July 1, 1997. How will the shareholder be taxed on the $60,000?

43. Indigo Corporation had a deficit of $60,000 in E & P at the beginning of its taxable year 1997. Its net profits for the period January 1, 1997, through June 30, 1997, were $75,000, but its E & P for the entire taxable year was only $5,000. Indigo Corporation made a distribution of $15,000 to its sole individual shareholder on December 31, 1997. How will the shareholder be taxed on the distribution?

44. The stock in White Corporation is owned equally by Fred and Red Corporation. On January 1, 1997, White had a deficit of $150,000. Its current E & P (for taxable year 1997) was $105,000. In 1997, White distributed cash of $45,000 to both Fred and Red Corporation. How will Fred and Red Corporation be taxed on the distribution? What is the accumulated E & P of White Corporation at the end of 1997?

45. Cardinal Corporation is the sole shareholder of Quail Corporation. Plover Corporation is a prospective buyer of Quail Corporation but can only pay $300,000 of the $350,000 price Cardinal wants for its stock in Quail. Quail Corporation has $50,000 cash on hand that it distributes to Cardinal Corporation. Cardinal then sells its stock to Plover Corporation for $300,000. Your client, Cardinal Corporation, asks you the tax consequences to it on the sale if it has a basis of $100,000 in the Quail Corporation stock.

(Assume Quail Corporation, has sufficient E & P to cover the $50,000 distribution.) Prepare a letter to your client and a memo for the file. Cardinal's address is 1010 Keystone Street, Middleton, PA 17057.

46. Wren Corporation loans its principal shareholder, James, $200,000 on January 3, 1997. The loan is interest-free. Assume the Federal rate is 10%. What are the tax consequences to Wren Corporation and to James with respect to the interest-free loan?

47. Myrtle Adams paid $180,000 for 15 shares of stock in Petrel Corporation five years ago. In November 1996, she received a nontaxable stock dividend of 5 additional shares in Petrel Corporation. She sells the 5 shares in March 1997 for $60,000. What is her gain, and how is it taxed? Prepare a letter to your client and a memo for the file. Myrtle's address is 14009 Pine Street, Dover, DE 19901.

48. Lark Corporation declares a nontaxable dividend payable in rights to subscribe to common stock. One right and $60 entitle the holder to subscribe to one share of stock. One right is issued for each share of stock owned. Karen, a shareholder, owns 100 shares of stock that she purchased two years ago for $3,000. At the date of distribution of the rights, the market value of the stock was $80 per share, and the market value of the rights was $20 per right. Karen received 100 rights. She exercises 60 rights and purchases 60 additional shares of stock. She sells the remaining 40 rights for $750. What are the tax consequences of these transactions to Karen?

49. Partridge Corporation has accumulated E & P of $300,000 as of January 1, 1997. During 1997, it expects to have earnings from operations of $240,000 and to make a cash distribution of $180,000. Partridge Corporation also expects to sell an asset for a loss of $300,000. Thus, it anticipates incurring a deficit of $60,000 for the year. What can Partridge do to cause its shareholders to have the least amount of dividend income?

50. Diver Corporation has a deficit in accumulated E & P of $200,000 as of January 1, 1997. Starting in 1997, Diver Corporation expects to generate annual E & P of $100,000 for the next four years and would like to distribute this amount to its shareholders. How should Diver Corporation distribute the $100,000 over the four-year period (for a total distribution of $400,000) to provide the least amount of dividend income to its shareholders (all individuals)? Prepare a letter to your client, Diver Corporation, and a memo for the file. Diver Corporation's address is 1010 Oak Street, Oldtown, MD 20742.

RESEARCH PROBLEMS

Note: ***West's Federal Taxation on CD-ROM*** *can be used in preparing solutions to the Research Problems. Alternatively, tax research materials contained in a standard tax library can be used.*

Research Problem 1. Wes and Edna entered into a separation agreement providing that Wes would purchase Edna's stock in Bunting Corporation. Wes and Edna were the sole shareholders of Bunting Corporation. In 1995, the court entered a judgment of divorce for Wes and Edna and incorporated their separation agreement, including the provision obligating Wes to purchase Edna's Bunting stock. On the same day, Edna and Bunting Corporation executed an agreement in which Bunting agreed to redeem Edna's stock. Bunting Corporation made one payment in redemption of Edna's stock in 1995 and a final payment in 1996. In 1996, the court that had entered the original judgment of divorce entered an order correcting the original judgment. The court changed the terms of the judgment requiring Wes to purchase Edna's Bunting stock and provided instead that Bunting Corporation agreed to redeem Edna's stock. In 1997, in auditing their returns, the IRS contended that the redemption of Edna's stock constituted a constructive dividend to Wes and increased his taxable income in 1995 and 1996 by the amount of the redemption payments paid to Edna in those two years. Wes seeks your advice. Do the payments constitute taxable income to him?

Research Problem 2. Jaime Martinez is the president and majority shareholder of Black Corporation. During 1994, Jaime was paid a salary of $50,000 and received a year-end bonus of $200,000. Upon audit of Black Corporation in 1995, the IRS disallowed $150,000

of the amount paid to Jaime as being unreasonable. Under a repayment agreement, Jaime reimbursed Black Corporation for the $150,000 in 1996. On his 1994 return, Jaime had included the $150,000 in gross income. On his 1996 return, he deducted none of the repayment but elected the option set forth in § 1341(a)(5). Thus, Jaime claimed a credit for the amount of tax that was generated by the inclusion of the $150,000 on his 1994 return. Upon audit of his 1996 return in 1997, the IRS did not accept the credit approach but did permit a deduction of $150,000 for 1996. Because Jaime was in a higher tax bracket in 1994, a deficiency resulted for 1996. Jaime comes to you, a senior for a CPA firm, for advice. Should he challenge the tax deficiency for tax year 1996?

a. Prepare a letter for Jaime as to his tax status. Jaime's address is 509 Maple Street, Camden, NJ 08102.

b. Prepare a memo for your firm's client files.

Research Problem 3. Mark, the principal shareholder of Condor Corporation, diverted sums totaling $60,000 from the corporation during tax year 1996. Upon audit of Mark's return, the IRS contended these sums were taxable income to Mark under § 61 of the Code. Mark disagrees, stating that such sums represent constructive dividends and are taxable only to the extent of Condor's E & P, which Mark argues had a deficit in 1995. The IRS contends that even if § 61 does not apply, the $60,000 would still be taxable income because Condor had income in 1996. Condor Corporation is on the cash basis. It had a deficit in its E & P account as of January 1, 1996. However, it had E & P of $65,000 in 1996. Its income tax liability for 1996 was $31,500. The IRS argues that $31,500 cannot be a charge against current E & P because the tax was not paid until 1997 and the corporation was on the cash basis. Consequently, the $60,000 would be taxable income to Mark in 1996, regardless of whether it is income under § 61 or under § 301. Mark comes to you for advice. What advice would you give him?

Partial list of research aids:
Charles Leaf, 33 T.C. 1093 (1960).
Weir v. Comm., 60–2 USTC ¶9763, 6 AFTR2d 5770, 283 F.2d 675 (CA–6, 1960).

Research Problem 4. Aaron Tuttle is the sole shareholder of Crimson Corporation, a profitable wholesaler of medical equipment and supplies. Aaron's daughter, Carol, majored in fashion design while in college and is currently unemployed. When the sole proprietor of a local fabric retail store is killed in an auto accident, the business is offered for sale by his estate. Carol is certain that she can operate the store successfully and convinces Aaron to this effect. To satisfy his daughter, Aaron proceeds as follows:

• Forms Azure Corporation with a $10,000 cash investment. Aaron makes himself chairman of the board and appoints Carol as CEO.

• Azure purchases the retail store from the estate of the owner for $100,000, using $10,000 cash as a downpayment and issuing its notes for the balance.

• Azure Corporation borrows $50,000 from Eagle Savings Association, pledging its assets as collateral for the loan. The funds are needed to meet operating expenses.

For the first year of its existence, Azure Corporation has an operating loss and ultimately is faced with the prospect of defaulting on its debt obligations. The creditors agree to refinance Azure's debt but only on condition that Aaron personally guarantee the loans. When losses continue and Azure still cannot service the debts, its creditors threaten action. Azure Corporation then borrows $300,000 from Crimson Corporation by issuing a note payable on demand and carrying an interest rate of 2% in excess of prime. Azure uses the loan funds to pay off all of its creditors and to satisfy the working capital needs of the business.

When Azure's financial situation further deteriorates, Crimson Corporation demands payment on its note. Unable to pay, Azure turns over its assets (realizable value of $35,000) to Crimson and ceases doing business. On its income tax return for the year, Crimson Corporate claims a bad debt deduction of $265,000.

Comment on the tax positions of Crimson Corporation and Aaron Tuttle.

Use the tax resources of the internet to address the following questions. Do not restrict your search to the World Wide Web, but include a review of newsgroups and general reference materials, practitioner sites and resources, primary sources of the tax law, chat rooms and discussion groups, and other opportunities.

Research Problem 5. Just how common is it to receive a dividend distribution? Are dividends concentrated in the companies traded on the New York Stock Exchange, or do closely held corporations pay dividends with the same frequency and at the same rates? Financial institutions and observers are acutely interested in these issues. Search for comments on such questions at various commercial web sites as well as one or two academic journals or newsgroups.

Research Problem 6. Financial planners have begun to tout Dividend Reinvestment Plans (DRIPs) as an effective way to hold down the costs of building a portfolio. Outline the key advantages and disadvantages of DRIPs, by reviewing analyses of them provided by investor organizations, brokerage houses, and corporations providing such plans themselves.

Research Problem 7. Which techniques have become popular in the last year or two as a means of working around the § 162(m) limitation on deductions for executive compensation?

CORPORATIONS: REDEMPTIONS AND LIQUIDATIONS

LEARNING OBJECTIVES

After completing Chapter 5, you should be able to:

1. Identify the various stock redemptions that cause payments to shareholders to be treated as sales or exchanges of stock rather than as dividend income.

2. Recognize that some redemption transactions do not qualify for sale or exchange treatment.

3. Understand the tax consequences when a parent corporation distributes stock and securities of its subsidiary.

4. Master the tax laws governing corporate liquidations and their impact on both the corporation and its shareholders.

5. Identify tax planning opportunities available to minimize the income tax impact in stock redemptions and in the complete liquidation of a corporation.

Chapter 4 considered the tax treatment of corporate distributions that represent a return *from* a shareholder's investment. Such distributions are taxed as dividends to the extent of the earnings and profits (E & P) of the corporation. For noncorporate shareholders, corporate earnings are subject to double taxation, first to the corporation and then as dividend income to the shareholders when the earnings are distributed. Shareholders obviously would prefer that such distributions not be taxed as dividends. Therefore, one aspect of tax planning involves considering alternatives to corporate distributions being treated as dividends.

Are there acceptable alternatives? One possibility is a qualified stock redemption. Another is a stock spin-off or split-off. Both these possibilities are discussed in this chapter.

Corporate distributions to noncorporate shareholders that are a return *of* a shareholder's investment, such as qualifying stock redemptions and complete liquidations, receive more favorable tax treatment than distributions that are a return *from* the shareholder's investment. Distributions that are a return *of* the shareholder's investment are treated as a sale or exchange of the investment. As a result, the shareholder recognizes income only to the extent that the amount realized exceeds the basis in the stock. An additional advantage of sale or exchange treatment is that any income recognized generally is treated as capital gain.

While a noncorporate shareholder receives less favorable tax treatment from a dividend distribution than from a qualifying stock redemption or a complete liquidation, the reverse is generally the case for a corporate shareholder. Because of the dividends received deduction for corporate shareholders, a corporate shareholder would report only a small portion of dividend income as taxable income. Thus, a corporate shareholder normally receives *more* favorable tax treatment from a dividend distribution than would result from a qualifying stock redemption or complete liquidation. Consequently, tax planning to provide alternatives to dividend treatment must consider the preferences of corporate shareholders as well.

Because corporate distributions that represent a return of a shareholder's investment have many tax ramifications, the transactions should be planned with a full understanding of those tax consequences. This chapter examines the tax implications of corporate distributions that are not dividend distributions.

EXAMPLE 1

Debra, who is in need of cash for personal purposes, owns a substantial portion of the stock of Brown Corporation. The logical place for Debra to acquire this needed cash is from Brown. Consequently, she causes the corporation to distribute $50,000 to her in exchange for stock in Brown that she purchased several years ago for $35,000. Debra continues to own stock in the corporation. If the distribution is treated as a return *from* her investment, Debra would report a dividend of $50,000, assuming ample E & P. On the other hand, if the transaction is treated as a return *of* her investment, the redemption is treated as a sale or exchange, and a gain of $15,000 ($50,000 − $35,000) is recognized. If the stock is a capital asset in Debra's hands, the gain is given beneficial capital treatment. Alternatively, if Debra decides to completely liquidate the corporation to obtain the cash she needs, this return *of* her investment would be taxed to her in the same manner as a qualifying redemption: gain or loss is recognized in an amount equal to the difference between the amount realized and her adjusted basis in the stock. ▼

STOCK REDEMPTIONS—IN GENERAL

1 LEARNING OBJECTIVE
Identify the various stock redemptions that cause payments to shareholders to be treated as sales or exchanges of stock rather than as dividend income.

In a **stock redemption**, a corporation purchases its stock from a shareholder. A stock redemption involves an exchange of a shareholder's stock in the corporation for property of the corporation. Except for the fact that the shareholder is selling the stock back to the corporation, the sale resembles a sale of the stock to an outsider, or third party. While a sale of stock to an outsider is invariably given sale or exchange treatment, only a *qualifying* stock redemption will be treated as a sale for tax purposes.

A stock redemption may have the same effect as a dividend. For example, if a shareholder owns all the stock of a corporation and sells a portion of that stock to the corporation, the shareholder's ownership percentage in the corporation will not change. After the redemption, the shareholder still owns all the outstanding stock of the corporation. In this situation, the stock redemption resembles a dividend distribution and is taxed as such.

Stock redemptions occur for numerous reasons. A shareholder may want to retire. Rather than the other shareholders purchasing the retiree's stock, the corporation simply redeems all of the shareholder's stock. Similarly, when a shareholder dies, the corporation may purchase the shareholder's stock from the estate. In both cases, having the corporation provide the funds to purchase the stock relieves the remaining shareholders of the need to use their own money. In addition, stock redemptions often occur with respect to property settlements in divorce actions. For example, in a divorce action involving joint ownership of corporate shares, one spouse will usually wind up owning all the stock. By having the corporation redeem the other spouse's shares, the spouse who remains as a shareholder is relieved of the need to obtain funds for the buyout. As a result, the departing spouse receives a part of the property settlement from the corporation.

Stock Redemptions—Sale or Exchange Treatment

A qualifying stock redemption provides *sale or exchange* treatment for the shareholder. Sale or exchange treatment permits a shareholder to recover his or her capital investment tax-free and permits the noncorporate shareholder to avoid dividend consequences. Generally, such treatment results in capital gain or loss to the shareholder, which is calculated by subtracting the redeemed stock's adjusted basis from the sum of any money received plus the fair market value of any property received. The shareholder's basis in any property received in exchange for his or her stock in the corporation is equal to the fair market value of the property.

A capital gain is beneficial for a noncorporate shareholder who is in the highest tax brackets as the tax is limited to 28 percent of the gain recognized, assuming the stock meets the long-term holding requirement. The capital gain also provides a benefit to a shareholder who has substantial capital losses.

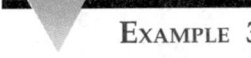

EXAMPLE 2   Abby, a corporate executive, is in the 39.6% tax bracket. She acquired stock in Bluejay Corporation five years ago for $100,000. In the current year, Bluejay Corporation redeems her shares for $200,000. If the redemption qualifies for sale or exchange treatment, Abby will have a long-term capital gain of $100,000 [$200,000 (redemption amount) − $100,000 (cost of the shares)]. Her income tax liability on the $100,000 capital gain will be $28,000 ($100,000 × 28%). If the $200,000 stock redemption does not qualify as a sale or exchange, it will be treated as dividend income, and Abby's tax liability will be $79,200 ($200,000 × 39.6%). Thus, Abby will save $51,200 ($79,200 − $28,000) in income taxes if the corporate payment is a qualifying stock redemption. ▼

EXAMPLE 3   Assume Abby, in Example 2, has a capital loss carryover of $80,000 in the current tax year. If the corporate payment is a qualifying stock redemption, Abby can offset the entire $80,000 capital loss against her $100,000 capital gain. As a result, only $20,000 of the gain will be taxed, and her tax liability will be only $5,600 ($20,000 × 28%). On the other hand, if the corporate payment does not qualify for sale or exchange treatment, the entire $200,000 will be taxed at 39.6%. In addition, assuming no other capital gains in the current year, Abby will be able to deduct only $3,000 of the $80,000 capital loss carryover to offset her other (ordinary) income. ▼

EXAMPLE 4   Assume Abby, in Example 2, is a corporation, that the stock represents a 40% ownership in Bluejay Corporation, and that Abby has corporate taxable income of $350,000 before the payment from Bluejay. If the corporate payment is a qualifying stock redemption for tax purposes, Abby will have a capital gain of $100,000 that will be subject to tax at 34% or $34,000. On the other hand, if the $200,000 payment is a dividend, Abby will have a dividends received deduction of $160,000 ($200,000 × 80%) so that only $40,000 of the payment will be taxed. Consequently, Abby's tax liability on the payment would be only $13,600 ($40,000 × 34%). ▼

To determine whether a redemption exists for tax purposes, a taxpayer must look to the Code. The label given to the transaction by the parties *or* by state law is not controlling. One Code section provides that if a corporation redeems its stock pursuant to one of four special rules, the redemption is treated as a sale or exchange of a shareholder's stock.[1] Another section provides that certain distribu-

---

[1] § 302(a).

tions of property to a shareholder in exchange for stock included in a decedent's estate are treated as qualifying stock redemptions.[2]

HISTORICAL BACKGROUND AND OVERVIEW

Under earlier law, stock redemptions that constituted ordinary taxable dividends were distinguished from those qualifying for capital gain by the so-called *dividend equivalency rule*. When a redemption was essentially equivalent to a dividend, it did not qualify for sale or exchange treatment. The entire amount received by the shareholder was subject to taxation as ordinary income to the extent of the corporation's E & P.

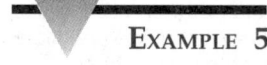

EXAMPLE 5

Adam owns 100% of the stock of White Corporation. White has E & P of $50,000. Adam sells one-half of his shares to the corporation for $50,000. His basis in the stock he sells is $10,000, and he has held the stock for five years. If the sale of the stock to White Corporation were treated as a qualifying stock redemption, Adam would have a long-term capital gain of $40,000. However, in reality, the distribution is essentially equivalent to a dividend because Adam's percentage of ownership in the corporation has not changed. Therefore, he is deemed to have received a taxable dividend of $50,000. ▼

Current Code provisions are designed to eliminate the uncertainty and subjectivity that resulted from reliance on the dividend equivalency rule. Under

[2]§ 303.

the Code, the following five major types of stock redemptions qualify for sale or exchange treatment and therefore avoid dividend income consequences:

- Distributions not essentially equivalent to a dividend (subsequently referred to as not essentially equivalent redemptions).
- Distributions substantially disproportionate in terms of shareholder effect (subsequently referred to as disproportionate redemptions).
- Distributions in complete termination of a shareholder's interest (subsequently referred to as complete termination redemptions).
- Distributions in partial liquidation of a corporation, but only to a noncorporate shareholder when (1) the distribution is not essentially equivalent to a dividend or (2) an active business is terminated (subsequently referred to as partial liquidations).
- Distributions to pay a shareholder's death taxes (subsequently referred to as redemptions to pay death taxes).

STOCK ATTRIBUTION RULES

A stock redemption that qualifies for sale or exchange treatment generally must result in a substantial reduction in a shareholder's ownership in the corporation. If this does not occur, proceeds received for a redemption of the shareholder's stock are taxed as ordinary dividend income. In determining whether a shareholder's interest has substantially decreased, the stock ownership of certain related parties is attributed to the shareholder whose stock is redeemed.[3] Thus, one should consider the stock **attribution** rules along with the stock redemption provisions. Under these stock attribution rules, related parties are defined to include immediate family, specifically, spouses, children, grandchildren, and parents. Attribution also takes place *from* and *to* partnerships, estates, trusts, and corporations (50 percent or more ownership required in the case of regular corporations). Exhibit 5–1 summarizes the relevant stock attribution rules.

▼ **EXHIBIT 5–1**
Stock Attribution Rules

	Deemed or Constructive Ownership
• Individual/family	Stock owned by the spouse, children, grandchildren, and parents (not siblings or grandparents) is considered to be owned by the individual.
• Partnership	A partner is deemed to be the owner of shares owned by a partnership to the extent of the partner's proportionate share in the partnership.
	Stock of a partner is deemed to be owned in full by a partnership.
• Estate or trust	A beneficiary or heir is deemed to be the owner of shares owned by an estate or trust to the extent of the beneficiary or heir's proportionate interest in the estate or trust.
	Stock of a beneficiary or heir is deemed to be owned in full by an estate or trust.
• Corporation	Stock owned by a corporation is considered to be owned proportionately by any shareholder owning 50% or more of the corporation's stock.
	All stock owned by a shareholder who owns 50% or more of a corporation is considered to be owned by the corporation.

---

[3] § 318.

EXAMPLE 6

Larry owns 30% of the stock in Blue Corporation, the other 70% being held by his children. For purposes of the stock attribution rules, Larry is treated as owning 100% of the stock in Blue Corporation. He owns 30% directly and, because of the family attribution rules, 70% indirectly. ▼

EXAMPLE 7

Chris owns 50% of the stock in Gray Corporation. The other 50% is owned by a partnership in which Chris has a 20% interest. Chris is deemed to own 60% of Gray Corporation: 50% directly and, because of the partnership interest, 10% indirectly. ▼

As discussed later, the *family* attribution rules (refer to Example 6) *may* not apply to stock redemptions in complete termination of a shareholder's interest. In addition, these stock attribution rules do not apply to stock redemptions to pay death taxes.

NOT ESSENTIALLY EQUIVALENT REDEMPTIONS

Section 302(b)(1) provides that a redemption qualifies for sale or exchange treatment if it is "not essentially equivalent to a dividend." Few objective tests exist to determine when a redemption is or is not essentially equivalent to a dividend. This provision was added to provide specifically for redemptions of preferred stock because shareholders often have no control over when corporations call in such stock.[4] Some courts concluded that such a redemption would receive capital gain treatment if the redemption had a **business purpose** and was not part of a tax avoidance scheme to bail out dividends at favorable tax rates.[5] However, an unresolved question was whether the stock attribution rules applied to this provision.

The interpretation of the statutory language on this point was settled by the Supreme Court in *U.S. v. Davis*.[6] The Court agreed with the IRS that the redemption of preferred stock in *Davis* was essentially equivalent to a dividend and was taxable as ordinary income because the attribution rules *should* apply. The Court reasoned that the business purpose of the transaction was not controlling in determining whether a stock redemption was "not essentially equivalent to a dividend." It ruled that a redemption would not qualify under this provision unless there was a "meaningful reduction" in the shareholder's ownership in the redeeming corporation.

Based upon this Supreme Court decision, a redemption will qualify as a **not essentially equivalent redemption** only when the shareholder's interest in the redeeming corporation has been meaningfully reduced. As a result, the facts and circumstances of each case must be assessed.[7] A decrease in the redeeming shareholder's voting control appears to be the most significant indicator of a meaningful reduction,[8] but reductions in the rights of redeeming shareholders to share in corporate earnings or to receive corporate assets upon liquidation are also considered.[9] The **meaningful reduction test** is applied whether common stock or preferred stock is being redeemed.

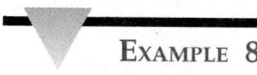

EXAMPLE 8

Pat owns 58% of the common stock of Green Corporation. After a redemption of part of Pat's stock, he owns 51% of the stock of Green. Pat continues to have dominant voting rights in Green; thus, the redemption is treated as essentially equivalent to a dividend, and Pat has ordinary income on the entire amount of the distribution assuming adequate E & P. ▼

---

[4] See S.Rept. No. 1622, 83d Cong., 2d Sess., at 44.
[5] See, for example, *Kerr v. Comm.*, 64–1 USTC ¶9186, 13 AFTR2d 386, 326 F.2d 225 (CA–9, 1964).
[6] 70–1 USTC ¶9289, 25 AFTR2d 70–827, 90 S.Ct. 1041 (USSC, 1970).

[7] Reg. § 1.302–2(b). See *Mary G. Roebling*, 77 T.C. 30 (1981).
[8] See *Jack Paparo*, 71 T.C. 692 (1979), and *Blanche S. Benjamin*, 66 T.C. 1084 (1976).
[9] See *Grabowski Trust*, 58 T.C. 650 (1972).

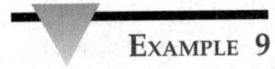

EXAMPLE 9

Brown Corporation redeems 2% of its stock from Maria. Before the redemption, Maria owned 10% of Brown Corporation. In this case, the redemption will likely qualify as not essentially equivalent to a dividend. Maria experiences a reduction in her voting rights, her right to participate in current earnings and accumulated surplus, and her right to share in net assets upon liquidation. ▼

If a redemption is treated as an ordinary dividend, the shareholder's basis in the stock redeemed attaches to the remaining stock (or to stock the shareholder owns constructively).[10]

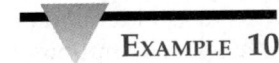

EXAMPLE 10

Floyd and Fran, husband and wife, each own 50 shares in Gray Corporation, representing 100% of the stock of Gray. All the stock was purchased for $50,000. Both Floyd and Fran serve as directors of the corporation. The corporation redeems Floyd's 50 shares. Floyd continues to serve as director of the corporation. The redemption would be treated as a taxable dividend because he constructively owns Fran's stock. Floyd's basis in the stock, $25,000, would attach to Fran's stock. She then would have a basis of $50,000 in the 50 shares she owns in Gray. ▼

DISPROPORTIONATE REDEMPTIONS

A redemption of stock qualifies for capital gain treatment under § 302(b)(2) as a **disproportionate redemption** if two conditions are met:

- The distribution must be substantially disproportionate. To be substantially disproportionate, the shareholder must own, after the distribution, *less than* 80 percent of the interest owned in the corporation before the redemption. For example, if a shareholder owns a 60 percent interest in a corporation that redeems part of the stock, the redemption is substantially disproportionate only if the percentage of ownership after the redemption is less than 48 percent (80 percent of 60 percent).
- The shareholder must own, after the distribution, *less than* 50 percent of the total combined voting power of all classes of stock entitled to vote.

Figure 5–1 provides a graphic presentation of qualifying disproportionate redemptions. In determining a shareholder's percentage of ownership, the attribution rules discussed earlier apply.

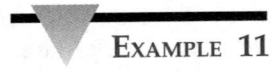

EXAMPLE 11

Bob, Carl, and Dan, unrelated individuals, own 30 shares, 30 shares, and 40 shares, respectively, in Wren Corporation. Wren has E & P of $200,000. The corporation redeems 20 shares of Dan's stock for $30,000. Dan paid $200 a share for the stock two years ago. Dan's ownership in Wren Corporation before and after the redemption is as follows:

	Total Shares	Dan's Ownership	Ownership Percentage	80% of Original Ownership
Before redemption	100	40	40% (40 ÷ 100)	32% (80% × 40%)
After redemption	80	20	25% (20 ÷ 80)*	

*Note that the denominator of the fraction is reduced after the redemption (from 100 to 80).

Dan's 25% ownership after the redemption meets both tests of § 302(b)(2). It is less than 80% of his original ownership and less than 50% of the total voting power. The distribution qualifies as a stock redemption that receives sale or exchange treatment. Therefore, Dan has a long-term capital gain of $26,000 [$30,000 − $4,000 (20 shares × $200)]. ▼

---

[10] Reg. § 1.302–2(c).

▼ **FIGURE 5–1**
Qualifying Disproportionate
Redemptions

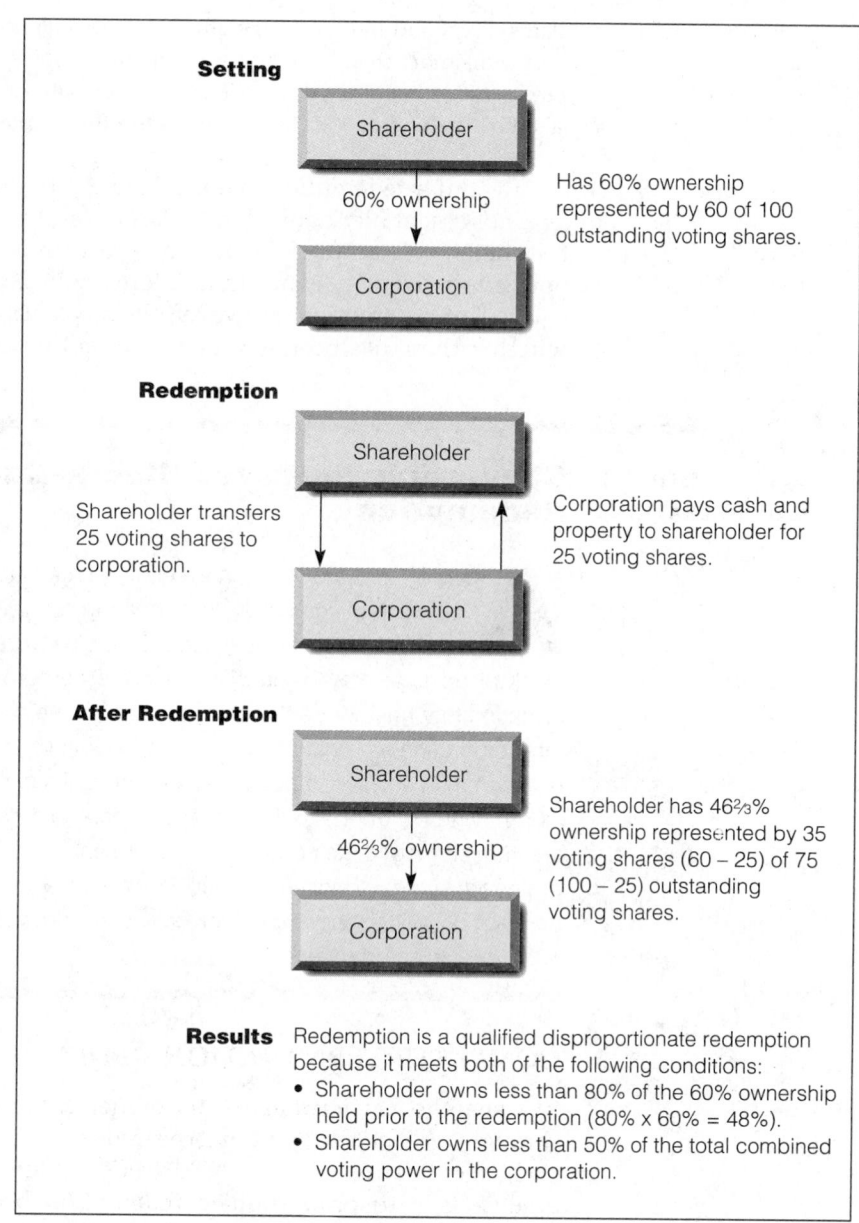

Setting

Shareholder

60% ownership

Corporation

Has 60% ownership
represented by 60 of 100
outstanding voting shares.

Redemption

Shareholder

Shareholder transfers
25 voting shares to
corporation.

Corporation pays cash and
property to shareholder for
25 voting shares.

Corporation

After Redemption

Shareholder

46⅔% ownership

Corporation

Shareholder has 46⅔%
ownership represented by 35
voting shares (60 – 25) of 75
(100 – 25) outstanding
voting shares.

Results   Redemption is a qualified disproportionate redemption
because it meets both of the following conditions:
- Shareholder owns less than 80% of the 60% ownership
  held prior to the redemption (80% x 60% = 48%).
- Shareholder owns less than 50% of the total combined
  voting power in the corporation.

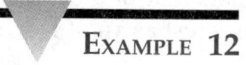

EXAMPLE 12

Assume that Carl and Dan are father and son. The redemption described above would not qualify for sale or exchange treatment because of the effect of the attribution rules. Dan is deemed to own Carl's stock so that after the redemption, Dan would have 50 shares of the total of 80 shares, a more than 50% ownership. He would also fail the 80% test. Dan's ownership in Wren Corporation is computed as follows:

	Total Shares	Dan's Direct Ownership	Carl's Ownership	Dan's Direct and Indirect Ownership	Ownership Percentage	80% of Original Ownership
Before redemption	100	40	30	70	70% (70 ÷ 100)	56% (80% × 70%)
After redemption	80	20	30	50	62.5% (50 ÷ 80)	

Dan's direct and indirect ownership of 62.5% fails to meet either of the tests of § 302(b)(2). Dan owns more than 80% of his original ownership and more than 50% of the voting stock. Thus, the redemption does not qualify for sale or exchange treatment and results in a taxable dividend of $30,000 to Dan, assuming ample E & P exists. ▼

Even if a redemption is not substantially disproportionate, it may still qualify as a not essentially equivalent redemption if it meets the "meaningful reduction" test. Refer to Example 9. A reduction in voting control when the shareholder does not have a majority controlling interest will generally qualify as a not essentially equivalent redemption. However, the stock attribution rules apply in determining whether there has been a reduction in voting control.

ETHICAL CONSIDERATIONS

Convertible Preferred Stock—Conversion versus Redemption

A corporation that does not sell its stock publicly sold some convertible preferred stock a few years ago to a small group of passive investors. The holders of the preferred stock have the option of converting the preferred stock into common stock at anytime they desire. Because the corporation has developed a successful new invention that has not become known outside the company, the board of directors expects the corporation's earnings will grow substantially in the future. The directors, all of whom own common stock in the corporation, would like to redeem the preferred stock so they can stop paying dividends to the preferred shareholders and prevent the preferred shareholders from sharing in the corporation's future earnings. The board of directors votes to pay the preferred shareholders a premium for redeeming their stock and notifies them that the corporation will redeem their stock unless they instruct otherwise. Did the board of directors act in an ethical manner?

COMPLETE TERMINATION REDEMPTIONS

If a shareholder terminates his or her *entire* stock ownership in a corporation through a stock redemption, the redemption generally will qualify for sale or exchange treatment under § 302(b)(3). Often a complete termination may not qualify as a disproportionate redemption because the constructive ownership rules are applied. The difference between the two provisions is that the *family* attribution rules do not apply to a **complete termination redemption.** This favorable treatment occurs only if *both* of the following conditions are met:

- The former shareholder has no interest, other than that of a creditor, in the corporation after the redemption (including an interest as an officer, director, or employee) for at least 10 years.
- The former shareholder files an agreement to notify the IRS of any acquisition within the 10-year period and to retain all necessary records pertaining to the redemption during this time period.

A shareholder can reacquire an interest in the corporation by bequest or inheritance, but in no other manner. The required agreement should be in the form of a separate statement signed by the shareholder and attached to the return for the year in which the redemption occurs. The agreement should state that the shareholder agrees to notify the appropriate District Director within 30 days of reacquiring an interest in the corporation within the 10-year period following the redemption.

EXAMPLE 13   Kevin owns 50% of the stock in Green Corporation while the remaining interest in Green is held as follows: 40% by Wilma (Kevin's wife) and 10% by Helen (a key employee). Green redeems all of Kevin's stock for its fair market value. As a result, Wilma and Helen are the only remaining shareholders, now owning 80% and 20%, respectively. This complete termination qualifies as a sale or exchange rather than as a dividend because the family attribution rules may be waived. If this waiver were not allowed, Kevin would have been deemed the owner of his wife's stock, and the distribution would have been treated as a dividend to the extent of Green's E & P. ▼

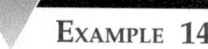

EXAMPLE 14   Assume Kevin, in Example 13, purchases the stock held by Helen seven years after the redemption of his original 50% ownership. The redemption of his original 50% ownership would be reclassified as a dividend, and Kevin would be required to pay additional taxes on the redemption due to this revised treatment. ▼

An estate or trust whose stock is redeemed also may waive family attribution. This occurs if, after the redemption, neither the entity nor its beneficiaries hold a prohibited interest in the corporation or acquire such an interest within the 10-year period. All parties involved must file an agreement to be jointly and severally liable for any taxes due if a reacquisition occurs.[11]

ETHICAL CONSIDERATIONS

A Friend in Need

Nine years ago, Orange Corporation redeemed all of Dan's shares in the corporation. Dan reported the transaction as a qualified complete termination redemption. At that time, Dan's children held the remaining shares in Orange. You were Dan's CPA at the time of the redemption.

Now you learn that Dan is currently unemployed and destitute and that he has received a prohibited interest in Orange Corporation during the current year. As Dan's former CPA and friend, you know that Dan should inform the IRS that the transaction of nine years ago should be recast as a dividend distribution. This will mean that Dan will owe additional income taxes, which will be a real problem because Dan has no cash. How should you proceed?

REDEMPTIONS IN PARTIAL LIQUIDATION

Under § 302(b)(4), a *noncorporate* shareholder is allowed sale or exchange treatment for a **partial liquidation.** A partial liquidation includes either of the following:

- A distribution not essentially equivalent to a dividend.
- A distribution pursuant to the termination of an active business.

To qualify as a partial liquidation, a distribution must be made within the taxable year in which the plan is adopted or within the succeeding taxable year.

Earlier, in the not essentially equivalent redemption discussion, it was noted that the not essentially equivalent to a dividend test is applied at the *shareholder* level. However, in the context of a partial liquidation, the not essentially equivalent to a dividend test looks to the effect of the distribution on the *corporation*.[12] In a partial liquidation, the test requires a *genuine contraction* of the business of the corporation.

---

[11] § 302(c)(2)(C).   [12] § 302(e).

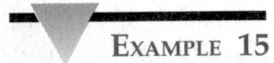

EXAMPLE 15

Cardinal Corporation owned a building with seven floors. Part of the building was rented, and part was used directly in Cardinal's business. A fire destroyed the two top floors, and Cardinal received insurance proceeds in reimbursement for the damage sustained. For business reasons, Cardinal did not rebuild the two floors, but chose to operate on a smaller scale than before the fire. With excess funds collected as insurance proceeds from the fire, the corporation redeemed some stock from its shareholders. The distribution made in exchange for the stock qualified as a partial liquidation.[13] ▼

Applying the genuine contraction of a corporate business concept has proved difficult due to the lack of objective tests. The IRS has ruled that proceeds from the sale of excess inventory distributed to shareholders in exchange for part of their stock will not qualify.[14] Because the genuine contraction of a corporate business test is so subjective, it should not be relied upon without a favorable ruling from the IRS.

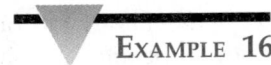

EXAMPLE 16

Red Corporation has been selling a single product to its customers. It loses its major customer, and a severe drop in sales results. The corporation reduces its inventory investment and has substantial cash on hand. It redeems 20% of its outstanding stock from all of its shareholders. Lynn, one of Red's shareholders, receives $10,000 for stock that cost $5,000 two years ago. The distribution will not qualify under § 302 as it is not a disproportionate redemption. Further, Lynn's interest has not been meaningfully reduced or completely terminated. Finally, the distribution does not qualify as a genuine contraction of a corporate business since it relates only to a reduction of excess inventory. Therefore, the $10,000 is a taxable dividend to Lynn, assuming adequate corporate E & P. ▼

In contrast to the genuine contraction test, the complete termination of a business test sets out objective requirements. A distribution will qualify as a partial liquidation under the complete termination of a business test if the following conditions are met:

- The corporation has more than one trade or business, and at least two of the trades or businesses have been in existence for more than five years.
- The corporation terminates one trade or business that has been in existence for more than five years while continuing a remaining trade or business that has been in existence for more than five years.
- The trade or business that was terminated was not acquired in a taxable transaction within the five-year period.

The five-year requirement prevents the bailout of E & P by the acquisition and subsequent distribution of another business within a short period of time.

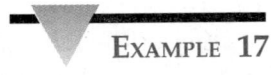

EXAMPLE 17

Bluejay Corporation, the owner and operator of a wholesale grocery business with a substantial amount of excess cash, purchased a freight-hauling concern. Three years later, Bluejay distributes the freight-hauling concern in kind on a pro rata basis to all its shareholders. The distribution does not satisfy the requirements of the complete termination of a business test because Bluejay had not conducted the freight-hauling business for more than five years. Thus, the distribution is treated as a dividend and not as a qualifying partial liquidation. ▼

REDEMPTIONS TO PAY DEATH TAXES

Section 303 provides sale or exchange treatment when an executor sells stock that represents a substantial amount of the estate of a shareholder-decedent back to a

---

[13] *Joseph W. Imler*, 11 T.C. 836 (1948).   [14] Rev.Rul. 60–322, 1960–2 C.B. 118.

corporation. The purpose of such a redemption is to provide the estate with liquidity. A redemption is often necessary because stock in a closely held corporation is generally not marketable. Although the stock could be redeemed under the other redemption rules, the transaction would run the risk of being treated as a dividend because of the attribution rules. The special rule under § 303, allowing sale or exchange treatment in a **redemption to pay death taxes,** alleviates this problem.

The rule providing for sale or exchange treatment in redemptions to pay death taxes is an exception to the redemption rules just discussed. If a stock redemption qualifies as a redemption to pay death taxes, the other redemption provisions do not apply. The distribution will be treated as a sale or exchange regardless of whether it is substantially disproportionate or not essentially equivalent to a dividend. However, this special treatment is limited to the sum of the death taxes and funeral and administration expenses. The redemption must be of stock held by the estate or by heirs who are liable for the death taxes and other administration expenses.

In a redemption to pay death taxes, the redemption price generally equals the basis of the stock. Under the step-up in basis rules, the income tax basis of property owned by a decedent's estate becomes the property's fair market value on the date of death (or alternate valuation date if available and if elected).[15] When this so-called step-up or step-down in basis that occurs at death (see Chapter 18) equals the redemption price, the exchange is free of any income tax consequences to the shareholder's estate.

Section 303 applies to a distribution made with respect to stock of a corporation when the value of the stock in the gross estate of a decedent exceeds 35 percent of the value of the adjusted gross estate. (For a definition of "gross estate" and "adjusted gross estate," see the Glossary of Tax Terms in Appendix C.)

EXAMPLE 18

Juan's adjusted gross estate is $900,000. The death taxes and funeral and administration expenses of the estate total $200,000. Included in the estate is stock in Yellow Corporation valued at $340,000. Juan had acquired the stock years ago at a cost of $60,000. Yellow redeems $200,000 of the stock from Juan's estate. Because the value of the Yellow stock in Juan's estate exceeds the 35% threshold ($340,000 ÷ $900,000 = 37.8%), the redemption qualifies under § 303 as a sale or exchange instead of being treated as a dividend to Juan's estate. The basis rules apply to give the stock a step-up in basis. Consequently, there is no recognized gain on the redemption [$200,000 (amount realized) – $200,000 (stock basis)]. ▼

In determining whether the value of stock in a corporation exceeds 35 percent of the value of the adjusted gross estate of a decedent, the stock of two or more corporations may be treated as the stock of a single corporation. Stock in corporations in which the decedent held a 20 percent or more interest is treated as stock in a single corporation for this purpose.[16]

EXAMPLE 19

The adjusted gross estate of a decedent is $300,000. The gross estate includes stock in Orange and Red Corporations valued at $100,000 and $80,000, respectively. Unless the two corporations are treated as a single corporation, § 303 does not apply to a redemption of the stock of either corporation. Assuming the decedent owned all the stock of Orange Corporation and 80% of the stock of Red, § 303 applies because 20% or more of the value of the stock of both corporations is included in the decedent's estate. The 35% test is met when the stock of Orange and Red is treated as that of a single corporation [($100,000 + $80,000) ÷ $300,000 = 60%]. ▼

---

[15]§ 1014.

[16]§ 303(b)(2)(B).

Qualifying redemptions to pay death taxes also are subject to time limitations. For example, sale or exchange treatment under this rule applies only to redemptions made within 90 days after the expiration of the period of limitations for the assessment of the Federal estate tax. If a petition for a redetermination of an estate tax deficiency is timely filed with the U.S. Tax Court, the applicable period for such a redemption is extended to 60 days after the Court's decision becomes final.[17]

CONCEPT SUMMARY 5–1

Summary of the Redemption Rules

Type of Redemption	Requirements to Qualify
Not essentially equivalent to a dividend	Meaningful reduction in shareholder's voting interest. If less than a majority interest, reduction in interest in assets and E & P also considered.
	Stock attribution rules apply.
Substantially disproportionate	Shareholder's interest in the corporation, after the redemption, must be less than 80% of interest before the redemption and less than 50% of total combined voting power of all classes of stock entitled to vote.
	Stock attribution rules apply.
Complete termination	Entire stock ownership terminated. Former shareholder must have no interest, other than as creditor, in the corporation for at least 10 years and must file agreement with IRS to notify IRS of any disallowed acquisition during 10-year period. Shareholder must retain all necessary records during 10-year period.
	Family stock attribution rules do not apply.
Partial liquidation	Not essentially equivalent to a dividend:
	• Genuine contraction of corporation's business.
	Complete termination of a business:
	• Corporation has more than one trade or business and at least two of the trades or businesses have been in existence for more than 5 years.
	• One of such trades or businesses in existence for at least 5 years is terminated, and other trade or business in existence for at least 5 years is continued.
Redemption to pay death taxes	If value of stock in estate exceeds 35% of value of adjusted gross estate, stock can be redeemed in qualified redemption to extent of death taxes and funeral and administration expenses.
	Stock of two or more corporations may be treated as stock of a single corporation in determining whether the value of the stock exceeds 35% of the value of the adjusted gross estate if decedent held a 20% or more interest in the stock of the corporations.
	Redemption is generally tax-free because tax basis of stock is FMV on date of decedent's death.

---

[17] § 303(b)(1). The latter extension of time applies only to contests in the Tax Court. It does not apply to a petition initiated solely for the purpose of extending the time period under § 303.

EFFECT ON THE CORPORATION REDEEMING ITS STOCK

Having considered the different types of stock redemptions that will produce sale or exchange treatment for a shareholder, what is the tax effect to the corporation redeeming its stock? If the corporation uses property to carry out the redemption, is gain or loss recognized on the distribution? Furthermore, what effect does the redemption have on the corporation's E & P? These matters are discussed in the following paragraphs.

Recognition of Gain or Loss by the Corporation.   Section 311 provides that corporations are taxed on all distributions of appreciated property whether in the form of a property dividend or a stock redemption. Losses, however, are not recognized.[18] When distributed property is subject to a corporate liability, the fair market value of that property is treated as not being less than the amount of the liability.

EXAMPLE 20

To carry out a stock redemption, Bluebird Corporation transfers land (basis of $80,000, fair market value of $300,000) to a shareholder. Bluebird has a recognized gain of $220,000 ($300,000 – $80,000). If the value of the property distributed was less than its adjusted basis, the realized loss would not be recognized. ▼

Because a loss is not recognized by a corporation redeeming its stock, a corporation should not use property that has depreciated in value as consideration in the redemption of a shareholder's stock. Instead, the corporation should sell the property in a taxable transaction in which it can recognize a loss.

Effect on Earnings and Profits.   The E & P account of a corporation is reduced by a qualified stock redemption in an amount not in excess of the ratable share of the E & P of the distributing corporation attributable to the stock redeemed.[19]

EXAMPLE 21

Green Corporation has 100 shares of stock outstanding. It redeems 30 shares for $100,000 at a time when it has paid-in capital of $120,000 and E & P of $150,000. The charge to E & P is 30% of the amount in the E & P account ($45,000), and the remainder of the redemption price ($55,000) is a reduction of the capital account. If instead the 30 shares were redeemed for $40,000, the charge to E & P would be limited to $40,000, the amount paid by the corporation for the stock. ▼

STOCK REDEMPTIONS—NO SALE OR EXCHANGE TREATMENT

2 LEARNING OBJECTIVE
Recognize that some redemption transactions do not qualify for sale or exchange treatment.

Stock redemptions that do not fall under any of the types provided for in the Code are treated as dividend distributions to the extent of E & P. Resourceful taxpayers, however, devised two ways to circumvent the redemption provisions. Both involved structuring what was, in effect, a stock redemption or a dividend distribution as a sale of the stock. The widespread use of these approaches to obtain capital gain treatment in the past led to the enactment of § 306, dealing with preferred stock bailouts, and § 304, dealing with sales of stock to related corporations.

---

[18]§ 311(a).   [19]§ 312(n)(7).

PREFERRED STOCK BAILOUTS

The Problem.   Suppose a shareholder wanted to bail out corporate profits as a long-term capital gain rather than as a dividend. Several possibilities exist:

- A redemption of stock by the corporation in a transaction that qualifies for sale or exchange treatment under one of the redemption rules discussed previously.
- A complete liquidation of the corporation, the rules for which are discussed later in this chapter.
- A sale of stock to third parties.

Generally, a qualifying stock redemption is difficult to carry out successfully in the case of a family corporation unless the shareholder completely terminates his or her interest in the corporation. A redemption of stock to pay death taxes is not available until after the death of a shareholder. Partial liquidations are limited to unique circumstances and are difficult to arrange. Complete liquidations are not feasible for going-concerns with good present and future profit potential. Lastly, the sale of stock to third parties may not be desirable if a shareholder wishes to maintain the same voting power in the corporation. Clever taxpayers devised the following scheme to bail out corporate profits.[20]

A corporation would issue a nontaxable (nonvoting) preferred stock dividend on common stock. The shareholder would assign a portion of his or her basis in the common stock to the preferred stock. The shareholder then would sell the preferred stock to a third party. Unlike a sale of common shares, the sale of preferred stock would not reduce the shareholder's percentage ownership in the corporation. The difference between the selling price and the shareholder's basis would be a capital gain. The result would be a bailout of corporate profits as a capital gain. No diminution in control of the corporation would occur because the voting common stock would remain intact. Not surprisingly, Congress found this scheme to be abusive.

The Statutory Solution to Preferred Stock Bailouts.   The tax avoidance possibilities of the **preferred stock bailout** approach led to the enactment of § 306. Although certain transactions are excepted,[21] this provision produces the following tax consequences:

- The shareholder has ordinary income (i.e., the § 306 taint) on the sale (but not the receipt) of the preferred stock to a third party. The amount of the ordinary income is the fair market value of the preferred stock (on the date of distribution), but is limited to the amount that would have been a dividend had the corporation distributed cash in lieu of stock.[22] If the selling price of the preferred stock exceeds the § 306 taint, the excess reduces the shareholder's basis in the preferred stock. Any excess received over the § 306 taint and the preferred stock's basis is capital gain.
- Ordinary income to the extent of the § 306 taint is *not a dividend* and has no effect on the issuing corporation's E & P. In this respect, the statutory solution leads to a harsher result than does a taxable dividend distribution.
- No loss is recognized on any sale of the preferred stock by the shareholder.
- If the shareholder does not sell the preferred stock to a third party but has it redeemed by the issuing corporation, a different rule applies. The redemption proceeds constitute dividend income to the extent of the

---

[20] *Chamberlin v. Comm.*, 53–2 USTC ¶9576, 44 AFTR 494, 207 F.2d 462 (CA–6, 1953), *cert. den.*, 74 S.Ct. 516 (USSC, 1954).

[21] § 306(b).

[22] § 306(a)(1).

corporation's E & P on the date of the redemption.[23] (Because the transaction is treated as a § 301 distribution, the corporation's E & P is reduced the same as in the case of an ordinary dividend.)

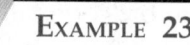

EXAMPLE 22

As of January 1 of the current year, Black Corporation has E & P of $150,000. Carol owns all of Black's common stock (100 shares) with a basis of $60,000. On that date, Black declares and pays a nontaxable preferred stock dividend of 100 shares.[24] After the dividend, the fair market value of one share of common is $2,000, and the fair market value of one share of preferred is $1,000. Two days later, Carol sells the 100 shares of preferred to Emily for $100,000. Section 306 produces the following results:

- After the distribution and before the sale, the preferred stock has a basis to Carol of $20,000 [($100,000 value of preferred ÷ $300,000 value of preferred and common) × $60,000 (the original basis of the common stock)].
- The sale of the preferred stock generates $100,000 of ordinary income to Carol. This is the amount of dividend income Carol would have recognized had cash been distributed instead of preferred stock.
- The $20,000 basis allocated to the preferred stock is not lost but is returned to the common stock.
- Black Corporation's E & P account is unaffected by either the stock distribution or its subsequent sale. ▼

EXAMPLE 23

Assume the same facts as in Example 22 with this exception: Black Corporation's E & P is only $50,000 on the date the preferred stock is distributed. Under these circumstances, the $100,000 sale proceeds are accounted for as follows: $50,000 ordinary income under § 306, $20,000 applied against the basis of the preferred stock, and $30,000 capital gain. Whether the capital gain is long term or short term depends upon the holding period of the underlying common stock. ▼

What Is § 306 Stock? Section 306 stock is stock other than common that (1) is received as a nontaxable stock dividend, (2) is received tax-free in a corporate reorganization or separation to the extent that either the effect of the transaction was substantially the same as the receipt of a stock dividend or the stock was received in exchange for § 306 stock, or (3) has a basis determined by reference to the basis of § 306 stock (e.g., such as a gift of § 306 stock). (Corporate reorganizations are discussed in Chapter 7.) If a corporation has no E & P on the date of distribution of a nontaxable preferred stock dividend, the stock will not be § 306 stock.

REDEMPTIONS THROUGH THE USE OF RELATED CORPORATIONS

Without the anti-abuse provisions of § 304, the redemption rules, which limit the situations where sale or exchange treatment is available, could be circumvented if a shareholder had a controlling interest in more than one corporation. For example, a shareholder controlling both Teal and Amber Corporations could sell the stock in one corporation to the other and receive capital gain treatment. This would be the case regardless of whether the proportionate interest in the corporation whose stock is sold changed substantially as a result of the sale. Section 304 closes the loophole. When a shareholder sells stock of one corporation to a related corporation, the sale is treated as a redemption subject to the rules discussed earlier in the chapter.

---

[23] § 306(a)(2).

[24] § 305.

Section 304 applies when one corporation acquires stock in another corporation from a shareholder in exchange for property and the shareholder controls both corporations. Section 304 is designed to "look through" the transaction to the realities of the situation. Sale or exchange treatment results only if the owner's control in the corporation whose stock is being sold is meaningfully or substantially reduced. This provision applies to transfers involving brother-sister corporations as well as to parent-subsidiary situations. To illustrate the concept and the consequences of this type of transaction, the provision's effect in brother-sister situations is discussed. This provision's application to parent-subsidiary situations is beyond the scope of this chapter.

The Code defines property to mean money, securities, and any other property.[25] Stock (or rights to acquire stock) in the corporation making the distribution is specifically excluded from the definition. Control for the purpose of this provision is defined as the ownership of stock possessing at least 50 percent of the total combined voting power of all classes of stock entitled to vote, or at least 50 percent of the total value of all classes of stock. For purposes of determining the degree of control, the constructive ownership rules described earlier in the chapter apply.[26]

If an individual controls two corporations (i.e., brother-sister corporations) and transfers stock in one corporation to the other for property, the exchange is treated as a redemption of the stock of the *acquiring* corporation. If the distribution is treated as a dividend under the general distribution rules, the stock received by the acquiring corporation is treated as a contribution to the corporation's capital. In that event, the basis of the stock to the acquiring corporation is the basis the shareholder had in the stock. The individual's basis in the stock of the acquiring corporation is increased by the basis of the stock surrendered. In applying the redemption provisions to the exchange, reference is made to the shareholder's ownership of stock in the *issuing* corporation and not to ownership of stock in the acquiring corporation.[27] The amount of dividend income is determined as if the property were distributed by the acquiring corporation to the extent of its E & P and then by the issuing corporation to the extent of its E & P.[28]

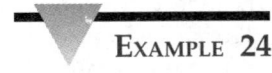

EXAMPLE 24

Ramon owns 100 shares of Bluejay Corporation stock and 200 shares of Redbird Corporation stock, representing 50% ownership in both corporations. Ramon sells 20 shares of Bluejay stock to Redbird Corporation for $30,000. Bluejay has E & P of $100,000, and Redbird has E & P of $20,000. Ramon purchased the 20 shares of stock two years ago for $5,000. ▼

What are the results of the sale in Example 24? Section 304 applies to the transaction. The sale is treated as a redemption of the stock of Redbird Corporation. If the redemption qualifies as a sale or exchange, Ramon will have a long-term capital gain of $25,000 on the sale. If not, the transaction will be considered a dividend to the extent of the corporations' E & P.

To determine whether the transaction qualifies for sale or exchange treatment, refer to Ramon's ownership in Bluejay Corporation before and after the redemption. Assuming the transaction would not qualify as a not essentially equivalent redemption, the disproportionate redemption provisions are considered.

- Ramon's ownership of Bluejay Corporation before and after the sale is determined as follows:

---

[25] § 317(a).
[26] §§ 304(c)(3) and 318(a).
[27] Reg. § 1.304–2(a).
[28] § 304(b)(2).

	Total Shares	Ramon's Shares	Redbird Corporation's Shares	Ramon's Direct and Indirect Ownership	Ownership Percentage	80% of Original Ownership
Before sale	200	100		100	50% (100 ÷ 200)	40%
After sale	200	80	20	90*	45% (90 ÷ 200)	

*Ramon constructively owns 50% of the 20 shares transferred to Redbird Corporation because he has a 50% ownership in Redbird. Thus, Ramon owns directly and indirectly 90 shares in Bluejay Corporation [80 + 10 (50% × 20) = 90].

- Ramon's deemed ownership of 45 percent of the stock in Bluejay Corporation does not meet the 80 percent test of a disproportionate redemption. Ramon does not own less than 80 percent of his interest in Bluejay prior to the sale. Therefore, the transaction does not qualify as a sale or exchange.
- Because the transaction does not qualify as a sale or exchange, Ramon will have dividend income of $30,000. Ramon's basis in his Redbird Corporation stock will increase by $5,000.
- Redbird Corporation will have a basis of $5,000 in the Bluejay Corporation stock it acquired from Ramon.

Transfers involving the application of § 304 to brother-sister corporations are summarized in Figure 5–2.

▼ **FIGURE 5–2**
Redemptions Involving
Brother-Sister Corporations

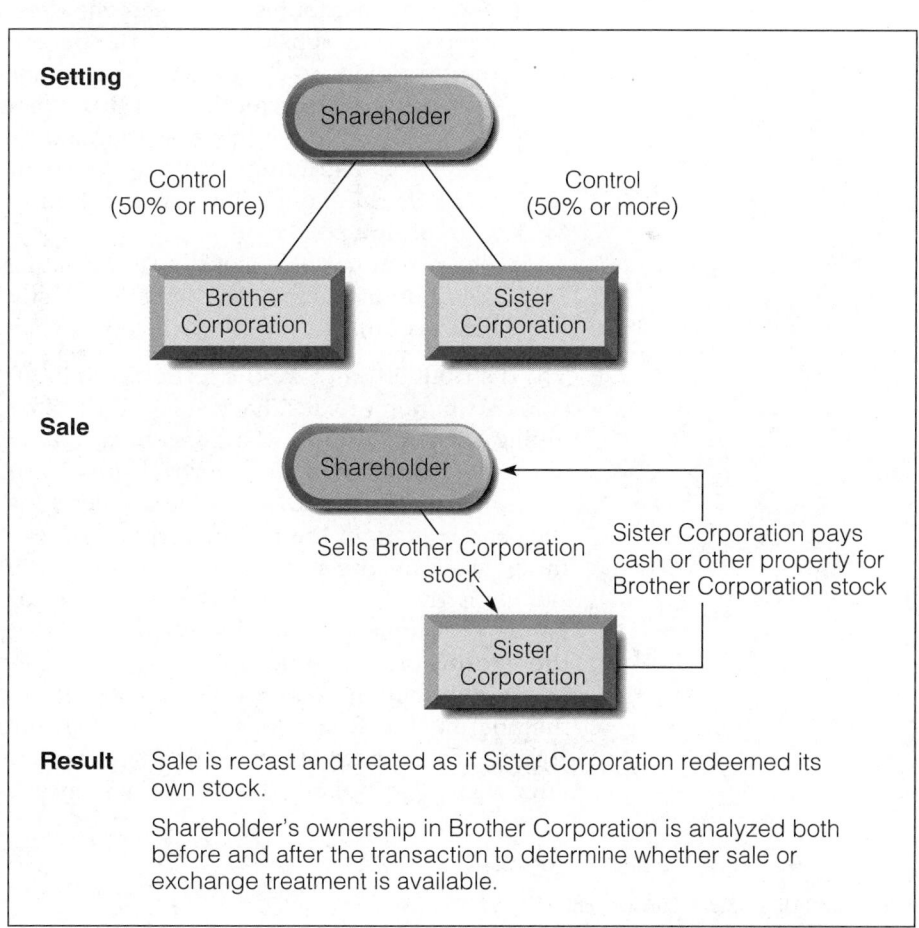

3 **LEARNING OBJECTIVE**
Understand the tax consequences when a parent corporation distributes stock and securities of its subsidiary.

If a corporation has control of another corporation, stock in the subsidiary corporation can be distributed to the shareholders of the parent corporation tax-free if the requirements of § 355 are met.[29] When a subsidiary is newly formed to perfect a corporate division, this provision applies through the divisive corporate reorganization rules discussed in Chapter 7. However, when a subsidiary already exists, § 355 alone applies. Although these rules are discussed further in Chapter 7 in connection with the corporate reorganization provisions, they are introduced here because, applied alone, they involve a transaction resembling either a dividend, a stock redemption, or a complete liquidation.

As discussed earlier, if a corporation discontinues a trade or business that it has conducted for at least five years, it can distribute the *assets* of that business to the shareholders in exchange for their stock as a partial liquidation. Recall that in a partial liquidation, the shareholders must recognize capital gain. However, in distributions of *stock* of a controlled corporation, under § 355, the shareholder recognizes *no* gain or loss.

GENERAL REQUIREMENTS

Section 355 applies only if the following conditions are met:

- A parent distributes to its shareholders at least an 80 percent controlling interest in its subsidiary (i.e., the parent transfers its controlling interest in the subsidiary to the parent's shareholders).
- Following the distribution, both the parent and the subsidiary continue to engage in a trade or business that had been conducted for at least five years before the distribution. This requirement is intended to deter the bailout of E & P by the acquisition and distribution of another business within a short span of time.
- The parent has held stock in the subsidiary for at least five years prior to the distribution (unless the subsidiary stock was acquired in a nontaxable transaction).

The distribution can take the form of a spin-off, a split-off, or a split-up. A *spin-off* is a distribution of subsidiary stock to the shareholders of the parent corporation giving them control of the subsidiary. The shareholders of the parent do not surrender any of their stock for the subsidiary stock. This distribution resembles an ordinary dividend distribution. A *split-off* is identical to a spin-off, except that the shareholders in the parent corporation exchange some of their parent corporation stock for the subsidiary stock. A split-off resembles a stock redemption. A *split-up* is the distribution of the stock of two subsidiaries to shareholders of the parent in complete liquidation of the parent. (See Chapter 7 for an illustration of these forms of distributions.)

A distribution under § 355 must not be used principally as a means of distributing the E & P of either the distributing corporation or the controlled corporation. If the stock or securities of the controlled corporation are sold shortly after their distribution, the sale is evidence that the transaction was used as a

---

[29] The control threshold is 80% as defined in § 368(c).

<table>
<tr><td>
TAX IN THE NEWS
</td></tr>
</table>

FAVORABLE TAX STATUS IS ONE FACTOR INFLUENCING CORPORATE SPIN-OFFS

Many financial analysts have observed that the favorable tax treatment of spin-offs has played a significant role in the decisions of many boards to break up corporate empires. The spin-off (or split-off) is the only way to distribute stock in a subsidiary tax-free to both the corporation and its shareholders.

Many companies now appear ready to break up their holdings. A spin-off permits a corporation to narrow its focus, reduce its debt, and maximize total shareholder value. For example, the recent announcement that AT&T would split into three publicly traded companies, in what was termed the largest voluntary corporate breakup in history, caused AT&T stock to increase substantially in value. After the spin-off, its shareholders owned stock in three companies instead of one.

means of distributing E & P. A distribution made under § 355 must also have a business purpose. Another issue, which is often the subject of litigation is what constitutes an active trade or business. The Regulations take the position that holding stock, securities, land, or other property, including casual sales of such properties, is not an active trade or business.[30]

EXAMPLE 25

Silver Corporation has operated an active business for the past 10 years. Six years ago it acquired all of the stock of Gold Corporation, which has been engaged in an active business for 8 years. Silver distributes all the Gold stock to its shareholders. Both corporations continue to operate their separate businesses. Assuming a business reason exists for the distribution, the distribution qualifies under § 355, and the receipt of the Gold stock is tax-free to the shareholders of Silver Corporation. This is a spin-off. ▼

TAX CONSEQUENCES OF A § 355 DISTRIBUTION AT THE SHAREHOLDER LEVEL

If the requirements of § 355 are met, the shareholders of the parent corporation recognize no gain on the receipt of the subsidiary corporation stock. A shareholder can receive only stock or securities tax-free. If other property is received, it is boot and is subject to taxation.[31]

To further qualify the exchange when securities are received, a § 355 distribution is tax-free only if certain conditions are met. The shareholder is considered to have received boot, which can trigger gain, if the principal amount of the securities received is greater than the principal amount of the securities surrendered or if no securities are surrendered. The amount of the boot is the fair market value of the excess principal amount determined on the date of the exchange.

---

[30] Regulations covering distributions of stock and securities of controlled corporations are at Reg. §§ 1.355–1 to –5.

[31] § 356.

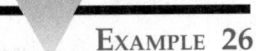

EXAMPLE 26

Tara exchanges stock in Wren Corporation (the parent corporation) for stock and securities in Cardinal Corporation (the subsidiary corporation) under § 355. The exchange is a tax-free split-off except to the extent of the securities received. The securities in Cardinal have a principal amount of $1,000 and a fair market value of $950 on the date of the exchange. Tara has boot of $950, which can lead to the recognition of realized gain. ▼

The basis of stock received by a shareholder under § 355 is determined by application of the carryover basis rules discussed in Chapter 3. The basis of the stock held before the exchange is allocated among the stock of all classes held immediately after the transaction in proportion to the fair market value of the stock of each class.[32]

EXAMPLE 27

Terry has a basis of $7,000 in her stock in Black Corporation (Red Corporation's parent). Terry receives stock in Red Corporation in a distribution that qualifies under § 355. The Black stock has a value of $30,000, and the Red stock has a value of $5,000. Terry's basis in the Black stock is allocated between the Black stock and the Red stock as follows:

Basis of Black Corporation stock:

$$\$7,000 \times \frac{\$30,000 \text{ (fair market value of Black stock)}}{\$35,000 \text{ (fair market value of Black and Red stock)}} = \$6,000$$

Basis of Red Corporation stock:

$$\$7,000 \times \frac{\$5,000 \text{ (fair market value of Red stock)}}{\$35,000 \text{ (fair market value of Black and Red stock)}} = \$1,000$$ ▼

EXAMPLE 28

Assume in Example 27 that Terry exchanges half of her shares in Black Corporation for the shares in Red Corporation. The remaining shares in Black Corporation have a basis of $5,250, and the basis of Terry's shares in Red Corporation is $1,750, computed as follows:

Basis of Black Corporation stock:

$$\$7,000 \times \frac{\$15,000 \text{ (fair market value of the remaining shares in Black)}}{\$20,000 \text{ (fair market value of Black stock and Red stock)}} = \$5,250$$

Basis of Red Corporation stock:

$$\$7,000 \times \frac{\$5,000 \text{ (fair market value of Red stock)}}{\$20,000 \text{ (fair market value of Black stock and Red stock)}} = \$1,750$$ ▼

If a distribution fails to meet the requirements of § 355, the distribution becomes taxable. In such a case, the transaction is taxed as an ordinary dividend, stock redemption, or complete liquidation, depending on the form of transaction.

LIQUIDATIONS—IN GENERAL

4   LEARNING OBJECTIVE
Master the tax laws governing corporate liquidations and their impact on both the corporation and its shareholders.

When a stock redemption occurs or a dividend is distributed, the assumption usually is that the corporation will continue as a going-concern. However, with a complete liquidation, corporate existence terminates. A complete liquidation, like a qualified stock redemption, produces sale or exchange treatment to the shareholder. However, the tax effects of a liquidation to the corporation vary somewhat from those of a stock redemption.

---

[32] § 358 and Reg. § 1.358–2(a)(2).

THE LIQUIDATION PROCESS

A **corporate liquidation** exists for tax purposes when a corporation ceases to be a going-concern. The corporation continues solely to wind up affairs, pay debts, and distribute any remaining assets to its shareholders.[33] Legal dissolution under state law is not required for the liquidation to be complete for tax purposes. A transaction will be treated as a liquidation even if the corporation retains a nominal amount of assets to pay remaining debts and preserve legal status.[34]

A liquidation may occur for one or more of several reasons. The corporate business may have been unsuccessful. But even when a corporation has been profitable, the shareholders may decide to terminate the corporation to acquire its assets. A liquidation often occurs when another person or corporation wants to purchase the assets of the corporation. The purchaser may buy the stock of the shareholders and then liquidate the corporation to acquire the assets. On the other hand, the purchaser may buy the assets directly from the corporation. After the assets are sold, the corporation distributes the sales proceeds to its shareholders and liquidates. As one may expect, the different means used to liquidate a corporation produce varying tax results.

ETHICAL CONSIDERATIONS

A Liquidating Corporation's Responsibilities

A corporation is considering closing its plant and liquidating. Researchers have reported that a parent's job loss has a huge impact on children and can be as traumatic for them as a divorce. Some outplacement firms have begun offering counseling to children as part of their services. Does the liquidating corporation have an obligation to provide outplacement services to its displaced workers and their families?

LIQUIDATIONS AND OTHER DISTRIBUTIONS COMPARED

A property distribution, whether in the form of a dividend or a stock redemption, produces gain (but not loss) to the distributing corporation. For the shareholder, the receipt of cash or property produces dividend income to the extent of the corporation's E & P. On the other hand, a qualifying stock redemption results in sale or exchange treatment.

The tax effects to the shareholder in a complete liquidation are similar to those in a qualifying stock redemption in that a liquidation also yields sale or exchange treatment. Still a complete liquidation produces somewhat different tax consequences to the liquidating corporation. With certain exceptions, a liquidating corporation recognizes gain *and* loss upon the distribution of its assets.

As in the case of a stock redemption, for the corporation undergoing liquidation, E & P has no tax impact on the gain or loss to be recognized by the shareholders. The provision governing dividend distributions does not apply to complete liquidations.[35]

EXAMPLE 29

Green Corporation, with E & P of $40,000, makes a cash distribution of $50,000 to its sole shareholder. Assume the shareholder's basis in the Green stock is $20,000 and the stock is

---

[33] Reg. § 1.332–2(c).
[34] Rev.Rul. 54–518, 1954–2 C.B. 142.

[35] § 331(b).

held as an investment. If the distribution is not in complete liquidation or is not a qualifying stock redemption, the shareholder recognizes dividend income of $40,000 (the amount of Green's E & P) and treats the remaining $10,000 of the distribution as a return of capital. If the distribution is pursuant to a complete liquidation or is a qualifying stock redemption, the shareholder has a capital gain of $30,000 [$50,000 (the amount of the distribution) − $20,000 (the basis in the stock)]. In the latter case, Green's E & P is of no consequence to the tax result to the shareholder. ▼

In the event the distribution results in a *loss* to the shareholder, an important distinction can exist between stock redemptions and liquidations. The distinction arises because losses between related parties in a redemption transaction are not allowed whereas losses may be recognized by shareholders in a complete liquidation.[36]

EXAMPLE 30

The stock of Robin Corporation is owned equally by three brothers, Rex, Sam, and Ted. When Ted's basis in his stock investment is $40,000, the corporation distributes $30,000 to him in cancellation of all his shares. If the distribution is a qualifying stock redemption, the $10,000 realized loss is not recognized.[37] Ted and Robin Corporation are related parties because Ted is deemed to own more than 50% in value of the corporation's outstanding stock. Ted's direct ownership is limited to 33⅓%, but through his brothers he owns indirectly another 66⅔% for a total of 100%. On the other hand, if the distribution qualifies as a complete liquidation, Ted's $10,000 realized loss is recognized. ▼

As to the basis of noncash property received from the corporation, the rules governing liquidations and stock redemptions are identical. Section 334(a) specifies that the basis of such property distributed in a taxable complete liquidation shall be the fair market value on the date of distribution.

In the following pages, the tax consequences of a complete liquidation of a corporation are examined first from the standpoint of the effect on the distributing corporation and then in terms of its effect on the shareholder. Because the tax rules differ when a controlled subsidiary is liquidated, the rules relating to the liquidation of a controlled subsidiary receive separate treatment.

LIQUIDATIONS—EFFECT ON THE DISTRIBUTING CORPORATION

A corporation in the process of complete liquidation may or may not be required to recognize gain or loss, depending on the nature of the transaction. The general rules relating to complete liquidations require the distributing corporation to recognize gain or loss. Loss is not recognized, however, for certain distributions of property to related shareholders and in the case of distributions or sales of built-in loss property. Under § 337, a subsidiary corporation does not recognize gain or loss for distributions to a parent corporation that owns 80 percent or more of the subsidiary's stock.

---

[36] § 267(a).
[37] *McCarthy v. Conley, Jr.,* 65–1 USTC ¶9262, 15 AFTR2d 447, 341 F.2d 948 (CA–2, 1965).

GENERAL RULE

Section 336 provides that a liquidating corporation recognizes gain or loss on the distribution of property in complete liquidation. The property is treated as if it were sold at its fair market value. This requirement is consistent with the notion of double taxation that is inherent in operating a business as a C corporation. As a result, liquidating distributions are subject to tax at both the corporate level and the shareholder level. As in a stock redemption, when property distributed in a complete liquidation is subject to a liability of the liquidating corporation, the fair market value of that property is treated as not being less than the amount of the liability.

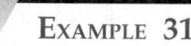

EXAMPLE 31

As part of a complete liquidation, Warbler Corporation distributes to its shareholders land held as an investment (basis of $200,000, fair market value of $300,000). The land is subject to a liability of $250,000. Warbler Corporation has a gain of $100,000 on the distribution ($300,000 − $200,000). If, instead, the liability were $350,000, Warbler's gain on the distribution would be $150,000 ($350,000 − $200,000). ▼

Limitation on Losses.   As a general rule, losses on the distribution of property in a complete liquidation are recognized. There are two exceptions, however. The first exception applies to certain distributions to related parties. The second exception prevents a loss deduction on certain sales and distributions of property that was contributed to the corporation with a built-in loss shortly before the adoption of a plan of liquidation. In this instance, the built-in loss may be disallowed as a deduction upon liquidation even if the distribution is to an unrelated party.

These two exceptions prohibiting loss recognition exist because Congress was concerned that taxpayers might attempt to create artificial losses at the corporate level. Taxpayers could otherwise have accomplished this by contributing property with built-in losses to the corporation before a liquidation. Recall from Chapter 3 that in § 351 transfers (nontaxable transfers to a corporation in exchange for stock when the transferor is in control of the corporation) and contributions to capital, the transferor's tax basis carries over to the transferee corporation. Thus, a taxpayer might transfer high-basis, low-fair market value property to a corporation contemplating liquidation in the hope that the built-in losses would neutralize expected gains from appreciated property distributed or sold in the liquidation process. Consequently, to prevent abuse, the deductibility of losses is limited by these "anti-stuffing" rules in certain related-party situations and in certain sales and distributions of built-in loss property.[38] A corporation and a shareholder are considered related if the shareholder owns (directly or indirectly) more than 50 percent in value of the corporation's outstanding stock.

Related-Party Situations.   Losses are disallowed on distributions to *related parties* in either of the following cases:

- The distribution is *not* pro rata.
- The property distributed is disqualified property.

A *pro rata distribution* is one where each shareholder receives his or her share of *each* corporate asset. *Disqualified property* is property acquired by the liquidating

---

[38] § 336(d). Section 267 provides the definition of related party for purposes of this provision.

corporation in a § 351 transaction or as a contribution to capital during a five-year period ending on the date of the distribution.

EXAMPLE 32

Bluebird Corporation's stock is held equally by three brothers. One year before Bluebird's liquidation, the shareholders transfer property (basis of $150,000, fair market value of $100,000) to the corporation in return for stock (a § 351 transaction). In liquidation, Bluebird transfers the property (still worth $100,000) back to the brothers. Because each brother owns directly and indirectly more than 50% (i.e., 100% in this situation) of the stock and disqualified property is involved, none of the $50,000 realized loss is recognized by Bluebird Corporation. ▼

EXAMPLE 33

Assume that Bluebird Corporation stock is owned by Lee and Terry, who are unrelated. Lee owns 80% and Terry owns 20% of the stock in the corporation. Bluebird has the following assets (none of which were acquired in a § 351 transaction or as a contribution to capital) that are distributed in complete liquidation of the corporation:

	Adjusted Basis	Fair Market Value
Cash	$600,000	$600,000
Equipment	150,000	200,000
Building	400,000	200,000

Assume Bluebird Corporation distributes the equipment to Terry and the cash and the building to Lee. Bluebird recognizes a gain of $50,000 on the distribution of the equipment. The loss of $200,000 on the building will be disallowed because the distribution is not pro rata and the loss property is distributed to a related party. ▼

EXAMPLE 34

Assume that Bluebird Corporation in Example 33 distributed the cash and equipment to Lee and the building to Terry. Again, Bluebird recognizes the $50,000 gain on the equipment. However, it can now recognize the $200,000 loss on the building because the loss property is not distributed to a related party (i.e., Terry does not own more than 50% of the stock in Bluebird Corporation). ▼

Built-in Loss Situations.   The loss limitation provisions are extended to distributions to *unrelated* parties when loss property is transferred to a corporation shortly before the corporation is liquidated. This second exception to the general rule likewise is imposed to prevent the doubling of losses.

EXAMPLE 35

Assume Nora, a shareholder in White Corporation, transfers property with a basis of $10,000, fair market value of $3,000, to the corporation in a transaction that qualifies under § 351. Nora's basis in the additional stock acquired in White Corporation, in exchange for the property, is $10,000. White Corporation's basis in the property is also $10,000. A few months after the transfer, White Corporation adopts a plan of complete liquidation. Upon liquidation, White distributes the property to Nora. If White were permitted a loss deduction of $7,000, there would be a double loss because Nora would also recognize a loss of $7,000 upon receipt of the property [$3,000 (fair market value of the property) – $10,000 (basis in Nora's stock)]. To prevent the doubling of losses, the law prohibits White Corporation from taking a loss on the distribution even if Nora is an unrelated party. ▼

Losses are disallowed on distributions to shareholders who are not related parties when the property distributed was acquired in a § 351 transaction or as a contribution to capital. Furthermore, it must have been contributed as part of a plan, whose principal purpose was to cause the corporation to recognize a loss in connection with the liquidation. Such a purpose will be presumed if the transfer occurs within two years of the adoption of the liquidation plan. However, losses can be recognized if a business purpose was associated with the earlier contribution of the property. Further, any *subsequent* decline in value after the property's contribution and prior to the distribution results in a deductible loss (as long as the property is not distributed to a related party).[39]

The prohibition against a loss deduction on distributions to unrelated parties is broader than the first exception, which disallows losses on certain distributions to related parties. The prohibition applies regardless of whether the shareholder is considered a related party. At the same time, however, the prohibition is narrower than the first exception since it applies only to property that had a built-in loss upon its acquisition by the corporation and only as to the amount of the built-in loss.

EXAMPLE 36

On January 2, 1997, in a transaction that qualifies under § 351, Brown Corporation acquires property with a basis of $10,000 and fair market value of $3,000. Brown adopts a plan of liquidation on July 1, 1997, and distributes the property to Rick, an unrelated party, on November 10, 1997, when the property is worth $1,000. Brown Corporation can recognize a loss of $2,000, the difference between the value of the property on the date of acquisition and the fair market value of the property on the date of distribution. Only the built-in loss of $7,000 [$3,000 (fair market value on date of acquisition) – $10,000 (basis)] is disallowed. ▼

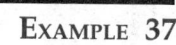

EXAMPLE 37

Assume the property in Example 36 was worth $12,000 on the date Brown Corporation acquired the property. However, the property is worth only $2,000 when Brown distributes the property upon the complete liquidation of the corporation. If the distribution is to an unrelated shareholder, Brown Corporation will recognize the entire $8,000 loss [$2,000 (fair market value on date of distribution) – $10,000 (basis)]. However, if the distribution is to a related party, Brown cannot recognize any of the loss because the property is disqualified property. When the distribution is to a related party, the loss is disallowed even though the entire decline in value occurred during the period the corporation held the property. ▼

The loss limitation can apply regardless of how long the corporation has held the property prior to liquidation. If the property is held for two years or less, a tax avoidance purpose is presumed. Still, if there is a clear and substantial relationship between the contributed property and the business of the corporation, a loss will be permitted on the *distribution* of the property to an unrelated party. When there was a business reason for transferring the loss property to the liquidating corporation, a loss will also be permitted on the *sale* of the property.

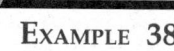

EXAMPLE 38

Cardinal Corporation's stock is held 60% by Manuel and 40% by Jack. One year before Cardinal's liquidation, property (basis of $150,000, fair market value of $100,000) is transferred to the corporation as a contribution to capital. There is no business reason for the transfer. In liquidation, Cardinal transfers the property (now worth $90,000) to Jack. Even though the distribution is to an unrelated party, the built-in loss of $50,000 is not recognized. However, Cardinal can recognize the loss of $10,000 ($90,000 – $100,000) that occurred while it held the property. (If the property is distributed to Manuel, a related party, even the $10,000 loss is disallowed.) ▼

---

[39] § 336(d)(2).

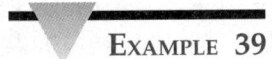

EXAMPLE 39

Assume in Example 38, that the property is transferred to Cardinal Corporation because a bank required the additional capital investment as a condition to making a loan to the corporation. Because there is a business purpose for the transfer, presumably all of the $60,000 loss is recognized if the property is distributed to Jack in liquidation. If the property is distributed to Manuel, a related party, the loss is disallowed. ▼

Distributions of loss property by a liquidating corporation are summarized in Figure 5–3.

Tax Paid on Net Gain.   To the extent that a corporation pays tax on the net amount of gain recognized at the corporate level, the proceeds available to be distributed to the shareholder are likewise reduced. This reduction for the payment of taxes will reduce the amount realized by the shareholder, which will then reduce the gain or increase the loss recognized.

▼ FIGURE 5–3
Distributions of Loss Property
by a Liquidating Corporation

```
┌────────────────────────────────────────────────────────────────────────────────┐
│                                                                                  │
│   ┌──────────────┐                                                               │
│   │ Liquidating  │      Was the distribution non–pro rata to a                   │
│   │ corporation  │      related party?                                           │
│   │ distributes  │                                                               │
│   │ loss         │            No          Yes                                    │
│   │ property.    │                                                               │
│   └──────────────┘                                                               │
│                                                                                  │
│                    Was the distributed property disqualified                     │
│                    property (property acquired by the                            │
│                    liquidating corporation in a § 351 transfer                   │
│                    or as a contribution to capital during the      ┌──────────────┐│
│                    five-year period ending on the date of the      │ Loss is      ││
│                    distribution)?                                   │ disallowed.  ││
│                                                                     └──────────────┘│
│                          No          Yes                                         │
│   ┌──────────────┐                                                               │
│   │ Loss is      │   Was the distribution to a related party?                    │
│   │ allowed.     │                                                               │
│   └──────────────┘         No          Yes                                       │
│                                                                                  │
│                    Was the principal purpose in transferring                     │
│                    the property to the liquidating corporation    ┌──────────────┐│
│                    the recognition of loss by the liquidating     │ Built-in loss││
│                    corporation (such purpose is presumed if       │ (loss that   ││
│                    the transfer occurred within two years of      │ occurred     ││
│                    the adoption of the plan of liquidation)?      │ prior to the ││
│                                                                   │ transfer of  ││
│                          No          Yes                          │ the property ││
│                                                                   │ to the       ││
│                                                                   │ corporation) ││
│                                                                   │ is           ││
│                                                                   │ disallowed.  ││
│                                                                   └──────────────┘│
└────────────────────────────────────────────────────────────────────────────────┘
```

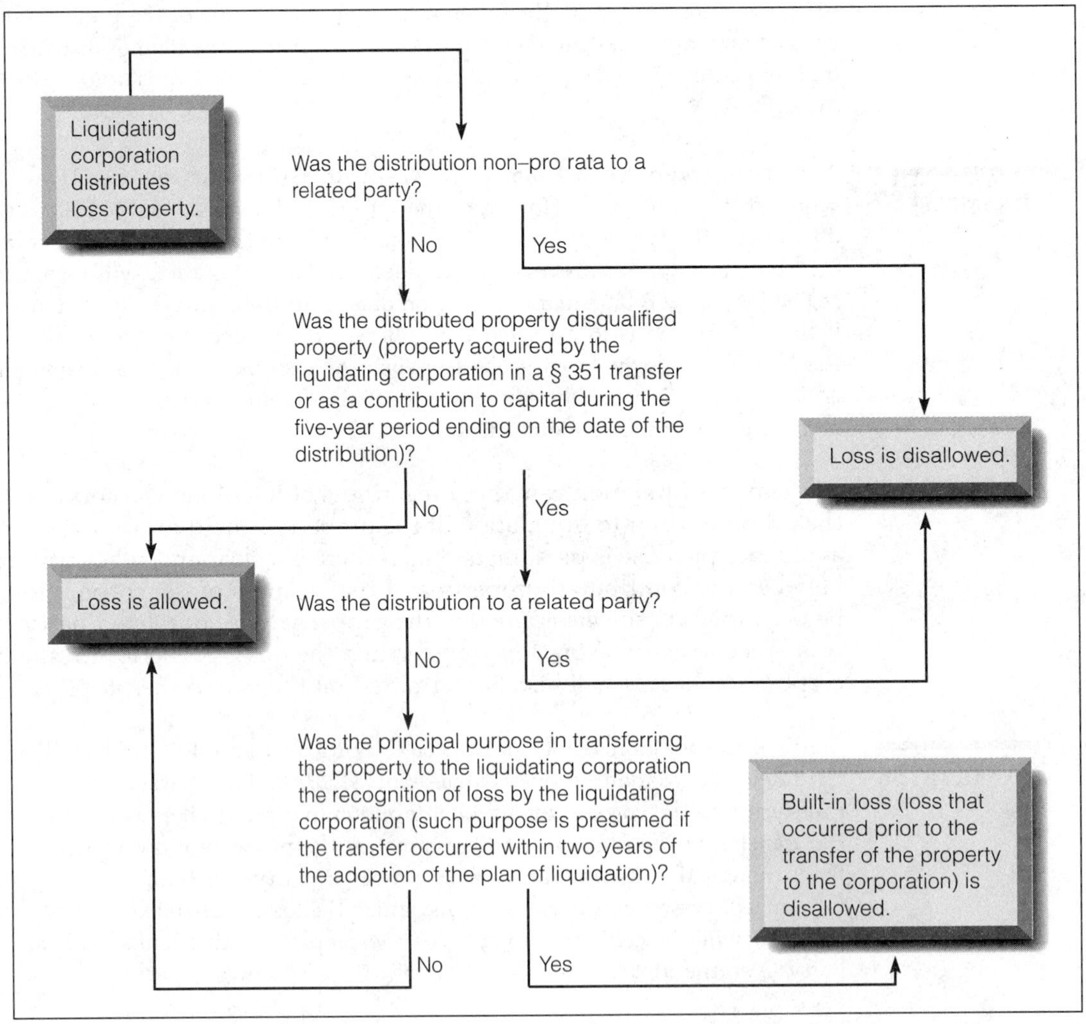

EXAMPLE 40

Blue Corporation's assets are valued at $2 million after payment of all corporate debts except for $300,000 of taxes payable on net gains it recognized on the liquidation. Therefore, the net amount realized by the shareholders is $1.7 million ($2 million − $300,000). As described below, in determining the gain or loss recognized by a shareholder, the net amount realized is offset by the stock's adjusted basis. ▼

LIQUIDATIONS—EFFECT ON THE SHAREHOLDER

The tax consequences to the shareholders of a corporation in the process of liquidation are governed either by the general rule of § 331 or by one of two exceptions relating to the liquidation of a subsidiary.

THE GENERAL RULE

In the case of a complete liquidation, the general rule of § 331 provides for sale or exchange treatment.[40] Since gain or loss must be recognized on the sale or exchange of property unless an exception applies, the shareholder is treated as having sold his or her stock to the liquidating corporation. The difference between the fair market value of the assets received from the corporation (which is net of the income tax paid by the corporation) and the adjusted basis of the stock surrendered becomes the gain or loss recognized by the shareholder. If the stock is a capital asset in the hands of the shareholder, capital gain or loss results. The burden of proof is on the taxpayer to furnish evidence as to the adjusted basis of the stock. In the absence of such evidence, the stock is deemed to have a zero basis, and the full amount of the liquidation proceeds becomes the amount of the gain recognized.[41]

Under the general liquidation provision, the shareholder's tax basis for property received in a liquidation is the property's fair market value on the date of distribution.[42]

SPECIAL RULE FOR CERTAIN INSTALLMENT OBLIGATIONS

The installment sale rules provide some relief from the bunching of gain that occurs when a liquidating corporation sells its assets. The liquidating corporation must recognize all gain on such sales. However, the *shareholders'* gain on the receipt of notes obtained by the corporation on the sale of its assets may be deferred to the point of collection.[43] Such treatment requires the shareholders to allocate their bases in the stock among the various assets received from the corporation.

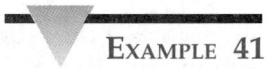

EXAMPLE 41

After a plan of complete liquidation has been adopted, Black Corporation sells its only asset, unimproved land held as an investment. The land has appreciated in value and is

---

[40] § 331(a)(1).
[41] *John Calderazzo*, 34 TCM 1, T.C.Memo. 1975–1.
[42] § 334.

[43] § 453(h). This provision does not apply to the sale of inventory and other property held by the corporation primarily for sale to customers in the ordinary course of its trade or business unless such property is sold in bulk to one person.

sold to Jane (an unrelated party) for $100,000. Under the terms of the sale, Black Corporation receives cash of $25,000 and Jane's notes for the balance of $75,000. The notes are payable over 10 years ($7,500 per year) and carry an appropriate rate of interest. Immediately after the sale, Black Corporation distributes the cash and notes to Earl, the sole shareholder. Earl has an adjusted basis of $20,000 in the Black stock, and the installment notes have a value equal to the face amount ($75,000). These transactions have the following tax result:

- Black Corporation recognizes gain on the sale of the land, measured by the difference between the $100,000 selling price and the basis Black had in the land.
- Earl may defer the gain on the receipt of the notes to the point of collection.
- Earl must allocate the adjusted basis in the stock ($20,000) between the cash and the installment notes as follows:

$$\frac{\text{Cash}}{\text{Total receipts}} = \frac{\$25,000}{\$100,000} \times \$20,000 = \begin{array}{c}\$5,000 \text{ basis} \\ \text{allocated to} \\ \text{the cash}\end{array}$$

$$\frac{\text{Notes}}{\text{Total receipts}} = \frac{\$75,000}{\$100,000} \times \$20,000 = \begin{array}{c}\$15,000 \text{ basis} \\ \text{allocated to} \\ \text{the notes}\end{array}$$

- Earl must recognize $20,000 of gain [$25,000 (cash received) − $5,000 (basis allocated to the cash)] in the year of liquidation.
- Earl must recognize gain on the notes, computed as follows:

$75,000 (contract price) − $15,000 (basis allocated to the notes) = $60,000 (gross profit)

- The gross profit percentage is 80%:

$$\frac{\$60,000 \text{ (gross profit)}}{\$75,000 \text{ (contract price)}} = 80\%$$

Thus, Earl must report a gain of $6,000 [$7,500 (amount of note) × 80% (gross profit percentage)] on the collection of each note over the next 10 years (i.e., $60,000 of gain in total).

- The interest element is accounted for separately.   ▼

LIQUIDATIONS—PARENT-SUBSIDIARY SITUATIONS

Section 332, an exception to the general rule, provides that a parent corporation does *not* recognize gain or loss on a liquidation of its subsidiary. In addition, the subsidiary corporation recognizes neither gain nor loss on distributions of property to its parent.[44]

The requirements for applying § 332 are as follows:

- The parent must own at least 80 percent of the voting stock of the subsidiary and at least 80 percent of the total value of the subsidiary's stock.
- The subsidiary must distribute all its property in complete cancellation of all its stock within the taxable year or within three years from the close of the tax year in which the first distribution occurred.
- The subsidiary must be solvent.[45]

---

[44] § 337.

[45] Reg. §§ 1.332–2(a) and (b).

If these requirements are met, nonrecognition of gains and losses becomes mandatory.

When a series of distributions occurs in the liquidation of a subsidiary corporation, the parent corporation must own the required amount of stock (80 percent) on the date the plan of liquidation is adopted. Such ownership must continue at all times until all property has been distributed.[46] If the parent fails to qualify at any time, the provisions for nonrecognition of gain or loss do not apply to any distribution.[47]

TAX TREATMENT WHEN A MINORITY INTEREST EXISTS

A distribution to a minority shareholder in a parent-subsidiary situation is treated in the same manner as one made pursuant to a nonliquidating redemption. That is, the distributing corporation recognizes gain (but not loss) on the property distributed to the minority shareholder.

EXAMPLE 42

The stock of Red Corporation is held as follows: 80% by Yellow Corporation and 20% by Dan. Red Corporation is liquidated on December 10, 1997, pursuant to a plan adopted on January 10, 1997. At the time of its liquidation, Red Corporation has assets with a basis of $100,000 and fair market value of $500,000. Red Corporation distributes the property pro rata to Yellow Corporation and to Dan. Red must recognize gain of $80,000 [($500,000 fair market value – $100,000 basis) × 20% minority interest]. The corporate tax due on this gain will most likely be deducted from the $100,000 distribution ($500,000 × 20%) going to the minority interest. The remaining gain of $320,000 is sheltered because it is related to property being distributed to Yellow, the parent corporation. ▼

The minority shareholder is subject to the general rule requiring the recognition of gain or loss. Accordingly, the difference between the fair market value of the assets received and the basis of the minority shareholder's stock is the amount of gain or loss recognized. The tax basis of property received by the minority shareholder is the property's fair market value on the date of distribution.[48]

INDEBTEDNESS OF THE SUBSIDIARY TO THE PARENT

If a subsidiary transfers appreciated property to the parent to satisfy a debt, it must recognize gain on the transaction unless § 332 applies. When § 332 applies, the subsidiary does not recognize gain or loss upon the transfer of properties to the parent.[49]

EXAMPLE 43

Green Corporation owes its parent, Gray Corporation, $20,000. It satisfies the obligation by transferring land (worth $20,000 with a tax basis of $8,000). Normally, Green would recognize a gain of $12,000 on the transaction. However, if the transfer is made pursuant to a liquidation under § 332, Green does not recognize a gain. ▼

The special provision noted above will not apply to the parent corporation. The parent corporation recognizes realized gain or loss on the satisfaction of indebtedness, even if property is received during liquidation of the subsidiary.

---

[46] Establishing the date of the adoption of a plan of complete liquidation could be crucial in determining whether § 332 applies. See, for example, *George L. Riggs, Inc.*, 64 T.C. 474 (1975).

[47] Reg. § 1.332–2(a).
[48] § 334(a).
[49] § 337(b).

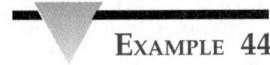

EXAMPLE 44

Redbird Corporation purchased bonds of its subsidiary, Bluebird Corporation, at a discount for $95,000. Upon liquidation of the subsidiary pursuant to § 332, Redbird receives payment for $100,000, the face amount of the bonds. The transaction has no tax effect on Bluebird. However, Redbird Corporation recognizes gain of $5,000—the difference between its basis in the bonds and the amount received in payment. ▼

BASIS OF PROPERTY RECEIVED BY THE PARENT CORPORATION—THE GENERAL RULE

Property received in the complete liquidation of a subsidiary has the same basis it had in the hands of the subsidiary unless a parent corporation elects under the exception discussed below.[50] Further, the parent's basis in the stock of the liquidated subsidiary disappears, even if some of the property is transferred to the parent in satisfaction of a debt owed to the parent by the subsidiary.

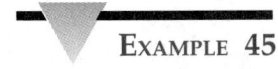

EXAMPLE 45

Wren, the parent corporation, has a basis of $20,000 in stock in Robin Corporation, a subsidiary in which it owns 85% of all classes of stock. Wren purchased the Robin stock 10 years ago. In the current year, Wren liquidates Robin Corporation and acquires assets worth $50,000 with a tax basis to Robin of $40,000. Wren Corporation takes a basis of $40,000 in the assets, with a potential gain upon their sale of $10,000. Wren's $20,000 basis in Robin's stock disappears. ▼

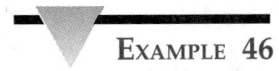

EXAMPLE 46

White Corporation has a basis of $60,000 in the stock of Gray Corporation, a subsidiary acquired 10 years ago. It liquidates Gray Corporation and receives assets worth $50,000 with a tax basis to Gray of $40,000. White Corporation takes a basis of $40,000 in the assets it acquired from Gray. If White sells the assets, it has a gain of $10,000 even though its basis in the Gray stock was $60,000. White's loss will never be recognized. ▼

Because the parent corporation takes the subsidiary's basis in its assets, the carryover rules of § 381 apply (see Chapter 7). The parent acquires any net operating loss of the subsidiary, any business credit carryover, any capital loss carryover, and a carryover of the subsidiary's E & P.

BASIS OF PROPERTY RECEIVED BY THE PARENT CORPORATION—THE EXCEPTION

Background.   Under the general rule described above, problems can develop when a subsidiary is liquidated shortly after acquisition by a parent corporation.

- When the basis of the subsidiary's assets is more than the purchase price of the stock, the parent receives a step-up in basis in the assets at no tax cost. If, for example, the parent pays $100,000 for the subsidiary's stock and the basis of the assets transferred to the parent is $150,000, the parent enjoys a $50,000 benefit without any gain recognition. The $50,000 increase in basis of the subsidiary's assets can lead to additional depreciation deductions and either more loss or less gain upon the later disposition of the assets by the parent.
- If the basis of the subsidiary's assets is below the purchase price of the stock, the parent suffers a step-down in basis in the assets with no tax benefit. Return to Example 46, but change the situation slightly so that the subsidiary is liquidated shortly after acquisition. The basic inequity of the

---

[50]§ 334(b)(1) and Reg. § 1.334–1(b).

"no loss" situation now develops. But why would a corporation pay more for the stock in another corporation than the latter's basis in the assets? One reason is that the basis of the assets is not necessarily related to the fair market value. The acquiring corporation may not have the option of purchasing the assets of the acquired corporation instead of its stock. Further, the shareholders in the acquired corporation may prefer to sell their stock rather than the assets of the corporation.

In the landmark decision of *Kimbell-Diamond Milling Co. v. Comm.*,[51] the courts considered these problems. The courts concluded that when a parent corporation liquidates a subsidiary shortly after acquiring its stock, the parent is really purchasing the assets of the subsidiary. Consequently, the basis of the assets should be the same as the cost of the stock. After this decision, § 338 was enacted, which provides for certain situations where the basis determination is made under the special rule of § 338 rather than the general rule.

Requirements for Application. Section 338 provides that an acquiring corporation may elect to treat the acquisition of stock in an acquired corporation as a purchase of the acquired corporation's assets. The **§ 338 election** must be made by the fifteenth day of the ninth month beginning after the month in which a *qualified stock purchase* occurs. If made, the election is irrevocable.

A purchasing corporation makes a qualified stock purchase if it acquires at least 80 percent of the voting power and at least 80 percent of the value of the acquired corporation within a 12-month period. The 12-month period begins with the first purchase of stock. The stock must be acquired in a taxable transaction (i.e., § 351 and other nonrecognition provisions do not apply). An acquisition of stock by any member of an affiliated group which includes the purchasing corporation is considered to be an acquisition by the purchasing corporation.

Tax Consequences. If the parent makes a qualified election under the special rule of § 338, the purchasing corporation has a basis in the subsidiary's assets equal to its basis in the subsidiary's stock. The subsidiary may, but need not, be liquidated.

Under § 338, the subsidiary corporation is *deemed* to have sold its assets for an amount equal to the purchasing corporation's grossed-up basis in the subsidiary's stock. This amount must be adjusted for liabilities of the subsidiary corporation. The grossed-up basis is the basis in the subsidiary stock multiplied by a fraction. The numerator of the fraction is 100 percent. The denominator is the percentage of value of the subsidiary's stock held by the purchasing corporation on the acquisition date.[52] The amount is allocated among the subsidiary's assets using the residual method described below.

The § 338 election produces gain or loss to the subsidiary. The subsidiary is treated as having sold all of its assets at the close of the acquisition date in a single transaction at the fair market value.[53] The subsidiary is then treated as a new corporation that purchased all of the assets as of the beginning of the day after the acquisition date.

EXAMPLE 47

White Corporation has an $800,000 basis in its assets and $500,000 of liabilities. It has E & P of $200,000, and the assets are worth $2,000,000. Black Corporation purchases 80% of the White stock on March 10, 1997, for $1,200,000 [(asssets worth $2,000,000 – liabilities of

---

[51] 14 T.C. 74 (1950), *aff'd.* in 51–1 USTC ¶9201, 40 AFTR 328, 187 F.2d 718 (CA–5, 1951), *cert. den.* 72 S.Ct. 50 (USSC, 1951).

[52] § 338(b)(4).
[53] § 338(a).

$500,000) × 80%]. Because the purchase price of the White stock exceeds White's basis in its assets, and to eliminate White's E & P, Black may choose to elect § 338 by December 15, 1997. White need not be liquidated for the provision to apply. If Black elects § 338, the tax consequences are as follows:

- White is deemed to have sold its assets for an amount equal to Black's grossed-up basis in the White stock.
- Black's grossed-up basis in the White stock is computed as follows: The basis of the White stock is multiplied by a fraction, with 100% the numerator and 80% the denominator. The basis of the White stock, $1,200,000, is multiplied by 100/80. The result is $1,500,000, which is adjusted for White's liabilities of $500,000 for a deemed selling price of $2,000,000.
- The $2,000,000 selling price less $800,000, the basis of White's assets, produces a recognized gain to White Corporation of $1,200,000. ▼

Because Black did not purchase 100 percent of the White stock, different results occur depending on whether or not White is liquidated. If White is not liquidated, it is treated as a new corporation as of March 11, 1997. The basis of White's assets is $2,000,000, and the E & P is eliminated. If White Corporation is liquidated, Black Corporation has a basis of $1,600,000 in White's assets, representing 80 percent of White's assets. White's E & P does not carry over to Black.

Note the results of the § 338 election. White Corporation's assets receive a stepped-up basis but at a substantial tax cost. White Corporation must recognize all of its realized gain. Any tax liability White incurs on its recognized gain causes Black Corporation to reduce the amount paid for White's assets.

Allocation of Purchase Price. The new stepped-up basis of the assets of a subsidiary when a § 338 election is in effect is allocated among the assets by the **residual method.**[54] The amount of the purchase price that exceeds the aggregate fair market values of the tangible and identifiable intangible assets must be allocated to goodwill or going-concern value. Goodwill and going-concern value are referred to as "§ 197 intangibles." Costs allocated to acquired § 197 intangibles are amortized over a 15-year period.

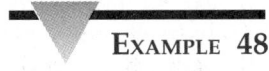

EXAMPLE 48

For $4,000,000, Red Corporation acquires all of the stock of Orange Corporation and elects the treatment under § 338. If the fair market value of Orange's physical assets is $3,500,000, Red must allocate $500,000 of the purchase price either to goodwill or to going-concern value, which may be amortized over a 15-year period. ▼

In Example 48, none of the purchase price must be allocated to goodwill or going-concern value if the physical assets are worth $4,000,000. However, the burden of proof of showing no residual amount is on the taxpayer, not on the IRS.

A Comparison of the General Rule and the § 338 Exception. Under the general rule, a subsidiary's basis in its assets carries over to the parent corporation upon liquidation. In addition, the subsidiary liquidation is completely tax-free (except for any minority interest). A liquidation under § 338, while tax-free to the parent, is taxable to the subsidiary. The subsidiary assets will have a stepped-up basis.

If a subsidiary liquidation qualifies under § 338 and a timely election is made, the holding period of the property received by the parent corporation begins on the date the parent acquired the subsidiary's stock. If the corporation is not

---

[54] § 1060.

CONCEPT SUMMARY 5–2

Summary of Liquidation Rules

Effect on the Shareholder	Basis of Property Received	Effect on the Corporation
§ 331—The general rule provides for capital gain treatment on the difference between the FMV of property received and the basis of the stock in the corporation.	§ 334(a)—Basis of assets received by the shareholder will be the FMV on the date of distribution (except for installment obligations in which gain is deferred to the point of collection).	§ 336—Gain or loss is recognized for distributions in kind and for sales by the liquidating corporation. Losses are not recognized for distributions to related parties if the distribution is not pro rata or if disqualified property is distributed. Losses may be disallowed on sales and distributions of certain other property even if made to unrelated parties.
§ 332—In liquidation of a controlled subsidiary, no gain or loss is recognized to the parent corporation. Subsidiary must distribute all of its property within the taxable year or within three years from the close of the taxable year in which the first distribution occurs.	§ 334(b)(1)—Property has the same basis as it had in the hands of the subsidiary. Parent's basis in the stock disappears. Carryover rules of § 381 apply.	§ 337—No gain or loss is recognized to the subsidiary on distributions to an 80% or more parent. Gain (but not loss) is recognized on distributions to minority shareholders.
	§ 338—Basis of assets takes the basis that the parent held in the stock in the subsidiary. Basis is allocated to assets using the residual method. Carryover rules of § 381 do not apply. Subsidiary need not be liquidated.	§ 338—Gain or loss is recognized to the subsidiary corporation.

---

liquidated, the holding period of the assets to the subsidiary starts anew on the day after the acquisition date.[55] In a liquidation under the general rule of § 332, the holding period of the subsidiary carries over to the parent. The rules regarding an election under § 338 as compared to other liquidation rules are set out in Concept Summary 5–2.

TAX PLANNING CONSIDERATIONS

STOCK REDEMPTIONS

Stock redemptions offer several possibilities for tax planning:

- A not essentially equivalent redemption provides minimal utility and generally should be relied upon only as a last resort. Instead, the redemption should be structured to fit one of the safe harbors. These include disproportionate redemptions, complete termination redemptions, or redemptions to pay death taxes.
- For a family corporation in which all of the shareholders are related to each other, the only hope of achieving sale or exchange treatment may lie in the

---

[55] § 338(a).

5 ▼ **LEARNING OBJECTIVE**
Identify tax planning opportunities available to minimize the income tax impact in stock redemptions and in the complete liquidation of a corporation.

use of a redemption that completely terminates a shareholder's interest or one that follows a shareholder's death. In a complete termination redemption, be careful that the family stock attribution rules are avoided. Here, strict compliance with the requirements (e.g., the withdrawing shareholder does not continue as an employee of the corporation and does not reacquire an interest in the corporation within 10 years) is crucial.

- The alternative to a qualifying stock redemption or partial liquidation is dividend treatment. But do not conclude that a dividend is always undesirable from a tax standpoint. Suppose the distributing corporation has little, if any, E & P or the distributee-shareholder is another corporation. In the latter situation, dividend treatment may be preferred due to the availability of the dividends received deduction.
- Recall that a stock redemption may be utilized to purchase the interest of a retiring or deceased shareholder. Rather than the remaining shareholders buying the stock of the retiring or deceased shareholder, the corporation uses its funds to redeem the stock from the shareholder or from the estate.
- A third party who wishes to purchase all the stock of a corporation can also use a stock redemption to obtain the needed purchase money. The third party purchases a small amount of stock from the shareholders. The corporation then redeems all the stock except that of the third party. The third party becomes the sole shareholder of the corporation, but the corporation furnished most of the needed purchase money.
- When using the special redemption rules following a shareholder's death, the amount to be sheltered from dividend treatment is limited to the sum of death taxes and certain estate administration expenses. However, a redemption in excess of the limitation does not destroy the applicability of this provision. Instead, any such excess (if properly structured) may qualify as a sale or exchange under one of the other redemption rules.
- The timing and sequence of a redemption should be handled carefully.

EXAMPLE 49

Bluejay Corporation's stock is held as follows: Abby (60 shares), Antonio (20 shares), and Ali (20 shares). Abby, Antonio, and Ali are not related to each other. The corporation redeems 24 of Abby's shares. Shortly thereafter, it redeems 5 of Antonio's shares. Does Abby's redemption qualify as a disproportionate redemption? Taken in isolation, it would appear to meet the 80% and 50% tests. Yet, if the IRS takes into account the later redemption of Antonio's shares, Abby has not satisfied the 50% test; she still owns 36/71 of the corporation after both redemptions. A greater time lag between the two redemptions places Abby in a better position to argue against collapsing the series of redemptions into one. ▼

CORPORATE LIQUIDATIONS

Liquidating distributions are taxed at both the corporate level and the shareholder level. When a corporation liquidates, it can, as a general rule, claim losses on assets that have depreciated in value. These assets should not be distributed in the form of a property dividend before liquidation because losses are not deductible on nonliquidating distributions of depreciated property. Thus, if such assets are distributed as property dividends, the corporation receives no tax benefit from the potential loss.

Under the general rule for corporate liquidations, shareholders recognize gain or loss equal to the difference between the liquidation proceeds and the basis of the stock given up. When the gain is large, a shareholder may consider shifting it to others. One approach is to give the stock to family members or donate it to charity. Whether this procedure will be successful depends on the timing of the transfer. If the donee of the stock is not in a position to prevent the liquidation of the corporation, the donor is deemed to have made an anticipatory assignment of income. As a result, the gain is still taxed to the donor. Hence, advance planning is crucial in arriving at the desired tax result.

Recall that the installment sale provisions provide some relief from the general corporate liquidation rule that the shareholder recognizes all gain upon receiving the liquidation proceeds. Assume that after a plan of liquidation has been adopted, corporate assets are sold in exchange for installment notes. The shareholders receiving the notes as liquidation distributions may be able to report the gain on the installment method. In that case, some gain can be deferred until the notes are collected.

The provision applicable to the liquidation of a subsidiary, § 332, is not elective. Nevertheless, some flexibility may be available:

- Whether § 332 applies depends on the 80 percent stock ownership test. Assuming the transaction has some substance, it may be avoided if a parent corporation reduces its stock ownership in the subsidiary below this percentage. On the other hand, the opposite approach may be desirable. A parent can make the provision applicable by acquiring enough additional stock in the subsidiary to meet the 80 percent test.
- Once § 332 becomes effective, less latitude is allowed in determining the parent's basis in the subsidiary's assets. If the general rule applies, the subsidiary's basis carries over to the parent. If the exception to the general rule is available and a timely § 338 election is made, the parent's basis equals the cost of the stock. (If the subsidiary is not liquidated, the basis of the assets to the subsidiary is the parent's cost of the stock.) The exception of § 338 can be avoided by failing to make a timely election.
- If a timely § 338 election is made, the parent corporation's basis in the stock of the subsidiary is allocated among the assets of the subsidiary by the residual method.
- The residual method requires the parent corporation's basis in excess of the aggregate fair market value of the physical assets to be allocated to goodwill or going-concern value (which can be amortized for tax purposes over a 15-year period). Appraisal data relating to the physical assets may be advisable to justify a higher allocation of the basis to shorter-lived assets. Recall that the burden of proof as to the value of the physical assets is on the taxpayer.
- An election to have the § 338 rules apply should be carefully weighed as the election can be detrimental. Any stepped-up basis in the subsidiary's assets produces immediate taxable gain to the subsidiary.
- Some nontax considerations may affect the form of a liquidation. The sale of a corporation's assets may take one of two forms. In one form, the corporation's stock is sold, and the purchaser then liquidates the corporation. In the other form, the corporation's assets are sold, and the sales proceeds are distributed to the shareholders who then liquidate the corporation. Selling the stock presents fewer problems. The transfer of assets requires that title be changed and that creditors be notified. Some corporations hold valuable nontransferable trademarks or licenses. In this case, only a sale of stock can be used. On the other hand, a sale of assets may be preferable if minority shareholders refuse to sell their stock and the purchaser wants full control.
- A sale of stock poses fewer tax problems to the seller. The buyer may prefer to receive a stepped-up tax basis through a purchase of the corporation's

assets. A purchase of the stock and an election under § 338 produce this result. However, there is a substantial tax cost since the purchased corporation must recognize a gain on the transaction. Still a purchase of the stock can be beneficial to the purchaser when the purchased corporation has a basis in its assets in excess of the value of the assets. In this case, a purchase of the stock generally permits the purchaser to retain the higher basis.

KEY TERMS

Attribution, 5–6

Business purpose,
5–7

Complete termination
redemption, 5–10

Corporate liquidation,
5–23

Disproportionate
redemption, 5–8

Meaningful reduction
test, 5–7

Not essentially
equivalent
redemption, 5–7

Partial liquidation,
5–11

Preferred stock
bailout, 5–16

Redemption to pay
death taxes, 5–13

Residual method,
5–34

Section 338 election,
5–33

Stock redemption,
5–3

PROBLEM MATERIALS

DISCUSSION QUESTIONS

1. Compare stock redemptions and liquidations with other corporate distributions in terms of the following:
   a. Recognition of gain to the shareholder.
   b. Recognition of gain or loss by the distributing corporation.
   c. Effect on the distributing corporation's E & P.

2. Shareholders of a corporation will always prefer that a corporate distribution be treated as a qualifying stock redemption for tax purposes rather than as a dividend. Evaluate this statement.

3. Lana wants to retire and sell her shares in Brown Corporation either to Brown's remaining shareholders, Jack and Ivan, or to a third party. What issues may support a preference for Brown Corporation to redeem Lana's shares rather than for Jack and Ivan or a third party to purchase them?

4. What effect does state law have on the determination of whether a corporate distribution qualifies as a stock redemption for tax purposes?

5. Under the attribution rules, a shareholder is deemed to own the stock of certain "related parties." What family members are included as "related parties" for this purpose?

6. Do the stock attribution rules apply to stock redemptions in complete termination of a shareholder's interest? Explain.

7. Wilma owns 200 shares in Cardinal Corporation, which represents a 60% interest in Cardinal. Wilma also owns 100 shares in Wren Corporation. Cardinal Corporation owns 100 shares in Wren Corporation. Compare Wilma's deemed stock ownership in Wren Corporation with Cardinal's deemed ownership in Wren.

8. When is a redemption considered to be a "not essentially equivalent to a dividend" redemption?

9. Two years ago, José transferred property he had used in his sole proprietorship to Cardinal Corporation, a newly formed corporation, for 50 shares of stock in Cardinal. The property had an adjusted basis of $300,000 and a fair market value of $800,000. Six

months later, José's friend, Peggy, transferred property she had used in her sole proprietorship to Cardinal Corporation for 50 shares of the stock in Cardinal and cash of $100,000. Her property had an adjusted basis of $150,000 and a value of $900,000. Both José and Peggy serve on the board of directors of Cardinal Corporation. In addition, Peggy has a contract with Cardinal to perform services for the corporation. In the current year, Cardinal Corporation redeems all of Peggy's shares in Cardinal for property with a probable value of $1,400,000. What issues must you consider?

10. Compare a stock redemption that would qualify as a not essentially equivalent redemption, a disproportionate redemption, or a complete termination redemption with a stock redemption pursuant to a partial liquidation.

11. Explain the application of the "not essentially equivalent to a dividend test" in a redemption that is a partial liquidation.

12. Under what circumstances is a redemption to pay death taxes available? What is the tax effect of such a transaction?

13. "A redemption to pay death taxes usually results in no gain or loss being recognized by the estate." Evaluate this statement.

14. Abby and her daughter, Ann, who are the only shareholders of Bluebird Corporation, each paid $100,000 four years ago for their shares in Bluebird. Abby also owns 20% of the stock in Redbird Corporation. The Redbird stock is worth $500,000, and Abby's basis in the stock is $50,000. Abby died in the current year leaving all her property to her husband, Gary, but Ann wants to be the sole shareholder of Bluebird Corporation. Bluebird has assets worth $2 million (basis of $700,000) and E & P of $1 million. Abby's estate is worth approximately $4 million. Abby has made gifts during her lifetime to Ann. Identify the relevant tax issues.

15. Cardinal Corporation desires to transfer cash of $10,000 or property worth $10,000 to its sole shareholder, Linda, in a transaction that will be treated as a dividend to Linda. Explain the general consequences to Cardinal if it distributes either cash, property whose fair market value exceeds its adjusted basis, or property whose adjusted basis exceeds its fair market value.

16. A corporation distributes $100,000 to a shareholder in complete redemption of the shareholder's stock. Can the corporation reduce its E & P by this amount? Explain.

17. Dan and Debra are married and have three minor children. Dan and Debra are the sole shareholders of Green Corporation. They each have an adjusted basis of $150,000 in their stock in Green. Green has E & P of $2 million, and its net assets are worth $3 million. It has had considerable earnings in the past few years and has substantial cash flow. Green pays Dan a salary of $200,000. Debra is unemployed. Dan and Debra have a home worth $300,000 with an adjusted basis of $100,000. The couple decides to divorce in the current year. They want to sell their residence and each purchase a new home. Dan wants to acquire Debra's stock in Green Corporation but does not have adequate cash to buy her one-half interest. Identify the relevant tax issues for Dan and Debra.

18. Pete, a 30% shareholder in Black Corporation, sells one-half of his preferred stock and one-half of his common stock to a third party. Is there any danger that § 306 could apply to the sale of the preferred stock? Why or why not?

19. It has been said that the operation of § 306 to a sale of preferred stock could have a harsher tax effect than if the corporation had distributed a taxable dividend in the first place. Explain.

20. What problems arise when a shareholder sells stock he or she owns in one corporation to a related corporation?

21. Describe a spin-off, a split-off, and a split-up.

22. Compare stock redemptions with liquidations in terms of the following:
    a. Possible disallowance of a loss (§ 267) to a shareholder.
    b. Basis of noncash property received from the corporation.

23. Can losses ever be recognized in a complete liquidation if disqualified property is involved? Explain.

24. Explain the tax consequences to a shareholder of a corporation in the process of liquidation under the general rule of § 331.

25. May a shareholder use the installment method to report gain on a complete liquidation? Explain.

26. In terms of the rules applying to the liquidation of a subsidiary by its parent, describe the effect of each of the following:
    a. The adoption of a plan of complete liquidation.
    b. The period of time in which the corporation must liquidate.
    c. The amount of stock held by the parent corporation.
    d. The solvency of the subsidiary being liquidated.

27. What are the tax consequences of a liquidation of a subsidiary by its corporate parent when a minority interest is involved?

28. Could a liquidation of one corporation involve both the general rule (§ 331) and the rule applicable to the liquidation of a controlled subsidiary (§ 332)?

29. Bluebird Corporation pays $1 million for 100% of the stock in Redbird Corporation. Redbird has a basis of $500,000 in its assets. If Bluebird liquidates Redbird and makes no special election, what basis will it have in Redbird's assets?

30. What are the requirements for the application of § 338?

31. Under what circumstances could the application of § 338 be beneficial to the parent corporation? Detrimental?

32. What is the tax treatment of goodwill and going-concern value when stock of a corporation is purchased and an election is made under § 338?

33. Compare the sale of a corporation's assets with a sale of its stock in terms of problems to the seller.

PROBLEMS

34. Black Corporation, with E & P of $1 million, distributes property with a basis of $100,000 and a fair market value of $250,000 to Grace, one of its three shareholders. Each shareholder has a one-third interest in the corporation.
    a. What are the tax consequences to Black Corporation and to Grace if the distribution is a property dividend?
    b. What are the tax consequences in (a) if Grace is a corporation?
    c. What are the tax consequences to Black Corporation and to Grace if the distribution is a qualified stock redemption? Assume Grace has a basis of $80,000 in the stock surrendered to Black Corporation.
    d. What are the tax consequences in (c) if Grace is a corporation?
    e. If the parties involved could choose from among the preceding options, which would they choose and why?

35. Juan is in the 39.6% tax bracket. He acquired 400 shares of stock in Gray Corporation three years ago at a cost of $100 per share. In the current year, Juan received a payment of $80,000 from Gray Corporation in exchange for 200 of his shares in Gray. What tax liability would Juan incur on the $80,000 payment in each of the following situations?
    a. The payment qualifies for stock redemption (i.e., sale or exchange) treatment.
    b. The payment does not qualify for stock redemption treatment.

36. How would your answer to Problem 35 differ if Juan were a corporate shareholder (in the 34% tax bracket) rather than an individual shareholder and the stock ownership in Gray Corporation represented a 30% interest?

37. Assume Juan in Problem 35 has a capital loss carryover of $50,000 in the current tax year. Juan has no other capital gain transactions during the year. What amount of the capital loss may Juan deduct in the current year in the following situations?

a. The $80,000 payment from Gray Corporation qualifies as a stock redemption for tax purposes (i.e., receives sale or exchange treatment).

b. The $80,000 payment from Gray Corporation does not qualify as a stock redemption for tax purposes (i.e., does not receive sale or exchange treatment).

c. If Juan had the flexibility to structure the transaction either as described in (a) or in (b), which form would he choose?

38. How would your answer to parts (a) and (b) of Problem 37 differ if Juan were a corporate shareholder (in the 34% tax bracket) rather than an individual shareholder and the stock ownership in Gray Corporation represented a 30% interest?

39. Black Corporation has 200 shares of common stock outstanding, owned as follows: Peggy, 100 shares; Carlos (unrelated to Peggy), 50 shares; estate of Vern (Peggy's father), 50 shares. Peggy is the beneficiary of Vern's estate. Determine whether the following redemptions of Black Corporation receive sale or exchange treatment:

a. Black Corporation redeems the stock of Vern's estate. Assume that § 303 (redemptions to pay death taxes) is not available.

b. Black Corporation redeems all of Peggy's 100 shares.

c. Black Corporation redeems all of Peggy's 100 shares and all of the 50 shares of Vern's estate. Assume that § 303 (redemptions to pay death taxes) is not available.

40. Rosa owns 110 shares of the 200 shares of Bluebird Corporation. Rosa paid $1,000 per share for the stock five years ago. The remaining stock in Bluebird Corporation is owned by several individuals, none of whom owns more than 10% of the stock. In the current year, Bluebird redeems 20 of Rosa's shares for $60,000 ($3,000 per share). Bluebird has E & P of $200,000. How must Rosa report the $60,000?

41. Robin Corporation has 1,000 shares of common stock outstanding. The shares are owned by unrelated shareholders as follows: Leo Jones, 400 shares; Lori Johnson, 400 shares; and Lana Pierce, 200 shares. The corporation redeems 100 shares of Lana's stock for $45,000. Lana paid $100 per share for her stock two years ago. Robin's E & P was $400,000 on the date of redemption. What is the tax effect to Lana of the redemption? Prepare a letter to Lana (1000 Main Street, Oldtown, MN 55166) and a memo for the file in which you explain your conclusions.

42. In Problem 41, assume Leo is Lana's father. How would this affect the tax status of the redemption? What if Leo were Lana's brother instead of her father?

43. Thrush Corporation is owned by José, Juan (José's son), and Carmen (José's daughter). José owns 50 shares in Thrush, Juan owns 25, and Carmen owns 25. In the current year, Thrush Corporation redeems all of José's shares. Determine whether the redemption qualifies under the favorable complete termination rules in the following circumstances:

a. José acquires 25 shares in Thrush Corporation when Juan dies two years later and leaves his property to José.

b. José does not file an agreement with his tax return to notify the IRS of any acquisition of stock in Thrush Corporation in the next 10 years.

c. José remains as a director in Thrush Corporation.

d. José resigns as director of Thrush Corporation; Carmen becomes a director of Thrush to replace José.

44. Hal and Hans own all the stock in Green Corporation. Each has a basis of $15,000 in his 50 shares. Green Corporation has accumulated E & P of $550,000. Hal wishes to retire in the current year and wants to sell his stock for $300,000, the fair market value. Hans would like to purchase Hal's shares and, thus, become the sole shareholder in Green Corporation, but Hans is short of funds. What are the tax consequences to Hal, to Hans, and to Green Corporation under the following circumstances?

a. Green Corporation distributes cash of $300,000 to Hans, and he uses the cash to purchase Hal's shares.

b. Green Corporation redeems all of Hal's shares for $300,000.

45. White Corporation, which has E & P of $6 million, manufactures widgets. In addition, it operates a separate division that sells farm machinery. White also owns stock in

several corporations that it purchased for investment purposes. The stock in White Corporation is held by Helen and Gray Corporation. Both Helen and Gray Corporation own 100 shares in White that were purchased 10 years ago at a cost of $10,000 per share. Determine whether the following transactions qualify as partial liquidations under § 302(b)(4). In each transaction, determine the tax consequences to White Corporation, to Gray Corporation, and to Helen, including the tax basis of any property received by Helen and Gray Corporation.

a. The division selling farm machinery is destroyed by fire. White Corporation decides to discontinue the business and distributes all the insurance proceeds collected as a result of the fire to Helen and to Gray Corporation in redemption of 20 shares of stock from each shareholder. The assets in the farm machinery division had a basis to White of $1 million and a fair market value of $4 million. The insurance recovery was $4 million.

b. White Corporation has manufactured widgets and sold farm machinery for 10 years. In the current year, it decides to discontinue selling farm machinery and distributes all the assets of the farm machinery division to Helen and Gray Corporation, equally, in redemption of 20 shares from each shareholder. The assets in the farm machinery division had a basis of $1 million to White and a fair market value of $4 million on the date of the distribution.

c. Assume that White Corporation had manufactured widgets for only 2 years but had sold farm machinery for the past 10 years. It distributes the farm machinery equally to Helen and to Gray Corporation as in (b) for half of the shares Helen and Gray hold in White.

d. White Corporation distributes the stock it holds in other corporations equally to Helen and to Gray Corporation in exchange for 10 shares of stock that Helen and Gray hold in White. The stock has a basis to White of $100,000 and a fair market value of $500,000 on the date of the distribution.

46. The gross estate of Debra, decedent, includes stock in Black Corporation and White Corporation valued at $150,000 and $250,000, respectively. Debra's adjusted gross estate is $900,000. She owned 30% of the Black stock and 60% of the White stock. Death taxes and funeral and administration expenses for Debra's estate are $100,000. Debra had a basis of $60,000 in the Black stock and $90,000 in the White stock. What are the tax consequences to Debra's estate if Black Corporation redeems one-third of Debra's stock for $50,000 and White Corporation redeems one-fifth of her stock for $50,000?

47. In the current year, Red Corporation transfers land to a shareholder's estate to carry out a § 303 redemption (redemption to pay death taxes). The land is worth $1 million and has a tax basis to Red Corporation of $400,000. The estate sells the land nine months later for $1,100,000. What are the tax results to Red Corporation and to the estate as a result of the transfer? The death taxes and funeral and administration costs for the estate total $2 million.

48. White Corporation has 100 shares of common stock outstanding owned as follows: Ann, 50 shares, and Bonnie (an unrelated party), 50 shares. Ann and Bonnie each paid $1,000 per share for the White Corporation stock 10 years ago. White has $100,000 of accumulated E & P and $20,000 of current E & P. White distributes land held as an investment (fair market value of $80,000, adjusted basis of $30,000) to Ann in redemption of 25 of her shares.

a. What are the tax results to Ann on the redemption of her stock in White Corporation?

b. What gain or loss results to White Corporation on the redemption?

c. What is White's E & P after the redemption?

49. Wren Corporation has 500 shares of stock outstanding. It redeems 50 shares for $90,000 when it has paid-in capital of $300,000 and E & P of $400,000. What is the reduction in the E & P of Wren Corporation as a result of the redemption? Prepare a letter to Wren Corporation (506 Wall St. Winona, MN 55987) and a memo for the file in which you explain your conclusions.

50. Brown Corporation has 1,000 shares of stock outstanding. It redeems 350 shares for $200,000 when it has paid-in capital of $100,000 and E & P of $700,000. What is the reduction in Brown's E & P as a result of the redemption?

51. Carl and Cora are the sole shareholders of Black Corporation, which has E & P of $500,000. Carl and Cora each have a basis of $50,000 in their 100 shares of Black common stock. Black Corporation issued a preferred stock dividend on the common shares of Carl and Cora. Carl and Cora each received 100 shares of preferred stock with a par value of $200 per share. Fair market value of one share of common was $300, and fair market value of one share of preferred was $200.
    a. What are the tax consequences of the distribution to Carl and Cora?
    b. What are the tax consequences to Carl if he later sells his preferred stock to Adam for $40,000? Adam is not related to Carl.

52. Bob owns 250 shares of stock in Black Corporation and 200 shares of stock in White Corporation, representing an 80% interest in each corporation. Bob sells 20 shares of White stock to Black Corporation for $20,000. The White stock was acquired 10 years ago; the tax basis to Bob of these 20 shares is $2,000. The E & P of Black Corporation is $10,000 on the date of sale, and the E & P of White Corporation is $15,000. What are the tax consequences of this transaction?

53. Gary, a shareholder in Yellow Corporation, exchanges stock in Yellow (the parent corporation) for all the stock and some securities in Blue Corporation. The transaction meets the requirement of § 355. The stock in Yellow that Gary exchanged had a fair market value of $5 million and a tax basis of $1 million. The stock he received in Blue had a fair market value of $3,750,000; the securities had a fair market value of $1,250,000, and a principal amount of $1,400,000. What gain, if any, is recognized by Gary?

54. Iris has a basis of $12,000 in her 50 shares in Brown Corporation. Iris receives 100 shares of stock in White Corporation pursuant to a distribution from Brown that qualifies under § 355. The stock in Brown Corporation has a value of $1,000 per share, and the stock in White Corporation has a value of $500 per share. What basis will Iris have in the stock of Brown Corporation and White Corporation after the distribution?

55. Wren Corporation is owned equally by José and Jill, who are not related. Each has a stock basis of $600,000. Wren Corporation has the following assets and no liabilities:

	Basis to Wren Corporation	Fair Market Value
Cash	$ 200,000	$ 200,000
Inventory	800,000	1,200,000
Equipment ($400,000 depreciation has been taken)	200,000	1,000,000
Building	800,000	2,400,000
Land	200,000	400,000
Stock in Gray Corporation (10% interest)	1,600,000	4,000,000
Total	$3,800,000	$9,200,000

Compute the tax liability to Wren Corporation and the taxable gain to José and Jill if Wren is liquidated in the current year after the corporation sells each asset for its fair market value and distributes the after-tax proceeds to José and Jill. Straight-line depreciation of $1,200,000 had been claimed on the building. The land was used in Wren Corporation's business.

56. After a plan of complete liquidation has been adopted, Green Corporation sells its only asset, land, to Rex (an unrelated party) for $250,000. Under the terms of the sale, Green receives cash of $50,000 and Rex's note in the amount of $200,000. The note is payable over five years ($40,000 per year) and carries an appropriate rate of interest. Immediately after the sale, Green distributes the cash and notes to Helen, the sole shareholder of Green Corporation. Helen has a basis of $60,000 in the Green stock. What are the tax results to Helen if she wishes to defer as much gain as possible on the transaction? Assume the installment notes possess a value equal to the face amount.

57. Green Corporation's stock is held equally by three sisters, Abby, Bonnie, and Carol. The three sisters owned, as tenants in common, a tract of land and a warehouse needed by the corporation. The land and warehouse had a basis of $325,000 and fair market value of $100,000. Three years prior to the complete liquidation of Green, the sisters transferred the land and warehouse to the corporation in return for stock. At the time of the liquidation, the land and warehouse had a fair market value of $60,000 and a tax basis of $322,000. In liquidation, Green Corporation transferred the land and warehouse equally to Abby, Bonnie, and Carol as tenants in common. How much loss would Green Corporation recognize on the distribution?

58. Robin Corporation distributes to its shareholders land held as an investment (basis of $100,000, fair market value of $600,000) pursuant to a complete liquidation. The land is subject to a liability of $700,000. How much gain does Robin Corporation recognize on a distribution of the land?

59. The stock in Gray Corporation is owned by Carol and Gail, unrelated individuals. Carol owns 80% and Gail owns 20% of the Gray stock. Gray Corporation has the following assets that are distributed in complete liquidation:

	Adjusted Basis	Fair Market Value
Cash	$600,000	$600,000
Inventory	80,000	200,000
Equipment	350,000	200,000

What gain or loss would Gray Corporation recognize on the liquidation if it distributes the cash and equipment to Carol and the inventory to Gail? What gain or loss would Gray Corporation recognize if it distributes the cash and inventory to Carol and the equipment to Gail?

60. Blue Corporation acquired land in a § 351 exchange in 1995. The land had a basis of $1,800,000 and a fair market value of $1,950,000 on the date of the transfer. Blue Corporation has two shareholders, Ann and Paul, unrelated individuals. Ann owns 80% of the stock in Blue Corporation and Paul owns 20%. The corporation adopts a plan of liquidation in 1997. On this date the value of the land has decreased to $600,000. In distributing the land either to Ann or to Paul, or to both, as part of liquidating distributions from Blue Corporation, should the corporation:
   a. Distribute all the land to Ann?
   b. Distribute all the land to Paul?
   c. Distribute 80% of the land to Ann and 20% to Paul?
   d. Distribute 50% of the land to Ann and 50% to Paul?
   e. Sell the land and distribute the proceeds of $600,000 proportionately to Ann and to Paul?

61. Assume in Problem 60 that the plan of liquidation is not adopted until 1998. In addition, assume the land had a fair market value of $1.5 million on the date of its transfer to Blue Corporation. On the date of the liquidation, the land's fair market value has decreased to $600,000. How would your answer to Problem 60 change if:
   a. All the land is distributed to Ann?
   b. All the land is distributed to Paul?
   c. The land is distributed 80% to Ann and 20% to Paul?
   d. The land is distributed 50% to Ann and 50% to Paul?
   e. The land is sold and the proceeds of $600,000 are distributed proportionately to Ann and to Paul?

62. The stock of Yellow Corporation is held as follows: 85% by Red Corporation and 15% by Fred. Yellow Corporation is liquidated on October 1, 1997, pursuant to a plan of liquidation adopted on January 15, 1997. At the time of its liquidation, Yellow's assets had a basis of $2 million and a fair market value of $18 million. Red Corporation has a

basis of $800,000 in its Yellow Corporation stock. The basis of the Yellow stock to Fred is $80,000.

   a. How much gain, if any, must Yellow Corporation recognize on the liquidation?
   b. How much gain, if any, is recognized on receipt of property from Yellow Corporation by Red Corporation? By Fred?

63. At the time of its liquidation under § 332, Cardinal Corporation had the following assets and liabilities:

	Basis to Cardinal Corporation	**Fair Market Value**
Cash	$120,000	$120,000
Marketable securities	90,000	240,000
Unimproved land	150,000	300,000
Unsecured bank loan	(30,000)	(30,000)
Mortgage on land	(90,000)	(90,000)

Wren Corporation, the sole shareholder of Cardinal Corporation, has a basis in its stock investment of $360,000. At the time of its liquidation, Cardinal's E & P was $200,000.

   a. How much gain (or loss) will Cardinal Corporation recognize if it distributes all of its assets and liabilities to Wren Corporation?
   b. How much gain (or loss) will Wren Corporation recognize?
   c. If the general rule of § 334(b)(1) applies, what will be Wren's basis in the marketable securities it receives from Cardinal Corporation?
   d. What will be Wren's basis in the unimproved land?

64. Orange Corporation, owned by two individual shareholders, has a basis of $450,000 (fair market value of $1 million) in its assets and E & P of $80,000. Its liabilities total $100,000. Green Corporation purchases 20% of all the stock of Orange Corporation for $180,000 on March 1, 1997; 15% for $135,000 on September 20, 1997; and 60% for $540,000 on December 1, 1997, for a total consideration of $855,000. Assume Orange's marginal tax rate is 34%.

   a. Is Green Corporation entitled to make an election under § 338?
   b. Assume Green Corporation may make an election under § 338. Should Green do so? When must Green make such an election?
   c. What are the tax consequences to Orange Corporation and to Green Corporation if Green makes a valid election under § 338 but does not liquidate Orange?
   d. What is the tax result if Orange Corporation is liquidated four months after a valid § 338 election? Eve, who holds the 5% minority interest in Orange Corporation, has a $10,000 basis in her stock in Orange. What is the tax result to Eve upon the liquidation?

65. Green Corporation paid $5,400,000 for all the stock of Gray Corporation 10 years ago. Gray Corporation's balance sheet reflects the following values:

Assets	
Cash	$ 135,000
Inventory	405,000
Machinery	270,000
Equipment	1,080,000
Land	1,350,000
	$3,240,000

Liabilities and Shareholders' Equity

Accounts payable	$ 5,400,000
Common stock	5,400,000
Deficit	(7,560,000)
	$ 3,240,000

What are the tax consequences to Green Corporation if it liquidates Gray Corporation? Prepare a letter to your client Green Corporation (1010 Cypress Lane, Community, MN 55166) and a memo for the file in which you explain your conclusions.

66. White Corporation is owned 90% by Black Corporation. The parent is contemplating a liquidation of White Corporation and the acquisition of its assets. Black Corporation purchased the White stock from White's two individual shareholders a month ago on January 1, 1997, for $400,000. The financial statement of White Corporation as of January 1, 1997, is as follows:

Assets

	Basis to White Corporation	Fair Market Value
Cash	$ 40,000	$ 40,000
Inventory	80,000	60,000
Accounts receivable	160,000	100,000
Equipment	400,000	320,000
Land	520,000	280,000
	$1,200,000	$800,000

Liabilities and Shareholders' Equity

Accounts payable	$ 120,000	$120,000
Mortgages payable	200,000	200,000
Common stock	1,000,000	480,000
Retained earnings	(120,000)	
	$1,200,000	$800,000

The management of Black Corporation asks your advice on the feasibility of an election under § 338.

a. Can Black Corporation make a § 338 election?

b. Assuming Black can make a § 338 election, is such an election feasible?

RESEARCH PROBLEMS

Note: **West's Federal Taxation on CD-ROM** *can be used in preparing solutions to the Research Problems. Alternatively, tax research materials contained in a standard tax library can be used.*

Research Problem 1.   Keith Magness (1400 Cedar Road, Belton, TX 76513) owned 80% of the common stock of Green Corporation. In 1995, when Green had E & P of $300,000, it issued a pro rata dividend of preferred stock on common stock worth $100,000. As a result of the distribution, Keith received 100 shares of preferred stock that he did not report as income. In 1996, Keith donated the preferred stock to his favorite charity, his alma mater. Keith deducted $100,000, the amount he determined to be the fair market value of the stock on the date of the gift, as a charitable contribution on his 1996 income tax return. Keith's adjusted gross income for 1996 was $500,000. Upon audit of Keith's return in 1997, the IRS disallowed the deduction contending that the preferred stock was § 306 stock. Thus, according to the IRS, the gift was subject to the provisions of § 170(e)(1)(A) of the Code. Keith seeks your advice. Prepare a letter to Keith and a memo for the file.

Research Problem 2. Dave Smith (1256 Pine Tree Lane, Waverly, MN 55390) owns 40% of Brown Corporation; his father owns the remaining 60%. Dave also owns 70% of White Corporation, with the remaining 30% being owned by his wife. Dave terminates his entire interest in Brown Corporation through a stock redemption that he reports as a long-term capital gain pursuant to § 302(b)(3). Three years later, White Corporation enters into a contract with Brown Corporation whereby White is given exclusive management authority over Brown's operations. Upon audit, the IRS disallowed long-term capital gain treatment on the stock redemption in Brown Corporation contending that Dave acquired an interest in Brown within 10 years from the date of the redemption because of White's management contract with Brown. What is the result? Prepare a letter to Dave and a memo to the file documenting your conclusions.

Research Problem 3. Green Corporation was liquidated two years ago. In the year of liquidation, Green reported taxable gain of $8 million, based upon a value in its assets of $10 million and a basis of $2 million. After paying its tax liability of $2,720,000, Green distributed its remaining assets, valued at $7,280,000 ($10 million – $2,720,000 tax paid), to its 10 shareholders. Shareholder Beth received $728,000 and reported a long-term capital gain of $628,000 ($728,000 distribution – $100,000 stock basis). In the current year, the IRS audited Green Corporation and determined that the corporation had an additional gain of $1 million in the year of liquidation. The IRS assessed additional tax of $340,000 plus penalties and interest against Green Corporation and then against Beth, based on transferee liability. Beth comes to you for advice. She is not certain where the other shareholders are located.

a. If Beth is required to pay all of the tax liability, will she be entitled to deduct the amount paid as a loss?
b. What is the nature of the loss—capital or ordinary?
c. Would § 1341 apply?
d. How can a shareholder be protected from the problem facing Beth?

Research Problem 4. The stock of Bluebird Corporation is held 15% by Rosa and 85% by Beth. José would like to purchase all the stock but has only enough cash to pay for 70%. Bluebird Corporation has enough cash on hand to redeem 30% of its shares. Consider and evaluate the following alternatives in terms of Bluebird Corporation, Rosa, and Beth:

a. Bluebird Corporation redeems 30% of the shares from Beth. José purchases the remaining 55% held by Beth and the 15% held by Rosa.
b. Bluebird distributes 85% of its cash to Beth and 15% to Rosa. This reduces the value of the stock to a level where José's cash is adequate to purchase Rosa's and Beth's shares.
c. Bluebird Corporation redeems all of Rosa's shares. José purchases 70% of the shares held by Beth. Bluebird Corporation then redeems the remainder of Beth's shares.
d. José borrows money from a bank to purchase all of Rosa's and Beth's shares. Later, José has Bluebird redeem 30% of the shares he purchased so that he can pay off the bank loan.

Partial list of research aids:
Bernard E. Niedermeyer, 62 T.C. 280 (1974).
Television Industries, Inc. v. Comm., 60–2 USTC ¶9795, 6 AFTR 2d 5864, 284 F.2d 322 (CA–2, 1960).

Use the tax resources of the internet to address the following questions. Do not restrict your search to the World Wide Web, but include a review of newsgroups and general reference materials, practitioner sites and resources, primary sources of the tax law, chat rooms and discussion groups, and other opportunities.

Research Problem 5.   The repeal of the *General Utilities* doctrine by the 1986 Tax Reform Act has been described as making corporate liquidations more expensive. Make a list of tax advisors on the internet who discuss this point in their solicitations and newsletters. Do they discuss *General Utilities* for C corporations only or also for S corporations and their shareholders?

Research Problem 6.   Publicly traded corporations often attempt to boost the value of their shares by repurchasing their own stock on the market. Review various financial news sites on the internet and find a capital transaction completed in the last year that appears to you to have been completed using the § 302 provisions. Diagram the transaction.

ALTERNATIVE MINIMUM TAX AND CERTAIN PENALTY TAXES IMPOSED ON CORPORATIONS

LEARNING OBJECTIVES

After completing Chapter 6, you should be able to:

1. Explain the reason for the alternative minimum tax.

2. Work with the alternative minimum tax applicable to corporations.

3. Understand the function of adjusted current earnings (ACE).

4. Appreciate the purpose of the accumulated earnings tax.

5. Determine the reasonable needs of the business.

6. Compute the accumulated earnings tax.

7. Discuss the reason for the personal holding company tax.

8. Recognize the requirements for personal holding company status.

9. Compute the personal holding company tax.

10. Compare the accumulated earnings and personal holding company taxes.

1   **LEARNING OBJECTIVE**
Explain the reason for the alternative minimum tax.

In the early 1980s, the perception that many large corporations were not paying their fair share of Federal income tax was widespread. A study released in 1986 reported that 130 of the 250 largest corporations in the United States paid zero or less in Federal taxes in at least one year between 1981 and 1985 (e.g., Reynolds Metals, General Dynamics, Georgia Pacific, and Texas Commerce Bankshares). Political pressure subsequently led to the adoption of an alternative minimum tax to ensure that corporations with substantial economic income pay a minimum amount of Federal taxes.

Corporations are now less able to use exclusions, deductions, and credits available under the law to pay no taxes. A separate tax system with a quasi-flat tax rate is applied each year to a corporation's economic income. If the tentative alternative minimum tax is greater than the regular corporate tax under § 11, then the corporation must pay the regular tax plus this excess, the **alternative minimum tax (AMT).**

The corporate AMT has become an important revenue raiser, accounting for 8 percent of corporate tax liabilities by 1991. Between 1987 and 1990, receipts from the corporate AMT increased from $2 billion to $8 billion, and the number of taxpayers almost doubled from 17,000 to 32,000. But in 1991, AMT receipts dropped to $5.3 billion, paid by 30,400 corporations; of that amount, 78 percent was paid by a few hundred large corporations with assets greater than $500 million. More than 64 percent of this $5.3 billion was paid by the capital-intensive manufacturing, mining, construction, transportation, and utility sectors.

In general, a corporation is likely to pay an AMT for one or more of three reasons:

- A high level of investment in assets such as equipment and structures.
- Low taxable income due to a cyclical downturn, strong international competition, or other factors.
- Investment at low real interest rates, which increases the company's deductions for depreciation relative to those for interest payments.

Presuming the AMT hurdle can be resolved, one major advantage of the corporate form is the opportunity to control the income tax burden of the owner(s). One way this control can be accomplished is to accumulate the earnings of the business at the corporate level. A temporary or permanent accumulation of earnings in a corporation results in a deferral of the second tax at the shareholder level. The corporation can invest the funds in tax-free vehicles or in other corporations to take advantage of the dividends received deduction. Accumulations at the corporate level could result in a *modest* tax benefit because dividend income would be converted into long-term capital gain. Long-term capital gains of noncorporate taxpayers cannot be taxed at a rate in excess of 28 percent. Dividend income is ordinary income and can be taxed at a rate as high as 39.6 percent.

Congress took steps to stem corporate accumulations as early as the first income tax law enacted under the Sixteenth Amendment. Today, in addition to the usual corporate income tax, an extra tax is imposed on earnings accumulated beyond the reasonable needs of the business. Also, a penalty tax may be imposed on undistributed personal holding company income.

This chapter explains how corporations can reduce or eliminate the AMT, which to a large degree taxes a company's economic income. Also, it demonstrates how closely held corporations can accumulate earnings without triggering the imposition of the accumulated earnings and personal holding company penalty taxes.

ALTERNATIVE MINIMUM TAX

The AMT applicable to regular corporations is similar to the AMT applicable to individuals.[1] Many of the adjustments and tax preference items necessary to arrive at **alternative minimum taxable income (AMTI)** are the same. The rates and exemptions are different, but the objective is identical—to force taxpayers who are more profitable than their taxable income reflects to pay additional income taxes.

The AMT is in addition to the regular corporate tax, but is computed in a manner wholly separate and independent from it. This truly alternative and parallel income tax system requires separate and independent calculations of the amount and character of all items affecting the computation of the AMT. The Code itself mandates separate and independent treatment of many items affecting the computation of the AMT. Regulations provide broad rules requiring separate and independent treatment of other items for AMT purposes. However, the Code and Regulations do not provide guidance for many items.

The formula for determining the AMT liability of corporate taxpayers appears in Figure 6–1 and follows the format of Form 4626 (Alternative Minimum Tax—Corporations).

AMT ADJUSTMENTS

2 **LEARNING OBJECTIVE**
Work with the alternative minimum tax applicable to corporations.

As Figure 6–1 indicates, the starting point for computing AMTI is the taxable income of the corporation before any net operating loss (NOL) deduction. Certain adjustments must be made to this amount. Unlike tax preference items, which are always additions, the adjustments may either increase or decrease taxable income.

The positive adjustments arise as a result of timing differences and are added back to the taxable income in computing AMTI. Since most preferences only defer taxes, a corporation may recoup AMT paid on tax preferences when the deferral of regular tax (that the preference created) is reversed and the regular tax is due. Once the preferences reverse themselves, they are deducted from taxable income to arrive at AMTI. This mechanism is called the *netting process*.

Although NOLs are separately stated in Figure 6–1, they are actually negative adjustments. They are separately stated in Figure 6–1 and on Form 4626 because they may not exceed more than 90 percent of AMTI. Thus, such adjustments cannot be determined until all other adjustments and tax preference items are considered.

---

[1] The AMT provisions are contained in §§ 55 through 59.

▼ **FIGURE 6–1**
AMT Formula for Corporations

Regular taxable income before NOL deduction

Plus/minus: AMT adjustments (except ACE adjustment)

Plus: Tax preferences

Equals: AMTI before AMT NOL deduction and ACE adjustment

Plus/minus: ACE adjustment

Equals: AMTI before AMT NOL deduction

Minus: AMT NOL deduction (limited to 90%)

Equals: Alternative minimum taxable income (AMTI)

Minus: Exemption

Equals: Tentative minimum tax base

Times: 20% rate

Equals: Tentative minimum tax before AMT foreign tax credit

Minus: AMT foreign tax credit (possibly limited to 90%)

Equals: Tentative minimum tax

Minus: Regular tax liability before credits minus regular foreign tax credit

Equals: Alternative minimum tax (AMT)

TAX IN THE NEWS

THE AMT UNDULY HARMS THE U.S. STEEL INDUSTRY

According to a recent release by the American Iron and Steel Institute, the AMT has had an adverse impact on steel and other marginally profitable capital-intensive industries. In one five-year period, a U.S. steel company reported $1.2 billion in losses to shareholders yet paid $200 million in AMT.

Besides being subject to 15-year capital cost recovery periods for most steel assets (versus 7 years under regular corporate tax), steel companies under the AMT have to use a 150 percent declining-balance method (versus 200 percent under the regular tax).

Because the U.S. tax law has the worst cost recovery system in the industrialized world, our businesses are placed in a competitive disadvantage in world trade. After five years and under the AMT, a U.S. steel company can recover only 37 percent of its investment in casting equipment. This is to be contrasted with 58 percent in Japan, 81 percent in Germany, 90 percent in Korea, and 100 percent in Brazil. In steel, advances in technology require a steady stream of investment in new equipment just to stay competitive. American companies have a more difficult time recovering their investment so that they can move to the next generation of technology.

Other adjustments include the following:

- A portion of depreciation on property placed in service after 1986. For realty, the adjustment amount is the difference between depreciation for regular tax purposes and ADS depreciation using a 40-year life. For personalty, the adjustment is the excess of accelerated depreciation over the amount determined using the 150 percent declining-balance method switching to straight-line. Thus, the depreciation allowances for purposes of the AMT are generally much less favorable than for the regular corporate income tax.

EXAMPLE 1

Purple Corporation placed an asset costing $10,000 in service on March 15, 1996. Based upon a three-year recovery class life, this personalty has the following effect upon the AMTI:

Year	Tax Deduction 200%	AMT Deduction 150%	Increase or (Decrease) AMT Adjustment
1996	$3,333	$2,500	$ 833
1997	4,445	3,750	695
1998	1,481	2,500	(1,019)
1999	741	1,250	(509)

- Since different depreciation methods are used for AMT and regular tax purposes, the adjusted bases for these depreciable assets are affected. When the bases are different and the asset is disposed of, a basis adjustment is necessary to reflect the difference in the AMT gain or loss *and* the regular tax gain or loss.

EXAMPLE 2

Assume the same facts as in Example 1, except that the asset is sold at the end of the second year for $4,000. For regular tax purposes, the basis is $2,222 ($10,000 − $3,333 − $4,445), and the basis for AMT purposes is $3,750 ($10,000 − $2,500 − $3,750). Thus, the regular tax gain is $1,778 ($4,000 − $2,222), and the AMT gain is $250 ($4,000 − $3,750). Consequently, a $1,528 negative basis adjustment is required when computing AMT ($1,778 − $250). ▼

- Passive activity losses of certain closely held corporations and personal service corporations.
- The excess of mining exploration and development costs over what would have resulted if the costs had been capitalized and written off over 10 years.
- For contracts entered into on or after March 1, 1986, the requirement that the percentage of completion method be used for AMTI purposes. Thus, corporations using the completed contract method must make the appropriate adjustment.
- For AMTI purposes, denial to dealers of the use of the installment method in accounting for sales. Consequently, gain must be reflected in the year the property is disposed of.
- A portion of the difference between **adjusted current earnings (ACE)** and unadjusted AMTI (post-1989).

ADJUSTED CURRENT EARNINGS (ACE)

3   **LEARNING OBJECTIVE**
Understand the function of adjusted current earnings (ACE).

The ACE rules are a separate parallel system to both AMT and taxable income. S corporations, real estate investment trusts, regulated investment companies, and real estate mortgage investment conduits are not subjected to the ACE provisions.

The purpose of the ACE adjustment is to ensure that the mismatching of financial statement income and taxable income will not produce inequitable results. The ACE adjustment is tax-based and can be a negative amount. AMTI is increased by 75 percent of the excess of ACE over unadjusted AMTI. Or, AMTI is reduced by 75 percent of the excess of unadjusted AMTI over ACE. This negative adjustment is limited to the aggregate of the positive adjustments under ACE for

▼ **FIGURE 6-2**
Determining the ACE
Adjustment*

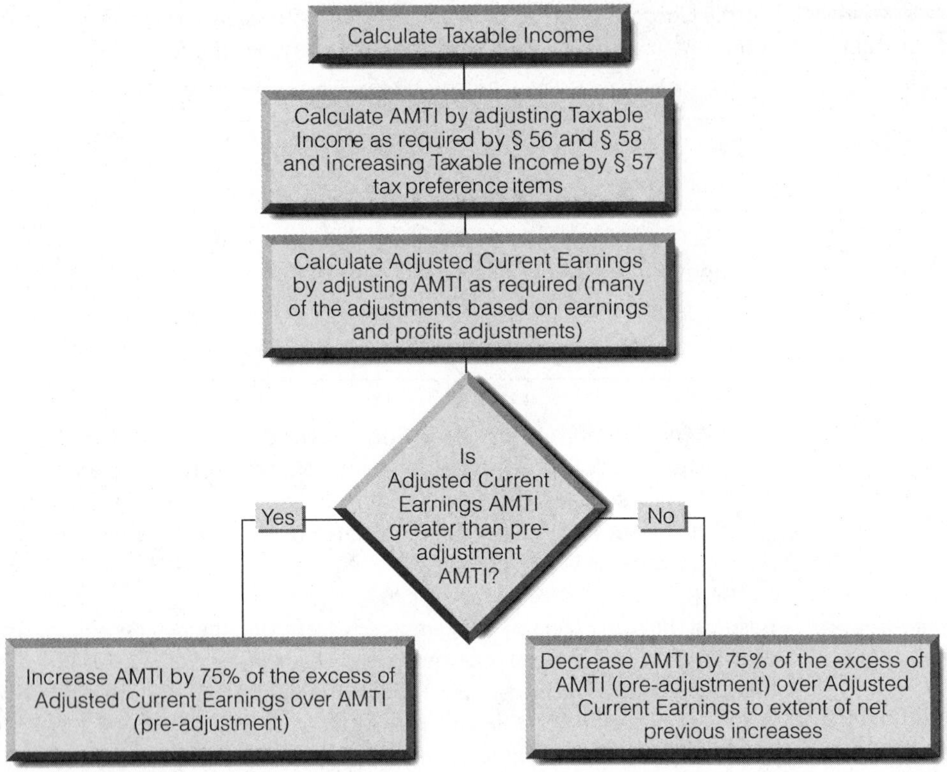

```
                    Calculate Taxable Income

            Calculate AMTI by adjusting Taxable
             Income as required by § 56 and § 58
            and increasing Taxable Income by § 57
                     tax preference items

            Calculate Adjusted Current Earnings
             by adjusting AMTI as required (many
            of the adjustments based on earnings
                   and profits adjustments)

                              Is
                        Adjusted Current
              Yes        Earnings AMTI          No
                       greater than pre-
                          adjustment
                            AMTI?

      Increase AMTI by 75% of the excess of      Decrease AMTI by 75% of the excess of
       Adjusted Current Earnings over AMTI       AMTI (pre-adjustment) over Adjusted
               (pre-adjustment)                   Current Earnings to extent of net
                                                         previous increases
```

*Adapted from "Corporate Alternative Minimum Tax: The Impact of Current Earnings Adjustment on Oil and Gas Companies"
by Gallun and Zachry, which appeared in the September 1989 issue of the *Oil and Gas Tax Quarterly*, published and
copyrighted 1989 by Matthew Bender & Co., and appears here with their permission.

prior years reduced by the previously claimed negative adjustments (see Figure
6-2). Thus, the ordering of the timing differences is crucial because any unused
negative adjustment is lost forever. Unadjusted AMTI is AMTI without the ACE
adjustment or the AMT NOL.[2]

EXAMPLE **3**

A calendar year corporation has the following data:

	1996	1997	1998
Unadjusted AMTI	$3,000	$3,000	$3,100
Adjusted current earnings	4,000	3,000	2,000

In 1996, since ACE exceeds unadjusted AMTI by $1,000, $750 (75% × $1,000) will be
included as a positive adjustment to AMTI. No adjustment is necessary for 1997. Unadjusted AMTI exceeds ACE by $1,100 in 1998, so there is a potential negative adjustment to
AMTI of $825. Since the total increases to AMTI for prior years equal $750 (and there are no
negative adjustments), only $750 of the potential negative adjustment will reduce AMTI for

---

[2] §§ 56(g)(1) and (2).

CONCEPT SUMMARY 6–1

Impact of Various Transactions on ACE and E & P

	Effect on Unadjusted AMTI in Arriving at ACE	Effect on Taxable Income in Arriving at E & P
Tax-exempt income (net of expenses)	Add	Add
Federal income tax	No effect	Subtract
Dividends received deduction (80% and 100% rules)	No effect	Add
Dividends received deduction (70% rule)	Add	Add
Exemption amount of $40,000	No effect	No effect
Key employee insurance proceeds	Add	Add
Excess charitable contribution	No effect	Subtract
Excess capital losses	No effect	Subtract
Disallowed travel and entertainment expenses	No effect	Subtract
Penalties and fines	No effect	Subtract
Intangible drilling costs deducted currently	Add	Add
Deferred gain on installment sales	Add	Add
Realized (not recognized) gain on an involuntary conversion	No effect	No effect
Loss on sale between related parties	Subtract	Subtract
Gift received	No effect	No effect
Net buildup on life insurance policy	Add	Add

Note: See also Concept Summary 4–1.

1998. Further, $75 of the negative amount is lost forever. Prior book income adjustments are ignored for limitation purposes. ▼

ACE should not be confused with current earnings and profits (E & P). Many items are treated in the same manner, but certain items that are deductible in computing E & P (but are not deductible in calculating taxable income) generally are not deductible in computing ACE (e.g., Federal income taxes). Concept Summary 6–1 compares the impact various transactions will have on the determination of ACE and E & P.

The starting point for computing ACE is AMTI, which is defined as regular taxable income after AMT adjustments (other than the NOL and ACE adjustments) and tax preferences.[3] The resulting figure is adjusted for the following items in order to determine ACE:

- *Exclusion items.* These are income items (net of related expenses) that are included in E & P, but will never be included in regular taxable income or AMTI (except on liquidation or disposal of a business). In essence, items that are permanently excluded from unadjusted AMTI but are included in E & P are therefore included in ACE (e.g., life insurance proceeds, interest on tax-exempt bonds, and tax benefit exclusions).

---
[3] § 56(g)(3).

- *Depreciation.* For property placed in service before 1994, the depreciation is calculated using the alternative depreciation system outlined in § 168(g). Thus, depreciation is based on acquisition costs using the straight-line method without regard to salvage value. For property placed in service after 1993, the ACE adjustment is eliminated. This change will speed up the depreciation allowance for capital-intensive industries. But computing the prior ACE depreciation adjustment for pre-1994 assets remains complex.
- *Disallowed items.* A deduction is not allowed in computing ACE if it is never deductible in computing E & P. Thus, the NOL deduction is not allowed. However, since the starting point for ACE is AMTI before the NOL, no adjustment is necessary for NOL. A deduction *is not allowed* for the dividends received deduction of 70 percent (less than 20 percent ownership). But a deduction *is allowed* for the dividends received deduction of 80 percent (20 percent but less than 80 percent ownership) and 100 percent (80 percent or more ownership).[4]
- *Other adjustments.* The following adjustments, which are required for regular E & P purposes, are necessary: intangible drilling costs, circulation expenditures, organization expense amortization, LIFO inventory adjustments, and installment sales.[5]
- *Both AMTI and ACE.* Deduction items must be deductible for both AMTI and E & P purposes in order to be deductible for ACE. For example, certain deductible items do not reduce ACE: excess charitable contributions, excess capital losses, disallowed travel and entertainment expenses, penalties, fines, bribes, and golden parachute payments.
- *Lessee improvements.* The value of improvements made by a lessee to a lessor's property that is excluded from the lessor's income is excluded from both unadjusted AMTI and ACE.
- *LIFO recapture adjustments.* An increase or decrease in the LIFO recapture amount will result in a corresponding increase or decrease in ACE.

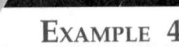

EXAMPLE 4

Crimson Corporation makes the ACE adjustment calculation as follows:

AMTI		$ 278,000
Plus:		
Municipal bond interest	$21,000	
Installment gain	14,000	
70% dividends received deduction	30,000	
Income element in cash surrender life insurance	6,000	
Organization expense amortization	7,000	78,000
		$ 356,000
Less:		
ACE depreciation in excess of amount allowed for AMTI (property placed in service before 1994)	$23,000	
Life insurance expense	1,000	24,000
Adjusted current earnings		$ 332,000
AMTI		−278,000
Base amount		$ 54,000
Times		.75
ACE adjustment (positive)		$ 40,500

[4] §§ 56(g)(4)(C)(i) and (ii).   [5] Reg. § 1.65(g)–1(f).

TAX PREFERENCES

AMTI includes designated **tax preference items.** In many cases, this inclusion has
the effect of subjecting nontaxable income to the AMT. Some of the most common
tax preferences include the following:

- Amortization claimed on certified pollution control facilities.
- Accelerated depreciation on real property in excess of straight-line (placed in
service before 1987).
- Tax-exempt interest on state and local bonds where the generated funds are
not used for an essential function of the government.
- Percentage depletion claimed in excess of the adjusted basis of property.
- For integrated oil companies (Exxon, Texaco) the excess of intangible drilling
costs over 10-year amortization if in excess of 65 percent of net oil and gas
income. This item is not a tax preference for independent oil and gas
producers and royalty owners.

COMPUTING ALTERNATIVE MINIMUM TAXABLE INCOME

The following example illustrates the effect of tax preferences and adjustments in
arriving at AMTI.

EXAMPLE 5

For 1997, Tan Corporation (a calendar year, integrated oil company) had the following
transactions:

Taxable income	$200,000
Mining exploration costs	50,000
Percentage depletion claimed (the property has a zero adjusted basis)	70,000
Donation of land held since 1980 as an investment (basis of $40,000 and fair market value of $50,000) to a qualified charity	50,000
Interest on City of Elmira (Michigan) bonds. The proceeds were used for nongovernmental purposes	30,000

Tan Corporation's AMTI for 1997 is determined as follows:

Taxable income		$200,000
Adjustments		
Excess mining exploration costs [$50,000 (amount expensed) − $5,000 (amount allowed over a 10-year amortization period)]		45,000
Tax preferences		
Excess depletion	$70,000	
Interest on bonds	30,000	100,000
AMTI		$345,000

EXEMPTION

The AMT is 20 percent of AMTI that exceeds the exemption amount. The
exemption amount for a corporation is $40,000 reduced by 25 percent of the
amount by which AMTI exceeds $150,000.

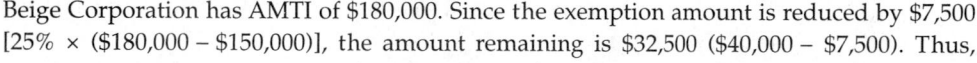

EXAMPLE 6

Beige Corporation has AMTI of $180,000. Since the exemption amount is reduced by $7,500
[25% × ($180,000 − $150,000)], the amount remaining is $32,500 ($40,000 − $7,500). Thus,

Beige Corporation's alternative minimum tax base (refer to Figure 6–1) is $147,500 ($180,000 − $32,500). ▼

Note that the exemption phases out entirely when AMTI reaches $310,000.

MINIMUM TAX CREDIT

The AMT is a separate tax system that is computed side-by-side with the regular tax. Along with the "netting concept," a **minimum tax credit** is available to eliminate the possibility of double taxation. Essentially, the AMT paid in one tax year may be carried forward indefinitely and used as a credit against the corporation's future *regular* tax liability that exceeds its tentative minimum tax. The minimum tax credit may not be carried back and may not be offset against any future *minimum* tax liability.

Unfortunately, the law does not cover the reverse situation (a preference item generates a regular tax in one year and results in an AMT in a later year). An example could be unearned income that is taxed in the year of receipt but is not recognized for book income purposes until the year earned. Consequently, it is entirely possible that the same income could be taxed twice.

EXAMPLE 7

In Example 5, the AMTI exceeds $310,000, so there is no exemption amount. The tentative minimum tax is $69,000 (20% of $345,000). Assuming the regular tax liability in 1997 is $68,000, the AMT liability is $1,000 ($69,000 − $68,000). The amount of the minimum tax credit carryover is $1,000, which is all of the current year's AMT. ▼

OTHER ASPECTS OF THE AMT

In addition to paying their regular tax liability, corporations have to make estimated tax payments of the AMT liability. Even corporations that prepare quarterly financial statements may find this requirement adds to compliance costs. Unfortunately, the estimated tax payment dates will not coincide with the dates of the financial statements. Accordingly, estimating book income accurately for AMT purposes from the information usually available may be difficult.

The AMT can be computed and reported by completing Form 4626.

PENALTY TAX ON UNREASONABLE ACCUMULATIONS

4   LEARNING OBJECTIVE
Appreciate the purpose of the accumulated earnings tax.

In a corporate situation, income is taxed at the corporation level and again when the income is distributed or the stock is sold or exchanged. One method of optimizing the distribution of corporate earnings is to accumulate the earnings until the most advantageous time to distribute them to shareholders. While the earnings are being accumulated, the corporation can invest in dividend-paying stocks and take advantage of the 70 percent dividends received deduction. Also, for corporate income below $75,000, the corporate rate may be below the individual tax rate.

If the board of directors is aware of the tax problems of the shareholders, it can channel earnings into the shareholders' pockets with a minimum of tax cost by using any of several mechanisms. The corporation can distribute dividends only in years when the major shareholders are in lower tax brackets. Alternatively, dividend distributions might be curtailed, causing the value of the stock to increase in a manner similar to a savings account. Later, the shareholders can sell their stock in the year of their choice at an amount that reflects the increased retained earnings and receive capital gain treatment. In this manner, the capital gain could be postponed to years when less tax results (e.g., the shareholders have capital losses to offset the gains). Alternatively, the shareholders can retain their shares. Upon death, the estate or heirs will receive a step-up in basis equal to the fair market value of the stock on the date of death or, if elected, on the alternate valuation date. The increment in value represented by the step-up in basis will be largely attributable to the earnings retained by the corporation and will not be subject to income taxation.

Accumulating corporate earnings always entails problems, however. A penalty tax may be imposed on accumulated taxable earnings, or a personal holding company tax may be levied on certain accumulated passive income. Consider first the 39.6 percent **accumulated earnings tax (AET).** The tax law is framed to discourage the retention of earnings that are unrelated to the business needs of the company. Earnings retained in the business to avoid the imposition of the tax that would have been imposed on distributions to the shareholder are subject to a 39.6 percent penalty tax.

EXAMPLE 8

Janet operated a consulting business as a sole proprietor in 1996. Assume she is in the 39.6% tax bracket in 1997, and she incorporates her business at the beginning of the year. Her business earns $120,000 in 1997, before her salary of $60,000. Since $60,000 of the income is accumulated, $13,760 of taxes are "saved" ($23,760 individual tax versus $10,000 corporate tax on the $60,000 accumulated). This accumulated savings could occur each year with the corporation reinvesting the saved taxes. Thus, without an accumulated earnings tax or personal holding company tax, Janet could use her corporation like a savings account. For example, the corporation could take advantage of the 70% dividends received deduction for dividend-paying stocks. With the top individual tax rate (39.6% for 1997) above the top corporate tax rate (35% for 1997), it is more attractive to hold investment property in a C corporation than in a flow-through entity (partnership, S corporation, or sole proprietor). However, the earnings are still at the corporate level, and Janet might be in a higher individual rate when the accumulated earnings are distributed. ▼

THE ELEMENT OF INTENT

Although the penalty tax is normally applied against closely held corporations, a corporation is not exempt from the tax merely because its stock is widely held.[6] For example, a Second Court of Appeals decision[7] imposed the tax upon a widely held corporation with over 1,500 shareholders. However, a much smaller group of shareholders actually controlled the corporation. As a practical matter, a widely held corporation that is not under the legal or effective control of a small group is unlikely to be suspected of accumulating earnings for the purpose of tax avoidance.

The key to imposition of the tax is not the number of the shareholders in the corporation but whether a shareholder group controls corporate policy. If such a group does exist and withholds dividends to protect its own tax position, an AET (§ 531) problem might materialize.

When a corporation is formed or used to shield its shareholders from individual taxes by accumulating rather than distributing earnings and profits, the

---

[6] § 532(c).

[7] *Trico Products v. Comm.*, 43–2 USTC ¶9540, 31 AFTR 394, 137 F.2d
424 (CA–2, 1943).

"bad" purpose for accumulating earnings is considered to exist under § 532(a). This subjective test, in effect, asks, Did the corporation and/or shareholder(s) *intend* to retain the earnings in order to avoid the tax on dividends? According to the Supreme Court, the tax avoidance motive need *not* be the dominant or controlling purpose to trigger application of the penalty tax; it need only be a contributing factor to the retention of earnings.[8] If a corporation accumulates funds beyond its reasonable needs, such action is determinative of the existence of a "bad" purpose, unless the contrary can be proven by the preponderance of the evidence. The fact that a business is a mere holding or investment company is *prima facie* evidence of this tax avoidance purpose.[9]

IMPOSITION OF THE TAX AND THE ACCUMULATED EARNINGS CREDIT

Contrary to its name, the accumulated earnings tax is not levied on the corporate accumulated earnings balance. Instead, the tax is imposed on the current year's addition to this balance not needed for a reasonable business purpose. The penalty tax is not imposed upon S corporations, personal holding companies, foreign personal holding companies, tax-exempt organizations, and passive foreign investment companies. The tax is in addition to the regular corporate tax and the 20 percent alternative minimum tax. For taxable years beginning after December 31, 1992, the rate is 39.6 percent.

Most corporations are allowed a **minimum credit** of $250,000 against accumulated taxable income, even when earnings are accumulating beyond reasonable business needs. However, certain personal service corporations in health, law, engineering, architecture, accounting, actuarial science, performing arts, and consulting are limited to a $150,000 accumulated earnings credit. Moreover, a nonservice corporation (other than a holding or investment company) may retain more than $250,000 ($150,000 for a service organization) of accumulated earnings if the company can justify the accumulation as necessary to meet the reasonable needs of the business.[10]

The **accumulated earnings credit** is the greater of the following:

1. The current E & P for the tax year that are needed to meet the reasonable needs of the business (see the subsequent discussion) *less* the net long-term capital gain for the year (net of any tax). In determining the reasonable needs for any one year, the accumulated E & P of past years must be taken into account.
2. The amount by which $250,000 exceeds the accumulated E & P of the corporation at the close of the preceding tax year (designated the *minimum credit*).

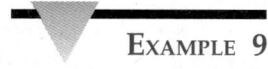

EXAMPLE 9

Yellow Corporation, a calendar year manufacturing concern, has accumulated E & P of $120,000 as of December 31, 1996. For 1997, it has no capital gains and current E & P of $140,000. A realistic estimate places Yellow Corporation's reasonable needs of the business for 1997 at $200,000.

---

[8] *U.S. v. The Donruss Co.*, 69–1 USTC ¶9167, 23 AFTR2d 69–418, 89 S.Ct. 501 (USSC, 1969).

[9] § 533. See, for example, *H. C. Cockrell Warehouse Corp.*, 71 T.C. 1036 (1979).

[10] §§ 535(c) and 537 and Reg. § 1.537–1.

The allowable credit is the greater of (1) or (2).

	(1)	(2)
Reasonable needs	$200,000	
Minimum credit		$250,000
Accumulated E & P	120,000	120,000
Potential credit	$ 80,000	$130,000

Thus, the credit becomes $130,000 (the greater of $80,000 or $130,000). ▼

Several observations can be made about the accumulated earnings credit. First, the minimum credit of $250,000 is of no consequence as long as the prior year's ending balance in accumulated E & P is $250,000 or more. Second, when the credit is based on reasonable needs, the credit is the amount that exceeds accumulated E & P. Third, a taxpayer must choose between the reasonable needs credit (item 1) and the minimum credit (item 2). Combining the two in the same year is not permissible. Fourth, although the § 531 tax is not imposed on accumulated E & P, the amount of the credit depends upon the balance of this account as of the end of the preceding year.

REASONABLE NEEDS OF THE BUSINESS

5 **LEARNING OBJECTIVE**
Determine the reasonable needs of the business.

If a corporation's funds are invested in assets essential to the needs of the business, the IRS will have a difficult time imposing the AET. "Thus, the size of the accumulated earnings and profits or surplus is not the crucial factor; rather it is the reasonableness and nature of the surplus."[11] What are the reasonable business needs of a corporation? This question is difficult to answer and creates controversy with the IRS.

Justifiable Needs—In General. The **reasonable needs of a business** include the business's reasonably anticipated needs.[12] These anticipated needs must be specific, definite, and feasible. A number of court decisions illustrate that indefinite plans referred to only briefly in corporate minutes merely provide a false feeling of security for the taxpayer.[13]

The Regulations list some legitimate reasons that could indicate that the earnings of a corporation are being accumulated to meet the reasonable needs of the business. Earnings may be allowed to accumulate to provide for bona fide expansion of the business enterprise or replacement of plant and facilities as well as to acquire a business enterprise through the purchase of stock or assets. Provision for the retirement of bona fide indebtedness created in connection with the trade or business (e.g., the establishment of a sinking fund for the retirement of bonds issued by the corporation) is a legitimate reason for accumulating earnings under ordinary circumstances. Providing necessary working capital for the business (e.g., to acquire inventories) and providing for investment or loans to suppliers or customers (if necessary to maintain the business of the corporation)

---

[11] *Smoot Sand & Gravel Corp. v. Comm.*, 60–1 USTC ¶9241, 5 AFTR 2d 626, 274 F.2d 495 (CA–4, 1960).
[12] § 537(a)(1).

[13] See, for example, *Fine Realty, Inc. v. U.S.*, 62–2 USTC ¶9758, 10 AFTR2d 5751, 209 F.Supp. 286 (D.Ct. Minn., 1962).

are valid grounds for accumulating earnings.[14] Funds may be retained for self-insurance[15] and realistic business contingencies (e.g., lawsuits, patent infringement).[16] Accumulations to avoid an unfavorable competitive position[17] and to carry key employee life insurance policies[18] are justifiable. Accumulation for the possible loss of a key customer or client is a reasonable need of the business.[19]

The reasonable business needs of a company also include the post-death § 303 redemption requirements of a corporation.[20] Accumulations for such purposes are limited to the amount needed (or reasonably anticipated to be needed) to redeem stock included in the gross estate of the decedent-shareholder.[21] This amount may not exceed the sum of the death taxes and funeral and administration expenses allowable under § 2053 or § 2106.[22]

Section 537(b) provides that reasonable accumulations to pay future product liability losses represent a reasonable anticipated need of the business. Guidelines for the application of this change are prescribed in Proposed Regulations.

Justifiable Needs—Working Capital Requirements for Inventory Situations. For many years the penalty tax on accumulated earnings was based upon the concept of retained earnings. The courts generally looked at retained earnings alone to determine whether there was an unreasonable accumulation. However, a corporation may have a large retained earnings balance and yet possess no liquid assets with which to pay dividends. Therefore, the emphasis should more appropriately be placed upon the liquidity of a corporation. Does the business have liquid assets *not* needed that could be used to pay dividends? The courts did not begin to use this liquidity approach until 1960, however.

The operating cycle of a business is the average time interval between the acquisition of materials (or services) entering the business and the final realization of cash. The courts seized upon the operating cycle because it had the advantage of objectivity for purposes of determining working capital. A normal business has two distinct cycles:

1. Purchase of inventory → the production process → finished goods inventory.
2. Sale of merchandise → accounts receivable → cash collection.

A systematic operating cycle formula was developed in *Bardahl Manufacturing Co.* and *Bardahl International Corp.*[23] The technique became known as the *Bardahl* formula. This formula is not a precise tool and is subject to various interpretations.

The following is the standard formula used to determine the reasonable working capital needs for a corporation:

$$\text{Inventory cycle} = \frac{\text{Average inventory}}{\text{Cost of goods sold}}$$

[14] Reg. § 1.537–2(b).

[15] *Halby Chemical Co., Inc. v. U.S.*, 67–2 USTC ¶9500, 19 AFTR2d 1589, 180 Ct.Cls. 584 (Ct.Cls., 1967).

[16] *Dielectric Materials Co.*, 57 T.C. 587 (1972).

[17] *North Valley Metabolic Laboratories*, 34 TCM 400, T.C.Memo, 1975–79.

[18] *Emeloid Co. v. Comm.*, 51–1 USTC ¶66,013, 40 AFTR 674, 189 F.2d 230 (CA–3, 1951). Key employee life insurance is a policy on the life of a key employee that is owned by and made payable to the employer. Such insurance enables the employer to recoup some of the economic loss that could materialize upon the untimely death of the key employee.

[19] *EMI Corporation*, 50 TCM 569, T.C.Memo. 1985–386 and *James H. Rutter*, 52 TCM 326, T.C.Memo. 1986–407.

[20] The § 303 redemption to pay death taxes and administration expenses of a deceased shareholder is discussed in Chapter 5. See § 537(a).

[21] §§ 537(a)(2) and (b)(1).

[22] § 303(a).

[23] *Bardahl Manufacturing Co.*, 24 TCM 1030, T.C.Memo. 1965–200; *Bardahl International Corp.*, 25 TCM 935, T.C.Memo. 1966–182. See also *Apollo Industries, Inc. v. Comm.*, 66–1 USTC ¶9294, 17 AFTR2d 518, 358 F.2d 867 (CA–1, 1966).

Plus

$$\text{Accounts receivable cycle} = \frac{\text{Average accounts receivable}}{\text{Net sales}}$$

Minus

$$\text{Accounts payable cycle} = \frac{\text{Average accounts payable}^{24}}{\text{Purchases} + \text{cash operating expenses}}$$

Equals

A decimal percentage

This imprecise formula assumes that working capital needs are computed on a yearly basis. However, this may not provide the most favorable result. A business that experiences seasonally based high and low cycles illustrates this point. For example, a construction company can justify a greater working capital need if computations are based on a cycle that includes the winter months only and not on an annual average.[25] In the same vein, an incorporated CPA firm would choose a cycle during the slow season.

The decimal percentage derived above, when multiplied by the cost of goods sold plus general, administrative, and selling expenses (not including unpaid Federal income taxes and depreciation),[26] equals the working capital needs of the business. Paid estimated Federal income taxes are treated as operating expenses, but profit sharing contributions and charitable contributions are not operating expenses.

If the statistically computed working capital needs plus any extraordinary expenses are more than the current year's net working capital, no penalty tax is imposed. Working capital is the excess of current assets over current liabilities. This amount is the relatively liquid portion of the total business capital that is a buffer for meeting obligations within the normal operating cycle of the business.

However, if working capital needs plus any extraordinary expenses are less than the current year's net working capital, the possibility of the imposition of a penalty tax does exist.[27]

The IRS normally takes the position that the operating cycle should be reduced by the accounts payable cycle. The IRS maintains that the payment of such expenses may be postponed by various credit arrangements that will reduce the operating capital requirements. However, a number of court decisions have omitted such a reduction. Some courts use all payables, while other courts use only material and trade payables. In any case, a corporate tax planner should not have to rely on creditors to avoid the accumulated earnings penalty tax. The corporation with the most acute working capital problem will probably have a large accounts payable balance. If the formula for determining reasonable working capital needs is used, a large accounts payable balance will result in a sizable reduction in the maximum working capital allowable before the tax is imposed. For tax planning purposes, a corporation should hold accounts payable at a reduced level.

---

[24] The accounts payable cycle was developed in *Kingsbury Investments, Inc.*, 28 TCM 1082, T.C.Memo. 1969–205. Some courts have used only purchases and not total operating expenses: *Suwannee Lumber Mfg. Co., Inc.*, 39 TCM 572, T.C.Memo. 1979–477. But see *Snow Manufacturing*, 86 T.C. 260 (1986).

[25] See *Audits of Construction Contracts*, AICPA, 1965, p. 25.

[26] In *W. L. Mead, Inc.*, 34 TCM 924, T.C.Memo. 1975–215, the Tax Court allowed depreciation to be included in the expenses of a service firm with no inventory. Likewise, in *Doug-Long, Inc.*, 72 T.C. 158 (1979), the Tax Court allowed a truck stop to include quarterly estimated tax payments in operating expenses.

[27] *Electric Regulator Corp. v. Comm.*, 64–2 USTC ¶9705, 14 AFTR2d 5447, 336 F.2d 339 (CA–2, 1964) used "quick assets" (current assets less inventory).

TAX IN THE NEWS

APPLYING THE BARDAHL FORMULA COULD BE MISLEADING

Experience in tax audits has shown that the *Bardahl* formula is a double-edged sword. The problem is that it measures working capital, not cash. In reality, the payment of dividends—which is the whole purpose of the AET provisions—can be made only in cash. When the *Bardahl* formula works to a corporation's disadvantage, it is important to determine how much cash, on average, is available for distribution. Case law has held that a corporation should not be forced to incur debt or sell off business assets merely to pay dividends so as to avoid the AET. The statement of cash flows may be useful in defending against an AET attack, because it highlights fixed assets acquired and other business investments made. Cash on hand at the end of the year may not be a fair reflection of the average of cash available during the year. In addition, bank covenants, which prevent the payment of dividends or require certain levels of working capital, should be taken into account since they evidence a nonprohibited purpose for accumulating earnings. However, lack of cash due to nonbusiness related activities, such as loans to shareholders, will not help avoid AET exposure.

On the other hand, when the *Bardahl* formula indicates that the working capital needs are greater than the working capital available, weary IRS agents are sometimes willing to accept this as dispositive that no AET should be assessed, rather than investigating the other aspects of potential AET exposure.

SOURCE: Excerpted by permission from Michael J. Goldberg, "The Accumulated Earnings Tax: A Practical Approach to a Subjective Assessment," *The Tax Adviser*, March 1993, p. 146.

Justifiable Needs—Working Capital Requirements for Noninventory Situations. A service business does not purchase inventories, so part of the operating cycle in the *Bardahl* formula is missing. However, a service business incurs certain costs such as salaries and overhead for a period of time before billing customers for services. Some courts have used a rough rule of thumb to determine an inventory equivalent cycle. Under certain circumstances, a human resource accounting (HRA) approach may be used to determine the working capital needs of a noninventory corporation. The use of an HRA approach is based on the contention that the strength of a service business—and its major asset—is its highly educated, skilled technicians. Such individuals must be available both to attract clients and to execute projects efficiently. In the event of a business downturn, it would be foolish to abruptly discharge highly paid specialists, recruited and trained at considerable expense. The business decline might prove to be of brief duration.

One court[28] allowed an engineering firm to add to the IRS's *Bardahl*-calculated operating reserve the reasonable professional and technical payroll for an additional period of two months (or 60 days). The Court felt that this extra amount would ". . . allow sufficient reserve for one cycle of full operation plus a reasonable period (60 days) of curtailed operation to recapture business or, in the alternative, to face up to hard decisions on reducing the scope of the entire operation or

---

[28] *Simons-Eastern Co. v. U.S.*, 73–1 USTC ¶9279, 31 AFTR2d 73–640, 354 F.Supp. 1003 (D.Ct. Ga., 1972). See also *Delaware Trucking Co., Inc.*, 32 TCM 105, T.C.Memo. 1973–29; *Magic Mart, Inc.*, 51 T.C. 775 (1969); and *Technalysis*, 101 T.C. 397 (1993), a three-month period.

CONCEPT SUMMARY 6–2

Reasonable Business Needs

Legitimate Reasons	Invalid Reasons
Expansion of a business.	Loans to shareholders.
Replacement of capital assets.	Loans to brother-sister corporations.
Replacement of plant.	Future depression.
Acquisition of a business.	Unrealistic contingencies.
Working capital needs.	Investment in assets unrelated to the business.
Product liability loss.	Retirement of stock without a curtailment of the business.*
Loans to suppliers or customers.	
Redemption under § 303 to pay death taxes and administration expenses of a shareholder.	
Realistic business hazards.	
Loss of a major customer or client.	
Reserve for actual lawsuit.	
To protect a family business from takeover by outsiders.	
Debt retirement.	
Self-insurance.	

*But see *Technalysis*, 101 T.C. 397 (1993).

abandoning it." Further, the Court expressed its opinion that a multiple of reasonable professional and technical salaries is a useful method for determining the amount to be included in an operating reserve. However, the Court did not indicate why it selected two months as the magic number. It can be anticipated that the courts will continue to evolve a *Bardahl*-like formula for noninventory corporations.

No Justifiable Needs. Certain situations do *not* call for the accumulation of earnings. For example, accumulating earnings to make loans to shareholders[29] or brother-sister corporations is not considered within the reasonable needs of the business.[30] Accumulations to retire stock without curtailment of the business and for unrealistic business hazards (e.g., depression of the U.S. economy) are invalid reasons for accumulating funds.[31] The same holds true for accumulations made to carry out investments in properties or securities unrelated to the corporation's activity.[32]

Concept Summary 6–2 reviews the previous discussion regarding what does and does not constitute a reasonable need of the business.

---

[29] Reg. §§ 1.537–2(c)(1), (2), and (3).
[30] See *Young's Rubber Corp.*, 21 TCM 1593, T.C.Memo. 1962–300.
[31] *Turnbull, Inc. v. Comm.*, 67–1 USTC ¶9221, 19 AFTR2d 609, 373 F.2d 91 (CA–5, 1967), and Reg. § 1.537–2(c)(5).

[32] Reg. § 1.537–2(c)(4).

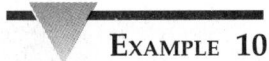

EXAMPLE 10

For a period of years, Brown, Inc., a trucking company, has considered the purchase of various vehicles and other facilities directly related to its business. It has, during the same time, also invested in oil and gas drilling projects (mostly wildcats). Despite substantial accumulated earnings, the corporation made no distributions of dividends during the same period of years. The Claims Court imposed the penalty tax because the plan to acquire vehicles and facilities was not supported by documents in existence or prepared during the taxable years at issue. Furthermore, accumulations to further the oil and gas investments were unjustified. Brown was not in the oil and gas business and was only a minor investor.[33] ▼

Measuring the Accumulation.   Should the cost or fair market value of assets be used to determine whether a corporation has accumulated E & P beyond its reasonable needs? This issue remains unclear. The Supreme Court has indicated that fair market value is to be used when dealing with marketable securities.[34] Although the Court admitted that the concept of E & P does not include unrealized appreciation, it asserted that the current asset ratio must be considered in determining if accumulated earnings are reasonable. Thus, the Court looked to the economic realities of the situation and held that fair market value is to be used with respect to readily marketable securities. The Court's opinion did not address the proper basis for valuation of assets other than marketable securities. However, the IRS may assert that this rule should be extended to include other assets. Therefore, tax advisers and corporate personnel should regularly check all security holdings to guard against accumulations caused by the appreciation of investments.

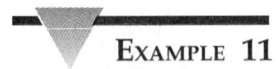

EXAMPLE 11

Robin Company had accumulated E & P of approximately $2,000,000. Five years ago, the company invested $150,000 in various stocks and bonds. At the end of the current tax year, the fair market value of these securities approximates $2,500,000. Two of Robin's shareholders, father and son, own 75% of the stock. If these securities are valued at cost, current assets minus current liabilities are deemed to be equal to the reasonable needs of the business. However, if the marketable securities are valued at their $2,500,000 fair market value, the value of the liquid assets greatly exceeds the corporation's reasonable needs. Under the Supreme Court's economic reality test, the fair market value is used. Consequently, the corporation is subject to the § 531 penalty tax. ▼

6 LEARNING OBJECTIVE
Compute the accumulated earnings tax.

MECHANICS OF THE PENALTY TAX

The taxable base of the AET is a company's accumulated taxable income (ATI). Taxable income of the corporation is modified as follows:[35]

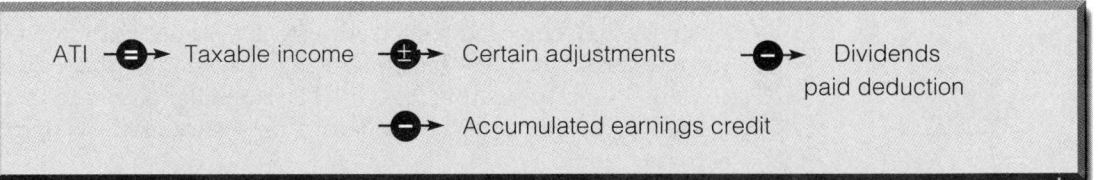

---

[33] *Cataphote Corp. of Miss. v. U.S.*, 75–2 USTC ¶9753, 36 AFTR2d 75–5990 (Ct.Cls., 1975).

[34] *Ivan Allen Co. v. U.S.*, 75–2 USTC ¶9557, 36 AFTR2d 75–5200, 95 S.Ct. 2501 (USSC, 1975).

[35] § 535(a).

The "certain adjustments" include the following items (for a corporation not a mere holding or investment company):

As deductions—

1. Corporate income tax accrued.
2. Charitable contributions in excess of 10 percent of adjusted taxable income.
3. Capital loss adjustment.[36]
4. Excess of net long-term capital gain over net short-term capital loss, diminished by the capital gain tax and reduced by net capital losses from earlier years.

And as additions—

5. Capital loss carryovers and carrybacks.
6. Net operating loss deduction.
7. The dividends received deduction.

The purpose of each of these adjustments is to produce an amount that more closely represents the dividend-paying capacity of the corporation. For example, the corporate income tax is deducted from taxable income because the corporation does not have this money to pay dividends. Conversely, the dividends received deduction is added to taxable income since the deduction has no impact upon the ability to pay a dividend. Note that item 4, in effect, allows a corporation to accumulate any capital gains without a penalty tax.

Payment of dividends reduces the amount of ATI subject to the penalty tax. The dividends paid deduction includes those dividends paid during the tax year that the shareholders must report as ordinary income *and* any dividends paid within 2½ months after the close of the tax year.[37] However, a nontaxable stock dividend does not affect the dividends paid deduction. Further, a shareholder may file a consent statement to treat as a dividend the amount specified in the statement. A consent dividend is taxed to the shareholder even though it is not actually distributed. The consent dividend is treated as a contribution to the capital of the corporation (paid-in capital) by the shareholder.[38]

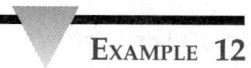

EXAMPLE 12

A nonservice closely held corporation that had no capital gains or losses in prior years has the following financial transactions for calendar year 1997:

Taxable income	$300,000
Tax liability	100,250
Excess charitable contributions	22,000
Short-term capital loss	(40,000)
Dividends received (less than 20% owned)	100,000
Research and development expenses	46,000
Dividends paid in 1997	40,000
Accumulated earnings (1/1/97)	220,000

[36] This deduction (item 3) and item 4 are either/or deductions, since a corporation would not have both in the same year. For the capital loss adjustment, see § 535(b)(5).

[37] §§ 535(a), 561(a), and 563(a).

[38] §§ 565(a) and (c)(2). The consent dividend procedure would be appropriate if the corporation is not in a position to make a cash or property distribution to its shareholders. The dividends paid deduction is discussed more fully later in the chapter.

Presuming the corporation is subject to the § 531 tax and has *no* reasonable business needs that justify its accumulations, the ATI is calculated as follows:

Taxable income		$300,000
Plus: 70% dividends received deduction		70,000
		$370,000
Less: Tax liability	$100,250	
Excess charitable contributions	22,000	
Net short-term capital loss adjustment	40,000	
Dividends paid	40,000	
Accumulated earnings minimum credit ($250,000 − $220,000)	30,000	232,250
Accumulated taxable income (ATI)		$137,750

Thus, the accumulated earnings penalty tax for 1997 would be $54,549 ($137,750 × 39.6%). ▼

EXAMPLE 13

In Example 12, assume that the reasonable needs of the business of § 535(c) amount to $270,000 in 1997. The current year's accumulated earnings are now reduced by $50,000, rather than the $30,000, of accumulated earnings minimum credit. ATI is $117,750, and the penalty tax is $46,629. Note that the first $220,000 of accumulated earnings *cannot* be omitted in determining whether taxable income for the current year is reasonably needed by the enterprise. ▼

PERSONAL HOLDING COMPANY PENALTY TAX

7 LEARNING OBJECTIVE
Discuss the reason for the personal holding company tax.

The personal holding company (PHC) tax was enacted to discourage the sheltering of certain types of passive income in corporations owned by high tax bracket individuals. These "incorporated pocketbooks" were frequently found in the entertainment and construction industries. For example, a taxpayer could shelter the income from securities in a corporation, which would pay no dividends, and allow the corporation's stock to increase in value. Like the accumulated earnings tax, the purpose of the 39.6 percent PHC tax is to force the distribution of corporate earnings to the shareholders. However, in any one year, the IRS cannot impose both the PHC tax and the accumulated earnings tax.[39]

EXAMPLE 14

Considerable tax savings could be achieved by incorporating a "pocketbook" if § 541 did not exist. Assume that investments that yield $50,000 a year are transferred to a corporation by a 39.6% income tax bracket shareholder. A tax savings of $12,300 will occur each year if no dividends are paid to the shareholder. With no corporation, there would be a total tax liability of $19,800, but with a corporation the tax liability is only $7,500 in 1996 (15% × $50,000). Further, if the yield of $50,000 is in the form of dividends, the corporate tax will be even less because of the dividends received deduction. ▼

Whether a corporation will be included within the statutory definition of a PHC for any particular year depends upon the facts and circumstances during that

---

[39] § 532(b)(1) and Reg. § 1.541–1(a).

year.[40] Therefore, PHC status may be conferred even in the absence of any avoidance intent on the part of the corporation. In one situation,[41] a manufacturing operation adopted a plan of complete liquidation, sold its business, and invested the proceeds of the sale in U.S. Treasury bills and certificates of deposit. During the liquidating corporation's last tax year, 100 percent of the corporation's adjusted ordinary gross income was interest income. Since the corporation was owned by one shareholder, the corporation was a PHC, even though in the process of liquidation.

Certain types of corporations are expressly excluded from PHC status in § 542(c):

- Tax-exempt organizations under § 501(a).
- Banks and domestic building and loan associations.
- Life insurance companies.
- Surety companies.
- Foreign personal holding companies.
- Lending or finance companies.
- Foreign corporations.
- Small business investment companies.

Without these exceptions, the business world could not perform necessary activities without a high rate of taxation. For example, a legitimate finance company should not be burdened by the PHC tax because it is performing a valuable business function of loaning money. In contrast, in the case of a classic incorporated pocketbook, the major purpose is to shelter the investment income from possible higher individual tax rates.

DEFINITION OF A PERSONAL HOLDING COMPANY

8 **LEARNING OBJECTIVE**
Recognize the requirements for personal holding company status.

The PHC provisions include two tests:

1. Was more than 50 percent of the *value* of the outstanding stock owned by five or fewer individuals at any time during the *last half* of the taxable year?
2. Is a substantial portion (60 percent or more) of the corporate income (adjusted ordinary gross income) composed of passive types of income such as dividends, interest, rents, royalties, or certain personal service income?

If the answer to *both* of these questions is yes, the corporation is classified as a **personal holding company (PHC).** Once classified as a PHC, the corporation must pay a 39.6 percent penalty tax in addition to the regular corporate income tax.

Stock Ownership Test. To meet the stock ownership test, more than 50 percent *in value* of the outstanding stock must be owned, directly or indirectly, by or for not more than five individuals sometime during the last half of the tax year. Thus, if the corporation has nine or fewer shareholders, it automatically meets this test. If 10 unrelated individuals own an *equal* portion of the value of the outstanding stock, the stock ownership requirement is not met. However, if these 10 individuals do not hold equal value, the test is met.

---

[40] *Affiliated Enterprises, Inc. v. Comm.*, 44–1 USTC ¶9178, 32 AFTR 153, 140 F.2d 647 (CA–10, 1944).

[41] *Weiss v. U.S.*, 75–2 USTC ¶9538, 36 AFTR2d 75–5186 (D.Ct. Ohio, 1975). See also *O'Sullivan Rubber Co., v. Comm.*, 41–2 USTC ¶9521, 27 AFTR 529, 120 F.2d 845 (CA–2, 1941).

The ownership test is based on fair market value and not on the number of shares outstanding. Fair market value is determined in light of all the circumstances and is based on the company's net worth, earning and dividend-paying capacity, appreciation of assets, and other relevant factors. If there are two or more classes of stock outstanding, the total value of all the stock is allocated among the various classes according to the relative value of each class.[42]

In determining the stock ownership of an individual, broad constructive ownership rules apply. Under § 544, the following attribution rules determine indirect ownership:

1. Any stock owned by a corporation, partnership, trust, or estate is considered to be owned proportionately by the shareholders, partners, or beneficiaries.
2. The stock owned by the members of an individual's family (brothers, sisters, spouse, ancestors, and lineal descendants) or by the individual's partner is considered to be owned by the individual.
3. If an individual has an option to purchase stock, the stock is regarded as owned by that person.[43]
4. Convertible securities are treated as outstanding stock.

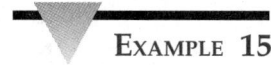

EXAMPLE 15   Aaron and Barbara, two individuals, are the equal beneficiaries of a trust that owns the entire capital stock of Wren Corporation. Wren Corporation owns all of the stock of New Corporation. All of the stock of Wren and New is considered to be owned equally by Aaron and Barbara by reason of indirect ownership under § 544(a)(1). ▼

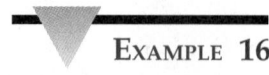

EXAMPLE 16   During the last half of the tax year, Azure Corporation has 1,000 shares of outstanding stock, 499 of which are held by various individuals having no relationship to one another and none of whom are partners. The remaining 501 shares are held by seven shareholders as follows:

Dana	100
Dana's spouse	50
Dana's brother	20
Dana's sister	70
Dana's father	120
Dana's son	80
Dana's daughter	61

Under the family attribution rules of § 544(a)(2), Dana owns 501 shares of Azure for purposes of determining stock ownership in a PHC. ▼

Attribution rules 2, 3, and 4 are applicable only for the purpose of classifying a corporation as a PHC and cannot be used to avoid the application of the PHC provisions. Basically, the broad constructive ownership rules make it difficult for a closely held corporation to avoid application of the stock ownership test. For example, convertible securities are treated as outstanding stock only if the effect of the inclusion is to make the corporation a PHC (and not to expand the total amount of stock in order to avoid PHC classification).

---

[42] Reg. § 1.542–3(c).

[43] For examples of how these constructive ownership rules operate, see Reg. §§ 1.544–2, –3(a), and –4.

▼ FIGURE 6–3
Adjusted Ordinary Gross
Income Determination

Gross income (defined in § 61)

Less: a. Capital gains.
              b. Section 1231 gains.

Equals: Ordinary gross income (OGI).

Less: c. Depreciation, property taxes, interest expense, and rental expenses
                  directly related to gross income from rents (not to exceed the income
                  from rents).
              d. Depreciation, property and severance taxes, interest expense, and
                  rental expenses directly related to gross income from mineral, oil, and
                  gas royalties (not to exceed gross income from the royalties).
              e. Interest on a condemnation award, a judgment, a tax refund, and an
                  obligation of the United States held by a dealer.

Equals: Adjusted ordinary gross income (AOGI).

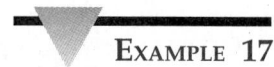

**ETHICAL
CONSIDERATIONS**

Staying Single for the Sake of the Company

Falcon Corporation is a closely held corporation, and for many years it has satisfied the gross income test. The company has avoided PHC status, however, by not meeting the stock ownership test.

Beth James and Harvey Mason, both shareholders in Falcon, have fallen in love and are considering marriage. When the other shareholders learn about the possible marriage and realize that it would cause Falcon to become a PHC, they suggest that Beth and Harvey live together and remain single.

Do you have any comment and advice regarding this moral and legal dilemma?

Gross Income Test.   The gross income test is met if 60 percent or more of the corporation's **adjusted ordinary gross income (AOGI)** consists of certain passive income items (PHC income). AOGI is calculated by subtracting certain items from gross income (as defined by § 61).[44] The adjustments required to arrive at AOGI appear in Figure 6–3.

In Figure 6–3, the deduction of items (a) and (b) from gross income results in the intermediate concept, **ordinary gross income (OGI),** the use of which is noted subsequently. The starting point, gross income, is not necessarily synonymous with gross receipts. In fact, for transactions in stocks, securities, and commodities, the term "gross income" includes only the excess of gains over any losses.[45]

PHC income includes income from dividends; interest; royalties; annuities;[46] rents; mineral, oil, and gas royalties; copyright royalties; produced film rents; computer software royalties; and amounts from certain personal service contracts.

EXAMPLE 17   Crow Corporation has four shareholders, and its AOGI is $95,000, consisting of gross income of $40,000 from a merchandising operation, interest income of $15,000, dividend

---

[44]§§ 543(b)(1) and (2).
[45]Reg. § 1.542–2.

[46]§ 543(a)(1).

income of $25,000, and adjusted income of $15,000 from rents. Total passive income is $55,000 ($15,000 + $25,000 + $15,000). Since 60% of AOGI ($57,000) is greater than the passive income ($55,000), the corporation is not a PHC. ▼

EXAMPLE 18

Assume in Example 17 that the corporation received $21,000 in interest income rather than $15,000. Total passive income is now $61,000 ($21,000 + $25,000 + $15,000). Since 60% of AOGI ($60,600) is less than passive income of $61,000, the corporation is a PHC. ▼

Most passive types of income such as dividends, interest, royalties, and annuities cause few classification problems. Certain income items, however, may or may not be classified as PHC income. Special rules apply to rent income, mineral, oil, and gas royalties, and personal service contracts.

Rent Income.   Although rent income is normally classified as PHC income, such income can be excluded from that category if two tests are met. The first test is met if a corporation's adjusted income from rents is 50 percent or more of the corporation's AOGI. The second test is satisfied if the total dividends for the tax year are equal to or greater than the amount by which the nonrent PHC income exceeds 10 percent of OGI.[47] Dividends for this purpose include those actually paid, those considered as paid on the last day of the tax year, and consent dividends (see the later discussion of the dividends paid deduction). The taxpayer must meet both tests for the rent income to be excluded from PHC income (see Figure 6–6 later in the chapter).

With respect to the 50 percent test, "adjusted income from rents" is defined as gross income from rents reduced by certain deductions. The deductions are depreciation, property taxes, interest, and rent. Generally, compensation is not included in the term "rents" and is not an allowable deduction. The final amount included in AOGI as adjusted income from rents cannot be less than zero.

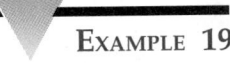

EXAMPLE 19

Assume that a corporation has rent income of $10,000 and the following business deductions:

Depreciation on rental property	$1,000
Interest on mortgage	2,500
Real property taxes	1,500
Salaries and other business expenses (§ 162)	3,000

The adjusted income from rents included in AOGI is $5,000 ($10,000 − $1,000 − $2,500 − $1,500). Salaries and other § 162 expenses do not affect the calculation of AOGI. ▼

A company deriving its income primarily from rental activities can avoid PHC status by merely distributing as dividends the amount of nonrental PHC income that exceeds 10 percent of its OGI.

EXAMPLE 20

During the tax year, Amber Corporation receives $15,000 in rent income, $4,000 in dividends, and a $1,000 long-term capital gain. Corporate deductions for depreciation, interest, and real estate taxes allocable to the rent income are $10,000. The company pays a total of $2,500 in dividends to its eight shareholders. To determine whether or not rent income is PHC income, OGI, AOGI, and adjusted income from rents must be calculated.

---
[47] § 543(a)(2).

Rent income	$15,000
Dividends	4,000
Long-term capital gain	1,000
Gross income	$20,000
Deduct: Gains from sale or disposition of capital assets	1,000
OGI	$19,000
Deduct: Depreciation, interest, and real estate taxes	10,000
AOGI	$ 9,000

First, adjusted income from rents must be 50% or more of AOGI.

Rent income	$15,000
Deduct: Depreciation, interest, and real estate taxes	10,000
Adjusted income from rents	$ 5,000
50% of AOGI	$ 4,500

Amber Corporation has satisfied the first test.

Second, total dividends paid for the year are $2,500. This figure must be equal to or greater than the amount by which nonrent PHC income exceeds 10% of OGI.

Nonrent PHC income	$4,000
Less: 10% of OGI	1,900
Excess	$2,100

Amber Corporation meets both tests, and the adjusted income from rents is not PHC income. ▼

Mineral, Oil, and Gas Royalties.

As with rent income, adjusted income from mineral, oil, and gas royalties can be excluded from PHC income if certain tests are met.[48] First, adjusted income from the royalties must constitute 50 percent or more of AOGI. Second, nonroyalty PHC income may not exceed 10 percent of OGI. Note that this 10 percent test is not accompanied by the dividend escape clause previously described in relation to rent income. Therefore, corporations receiving income from mineral, oil, or gas royalties must be careful to minimize nonroyalty PHC income. Furthermore, adjusted income from rents and copyright royalties are considered to be nonroyalty PHC income whether or not treated as such by §§ 543(a)(2) and (4). Third, the company's business expenses under § 162 (other than compensation paid to shareholders) must be at least 15 percent of AOGI.

EXAMPLE 21   Lark Corporation has gross income of $4,000, which consists of gross income from oil royalties in the amount of $2,500, $400 of dividends, and $1,100 from the sale of merchandise. The total amount of the deductions for depletion, interest, and property and severance taxes allocable to the gross income from oil royalties equals $1,000. Deductions allowable under § 162 are $450. Lark Corporation's adjusted income from oil royalties will not be PHC income if the three tests are met. Therefore, OGI, AOGI, and adjusted income from oil royalties must be determined:

---

[48] § 543(a)(3).

Oil royalties income	$2,500
Dividends	400
Sale of merchandise	1,100
Gross income (*and* OGI)	$4,000
Deduct: Depletion, interest, and property and severance taxes	1,000
AOGI	$3,000

Adjusted income from oil royalties must be 50% or more of AOGI.

Oil royalties income	$2,500
Deduct: Depletion, interest, and property and severance taxes	1,000
Adjusted income from oil royalties	$1,500
50% of AOGI	$1,500

The first test is met. Since nonroyalty PHC income is $400 (composed solely of the $400 of dividends) and this amount is not more than 10% of OGI, the second test is also satisfied. The third requirement is satisfied if deductible expenses under § 162 amount to at least 15% of AOGI.

§ 162 expenses	$450
15% of $3,000 (AOGI)	$450

Lark Corporation's adjusted income from oil royalties is *not* PHC income. ▼

Personal Service Contracts. Any amount from personal service contracts is classified as PHC income only if (1) some person other than the corporation has the right to designate, by name or by description, the individual who is to perform the services and (2) the person so designated owns, directly or indirectly, 25 percent or more in value of the outstanding stock of the corporation at some time during the taxable year.[49]

EXAMPLE 22

Blair, Cody, and Dana (all attorneys) are equal shareholders in Canary Company, a professional association engaged in the practice of law. Irene, a new client, retains Canary Company to pursue a legal claim. Under the terms of the retainer agreement, Irene designates Blair as the attorney who will perform the legal services. The suit is successful, and 30% of the judgment Irene recovers is paid to Canary Company as a fee. Since the parties have met all of the requirements of § 543(a)(7), the fee received by Canary is PHC income.[50] ▼

The result reached in Example 22 could have been avoided had Blair not been specifically named in the retainer agreement as the party to perform the services.

CALCULATION OF THE PHC TAX

9   LEARNING OBJECTIVE
Compute the personal holding company tax.

To this point, the discussion has focused on the determination of PHC status. Once a corporation is classified as a PHC, the amount upon which the 39.6 percent penalty tax is imposed must be computed. The tax base is called undistributed PHC income (UPHC income). Basically, this amount is taxable income, subject to

---

[49] § 543(a)(7). For an application of the "right to designate," see *Thomas P. Byrnes, Inc.*, 73 T.C. 416 (1979).

[50] The example presumes Canary Company will be treated as a corporation for Federal tax purposes. As noted in Chapter 2, this is the usual result of professional association status.

▼ **FIGURE 6–4**
Undistributed PHC Income
Determination

Taxable income		
Plus:	a.	Dividends received deduction.
	b.	Net operating loss (NOL), other than the NOL from the preceding year (computed without the dividends received deduction).
	c.	Certain business expenses and depreciation attributable to nonbusiness property owned by the corporation that exceed the income derived from such property (unless taxpayer proves that the rent was the highest obtainable and the rental business was a bona fide business activity).*
Less:	d.	Federal income tax accrual (other than the PHC tax and the accumulated earnings tax).
	e.	Excess charitable contributions beyond the 10% corporate limitation (with a maximum of the 20%, 30%, or 50% limitation imposed on individuals).**
	f.	Excess of long-term capital gain over short-term capital loss (net of tax).
Equals:		Adjusted taxable income.
Less:		Dividends paid deduction.
Equals:		Undistributed PHC income.

*§ 545(b).
**Reg. § 1.545–2.

certain adjustments, minus the dividends paid deduction. After the adjustments, UPHC income more clearly represents the corporation's dividend-paying capacity. Figure 6–4 shows how this amount is determined.

Dividends Paid Deduction. Since the purpose of the PHC penalty tax is to force a corporation to pay dividends, five types of **dividends paid deductions** reduce the amount subject to the penalty tax (see Table 6–1). First, dividends actually paid during the tax year ordinarily reduce UPHC income.[51] However, such distributions must be pro rata. They must exhibit no preference to any shares of stock over shares of the same class or to any class of stock over other classes outstanding.[52] The prohibition is especially harsh when portions of an employee-shareholder's salary are declared unreasonable and classified as a disguised or constructive dividend.[53] In the case of a property dividend of appreciated property, the dividends paid deduction is the fair market value of the property (not adjusted basis).

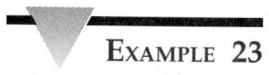

EXAMPLE 23

Three individuals are equal shareholders in a PHC. A property dividend is paid to the three shareholders in the following proportion: 25%, 35%, and 40%. This dividend is not a pro rata distribution, and the dividends are not deductible from UPHC income. ▼

A 2½-month grace period exists following the close of the tax year. Dividends paid during this period may be treated as paid during the tax year just closed. However, the amount allowed as a deduction from UPHC income cannot exceed either (1) the UPHC income for the tax year or (2) 20 percent of the total dividends distributed during the tax year.[54] Reasonable cause may not be used to overcome the 20 percent limitation even if the taxpayer relied upon incorrect advice given by an accountant.[55]

---

[51] §§ 561(a)(1) and 562.
[52] § 562(c).
[53] Refer to Chapter 4 and *Henry Schwartz Corp.*, 60 T.C. 728 (1973).

[54] §§ 563(b) and 543(a)(2)(B)(ii).
[55] *Kenneth Farmer Darrow*, 64 T.C. 217 (1975).

▼ **TABLE 6–1**
Dividends Paid Deductions

Type of Dividend	Availability	Timing	Statutory Location	Effect on Shareholders
Current year	Both § 531 and § 541	By end of year.	§ 561(a)(1)	Reduction in ATI and UPHC income.
2½-month grace period	Both § 531 and § 541*	On or before the 15th day of the 3rd month after end of year.	§§ 563(a) and (b)	Reduction in ATI and UPHC income.
Consent dividend	Both § 531 and § 541	Not later than due date of the corporate tax return.	§ 565(a)	Treated as a dividend as of end of tax year and given back as a contribution to capital.
Dividend carryover	§ 541	Not later than due date of the corporate tax return.	§ 564	Reduction in UPHC income.
Deficiency dividend	§ 541	Within 90 days after determination of PHC tax deficiency.	§ 547	Treated as if dividend paid in offending year. No impact on interest and penalties.

*Limited to 20% of current-year dividends paid for a PHC.

The **consent dividend** procedure[56] involves a hypothetical distribution of the corporate income to be taxed to the shareholders. Since the consent dividend is taxable, a dividends paid deduction is allowed. The shareholder's basis in his or her stock is increased by the consent dividend (a contribution to capital), and a subsequent actual distribution of the consent dividend might be taxed. The consent election is filed by the shareholders at any time not later than the due date of the corporate tax return. The consent dividend is considered distributed by the corporation on the last day of the tax year and is included in the gross income of the shareholder in the tax year in which or with which the tax year of the corporation ends. The disadvantage of this special election is that the shareholders must pay taxes on dividends they do not actually receive. However, if cash is not available for dividend distributions, the consent dividend route is a logical alternative.

EXAMPLE 24

Snipe Corporation, a calendar year taxpayer solely owned by Tracy, is a PHC. Dividends of $30,000 must be paid to avoid the PHC tax, but the company has a poor cash position. Tracy elects the consent dividend treatment under § 565 and is taxed on $30,000 of dividends. Her basis in Snipe Corporation stock is increased by $30,000 as a result of this special election. Thus, Snipe does not incur the PHC tax, but Tracy is taxed even though she receives no cash from the corporation with which to pay the tax. ▼

Even after a corporation has been classified as a PHC, a delayed dividend distribution made in a subsequent tax year can avoid the PHC penalty tax. This **deficiency dividend** provision[57] allows a dividend to be paid within 90 days after the determination of the PHC tax deficiency for a prior tax year. A determination occurs when a decision of a court is final, a closing agreement under § 7121 is signed, or a written agreement is signed between the taxpayer and a District

---

[56] Reg. § 1.565–1.   [57] § 547.

▼ **FIGURE 6–5**
Personal Holding Company
Planning Model

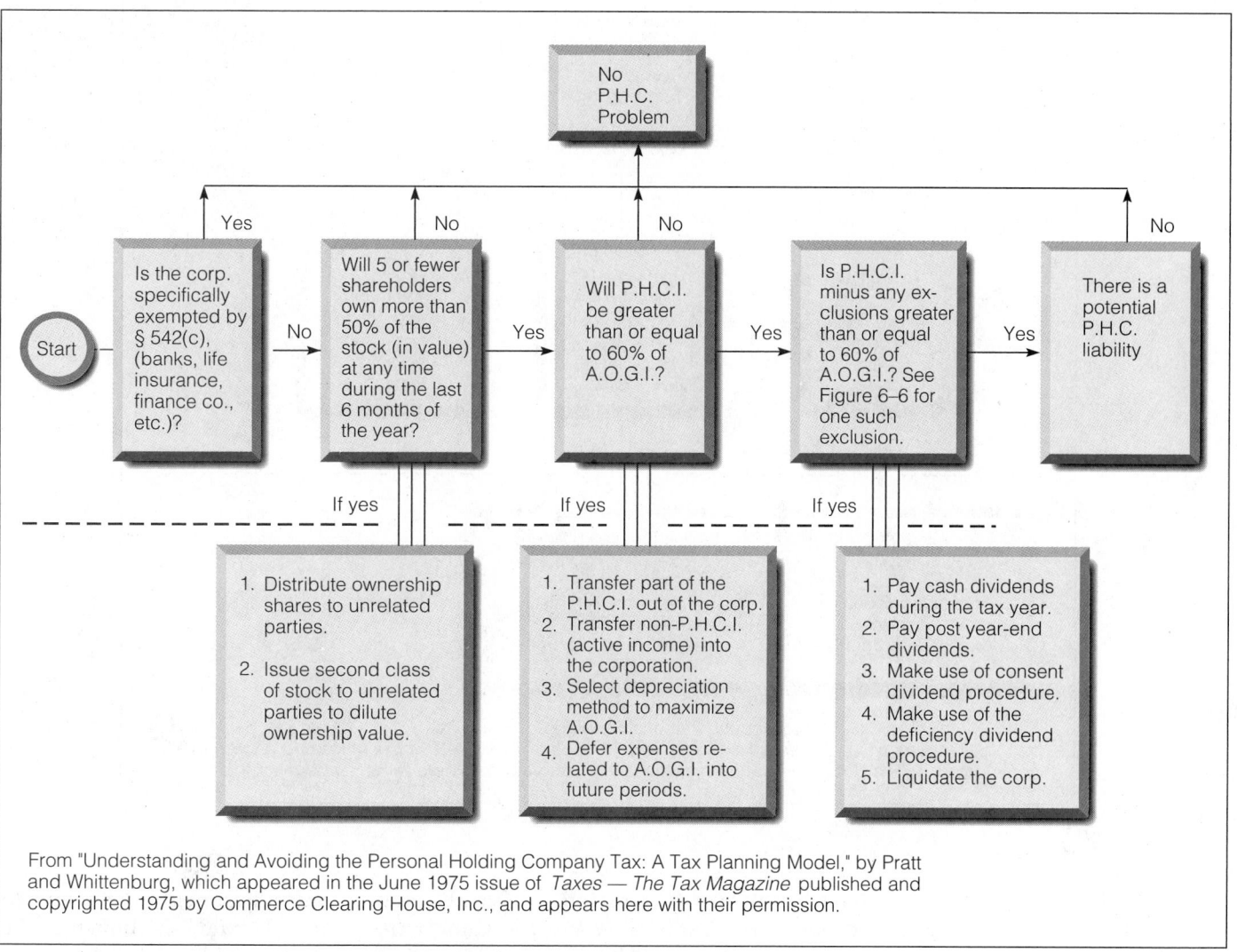

From "Understanding and Avoiding the Personal Holding Company Tax: A Tax Planning Model," by Pratt and Whittenburg, which appeared in the June 1975 issue of *Taxes — The Tax Magazine* published and copyrighted 1975 by Commerce Clearing House, Inc., and appears here with their permission.

Director. The dividend distribution *cannot be made* before the determination or after the running of the 90-day time period. Furthermore, the deficiency dividend procedure does not relieve the taxpayer of interest, additional amounts, or assessable penalties computed with respect to the PHC tax.

A dividend carryover from two prior years may be available to reduce the UPHC income. When the dividends paid by a company in its prior years exceed the company's UPHC income for those years, the excess may be deducted in the current year. See § 564(b) for the computation of this dividend carryover and Table 6–1 for a listing of dividends paid deductions.

Personal Holding Company Planning Model. Some of the complex PHC provisions may be developed into a flow chart format. Figures 6–5 and 6–6 provide a PHC planning model and the rules for the rent exclusion test.

▼ **FIGURE 6–6**
Rent Exclusion Test

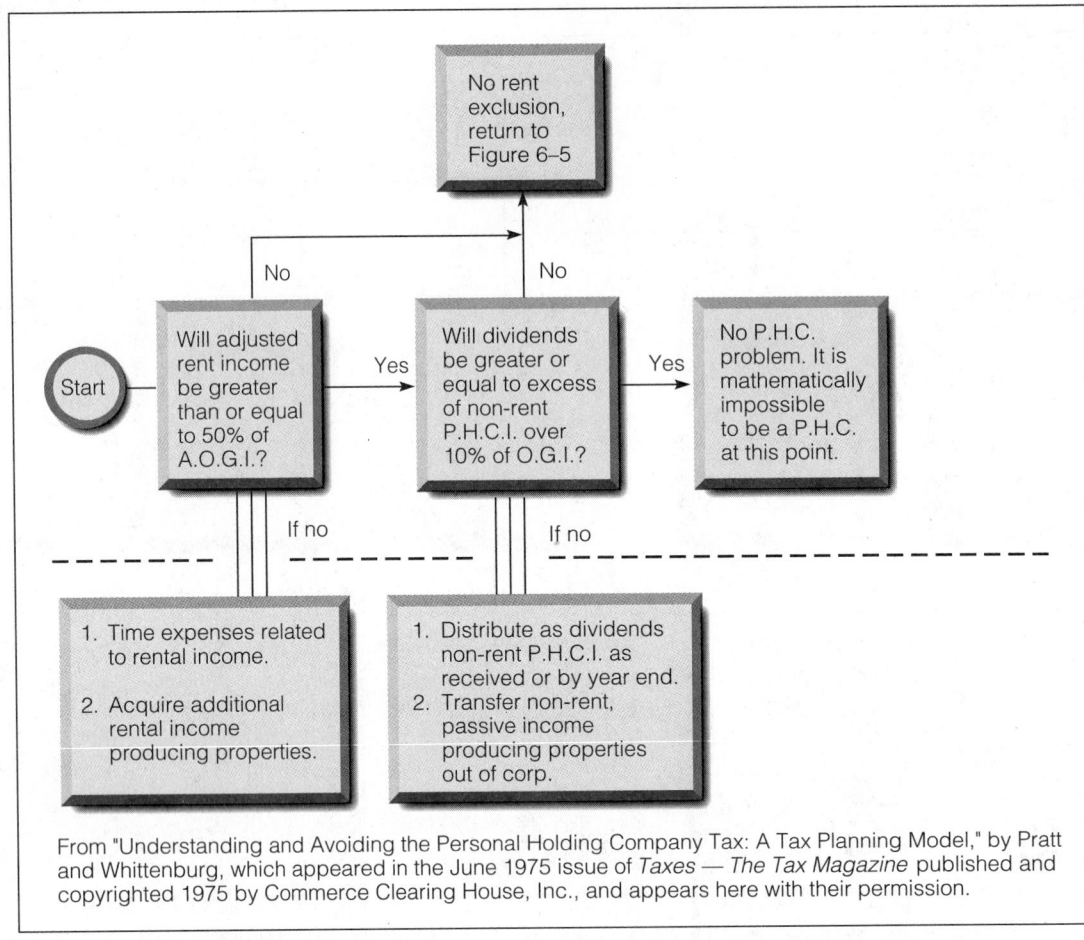

From "Understanding and Avoiding the Personal Holding Company Tax: A Tax Planning Model," by Pratt and Whittenburg, which appeared in the June 1975 issue of *Taxes — The Tax Magazine* published and copyrighted 1975 by Commerce Clearing House, Inc., and appears here with their permission.

Computations Illustrated. After the appropriate adjustments are made to corporate taxable income and the sum of the dividends paid is subtracted, the resulting figure is UPHC income. This amount is multiplied by the 39.6 percent penalty tax rate to obtain the PHC tax. Although the tax revenue from the PHC tax is small, the consequences of this confiscatory tax can be severe. Taxpayers should monitor their corporations and take the necessary steps to avoid the tax.

EXAMPLE 25

Bluebird Corporation had the following items of income and expense in the current year:

Dividend income (less than 20% owned)	$ 40,000
Rent income	150,000
Depreciation expense	40,000
Mortgage interest	30,000
Real estate taxes	30,000
Salaries	20,000
Dividends paid (three shareholders)	20,000
Corporate income tax liability (§ 11)	6,300

OGI is $190,000 ($40,000 + $150,000), and AOGI is $90,000 ($190,000 – $40,000 – $30,000 – $30,000). Taxable income is $42,000, computed as follows:

Rent income		$ 150,000
Dividend income		40,000
		$ 190,000
Less: Depreciation expense	$40,000	
Mortgage interest	30,000	
Real estate taxes	30,000	
Salaries	20,000	(120,000)
		$ 70,000
Less: Dividends received deduction ($40,000 × 70%)		(28,000)
Taxable income		$ 42,000

The adjusted income from rents is $50,000 ($150,000 – $100,000). Bluebird does meet the 50% rent income test, since $50,000 is greater than 50% of AOGI ($90,000 × 50% = $45,000). But the corporation did not pay at least $21,000 of dividends (nonrent PHC income $40,000 – $19,000 = $21,000). Therefore, the 10% rent income test is not met, and the rent income is classified as PHC income. Since all income is passive, Bluebird Corporation is a PHC. The PHC tax of $17,305 is calculated as follows:

Taxable income	$ 42,000
Plus: Dividends received deduction ($40,000 × 70%)	28,000
	$ 70,000
Less: § 11 tax	(6,300)
	$ 63,700
Less: Dividends paid	(20,000)
UPHC income	$ 43,700
	× .396
PHC tax liability	$ 17,305

▼

EXAMPLE 26 Assume in Example 25 that dividends of $22,000 (instead of $20,000) are paid to the shareholders. In this case, the rent income is not PHC income because the 10% test is met ($22,000 is equal to or greater than the nonrent PHC income in excess of 10% of OGI). Thus, an increase of at least $2,000 in the dividends paid in Example 25 avoids the $17,305 PHC tax liability. ▼

COMPARISON OF §§ 531 AND 541

10 LEARNING OBJECTIVE
Compare the accumulated earnings and personal holding company taxes.

A review of several important distinctions between the penalty tax on the unreasonable accumulation of earnings (§ 531) and the tax on PHCs (§ 541) sets the stage for the presentation of tax planning considerations applicable to these taxes.

• Unlike § 531, no element of intent is necessary for the imposition of the § 541 tax.[58] Consequently, § 541 can be a real trap for the unwary.

---

[58] In light of the Supreme Court decision in *Donruss* (refer to Footnote 8 and the related text), what role, if any, will intent play in the future in helping taxpayers avoid the § 531 tax? In this connection, see the dissenting opinion issued by Justice Harlan.

- The imposition of the § 541 tax is not affected by the past history of the corporation. Thus, the tax could be just as applicable to a newly formed corporation as to one that has been in existence for many years. This is not the case with the § 531 tax. Past accumulations have a direct bearing on the determination of the accumulated earnings credit. In this sense, younger corporations are less vulnerable to the § 531 tax since complete insulation generally is guaranteed until accumulations exceed $250,000.

- Although both taxes pose threats for closely held corporations, the § 541 tax presents the more explicit threat due to the constructive stock ownership rules. However, publicly held corporations can be subject to the § 531 tax if corporate policy is dominated by certain shareholders who are using the corporate form to avoid income taxes on dividends through the accumulation of corporate profits.

- Sufficient dividend distributions can eliminate both taxes. In the case of § 531, however, such dividends must be distributed on a timely basis. Both taxes allow a 2½-month grace period and provide for the consent dividend procedure.[59] Only the § 541 tax allows the deficiency dividend procedure.

- Differences in reporting procedures arise because the § 541 tax is a self-assessed tax and the § 531 tax is not. For example, if a corporation is a PHC, the company must file a Schedule PH along with its Form 1120 (the corporate income tax return) for the year involved. Failure to file the Schedule PH can result in the imposition of interest and penalties and also brings into play a special six-year statute of limitations for the assessment of the § 541 tax.[60] On the other hand, the § 531 tax is assessed by the IRS and consequently requires no reporting procedures on the part of the corporate taxpayer.

TAX PLANNING CONSIDERATIONS

ALTERNATIVE MINIMUM TAX

Planning for the AMT is complicated by the fact that many of the procedures recommended run counter to what is done to reduce the regular corporate income tax. Further, the AMT has the perverse effect of increasing a company's effective tax rate during economic slowdowns.

Avoiding Preferences and Adjustments. Investments in state and local bonds are attractive for income tax purposes because the interest is not included in gross income. Some of these bonds are issued to generate funds that are not used for an essential function of the government. The interest on such bonds is a tax preference item and could lead to the imposition of the AMT. When the AMT applies, investors should take this factor into account. Perhaps an investment in regular tax-exempt bonds or even fully taxed private-sector bonds might yield a higher after-tax rate of return.

For a corporation anticipating AMT problems, capitalizing rather than expensing certain costs can avoid generating preferences and adjustments. The decision should be based on the present discounted value of after-tax cash flows under the available alternatives. Costs that may be capitalized and amortized, rather than expensed, include circulation expenditures, mining exploration and development costs, and research and experimentation expenditures.

---

[59] Under the § 531 tax, dividends paid within the first 2½ months of the succeeding year *must* be carried back to the preceding year. In the case of the § 541 tax, the carryback is optional—some or all of the dividends can be deducted in the year paid. The 20% limit on carrybacks applicable to § 541 [see § 563(a)] does not cover § 531 situations.

[60] § 6501(f).

Controlling the Timing of Preferences and Adjustments. In many situations, smaller corporations may be able to avoid the AMT by making use of the exemption. To maximize the exemption, taxpayers should attempt to avoid bunching positive adjustments and tax preferences in any one year. When the expenditure is largely within the control of the taxpayer, timing to avoid bunching is more easily accomplished.

Optimum Use of the AMT and Regular Corporate Income Tax Rate Difference. A corporation that cannot avoid the AMT in a particular year can often save taxes by taking advantage of the difference between the AMT and the regular tax rates. In general, a corporation that expects to be subject to the AMT should accelerate income and defer deductions for the remainder of the year. Since the difference between the regular tax and the AMT may be as much as 14 or 15 percent, this strategy results in the income being taxed at less than it would be if reported in the next year. There is always the risk that the regular corporate rates may increase in future years. If the same corporation expects to be subject to the AMT for the next year (or years), this technique must be reversed. The corporation should defer income and accelerate deductions. The strategy delays the date the corporation has to pay the tax.

EXAMPLE 27

Falcon Corporation expects to be in the 34% tax bracket in 1998 but is subject to the AMT in 1997. In late 1997, Falcon is contemplating selling a tract of unimproved land (basis of $20,000 and fair market value of $100,000). Under these circumstances, it is preferable to sell the land in 1997. The gain of $80,000 ($100,000 – $20,000) generates a tax of $16,000 [$80,000 (recognized gain) × 20% (AMT rate)]. However, if the land is sold in 1998, the resulting tax is $27,200 [$80,000 (recognized gain) × 34% (regular corporate income tax rate)]. A saving of $11,200 ($27,200 – $16,000) materializes by making the sale in 1997. ▼

Key Employee Insurance Proceeds. A corporation may pay 15 percent AMT on key employee life insurance proceeds (.75 × .20). By selling its life insurance policies at their reserve value to a partnership, this tax can be avoided. The partners of the partnership are the corporate shareholders/employees covered by the policies. When the partner/shareholder dies, AMT is not affected because a partnership does not have an ACE adjustment. The partners may withdraw the proceeds and contribute them to the corporation as a capital contribution. The remaining shareholders get a step-up in their stock basis, and the corporation can use the funds to redeem the deceased shareholder's stock (possibly receiving § 303 treatment).

The Subchapter S Option. Corporations that make the S election will not be subject to the corporate AMT. As noted in Chapter 12, however, various AMT adjustments and preferences pass through to the individual shareholders. But one troublesome adjustment, the one involving the ACE adjustment, is eliminated since it does not apply to individual taxpayers.

THE § 531 TAX

The modification of capital gain rates has made most corporate distributions less attractive, and many companies prefer permanent rather than temporary deferral of accumulated earnings. Even when corporate rates are higher than individual rates, a corporation can invest accumulated funds in tax-free securities or purchase high-yield corporate stocks to take advantage of the dividends received deductions. Thus, the threat of the accumulated earnings tax and the PHC tax continues to be a prime concern of many corporations.

Justifying the Accumulations.   The key defense against imposition of the § 531 tax is to show that the accumulations are necessary to meet the reasonable needs of the business. Several points should be kept in mind:

- To the extent possible, the justification for the accumulation should be documented. If, for example, the corporation plans to acquire additional physical facilities for use in its trade or business, the minutes of the board of directors' meetings should reflect the decision. Furthermore, such documentation should take place during the period of accumulation. This planning may require some foresight on the part of the taxpayer. Meaningful planning to avoid a tax problem should not be based on what happens after the issue has been raised by an agent as the result of an audit. In the case of a profitable closely held corporation that accumulates some or all of its profits, the parties should operate under the assumption that § 531 is always a potential issue. Recognition of a tax problem at an early stage is the first step in a satisfactory resolution.
- Multiple reasons for making an accumulation are not only permissible but invariably advisable. Suppose, for example, a manufacturing corporation plans to expand its plant. It would not be wise to stop with the cost of the expansion as the only justification for all accumulations. What about further justification based on the corporation's working capital requirements as determined under the *Bardahl* formula or some variation? Other reasons for making the accumulation may be present and should be recognized.
- The reasons for the accumulation should be sincere and, once established, pursued to the extent feasible.

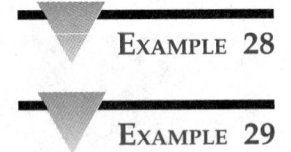

EXAMPLE 28   In 1992, the directors of Gull Corporation decide to accumulate $1 million to fund the replacement of Gull's plant. Five years pass, and no steps are taken to begin construction. ▼

EXAMPLE 29   In 1992, the directors of Grouse Corporation decide to accumulate $1 million to fund the replacement of Grouse's plant. In the ensuing five-year period, the following steps are taken: a site selection committee is appointed (1992); a site is chosen (1993); the site (land) is purchased (1994); an architect is retained, and plans are drawn up for the new plant (1996); bids are requested and submitted for the construction of the new plant (1997). ▼

Compare Examples 28 and 29. Grouse Corporation is in a much better position to justify the accumulation. Even though the plant has not yet been replaced some five years after the accumulations began, the progress toward its ultimate construction speaks for itself. Gull Corporation may be hard-pressed to prove the sincerity of its objective for the accumulations in light of its failure to follow through on the projected replacement.

- The amount of the accumulation should be realistic under the circumstances.

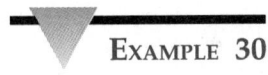

EXAMPLE 30   Bunting Corporation plans to replace certain machinery at an estimated cost of $500,000. The original machinery was purchased for $300,000 and, because $250,000 in depreciation was deducted for tax purposes, has a present book value of $50,000. How much of an accumulation can be justified for the replacement to avoid the § 531 tax? Initially, $500,000 seems to be the appropriate amount since this represents the estimated replacement cost of the machinery. But what about the $250,000 in depreciation that Bunting already deducted? If it is counted again as part of a reasonable accumulation, a double tax benefit results. Only $250,000 [$50,000 (the unrecovered cost of the old machinery) + $200,000 (the additional outlay necessary)] can be justified as the amount for an accumulation.[61] ▼

---

[61] *Battelstein Investment Co. v. U.S.*, 71–1 USTC ¶9227, 27 AFTR2d 71–713, 442 F.2d 87 (CA–5, 1971).

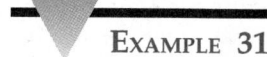

EXAMPLE 31

During the current year, a competitor files a $2 million patent infringement suit against Egret Corporation. Competent legal counsel advises Egret that the suit is groundless. Under such conditions, the corporation can hardly justify accumulating $2 million because of the pending lawsuit. ▼

- Since the § 531 tax is imposed on an annual basis, justification for accumulations may vary from year to year.[62]

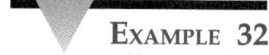

EXAMPLE 32

For calendar years 1996 and 1997, Red Corporation was able to justify large accumulations due to a pending additional income tax assessment. In early 1998, the assessment is settled and paid. After the settlement, Red Corporation can no longer consider the assessment as a reasonable anticipated need of the business. ▼

Danger of Loans to Shareholders.   The presence of loans made by a corporation to its shareholders often raises the § 531 issue. If this same corporation has a poor dividend-paying record, the company becomes particularly vulnerable. The avowed goal of the § 531 tax is to force certain corporations to distribute dividends. If a corporation can spare funds for loans to shareholders, the company certainly has the capacity to pay dividends. Unfortunately, the presence of such loans can cause other tax problems for the parties.

EXAMPLE 33

During the year in question, Quail Corporation made advances of $120,000 to its sole shareholder, Tom. Although prosperous and maintaining substantial accumulations, Quail has never paid a dividend. Under these circumstances, the IRS could move in either of two directions. The Service could assess the § 531 tax against Quail Corporation for its unreasonable accumulation of earnings. Alternatively, the IRS could argue that the advances were not bona fide loans but, instead, taxable dividends.[63] The dual approach places the taxpayers in a difficult position. If, for example, they contend that the advance was a bona fide loan, Tom avoids dividend income but Quail becomes vulnerable to the imposition of the § 531 tax.[64] On the other hand, a concession that the advance was not a loan hurts Tom but helps Quail avoid the penalty tax. ▼

Role of Dividends.   The relationship between dividend distribution and the § 531 tax can be further clarified. First, can the payment of enough dividends completely avoid the § 531 tax? The answer must be *yes* due to the operation of § 535. This provision defines accumulated taxable income as *taxable income* (adjusted by certain items) *minus the sum of the dividends paid deduction and the accumulated earnings credit.* Since the § 531 tax is imposed on accumulated taxable income, no tax is due if the taxable dividends paid and the accumulated earnings credit are large enough to offset taxable income. The payment of sufficient taxable dividends, therefore, avoids the tax. Second, can the payment of *some* dividends completely avoid the § 531 tax? As the question is worded, the answer must be *no*. Theoretically, even significant dividend distributions will not insulate a corporation from the tax. From a practical standpoint, however, the payment of dividends indicates that the corporation is not being used exclusively to shield its shareholders from tax consequences. In applying § 531, the IRS will consider such payments to the extent that they reflect the good faith of the parties and the lack of tax avoidance motivation.

---

[62] Compare *Hardin's Bakeries, Inc. v. Martin, Jr.,* 67–1 USTC ¶9253, 19 AFTR2d 647, 293 F.Supp. 1129 (D.Ct. Miss., 1967), with *Hardin v. U.S.,* 70–2 USTC ¶9676, 26 AFTR2d 70–5852 (D.Ct. Miss., 1970), *aff'd., rev'd., rem'd.* by 72–1 USTC ¶9464, 29 AFTR2d 72–1446, 461 F.2d 865 (CA–5, 1972).

[63] Refer to the discussion of constructive dividends in Chapter 4.
[64] *Ray v. U.S.,* 69–1 USTC ¶9334, 23 AFTR2d 69–1141, 409 F.2d 1322 (CA–6, 1969).

Role of the S Corporation Election. An S corporation election circumvents the application of the § 531 tax. However, the protection only covers the period of S corporation status and is not retroactive to years during which the entity was a regular corporation.

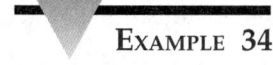

EXAMPLE 34

Eagle Corporation, a calendar year taxpayer, makes a timely and proper election under Subchapter S effective for tax year 1998. Since its formation in 1984, Eagle has accumulated significant earnings and has never paid a dividend. The election protects the corporation from the imposition of the § 531 tax for year 1998 and for any subsequent years it remains in effect. The S election does not, however, preclude the IRS from assessing the tax on Eagle for those years open under the statute of limitations in which it qualified as a regular corporation. ▼

AVOIDING THE § 541 TAX

The classification of a corporation as a personal holding company requires the satisfaction of *both* the stock ownership and the gross income tests. Failure to meet either of these two tests avoids PHC status and the § 541 tax.

- The stock ownership test can be handled through a dispersion of stock ownership. In this regard, however, watch the application of the stock attribution rules.
- Remember the following relationship when working with the gross income test:

$$\frac{\text{PHC income}}{\text{AOGI}} = 60\% \text{ or more}$$

Decreasing the numerator (PHC income) or increasing the denominator (AOGI) of the fraction reduces the resulting percentage. Keeping the percentage below 60 percent precludes classification as a PHC. To control PHC income, investments in low-yield growth securities are preferable to those that generate heavy interest or dividend income. Capital gains from the sale of such securities will not affect PHC status since they are not included in either the numerator or the denominator of the fraction. Investments in tax-exempt securities are attractive because the interest income, like capital gains, has no effect in applying the gross income test.

- Income from personal service contracts may, under certain conditions, be PHC income. Where a 25 percent or more owner of a PHC is specifically designated in a retainer agreement as the party to perform the services, the personal service contract income will be PHC income. See Example 22 earlier in the chapter.
- Rent income may or may not be PHC income. The relative amount of rent income is the key consideration. If

$$\frac{\text{Adjusted income from rents}}{\text{AOGI}} = 50\% \text{ or more}$$

and nonrent PHC income less 10 percent of OGI is distributed as a dividend, rent income is not PHC income. Maximizing adjusted income from rents clearly improves the situation for taxpayers. Since adjusted income from rents represents gross rents less attributable expenses, a conservative approach in determining such expenses is helpful. The taxpayer should minimize depreciation (e.g., choose straight-line over accelerated cost recovery method). This approach to the handling of expenses attributable to

rental property is confusing to many taxpayers because it contradicts what is normally done to reduce income tax consequences.
- In some cases, a company may reduce PHC exposure by readjusting its corporate structure. Business combinations (e.g., mergers and consolidations) or the filing of a consolidated return by an affiliated group of corporations can be used to dilute the PHC income of one corporation with the income from operations of another to avoid meeting the gross income test.

Corporations in the process of liquidation can be particularly susceptible to the PHC tax for two reasons. Operating income may be low because the corporation is in the process of winding up its business. If passive investment income remains at the level maintained during periods of normal operations or perhaps increases, the corporation might satisfy the gross income test.[65] In addition, the parties may never realize that the corporation was a PHC until it has been completely liquidated. At this point, the tax can no longer be neutralized through the issuance of a deficiency dividend.[66] The solution to the problem is to recognize the vulnerability of the corporation and keep it on the safe side of the gross income test. Good control can be obtained over the situation if the earlier corporate distributions in liquidation include those assets that generate PHC income.

PHC status need not carry tragic tax consequences if the parties are aware of the issue and take appropriate steps. Since the tax is imposed on UPHC income, properly timed dividend distributions neutralize the tax and avoid interest and penalties. Also, as long as a corporation holds PHC status, the § 531 tax cannot be imposed.

KEY TERMS

Accumulated earnings credit, 6–12

Accumulated earnings tax (AET), 6–11

Adjusted current earnings (ACE), 6–5

Adjusted ordinary gross income (AOGI), 6–23

Alternative minimum tax (AMT), 6–2

Alternative minimum taxable income (AMTI), 6–3

Consent dividend, 6–28

Deficiency dividend, 6–28

Dividends paid deduction, 6–27

Minimum credit (AET), 6–12

Minimum tax credit (AMT), 6–10

Ordinary gross income (OGI), 6–23

Personal holding company (PHC), 6–21

Reasonable needs of the business, 6–13

Tax preference items, 6–9

---

[65] Investment or PHC income might increase if the corporation, pending complete dissolution, invested some or all of the proceeds from the sale of its operating assets.

[66] *Michael C. Callan*, 54 T.C. 1514 (1970), and *L. C. Bohart Plumbing & Heating Co., Inc.*, 64 T.C. 602 (1975).

PROBLEM MATERIALS

DISCUSSION QUESTIONS

1. If the tentative AMT is greater than the regular tax under § 11, then a corporation must pay the larger AMT. Discuss.

2. What is meant by the netting process?

3. Taxable income – AMT adjustments (except ACE) + tax preferences = tentative AMTI – ACE adjustment = AMTI before NOL deduction. Please comment.

4. In arriving at AMTI, why are NOLs stated separately instead of being included with other adjustments?

5. Using the legend provided, classify the impact each of the following items has upon unadjusted AMTI in arriving at ACE:

Legend		
I	=	Increase in AMTI
D	=	Decrease in AMTI
E	=	Either an increase or a decrease in AMTI
N	=	No impact

    a. Loss on sale of a piece of equipment to a related party.
    b. Currently deducted intangible drilling costs.
    c. Purchase of raw materials.
    d. Nondeductible transportation fines.
    e. Proceeds from a key employee insurance policy.
    f. Dividends received deduction for a 15%-owned business.
    g. Tax-exempt interest.
    h. Gift received from grandmother.

6. Does the AMT exemption favor smaller corporations over larger corporations? Why or why not?

7. What purpose is served by the AMT credit for prior-year minimum tax?

8. Using the legend provided, classify the impact each of the following items has upon taxable income or loss for purposes of determining AMTI:

Legend		
I	=	Increase in taxable income
D	=	Decrease in taxable income
E	=	Either an increase or a decrease in taxable income
N	=	No impact

    a. Amortization claimed on certified pollution control facilities.
    b. Adjusted current earnings (ACE) adjustment.
    c. Excess mining exploration and development costs.
    d. AMT net operating loss deduction.
    e. Statutory exemption.
    f. Accelerated depreciation on post-1986 property acquisitions.
    g. Tax-exempt interest on private activity bonds.
    h. LIFO inventory.
    i. Excess percentage depletion of an integrated oil company.

9. Robert Barrack calls you to discuss the possibility that his company will have to make estimated tax payments of its AMT liability of approximately $96,500. Prepare a tax file memo dated February 12, 1998, indicating what you told Mr. Barrack.

10. A regular corporation is anticipating AMT problems during 1997. Point out some strategies available to help this corporation avoid or minimize the AMT.

11. Charlene creates a corporation in order to obtain limited liability. She would prefer to avoid the second shareholder tax. Suggest some techniques that would help Charlene avoid double taxation.

12. Explain the purpose(s) underlying the creation of the accumulated earnings penalty tax and the PHC tax.

13. Omar is considering merging two of his brother-sister corporations. Outline any relevant tax issues facing this merger.

14. How can human resource accounting be used in an accumulated earnings situation?

15. Cecil McDowell is preparing *Bardahl* calculations for his closely held corporation. Should he include other operating expenses in the calculation of the accounts payable cycle?

16. Determine whether the following factors or events will increase (+), decrease (–), or have no effect (NE) on the working capital needs of a corporation when calculating the *Bardahl* formula:
    a. A decrease in depreciation deduction.
    b. Use of peak inventory figure rather than average inventory.
    c. An increase in the annual cost of goods sold.
    d. Purchase of a tract of land for a future parking lot.
    e. Use of average receivables rather than peak receivables.
    f. An increase in annual net sales.
    g. An increase in accounts payable.
    h. An increase in the annual expenses.
    i. A gain on the sale of treasury stock.

17. ATI = taxable income – certain adjustments + the dividends paid deduction – the accumulated earnings credit. Please comment.

18. In making the "certain adjustments" (refer to Question 17) necessary in arriving at ATI, which of the following items should be added (+), should be subtracted (–), or will have no effect (NE) on taxable income?
    a. A nontaxable stock dividend distributed by the corporation to its shareholders.
    b. Corporate income tax incurred and paid.
    c. Charitable contributions paid in the amount of 10% of taxable income.
    d. Deduction of an NOL carried over from a prior year.
    e. The dividends received deduction.

19. Can the IRS impose both the accumulated earnings tax *and* the PHC tax upon a manufacturing company?

20. Ms. Janson (a widow) and Mr. Kimbell (a bachelor) are both shareholder-employees in Tern Corporation (closely held). If they elope during the year, what are the relevant tax issues with respect to Tern Corporation's vulnerability to the accumulated earnings tax or the PHC tax?

21. Jay Corporation is a consulting firm. Its entire outstanding stock is owned by three individuals. Jay enters into a contract with Warbler Corporation to perform certain consulting services in consideration of which Warbler is to pay Jay $35,000. The individual who is to perform the services is not designated by name or description in the contract, and no one but Jay has the right to designate such person. Does the $35,000 constitute PHC income?

22. Why is the designation of capital gain income important for PHC purposes?

23. Which of the following income items could be PHC income?
    a. Annuities.
    b. Interest.
    c. Rent income.
    d. Sales of inventory.
    e. Dividends.
    f. Coal royalties.
    g. Copyright royalties.
    h. Produced film rents.
    i. Gain from sale of farmland.
    j. Gas royalties.

24. The election to capitalize (rather than to depreciate) certain expenses for rental property could make a difference in determining whether or not the corporate lessor is a PHC. How could this be so?

25. Explain the deficiency dividend procedure for purposes of the accumulated earnings tax and the PHC tax.

26. If a corporation has an effective Federal income tax rate of 34% and also incurs a PHC tax, what is the company's aggregate tax rate in 1997?

27. The payment of enough dividends can avoid either the accumulated earnings tax or the PHC tax. Explain.

28. Ford Motor Corporation has no difficulty avoiding both the accumulated earnings tax and the PHC tax. Explain.

29. Which of the following purposes can be used to justify accumulations to meet the reasonable needs of the business?
    a. A corporation creates a reserve for a depression that might occur in 1999.
    b. A corporation has an extraordinarily high working capital need.
    c. A manufacturing corporation invests in several oil and gas drilling funds.
    d. A hotel corporation is being sued because of a structural accident that injured 32 people.
    e. A corporation is considering establishing a sinking fund to retire some bonds.
    f. A corporation carries six key employee life insurance policies.
    g. Robin Corporation makes loans to Crane Corporation, an unrelated party that is having financial problems and is a key customer.
    h. A corporation agrees to retire 20% of its outstanding stock without curtailing its business.

30. Relate the following points to the avoidance of the PHC tax:
    a. Sale of stock to outsiders.
    b. An increase in AOGI.
    c. A decrease in PHC income.
    d. Long-term capital gains recognized by the corporation.
    e. Corporate investment in tax-exempt bonds.
    f. Income from personal service contracts.
    g. The choice of straight-line depreciation for rental property owned by the corporation.
    h. A merger of several corporations.
    i. The liquidation of a corporation. Prepare a short discussion paper for your managing partner, Cora Zicko, on item (i).

31. Compare the accumulated earnings tax to the PHC tax on the basis of the following items:
    a. The element of intent.
    b. Applicability of the tax to a newly created corporation.
    c. Applicability of the tax to a publicly held corporation.
    d. The 2½-month rule with respect to the dividends paid deduction.
    e. The availability of the deficiency dividend procedure.
    f. Procedures for reporting and paying the tax.

PROBLEMS

32. In each of the following independent situations, determine the tentative minimum tax:

	AMTI (Before the Exemption Amount)
Crane Corp.	$120,000
Rider Corp.	170,000
Mallard Corp.	340,000

33. For 1997, Peach Corporation (a calendar year integrated oil company) had the following transactions:

Taxable income	$100,000
Regular tax depreciation on realty in excess of ADS (placed in service in 1989)	170,000
Amortization of certified pollution control facilities	20,000
Tax-exempt interest on municipal bonds (funds were used for nongovernmental purposes)	30,000
Percentage depletion in excess of the property's adjusted basis	70,000

   a. Determine Peach Corporation's AMTI for 1997.
   b. Determine the tentative minimum tax base (refer to Figure 6–1).
   c. Determine the tentative minimum tax.
   d. What is the amount of the AMT?

34. Maize Corporation (a calendar year corporation) reports the following information for the years listed below:

	1996	1997	1998
Unadjusted AMTI	$3,000	$3,000	$7,000
Adjusted current earnings	5,000	3,000	3,000

Compute the ACE adjustment for each year.

35. Based upon the following facts, calculate adjusted current earnings (ACE):

Alternative minimum taxable income (AMTI)	$120,000
Municipal bond interest	63,000
Expenses related to municipal bonds	5,000
Key employee life insurance proceeds in excess of cash surrender value	200,000
Excess of FIFO over LIFO	16,000
Organization expense amortization	10,000
Cost of goods sold	622,000
Advertising expenses	76,000
Loss between related parties	26,000
Life insurance expense	30,000

36. Orange Corporation, a calendar year taxpayer, has the following preadjusted AMTI and ACE for 1995 through 1998:

	Preadjusted AMTI	ACE
1995	$80,000	$70,000
1996	60,000	90,000
1997	50,000	40,000
1998	50,000	10,000

Calculate Orange's positive and negative adjustments, if any, for ACE.

37. Determine whether each of the following transactions is a preference (P), an adjustment (A), or not applicable (NA) for purposes of the corporate AMT:
    a. Depletion in excess of basis of an integrated oil company.
    b. Accelerated depreciation on property placed in service after 1986.
    c. Mining exploration and development costs.
    d. Adjusted current earnings.
    e. Certain tax-exempt interest.
    f. Untaxed appreciation on property donated to charity.
    g. Dividends received deduction.

38. Diver, Inc., a calendar year consulting corporation, has accumulated E & P of $90,000 on January 1, 1998. For the calendar year 1998, the corporation has taxable income of $100,000. Diver has no reasonable needs that justify an accumulation of its E & P. Calculate the amount vulnerable to the accumulated earnings penalty tax.

39. A nonservice corporation has accumulated E & P of $225,000 as of December 31, 1997. The company has earnings of $100,000 for the taxable year 1998 and has a dividends paid deduction of $30,000 (paid during the last half of the tax year). The corporation determines that the earnings for the tax year that may be retained for the reasonable needs of the business are $65,000 over the $250,000 minimum credit, and that it is entitled to a $6,000 deduction for net capital gain (after adjustment for attributable tax and prior capital losses). Calculate the accumulated earnings credit for the tax year ending December 31, 1998.

40. In 1997, Finch Corporation, a manufacturing company, retained $60,000 for its reasonable business needs. The company had a long-term capital gain of $20,000 and a short-term capital loss of $15,000, with a resulting capital gain tax of $1,250. The accumulated E & P at the end of 1996 was $260,000. On January 25, 1997, Finch paid a taxable dividend of $90,000. Calculate the accumulated earnings credit for 1997.

41. A retail corporation had accumulated E & P of $250,000 on January 1, 1997. Its taxable income for the year 1997 was $75,000. The corporation paid no dividends during the year. There were no other adjustments to determine accumulated taxable income. Assume that a court determined that the corporation is subject to the accumulated earnings tax and that the reasonable needs of the business required E & P in the total amount of $270,500. Determine the accumulated earnings tax and explain your calculations.

42. A manufacturing corporation in Oxford, Mississippi, is accumulating a significant amount of E & P. Although the corporation is closely held, it is not a PHC. The following facts relate to the tax year 1997:
    - Taxable income, $450,000.
    - Federal income tax, $153,000.
    - Dividend income from a qualified domestic corporation (less than 20% owned), $40,000.
    - Dividends paid in 1997, $70,000.
    - Consent dividends, $35,000.
    - Dividends paid on 2/1/98, $5,000.
    - Accumulated earnings credit, $10,000.

- Excess charitable contributions of $12,000 (the portion in excess of the amount allowed as a deduction in computing the corporate income tax).

- Net capital loss adjustment, $6,000.

Compute the accumulated earnings tax, if any.

43. The following data relate to a closely held manufacturing corporation's 1997 tax year:

Net taxable income	$500,000
Federal income taxes	170,000
Excess charitable contributions	30,000
Capital loss adjustment	20,000
Dividends received (14% owned)	140,000
Dividends paid	60,000
Accumulated earnings, 1/1/97	130,000

   a. Assume that the corporation is not a PHC. Calculate any accumulated earnings tax and total tax payable in 1997.
   b. Can the deficiency dividend procedure be used to avoid this accumulated earnings tax?

44. Indicate in each of the following independent situations whether or not the corporation involved has any accumulated taxable income and, if so, the amount (assume the corporation is not a mere holding or investment company):

	Silver Corporation	Gold Corporation
Taxable income	$150,000	$500,000
Accrued Federal income taxes	41,750	170,000
Capital loss adjustment	1,000	
Net LTCG		42,000
Tax on LTCG		14,280
Contributions in excess of 10%	10,000	
NOL deduction	24,000	
70% dividends received deduction		35,000
Dividends paid deduction	4,000	8,000
Accumulated earnings credit	60,000	110,000

45. Garcia Pullig, CEO for a local company, asks you to calculate his company's operating cycle needs without considering accrued Federal income taxes as an operating expense. March is the longest operating cycle for the company, which has reasonable business needs of $40,000 in addition to the working capital required for one operating cycle. Additional information is provided as follows:

Accounts receivable—March	$ 120,000
Inventory—March	160,000
Accounts payable—March	101,000
Cost of goods sold	1,000,000
Other expenses (less depreciation)	100,000
Depreciation	90,000
Sales	2,000,000
Dividends paid	7,000
Accumulated earnings (beginning)	180,000
Accrued Federal income taxes	220,000

Respond to Mr. Pullig in a letter dated June 2, 1998. Mr. Pullig's address is 451 Maple St., Athens OH 45701.

46. Agnes, an accountant for a local building supply store in Memphis, Tennessee, is asked by her president to determine if the corporation is susceptible to the accumulated earnings tax. Agnes calculates, as a fraction of the year, the inventory cycle (.21), the receivable cycle (.11), and the payable cycle (.10). Operating expenses are $525,000. Current assets at fair market value are $285,000, and current liabilities are $200,000. If the corporation has no other reasonable business needs, is it susceptible to the penalty tax?

47. A wholly owned motor freight corporation has permitted its earnings to accumulate. The company has no inventory but wishes to use the *Bardahl* formula to determine the amount of operating capital required for a business cycle. The following facts are relevant:

Yearly revenues	$3,300,000
Average accounts receivable	300,000
Yearly expenses	3,500,000
Average accounts payable	213,000

   a. Determine the turnover rate of average accounts receivable.
   b. Determine the number of days in the accounts receivable cycle.
   c. Determine the expenses for one accounts receivable cycle.
   d. Determine the number of days in the accounts payable cycle.
   e. Determine the operating capital needed for one business cycle.
   f. Explain why the time allowed a taxpayer for the payment of accounts payable should be taken into consideration in applying the *Bardahl* formula.

48. The stock of Dove Corporation is owned as follows:

Sand Corporation (wholly owned by Karl)	100 shares
Karl's wife	100 shares
Karl's partner	100 shares
Karl's wife's sister	100 shares
Abe	50 shares
Beth	30 shares
Charles	20 shares
Unrelated individuals with 10 or fewer shares	500 shares
Total	1,000 shares

   Do five or fewer individuals own more than 50% of Dove Corporation?

49. Teal Corporation has gross income of $200,000, which consists of $110,000 of rent income and $90,000 of interest income. The corporation has $30,000 of rent income adjustments and pays $80,000 to its nine shareholders.
   a. Calculate adjusted income from rents.
   b. Calculate AOGI.
   c. Is the so-called 50% test met? Show calculations.
   d. Is the 10% rent income test met? Show calculations.
   e. Is the corporation a PHC?

50. Assume the same facts as in Problem 49, except that rent income adjustments decrease from $30,000 to $20,000. Answer the same questions as in Problem 49.

51. Sally Segal, the president of a local company, asks you to determine if her corporation is a PHC. The company has $20,000 of interest income, $40,000 of gross income from rents, and $20,000 of personal service income (not PHC income). Expenses in the amount of $20,000 relate directly to the rent income. Assume there are eight shareholders and the 10% test is met.

   Communicate your answer to Ms. Segal in a letter dated January 18, 1998. Ms. Segal's address is 152 Redwood Drive, Eugene, OR 97331.

52. Harrier Corporation has gross income of $165,000, which consists of gross income from rent of $100,000, $40,000 from the sale of merchandise, interest of $15,000, and income from annuities of $10,000. Deductions directly related to the rent income total $28,000.

a. Calculate OGI.
b. Calculate AOGI.
c. Calculate adjusted income from rent.
d. Does the rent income constitute PHC income? Explain.
e. Is this corporation a PHC (assuming there are seven shareholders)?
f. Should the company pay $9,000 of dividends?

53. Daryl is the sole owner of a corporation in Raleigh, North Carolina. The following information is relevant to the corporation's tax year just ended:

Capital gain	$ 20,000
Dividend income	30,000
Rent income	130,000
Rent expenses	40,000
Section 162 business expenses	15,000
Dividends paid	12,000

a. Calculate OGI.
b. Calculate AOGI.
c. Calculate adjusted income from rents.
d. Calculate nonrent PHC income.
e. Does this corporation meet the 50% rent income test? Explain.
f. Does this corporation meet the 10% rent income test? Explain.
g. Is this company a PHC?
h. Should $15,000 of dividends be paid?

54. Blue Corporation has the following financial data for the tax year 1997:

Rent income	$430,000
Dividend income	2,900
Interest income	50,000
Operating income	9,000
Depreciation (rental warehouses)	100,000
Mortgage interest	125,000
Real estate taxes	35,000
Officers' salaries	85,000
Dividends paid	2,000

a. Calculate OGI.
b. Calculate AOGI.
c. Does Blue's adjusted income from rents meet the 50%-or-more-of-AOGI test?
d. Does Blue Corporation meet the 10% dividend test?
e. How much in dividends could Blue pay within the 2½-month grace period during 1998?
f. If the 1997 corporate income tax return has not been filed, what would you suggest for Blue Corporation?

55. Using the legend provided, classify each of the following statements accordingly:

Legend

A = Relates only to the tax on unreasonable accumulation of earnings (the § 531 tax)

P = Relates only to the PHC tax (the § 541 tax)

B = Relates to both the § 531 tax and the § 541 tax

N = Relates to neither the § 531 tax nor the § 541 tax

a. The tax is applied to taxable income after adjustments are made.
b. The tax is a self-assessed tax.
c. An accumulation of funds for reasonable business purposes will help avoid the tax.
d. A consent dividend mechanism can be used to avoid the tax.
e. If the stock of the corporation is equally held by 10 unrelated individuals, the tax cannot be imposed.
f. Any charitable deduction in excess of the 10% limitation is allowed as a deduction before the tax is imposed.
g. Gains from the sale or disposition of capital assets are *not* subject to the tax.
h. A sufficient amount of rent income will cause the tax *not* to be imposed.
i. A life insurance company would *not* be subject to the tax.
j. A corporation with only dividend income would avoid the tax.

56. The PHC tax is computed on an amount called undistributed personal holding company (UPHC) income. To arrive at UPHC income, certain adjustments are made to taxable income. Determine whether the following independent items are positive (+), negative (–), or no adjustment (NA):
    a. Federal income taxes on the accrual basis.
    b. Tax-free interest from municipal bonds.
    c. Charitable deductions in excess of 10%.
    d. Net capital gain minus any taxes.
    e. Dividends paid during the taxable year.
    f. Dividends received deduction.
    g. NOL carryforward from three tax years ago.
    h. Consent dividends under § 565.

57. Indicate in each of the following independent situations whether or not the corporation involved is a PHC (assume the stock ownership test is met):

	Whistler Corporation	Wren Corporation	Stork Corporation	Swallow Corporation
Sales of merchandise	$ 8,000	$ –0–	$ –0–	$ 2,500
Capital gains	–0–	–0–	–0–	1,000
Dividend income	15,000	5,000	1,000	2,500
Gross rent income	10,000	5,000	9,000	15,000
Expenses related to rents	8,000	2,500	8,000	10,000
Dividends paid	–0–	–0–	–0–	500
Personal holding company? (Circle Y for yes or N for no.)	Y N	Y N	Y N	Y N

58. Indicate in each of the following independent situations whether or not the corporation involved is a PHC (assume the stock ownership test is met):

	White Corporation	Red Corporation	Lavender Corporation	Aqua Corporation
Sales of merchandise	$ –0–	$3,000	$ –0–	$ –0–
Capital gains	–0–	–0–	1,000	–0–
Interest income	20,000	4,800	2,000	60,000
Gross rent income	80,000	1,200	20,000	50,000
Expenses related to rents	60,000	1,000	10,000	–0–
Dividends paid	12,000	–0–	–0–	20,000
Personal holding company? (Circle Y for yes or N for no.)	Y N	Y N	Y N	Y N

59. Calculate in each of the following independent situations the PHC tax liability in 1997:

	Flamingo Corporation	Pidgeon Corporation
Taxable income	$140,000	$580,000
Dividends received deduction	37,000	90,000
Contributions in excess of 10%	3,000	10,000
Federal income taxes	37,850	197,200
Net capital gain	70,000	40,000
Capital gain tax	25,350	13,600
NOL under § 172		12,000
Current-year dividends paid	14,000	120,000
Consent dividends		40,000
Two and one-half month dividends	4,000	

RESEARCH PROBLEMS

*Note: **West's Federal Taxation on CD-ROM** can be used in preparing solutions to the Research Problems. Alternatively, tax research materials contained in a standard tax library can be used.*

Research Problem 1. Snap, Inc., was owned entirely by Jeri Belk and Jerry Gore, each owning 620,000 of the 1.24 million shares of common stock outstanding. On January 1, 1997, Snap established an ESOP, which later received a favorable determination letter from the IRS.

On February 1, 1997, Belk and Gore each sold 500,000 of their shares to the ESOP, each receiving $2.5 million. To facilitate the transaction, the ESOP borrowed $5 million from a local bank; the loan was guaranteed by Snap, Inc. During the year, Snap paid $1.4 million in cash dividends to the ESOP with respect to its stock. The ESOP transferred the cash to the bank as payment of principal and interest under the note.

Jeri Belk calls you and asks if Snap may claim a deduction under § 404(k) for the $1.4 million cash dividends. Does Snap have to include the dividends in its computation of ACE, thus avoiding any AMT? Write a memo dated March 23 for the tax files in response to Ms. Belk.

Research Problem 2. In 1997, Ganz Corporation lost a Tax Court decision upholding the following deficiencies in income tax and accumulated earnings tax:

Year	Deficiency in Income Tax	Accumulated Earnings Tax
1986	$ 360,000	$ –0–
1987	200,000	450,000
1988	201,000	600,000

May Ganz Corporation deduct the deficiency in income taxes for 1987 and 1988 from accumulated taxable income in order to determine the accumulated earnings tax in 1987 and 1988?

Research Problem 3. Vechnalysis was a computer programming services business listed on the National Market System of the over-the-counter market. Pamela Wilson, the president, and three other members of the company's board of directors owned about 25% of the company's stock. The company had accumulated earnings and profits of $5.3, $6, and $7 million in 1988, 1989, and 1990, respectively.

The Tax Court agreed with the IRS that Vechnalysis had unreasonable accumulated earnings and profits to the extent of $1.77 million in 1988 and $600,000 in 1990. The Tax Court applied the *Bardahl* formula using a 22-day business cycle and the succeeding year's operating expenses to compute the company's working capital needs. To reach excess working capital where net liquid assets exceeded accumulated earnings and profits, the Tax Court subtracted the working capital needs from accumulated earnings and profits. The excess working capital was thus computed as follows:

Year	Excess Working Capital	Accumulated E & P Less Working Capital
1988	$2,820,193	($5,346,888 – $2,526,695)
1989	2,902,809	($6,082,042 – $3,179,233)
1990	3,484,041	($7,062,764 – $3,578,723)

The company had adopted a stock purchase plan, which the directors believed would arouse interest in Vechnalysis shares and maintain the shareholders' confidence in their investment. Based upon these facts, calculate the Tax Court's eventual accumulated earning tax for this corporation.

Research Problem 4. Dr. Bob owns 90% of the stock of Dental Services, Inc. Dr. Bob performs medical services under an employment contract with the corporation. He is the only dentist employed and is the only officer of the corporation actively engaged in the production of income. Dental Services, Inc., furnishes office space and equipment and employs a dental hygienist and a receptionist to assist Dr. Bob.
a. Various patients receive dental care from Dr. Bob. Does Dental Services have PHC income under § 543(a)(7)?
b. Suppose Jack, a patient, secures an absolute binding promise from Dr. Bob that the dentist will personally perform a root canal operation and that the dentist has no right to substitute another dentist. Would your answer change?

Research Problem 5. During early 1998, Conchita Power Corporation's controller, discovers that the corporation is a PHC for 1997. She decides to use the deficiency dividend procedure under § 547 for avoiding the PHC tax. The company is short of cash. Can a consent dividend qualify for deficiency dividend treatment? Should Conchita make a full disclosure of the liability for the PHC tax on the 1997 corporate tax return by filing a Schedule PH?

Research Problem 6. Adolph, Inc., has six shareholders, and most of its income is from a grant of a trademark by Adolph to Pac Company. The contract grant can be summarized as follows:
a. The grant of the trademark by Adolph to Pac was exclusive, worldwide, and forever as long as Pac made the required production payments.
b. At such time as Pac had made production payments to Adolph of $1 million, Adolph was required to transfer legal title to the trademark to Pac (as distinguished from Pac's mere option to acquire the title).
c. Adolph had no right to terminate the agreement except upon Pac's failure to make the required periodic payments. Furthermore, after the transfer of title to the trademark from Adolph to Pac, the termination rights no longer applied even if Pac failed to make the required continuing payments.
d. Although Pac was not permitted to dispose of the portion of the business using the trademark "MYCLO" separately from a sale of Pac's entire business without Adolph's prior approval, "said approval shall not be unreasonably withheld."
e. Adolph retained the right to inspect Pac's business operations to ensure continuing quality control.
f. Adolph agreed that it would not use the trademark any further or engage in any business involving the products covered by the trademark that was conveyed to Pac.

If most of Adolph's income is from the trademark, would Adolph be subject to the PHC tax?

Use the tax resources of the internet to address the following questions. Do not restrict your search to the World Wide Web, but include a review of newsgroups and general reference materials, practitioner sites and resources, primary sources of the tax law, chat rooms and discussion groups, and other opportunities.

Research Problem 7. The U.S. government believes that the imposition of the alternative minimum tax (AMT) has forced corporations in several key industries, such as defense and oil exploration, to pay taxes for the first time in decades. Summarize these findings, examining both government and press sites on the internet.

Research Problem 8. Owners of closely held businesses and their tax advisors make available substantial in-depth information about the dangers of the accumulated earnings tax and the best means by which to avoid the tax. Outline the key techniques promoted by these sources as effective in minimizing § 531 exposure.

Research Problem 9. Locate an outstanding proposal to modify the structure or scope of the AMT on corporations. Describe the proposal, the party making the proposal, and potential motivations for submitting the modification to Congress.

CORPORATIONS: REORGANIZATIONS

LEARNING OBJECTIVES

After completing Chapter 7, you should be able to:

1. Understand the vocabulary used in discussing corporate takeovers.

2. Identify and apply the tax consequences of a corporate reorganization.

3. Identify the statutory requirements for the different types of reorganizations.

4. Recognize the judicial and administrative conditions that complement the statutory requirements for a nontaxable corporate reorganization.

5. Use the rules applicable to the carryover of tax attributes in a corporate reorganization.

6. Structure corporate reorganizations to obtain the desired tax consequences.

OUTLINE

Corporations often engage in capital restructurings, ranging from complicated mergers and acquisitions to simpler recapitalizations and corporate divisions. The 1980s saw a dramatic surge in takeover activity, marked by intense battles for corporate control. The 1980s merger craze reached a pinnacle in 1988 with the $25 billion takeover of RJR Nabisco by Kohlberg Kravis Roberts, which remains the largest takeover in history. In the late 1980s and early 1990s, the number of takeovers declined, largely due to recession-related problems. By the mid-1990s, however, as large corporations began to recover from the business slump, they again started to look for smaller companies to acquire, offering prices that were comparable to the amounts the smaller companies could raise by going public but without the bother and inconvenience. At present, with relatively low interest rates in effect and banks and other lenders willing to provide financing, acquisitions again are highly popular.

Mergers in the 1990s have involved a wide and diverse list of corporate giants, including the entertainment industry (Walt Disney snatching ABC), utility companies (Southwestern Public Service swapping stock with Public Service Co. of Colorado), banks (Chemical Banking Corporation combining with rival Chase Manhattan to form a banking giant), drug firms (Pharmacia joining forces with Upjohn, Inc.), and even paper companies (Kimberly-Clark and Scott Paper Co. wiping up the market).

The market for mergers and acquisitions often is steered by strategic buyers who push up the selling prices for small and average-size businesses. Some companies have sold for 7 to 10 times their earnings before interest and taxes. For example, the announcement of AT&T's agreement to buy McCaw Cellular Communications in a one-for-one stock swap valued at $12.6 billion sent McCaw's Class A shares surging from $5.00 to $56.25 in national over-the-counter trading. The disclosure of IMR Fund L.P.'s $13.50 per share bid for Mayflower Group, Inc., caused Mayflower's normally thinly traded stock to increase over 30 percent in national over-the-counter trading.

Although many mergers are the result of a mutual agreement between two companies, the 1980s saw a number of unwelcome acquisitions triggered by so-called corporate raiders seeking to profit from hostile tender offers. The trend in the 1990s has been toward more friendly mergers, prompting speculation that the corporate raider has disappeared. Nevertheless, small businesses with substantial liquidity must continue to be alert to the possibility of a hostile takeover. One legacy of the attempted hostile takeovers of the 1980s and the defensive measures adopted by merger candidates was a whole new vocabulary. Terms such as "greenmail," "golden parachute," "tin parachute," "poison pill," "white knight," "junk bond," and "Pac-Man" have special meanings in corporate finance. These terms are defined later in the chapter.

Taxes play an important role in corporate restructurings. The type of compensation a target corporation's shareholders receive often is dictated by tax provisions. For example, merger transactions and corporate divisions that are accomplished using stock or securities as consideration generally are wholly or partly tax-free. If the acquired company's shareholders receive cash or other property, their gains are taxed at the time of the transaction. Most corporate acquisitions are structured so that they are tax-free and involve only stock-for-stock or assets-for-stock exchanges. For example, the merger of Kimberly-Clark and Scott Paper Co. took the form of a tax-free stock swap.

Courts originally concluded that even minor changes in the form of a corporation's structure would produce taxable gain to the shareholders involved.[1] Congress, however, determined that businesses should be permitted to proceed with necessary capital adjustments without being subject to taxation.[2] The theory for the nonrecognition of gain on a corporate acquisition or division is similar to the theory underlying like-kind exchanges and other nonrecognition transactions. Sections 361 and 368 provide for nonrecognition of gain in certain corporate restructurings or "reorganizations." The Regulations state the underlying assumption behind the nonrecognition of gain or loss.

> . . . the new property is substantially a continuation of the old investment . . . and, in the case of reorganizations, . . . the new enterprise, the new corporate structure, and the new property are substantially continuations of the old . . .[3]

GENERAL CONSIDERATIONS

1 LEARNING OBJECTIVE
Understand the vocabulary used in discussing corporate takeovers.

Although the term **reorganization** commonly is associated with a corporation in financial difficulty, for tax purposes the term refers to any corporate adjustment or combination that is tax-free under § 368. To qualify as a tax-free reorganization, a corporate restructuring transaction must meet not only the specific requirements of § 368 but also several general requirements. These requirements variously are set out in the Regulations or are judicially imposed. For example, a tax-free reorganization must meet the *continuity of interest* and *continuity of business enterprise* tests set out in the Regulations. It must meet the judicial condition that it have a *sound business purpose*, and it can be denied tax-free status because of the court-imposed *step transaction* doctrine. There must be a *plan of reorganization*, and tax-free status is only available to *parties to the reorganization*. All of these concepts are discussed later in the chapter. The initial and most important consideration is whether the transaction qualifies for nonrecognition status under § 368.

---

[1] *U.S. v. Phellis*, 1 USTC ¶54, 3 AFTR 3123, 42 S.Ct. 63 (USSC, 1921).

[2] Reg. § 1.368–1(b). See S.Rept. No. 275, 67th Cong., 1st Sess. (1921), at 1939–1 C.B. 181.

[3] Reg. § 1.1002–1(c).

SUMMARY OF THE DIFFERENT TYPES OF REORGANIZATIONS

Section 368(a) of the Code specifies seven corporate restructurings or *reorganizations* that will qualify as nontaxable exchanges. The planner of a nontaxable business combination must determine in advance that the proposed transaction falls specifically within one of these seven types. If the transaction fails to qualify, it will not be granted special tax treatment. In certain situations, the parties should obtain a letter ruling from the IRS that the proposed combination qualifies as a tax-free reorganization under § 368.

Section 368(a)(1) states that the term *reorganization* applies to any of the following.

A. A statutory merger or consolidation.
B. The acquisition by one corporation, in exchange solely for all or a part of its voting stock, of stock of another corporation.
C. The acquisition by one corporation, in exchange solely for all or a part of its voting stock, of substantially all of the properties of another corporation.
D. A transfer by a corporation of all or a part of its assets to another corporation if, immediately after the transfer, the transferor or one or more of the shareholders, or any combination thereof, is in control of the corporation to which the assets are transferred.
E. A recapitalization.
F. A mere change in identity, form, or place of organization.
G. A transfer by a corporation of all or a part of its assets to another corporation in a bankruptcy or receivership proceeding.

These seven types of tax-free reorganizations typically are designated by their identifying letters: "Type A," "Type B," "Type C," and so on. For the most part, excepting the recapitalization (E), the change in form (F), and the insolvent corporation (G) provisions, a tax-free reorganization is (1) a statutory merger or consolidation, (2) an exchange of stock for voting stock, (3) an exchange of assets for voting stock, or (4) a divisive reorganization (the so-called spin-off, split-off, or split-up).

Familiarity with the corporate finance vocabulary can be helpful in understanding the reorganization provisions. Concept Summary 7–1 defines terms that often appear when a corporate restructuring is discussed.

SUMMARY OF TAX CONSEQUENCES IN A TAX-FREE REORGANIZATION

The exchange of stock in one corporation for stock in another corporation pursuant to a tax-free reorganization parallels almost exactly the like-kind exchange provisions of § 1031. In the simplest like-kind exchange, neither gain nor loss is recognized on the exchange of investment property or property used in a trade for property of a "like kind" that will also be held for investment purposes or used in a trade or business. For example, the exchange of a truck used in a trade or business for another truck also used in the trade or business is a tax-free exchange if no "boot," or property not of a like kind, is received.

However, the like-kind provisions of § 1031 do not apply to the exchange of securities. Thus, an investor's exchange of stock in Cardinal Corporation for another investor's stock in Redbird Corporation is a taxable exchange. But, if the exchange of Cardinal stock for Redbird stock is pursuant to a merger at the corporate level that qualifies as a tax-free reorganization under § 368, the exchange

CONCEPT SUMMARY 7–1

Terms Used in Corporate Takeovers

- **Acquiring corporation.** The corporation that receives the assets of another corporation in a corporate acquisition or combination.
- **Exclusive merger agreement.** An agreement that prevents the corporations involved from negotiating or accepting competing offers, pending submission of a merger agreement for shareholder approval.
- **Golden parachutes.** Executive employment contracts that provide substantial postemployment compensation for corporate executives who lose their positions without sufficient cause after a merger.
- **Goodwill.** An intangible asset that represents the premium paid for the assets of an acquired corporation. It is the excess of the amount paid for the assets over their fair market value.
- **Greenmail.** The practice of purchasing a large block of stock while at the same time threatening a proxy battle or tender offer that will force the target corporation to buy back the stock at a premium. The term also refers to the payments made by the target corporation to purchase or redeem one shareholder's stock on terms that are not offered to all shareholders.
- **Junk bonds.** High-yield securities used by parties initiating a tender offer. The bonds are speculative and are secured by the target company's assets. Repayment is usually dependent upon the cash flow of the target business. Often the acquiror contemplates the sale of the target company's assets. Lending institutions make loans or purchase these debt securities because of the high interest rates and high commitment fees that are promised.
- **Leveraged buyout.** A method of buying a corporation or a division of a corporation in which the buyer borrows most of the purchase price using the purchased assets as collateral for the loan. Often the buyers are managers of the divisions that are being sold.
- **Merger.** A combination of two or more corporations into one surviving corporation. The surviving corporation acquires the assets and the liabilities of the merged corporations as a matter of law.
- **Other property.** Consideration other than stock or securities in a corporate combination or division. To the extent of "other property," as with boot received in a like-kind exchange, the shareholders of the corporations involved recognize taxable gain.
- **Pac-Man.** A defense to an unsolicited takeover bid in which the target corporation makes a counter tender offer for the stock of the raider corporation. The

target corporation attempts to gain control of the raider before the raider gains control of the target. This is known as the "I'll eat you before you eat me" defense.
- **Poison pill.** A defensive weapon against a hostile takeover attempt. The target passes a resolution stating that common shareholders will be issued a pro rata dividend of stock or rights to acquire stock of the target if a raider obtains a certain percentage of the target's common stock. By diluting the target's stock, a poison pill makes a hostile acquisition too expensive for the raider.
- **Raider.** A person or corporation that seeks to gain control of another corporation in an unwelcome acquisition.
- **Self-tender.** A defensive measure to ward off a hostile takeover bid. The target corporation purchases its own shares for cash or debt securities at a price in excess of the raider's bid.
- **Standstill agreement.** An agreement that limits the percentage of shares a given shareholder may hold. The agreement generally prohibits a shareholder from making a tender offer for the corporation's stock during the term of the agreement. It may provide for a right of first refusal to the corporation to restrict the shareholder's ability to transfer his or her shares.
- **Target.** The corporation that transfers business assets in a merger or acquisition.
- **Target shareholders.** Shareholders of the acquired or transferor corporation who receive stock in the acquiring corporation in a merger or acquisition.
- **Tender offer.** An offer made by an acquiring corporation to obtain stock of a target corporation in an unfriendly acquisition. The acquiring corporation agrees to pay a stated price above the then-existing market price for any stock of the target's shareholders that is "tendered" to it before a particular date.
- **Tin parachute.** A defensive measure by management to discourage a hostile takeover. The target company's executives negotiate contracts with the company's salaried employees under which the employees will receive severance pay, health and life insurance benefits, and outplacement services if they lose their jobs as a result of a proxy fight or a takeover.
- **White knight.** An acquiring company that is more friendly to the target. Often the target looks for a company to enter into a bidding war with the unfriendly acquiring company.

HOW TO CHECK OUT A TAKEOVER RUMOR

Is it possible for an investor to predict a takeover? Financial analysts tell investors to look at the trading activity of corporate insiders. Insiders will not be buying stock in anticipation of a merger because that is illegal insider trading, but they will halt the sale of their stock. Insiders who know a bid is "percolating" will hold on to their shares in anticipation of a "premium offer price from the prospective bidder." Analysts point to an announcement that Grand Metropolitan would acquire Pet, Inc., for $2.6 billion in a friendly takeover. A review of SEC data on insider trading revealed that insider selling at Pet had "all but dried up" in the months prior to the announcement. When ITT announced that it would buy gambling giant Caesar's World, Inc., in a friendly tender offer, SEC data indicated that insider selling at Caesar's fell off as its stock price rose.

Insider activity can also squelch a takeover rumor. If there are takeover rumors but senior insiders continue to sell their shares, the likelihood of a bid is "fairly slim," according to analysts. Studies reveal that insider selling typically drops off some three months ahead of any announcement of either a takeover or talks about a takeover.

of the stock at the shareholder level also qualifies as a nontaxable exchange. As a result, when Cardinal stock is exchanged for Redbird stock at the shareholder level as a result of a tax-free reorganization at the corporate level, the exchange of stock is similar to and is treated in the same manner as a like-kind exchange. In substance, then, a reorganization is a nontaxable exchange of like-kind property at the shareholder level.

Gain or Loss. In a corporate restructuring that qualifies as a tax-free reorganization, the acquiring corporation does not recognize gain or loss unless it transfers appreciated property along with its stock and securities to the target corporation.[4] No gain or loss is recognized by the target corporation on the exchange of property pursuant to a tax-free reorganization unless the target (1) fails to distribute *other property* received in the exchange or (2) distributes its own appreciated property to its shareholders.[5]

Generally, the security holders of the various corporations involved in a tax-free reorganization do not recognize gain or loss on the exchange of their stock and securities unless they receive cash or other consideration in addition to stock and securities.[6] Investors recognize gain only if the principal amount of the securities surrendered is less than the principal amount of the securities received.

If the security holders receive additional consideration, they recognize gain, but not more than the sum of money and the fair market value of other property received. If a shareholder does not surrender any stock, the additional consideration generally is treated as a dividend to the extent of the shareholder's share of

2   **LEARNING OBJECTIVE**
Identify and apply the tax consequences of a corporate reorganization.

---

[4] § 1032.
[5] §§ 361(a) and (b).

[6] § 356(a).

CONCEPT SUMMARY 7–2

Basis Rules for a Tax-Free Reorganization

Basis to Acquiring Corporation of Property Received

Target's basis in property transferred	$xx,xxx
Plus: Gain recognized by Target on the transaction	x,xxx
Equals: Basis of property to Acquiring Corporation	$xx,xxx

Basis to Target Shareholders of Stock and Securities Received

Basis of stock and securities transferred	$xx,xxx
Plus: Gain and dividend income recognized	x,xxx
Minus: Money and fair market value of other property received	(x,xxx)
Equals: Basis of stock and securities received	$xx,xxx

the corporation's earnings and profits (E & P).[7] The remainder is treated as an exchange of property.

Basis.   Property received by the acquiring corporation from the target corporation retains the basis it had in the hands of the target, increased by the amount of gain recognized to the target on the transfer.[8] The tax basis of stock and securities received by a shareholder pursuant to a tax-free reorganization is the same as the basis of those surrendered. This amount is decreased by the amount of boot received and increased by the amount of gain and dividend income, if any, recognized on the transaction.[9] Because of the substituted basis, the gain or loss effectively is deferred until the new stock or securities are disposed of in a taxable transaction. Concept Summary 7–2 summarizes the basis rules.

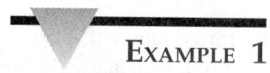

EXAMPLE 1

Quinn exchanges stock he owns in Target Corporation for stock in Acquiring Corporation plus $2,000 cash. The exchange is pursuant to a tax-free reorganization of both corporations. Quinn paid $10,000 for the stock in Target two years ago. The stock in Acquiring has a fair market value of $12,000. Quinn has a realized gain of $4,000 ($12,000 + $2,000 – $10,000), which is recognized to the extent of the boot received, $2,000.

Assume the distribution has the effect of a dividend. If Quinn's share of E & P in Target is $800, that amount is a taxable dividend. The remaining $1,200 is treated as capital gain.

---

[7] § 356. Compare *Shimberg v. U.S.*, 78–2 USTC ¶9607, 42 AFTR2d 78–5575, 577 F.2d 283 (CA–5, 1978), with *Comm. v. Clark*, 89–1 USTC ¶9230, 63 AFTR2d 89–860, 109 S.Ct. 1455 (USSC, 1989). In *Comm. v. Clark*, the Supreme Court ruled that the question of whether the payment of boot in a shareholder exchange pursuant to a tax-free reorganization has the effect of a dividend distribution is answered by examining the effect of the exchange as a whole. Boot can be characterized as capital gain if the requirements relating to qualified redemptions (see Chapter 5) are met. In applying the qualified redemption rules, the Court held that stock ownership reduction is determined by reference to ownership in the acquiring corporation.

[8] § 362(b).

[9] § 358.

Quinn's basis in the Acquiring stock is $10,000 [$10,000 (basis in stock surrendered) − $2,000 (boot received) + $2,000 (gain and dividend income recognized)]. ▼

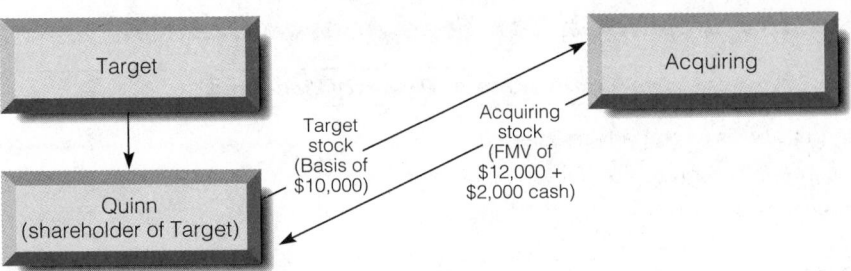

EXAMPLE 2

Assume the same facts as in Example 1 except that Quinn's basis in the Target stock was $15,000. Quinn realizes a loss of $1,000 on the exchange, none of which is recognized. His basis in the Acquiring stock is $13,000 [$15,000 (basis in stock surrendered) − $2,000 (boot received)]. ▼

TYPES OF TAX-FREE REORGANIZATIONS

TYPE A

3
LEARNING OBJECTIVE
Identify the statutory requirements for the different types of reorganizations.

Although the terms are not analogous, "Type A" reorganizations include both mergers and consolidations. A **merger** is the union of two or more corporations, in which one of the corporations retains its corporate existence and absorbs the other or others. The other corporations lose their corporate existence by operation of law. A **consolidation** occurs when a new corporation is created to take the place of two or more corporations. The "Type A" reorganization is illustrated in Figure 7–1.

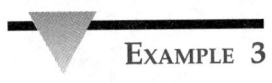
EXAMPLE 3

Acquiring Corporation acquires all the properties of Target Corporation in exchange for 5,000 shares of Acquiring stock. The Acquiring stock is distributed to Target's shareholders, in complete liquidation of Target. This transaction qualifies as an "A" reorganization (assuming that all other requirements of state law are met). It is a statutory merger. ▼

EXAMPLE 4

Brown and Black Corporations are consolidated under state law into a new corporation, Gray Corporation. Gray stock is distributed to the shareholders of Brown and Black, in complete liquidation of each. This is an "A" reorganization in the form of a consolidation. ▼

Advantages and Disadvantages.   The "A" reorganization allows more flexibility than the other types of reorganizations. Unlike both the "B" and "C" reorganizations, the consideration need not be voting stock. Further, the "A" reorganization allows money or property to change hands without disqualifying the business combination as a tax-free reorganization. The money or property constitutes boot, though, and some gain may be recognized. However, the receipt of this boot will not destroy the tax-free treatment of stock received as consideration.

If consideration other than stock is to be used, one must not run afoul of the **continuity of interest test.** This test, promulgated by the courts, requires that at least 50 percent of the consideration used in a reorganization be stock.

Definite disadvantages should be considered before an "A" reorganization is carried out. In almost all states, shareholders of all corporations participating in a

▼ **FIGURE 7–1**
"A" Reorganization

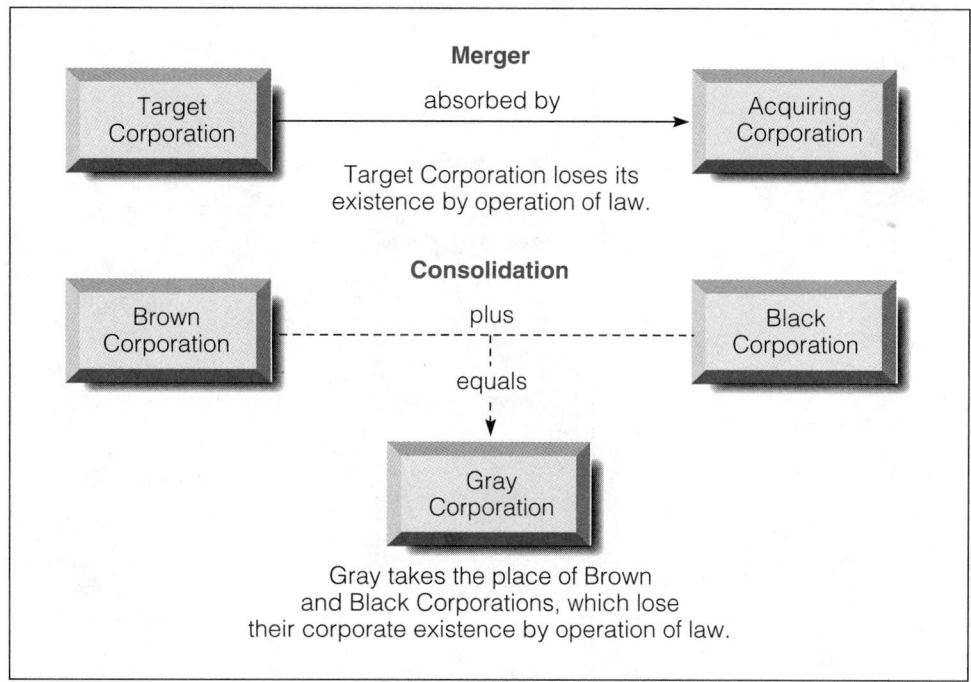

merger or consolidation have the right to dissent and have their shares appraised and bought. Meeting the demands of objecting shareholders can become so cumbersome and expensive that the parties may be forced to abandon the "A" reorganization.

Another disadvantage of the "A" reorganization is that the acquiring corporation is required to assume *all* liabilities (including unknown and contingent liabilities) of the target corporation. The surviving corporation assumes the liabilities of the target corporation as a matter of law.

The Use of a Subsidiary in a "Type A" Reorganization. Many of the problems with state law in the "Type A" reorganization can be reduced if a subsidiary becomes the acquiring corporation. When a subsidiary acquires the assets of another corporation and gives its own voting stock as consideration, most problems regarding the validity of the stock transfer are solved. However, the parent corporation may want the shareholders of the target corporation to hold the parent's stock rather than that of the subsidiary. This enables the parent to retain control over the subsidiary. Moreover, the assets of the parent are protected from the liabilities of the target.

A major problem of the "A" reorganization is the need to secure the approval of a majority of the shareholders of the acquiring corporation. Because the parent corporation is the majority shareholder, this problem is lessened.[10] Only the approval of the board of directors of the parent corporation need be obtained. For these reasons, the use of a subsidiary corporation to effect the "A" reorganization offers advantages.

---

[10]The approval of a majority of the shareholders of the target corporation still is required.

▼ FIGURE 7–2
Use of a Subsidiary in an "A"
Reorganization

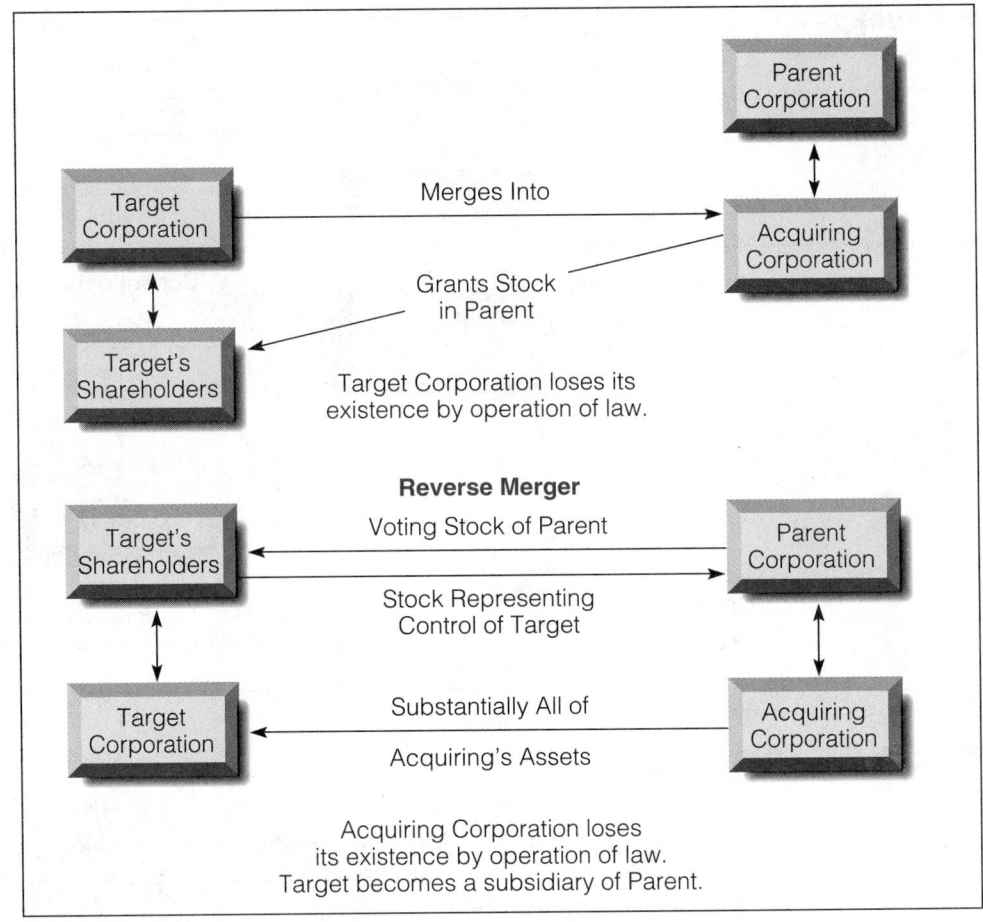

The exchange of a parent's stock by a subsidiary in a statutory merger qualifies the reorganization as a tax-free "A" reorganization if (1) no subsidiary stock is used and (2) the exchange would have been an "A" reorganization had the merger been into the parent.[11]

Under § 368(a)(2)(E), a so-called *reverse merger* is permitted. To qualify as a tax-free reorganization under this provision, the surviving corporation must hold, in addition to its own assets, substantially all of the properties of the merged corporation. The former shareholders of the surviving corporation must receive voting stock of the controlling corporation in exchange for control (80 percent) of the surviving corporation. The use of a subsidiary in an "A" reorganization and a reverse merger are illustrated in Figure 7–2.

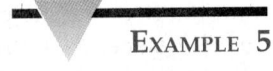

EXAMPLE 5

Acquiring Corporation is a subsidiary of Parent Corporation. It also holds some stock in Parent. Acquiring transfers the Parent stock it owns to the shareholders of Target Corporation for substantially all the assets of Target. Target is liquidated. This is an "A" reorganization using parent company stock. If Parent Corporation is Acquiring's only shareholder, the merger can be effected by securing approval of Parent's board of directors. Because the vote of Parent's shareholders is not required, considerable time and expense are avoided. Further, Parent's assets are protected from Target's creditors. ▼

_____
[11] § 368(a)(2)(D).

▼ FIGURE 7–3
"B" Reorganization

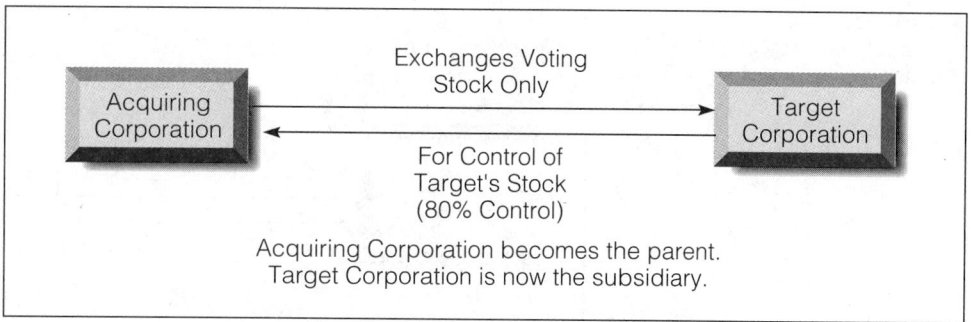

In a reverse merger, Target Corporation, rather than Acquiring Corporation, would survive. Further, the Parent stock must be voting stock. Target's shareholders must surrender their stock representing 80% control of Target to Parent for its voting stock. Acquiring transfers all its assets to Target and is liquidated. Target then is the subsidiary of Parent. ▼

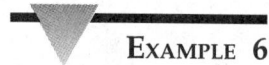

EXAMPLE 6

Two disadvantages of the reverse merger are the requirements that voting stock of the parent corporation be used, and that at least 80 percent of the stock of the target corporation be obtained. These requirements severely limit the flexibility present in the regular "A" reorganization.

TYPE B

In a "Type B" reorganization, a corporation acquires the stock of another corporation solely in exchange for its voting stock. Immediately after the acquisition, the acquiring corporation must be in control of the target corporation. In simple terms, this transaction is an exchange of stock for voting stock. Voting stock must be the sole consideration, and the requirement is strictly construed. The "Type B" reorganization is illustrated in Figure 7–3.

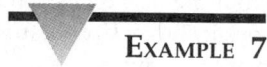

EXAMPLE 7

Acquiring Corporation exchanges 20% of its voting stock for 80% of all classes of stock in Target Corporation. The exchange qualifies as a "B" reorganization. Acquiring becomes the parent of Target. The "B" reorganization precludes the use of boot. Consequently, gain is never recognized in a "B" reorganization. If Acquiring exchanges nonvoting preferred stock or bonds in addition to voting stock, the transaction does not qualify as a "B" reorganization. ▼

The Eighty Percent Control Requirement.   Stock may be acquired from the shareholders or directly from the corporation in obtaining control of the target. For example, if Black Corporation has 100 shares outstanding, White Corporation must acquire, in exchange for its voting stock, at least 80 of those shares. Alternatively, White could acquire 400 newly issued shares directly from Black Corporation. It would then own 400 shares of 500 outstanding shares, an 80 percent ownership.

To obtain control, the parent, or acquiring corporation, must hold at least 80 percent of the total combined voting power of all classes of stock entitled to vote. It also must acquire at least 80 percent of the total number of shares of all other classes of stock of the corporation. This does not mean that the acquiring corporation must actually "acquire" 80 percent of the target corporation. Rather, after the acquisition, it must have an 80 percent ownership. A previous cash

▼ **FIGURE 7–4**
Use of a Subsidiary in a "B"
Reorganization

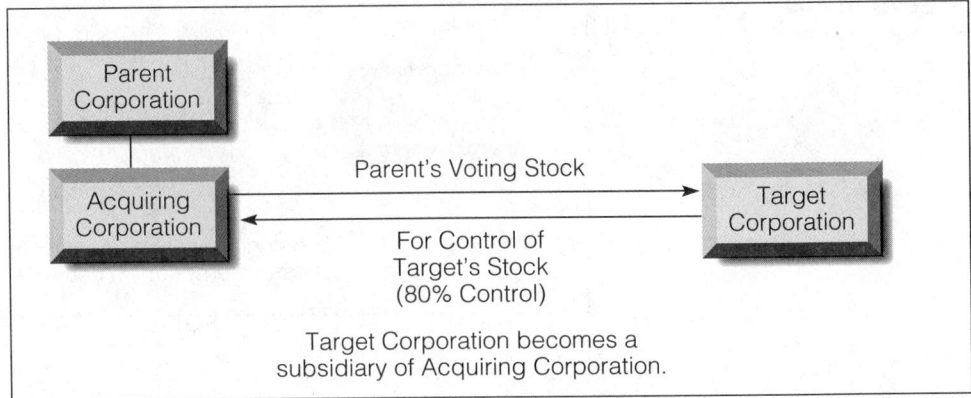

purchase can be counted in determining the 80 percent ownership, if the purchase was a separate transaction.[12]

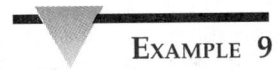

EXAMPLE 8

Acquiring Corporation purchased 30% of Target for cash six years ago. It acquires another 50% in the current year, through the issuance of voting stock. Thus, even though some of the shares of Target were acquired with cash, the requirements of a "B" reorganization are satisfied.

What if Acquiring Corporation purchased 30% of Target's stock for cash three months ago? Now the acquisition of the additional 50% of Target's stock for voting stock seems to be part of a two-step transaction. The acquisition of the remaining stock for voting stock is probably not tax-free. ▼

The Use of a Subsidiary in a "Type B" Reorganization.   In the "Type B" as in the "Type A" reorganization, voting stock of the acquiring corporation's parent may be used. The use of a parent's stock by a subsidiary in a "Type B" reorganization is illustrated in Figure 7–4.

EXAMPLE 9

Blue Corporation is the parent of Acquiring Corporation. Acquiring also owns some stock in Blue. It exchanges voting stock in Blue for control of the stock in Target Corporation. This qualifies as a "B" reorganization. Target is now the subsidiary of Acquiring. ▼

The "Solely for Voting Stock" Requirement.   The "B" reorganization is limited in that the *sole* consideration must be voting stock. Voting stock plus some other consideration does not meet the statutory requirement.[13] This limitation on consideration is a great disadvantage of the "B" reorganization. Another disadvantage is that, if the acquiring corporation does not obtain 100 percent control of the target corporation, problems may arise with the minority interest remaining in the target.

Nevertheless, the stock-for-voting-stock acquisition has the advantage of simplicity. Generally, the shareholders of the target corporation act individually in transferring their stock, so the affairs of the corporation itself are not directly involved. This assumes there are sufficient treasury or unissued shares to effect the transaction without any formal shareholder action to increase authorized shares.[14]

[12] Reg. § 1.368–2(c).
[13] *Helvering v. Southwest Consolidated Corporation*, 41–1 USTC ¶9402, 27 AFTR 160, 119 F.2d 561 (CA–5, 1941), *rev'd.* in 42–1 USTC ¶9248, 28 AFTR 573, 62 S.Ct. 546 (USSC, 1942).

[14] Though shareholders in the "B" reorganization normally do not act through the corporation, this is subject to legal or other restrictions on transfers of shares.

▼ **FIGURE 7–5**
"C" Reorganization

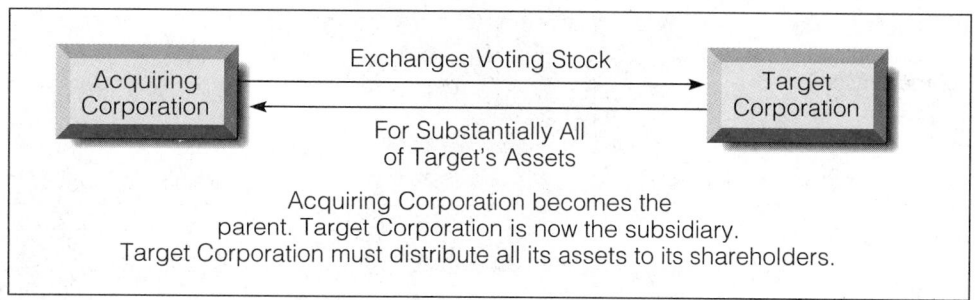

Exchanges Voting Stock

Acquiring Corporation → Target Corporation

For Substantially All of Target's Assets

Acquiring Corporation becomes the parent. Target Corporation is now the subsidiary. Target Corporation must distribute all its assets to its shareholders.

EXAMPLE 10

Target has assets with an adjusted basis of $400,000 and liabilities of $100,000. Its common stock consists of 2,000 shares with a par value of $100 per share. It has no other classes of stock and E & P of $100,000. Target's assets are worth $500,000. Acquiring Corporation obtains the assets of Target in a tax-free "A" reorganization. Acquiring takes a basis of $400,000 in Target's assets.

If Acquiring takes over Target by exchanging with Target's shareholders 30% of its voting stock (worth $320,000) for 1,600 shares of Target stock, the reorganization qualifies as a "B" reorganization. Target becomes the subsidiary of Acquiring. Acquiring's basis in the Target stock is the same basis Target's shareholders had in the stock. ▼

TYPE C

In the "Type C" reorganization, the acquiring corporation obtains substantially all of the assets of the target corporation solely in exchange for voting stock. It is essentially an exchange of assets for voting stock.

A transaction does not qualify as a "C" reorganization unless the target corporation distributes to its shareholders the stock, securities, and other properties it receives in the reorganization as well as any of its own properties.[15] The "Type C" reorganization is illustrated in Figure 7–5.

EXAMPLE 11

Acquiring Corporation transfers voting stock representing a 30% ownership interest to Target Corporation for substantially all of the assets of Target. After the exchange, Target's only assets are the voting stock of Acquiring. This exchange qualifies as a "C" reorganization if Target distributes the voting stock to its shareholders. ▼

"Type A" and "Type C" Reorganizations Compared. The "Type C" reorganization has almost the same consequences as the "Type A," but the rule on consideration is more exacting for the "Type C." However, the "C" reorganization is preferable to the "A" in many circumstances. In the "C" reorganization, the acquiring corporation assumes only the liabilities it chooses to assume. It is normally not liable for unknown or contingent liabilities. Further, in some states, only the approval of the shareholders in the target corporation is required in the "C" reorganization.

The "C" reorganization also can be carried out by the use of a subsidiary, as illustrated in Figure 7–6.

EXAMPLE 12

Parent Corporation is in control of Acquiring Corporation. Acquiring also owns some stock in Parent. It transfers the Parent (voting) stock to Target Corporation for substantially all of the assets of Target. Target is then liquidated. The transaction qualifies as a "C" reorganization. ▼

---

[15] § 368(a)(2)(G).

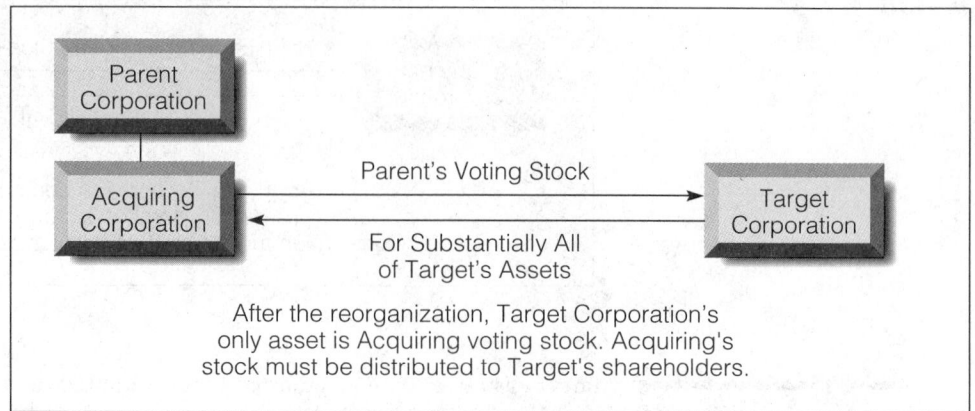

After the reorganization, Target Corporation's
only asset is Acquiring voting stock. Acquiring's
stock must be distributed to Target's shareholders.

Consideration in the "Type C" Reorganization.   Consideration in the "C"
reorganization normally consists of voting stock, as in the "B" reorganization.
However, there are exceptions to this rule. Cash and other property do not disrupt
the tax-free status of the reorganization if at least 80 percent of the fair market
value of all the property of the target corporation is obtained by the use of voting
stock. An assumption of the liabilities of the target corporation is disregarded in
determining whether the transaction is solely for voting stock.[16]

The "C" reorganization has a slight degree of freedom in reference to
consideration, while the "B" does not. But in making the statutory computation
that *other property* does not exceed 20 percent of the fair market value of the
property transferred, a restriction is imposed. Liabilities assumed by the acquiring
corporation are treated as *other property* if the corporation receives other consideration. Liabilities assumed by the acquiring corporation normally exceed 20 percent
of the fair market value of the assets acquired.

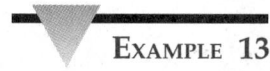

EXAMPLE 13

Target Corporation transfers assets with a fair market value of $200,000 to Acquiring
Corporation for voting stock valued at $160,000 and cash of $40,000. No liabilities are
assumed. Target distributes the cash and stock to its shareholders and liquidates. The
transaction qualifies as a "C" reorganization since *other property* received is exactly 20% of
$200,000.

If Target had transferred assets for stock valued at $140,000, cash of $40,000, and the
assumption of $20,000 of its liabilities by Acquiring, the liabilities would be counted as *other
property* because Target also received cash. *Other property* amounts to $60,000, which exceeds
20% of the fair market value of Target's assets. The transaction does not qualify as a "C"
reorganization.

Had Acquiring given Target voting stock worth $120,000 and assumed $80,000 of
Target's liabilities, the transaction would qualify as a "C" reorganization. Liabilities
assumed by the acquiring corporation are disregarded as boot, when no additional
consideration (other than stock) is used. ▼

Asset Transfers.   The "C" reorganization requires that substantially all of the
assets of the target corporation be transferred. Numerous problems arise in
determining whether the *substantially all* requirement has been met. There is no
statutory definition of "substantially all." To obtain a favorable ruling from the
IRS, assets representing at least 90 percent of the fair market value of the net assets
and at least 70 percent of the fair market value of the gross assets held by the

---

[16] §§ 368(a)(1)(C) and (a)(2)(B).

target corporation must be transferred.[17] Smaller percentages may still qualify. However, the parties must rely on case law to obtain a favorable decision.[18]

TYPE D

The first three types of tax-free corporate reorganizations are designed for corporate combinations. The "D" reorganization is different, in that it is generally a mechanism for corporate division. However, the "D" reorganization also can be used to carry out a corporate combination.

There are two types of "D" reorganizations. In the acquisitive "D" reorganization, an acquiring corporation transfers all or substantially all of its assets to a target corporation, in exchange for control of the target. In the **divisive reorganization,** an acquiring corporation transfers part of its assets for controlling stock of the target. The controlling stock of the target is distributed to the shareholders of the acquiring corporation. Thus, in a "D" reorganization, the target transfers a controlling interest in its stock, rather than transferring its assets. The acquiring corporation is the entity that transfers assets in a "D" reorganization.

Acquisitive "D" Reorganization.   Section 354 applies to a "D" reorganization that is a corporate combination. Substantially all the property of one corporation must be transferred to the second corporation for control (50 percent) of the second corporation. All stock and other property received by the transferor corporation must be distributed to the transferor's shareholders. If any assets remain in the transferor corporation, the requirements of § 354 are not met. This transaction can also meet the requirements of a "C" reorganization. If a transaction can be both a "C" and a "D" reorganization, it is treated as a "D" reorganization.

EXAMPLE 14

Acquiring Corporation wishes to acquire Target Corporation, but Target holds a nontransferable license. Thus, Target must be the surviving corporation. Acquiring transfers all its assets to Target for 80% of the stock of Target. Acquiring then distributes all the Target stock to its shareholders and is liquidated. The transaction qualifies as a "D" reorganization. ▼

Divisive "D" Reorganization.   In the more typical "D" reorganization, a corporation is divided. Shareholders of a corporation may wish to divide corporate assets and split the business of a corporation for many reasons. Antitrust problems may have arisen. The shareholders may have differences of opinion. Family tax planning may enter the picture.

A corporate division can be accomplished in several ways. The old corporation can be liquidated and the assets distributed to the various shareholders. Then, those wishing to continue the business in corporate form can establish a new entity. Assets can be transferred to a controlled corporation tax-free under § 351. However, problems arise upon liquidation of the old corporation. Shareholders recognize gain upon the liquidation, and § 336 generates tax at the corporate level. Consequently, this route may not be the best. A stock redemption is another possibility. However, gain usually is also recognized at both the shareholder level and the corporate level.

The better alternative would be to effect a split-up and distribute stock and securities in the new corporation pursuant to § 355. Utilizing the "D" reorganization, the shareholders of a corporation can divide the corporation tax-free.

---

[17] Rev.Rul. 77–37, 1977–2 C.B. 568, amplified by Rev.Proc. 86–42, 1986–2 C.B. 722.

[18] See, for example, *National Bank of Commerce of Norfolk v. U.S.,* 58–1 USTC ¶9278, 1 AFTR2d 894, 158 F.Supp. 887 (D.Ct.Va., 1958).

EXAMPLE 15

Iris and Ivan are the sole shareholders of Manufacturing Corporation. Manufacturing was organized 10 years ago and has been actively engaged in development, manufacturing, and sales of two products, widgets and bolts. Considerable friction has developed between Iris and Ivan, who now wish to divide the business. Iris wants the assets used in manufacturing widgets, and Ivan wants to continue manufacturing bolts.

A new corporation, Developer, is formed. All the assets relating to the manufacture of widgets are transferred to Developer. All the stock in Developer is distributed to Iris in exchange for all of her stock in Manufacturing. After the reorganization, Ivan owns all the stock in Manufacturing, and Iris owns all the stock in Developer. By virtue of § 355, no gain or loss is recognized by either Iris or Ivan upon the exchange of Iris's stock in Manufacturing for all the stock in Developer. Gain or loss is not recognized to Manufacturing under § 361. Developer receives the assets of Manufacturing tax-free under § 1032 (a corporation does not recognize gain or loss on the receipt of money or property in exchange for its stock). ▼

Spin-Offs, Split-Offs, and Split-Ups.   To qualify as a tax-free reorganization, the transferor corporation must obtain stock representing control (80 percent) in the transferee corporation. Then, the stock received in the new corporation must be distributed to the shareholders of the transferor corporation either as a spin-off or as a split-off. In a spin-off, the shareholders do not surrender any stock in the distributing corporation. In a split-off, the shareholders do surrender stock in the distributing corporation in exchange for stock in the new corporation. In a split-up, the assets of one corporation are transferred to two or more new corporations. Stock in the new corporations is distributed to the transferor's shareholders. The transferor corporation is liquidated. The spin-off, split-off, and split-up are illustrated in Figure 7–7.

EXAMPLE 16

Nina owns 200 shares of Paramount stock with a basis of $40,000 (value of $60,000). In a "D" reorganization (spin-off), she receives a distribution of 50 shares of Viacom stock valued at $20,000. Nina surrenders none of her Paramount stock. The basis she had in her Paramount stock is allocated between the Paramount stock and Viacom stock, using the fair market value of each. Thus, $20,000/$80,000 of the $40,000 basis, or $10,000, is allocated to the Viacom stock, and $60,000/$80,000 of the $40,000 basis, or $30,000, is allocated to the Paramount stock.

Assume instead that a split-off occurred. Nina surrenders 100 shares of Paramount stock for 50 shares of Viacom stock. Again, her basis of $40,000 is allocated between the Paramount and Viacom stock using the fair market value of each. The fair market value of the retained Paramount stock is $30,000. Thus, $30,000/$50,000 of the $40,000, or $24,000, is allocated to the Paramount stock, and $20,000/$50,000 of the $40,000, or $16,000, is allocated to the Viacom stock. ▼

EXAMPLE 17

Gail and Gary are the sole shareholders of Books, a publishing corporation. Books was organized six years ago and has been actively engaged in publishing both books and periodicals. Because of antitrust problems, Books wishes to divide the business. Two new corporations are formed, Books II and Periodicals. All the assets relating to the book-publishing business are transferred to Books II. All assets relating to the publishing of periodicals are transferred to Periodicals. Gail exchanges all her stock in Books for the stock in Books II. Gary exchanges all his stock in Books for the stock in Periodicals. Books is liquidated. The transaction qualifies as a "D" reorganization split-up. Neither Gail nor Gary recognizes gain on the exchange. Gail's basis in her stock in Books becomes the basis for her stock in Books II. Gary's basis in his stock in Books becomes his basis for his stock in Periodicals. ▼

▼ **FIGURE 7–7**
"D" Reorganization

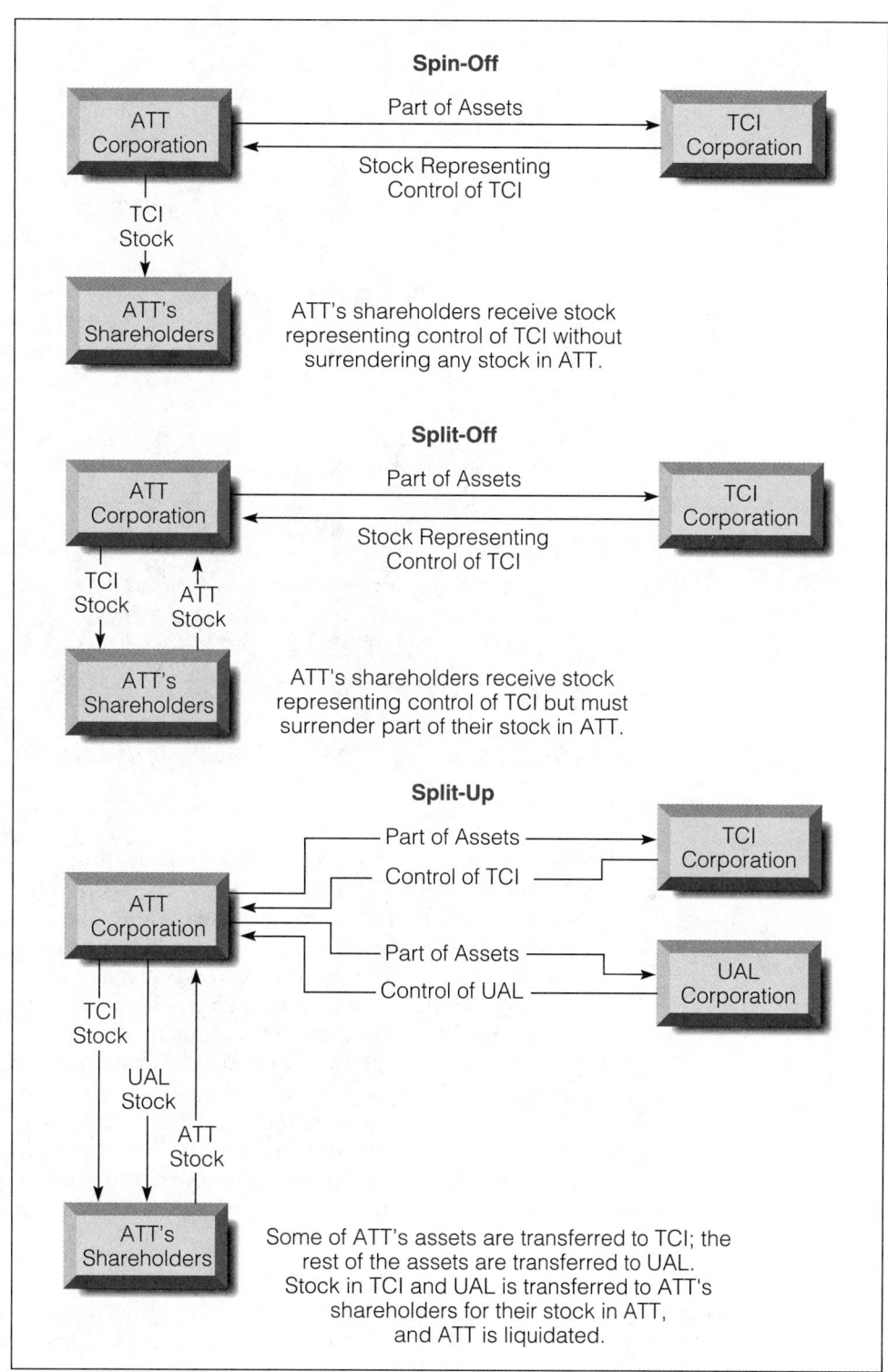

THE NEW SPIN-OFF RAGE

The tax advantage of spin-offs has become a major factor in the growing trend to break up corporate giants. Currently, the only tax-free avenue for shedding assets is to spin them off to shareholders. As financial advisers point out, there is no tax cost to either the parent corporation or its shareholders.

Recent years have seen a new wave of spin-offs. ITT announced that it would break up into three publicly traded companies in the largest corporate divestiture since the AT&T spin-off of local phone companies in 1984. Sprint Corporation announced it was considering the spin-off of its cellular business, rather than selling assets from that business, because it could avoid paying a substantial capital gains tax. W. R. Grace & Co. decided to spin off its dialysis division to its shareholders. It received a $3.5 billion bid for its medical unit but favored the spin-off because of an estimated "tax bite" of $850 million to $1 billion on a cash sale. Times Mirror spun off 20 percent of its cable business to its shareholders. Banks have spun off credit-card operations, and some energy companies have considered spinning off chemical businesses.

As one reporter noted, it takes years to build corporate giants, "but only a single board meeting to bust them up."

SOURCE: Information from Steven Lipin and Randall Smith, "Spinoffs Burgeon, Fueled by Tax Status, Investor Pressure and Stock Performance," *Wall Street Journal*, June 15, 1995, pp. C1 and C15.

Requirements of § 355.   Stock representing control [80 percent ownership, as defined in § 368(c)(1)] of the transferee corporation must be distributed to the shareholders of the transferor corporation. The assets transferred (plus those retained) must represent an active business that has been owned and conducted by the transferor corporation for at least five years before the transfer. A distribution under § 355 must not be used principally as a device for distributing the E & P of either the distributing corporation or the controlled corporation.

Note that *control* in a "D" reorganization has different meanings depending upon whether the reorganization is a corporate combination or a corporate division. In a corporate combination, control is ownership of at least 50 percent of the total voting stock *or* 50 percent of the total *value* of all classes of stock.[19] If the reorganization is a corporate division, control is ownership of at least 80 percent of the total voting stock *and* at least 80 percent of the total *number* of shares of all other classes of stock.[20]

EXAMPLE 18

Bell Atlantic has been engaged in the manufacture of certain products. It also owns investment securities. Bell Atlantic transfers the investment securities to a newly formed corporation and distributes the stock of the new corporation to its shareholders. The transaction does not qualify as a "D" reorganization. Holding investment securities does not constitute a trade or business. The shareholders of Bell Atlantic Corporation are taxed on the receipt of the stock. ▼

---

[19] § 368(a)(2)(H).

[20] § 368(c).

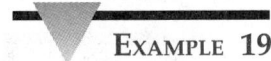

EXAMPLE 19

Assume Bell Atlantic Corporation of Example 18 has a separate research department. It transfers the research department to a new corporation and distributes the stock of the new corporation to its shareholders. The activities of the research department do not constitute a trade or business. The transaction does not qualify as a "D" reorganization. ▼

EXAMPLE 20

QVC, Inc., manufactures a single product, but it has had two plants for the past 10 years. It transfers one plant and related activities to a new corporation and distributes the stock of the new corporation to its shareholders. The activities of each plant constitute a trade or business. The transaction qualifies as a "D" reorganization. ▼

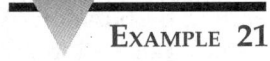

EXAMPLE 21

Assume that one of the plants in Example 20 has been in existence for only two years. QVC transfers one plant and related activities to a new corporation and distributes the stock of the new corporation to its shareholders. Though the activities of each plant constitute a trade or business, one of them has not been in existence for at least five years. Consequently, the transaction does not qualify as a "D" reorganization. It does not matter which plant is transferred. Both the transferred plant and the one retained must have been in existence for at least five years before the transfer. ▼

TYPE E

The "Type E" reorganization is a **recapitalization**—a major change in the character and amount of outstanding capital stock or paid-in capital of a corporation. The transaction is significant only for the shareholders who exchange stock or securities. The corporation itself exchanges no property.

The following types of exchanges qualify for nonrecognition treatment as an "E" reorganization: bonds for stock, stock for stock, and bonds for bonds.[21] A corporation can exchange its common stock for preferred stock or its preferred stock for common stock tax-free. The exchange of bonds for other bonds is tax-free if the principal amount of the debt surrendered is not less than that of the debt received.

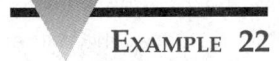

EXAMPLE 22

Half of the stock in Blue Corporation is owned by Wade and half by his children, Mark and Marcia. Wade wishes to retire and relinquish control of the corporation. He exchanges his common voting stock for nonvoting preferred stock. The exchange qualifies as an "E" reorganization. However, any difference in value between stock received and stock surrendered could be treated as compensation or as a gift. ▼

TYPE F

The "Type F" reorganization is "a . . . mere change in identity, form or place of organization, however effected."[22] The IRS has ruled that if a reorganization qualifies as an "A," "C," or "D" reorganization and as an "F" reorganization, "Type F" reorganization treatment prevails.[23]

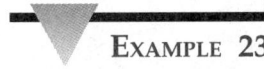

EXAMPLE 23

Black Corporation changes its name to Gray Corporation. This is an "F" reorganization. ▼

The "F" reorganization is illustrated in Figure 7–8.

The surviving corporation in an "F" reorganization is the same corporation as its predecessor. Consequently, the tax characteristics of the predecessor carry over to the successor. Such a reorganization is a mere change in identity or form, and net operating losses can be carried back as well as forward.

---

[21] Reg. § 1.368–2(e).
[22] § 368(a)(1)(F).

[23] Rev.Rul. 57–276, 1957–1 C.B. 126.

▼ **FIGURE 7–8**
"F" Reorganization

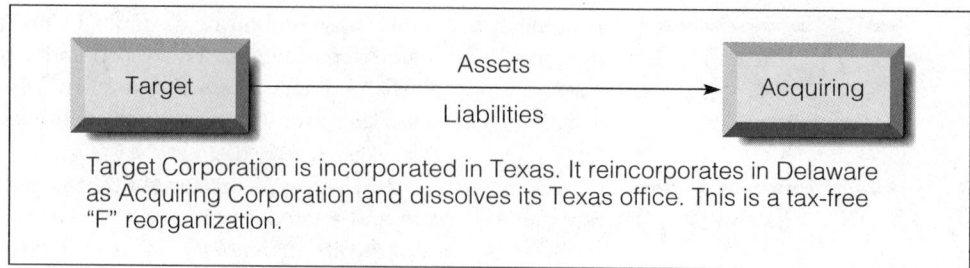

Target Corporation is incorporated in Texas. It reincorporates in Delaware as Acquiring Corporation and dissolves its Texas office. This is a tax-free "F" reorganization.

An "F" reorganization is restricted to a *single* operating corporation. An "F" reorganization does not jeopardize the status of § 1244 stock, nor will it terminate a valid S corporation election.[24] There is no significant change in stock ownership in the "F" reorganization.[25]

TYPE G

Bankruptcy legislation introduced the "G" reorganization. In this type of reorganization, all or a part of the assets of a debtor corporation are transferred to an acquiring corporation in a bankruptcy or similar proceeding of a Federal or state court. The debtor corporation's creditors must receive voting stock of the acquiring corporation in exchange for debt representing 80 percent or more of the total fair market value of the debt of the debtor corporation.

ETHICAL CONSIDERATIONS

Who Benefits from a Corporate Merger?

Mega Bank merges with National Bank in a $70 million stock swap. The new surviving bank, MegaNational, will virtually control the banking industry in the states where it does business. Ralph, the CEO of Mega Bank who will receive a bonus of $100 million for his part in structuring the merger, has cited the enormous cost reductions accruing from the merger. Part of the cost savings will result from the ability of the new bank to cut 12,000 jobs. In addition, by controlling the banking market, MegaNational will be able to raise its fees for providing banking services to its customers. The shareholders of the merged banks reaped a substantial profit from later sales of their stock. Does the merger present any ethical problems?

JUDICIAL CONDITIONS

4   LEARNING OBJECTIVE
Recognize the judicial and administrative conditions that complement the statutory requirements for a nontaxable corporate reorganization.

A discussion of reorganizations must consider certain basic conditions that pervade the entire field. Various judicially created doctrines—sound business purpose, continuity of interest, and continuity of business enterprise—have become basic requirements for the tax-free status of corporate reorganizations. The courts have also formulated the so-called step transaction doctrine to determine the tax status of a reorganization effected through a series of related transactions.

---

[24] Reg. § 1.1244(d)–3(d)(1) and Rev.Rul. 64–250, 1964–2 C.B. 333.   [25] Rev.Rul. 66–284, 1966–2 C.B. 115.

CONCEPT SUMMARY 7–3

Corporate Reorganizations

Reorganization	Type	Advantages	Disadvantages
A	Merger or consolidation.	• No requirement that consideration be voting stock.	• State law must be followed—dissenters' rights and required shareholder meetings may present problems.
		• As much as 50% of consideration can be cash without tax consequences for receipt of stock (cash and other property received *is* taxed).	• All liabilities of target corporation are assumed by acquiring corporation as a matter of law.
	Subsidiary "A."	• As parent is majority stockholder, problem of securing approval of majority shareholder is removed.	• For "reverse merger," must have 80% control of target corporation.
		• Subsidiary, rather than parent, assumes liabilities of target corporation.	• For "reverse merger," only voting stock of the parent may be used.
B	Stock-for-stock exchange.	• Stock may be acquired from shareholders.	• *Only* voting stock of acquiring corporation may be used.
		• Procedures to effect reorganization are not complex.	• Must have 80% control of a target corporation.
			• May have minority interest remaining in target corporation.
C	Assets-for-stock exchange.	• Less complex as to state law than "A."	• *Substantially all* assets of target corporation must be transferred.
		• Cash or property can be used as consideration if 20% or less of fair market value of property transferred.	• Liabilities count as *other property* for 20% rule if any consideration other than stock and liabilities is used.
			• The target corporation must distribute the stock, securities, and other properties it receives in the reorganization to its shareholders.
D	Usually corporate division (spin-off, split-off, or split-up).	• Permits corporate division without tax consequences if no *boot* is involved.	
E	Recapitalization.	• Allows for major change in makeup of shareholders' equity.	
F	Change in identity, form, or place of organization.	• Survivor is treated as same entity as predecessor; thus, tax attributes of predecessor can be carried back as well as forward.	
G	Court-approved reorganization of debtor corporation.	• Creditors can exchange notes for stock tax-free.	
		• State merger laws need not be followed.	

In addition, a plan of reorganization is required. In essence, these doctrines have imposed additional requirements for attaining the tax-favored status of corporate reorganizations.

SOUND BUSINESS PURPOSE

Even if the statutory requirements of a reorganization have been literally followed, a transaction will not be tax-free unless it exhibits a **business purpose.**[26] The Regulations have followed the courts in recognizing this requirement.[27]

The test of business purpose, and whether it may reflect the shareholder's purpose rather than that of the corporation, is not well-defined. In one case, the Court implied that the resulting benefits from the capital change to the corporation must be direct and substantial.[28] In more recent cases, though, courts have conceded that it is sometimes impossible to draw a line between the purpose of the corporation and that of the shareholders.[29]

Cases indicate that the business purpose doctrine does not operate in reverse. It is normally the revenue agent who asserts lack of business purpose to deny tax-free status to a corporate reorganization. Occasionally, however, the taxpayer may want the transaction to be taxable so as to receive a step-up in basis in assets or to recognize a loss. Taxpayers have attempted to employ the business purpose doctrine to prevent the transaction from being considered a reorganization. In those instances, however, the courts have required the taxpayers to abide by the form of the transaction and have agreed with the IRS that a reorganization was involved.[30]

CONTINUITY OF INTEREST

The continuity of interest doctrine is founded in the philosophy of the tax-free reorganization. If a shareholder or corporation has substantially the same investment after a corporate exchange as before, no tax should be imposed upon the transaction. Thus, the courts imposed what has been termed the *continuity of interest* test. To qualify for tax-favored reorganization status, the seller must acquire an equity interest in the purchasing corporation.[31]

The IRS has attempted to define exactly how much equity shareholders of the target corporation must receive in the acquiring corporation. The IRS deems the test met if shareholders of the target corporation, in the aggregate, receive stock in the acquiring corporation equal in value to at least 50 percent of all formerly outstanding stock of the target corporation.[32] Not all shareholders of the target corporation need to have a proprietary interest in the surviving corporation. The requirement is applied to the total consideration given in the acquisition.

---

[26] *Gregory v. Helvering,* 35–1 USTC ¶9043, 14 AFTR 1191, 55 S.Ct. 266 (USSC, 1935). The doctrine as developed in the *Gregory* case became a precedent for all transactions that might be shams devised merely for tax avoidance purposes. It brought about the principle of substance over form. The IRS and the courts look through the form of a transaction to determine what really took place. All business transactions must have a sound business purpose.

[27] Reg. § 1.368–1(c).

[28] *Bazley v. Comm.,* 47–1 USTC ¶9288, 35 AFTR 1190, 67 S.Ct. 1489 (USSC, 1947).

[29] *Estate of Parshelsky v. Comm.,* 62–1 USTC ¶9460, 9 AFTR2d 1382, 303 F.2d 14 (CA–2, 1962).

[30] *Survaunt v. Comm.,* 47–2 USTC ¶9344, 35 AFTR 1557, 162 F.2d 753 (CA–8, 1947).

[31] *Pinellas Ice & Cold Storage v. Comm.,* 3 USTC ¶1023, 11 AFTR 1112, 53 S.Ct. 257 (USSC, 1933), and *LeTulle v. Scofield,* 40–1 USTC ¶9150, 23 AFTR 789, 60 S.Ct. 313 (USSC, 1940). In *LeTulle,* a corporation transferred all its assets to another corporation for cash and bonds. The Court held that the transaction was not a tax-free reorganization if the transferor's only retained interest was that of a creditor. This concept is now in Reg. § 1.368–2(a).

[32] Rev.Proc. 74–26, 1974–2 C.B. 478, § 3.02, updated by Rev.Proc. 77–37, 1977–2 C.B. 568.

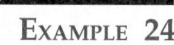

EXAMPLE 24   Target Corporation, with 50 shareholders, merges into Acquiring Corporation, pursuant to state statute. Under the merger plan, the shareholders of Target can elect to receive either cash or stock in Acquiring. Thirty of the shareholders (holding 40% of Target's outstanding stock) elect to receive cash; the remaining 20 shareholders of Target (holding 60% of the stock) elect to receive stock in Acquiring. This plan satisfies the continuity of interest test. The shareholders receiving cash are taxed on the transaction. Those receiving stock are not. ▼

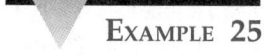

EXAMPLE 25   Jaime and Pedro each hold 50% of the stock of Target Corporation. Target merges into Acquiring Corporation. Jaime receives cash for his stock in Target, while Pedro receives stock in Acquiring equal in value to at least 50% of the formerly outstanding stock in Target. Jaime is taxed on the transaction, but Pedro is not. ▼

CONTINUITY OF BUSINESS ENTERPRISE

The Regulations refer to a **"continuity of business enterprise** under the modified form" as a prerequisite for a statutory reorganization.[33] Originally, this test was interpreted to mean that the acquiring corporation must conduct business activities of the same type as the target corporation.[34] Now, this test is satisfied if the transferee continues the historic business of the transferor or uses a significant portion of the assets of the transferor in its business.[35]

STEP TRANSACTION

The court-imposed **step transaction** doctrine is employed to determine whether a reorganization is tax-favored when a series of related transactions is involved. The courts look at the conditions before and after the change in ownership. Assuming the transactions in the series are related, all will be considered as one for tax purposes. In one case, the Court advanced a test for determining whether a series

---

[33] Reg. § 1.368–1(b).
[34] Rev.Rul. 56–330, 1956–2 C.B. 204.

[35] Reg. § 1.368–1(d).

of steps is to be treated as a single indivisible transaction: "Were the steps so interdependent that the legal relations created by one transaction would have been fruitless without a completion of the series?"[36]

The step transaction doctrine presents complications for reorganizations when *unwanted* assets are involved. If the target corporation attempts to dispose of its unwanted assets before a reorganization, the doctrine could be used to defeat the tax-favored status of the reorganization. A *substantially all* requirement is present in the "C," "D," and subsidiary "A" reorganizations. Assuming application of the doctrine is appropriate, a prior nontaxable disposition of unwanted assets and a later reorganization are treated as a single transaction. Consequently, the acquiring corporation has failed to acquire substantially all of the target corporation's assets.

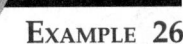

EXAMPLE 26

Acquiring Corporation wants to obtain certain, but not all, of the assets of Target Corporation. A direct conveyance of the desired property to Acquiring is not a tax-free reorganization, because the unwanted assets make up a substantial portion of Target's total assets. A valid "C" reorganization is not possible, as substantially all of Target's assets will not be conveyed. A possible solution would be to organize a new corporation, transfer the unwanted assets to the new corporation for all of its stock, and distribute the stock to Target's shareholders. Then, the remaining assets in Target Corporation would be transferred to Acquiring Corporation in return for stock. What has been accomplished?

- The first transfer would be tax-free under § 351 as a transfer to a corporation in exchange for at least 80% of the new company's stock.
- The second transfer of Target's remaining assets to Acquiring in return for stock is a tax-free "C" reorganization.

What could go wrong with the results? One court agreed with the IRS that the first transfer was equivalent to a retention of assets by Target.[37] If the unwanted assets had remained in Target, the transfer to Acquiring would not have met the *substantially all* test. Consequently, the court held that transferring the assets solely to make a "C" reorganization possible constituted tax avoidance. ▼

The IRS generally views any transaction occurring within one year of the reorganization as part of the acquisition. This assumes there is no other direct proof that the transaction was, in fact, unrelated.[38]

OTHER CONSIDERATIONS

ASSUMPTION OF LIABILITIES

Because a corporate reorganization normally results in a continuation of the business activities of the previous corporations, liabilities are seldom liquidated. The acquiring corporation either assumes the liabilities of the acquired organization or takes property subject to liabilities. In a regular sale or purchase of

---

[36] *American Bantam Car Co.*, 11 T.C. 397 (1948), *aff'd.* in 49–2 USTC ¶9471, 38 AFTR 820, 177 F.2d 513 (CA–3, 1949), *cert. den.* 70 S.Ct. 622 (USSC, 1950). If the steps are not related, the doctrine does not apply. See *Esmark, Inc.*, 90 T.C. 171 (1988).

[37] *Helvering v. Elkhorn Coal Co.*, 38–1 USTC ¶9238, 20 AFTR 1301, 95 F.2d 732 (CA–4, 1938), *cert. den.* 59 S.Ct. 65 (USSC, 1938).

[38] In Rev.Rul. 69–48, 1969–1 C.B. 106, the IRS applied the step transaction doctrine to transactions that were 22 months apart.

properties, the assumption of liabilities by the purchaser is part of the selling price.[39] As noted in Chapter 3, in some nonrecognition transactions, assumption of liabilities is considered boot and is taxable. In a "C" reorganization, assumed liabilities are, for the most part, disregarded in computing taxable gain to the transferor corporation.[40]

A transferor corporation must not take back liabilities in a "B" reorganization. Any debt assumption violates the *solely for voting stock* requirement.

ETHICAL CONSIDERATIONS

Switching from Defender to Raider

Pat, a partner in an accounting and consulting firm, has been instrumental in her firm's helping target corporations avoid corporate raids in the past by inventing a variety of popular takeover defenses, including the so-called poison pill. As a result of Pat's efforts, the firm's reputation for skillful and principled antitakeover work brought it several corporate clients and provided it with substantial profits, in which Pat generously shared.

Now Pat's firm wants to represent hostile bidders and help them in their takeover fights. The firm wants Pat to advise the new clients on how to structure hostile takeovers. Pat has several creative ideas as to how to accomplish these goals in a manner that other advisers have yet to discover. Does Pat have an ethical problem in switching positions?

UNFRIENDLY TAKEOVERS

As a result of the dramatic increase in unfriendly corporate takeover attempts, directors of target corporations must be prepared to contend with a whole new array of complex issues and options. Many companies have taken various measures to discourage unfriendly takeovers. These defensive measures include staggering the terms of the board of directors over several years instead of having the entire board up for election at one time. This makes it more difficult for the acquiring corporation to gain control by electing its own board of directors.

Some corporations have given key employees golden parachute contracts that will pay them large benefits if they are terminated after an unfriendly merger. Poison pills, tin parachutes, self-tender offers, Pac-Man defenses, exclusive merger agreements, and standstill agreements are some of the more recent defensive weapons adopted to ward off hostile takeover attempts.

Members of the board of directors of a target corporation face complex legal issues when they adopt defensive measures. Are the directors serving their own interests and not considering the benefits that might accrue to the target's shareholders if a takeover attempt is successful? Directors of the target corporation must take some position in a hostile takeover attempt; they cannot remain neutral. In considering the available alternatives, directors must adopt measures that are beneficial to the corporation. Their own private interests cannot be considered.

---

[39] *Crane v. Comm.*, 47–1 USTC ¶9217, 35 AFTR 776, 67 S.Ct. 1047 (USSC, 1947).

[40] § 357.

┌───┐
│ TAX IN THE NEWS   │
└───┘

A Poison Pill That Pleased Some Shareholders

Time Warner, Inc., in a move designed to keep its new investor Seagram Company "at bay," reinstituted a poison-pill provision that effectively limited an outside investor's ownership to 15 percent of Time Warner's stock. The pill made it prohibitively expensive for a hostile acquirer to take over the company. The move was approved by Time Warner's board just a day after Seagram became Time Warner's largest shareholder.

Seagram criticized the move, stating that such plans are not in the best interest of public shareholders. According to Seagram, poison pills "can interfere with shareholder choice and adversely affect shareholder values." Although large institutional investors typically are opposed to poison pills, in Time Warner's case some of the company's largest shareholders, including Capital Group, Inc., with an 11 percent stake, endorsed the plan. Time Warner announced that although it had dropped a similar poison pill three years ago, it decided to adopt a new one after several institutional investors expressed concern that the company might be vulnerable to "abusive takeover tactics," including acquisition of control without paying all shareholders a fair premium.

SOURCE: Information from Laura Landro and Eben Shapiro, "Time Warner Moves to Keep Seagram at Bay," *Wall Street Journal*, January 21, 1994, pp. A3 and A4.

ETHICAL CONSIDERATIONS

Poison Pills and Golden Parachutes

White Corporation is engaged in commercial development. Julio, its chief executive officer, has been referred to as a financial wizard. Sales of commercial properties were down in the current year, and White suffered a small loss for the year.

Some national developers have been considering purchasing the stock of White Corporation because of its demonstrated success in the past. As rumors of a takeover appeared in the media, Julio directed the company's attorneys to create golden parachutes for all of White's officers and tin parachutes for the company's employees. He also directed the attorneys to develop a poison pill that would take effect if a takeover was successful. Under the plan developed by the attorneys, in the event of a takeover, all shareholders would immediately be issued shares as a dividend in the form of a special class of stock. Should a takeover occur, the special stock would have to be repurchased at a cost of $100 per share. The effect of the plan was to triple the cost of a takeover.

Julio presented the parachute plans and the poison pill to White's board of directors. One director asked if the shareholders of White would not be better off to sell their shares in a tender offer. The director was also curious about the parachute payments and asked why the corporation should try to keep its management. Whose interests should be considered in a takeover?

Congress has entered the corporate-control arena by adding several new provisions to tax some of the measures adopted in unfriendly merger transactions. One such provision is § 5881, which imposes a 50 percent tax on any gain realized, whether it is recognized or not, by anyone receiving greenmail.

Gain realized by a white knight, the friendly bidder who enters the bidding war in response to the target corporation's attempt to find a more compatible acquiring company, may also be subject to the penalty tax.

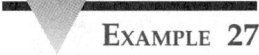

EXAMPLE 27

Jack, a corporate raider, buys 20% of the stock of Target Corporation, or 15,000 shares, in the open market on November 10, 1996, for $10 per share. Jack then makes a public tender offer to the remaining shareholders of Target to buy their shares for $14 per share. Target's directors seek a white knight to ward off a hostile takeover by Jack. Knight, a corporation that is friendly to Target, agrees to purchase Target stock. In 1997, Knight offers Target's shareholders $15 per share to be paid in the form of Knight stock. Then, to prevent any disagreements with Jack, Knight offers to pay Jack $16 per share in voting stock in Knight for the 15,000 shares he purchased.

After purchasing Jack's 15,000 shares, or 20% of Target's shares, Knight acquires an additional 45,000 shares, or 60% of Target's shares. The transaction qualifies as a "B" reorganization because control of Target was obtained solely for voting stock in Knight.

- Because Jack was paid more than other Target shareholders, he is subject to the greenmail tax. The tax is applicable to gain *realized* even though the gain is not *recognized*.
- Jack must pay a penalty tax of $45,000 (50% of realized gain of $90,000). Jack paid $150,000 for the Target stock (15,000 shares at $10 per share) and realized $240,000 on the exchange (15,000 shares at $16 per share). The § 5881 penalty tax applies to the total gain realized, not just the excess of the price Jack received over the price paid other shareholders.
- Had Jack transferred the Target stock for $15 per share, the price other shareholders received, he would have escaped the 50% penalty tax. His consideration at $15 per share would be $225,000. After paying the $45,000 penalty tax, Jack has received only $195,000 ($240,000 – $45,000). ▼

Tax problems arise in other contexts when unfriendly mergers or measures to ward off hostile takeovers occur. For example, golden parachutes are not deductible to the extent of the *excess parachute payment*. Further, the person receiving a golden parachute is subject to an excise tax of 20 percent[41] of the excess payment, in addition to income and Social Security taxes. In addition, the use of a poison pill to ward off hostile takeovers can keep the corporation from acquiring another corporation in a tax-free "B" or "C" reorganization.

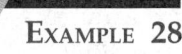

EXAMPLE 28

Gina is president of Target Corporation. Her average salary for the past five years was $150,000. In 1997, Target Corporation is taken over, and Gina loses her position. Under her employment contract, she is paid $1 million in 1997. A parachute payment has occurred because the $1 million payment exceeds $450,000 (three times the base amount of $150,000, Gina's average salary for the past five years). The excess of the $1 million payment over the base amount of $150,000, or $850,000, is not deductible by Target. Further, Gina is subject to an excise tax of $170,000 ($850,000 × 20%). ▼

---

[41] § 4999.

EXAMPLE 29

Parent Corporation adopts a poison pill as a preventive measure in case a corporate raider attempts a hostile takeover. Parent's shareholders are given rights to purchase one preferred share for each share of Parent's voting stock. Later, Parent decides to acquire Target Corporation, believing that the combination of the two businesses will increase sales and produce greater market penetration. Parent issues 10% of its voting stock to the shareholders of Target in exchange for 80% of the stock in Target. The shareholders of Target also are given rights to purchase one preferred share in Parent for each share of voting stock acquired in the exchange. The IRS may take the position that the rights constitute boot.[42] Thus, the exchange may not qualify as a "B" reorganization, as the consideration for the exchange was not solely voting stock in Parent. ▼

CARRYOVER OF CORPORATE TAX ATTRIBUTES

5 LEARNING OBJECTIVE
Use the rules applicable to the carryover of tax attributes in a corporate reorganization.

Some tax features of an acquired corporation (the carryover of losses, tax credits, and E & P deficits) are welcomed by a successor corporation. Others may prove less desirable. The mandatory carryover rules should be carefully considered in every corporate acquisition; they may, in fact, determine the form of the acquisition.

THEORY OF CARRYOVERS

Before the enactment of § 381, case law determined which tax benefits of an acquired corporation could be carried over to the successor. With respect to net operating losses, general theory held that only the corporation sustaining the loss could take the deduction. As a result, the form of a corporate acquisition largely determined whether a tax loss could be carried over to the acquiring corporation. If a statutory merger or consolidation occurred, the courts permitted the carryover of the predecessor corporation's deductions. Since the assets and liabilities of the two corporations were amalgamated by operation of law, a carryover was justified. Carryovers were not permitted in other forms of corporate acquisitions.[43]

The courts held that although a credit balance in the target corporation's E & P carries over to the successor corporation, a deficit does not.[44] This rule was designed to prevent any E & P from escaping taxation.

Section 381 now determines which tax benefits of an acquired corporation can be carried over to the successor, but the statute does not apply to all transactions. In instances where it does not apply, case law may still apply.

Allowance of Carryovers. Section 381 provides for the carryover of various specific tax attributes from one corporation to another in certain tax-free liquidations and reorganizations. Section 381(c) lists the tax features of an acquired corporation that can be carried over to a successor corporation. Section 381 does not apply to any other items. Only the "A," "C," "F," nondivisive "D," and "G" reorganizations are subject to the rules. The rule also is used in the liquidation of a controlled subsidiary under § 332 where the subsidiary's basis in its assets carries over to the parent.

---

[42] See Ltr.Ruls. 8808081, 8925087, and 9125013.
[43] *New Colonial Ice Co. v. Helvering*, 4 USTC ¶1292, 13 AFTR 1180, 54 S.Ct. 788 (USSC, 1934).

[44] *Comm. v. Sansome*, 3 USTC ¶978, 11 AFTR 854, 60 F.2d 931 (CA–2, 1931), *cert. den.* 53 S.Ct. 291 (USSC, 1932), and *Comm. v. Phipps*, 49–1 USTC ¶9204, 37 AFTR 827, 69 S.Ct. 616 (USSC, 1949).

NET OPERATING LOSS CARRYOVERS

A net operating loss (NOL) carryover is permitted as a deduction of the successor corporation. However, the amount of the carryover can be limited.

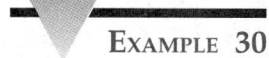

EXAMPLE 30

Target Corporation has an NOL of $3,000,000. It advertises its NOL as an asset it would "sell" to another corporation having substantial taxable income.

Acquiring Corporation has taxable income of $5,000,000 in 1997. It expects about the same amount of taxable income in 1998. Acquiring's tax liability for 1997 is $1,700,000 ($5,000,000 × 34%). Acquiring undoubtedly will incur approximately the same tax liability in 1998 unless it can use Target's NOL. If Target is merged into Acquiring and Target's NOL carries over to offset Acquiring's taxable income for 1998, Acquiring's taxable income would be only $2,000,000 [$5,000,000 (taxable income before reduction for NOL) – $3,000,000 (NOL carryover)]. Acquiring will save approximately $1,020,000 in tax liability [$1,700,000 (tax on $5,000,000) – $680,000 (tax on $2,000,000 at 34%)].

Target's NOL is indeed an "asset" that is worth approximately $1,020,000 to Acquiring. But will the NOL carry over to offset Acquiring's taxable income? ▼

Limitation of Carryover for Year of Transfer. The amount of the current-year NOL that can be used in the first tax year ending after the transfer date is limited to a percentage representing the remaining days in that tax year.[45] For example, if two calendar year corporations merged on April 1, only a portion of an NOL of the acquired corporation can be used to offset income for that tax year. The amount is limited to three-fourths of the taxable income of the acquiring corporation.

EXAMPLE 31

Target Corporation merges into Acquiring Corporation on December 16, 1997. Target had an NOL of $73,000, while Acquiring had taxable income of $100,000 for 1997. Only $4,110 [$100,000 × (15/365) = $4,110] of the $73,000 NOL can be used to offset Acquiring's taxable income. Acquiring's taxable income is $95,890 ($100,000 – $4,110). The remainder of Target's 1997 loss, $68,890, is carried forward to offset Acquiring's 1998 or later taxable income. ▼

Ownership Changes. The carryover of NOLs is also limited by § 382, which may prevent prior-year losses from being used as in the following example.

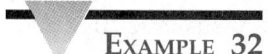

EXAMPLE 32

Target Corporation has an NOL of $3,000,000. On January 1, 1998, Target is merged into Acquiring Corporation. Acquiring has taxable income of $3,500,000 in 1998. Because the merger occurred on the first day of the year, Acquiring could use all of Target's $3,000,000 NOL to offset its taxable income of $3,500,000 in 1998, if no other provision in the Code limited the carryover. But Acquiring must also consider § 382, which may limit the amount of the carryover, not only in the year of the acquisition but in succeeding years as well. ▼

The *§ 382 limitation* on the carryover of an NOL provides that the taxable income of the new corporation may be reduced each year by a portion of the NOL carryover. The reduction is available only to the extent of the value of the loss corporation's stock on the date of the ownership change multiplied by the **long-term tax-exempt rate.** This is the highest of the Federal long-term rates for the three calendar months before the exchange.

The objective of the § 382 limitation is to restrict the use of NOLs to a hypothetical future income stream, which is to be measured by the yield that would have been received had the value of the stock been invested in long-term

---

[45] § 381(c)(1)(B).

securities. Section 382 does not disallow an NOL. It merely limits the amount of NOL carryover that the new loss or surviving corporation can utilize on an annual basis.

Section 382 imposes limitations on the carryover of an NOL only if there is (1) an *owner shift* or (2) an *equity structure shift*:

- An **owner shift** is any change in the respective ownership of stock by a 5 percent shareholder. The change is determined by looking to a testing period that is the shorter of the prior three years or the period following the most recent ownership change. All less-than-5 percent shareholders are treated as a single 5 percent shareholder.
- An **equity structure shift** occurs with any tax-free reorganization other than a divisive reorganization or an "F" reorganization.

If neither an owner shift nor an equity structure shift occurs, no limitation is placed on the amount of the carryover. If either the owner shift or the equity structure shift causes a more-than-50 percent change in the ownership of the loss corporation, the NOL carryover is subject to the § 382 limitation.

EXAMPLE 33 The stock of Black Corporation is publicly traded, and no shareholder holds 5% or more of the stock. During the three-year period between January 1, 1995, and January 1, 1998, numerous trades are made involving Black stock, but no person (or persons) becomes a 5% shareholder (either directly or indirectly) and increases his or her (or their) ownership by more than 50 percentage points. No ownership change takes place that results in § 382 limitations to any NOL carryovers. No ownership shift has occurred, as the less-than-5% shareholders are aggregated. They own 100% before the trades and 100% after the trades. ▼

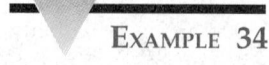

EXAMPLE 34 Brown Corporation, a calendar year taxpayer, has a more-than-50% ownership change on January 1, 1998. At this point, it has an NOL carryover of $500,000. The value of the Brown stock is $1 million, and the long-term tax-exempt rate is 10%. Brown's § 382 limitation for 1998 is $100,000 ($1 million × 10%). If, in 1998, Brown Corporation has taxable income of $70,000 (before any NOL carryover), $70,000 of the loss can be used. The $30,000 remaining portion ($100,000 – $70,000) is carried over and increases the § 382 limitation for 1999 to $130,000 ($30,000 + $100,000). ▼

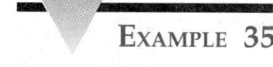

EXAMPLE 35 Target Corporation is merged into Acquiring Corporation in an "A" reorganization. At the time of the merger, Target had an NOL of $100,000. Pursuant to the merger, the shareholders of Target receive 40% of the stock of Acquiring. An equity structure shift has taken place. If the value of Target is $50,000 and the applicable rate is 10%, the § 382 limitation on Target's NOL is $5,000 ($50,000 × 10%). ▼

EARNINGS AND PROFITS

The Supreme Court held in an early case that the E & P of an acquired corporation carries over to a successor corporation. However, the Court later held that a successor corporation was not permitted to apply a deficit in the acquired corporation's E & P against its own E & P.[46] The result was confusion in applying these general rules. Earnings and profits of a predecessor corporation are now deemed to have been received by the successor corporation as of the date of the distribution or transfer. A deficit may only be used to offset E & P accumulated by the successor corporation after the date of the transfer.[47]

---

[46] *Comm. v. Sansome* and *Comm. v. Phipps,* both cited in Footnote 44.   [47] § 381(c)(2) and Reg. § 1.381(c)(2)–1(a)(5).

If one corporation has accumulated E & P and the other has a deficit, the deficit can be used only to offset E & P accumulated after the date of the transfer. The acquiring corporation essentially has two separate E & P accounts after the date of the transfer. One account contains the total accumulated E & P as of the date of the transfer. The other contains the total deficits as of the date of the transfer. The deficit in one account may not be used to reduce accumulated E & P in the other account.

CAPITAL LOSS CARRYOVERS

The carryover of capital losses of the predecessor corporation is subject to the same limitations as the carryover of NOLs. The capital loss carryover is a short-term capital loss to the acquiring corporation. The amount deductible in the year of transfer is limited to a percentage of the net capital gains of the successor corporation computed with reference to the number of days remaining in the tax year.

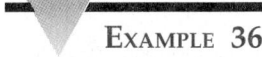

EXAMPLE 36

Target Corporation has a capital loss in the amount of $30,000. Target transfers all its assets to Acquiring Corporation on July 1. Acquiring files a calendar year return. Acquiring has net capital gains (computed without regard to any capital loss carryovers) for that year of $40,000. The amount of capital loss carryover available in the current year is $20,000 ($40,000 × ½). ▼

OTHER CARRYOVERS

Numerous other carryover items are addressed in § 381. The successor corporation determines depreciation on acquired assets in the same manner as did the predecessor corporation. Should installment obligations pass to a transferee corporation in a reorganization, the transferee corporation reports the income from the obligations on the installment method.

Section 383 limits the amount of unused foreign tax credits and other credits that may be carried over in the context of an owner shift or an equity structure shift. The limitation is applied to these credits in the same manner as it is applied to capital loss carryovers.

DISALLOWANCE OF CARRYOVERS

Irrespective of § 381, the IRS can utilize § 269 to disallow the carryover of tax benefits if a tax avoidance scheme is apparent. Such items are disallowed if a corporation acquires property of another corporation primarily to evade or avoid Federal income tax by securing the benefit of a deduction, credit, or other allowance that the acquiring corporation would not otherwise enjoy. Whether the principal purpose is the evasion or avoidance of taxes becomes a question of fact. If the business of the loss corporation is promptly discontinued after a corporate reorganization, the IRS may use § 269 in an attempt to disallow the loss carryover.

TAX PLANNING CONSIDERATIONS

ASSESSING THE POSSIBLE ALTERNATIVES

The various types of corporate reorganizations should not be considered in isolation. Often the parties involved can achieve the desired tax result through more than one type of reorganization.

CONCEPT SUMMARY 7–4

Summary of Carryover Rules

Tax attributes carry over in tax-free liquidations and in tax-free reorganizations as follows.

1. Net operating losses and capital losses.
   A. Year of transfer.
      The amount of the loss in the year of transfer is limited to the taxable income of the surviving corporation (capital gain in the case of a carryover of a capital loss) multiplied by a percentage representing the remaining days in the year of transfer.
   B. Ownership changes.
      - Section 382 imposes an annual limitation on the amount of loss carryover if an owner shift or an equity structure shift occurs.
      - An owner shift is a more-than-50% change in the ownership of shareholders owning 5% or more of the corporate stock.
      - An equity structure shift is a tax-free reorganization, other than a divisive "D" or an "F," in which a more-than-50% change occurs in the ownership of the loss corporation.
      - The § 382 limitation provides that the annual carryover may not exceed the value of the old loss corporation's stock on the date of the transfer multiplied by the Federal long-term rate.
      - The Federal long-term rate is the highest such rate in the three-calendar-month period before the stock change.

2. Earnings and profits.
   A. E & P of an acquired corporation carries over.
   B. If either corporation has a deficit in E & P, the surviving corporation will have two E & P accounts. One account contains the total accumulated E & P as of the date of the transfer. The other contains the total deficit as of the date of the transfer.

3. Other tax attributes.
   A. Depreciation and cost recovery methods carry over.
   B. The installment method of reporting carries over.
   C. Credits carry over, but they are limited in the acquisition year.
   D. The acquiring corporation uses the method of accounting used by the acquired corporation.

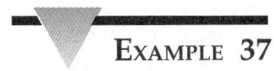

EXAMPLE 37

Black Corporation operates two businesses, both of which have been in existence for five years. One business is a manufacturing operation; the other is a wholesale distributorship. White Corporation wishes to acquire only the former business and does not wish to purchase all of Black's assets. Black has an NOL, a deficit in E & P, and a basis in its assets in excess of their fair market value. ▼

6   LEARNING OBJECTIVE
Structure corporate reorganizations to obtain the desired tax consequences.

What course of action might be advisable to transfer the manufacturing operation from Black to White with the least, if any, tax consequences? Compare the following three possibilities.

1. Black Corporation transfers the manufacturing operation to White Corporation in return for some of the latter's stock.
2. Black Corporation forms Brown Corporation and transfers the wholesale distributorship to it in return for all of Brown's stock. The Brown stock is then distributed to Black's shareholders. This portion of the arrangement is a nontaxable spin-off. Black now transfers the manufacturing operation to White Corporation in exchange for some of the latter's stock.

3. After the nontaxable spin-off described in possibility 2, White acquires all of the Black stock in exchange for some of White's voting stock. Black is now a subsidiary of White.

Possibility 1 probably will not fit within the definition of a "C" reorganization, because substantially all of the assets are not transferred by Black in return for White stock. The manufacturing operation (the "wanted" assets) is transferred, the wholesale distributorship ("unwanted" assets) is not.

Possibility 2 suffers from these same shortcomings. If the spin-off is disregarded, the transaction becomes an unsuccessful attempt to carry out a "C" reorganization (possibility 1). Disregarding the spin-off is the natural result of following the step transaction doctrine.[48]

Possibility 3 follows a different approach. It starts with the spin-off of the *unwanted* assets and concludes with White obtaining the *wanted* assets by purchasing the Black stock. Taken by itself, this last step satisfies the stock-for-stock requirement of a "B" reorganization. If, however, the step transaction doctrine is applied and the spin-off is disregarded, the Brown stock distributed to Black's shareholders might be considered as property *other than voting stock* in White. The IRS has not chosen to take this position and probably will recognize the nontaxability of a spin-off of *unwanted* assets followed by a "B" reorganization.[49]

RESOLVING SHAREHOLDER DISPUTES

The use of a split-off under the "D" reorganization should not be overlooked as a means of resolving shareholder disputes.

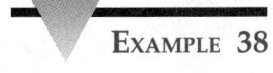

EXAMPLE 38

Target Corporation was organized 10 years ago; since that time, it has operated retail and wholesale businesses. Target's two shareholders, Maggie and Carl, each manage one of the businesses. Due to a difference of opinion over corporate policy, Maggie and Carl decide to separate the two businesses. ▼

Presuming Maggie and Carl plan to continue operating each business in the corporate form, any tax consequences on the division can be avoided by pursuing a "D" reorganization. Target could form Acquiring Corporation by transferring to it one of the businesses, say, the wholesale operation, in return for all the Acquiring stock. Next the Acquiring stock is distributed to the manager of the wholesale business, Maggie, in exchange for all of the Target stock. After the nontaxable split-off, Carl has the retail business through his sole ownership in Target, and Maggie has control of the wholesale operation through the ownership of Acquiring.

REORGANIZATIONS COMPARED WITH STOCK REDEMPTIONS AND LIQUIDATIONS

Example 38 presents an opportunity to review certain other possibilities discussed in previous chapters.

- If, for example, Carl wishes to continue operating in the corporate form while Maggie does not, the stock redemption approach can be used (refer to Chapter 5). Maggie could exchange all of her Target stock for the wholesale business. This would qualify as a complete termination redemption of a

---

[48] *Helvering v. Elkhorn Coal Co.*, cited in Footnote 37.   [49] Rev.Rul. 70–434, 1970–2 C.B. 83.

shareholder's interest. Maggie recognizes a capital gain or loss, measured by the difference between the fair market value of the wholesale business and her basis in the surrendered Target stock.

- If both shareholders are indifferent about whether the businesses should continue to operate in the corporate form, a complete liquidation of Target may be appropriate. The liquidation is carried out by making a distribution in kind of the wholesale business to Maggie and of the retail business to Carl. As was true in the stock redemption alternative, the shareholders recognize a capital gain or loss, measured by the difference between the fair market value of the property received and the basis of the stock given up.

The stock redemption and liquidation approaches produce gain at both the corporate and the shareholder level. The "D" reorganization postpones the recognition of *any* gain on the division of the businesses. In a purely tax-free exchange, no change takes place in income tax basis. Thus, Carl's basis in the Target stock remains the same, while Maggie's basis in the Target stock surrendered carries over to the new Acquiring stock received. At the corporate level, Target retains the same basis it had in the retail business, and Acquiring assumes Target's basis in the wholesale operation. Figure 7–9 illustrates the various alternatives.

Carryover Considerations.   The tax differences between corporate reorganizations and liquidations are significant in other respects.

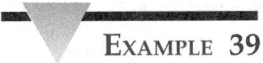
EXAMPLE 39

Acquiring Corporation wants to acquire the assets of Target Corporation. These assets have a basis to Target of $300,000 and a fair market value of $200,000. Target has incurred losses in its operations during the past several years and possesses unabsorbed NOLs of $250,000. Acquiring plans to continue the business conducted by Target, hoping to do so on a profitable basis. ▼

To carry out the acquisition planned by Acquiring Corporation, the tax consequences of various available alternatives must be assessed. In this connection, consider the following.

1. Using cash and/or other property, Acquiring purchases the assets directly from Target. Following the purchase, Target liquidates and distributes the cash and/or property to its shareholders.
2. Acquiring purchases all of the stock in Target from its shareholders. Shortly thereafter, Acquiring liquidates Target.
3. Utilizing an "A" reorganization, Target merges into Acquiring. In exchange for their stock, the shareholders of Target receive stock in Acquiring.
4. Under a "C" reorganization, Target transfers all of its assets to Acquiring in return for the latter's voting stock. Target distributes the Acquiring stock to its shareholders.

A satisfactory solution must center around the preservation of Target Corporation's favorable tax attributes—the high basis in the assets and the NOL carryovers. Alternative 1 is highly unsatisfactory. The purchase price (probably $200,000) becomes the basis of the assets in the hands of Acquiring Corporation. Further, any unused NOLs disappear upon the liquidation of Target. Target has a realized loss of $100,000 [$300,000 (basis in the assets) – $200,000 (sale proceeds)] from the sale of its assets. Yet the realized loss may generate little, if any, tax savings to Target. In view of Target's history (unabsorbed NOL carryovers), it appears doubtful that the company will generate much income in the year of sale.

Alternative 2 also suffers from shortcomings. When a subsidiary is liquidated under § 332, the general rule of § 334(b)(1) applies for basis determination

▼ **FIGURE 7–9**
Three Alternatives for Separating
the Businesses of Target
Corporation

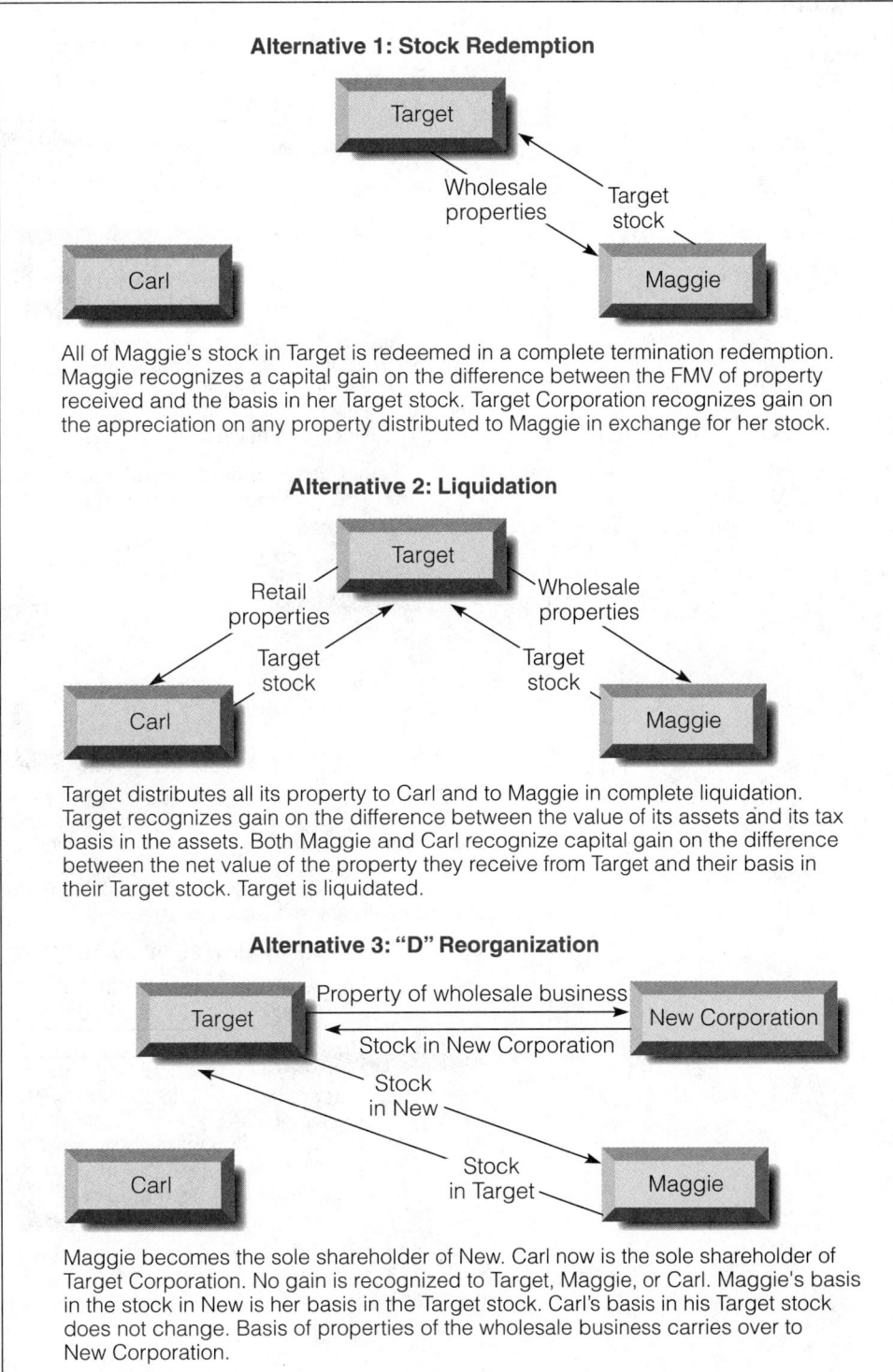

Alternative 1: Stock Redemption

All of Maggie's stock in Target is redeemed in a complete termination redemption. Maggie recognizes a capital gain on the difference between the FMV of property received and the basis in her Target stock. Target Corporation recognizes gain on the appreciation on any property distributed to Maggie in exchange for her stock.

Alternative 2: Liquidation

Target distributes all its property to Carl and to Maggie in complete liquidation. Target recognizes gain on the difference between the value of its assets and its tax basis in the assets. Both Maggie and Carl recognize capital gain on the difference between the net value of the property they receive from Target and their basis in their Target stock. Target is liquidated.

Alternative 3: "D" Reorganization

Maggie becomes the sole shareholder of New. Carl now is the sole shareholder of Target Corporation. No gain is recognized to Target, Maggie, or Carl. Maggie's basis in the stock in New is her basis in the Target stock. Carl's basis in his Target stock does not change. Basis of properties of the wholesale business carries over to New Corporation.

purposes. Target's basis in its assets carries over to Acquiring. What Acquiring paid for the Target stock becomes irrelevant. Other tax attributes of Target (e.g., NOLs) carry over to Acquiring. Section 269 (dealing with the disallowance of any deduction or credit when the acquisition was made to evade or avoid income tax) could present a problem, however. Section 269(b) specifically applies to a liquidation

▼ FIGURE 7–10
Three Alternatives for Acquiring
Corporate Assets

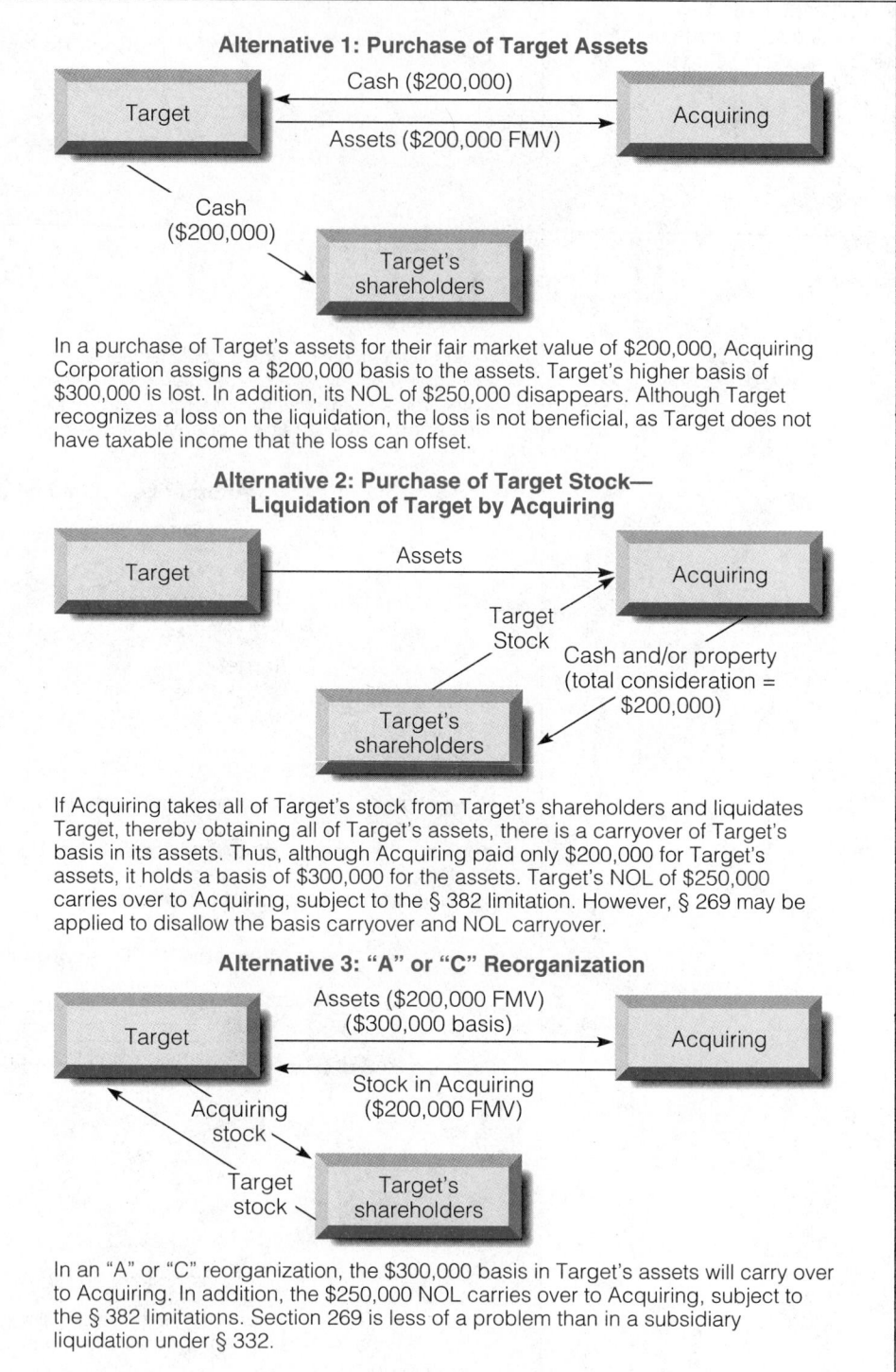

within two years after the acquisition date. It provides that, if the principal purpose of the liquidation is the evasion or avoidance of income tax by securing the benefit of a deduction, credit, or other allowance, the items involved may be disallowed.

Alternatives 3 and 4 should accomplish the same tax result, but with less tax risk. Presuming Acquiring can establish a business purpose for the "A" or "C" reorganization, § 269 can be avoided. The alternatives are illustrated in Figure 7–10.

The preservation of favorable tax attributes, such as the NOL carryover and any capital loss or investment credit carryovers, should be considered in the context of the sale of a small corporation.

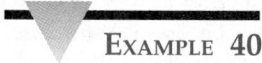

EXAMPLE 40

Cardinal Corporation, worth $200,000, has an NOL of $150,000. The stock in Cardinal is owned by Kevin, 55%, and Fran, 45%. Kevin wants to sell his interest in Cardinal and retire. But what happens to the NOL if Kevin sells his entire interest? There would be a more-than-50% change in the ownership of Cardinal Corporation. Therefore, the § 382 limitation would be $200,000 times the long-term tax-exempt rate. Assume the rate is 10%. The loss of $150,000 is now limited to $20,000 annually. Can a sale be structured so that the NOL is not so limited?

An owner shift is determined by looking to a three-year testing period. Kevin could sell 15% of his stock in Year 1, 15% in Year 2, 15% in Year 3, and 10% in Year 4. In neither of the three-year testing periods (Years 1 through 3 or Years 2 through 4) is there a more-than-50% change in the ownership of the corporation. Thus, there is no § 382 limitation. Cardinal can deduct the entire $150,000 NOL sooner rather than later. ▼

THE ROLE OF THE LETTER RULING

When feasible, the parties contemplating a corporate reorganization should apply for and obtain from the IRS a letter ruling concerning the income tax effect of the transaction(s). Assuming the parties carry out the transfers as proposed in the ruling request, a favorable ruling provides, in effect, an insurance policy. If the tax implications are significant, as they often are with corporate reorganizations, the advantage of obtaining prior IRS approval is clear.

KEY TERMS

Business purpose, 7–22	Divisive reorganization, 7–15	Owner shift, 7–30
Consolidation, 7–8	Equity structure shift, 7–30	Recapitalization, 7–19
Continuity of business enterprise, 7–23	Long-term tax-exempt rate, 7–29	Reorganization, 7–3
Continuity of interest test, 7–8	Merger, 7–8	Step transaction, 7–23

PROBLEM
MATERIALS

DISCUSSION QUESTIONS

1. What is the theory underlying nonrecognition of gain or loss in a corporate reorganization?

2. Briefly explain the seven forms of corporate reorganizations that qualify for nonrecognition treatment.

3. Compare "golden parachute" and "tin parachute" payments.

4. How does the receipt of boot affect the tax-free status of a corporate reorganization?

5. What are the advantages of effecting a business combination through a "Type A" reorganization?

6. What problems exist in effecting a business combination through a "Type A" reorganization?

7. How can the use of a subsidiary corporation in a "Type A" reorganization solve some of the problems inherent in such a reorganization?

8. Ann purchased 200 shares of stock in Gray Corporation five years ago for $50 per share. Two years ago, Gray redeemed 50 of Ann's shares for $100 per share. In the current year, all of Gray's shareholders exchanged their shares in Gray for voting stock in Blue Corporation. The agreement provided that a sufficient number of shares in Blue, valued at $95 per share, would be issued to the Gray shareholders to equal the value of their Gray shares. In the event the purchase price was not evenly divisible by shares at $95 per share, the difference would be paid in cash. Ann was paid $15 cash and one share of Blue stock for each of her remaining shares in Gray. What are the tax issues to be considered in this situation?

9. Compare a "Type B" reorganization with a "Type C" reorganization in terms of consideration.

10. Submit an outline for a talk on the "D" reorganization to be given to your tax department colleagues.

11. What type of exchanges qualify for nonrecognition treatment as "Type E" reorganizations?

12. Red Corporation has 1,000 shares of $100 par value preferred stock and 2,000 shares of $100 par value common stock outstanding. Iris, a highly valued Red employee, owns 200 shares of preferred stock and 400 shares of common, or 20% of each. Lynn owns the remaining shares, or 80% of each. To retain Iris as an employee, Lynn agrees to surrender 1,400 of her shares of common stock for 1,000 newly issued shares of preferred stock; as a result, Iris will have a 66⅔% ownership in Red Corporation. What are the tax issues in this transaction?

13. Two years ago, Ted transferred property worth $100,000, basis of $40,000, to a state-chartered savings and loan association for guaranty stock in the savings and loan. In the current year, the state-chartered savings and loan association merged with a Federal savings and loan association. Ted and the other shareholders of the state savings and loan exchange their guaranty stock in the state savings and loan for passbook savings accounts and certificates of deposit in the Federal savings and loan association. The savings accounts and certificates of deposit were the only form of equity in the Federal savings and loan. What are the tax issues associated with this situation?

14. Four years ago, Pat transferred all the property of his individual proprietorship, basis of $600,000 and fair market value of $2 million, to Yellow Corporation for 50% of the stock in Yellow. Pat's Yellow stock has a fair market value of $3 million in the current year, when Yellow is merged into Green Corporation. What tax issues come to mind if:
    a. Pat receives a 20% interest in Green?
    b. Pat receives preferred stock in Green worth $1 million and bonds in Green worth $2 million, but with a principal amount of $2,500,000?

15. Must an acquiring corporation conduct the same business activities as the target corporation to satisfy the continuity of business enterprise test?

16. When does the step transaction doctrine present complications for reorganizations?

17. What are the tax consequences of a corporation's payment for a "golden parachute"?

18. Is there a limitation on the amount of NOL carryover that can be deducted in the year of the reorganization?

19. Explain the terms *owner shift* and *equity structure shift.*

20. Warbler Corporation acquired Wren Corporation in an exchange of assets for stock. Warbler transferred 55% of its voting stock to Wren for substantially all of Wren's assets. Wren had an NOL carryover of $1 million. Wren did not liquidate, and it retained the Warbler stock as its only asset. Warbler deducted Wren's NOL on its income tax returns filed after the date of the reorganization. What are the tax issues presented by this scenario?

21. Does the E & P of an acquired corporation, whether a positive balance or a deficit, carry over to an acquiring corporation in a tax-free reorganization?

 22. Bluebird Corporation is interested in acquiring the assets of Redbird Corporation. Redbird has a basis of $1 million in its assets (fair market value of Redbird's assets is $300,000). Redbird has incurred substantial losses in the last few years and has a $250,000 NOL carryover. Bluebird believes that by making some changes in operations, Redbird could be a successful corporation. What is the best alternative for tax purposes for acquiring either the assets or the stock of Redbird?

PROBLEMS

 23. What type of reorganization is effected in the following transactions?

   a. Black Corporation acquires all the assets of White Corporation in exchange for newly issued nonvoting preferred stock of Black. White distributes the preferred stock in Black to its shareholders in exchange for their common stock in White. White then is dissolved.

   b. Gray Corporation transfers Gray voting stock to Black Corporation in exchange for preferred stock in Black. Gray owns 85% of the voting stock in Black. Black exchanges the voting stock in Gray with shareholders in Brown Corporation holding 95% of the stock in Brown.

   c. The shareholders of Blue and White Corporations agree to form Gray Corporation. All the assets of Blue and White are transferred to Gray in exchange for common stock in Gray. The common stock in Gray is then distributed to the shareholders of Blue and White in exchange for all of their stock in Blue and White. Blue and White are then dissolved.

   d. Assume in (c) that the shareholders of Blue and White receive stock in Gray worth $400,000 and long-term bonds worth $200,000.

   e. Assume in (c) that the shareholders of Blue and White receive stock in Gray worth $100,000 and long-term bonds worth $300,000.

   f. Green Corporation transfers voting stock in Brown Corporation, its parent, to Red Corporation for substantially all of Red's assets. Red then distributes the Brown stock and its remaining property to its shareholders.

   g. Robin Corporation transfers all of its assets to Wren Corporation. Bluejay, the parent of Robin, transfers its voting stock to the shareholders of Wren for 80% control of Wren. Robin then is liquidated.

   h. Black Corporation transfers assets worth $300,000 to Brown Corporation for voting stock worth $200,000, the assumption of liabilities in the amount of $40,000, and cash of $60,000.

   i. Green Corporation has been actively engaged in two businesses for the past 10 years. It transfers assets of one business to a newly formed corporation and distributes stock in the new corporation, representing control of the corporation, to the shareholders of Green.

   j. White Corporation manufactures a single product but has two plants. One plant was established three years ago; the other has been in existence since the corporation was organized eight years ago. White transfers the older plant to a new corporation and distributes stock in the new corporation to half its shareholders in exchange for all of their White stock.

   k. Common shares in Blue Corporation are owned by father and son. The father exchanges his common stock in Blue for newly issued nonvoting cumulative preferred stock.

   l. Black, a New York corporation, incorporates White in Delaware and transfers all of its assets to White in exchange for White's stock. Black subsequently is liquidated.

24. a. José, a shareholder of White Corporation, exchanges his White stock for stock in Green Corporation. The exchange is pursuant to a tax-free reorganization of White and Green. José paid $150,000 for his stock in White three years ago. The White stock is worth $300,000, and the stock José receives in Green is worth $240,000. What is José's basis in the Green stock?

b. Assume José receives $60,000 cash in addition to the Green stock. What are the tax consequences to José, and what basis does he have in the Green stock?

25. Quinn exchanges stock he owns in Redbird Corporation for stock in Bluebird Corporation and additionally receives $80,000 cash. The exchange is pursuant to a tax-free reorganization of both corporations. Quinn paid $40,000 five years ago for the stock in Redbird. The stock in Bluebird has a fair market value of $240,000. Quinn's share of Redbird's E & P is $70,000. How will Quinn treat this transaction for tax purposes?

26. Assume the same facts as in Problem 25, except that Quinn paid $360,000 (instead of $40,000) for his stock in Redbird Corporation. How would Quinn treat the transaction for tax purposes?

27. Target Corporation has assets with a fair market value of $4 million, adjusted basis of $1 million, and liabilities of $500,000. It transfers assets worth $3,700,000 in a "C" reorganization to Acquiring Corporation in exchange for Acquiring voting stock and Acquiring's assumption of its liabilities. Target retained a building worth $300,000, basis of $150,000. Target distributes the voting stock in Acquiring and the building to Wanda, its sole shareholder. How much gain does Target recognize on the reorganization?

28. Assume in Problem 27 that the consideration Acquiring Corporation gives for all of the assets of Target Corporation is voting stock worth $3,200,000, a building worth $300,000, basis of $150,000, and the assumption of Target's liabilities. Target distributes the stock and the building to its sole shareholder, Wanda. Will either Target or Acquiring recognize any gain on the reorganization?

29. Target Corporation has assets worth $5 million and liabilities totaling $1 million. Acquiring Corporation is interested in acquiring either the assets or the stock of Target. Target wants the acquisition to be tax-free. Discuss whether the parties can arrange an "A," "B," or "C" reorganization under the following circumstances.
   a. Dissenting Target shareholders own 15% of the Target stock.
   b. Dissenting Target shareholders own 35% of the Target stock.

30. Target Corporation has assets with a fair market value of $1 million and a basis of $500,000. Target transfers the assets to Acquiring Corporation for voting stock valued at $800,000, cash of $50,000, and the assumption of $150,000 of Target's liabilities. Target distributes the voting stock in Acquiring and the cash of $50,000 to Alice, its sole shareholder, and liquidates. Alice had a basis of $40,000 in her stock in Target. Discuss the tax consequences of the transfer to Target, Acquiring, and Alice.

31. Target Corporation has assets worth $1,500,000 and liabilities of $200,000. Acquiring Corporation, a white knight, wants to acquire assets in Target worth $1,400,000. (Acquiring does not want a specific group of assets worth $100,000.) It agrees to assume all of Target's liabilities. Target's shareholders are agreeable to the takeover if they receive some cash, but they want the takeover to qualify as a tax-free reorganization. How much cash may Acquiring pay Target's shareholders in addition to distributing its voting stock to them without disqualifying the takeover as a tax-free "C" reorganization?

32. Cardinal Corporation has two shareholders, Cliff and Debra. Cliff and Debra purchased their stock in Cardinal eight years ago at a cost of $100,000 each. Cardinal Corporation has been engaged in two businesses for the past eight years, a wholesale manufacturing business and a retail merchandising business. Cardinal also has substantial investments. To avoid antitrust problems, Cardinal transfers all the assets of the wholesale manufacturing business to Wren Corporation for all the stock in Wren. The assets transferred to Wren have a fair market value of $1 million and a tax basis of $400,000. Cardinal Corporation distributes all the stock in Wren to Cliff in exchange for all his stock in Cardinal. The stock in Wren has a value of $1 million. Cardinal will continue its retail merchandising business, and Wren will continue the wholesale manufacturing business. Discuss the tax consequences to Cardinal Corporation and to its shareholders, Cliff and Debra.

33. Would your answer to Problem 32 change if Cardinal had acquired the retail business three years ago? Explain.

34. Assume Cardinal, in Problem 32, transfers its investments, fair market value of $1 million, to Wren in exchange for all the stock in Wren. It then distributes the Wren stock to Cliff in exchange for all of Cliff's stock in Cardinal. Discuss the tax consequences to Cardinal Corporation and to its shareholders, Cliff and Debra.

35. Kate owns half of the stock in Red Corporation. Her children, Mark, Matt, and Melissa, own the other half. Kate has a basis of $80,000 in her stock. The stock is worth $500,000. Kate wishes to retire and relinquish control of Red to her children. She exchanges her common voting stock for bonds issued to her by Red Corporation in the amount of $500,000. Discuss the tax consequences to Kate.

36. Assume Kate, in Problem 35, receives nonvoting preferred stock in Red Corporation worth $500,000 instead of bonds. What are the tax consequences to Kate?

37. Target Corporation is merged into Acquiring Corporation. Target's assets had a tax basis to Target of $800,000 and a fair market value of $3 million. Target had liabilities of $500,000, which Acquiring assumed. Target received voting stock in Acquiring Corporation worth $2,500,000, which it distributed to Eduardo, its sole shareholder. Eduardo has a basis of $200,000 in his stock in Target. Target is liquidated after it distributes the stock in Acquiring to Eduardo. Immediately after the merger, Acquiring sells Target's assets for $2,500,000. Discuss the tax consequences to Target and to Eduardo.

38. On June 1, 1997, Maria, a corporate raider, buys 20% of the stock of Target Corporation, or 10,000 shares, in the open market for $9 per share. Maria then threatens to make a public tender offer to Target's remaining shareholders to buy their shares for $10 per share.
    a. Upon learning of the threatened public tender offer, Target's board of directors offers the remaining shareholders $10.50 per share for their stock. On December 1, 1998, to eliminate Maria as a shareholder, the board of directors offers to pay her $11 per share. Maria accepts the offer and sells the 10,000 shares she had purchased at $9 per share for $11 per share. How much gain does Maria recognize on the sale of the stock, after any penalties?
    b. After Maria's threatened public tender offer, Target instead offers to pay all its shareholders, including Maria, $10.50 per share. How much gain must Maria recognize if she accepts the offer and sells the 10,000 shares for $10.50 per share?

39. Ted is president of Target Corporation. His average annual salary for the past five years has been $200,000. Acquiring Corporation gains control of Target in a hostile takeover, and Ted loses his position. Pursuant to an employment contract with Target, Ted is paid $1,500,000 in the year of the takeover.
    a. What are the tax consequences to Ted of the $1,500,000 payment?
    b. Can Target, now controlled by Acquiring, deduct the $1,500,000 payment?

40. Target Corporation merges into Acquiring Corporation on June 30, 1998. Both corporations use a calendar year. Target has an NOL of $900,000. Acquiring's taxable income for 1998 is $1,080,000. How much of the loss can be used to offset Acquiring's 1998 taxable income? (Assume § 382 is not applicable.)

41. Target Corporation is merged into Acquiring Corporation on January 1 this year. At the time of the merger, Target had an NOL of $300,000. Pursuant to the merger, the shareholders of Target receive 30% of the stock of Acquiring. Target has a value of $250,000 on the date of the merger, and the long-term tax-exempt rate is 10%. How much of Target's NOL can be used this year to offset Acquiring's $500,000 taxable income?

42. Assume the shareholders in Problem 41 receive 60% of the stock of Acquiring Corporation. How much of Target Corporation's NOL can be used to offset Acquiring's taxable income in the current year?

43. Target Corporation, which has an NOL of $5 million, is merged into Acquiring Corporation in an "A" reorganization. Acquiring obtained Target for the principal purpose of utilizing the NOL. After the merger, Target's former shareholders own 55% of the fair market value of the stock in Acquiring. The value of Target stock on the date of the merger is $500,000, and the long-term tax-exempt rate is 7%. How much of the NOL can be used by Acquiring?

44. Target Corporation had accumulated E & P of $210,000 on January 1, 1998, when it merged into Acquiring Corporation. Acquiring had an accumulated deficit in E & P of $30,000 on January 1, 1998. In 1998, Acquiring had an NOL of $180,000, producing a current deficit in E & P of $180,000. On December 30, 1998, Acquiring distributed $90,000 to its shareholders. How are the Acquiring shareholders taxed on the $90,000 distribution? May the 1998 NOL be carried back to offset Target's taxable income for the past three years?

45. Acquiring Corporation has a deficit in E & P of $120,000. It acquires the assets of Target Corporation in a statutory merger. Target has E & P of $600,000. After the merger, Acquiring distributes $340,000 to its shareholders. How is the $340,000 treated for tax purposes?

46. Crow Corporation, worth $2,100,000, has an NOL of $600,000. The Crow stock is owned by Abby, 55%, and José, 45%. Abby wants to sell her interest in Crow to José in 1998. The long-term tax-exempt rate is 6%.
    a. If Abby sells her entire interest in Crow to José, how much of its NOL may Crow deduct thereafter?
    b. How should the sale of Abby's interest to José be structured to produce the best tax results for Crow?

47. Yellow Corporation has assets with a basis of $1,800,000 and a fair market value of $5 million. Yellow has liabilities of $400,000. Ann, who owns 100% of the stock in Orange Corporation, has a 20% common stock interest in Yellow. Orange wants to acquire some, but not all, of Yellow's assets. Orange is willing to assume all of Yellow's liabilities.

    Although Yellow's shareholders would like to receive some cash from a disposition of the corporation's assets, they would like to receive Orange stock as part of the consideration, and they prefer that the entire transaction be nontaxable to them. Yellow's shareholders certainly do not want to be taxed on the receipt of Orange stock.

    Demonstrate to the parties several alternative transactions in which Yellow can dispose of its unwanted assets, worth $2 million and basis of $1 million, and then transfer the remaining assets and liabilities to Orange. Because of the substantial appreciation in Yellow's assets, its shareholders are concerned that a transfer of assets to Orange will be a taxable event.

    Calculate the gain realized and recognized to Yellow in each of the alternatives you propose. Indicate whether Orange and Ann, its sole shareholder, recognize gain on the transactions you have proposed, and derive the basis Orange assigns to the assets it acquires from Yellow.

48. Redbird Corporation has two shareholders, Juan and Juanita. Juan and Juanita purchased their stock in Redbird 10 years ago at a cost of $200,000 each. Redbird is involved in two businesses, construction and retail selling. Redbird has suffered financial difficulties in the past 5 years. The assets of its construction company have a basis of $2 million and a fair market value of only $1 million. The assets of its retail sales division have a basis of $2,400,000 and a fair market value of $800,000. Redbird has an NOL carryover of $1,200,000.

    Juan and Juanita have had serious disagreements since Redbird began losing money, and they want to sever their relationship. Wren Corporation would like to acquire Redbird. Wren believes it can conduct the businesses on a profitable basis. Juanita would like to continue the construction business. She thinks that the business would become profitable if Juan were no longer involved in its operations.

    Juan would like to remain involved in the retail selling business and is willing to transfer the assets of this division to Wren if he would be Wren's controlling shareholder. Juan wants to hold a 52% stock ownership in Wren after the transfer.

    Demonstrate various available alternatives to the parties. Propose to the parties the alternative that would produce the most favorable tax results.

49. The board of directors of Red Corporation wants to acquire the assets of Blue Corporation. Blue's assets have a basis of $4 million and a fair market value of $1,600,000. Blue has incurred losses in its operations during the past several years and

possesses unabsorbed NOLs of $3 million. Red plans to continue the business conducted by Blue, hoping to do so at a profitable basis. Diagram the alternatives for a takeover by Red, to present to the board's Finance Committee.

RESEARCH PROBLEMS

Note: West's Federal Taxation on CD-ROM can be used in preparing solutions to the Research Problems. Alternatively, tax research materials contained in a standard tax library can be used.

Research Problem 1. Target Corporation has two shareholders, Diego Martinez and Carmen Smith, who acquired their stock in Target six years ago. Diego paid $300,000 for 60% of the stock in Target, and Carmen paid $200,000 for 40% of the stock.

Acquiring Corporation takes all the properties of Target Corporation, basis of $1 million and worth $4 million, in a statutory merger in exchange for 2,500 shares of Acquiring stock worth $2,500,000, the assumption of Target's liabilities in the amount of $500,000, and newly issued bonds of Acquiring in the amount of $1 million and worth $1 million. Target is liquidated after the merger. Diego receives 2,100 shares of Acquiring stock, worth $2,100,000, and Carmen receives 400 shares of Acquiring stock, worth $400,000, and the bonds worth $1 million.

Diego asks you what tax consequences the transaction creates for himself, for the corporations, and for Carmen. Prepare a letter to Diego and a memo for the tax research file. (Your citations should be only to the Code and Regulations.) Diego's address is 1400 Hancock Street, Lincoln, IL 60440.

Research Problem 2. Bluebird Corporation wanted to take over Redbird Corporation and commenced a cash tender offer for Redbird stock. Shortly thereafter, Yellowbird Corporation and Redbird entered into an agreement under which Yellowbird would acquire all of Redbird's stock in a tax-free "A" reorganization and Redbird would be merged into Yellowbird's subsidiary, Wren Corporation. The agreement was subject to the condition that Yellowbird would acquire at least 51% of Redbird's stock.

Another corporation, Cardinal, also initiated a cash tender offer for the Redbird stock. After the various tender offers expired, Bluebird acquired 32% of Redbird stock, but Yellowbird acquired more than 50% through its tender offer. The reorganization concluded when Redbird was merged into Wren. Bluebird then congratulated Yellowbird and offered to exchange its Redbird stock for Yellowbird stock. Yellowbird accepted the offer, and the two corporations exchanged their stock. Bluebird incurred an economic loss of $400 million on the exchange.

Although Bluebird Corporation did not report a loss on the exchange of its Redbird stock for Yellowbird stock for financial accounting purposes, it did deduct the loss on its tax return filed in the year of the exchange. The IRS disallowed the loss, contending the transaction was part of the tax-free reorganization between Redbird and Yellowbird.

Bluebird Corporation asks your advice. It contends that Yellowbird, in effect, sold its stock in Redbird to Bluebird after the reorganization and, thus, the continuity of interest test was not met. What would you advise Bluebird?

Partial list of research aids:
Rev.Proc. 77–37, 1977–2 C.B. 568, § 3.02.
Yoc Heating Corp. v. Comm., 61 T.C. 168 (1973).

Research Problem 3. Black Corporation had a large NOL. Rosa Loya, the sole shareholder and president of White Corporation, purchased all the stock of Black on January 10. On December 15 of the same year, White adopted a plan to merge Black and White. After the merger on January 5 of the following year, Black was liquidated. White offset Black's NOL against its income from operations in the later year. Upon audit of White's return, the IRS disallowed the carryover of Black's loss to White. Rosa seeks your advice. Rosa's argument is that she was the sole shareholder of both Black and White on the date of the merger. Thus, the provisions of § 382 provide that all Black's loss can be carried over to White. What would you advise Rosa? Prepare a letter to her, and a memo for your firm's files. Rosa's address is 348 Grand Avenue, Mesa, AZ 85201.

Use the tax resources of the internet to address the following questions. Do not restrict your search to the World Wide Web, but include a review of newsgroups and general reference materials, practitioner sites and resources, primary sources of the tax law, chat rooms and discussion groups, and other opportunities.

Research Problem 4.   The acquisition of Snapple has been used as an illustration of "how not to do" a corporate takeover. Some of the difficulties encountered by the parties are traceable to Internal Revenue Code provisions. Summarize the reactions of observers to this merger, concentrating on the related tax effects, but not restricting your review to them.

Research Problem 5.   Find materials prepared on the internet by attorneys, accountants, and other advisors who work with merger and acquisition candidates. Write an e-mail message to one of them, mentioning a tax planning opportunity that their materials do not fully explain.

Research Problem 6.   How many letter rulings did the Treasury issue this month addressing issues related to the § 368 definitions of tax-favored reorganizations? Summarize one such ruling, providing full citations to pertinent cases and Regulations.

CONSOLIDATED TAX RETURNS

LEARNING OBJECTIVES

After completing Chapter 8, you should be able to:

1. Apply the fundamental concepts of consolidated tax returns.

2. Identify the sources of the rules for consolidated taxable income.

3. Recognize the major advantages and disadvantages of filing consolidated tax returns.

4. Describe the corporations that are eligible to file on a consolidated basis.

5. Explain the compliance aspects of consolidated returns.

6. Compute a parent's investment basis in a subsidiary.

7. Account for intercompany transactions of a consolidated group.

8. Identify limitations that restrict the use of losses and credits of group members derived in separate return years.

9. Derive deductions and credits on a consolidated basis.

10. Demonstrate tax planning opportunities available to consolidated groups.

CONTEXT OF THE CONSOLIDATED RETURN RULES

To this point, the discussion has centered on the computation of the tax liability of individual corporations under the regular tax calculation, along with specific penalty taxes and the alternative minimum tax. This is an appropriate approach to the study of corporate taxation, as more than 90 percent of all U.S. corporations (almost 4 million) are closely held (i.e., either by a small group of operators/investors or by members of the same family).

Although some of these family businesses operate in a multiple-corporation environment, the vast majority of the assets held by businesses nationwide are owned by no more than 10,000 large corporate conglomerates. These corporations conduct the bulk of the country's "big business" and generate most of the taxable income earned by corporate taxpayers.

MOTIVATIONS TO CONSOLIDATE

Corporate conglomerates are present in every aspect of life. The local dairy or bakery is likely to be owned by General Mills or General Foods. Oil and insurance companies own movie-making corporations. Professional sports teams are corporate cousins of the newspapers and television/radio stations that carry their games. The same corporate group that produces night lights for a child's nursery may manufacture control equipment for bombers and other elements of the Defense Department's arsenal.

What brings together these sometimes strange corporate bedfellows? For the most part, nontax motivations provide the strongest incentives for multiple-corporation acquisitions and holdings. Among the many commonly encountered motivations are the following.

- A desire to isolate assets of other group members from the liabilities of specific operating divisions (e.g., to gain limited liability for a tobacco or asbestos company within an operating conglomerate).
- A need to carry out specific estate planning objectives (e.g., by transferring growth or high-risk assets to younger-generation shareholders).
- A preference to isolate the group's exposure to losses and liabilities incurred in joint ventures with "outside" entities (especially when such venturers are not based in the United States).

TAX IN THE NEWS

OWNING A WINNING TEAM

Tribune Entertainment, based in Chicago, has taken an aggressive path to growth since the 1970s, acquiring successful businesses that fit into the corporate long-range plan. The newspaper publisher owns several radio and television stations and production companies, book publishers, and on-line and multimedia high-tech product developers. Most observers regard the corporation as one that is willing to invest capital in its subsidiaries to assure a clear path to success.

Tribune Entertainment also owns the Chicago Cubs. When the Cubs won a division title several years ago, its parent took out full-page ads in various newspapers around the country, celebrating the team's good fortune with the theme "Just Another One of Our Subsidiaries Having a Good Year."

• A perception that separate divisions/group members will be worth more on the market if they maintain unique identities or otherwise avoid a commingling of assets and liabilities with other group members (e.g., where a trade name or patent is especially valuable or carries excessive goodwill in the marketplace).
• Conversely, an attempt to shield the identities of a subsidiary's true owners from the public where negative goodwill exists (e.g., with respect to the consequences of a nuclear or industrial accident).
• A desire to optimize negotiations with labor unions, suppliers, or governmental units (e.g., where annual negotiations are likely to be lengthy or costly, an operating division might be set up in each state or for each trade to isolate the potential for disruption of the entire group's operations).

ETHICAL CONSIDERATIONS

Sheltering Corporate Assets

Should corporations be able to shelter their assets from marketplace liabilities through a capital restructuring? The first large corporations to spin off subsidiaries to isolate high-risk assets and their related liabilities from the main business were financial institutions (e.g., risky loans to debtors in exploratory industries or underdeveloped countries) and utilities (e.g., nuclear power facilities). Today, conglomerates involved in developing health care procedures or turning out such products as tobacco and industrial equipment protect the bulk of the entity's assets by isolating product-liability risks in subsidiaries.

Given the "deep pockets" mentality of many juries and government agencies, this is a prudent reaction by the corporate community. But should not a society's largest risks be shared among all of its players? And should the tax laws be used to foster the isolation of such risk into shallow and insulated corporate pockets?

In many states, "tort reform" would further limit the business entity's exposure to/ accountability for malpractice and product warranty claims. Your state's CPA society asks you to lobby legislators in favor of such a measure. Can you take the assignment?

1 LEARNING OBJECTIVE
Apply the fundamental concepts of consolidated tax returns.

Although nontax concerns may be the primary reason for the creation of many conglomerates, tax incentives may also play a role. To a large extent, these incentives can be found in the rules that control the filing of **consolidated returns.** In general terms, the IRS allows certain corporate groups to be treated as a single entity for Federal income tax purposes. This enables the group to use available tax exemptions and brackets optimally among its members and to shelter the income of profitable members with the losses of other members. Thus, through the consolidated return rules, corporate taxpayers have an opportunity to manage the combined tax liability of the members of the group.

The consolidated return rules may be available to a taxpayer as a result of various business decisions.

- Consolidated returns may be the result of a merger, acquisition, or other corporate combination (discussed in Chapter 7).

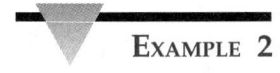

EXAMPLE 1

When Dover Corporation acquires all of the stock of Edwards Corporation, a new corporate group, Dover and Edwards Corporation, is formed. The two group members can elect to file their tax return on a consolidated basis. ▼

- A group of business taxpayers may be restructured to comply with changes in regulatory requirements, meet the demands of a competitive environment, or gain economies of scale and operate more efficiently in a larger arrangement. Consequently, an election to file a consolidated return becomes available.

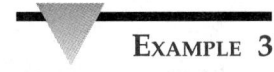

EXAMPLE 2

External Corporation, a retailer, acquires Internal Corporation, a wholesaler, in an effort to control its flow of inventory in unstable economic times. The two group members can elect to file their tax returns on a consolidated basis. ▼

- The taxpayers may be seeking to gain tax and other financial advantages that are more readily available to corporate combinations.

EXAMPLE 3

Over the next three years, Mary Corporation will be selling a number of its business assets at a loss. If Norbert Corporation acquires all of Mary's stock and the group elects to file its tax returns on a consolidated basis, Norbert will be able to combine its gains from the sale of business property with Mary's losses in computing the group's consolidated § 1231 gain/loss for the year. ▼

SOURCE AND PHILOSOPHY OF CONSOLIDATED RETURN RULES

Some form of consolidated corporate tax return has been allowed for Federal purposes since World War I. At that time, the Treasury became suspicious that conglomerates were shifting taxable income to a number of smaller entities to avoid the high marginal rates of the excess profits tax that had been imposed to finance the war effort. Thus, the consolidated return rules can be seen as perhaps the earliest effort of the IRS to limit the tax benefits available to multiple corporations.

EXAMPLE 4

Assume that the marginal Federal income tax rate is 10% on the first $100,000 of taxable income and 15% on any taxable income in excess of $100,000. The additional five percentage points constitute a war profits tax, and the revenue raised is used for the war effort.

Further assume that the tax law includes no restrictions on the tax computations of related corporations. A corporation with annual taxable income of $1 million can eliminate its entire exposure to the war profits tax by splitting its business evenly among 10 separate corporations. ▼

2 **LEARNING OBJECTIVE**
Identify the sources of the rules for consolidated taxable income.

At various times since World War I, Congress has modified the pertinent Regulations and imposed a higher tax rate on consolidated groups to increase the cost of making the consolidation election. During the Great Depression, when it feared "too much" income was being sheltered within consolidated groups, Congress suspended the application of the rules for most taxpayers. On other occasions, complex limitations were placed upon the use and timing of positive tax benefits, such as net operating loss carryovers, that were acquired in a corporate consolidation. Congress imposed these limits to discourage profitable corporations from "trafficking" in businesses that had generated net losses.

Currently, Congress has delegated most of its legislative authority involving consolidated returns to the Treasury. As a result, the majority of the rules that affect consolidated groups are found in the Regulations. The Code provisions dealing with consolidated returns are strictly definitional in nature and broad in scope,[1] while the related Regulations dictate the computational and compliance requirements of the group.[2]

The length and detail of these Regulations make the consolidated return rules among the most complex in the entire Federal income tax law. For the most part, the underlying purpose of the rules remains one of organizational neutrality; that is, a group of closely related corporations should have neither a tax advantage nor a disadvantage relative to taxpayers who file separate corporate returns.

ETHICAL CONSIDERATIONS

Delegating Authority to the Nonelected

In no other area of the tax law has Congress given the Treasury such leeway in crafting both major principles and details as in the area of consolidated returns. Since Treasury staff members are not elected officials, this delegation of authority might appear to be a shirking of congressional duty and a dangerous assignment of legislative power to an isolated group of individuals.

To what extent should Congress delegate its powers over the country's largest businesses (not only the largest players in the global economy but also the largest contributors to campaign and reelection funds)? Can the delegation of congressional powers to Washington-based civil servants, who are virtually immune to the checks and balances of the election process, be healthy for all taxpayers?

You are a member of the House Ways and Means Committee, and your chances of reelection are jeopardized when you must take a position on a consolidated tax return issue: Taxes on old-line manufacturers would increase, while those on more environmentally friendly, high-tech industries would fall. Are you tempted to avoid the debate altogether by deferring the issue to the Regulations process?

The derivation of a set of consolidated financial statements for a conglomerate and the computation of its consolidated taxable income correspond only slightly. The equity approach followed for financial accounting purposes has a role in the

---

[1] §§ 1501–1505.

[2] Reg. §§ 1.1501–1, 1.1502–0 through 1.1502–100, 1.1503–1 through 1.1503–2T, and 1.1504–1.

consolidated return rules, but exceptions to accounting conventions are both critical and numerous. Thus, a knowledge of financial accounting consolidation procedures will not necessarily be of great assistance in computing consolidated taxable income, nor will a lack of familiarity with accounting conventions be a hindrance.

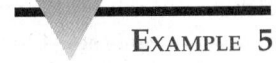

EXAMPLE 5

Dividends paid by SubCo to its 100% owner, Parent Corporation, are eliminated from the separate taxable income computations of both group members in deriving consolidated taxable income. This treatment parallels the eliminating entry that is made in developing the group's consolidated financial statements. ▼

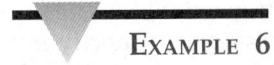

EXAMPLE 6

SubCo sells an asset to its 100% owner, Parent Corporation, at a tax and accounting gain of $100,000. The asset appreciates by another $20,000 before Parent sells it to an unrelated party, Outsider Corporation.

No tax or accounting gain is reported by the group members until the ultimate sale by Parent to Outsider. In constructing the consolidated financial statements, Parent realizes a $120,000 gain. For tax purposes, however, SubCo is assigned $100,000 of the gain, and Parent recognizes only "its" $20,000. ▼

INTERNATIONAL PERSPECTIVES

The United States is one of the few Western countries that allows consolidated returns. Most of its trading partners allow their taxing authority to recompute the taxable income of the members of a conglomerate,[3] but require the members to file separate tax returns. Net operating losses are allowed only if they are attributable to local enterprise. Even then, unused losses seldom can be carried back or forward to other years. Group members that are incorporated outside the host country are especially likely to be subject to such limitations.

Thus, in the view of these more restrictive countries, the ability of a taxpayer to shelter taxable income among multiple corporations, jurisdictions, and time periods should be eliminated. Although U.S. rules also preclude most foreign corporations from joining in a consolidated return,[4] even where consolidated financial statements are prepared, there appears to be no current trend toward the abolition of the consolidated return rules for domestic corporations.

ASSESSING CONSOLIDATED RETURN STATUS

3   LEARNING OBJECTIVE
Recognize the major advantages and disadvantages of filing consolidated tax returns.

As Concept Summary 8–1 illustrates, all of the members of a corporate group must meet three broad requirements to be eligible to elect to file consolidated income tax returns: (1) The corporations must meet the statutory ownership requirements to be classified as an affiliated group.[5] (2) The corporations must be eligible to make a consolidation election.[6] (3) The group must meet various tax accounting and compliance requirements in making and maintaining the election.[7]

Before making an election to file consolidated tax returns, related taxpayers must weigh the related advantages and disadvantages.

---

[3] This is similar to the powers assigned to the IRS under § 482.
[4] § 1504(b)(3).
[5] §§ 1504(a)(1) and (2).

[6] This is a negative definition, rooted in §§ 1504(b) through (f).
[7] See especially Reg. §§ 1.1502–75, –76, and –77.

TAX IN THE NEWS

INTERNATIONAL USE OF CONSOLIDATED RETURNS

Very few countries besides the United States allow the use of consolidated returns. In the view of most countries, tax deductions for operating losses should be used only by those who generated them, not by some sister or other related corporation. This is as much a social principle (the sanctity of the corporate entity) as a revenue-raising provision (NOL deductions mean lower tax collections).

The way European business is conducted makes this result more understandable, as the tax laws of the various countries must ensure that operating losses generated in Tedesco, for instance, are not shifted to Cadenza and converted to deductions there. When a large number of sometimes combative jurisdictions occupy a small geographical area, even the tax laws can be expected to reflect some degree of border consciousness. Eventually, the European Community will address this difficult parochial issue, but it will be a while before new tax laws are drafted and accepted by the business community.

This restrictive approach to the trading of operating loss deductions is found in U.S. multistate tax law as well, where tax-oriented border incentives can be especially important. Some states (like Pennsylvania) have, over a specified time period, disallowed the use of loss carryovers of any sort, whereas others (like Ohio) require the taxpayer to deduct only losses assigned to the taxpayer's in-state operations.

The potential advantages of filing consolidated returns are many.

- The operating and capital loss carryovers of one group member may be used to shelter the corresponding income of other group members.
- The taxation of all intercompany dividends may be eliminated.
- Recognition of income from certain intercompany transactions can be deferred.
- Certain deductions and credits may be optimized by using consolidated amounts in computing pertinent limitations (e.g., the deductions for charitable contributions and dividends received, and foreign tax credits).
- The tax basis of investments in the stock of subsidiaries is increased as the members contribute to consolidated taxable income.
- The alternative minimum tax (AMT) attributes of all group members can be used in deriving consolidated alternative minimum taxable income (AMTI). This can reduce the adjusted current earnings (ACE) adjustment and optimize other AMT preferences and adjustments.
- The share holdings of all group members can be used in meeting other statutory requirements.[8]
- The adjusted ordinary gross income of all group members can be used in avoiding the personal holding company tax.

---

[8] E.g., for purposes of the § 165(g)(3) ordinary deduction for losses from worthlessness of securities. For the 80% corporate control requirement of § 351, see the discussion in Chapter 3.

- Current-year operating losses of one group member can be used to defer or reduce the (regular or AMT) estimated tax payments of the entire group.

Consolidated returns also have a number of potential disadvantages.

- The election is binding on all subsequent tax years of the group members, unless either the makeup of the affiliated group changes or the IRS consents to a revocation of the election.
- Capital and operating losses of one group member are applied against the corresponding income of the other group members even when assigning the losses to separate return years would produce a greater tax benefit. The benefit might be due, for instance, to rate discounts or changes in tax rates.
- Recognition of losses from certain intercompany transactions is deferred.
- Using consolidated amounts in computing the limitations may decrease the amounts of certain deductions and credits.
- Return elections made by the parent (e.g., to claim a § 901 credit for foreign tax payments rather than a deduction) are binding on all members of the filing group for the year.
- The tax basis of investments in the stock of subsidiaries is decreased when the members generate operating losses and by distributions from members' E & P.
- The requirement that all group members use the parent's tax year creates short tax years for the subsidiaries. As a result, a subsidiary's income may be bunched together needlessly, and one of the years of its charitable contribution and loss carryforward periods may be lost.
- Recognition of legal and other rights of minority shareholders may be more restrictive in the context of a consolidated group.

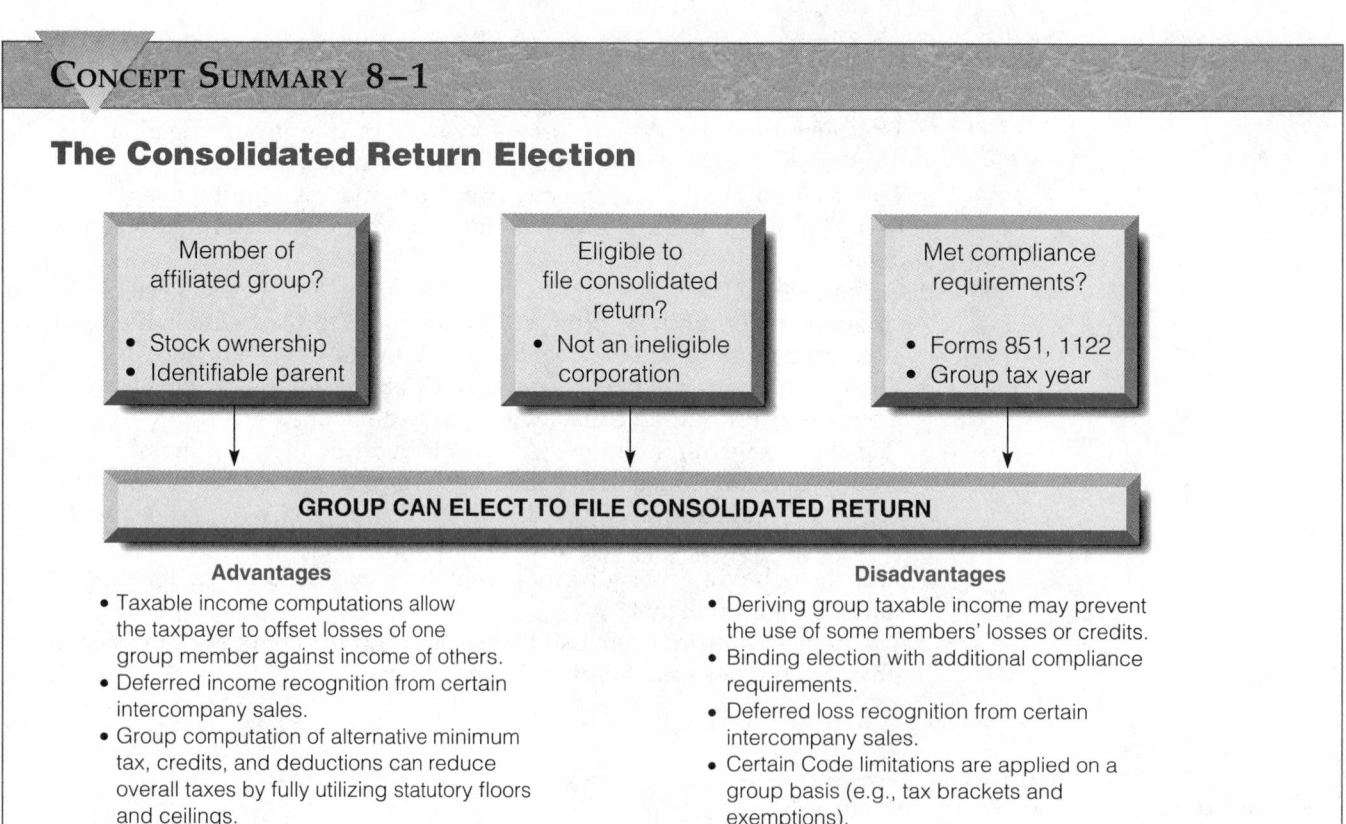

CONCEPT SUMMARY 8–1

The Consolidated Return Election

Member of affiliated group?	Eligible to file consolidated return?	Met compliance requirements?
• Stock ownership • Identifiable parent	• Not an ineligible corporation	• Forms 851, 1122 • Group tax year

GROUP CAN ELECT TO FILE CONSOLIDATED RETURN

Advantages
- Taxable income computations allow the taxpayer to offset losses of one group member against income of others.
- Deferred income recognition from certain intercompany sales.
- Group computation of alternative minimum tax, credits, and deductions can reduce overall taxes by fully utilizing statutory floors and ceilings.

Disadvantages
- Deriving group taxable income may prevent the use of some members' losses or credits.
- Binding election with additional compliance requirements.
- Deferred loss recognition from certain intercompany sales.
- Certain Code limitations are applied on a group basis (e.g., tax brackets and exemptions).

- Additional administrative costs may be incurred in complying with the consolidated return Regulations.

ELECTING CONSOLIDATED RETURN STATUS

As Concept Summary 8–1 illustrates, the election to file on a consolidated basis is restricted to certain groups of corporations.

CONTROLLED AND AFFILIATED GROUPS

The Code defines two groups of multiple corporations, namely, the controlled group[9] and the affiliated group.[10] Broadly, a controlled group refers to both parent-subsidiary and brother-sister corporations, while an affiliated group includes only parent-subsidiary groups (see Figure 8–1). Thus, the affiliated group definition essentially describes a subset of the controlled group specification; rules that apply to controlled groups are effective for nearly all affiliated groups, but not vice versa.

Controlled Groups.   As Chapter 2 explained, a controlled group is treated as one corporation for purposes of assigning a number of tax benefits, including:

- Discounted marginal tax rates on the first $75,000 of taxable income.[11]
- The $150,000 or $250,000 accumulated earnings credit.[12]

▼ **FIGURE 8–1**
Controlled and Affiliated Groups

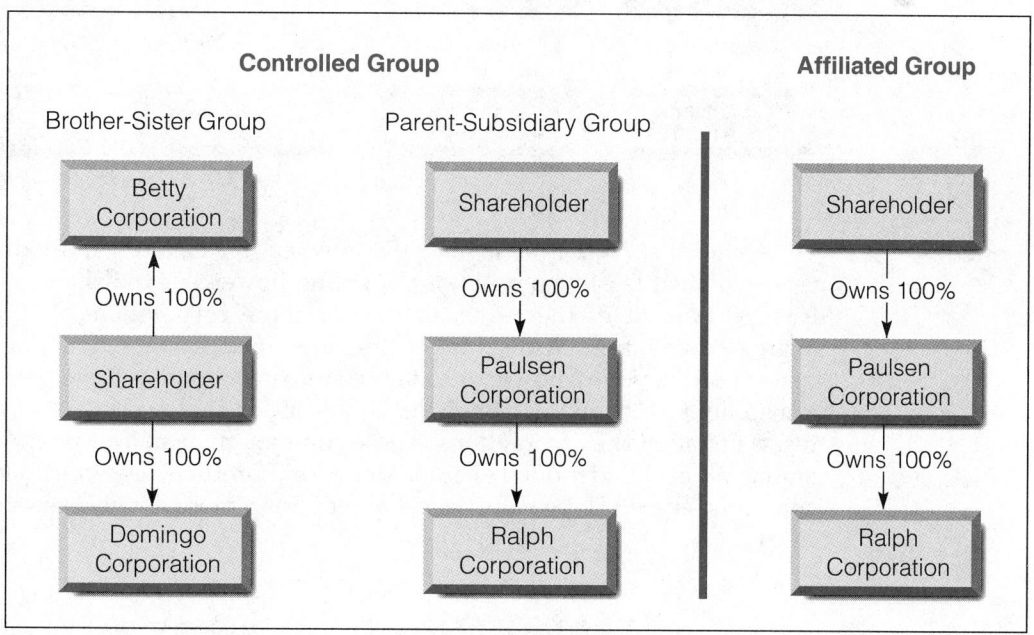

[9] §§ 1563(a)(1) and (2).
[10] § 1504.

[11] §§ 11(b)(1) and 1561(a)(1).
[12] §§ 535(c)(2) and (3) and 1561(a)(2).

- The $40,000 exemption in computing AMTI.[13]
- The $2 million exemption in computing the environmental superfund tax (as applicable before January 1, 1996).[14]

In addition, members of a controlled group must defer the recognition of any realized loss on intercompany sales until a sale is made at a gain to a nongroup member.[15] Similarly, any gain on the sale of depreciable property between members of a controlled group is recognized as ordinary income.[16]

These restrictions are imposed to limit taxpayers' ability to minimize a group's tax liability by creating multiple corporations. Each member of the group is assigned an equal share of the above benefits every taxable year, unless all members consent to some other apportionment method.

A *parent-subsidiary controlled group* exists when one corporation owns at least 80 percent of the voting power of another corporation or holds shares representing at least 80 percent of the value thereof.[17] Multiple tiers of subsidiaries and chains of ownership are allowed, as long as the group has an identifiable parent corporation (i.e., after attribution, at least 80 percent of one corporation must be owned by another).

EXAMPLE 7

In the following figure, a parent-subsidiary controlled group exists in the first ownership structure, but not in the second (inadequate ownership level) or third (no identifiable parent).

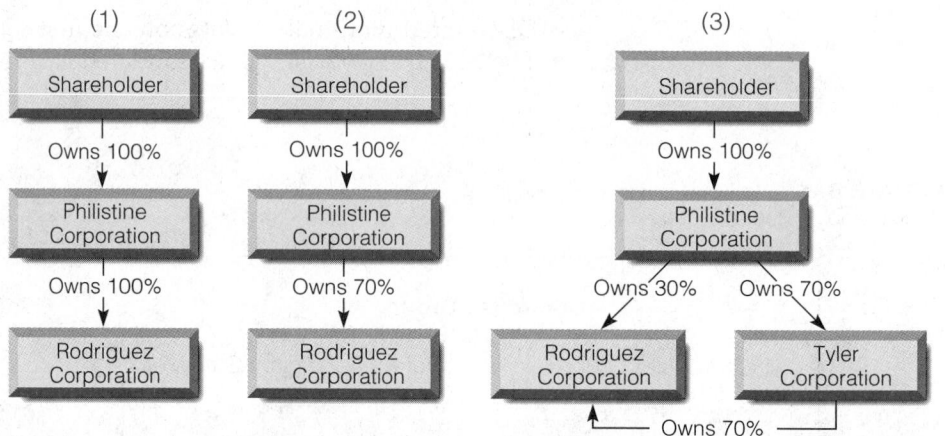

A *brother-sister controlled group* exists when five or fewer individuals, trusts, or estates own at least 80 percent of the voting power, or hold shares representing at least 80 percent of the value, of two or more corporations.[18] In addition, the aggregate common ownership of the identified shareholders must exceed 50 percent of the voting power or value of the corporation's shares. For this purpose, a shareholder's common ownership equals his or her lowest level of holdings with respect to all of the corporations. These common ownership values are aggregated among all of the identified shareholders; for a brother-sister controlled group, the sum must exceed 50 percent. See Chapter 2 for a more detailed discussion of these rules.

---

[13] §§ 55(d)(2) and 1561(a)(3).
[14] §§ 59A(a) and 1561(a)(4).
[15] §§ 267(a)(1), (b)(3), and (f).
[16] §§ 1239(a) and (c).

[17] § 1563(a)(1). For this purpose, certain attribution rules apply. In addition, all stock options are considered to be exercised by their holders. §§ 1563(d)(1) and (e)(1) through (3).
[18] § 1563(a)(2). Certain attribution rules apply. In addition, all stock options are considered to be exercised by their holders. §§ 1563(d)(2) and (e).

Affiliated Groups. An *affiliated group* exists when one corporation owns at least 80 percent of the voting power of another corporation and holds shares representing at least 80 percent of its value.[19] This definition is very similar to that of the parent-subsidiary controlled group. Again, multiple tiers and chains of corporations are allowed as long as the group has an identifiable parent corporation.

The following are the most important differences between the definitions of parent-subsidiary controlled groups and affiliated groups. In each case, the affiliated group definition is more difficult to meet.

- An affiliated group must have 80 percent of the voting power *and* value of the members of the group, whereas a controlled group needs only 80 percent of the voting power *or* value. This difference can be important when preferred stock or other shares with voting or liquidation limitations are involved.
- The stock attribution rules that must be applied to a controlled group are not required for an affiliated group. Thus, in an affiliated group, the identifiable parent corporation itself must own at least 80 percent of the voting power and value of the shares of at least one subsidiary.
- The corporations must meet the stock ownership tests of the affiliated group rule on *every day* of the tax year, whereas the corresponding controlled group tests are applied only on the last day of the year.[20]

Members of an affiliated group are allowed to either (1) claim on their separately filed tax returns a 100 percent dividends received deduction for payments passing between them[21] or (2) elect to file income tax returns on a consolidated basis. Other critical tax effects available to an affiliated group are described in Table 8–1.

ELIGIBILITY FOR THE CONSOLIDATION ELECTION

4   **LEARNING OBJECTIVE**
Describe the corporations that are eligible to file on a consolidated basis.

The Code lists a number of corporations that may *not* use a consolidated return to report their taxable income.[22] Thus, these corporations cannot be used to meet the stock ownership tests, and their taxable incomes cannot be included in a consolidated return. Some of the most frequently encountered entities that are ineligible for consolidated return status include:

- Corporations established outside the United States or in a U.S. possession.
- Tax-exempt (charitable) corporations.[23]
- Insurance companies.
- Partnerships, trusts, estates, and any other noncorporate entities.[24]

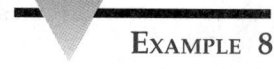

EXAMPLE 8

In the first ownership structure in the accompanying figure, Phillips, Rhesus, Todd, and Valiant form an affiliated group, with Phillips as the parent, under the stock ownership rules. Valiant cannot be included in a consolidated return, however, so the consolidation election is available only to Phillips, Rhesus, and Todd. In the second structure, Phillips, Rhesus, and Todd form an affiliated group, and all of them can be included in a properly

---

[19] §§ 1504(a)(1) and (2).
[20] §§ 1501 and 1563(b)(1).
[21] § 243(b)(1).
[22] § 1504(b).
[23] This includes any entity that is exempt from tax under § 501. See Chapter 14 for a discussion of the qualification of organizations for exempt status.

[24] Some less frequently encountered entities also are prohibited from filing on a consolidated basis. These include domestic international sales corporations and possessions corporations, regulated investment companies, and real estate investment trusts. §§ 1504(b)(4) through (7).

executed consolidated return. Phillips is the identifiable parent of the group. Rhesus and Todd essentially form a brother-sister group below Phillips.

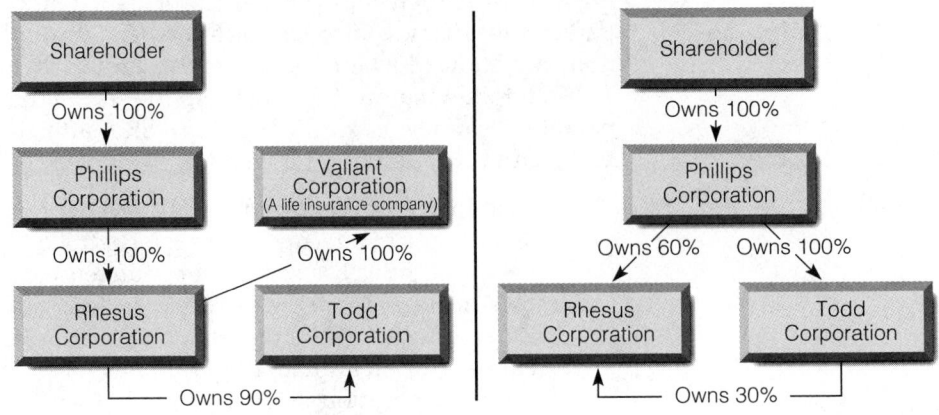

▼ **TABLE 8–1**
Comparison of Tax Effects
Available to Affiliated Group

Attribute	Treatment if Consolidated Returns Are Filed	Treatment if Separate Returns Are Filed
Tax year	All companies use the parent's tax year.	Companies use various tax years.
Change to common tax year	Required, no IRS permission needed.	Requires IRS permission.
Returns of acquired companies	Separate returns through date of consolidation, then join in consolidated return.	Continue filing for each company's tax year. No extra returns needed.
Intercompany dividend	Eliminated, not taxed.	Include in taxable income, then claim dividends received deduction.
Lower tax brackets	Share one set of rates among the group.	Share one set of rates among the group.
Accumulated earnings credit, $150,000/$250,000 floor	Share one floor among the group.	Share one floor among the group.
Liability for tax	Each company liable for the entire consolidated tax liability.	Each company liable only for its own tax.
Statute of limitations	Extension for one company applies to all in the group.	Each company retains its own statute of limitations.
Accounting methods	Need not conform.	Need not conform.
NOLs, capital gains/losses, § 1231 gains/losses, charitable contribution deductions, dividends received deductions, foreign tax credit payments and baskets, etc.	Computed on a consolidated basis.	Computed separately for each company.
Gain/loss on intercompany transactions	Deferred.	Not deferred.
Basis of parent's investment	Changes due to subsidiary operating gain/loss, taxes, and distributions.	No adjustments.

COMPLIANCE REQUIREMENTS

5 **LEARNING OBJECTIVE**
Explain the compliance aspects of consolidated returns.

An eligible entity that meets the stock ownership test can be included in a consolidated group if several compliance requirements are met.

The Initial Consolidated Return.   The first consolidated tax return must meet certain requirements.

- The Form 1120 for the tax year of the consolidated group should include the taxable results of the operations of all of the members of the consolidated group.[25] This return is filed in lieu of the separate returns of the group members.[26] The identified group then continues to file on a consolidated basis until an eligible group no longer exists, or an election to "de-consolidate" is made.[27]
- A Form 1122 should be attached to the first consolidated tax return for all of the subsidiaries included in the group.[28] This form represents a consent by all of the entities to be included in the consolidated group.

The election must be made no later than the extended due date of the parent's return for the year. Only in the case of an inadvertent error can the election to consolidate be rescinded once this extended due date passes.[29]

EXAMPLE 9

Parent Corporation owns 100% of the stock of SubCo. Both corporations use calendar tax years and file separate returns. The entities wish to file on a consolidated basis starting with the tax return for 1998. Parent Corporation does not file to obtain an extended due date for its 1998 return.

If the consolidation election is to be effective, Parent must file a Form 1120 that includes the taxable income of the two corporations by March 15, 1999. SubCo must execute a Form 1122 and attach it to the consolidated Form 1120. ▼

EXAMPLE 10

Continue with the facts of the previous example. Parent Corporation files a complete consolidated Form 1120 on March 1, 1999. On March 5, 1999, the Supreme Court issues a decision that will have a considerable adverse effect on the group's 2000–2004 taxable incomes. If Parent and SubCo file separate 1998 returns by March 15, 1999 (or by some later date if an extension to file is obtained in a timely fashion), the IRS will ignore the consolidation election.

If Parent and SubCo fail to file separate returns in this manner, the election to consolidate is in force for all future years, or until the IRS approves Parent's application to revoke it. ▼

An application to terminate the consolidation election must be filed at least 90 days prior to the extended due date of the consolidated return.[30] Generally, when a subsidiary leaves an ongoing consolidated group, it must wait five years before it can reenter the group.[31]

Subsequent Consolidated Returns.   Each consolidated tax return must include Form 851, Affiliations Schedule, reproduced in Appendix B of this text. This

---

[25] A consolidation election is inferred, even when specific aspects of pertinent forms are completed incorrectly, as long as the members' combined operations are reported on the Form 1120. *American Pacific Whaling Co.*, 74 F.2d 613 (CA–9, 1935).

[26] Reg. § 1.1502–75(a)(1).

[27] Reg. § 1.1502–75(c). The IRS permits such an election only rarely, on the parent's assertion of (1) a good-cause reason to disengage

from consolidated status or (2) a substantial change in the tax law that adversely affects the consolidated tax liability.

[28] Reg. § 1.1502–75(b). A specimen Form 1122 is included in Appendix B of this text.

[29] Reg. §§ 1.1502–75(b)(3) and 301.9100–1T(a).

[30] Reg. § 1.1502–75(c)(1)(i).

[31] § 1504(a)(3).

report identifies all of the corporations in the electing group, summarizes pertinent shareholdings and stock ownership changes that occurred during the tax year, and lists the estimated tax payments made by the group members for the year.

Consolidated tax returns are due on the fifteenth day of the third month following the close of the group's tax year (this is March 15 for a calendar year taxpayer). A six-month extension to file the return can be obtained by executing Form 7004, but an estimated payment of the remaining tax liability for the group must accompany the extension application.

Liability for Taxes.   Group members are jointly and severally liable for the entire consolidated tax liability.[32] This rule applies to interest and penalties imposed as a result of audits as well as to tax liabilities. Furthermore, the IRS is not bound to follow internal agreements among group members in apportioning the liability.[33]

EXAMPLE 11

Parent Corporation, a calendar year taxpayer, acquired 100% of the stock of calendar year SubCo on December 20, 1995. The group filed on a consolidated basis from that date until December 31, 1997, when all of the SubCo stock was sold to Foreign Corporation.

A 1997 IRS audit determined that Parent owed an additional $10 million in Federal income taxes, relating to a sale it made on December 30, 1995. By mid-1998, however, Parent's cash-flow difficulties had brought it close to bankruptcy and forced it to cease activities.

Due to the consolidation election, the IRS can assess the delinquent taxes from SubCo (and Foreign Corporation) in 1997.[34] SubCo is liable for the full amount of any consolidated tax liability, even when it is not the source of the income that led to the tax. ▼

Starting with the third consolidated return year, estimated tax payments must be made on a consolidated basis.[35] Prior to that year, estimates can be computed and paid on either a separate or a consolidated basis.

Regular tax liability is computed applying the graduated tax rates to consolidated taxable income, following the requirements of controlled group status. In this regard, contributions to the actual payment of the tax liability often are arranged to correspond to contributions to consolidated taxable income. Benefits accruing from the graduated corporate tax rates are apportioned equally among the group members unless all members consent to some other method through an annual election.

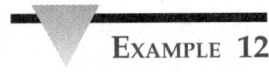

EXAMPLE 12

Parent Corporation owns 100% of the stock of SubCo, and the two corporations file a consolidated tax return. Over the course of a five-year period, the corporations generate the following taxable income/(loss). The low marginal rates that apply to the group's first $75,000 of taxable income might be assigned in various ways.

---

[32] Reg. § 1.1502–6(a).
[33] Reg. § 1.1502–6(c).
[34] The assessment is limited to SubCo's allocable share of the tax (here, probably zero) if the election occurred after the sale of the shares to Foreign Corporation. Reg. § 1.1502–6(b).

[35] Reg. § 1.1502–5(a)(1).

Year	Parent's Taxable Income	SubCo's Taxable Income	Low Brackets Assigned to Parent	Low Brackets Assigned to SubCo
1*	$100,000	($ 10,000)	$37,500	$37,500
2**	100,000	(10,000)	75,000	–0–
3	50,000†	10,000	65,000	10,000
4	(15,000)†	10,000	65,000	10,000
5	100,000	100,000	37,500	37,500

*No election to consolidate is made by group members; brackets are allocated equally between them.

**The indicated election was made for each of the following years.

†The taxpayer believes that Parent's taxable income is more likely to be adjusted on audit. ▼

Alternative minimum tax (AMT) liability is computed on the basis of consolidated AMTI.[36] The group is allowed only one $40,000 AMT exemption, which is phased out at a rate of 25 percent of the amount by which consolidated AMTI exceeds $150,000. Similarly, the AMT adjustment for adjusted current earnings (ACE), which is 75 percent of the excess of ACE over pre-ACE AMTI, is computed using consolidated amounts.

Tax Accounting Periods and Methods. All the members of a consolidating group must use the parent's tax year.[37] As a result, the group may be required to file a short-year return for the first year a subsidiary is included in the consolidated return, so that the parent's year-end can be adopted.[38]

When a mid-year acquisition occurs, both short years are used in tracking the carryforward period of unused losses and credits.[39] Short-year income and deductions are apportioned between the pre- and postacquisition periods. The apportionment may be done either on a daily basis or as the items are recorded for financial accounting purposes, at the election of the corporation being acquired.[40]

EXAMPLE 13 All of the stock of calendar year SubCo is acquired by Parent Corporation on July 15, 1997. The corporations elect to file a consolidated return immediately upon the acquisition.

SubCo had generated a long-term capital loss in its 1994 tax year. As of January 1, 1998, only one year remains in the carryforward period for the capital loss. ▼

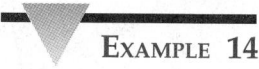

EXAMPLE 14 Continue with the facts of the previous example. According to SubCo's financial accounting records, $400,000 of its $1 million accounting and taxable income for the year was generated after the acquisition. At SubCo's election, either $400,000 (the "books" apportionment method) or $465,753 [(170 postacquisition days/365 days) × $1 million income] (the "daily" method) can be included in the first consolidated return. ▼

Members of a consolidated group can continue to use the tax accounting methods that were in place prior to the consolidation election.[41] Thus, the members of a

---

[36] See Chapter 6 for a full discussion of AMT computations.
[37] Reg. § 1.1502–76(a)(1).
[38] Reg. § 1.1502–76(b)(2).

[39] Reg. § 1.1502–76(d).
[40] Reg. § 1.1502–76(b)(4).
[41] Reg. § 1.1502–17(a).

consolidated group may use different accounting methods.[42] On the other hand, because the $5 million gross-receipts test with respect to use of the cash method of accounting is applied on a consolidated basis,[43] some of the group members may need to switch from the cash to the accrual method of tax accounting. If the members of the consolidated group are treated as personal service corporations, however, their gross receipts are not aggregated, unless the parent so elects; by using this election in an optimal manner, the cash method may be available to some or all of the members.[44]

STOCK BASIS OF SUBSIDIARY

6   **LEARNING OBJECTIVE**
Compute a parent's investment basis in a subsidiary.

Upon acquiring a subsidiary, the parent corporation records a stock basis on its tax balance sheet equal to the acquisition price. At the end of every consolidated return year, the parent records one or more adjustments to this stock basis, as in the financial accounting "equity" method. This treatment prevents double taxation of gain (or deduction of loss) upon the ultimate disposal of the subsidiary's shares.[45] The adjustments are recorded on the last day of the consolidated return year or on the (earlier) date of the disposal of the shares.[46]

In this regard, positive adjustments to stock basis include:

- An allocable share of consolidated taxable income for the year.
- An allocable share of the consolidated operating or capital loss of a subsidiary that could not utilize the loss through a carryback to a prior year.

Negative adjustments to stock basis include:

- An allocable share of a consolidated taxable loss for the year.
- An allocable share of any carryover operating or capital losses that are deducted on the consolidated return and have not previously reduced stock basis.
- Dividends paid by the subsidiary to the parent out of E & P.

EXAMPLE 15

Parent Corporation acquired all of the stock of SubCo on January 1, 1995, for $1 million. The parties immediately elected to file consolidated tax returns. SubCo had a taxable loss of $100,000 in 1995, but it generated $40,000 taxable income in 1996 and $65,000 in 1997. SubCo paid a $10,000 dividend in mid-1997.

Parent has the following stock bases in SubCo on the last day of each of the indicated years.

1995 $900,000   **1996** $940,000   **1997** $995,000 ▼

When accumulated postacquisition taxable losses of the subsidiary exceed the acquisition price, an **excess loss account** is created.[47] This account (1) allows the

---

[42] A series of complex adjustments to inventory values are required where a group member (1) filed a separate return in the preceding tax year; (2) sold inventory assets to another group member in that year, and the goods remained unsold at the end of the separate return year; and (3) otherwise was eligible to file on a consolidated basis with the purchaser for that year. Reg. § 1.1502–18(b). These adjustments override the usual intercompany transaction rules discussed later in the chapter. Essentially, built-in gain from such inventory is recognized immediately upon the consolidation.

[43] §§ 448(a)(1) and (c)(2).

[44] §§ 448(d)(2) and (4)(C).

[45] This procedure parallels the accounting for tax basis in a partnership or S corporation. See Chapters 10 and 12.

[46] Reg. § 1.1502–32(a). Basis adjustments also are allowed when necessary to determine a tax liability (e.g., when member stock is bought or sold). Prop.Reg. § 1.1502–32(c)(4).

[47] Reg. § 1.1502–19.

consolidated return to recognize the losses of the subsidiary in the current year and (2) enables the group to avoid the need to reflect a negative stock basis on its tax-basis balance sheet. If the subsidiary stock is redeemed or sold to a nongroup member while an excess loss account exists, the seller recognizes the balance of the account as capital gain income.[48]

EXAMPLE 16

Parent Corporation acquired all of the stock of SubCo on January 1, 1995, for $100,000. As a result of SubCo's operations, the group records the amounts listed.

Year	Operating Gain/(Loss)	Stock Basis	Excess Loss Account
1995	($ 40,000)	$60,000	$ –0–
1996	(80,000)	–0–	20,000
1997	30,000	10,000	–0–

If Parent sells the SubCo stock for $50,000 at the end of 1996, Parent recognizes a $70,000 capital gain ($50,000 amount realized – $0 adjusted basis in stock + $20,000 recovery of excess loss account). If the sale takes place at the end of 1997, the capital gain is $40,000.[49] ▼

To limit the recognition effects of an excess loss account, the group may elect to reduce the parent's basis of any remaining stock or indebtedness of the subsidiary that is held after the triggering disposition.[50] After the bases of these other investments have been reduced to zero, the seller must recognize the balance of the excess loss account.

In a chain of more than one tier of subsidiaries, the computation of the stock basis amounts starts with the lowest-level subsidiary, then proceeds up the ownership structure to the parent's holdings. In this regard, there is no such concept as consolidated E & P. Rather, each entity accounts for its own share of consolidated taxable income on an annual basis, immediately recognizing within E & P any gain or loss on intercompany transactions and reducing E & P by an allocable share of the consolidated tax liability.[51]

COMPUTING CONSOLIDATED TAXABLE INCOME

Derivation of annual consolidated taxable income involves more than a mere summing of the members' separate taxable income amounts. As Figure 8–2 shows, a number of additional steps are required for several reasons: (1) a few intercompany transactions are directly eliminated from the computation; (2) several transactions are accounted for on a consolidated basis and are therefore removed from the members' computations and treated using group amounts; and (3) certain

---

[48] Reg. §§ 1.1502–19(a)(1) and (2).

[49] Technically, the 1997 subsidiary income is first used to eliminate the excess loss account (i.e., before it creates new stock basis). Reg. § 1.1502–32(e)(3).

[50] Reg. § 1.1502–19(a)(6).

[51] Reg. § 1.1502–33(d). In the absence of an election to use some other allocation method, the consolidated tax liability is allocated to each group member in proportion to its contribution to consolidated taxable income. § 1552(a) and Reg. §§ 1.1552–1(a)(2) and (3)(i).

▼ **FIGURE 8–2**
Computing Consolidated
Taxable Income

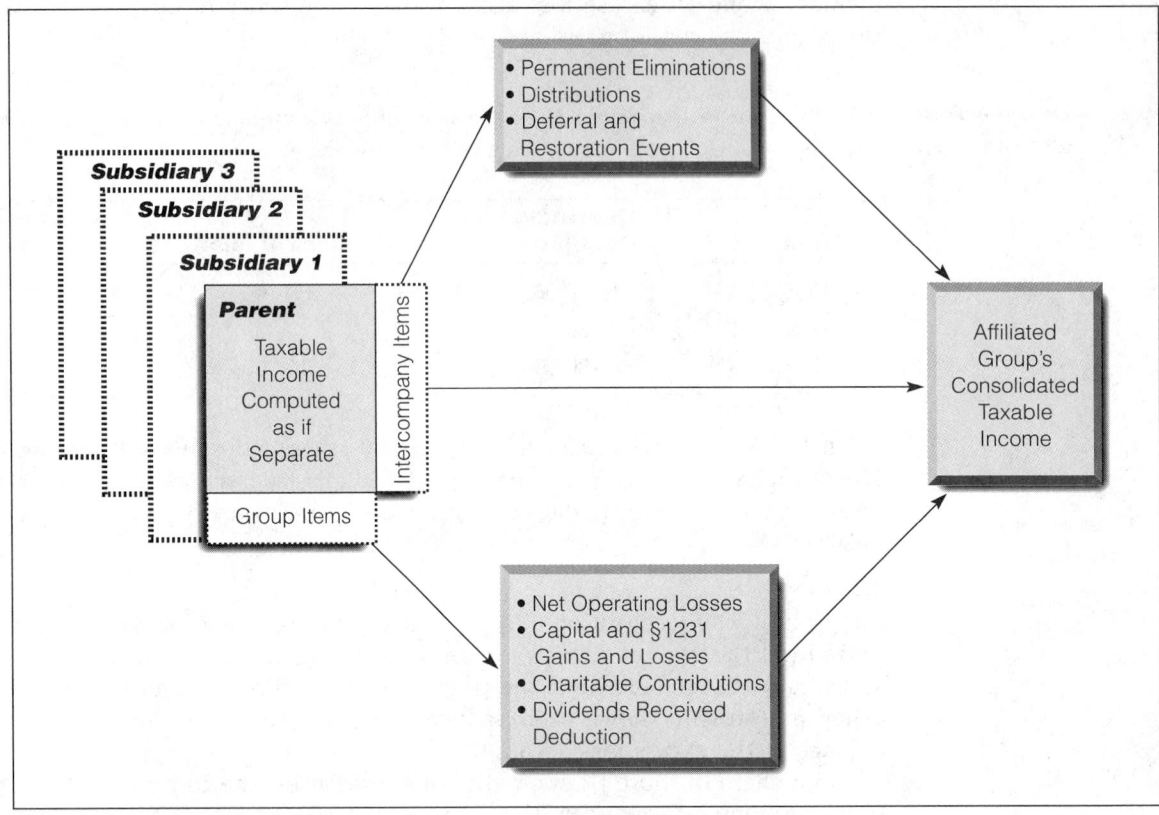

transactions receive special deferral treatment under the Code, so they are removed from further computations until the deferral period ends.

Specifically, each group member splits several items off from its separately computed taxable income. Thus, consolidated taxable income becomes a combination of the revised separate taxable incomes and the resulting income/loss from group items and deferral/restoration events.

COMPUTATIONAL PROCEDURE

The remainder of this chapter will follow the computational procedure suggested in Figure 8–2.[52] Figure 8–3 presents a skeleton worksheet for this computational procedure. Additional information is added to the worksheet for every additional subsidiary. In each case, the starting point for this procedure is the separate taxable incomes of all the group members.

EXAMPLE 17

Parent Corporation owns 100% of the stock of SubCo. This year, Parent's taxable income amounted to $100,000, while SubCo generated a $40,000 taxable loss. There were no transactions between the two corporations, and they incurred no capital or §1231 gains/losses, charitable contributions, dividend income, or other items that are accounted for on a group basis. Accordingly, consolidated taxable income was $60,000.

---

[52] Inventory adjustments, recovery of excess loss accounts, and treatment of depletion deductions, among other items, also are included at an appropriate point in these computations.

	Separate Taxable Income	Adjustments	Post-adjustment Amounts
Parent information	$100,000	_____	$100,000
SubCo information	(40,000)	_____	(40,000)
Group-basis transactions	_____	_____	_____
Deferral/restoration events	_____	_____	_____
Consolidated taxable income			$ 60,000

  *Permanent eliminations.
 **Group-basis transaction.
  †Deferral/restoration event.

TYPICAL INTERCOMPANY TRANSACTIONS

7 **LEARNING OBJECTIVE**
Account for intercompany transactions of a consolidated group.

General Rules. When one member of a consolidated group engages in a transaction with another member of the group, an intercompany transaction occurs. In contrast to the financial accounting treatment of most such transactions, the most commonly encountered items *remain in* the members' separate taxable incomes and therefore cancel each other out on a consolidated basis.[53] For instance, when one group member performs services for another member during the year, the purchaser of the services incurs a deductible expenditure, while the service provider generates includible income. The net result is a zero addition to consolidated taxable income.[54]

This two-step procedure prevents the group from avoiding any § 267 loss disallowances. Furthermore, when the members involved in the transaction are using different tax accounting methods, the payor's deduction for the expenditure is deferred until the year in which the recipient recognizes the related gross income.[55]

▼ **FIGURE 8–3**
Consolidated Taxable Income Worksheet

	Separate Taxable Income	Adjustments	Post-adjustment Amounts
Parent information	_____	_____	_____
Subsidiary information	_____	_____	_____
Group-basis transactions	_____	_____	_____
Deferral/restoration events	_____	_____	_____
Consolidated taxable income			_____

  *Permanent eliminations.
 **Group-basis transaction.
  †Deferral/restoration event.

---

[53] Reg. § 1.1502–13(b)(1).
[54] Reg. §§ 1.1502–13(a)(1)(i) and (b)(1).

[55] §§ 267(a)(2) and (b)(3); Reg. § 1.1502–13(b)(2).

EXAMPLE 18

In the current year, Parent Corporation provided consulting services to its 100%-owned subsidiary, SubCo, under a contract that requires no payments to Parent until next year. Both parties use the accrual method of tax accounting. The services that Parent rendered are valued at $100,000. In addition, Parent purchased $15,000 of supplies from SubCo.

Including these transactions, Parent's taxable income for the year amounted to $500,000. SubCo reported $150,000 separate taxable income. The group is not required to make any eliminating adjustments. The members' deductions incurred offset the income included by the other party to the intercompany transaction. The consolidated taxable income includes both Parent's $15,000 deduction for supplies and SubCo's $15,000 gross receipts therefrom, so the consolidated taxable income computation *de facto* results in an elimination similar to the kind made in financial accounting.

	Separate Taxable Income	Adjustments	Post-adjustment Amounts
Parent information	$500,000	_____	$500,000
SubCo information	150,000	_____	150,000
Group-basis transactions	_____	_____	_____
Deferral/restoration events	_____	_____	_____
Consolidated taxable income			$650,000

*Permanent eliminations.
**Group-basis transaction.
†Deferral/restoration event.

EXAMPLE 19

Continue with the facts of the previous example, except that Parent is a cash basis taxpayer. Since Parent will not recognize the $100,000 of service income earned in the current year until the next tax period, SubCo's related deduction also is deferred until the following year. Thus, the intercompany item—SubCo's deduction—must be eliminated from consolidated taxable income. Additional record keeping is required to keep track of this intercompany transaction (and all others like it), so that the deduction is claimed in the appropriate year.

	Separate Taxable Income	Adjustments	Post-adjustment Amounts
Parent information	$500,000	_____	$500,000
SubCo information	150,000	+ $100,000 due to use of different tax accounting methods	250,000
Group-basis transactions	_____	_____	_____
Deferral/restoration events	_____	_____	_____
Consolidated taxable income			$750,000

*Permanent eliminations.
**Group-basis transaction.
†Deferral/restoration event.

Several other rules also apply to intercompany transactions. Certain deferral/ restoration events require adjusting computations among tax years; these provisions are addressed in a later section of the chapter. Dividends received from other group members are eliminated from the recipients' separate taxable incomes, and no dividends received deduction is allowed.[56] When the distribution is comprised of noncash assets, the subsidiary payor realizes (and defers) any gain on the distributed property, and the (eliminated) dividend amount equals the fair market value of the asset.[57]

EXAMPLE 20

Parent Corporation received a $50,000 cash dividend from 100%-owned SubCo in the current year. Including this item, Parent's separate taxable income amounted to $200,000, and SubCo reported $240,000 separate taxable income.

Parent cannot claim a dividends received deduction for this payment, but the dividend is eliminated in computing consolidated taxable income. No elimination is required for SubCo, as dividend payments are nondeductible.

	Separate Taxable Income	Adjustments	Post-adjustment Amounts
Parent information	$ 200,000	− $50,000 dividend received from SubCo*	$150,000
SubCo information	240,000		240,000
Group-basis transactions	_____	_____	_____
Deferral/restoration events	_____	_____	_____
Consolidated taxable income			$390,000

*Permanent eliminations.
**Group-basis transaction.
†Deferral/restoration event.

Realized gains and losses from other intercompany transactions involving stock or debt of group members are treated as deferral events, which are discussed later in the chapter.[58] Several other permanent eliminations are delineated in the Regulations.[59]

8 LEARNING OBJECTIVE
Identify limitations that restrict the use of losses and credits of group members derived in separate return years.

Members' Net Operating Losses.   Most often, the election to file consolidated returns is motivated by the parent corporation's desire to gain access to the positive tax attributes of the subsidiary corporation, especially its net operating losses (NOLs). Congress has enacted a number of provisions, however, to discourage corporate acquisitions that are solely tax motivated. These include §§ 381 and 382, which limit the current-year and overall use of NOL carryovers by parties in a tax-favored reorganization (see Chapter 7), and §§ 269 and 482, which allow the

[56] Reg. § 1.1502–14(a)(1). If the distribution exceeds the payor's E & P, the stock basis of the payor is reduced. When the basis reaches zero, an excess loss account is created. Reg. § 1.1502–14(a)(2). Dividends received from nongroup members may result in a dividends received deduction; they constitute a group-basis item (discussed later in the chapter).

[57] §§ 301(b)(1) and (d); 311(b)(1); Reg. §§ 1.1502–14(c)(1) and –14T; Ltr.Rul. 8922096.
[58] Reg. §§ 1.1502–14(b) through (e).
[59] Reg. §§ 1.1502–15 through 19.

IRS to reallocate income and deduction items of related parties that allegedly distort taxable income.

The usual corporate NOL computations are available to the losses of the consolidated group. Excessive losses are carried back 3 years and then forward 15 years, although the parent may elect to forgo the carryback deductions for all members of the group.[60] The NOL is derived after removing any consolidated charitable contribution deduction and capital gain or loss from consolidated taxable income. These items are removed because they have their own carryover periods and rules.[61] The consolidated dividends received deduction remains a part of the consolidated NOL.[62]

EXAMPLE 21

Parent Corporation and SubCo have filed consolidated returns since both entities were incorporated in 1995. Neither group member incurred any capital gain or loss transactions during 1995–1998, nor did they make any charitable contributions. Taxable income computations for the members include the following.

Year	Parent's Taxable Income	SubCo's Taxable Income	Consolidated Taxable Income
1995	$100,000	$ 40,000	$140,000
1996	100,000	(40,000)	60,000
1997	100,000	(140,000)	?
1998	100,000	210,000	?

The 1997 consolidated loss of $40,000 can be carried back to offset 1995 consolidated taxable income. Alternatively, Parent can elect to carry the loss forward to 1998, forgoing any carryback computation. This might be appropriate given an increase in statutory tax rates effective for 1998 or an application of the AMT in 1995 and 1996. ▼

Complications arise, however, when the corporations enter or depart from a consolidated return election, so that members' operating losses are either incurred in a "separate return year" and deducted in a "consolidated return year," or vice versa. Congress has imposed a variety of restrictions on the availability of such deductions to discourage profitable corporations from acquiring unprofitable entities simply in order to file immediate refund claims based on loss and credit carryforwards. Figure 8–4 summarizes the applicable limitations.

In any case where the members of a consolidated group change over time, the taxpayer must apportion the consolidated NOL among the group members. When more than one group member generated a loss for the consolidated year, the following formula is used to apportion the loss among the electing group's members.

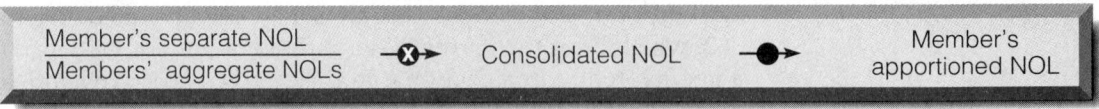

$$\frac{\text{Member's separate NOL}}{\text{Members' aggregate NOLs}} \; \otimes \; \text{Consolidated NOL} \; \longrightarrow \; \text{Member's apportioned NOL}$$

---

[60] Prop.Reg. § 1.1502–21(b)(3)(i).

[61] For instance, there is no election available that would enable the parent to forgo the net capital loss carryback.

[62] Reg. § 1.1502–21(f).

▼ **FIGURE 8–4**
Limitations on Use of Net
Operating Losses

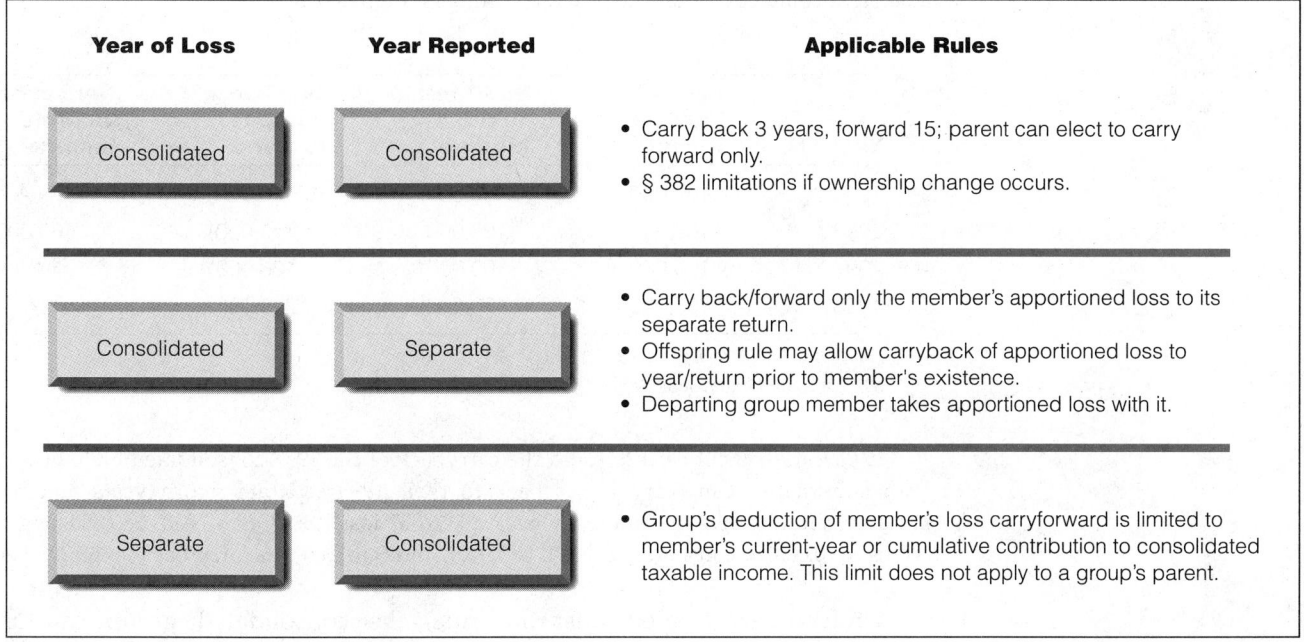

Year of Loss	Year Reported	Applicable Rules
Consolidated	Consolidated	• Carry back 3 years, forward 15; parent can elect to carry forward only. • § 382 limitations if ownership change occurs.
Consolidated	Separate	• Carry back/forward only the member's apportioned loss to its separate return. • Offspring rule may allow carryback of apportioned loss to year/return prior to member's existence. • Departing group member takes apportioned loss with it.
Separate	Consolidated	• Group's deduction of member's loss carryforward is limited to member's current-year or cumulative contribution to consolidated taxable income. This limit does not apply to a group's parent.

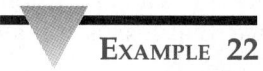

EXAMPLE 22

Parent Corporation and SubCo have filed consolidated returns since 1996. Both entities were incorporated in 1995. Neither group member incurred any capital gain or loss transactions during 1995–1998, nor did they make any charitable contributions. Taxable income computations for the members are listed below.

Year	Parent's Taxable Income	SubCo's Taxable Income	Consolidated Taxable Income
1995*	$100,000	$ 40,000	N/A
1996**	100,000	(40,000)	$60,000
1997**	100,000	(140,000)	?
1998**	100,000	210,000	?

*Separate return year.
**Consolidated return year.

In 1997, SubCo can carry back the entire $40,000 consolidated NOL to its separate 1995 tax year, because it is solely responsible for generating the loss. SubCo files for the refund of taxes that result from the carryback, and it alone receives the refund.[63]

Alternatively, Parent could elect to forgo the carryback of the 1997 consolidated loss, thereby preserving the loss deduction for the group's subsequent years. In that case, the 1998 tax reduction would be claimed by filing the 1998 consolidated tax return, and Parent would receive the refund on behalf of the group. ▼

---

[63] Reg. §§ 1.1502–78(b)(1) and (c), Example 4.

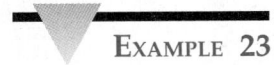

EXAMPLE 23

Parent Corporation, SubOne, and SubTwo have filed consolidated returns since 1996. All of the entities were incorporated in 1995. None of the group members incurred any capital gain or loss transactions during 1995–1998, nor did they make any charitable contributions. Taxable income computations for the members are listed below.

Year	Parent's Taxable Income	SubOne's Taxable Income	SubTwo's Taxable Income	Consolidated Taxable Income
1995*	$100,000	$100,000	$ 40,000	N/A
1996**	100,000	100,000	(40,000)	160,000
1997**	100,000	(60,000)	(120,000)	?
1998**	100,000	100,000	210,000	?

*Separate return year.
**Consolidated return year.

If Parent does not elect to forgo the carryback of the 1997 consolidated NOL of $80,000, both subsidiaries can carry losses back to their 1995 separate return years and receive separate refunds. SubOne can carry back a $26,667 loss [(SubOne's NOL $60,000/aggregate NOLs $180,000) × consolidated NOL $80,000], and SubTwo can carry back a $53,333 loss. ▼

Under the so-called offspring rule, the consolidated group can use a carryback loss that is apportioned to a member of the electing group, even though that member was not in existence in the carryback year.[64] If the member joined the group immediately upon its incorporation, but cannot use an apportioned loss in the carryback period because it was not in existence, that loss is still available to the group.[65]

EXAMPLE 24

Parent Corporation, SubOne, and SubTwo have filed consolidated returns since 1996. The first two entities were incorporated and consolidated in 1995, and SubTwo came into existence in 1996 through an asset spin-off from Parent. None of the group members incurred any capital gain or loss transactions during 1995–1998, nor did they make any charitable contributions. Taxable income computations for the members are listed below.

Year	Parent's Taxable Income	SubOne's Taxable Income	SubTwo's Taxable Income	Consolidated Taxable Income
1995*	$100,000	$ 40,000	—	$140,000
1996*	100,000	100,000	($ 40,000)	160,000
1997*	100,000	(60,000)	(120,000)	?
1998*	100,000	100,000	210,000	?

*Consolidated return year.

---

[64] Reg. § 1.1502–79(a)(2).
[65] Prop.Reg. § 1.1502–21(b)(2)(ii)(B) restricts the use of this loss to the parent, if the carryback year is a separate return year for the parties.

If Parent does not elect to forgo the carryback of the 1997 consolidated NOL of $80,000, SubOne can carry its $26,667 loss back to 1995. SubTwo's $53,333 share of the loss can also be carried back to 1995 and used by members of the consolidated group. Under the offspring rule, SubTwo is treated as being a member of the group for the entire *group* carryback period because its existence is rooted in Parent's assets. ▼

When a corporation leaves a consolidated group, it takes with it any apportioned share of any unused loss carryforwards, to be used on its subsequent separate returns.

EXAMPLE 25

Parent Corporation, SubOne, and SubTwo have filed consolidated returns since 1995, the year in which all of the entities were incorporated. None of the group members incurred any capital gain or loss transactions during 1995–1998, nor did they make any charitable contributions. Taxable income computations for the members are listed below.

Year	Parent's Taxable Income	SubOne's Taxable Income	SubTwo's Taxable Income	Consolidated Taxable Income
1995*	$100,000	$100,000	$ 40,000	$240,000
1996*	100,000	100,000	(40,000)	160,000
1997*	100,000	(60,000)	(120,000)	?
1998**	100,000	100,000	210,000	N/A

*Consolidated return year.
**Separate return year.

Parent elects to forgo any loss carryback for the group's 1997 operations. On the first day of the 1998 tax year, a foreign investor purchases all of the stock of SubTwo. On its 1998 separate return, SubTwo can deduct its $53,333 share of the 1997 NOL carryforward.[66] ▼

When an NOL is carried forward from a separate return year onto a consolidated return, another set of limitations, known as the **separate return limitation year (SRLY)** rules, applies.[67] The consolidated return can include an NOL carryforward from the member's SRLY period only to the extent of the lesser of its (1) current-year or (2) cumulative positive contribution to current-year consolidated income.[68]

The SRLY limitations never apply to the electing group's identifiable parent.[69] Nor do they apply to a member that met all of the eligibility and stock ownership tests for consolidated return status, but never was included in a consolidation election.[70]

EXAMPLE 26

Parent Corporation and SubCo have filed consolidated returns since 1996. Both entities were incorporated in 1995. Neither group member incurred any capital gain or loss

---

[66] SubTwo cannot take the entire $120,000 NOL that is attributable to it. Reg. §§ 1.1502–79(a)(1)(ii) and (b)(2)(ii). Losses and carryovers must first be absorbed within the current consolidated return year before any loss apportionment occurs.

[67] Reg. § 1.1502–21(c). The SRLY rules apply to capital loss and credit carryforwards as well.

[68] Prop.Reg. § 1.1502–21(c).

[69] Reg. § 1.1502–1(f)(2)(i), known as the "lonely parent" rule.

[70] Reg. § 1.1502–1(f)(2)(ii).

transactions during 1995–1998, nor did they make any charitable contributions. Taxable income computations for the members are listed below.

Year	Parent's Taxable Income	SubCo's Taxable Income	Consolidated Taxable Income
1995*	$100,000	($ 40,000)	N/A
1996**	100,000	(10,000)	$90,000
1997**	100,000	15,000	?
1998**	100,000	70,000	?

*Separate return year.

**Consolidated return year.

The thrust of the SRLY rules is to presume that Parent acquired SubCo so that it could deduct losses from a separate return year against consolidated income. Accordingly, none of SubCo's separate return loss from 1995 can be deducted in computing 1996 consolidated taxable income; the deduction is limited to the lesser of SubCo's current-year (zero) or cumulative (zero) contribution to consolidated taxable income.

In computing 1997 consolidated taxable income, the SubCo SRLY loss deduction is limited to $5,000, the lesser of SubCo's current-year ($15,000) or cumulative ($5,000) contribution to consolidated taxable income. ▼

EXAMPLE 27

Parent Corporation and SubCo have filed consolidated returns since 1996. Both entities were incorporated in 1995. Neither group member incurred any capital gain or loss transactions during 1995–1998, nor did they make any charitable contributions. Taxable income computations for the members are listed below.

Year	Parent's Taxable Income	SubCo's Taxable Income	Consolidated Taxable Income
1995*	($ 40,000)	$100,000	N/A
1996**	(100,000)	(10,000)	($110,000)
1997**	20,000	165,000	?
1998**	100,000	70,000	?

*Separate return year.

**Consolidated return year.

The 1997 consolidated return can include a deduction for Parent's entire 1995 NOL of $40,000. The deduction is not limited to the lesser of Parent's current-year ($20,000) or cumulative (zero) contribution to consolidated taxable income. ▼

COMPUTATION OF GROUP ITEMS

9   LEARNING OBJECTIVE
Derive deductions and credits on a consolidated basis.

Several income and deduction items are derived on a consolidated-group basis. Therefore, statutory limitations and allowances are applied to the group as though it were a single corporation. This computational convention allows group members to match various types of gains and losses and to increase specific limitations, required by the Code, in a manner that optimizes the overall tax benefit.

Specifically, the following items are computed on a group basis with the usual C corporation tax effects applied on a group basis (see Chapter 2).

- Net capital gain/loss.
- Section 1231 gain/loss.
- Casualty/theft gain/loss.

- Charitable contributions.
- Dividends received deduction.
- Net operating loss.

Following the computational procedure of Figures 8–2 and 8–3, all of the group-basis items are removed from each member's separate taxable income. Then, using the consolidated taxable income figure to that point, statutory limitations are applied to the aggregate income and expenditures of the group, and group-basis gains, losses, income, and deductions are derived.

EXAMPLE 28

Parent Corporation's current-year taxable income included $300,000 net income from operations and a $50,000 net long-term capital gain. Parent also made a $40,000 contribution to State University. Accordingly, its separate taxable income amounted to $315,000.

Income from operations	$300,000
Capital gain income	+50,000
Charitable contribution (maximum)	−35,000
Separate taxable income	$315,000

SubCo generated $170,000 income from operations and incurred a $45,000 short-term capital loss. Thus, its separate taxable income was $170,000, and aggregate separate taxable income for the group amounted to $485,000.

Upon consolidation, a larger amount of Parent's charitable contribution is deductible, and its capital gain is almost fully sheltered from current-year tax.

	Separate Taxable Income	Adjustments	Post-adjustment Amounts
Parent information	$315,000	− $50,000 capital gain income** + $35,000 charitable contribution deduction**	$300,000
SubCo information	170,000	$45,000 short-term capital loss**	170,000
Group-basis transactions		+ $5,000 net long-term capital gain − $40,000 charitable contribution deduction (maximum for group is $47,500)	−35,000
Deferral/restoration events			————
Consolidated taxable income			$435,000

*Permanent eliminations.
**Group-basis transaction.
†Deferral/restoration event.

Computing these items on a group basis does not always result in a reduction of aggregate group taxable income. Nevertheless, the possibility of using the group-basis computations may affect transactions by group members late in the tax year when it becomes apparent that planning opportunities may be available. It may also encourage the taxpayer to seek fellow group members that bring complementary tax attributes to the consolidated return.

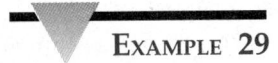

EXAMPLE 29

Parent Corporation owns 15% of the stock of Outsider Corporation throughout the year. Outsider paid a $150,000 dividend to Parent during the year. Parent also generated $400,000 of taxable operating income and sold a § 1231 asset at a $10,000 gain. Parent's separate taxable income is computed below.

Operating income	$ 400,000
Dividend income	+150,000
§ 1231 gain	+10,000
Dividends received deduction (70%)	−105,000
Separate taxable income	$ 455,000

A 10% owner of Outsider, SubCo also received a $100,000 dividend. SubCo's operations produced a $20,000 net taxable loss for the year, and it sold a § 1231 asset at a $4,000 loss. Thus, SubCo's separate taxable income is computed as follows.

Operating income	($ 20,000)
Dividend income	+100,000
§ 1231 loss	−4,000
Dividends received deduction[71]	−53,200
Separate taxable income	$ 22,800

A consolidated return increases the group's dividends received deduction,[72] but it wastes the opportunity to claim SubCo's § 1231 loss as an ordinary deduction.

	Separate Taxable Income	Adjustments	Post-adjustment Amounts
Parent information	$455,000	− $150,000 dividend received from Outsider** − $10,000 § 1231 gain** + $105,000 dividends received deduction**	$400,000
SubCo information	22,800	− $100,000 dividend received from Outsider** + $4,000 § 1231 loss + $53,200 dividends received deduction	(20,000)
Group-basis transactions		+ $250,000 dividend received from Outsider − $175,000 dividends received deduction (70% × $250,000) + $6,000 § 1231 gain	+81,000
Deferral/restoration events			
Consolidated taxable income			$461,000

*Permanent elimination.

**Group-basis transaction.

†Deferral/restoration event.

---

[71] Limited to 70% of taxable income before the deduction. § 246(b)(1).

[72] The group cannot apply an 80% rate for the dividends received deduction, even though aggregate group ownership in Outsider Corporation now exceeds 20%. Reg. § 1.1502–26(a)(1)(i).

Other items computed on a consolidated basis include all elements of the general business and research credits, any recapture of those credits, the foreign tax credit, the percentage depletion deduction, and all elements of AMTI.

DEFERRAL AND RESTORATION EVENTS

A special class of intercompany transactions receives deferral treatment under the Regulations.[73] The gain or loss realized on these transactions is removed from consolidated taxable income until a **restoration event** occurs. The purpose of these rules is to prevent group members from accelerating loss deductions that relate to sales of assets within the group. Generally, the loss is deductible only when control of the asset leaves the electing group.

Deferral/restoration treatment applies to sales of assets or the performance of services among group members. The entire deferred gain or loss is restored to the consolidated taxable income computation when, say, the asset is transferred outside the group through a subsequent sale. Full gain or loss restoration can also be triggered when the transferor of the property leaves the group or the consolidation election is terminated. Generally, the restored gain or loss is recognized in the same manner as it would have been on the initial transfer.[74] Asset basis and holding periods "start over," reflecting the purchaser's intermediary acquisition.[75] The installment method is not available for any deferral/restoration transaction.[76]

EXAMPLE 30

Parent Corporation sold a plot of land to SubCo in the current year for $100,000. Parent had acquired the land 10 years ago for $40,000. The consolidated return also reflects the operating results of the parties: Parent generated a $10,000 gain, and SubCo produced a $100,000 gain.

This intercompany transaction is a deferral event: Parent's $60,000 realized gain is deferred through an elimination in the computation of consolidated taxable income. SubCo's basis in the land is $100,000, and its holding period in the land begins with this year's purchase. The $60,000 gain is recognized when SubCo sells the land to Outsider Corporation.

	Separate Taxable Income	Adjustments	Post-adjustment Amounts
Parent information	$ 70,000	_____	$ 70,000
SubCo information	100,000	_____	100,000
Group-basis transactions			
Deferral/restoration events		– $60,000 gain on intercompany sale to SubCo†	–60,000
Consolidated taxable income			$110,000

*Permanent elimination.

**Group-basis transaction.

†Deferral/restoration event.

---

[73] Reg. §§ 1.1502–13(c) through (h) and –13T.

[74] Sections 267 and 1239 may convert other types of gain into ordinary income. See especially Reg. §§ 1.267(f)–1T and –2T and 1.1239–1(a) and (b)(3).

[75] Reg. § 1.1502–13(g).

[76] Reg. § 1.1502–13(c)(1)(ii).

SubCo sold the land to Outsider for $110,000 in a year in which its operating income totaled $60,000 (exclusive of the restoration event, the sale of the land), and Parent's operating income amounted to $170,000.

	Separate Taxable Income	Adjustments	Post-adjustment Amounts
Parent information	$170,000	————	$170,000
SubCo information	70,000	————	70,000
Group-basis transactions			
Deferral/restoration events		+ $60,000 restored gain on Parent's sale to SubCo†	+60,000
Consolidated taxable income			$300,000

*Permanent elimination.

**Group-basis transaction.

†Deferral/restoration event.

Any deferred gain or loss on a transfer is recognized upon the earliest restoration event to occur. Other potential restoration events include the following.

- The acquiring group member claims a cost recovery deduction for the asset.[77]
- A nongroup member's installment note is transferred among group members (e.g., with the transferred asset itself).
- The transferred inventory is written down from its purchase price to fair market value.[78]

Generally, the deferral/restoration rules are attractive to the group when intercompany sales take place at a gain. When such sales generate losses, however, the mandatory nature of the rules may become burdensome. Consequently, the Regulations allow an election that overrides the deferral/restoration rules. With the election, all intercompany gains and losses are immediately includible or deductible.[79] The election remains in force until the IRS consents to its revocation.

TAX PLANNING CONSIDERATIONS

CHOOSING CONSOLIDATED RETURN PARTNERS

Taxpayers should optimize their overall tax benefits when choosing consolidated return partners. Within the limitations of the rules discussed earlier in the chapter, target corporations might include some of the following.

10   **LEARNING OBJECTIVE**
Demonstrate tax planning opportunities available to consolidated groups.

- Loss and credit carryovers.
- Passive activity income, loss, or credits.
- Gains that can be deferred through intercompany sales.
- Contributions to consolidated ACE adjustments.
- Excess limitation amounts (e.g., with respect to charitable contributions).
- Section 1231 gains, losses, and look-back profiles.

---

[77] Reg. §§ 1.1502–13(d)(1) and –13T(l). The deferred gain is restored to consolidated taxable income over a period of years, using the ACRS, MACRS, or other cost recovery method that the acquiring group member employs. Thus, the present value of the tax on

this restored gain is reduced when the purchaser uses slower methods of cost recovery.

[78] Reg. § 1.1502–13(f)(1)(viii).

[79] Reg. § 1.1502–13(c)(3).

CONCEPT SUMMARY 8–2

The Consolidated Tax Return

1. Groups of corporations form for a variety of tax and nontax reasons. The election to file Federal income tax returns on a consolidated basis allows certain group members to use their positive tax attributes (e.g., loss or credit carryovers) to offset negative tax attributes (e.g., positive taxable income) of other members.
2. Consolidated tax returns are limited to eligible corporations that satisfy stock ownership tests and meet various compliance requirements. For instance, all group members must conform their tax years to that of the parent of the group. Group members may use different tax accounting methods, however.
3. Group members are jointly and severally liable for the overall tax liability of the group. For the most part, computations of estimated tax liabilities must be made on a consolidated basis.
4. The stock basis of a subsidiary is derived from the acquisition price of the stock, increased by the taxable income (or decreased by the losses) of the subsidiary, and decreased by dividend distributions. An excess loss account is created when aggregate losses of the subsidiary exceed both the purchase price and ensuing income amounts. The excess loss account is recaptured as capital gain when the subsidiary stock is disposed of.
5. In computing consolidated taxable income, certain items, such as charitable contributions and § 1231 gains and losses, are computed on a consolidated basis, while other gains and losses are deferred until later tax periods. The group is subject to severe restrictions in using any operating losses of a subsidiary that has been acquired or disposed of.

CONSOLIDATION VERSUS 100 PERCENT DIVIDENDS RECEIVED DEDUCTION

When adequate ownership is held, a 100 percent dividends received deduction is available for payments received from subsidiaries with whom a consolidated return is *not* filed. Thus, this tax benefit is still available when the taxpayer wishes to affiliate with an insurance company, foreign entity, or other ineligible corporation. A taxpayer that cannot find potential group partners with the desired level of complementary tax attributes may also take advantage of this benefit.

PROTECTING THE GROUP MEMBER'S LIABILITY FOR TAX PAYMENTS

Because all group members are responsible for consolidated tax liabilities, interest, and penalties, target subsidiaries and their (present and potential) shareholders should take measures to protect their separate interests.

EXAMPLE 31

Return to the facts of Example 11. Exposure by SubCo and its successive shareholders to tax (and all other) liabilities of Parent Corporation should be minimized by including appropriate clauses in purchase contracts and related documents. For instance, (1) Foreign Corporation could alter its negotiating position so that it pays less to acquire the SubCo stock, or (2) SubCo might attempt to recover any Parent taxes that it pays through courts other than the Tax Court. ▼

A short tax year may be created when a member with a nonmatching tax year joins or leaves the group. When this occurs, the group should consider measures to limit the ensuing negative tax consequences. For instance, additional income can be accelerated into the short year of acquisition. This will reduce any loss carryforwards when the carryover period effectively is shortened due to the takeover. The group should also make suitable income-allocation elections in assigning income to the short year. Finally, group estimated tax payments should be computed using both consolidated and separate liability amounts to determine the more beneficial method. In this way, only the minimum quarterly tax payments are made, and the benefits of the time value of money are maximized.

ELECTING TO POSTPONE RECOGNITION OF THE EXCESS LOSS ACCOUNT

An election to reduce the investment basis of remaining subsidiary stock and debt (i.e., upon disposition of shares when an excess loss account exists) may be attractive when the remaining shares are not likely to be sold in the near future. In that case, the present value of the tax on any resulting increased gain will be low. The election may also be used to offset any recognition of the postponed gain upon debt repayments or stock sales when future operating losses are anticipated. The election generally is not attractive when operating loss carryforwards are available in the current year. These can be used to shelter the gain recognized on recovery of the excess loss account.

EXAMPLE 32

Parent Corporation owns preferred stock of SubCo with a basis of $10,000. Parent's basis in its common stock investment in SubCo has been eliminated through SubCo's operating losses; in fact, Parent holds a $6,000 excess loss account for SubCo.

Parent sells the SubCo common for $9,000. Thus, it must recognize a $15,000 capital gain on the sale. Alternatively, Parent can elect to recognize only a $9,000 gain on the sale and to reduce its basis in the SubCo preferred to $4,000. ▼

ELECTION TO OVERRIDE DEFERRAL AND RESTORATION RULES

An election to make all intercompany transactions includible or deductible upon completion of the intragroup transaction may be especially attractive in the following circumstances: (1) due to market or other conditions, the transfers generate realized losses that the taxpayer wishes to deduct; (2) the transactions occur frequently, making record keeping burdensome (particularly for cost recovery assets that are exchanged in midrecovery life); and (3) intercompany transactions produce ordinary income under §§ 1239, 1245, or some other provision in years for which sufficient operating loss carryforwards are available.

Recall, however, that the § 267(f) rules may further limit the seller's ability to deduct a loss from a sale to a fellow *controlled* group member.[80] In fact, such a loss remains nondeductible even when the purchasing group member disengages from the consolidation election, but remains a member of a controlled group with the internal seller.

EXAMPLE 33

SubCo purchased an asset from Parent Corporation last year, with Parent incurring a $10,000 realized loss that was nondeductible under the deferral/restoration rules. This year, SubCo sold the asset to Foreign Corporation, also a 100%-owned subsidiary of Parent. Foreign cannot be a member of the affiliated group because it is not incorporated in the United States. The sale is not a restoration event, however, because Foreign is a member of a controlled group with the other two entities. ▼

---

[80] Reg. § 1.267(f)–2T(c).

KEY TERMS

Consolidated return,
8–4

Excess loss account,
8–16

Restoration event,
8–29

Separate return
limitation year (SRLY),
8–25

**PROBLEM
MATERIALS**

DISCUSSION QUESTIONS

1. List some of the nontax motivations for arranging corporate holdings so that a consolidated return is available.

2. Identify several business decisions that might trigger a consolidation election.

3. Describe the organization of the rules that govern consolidated returns.

4. Does familiarity with the financial accounting rules for consolidations help in analyzing the tax law's consolidated return rules?

5. How do the tax laws of other countries treat the issues raised by consolidated returns?

6. Prepare an outline of a talk that you are to give to your fellow students, identifying the chief advantages and disadvantages of filing consolidated returns.

7. Identify the three major requirements that must be met before a consolidated return election can be made.

8. What are the chief differences between the definitions of affiliated groups and parent-subsidiary controlled groups?

9. What are the major tax effects available to members of an affiliated group? A controlled group?

10. Identify several types of corporate entities that cannot participate in a consolidated return.

11. Parent Corporation and its wholly owned subsidiary, Child Corporation, file Federal tax returns on a separate basis. Parent uses a calendar tax year, while Child files using an April 30 year-end. If the corporations wish to elect to file on a consolidated basis as of January 1, 1997, how long do they have to decide to consolidate?

12. Parent Corporation and its wholly owned subsidiary, Child Corporation, file Federal tax returns on a consolidated basis. The group uses a calendar tax year. If the corporations wish to apply to terminate the group's filing on a consolidated basis as of January 1, 1998, how long do they have to decide to de-consolidate?

13. Parent Corporation and its wholly owned subsidiary, Child Corporation, file Federal tax returns on a separate basis. Parent manufactures postage meters, and Child provides mail-order services to a cross section of clients in the state.

    Parent uses a calendar tax year, while Child files using an April 30 year-end. Parent's gross receipts for the year total $10 million, and Child's are $2.5 million. Identify some tax issues as to accounting periods and methods that the group would face if the corporations elect to consolidate.

14. In a memo to the tax research file, summarize the positive and negative adjustments made by a parent corporation to the stock basis of its subsidiary.

15. Describe the process of determining the taxable income of a consolidated group. Use a diagram to illustrate your methodology.

16. How does tax law treat the "eliminating entries" used to apply generally accepted accounting procedures to a consolidated group?

17. In December 1997, Parent Corporation renders services worth $250,000 to its wholly owned subsidiary, Child Corporation. Both entities use calendar tax years. Parent uses accrual tax accounting, while Child employs the cash method of accounting. The entities have been filing on a consolidated basis since Child was incorporated many years ago.

    Parent's operations for 1997 resulted in a $2 million loss. Parent sends Child an invoice for the services in December 1997, and Child pays it in January 1998. What tax consequences are the parties trying to accomplish?

18. SubOne Corporation brought a $2 million NOL carryforward into a group of corporations that elected to file on a consolidated basis as of the beginning of this year. Combined results for the year generated $10 million taxable income, $500,000 of which was attributable to SubOne's activities for the year. Has SubOne been a good consolidation partner?

19. Prepare for a presentation to the local Tax Club on consolidated tax return rules by listing the most commonly encountered items accounted for on a group basis.

20. Do most consolidated groups prefer that their intercompany sales result in a net gain or a loss? Why?

PROBLEMS

21. SubCo sold an asset to Parent at a tax and accounting gain of $200,000. The asset appreciated by another $30,000 before Parent sold it to an unrelated party, Outsiders, Inc.
    a. Compute the realized financial accounting and recognized taxable income of the group members for these transactions, indicating the date upon which the gain is triggered and the member that includes the gain.
    b. Same as (a), except that the asset declines in value by $30,000 while it is in Parent's hands.

22. Indicate whether each of the following independent situations is a controlled group (C) and/or an affiliated group (A).
    a. ParentCo holds 90% of the common shares of SubCo and all of the preferred shares. _____
    b. ParentCo holds 90% of the common shares of SubCo and half of the preferred shares. _____
    c. ParentCo holds 60% of the shares of SubCoA and 60% of the shares of SubCoB. SubCoA holds the "other" 40% of the SubCoB shares. _____
    d. At the beginning of the year, ParentCo held 90% of the shares of SubCo. It sold half of those shares on the market on July 14, but bought them all back on September 1. _____
    e. ParentCo holds 90% of the shares of SubCoA and 60% of the shares of SubCoB. SubCoA holds the "other" 40% of the SubCoB shares. _____

23. Mother Corporation, a service provider, has the following stock holdings. With which of the related corporations can Mother file a consolidated return?

Company	Percentage of Voting Power Owned by Mother	Percentage of Value Owned by Mother
Brother, manufacturer	65%	75%
Sister, processor	85	89
Nephew, insurance company	90	87
Niece, marketing firm	78	85
Cousin, food producer	82	83

24. Parent purchased all of SubCo's stock on January 2, 1997. The group intends to file on a consolidated basis for 1997 and thereafter. The following estimated payment compu-

tations pertain to the affiliates, who come to you looking for advice. What are the lowest estimated payments that the group can make without incurring penalties for the years at issue?

Year	ParentCo's Separate Estimated Tax Payment	SubCo's Separate Estimated Tax Payment	Consolidated Estimated Tax Payment
1997	$10,000	$7,000	$14,000
1998	10,000	3,000	14,000
1999	10,000	3,000	14,000

25. ParentCo owns all of DaughterCo, and the group files its Federal income tax returns on a consolidated basis. Both taxpayers are subject to the alternative minimum tax (AMT) this year due to active operations in the oil and gas development industry. No intercompany transactions were incurred this year. If the affiliates filed separate returns, they would report the following amounts. How does the consolidation election affect the overall AMT liability of the group?

Company	Adjusted Current Earnings (ACE)	AMT Income before the ACE Adjustment
ParentCo	$1,500,000	$900,000
DaughterCo	200,000	300,000

26. LargeCo files on a consolidated basis with LittleCo. The subsidiary was acquired for $250,000 on January 1, 1997, and it paid a $30,000 dividend to LargeCo at the end of both 1998 and 1999.
    a. Given the following information about the subsidiary's operating results, derive the requested amounts as of December 31 of each year. The group files using a calendar year.

Year	LittleCo's Operating Gain/(Loss)	LargeCo's Investment in LittleCo	
		Stock Basis	Excess Loss Account
1997	($140,000)	?	?
1998	(125,000)	?	?
1999	15,000	?	?

    b. LargeCo sold LittleCo to an unrelated competitor for $150,000 on December 31, 1999. How will LargeCo account for this sale?

27. Compute consolidated taxable income for the calendar year Moose group, which elected consolidated status immediately upon the creation of the two member corporations on January 1, 1997. All recognized income is ordinary in nature, and no intercompany transactions were completed during the indicated years.

Year	Moose Corporation	Goose Corporation
1997	$250,000	$ 10,000
1998	250,000	(100,000)
1999	250,000	(300,000)
2000	250,000	15,000

28. Parent Corporation, SubOne, and SubTwo have filed consolidated returns since 1996. All of the entities were incorporated in 1995. None of the group members incurred any capital gain or loss transactions during 1995–1998, nor did they make any charitable contributions. Taxable income computations for the members are listed below.

Year	Parent's Taxable Income	SubOne's Taxable Income	SubTwo's Taxable Income	Consolidated Taxable Income
1995*	$100,000	$100,000	$ 40,000	N/A
1996**	100,000	100,000	(40,000)	$160,000
1997**	100,000	(80,000)	(240,000)	?
1998**	100,000	100,000	210,000	?

*Separate return year.
**Consolidated return year.

a. How much of the 1997 loss is apportioned to SubOne and SubTwo? How is this loss treated in generating a refund of prior tax payments?
b. Why would Parent consider electing to forgo the carryback of the 1997 consolidated NOL?
c. In this light, analyze the election to consolidate.

29. The group of Parent Corporation, SubOne, and SubTwo has filed a consolidated return since 1996. The first two entities were incorporated in 1995, and SubTwo came into existence in 1996 through an asset spin-off from Parent. Taxable income computations for the members are shown below. None of the group members incurred any capital gain or loss transactions during 1995–1998, nor did they make any charitable contributions.

Describe the treatment of the group's 1997 consolidated NOL.

Year	Parent's Taxable Income	SubOne's Taxable Income	SubTwo's Taxable Income	Consolidated Taxable Income
1995*	$200,000	$ 70,000	—	$270,000
1996*	100,000	20,000	($ 40,000)	80,000
1997*	100,000	(90,000)	(180,000)	?
1998*	100,000	100,000	210,000	?

*Consolidated return year.

30. Parent Corporation and SubCo have filed consolidated returns since 1996. Both entities were incorporated in 1995. Taxable income computations for the members are shown below. Neither group member incurred any capital gain or loss transactions during 1995–1998, nor did they make any charitable contributions.

Compute the group's 1996, 1997, and 1998 loss carryforward deductions related to SubCo's 1995 NOL.

Year	Parent's Taxable Income	SubCo's Taxable Income	Consolidated Taxable Income
1995*	$100,000	($ 60,000)	N/A
1996**	100,000	(30,000)	$70,000
1997**	100,000	12,000	?
1998**	100,000	70,000	?

*Separate return year.
**Consolidated return year.

31. Parent Corporation's current-year taxable income included $100,000 net income from operations and a $50,000 net long-term capital gain. Parent also made a $40,000 contribution to State University. SubCo produced $70,000 income from operations and incurred a $65,000 short-term capital loss.

    Use the computational worksheet of Figure 8–3 to derive the group members' separate taxable incomes and the group's consolidated taxable income.

32. Parent Corporation sold a plot of undeveloped land to SubCo this year for $100,000. Parent had acquired the land several years ago for $20,000. The consolidated return also reflects the operating results of the parties: Parent generated $130,000 income from operations, and SubCo produced a $20,000 operating loss.
    a. Use the computational worksheet of Figure 8–3 to derive the group members' separate taxable incomes and the group's consolidated taxable income.
    b. Same as (a), except that SubCo sold the land to Outsider Corporation for $110,000 in a subsequent year, when its operating income totaled $30,000 (exclusive of the sale of the land), and Parent's operating income amounted to $90,000.

RESEARCH PROBLEMS

Research Problem 1.   Parent Corporation (3 Noll Street, Shreveport, LA 71102) purchased all of the stock of SubCo in the current year. The parties intend to file their Federal income tax returns on a consolidated basis, effective immediately.

   One of the assets on SubCo's balance sheet was an investment in undeveloped land, acquired by SubCo seven years ago for $50,000. The land now is worth $20,000, and Parent would like to sell the land in the current year to offset its other § 1231 gains that would be fully taxable on the consolidated return.

   It is likely that SubCo will continue to generate small NOLs for the next five years, until the additional investment associated with being a member of a conglomerate enables SubCo to turn a profit.

   Advise Parent on the deductibility of this loss in the current year by summarizing your findings in a letter to the board of directors. *This problem can be solved solely by reviewing materials from the Code and Regulations.*

Partial list of research aids:
Reg. § 1.1502–15.
Prop.Reg. § 1.1502–15.

Research Problem 2.   This is the second year in which Parent and Junior Corporations have filed on a consolidated basis. Both companies have existed for many years, but the common ownership necessary to consolidate was first reached at the end of the second prior tax year. The advantages of consolidation were so strong—the two firms operate in industries that are countercyclical to each other—that the election to file as a group was made almost immediately.

   Now trouble has arisen because a Federal income tax audit of Junior's tax return of three years ago has produced a sizable deficiency. The auditor has asked for an eight-month extension of the statute of limitations to finish her work.

   Jill Robertson, Parent's tax director, wonders whether to agree to the request. Not yet discovered on Parent's own tax return of three years ago is an item that is legitimately deductible but will be difficult to substantiate to the extent expected by the IRS. As a result, Robertson looks forward to the expiration of the three-year statute of limitations on Parent's return. Its expiration will preclude the IRS from ever questioning this item and exposing it to further review.

   Does an extension of the statute of limitations, agreed to with respect to a separate return year of one affiliate member of a consolidated filing group, apply to the entire group? Or will Parent's statute of limitations expire on its own as scheduled? *This problem can be solved solely by reviewing material from the Code and Regulations.*

Research Problem 3.   Eastern Trails (ET) manufactures passenger buses. Its fully owned subsidiary, Eastern Ways (EW), operates a transportation business, running a full schedule of buses to various destinations east of the Mississippi River. Western Trails (WT) is organized similarly (i.e., with the parent manufacturing buses and the 100% subsidiary, Western Ways [WW], operating a transportation line to various stations west of the Mississippi).

The Eastern group is owned by the Eastman family, and the Western group is owned by the Westwood family. Both affiliated groups have filed consolidated returns since inception.

To obtain economies of scale and compete more effectively in a regulated environment, Eastern Trails acquires the Western group in a merger qualifying for favorable tax treatment under § 368(a)(1)(A). After the takeover, ET owns EW and WT, while WT still owns WW, all at 100% ownership levels.

Eastern Trails, the continuing common parent, wants to file a consolidated return including all four companies. ET's controller, Karla Benton, CPA, believes that this is not possible, however. Under § 1504(a)(3)(A), members of one consolidated return group must wait five years before being included in another affiliated group's consolidated return. Analyze the situation for Benton in a memo to the client's file.

Use the tax resources of the internet to address the following questions. Do not restrict your search to the World Wide Web, but include a review of newsgroups and general reference materials, practitioner sites and resources, primary sources of the tax law, chat rooms and discussion groups, and other opportunities.

Research Problem 4.   Most of the controlling law relative to consolidated returns is found in the income tax regulations. Prepare a table of contents for the most important such regulations, currently in effect.

Research Problem 5.   Summarize a ruling issued by the Treasury in the last two years concerning a consolidated return issue. Send an e-mail message to the author of the ruling asking a follow-up question, or clarifying a point addressed in the ruling.

Research Problem 6.   Summarize the income tax treatment of consolidated returns in three other countries. Provide full citations to support your observations. Comment on how and why the laws of those countries might have evolved differently than did the corresponding U.S. provision.

TAXATION OF INTERNATIONAL TRANSACTIONS

LEARNING OBJECTIVES

After completing Chapter 9, you should be able to:

1. Use the foreign tax credit provisions.

2. Apply the rules for sourcing income and allocating deductions into U.S. and foreign categories.

3. Utilize the U.S. tax provisions concerning nonresident alien individuals and foreign corporations.

4. Appreciate the tax benefits available to certain U.S. individuals working abroad.

5. Apply the U.S. tax rules for foreign corporations controlled by U.S. persons.

6. Explain how foreign currency exchange affects the tax consequences of international transactions.

OVERVIEW OF INTERNATIONAL TAXATION

International taxation is an integral part of the U.S. involvement in the world economy. In an age when economic isolation is no longer feasible for most countries, the United States, as a large and influential nation, plays a particularly important role in the global economy. In 1995, U.S. holdings of foreign stocks amounted to $411.1 billion, and U.S. banks reported $809 billion in liabilities to foreigners and international financial institutions. As Table 9–1 shows, both U.S. investment abroad and foreign investment in the United States increased significantly from 1986 through 1994.

The world economy also has implications for the U.S. domestic economy. The global economy influences the interest rate that a small U.S. business pays for new equipment or a U.S. family pays for a new home, automobile, or television set.

▼ **TABLE 9–1**
U.S. Assets Abroad and Foreign Assets in the United States (in Billions at Current Cost)

	U.S. Assets Abroad	Foreign Assets in United States
1986	$1,479.1	$1,434.2
1990	2,066.4	2,317.5
1994	2,477.7	3,158.6

SOURCE: U.S. Department of Commerce, Bureau of Economic Analysis.

More and more U.S. corporations are developing international ties. Even the local oil company and cotton cooperative in a city of less than 200,000 are entering into negotiations with former Soviet bloc nations. For 1992, the 7,500 largest U.S.-controlled foreign corporations (CFCs) held $1.6 trillion in total assets and reported receipts of $1.2 trillion. These CFCs are incorporated in countries around the world, including Europe, Latin America, Africa, Asia, Oceania, and Canada. In 1995, the market value of U.S. investment abroad was almost $2.5 trillion.

As a result of this growing globalization of business, tax practitioners who are employed by a company with even a small amount of foreign-source income or who have clients generating foreign-source income must deal with (at minimum) the foreign tax credit and U.S. income tax treaties. More complex international transactions require an in-depth knowledge of international taxation.

U.S. persons with international transactions encounter many of the same Federal tax laws as any U.S. taxpayer. Income is subject to U.S. taxation, certain expenses and losses are deductible, and credits are available. Earnings of domestic corporations face double taxation. However, U.S. taxpayers with international transactions face another set of provisions that apply to international business. These laws are meant to prevent double (two-country) taxation, allow the United States to remain competitive internationally, and prevent taxpayers from evading U.S. taxes by moving income-producing activities abroad.

▼

EXAMPLE 1

Jorge Ramirez is a U.S. citizen working as chief accountant for a U.S. corporation's bridge building project in Brazil. His annual salary is $120,000, and the company annually provides $35,000 of living expenses for Jorge and his family. Jorge has U.S. investments that earn about $2,500 a year, and he is a shareholder in a Brazilian corporation that is controlled by U.S. persons.

Without special provisions to deal with Jorge's foreign-earned income, he would be subject to double taxation—once by the United States, which taxes worldwide income on the basis of citizenship or residency, and once by Brazil, which taxes on the basis of residency. Additionally, Jorge's company might be at a competitive disadvantage when bidding on such contracts. If the company compensated its employees for this double taxation, it would incur a greater wage and salary expense than companies from countries where double taxation was not a problem. Further, without special U.S. tax provisions, Jorge and the other U.S. shareholders could invest in the Brazilian corporation, which would not incur any U.S. taxation until distributions were made to shareholders. ▼

THE FOREIGN TAX CREDIT

1 LEARNING OBJECTIVE
Use the foreign tax credit provisions.

The United States retains the right to tax its citizens and residents on their worldwide taxable income. This approach can result in double taxation and presents a potential problem to U.S. persons who invest abroad.

To reduce the possibility of double taxation, the U.S. Congress enacted the **foreign tax credit (FTC)** provisions. Under these provisions, a qualified taxpayer is allowed a tax credit for foreign income taxes paid. The credit is a dollar-for-dollar reduction of U.S. income tax liability. For 1992, the more than 5,000 U.S. corporations claiming the FTC reported worldwide taxable income of $194.2 billion. Approximately 45 percent of this income (or $86.9 billion) was from foreign sources. The FTC reduced 1992 U.S. taxes from $65.5 billion to $44 billion for these U.S. corporations. In the first quarter of 1996, income receipts on U.S. direct investment abroad were $24 billion. Without the benefit of the FTC, much of this income would be subject to double taxation.

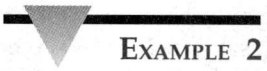

EXAMPLE 2

Ace Tools, Inc., a U.S. corporation, has a branch operation in Mexico, from which it earns taxable income of $750,000 for the current year. Ace pays income tax of $150,000 on these earnings to the Mexican tax authorities. Ace must also include the $750,000 in gross income for U.S. tax purposes. Assume that, before considering the FTC, Ace would owe $255,000 in U.S. income taxes on this foreign-source income. Thus, total taxes on the $750,000 could equal $405,000 ($150,000 + $255,000), a 54% effective rate. But Ace takes an FTC of $150,000 against its U.S. tax liability on the foreign-source income. Ace Tools' total taxes on the $750,000 now are $255,000 ($150,000 + $105,000), a 34% effective rate. ▼

THE CREDIT PROVISIONS

The Direct Credit.   Section 901 provides a direct FTC to U.S. taxpayers who pay or incur a foreign income tax. For purposes of the direct credit, only the taxpayer who bears the legal incidence of the foreign tax is eligible for the credit. Ace Tools, in Example 2 above, would be eligible for the direct credit.

The Indirect Credit.   If a U.S. corporation operates in a foreign country through a branch, the direct credit is available for foreign taxes paid. If, however, a U.S. corporation operates in a foreign country through a foreign subsidiary, the direct credit is not available for foreign taxes paid by the foreign corporation. An indirect credit is available to U.S. corporate taxpayers who receive actual or constructive dividends from foreign corporations that have paid a foreign tax on earnings. These foreign taxes are deemed paid by the corporate shareholders in the same proportion as the dividends actually or constructively received bear to the foreign corporation's post-1986 undistributed earnings and profits (E & P). Section 78 requires a domestic corporation that chooses the FTC for deemed-paid foreign taxes to *gross up* dividend income by the amount of deemed-paid taxes.

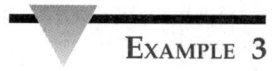

EXAMPLE 3

Wren, Inc., a domestic corporation, owns 50% of Finch, Inc., a foreign corporation. Wren receives a dividend of $120,000 from Finch. Finch paid foreign taxes of $500,000 on post-1986 E & P. Finch's post-1986 E & P (after taxes) totals $1,200,000. Wren's deemed-paid foreign taxes for FTC purposes are $50,000.

Cash dividend from Finch	$120,000
Deemed-paid foreign taxes $\left(\$500,000 \times \dfrac{\$120,000}{\$1,200,000}\right)$	50,000
Gross income to Wren	$170,000

Wren must include the $50,000 in gross income for the gross-up adjustment if the FTC is elected. ▼

Certain ownership requirements must be met before the indirect credit is available to a domestic corporation. The domestic corporation must own 10 percent or more of the voting stock of the foreign corporation. The credit is also available for deemed-paid foreign taxes of second- and third-tier foreign corporations if the 10 percent ownership requirement is met at the second- and third-tier level. A 5 percent indirect ownership requirement must also be met. The § 902 ownership requirements are summarized in Figure 9–1.

FTC Limitations.   To prevent foreign taxes from being credited against U.S. taxes levied on U.S.-source taxable income, the FTC is subject to a limitation. The FTC for any taxable year cannot exceed the lesser of the actual foreign taxes paid

▼ **FIGURE 9–1**
Section 902 Ownership
Requirements

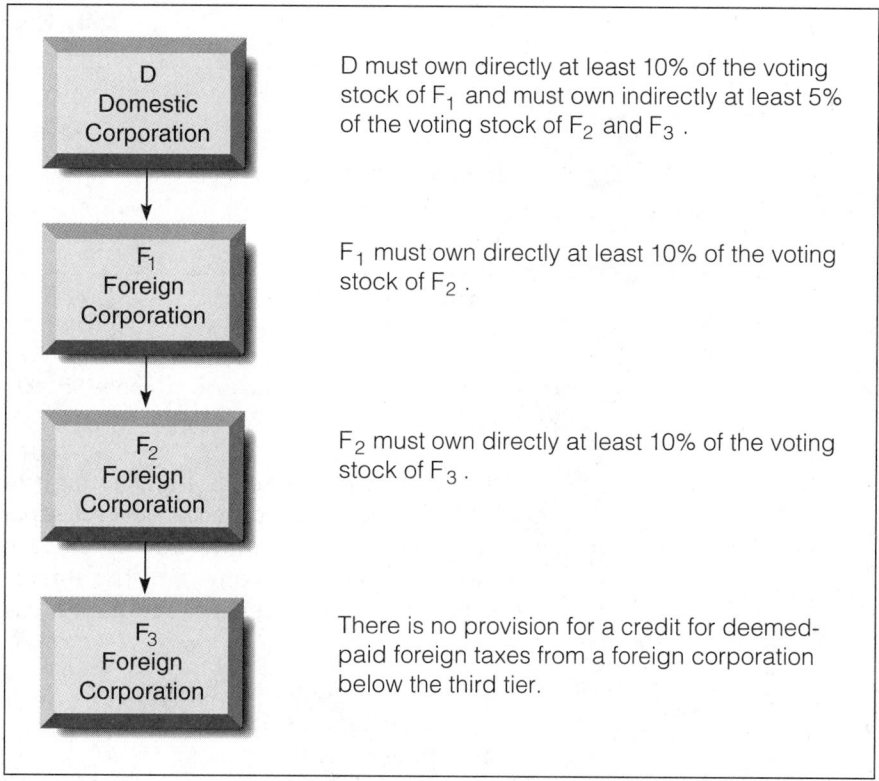

D must own directly at least 10% of the voting stock of F_1 and must own indirectly at least 5% of the voting stock of F_2 and F_3.

F_1 must own directly at least 10% of the voting stock of F_2.

F_2 must own directly at least 10% of the voting stock of F_3.

There is no provision for a credit for deemed-paid foreign taxes from a foreign corporation below the third tier.

or accrued, or the U.S. taxes (before the FTC) on foreign-source taxable income (the general limitation). The latter limitation formula is derived in the following manner.

$$\text{U.S. tax} \atop \text{before FTC} \times \frac{\text{Foreign-source taxable income}}{\text{Worldwide taxable income}^1}$$

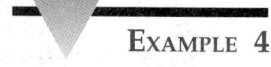

EXAMPLE 4

Terry, a U.S. resident, invests in foreign securities. Her worldwide taxable income for the tax year is $120,000, consisting of $100,000 in salary from a U.S. employer and $20,000 of income from foreign sources. Foreign taxes of $6,000 were withheld by foreign tax authorities. Assume that Terry's U.S. tax before the FTC is $33,600. Her FTC is $5,600 [$33,600 × ($20,000/$120,000)]. Her net U.S. tax liability is $28,000. ▼

As Example 4 illustrates, the limitation can prevent the total amount of foreign taxes paid in high-tax jurisdictions from being credited. Taxpayers could overcome this problem by generating additional foreign-source income that is subject to no, or low, foreign taxation.

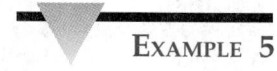

EXAMPLE 5

Compare Domestic Corporation's FTC situation when the corporation has only $500,000 of highly taxed foreign-source income with the situation where Domestic also has $100,000 of low-taxed foreign-source interest income.

---

[1] For FTC purposes, the taxable income of an individual, estate, or trust is computed without any deduction for personal exemptions. §904(b)(1).

	Only Highly Taxed Income	With Low-Taxed Interest
Foreign-source income	$500,000	$600,000
Foreign taxes	275,000	280,000
U.S.-source income	700,000	700,000
U.S. taxes (34%)	408,000	442,000
FTC limitation	170,000*	204,000**

*$408,000 × ($500,000/$1,200,000).

**$442,000 × ($600,000/$1,300,000).

Domestic's foreign taxes increase by only $5,000, while its FTC limitation increases by $34,000. ▼

To prevent the *cross-crediting* of foreign taxes as in Example 5, Congress has enacted legislation providing for several separate limitation *baskets*. These provisions require that a separate limitation be calculated for certain categories of foreign-source taxable income and the foreign taxes attributable to that income. Section 904(d) provides separate limitation baskets for the following.

- Passive income.
- High withholding tax income.
- Financial services income.
- Shipping income.
- Dividends from each noncontrolled § 902 corporation.
- Dividends from a domestic international sales corporation (DISC) or former DISC to the extent they are treated as foreign-source income.
- Taxable income attributable to foreign trade income under § 923(b).
- Distributions from a foreign sales corporation (FSC) or former FSC out of E & P attributable to foreign trade income or qualified interest and carrying charges under § 263(c).

All other foreign-source income is included in a general (or overall) limitation basket. These separate limitations are diagrammed in Concept Summary 9–1.

EXAMPLE 6

Wood Products, Inc., a U.S. corporation, has a foreign branch in Canada that earns taxable income of $1,000,000 from manufacturing operations and $500,000 from shipping operations. Wood Products also earns Canada-source high withholding tax interest of $100,000. Wood Products pays foreign taxes of $400,000 (40%), $250,000 (50%), and $15,000 (15%), respectively, on this foreign-source income. The corporation also earns $4,000,000 of U.S.-source taxable income, resulting in worldwide taxable income of $5,600,000. The U.S. taxes before the FTC are $1,904,000 (at 34%). The following tabulation illustrates the effect of the separate limitation baskets on cross-crediting.

Foreign Income Category	Net Taxable Amount	Foreign Taxes	U.S. Tax before FTC at 34%	FTC with Separate Limits
Manufacturing	$1,000,000	$400,000	$340,000	$340,000
Shipping	500,000	250,000	170,000	170,000
High withholding tax interest	100,000	15,000	34,000	15,000
Total	$1,600,000	$665,000	$544,000	$525,000

Concept Summary 9–1

Foreign Tax Credit: Separate Income Limitations

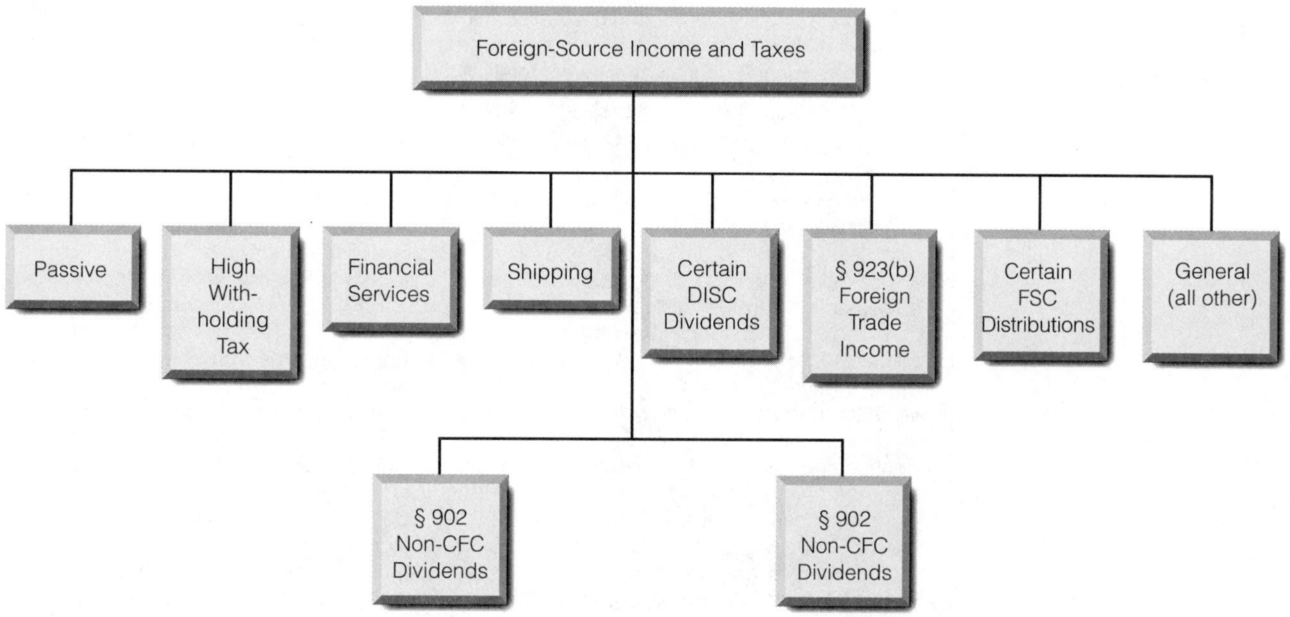

Foreign-Source Income and Taxes

- Passive
- High With-holding Tax
- Financial Services
- Shipping
- Certain DISC Dividends
- § 923(b) Foreign Trade Income
- Certain FSC Distributions
- General (all other)

- § 902 Non-CFC Dividends
- § 902 Non-CFC Dividends

Without the separate limitation provisions, the FTC would be the lesser of $665,000 foreign taxes paid or accrued, or $544,000 [i.e., $1,904,000 × ($1,600,000/$5,600,000)]. The separate limitation provisions reduce the total FTC by $19,000 ($544,000 − $525,000). The foreign-source income taxed at the foreign tax rates of 40% and 50% cannot be aggregated with foreign-source income taxed at only 15%.

See Exhibit 9–1 for Wood Products' Form 1118 for its general limitation basket. ▼

The limitations can result in unused (noncredited) foreign taxes for the tax year. A two-year carryback and a five-year carryover of excess foreign taxes are allowed. The taxes can be credited in years when the formula limitation for that year exceeds the foreign taxes attributable to the same tax year. The carryback and carryover provision is available only within the separate baskets. In other words, excess foreign taxes in one basket cannot be carried over unless there is an excess limitation in the same basket for the carryover year.

ETHICAL CONSIDERATIONS

More Effort Than It's Worth?

Studies have shown that the record keeping required to comply with the § 902 non-CFC dividend income basket can consume many staff-hours and, thus, be very expensive for companies. It has been suggested that some companies' compliance with this provision may be limited, especially where dividend income is received from 50 to 200 separate § 902 non-CFCs. A tax provision is a "good law" when, among other considerations, it is fair and efficient. Is the separate limitation for dividend

▼ **EXHIBIT 9–1**
Form 1118 Illustrated

The following Form 1118 has been completed using the information from Example 6. Additional pertinent information regarding Wood Products, Inc., follows.

- The taxpayer's employer identification number is 75–2837157; the country of incorporation is the United States.
- Gross income from the manufacturing operations of the Canadian branch is $5,000,000. Deductions definitely allocable to the branch's manufacturing operations total $3,700,000; the apportioned share of deductions not definitely allocable to the branch's manufacturing operations totals $300,000.
- Wood Products accrues its foreign taxes for purposes of the FTC.

This Form 1118 is completed for the general limitation category (basket) of income. A summary of the separate limitation FTCs from Part II, Schedule B, of each separate Form 1118 is given on Part III, Schedule B, of the Form 1118. Form 1118 actually contains 6 pages, but pages 3 through 6 have been omitted from this illustration. They are used for calculating deemed-paid FTCs and making certain adjustments to the FTC.

Schedule A of Form 1118 is used to report the separate limitation income and/or losses from operations in each country. This Form 1118, Schedule A, presents information for the manufacturing income (general limitation income). The country code for Canada (CA) is given on Line 1A. Line 7A lists the gross income from the manufacturing operations in Canada. Line 8A shows total gross income from Canada for this separate limitation basket. Line 9A, column (d) is used to report expenses definitely allocable to manufacturing income, i.e., $3,700,000. Line 10A shows the apportioned share of deductions not directly allocable to the manufacturing income, i.e. $300,000. Total deductions are summarized on Line 11A. Line 12A is used to determine net separate limitation income or loss, in this case, $1,000,000 [$5,000,000 (Line 8 total) − $4,000,000 (Line 11 total)]. Schedule B, Part I, is a summary of the foreign taxes paid, accrued, or deemed paid on the separate category income—manufacturing income on the Schedule B shown. Part II of Schedule B is used to calculate the FTC limitation and determine the credit.

Part III of Form 1118 is used to summarize all of the separate limitation basket FTCs. Line 2 on Schedule B, Part III, shows the $15,000 FTC allowed for high withholding tax interest, Line 4 is used to report the $170,000 FTC for the shipping income, and Line 9 is used to report the $340,000 FTC for the general limitation income (manufacturing in this case). The total FTC of $525,000 is the sum of these amounts and is reported on Line 12 of Part III. This amount is then entered on the corporation's Schedule J, Line 4a of Form 1120.

continued

income from each § 902 non-CFC fair when some companies comply, while others may not due to the expense of adequate record keeping? Can a provision that is so costly to companies be considered efficient?

Foreign Losses. Citizens and residents of the United States who hold foreign investments or operations directly (e.g., through a branch operation) or through a conduit entity (e.g., a partnership) have the opportunity to offset foreign losses against U.S.-source income, thereby reducing the U.S. income tax due on U.S.-source income. If the foreign country in which the loss is generated (sourced) taxes subsequent income from these foreign operations, the FTC could reduce or eliminate any U.S. tax on the income.

To prevent this loss of tax revenue to the United States, tax law provides that the overall foreign losses should be recaptured as U.S.-source income for FTC purposes.[2] This is accomplished by reducing the numerator of the FTC limitation

[2] § 904(f)(1).

Form 1118
(Rev. July 1994)

Internal Revenue Service
Department of the Treasury

Foreign Tax Credit—Corporations

▶ Attach to the corporation's tax return.

OMB No. 1545-0122

Name: *Wood Products, Inc.*

Employer identification number: 75 : 283 : 7157

Complete this form for credit for taxes paid on the following separate limitation categories of income. See instructions. **Use a separate Form 1118 for each category.** Check only one box on each form.

- ☐ Passive Income
- ☐ High Withholding Tax Interest
- ☐ Financial Services Income
- ☐ Shipping Income
- ☐ Dividends From a DISC or Former DISC
- ☐ Taxable Income Attributable To Foreign Trade Income
- ☐ Certain Distributions From a FSC or Former FSC
- ☒ General Limitation Income (see instructions)
- ☐ Dividends From **Each** Noncontrolled Section 902 Corporation (see instructions):

For calendar year 19 ___, or other tax year beginning ___, 19 ___, and ending ___, 19 ___

Name of Foreign Corporation ▶ ___ Country of Incorporation ▶ ___

Schedule A — Separate Limitation Income or (Loss) Before Adjustments

Separate Limitation Gross Income or (Loss) From Sources Outside the United States
(*INCLUDE* Foreign Branch and Section 863(b) Gross Income here *and* on Schedule F—See instructions)

1. Foreign Country or U.S. Possession (Enter two-letter code from page 8 of instructions. Use a separate line for each.)	2. Deemed Dividends (see instructions)		3. Other Dividends		4. Interest	5. Gross Rents, Royalties, and License Fees	6. Gross Income From Performance of Services	7. Other (attach schedule)	8. Total (add columns 2a through 7)
	(a) Exclude gross-up	(b) Gross-up (sec. 78)	(a) Exclude gross-up	(b) Gross-up (sec. 78)					
A CA	-0-	-0-	-0-	-0-	-0-	-0-	-0-	5,000,000	5,000,000
B									
C									
D									
E									
F									
G									
H									
Totals (add lines A through H)	-0-	-0-	-0-	-0-	-0-	-0-	-0-	5,000,000	5,000,000

Separate Limitation Deductions
(*INCLUDE* Foreign Branch and Section 863(b) Deductions here *and* on Schedule F—See instructions)

	9. Definitely Allocable Deductions					10. Apportioned Share of Deductions Not Definitely Allocable (enter amount from applicable line of Schedule H, Part II, column (d))	11. Total Deductions (add columns 9e and 10)	12. Total Separate Limitation Income or (Loss) Before Adjustments (subtract column 11 from column 8)
	Rental, Royalty, and Licensing Expenses		(c) Expenses Related to Gross Income From Performance of Services	(d) Other Definitely Allocable Deductions	(e) Total Definitely Allocable Deductions (add columns 9a through 9d)			
	(a) Depreciation, Depletion, and Amortization	(b) Other Expenses						
A	-0-	-0-	-0-	3,700,000	3,700,000	300,000	4,000,000	1,000,000
B								
C								
D								
E								
F								
G								
H								
Totals	-0-	-0-	-0-	3,700,000	3,700,000	300,000	4,000,000	1,000,000

For Paperwork Reduction Act Notice, see page 1 of the Instructions.   Cat. No. 10900F   Form **1118** (Rev. 7-94)

continued

Schedule B   Foreign Tax Credit

Part I—Foreign Taxes Paid, Accrued, and Deemed Paid

1. Credit is Claimed for Taxes: ☐ Paid ☒ Accrued		2. Foreign Taxes Paid or Accrued (attach schedule showing amounts in foreign currency and conversion rate(s) used)							3. Tax Deemed Paid (from Schedule C, Part I, column 9, and Schedule C, Part II, column 10)
		Tax Withheld at Source on:			Other Foreign Taxes Paid or Accrued on:			(h) Total Foreign Taxes Paid or Accrued (add columns 2a through 2g)	
	Date Paid / Date Accrued	(a) Dividends	(b) Interest	(c) Rents, Royalties, and License Fees	(d) Section 863(b) Income	(e) Foreign Branch Income	(f) Services Income	(g) Other	
A	12-31-96	-0-	-0-	-0-	-0-	400,000	-0-	-0-	400,000	400,000
B										
C										
D										
E										
F										
G										
H										
Totals (add lines A through H)		-0-	-0-	-0-	-0-	400,000	-0-	-0-	400,000	400,000

Part II—Separate Limitation Foreign Tax Credit

Foreign Tax Credit Limitation:

1	Total foreign taxes paid or accrued (from Part I, column 2h, "Totals" line)	400,000
2	Total taxes deemed paid (from Part I, column 3, "Totals" line)	-0-
3	Reductions of taxes paid, accrued, or deemed paid (enter total from Schedule G, Part II)	(-0-)
4	Carryback or carryover (attach schedule showing computation in detail—see **Carryback and Carryover of Excess Foreign Taxes** on page 3 of the instructions)	-0-
5	Total foreign taxes (combine lines 1 through 4)	400,000
6	*Numerator of Limitation Fraction.*—If required to complete Schedule J, enter the result from the applicable column of Schedule J, Part I, line 11. If **not** required to complete Schedule J, enter the result from the "Totals" line of column 12 of the applicable Schedule A	100,000
7a	Total taxable income from all sources (enter taxable income from the corporation's tax return)	5,600,000
b	Adjustments to line 7a. (See instructions.)	-0-
c	*Denominator of Limitation Fraction.*—Subtract line 7b from line 7a	5,600,000
8	Divide line 6 by line 7c. (Enter the resulting fraction as a decimal less than 1.00000. If line 6 is greater than line 7c, enter 1.)	.17857
9	Total U.S. income tax against which credit is allowed (regular tax liability (as defined in section 26(b)) minus possessions tax credit determined under section 936)	1,904,000
10	Limitation (multiply line 8 by line 9). (See instructions.)	340,000
11	Foreign tax credit (enter the smaller of line 5 or line 10 here and on the appropriate line of Part III)	340,000

Part III—Summary of Separate Limitation Foreign Tax Credits from Schedule B, Part II of Separate Forms 1118 (Complete Only Once)

1	Credit for taxes on passive income	15,000
2	Credit for taxes on high withholding tax interest	
3	Credit for taxes on financial services income	170,000
4	Credit for taxes on shipping income	
5	Credit for taxes on dividends from each noncontrolled section 902 corporation (combine all such credits on this line)	
6	Credit for taxes on dividends from a DISC or former DISC	
7	Credit for taxes on taxable income attributable to foreign trade income	
8	Credit for taxes on certain distributions from a FSC or former FSC	
9	Credit for taxes on General Limitation Income	340,000
10	Total (add lines 1 through 9)	525,000
11	Reduction in credit for international boycott operations (see instructions)	-0-
12	**Total foreign tax credit** (subtract line 11 from line 10). Enter here and on the corporation's tax return	525,000

TAX IN THE NEWS

FOREIGN TAXES AND THE FTC—SOME STATISTICS

The United Kingdom, Germany, Japan, and Canada accounted for approximately 35 percent of the foreign-source income earned and 41 percent of the foreign taxes paid by U.S. corporations for 1992. U.S. manufacturers claimed more than 68 percent of the FTCs taken for 1992. U.S. banks showed the largest increase in FTCs, however, increasing from $0.4 billion for 1991 to $1.3 billion for 1992.

SOURCE: *SOI Bulletin*, Winter 1995–96, p. 111.

formula. Foreign-source taxable income is reduced by the lesser of (1) the remaining unrecaptured overall foreign loss or (2) 50 percent of foreign-source taxable income for the taxable year (unless the taxpayer elects to recapture a greater percentage). Unrecaptured foreign losses are carried over indefinitely until recaptured. Losses incurred before 1976 are not subject to recapture.

EXAMPLE 7

Dual, Inc., a domestic corporation, operates a branch in Japan. The earnings record of the branch is as follows.

Year	Taxable Income (Loss)	Foreign Taxes Paid
1994	($15,000)	–0–
1995	(20,000)	–0–
1996	(20,000)	–0–
1997	40,000	$20,000

For 1994–1997, Dual has U.S.-source taxable income of $300,000 each year. Dual's 1997 U.S. tax liability before the FTC is $115,600. Its overall foreign loss is $55,000 for 1994–1996. The FTC limitation for 1997 is $6,800, $115,600 × {[$40,000 – (50% × $40,000)]/$340,000}. ▼

These provisions will not necessarily reach the situation where overall foreign losses have been incurred and the U.S. taxpayer disposes of trade or business property used predominantly outside the United States before any or all of the loss is recaptured. The statutory solution to this problem is that the U.S. taxpayer generates U.S.-source income in the amount of the lesser of the fair market value of the property less its adjusted basis, or the remaining amount of unrecaptured foreign losses.

When a taxpayer has a loss for the tax year in one or more foreign-source categories (baskets), the loss must be apportioned pro rata to foreign-source categories with income for the tax year. If there is an excess foreign loss (i.e., foreign losses exceed foreign income in all categories), the excess foreign loss then reduces U.S.-source income. A U.S. loss for the tax year is apportioned pro rata to foreign-source income in each category, but only after the apportionment of any foreign losses to those income categories.

The Alternative Minimum Tax FTC. For purposes of the alternative minimum tax, the FTC is limited to the lesser of the credit for regular tax purposes or

90 percent of the tentative minimum tax before the credit.[3] The 10 percent cutback is calculated on the tentative minimum tax without regard to the alternative tax NOL deduction. The general FTC limitation is calculated by using alternative minimum taxable income rather than taxable income in the denominator of the formula and the tentative minimum tax rather than the regular tax. The source of alternative minimum taxable income must be determined for the purpose of foreign-source taxable income.

Other Considerations.   In order for a foreign levy to qualify for the FTC, it must be a tax, and its predominant character must be that of an income tax in the U.S. sense.[4] A levy is a tax if it is a compulsory payment, as contrasted with a payment for a specific economic benefit such as the right to extract oil. A tax's predominant character is that of an income tax in the U.S. sense if it reaches realized net gain and is not dependent on being credited against the income tax of another country (not a *soak-up* tax). Persons whose foreign taxes are partially creditable because only a portion of the foreign levy is considered an income tax in the U.S. sense are dual-capacity taxpayers.[5] A tax that is levied in lieu of an income tax is also creditable.[6]

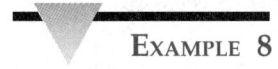

EXAMPLE 8

Rigs, a domestic corporation, receives oil extraction income from operations in a foreign country. The other country levies a 50% tax on extraction income and a 30% tax on all other taxable income derived within the country. If Rigs pays $700,000 in taxes on its extraction income to the foreign country, only $420,000 [$700,000 × (30% ÷ 50%)] of that amount is creditable as an income tax. ▼

EXAMPLE 9

Hoops, a domestic corporation, generates $2 million of taxable income from operations in Larissa, a foreign country. Larissan law levies a tax on income generated in Larissa by foreign residents only in cases in which the country of residence (such as the United States) allows a tax credit for foreign taxes paid. Hoops will not be allowed an FTC for taxes paid to Larissa, because the foreign tax is a soak-up tax. ▼

For purposes of the FTC, foreign taxes are attributable to the year in which they are paid or accrued. Under § 905, taxpayers using the cash method of accounting for tax purposes may elect to take the FTC in the year in which the foreign taxes accrue. The election is binding on the taxpayer for the year in which it is made, and for all subsequent years. Taxes paid in a foreign currency are translated to U.S. dollars for FTC purposes at the exchange rate in effect when the taxes are actually paid.[7] Any adjustment of foreign taxes paid by a foreign corporation is translated at the rate in effect at the time of adjustment. Any refund or credit is translated at the rate in effect at the time the foreign taxes were originally paid.

The FTC is elective for any particular tax year. If the taxpayer does not "choose" to take the FTC, § 164 allows a deduction for foreign taxes paid or incurred. However, a taxpayer cannot take a credit and a deduction for the same foreign income taxes.[8] A taxpayer can take a deduction in the same year as an FTC for foreign taxes that are not creditable (e.g., soak-up taxes).

---

[3] § 59. A "small corporation" exception is available.
[4] Reg. § 1.901–2.
[5] Reg. § 1.901–2A.

[6] § 903 and Reg. § 1.903–1.
[7] §§ 986(b) and 987.
[8] § 275.

ETHICAL CONSIDERATIONS

Taxes on Foreign Investments and the Public Good

The decision to invest abroad is strongly influenced by the availability of the FTC. Without the FTC, U.S. investors, in many cases, would incur double taxation—once by the United States (based on residency or citizenship) and then by the country in which the investment is made (based on source). The FTC generally allows the U.S. investor, with regard to tax consequences, to be indifferent between investment abroad and in the United States when the tax rates are equal. As a result of the FTC, the investor will receive the same net return (after taxes).

You are the CEO of a multinational corporation based in Iowa. Your Vice President of Taxation brings you a draft of a position paper prepared by a national tax policy think tank of which she is a member. The paper argues that only a deduction should be allowed for foreign taxes incurred by U.S. taxpayers. The argument is based on "public good" considerations. Even though investors may be indifferent to the location of their investments, the U.S. "public good" is not served when the taxes paid on those investments remain offshore. Do you agree? How would you propose to modify the association's position?

POSSESSIONS CORPORATIONS

To encourage the economic development of U.S. possessions, Congress enacted a credit provision for income from operations in U.S. possessions. Domestic corporations could elect to receive a § 936 credit against U.S. taxes. The credit is equal to the portion of the U.S. tax attributable to the sum of possession-source taxable income and qualified investment income, even if no tax is paid or due to the possession. This is referred to as a *tax-sparing* credit. No additional credit or deduction is allowed for income taxes actually paid to the possession. A number of pharmaceutical companies, including Eli Lilly Company, have used subsidiaries with operations in Puerto Rico to take advantage of this and local tax benefits. The pharmaceutical and electrical machinery industries receive more than 60 percent of the total § 936 credits allowed. The Congressional Budget Office estimated that the § 936 incentive would result in $15 billion of tax revenue losses between 1993 and 1997. For this reason, in 1996 Congress enacted legislation that repealed the credit except for existing claimants. For § 936 corporations conducting an active trade or business in a possession on October 13, 1995, the credit will be phased out by January 1, 2006. A § 936 corporation that adds a new line of business after October 13, 1995, will cease to be eligible for the credit.

The phase-out period rules apply differently to corporations in different circumstances. For example, credit claimants in Puerto Rico that use the economic activity limitation will calculate the credit under new § 30A, which provides a cap on the credit based on possession income over the five preceding tax years. In some cases, the phase-out period will end before 2006.

The credit is allowed against the U.S. tax attributable to foreign-source taxable income from the active conduct of a trade or business in a U.S. possession. It is also allowed on the sale or exchange of substantially all the assets used by the domestic corporation in that active trade or business. The credit is not allowed against certain taxes, though, such as the accumulated earnings tax under § 531 and the personal holding company tax under § 541.

The credit is not available for income received in the United States unless it is possession-source income received from an unrelated person and is attributable to an active trade or business conducted in a possession.

The credit is not available for income from intangible assets, such as formulas and patents. Intangible property income is includible in taxable income by a domestic corporation as U.S.-source income. If a domestic corporation elects the credit, however, all of its shareholders who are U.S. persons include their pro rata share of that item in gross income as U.S.-source income. In this case, the domestic corporation is not taxed on such income.

EXAMPLE 10

A qualified possessions corporation generates the following foreign-source income on which it pays the following foreign taxes.

Taxable Income	Source	Foreign Taxes
$450,000 active trade or business income	Possession	$40,000
10,000 passive investment income	Possession	–0–
40,000 investment income	Nonpossession	16,000

Assume that the corporation's worldwide taxable income is $500,000 and its U.S. tax before the FTC is $170,000. The § 936 possessions corporation credit is $153,000 (34% × $450,000) before consideration of the § 936 limitation, and the direct FTC is $13,600, the lesser of $16,000 or $13,600 [$170,000 × ($40,000/$500,000)]. ▼

The 1993 tax act initiated two alternative limits on the credit. The taxpayer makes an irrevocable election to apply one of these limitations.

SOURCING OF INCOME AND ALLOCATION OF DEDUCTIONS

2 LEARNING OBJECTIVE
Apply the rules for sourcing income and allocating deductions into U.S. and foreign categories.

The sourcing of income within or without the United States has a direct bearing on a number of tax provisions. The numerator of the FTC limitation formula is foreign-source taxable income. Generally, **nonresident aliens** and foreign corporations are subject to Federal taxation only on U.S.-source income. The foreign earned income exclusion is available only for foreign-source income.

INCOME SOURCED WITHIN THE UNITED STATES

The determination of the source depends on the type of income realized. This makes the classification of income an important consideration (e.g., income from the sale of property versus income for the use of property). A detailed discussion of the characterization of income, however, is beyond the scope of this chapter. Section 861 contains source rules for most types of income. Other rules pertaining to the source of income are found in §§ 862–865.

Interest.   Interest income received from the U.S. government, from the District of Columbia, and from noncorporate U.S. residents or domestic corporations is sourced within the United States. There are a few exceptions to this rule, most notably, certain interest received from a resident alien individual or domestic corporation. This exception applies if an 80 percent foreign business requirement is met. Interest received on amounts deposited with a foreign branch of a U.S. corporation is also treated as foreign-source income if the branch is engaged in the commercial banking business.

EXAMPLE 11

John holds a bond issued by Delta, a domestic corporation. For the immediately preceding three tax years, 82% of Delta's gross income was active foreign business income. The interest income that John receives for the tax year from Delta is foreign-source income. ▼

Dividends. Dividends received from domestic corporations (other than certain possessions corporations) are sourced within the United States. Generally, dividends paid by a foreign corporation are foreign-source income. An exception to this rule applies, however, if 25 percent or more of a foreign corporation's gross income for the immediately preceding three tax years was effectively connected with the conduct of a U.S. trade or business. In this case, the dividends received in the taxable year are U.S.-source income to the extent of the proportion of gross income that was **effectively connected** with the conduct of a U.S. trade or business for the immediately preceding three-year period. Dividends from **foreign sales corporations (FSCs)** and domestic international sales corporations (DISCs) can be treated as U.S.-source income.

EXAMPLE 12

Ann receives dividend income from the following corporations for the tax year.

Amount	Corporation	Effectively Connected Income for Past 3 Years	Active Foreign Business Income for Past 3 Years	U.S.-Source Income
$500	Green, domestic	85%	15%	$500
600	Brown, domestic	13%	87%	600
300	Orange, foreign	80%	20%	240

The 80% active foreign business requirement affects only interest income received from Green Corporation and Brown Corporation, not dividend income. The dividends received from Green and Brown are U.S.-source income. Since Orange Corporation is a foreign corporation meeting the 25% test, 80% of the dividend from Orange is U.S.-source income. ▼

Personal Services Income. The source of income from personal services is determined by the location in which the services are performed (within or without the United States). A limited *commercial traveler* exception is available. Personal services income must meet the following requirements to avoid being classified as U.S.-source income.

- The services must be performed by a nonresident alien who is in the United States for 90 days or less during the taxable year;
- The compensation may not exceed $3,000 in total for the services performed in the United States; and
- The services must be performed on behalf of
  - a nonresident alien, foreign partnership, or foreign corporation that is not engaged in a U.S. trade or business, or
  - an office or place of business maintained in a foreign country or possession of the United States by an individual who is a citizen or resident of the United States, a domestic partnership, or a domestic corporation.

EXAMPLE 13

Mark, a nonresident alien, is an engineer employed by a foreign oil company. He spent four weeks in the United States arranging the purchase of field equipment for his company. His salary for the four weeks was $3,500. Even though the oil company is not engaged in a U.S. trade or business, and Mark was in the United States for less than 90 days during the taxable year, the income is U.S.-source income because it exceeds $3,000. ▼

The issue of whether income is derived from the performance of personal services is important in determining the income's source. The courts have held that a corporation can perform personal services[9] and that, in the absence of capital as an income-producing factor, personal services income can arise even though there is no recipient of the services.[10] If payment is received for services performed partly within and partly without the United States, the income must be allocated for source purposes on some reasonable basis, such as days worked.[11]

Rents and Royalties.   The source of income received for the use of tangible property is the country in which the property producing the income is located. The source of income received for the use of intangible property (e.g., patents, copyrights, secret processes and formulas) is the country in which the property producing the income is used.

Sale or Exchange of Property.   Income from the disposition of U.S. real property interests is U.S.-source income. The definition of a U.S. real property interest is discussed subsequently under the Foreign Investment in Real Property Tax Act (FIRPTA). Generally, the location of real property determines the source of any income derived from the property.

The source of income from the sale of personal property (assets other than real property) depends on several factors, including whether the property was produced by the seller, the type of property sold (e.g., inventory or a capital asset), and the residence of the seller. Income, gain, or profit from the sale of personal property is sourced according to the residence of the seller. Income from the sale of purchased inventory, however, is sourced in the country in which the sale takes place.[12]

When the seller has produced the property, the income must be apportioned between the country of production and the country of sale. If the manufacturer or producer regularly sells to wholly independent distributors, this can establish an *independent* factory or production price that can be used to determine the split between production and sales income. However, if an independent price has not been established, taxable income from production and sales must be apportioned.[13]

Losses from the sale of personal property are sourced according to the source of any income that may have been generated by the property prior to its disposition. This provision discourages the manipulation of the source of losses for tax purposes.[14]

The general rule for the sourcing of income from the sale of personal property has several exceptions.

- Gain on the sale of depreciable personal property is sourced according to prior depreciation deductions to the extent of the deductions. Any excess gain is sourced as the sale of inventory.
- Gain attributable to an office or fixed place of business maintained outside the United States by a U.S. resident is foreign-source income.

[9] See *British Timken Limited*, 12 T.C. 880 (1949), and Rev.Rul. 60–55, 1960–1 C.B. 270.

[10] See *Robida v. Comm.*, 72–1 USTC ¶9450, 29 AFTR2d 72–1223, 460 F.2d (CA–9, 1972). The taxpayer was employed in military PXs around the world. He had large slot machine winnings and claimed the foreign earned income exclusion. The IRS challenged the exclusion on the grounds that the winnings were not earned income because there was no recipient of Robida's services. The Court, however, found that, even in the absence of capital, the winnings were earned income.

[11] Reg. § 1.861–4(b).

[12] §§ 861(a)(6) and 865. The sale is deemed to take place where title passes. See Reg. § 1.861–7(c) regarding title passage. There has been considerable conflict in this area of tax law. See, for example, *Kates Holding Company, Inc.*, 79 T.C. 700 (1982) and *Miami Purchasing Service Corporation*, 76 T.C. 818 (1981).

[13] § 863(b)(2) and Reg. § 1.863–3.

[14] The Treasury has issued Prop.Reg. § 1.865–2 dealing with the source of losses on the disposition of stock of a foreign corporation.

- Income or gain attributable to an office or fixed place of business maintained in the United States by a nonresident is U.S.-source income.
- Gain on the sale of intangibles is sourced according to prior amortization deductions to the extent of the deductions. Contingent payments, however, are sourced as royalty income.

Transportation and Communication Income.   Income from transportation beginning *and* ending in the United States is U.S.-source income. Fifty percent of the income from transportation beginning *or* ending in the United States is U.S.-source income, unless the U.S. point is only an intermediate stop. This rule does not apply to personal services income unless the transportation is between the United States and a possession. Income from space and ocean activities conducted outside the jurisdiction of any country is sourced according to the residence of the person conducting the activity.

International communication income derived by a U.S. person is sourced 50 percent within the United States in cases where transmission is between the United States and a foreign country. International communication income derived by foreign persons is foreign-source income unless it is attributable to an office or other fixed place of business within the United States. In that case, it is U.S.-source income.

INCOME SOURCED WITHOUT THE UNITED STATES

The provisions for sourcing income without the United States are not as detailed and specific as those for determining U.S.-source income. Basically, § 862 provides that if interest, dividends, compensation for personal services, income from the use or sale of property, and other income is not U.S.-source income, then it is foreign-source income.

ALLOCATION AND APPORTIONMENT OF DEDUCTIONS

The United States levies a tax on *taxable income.* The FTC limitation is based on taxable income. Deductions and losses, therefore, must be allocated and apportioned between U.S.- and foreign-source gross income to determine U.S.- and foreign-source taxable income. Deductions directly related to an activity or property are allocated to classes of income. This is followed by apportionment between the statutory and residual groupings on some reasonable basis. For FTC purposes, U.S.-source income is the residual grouping.[15]

EXAMPLE 14

Ace, Inc., a domestic corporation has $2 million gross income and a $50,000 expense, all related to real estate activities. The expense is allocated and apportioned as follows.

| | Gross Income | | | Apportionment | |
	Foreign	U.S.	Allocation	Foreign	U.S.
Sales	$1,000,000	$500,000	$37,500*	$25,000	$12,500**
Rentals	400,000	100,000	12,500	10,000	2,500
			$50,000	$35,000	$15,000

*$50,000 × ($1,500,000/$2,000,000).

**$37,500 × ($500,000/$1,500,000).

---

[15]Reg. § 1.861–8.

If Ace could show that $45,000 of the expense was directly related to sales income, the $45,000 would be allocated to that class of gross income, with the remainder allocated ratably. ▼

Interest expenses are allocated and apportioned based on the theory that money is fungible. With limited exceptions, interest expense is attributable to all the activities and property of the taxpayer, regardless of the specific purpose for incurring the debt on which interest is paid.[16] Taxpayers must allocate and apportion interest expense on the basis of assets, using either the fair market value or the tax book value of the assets.[17] Once the fair market value is used, the taxpayer must continue to use this method. Special rules apply in allocating and apportioning interest expense in an affiliated group of corporations.

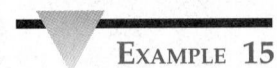

EXAMPLE 15

Black, Inc., a domestic corporation, generates U.S.-source and foreign-source gross income for 1997. Black's assets (tax book value) are as follows.

Generating U.S.-source income	$18,000,000
Generating foreign-source income	5,000,000
	$23,000,000

Black incurs interest expense of $800,000 for 1997. Using the asset method and the tax book value, interest expense is apportioned to foreign-source income as follows.

$$\frac{\$5,000,000 \text{ (foreign assets)}}{\$23,000,000 \text{ (total assets)}} \times \$800,000 = \underline{\$173,913} \qquad ▼$$

Specific rules also apply to research and development (R & D) expenditures, certain stewardship expenses, legal and accounting fees and expenses, income taxes, and losses. U.S. companies incur about 90 percent of their R & D expenditures at U.S. facilities. Nevertheless, U.S. companies spent $9.8 billion in 1993 on foreign R & D, most of which was performed in Germany, the United Kingdom, Canada, France, and Japan. The Regulations provide that a portion of a U.S. company's R & D expenditures must be apportioned to foreign-source income at least indirectly attributable to that R & D.

A deduction not definitely related to any class of gross income is ratably allocated to all classes of gross income and apportioned between U.S.- and foreign-source income.

SECTION 482 CONSIDERATIONS

Taxpayers may be tempted to manipulate the source of income and the allocation of deductions arbitrarily to minimize taxation. This manipulation is more easily accomplished between or among related persons. The IRS uses § 482 to counter such actions. The provision gives the IRS the power to reallocate gross income, deductions, credits, or allowances between or among organizations, trades, or businesses owned or controlled directly or indirectly by the same interests. This can be done whenever the IRS determines that reallocation is necessary to prevent

---

[16] Reg. § 1.861–10T(b) describes circumstances where interest expense can be directly allocated to specific debt. This exception to the fungibility concept is limited to cases in which specific property is purchased or improved with nonrecourse debt.

[17] Reg. § 1.861–9T.

> ## TAX IN THE NEWS
>
> ### RESEARCH AND DEVELOPMENT EXPENSES OF MULTINATIONALS
>
> The Treasury has been reluctant to allow 100 percent of R & D expenses to be allocated against U.S.-source income, based on the premise that the results of this R & D, in certain cases, benefit the taxpayer's U.S. and foreign operations. Such an application would also likely overstate foreign-source income.
>
> Much of the R & D of U.S. companies is performed in the United States. For foreign income tax purposes, other countries are hesitant to allow a deduction for R & D expenses against income sourced in their country when none of the R & D is performed there. This poses a problem for U.S. multinationals because the absence of a deduction increases foreign-source income for foreign tax purposes, but reduces it for purposes of the FTC limitation. Foreign taxes in excess of the FTC limitation tend to build up for companies that perform extensive R & D.

the evasion of taxes or to reflect income more clearly. Section 482 is a "one-edged" sword available only to the IRS. The taxpayer cannot invoke it to reallocate income and expenses.[18]

The reach of § 482 is quite broad. The IRS takes the position that a corporation and its sole shareholder who works full-time for the corporation can be treated as two separate trades or businesses for purposes of § 482.[19] Two unrelated shareholders who each owned 50 percent of a corporation were held to be acting in concert for their common good and, thus, together controlled the corporation.[20]

One of six methods can be used in determining an arm's length price on the sale of tangible property: the comparable uncontrolled price method, the resale price method, the cost plus method, the comparable profits method, the profit split method, and other unspecified methods. Methods available for pricing intangible property include the comparable uncontrolled transactions method, the comparable profits method, the profit split method, the cost-sharing method, and other unspecified methods. The major problem with most pricing methods is that uncontrolled comparable transactions are needed as a benchmark.

An accuracy-related penalty of 20 percent is provided by § 6662 for net § 482 transfer price adjustments for a taxable year that exceed the lesser of $5 million or 10 percent of the taxpayer's gross receipts. In addition, there is a 40 percent penalty for "gross misstatements."

As a further aid to reducing pricing disputes, the IRS has initiated an Advanced Pricing Agreement (APA) program whereby the taxpayer can propose a transfer pricing method for certain international transactions.[21] The taxpayer provides relevant data, which is then evaluated by the IRS. If accepted, the APA provides a safe harbor transfer pricing method for the taxpayer. Apple Computer, Inc., accomplished the first successful APA submission.

---

[18] Reg. § 1.482–1(b)(3).

[19] Rev.Rul. 88–38, 1988–1 C.B. 246. But see *Foglesong v. Comm.*, 82–2 USTC ¶9650, 50 AFTR2d 82–6016, 691 F.2d 848 (CA–7, 1982), *rev'g.* 77 T.C. 1102 (1981).

[20] See *B. Forman Company, Inc. v. Comm.*, 72–1 USTC ¶9182, 29 AFTR2d 72–403, 453 F.2d 1144 (CA–2, 1972).

[21] Rev.Proc. 91–22, 1991–1 C.B. 526.

The Pros and Cons of APAs

The APA program is intended to alleviate the concern that price setting for transactions between related parties may give rise to tax audits. Reducing this uncertainty can be very beneficial to multinational corporations selling products in the international market. The government also benefits because its court case load is reduced.

As the price of this security, however, the taxpayer must disclose sensitive corporate data. A taxpayer that fails to reach an agreement with the IRS may be in a worse position than prior to seeking the APA. Furthermore, the APA may cause retroactive problems for open years.

How would you, as the Director of International Taxes for a large firm, advise the board of directors as to the use of an APA for the company's line of proprietary communications software products?

U.S. TAXATION OF NONRESIDENT ALIENS AND FOREIGN CORPORATIONS

3   LEARNING OBJECTIVE
Utilize the U.S. tax provisions concerning nonresident alien individuals and foreign corporations.

Generally, only the U.S.-source income of nonresident aliens (NRAs) and foreign corporations is subject to U.S. taxation. This reflects the reach of U.S. tax jurisdiction. The constraint, however, does not prevent the United States from also taxing the foreign-source income of NRAs and foreign corporations, when that income is effectively connected with the conduct of a U.S. trade or business.[22]

NONRESIDENT ALIEN INDIVIDUALS

An NRA individual is an individual who is not a citizen or resident of the United States. For example, Queen Elizabeth is an NRA since she is not a citizen or resident of the United States. Citizenship is determined under the immigration and naturalization laws of the United States.[23] Basically, the citizenship statutes are broken down into two categories: nationality at birth and nationality through naturalization.

Residency.   For many years, the definition of residency for Federal income tax purposes was very subjective, requiring an evaluation of a person's intent and actions with regard to the length and nature of stay in the United States. In 1984, Congress enacted a more objective test of residency. Under § 7701(b), a person is a resident of the United States for income tax purposes if he or she meets either the **green card test** or the substantial presence test. If either of these tests is met for the calendar year, the individual is deemed a U.S. resident for the year.

An alien issued a green card is considered a U.S. resident on the first day he or she is physically present in the United States after issuance. The green card is Immigration Form I–551. Newly issued cards are now rose (off-pink), but the form is still referred to as the "green card." Status as a U.S. resident remains in effect until the green card has been revoked or the individual has abandoned lawful permanent resident status.

---

[22] §§ 871, 881, and 882.

[23] Title 8, Aliens and Nationality, *United States Code.*

The substantial presence test is applied to an alien without a green card. It is a mathematical test involving physical presence in the United States. An individual who is physically present in the United States for at least 183 days during the calendar year is a U.S. resident for income tax purposes. This 183-day requirement can also be met over a three-year period that includes the two immediately preceding years and the current year. For this purpose, each day of the current calendar year is counted as a full day, each day of the first preceding year as one-third day, and each day of the second preceding year as one-sixth day.

▼

EXAMPLE 16

Li, an alien, was present in the United States for 90 days in 1995, 180 days in 1996, and 110 days in 1997. For Federal income tax purposes, Li is a U.S. resident for 1997, since she was physically present for 185 days [(90 days × ⅙) + (180 days × ⅓) + (110 days × 1)] during the three-year period. ▼

The substantial presence test allows for several exceptions. Commuters from Mexico and Canada who are employed in the United States, but return home each day, are excepted. Also excepted are individuals who are prevented from leaving the United States due to a medical condition that arose while in the United States. Some individuals are exempt from the substantial presence test, including foreign government-related individuals (e.g., diplomats), qualified teachers, trainees and students, and certain professional athletes.

There is a 31-day per year exception and a 183-day current year exception that may apply to prevent residence.[24] Under the substantial presence test, residence begins the first day the individual is physically present in the United States and ends the last day of physical presence for the calendar year. This assumes the substantial presence test is not satisfied for the next calendar year. Nominal presence of 10 days or less can be ignored in determining whether the substantial presence test is met.

Nonresident Aliens Not Engaged in a U.S. Trade or Business. Certain U.S.-source income that is *not* effectively connected with the conduct of a U.S. trade or business is subject to a flat 30 percent tax. This income includes dividends, interest, rents, royalties, certain compensation, premiums, annuities, and other fixed, determinable, annual or periodic (FDAP) income. This tax generally is levied by a withholding mechanism that requires the payors of the income to withhold 30 percent of gross amounts.[25] This method eliminates the problems of assuring payment by nonresidents, determining allowable deductions, and, in many instances, the filing of tax returns by nonresidents. NRAs are allowed a deduction for casualty and theft losses related to property located within the United States, a deduction for qualified charitable contributions, and one personal exemption. Residents of countries contiguous to the United States (e.g., Canada and Mexico) are allowed dependency exemptions as well. Interest received from certain portfolio debt investments, even though U.S.-sourced is exempt from taxation. Interest earned on deposits with banking institutions is also exempt as long as it is not effectively connected with the conduct of a U.S. trade or business.

Capital gains *not* effectively connected with the conduct of a U.S. trade or business are exempt from tax, as long as the NRA individual was not present in the United States for 183 days or more during the taxable year. If an NRA has not established a taxable year, the calendar year is used. NRAs are not permitted to carry forward capital losses.[26]

---

[24] § 7701(b)(3).
[25] §§ 873 and 1441.

[26] § 871(a)(2).

Nonresident Aliens Engaged in a U.S. Trade or Business. As long as FDAP income and capital gains are not effectively connected income, the tax treatment of these income items is the same, whether NRAs are engaged in a U.S. trade or business or not. Effectively connected income, however, is taxed at the same rates that apply to U.S. citizens and residents, and deductions for expenses attributable to that income are allowed. NRAs with income effectively connected with the conduct of a U.S. trade or business may also be subject to the alternative minimum tax.

Two important definitions determine the U.S. tax consequences to NRAs with U.S.-source income: "the conduct of a U.S. trade or business" and "effectively connected income." General criteria for determining if a U.S. trade or business exists include the location of production activities, management, distribution activities, and other business functions. Trading in commodities and securities ordinarily does not constitute a trade or business. Dealers, however, need to avoid maintaining a U.S. trading office and trading for their own account. Corporations (other than certain personal holding companies) that are not dealers can trade for their own account as long as their principal office is located outside the United States. There are no restrictions on individuals who are not dealers. An NRA who performs services in the United States for a foreign employer is not engaged in a U.S. trade or business.

A U.S. trade or business is a prerequisite to having effectively connected income. Income is effectively connected with a U.S. trade or business if it is derived from assets used in, or held for use in, the trade or business (asset-use test) or if the activities of the trade or business were a material factor in the production of the income (business-activities test).[27]

EXAMPLE 17

Ingrid, an NRA, operates a U.S. business. During the year, excess cash funds accumulate. Ingrid invests these funds on a short-term basis so that they remain available to meet her business needs. Any income earned from these investments is effectively connected income, under the asset-use test. ▼

Withholding Provisions. The 30 percent U.S. tax on FDAP is generally administered by requiring the payor of the income to withhold the tax and remit it to the U.S. tax authorities. This assures the government of timely collection and relieves it of jurisdictional problems that could arise if it had to rely on recipients residing outside the United States to pay the tax. As of March 1996, the United States had 44 income tax treaties with other countries. Most of these treaties provide for reduced withholding on certain types of income. For example, the new income tax treaty with Austria, signed on May 31, 1996, reduces the withholding tax on dividends to 5 or 15 percent, depending on the circumstances.

FOREIGN CORPORATIONS

Definition. The classification of an entity as a foreign corporation for U.S. tax purposes is an important consideration. Section 7701(a)(5) defines a foreign corporation as one that is not domestic. A domestic corporation is a corporation that is created or organized in the United States. Even though McDonald's is, in reality, a multinational corporation, it is considered a domestic corporation for U.S. tax purposes, solely because it was organized in the United States.

Income Not Effectively Connected with a U.S. Trade or Business. U.S.-source FDAP income of foreign corporations is taxed by the United States in the

---

[27] § 864(c).

same manner as that of NRA individuals—at a flat 30 percent rate. Basically, foreign corporations qualify for the same exemptions from U.S. taxation for interest and dividend income as do NRA individuals. The U.S.-source capital gains of foreign corporations are exempt from the Federal income tax if they are not effectively connected with the conduct of a U.S. trade or business.

Effectively Connected Income. Foreign corporations conducting a trade or business within the United States are subject to Federal income taxation on effectively connected income. Additionally, any U.S.-source income attributable to the U.S. office of a foreign corporation is deemed to be effectively connected.[28] For such purposes, foreign corporations are subject to the same tax rates as domestic corporations.

Branch Profits Tax. In addition to the income tax imposed under § 882 on effectively connected income of a foreign corporation, a tax equal to 30 percent of the **dividend equivalent amount (DEA)** for the taxable year is imposed on *any* foreign corporation.[29]

The objective of the **branch profits tax** is to afford equal tax treatment to income generated by a domestic corporation controlled by a foreign corporation and to income generated by other U.S. operations controlled by foreign corporations. If the foreign corporation operates through a U.S. subsidiary (a domestic corporation), the income of the subsidiary is taxable by the United States when derived and is also subject to a withholding tax when repatriated (returned as dividends to the foreign parent). Before the branch profits tax was enacted, a foreign corporation with a branch in the United States paid only the initial tax on its U.S. earnings; remittances were not taxed.

The DEA is the foreign corporation's effectively connected earnings for the taxable year, adjusted for increases and decreases in the corporation's U.S. net equity (investment in the U.S. operations). The DEA is limited to current E & P and post-1986 accumulated E & P that is effectively connected, or treated as effectively connected, with the conduct of a U.S. trade or business. U.S. net equity is the sum of money and the aggregate adjusted basis of assets and liabilities directly connected to U.S. operations that generate effectively connected income.

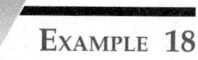

EXAMPLE 18   Robin, Inc., a foreign corporation, has a U.S. branch operation with the following tax results and other information for the year.

E & P effectively connected with a U.S. trade or business	$2,000,000
U.S. corporate tax (at 34%)	680,000
Remittance to home office	1,000,000
Increase in U.S. net equity	320,000

Robin's DEA and branch profits tax are computed as follows.

After-tax E & P effectively connected with a U.S. trade or business	$1,320,000
Less increase in U.S. net equity	(320,000)
Dividend equivalent amount	$1,000,000
Branch profits tax rate	× 30%
Branch profits tax	$ 300,000

---

[28] § 865(e)(2).

[29] § 884.

The 30 percent rate of the branch profits tax may be reduced or eliminated by a treaty provision. If a foreign corporation is subject to the branch profits tax, no other tax is levied on the dividend actually paid by the corporation during the taxable year.

THE FOREIGN INVESTMENT IN REAL PROPERTY TAX ACT

Under prior law, NRAs and foreign corporations could avoid U.S. taxation on gains from the sale of U.S. real estate if the gains were treated as capital gains and were not effectively connected with the conduct of a U.S. trade or business. Furthermore, the United States has a number of income tax treaties that allow for an annual election to treat real estate operations as a trade or business. Persons who were residents of the treaty countries could take advantage of the election for tax years prior to the year of sale and then revoke the election for the year in which the sale took place. In the mid-1970s, midwestern farmers put pressure on Congress to eliminate what they saw as a tax advantage that would allow nonresidents to bid up the price of farmland. This and other concerns regarding the foreign ownership of U.S. real estate led to enactment of the Foreign Investment in Real Property Tax Act (FIRPTA) of 1980.

Under **FIRPTA,** gains and losses realized by NRAs and foreign corporations from the sale or other disposition of U.S. real property interests are treated as effectively connected with the conduct of a U.S. trade or business even where those persons are not actually so engaged. NRA individuals must pay a tax equal to at least 26 (or 28) percent of the lesser of their alternative minimum taxable income, or regular U.S. rates on the net U.S. real property gain for the taxable year.[30]

For purposes of this provision, losses of individual taxpayers are taken into account only to the extent they are deductible as business losses, losses on transactions entered into for profit, and losses from casualties and thefts.

U.S. Real Property Interest (USRPI). Any direct interest in real property situated in the United States and any interest in a domestic corporation (other than solely as a creditor) are U.S. real property interests (USRPIs). This definition applies unless the taxpayer can establish that a domestic corporation was not a U.S. real property holding corporation (USRPHC) during the shorter of the period during which the taxpayer held an interest in the corporation, or for the five-year period ending on the date on which the interest was disposed of (the base period). A domestic corporation is not a USRPHC if it holds no USRPIs on the date of disposition of its stock and if any USRPIs held by the corporation during the base period were disposed of in a transaction in which gain, if any, was fully recognized.

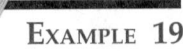

EXAMPLE 19

From January 1, 1992, through January 1, 1997, Francis (a foreign investor) holds shares in Door, Inc., a U.S. corporation. During this period, Door holds two parcels of U.S. real estate and stock of Sash, Inc., another U.S. corporation. Sash also owns U.S. real estate. The two parcels of real estate held directly by Door were disposed of on December 15, 1993, in a nontaxable transaction. Sash disposed of its U.S. real estate in a taxable transaction on January 1, 1997.

An interest in Door is treated as a USRPI because Door did not recognize gain on the December 15, 1993, disposition of the USRPIs. If Door's ownership of U.S. real estate had

---

[30] § 897.

CONCEPT SUMMARY 9–2

U.S. Taxation of NRAs and Foreign Corporations (FCs)

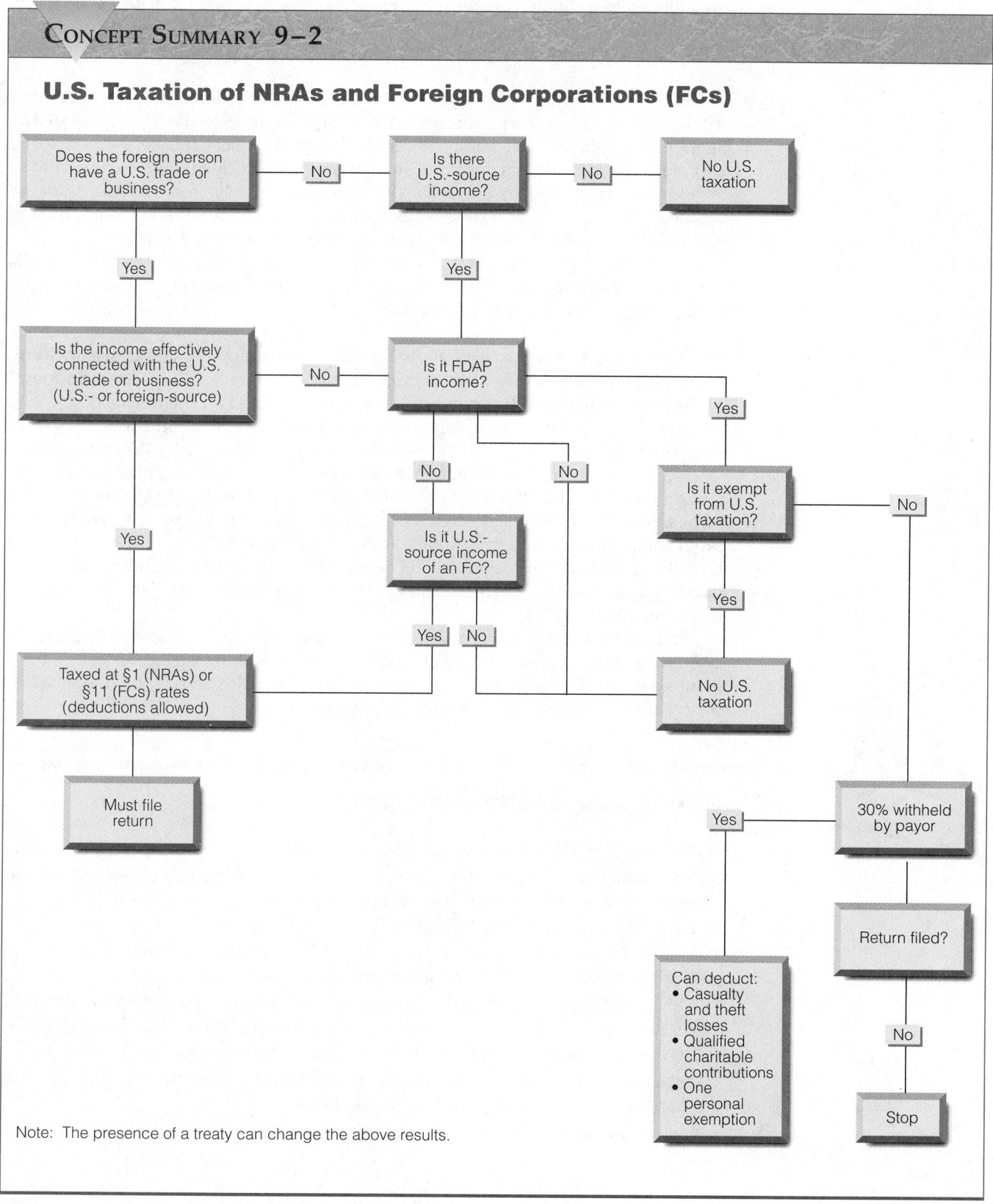

Note: The presence of a treaty can change the above results.

been limited to its indirect ownership through Sash, as of January 2, 1997, an interest in Door would not constitute a USRPI. This result would occur because Sash disposed of its USRPIs in a taxable transaction in which gain was fully recognized. ▼

A USRPHC is any corporation (whether foreign or domestic) where the fair market value of the corporation's USRPIs equals or exceeds 50 percent of the aggregate of fair market value of certain specified assets. These assets are the corporation's USRPIs, its interests in real property located outside the United States, plus any other of its assets that are used or held for use in a trade or business. Stock regularly traded on an established securities market is not treated as a USRPI where a person holds no more than 5 percent of the stock.

Gain on a disposition of stock of a foreign real property holding corporation is not subject to tax under FIRPTA. However, gain on a disposition of a USRPI by such a foreign corporation is subject to FIRPTA.

Withholding Provisions. Following the same rationale as the withholding provisions for FDAP, any purchaser or agent acquiring a USRPI from a foreign person must withhold 10 percent of the amount realized on the disposition.[31] The amount withheld must be submitted along with Form 8288 within at least 20 days after the transfer. A domestic partnership, trust, or estate with a foreign partner, foreign grantor treated as owner, or foreign beneficiary must withhold 35 percent (or 28 percent where allowed by the IRS) of the gain allocable to that person on a disposition of a USRPI. Foreign corporations are also subject to withholding provisions on certain distributions. Without this withholding, NRAs could sell USRPIs, receiving the sales proceeds outside the United States, and jurisdictional issues could make it difficult for the U.S. tax authorities to collect any U.S. tax that might be due on gains.

Failure to withhold can subject the purchaser or the purchaser's agent to interest on any unpaid amount.[32] A civil penalty of 100 percent of the amount required to be withheld and a criminal penalty of up to $10,000 or five years in prison can be imposed for willful failure to withhold.[33]

ETHICAL CONSIDERATIONS

Maintaining Equity in the Tax Law

Equity is one of the basic tenets of U.S. taxation that policy makers consider when advocating changes in the tax law. In some cases, equity considerations have resulted in more equitable treatment, under U.S. tax law, of NRAs and foreign corporations (e.g., before the Tax Reform Act of 1986 lowered income tax rates for U.S. individuals, the 30 percent withholding tax on FDAP income equaled the effective tax rate paid by the average U.S. taxpayer with dividend and interest income).

FIRPTA was enacted to improve tax equity for U.S. persons. When NRAs and foreign corporations were able to dispose of appreciated U.S. real estate without being subject to U.S. taxation, they could pay more initially for the real estate because a subsequent sale of the property would not incur a tax liability. Congress sought to remedy this inequity to U.S. persons dealing in U.S. real estate by enacting FIRPTA.

---

[31] § 1445.
[32] §§ 6601, 6621, and 6651.

[33] §§ 6672 and 7202.

EXPATRIATION TO AVOID U.S. TAXATION

Section 877 provides for U.S. taxation of U.S.-source income earned by persons who relinquished their U.S. citizenship within 10 years of deriving that income if those persons gave up their U.S. citizenship to avoid U.S. taxation. Tax legislation enacted in 1996 expanded these provisions.

NRAs who lost U.S. citizenship within a 10-year period immediately preceding the close of the tax year must pay taxes on their U.S.-source income as though they were still U.S. citizens. This provision applies only if the NRA's expatriation had as one of its principal purposes the avoidance of U.S. taxes. Individuals are presumed to have a tax avoidance purpose if they meet either of the following criteria.

- Average annual net income tax for the five taxable years ending before the date of loss of U.S. citizenship is more than $100,000.
- Net worth as of that date is $500,000 or more.

This provision applies to loss of U.S. citizenship at any time on or after February 6, 1995. The dollar amounts will be adjusted for inflation after 1996. These provisions also apply to "long-term lawful permanent residents" who cease to be taxed as U.S. residents. A long-term permanent resident is an individual (other than a citizen of the United States) who is a lawful permanent resident of the United States in at least 8 taxable years during the 15-year period ending with the taxable year in which the individual either ceases to be a lawful permanent resident of the United States or begins to be treated as a resident of another country under an income tax treaty between the United States and the other country (and does not waive the benefits of the treaty to residents of that country). An exception applies to certain individuals with dual citizenship. Special source rules also apply for purposes of expatriate taxation. The expatriate tax will not apply if U.S. taxation of the NRA under the normal provisions applicable to NRAs results in a greater tax liability. Certain expatriate provisions also apply for estate and gift tax purposes.

TAX TREATIES

Income Tax. Over 40 income **tax treaties** between the United States and other countries are in effect (see Exhibit 9–2). These treaties generally provide *taxing rights* with regard to the taxable income of residents of one treaty country who have income sourced in the other treaty country. For the most part, neither country is prohibited from taxing the income of its residents. The treaties generally provide for primary taxing rights that require the *other* treaty partner to allow a credit for the taxes paid on the twice-taxed income.

EXAMPLE 20

Caterina, a resident of a foreign country with which the United States has an income tax treaty, earns income attributable to a permanent establishment (e.g., place of business) in the United States. Under the treaty, the United States has primary taxing rights with regard to this income. The other country can also require that the income be included in gross income and subject to its income tax, but must allow a credit for the taxes paid to the United States on the income. ▼

Primary taxing rights usually depend on the residence of the taxpayer or the presence of a permanent establishment in a treaty country to which the income is attributable. Generally, a permanent establishment is a branch, office, factory, workshop, warehouse, or other fixed place of business.

TAX IN THE NEWS

WHY THE TREATY PROCESS STALLS

The United States has negotiated several income tax treaties that have never been signed or ratified (e.g., with Argentina, Bangladesh, and Brazil). The treaty process sometimes stalls for several reasons. One is the desire (on the part of some less developed countries) for a tax-sparing provision in the treaty. In other words, the United States would allow an FTC against U.S. taxes even though the treaty partner had a lower tax rate or even gave a tax holiday to U.S. companies operating there.

Another reason is the exchange of information provision. Some countries, for example, have anonymous bank rules that would preclude the exchange of information. In September 1996, the Parliament of Kazakhstan voted on a provision to eliminate anonymous bank accounts so that the United States–Kazakhstan income tax treaty could be ratified.

▼ EXHBIIT 9–2
U.S. Income Tax Treaties in Force as of 1996

Australia	Hungary	New Zealand
Austria	Iceland	Norway
Barbados	India	Pakistan
Belgium	Indonesia	Philippines
Canada	Ireland	Poland
China	Israel	Portugal
Cyprus	Italy	Romania
Czech Republic	Jamaica	Russia
Denmark	Japan	Slovakia
Egypt	Korea (South)	Spain
Finland	Luxembourg	Sweden
France	Malta	Switzerland
Germany	Mexico	Trinidad and Tobago
Greece	Morocco	Tunisia
	Netherlands*	United Kingdom

*Aruba and the Netherlands Antilles were covered under the United States–Netherlands treaty until January 1, 1988, when this coverage was terminated except for Article VIII (which generally allows a U.S. tax exemption for interest paid from domestic sources to residents of these countries) and certain ancillary provisions.

Most U.S. income tax treaties reduce the withholding rate on certain items of FDAP income, such as interest and dividends. For example, treaties with France and Sweden reduce the withholding on portfolio dividends to 15 percent and on certain interest income to zero. The United States has developed a Model Income Tax Treaty[34] as the starting point for negotiating income tax treaties with other countries.

---

[34] Treasury Department Model Income Tax Treaty (September 20, 1996).

U.S. Taxpayers Abroad

4 LEARNING OBJECTIVE
Appreciate the tax benefits available to certain U.S. individuals working abroad.

Citizens and residents of the United States are subject to Federal taxation on their worldwide taxable income. U.S. taxpayers who operate in a foreign country as a sole proprietor, or through a foreign branch or foreign partnership, must include foreign-source income in gross income for U.S. tax purposes. They are allowed a deduction for related expenses and losses. An FTC is available for foreign income taxes paid.

Income tax treaties can reduce or eliminate the taxation of the income by the foreign country party to the treaty. Since, under the treaty, the United States reserves the right to tax its citizens and residents, relief from double taxation is achieved with the FTC. In addition to the FTC, several other tax provisions involve certain foreign-source income of U.S. citizens and residents.

THE FOREIGN EARNED INCOME EXCLUSION

To help U.S. multinational entities be competitive in the world market, Congress enacted legislation granting an exclusion (from U.S. gross income) for a certain amount of qualified foreign *earned* income. This exclusion allows multinational entities to employ U.S. citizens and residents for foreign operations without having to pay them a wage or salary far in excess of that paid to nationals of the particular foreign country or countries. As Example 1 illustrates, the tax burden on a U.S. taxpayer working abroad could be much greater than that on a native of the foreign country. The **foreign earned income exclusion** reduces this problem.

For 1991, U.S. taxpayers filed approximately 220,000 Form 2555s claiming exclusions totaling almost $9.7 billion. Salaries and wages made up 71 percent of total foreign earned income for 1991. The average salary or wages earned was $46,000. Actual per country averages varied widely, however; for example, $28,000 for Peru and $65,000 for Singapore.

Currently, § 911 allows a foreign earned income exclusion for (1) a qualified housing cost amount and (2) foreign earned income not in excess of $70,000. The exclusion is elective and is made by filing Form 2555 with the income tax return, or with an amended return, for the first taxable year for which the election is to be effective. An election once made remains in effect for that year and for all subsequent years, unless revoked. If the election is revoked for any taxable year, the taxpayer may not make the election again (without consent of the IRS) until the sixth taxable year following the taxable year for which revocation was first effective.[35]

Qualified Individuals. The exclusion is available to an individual whose tax home is in a foreign country and who is either (1) a U.S. citizen and bona fide resident of a foreign country or countries or (2) a citizen or resident of the United States who, during any 12 consecutive months, is physically present in a foreign country or countries for at least 330 full days. *Tax home* has the same meaning as for U.S. cases relating to travel expenses while away from home.[36] The issue of whether a stay abroad is temporary can be troublesome. If the stay abroad is deemed to be temporary, the taxpayer's tax home has not shifted to the foreign country. A stay that exceeds one year is not temporary.

Only whole days count for the physical presence test. The taxpayer has some flexibility in choosing the 12-month period.

---

[35] Reg. § 1.911–7.

[36] § 162(a)(2).

EXAMPLE 21

Carla, a U.S. citizen, arrived in Ireland from Boston at 3 P.M. on March 28, 1996. She remained in Ireland until 8 A.M. on March 1, 1997, when she departed for the United States. Among other possible 12-month periods, Carla was present in a foreign country an aggregate of 331 full days during each of the following 12-month periods: March 1, 1996, through February 28, 1997, and March 29, 1996, through March 28, 1997.[37] ▼

The General Exclusion. The foreign earned income (general) exclusion is available for foreign earned income and is limited to the lesser of (1) $70,000 or (2) foreign earned income less the housing cost amount exclusion. The exclusion is available for the tax year in which the income would be recognized. The limitation, however, is determined for each tax year in which services were performed. Income received after the close of the taxable year following the taxable year in which the services were performed does not qualify for the exclusion.

EXAMPLE 22

Tom, a U.S. resident, is present in a foreign country for all of 1996. He earns $100,000 from the performance of personal services. On January 1, 1997, he returns to the United States and remains there. Of the $100,000 foreign earned income, Tom receives $60,000 in 1996 and $40,000 in 1997. Tom can take a foreign earned income exclusion of $60,000 for 1996 and $10,000 for 1997 ($70,000 statutory limit – $60,000 excluded for 1996). If Tom did not receive the $40,000 until 1998, no exclusion would be allowed for 1998 because the $40,000 was received after the close of the taxable year following the taxable year in which the services were performed. ▼

The $70,000 statutory amount is prorated on a daily basis where the taxpayer does not qualify for the exclusion for the full tax year. If Tom in Example 22 qualified for only 11 months of the year, the $70,000 statutory amount would be $63,880 [$70,000 × (334 days/366 days)].

The Housing Cost Amount. The housing cost amount is equal to the qualified housing expenses of an individual for the tax year less a base amount. The base amount is 16 percent of the salary of an employee of the United States for Step 1 Grade GS–14. The base amount is determined on a daily basis. For 1996, the base amount for a full year was $9,426. For a qualified individual employed overseas for 250 days of the year, the applicable base amount would be $6,439 [$9,426 × (250 days/366 days)]. The housing cost amount exclusion is limited to foreign earned income.

EXAMPLE 23

Charles, a U.S. citizen, works as an engineer for a U.S. multinational company in Bahrain. He is a bona fide resident of Bahrain for the entire calendar and tax year and earns a salary of $80,000. In addition, his employer provides $16,000 in housing costs. If the base amount is $9,426 and Charles elects both exclusions, the housing cost amount exclusion is $6,574 ($16,000 – $9,426), and the foreign earned income exclusion is $70,000 (the lesser of $96,000 foreign earned income – $6,574 housing cost amount exclusion, or the $70,000 statutory limit). Charles's gross income includes $19,426 of foreign earned income ($80,000 + $16,000 – $6,574 – $70,000). ▼

A self-employed individual is not eligible to exclude housing expenses, but can elect to deduct them. For 1991, taxpayers claimed $43.5 million in housing cost deductions on approximately 3,000 returns.

---

[37] Reg. § 1.911–2(d).

FOREIGN CORPORATIONS CONTROLLED BY U.S. PERSONS

5 LEARNING OBJECTIVE
Apply the U.S. tax rules for foreign corporations controlled by U.S. persons.

To minimize current tax liability, taxpayers often attempt to defer the recognition of taxable income. As Example 1 suggests, one way of trying to defer income recognition is to shift the income-generating activity to a foreign entity that is not within the U.S. tax jurisdiction. A foreign corporation is the most suitable entity for such an endeavor since, unlike a partnership, it is not a conduit through which income is taxed directly to the owner.

CONTROLLED FOREIGN CORPORATIONS

Subpart F, §§ 951–964 of the Code, provides that certain types of income generated by **controlled foreign corporations (CFCs)** are currently included in gross income by the **U.S. shareholders.** For Subpart F to apply, the foreign corporation must have been a CFC for an uninterrupted period of 30 days or more during the taxable year. When this is the case, U.S. shareholders must include in gross income their pro rata share of Subpart F income, earnings invested in excess passive assets, and increase in earnings that the CFC has invested in U.S. property for the tax year. This rule applies to U.S. shareholders who own stock in the corporation on the last day of the tax year on which the corporation is a CFC. The gross income inclusion must be made for their taxable year in which or with which the taxable year of the corporation ends.

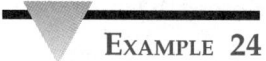
EXAMPLE 24

Gray, Inc., a calendar year corporation, is a CFC for the entire tax year. Chance Company, a U.S. corporation, owns 60% of Gray's one class of stock for the entire year. Subpart F income is $100,000, investment in U.S. property has not increased, and no distributions have been made during the year. Chance, a calendar year taxpayer, includes $60,000 in gross income as a constructive dividend for the tax year. ▼

EXAMPLE 25

Gray, Inc., is a CFC until July 1 of the tax year (a calendar year). Terry, a U.S. citizen, owns 30% of its one class of stock for the entire year. She includes $14,877 [$100,000 × 30% × (181 days/365 days)] in gross income as a constructive dividend for the tax year. ▼

A CFC is any foreign corporation in which more than 50 percent of the total combined voting power of all classes of stock entitled to vote or the total value of the stock of the corporation is owned by U.S. shareholders on any day during the taxable year of the foreign corporation. For purposes of determining if a foreign corporation is a CFC, a *U.S. shareholder* is defined as a U.S. person who owns, or is considered to own, 10 percent or more of the total combined voting power of all classes of voting stock of the foreign corporation. Stock owned directly, indirectly, and constructively is counted. The foreign subsidiaries of most multinational U.S. parent corporations are CFCs. Hallmark Cards, Inc., has a Canadian subsidiary that is a CFC.

Indirect ownership involves stock held through a foreign entity, such as a foreign corporation, foreign partnership, or foreign trust. This stock is considered as actually owned proportionately by the shareholders, partners, or beneficiaries. Constructive ownership rules, with certain modifications, apply in determining if a U.S. person is a U.S. shareholder, in determining whether a foreign corporation is a CFC, and for certain related-party provisions of Subpart F.[38] Some of the modifications include the following.

---

[38] §§ 958 and 318(a).

- Stock owned by a nonresident alien individual is not considered constructively owned by a U.S. citizen or resident alien individual.
- If a partnership, estate, trust, or corporation owns, directly or indirectly, more than 50 percent of the voting power of a corporation, it is deemed to own all of its stock.
- The threshold for corporate attribution is 10 percent rather than 50 percent.

EXAMPLE 26

Shareholders of Foreign Corporation	Voting Power	Classification
Alan	30%	U.S. person
Bill	9%	U.S. person
Carla	41%	Foreign person
Dora	20%	U.S. person

Bill is Alan's son. Alan, Bill, and Dora are *U.S. shareholders.* Alan owns 39%, 30% directly and 9% constructively through Bill. Bill also owns 39%, 9% directly and 30% constructively through Alan. Thus, Bill is a U.S. shareholder. Dora owns 20% directly. The corporation is a CFC because U.S. shareholders own 59% of the voting power. If Bill were not related to Alan or to any other U.S. persons who were shareholders, Bill would not be a U.S. shareholder, and the corporation would not be a CFC. ▼

U.S. shareholders must include their pro rata share of the applicable income in their gross income only to the extent of their actual ownership. Stock held indirectly is considered actually owned for this purpose.

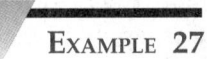

EXAMPLE 27

Bill, in Example 26, would recognize only 9% of the Subpart F income as a constructive dividend. Alan would recognize 30% and Dora would recognize 20%. If Bill were a foreign corporation wholly owned by Alan, Alan would recognize 39% as a constructive dividend. If Carla owned only 40% of the stock and Ed, a U.S. person, owned 1% and was not related to any of the other shareholders, Ed would not be a *U.S. shareholder* and would not have to include any of the Subpart F income in gross income. ▼

Subpart F Income.   Subpart F income consists of the following.

- Insurance income (§ 953).
- Foreign base company income (§ 954).
- International boycott factor income (§ 999).
- Illegal bribes.
- Income derived from a § 901(j) foreign country.

Foreign Base Company Income.   There are five categories of foreign base company income (FBCI).

- Foreign personal holding company income.
- Foreign base company sales income.
- Foreign base company services income.
- Foreign base company shipping income.
- Foreign base company oil-related income.

A *de minimis* rule provides that if the total amount of a foreign corporation's FBCI and gross insurance income for the taxable year is less than the lesser of 5 percent of gross income or $1 million, none of its gross income is treated as FBCI for the tax year. The *de minimis* rule does not apply to other types of income under Subpart F, such as increases in investment in U.S. property. However, if a foreign corporation's FBCI and gross insurance income exceed 70 percent of total gross income, all the corporation's gross income for the tax year is treated as FBCI or insurance income.

FBCI and insurance income subject to high foreign taxes are not included under Subpart F if the taxpayer establishes that the income was subject to an effective rate, imposed by a foreign country, of more than 90 percent of the maximum corporate rate under § 11. For example, this rate must be greater than 31.5 percent (90% × 35%), where 35 percent represents the highest U.S. corporate rate.

Foreign personal holding company (FPHC) income consists of the following.

- Dividends, interest, royalties, rents, and annuities.
- Excess gains over losses from the sale or exchange of property (including an interest in a trust or partnership) that gives rise to FPHC income or that does not give rise to any income.
- Excess of foreign currency gains over foreign currency losses (other than any transaction directly related to the business needs of the CFC).

Foreign base company (FBC) sales income is income derived from the purchase of personal property from or on behalf of a related person, or from the sale of personal property to or on behalf of a related person.

EXAMPLE 28

A CFC owned 100% by Romus, a U.S. corporation, generates FBC sales income in any one of the following situations.

- Purchase of widgets from anyone as commission agent for Romus Corporation.
- Purchase of widgets from Romus and sale to anyone.
- Purchase of widgets from anyone and sale to Romus Corporation.
- Sale of widgets to anyone as commission agent for Romus.   ▼

An exception applies to property that is manufactured, produced, grown, or extracted in the country in which the CFC was organized or created and also to property sold for use, consumption, or disposition within that country. Certain income derived by a branch of the CFC in another country can be deemed FBC sales income. This would be the case if the effect of using the branch is the same as if the branch were a wholly owned subsidiary.[39]

FBC services income is income derived from the performance of services for or on behalf of a related person and performed outside the country in which the CFC was created or organized. Income from services performed before and in connection with the sale of property by a CFC that has manufactured, produced, grown, or extracted such property is not FBC services income.

FBC shipping income includes several classifications of income, including dividends and interest received from a foreign corporation, to the extent that income is attributable to, or is derived from or in connection with, the shipping activity. Thus, income attributable to the use of any aircraft or vessel in foreign commerce, performance of services directly related to the use of that aircraft or vessel, or sale or exchange of any such aircraft or vessel is FBC shipping income.

FBC oil-related income is income, other than extraction income, derived in a foreign country in connection with the sale of oil and gas products and sold by the CFC or a related person for use or consumption within the country in which the oil or gas was extracted. Only corporations with production of at least 1,000 barrels per day are treated as deriving FBC oil-related income.

U.S. shareholders must include in gross income their pro rata share of the CFC's increase in investment in U.S. property for the taxable year. Subpart F income is considered attributable first to the increase in investment in U.S. property and thus is not taxed twice.

Distributions of Previously Taxed Income. Distributions from a CFC are treated as being first from E & P attributable to increases in investment in U.S. property previously taxed as a constructive dividend, second from E & P attributable to excess passive assets previously taxed as a constructive dividend, third from E & P attributable to previously taxed Subpart F income other than that described above, and last from other E & P. Thus, distributions of previously taxed income are not taxed as a dividend but reduce E & P.

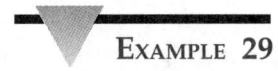

EXAMPLE 29

In 1997, Jet, Inc., a U.S. shareholder, owns 100% of a CFC, from which Jet receives a $100,000 distribution. The CFC's E & P is composed of the following amounts.

- $50,000 attributable to previously taxed increases in investment in U.S. property.
- $30,000 attributable to previously taxed Subpart F income.
- $40,000 attributable to other E & P.

Jet has a taxable dividend of only $20,000, all attributable to other E & P. The remaining $80,000 is previously taxed income. The CFC's E & P is reduced by $100,000. The remaining E & P is all attributable to other E & P. ▼

A U.S. shareholder's basis in CFC stock is increased by constructive dividends included in income under Subpart F and decreased by subsequent distributions of previously taxed income. U.S. corporate shareholders who own at least 10 percent of the voting stock of a foreign corporation are allowed an indirect FTC for foreign taxes deemed paid on constructive dividends included in gross income under Subpart F. The indirect credit also is available for Subpart F income attributable to second- and third-tier foreign corporations as long as the 10 percent ownership requirement is met from tier to tier.

Dispositions of Stock of a CFC. The Subpart F provisions provide for the current taxation of Subpart F income of a CFC to U.S. shareholders to the extent of

---

[39] § 954(d)(2).

CONCEPT SUMMARY 9–3

Income of a CFC That Is Included in Gross Income of a U.S. Shareholder

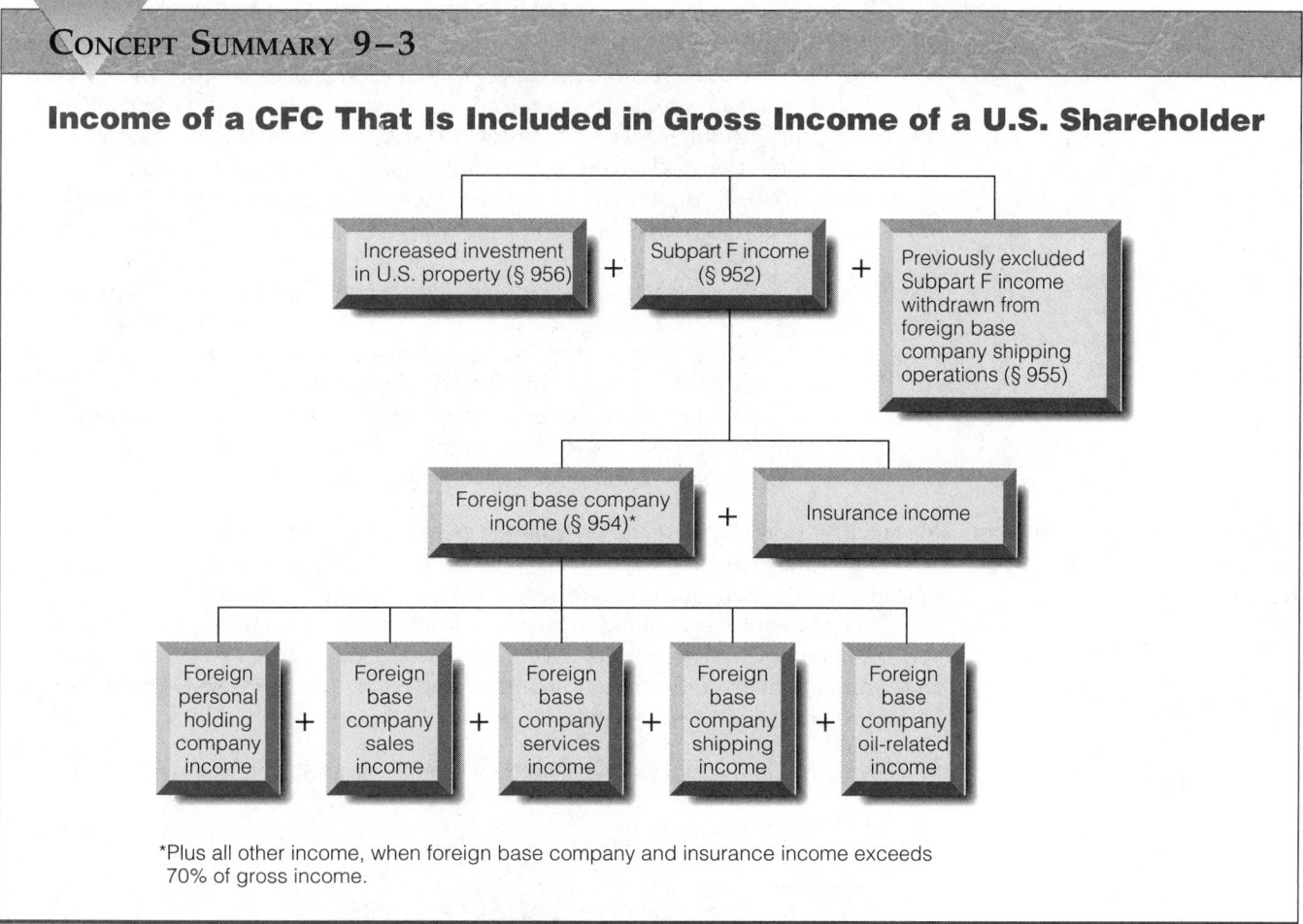

*Plus all other income, when foreign base company and insurance income exceeds 70% of gross income.

their pro rata share. This, however, does not reach the earnings of the CFC that are not included in the taxable income of the shareholders under Subpart F (e.g., active trade or business income not involving related persons). Section 1248 prevents the gain from the disposition of CFC stock from escaping taxation as ordinary income to the extent that it previously had not been taxed.

This provision requires that gain on the sale or other disposition of stock of a CFC by a U.S. shareholder be treated as dividend income to the extent of the transferor's share of undistributed nonpreviously taxed E & P of the corporation.

The various constructive dividend possibilities for CFC income appear in Concept Summary 9–3.

THE FOREIGN PERSONAL HOLDING COMPANY (FPHC) TAX

The major distinction between the FPHC tax and the personal holding company (PHC) tax (see Chapter 6) is that the FPHC tax is levied on the U.S. shareholders of an FPHC rather than on the corporation. A pro rata share of the undistributed FPHC income (a deemed dividend) is included in the gross income of U.S. persons who are shareholders of the FPHC. Only persons who are shareholders on the last day in the taxable year in which a *U.S. group* existed must include this deemed dividend in gross income. The undistributed FPHC income for the taxable year is limited to current E & P. The amount taxable as a deemed dividend to a U.S. shareholder is treated as a contribution to the capital of the corporation and increases the shareholder's basis in the corporation's stock.

A foreign corporation is an FPHC if it meets two requirements. First, 60 percent or more of the gross income of the foreign corporation for the taxable year must be FPHC income. This percentage drops to 50 percent or more after the 60 percent requirement has been met for a tax year. The percentage remains at 50 percent until the foreign corporation does not meet the 50 percent test for three consecutive years or does not meet the stock ownership requirement for an entire tax year.

Second, more than 50 percent of the total combined voting power or the total value of the stock of the corporation must be owned, directly or indirectly, by five or fewer individuals who are U.S. persons (the U.S. group) at any time during the taxable year. Attribution rules for determining constructive ownership are provided in § 554. Furthermore, stock held through a domestic or foreign entity is considered owned proportionately by its partners, beneficiaries, or shareholders.

The amount of the deemed dividend included in gross income by the U.S. shareholders is equal to each shareholder's pro rata share of undistributed FPHC income for the portion of the year the stock ownership test was satisfied. A U.S. shareholder need not be a member of the U.S. group to be taxed.

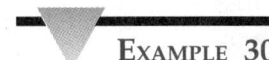

EXAMPLE 30

Mr. and Mrs. Cordero, Mr. and Mrs. Estevez, and Mr. Estevez, Jr., (the U.S. group) each own 11 shares of the 100 outstanding shares of Gold, Inc., a foreign corporation. Ms. Santos, an unrelated U.S. person, owns 5 shares, and NRAs own the remaining 40 shares. If Gold is an FPHC for the entire tax year, all of the U.S. shareholders hold their shares all year, and undistributed FPHC income for the tax year is $100,000, each U.S. shareholder includes his or her pro rata share of the $100,000 in gross income as a dividend for the taxable year. Ms. Santos includes $5,000 in gross income. ▼

FPHC income consists of passive income such as the following.

- Dividends.
- Interest.
- Royalties.
- Gains from the sale or exchange of securities.
- Certain personal service contract income.
- Certain rents constituting less than 50 percent of the foreign corporation's gross income.

Dividends paid can reduce the amount taxable as undistributed FPHC income. In addition, certain income otherwise qualifying as FPHC income is ignored if it is received from a related corporation. U.S. shareholders of a CFC that is also an FPHC are not taxed on the same income under Subpart F and the FPHC provisions. Income falling within both provisions is taxed only under Subpart F.[40]

FOREIGN SALES CORPORATIONS

Prior to 1985, the Domestic International Sales Corporations (DISC) provisions (§§ 991–997) allowed for a deferral of the tax on a portion of the export income of a DISC until actual repatriation of the earnings. Over the years, Congress cut the amount of export income on which deferral was allowed. As the result of charges by the General Agreement on Trade and Tariffs (GATT—whose members include some of the United States' major trading partners) that the DISC provisions were a prohibited *export subsidy*, the DISC provisions were curtailed. As an alternative, the Foreign Sales Corporation (FSC) provisions (§§ 921–927) were enacted. Most remaining DISCs are "interest charge DISCs"—the price of deferral is an annual interest charge on the deferred taxes.[41] Only export sales up to $10 million qualify for deferral. Amounts in excess of $10 million are deemed distributed.

---

[40] § 951(d).   [41] § 995(f).

Most large multinational firms prefer CFCs to FSCs because they establish a more permanent active foreign presence, as in manufacturing. Mid-sized companies, such as Convex, often use FSCs, however, as do companies with very high profit margins (e.g., 50 to 60 percent). In addition, the FSC has been used as a lessor that receives lease income, a portion of which will be exempt from U.S. taxation. Some large airlines, such as KLM, have entered into long-term leasing agreements with FSCs.

FSCs are not allowed a tax deferral on export income. Instead, a certain percentage (about 15 or 16 percent, depending on taxpayer status) of export income is exempt from U.S. taxation (exempt foreign trade income). Pricing methods are provided for determining exempt foreign trade income.

To elect FSC status, a foreign corporation must meet a foreign presence requirement. An exception to this requirement is provided if the foreign corporation's export receipts do not exceed $5 million (the small FSC). The foreign presence requirement includes the following.

- Maintaining a foreign office.
- Operating under foreign management.
- Keeping a permanent set of books at the foreign office.
- Conducting foreign economic processes (e.g., selling activities).
- Being a foreign corporation.[42]

In addition, the corporation must have no more than 25 shareholders at any time during the taxable year and have no preferred stock outstanding at any time during the taxable year.

Most FSCs operate as commission FSCs. Rather than buying the item produced by the parent and then reselling it, they receive a commission for "arranging sales." Smiths Industries, a Florida corporation that does no business in the United States, has a commission FSC organized in the Virgin Islands. The maximum profit allowed the FSC cannot exceed the greater of the following.

- 23 percent of combined taxable income (CTI) of the related exporter and the FSC.
- 1.83 percent of foreign trade gross receipts (not exceeding 46 percent of CTI).
- Taxable income using § 482 arm's length pricing provisions.[43]

EXAMPLE 31

In 1990, an FSC was incorporated in a U.S. possession by DOMI, the U.S. parent. The FSC operates as a commission FSC for DOMI's export sales of product X. Sales results this year are as follows.

DOMI's gross sales	$ 80,000
Cost of goods sold	(44,000)
DOMI's gross income from sales	$ 36,000
Expenses attributable to export sales	(9,500)
Net income from sales before FSC considerations	$ 26,500
Expenses paid by FSC	(2,000)
CTI	$ 24,500
FSC's profit under CTI method (23%)	$ 5,635
FSC's profit under gross receipts method (1.83% of gross receipts)	$ 1,464

[42] § 922.   [43] § 925.

```
┌─────────────────────────────────────────────────────────────┐
│  TAX  IN  THE  NEWS                                          │
├─────────────────────────────────────────────────────────────┤
│                                                             │
│  THE BENEFITS OF LOCATING AN FSC IN GUAM                    │
│                                                             │
│      Since the FSC provisions were enacted in 1984,         │
│      approximately 500 FSCs have been created in Guam.      │
│      Companies such as Boeing, Exxon, General Electric,     │
│      and Computerland have FSCs located there. The tax      │
│  climate of Guam makes such a location very attractive.     │
│  For example, there are no registration fees for            │
│  incorporating in Guam. In contrast, registration fees in   │
│  Bermuda range from $1,600 to $8,000, and the franchise     │
│  tax in the Virgin Islands can run as high as $25,000.      │
│      Guam recently has enhanced the tax benefits of         │
│  locating there by extending FSC licenses for an            │
│  additional 30 years and expanding the tax exemption.       │
│  FSCs are completely exempt from taxation in Guam.          │
│  Furthermore, the government of Guam has made it easy       │
│  for U.S. corporations to form and operate an FSC there.    │
│  The political climate is stable, and communication with    │
│  the U.S. mainland is not complicated.                      │
│                                                             │
│  SOURCE: Tax Notes International 9, No. 10 (September 5,     │
│  1994), p. 719.                                             │
│                                                             │
└─────────────────────────────────────────────────────────────┘
```

Since the CTI method results in more profit to the FSC than the gross receipts method, the FSC is allowed to earn a profit of $5,635. The FSC's commission is determined as follows.

Maximum profit allowed	$5,635
Expenses incurred by FSC	2,000
FSC commission	$7,635

The tax attributable to FSC activity is calculated as follows.

Commission income	$7,635	
$8/23$ of commission income		$2,656
Expenses incurred by FSC	$2,000	
$8/23$ of FSC's expenses		(696)
Taxable income		$1,960
U.S. tax (at 34%)		$ 666

The exempt foreign trade income is $3,675 [($7,635 – $2,000) × $15/23$]. This is equal to 15% of $24,500. ▼

TAX HAVENS

All other considerations being equal, a U.S. corporation generally would prefer to make its foreign investment in (or through) a **tax haven.** A tax haven can be described as a country in which either locally sourced income or residents of the country are subject to no or low internal taxation. One method of avoiding taxation is to invest through a foreign corporation incorporated in a tax haven. Since the foreign corporation is a resident of the tax haven, the income it earns is subject to no or low internal taxes. Tax haven countries may also require the confidentiality of financial and commercial information. Exhibit 9–3 lists countries classified as tax havens.

▼ **EXHIBIT 9–3**
Countries Classified as Tax
Havens* (1992)

Antigua and Barbuda	Leeward Islands
Aruba	Liberia
Austria	Liechtenstein
Bahamas	Luxembourg
Bahrain	Monaco
Barbados	Netherlands
Belize	Netherlands Antilles
Bermuda	Panama
Cayman Islands	Singapore
Costa Rica	Switzerland
Gibraltar	Turks and Caicos Islands
Hong Kong	Windward Islands

*The United States classifies a country as a tax haven if its income tax rates are lower than U.S. rates.
SOURCE: *SOI Bulletin*, Winter 1995–96, p. 114.

A tax haven can, in effect, be created by an income tax treaty. For example, under an income tax treaty between Country A and Country B, residents of A are subject to a withholding tax of only 5 percent on dividend and interest income sourced in B. The United States and A have a similar treaty. The United States does not have a treaty with Country B. A U.S. corporation can create a foreign subsidiary in Country A and use that subsidiary to make investments in Country B. This is referred to as **treaty shopping.** If the Country B investment income had been earned directly by the U.S. corporation, it would be subject to a 30 percent withholding tax. By investing through the foreign subsidiary created in Country A, the U.S. parent corporation pays only 10 percent in foreign taxes on the income earned, i.e., 5 percent to B and 5 percent to A.

In recent years, many countries have enacted "treaty shopping" provisions that provide that treaty benefits for withholding taxes are not available to a resident corporation unless a certain percentage of its beneficial interests are owned, directly or indirectly, by one or more individual residents of the country in which the corporation is resident. The most controversial article in the U.S. Model Treaty is Article 16, Limitation on Benefits, which is meant to prevent treaty shopping. Article 16 disallows treaty benefits to an entity unless more than 75 percent of the beneficial interest in the entity is owned, directly or indirectly, by one or more individual residents of the same treaty country in which the entity is resident.

U.S. owners of 749 of the largest CFCs filed information returns (Form 5471) reporting more than $13.2 billion of Subpart F income for 1992. More than 400 of these CFCs with Subpart F income were based in tax havens; for example, Switzerland was the home of 114 of these CFCs. Among the non-tax haven countries, Canada had the largest number, with 408 large CFCs filing 1992 U.S. tax returns.

OTHER CONSIDERATIONS

Interest expense deductions are limited for certain foreign-controlled U.S. corporations. While primarily aimed at these foreign-controlled entities, this provision can also apply to U.S. parent corporations paying interest to their foreign subsidiaries. This rule is referred to as the "earnings stripping" provision, since it applies only if the payor's debt-to-equity ratio exceeds 1.5 to 1, and a high proportion of earnings is paid out as interest expense. Disallowed amounts can be carried over to future years.

The tax years of CFCs and FPHCs must conform to that of a more-than-50 percent U.S. owner. Additionally, a CFC is allowed to use a tax year ending such that no more than one month's deferral of income recognition is provided to the majority U.S. shareholder.

TRANSFERRING OWNERSHIP TO A FOREIGN PERSON

This chapter has illustrated a number of tax motives for investing or operating overseas through a foreign entity. To originate investment through, or transfer investment to, a foreign entity, the U.S. taxpayer must make some sort of transfer to the foreign entity. This may be in the form of a cash investment, or it may be the transfer of all the assets of a U.S. entity.

EXAMPLE 32

Jorge, the U.S. citizen of Example 1, exchanges $500,000 for 50% of the stock of Brazil Stores, Inc., a newly formed foreign corporation. ▼

EXAMPLE 33

Parts Company, a U.S. partnership, transfers its assets to a newly formed foreign corporation in exchange for 100% of its stock. The stock is transferred to Parts' partners in complete liquidation of the partnership. ▼

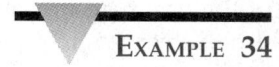

EXAMPLE 34

Wheels, Inc., a U.S. corporation, transfers all of the assets of its foreign branch to a newly formed foreign corporation in exchange for 100% of its stock. ▼

In each of the above cases, U.S. property has been exchanged for foreign property. In situations where potential taxable income is transferred to a corporation outside the U.S. Federal tax jurisdiction, the transfer may incur a tax. The tax result of transferring property to a foreign corporation depends on the income potential of the property and the character of the property in the hands of the transferor or transferee. Generally, the tax treatment of outbound transfers such as those described in Examples 32 through 34 is addressed in § 367(a) or § 1491.

SECTION 367

Outbound Transfers. The tax treatment of transfers of property by a U.S. person to a foreign corporation is prescribed in § 367(a). These *outbound* transfers include (1) transfer of property to a CFC under § 351, (2) liquidation of a domestic subsidiary into a foreign parent corporation under § 332, (3) acquisition of stock in a domestic corporation by a foreign corporation in a "B" reorganization, and (4) acquisition of a domestic corporation's assets by a foreign corporation in a "C" reorganization. The incorporation of a U.S. corporation's foreign branch may be taxable under this provision.

The transferor must recognize any realized gain on the transfer. The character of any gain recognized depends on the character of the property transferred.[44]

Because several exceptions apply, only the gain in what have been termed *tainted* assets is subject to taxation under § 367(a). Excluded from the tainted asset category are property to be used by the foreign corporation in the active conduct of a trade or business outside the United States and stock or securities of a foreign corporation that is a party to the exchange or reorganization. Certain property to

---

[44] See Reg. §§ 1.367(a)–1T through –6T.

be used by the foreign corporation in the active conduct of a trade or business outside the United States, however, is *tainted* and, thus, subject to § 367. In effect, a *deemed sale* is treated as having occurred when the following assets are transferred.

- Inventory (raw goods, work-in-process, and finished goods).
- Installment obligations and accounts receivable.
- Foreign currency or other property denominated in foreign currency.
- Property leased by the transferor unless the transferee is the lessee.

In addition to gain on the *tainted* assets listed above, any *U.S. depreciation* (§§ 1245 and 1250) and other type recapture potential (e.g., §§ 617, 1252, and 1254) in the assets transferred must be recognized to the extent of gain realized. This provision applies only to appreciated assets for which the depreciation or other deduction has resulted in a tax benefit. The U.S. depreciation is the portion of the depreciation attributable to use of the property in the United States.

The transfer of intangibles is treated separately as a transfer pursuant to a sale for contingent payments.[45] These amounts are treated as received by the transferor over the life of the intangible and are U.S.-source ordinary income. They are recognized by the transferor and must be commensurate with the income attributable to the intangible. A subsequent disposition by the transferee triggers income recognition to the initial transferor under § 367.

Inbound and Offshore Transfers. As previously illustrated, one objective of Federal tax law is to prevent E & P that has accumulated in U.S.-owned foreign corporations from escaping U.S. taxation. Section 367(b) covers the tax treatment of inbound and offshore transfers with regard to stock of a CFC. Examples of inbound transactions include the liquidation of a foreign corporation into a domestic parent under § 332, and acquisition of the assets of a foreign corporation by a domestic corporation in a "C" or "D" reorganization. Offshore transfers include a foreign corporate "B" acquisition of a first- or lower-tier foreign corporation in exchange for stock of a non-CFC; foreign corporate "B," "C," or "D" acquisition of a foreign corporation in exchange for CFC stock; and a foreign § 351 transfer of stock or other property in a foreign corporation having a U.S. shareholder.

U.S. persons directly or indirectly a party to an inbound or offshore transfer involving stock of a CFC recognize dividend income to the extent of their pro rata share of the previously untaxed E & P of the foreign corporation.

SECTION 1491

Section 367 covers only certain otherwise tax-free outbound transfers to foreign corporations. Congress has dealt with similar but complementary situations in § 1491.

Any U.S. person who transfers appreciated property to a foreign corporation as paid-in surplus or as a contribution to capital to a foreign partnership, or to a foreign estate or trust, must pay an excise tax on the transfer. The tax is equal to 35 percent of the excess of the fair market value of the property over the sum of its adjusted basis and any gain recognized to the U.S. person on the transfer. Under § 1057, the transferor can elect to treat the transfer as a sale or exchange at fair market value. In this case, the transferor recognizes gain equal to the excess of the fair market value over the adjusted basis of the property in the hands of the transferor.

---

[45] § 367(d)(2).

▼ **FIGURE 9–2**
Taxation of Asset Transfers

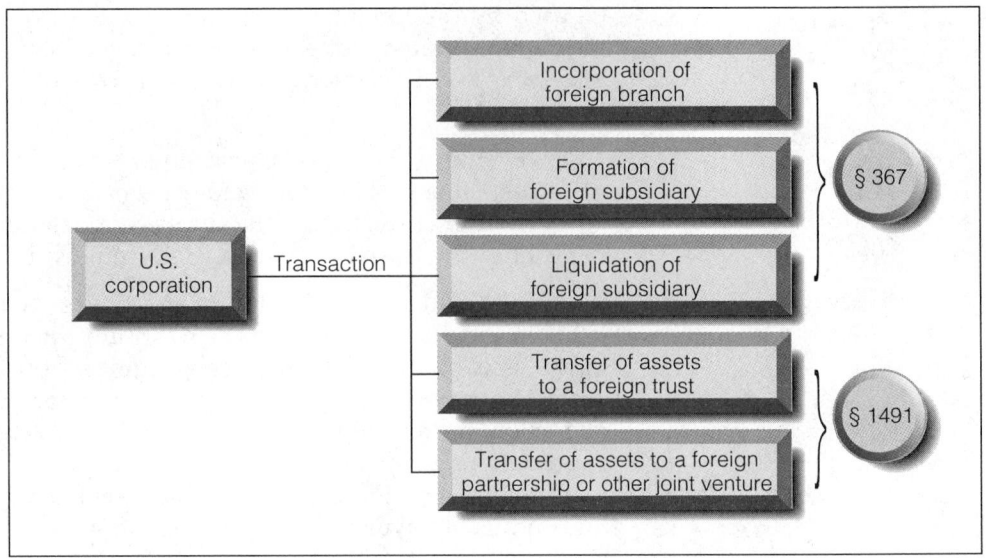

The § 1491 tax is an excise tax. The significance of this distinction is that the transferee does not increase the basis of the property by the appreciation subject to the excise tax. The parties to the transfer can overcome this result if the transferor elects § 1057 treatment.

Figure 9–2 summarizes the taxation of asset transfers.

FOREIGN CURRENCY TRANSACTIONS

6   LEARNING OBJECTIVE
Explain how foreign currency exchange affects the tax consequences of international transactions.

Changes in the relative value of a foreign currency and the U.S. dollar (the foreign exchange rate) affect the dollar value of foreign property held by the taxpayer, the dollar value of foreign debts, and the dollar amount of gain or loss on a transaction denominated in a foreign currency.

EXAMPLE 35

Dress, Inc., a domestic corporation, purchases merchandise for resale from Fiesta, Inc., a foreign corporation, for 50,000K. On the date of purchase, 1K (a foreign currency) is equal to $1 U.S. (1K:$1). At this time, the account payable is $50,000. On the date of payment by Dress (the foreign exchange date), the exchange rate is 1.25K:$1. In other words, the foreign currency has devalued in relation to the U.S. dollar, and Dress will pay Fiesta 50,000K, which cost Dress only $40,000. Dress must record the purchase of the merchandise at $50,000 and recognize a foreign currency gain of $10,000 ($50,000 – $40,000). ▼

Taxpayers may find it necessary to translate amounts denominated in foreign currency into U.S. dollars for any of the following purposes.

• Purchase of goods, services, and property.
• Sale of goods, services, and property.
• Collection of foreign receivables.
• Payment of foreign payables.
• FTC calculations.
• Recognition of income or loss from foreign branch activities.

The foreign currency exchange rates, however, have no effect on the transactions of a U.S. person who arranges all international transactions in U.S. dollars.

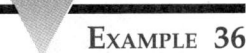

EXAMPLE 36

Sellers, Inc., a domestic corporation, purchases goods from Rose, Inc., a foreign corporation, and pays for these goods in U.S. dollars. Rose then exchanges the U.S. dollars for the currency of the country in which it operates. Sellers has no foreign exchange considerations with which to contend. If Sellers purchased goods from Rose and was required to pay Rose in a foreign currency, Sellers would have to exchange U.S. dollars for the foreign currency in order to make payment. If the exchange rate had changed from the date of purchase to the date of payment, Sellers would have a foreign currency gain or loss on the currency exchange. ▼

TAX ISSUES

The following are the major tax issues that must be considered in the taxation of foreign currency exchange.

- The character of the gain or loss (ordinary or capital).
- The date of recognition of any gain or loss.
- The source (U.S. or foreign) of the foreign currency gain or loss.

EXAMPLE 37

Batch, Inc., a domestic corporation, purchases computer parts for resale from Chips, a foreign corporation, for 125,000K. On the date of purchase, .75K (a foreign currency) is equal to $1 U.S. (.75K:$1). On the date of payment by Batch (the foreign exchange date), the exchange rate is .8K:$1. In other words, Batch paid 125,000K, which cost Batch $156,250 in U.S. dollars (125,000K/.8K). Batch, however, must record the purchase of the computer parts for inventory purposes at $166,667 (125,000K/.75K) and recognize a foreign currency gain of $10,417 ($166,667 – $156,250). ▼

The following concepts are important when dealing with the tax aspects of foreign exchange.

- Foreign currency is treated as property other than money.
- Gain or loss on the exchange of foreign currency is considered separately from the underlying transaction (e.g., the purchase or sale of goods).
- No gain or loss is recognized until a transaction is closed.

FUNCTIONAL CURRENCY

Prior to 1987, the Code contained no provisions for determining tax results when foreign operations could be recorded in a foreign currency. However, in 1981, the Financial Accounting Standards Board adopted FAS 52 on foreign currency translation. FAS 52 introduced the **functional currency** approach (the currency of the economic environment in which the foreign entity operates generally is to be used as the monetary unit to measure gains and losses). TRA of 1986 adopted this approach for the most part.

Under § 985, all income tax determinations are to be made in the taxpayer's functional currency. Generally, a taxpayer's functional currency is the U.S. dollar. In certain circumstances, a qualified business unit (QBU) may be required to use a foreign currency as its functional currency. A QBU is a separate and clearly identified unit of a taxpayer's trade or business (e.g., a foreign branch). An individual is not a QBU; however, a trade or business conducted by an individual may be a QBU.[46]

---

[46] Reg. § 1.989(a)–1(b).

SECTION 988 TRANSACTIONS

The disposition of a nonfunctional currency can result in a foreign currency gain or loss under § 988. Section 988 transactions include those in which gain or loss is determined with regard to the value of a nonfunctional currency, such as the following.

- Acquisition of (or becoming obligor under) a debt instrument.
- Accruing (or otherwise taking into account) any item of expense or gross income or receipts that is to be paid or received at a later date.
- Entering into or acquiring nearly any forward contract, futures contract, option, or similar investment position.
- Disposition of nonfunctional currency.

Section 988 generally treats exchange gain or loss falling within its provisions as ordinary income or loss. Certain exchange gain or loss is apportioned in the same manner as interest expense.[47] Capital gain or loss treatment may be elected with regard to forward contracts, futures contracts, and options that constitute capital assets in the hands of the taxpayer.

A closed or completed transaction is required. The residence of the taxpayer generally determines the source of a foreign exchange gain or loss.

BRANCH OPERATIONS

Where a QBU (a foreign branch, in this case) uses a foreign currency as its functional currency, the profit or loss is computed in the foreign currency each year and translated into U.S. dollars for tax purposes. The entire amount of profit or loss, without taking remittances into account, is translated using a weighted-average exchange rate for the taxable year. Exchange gain or loss is recognized on remittances from the QBU. One compares the U.S. dollar amount of the remittance at the exchange rate in effect on the date of remittance with the U.S. dollar value (basis pool) of the equity pool of the branch (i.e., initial capitalization plus contributions to the branch plus undistributed profits minus remittances and losses—all measured in the QBU's functional currency).[48] This gain or loss is ordinary, and it is sourced according to the income to which the remittance is attributable.

 **EXAMPLE 38**

Icon, a domestic corporation, began operation of a QBU (foreign branch) in 1995. The functional currency of the QBU is the K. The QBU's profits for 1995–1997 are as follows.

	Income (in Ks)	Weighted-Average Exchange Rate	Income in U.S. Dollars
1995	200K	1K:$1	$200
1996	200K	1.25K:$1	160
1997	200K	1.6K:$1	125
	600K		$485

The income is taxed to Icon in the year earned, regardless of whether any remittances take place. ▼

---

[47] Temp.Reg. § 1.861–9T(b).   [48] Prop.Reg. § 1.987–2.

Recognition of Foreign Exchange Gain or Loss

Transaction	Date of Recognition
Purchase or sale of inventory or business asset	Date of disposition of foreign currency
Branch profits	Remittance of branch profits
Subpart F income	Receipt of previously taxed income (accumulated E & P)
Dividend from current E & P or untaxed accumulated E & P	No gain or loss to recipient

DISTRIBUTIONS FROM FOREIGN CORPORATIONS

An actual distribution of E & P from a foreign corporation is included in income by the U.S. recipient at the exchange rate in effect on the date of distribution. Thus, no exchange gain or loss is recognized. Deemed dividend distributions under Subpart F are translated at the weighted-average exchange rate for the CFC's tax year to which the deemed distribution is attributable, similar to Example 38 above. Exchange gain or loss can result when an actual distribution of this previously taxed income is made.

For FTC purposes, foreign taxes are translated at the exchange rate in effect when the foreign taxes were paid. For purposes of the indirect FTC, any adjustment of foreign taxes paid by the foreign corporation is translated at the rate in effect at the time of adjustment. Any refund or credit is translated at the rate in effect at the time the foreign taxes were originally paid.

EXAMPLE 39

Music, Inc., a foreign subsidiary of Keyboard, a U.S. corporation, has pre-tax income of 300K. Music pays 100K in foreign taxes. The exchange rate was .5K:$1 when the income was earned and the foreign taxes paid. None of the income is Subpart F income. If the 200K net earnings are distributed when the exchange rate is .4K:$1, the deemed-paid taxes are $200 [($500/$500) × $200]. The effective tax rate is 40%. ▼

REPORTING REQUIREMENTS

The U.S. tax provisions in the international area include numerous reporting requirements. Furthermore, civil and criminal penalties for noncompliance can apply.[49]

A domestic corporation that is 25 percent or more foreign owned must file an information return and maintain certain records where they will be accessible to the IRS.[50] Additionally, any foreign corporation carrying on a trade or business in the United States must file an information return and maintain records in a similar manner.[51] Form 5472 is used for these purposes.

U.S. persons who acquire or dispose of an interest in a foreign partnership must file an information return disclosing information regarding the transfer.[52]

---

[49] See Chapter 14.
[50] § 6038A.
[51] § 6038C.
[52] § 6046A.

Creation of, or a transfer to, a foreign trust by a U.S. person necessitates the filing of a Form 3520.[53] Information returns are also required in connection with foreign investment in U.S. real property interests.[54]

TAX PLANNING CONSIDERATIONS

Tax legislation tends progressively to reduce the ability to plan transactions and operations in a manner that minimizes tax liability. However, taxpayers who are not limited by the constraints of a particular transaction or operation can use the following suggestions to plan for maximum tax benefits.

THE FOREIGN TAX CREDIT LIMITATION AND SOURCING PROVISIONS

The FTC limitation is partially based on the amount of foreign-source taxable income in the numerator of the limitation ratio. Consequently, the sourcing of income is extremely important. Income that is taxed by a foreign tax jurisdiction benefits from the FTC only to the extent that it is classified as foreign-source income under U.S. tax law. Thus, elements that affect the sourcing of income, such as the place of title passage, should be considered carefully before a transaction is undertaken.

After the 1986 tax act, which added several limitation basket computations to the FTC, many companies generated excess foreign taxes. These companies have not been able to take advantage of the carryback and carryover provision for the FTC. It may be possible for a U.S. corporation to alleviate the problem of excess foreign taxes by using the following techniques.

- Generate "same basket" foreign-source income that is subject to a tax rate lower than the U.S. tax rate.
- Reduce highly taxed foreign-source income in favor of foreign-source income that is taxed at a lower rate.
- Time the repatriation of foreign-source earnings to coincide with excess limitation years.
- Deduct foreign taxes for years in which the deduction benefit would exceed the FTC benefit.

A taxpayer who can control the timing of income and loss recognition will want to avoid recognizing losses in years in which the loss is apportioned among the FTC limitation baskets. Otherwise, the foreign taxes for which a credit is allowed for the tax year are reduced.

EXAMPLE 40

Della, a U.S. person, has U.S.-source taxable income of $200,000, worldwide taxable income of $300,000, and a U.S. tax liability (before FTC) of $84,000. She receives foreign-source taxable income, pays foreign income taxes, and has an FTC as shown.

Basket	Amount	Foreign Taxes	FTC Limitation	FTC
Passive	$ 20,000	$ 800	$ 5,600	$ 800
General	50,000	20,500	14,000	14,000
Non-CFC § 902 corporation #1	15,000	3,000	4,200	3,000
Non-CFC § 902 corporation #2	15,000	4,500	4,200	4,200
	$100,000	$28,800		$22,000

---

[53] § 6048.   [54] § 6039C.

If Della had a foreign-source loss of $10,000 in the shipping limitation basket, the FTC is reduced by $1,820. The U.S. tax liability before the FTC is $81,200; 50% of the loss would be apportioned to the general limitation basket, reducing the FTC limitation for this basket to $12,600 [$81,200 × ($45,000/$290,000)]; and 15% is apportioned to the non-CFC § 902 corporation #2 basket, reducing the FTC limitation for this basket to $3,780 [$81,200 × ($13,500/$290,000)]. Della would avoid this result if she could defer recognition of the loss to a tax year in which it would not have a negative effect on the FTC. ▼

THE FOREIGN CORPORATION AS A TAX SHELTER

An NRA who is able to hold U.S. investments through a foreign corporation can accomplish much in the way of avoiding U.S. taxation. Capital gains (other than dispositions of U.S. real property interests) are not subject to U.S. taxation. This assumes that they are not effectively connected with a U.S. trade or business and are not gains from commodity transactions entered into by a foreign corporation with its principal place of business in the United States. The NRA can dispose of the stock of a foreign corporation that holds U.S. real property and not be subject to taxation under § 897 (FIRPTA). Furthermore, the stock of a foreign corporation is not included in the U.S. gross estate of a deceased NRA, even if all the assets of the foreign corporation are located in the United States.

Caution is advised where the foreign corporation may generate income effectively connected with the conduct of a U.S. trade or business. The income may be taxed at a higher rate than if the NRA individually generated the income. The tradeoff between a higher U.S. tax on this income and protection from the U.S. estate tax and § 897 must be weighed.

PLANNING UNDER SUBPART F

The *de minimis* rule allows a CFC to avoid the classification of income as FBC income or insurance income and prevents the U.S. shareholder from having to include it in gross income as a constructive dividend. Thus, a CFC with total FBC income and insurance income in an amount close to the 5 percent or $1 million level should monitor income realization to assure that the *de minimis* rule applies for the tax year. At least as important is avoiding the classification of all the gross income of the CFC as FBC income or insurance income. This happens when the sum of the FBC income and gross insurance income for the taxable year exceeds 70 percent of total gross income.

Careful timing of increases in investment in U.S. property can reduce the potential for constructive dividend income to U.S. shareholders. The gross income of U.S. shareholders attributable to increases in investment in U.S. property is limited to the E & P of the CFC.[55] E & P that is attributable to amounts that have been included in gross income as Subpart F income in either the current year or a prior tax year is not taxed again when invested in U.S. property.

THE FOREIGN EARNED INCOME EXCLUSION

The tax benefit of the foreign earned income exclusion depends on the tax the income will incur in the country in which earned and the year in which received. If the foreign country levies little or no tax on the income, the U.S. taxpayer can exclude the housing cost amount plus up to $70,000 of foreign earned income and pay little or no tax on the income to the foreign tax jurisdiction. Since foreign

---

[55] §§ 959(a)(1) and (2).

earned income qualifies for the exclusion only if received in the year in which earned or the immediately succeeding tax year, the timely payment of such income is necessary.

In high-tax jurisdictions, the taxpayer may benefit more from taking the FTC than from excluding the earnings from gross income. The taxpayer earning income in a high-tax jurisdiction should compare the tax result of taking the exclusion with the tax result of forgoing either or both exclusions for the FTC. If U.S. taxes on the income are eliminated under all options and the taxpayer has excess foreign taxes to carry back or carry forward, then the FTC generally is more beneficial than the exclusion.

Taxpayers must also carefully monitor trips to the United States when attempting to qualify for the exclusion under the physical presence test. Taxpayers who are attempting to establish a bona fide foreign residence must make sure that their ties to the foreign country predominate over their ties to the United States for the period for which bona fide foreign residence is desired.

KEY TERMS

Branch profits tax, 9–23

Controlled foreign corporation (CFC), 9–31

Dividend equivalent amount (DEA), 9–23

Effectively connected income, 9–15

FIRPTA, 9–26

Foreign earned income exclusion, 9–29

Foreign sales corporation (FSC), 9–15

Foreign tax credit (FTC), 9–3

Functional currency, 9–43

Green card test, 9–20

Nonresident alien, 9–14

Subpart F, 9–31

Tax haven, 9–38

Tax treaty, 9–27

Treaty shopping, 9–39

U.S. shareholder, 9–31

PROBLEM MATERIALS

DISCUSSION QUESTIONS

1. Why is the FTC generally more beneficial to the taxpayer than a deduction of foreign taxes paid by the taxpayer?

2. What income tax consequences need to be considered by a corporate shareholder who takes the indirect credit?

3. Anchor, Inc., a domestic corporation, owns 15% of Dorkin, Inc., and 12% of Felton, Inc., both foreign corporations. Anchor is paid gross dividends of $35,000 and $18,000 from Dorkin and Felton, respectively. Dorkin withheld and paid more than $10,500 in foreign taxes on the $35,000 dividend. Dorkin's country of residence levies a 20% tax on dividends paid to nonresident corporations. However, the tax rate is increased to 30% if the recipient is a resident of a country that provides an FTC. Taxes of $3,600 are withheld on the dividend from Felton. What tax issues must be considered in determining the availability and amount of the FTC allowed to Anchor?

4. For FTC purposes, how must the taxpayer apportion a foreign loss in one category when there is foreign-source income in other categories and also U.S.-source income?

5. What are some of the tax consequences affected by the sourcing of income as within or without the United States?

6. Will interest paid by a U.S. corporation be treated as U.S.-source in all cases? Explain.

7. Generally, U.S. taxpayers with foreign operations desire to increase foreign-source income and reduce deductions against that foreign-source income in order to increase their FTC limitations. What provision enables the IRS to prevent taxpayers from manipulating the source of income and allocation of deductions? Explain.

8. May Lyle, an alien, overcome classification as a U.S. resident under the substantial presence test if he is physically present in the United States for 183 days during 1997?

9. Trader, Inc., a foreign corporation, sells transistors in several countries, including the United States. In fact, currently 18% of Trader's sales income is sourced in the United States (through branches in New York and Miami). Trader is considering opening additional branches in San Francisco and Houston in order to increase U.S. sales. What tax issues must Trader consider before making this move?

10. Explain why the following statement is false: Income tax treaties between the United States and foreign countries allow only one of the treaty partners (either the United States or the foreign country) to tax income earned in one treaty country by residents of the other treaty country.

11. Why can stock of a foreign corporation held by NRA individuals be considered a tax shelter for U.S. tax purposes?

12. How does the U.S. tax law attempt to assure that the tax will be paid when nonresident aliens and foreign corporations dispose of U.S. real property interests at a gain?

13. Do self-employed individuals receive the same benefits under § 911 (foreign-earned income exclusion provisions) as do individuals classified as "employees"? Explain.

14. Joanna owns 5% of Axel, a foreign corporation. Joanna's son, Fred, is considering acquiring 15% of Axel from an NRA. The remainder of Axel is owned 34% by unrelated U.S. persons and 53% by unrelated NRAs. Currently, Fred operates a manufacturing business (as a sole proprietorship) that sells goods to Axel for resale outside the United States and outside Axel's country of residence. Joanna is not concerned about the concentration of investment since she expects to sell her stock in Axel in three years at a significant capital gain. Are there tax issues that Joanna and Fred need to address?

15. How does the tax law prevent Subpart F income from being taxed more than once to the U.S. shareholders?

16. Describe the foreign presence requirement of the FSC provisions.

17. LeBlanc, Inc., a foreign sales corporation, is having trouble raising additional needed capital. Its only stock issue, common stock, is currently owned by 20 U.S. corporations. LeBlanc is considering an additional issue of common or preferred stock. LeBlanc is also considering a takeover bid made by one of its corporate shareholders in which LeBlanc's shareholders would receive shares of the U.S. corporation in exchange for their shares in LeBlanc. LeBlanc would be merged into the U.S. corporation. Does LeBlanc face any FSC issues in making these decisions?

18. Describe a tax haven.

19. What are the important concepts when dealing with the tax aspects of foreign exchange?

20. When would the U.S. recipient of a constructive dividend (for example, under Subpart F) have a foreign exchange gain or loss?

PROBLEMS

21. Ellen, a U.S. resident, operates an import/export company. This year, the business generated taxable income of $120,000 from foreign sources and $90,000 from U.S. sources. All of Ellen's foreign-source income is in the general limitation basket. The remainder of her taxable income is from U.S. investments. Her total worldwide taxable income (before personal exemptions) is $250,000. Ellen pays foreign taxes of $48,000. Her U.S. income taxes (before FTC) are $70,000. What is Ellen's FTC for the tax year?

22. Space, Inc., a domestic corporation, owns 40% of Satellite, Inc., a foreign corporation. Space receives a gross dividend of $42,000 from Satellite. Satellite's after-tax post-1986 E & P is $320,000, and its post-1986 foreign taxes total $96,000. Space's taxable income before consideration of the dividend is $300,000. Assume that Space is subject to a flat U.S. tax rate of 34%.

    a. What are Space's deemed-paid foreign taxes with respect to the dividend from Satellite?

    b. What is Space's FTC?

23. Prepare a flowchart for your colleagues in the Tax Department, illustrating the steps in determining a company's FTC.

24. Parent, Inc., a U.S. corporation, owns an interest in a chain of foreign corporations. Given the following chains of ownership, from which foreign corporation(s) is it possible for Parent to claim the deemed-paid (indirect) FTC?

    a. Parent owns 45% of FC1, FC1 owns 90% of FC2, FC2 owns 25% of FC3, and FC3 owns 50% of FC4.

    b. Parent owns 30% of FC1, FC1 owns 30% of FC2, and FC2 owns 15% of FC3.

25. Cotton Export, Inc., a domestic corporation, has the following taxable income amounts for the tax year and incurs foreign income taxes as shown.

Type of Income	Source	Amount	Foreign Taxes
Sales	Canada	$ 800,000	$336,000
	U.S.	300,000	–0–
Financial services income	Canada	30,000	3,000
	U.S.	–0–	–0–
Dividends*	Canada	12,000	3,900**
	U.S.†	15,000	–0–
Other interest	Canada	8,000	1,200††
	U.S.	10,000	–0–
		$1,175,000	$344,100

U.S. taxes before FTC = $399,500.

*From one § 902 non-CFC foreign corporation.
**Included in dividend amount.
†Net of dividend received deduction.
††High withholding tax.

Gross foreign-source sales income is $1,200,000. Deductions allocable to foreign sales income total $350,000, and the apportioned share of deductions not definitely allocable to foreign sales income is $50,000.

Gross foreign-source financial services income is $40,000. Deductions definitely allocable to foreign-source financial services income total $7,000, and the apportioned share of deductions not definitely allocable to foreign sales income is $3,000.

Gross foreign-source dividend income is $13,000. There are no deductions definitely allocable to dividend income. The apportioned share of deductions not definitely allocable to foreign-source dividend income is $1,000. Gross foreign-source "other interest" is $8,700. There are no deductions definitely allocable to other interest income. The apportioned share of deductions not definitely allocable to foreign-source other interest income is $700.

Determine Cotton's FTC by filling out the appropriate Form 1118s.

26. Jasper, a U.S. resident, received the following income items for the current tax year. What is the source (U.S. or foreign) of each income item?

    a. $800 dividend from U.S. Power Company, a U.S. corporation, that operates solely in the western United States.

    b. $1,200 dividend from Star Trading Corporation, a U.S. corporation that had total gross income of $2,100,000 from the active conduct of a foreign trade or business for the immediately preceding three tax years. Star's worldwide gross income for the same period was $2,600,000.

    c. $750 dividend from International Consolidated, Inc., a foreign corporation that had gross income of $800,000 effectively connected with the conduct of a U.S. trade or business for the immediately preceding three tax years. International's worldwide gross income for the same period was $3,000,000.

    d. $300 interest from a savings account at a Houston bank.

    e. $2,500 interest on Rolan Corporation bonds. Rolan is a U.S. corporation that derived $3,000,000 of its gross income for the immediately preceding three tax years from operation of an active foreign business. Rolan's worldwide gross income for this same period was $3,600,000.

27. Rita, an NRA, is a professional golfer. She played in 7 tournaments in the United States in the current year and earned $50,000 in prizes from these tournaments. She deposited the winnings in a bank account she opened in Mexico City after she won her first tournament money for the year. Rita played a total of 30 tournaments for the year and earned $200,000 in total prize money. She spent 40 days in the United States, 60 days in England, 20 days in Scotland, and the rest of the time in South America. How much U.S.-source income, if any, does Rita have from her participation in these tournaments, and is she subject to U.S. taxation on any of her winnings?

28. Determine the source of income (U.S. or foreign) of the following sales.
    a. Robert, an NRA, sells Wal-Mart stock at a gain on the New York Stock Exchange.
    b. Jennifer, a resident of El Paso, Texas, sells equipment used in her trade or business, which is operated in Juarez, Mexico. Title passes in El Paso.
    c. A U.S. company sells inventory purchased from a New Hampshire manufacturer to a Canadian company, title passing on shipment from Kennedy Airport in New York.
    d. A U.S. corporation manufactures inventory in Mexico and sells it to wholesale customers in Australia, title passing on delivery in Sydney.

29. Determine the source of income (U.S. or foreign) in each of the following situations.
    a. Development, Inc., a U.S. corporation, earns $150,000 in royalty income from Far East, Ltd., a foreign corporation, for the use of several patented processes in Far East's manufacturing business located in Singapore.
    b. Dora, an NRA, is an employee of a foreign corporation. During the tax year, she spends 50 days in the United States purchasing cloth for her employer, a clothing manufacturer. Her yearly salary is $80,000 (translated to U.S. dollars). She spends a total of 250 days working during the year. Her employer has no other business contacts with the United States.
    c. An NRA sells an apartment building to a U.S. resident. The building is located in Chicago. The closing takes place in the NRA's country of residence.
    d. A domestic corporation sells depreciable personal property that it has been using in its foreign branch operations. The property sells for $180,000, has a tax basis of $75,000, and has been depreciated for tax purposes to the extent of $77,000. The property is located in a foreign country, but is sold to another domestic corporation. The sales transaction takes place in the United States.

30. Jeanette, a citizen and resident of France, comes to the United States on March 3, 1997, and remains until July 20 of the same year, at which time she returns to France. Jeanette comes back to the United States on November 15, 1997, and remains until December 20, 1997, when she again returns to France. Jeanette does not possess a green card, but she was a U.S. resident for 1996 under the substantial presence test, spending 210 days in the United States in that year. Jeanette was never physically present in the United States before 1996. Is Jeanette a U.S. resident for 1997 under the physical presence test? If so, is there any way that she can overcome the presumption of residence?

31. For the current year, Carla, an NRA, has the U.S.-source income shown below. Determine Carla's U.S. tax liability, assuming that she is single and has no allowable itemized deductions. Assume the personal exemption amount is $2,650. Also assume that the 28% bracket for a single taxpayer begins at taxable income of $24,650.

Dividend from U.S. corporation*	$ 1,200
Interest from U.S. bank account**	1,500
Capital gain from sale of U.S. corporate stock†	6,000
Share of partnership taxable income††	20,000

*Carla owns less than 1% of the corporate stock.
**Not effectively connected with a U.S. trade or business.
†Carla was in the United States 25 days during the tax year, and the gain is not effectively connected with a U.S. trade or business.
††Carla is an investor in a U.S. partnership.

32. Toma, a resident of France, is sent to the United States by Felp Corporation, a foreign employer, to arrange the purchase of some machine tools. Toma spends three weeks in the United States. This is her only trip to the United States during the year.

    Toma's gross monthly salary is $3,500. Her paycheck is deposited in her French bank account while she is in the United States. The salary is attributable to 15 U.S. and 6 French working days. The foreign employer does not have a U.S. trade or business. What is the amount of Toma's U.S.-source income?

33. Provo Corporation, a pharmaceutical corporation resident in Switzerland, sells certain products through a U.S. office. Current-year taxable income from such sales in the United States is $3,500,000. Provo's U.S. office deposits working capital funds short term in certificates of deposit with U.S. banks. Current-year income from these deposits is $25,000.

    Provo also invests in U.S. securities traded on the New York Stock Exchange. This investing is done by the home office. For the current year, Provo has realized capital gains of $35,000 and dividend income of $18,000 from these stock investments. Compute Provo's U.S. tax liability, assuming that the U.S.-Switzerland income tax treaty reduces withholding on dividends to 15% and on interest to 5%.

34. Flipp, a foreign corporation, operates a trade or business in the United States. Flipp's U.S.-source taxable income effectively connected with this trade or business is $300,000 for the current tax year. Flipp's current E & P is $250,000. Net U.S. equity was $1.5 million at the beginning of the year and $1.4 million at the end of the year. Flipp is resident in a country with which the United States does not have an income tax treaty. What is the effect of the branch profits tax on Flipp for the current tax year?

35. Niles, a NRA individual, owns 20% of the stock of Sandstone, a U.S. corporation. Sandstone's balance sheet on the last day of the taxable year is as follows.

		Adjusted Basis	Fair Market Value
Cash (used as working capital)		$ 500,000	500,000
Investment in foreign land		200,000	400,000
Investment in U.S. real estate:			
Land		100,000	150,000
Buildings	$1,400,000		
Less depreciation	300,000	1,100,000	1,500,000
		$1,900,000	$2,550,000
Accounts payable		$ 300,000	$ 300,000
Notes payable		500,000	500,000
Capital stock		400,000	800,000
Retained earnings		700,000	950,000
		$1,900,000	$2,550,000

Niles was in the United States only 50 days in the tax year. He sold 70% of his stock in Sandstone on the last day of the tax year for $350,000. Niles's adjusted basis in the stock sold was $245,000. He sold the stock for cash. What are the U.S. tax consequences, if any, to Niles?

36. In Problem 35, what would be the U.S. tax consequences, if any, to Niles if Sandstone was a foreign corporation instead of a domestic corporation?

37. Linda is single, a chemist, and a U.S. citizen. For the past three years, she has worked in the lab of a foreign refinery owned by a U.S. corporation. She is a bona fide resident of a foreign country. This year, Linda received $75,000 in foreign earned income (FEI) and has qualified housing benefits provided by her employer of $35,000. Assuming that the base amount is $9,500, the personal exemption is $2,650, the standard deduction for a single taxpayer is $4,150, the 28% tax bracket for a single taxpayer begins at $24,650, and the 31% bracket begins at $59,750, compute Linda's U.S. tax liability (a) taking both the FEI exclusion and the housing exclusion, (b) taking only the FEI exclusion, and (c) taking only the housing exclusion. Linda does not pay any foreign taxes.

38. Dart is a U.S. corporation. Three of the company's engineers have been working in Bahrain for 18 months as of January 1, 1996. They are U.S. citizens who have worked for Dart for 8 to 12 years. The company controller asks you to summarize the tax provisions of the foreign earned income exclusion for these employees. In writing this summary, include Code sections and subsections where appropriate.

39. In each of the following independent cases, determine, under the stock ownership requirement, whether Steelmark, a foreign corporation, is a CFC and/or an FPHC. Steelmark has only one class of stock outstanding.
    a. Steelmark stock is directly owned 10% by Anna, 12% by Bart, 15% by Chris, 12% by Dave, 8% by Edith, and 43% by George. Anna, Bart, Chris, and Dave are U.S. residents. Edith and George are NRAs. Edith is Dave's daughter.
    b. Steelmark stock is directly owned 10% by Anna, 12% by Bart, 15% by Chris, 12% by Dave, 8% by Edith, and 43% by George. Anna, Bart, Chris, Dave, and Edith are all unrelated U.S. residents. George is an NRA.
    c. Steelmark stock is directly owned 20% by Anna, 15% by Bart, 10% by Chris, 30% by Dave, and 25% by Link, another foreign corporation. Anna, Bart, and Chris are U.S. residents. Dave is an NRA. Anna owns 50% of Link.

40. Profit, Inc., a foreign corporation resident in Ireland, is owned 100% by Balance, Inc., a domestic corporation. Profit is a CFC. Determine Profit's Subpart F income (before expenses and cost of goods sold) for the tax year, given the following items of income.
    a. $120,000 from the sale of merchandise to Balance. The merchandise was purchased from an unrelated manufacturer resident in Italy.
    b. $240,000 from the sale of merchandise (purchased from Balance) to customers in France.
    c. $80,000 commissions from the sale of merchandise on behalf of Balance to residents of Ireland, for use within Ireland.
    d. $250,000 from the performance on a construction contract entered into by Balance. The services were performed by Profit's personnel in Italy.

41. Box, Inc., a U.S. corporation, owns 30% of the only class of stock of Jewel, Inc., a CFC. Jewel is a CFC until July 1 of the current tax year. Box has held the stock since Jewel was organized and continues to hold it for the entire year. Box and Jewel are both calendar year taxpayers. If Jewel's Subpart F income for the tax year is $400,000, current E & P is $600,000, and no distributions have been made for the tax year, what is the amount, if any, that Box must include in gross income under Subpart F for the tax year?

42. The following persons own stock in Flint, Inc., a foreign personal holding company. If undistributed FPHC income is $400,000 for the tax year, how much of this amount must each shareholder include in U.S. gross income as a constructive dividend?

Mr. Brent, U.S. individual	25%
Mrs. Chan, U.S. individual	5%
Mr. Lin, U.S. individual	15%
Mrs. Lin, U.S. individual	5%
Ms. LeCreaux, U.S. individual	5%
Marc, Inc., a U.S. corporation	20%
Donre, Inc., a foreign corporation	25%

Only the Lins are related persons.

43. An FSC and its U.S. parent have gross receipts of $950,000 and combined taxable income (CTI) of $460,000 related to the export sales of a particular product. What is the FSC's profit allowed under (a) the gross receipts method and (b) the CTI method?

44. Plum, Inc., a U.S. corporation, and its commission foreign sales corporation (FSC), have the following profit picture with regard to Plum's export product.

Plum's gross sales	$550,000
Plum's gross income from sales	220,000
Plum's net income from sales before FSC considerations	132,000
Expenses incurred by FSC	14,000

Using the administrative pricing rules, calculate the FSC's taxable income.

45. For each of the following situations, determine whether § 367 or § 1491 would apply.
    a. Liquidation of a foreign subsidiary by a U.S. corporation.
    b. Transfer of assets by a U.S. individual to a foreign trust.
    c. Incorporation of a foreign branch by a U.S. corporation.

46. You are the head tax accountant for the Venture Company, a U.S. corporation. The board of directors is considering expansion overseas and asks you to present a summary of the U.S. tax consequences of investing overseas through a foreign subsidiary. Prepare a detailed outline of the presentation you will make to the board.

47. Weight, Inc., a domestic corporation, purchases weight-lifting equipment for resale from HiDisu, a Japanese corporation, for 75 million yen. On the date of purchase, 150 yen is equal to $1 U.S. (Y150:$1). The purchase is made on December 15, 1997, with payment due in 60 days. Weight is a calendar year taxpayer. On December 31, 1997, the foreign exchange rate is Y140:$1. What amount of foreign currency gain or loss, if any, must Weight recognize for 1997 as a result of this transaction?

48. Health, Inc., a domestic corporation, sells vitamins (inventory) to Svent, a Swiss drugstore chain, for 1,000,000 Swiss francs (Sf). The sale is made on January 15, with payment on the sale due in 180 days. On the date of sale, the exchange rate is .8125Sf:$1. On the date of collection, the exchange rate is .8640Sf:$1. Assuming that Health, Inc., converts the Swiss francs to U.S. dollars on the date of collection, what is the exchange gain or loss, if any?

49. Delane, Inc., a domestic corporation, organized a foreign branch in 1994. The branch is a QBU and uses the K (a foreign currency) as its functional currency. The following income and taxes resulted in 1995–1997. The branch income is all in the general limitation basket.

	Income	**Foreign Taxes**	**Exchange Rate**
1995	240K/$400	60K/$100	.6K:$1
1996	210K/$300	87.5K/$125	.7K:$1
1997	400K/$400	120K/$120	1K:$1

Assuming the maximum corporate rate of 35% applies for U.S. tax purposes, determine the net U.S. tax for each year with respect to the branch income.

50. Clarey, Inc., a domestic corporation, began operating a CFC (QBU) in 1996. The functional currency of the CFC is the rale (R). The CFC made no distributions for 1996 or 1997. Its E & P exceeded its Subpart F income for these years. Subpart F income and exchange rates are as follows.

	Subpart F Income (in R)	Exchange Rate
1996	270,000R	.9R:$1
1997	480,000R	1.2R:$1

If Clarey owns 100% of the CFC, what is the dollar amount of income that Clarey must recognize under Subpart F for 1996 and 1997?

51. Market, Inc., a foreign subsidiary of Export, Inc., a U.S. corporation, has pretax income of FF75,000 for 1997. Market pays FF18,750 in foreign taxes on this income. The exchange rate was FF.1961:$1 when the income was earned and the foreign taxes paid. None of the income is Subpart F income. If the net earnings of FF56,250 are distributed when the exchange rate is FF.2152:$1, what are the deemed-paid taxes available to Export? Assume that 1997 is Market's first year of operation.

52. Mega Corporation, a foreign corporation, is owned by Multi Corporation, a domestic corporation. Mega earns income of 3 million K (Mega's functional currency) and pays foreign taxes of 750,000K when the exchange rate is .3K:$1. If none of Mega's income is Subpart F income and Multi receives a dividend of 1.5 million K when the exchange rate is .5K:$1, what is the dollar amount of the dividend and of the deemed-paid foreign taxes to Multi?

53. Money, Inc., a U.S. corporation, has $500,000 to invest overseas for 1997. For U.S. tax purposes, any additional income earned by Money will be taxed at 34%. Two possibilities for investment are:
    a. Invest the $500,000 in Exco (a foreign corporation) common stock. Exco common stock pays a dividend of $3 per share each year. The $500,000 would purchase 10,000 shares (or 10%) of Exco's only class of stock (voting common). Exco expects to earn $10,000,000 before taxes for 1997 and to be taxed at a flat rate of 40%. Its 1997 E & P before taxes is estimated to be $9,400,000. Exco's government does not withhold on dividends paid to foreign investors.
    b. Invest the $500,000 in Exco bonds which pay interest at 7% per year. Assume that the bonds will be acquired at par, or face, value. Exco's government withholds 25% on interest paid to foreign investors.

    Analyze these two investment opportunities and determine which would give Money the best return after taxes. Be sure to consider the effect of the foreign tax credit.

54. Georgia Calder is considering two offers that she has received from prospective employers. Overseas Projects, Inc., has offered Calder a position in Istanbul that will last for a minimum of three years. She will earn approximately $130,000 a year, which includes employer-provided housing costs of $28,000. During this period, she is required to return to the United States for two-week executive meetings at least three times a year. She also will receive a three-week vacation that she can spend anywhere she chooses.

    Foreign Lands, Inc., has offered Calder a position in New Delhi that also will last for approximately three years. She will earn $110,000 a year, which does not include housing costs. However, her employer will reimburse her for up to $25,000 of qualified housing expenses. There is no requirement that she return to the United States for meetings. She will receive a four-week vacation that she can spend as she chooses. However, Foreign Lands will provide for her transportation if she wishes to spend her vacation in the United States.

Write a detailed memo to Ms. Calder explaining the tax consequences that she should consider in making her decision. Be sure to include a discussion of the bona fide residence versus physical presence rules. In your deliberations, use $9,500 as the base amount. Be careful not to overwhelm Ms. Calder with tax jargon such as "expatriate" and "outbound." Use plain language that a novice would understand. Do not let your tax knowledge cause you to use a "superior" attitude when addressing Ms. Calder.

RESEARCH PROBLEMS

*Note: **West's Federal Taxation on CD-ROM** can be used in preparing solutions to the Research Problems. Alternatively, tax research materials contained in a standard tax library can be used.*

Research Problem 1.   A U.S. corporation had the following net taxable income (loss) for the tax year. Its U.S. taxes before the foreign tax credit (FTC) are $6,750. Determine the FTC limitation for each basket of foreign-source income.

Source (Basket)	Income (Loss)	Foreign Taxes
U.S.-source	($ 54,000)	–0–
Foreign-source passive	80,000	$24,000
Foreign-source shipping	40,000	14,800
Foreign-source overall	(21,000)	–0–

Partial list of research aids:
§ 904(f)(5).

General Explanation of the Tax Reform Act of 1986 (the Bluebook), Joint Committee on Taxation, pp. 909–912.

Instructions accompanying Form 1118, Foreign Tax Credit—Corporations, Dept. of the Treasury, Internal Revenue Service.

Research Problem 2.   John and Marla Mayor, U.S. citizens, file a joint income tax return. They have two dependent children. John is an engineer for a multinational oil company and works primarily in Myanmar (formerly Burma) for the entire tax year. Because of adverse conditions in Myanmar, Marla and the children live in Kuala Lumpur, Malaysia, while John works in Myanmar. Marla works at the same company's corporate office in Kuala Lumpur.

John and Marla each meet the physical presence test for 1996 and each has a tax home in a foreign country. In addition, John's employer provides housing costs for him in Myanmar. On some occasions, John must go into the interior of the country. At such times, his employer provides meals and lodgings for him at nearby camps (which meet the requirements of § 119). Marla's employer provides a portion of her housing costs in Kuala Lumpur, and Marla pays the remainder.

John and Marla's salaries are entirely from foreign sources. John and Marla receive income and incur expenses as follows.

John's salary		$110,000
Marla's salary		60,000
Meals and lodgings provided to John in camps		4,800
Employer-provided housing costs (John):		
Apartment rent supplement	$6,000	
Utility bill* supplement	900	
Telephone charge supplement	672	
Apartment insurance	425	7,997

Employer-provided housing costs (Marla):

Apartment rent supplement	$9,000	
Utility bill* supplement	300	
Telephone charge supplement	275	
Apartment insurance	320	
Residential parking	700	10,595
Housing costs paid by Marla:		
Remainder of apartment rent	$4,800	
Remainder of utility bill*	1,200	
Remainder of telephone charges	500	
Rental of furniture	3,000	
Pay television subscription	400	
Maid service	3,500	13,400
Dividend income:		
John: From IBM, a U.S. corporation		750
From BAT Industries, a U.K. corporation		520
Marla: From K-Mart, a U.S. corporation		125
From Glaxo, a U.K. corporation		416
Interest income:		
John: Barclays (London)		3,200
Marla: First State Bank (Kuala Lumpur)		2,700
Chase Manhattan (New York)		1,800

*Other than telephone charges.

The Mayors elect to compute their housing cost amount jointly, with John claiming the exclusion for the second household maintained by Marla. They do not itemize deductions. Determine their taxable income for U.S. tax purposes, using a base housing amount of $9,500. Assume that the Mayors are calendar year taxpayers and the tax year is 1996.

Partial list of research aids
Reg. § 1.911–3.
Reg. § 1.911–4.
Reg. § 1.911–5.
IRS Publication 54, *Tax Guide for U.S. Citizens and Resident Aliens Abroad*, Department of the Treasury. This publication can be accessed on the Internet at **http://www.irs.ustreas.gov.**

Research Problem 3.   Fronig, Inc., a foreign corporation, is owned as follows.

- Mr. Allen, a U.S. resident   9%
- Ms. Bella, a U.S. resident   32%
- Mr. and Mrs. Cortez, NRAs   59%

Fronig has only one class of stock outstanding—voting common stock. Mander Corporation, a U.S. corporation, is considering the purchase of 10% of Fronig, Inc., from the Cortezes, which will leave them with 49% ownership. Mr. Allen owns 10% of Mander Corporation. Will Fronig become a CFC if Mander Corporation makes the purchase? Summarize your conclusions in a memo to Mander Corporation.

Partial list of research aids
§ 958(a) and (b) and Reg. § 1.958–2, Ex. 1.

Research Problem 4.   At the beginning of 1995, Monitor Corporation (a CFC) purchases a building for investment. During 1995 and 1996, Monitor derives rental income from this building that is included in the computation of foreign personal holding company income. At the beginning of 1997, Monitor changes the use of the building to active trade or business use. At the beginning of 1998, Monitor sells the building for a gain of $200,000. What is the characterization of the gain for purposes of determining foreign personal holding company income for the year of disposition?

Partial list of research aids
§ 954.
Reg. § 4.954–2.

Research Problem 5.   Jay, a U.S. citizen, lives in Switzerland. He is an artist who sells his paintings throughout the world. As a U.S. citizen, he is subject to taxation on his worldwide income. Jay seeks to take a foreign earned income exclusion with regard to the income he receives from the sales of the paintings. An IRS agent questions the claim that the income from sale of the paintings is "earned" income for purposes of the exclusion. How would you advise Jay?

Partial list of research aids
Mark Tobey, 60 T.C. 227 (1973), *acq.* 1979–1 C.B. 1.
Robida, 72–1 USTC ¶9450, 29 AFTR2d 72–1223, 460 F.2d (CA–9, 1972).
Ingram v. Bowers, 3 USTC ¶915, 10 AFTR 1513, 57 F.2d 65 (CA–2, 1932).

Use the tax resources of the internet to address the following questions. Do not restrict your search to the World Wide Web, but include a review of newsgroups and general reference materials, practitioner sites and resources, primary sources of the tax law, chat rooms and discussion groups, and other opportunities.

Research Problem 6.   What is the current exchange rate between the U.S. dollar and the currency of each of the following countries?
   a. Germany
   b. England
   c. South Africa
   d. Japan
   e. Russia

Research Problem 7.   Download a Form 2555 and use it to report your solution to Problem 37 of this chapter.

Research Problem 8.   Find the text of various tax treaties currently in force in the U.S.
   a. How does the U.S. income tax treaty with Germany define "permanent establishment" for multinational businesses?
   b. How does the U.S. income tax treaty with Japan treat the branch profits tax?
   c. List five countries with which the U.S. has entered into an estate tax treaty.

Unlike C Corporations, some business entities are taxed under the conduit principle. Generally, this means the tax attributes of various transactions are retained as they flow through the entity to the owners. With limited exceptions, no tax is imposed at the entity level. Part III discusses two types of flow-through entities—partnerships and corporations that make the Subchapter S election.

PARTNERSHIPS: FORMATION, OPERATION, AND BASIS

LEARNING OBJECTIVES

After completing Chapter 10, you should be able to:

1. Discuss governing principles and theories of partnership taxation.

2. Describe the tax effects of forming a partnership with cash and property contributions.

3. Examine the tax treatment of expenditures of a newly formed partnership and identify elections the partnership should make.

4. Specify the methods of determining a partnership's tax year.

5. Calculate partnership taxable income and describe how partnership items affect a partner's income tax return.

6. Determine a partner's basis in the partnership interest.

7. Explain how liabilities affect a partner's basis.

8. Describe the limitations on deducting partnership losses.

9. Review the treatment of transactions between a partner and the partnership.

10. Provide insights regarding advantageous use of a partnership.

OVERVIEW OF PARTNERSHIP TAXATION

FORMS OF DOING BUSINESS—FEDERAL TAX CONSEQUENCES

This chapter and the next two chapters analyze two entity structures that offer certain advantages over the regular corporate structure. These entities are partnerships and S corporations, which are called *flow-through* or *pass-through* entities because the owners of the trade or business elect to avoid treating the enterprise as a separate taxable entity. Instead, the owners are taxed on a proportionate share of the entity's taxable income at the end of each of its taxable years, regardless of the amount of cash or property distributions the owners receive from the entity during the year. The entity serves as an information provider to the IRS and its owners with respect to the proportionate income shares, and the tax falls directly upon the owners of those shares.

A partnership may be an especially advantageous entity form in many cases. A partnership is subject to only a single level of taxation, whereas C corporation income is subject to *double taxation*. Corporate income is taxed at the entity level at rates up to 35 percent. Any after-tax income that is distributed to corporate owners is taxed again as a dividend at the owner level. Though partnership income may be subject to high individual rates (currently up to 39.6 percent), the resulting tax will likely be lower than a combined corporate-level tax and a second tax on a dividend distribution.

In addition, administrative and filing requirements are relatively simple for a partnership, and it offers certain planning opportunities not available to other entity forms. Both the C and S corporate structures are subject to rigorous allocation and distribution requirements (generally, each allocation or distribution is proportionate to the ownership interest of the shareholder). A partnership, though, may adjust its allocations of income and cash flow among the partners each year according to their needs, as long as certain standards (discussed later in this chapter) are met. Also, any previously unrealized income (such as appreciation of corporate assets) of an S or C corporation is taxed at the entity level when

TAX IN THE NEWS

PARTNERSHIPS IN THE MOVIES

As movies have become more expensive to produce, many production studios have turned to limited partnerships as a lucrative source of investment capital. For example, the Walt Disney Company has sold limited partnership interests in Silver Screen Partnerships I, II, III, and IV and in Touchwood Pacific Partners I, L.P. Other studios have formed similar production partnerships.

In most cases the sponsoring studio injects capital for a small (1–5 percent) general partnership interest, and the investors contribute the remaining capital—hundreds of millions of dollars or more. The partnership agreement spells out the number and types of films the partnership intends to produce and provides a formula for allocating cash flows to the partners. Often the partnership agreement includes various benefits for the general partner (studio), such as a preferred allocation of cash flows (the first $1 million per year, for example), distribution fees for marketing the movies, and/or reimbursement of specified amounts of corporate overhead. Any cash remaining after these expenses is allocated under a fixed formula between the general and limited partners (for example, the limited partners may receive 90 percent of remaining cash flows).

Think about bank financing in comparison, and you will see why the studio finds partnerships so appealing: How many banks would allow the general partner to receive reimbursements and allocations before debt principal and interest are paid?

This capital-raising technique has proved so advantageous to the studios that some related industries, such as movie lighting contractors and special effects companies, have also used limited partnerships to raise capital. The next time you go to a movie, watch the credits at the end and think about the tremendous number of people who invested cash in the movie hoping for a blockbuster!

the corporation liquidates, but a partnership generally may liquidate tax-free. Finally, many states impose reporting and licensing requirements on corporate entities, including S corporations. These include franchise or capital stock tax returns that may require annual assessments and costly professional preparation assistance. Partnerships, on the other hand, often have no reporting requirements beyond Federal and state informational tax returns.

For smaller business operations, a partnership enables several owners to combine their resources at low cost. It also offers simple filing requirements, the taxation of income only once, and the ability to discontinue operations relatively inexpensively.

For larger business operations, a partnership offers a unique ability to raise capital with low filing and reporting costs (compared to corporate bond issuances, for example). Special allocations of income and cash-flow items are available in all partnerships to meet the objectives of the owners. The accompanying Tax in the News describes how one industry has used the partnership form as a means of raising capital.

This chapter addresses partnership formation and operations. Chapter 11 focuses on dispositions of partnership interests, partnership distributions, and optional basis adjustments. Chapter 12 discusses the taxation of S corporations.

WHAT IS A PARTNERSHIP?

A partnership is an association of two or more persons to carry on a trade or business, with each contributing money, property, labor, or skill, and with all expecting to share in profits and losses.[1] For Federal income tax purposes, a partnership includes a syndicate, group, pool, joint venture, or other unincorporated organization, through which any business, financial operation, or venture is carried on. The entity must not be otherwise classified as a corporation, trust, or estate.

The IRS has issued new Regulations that allow an eligible entity to "check the box" on the partnership tax return indicating that the entity wants to be taxed as a partnership.[2] This procedure provides certainty that the entity will be taxed as a partnership. The Regulations do not apply to publicly traded partnerships, which must be taxed as corporations under § 7704, but they do apply to most limited liability companies (discussed below).

An entity that would otherwise be classified as a partnership may be excluded from partnership taxation rules if it is used for the following purposes:

- Investment (rather than the active conduct of a trade or business).
- Joint production, extraction, or use of property.
- Underwriting, selling, or distributing a specific security issue.[3]

The key to the availability of this election is that the venturers act more as expense-sharing associates than as proprietors working for joint profit maximization.

Four types of entities are taxed as partnerships: general partnerships, limited liability partnerships, limited partnerships, and limited liability companies. A partnership that conducts a service business, such as accounting, law, or medicine, is usually established as either a **general partnership** or a **limited liability partnership (LLP).** A general partnership consists of one or more general partners. Creditors of a general partnership can collect amounts owed them from both the partnership assets and the personal assets of the owner-partners. A general partner can be bankrupted by a malpractice judgment brought against the partnership, even though the partner was not personally involved in the malpractice.

An LLP is a recently created form of entity. Owners of an LLP are also general partners. The primary difference between an LLP and a general partnership is that an LLP partner is not liable for any malpractice committed by his or her partners. LLPs are discussed in more detail in Chapter 11. The LLP is currently the organizational form of choice for the Big Six accounting firms.

A **limited partnership** is often used for acquiring capital in activities such as real estate development. A limited partnership is comprised of at least one general partner and often many limited partners. Typically, only the general partners are liable to creditors; each limited partner's risk of loss is restricted to his or her equity investment in the entity.

An alternative entity form, the **limited liability company (LLC),** is now permitted to operate in all states and the District of Columbia. An LLC combines the corporate benefit of limited liability of owners with the benefits of partnership

---

taxation, including the single level of tax and special allocations of income, losses, and cash flows. Owners are technically considered to be "members" rather than partners, but a properly structured LLC is treated as a partnership for all tax purposes. Almost all states permit capital-intensive companies as well as service-oriented businesses and some professional service-providing entities to operate as LLCs. This is highly advantageous to a service entity since the LLC can protect each member from malpractice committed by other members. As discussed in Chapter 11, application of the partnership tax rules to an LLC can produce unusual results.

PARTNERSHIP TAXATION AND REPORTING

1 **LEARNING OBJECTIVE**
Discuss governing principles and theories of partnership taxation.

A partnership is not a taxable entity.[4] Rather, the taxable income or loss of the partnership flows through to the partners at the end of the entity's tax year.[5] Partners report their allocable share of the partnership's income or loss for the year on their tax returns. As a result, the partnership itself pays no Federal income tax on its income; instead, the partners' individual tax liabilities are affected by the activities of the entity.

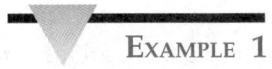

EXAMPLE 1

Adam is a 40% partner in the ABC Partnership. Both Adam's and the partnership's tax years end on December 31. In 1997, the partnership generates $200,000 of ordinary taxable income. However, because the partnership needs capital for expansion and debt reduction, Adam makes no cash withdrawals during 1997. He meets his living expenses by reducing his investment portfolio. Adam is taxed on his $80,000 allocable share of the partnership's 1997 income, even though he received no distributions from the entity during 1997. This allocated income is included in Adam's gross income. ▼

EXAMPLE 2

Assume the same facts as in Example 1, except the partnership recognizes a 1997 taxable loss of $100,000. Adam's 1997 adjusted gross income is reduced by $40,000 because his proportionate share of the loss flows through to him from the partnership. He claims a $40,000 partnership loss for the year. (Note: Loss limitation rules discussed later in the chapter may result in some or all of this loss being deferred to a later year.) ▼

Many items of partnership income or expense retain their identity as they flow through to the partners. When preparing a personal tax return, a partner may have to take into account several items rather than a single share of net partnership ordinary income or loss. Any item that *might* affect any two partners' tax liabilities in different ways is reported separately to the partners as a **separately stated item.**[6]

Ordinary partnership income or loss includes only the income and expenses related to partnership trade or business activities. These income and expense items are netted to produce a single income or loss amount that is passed through to the partners. Separately stated items (such as capital gains or losses, interest income, and charitable contributions) are reported separately to the partner by the partnership. Each partner combines his or her share of these partnership items with similar items the partner may have earned outside the partnership. Tax limitations or separate calculations (e.g., net capital gain or loss) are determined at the partner level.

---

[4] § 701.
[5] § 702.

[6] § 703(a)(1).

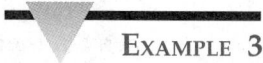

EXAMPLE 3

Beth is a 25% partner in the BR Partnership. The cash basis entity collected sales income of $60,000 during 1996 and incurred $15,000 in business expenses. In addition, it sold a corporate bond for a $9,000 long-term capital gain. Finally, the partnership made a $1,000 contribution to the local Performing Arts Fund drive. The fund is a qualifying charity. BR and all of its partners use a calendar tax year.

For 1996, Beth is allocated ordinary taxable income of $11,250 [($60,000 – $15,000) × 25%] from the partnership. She also is allocated a flow-through of a $2,250 long-term capital gain and a $250 charitable contribution deduction. The ordinary income increases Beth's gross income, and the capital gain and charitable contribution are combined with her other similar activities for the year as though she had incurred them herself. These items could be treated differently on the individual tax returns of the various partners (e.g., because a partner may be subject to a percentage limitation on charitable contribution deductions for 1996), so they are not included in the computation of ordinary partnership income. Instead, the items flow through to the partners separately. ▼

Other items that are allocated separately to the partners[7] include recognized gains and losses from property transactions; dividend income; tax preferences and adjustments for the alternative minimum tax; expenditures that qualify for the foreign tax credit; and expenditures that the partners would treat as itemized deductions.

Even though it is not a taxpaying entity, a partnership must file an information tax return, Form 1065. Look at Form 1065 in Appendix B, and refer to it during the following discussion. The partnership reports the results of its trade or business activities (ordinary income or loss) on Form 1065, page 1. Schedule K (page 3 of Form 1065) accumulates all items that must be separately reported to the partners, including net trade or business income or loss (from page 1). The amounts on Schedule K are allocated to all the partners. Each partner receives a Schedule K–1, which shows that partner's share of partnership items.

EXAMPLE 4

The BR Partnership in Example 3 reports its $60,000 sales income on Form 1065, page 1, line 1. The $15,000 of business expenses are reported in the appropriate amounts on page 1, line 2 or lines 9–20. Partnership ordinary income of $45,000 is shown on page 1, line 22, and on Schedule K, line 1. The $9,000 capital gain and the $1,000 charitable contribution are reported only on Schedule K, on lines 4e and 8, respectively.

Beth receives a Schedule K–1 from the partnership that shows her shares of partnership ordinary income of $11,250, long-term capital gain of $2,250, and charitable contributions of $250 on lines 1, 4e, and 8, respectively.

She combines these amounts with similar items from sources other than BR in her personal tax return. For example, if she has a $5,000 long-term capital loss from a stock transaction in 1996, her overall net capital loss is $2,750. She then evaluates this net amount to determine the amount she may deduct on her Form 1040. ▼

As this example shows, one must look at both page 1 and Schedule K to get complete information regarding a partnership's operations for the year. Schedule K accumulates all partnership tax items and arrives at a total amount on line 25a. Schedule M–1, page 4, reconciles accounting income with this total of partnership tax items on Schedule K (line 25a). Schedule L generally shows an accounting-basis balance sheet, and Schedule M–2 reconciles beginning and ending partners' capital accounts.

---

[7] § 702(a).

PARTNER'S OWNERSHIP INTEREST IN A PARTNERSHIP

Each partner owns both a **capital interest** and a **profits (loss) interest** in the partnership. A capital interest is measured by a partner's **capital sharing ratio,** which is the partner's percentage ownership of the capital of the partnership. A partner's capital interest can be determined in several ways. The most widely accepted method measures the capital interest as the percentage of net assets (assets remaining after payment of all partnership liabilities) a partner would receive on immediate liquidation of the partnership.

A profits (loss) interest is simply the partner's percentage allocation of current partnership operating results. **Profit and loss sharing ratios** are usually specified in the partnership agreement and are used to determine each partner's allocation of partnership ordinary taxable income and separately stated items.[8] The partnership can change its profit and loss allocations at any time simply by amending the partnership agreement.

Each partner's profit, loss, and capital sharing ratios may appear on the partner's Schedule K–1. In many cases, the three ratios are the same. A partner's capital sharing ratio generally equals the profit and loss sharing ratios if all profit and loss allocations, for each year of the partnership's existence, are in the same proportion as the partner's initial contributions to the partnership.

The partnership agreement may, in some cases, provide for a **special allocation** of certain items to specified partners, or it may allocate items in a different proportion from general profit and loss sharing ratios. These items are separately reported to the partner receiving the allocation. For a special allocation to be recognized for tax purposes, it must produce nontax economic consequences to the partners receiving the allocation.[9]

EXAMPLE 5 When the George-Helen Partnership was formed, George contributed cash and Helen contributed some City of Iuka bonds that she had held for investment purposes. The partnership agreement allocates all of the tax-exempt interest income from the bonds to Helen as an inducement for her to remain a partner. This is an acceptable special allocation for income tax purposes; it reflects the differing economic circumstances that underlie the partners' contributions to the capital of the entity. Since Helen would have received the exempt income if she had not joined the partnership, she can retain the tax-favored treatment via the special allocation. ▼

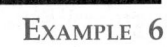

EXAMPLE 6 Assume the same facts as in Example 5. Three years after it was formed, the George-Helen Partnership purchased some City of Butte bonds. The municipal bond interest income of $15,000 flows through to the partners as a separately stated item, so it retains its tax-exempt status. The partnership agreement allocates all of this income to George because he is subject to a higher marginal income tax bracket than is Helen. The partnership also allocates $15,000 more of the partnership taxable income to Helen than to George. These allocations are not effective for income tax purposes because they have no purpose other than reduction of the partners' combined income tax liability. ▼

A partner has a **basis in the partnership interest,** just as he or she would have a tax basis in any asset owned. When income flows through to a partner from the partnership, the partner's basis in the partnership interest increases accordingly. When a loss flows through to a partner, basis is reduced.

---

[8] § 704(a). [9] § 704(b).

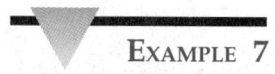

EXAMPLE 7   Paul contributes $20,000 cash to acquire a 30% capital and profits interest in the Red Robin Partnership. In its first year of operations, the partnership earns ordinary income of $40,000 and makes no distributions to Paul. Paul's initial basis is the $20,000 he paid for the interest. He reports ordinary income of $12,000 (30% × $40,000 partnership income) on his individual return and increases his basis by the same amount, to $32,000. ▼

In allowing increases and decreases in a partner's basis in a partnership interest, the Code ensures that only one level of tax arises on the income or loss from partnership operations. In Example 7, if Paul sold his interest at the end of the first year for $32,000, he would have no gain or loss. If the Code did not provide for an adjustment of a partner's basis, Paul's basis would be $20,000, and he would be taxed on the gain of $12,000 in addition to being taxed on his $12,000 share of income. In other words, without the basis adjustment, partnership income would be subject to double taxation.

As the following sections discuss in detail, a partner's basis is important for determining the treatment of distributions from the partnership to the partner, establishing the deductibility of partnership losses, and calculating gain or loss on the partner's disposition of the partnership interest.

A partner's basis is not reflected anywhere on the Schedule K–1. Instead, each partner should maintain a personal record of adjustments to basis. Schedule K–1 does reconcile a partner's **capital account,** but the ending capital account balance is rarely the same amount as the partner's basis. Just as the tax and accounting bases of a specific asset may differ, a partner's capital account and basis in partnership interest may not be equal for a variety of reasons. For example, a partner's basis also includes the partner's share of partnership liabilities. These liabilities are not reported as part of the partner's capital account but are included in question F at the top of the partner's Schedule K–1.

CONCEPTUAL BASIS FOR PARTNERSHIP TAXATION

The unique tax treatment of partners and partnerships can be traced to two legal concepts that evolved long ago: the **aggregate** (or conduit) **concept** and the **entity concept.** These concepts have been used in both civil and common law and have influenced practically every partnership tax rule.

Aggregate (or Conduit) Concept.   The aggregate (or conduit) concept treats the partnership as a channel through which income, credits, deductions, and the like flow to the partners. Under this concept, the partnership is regarded as a collection of taxpayers joined in an agency relationship with one another. The imposition of the income tax on individual partners reflects the influence of this doctrine. The aggregate concept has influenced the tax treatment of other pass-through entities, such as S corporations (Chapter 12) and trusts and estates (Chapter 19).

Entity Concept.   The entity concept treats partners and partnerships as separate units and gives the partnership its own tax "personality" by (1) requiring a partnership to file an information tax return and (2) treating partners as separate and distinct from the partnership in certain transactions between a partner and the entity. A partner's recognition of capital gain or loss on the sale of the partnership interest illustrates this doctrine.

Combined Concepts.   Some rules such as the various provisions governing the formation, operation, and liquidation of a partnership contain a blend of both the entity and aggregate concepts.

ANTI-ABUSE PROVISIONS

As Chapters 10 and 11 describe, partnership taxation is often flexible. For example, partnership operating income or losses can sometimes be shifted among partners, and partnership property gains and losses can sometimes be shifted from one partner to another. The Code contains many provisions designed to thwart unwarranted allocations, but the IRS believes opportunities still abound for tax avoidance. As Chapter 11 notes, the IRS has adopted Regulations that allow it to recharacterize transactions that it considers to be "abusive."[10]

FORMATION OF A PARTNERSHIP: TAX EFFECTS

GAIN OR LOSS ON CONTRIBUTIONS TO THE PARTNERSHIP

2 **LEARNING OBJECTIVE**
Describe the tax effects of forming a partnership with cash and property contributions.

When a taxpayer transfers property to an entity in exchange for valuable consideration, a taxable exchange normally results. Typically, both the taxpayer and the entity realize and recognize gain or loss on the exchange.[11] The gain or loss recognized by the transferor is the difference between the fair market value of the consideration received and the adjusted basis of the property transferred.[12]

In most situations, however, neither the partner nor the partnership recognizes the gain or loss that is realized when a partner contributes property to a partnership in exchange for a partnership interest. Instead, the realized gain or loss is deferred.[13]

There are two reasons for this nonrecognition treatment. First, forming a partnership allows investors to combine their assets toward greater economic goals than could be achieved separately. Only the form of ownership, rather than the amount owned by each investor, has changed. Requiring that gain be recognized on such transfers would make the formation of some partnerships economically unfeasible (e.g., two existing proprietorships are combined to form one larger business). Congress does not want to hinder the creation of valid economic partnerships by requiring gain recognition when a partnership is created. Second, because the partnership interest received is typically not a liquid asset, the partner may not be able to find the cash to pay the tax. Thus, deferral of the gain recognizes the economic realities of the business world and follows the wherewithal to pay principle of taxation.

EXAMPLE 8

Alicia transfers two assets to the Wren Partnership on the day the entity is created, in exchange for a 60% profit and loss interest (worth $60,000). She contributes cash of $40,000 and retail display equipment (basis to her as a sole proprietor, $8,000; fair market value, $20,000). Since an exchange has occurred between two parties, Alicia *realizes* a $12,000 gain on this transaction. The gain realized is the fair market value of the partnership interest of $60,000 less the basis of the assets that Alicia surrendered to the partnership [$40,000 (cash) + $8,000 (equipment)].

Under § 721, Alicia *does not recognize* the $12,000 realized gain in the year of contribution. Alicia might have been pressed for cash if she had been required to pay tax on the $12,000 gain. All that she received from the partnership was an illiquid partnership interest; she received no cash with which to pay any resulting tax liability. ▼

[10]Reg. § 1.701–2.
[11]§ 1001(c).

[12]§ 1001(a).
[13]§ 721.

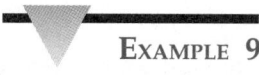

EXAMPLE 9

Assume the same facts as in Example 8, except that the equipment Alicia contributes to the partnership has an adjusted basis of $25,000. She has a $5,000 *realized* loss [$60,000 − ($40,000 + $25,000)], but she cannot deduct the loss. Realized losses, as well as realized gains, are deferred by § 721.

Unless it was essential that the partnership receive Alicia's display equipment rather than similar equipment purchased from an outside supplier, Alicia should have considered selling the equipment to a third party. This would have allowed her to deduct a $5,000 loss in the year of the sale. Alicia then could have contributed $60,000 cash (including the proceeds from the sale) for her interest in the partnership, and the partnership would have funds to purchase similar equipment. ▼

EXAMPLE 10

Five years after the Wren Partnership (Examples 8 and 9) was created, Alicia contributes another piece of equipment to the entity from her sole proprietorship. This property has a basis of $35,000 and a fair market value of $50,000. Alicia can defer the recognition of the $15,000 realized gain. Section 721 is effective whenever a partner makes a contribution to the capital of the partnership. ▼

If a partner contributes only capital and § 1231 assets, the partner's holding period in the partnership interest is the same as the partner's holding period for these assets. If assets that are not capital or § 1231 assets (including cash) are contributed, the holding period in the partnership interest begins on the date the partnership interest is acquired. If multiple assets are contributed, the partnership interest is apportioned, and a separate holding period applies to each portion.

EXCEPTIONS TO § 721

The nonrecognition provisions of § 721 do not apply where

- appreciated stocks are contributed to an investment partnership;
- the transaction is essentially a taxable exchange of properties;
- the transaction is a disguised sale of properties; or
- the partnership interest is received in exchange for services rendered to the partnership by the partner.

Investment Partnership. If the transfer consists of appreciated stocks and securities and the partnership is an investment partnership, it is likely that the realized gain on the stocks and securities will be recognized by the contributing partner at the time of contribution.[14] This provision prevents multiple investors from using the partnership form to diversify their investment portfolios on a tax-free basis.

Exchange. If a transaction is essentially a taxable exchange of properties, the tax is not deferred under the nonrecognition provisions of § 721.[15]

EXAMPLE 11

Sara owns land, and Bob owns stock. Sara would like to have Bob's stock, and Bob wants Sara's land. If Sara and Bob both contribute their property to newly formed SB Partnership in exchange for interests in the partnership, the tax on the transaction appears to be deferred under § 721. The tax on a subsequent distribution by the partnership of the land to Bob and the stock to Sara also appears to be deferred under § 731 (discussed in Chapter 11). According to a literal interpretation of the statutes, no taxable exchange has occurred. Sara

---

[14]§ 721(b).

[15]Reg. § 1.731–1(c)(3).

and Bob will find, however, that this type of tax subterfuge is not permitted. The IRS will disregard the passage of the properties through the partnership and will hold, instead, that Sara and Bob exchanged the land and stock directly. Thus, the transactions will be treated as any other taxable exchange. ▼

Disguised Sale. A similar result occurs in a **disguised sale** of properties. A disguised sale is deemed to occur where a partner contributes property to a partnership and soon thereafter receives a distribution from the partnership. This distribution could be viewed as a payment by the partnership for purchase of the property.[16]

EXAMPLE 12

Kim transfers property to the KLM Partnership. The property has an adjusted basis of $10,000 and a fair market value of $30,000. Two weeks later, the partnership makes a distribution of $30,000 cash to Kim. Under the distribution rules of § 731, the distribution would not be taxable to Kim if the basis for her partnership interest prior to the distribution was greater than the $30,000 cash distributed. However, the transaction appears to be a disguised purchase-sale transaction, rather than a contribution and distribution. Therefore, Kim must recognize gain of $20,000 on transfer of the property, and the partnership is deemed to have purchased the property for $30,000. ▼

Extensive Regulations under § 707 outline situations in which the IRS will presume a disguised sale has occurred. For example, if both the following occur, a disguised sale is presumed to exist:

- A contractual agreement requires a contribution by one partner to be followed within two years by a specified distribution from the partnership.
- The distribution is to be made without regard to partnership profits. In other words, the forthcoming distribution is not subject to significant "entrepreneurial risk."

In some cases, assumption of the partner's liabilities by the partnership may be treated as a purchase price paid by the partnership. The IRS can also use a facts and circumstances test to treat a transaction as a disguised sale.

The Regulations also outline situations in which a distribution generally will *not* be deemed to be part of a disguised sale. They include a distribution that occurs more than two years after the property is contributed and a distribution that is deemed "reasonable" in relation to the capital invested by the partner and in relation to distributions made to other partners.

Services. A final exception to the nonrecognition provision of § 721 occurs when a partner receives an interest in the partnership as compensation for services rendered to the partnership. This is not a tax-deferred transaction because services are not treated as "property" that can be transferred to a partnership on a tax-free basis. Instead, the partner performing the services recognizes ordinary compensation income equal to the fair market value of the partnership interest received.[17]

The partnership may deduct the amount included in the service partner's income if the services are of a deductible nature. If the services are not deductible to the partnership, they must be capitalized to an asset account. For example, architectural plans created by a partner are capitalized to the structure built with those plans. Alternatively, day-to-day management services performed by a partner for the partnership are usually deductible by the partnership.

---

[16] § 707(a)(2)(B).   [17] § 83(a).

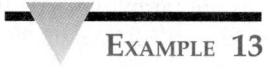

EXAMPLE 13

Bill, Carl, and Dave form the BCD Partnership, with each receiving a one-third interest in the entity. Dave receives his one-third interest as compensation for the accounting and tax planning services he rendered during the formation of the partnership. The value of a one-third interest in the partnership (for each of the parties) is $20,000. Dave recognizes $20,000 of compensation income, and he has a $20,000 basis in his partnership interest. The same result would occur if the partnership had paid Dave $20,000 for his services and he immediately contributed that amount to the entity for a one-third ownership interest. ▼

TAX ISSUES RELATIVE TO CONTRIBUTED PROPERTY

When a partner makes a tax-deferred contribution of an asset to the capital of a partnership, the entity assigns a carryover basis to the property.[18] The entity's basis in the asset is equal to the basis the partner held in the property prior to its transfer to the partnership. The partner's basis in the new partnership interest equals the prior basis in the contributed asset. The tax term for this basis concept is substituted basis. Thus, two assets are created out of one when a partnership is formed, namely, the property in the hands of the new entity and the new asset (the partnership interest) in the hands of the partner. Both assets are assigned a basis that is derived from the partner's basis in the contributed property.

To understand the logic of these rules, consider what Congress was attempting to accomplish in this deferral transaction. Recall that gain or loss is deferred when property is contributed to a partnership in exchange for a partnership interest. The deferral is implemented by calculating the partnership's basis in the transferred property and the partner's basis for the partnership interest. The basis amounts are the amounts necessary to allow for recognition of the deferred gain or loss if the property or the partnership interest is subsequently disposed of in a taxable transaction. This treatment is similar to the treatment of assets transferred to a controlled corporation[19] and the treatment of like-kind exchanges.[20]

EXAMPLE 14

On June 1, 1997, José transfers property to the JKL Partnership in exchange for a one-third interest in the partnership. The property has an adjusted basis to José of $10,000 and a fair market value of $30,000 on June 1. José has a $20,000 realized gain on the exchange ($30,000 − $10,000), but under § 721, he does not recognize any of the gain. José's basis for his partnership interest is the amount necessary to recognize the $20,000 deferred gain if his partnership interest is subsequently sold for its $30,000 fair market value. This amount, $10,000, is referred to as substituted basis. The basis of the property contributed to the partnership is the amount necessary to allow for the recognition of the $20,000 deferred gain if the property is subsequently sold for its $30,000 fair market value. This amount, also $10,000, is referred to as carryover basis. ▼

The holding period for the contributed asset also carries over to the partnership. Thus, the partnership's holding period for the asset includes the period during which the partner owned the asset individually.

Depreciation Method and Period. If depreciable property is contributed to the partnership, the partnership is usually required to use the same cost recovery method and life used by the partner. The partnership merely "steps into the shoes" of the partner and continues the same cost recovery calculations. If the property is not MACRS or ACRS property, the partnership must treat the property

---

[18] § 723.
[19] § 351.

[20] § 1031.

as used property for depreciation purposes. The partnership may not immediately expense any part of the basis of depreciable property it receives from the transferor partner under § 179.

Receivables, Inventory, and Losses.   To prevent ordinary income from being converted into capital gain, gain or loss is treated as ordinary when the partnership disposes of either of the following:[21]

- Contributed receivables that were unrealized in the contributing partner's hands at the contribution date. Such receivables include the right to receive payment for goods or services delivered (or to be delivered).
- Contributed property that was inventory in the contributor's hands on the contribution date, if the partnership disposes of the property within *five years of the contribution*. For this purpose, inventory includes all property except capital and real or depreciable business assets.

EXAMPLE 15

Tyrone operates a cash basis retail electronics and television store as a sole proprietor. Ramon is an enterprising individual who likes to invest in small businesses. On January 2 of the current year, Tyrone and Ramon form the TR Partnership. Their partnership contributions are as follows:

	Adjusted Basis	Fair Market Value
From Tyrone:		
Receivables	$ –0–	$ 2,000
Land used as parking lot*	1,200	5,000
Inventory	2,500	5,000
From Ramon:		
Cash	12,000	12,000

*The parking lot had been held for five months at the contribution date.

Within 30 days of formation, TR collects the receivables and sells the inventory for $5,000 cash. It uses the land for the next 10 months as a parking lot, then sells it for $3,500 cash. TR realized the following income in the current year from these transactions:

- Ordinary income of $2,000 from collecting receivables.
- Ordinary income of $2,500 from sale of inventory.
- § 1231 gain of $2,300 from sale of land.

Since the land takes a carryover holding period, it is treated as having been held 15 months at the sale date. ▼

A similar rule is designed to prevent a capital loss from being converted into an ordinary loss. Under the rule, if contributed property is disposed of at a loss and the property had a "built-in" capital loss to the contributing partner at the contribution date, the loss is treated as a capital loss if the partnership disposes of the property *within five years of the contribution*. The capital loss is limited to the "built-in" loss on the date of contribution.

---

[21] § 724. For this purpose, § 724(d)(2) waives the holding period requirement in defining § 1231 property.

EXAMPLE 16

Assume the same facts as Example 15, except for the following:

- Tyrone held the land he contributed for investment purposes. It had a fair market value of $800 at the contribution date.
- TR used the land as a parking lot for 11 months and sold it for $650.

TR realizes the following income and loss from these transactions:

- Ordinary income of $2,000 from collecting receivables.
- Ordinary income of $2,500 from sale of inventory.
- Capital loss of $400 from sale of land ($1,200 – $800).
- § 1231 loss of $150 from sale of land ($800 – $650).

Since the land was sold within five years of the contribution date, the $400 built-in loss is a capital loss. The postcontribution loss of $150 is a § 1231 loss since TR used the property in its business. ▼

INSIDE AND OUTSIDE BASES

Throughout these chapters, reference is made to the partnership's inside basis and the partners' outside basis. **Inside basis** refers to the adjusted basis of each partnership asset, as determined from the partnership's tax accounts. **Outside basis** represents each partner's basis in the partnership interest. Each partner "owns" a share of the partnership's inside basis for all its assets and should maintain a record of the outside basis.

In many cases—especially on formation of the partnership—the total of all partners' outside bases equals the partnership's inside bases for all its assets. Differences between inside and outside basis arise when a partner's interest is sold to another person for more or less than the selling partner's share of the inside basis of partnership assets. The buying partner's outside basis equals the price paid for the interest, but the buyer's share of the partnership's inside basis is the same amount as the seller's share of the inside basis.

Concept Summary 10–1 reviews the rules that apply to partnership asset contribution and basis adjustments.

TAX ACCOUNTING ELECTIONS

A newly formed partnership must make numerous tax accounting elections. These elections are formal decisions on how a particular transaction or tax attribute should be handled. Most of these elections must be made by the partnership rather than by the partners individually.[22] The *partnership* makes the elections involving the following items:

- Inventory method.
- Cost or percentage depletion method, excluding oil and gas wells.
- Accounting method (cash, accrual, or hybrid).
- Cost recovery methods and assumptions.
- Tax year.
- Amortization of organizational costs and amortization period.
- Amortization of start-up expenditures and amortization period.
- Optional basis adjustments for property (§ 754, discussed in Chapter 11).
- Section 179 deductions for certain tangible personal property.
- Nonrecognition treatment for involuntary conversions gains.
- Election out of partnership rules.

---

[22] § 703(b).

> ### CONCEPT SUMMARY 10–1
>
> ## Partnership Formation and Basis Computation
>
> 1. The *entity concept* treats partners and partnerships as separate units. The nature and amount of gains and losses are determined at the partnership level.
> 2. The *aggregate concept* is used to connect partners and partnerships. It allows income, gains, losses, credits, deductions, etc., to flow through to the partners for separate tax reporting.
> 3. Sometimes both the *aggregate* and the *entity* concepts apply, but one usually dominates.
> 4. Generally, partners or partnerships do not recognize gain or loss when property is contributed for capital interests.
> 5. Partners contributing property for partnership interests take the contributed property's adjusted basis for their *outside basis* in their partnership interest. The partners are said to take a substituted basis in their partnership interest.
> 6. The partnership will continue to use the contributing partner's basis for the *inside basis* in property it receives. The contributed property is said to take a carryover basis.
> 7. The holding period of a partner's interest includes that of contributed property when the property was a § 1231 asset or capital asset in the partner's hands. Otherwise, the holding period starts on the day the interest is acquired. The holding period of an interest acquired by a cash contribution starts at acquisition.
> 8. The partnership's holding period for contributed property includes the contributing partner's holding period.

Each partner is bound by the decisions made by the partnership relative to the elections. If the partnership fails to make an election, a partner cannot compensate for the error by making the election individually.

Though most elections are made by the partnership, each *partner* individually is required to make a specific election on the following relatively narrow tax issues:

- Whether to reduce the basis of depreciable property first when excluding income from discharge of indebtedness.
- Whether to claim cost or percentage depletion method for oil and gas wells.
- Whether to take a deduction or a credit for taxes paid to foreign countries and U.S. possessions.

INITIAL COSTS OF A PARTNERSHIP

3   LEARNING OBJECTIVE
Examine the tax treatment of expenditures of a newly formed partnership and identify elections the partnership should make.

In its initial stages, a partnership incurs expenses relating to some or all of the following: forming the partnership (organization costs), admitting partners to the partnership, marketing and selling partnership units to prospective partners (syndication costs), acquiring assets, starting business operations (start-up costs), negotiating contracts, and other items. Many of these expenditures are not currently deductible. However, the Code permits a ratable amortization of "organization" and "start-up" costs; acquisition costs for depreciable assets are included in the initial basis of the acquired assets; and costs related to some intangible assets may be amortized. "Syndication costs" may be neither amortized nor deducted.

Organization Costs.   The partnership may elect to amortize organization costs ratably over a period of 60 months or more, starting with the month in which it began business.[23] The election must be made by the due date (including extensions) of the partnership return for the year it began business.

---

[23] § 709.

Organization costs include expenditures that are (1) incident to the creation of the partnership; (2) chargeable to a capital account; and (3) of a character that, if incident to the creation of a partnership with an ascertainable life, would be amortized over that life. These expenditures include accounting fees and legal fees connected with the partnership's formation. To be amortizable, the expenditures must be incurred within a period that starts a reasonable time before the partnership begins business. The period ends with the due date (without extensions) of the tax return for the initial tax year.

Cash method partnerships are not allowed to deduct *in the year incurred* the portion of organization costs that are paid after the end of the first year. The partnership can deduct, in the year of payment, the portion of the expenditures that would have been deductible in a prior year, if they had been paid before that year's end.

EXAMPLE 17

The calendar year Bluejay Partnership is formed on May 1 of the current year and immediately starts business. Bluejay incurs $720 in legal fees for drafting the partnership agreement and $480 in accounting fees for tax advice of an organizational nature. The legal fees are paid in October of the current year. The accounting fees are paid in January of the following year. The partnership selects the cash method of accounting and elects to amortize its organization costs.

On its first tax return, Bluejay deducts $96 of organization costs [($720 legal fees/60 months) × 8 months]. No deduction is taken for the accounting fees since the partnership selected the cash method and the fees were paid the following year. On its tax return for next year, Bluejay deducts organization costs of $304 {[($720 legal fees/60 months) × 12 months] + [($480 accounting fees/60 months) × 20 months]}. Note that the second-year deduction ($304) includes the $64 of accounting fees [($480/60) × 8] that could have been deducted on Bluejay's first tax return if they had been paid by the end of that year. ▼

Costs incurred for the following items are not organization costs:

- Acquiring assets for the partnership.
- Transferring assets to the partnership.
- Admitting partners, other than at formation.
- Removing partners, other than at formation.
- Negotiating operating contracts.
- Syndication costs.

Start-up Costs.   Operating costs that are incurred after the entity is formed but before it begins business may not be deducted. Instead, these costs are capitalized. If so elected, they may be amortized over a period of 60 months or more, starting with the month in which the partnership begins business.[24] Such costs include marketing surveys prior to conducting business, pre-operating advertising expenses, costs of establishing an accounting system, and salaries paid to executives and employees before the start of business.

Acquisition Costs of Depreciable Assets.   Expenses may be incurred in changing the legal title in which certain assets are held from that of the contributing partner to the partnership name. These costs include legal fees incurred to transfer assets or transfer taxes imposed by states. Such costs are added to the basis of the assets in the hands of the partnership and are included in the basis the partnership may depreciate. As mentioned earlier, the partnership

[24]§ 195.

typically determines its depreciation deductions by "stepping into the shoes" of the contributing partner. If additional costs are incurred, though, the additional basis is treated as a new MACRS asset, placed in service on the date the cost is incurred (e.g., the date the asset is transferred to the partnership).

Intangible Assets.   Intangible assets that are considered "§ 197 intangibles" are amortized over a 15-year period regardless of the actual useful life of the property and without regard to whether a useful life is determinable.[25] Intangible assets that do not qualify as § 197 intangibles are only amortizable if a useful life is determined; related amortization deductions are claimed over that useful life. Amortization under § 197 is treated as depreciation, so it is subject to recapture under § 1245 or § 1250. A § 197 intangible is not eligible for an immediate expensing election under § 179.

Section 197 intangible assets include goodwill, going-concern value, information systems, customer- or supplier-related intangible assets, patents, licenses obtained from a governmental unit, franchises, trademarks, covenants not to compete, and other items. However, patents, copyrights, leasehold rights, licenses or contractual rights extending less than 15 years, and rights under an existing indebtedness are not considered § 197 intangibles unless they are included as part of an acquisition of an entire trade or business. Also, § 197 never applies to equity interests (such as a partnership interest or corporate stock), land, or computer software that may readily be purchased by the public.

To qualify under § 197, an intangible must be acquired after August 10, 1993, and must be held for use in a trade or business. An election was also available to apply § 197 to all eligible assets acquired after July 25, 1991. Goodwill and going-concern value cannot be amortized if they are "self-created." So-called antichurning conditions, which are beyond the scope of this discussion, must also be met.

If a partner contributes an existing § 197 intangible asset to the partnership, the partnership will "step into the shoes" of the partner in determining future amortization deductions.

EXAMPLE 18

On September 1, 1996, at a cost of $120,000, James obtained a license to operate a television station from the Federal Communications Commission. The license is effective for 20 years. On January 1, 1998, he contributes the license to the JS Partnership in exchange for a 60% interest. The value of the license is still $120,000 at that time.

The license is a § 197 asset since it is a license with a term greater than 15 years. The cost is amortized over 15 years. James claims amortization for 4 months in 1996 and 12 months in 1997. Thereafter, the partnership steps into James's shoes in claiming amortization deductions. ▼

Intangible assets that do not fall under the § 197 rules are treated under rules in effect prior to the RRA 1993. To claim an amortization deduction under these guidelines, a useful life must be adequately substantiated for the asset.[26]

Syndication Costs.   **Syndication costs** are capitalized, but no amortization election is available. Syndication costs include the following expenditures incurred for promoting and marketing partnership interests:

- Brokerage fees.
- Registration fees.

---

[25] § 197(a).

[26] Reg § 1.167(a)–3.

- Legal fees paid to the underwriter, placement agent, and issuer (general partner or the partnership) for security advice or advice on the adequacy of tax disclosures in the prospectus or placement memo for securities law purposes.
- Accounting fees related to offering materials.
- Printing costs of prospectus, placement memos, and other selling materials.

TAXABLE YEAR OF THE PARTNERSHIP

4 **LEARNING OBJECTIVE**
Specify the methods of determining a partnership's tax year.

Partnership taxable income (and any separately stated items) flows through to each partner at the end of the *partnership's* taxable year. A *partner's* taxable income, then, includes the distributive share of partnership income for any *partnership* taxable year that ends within the partner's tax year.

When all partners use the calendar year, it would be beneficial in present value terms for a profitable partnership to adopt a fiscal year ending with January 31. Why? As Figure 10–1 illustrates, when the adopted year ends on January 31, the reporting of income from the partnership and payment of related taxes can be deferred for up to 11 months. For instance, income earned by the partnership in September 1997 is not taxable to the partners until January 31, 1998. It is reported in the partner's tax return for the year ended December 31, 1998, which is not due until April 15, 1999. Even though each partner may be required to make quarterly estimated tax payments, some deferral is still possible.

Required Taxable Years.   To prevent excessive deferral of taxation of partnership income, Congress and the IRS have adopted a series of rules that prescribe the *required* taxable year an entity must adopt if no alternative tax years (discussed below) are available. Three rules are presented in Figure 10–2.[27] The partnership must consider each rule in order. If a taxable year is available under a given rule, that is the partnership's required taxable year.

The first two rules are relatively self-explanatory. Under the **least aggregate deferral rule,** the partnership tests the year-ends that are used by the various partners to determine the weighted-average deferral of partnership income. The year-end that offers the least amount of deferral is the *required tax year* for the partnership.

▼ **FIGURE 10–1**
Deferral Benefit When Fiscal Year Is Used and All Partners Are on the Calendar Year

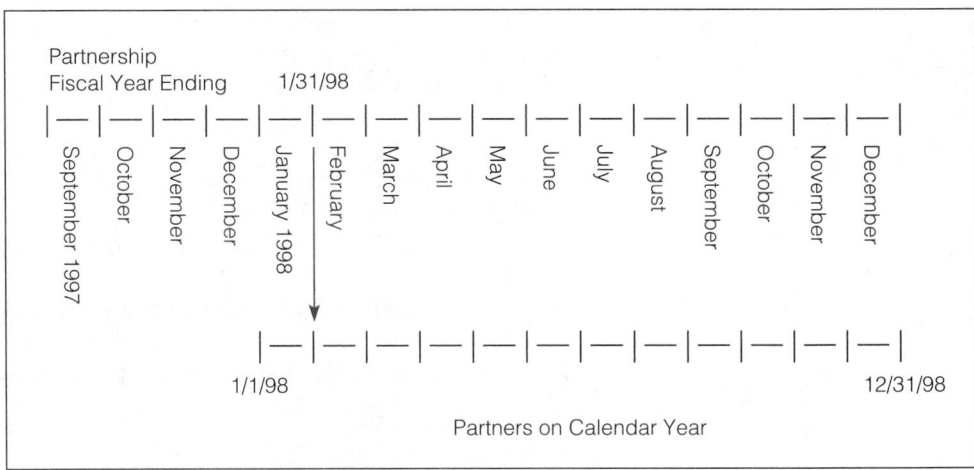

---

[27] § 706(b).

In Order, Partnership Must Use	Requirements
Majority partners' tax year	• More than 50% of capital *and* profits is owned by partners who have the same taxable year.
Principal partners' tax year	• All partners who own 5% or more of capital *or* profits are principal partners.
	• All principal partners must have the same tax year.
Year with smallest amount of income deferred	• "Least aggregate deferral" method (Example 19).

EXAMPLE 19

Anne and Bonnie are equal partners in the AB Partnership. Anne uses the calendar year, and Bonnie uses a fiscal year ending August 31. Neither Anne nor Bonnie is a majority partner since neither owns more than 50%. Although Anne and Bonnie are both principal partners, they do not have the same tax year. Therefore, the general rules indicate that the partnership's required tax year must be determined by the "least aggregate deferral" method. The following computations support August 31 as AB's tax year, since the 2.0 product using that year-end is less than the 4.0 product when December 31 is used.

Test for 12/31 Year-End

Partner	Year Ends	Profit Interest		Months of Deferral		Product
Anne	12/31	50%	×	–0–	=	0.0
Bonnie	8/31	50%	×	8	=	4.0
Aggregate number of deferral months						4.0

Test for 8/31 Year-End

Partner	Year Ends	Profit Interest		Months of Deferral		Product
Anne	12/31	50%	×	4	=	2.0
Bonnie	8/31	50%	×	–0–	=	0.0
Aggregate number of deferral months						2.0

Alternative Tax Years.   If the required tax year is undesirable to the entity, three other alternative tax years may be available:

• Establish to the IRS's satisfaction that a *business purpose* exists for a different tax year (a natural business year at the end of a peak season or shortly thereafter). It is difficult to obtain IRS approval when using the business purpose exception unless the 25 percent, two-month test described next can be satisfied.

• Follow IRS procedures to obtain approval for using a *natural business tax year.* The IRS has stated that a natural business year exists when 25 percent or more of the partnership's gross receipts were recognized during the last

2 months of the same 12-month period for three consecutive years.[28] New partnerships cannot use this natural business year justification because they lack the required three-year history.

- Elect a tax year so that taxes on partnership income are deferred for not more than *three months* from the *required* tax year.[29] Then, have the partnership maintain with the IRS a prepaid, non-interest-bearing deposit of estimated deferred taxes.[30] This alternative may not be desirable since the deposit is based on the highest individual tax rate plus one percent, or 40.6 percent.

OPERATIONS OF THE PARTNERSHIP

5   LEARNING OBJECTIVE
Calculate partnership taxable income and describe how partnership items affect a partner's income tax return.

An individual, corporation, trust, estate, or another partnership can become a partner in a partnership. Since a partnership is a tax-reporting, rather than a taxpaying, entity for purposes of its Federal (and state) income tax computations, the partnership's income, deductions, credits, and alternative minimum tax (AMT) preferences and adjustments can ultimately be reported and taxed on any of a number of income tax returns (e.g., Forms 1040 [individuals], 1041 [fiduciaries, see Chapter 19], 1120 [C corporations], and 1120S [S corporations]).

A partnership is subject to all other taxes in the same manner as any other business. Thus, the partnership files returns and pays the outstanding amount of pertinent sales taxes, property taxes, and Social Security, unemployment, and other payroll taxes.

MEASURING AND REPORTING INCOME

The partnership's Form 1065 organizes and reports the transactions of the entity for the tax year, and each of the partnership's tax items is reported on Schedule K of that return. Each partner, and the IRS, receives a Schedule K–1 that reports the partner's allocable share of partnership income, credits, and preferences for the year. Form 1065 is due on the fifteenth day of the fourth month following the close of the partnership's tax year; for a calendar year partnership, this is April 15.

Income Measurement.   The measurement and reporting of partnership income require a two-step approach. Certain items must be segregated and reported separately on the partnership return and each partner's Schedule K–1.

Items that are not separately reported are netted at the partnership level. Items passed through separately include the following:

- Short- and long-term capital gains and losses.
- Section 1231 gains and losses.
- Charitable contributions.
- Portfolio income items (dividends, interest, and royalties).
- Immediately expensed tangible personal property (§ 179).
- Items allocated differently from the general profit and loss ratio.

---

[28] Rev.Proc. 74–33, 1974–2 C.B. 489; Rev.Rul. 87–57, 1987–2 C.B. 117; and Rev.Proc. 87–32, 1987–1 C.B. 396.

[29] § 444.

[30] § 7519.

- Recovery of items previously deducted (tax benefit items).
- AMT preference and adjustment items.
- Passive activity items (rental real estate income or loss).
- Expenses related to portfolio income.
- Intangible drilling and development costs.
- Taxes paid to foreign countries and U.S. possessions.
- Nonbusiness and personal items (e.g., alimony, medical, and dental).[31]

The reason for separately reporting the preceding items is rooted in the aggregate or conduit concept. These items affect various exclusions, deductions, and credits at the partner level and must pass through without loss of identity so that the proper tax for each partner may be determined.[32]

A partnership is not allowed the following deductions:

- Net operating losses.
- Depletion of oil and gas interests.
- Dividends received deduction.

In addition, items that are only allowed by legislative grace to individuals, such as standard deductions or personal exemptions, are not allowed to the partnership. Also, if a partnership makes a payment on behalf of a partner, such as for alimony, medical expenses, or other items that constitute itemized deductions to individuals, the partnership treats the payment as a distribution or guaranteed payment (discussed later) to the partner, and the partner determines whether he or she may claim the deduction.

EXAMPLE 20

Tiwanda is a one-third partner in the TUV Partnership. This year, the partnership entered into the following transactions:

Fees received	$100,000
Salaries paid	30,000
Cost recovery deductions	10,000
Supplies, repairs	3,000
Payroll taxes paid	9,000
Contribution to art museum	6,000
Short-term capital gain	12,000
Passive income (rental operations)	7,500
Portfolio income (dividends received)	1,500
Exempt income (bond interest)	2,100
AMT adjustment (cost recovery)	3,600
Payment of partner Vern's alimony obligations	4,000

The partnership experienced a $20,000 net loss from operations last year, its first year of business.

The two-step computational process that is used to determine partnership income is applied in the following manner:

---

[31] § 702(a).　　　　　　　　　　[32] § 702(b).

Nonseparately Stated Items (Ordinary Income)	
Fee income	$100,000
Salaries paid	–30,000
Cost recovery deductions	–10,000
Supplies, repairs	–3,000
Payroll taxes paid	–9,000
Ordinary income	$ 48,000

Separately Stated Items	
Contribution to art museum	$ 6,000
Short-term capital gain	12,000
Passive income (rental operations)	7,500
Portfolio income (dividends received)	1,500
Exempt income (bond interest)	2,100
AMT adjustment (cost recovery)	3,600

Each of the separately stated items passes through proportionately to each partner and is included on the appropriate schedule or netted with similar items that the partner generated for the year. Thus, in determining what her tax liability will be on her Form 1040, Tiwanda includes a $2,000 charitable contribution, a $4,000 short-term capital gain, $2,500 of passive rent income, $500 of dividend income, and a $1,200 positive adjustment in computing alternative minimum taxable income. Tiwanda treats these items as if she had generated them herself. She must disclose her $700 share of exempt interest on the first page of her Form 1040. In addition, Tiwanda reports $16,000 as her share of the partnership's ordinary income, the net amount of the nonseparately stated items.

The partnership is not allowed a deduction for last year's $20,000 net operating loss—this item was passed through to the partners in the previous year. Moreover, the partnership is not allowed a deduction for personal expenditures (payment of Vern's alimony). ▼

Withdrawals.   Capital withdrawals by partners during the year do not affect the partnership's income measuring and reporting process. These items usually are treated as distributions made on the last day of the partnership's tax year. Thus, in Example 20 above, the payment of Vern's alimony by the partnership is probably treated as a distribution from the partnership to Vern. Distributions are discussed in Chapter 11.

Penalties.   Each partner's share of partnership items should be reported on his or her individual tax return in the same manner as presented on the Form 1065. If a partner treats an item differently, the IRS must be notified of the inconsistent treatment.[33] If a partner fails to notify the IRS, a negligence penalty may be added to the tax due.

To encourage the filing of a partnership return, a penalty of $50 per month (or fraction thereof), but not to exceed five months, is imposed on the partnership for failure to file a complete and timely information return without reasonable cause.[34]

---

[33] § 6222.   [34] § 6698.

A partnership with 10 or fewer "natural persons" as partners, where each partner's share of partnership items is the same for all items, is automatically excluded from these penalties.[35]

ETHICAL CONSIDERATIONS

A Preparer's Responsibility for Partners' Tax Returns

A partnership's tax return preparer is responsible for accurately presenting information supplied by the partnership in that return. If a flow-through amount is significant to a certain partner, the preparer of the *partnership* return can be treated as the preparer of the *partner's* tax return with respect to that item.

If a preparer misstates an item on a partnership return either by taking a position that is not supportable under current law or by willfully misreporting the item, "preparer penalties" can be assessed. Although these penalties are relatively small, their imposition may lead to the preparer's suspension from practice before the IRS or by a state accountancy board.

As an example, assume Stan, a CPA, knowingly reported a $20,000 deduction for fines and penalties (nondeductible items) in determining the JB Partnership's $30,000 income from operations. This amount is allocated equally to partners Joe and Barb. Joe has other income of $35,000; Barb has other income of $1 million. Stan is treated as the preparer of Joe's tax return with respect to the improper $10,000 flow-through item since the fines and penalties are significant relative to Joe's income. Stan is not the preparer of Barb's return since the fines and penalties are not significant to her income.

In a recent case, the preparer of a partnership return was considered to be the preparer of several partners' returns with respect to partnership items flowing through to the partners. The court reached this decision even though the return preparer never met the individual partners, received any direct fees from the partners, or otherwise performed services for them.

Do you believe this is a reasonable approach for allocating responsibility for accurate preparation of a partner's tax return? Why or why not?

PARTNERSHIP ALLOCATIONS

So far, all examples in this chapter have assumed that the partner has the same percentage interest in capital, profits, and losses. Thus, a partner who owns a 25 percent interest in partnership capital has been assumed to own 25 percent of partnership profits and 25 percent of partnership losses.

Economic Effect.   The partnership agreement can provide that any partner may share capital, profits, and losses in different ratios. For example, a partner could have a 25 percent capital sharing ratio, yet be allocated 30 percent of the profits and 20 percent of the losses of the partnership. Such special allocations are permissible if they follow certain rules contained in the Regulations under § 704(b).[36] Although these rules are too complex to discuss in detail, the general outline of one of these rules—the **economic effect test**—can be easily understood.

---

[35] §§ 6231(a)(1)(B) and (I). Natural persons for this purpose include individuals who are not nonresident aliens, as well as the estate of a decedent who was not a nonresident alien.

[36] Reg. § 1.704–1(b).

In general, the economic effect test requires the following:

- An allocation of income or gain to a partner must increase the partner's capital account, and an allocation of deduction or loss must decrease the partner's capital account.
- When the partner's interest is liquidated, the partner must receive assets that have a fair market value equal to the positive balance in the capital account.
- A partner with a negative capital account must restore that account upon liquidation of the interest. Restoration of a negative capital account can best be envisioned as a contribution of cash to the partnership equal to the negative balance.

These requirements are designed to ensure that a partner bears the economic burden of a loss or deduction allocation and receives the economic benefit of an income or gain allocation.

EXAMPLE 21

Eli and Sanjay each contribute $20,000 cash to the newly formed ES Partnership. The partnership uses the cash to acquire a depreciable asset for $40,000. The partnership agreement provides that the depreciation is allocated 90% to Eli and 10% to Sanjay. Other items of partnership income, gain, loss, or deduction are allocated equally between the partners. Upon liquidation of the partnership, property will be distributed to the partners in accordance with their positive capital account balances. Any partner with a negative capital account must restore the capital account upon liquidation. Assume the first-year depreciation on the equipment is $4,000. Also, assume nothing else happens in the first year that affects the partners' capital accounts.

Eli's capital account is $16,400 ($20,000 – $3,600), and Sanjay's capital account has a balance of $19,600 ($20,000 – $400) after the first year of partnership operations. The Regulations require that a hypothetical sale of the asset for its $36,000 adjusted basis on the last day of the year and an immediate liquidation of the partnership should result in Eli and Sanjay receiving distributions equal to their capital accounts. According to the partnership agreement, Eli would receive $16,400, and Sanjay would receive $19,600 of the cash in a liquidating distribution. Eli, therefore, bears the economic burden of $3,600 depreciation since he contributed $20,000 to the partnership and would receive only $16,400 upon liquidation. Likewise, Sanjay's economic burden is $400 since he would receive only $19,600 of his original $20,000 investment. The agreement, therefore, has economic effect.

If the partnership agreement had provided that Eli and Sanjay should each receive $18,000 of the liquidation proceeds, the "special" allocation of the depreciation would be defective. The IRS would require that the depreciation be allocated equally ($2,000 each) to the two partners to reflect the $2,000 economic burden borne by each partner. ▼

Precontribution Gain or Loss.   Income, gain, loss, and deductions relative to contributed property may not be allocated under the § 704(b) rules described above. Instead, **precontribution gain or loss** must be allocated among the partners to take into account the variation between the basis of the property and its fair market value on the date of contribution.[37] For nondepreciable property, this means that *built-in* gain or loss on the date of contribution must be allocated to the contributing partner when the property is eventually disposed of by the partnership in a taxable transaction.

---

[37] § 704(c)(1)(A).

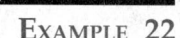

EXAMPLE 22

Seth and Tim form the equal profit and loss sharing ST Partnership. Seth contributes cash of $10,000, and Tim contributes land purchased two years ago and held for investment. The land has an adjusted basis of $6,000 and fair market value of $10,000 at the contribution date. For accounting purposes, the partnership records the land at its fair market value of $10,000. For tax purposes, the partnership takes a carryover basis of $6,000 in the land. After using the land as a parking lot for five months, ST sells it for $10,600. No other transactions have taken place.

The accounting and tax gain from the land sale are computed as follows:

	Accounting	Tax
Amount realized	$10,600	$10,600
Less: Adjusted basis	10,000	6,000
Gain realized	$ 600	$ 4,600
Gain at contribution date to Tim	–0–	4,000
Remaining gain (split equally)	$ 600	$ 600

Seth recognizes $300 of the gain ($600 remaining gain ÷ 2), and Tim recognizes $4,300 [$4,000 built-in gain + ($600 ÷ 2)]. ▼

Regulations outline specific allocation calculations that may be used and describe allowable methods of allocating depreciation deductions if the property is depreciable.[38]

Concept Summary 10–2 reviews the tax reporting rules for partnership activities.

ETHICAL CONSIDERATIONS

Built-in Appreciation on Contributed Property

In the "old days," one partner could contribute cash and another partner could contribute appreciated property with no subsequent record-keeping requirements. Future depreciation deductions and gains on sale of the property could be allocated to both partners equally, thereby shifting income from one taxpayer to another. A partner in a lower tax bracket (or with expiring net operating losses and the like) could report his or her share of the gain on sale of the asset with a relatively low corresponding tax burden.

Section 704(c)(1)(A) was added to the Code to ensure that the partner contributing the property pays tax on his or her own built-in gain. This prevents income shifting among taxpayers and loss of revenue to the IRS.

There is no corresponding provision for S corporations—gains and losses and depreciation expense are allocated among the shareholders without regard to any built-in appreciation on contributed property.

What theory of partnership taxation supports this difference in treatment?

---

[38] Reg. § 1.704–3. The three allowable methods are the "traditional method," the "traditional method with curative allocations," and the "remedial allocation method." See footnote 42.

CONCEPT SUMMARY 10–2

Tax Reporting of Partnership Activities

Event	Partnership Level	Partner Level
1. Compute partnership ordinary income.	Form 1065, line 22, page 1.	Schedule K–1 (Form 1065), line 1, page 1.
	Schedule K, Form 1065, line 1, page 3.	Each partner's share is passed through for separate reporting.
		Each partner's basis is increased.
2. Compute partnership ordinary loss.	Form 1065, line 22, page 1.	Schedule K–1 (Form 1065), line 1, page 1.
	Schedule K, Form 1065, line 1, page 3.	Each partner's share is passed through for separate reporting.
		Each partner's basis is decreased.
		The amount of a partner's loss deduction may be limited.
		Losses that may not be deducted are carried forward for use in future years.
3. Separately reported items like portfolio income, capital gain and loss, and § 179 deductions.	Schedule K, Form 1065, various lines, page 3.	Schedule K–1 (Form 1065), various lines, pages 1 and 2.
		Each partner's share of each item is passed through for separate reporting.
4. Net earnings from self-employment.	Schedule K, Form 1065, line 15, page 3.	Schedule K–1 (Form 1065), line 15, page 2.

BASIS OF A PARTNERSHIP INTEREST

6 **LEARNING OBJECTIVE**
Determine a partner's basis in the partnership interest.

Previously, this chapter discussed how to compute a partner's adjusted basis when the partnership is formed. It was noted that the partner's adjusted basis in the newly formed partnership usually equals (1) the adjusted basis in any property contributed to the partnership plus (2) the fair market value of any services the partner performed for the partnership (i.e., the amount of ordinary income reported by the partner for services rendered to the partnership).

A partnership interest also can be acquired after the partnership has been formed. The method of acquisition controls how the partner's initial basis is computed. If the partnership interest is purchased from another partner, the purchasing partner's basis is the amount paid (cost basis) for the partnership interest. The basis of a partnership interest acquired by gift is the donor's basis for the interest plus, in certain cases, some or all of the transfer (gift) tax paid by the donor. The basis of a partnership interest acquired through inheritance is the fair market value of the interest on the date the partner dies (or alternate valuation date).

After the partnership begins its activities, or after a transferee partner is admitted to the partnership, the partner's basis is adjusted for numerous items. The following operating results *increase* a partner's adjusted basis:

- The partner's proportionate share of partnership income (including capital gains and tax-exempt income).
- The partner's proportionate share of any increase in partnership liabilities.

The following operating results *decrease* the partner's adjusted basis in the partnership:

- The partner's proportionate share of partnership deductions and losses (including capital losses).
- The partner's proportionate share of nondeductible expenses.
- The partner's proportionate share of any reduction in partnership liabilities.[39]

Under no circumstances can the partner's adjusted basis for the partnership interest be reduced below zero.

Increasing the adjusted basis for the partner's share of partnership taxable income is logical since the partner has already been taxed on the income. By increasing the partner's basis, the Code ensures that the partner is not taxed again on the income when the interest is sold or a distribution is received from the partnership.

It is also logical that the tax-exempt income should increase the partner's basis. If the income is exempt in the current period, it should not contribute to the recognition of gain when the partner either sells the interest or receives a distribution from the partnership.

▼
EXAMPLE 23

Yuri is a one-third partner in the XYZ Partnership. His proportionate share of the partnership income during the current year consists of $20,000 of ordinary taxable income and $10,000 of tax-exempt income. None of the income is distributed to Yuri. The adjusted basis of Yuri's partnership interest before adjusting for his share of income is $35,000, and the fair market value of the interest before considering the income items is $50,000.

The unrealized gain inherent in Yuri's investment in the partnership is $15,000 ($50,000 – $35,000). Yuri's proportionate share of the income items should increase the fair market value of the interest to $80,000 ($50,000 + $20,000 + $10,000). By increasing the adjusted basis of Yuri's partnership interest to $65,000 ($35,000 + $20,000 + $10,000), the Code ensures that the unrealized gain inherent in Yuri's partnership investment remains at $15,000. This makes sense because the $20,000 of ordinary taxable income is taxed to Yuri this year and should not be taxed again when Yuri either sells his interest or receives a distribution. Similarly, the exempt income is exempt this year and should not increase Yuri's gain when he either sells his interest or receives a distribution from the partnership. ▼

Decreasing the adjusted basis for the partner's share of deductible losses, deductions, and noncapitalizable, nondeductible expenditures is logical for the same reasons. An item that is deductible currently should not contribute to creating a loss when the partnership interest is sold or a distribution is received from the partnership. Similarly, a noncapitalizable, nondeductible expenditure should never be deductible nor contribute to a loss when a subsequent sale or distribution transaction occurs.

7   **LEARNING OBJECTIVE**
Explain how liabilities affect a partner's basis.

Liability Sharing.   A partner's adjusted basis is affected by the partner's share of partnership debt.[40] Partnership debt includes any partnership obligation that creates an asset, results in a deductible expense, or results in a nondeductible, noncapitalizable item at the partnership level. The definition of partnership debt includes most debt that is considered a liability under financial accounting rules except for accounts payable of a cash basis partnership and certain contingent liabilities.

---

[39] §§ 705 and 752.   [40] § 752.

Under § 752, an increase in a partner's share of partnership debt is treated as a cash contribution by the partner to the partnership. A partner's share of debt increases as a result of (1) increases in partnership debt and (2) assumption of a partner's individual debt by the partnership. A decrease in a partner's share of partnership debt is treated as a cash distribution from the partnership to the partner. A partner's share of debt decreases as a result of (1) decreases in partnership debt and (2) assumption of partnership debt by a partner.

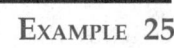

EXAMPLE 24

Jim and Becky contribute property to form the JB Partnership. Jim contributes cash of $30,000. Becky contributes land with an adjusted basis and fair market value of $45,000, subject to a liability of $15,000. The partnership borrows $50,000 to finance construction of a building on the contributed land. At the end of the first year, the accrual basis partnership owes $3,500 in trade accounts payable to various vendors. Assume no other operating activities occurred.

Partnership debt sharing rules are discussed later in this section, but assuming for simplicity that Jim and Becky share equally in liabilities, the partners' bases in their partnership interests are determined as follows:

Jim's Basis		Becky's Basis	
Contributed cash	$30,000	Basis in contributed land	$ 45,000
Share of construction loan	25,000	Less: Debt assumed by partnership	(15,000)
Share of trade accounts payable	1,750	Share of construction loan	25,000
Share of debt on land (assumed by partnership)	7,500	Share of trade accounts payable	1,750
		Share of debt on land (assumed by partnership)	7,500
	$64,250		$ 64,250

In this case, it is reasonable that the parties have an equal basis after contributing their respective properties, because each is a 50% owner and they contributed property with identical bases and identical *net* fair market values. ▼

Decreases in a partner's share of partnership liabilities are treated as cash distributions and can result in extremely negative tax consequences. Liability balances should be reviewed carefully near the partnership's year-end to ensure the partners have no unanticipated tax results.

EXAMPLE 25

Assume the same facts as in Example 24, except the partnership reported an ordinary loss of $100,000 in its first year of operations. Ignoring possible loss deduction limitations, Jim and Becky each deduct a $50,000 ordinary loss, and their bases in their respective partnership interests are reduced to $14,250 (including a $34,250 share of liabilities).

In the second year, the partnership generated no taxable income or loss from operations, but repaid the $50,000 construction loan (assume from collection of accounts receivable reported as income in the prior year). The $25,000 reduction of each partner's share of partnership liabilities is treated as a cash distribution by the partnership to each partner. As Chapter 11 notes, a cash distribution in excess of basis usually results in a capital gain (in this case $10,750) to each partner. The partners must pay tax on $10,750 of capital gain even though the partnership reported no taxable income. This gain can be thought of as a recapture of loss deductions the partners claimed during the first year. Such gains cause cash-flow difficulties to partners who are unaware that such a gain may occur. ▼

Two types of partnership debt exist. **Recourse debt** is partnership debt for which the partnership or at least one of the partners is personally liable. This liability can exist, for example, through the operation of state law or through personal guarantees that a partner makes to the creditor. Personal liability of a party related to a partner (under attribution rules) is treated as the personal liability of the partner. **Nonrecourse debt** is debt for which no partner (or party related to a partner) is personally liable. Lenders of nonrecourse debt generally require that collateral be pledged against the loan. Upon default, the lender can claim only the collateral, not the partners' personal assets.

How liabilities are shared among the partners depends upon whether the debt is recourse or nonrecourse and when the liability was incurred. For most debt *created* before January 29, 1989, the rules are relatively straightforward. Recourse debt is shared among the partners in accordance with their loss sharing ratios while nonrecourse debt is shared among the partners in accordance with the way they share partnership profits. Although questions arise about the calculation of the profit or loss sharing ratios and the treatment of personal guarantees of debt, the rules for sharing this earlier debt are easy to apply.

The rules for sharing partnership debt created after January 29, 1989, are much more complex. A complete analysis of these rules is beyond the scope of this text. The basic principles of these rules can be illustrated, however.

Current Recourse Debt Rules. Recourse debt created after January 29, 1989, is shared in accordance with a **constructive liquidation scenario.**[41]

Under this scenario, the following events are *deemed* to occur at the end of each taxable year of the partnership:

1. Most partnership assets (including cash) become worthless.
2. The worthless assets are sold at fair market value ($0), and losses on the deemed sales are determined.
3. These losses are allocated to the partners according to their loss sharing ratios. These losses reduce the partners' capital accounts.
4. Any partner with a (deemed) negative capital account balance is treated as contributing cash to the partnership to restore that negative balance to zero.
5. The cash deemed contributed by the partners with negative capital balances is used to pay the liabilities of the partnership.
6. The partnership is deemed to be liquidated immediately, and any remaining cash is distributed to partners with positive capital account balances.

The amount of a partner's cash contribution that would be used (in step 5 above) to pay partnership recourse liabilities is that partner's share of these partnership recourse liabilities.

EXAMPLE 26   On January 1 of the current year, Nina and Otis each contribute $20,000 cash to the newly created NO General Partnership. Each partner has a 50% interest in partnership capital, profits, and losses. The first year of partnership operations resulted in the following balance sheet as of December 31:

---

[41] Transition rules (beyond the scope of this text) apply to debt created between January 29, 1989, and December 28, 1991.

	Basis	Fair Market Value
Cash	$12,000	$12,000
Receivables	7,000	7,000
Land and buildings	50,000	50,000
	$69,000	$69,000
Recourse payables	$30,000	$30,000
Nina, capital	19,500	19,500
Otis, capital	19,500	19,500
	$69,000	$69,000

The recourse debt is shared in accordance with the constructive liquidation scenario. All of the partnership assets (including cash) are deemed to be worthless and sold for $0. This creates a loss of $69,000 ($12,000 + $7,000 + $50,000), which is allocated equally between the two partners. The $34,500 loss allocated to each partner creates negative capital accounts of $15,000 each for Nina and Otis. If the partnership were actually liquidated, each partner would contribute $15,000 cash to the partnership; the cash would be used to pay the partnership recourse payables; and the partnership would be liquidated. Because each partner would be required to contribute $15,000 to pay the liabilities, each shares in $15,000 of the recourse payables. Accordingly, Nina and Otis will each have an adjusted basis for their partnership interests of $34,500 ($19,500 + $15,000) on December 31. ▼

EXAMPLE 27

Assume the same facts as in Example 26, except that the partners allocate partnership losses 60% to Nina and 40% to Otis. The constructive liquidation scenario results in the $69,000 loss being allocated $41,400 to Nina and $27,600 to Otis. As a consequence, Nina's capital account has a negative balance of $21,900, and Otis's account has a negative balance of $8,100. Each partner is deemed to contribute cash equal to these negative capital accounts, and the cash would be used to pay the recourse liabilities under the liquidation scenario. Accordingly, Nina and Otis share $21,900 and $8,100, respectively, in the recourse debt. Note that the debt allocation percentages (73% to Nina and 27% to Otis) bear no relation to the partners' 60%/40% loss sharing ratios. ▼

Current Nonrecourse Debt Rules.   Nonrecourse debt is allocated in three stages. First, an amount of debt equal to the amount of *minimum gain* is allocated to partners who share in minimum gain. The calculation of minimum gain is complex, and details of the calculation are beyond the scope of this text. In general, minimum gain approximates the amount of nonrecourse (mortgage) liability on a property in excess of the "book" basis of the property. Generally, the "book" basis for a property item is the same as the "tax" basis, although sometimes the amounts are different. For example, the "book" basis for contributed property on the date of contribution is its fair market value at that date, not its "tax" basis.

If a lender forecloses on partnership property, the result is treated as a deemed sale of the property for the mortgage balance. Gain is recognized for at least the amount of the liability in excess of the property's "book" basis—hence, minimum gain. Allocation of minimum gain among the partners should be addressed in the partnership agreement.

Second, the amount of nonrecourse debt equal to a *precontribution gain* under § 704(c) is allocated to the partner who contributed the property and debt to the partnership. For this purpose, the § 704(c) amount is the excess of the nonrecourse debt assumed by the partnership over the tax basis of the property.[42] Note that this calculation is only relevant when the "book" and "tax" bases are different.

Third, any remaining nonrecourse debt is allocated to the partners in accordance with either their profit sharing ratios or the manner in which they share in nonrecourse deductions. The partnership agreement should specify which allocation method is used.

EXAMPLE 28

Ted contributes a nondepreciable asset to the TK Partnership in exchange for a one-third interest in the capital, profits, and losses of the partnership. The asset has an adjusted tax basis to Ted and the partnership of $24,000 and a fair market value and "book" basis on the contribution date of $50,000. The asset is encumbered by a nonrecourse note (created January 1, 1995) of $35,000. Because the "book" basis exceeds the nonrecourse debt there is no minimum gain. Under § 704(c) principles, the Regulations provide that the first $11,000 of the nonrecourse debt ($35,000 debt − $24,000 basis) is allocated to Ted. The remaining $24,000 nonrecourse debt is shared according to the profit sharing ratio, of which Ted's share is $8,000. Therefore, Ted shares in $19,000 ($11,000 + $8,000) of the nonrecourse debt.

Ted's basis in his partnership interest is determined as follows:

Substituted basis of contributed property	$ 24,000
Less: Liability assumed by partnership	(35,000)
Plus: Allocation of § 704(c) debt	11,000
Basis before remaining allocation	$ –0–
Plus: Allocation of remaining nonrecourse debt	8,000
Basis in partnership interest	$ 8,000

The § 704(c) allocation of nonrecourse debt prevents Ted from receiving a deemed distribution $35,000 in excess of his basis in property he contributed ($24,000). Without this required allocation of nonrecourse debt, in some cases, a contributing partner would be required to recognize gain on a contribution of property encumbered by nonrecourse debt. ▼

Other Factors Affecting Basis Calculations. The partner's basis is also affected by (1) postacquisition contributions of cash or property to the partnership; (2) postacquisition distributions of cash or property from the partnership; and (3) special calculations that are designed to allow the full deduction of percentage depletion for oil and gas wells. Postacquisition contributions of cash or property affect basis in the same manner as contributions made upon the creation of the partnership. Postacquisition distributions of cash or property reduce basis.

EXAMPLE 29

Ed is a one-third partner in the ERM Partnership. On January 1, 1997, Ed's basis in his partnership interest was $50,000. During 1997, the calendar year, accrual basis partnership generated ordinary taxable income of $210,000. It also received $60,000 of interest income from City of Buffalo bonds. It paid $3,000 in nondeductible bribes to local law enforcement officials, so that the police would not notify the Federal government about the products that the entity had imported without paying the proper tariffs. On July 1, 1997, Ed contributed $20,000 cash and a computer (zero basis to him) to the partnership. Ed's monthly draw from the partnership is $3,000; this is not a guaranteed payment. The only liabilities that the partnership has incurred are trade accounts payable. On January 1, 1997,

[42] A more complex calculation applies when the partnership allocates built-in gain under the "remedial allocation" method. (See footnote 38.)

the trade accounts payable totaled $45,000; this account balance was $21,000 on January 1, 1998. Ed shares in one-third of the partnership liabilities for basis purposes.

Ed's basis in the partnership on December 31, 1997, is $115,000, computed as follows:

Beginning balance	$ 50,000
Share of ordinary partnership income	70,000
Share of exempt income	20,000
Share of nondeductible expenditures	(1,000)
Ed's basis in noncash capital contribution	–0–
Additional cash contributions	20,000
Capital withdrawal	(36,000)
Share of net decrease in partnership liabilities [⅓ × ($45,000 – $21,000)]	(8,000)
	$115,000

▼

EXAMPLE 30

Assume the same facts as in Example 29. If Ed withdraws cash of $115,000 from the partnership on January 1, 1998, the withdrawal is tax-free to him and reduces his basis to zero. The distribution is tax-free because Ed has recognized his share of the partnership's net income throughout his association with the entity via the annual flow-through of his share of the partnership's income and expense items. Note that the $20,000 cash withdrawal of his share of the municipal bond interest retains its nontaxable character in this distribution. Ed receives the $20,000 tax-free because his basis was increased in 1997 when the partnership received the interest income. ▼

A partner is required to compute the adjusted basis only when necessary and thus can avoid the inconvenience of making day-to-day calculations of basis. When a partnership interest is sold, exchanged, or retired, however, the partner must compute the adjusted basis as of the date the transaction occurs. Computation of gain or loss requires an accurate calculation of the partner's adjusted basis on the transaction date.

Figure 10–3 summarizes the rules for computing a partner's basis in a partnership interest.

LOSS LIMITATIONS

8   **LEARNING OBJECTIVE**
Describe the limitations on deducting partnership losses.

Partnership losses flow through to the partners for use on their tax returns. However, the amount and nature of the losses that may be used in a partner's tax computations may be limited. When limitations apply, all or a portion of the losses are held in suspension until a triggering condition occurs. Only then can the losses be used to determine the partner's tax liability.

Three different limitations may apply to partnership losses that are passed through to a partner. The first is the overall limitation contained in § 704(d). This limitation allows the deduction of losses only to the extent the partner has adjusted basis for the partnership interest. Losses that are deductible under the overall limitation may then be subject to the at-risk limitation of § 465. Losses are deductible under this provision only to the extent the partner is at risk for the partnership interest. Any losses that survive this second limitation may be subject to a third limitation, the passive loss rules of § 469. Only losses that make it through all these applicable limitations are eligible to be deducted on the partner's tax return.

▼ **FIGURE 10–3**
Partner's Basis
in Partnership Interest

Basis is generally adjusted in the following order:

Initial basis. Amount paid for interest, or gift or inherited basis (including share of partnership debt). Amount paid can be amount contributed to partnership or amount paid to another partner or former partner.

+ Partner's contributions

+ Since interest acquired, partner's share of partnership's
  • Debt increase
  • Income items
  • Exempt income items
  • Excess of depletion deductions over adjusted basis of property subject to depletion

– Partner's distributions and withdrawals

– Since interest acquired, partner's share of partnership's
  • Debt decrease
  • Nondeductible items not chargeable to a capital account
  • Special depletion deduction for oil and gas wells
  • Loss items

The basis of a partner's interest can never be negative.

EXAMPLE 31

Meg is a partner in a partnership that does not invest in real estate. On January 1, 1997, Meg's adjusted basis for her partnership interest is $50,000, and her at-risk amount is $35,000. Her share of losses from the partnership for 1997 is $60,000, all of which is passive. She has one other passive income-producing investment that produced $25,000 of passive income during 1997.

Meg will be able to deduct $25,000 of partnership losses on her Form 1040 for 1997. Her deductible loss is calculated as follows:

Applicable Provision	Deductible Loss	Suspended Loss
Overall limitation	$50,000	$10,000
At-risk limitation	35,000	15,000
Passive loss limitation	25,000	10,000

Meg can deduct only $50,000 under the overall limitation. Of this $50,000, only $35,000 is deductible under the at-risk limitation. Under the passive loss limitation, passive losses can only be deducted against passive income. Thus, Meg can deduct only $25,000 on her return in 1997. ▼

Overall Limitation.   A partner may only deduct losses flowing through from the partnership to the extent of the partner's adjusted basis in the partnership. A partner's adjusted basis in the partnership is determined at the end of the partnership's taxable year. It is adjusted for distributions and any partnership gains during the year, but it is determined *before considering any losses for the year.*

Losses that cannot be deducted because of this rule are suspended and carried forward (never back) for use against future increases in the partner's adjusted basis. Such increases might result from additional capital contributions or from sharing in additional partnership debts or future partnership income.

EXAMPLE 32

Carol and Dan do business as the CD Partnership, sharing profits and losses equally. All parties use the calendar year. At the start of the current year, the basis of Carol's partnership interest is $25,000. The partnership sustains an operating loss of $80,000 in the current year. For the current year, only $25,000 of Carol's $40,000 allocable share of the partnership loss (one-half of $80,000 loss) can be deducted under the overall limitation. As a result, the basis of Carol's partnership interest is zero as of January 1 of the following year, and Carol must carry forward the remaining $15,000 of partnership losses. ▼

EXAMPLE 33

Assume the same facts as in Example 32, and that the partnership earns a profit of $70,000 for the next calendar year. Carol reports net partnership income of $20,000 ($35,000 distributive share of income – the $15,000 carryforward loss). The basis of Carol's partnership interest becomes $20,000. ▼

In Example 32, Carol's entire $40,000 share of the current-year partnership loss could have been deducted under the overall limitation in the current year if she had contributed an additional $15,000 or more in capital by December 31. Alternatively, if the partnership had incurred additional debt by the end of the current year, Carol's basis might have been increased to permit some or all of the loss to be deducted in that year. Thus, if partnership losses are projected for a given year, careful tax planning can ensure their deductibility under the overall limitation.

Notice that in Figure 10–3, contributions to capital, distributions from the partnership, and partnership income items are taken into account before loss items. This ordering produces some unusual results in taxation of partnership distributions and deductibility of losses.

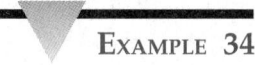

EXAMPLE 34

The Ellen-Glenn Partnership is owned equally by partners Glenn and Ellen. At the beginning of the year, Ellen's basis in her partnership interest is exactly $0. Her share of partnership income is $10,000 for the year, and she receives a $10,000 distribution from the partnership.

Under the basis adjustment ordering rules of Figure 10–3, Ellen's basis is first increased by the $10,000 of partnership income; then it is decreased by her $10,000 distribution. She reports her $10,000 share of partnership taxable income. Her basis at the end of the year is again exactly $0 ($0 + $10,000 income – $10,000 distribution). ▼

EXAMPLE 35

Assume the same facts as in Example 34, except that Ellen's share of partnership operating results is a $10,000 loss instead of $10,000 income. She again receives a $10,000 distribution.

As mentioned earlier, a distribution of cash in excess of basis in the partnership interest results in a gain to the distributee partner (for additional discussion, see Example 25 and Chapter 11). Under the basis adjustment ordering rules of Figure 10–3, Ellen's distribution is considered before the deductibility of the loss is evaluated under the overall limitation.

Ellen recognizes gain on the $10,000 distribution because she has no basis in her partnership interest. The gain effectively ensures that she still has a $0 basis after the distribution. The loss cannot be deducted under the overall loss limitation rule because Ellen has no basis in her partnership interest. ▼

Given this $20,000 swing in partnership earnings in the two examples ($10,000 income to $10,000 loss), does income taxed to Ellen exhibit a similar swing? Actually, she reports $10,000 of income (gain) in each case: ordinary income in Example 34, and (probably) a capital gain from the distribution in Example 35. In Example 35, she also has a $10,000 suspended loss carryforward. These results are due solely to the basis adjustment ordering rules. Remember these rules, and the appropriate results can be determined. Income and contributions are considered first, then distributions—and *last*, loss items.

At-Risk Limitation. Under the at-risk rules, the partnership losses from business and income-producing activities that individual partners and closely held C corporation partners can deduct are limited to amounts that are economically invested in the partnership. Invested amounts include the adjusted basis of cash and property contributed by the partner and the partner's share of partnership earnings that has not been withdrawn.[43] A closely held C corporation exists when five or fewer individuals own more than 50 percent of the entity's stock under appropriate attribution and ownership rules.

When some or all of the partners are personally liable for partnership recourse debt, that debt is included in the adjusted basis of those partners. Usually, those partners also include the debt in their amount at risk.

No partner, however, carries any financial risk on nonrecourse debt. Therefore, as a general rule, partners cannot include nonrecourse debt in their amount at risk even though that debt is included in the adjusted basis of their partnership interest. This rule has an exception, however, that applies in many cases. Real estate nonrecourse financing provided by a bank, retirement plan, or similar party or by a Federal, state, or local government generally is deemed to be at risk.[44] Such debt is termed **qualified nonrecourse debt.** In summary, although the general rule provides that nonrecourse debt is not at risk, the overriding exception may provide that it is deemed to be at risk.

When determining a partner's loss deduction, the overall limitation rule is invoked first. That is, the deduction is limited to the partner's outside basis at the end of the partnership year. Then, the at-risk provisions are applied to see if the remaining loss is still deductible. Suspended losses are carried forward until a partner has a sufficient amount at risk in the activity to absorb them.[45]

EXAMPLE 36

Kelly invests $5,000 in the Kelly Green Limited Partnership as a 5% general partner. Shortly thereafter, the partnership acquires the master recording of a well-known vocalist for $250,000 ($50,000 from the partnership and $200,000 secured from a local bank via a *recourse* mortgage). Assume Kelly's share of the recourse debt is $10,000, and her basis in her partnership interest is $15,000 ($5,000 cash investment + $10,000 debt share). Since the debt is recourse, Kelly's at-risk amount is also $15,000. Kelly's share of partnership losses in the first year of operations is $11,000. Kelly is entitled to deduct the full $11,000 of partnership losses under both the overall and the at-risk limitations because this amount is less than both her outside basis and at-risk amount. ▼

EXAMPLE 37

Assume the same facts as in Example 36, except the bank loan is nonrecourse (the partners have no direct liability under the terms of the loan in the case of a default). Kelly's basis in her partnership interest still is $15,000, but she can deduct only $5,000 of the flow-through loss. The amount she has at risk in the partnership does not include the nonrecourse debt. (The debt does not relate to real estate so it is not qualified nonrecourse debt.) ▼

Passive Activity Rules. A partnership loss share may be disallowed under the passive activity rules. These rules apply to partners who are individuals, estates, trusts, closely held C corporations, or personal service corporations. The rules require the partners to separate their interests in partnership activities into three groups:

- *Active.* Earned income, such as salary and wages; income or loss from a trade or business in which the partner materially participates; and guaranteed payments from a partnership for services.

---

[43] § 465(a).
[44] § 465(b)(6).

[45] § 465(a)(2).

- *Portfolio.* Annuity income, interest, dividends, guaranteed payments from a partnership for interest on capital, royalties not derived in the ordinary course of a trade or business, and gains and losses from disposal of investment assets.
- *Passive.* Income from a trade or business activity in which the partner does not materially participate on a regular, continuous, and substantial basis,[46] or income from a rental activity.

Material participation in an activity is determined annually. The burden is on the partner to prove material participation. The IRS has provided a number of objective tests for determining material participation. In general, these tests require the partner to have substantial involvement in daily operations of the activity. Thus, a Maine vacation resort operator investing in a California grape farm or an electrical engineer employed in Virginia investing in an Iowa corn and hog farm may have difficulty proving material participation in the activities.

Rent income from real or personal property generally is passive income, regardless of the partner's level of participation. Exceptions are made for rent income from activities where substantial services are provided (e.g., certain developers, resorts); from hotels, motels, and other transient lodging; from short-term equipment rentals; and from certain developed real estate.

Usually, passive activity losses can be offset only against passive activity income.[47] In determining the net passive activity loss for a year, losses and income from all passive activities are aggregated. The amount of suspended losses carried forward from a particular activity is determined by the ratio of the net loss from that activity to the aggregate net loss from all passive activities for the year. A special rule for rental real estate (discussed in the following section) allows a limited $25,000 offset against nonpassive income.[48]

A partner making a taxable disposition of an entire interest in a passive activity takes a full deduction for suspended passive activity losses from that activity in the year of disposal.[49] Suspended losses are deductible against income in the following order: income or gain from the passive activity, net income or gain from all passive activities, and other income. When a passive activity is transferred in a primarily nontaxable exchange (e.g., a like-kind exchange or contribution to a partnership), suspended losses are deductible only to the extent of gains recognized on the transfer. Remaining losses are deducted on disposal of the activity received in the exchange.

EXAMPLE 38

Debra has several investments in passive activities that generate aggregate losses of $10,000 in the current year. Debra wants to deduct all of these losses in the current year. To assure a loss deduction, she needs to invest in some passive activities that generate income. One of her long-time friends, an entrepreneur in the women's apparel business, is interested in opening a new apparel store in a nearby community. Debra is willing to finance a substantial part of the expansion but does not want to get involved with day-to-day operations. Debra also wants to limit any possible loss to her initial investment.

After substantial discussions, Debra and her friend decide to form a limited partnership, which will own the new store. Debra's friend will be the general partner, and Debra will be a limited partner. Debra invests $100,000, and her friend invests $50,000 and sweat equity (provides managerial skills and know-how). Each has a 50% interest in profits and losses. In the first year of operations, the store generates a profit of $30,000. Since Debra's

[46] §§ 469(c)(1) and (2).
[47] § 469(a)(1).
[48] § 469(i).
[49] § 469(g).

share of the profit ($15,000) is passive activity income, it can be fully utilized against any of her passive activity losses on other investments. Thus, via her share of the apparel store profits, Debra assures a full deduction of her $10,000 of passive activity losses. ▼

Rental Real Estate Losses.   Individuals can offset up to $25,000 of passive losses from rental real estate against active and portfolio income in any one year. The $25,000 maximum is reduced by 50 percent of the difference between the taxpayer's modified adjusted gross income (AGI) and $100,000. Thus, when the taxpayer's modified AGI reaches $150,000, the offset is eliminated.

The offset is available to those who actively (rather than materially) participate in rental real estate activities. Active participation is an easier test to meet. Unlike material participation, it does not require regular, continuous, and substantial involvement with the activity. However, the taxpayer must own at least 10 percent of the fair market value of all interests in the rental property and either contribute to the activity's management decisions in a significant and bona fide way or actively participate in arranging for others to make such decisions.

▼
EXAMPLE 39

Raoul invests $10,000 cash in the Sparrow Limited Partnership in the current year for a 10% limited interest in capital and profits. Shortly thereafter, the partnership purchases rental real estate subject to a qualified nonrecourse mortgage of $120,000 obtained from a commercial bank. Raoul has no other passive loss activities during the current year.

Raoul does not participate in any of Sparrow's activities. His share of losses from Sparrow's first year of operations is $27,000. His AGI before considering the loss is $60,000. Before considering the loss, Raoul's basis in the partnership interest is $22,000 [$10,000 cash + (10% × $120,000 debt)], and his loss deduction is limited to this amount under the overall limitation. The debt is included in Raoul's amount at risk because it is qualified nonrecourse financing. It may seem that Raoul should be allowed to deduct the $22,000 loss share from portfolio or active income under the rental real estate exception to the passive losses. However, the loss may not be offset against this income because Raoul is not an active participant in the partnership. ▼

▼ TRANSACTIONS BETWEEN PARTNER AND PARTNERSHIP

9 ▼ LEARNING OBJECTIVE
Review the treatment of transactions between a partner and the partnership.

Many types of transactions occur between a partnership and one of its partners. The partner may contribute property to the partnership, perform services for the partnership, or receive distributions from the partnership. The partner may borrow money from or lend money to the partnership. Property may be bought and sold between the partner and the partnership. Several of these transactions were discussed earlier in the chapter. The remaining types of partner-partnership transactions are the focus of this section.

GUARANTEED PAYMENTS

If a partnership makes a payment to a partner in his or her capacity as a partner, the payment may be a draw against the partner's share of partnership income; a return of some or all of the partner's original capital contribution; or a guaranteed payment, among other treatments. A **guaranteed payment** is a payment for services performed by the partner or for the use of the partner's capital. The payment may not be determined by reference to partnership income. Guaranteed payments are usually expressed as a fixed-dollar amount or as a percentage of capital that the partner has invested in the partnership. Whether the partnership deducts or capitalizes the guaranteed payment depends on the nature of the payment.

EXAMPLE 40

David, Donald, and Dale formed the accrual basis DDD Partnership in 1997. According to the partnership agreement, David is to manage the partnership and receive a $21,000 distribution from the entity every year, payable in 12 monthly installments. Donald is to receive an amount that is equal to 18% of his capital account, as it is computed by the firm's accountant at the beginning of the year, payable in 12 monthly installments. Dale is the partnership's advertising specialist. He withdraws 3% of the partnership's net income every month for his personal use. David and Donald receive guaranteed payments from the partnership, but Dale does not. ▼

Guaranteed payments resemble the salary or interest payments of other businesses and receive somewhat similar treatment under partnership tax law.[50] In contrast to the provision that usually applies to withdrawals of assets by partners from their partnerships, guaranteed payments are deductible (or capitalized) by the entity; on the last day of the partnership's tax year, the recipients must report such income separately from their usual partnership allocations. Deductible guaranteed payments, like any other deductible expenses of a partnership, can create an ordinary loss for the entity.

EXAMPLE 41

Continue with the situation introduced in Example 40. For calendar year 1997, David receives the $21,000 as provided by the partnership agreement, Donald's guaranteed payment for 1997 is $17,000, and Dale withdraws $20,000 under his personal expenditures clause. Before considering these amounts, the partnership's ordinary income for 1997 is $650,000.

The partnership can deduct its payments to David and Donald, so the final amount of its 1997 ordinary income is $612,000 ($650,000 − $21,000 − $17,000). Thus, each of the equal partners is allocated $204,000 of ordinary partnership income for their 1997 individual income tax returns ($612,000 ÷ 3). In addition, David reports the $21,000 guaranteed payment as income, and Donald includes the $17,000 guaranteed payment in his 1997 income. Dale's partnership draw is deemed to have come from his allocated $204,000 (or from the accumulated partnership income that was taxed to him in prior years) and is not taxed separately to him. ▼

EXAMPLE 42

Assume the same facts as in Example 40, except that the partnership's tax year ends on March 31, 1998. The total amount of the guaranteed payments is taxable to the partners on that date. Thus, even though David received 9 of his 12 payments for fiscal 1998 in calendar 1997, all of his guaranteed payments are taxable to him in 1998. Similarly, all of Donald's guaranteed payments are taxable to him in 1998 and not when they are received. The deduction for, and the gross income from, guaranteed payments is allowed on the same date that all of the other income and expense items relative to the partnership are allocated to the partners (on the last day of the entity's tax year). ▼

OTHER TRANSACTIONS BETWEEN A PARTNER AND A PARTNERSHIP

Certain transactions between a partner and the partnership are treated as if the partner were an outsider, dealing with the partnership at arm's length.[51] Loan transactions, rental payments, and sales of property between the partner and the

---

[50] § 707(c).

[51] § 707(a).

partnership are generally treated in this manner. In addition, payments for services are treated this way when the services are short-term technical services that the partner also provides for parties other than the partnership.

EXAMPLE 43

Emilio, a one-third partner in the ABC Partnership, owns a tract of land that the partnership wishes to purchase. The land has a fair market value of $30,000 and an adjusted basis to Emilio of $17,000. If Emilio sells the land to the partnership, he recognizes a $13,000 gain on the sale, and the partnership takes a $30,000 cost basis in the land. If the land has a fair market value of $10,000 on the sale date, Emilio recognizes a $7,000 loss. ▼

The timing of the deduction for a payment by an accrual basis partnership to a cash basis service partner depends upon whether the payment is a guaranteed payment or a payment to a partner who is treated as an outsider. A guaranteed payment is includible in the partner's income on the last day of the partnership year when it is properly accrued by the partnership, even though the payment may not be made to the partner until the next taxable year. Conversely, the partner's method of accounting controls the timing of the deduction if the payment is treated as made to an outsider. This is because a deduction cannot be claimed for such amounts until the recipient partner is required to include the amount in income under the partner's method of accounting.[52] Thus, a partnership cannot claim a deduction until it actually makes the payment to the cash basis partner, but it could accrue and deduct a payment due to an accrual basis partner even if payment was not yet made.

EXAMPLE 44

Rachel, a cash basis taxpayer, is a partner in the accrual basis RTC Partnership. On December 31, 1997, the partnership accrues but does not pay $10,000 for deductible services that Rachel performed for the partnership during the year. Both Rachel and the partnership are calendar year taxpayers.

If the $10,000 accrual is a guaranteed payment, the partnership deducts the $10,000 in its calendar year ended December 31, 1997, and Rachel includes the $10,000 in her income for the 1997 calendar year. That Rachel is a cash basis taxpayer and does not actually receive the cash in 1997 is irrelevant.

If the payment is classified as a payment to an outsider, the partnership cannot deduct the payment until Rachel actually receives the cash. If, for example, Rachel performs janitorial services (i.e., not in her capacity as a partner) and receives the cash on March 25, 1998, the partnership deducts the payment and Rachel recognizes the income on that date. ▼

Sales of Property. Certain sales of property fall under special rules. No loss is recognized on a sale of property between a person and a partnership when the person owns, directly or indirectly, more than 50 percent of partnership capital or profits.[53] The disallowed loss may not vanish entirely, however. If the transferee eventually sells the property at a gain, the disallowed loss reduces the gain that the transferee would otherwise recognize.

EXAMPLE 45

Barry sells land (adjusted basis to him, $30,000; fair market value, $45,000) to a partnership in which he controls a 60% capital interest. The partnership pays him $20,000 for the land. Barry cannot deduct his $10,000 realized loss. The sale apparently was not at arm's length, but the taxpayer's intentions are irrelevant. Barry and the partnership are related parties, and the loss is disallowed.

---

[52] § 267(a)(2).

[53] § 707(b).

When the partnership sells the land to an outsider at a later date, it receives a sales price of $44,000. The partnership can offset the recognition of its $24,000 realized gain on the subsequent sale ($44,000 sales proceeds − $20,000 adjusted basis) by the amount of the $10,000 prior disallowed loss ($30,000 − $20,000). Thus, the partnership recognizes a $14,000 gain on its sale of the land. ▼

Using a similar rationale, any gain that is realized on a sale or exchange between a partner and a partnership in which the partner controls a capital or profit interest of more than 50 percent must be recognized as ordinary income, unless the asset is a capital asset to both the seller and the purchaser.[54]

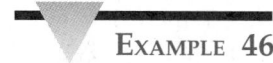

EXAMPLE 46

Kristin purchases some land (adjusted basis, $30,000; fair market value, $45,000) for $45,000 from a partnership in which she controls a 90% profit interest. The land was a capital asset to the partnership. If Kristin holds the land as a capital asset, the partnership recognizes a $15,000 capital gain. However, if Kristin is a land developer and the property is not a capital asset to her, the partnership must recognize $15,000 ordinary income from the sale, even though the property was a capital asset to the partnership. ▼

PARTNERS AS EMPLOYEES

A partner usually does not qualify as an employee for tax purposes. Thus, a partner receiving guaranteed payments is not regarded as an employee of the partnership for purposes of withholding taxes. Moreover, since a partner is not an employee, the partnership cannot deduct its payments for the partner's fringe benefits. A general partner's distributive share of ordinary partnership income and guaranteed payments for services are generally subject to the Federal self-employment tax.[55]

Concept Summary 10–3 reviews partner-partnership transactions.

CONCEPT SUMMARY 10–3

Partner-Partnership Transactions

1. Partners can transact business with their partnerships in a nonpartner capacity. These transactions include such things as the sale and exchange of property, rentals, loans of funds, etc.
2. A payment to a partner may be classified as a guaranteed payment if it is for services or use of the partner's capital and is not based on partnership income. A guaranteed payment may be deductible by the partnership and is included in the partner's income on the last day of the partnership's taxable year.
3. A payment to a partner may be treated as being to an outside (though related) party. Such a payment is deductible or capitalizable by the partnership at the time it must be included in income under the partner's method of accounting.
4. Guaranteed payments and payments to a partner that are treated as being to an outside party are only deductible if the underlying reason for the payment constitutes an ordinary and necessary (rather than capitalizable) business expense.
5. Losses are disallowed between a partner or related party and a partnership when the partner or related party owns more than a 50% interest in the partnership's capital or profits.
6. When there is income from a related-party sale, it is treated as ordinary income if the property is not a capital asset to both the transferor and the transferee.

---

[54]§ 707(b)(2).   [55]§ 1402(a).

CONCEPT SUMMARY 10–4

Advantages and Disadvantages of the Partnership Form

The partnership form may be attractive when one or more of the following factors is present:

- The entity is generating net taxable losses and/or valuable tax credits, which will be of use to the owners.
- Other means of reducing the effects of the double taxation of business income (e.g., compensation to owners, interest, and rental payments) have been exhausted.
- The entity does not generate material amounts of tax preference and adjustment items, which increase the alternative minimum tax liabilities of its owners.
- The entity is generating net passive income, which its owners can use to claim immediate deductions for net passive losses that they have generated from other sources.
- Given the asset holdings and distribution practices of the entity, the possibility of liability under the accumulated earnings and personal holding company taxes is significant.
- The owners wish to make special allocations of certain income or deduction items that are not possible under the C or S corporation forms.
- The owners anticipate liquidation of the entity within a short period of time. Liquidation of a C or S corporation would generate entity-level recognized gains on appreciated property distributed.
- The owners have adequate bases in their partnership interests to facilitate the deduction of flow-through losses and the assignment of an adequate basis to assets distributed in-kind to the partners.

The partnership form may be less attractive when one or more of the following factors is present:

- The maximum marginal tax rate applicable to individuals is higher than the rate applicable to C corporations. Currently, marginal tax rates for individuals may exceed rates applicable to corporations.
- The entity is generating net taxable income, which is taxed directly to the owners who do not necessarily receive any funds from the entity with which to pay the tax.
- The type of income that the entity is generating (e.g., business and portfolio income) is not as attractive to its owners as net passive income would be because the owners could use net passive income to offset the net passive losses that they have generated on their own.
- The entity is in a high-exposure business, and the owners desire protection from personal liability. An LLC or LLP structure may be available, however, to limit personal liability.
- The owners want to avoid Federal self-employment tax.

TAX PLANNING CONSIDERATIONS

10 LEARNING OBJECTIVE
Provide insights regarding advantageous use of a partnership.

CHOOSING PARTNERSHIP TAXATION

Concept Summary 10–4 enumerates various factors that the owners of a business should consider in deciding whether to use a C corporation, S corporation, or partnership as a means of doing business. The reader should refer back to this list after reading Chapters 11 (advanced partnership topics) and 12 (S corporations). Chapter 13 includes a more elaborate discussion of the tax effects of various forms of conducting business.

FORMATION AND OPERATION OF A PARTNERSHIP

Potential partners should be cautious in transferring assets to a partnership to ensure that they are not required to recognize any gain upon the creation of the entity. The nonrecognition provisions of § 721 are relatively straightforward and resemble the provisions under § 351. However, any partner can make a tax-deferred contribution of assets to the entity either at the inception of the

TAX IN THE NEWS

PARTNERSHIPS AROUND THE WORLD—AND BEYOND

Technology continues to act as a catalyst—and incentive—for the creation of multinational joint ventures. AT&T, MCI, and Sprint are racing each other to align with partners in foreign telecommunications markets: each wants to have the widest service coverage area so it can offer efficient communications and computer networking to business clients with a global presence.

Pharmaceutical companies find it advantageous to allow foreign partners to promote and distribute such products as imaging agents used in the detection of various cancers. Reciprocal agreements sometimes give each partner exclusive distribution rights for products created in the partners' separate research facilities.

Finally, there's Lockheed, which plans to use joint venture capital to take technology to the skies. The company will sell high-resolution images produced by satellites funded by the venture.

At least one country, Bermuda, has recognized this trend and is trying to lure multinational joint ventures to its shores. In 1995, it passed the Overseas Partnerships Act and other legislation designed to encourage foreign investment.

partnership or later. This possibility is not available to less-than-controlling shareholders in a corporation.

The partners should anticipate the tax benefits and pitfalls that are presented in Subchapter K and should take appropriate actions to resolve any resulting problems. Typically, all that is needed is an appropriate provision in the partnership agreement (e.g., with respect to differing allocation percentages for gains and losses). Recall, however, that a special allocation of income, expense, or credit items in the partnership agreement must satisfy certain requirements before it is acceptable to the IRS.

TRANSACTIONS BETWEEN PARTNERS AND PARTNERSHIPS

Partners should be careful when engaging in transactions with the partnership to ensure that no negative tax results occur. A partner who owns a majority of the partnership generally should not sell property at a loss to the partnership because the loss is disallowed. Similarly, a majority partner should not sell a capital asset to the partnership at a gain, if the asset is to be used by the partnership as other than a capital asset. The gain on this transaction is taxed as ordinary income to the selling partner rather than as capital gain.

As an alternative to selling property to a partnership, the partner may lease it to the partnership. The partner recognizes rent income, and the partnership has a rent expense. A partner who needs more cash immediately can sell the property to an outside third party; then the third party can lease the property to the partnership for a fair rental.

The timing of the deduction for payments by accrual basis partnerships to cash basis partners varies depending on whether the payment is a guaranteed payment or is treated as a payment to an outsider. If the payment is a guaranteed payment, the deduction occurs when the partnership properly accrues the payment. If the payment is treated as a payment to an outsider, the actual date the payment is made controls the timing of the deduction.

DRAFTING THE PARTNERSHIP AGREEMENT

Although a written partnership agreement is not required, many rules governing the tax consequences to partners and their partnerships refer to such an agreement. Remember that a partner's distributive share of income, gain, loss, deduction, or credit is determined in accordance with the partnership agreement. Consequently, if taxpayers operating a business in partnership form want a measure of certainty as to the tax consequences of their activities, a carefully drafted partnership agreement is crucial. An agreement that sets forth the obligations, rights, and powers of the partners should prove invaluable in settling controversies among them and provide some degree of certainty as to the tax consequences of the partners' actions.

KEY TERMS

Aggregate concept, 10–8

Basis in partnership interest, 10–7

Capital account, 10–8

Capital interest, 10–7

Capital sharing ratio, 10–7

Constructive liquidation scenario, 10–29

Disguised sale, 10–11

Economic effect test, 10–23

Entity concept, 10–8

General partnership, 10–4

Guaranteed payment, 10–37

Inside basis, 10–14

Least aggregate deferral rule, 10–18

Limited liability company (LLC), 10–4

Limited liability partnership (LLP), 10–4

Limited partnership, 10–4

Nonrecourse debt, 10–29

Outside basis, 10–14

Precontribution gain or loss, 10–24

Profit and loss sharing ratios, 10–7

Profits (loss) interest, 10–7

Qualified nonrecourse debt, 10–35

Recourse debt, 10–29

Separately stated item, 10–5

Special allocation, 10–7

Syndication costs, 10–17

PROBLEM MATERIALS

DISCUSSION QUESTIONS

1. What is a partnership for Federal income tax purposes?

2. Compare the nonrecognition of gain or loss provision on contributions to a partnership with the similar provision with respect to corporate formation. What are the major differences and similarities?

3. Harlen will contribute $50,000 cash to the HJ Partnership. Jane currently operates a sole proprietorship with assets valued at $50,000. Jane's tax basis in these assets is $75,000. Jane will either contribute these assets to the partnership in exchange for a 50% interest, or she will sell the assets to Brady Salvage (a third party) for their $50,000 fair market value and contribute that cash to the partnership. The partnership needs assets similar to those Jane owns, but it can purchase new assets from a third party for $60,000. Describe the tax consequences of each alternative to both Jane and the partnership.

4. Block, Inc., a calendar year general contractor, and Strauss, Inc., a development corporation with a July 31 year-end, formed the equal SB Partnership on January 1 of the current year. The partnership was formed to construct and lease shopping centers in Wilmington, Delaware. Block contributed equipment (basis of $650,000, fair market value of $650,000), building permits, and architectural designs that had been created by Block's employees (basis of $0, fair market value of $100,000).

Strauss contributed land (basis of $50,000, fair market value of $250,000) and cash of $500,000. The cash was used as follows:

Legal fees for drafting partnership agreement	$ 10,000
Materials and labor costs for construction in progress on shopping center	400,000
Office expense (utilities, rent, overhead, etc.)	90,000

What issues must the partnership address in preparing its initial tax return?

5. Describe the three tests a partnership must use to determine its required taxable year, and list alternative years that may be available to the partnership.

6. What effect does the contribution of property subject to a liability have on the basis of the contributing partner's interest? What is the effect on the basis of the other partners' interests?

7. What is the purpose of the three rules that implement the economic effect test?

8. Describe the procedure for allocating a nonrecourse debt related to appreciated property contributed by a partner, where the debt exceeds the partner's basis in the contributed property. What is the purpose of this allocation system?

9. Discuss the adjustments that must be made to a partner's basis in his or her partnership interest. When are such adjustments made?

10. To what extent can partners deduct their distributive shares of partnership losses? What happens to any unused losses?

11. Discuss the applicability of the at-risk rules to a partnership and its partners.

12. Discuss the advantages and disadvantages of the partnership entity form.

13. Sam has operated a microbrewery (sole proprietorship) in southern Oregon for the past 15 years. The business has been highly profitable lately, and demand for the product will soon exceed the amount Sam can produce with his present facilities. Marcie, a long-time fan of the brewery, has offered to invest $1,500,000 for equipment to expand production. The assets and goodwill of the brewery are currently worth $1,000,000 (tax basis is only $200,000). Sam will continue to manage the business. He is not willing to own less than 50% of whatever arrangement they arrive at. What issues should Sam and Marcie address and document before finalizing their venture?

PROBLEMS

14. Dan is an attorney who is financially quite successful. Mary is a real estate developer who has little cash for investment. The two decide to buy some real estate. Dan will contribute the money to buy the properties and have veto power over which properties to purchase. Mary will make all other decisions. Profits and losses from the operation will be shared equally.
    a. Is this a partnership for tax purposes? Why or why not?
    b. Would your answer change if Dan had no veto power and was to receive a guaranteed 10% annual return on his money?

15. Larry and Ken form an equal partnership with a cash contribution of $50,000 from Larry and a property contribution (adjusted basis of $30,000 and a fair market value of $50,000) from Ken.
    a. How much gain, if any, must Larry recognize on the transfer? Must Ken recognize any gain?

   b. What is Larry's interest basis in the partnership?

   c. What is Ken's interest basis in the partnership?

   d. What basis does the partnership take in the property transferred by Ken?

16. Three years after the S&P Partnership is formed, Sylvia, a 25% partner, contributes an additional $25,000 cash and land she has held for investment. Sylvia's basis in the land is $15,000, and its fair market value is $10,000. Her basis in the partnership interest was $50,000 before this contribution. The partnership uses the land as a parking lot for four years and then sells it for $8,000.

   a. How much gain or loss does Sylvia recognize on the contribution?

   b. What is Sylvia's basis in her partnership interest immediately following this contribution?

   c. How much gain or loss does S&P recognize on this contribution?

   d. What is S&P's basis in the property it receives from Sylvia?

   e. How much gain or loss does the partnership recognize on the later sale of the land, and what is the character of the gain or loss? How much is allocated to Sylvia?

17. Craig and Beth are equal members of the CB Partnership, formed on June 1 of the current year. Craig contributed land that he inherited from his father three years ago. Craig's father purchased the land in 1946 for $6,000. The land was worth $50,000 when the father died. The fair market value of the land was $75,000 at the date it was contributed to the partnership.

   Beth has significant experience developing real estate. After the partnership is formed, she will prepare a plan for developing the property and secure zoning approvals for the partnership. She would normally bill a third party $25,000 for these efforts. Beth will also contribute $50,000 cash in exchange for her 50% interest in the partnership. The value of her 50% interest is $75,000.

   a. How much gain or income will Craig recognize on his contribution of the land to the partnership? What is the character of any gain or income recognized?

   b. What basis will Craig take in his partnership interest?

   c. How much gain or income will Beth recognize on the formation of the partnership? What is the character of any gain or income recognized?

   d. What basis will Beth take in her partnership interest?

   e. Construct an opening balance sheet for the partnership reflecting the partnership's basis in assets and the fair market value of these assets.

   f. Outline any planning opportunities that may minimize current taxation to any of the parties.

18. Continue with the facts presented in Problem 17. At the end of the first year, the partnership distributes the $50,000 cash to Craig. No distribution is made to Beth.

   a. Under general tax rules, how would the payment to Craig be treated?

   b. How much income or gain would Craig recognize as a result of the payment?

   c. Under general tax rules, what basis would the partnership take in the land Craig contributed?

   d. What alternate treatment might the IRS try to impose?

   e. Under the alternate treatment, how much income or gain would Craig recognize?

   f. Under the alternate treatment, what basis would the partnership take in the land contributed by Craig?

   g. How can the transaction be restructured to minimize risk of IRS recharacterization?

19. The MDB Partnership was formed to acquire land and subdivide it as residential housing lots. On March 1, 1996, Maria contributed land valued at $60,000 to the partnership in exchange for a one-third interest. She had purchased the land in 1991 for $76,000 and held it for investment purposes (capital asset). The partnership holds the land as inventory.

   On the same date, Barry contributed land valued at $60,000 that he had purchased in 1989 for $48,000. He also became a one-third owner. Barry is a real estate developer, but he held this land personally for investment purposes. The partnership also holds this land as inventory.

   In 1994, Deborah had sold a parcel of land held for development purposes on the installment basis. She, too, is a real estate developer. The note has a fair market value and remaining principal balance of $60,000. She contributed this note to the partnership in exchange for her one-third interest. Deborah's basis in the note was $36,000 on the contribution date; the deferred gain on the installment sale is $24,000.

From 1996 to 2001, the partnership collects $10,000 per year on the installment obligation (plus adequate interest on the unpaid balance).

In 1997, the partnership sells half of the land contributed by Maria for $27,000. In 2002, MDB sells the other half of the land contributed by Maria for $36,000.

In 1999, the partnership sells half of the subdivided real estate contributed by Barry for $33,000. The other half is finally sold in 2005 for $42,000.

a. What is each partner's initial basis in his or her partnership interest?

b. What is the amount of gross profit recognized each year on collection of the installment proceeds? What is the character of the gain or loss?

c. What is the amount of gain or loss recognized each year on the sale of the land contributed by Maria? What is the character of this gain or loss?

d. What is the amount of gain or loss recognized each year on the sale of the land contributed by Barry? What is the character of this gain or loss?

20. The partnership agreement for the MDB Partnership in Problem 19 provides that all gains and losses are allocated equally among the partners unless otherwise required under the tax law.

a. How will the gains or losses determined in (b), (c), and (d) in Problem 19 be allocated to each of the partners?

b. If the partnership earns $15,000 of interest income on the installment note, how will this income be allocated to the partners? Assume no accrued interest existed on the day the note was contributed.

c. Calculate each partner's basis in his or her partnership interest at December 31, 2005. Assume the partnership has no transactions through the end of the year 2005 other than the transactions described in Problem 19 and the collection of $15,000 of interest income in (b) above. Why are these balances the same or different?

21. The cash basis Thrush Partnership incurred the following organization and syndication costs in calendar 1997:

Attorney fees for preparing partnership agreement	$2,100
Printing costs for preparing documents that were used to help sell the partnership interests	4,000
Accounting fees for tax advice of an organizational nature	2,400

The attorney fees and printing costs were incurred and paid in 1997. The accounting fees were incurred in December 1997 and paid in February 1998. If the partnership begins business in July 1997, how much of the organization costs can be amortized in 1997? In 1998?

22. Jim, John and Judy form the JJJ Partnership on January 1 of the current year. Jim is a 50% partner, and John and Judy are each 25% partners. Each partner and JJJ use the cash method of accounting. For reporting purposes, Jim uses a calendar year, John uses an August 31 fiscal year, and Judy uses a May 31 fiscal year. What is JJJ's required tax year under the least aggregate deferral method?

23. Lisa and Lori are equal members of the Redbird Partnership. They are real estate investors who formed the partnership several years ago with equal cash contributions. Redbird then purchased a piece of land.

On January 1 of the current year, to acquire a one-third interest in the entity, Lana contributed some land she had held for investment to the partnership. Lana purchased the land three years ago for $30,000; its fair market value at the contribution date was $40,000. No special allocation agreements were in effect before or after Lana was admitted to the partnership. The Redbird Partnership holds all land for investment.

Immediately before Lana's property contribution, the balance sheet of the Redbird Partnership was as follows:

	Basis	FMV		Basis	FMV
Land	$5,000	$80,000	Lisa,capital	$2,500	$40,000
			Lori,capital	2,500	$40,000
	$5,000	$80,000		$5,000	$80,000

a. At the contribution date, what is Lana's basis in her interest in the Redbird Partnership?

b. When does the partnership's holding period begin for the contributed land?

c. On June 30 of the current year, the partnership sold the land contributed by Lana for $40,000. How much is the recognized gain or loss, and how is it allocated among the partners?

d. Prepare a balance sheet reflecting basis and fair market value for the partnership immediately after the land sale.

24. Assume the same facts as in Problem 23, with the following exceptions.

   • Lana purchased the land three years ago for $50,000. Its fair market value was $40,000 when it was contributed to the partnership.

   • Redbird sold the land contributed by Lana for $34,000.

   a. How much is the recognized gain or loss, and how is it allocated among the partners?

   b. Prepare a balance sheet reflecting basis and fair market value for the partnership immediately after the land sale, along with schedules that support the amount in each partner's capital account.

25. Carrie and Fred are equal partners in the accrual basis CF Partnership. At the beginning of the current year, Fred's capital account has a balance of $60,000, and the partnership has recourse debts of $90,000 payable to unrelated parties. All partnership recourse debt is shared equally between the partners. The following information about CF's operations for the current year is obtained from the partnership's records.

Taxable income	$80,000
Tax-exempt interest income	5,000
§ 1231 gain	6,000
Long-term capital gain	2,000
Long-term capital loss	3,000
IRS penalty	2,000
Charitable contribution to Girl Scouts	6,000
Guaranteed payment to Carrie	14,000.
Payment of Fred's medical expenses	10,000

Assume that year-end partnership debt payable to unrelated parties is $40,000.

   a. If all transactions are reflected in his beginning capital and basis in the same manner, what is Fred's basis in the partnership interest at the beginning of the year?

   b. If all transactions are reflected in his beginning capital and basis in the same manner, what is Fred's basis in the partnership interest at the end of the current year?

26. The RUB Partnership reported the following items during the current tax year:

Taxable income	$120,000
Municipal bond interest income	10,000
Gain on sale of real estate	60,000

Taxable income includes $20,000 of income from collection of cash basis accounts receivable contributed by 25% partner Rolfe at the beginning of the year.

The municipal bond income was earned on bonds contributed by 50% partner Una. None of the interest was accrued on the contribution date. The partnership agreement provides that all this income will be specially allocated to Una this year, and no offsetting allocation will be made now or later.

The real estate gain resulted from the sale of a parcel of land contributed by 25% partner Bart. When the property was contributed, it was valued at $100,000 and Bart's basis was $80,000. Assume the real estate is a capital asset to both Bart and the partnership.

Prepare a schedule showing how each item is allocated to each of the three partners. Assume the partnership will maintain capital account balances and perform all other record keeping required to meet the substantial economic effect requirements of § 704(b).

27. The RB Partnership is owned equally by Rob and Bob. Bob's basis is $15,000 at the beginning of the tax year. Rob's basis is $6,000 at the beginning of the year. RB reported the following income and expenses for the current tax year:

Sales revenue	$130,000
Cost of sales	45,000
Guaranteed payment to Rob	24,000
Depreciation expense	12,500
Utilities	15,000
Rent	16,000
Interest income	3,000
Tax-exempt interest income	4,500
Long-term capital loss	3,200
Payment to Mount Vernon Hospital for Bob's medical expenses	10,000

a. Determine the ordinary partnership income and separately stated items for the partnership.

b. Calculate Bob's basis in his partnership interest at the end of the tax year. What items should Bob report on his Federal income tax return?

c. Calculate Rob's basis in his partnership interest at the end of the tax year. What items should Rob report on his Federal income tax return?

28. Assume the same facts as in Problem 27, except for the following:

• Partnership revenues were $90,000 instead of $130,000.

• Rob also received a distribution of $10,000 cash.

a. Redetermine the ordinary income and separately stated items for the partnership.

b. Calculate Bob's basis in his partnership interest at the end of the tax year. How much income or loss should Bob report on his Federal income tax return?

c. Calculate Rob's basis in his partnership interest at the end of the tax year. How much income or loss should Rob report on his Federal income tax return?

29. At the beginning of the current year, Bill's basis in his 50% interest in the BP Partnership is $10,000, including an $85,000 share of partnership recourse debt. Near the beginning of the year, he contributed land valued at $180,000 to the partnership. Bill's basis in the land was $76,000, and a nonrecourse liability on the land (assumed by the partnership) was $90,000. The value of the land rose sharply when plans for a new freeway nearby were approved during the year, and the partnership sold the land near the end of the year for $260,000. The gain on the land sale is a capital gain since the land was held for investment purposes by both Bill and the partnership. BP used the proceeds from the land sale to pay the partnership's recourse and nonrecourse debts. Other than the gain on the land sale, the partnership reported an ordinary loss of $150,000 from operations. Bill is an active partner in the partnership.

It is the last day of the current tax year. Bill has just called to ask you to help determine how his ownership interest in the partnership will affect his personal tax and financial situation this year.

a. What issues related to each of the above transactions must be addressed to determine the tax consequences of owning the partnership interest for the current year?

b. Make any necessary calculations and advise Bill regarding any year-end action you feel might be advisable.

30. Assume the same facts as in Problem 29, except as indicated below. Situations (a) and (b) are independent fact patterns.

a. How would your advice to Bill change if he was not an active partner in the partnership and had no other passive activities? Identify the additional issues that arise in this situation.

b. How would your advice to Bill change if his $10,000 basis included all $170,000 of partnership recourse debt (under a constructive liquidation calculation)? Identify the additional issues that arise in this situation. (Assume the partnership repaid all debt before year-end and Bill is still an active partner.)

31. The MGP General Partnership was created on January 1, 1997, by having Miguel, George, and Pat each contribute $10,000 cash to the partnership in exchange for a one-third interest in partnership income, gains, losses, deductions, and credits. On December 31, 1997, the partnership balance sheet reads as follows:

	Basis	FMV
Assets	$40,000	$55,000
Recourse debt	$12,000	$12,000
Miguel, capital	11,000	16,000
George, capital	11,000	16,000
Pat, capital	6,000	11,000
	$40,000	$55,000

Pat's capital account is less than Miguel's and George's capital accounts because Pat has withdrawn more cash than the other partners.

How do the partners share the recourse debt as of December 31, 1997?

32. Your client, the Williams Institute of Technology (WIT), is a 60% partner in the Research Industries Partnership (RIP). WIT is located at 76 Bradford Lane, St. Paul, MN 55164. The controller, Jeanine West, has sent you the following note and a copy of WIT's 1997 Schedule K–1 from the partnership.

Excerpt from client's note:
"RIP expects its 1998 operations to include the following:

Net loss from operations	$200,000
Capital gain from sale of land	100,000

The land was contributed by DASH, the other partner, when its value was $260,000. The partnership sold the land for $300,000. The partnership used this cash to repay all the partnership debt and pay for research and development expenditures, which a tax partner in your firm has said RIP can deduct this year.

We want to be sure we can deduct our full share of this loss, but we do not believe we will have enough basis. We are a material participant in this partnership's activities."

Items Reported on the 1997 Schedule K–1	
WIT's share of partnership recourse liabilities	$90,000
WIT's ending capital account balance	30,000

Draft a letter to the controller that describes the following:

- WIT's allocation of partnership items.

- WIT's basis in the partnership interest following the allocation.

- Any limitations on loss deductions.

- Any recommendations you have that would allow WIT to claim the full amount of losses in 1998.

Assume WIT's 1997 K–1 accurately reflects the information needed to compute its basis in the partnership interest. Also assume the research expenditures are fully deductible this year, as the partner said.

Your client has experience researching issues in the Internal Revenue Code, so you may use some citations. However, be sure the letter is written in layperson's terms and cites are minimized.

33. Lee, Brad, and Rick form the LBR Partnership on January 1 of the current year. In return for a 25% interest, Lee transfers property (basis of $15,000, fair market value of $17,500) subject to a nonrecourse liability of $10,000. The liability is assumed by the partnership. Brad transfers property (basis of $16,000, fair market value of $7,500) for a 25% interest, and Rick transfers cash of $15,000 for the remaining 50% interest. (See Example 24.)
   a. How much gain must Lee recognize on the transfer?
   b. What is Lee's basis in his interest in the partnership?
   c. How much loss may Brad recognize on the transfer?
   d. What is Brad's basis in his interest in the partnership?
   e. What is Rick's basis in his interest in the partnership?
   f. What basis does the LBR Partnership take in the property transferred by Lee?
   g. What is the partnership's basis in the property transferred by Brad?

34. Assume the same facts as in Problem 33, except that the property contributed by Lee has a fair market value of $27,500 and is subject to a nonrecourse mortgage of $20,000. (See Example 28.)
   a. What is Lee's basis in his partnership interest?
   b. How much gain must Lee recognize on the transfer?
   c. What is Brad's basis in his partnership interest?
   d. What is Rick's basis in his partnership interest?
   e. What basis does the LBR Partnership take in the property transferred by Lee?

35. Kim and Craig plan to form the KC General Partnership by the end of the current year. The partners will each contribute $30,000 cash to the venture. In addition, the partnership will borrow $140,000 from First State Bank. The partnership's land will serve as collateral, and both partners will be required to personally guarantee the debt.

   The tentative partnership agreement provides that 75% of operating income, gains, losses, deductions, and credits will be allocated to Kim for the first five years the partnership is in existence. The remaining 25% is allocated to Craig. Thereafter, all partnership items will be allocated equally. The agreement also provides that capital accounts will be properly maintained, and each partner must restore any deficit in the capital account upon the partnership's liquidation.

   The partners would like to know, before the end of the tax year, how the $140,000 liability will be allocated for basis purposes. Using the format (1) facts, (2) issues, (3) conclusion, and (4) law and analysis, draft a memo to the tax planning file for the KC Partnership that describes how the debt will be shared between the partners for purposes of computing the adjusted basis of each partnership interest.

36. Chris Elton is a 15% partner in the Cardinal Partnership, which is a lessor of residential rental property. Her share of the partnership's losses for the current year is $70,000. Immediately before considering the deductibility of this loss, Chris's capital account (which, in this case, corresponds to her basis excluding liabilities) reflected a balance of $40,000. Her share of partnership recourse liabilities is $10,000, and her share of the nonrecourse liabilities is $6,000. The nonrecourse liability was obtained from an

unrelated bank and is secured solely by the real estate. Chris is also a partner in the Bluebird Partnership, which has generated income from long-term (more than 30 days) equipment rental activities. Chris's share of Bluebird's income is $23,000. Chris performs substantial services for Bluebird and spends several hundred hours a year working for the Cardinal Partnership. Chris's modified adjusted gross income before considering partnership activities is $100,000. Your manager has asked you to determine how much of the $70,000 loss Chris can deduct on her current calendar year return. Using the format (1) facts, (2) issues, (3) conclusion, and (4) law and analysis, draft a memo to the client's tax file describing the loss limitations. Be sure to identify the Code Sections under which losses are suspended.

37. Fred and Fran are equal partners in the calendar year F & F Partnership. Fred uses a fiscal year ending June 30, and Fran uses a calendar year. Fred receives an annual guaranteed payment of $50,000 from F & F. F & F's taxable income (after deducting Fred's guaranteed payment) was $40,000 for 1997 and $50,000 for 1998.
    a. What is the aggregate amount of income from the partnership that Fred must report for his tax year ending June 30, 1998?
    b. What is the aggregate amount of income from the partnership that Fran must report for her tax year ending December 31, 1998?
    c. If Fred's annual guaranteed payment is increased to $60,000 starting on January 1, 1998, and the partnership's taxable income for 1997 and 1998 is the same (i.e., $40,000 and $50,000, respectively), what is the aggregate amount of income from the partnership that Fred must report for his tax year ending June 30, 1998?

38. Ned, a 50% partner in the MN Partnership, is to receive a payment of $35,000 for services. He will also be allocated 50% of the partnership's profits or losses. After deducting the payment to Ned, the partnership has a loss of $25,000. Ned's basis in his partnership interest was $10,000 before these items.
    a. How much, if any, of the $25,000 partnership loss will be allocated to Ned?
    b. What is the net income from the partnership that Ned must report on his Federal income tax return?
    c. What is Ned's basis in his partnership interest following the guaranteed payment and loss allocation?

39. Four Lakes Partnership is owned by four sisters. Anne holds a 70% interest; each of the others owns 10%. Anne sells investment property to the partnership for its fair market value of $100,000 (Anne's basis is $150,000).
    a. How much loss, if any, may Anne recognize?
    b. If the partnership later sells the property for $160,000, how much gain must it recognize?
    c. If Anne's basis in the investment property was $20,000 instead of $150,000, how much, if any, capital gain would she recognize on the sale?

40. Comment on the validity of the following statements:
    a. Since a partnership is not a taxable entity, it is not required to file any type of tax return.
    b. Each partner can choose a different method of accounting and depreciation computation in determining the gross income from the entity.
    c. Generally, a transfer of appreciated property to a partnership results in recognized gain to the contributing partner at the time of the transfer.
    d. A partner can carry forward, for an unlimited period of time, the partner's share of any partnership operating losses that exceed the partner's basis in the entity, provided the partner retains an ownership interest in the partnership.
    e. When a partner renders services to the entity in exchange for an unrestricted interest, that partner does not recognize any gross income.
    f. Losses on sales between a partner and the partnership always are nondeductible.
    g. A partnership may choose a year that results in the least aggregate deferral of tax to the partners, unless the IRS requires the use of a natural business year.
    h. A partner's basis in a partnership interest includes that partner's share of partnership recourse and nonrecourse liabilities.

     i. Built-in loss related to nondepreciable property contributed to a partnership must be allocated to the contributing partner to the extent the loss is eventually recognized by the partnership.

    j. Property that was held as inventory by a contributing partner, but is a capital asset in the hands of the partnership results in a capital gain if the partnership immediately sells the property.

COMPREHENSIVE TAX RETURN PROBLEM

Ben Boyle (256–99–0206), Anne Brophy (423–96–9943), and James Bierd (923–67–1969) are partners in the BBB Partnership—for "Bake-a-Better-Bagel"—a general partnership that operates a bakery in a waterfront retail area in Mobile, Alabama. BBB's Federal I.D. number is 63–0234576. The partnership uses the accrual method of accounting and the calendar year for reporting purposes. It began business operations on June 6, 1994. Its current address is 5816 North Crestline Boulevard, Mobile, AL 36609. The 1996 income statement for the partnership reflected net income of $63,045. The following information was taken from the partnership's financial statements for the current year:

Receipts	
Sales revenues	$309,800
Promotion revenues (advertising revenues from vendors)	10,600
Taxable interest from investments	1,200
Tax-exempt interest	1,500
Long-term capital gain	2,100
Long-term capital loss	(300)
§ 1231 gain	2,400
Total revenues	$327,300

Cash payments	
Purchases	$132,250
Rent	16,800
Utilities	16,530
Employee salaries	25,400
Contribution to Girl Scouts	330
Meals and entertainment, subject to 50% disallowance	1,200
Guaranteed payment, James Bierd, managing partner	23,000
Office expense	920
Accounting fees	1,225
Payroll taxes	2,680
Sales tax	22,540
Business interest on mortgage on leasehold improvements	7,500
Repairs	1,200
Payment of beginning accounts payable	7,300
Commercial oven	8,600
Total cash disbursements	$267,475

Noncash expenses	
Amortization	$ 600
Depreciation (including depreciation on commercial oven)	18,140
Accrual of ending accounts payable	–0–

The beginning and ending balance sheets for the partnership were as follows for 1996:

	Beginning	Ending
Cash	$ 15,505	$ 12,330
Inventory	36,875	42,935
U.S. Treasury notes	20,000	12,000
Short-term investments	26,000	25,000
Leasehold improvements	65,000	65,000
Equipment	30,000	38,600
Accumulated depreciation	(16,830)	(34,970)
Organization fees	3,000	3,000
Accumulated amortization	(950)	(1,550)
Total assets	$178,600	$162,345
Accounts payable	$ 7,300	0
Mortgage payable on leasehold improvements	75,000	75,000
Capital, Boyle	32,100	29,115
Capital, Brophy	32,100	29,115·
Capital, Bierd	32,100	29,115
Total liabilities and capital	$178,600	$162,345

The partnership uses the lower of cost or market method for valuing inventory. It is not subject to the provisions of § 263A. The partnership claimed $18,140 depreciation for both tax and financial accounting purposes. Assume none of the depreciation creates a tax preference.

No guaranteed payments were paid to partners other than James Bierd. Instead, each partner (including Bierd) withdrew $2,000 per month as a distribution (draw) of operating profits. The partners share equally in all partnership liabilities, since all initial contributions and all ongoing allocations and distributions are pro rata. All partners are considered "active" for purposes of the passive loss rules.

None of the partners sold any portion of their interests in the partnership during 1996. The partnership's operations are entirely restricted to the Mobile metropolitan area. All partners are U.S. citizens. The partnership had no foreign operations, no foreign bank accounts, and no interest in any foreign trusts or other partnerships. The partnership is not publicly traded and is not a statutory tax shelter.

The IRS's business code for the partnership operations is 5460. The partnership is not subject to the consolidated audit procedures and does not have a tax matters partner. The partnership files its tax return in Memphis, Tennessee. Partner James Bierd lives at 297 E. Ball Road, Mobile, AL 36609.

a. Prepare Form 1065 and Schedule K for the BBB Partnership, leaving blank any items where insufficient information has been provided. Prepare any supporting schedules necessary. *Hint:* Prepare Schedule A first to determine cost of goods sold.

b. Prepare Schedule K–1 for James Bierd.

RESEARCH PROBLEMS

Note: **West's Federal Taxation on CD-ROM** *can be used in preparing solutions to the Research Problems. Alternatively, tax research materials contained in a standard tax library can be used.*

Research Problem 1. Your clients, Mark Henderson and John Burton, each contributed $10,000 cash to form the Realty Management Partnership, a limited partnership. Mark is the general partner, and John is the limited partner. The partnership used the $20,000 cash to make a down payment on a building. The rest of the building's $200,000 purchase price was financed with an interest-only nonrecourse loan of $180,000, which was obtained from an independent third-party bank. The partnership allocates all partnership items equally between the partners except for the MACRS deductions and building maintenance, which are allocated 70% to John and 30% to Mark. The partnership definitely wishes to satisfy the "economic effect" requirements of Reg. § 1.704–1 and Reg. § 1.704–2 and will reallocate MACRS, if necessary, to satisfy the requirements of the Regulations. Under the partnership agreement, liquidation distributions will be paid in proportion to the partners' positive capital account balances. Capital accounts are maintained as required in the Regulations. Mark has an unlimited obligation to restore his capital account while John is subject to a qualified income offset provision. Assume all partnership items, except for MACRS, will net to zero throughout the first three years of the partnership operations. Also, assume that each year's MACRS deduction will be $10,000 (to simplify the calculations).

Draft a letter to the partnership evaluating the allocation of MACRS in each of the three years under Reg. § 1.704–1 and Reg. § 1.704–2. The partnership's address is 53 East Marsh Ave., Smyrna, Georgia 30082. Do not address the "substantial" test.

Research Problem 2.   Harrison has considerable experience as a leasing agent for residential rental properties. He is disappointed, though, that his salary with his present employer does not reflect the effort he puts forth.

Alameda Properties has offered Harrison a position handling leasing activities for a new limited partnership that is being formed to construct and manage three apartment complexes in southern California. Alameda is willing to hire Harrison for two years to lease the properties, but is unable to pay the $60,000 salary Harrison requires without impairing its ability to pay necessary cash distributions to the limited partners.

Alameda is willing to pay a $30,000 salary for two years, increasing to a market salary thereafter. Alameda is also willing to allow Harrison to purchase a 10% interest in the partnership, but Harrison cannot afford the required $20,000 capital contribution.

The partnership expects to distribute cash flows from operations of approximately $150,000 per year, for an estimated seven-year holding period (taxable income will be much lower because depreciation and interest deductions will be greater than mortgage payments).

Harrison and Alameda Properties have approached you for assistance in structuring a mutually satisfactory arrangement. You are aware that a partner can be awarded an interest in the future profits of a partnership and have learned from a colleague that in 1993 the IRS issued a Revenue Procedure that outlines the types of profits interests that will not be subject to current taxation. Present a structure to Harrison and Alameda Properties that meets their respective goals, and outline the advantages and disadvantages to each party.

Research Problem 3.   Fred and Grady have formed the FG Partnership to operate a retail establishment selling antique household furnishings. Fred is the general partner, and Grady is the limited partner. Both partners contribute $15,000 to form the partnership. The partnership uses the $30,000 contributed by the partners and a recourse loan of $100,000 obtained from an unrelated third-party lender to acquire $130,000 of initial inventory.

The partners believe they will have extensive losses in the first year due to advertising and initial cash-flow requirements. Fred and Grady have agreed to share losses equally. To make sure the losses can be allocated to both partners, they have included a provision in the partnership agreement requiring each partner to restore any deficit balance in his partnership capital account upon liquidation of the partnership.

Fred was also willing to include a provision that requires him to make up any deficit balance within 90 days of liquidation of the partnership. As a limited partner, Grady argued that he should not be subject to such a time requirement. The partners compromised and included a provision that requires Grady to restore a deficit balance in his capital account within two years of liquidation of the partnership. No interest will be owed on the deferred restoration payment.

Determine whether FG will be able to allocate the $100,000 recourse debt equally to the two partners to ensure they will be able to deduct their respective shares of partnership losses.

Use the tax resources of the internet to address the following questions. Do not restrict your search to the World Wide Web, but include a review of newsgroups and general reference materials, practitioner sites and resources, primary sources of the tax law, chat rooms and discussion groups, and other opportunities.

Research Problem 4. Find a discussion group that concentrates on the taxation of partners and partnerships. Post to the group a message defining the terms "inside and outside basis" and illustrating why the distinction between them is important. Respond to any replies you receive. Print your message and one or two of the replies.

Research Problem 5. Find the home page of a partnership that seems to be soliciting financing from new partners. Comment on the portrayal of the pertinent tax law that is included in the materials, especially with respect to the at-risk rules and the passive activity limitations.

Research Problem 6. Print an article posted by a law firm, commenting on pitfalls to avoid in drafting partnership agreements. Ideally, use the home page of a firm that has offices in your state.

PARTNERSHIPS: DISTRIBUTIONS, TRANSFER OF INTERESTS, AND TERMINATIONS

LEARNING OBJECTIVES

After completing Chapter 11, you should be able to:

1. Determine the tax treatment of proportionate nonliquidating distributions from a partnership to a partner.

2. Determine the tax treatment of proportionate distributions that liquidate a partnership.

3. Describe the general concepts governing tax treatment of disproportionate distributions.

4. Determine the tax treatment under § 736 of payments from a partnership to a retiring or deceased partner.

5. Calculate the selling partner's amount and character of gain or loss on the sale or exchange of a partnership interest.

6. Describe the different tax results that might arise on a sale of a partnership interest versus liquidation of the interest under § 736.

7. Calculate the optional adjustments to basis under § 754.

8. Outline the methods of terminating a partnership.

9. Describe the special considerations of a family partnership.

10. Describe the application of partnership provisions to limited liability companies (LLCs) and limited liability partnerships (LLPs).

After a partnership is established, many of its day-to-day transactions create no unusual tax problems. Under the aggregate theory of partnership taxation, revenue earned and expenses paid by the partnership are typically handled for tax purposes in the same manner as they are handled for individuals. Certain transactions, however, can have some surprising results. When a partnership interest is sold or exchanged for more or less than its basis, capital gain or loss is recognized. This is consistent with the entity theory treatment of a sale of stock by a shareholder in a C or S corporation. Under certain conditions, however, aggregate treatment may partially govern the results, and the disposal of a partnership interest may create some ordinary income, *even when* the overall result is a loss. Moreover, ordinary income can arise when a partnership simply distributes assets to its partners. Here, either the receiving partner or the partnership can have ordinary income.

This chapter discusses such transactions as sales of partnership interests, liquidation of interests by the partnership, and transfers of interests by gift or death of the partner. Situations where the expected result differs from the actual treatment are highlighted.

This chapter also discusses the taxation of partnership distributions. Unlike corporate distributions, which may result in dividend income to the shareholder, most proportionate distributions of partnership property create no recognized gain or loss to the distributee partner. Instead, the distributee partner's realized gain or loss is deferred until the partner subsequently disposes of the distributed property in a taxable transaction. This treatment is another application of the aggregate theory.

This chapter also addresses optional adjustments to the basis of partnership property, partnership terminations, and special problems associated with family partnerships. The chapter closes with discussions of limited liability companies and limited liability partnerships.

DISTRIBUTIONS FROM A PARTNERSHIP

The tax treatment of distributions from a partnership to a partner was introduced in Chapter 10 in the context of routine cash withdrawals (or "draws") and cash distributions from a continuing partnership to a partner who remains a member of the partnership. These draws and distributions reduce the partner's outside basis by the amount of the cash received. The partnership's inside basis in assets is similarly reduced.

EXAMPLE 1

Bill is a partner in the BB Partnership. The basis in his partnership interest is $10,000. The partnership distributes $3,000 cash to Bill at the end of the year. Bill does not recognize any gain on the distribution and reduces his basis by $3,000 (the amount of the distribution) to $7,000. Bill's basis in the cash he received is $3,000, and the partnership's inside basis for its assets is reduced by the $3,000 cash distributed. ▼

The result in Example 1 arises whether or not a similar distribution is made to other partners. In a partnership, it is not critical that all partners receive a distribution at the same time as long as capital account balances are maintained appropriately, and final distributions are in accordance with ending capital account balances (see Chapter 10). Capital account maintenance requirements ensure that each partner eventually receives the amount to which he or she is entitled, even though current distributions are not in accordance with ownership percentages.

A distribution from the partnership to a partner may consist of cash or partnership property. All distributions, cash and property, fall into two distinct categories:

- Liquidating distributions.
- Nonliquidating distributions.

Whether a distribution is a **liquidating** or **nonliquidating distribution** depends solely on whether the partner remains a partner in the partnership after the distribution is made. A *liquidating* distribution occurs either (1) when a partnership itself liquidates and distributes all of its property to its partners or (2) when an ongoing partnership redeems the interest of one of its partners. This second type of liquidating distribution occurs, for example, when a partner retires from a partnership, or when a deceased partner's interest is liquidated. The two types of liquidating distributions receive differing tax treatment, as later sections of the chapter will explain.

A *nonliquidating* distribution is any distribution from a continuing partnership to a continuing partner—that is, any distribution that is not a liquidating distribution. Nonliquidating distributions are of two types: draws or partial liquidations. A *draw* is a distribution of a partner's share of current or accumulated partnership profits that have been taxed to the partner in current or prior taxable years of the partnership. A *partial liquidation* is a distribution that reduces the partner's interest in partnership capital but does not liquidate the partner's entire interest in the partnership. The distinction between the two types of nonliquidating distributions is largely semantic, since the basic tax treatment typically does not differ.

EXAMPLE 2

Kay joins the calendar year KLM Partnership on January 1, 1997, by contributing $40,000 cash to the partnership in exchange for a one-third interest in partnership capital, profits, and losses. Her distributive share of partnership income for the year is $25,000. If the partnership distributes $65,000 ($25,000 share of partnership profits + $40,000 initial capital contribution) to Kay on December 31, 1997, the distribution is a nonliquidating distribution as long as Kay continues to be a partner in the partnership. This is true even though Kay receives her share of profits plus her entire investment in the partnership. In this case, $25,000 is considered a draw, and the remaining $40,000 is a partial liquidation of Kay's interest. If, instead, the partnership is liquidated or Kay ceases to be a partner in the ongoing partnership, the $65,000 distribution is a liquidating distribution. The two types of liquidating distributions receive differing tax treatment. ▼

A payment from a partnership to a partner is not necessarily treated as a distribution. For example, as discussed in Chapter 10, a partnership may pay interest or rent to a partner for use of the partner's capital or property, make a guaranteed payment to a partner, or purchase property from a partner. If a payment *is* treated as a distribution, it is not necessarily treated under the general tax deferral rules that apply to most partnership distributions. In certain circumstances, the partner may recognize gain when marketable securities are received from the partnership.

Finally, a distribution may be either proportionate or disproportionate. In a **proportionate distribution,** a partner receives his or her respective share of certain ordinary income-producing assets of the partnership. A **disproportionate distribution** occurs when the distribution increases or decreases the distributee partner's proportionate interest in certain ordinary income-producing assets. The tax treatment of disproportionate distributions is very complex.

The initial discussion and examples in this chapter describe the treatment of proportionate current and liquidating distributions. Special rules related to property distributions are discussed next. Then a brief overview of the rules pertaining to disproportionate distributions is presented.

PROPORTIONATE NONLIQUIDATING DISTRIBUTIONS

1 ▼ **LEARNING OBJECTIVE**
Determine the tax treatment of proportionate nonliquidating distributions from a partnership to a partner.

In general, neither the partner nor the partnership recognizes gain or loss when a proportionate nonliquidating distribution occurs.[1] The partner usually takes a carryover basis for the assets distributed.[2] The distributee partner's outside basis is reduced (but not below zero) by the amount of cash and the adjusted basis of property distributed to the partner by the partnership.[3]

Note the difference between the tax theory governing distributions from C corporations and partnerships. In a C corporation, a distribution from current or accumulated income (earnings and profits) is taxable as a dividend to the shareholder, and the corporation does not receive a deduction for the amount distributed. This is an example of corporate income being subject to double taxation. In a partnership, a distribution from current or accumulated profits is not taxable because Congress has decided that partnership income should be subject to only a single level of taxation. If a partner pays taxes on the share of income earned by the partnership, this income is not taxed again when it is distributed to the partner.

These results make sense under the entity and aggregate concepts. The entity concept is applicable to corporate dividends, so any amount paid as a dividend is treated as a transfer by the corporate entity to the shareholder and is taxed accordingly. Under the aggregate theory, though, a partner receiving a distribution of partnership income is treated as merely receiving something already owned. Whether the partner chooses to leave the income in the partnership or receive it in a distribution makes no difference. The following examples illustrate that a distribution does not change a partner's economic position.

---

[1] § 731(a)(1).
[2] § 732(a)(1).

[3] § 733.

EXAMPLE 3   Jay is a one-fourth partner in the SP Partnership. His basis in his partnership interest is $40,000 on December 31, 1997. The fair market value of the interest is $70,000. The partnership distributes $25,000 cash to him on that date. The distribution is not taxable to Jay or the partnership. The distribution reduces Jay's adjusted basis in the partnership to $15,000 ($40,000 − $25,000), and the fair market value of his partnership interest is, arguably, reduced to $45,000 ($70,000 − $25,000). ▼

EXAMPLE 4   Assume the same facts as in Example 3, except that, in addition to the $25,000 cash, the partnership distributes land with an adjusted basis to the partnership of $13,000 and a fair market value of $30,000 on the date of distribution. The distribution is not taxable to Jay or the partnership. Jay reduces his basis in the partnership to $2,000 [$40,000 − ($25,000 + $13,000)] and takes a carryover basis of $13,000 in the land. The fair market value of Jay's remaining interest in the partnership is, arguably, reduced to $15,000 [$70,000 − ($25,000 + $30,000)].

If Jay had sold his partnership interest for $70,000 rather than receiving the distributions, he would have realized and recognized gain of $30,000 ($70,000 selling price − $40,000 outside basis). Because he has not recognized any gain or loss on the distribution of cash and land, he should still have the $30,000 of deferred gain to recognize at some point in the future. This is exactly what will happen. If Jay sells the cash, land, and remaining partnership interest on January 1, 1998, the day after the distribution, he realizes and recognizes gains of $17,000 ($30,000 − $13,000) on the land and $13,000 ($15,000 − $2,000) on the partnership interest. These gains total $30,000, which is the amount of the original deferred gain. ▼

Gain Recognition.   A partner recognizes gain from a nonliquidating distribution to the extent that the cash received exceeds the outside basis of the partner's interest in the partnership.[4]

EXAMPLE 5   Samantha is a one-third partner in the SMP Partnership. Her basis in this ownership interest is $50,000 on December 31, 1997, after accounting for the calendar year partnership's 1997 operations and for Samantha's 1997 capital contributions. On December 31, 1997, the partnership distributes $60,000 cash to Samantha. She recognizes a $10,000 gain from this distribution ($60,000 cash received − $50,000 basis in her partnership interest). Most likely, this gain is taxed as a capital gain.[5] ▼

While distributions *from* accumulated earnings are taxed differently to shareholders and partners, cash distributions *in excess* of accumulated profits are taxed similarly for corporate shareholders and partners in partnerships. Both shareholders and partners are allowed to recover the cumulative capital invested in the entity tax-free.

Recall from Chapter 10 that the reduction of a partner's share of partnership debt is treated as a distribution of cash from the partnership to the partner. A reduction of a partner's share of partnership debt, then, first reduces the partner's basis in the partnership. Any reduction of a share of debt in excess of a partner's basis in the partnership is taxable as a gain.

EXAMPLE 6   Returning to the facts of Example 5, assume that Samantha's $50,000 basis in her partnership interest included a $60,000 share of partnership liabilities. If the partnership repays all of its liabilities, Samantha is treated as receiving a $60,000 distribution from the

---

[4]§ 731(a)(1).
[5]§ 731(a). If the partnership holds any "hot assets," however, Samantha will probably recognize some ordinary income. See

§ 751(b) and the related discussion of ordinary income ("hot") assets and disproportionate distributions later in this chapter.

partnership. The first $50,000 of this distribution reduces her basis to $0. The last $10,000 distributed creates a taxable gain to her of $10,000. ▼

A distribution of marketable securities can also be treated as a distribution of cash. Determining treatment of such distributions is complicated, though, since several exceptions may apply and the basis in the distributed stock must be calculated. Such distributions are discussed later under Property Distributions with Special Tax Treatment: Marketable Securities.

Loss Recognition. The distributee partner cannot recognize a loss in a nonliquidating distribution. This loss is deferred because tax law typically does not permit losses to be recognized until the loss is certain to occur and the amount is known. After the nonliquidating distribution, the partner still owns the partnership interest, which has an indeterminate future value. Only when a final liquidating distribution is received is the loss certain and known in amount—and potentially deductible.

EXAMPLE 7 Henry has a $50,000 basis in his partnership interest. Assume that on December 31 he receives a distribution of $10,000 cash. He knows the partnership has fallen on hard times and that future distributions will probably not amount to more than a few hundred dollars. As a result of the distribution, the basis in the partnership interest is reduced to $40,000. Henry does not recognize a loss, even though a loss probably exists. The amount of the loss is not fixed and determinable since he still owns the partnership interest. ▼

Property Distributions. In general, a distributee partner does not recognize gain from a property distribution. If the basis of property distributed by a partnership exceeds the partner's basis in the partnership interest, the distributed asset takes a substituted basis. This ensures that the partner does not receive asset basis that is not "paid for."

EXAMPLE 8 Mary has a $50,000 basis in her partnership interest. The partnership distributes land it owns with a basis and a fair market value of $60,000. Mary does not recognize any gain on this distribution because it is a distribution of property. However, Mary should not be allowed to take a carryover basis of $60,000 in the land, when her basis in her partnership interest is only $50,000. Therefore, the Code provides that Mary takes a substituted basis of $50,000 in the land. Her basis in her partnership interest is reduced by the basis she takes in the asset received, or $50,000. Therefore, Mary has a $50,000 basis in the land and a $0 basis in her partnership interest, and she recognizes no gain on this distribution. ▼

The rule that no gain or loss is recognized on a property distribution from a partnership has several exceptions. These situations may arise for either a current or a liquidating distribution, so discussion of these exceptions is deferred until all the general rules are discussed (see Property Distributions with Special Tax Treatment later in the chapter).

Ordering Rules. When the inside basis of the distributed assets exceeds the distributee partner's outside basis, the Code requires that the assets be deemed distributed in the following order:

- Cash is distributed first.
- Unrealized receivables and inventory are distributed second.
- All other assets are distributed last.

Unrealized receivables are receivables that have a value to the partnership, but for which the related income has not yet been realized or recognized under the partnership's method of accounting. Unrealized receivables include receivables from the sales of ordinary income property and rights to payments for services. For most purposes, unrealized receivables also include ordinary recapture income that would arise if the partnership sold its depreciable assets. The term *unrealized receivables* applies only to amounts that will ultimately be realized and recognized as ordinary income. If the partnership uses the cash method of accounting, trade receivables from services or sales are unrealized receivables. If the partnership uses the accrual method, they are not. Installment gains are unrealized receivables if the gain will be taxed as ordinary income when realized.

Inventory, for purposes of these ordering rules, includes any partnership assets except cash, capital, or § 1231 assets. For example, all accounts receivable are considered to be inventory, although only cash basis receivables are "unrealized receivables." In the discussions of disproportionate distributions and sales of a partnership interest later in this chapter, **substantially appreciated inventory** is important, but for proportionate distributions, all inventory (whether appreciated or not) is included in the second distribution classification.

Since the partner typically does not recognize a gain from a *property* distribution, the Code provides that the partner's basis for property received cannot exceed the partner's basis in the partnership interest immediately before the distribution. For each level of asset distribution, the relevant adjustments are made to the partner's basis in the interest. In other words, after a cash distribution, the partner's basis in the interest is recomputed before determining the effect of a distribution of unrealized receivables or inventory. The basis is again recomputed before determining the effect of a distribution of other assets. If the remaining outside basis at any step is insufficient to cover the entire inside basis of the assets in the next step, that remaining outside basis is allocated pro rata among the assets within that class in accordance with the relative inside bases of the assets.[6]

EXAMPLE 9

Sally has a $50,000 basis in her partnership interest. Assume the partnership distributes cash of $12,000, cash basis receivables with an inside basis of $0 and fair market value of $10,000, and two parcels of land to Sally. The partnership has a basis of $15,000 in one of these parcels and $45,000 in the other. Each parcel has a fair market value of $50,000.

Step 1. Determine the order in which these assets are distributed. According to the Code, the cash is treated as being distributed first, the unrealized receivables second, and the two parcels of land last.

Step 2. Determine whether Sally recognizes any gain on the distribution. Since the $12,000 cash that Sally received does not exceed the basis for her partnership interest, she recognizes none of the $72,000 gain realized on the transfer [$122,000 amount realized ($12,000 + $10,000 + $50,000 + $50,000) − $50,000 basis in the partnership interest].

Step 3. Determine the basis Sally takes in each distributed asset and the effect of the distribution on her outside basis. Sally first assigns a $12,000 basis to the cash. After the cash distribution, her basis in the partnership interest is $38,000 ($50,000 − $12,000). Next, she assigns a $0 carryover basis to the unrealized receivables. Her remaining outside basis is still $38,000 [$50,000 − ($12,000 + $0)]. The land parcels are deemed distributed last. Sally's remaining basis of $38,000 is less than the partnership's inside basis of $60,000 ($15,000 + $45,000) in the land parcels. Therefore, she must take a substituted basis of $38,000 in the land.

Sally allocates the $38,000 outside basis to the land parcels pro rata based on their adjusted inside *bases* to the partnership (and not according to their

[6]§ 732 and Reg. § 1.732–1(c)(1).

relative fair market values). Sally takes a $9,500 basis in the first parcel of land, computed as follows:

$$\$38,000 \times \frac{\$15,000}{\$60,000} = \underline{\underline{\$9,500}}$$

She takes a basis of $28,500 in the second parcel of land, computed as follows:

$$\$38,000 \times \frac{\$45,000}{\$60,000} = \underline{\underline{\$28,500}}$$ ▼

 **EXAMPLE 10**   Assume the same facts as in Example 9, and that Sally sells both parcels of land early the following year at their fair market values, receiving proceeds of $100,000 ($50,000 + $50,000). She also collects $10,000 for the cash basis receivables. Now she recognizes all of the $72,000 gain that she deferred upon receiving the property from the partnership [$100,000 amount realized – $38,000 adjusted basis for the two parcels ($9,500 + $28,500) + $10,000 received – $0 basis for the receivables]. ▼

Review the tax results of Example 9. Although Sally does not recognize any of the gain she realizes from the distribution, she has a zero outside basis for her partnership interest. If Sally expects the partnership to generate net losses in the near future, she will *not* find this zero basis attractive. She will be unable to deduct her share of the losses when they flow through to her on the last day of the partnership's tax year.

The low basis that Sally has assigned to the parcels of land is of no tax detriment to her if she does not intend to sell the land in the near future. Since land does not generate cost recovery deductions, the substituted basis is used only to determine Sally's gain or loss upon her disposition of the land in a taxable sale or exchange.

Concept Summary 11–1 reviews the general rules that apply to proportionate nonliquidating partnership distributions.

ETHICAL CONSIDERATIONS

Arranging Tax-Advantaged Distributions

The Sparrow Partnership plans to distribute $200,000 cash to its partners at the end of the year. Marjorie is a 40 percent partner and would receive $80,000. Her basis in the partnership is only $10,000, however, so she would be required to recognize a $70,000 gain if she receives a cash distribution. She has asked the partnership instead to purchase a parcel of land she has found on which she will build her retirement residence. The partnership will then distribute that land to her. Under the partnership distribution rules, Marjorie would take a $10,000 basis in land worth $80,000. Her basis in the partnership would be reduced to $0, and the $70,000 deferred gain would only be recognized if she sells the land. Do you think this is an appropriate transaction?

PROPORTIONATE LIQUIDATING DISTRIBUTIONS

2   LEARNING OBJECTIVE
Determine the tax treatment of proportionate distributions that liquidate a partnership.

Proportionate liquidating distributions consist of a single distribution or a series of distributions that result in the termination of the partner's entire interest in the partnership. If the partnership continues in existence after the partner's interest is liquidated, the rules of § 736 govern the classification of the liquidating payments. These rules are discussed later in the chapter. Other rules apply, however, if the

CONCEPT SUMMARY 11–1

Proportionate Nonliquidating Distributions (General Rules)

1. Neither the distributee partner nor the partnership recognizes any gain or loss on a nonliquidating distribution. However, if cash distributed exceeds the distributee partner's outside basis, gain is recognized. Property distributions generally do not result in gain recognition.
2. The distributee partner usually takes the same basis the distributed property had to the partnership (carryover basis). However, where the inside basis of distributed property exceeds the partner's outside basis, the basis assigned to the distributed property cannot exceed that outside basis (substituted basis).
3. Gain recognized by the distributee partner on a nonliquidating distribution is usually capital in nature.
4. Loss is never recognized on a proportionate nonliquidating distribution.

Calculations

1. Partner's outside basis.   _____
2. Less: Cash distributed to partner.   _____
3. Gain recognized by partner (excess of Line 2 over Line 1).   _____
4. Partner's remaining outside basis (Line 1 – Line 2). If less than $0, enter $0.   _____
5. Partner's basis in unrealized receivables and inventory distributed (enter lesser of Line 4 or the partnership's inside basis in the unrealized receivables and inventory).   _____
6. Basis available to allocate to other property distributed (Line 4 – Line 5).   _____
7. Partnership's inside basis of other property distributed.   _____
8. Basis to partner of other property distributed (enter lesser of Line 6 or Line 7).   _____
9. Partner's remaining outside basis (Line 6 – Line 8).   _____

partner's interest is liquidated because the partnership is also liquidating. This section examines the latter type of liquidating distribution.

Gain Recognition and Ordering Rules.   When a partnership liquidates, the liquidating distributions to a partner usually consist of an interest in several or all of the partnership assets. The gain recognition and ordering rules parallel those for nonliquidating distributions, except that the partner's *entire* basis in the partnership interest is allocated to the assets received in the liquidating distribution, unless the partner is required to recognize a loss. A loss may be recognized when *only* cash, unrealized receivables, or inventory is received in the distribution. As a result of the ordering rules, the basis of some assets may be adjusted upward or downward to absorb the partner's remaining outside basis. Unrealized receivables or inventory are never "stepped up," although they may be "stepped down." The partnership itself typically does not recognize either gain or loss on a liquidating distribution.

The general ordering and gain recognition rules for a proportionate liquidating distribution are summarized as follows:

- Cash is distributed first and results in a capital gain to the extent the distribution exceeds the partner's basis in the partnership interest. The amount distributed reduces the liquidated partner's outside basis dollar for dollar. The partner's basis cannot be reduced below zero.

- The partner's remaining outside basis is then allocated to unrealized receivables and inventory up to an amount equal to the partnership's adjusted bases in that property. If the partnership's bases in the unrealized receivables and inventory exceed the partner's remaining outside basis, the remaining outside basis is allocated to the unrealized receivables and inventory in the ratio of their inside bases to the partnership.
- Finally, if the liquidating partner has any outside basis left, that basis is allocated pro rata to any other assets received according to their inside bases to the partnership.[7]

EXAMPLE 11

When Tara's basis in her partnership interest is $25,000, she receives cash of $15,000 and a proportionate share of inventory and buildings in a distribution that liquidates both the partnership and her entire partnership interest. The inventory has a basis to the partnership of $20,000 and a fair market value of $30,000. The building's basis is $8,000, and the fair market value is $12,000. The building is not subject to depreciation recapture. Under these circumstances, Tara recognizes no gain or loss. After reducing Tara's $25,000 basis by the $15,000 cash received, the remaining $10,000 is allocated to the inventory. The basis of the inventory in Tara's hands is $10,000, and the basis of the building is zero.

Of the partnership's original bases of $20,000 in the inventory and $8,000 in the building, Tara is allocated only $10,000 in the inventory. The remaining $10,000 basis in inventory and $8,000 basis in the building appear to have been "lost" in the liquidating distribution. The partnership may be able to "save" this portion of the basis by making an election to adjust the basis of its remaining property upward. This concept is discussed later in the chapter. ▼

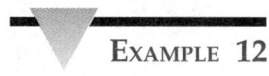

EXAMPLE 12

Assume the same facts as in Example 11, except that there was no inventory and Tara received two buildings (neither of which is subject to depreciation recapture). Building 1 had a basis of $6,000 to the partnership, and Building 2 had a basis of $9,000. Again, no gain or loss is recognized. The $10,000 basis of Tara's interest after reduction for the $15,000 cash received is allocated to the buildings in the ratio of their bases to the partnership. Tara's basis in Building 1 is $4,000 ($6/15 \times $10,000$), and her basis in Building 2 is $6,000 ($9/15 \times $10,000$). ▼

Loss Recognition.   The distributee partner may also recognize a *loss* on a liquidating distribution. The partner recognizes a loss if both of the following are true:

1. The partner receives *only* money, unrealized receivables, or inventory.
2. The partner's outside basis in the partnership interest exceeds the partnership's inside basis for the assets distributed. This excess amount is the loss recognized by the distributee partner.[8]

The word "only" is important. A distribution of any other property postpones recognition of the loss.

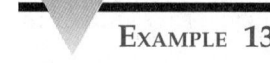

EXAMPLE 13

When Ramon's outside basis is $40,000, he receives a liquidating distribution of $7,000 cash and a proportionate share of inventory having a partnership basis of $3,000 and a fair market value of $10,000. Ramon is not allowed to "step up" the basis in the inventory, so it is allocated a $3,000 carryover basis. Ramon's unutilized outside basis is $30,000. Since he received a liquidating distribution of *only* cash and inventory, he recognizes a capital loss of $30,000 on the liquidation. ▼

---

[7] §§ 731 and 732.   [8] § 731(a)(2).

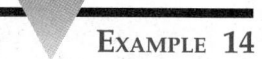

EXAMPLE 14

Assume the same facts as in Example 13, except that in addition to the cash and inventory, Ramon receives the desk he used in the partnership. The desk has an adjusted basis of $100 to the partnership. Applying the rules outlined above to this revised fact situation produces the following results:

Step 1. Cash of $7,000 is distributed to Ramon and reduces his outside basis to $33,000.

Step 2. Inventory is distributed to Ramon. He takes a $3,000 carryover basis in the inventory and reduces his outside basis in the partnership to $30,000.

Step 3. The desk is distributed to Ramon. Since the desk is a § 1231 asset and not cash, an unrealized receivable, or inventory, he cannot recognize a loss. Therefore, Ramon's remaining basis in his partnership interest is allocated to the desk. He takes a $30,000 basis for the desk. ▼

What can Ramon do with a $30,000 desk? If he continues to use it in a trade or business, he can depreciate it. Once he has established his business use of the desk, he could sell it and recognize a large § 1231 loss. If the loss is isolated in the year of the sale, it is an ordinary loss. Thus, with proper planning, no liquidated partner should be forced to recognize a capital loss.

Gain recognized by the withdrawing partner on the subsequent disposition of inventory is always ordinary income, unless the disposition occurs more than five years after the distribution.[9] The withdrawing partner's holding period for all other property received in a liquidating distribution includes the partnership's related holding period.

Concept Summary 11–2 outlines the general rules that apply to proportionate liquidating partnership distributions.

PROPERTY DISTRIBUTIONS WITH SPECIAL TAX TREATMENT

Recall that a distribution from a partnership to a partner usually does not result in taxable gain. This section discusses three exceptions in which a distribution of property to a partner may result in a gain. These exceptions can occur in either a current or a liquidating distribution.

Disguised Sales.   As discussed in Chapter 10, a disguised sale is a transaction in which a partner contributes appreciated property to a partnership and soon thereafter receives a distribution of cash or property from the partnership. If the IRS determines the payment is part of a "purchase" of the property, rather than a distribution from the partnership, the usual sale or exchange rules apply. The partner is treated as having sold the property and must report a gain on the sale. The partnership takes a cost basis in the property purchased. See Chapter 10 for additional discussion.

Marketable Securities.   For a distribution after December 8, 1994, the fair market value of a marketable security distributed to a partner is generally treated as a cash distribution.[10] The excess of the value of the security over the partner's outside basis prior to the distribution is a taxable gain. The partner must assign a basis to the security received in the distribution, so the distribution ordering rules must be taken into account.

The term *marketable securities* is broadly defined and includes almost any debt or equity interest that is actively traded, including options, futures contracts, and

---

[9] § 735(a)(2).

[10] § 731(c).

CONCEPT SUMMARY 11–2

Proportionate Liquidating Distributions When the Partnership Also Liquidates (General Rules)

1. Generally, neither the distributee partner nor the partnership recognizes gain or loss when a partnership liquidates. However, a partner recognizes gain if the cash received exceeds the outside basis. A distributee partner recognizes loss when (a) only money, unrealized receivables, or inventory is received and (b) the partner's outside basis is greater than the partnership's inside basis of the assets distributed.
2. Distributed assets must be treated as being distributed in a certain order. Cash is distributed first, inventory and unrealized receivables second, and all other assets last. Assets in the last category take a substituted basis equal to the distributee partner's remaining outside basis.
3. Gain or loss recognized by a distributee partner in a distribution that liquidates a partnership is usually capital in nature.

Calculations

1. Partner's outside basis. _____
2. Less: Cash distributed to partner. _____
3. Gain recognized by partner (excess of Line 2 over Line 1). _____
4. Partner's remaining outside basis (Line 1 – Line 2). If less than $0, enter $0. _____
5. Partner's basis in unrealized receivables and inventory distributed (enter lesser of Line 4 or the inside basis in the unrealized receivables and inventory). _____
6. Basis to partner of other property distributed (Line 4 – Line 5). _____
7. Loss recognized by partner (if no other property was distributed, enter amount from Line 6). _____
8. Partner's remaining outside basis. _____ $0 _____

derivatives. Marketable securities are *not* treated as cash if (1) they were originally contributed by the partner to whom they are now distributed (certain exceptions apply to this provision), (2) the property was not a marketable security when acquired by the partnership, or (3) the partner is an eligible partner of an investment partnership, as defined. Certain transitional rules apply if the partnership had an obligation to distribute marketable securities as of December 8, 1994.

The primary purpose of this rule is to stop the tax avoidance that otherwise would occur if a partnership purchased marketable securities with the intent of immediately distributing them to the partner. As the preceding Ethical Considerations indicated, a partnership can purchase property desired by a partner, distribute that property to the partner, and allow the partner to defer tax on any appreciation inherent in the partnership interest. Section 731(c) was enacted to prevent a partnership from arranging such a transaction with marketable securities.

If a marketable security is appreciated, however, it probably was not acquired by the partnership in an effort to assist the distributee partner in reducing his or her tax on the distribution. The portion of the security value treated as cash is reduced by a proportionate share of the appreciation inherent in the distributed security. This results in a deferral of gain for this portion of the appreciation. The "reduction" is intended to take into account the partnership's intent, or lack thereof, to reduce the partner's gains.

The amount of the reduction in fair market value is the excess of (1) the partner's share of appreciation in this particular security before the distribution over (2) the partner's share of appreciation in the portion of the security retained by the partnership.

▼ **EXAMPLE 15**

Assume the A to Z Partnership has the following balance sheet:

	Basis	**Fair Market Value**		**Basis**	**Fair Market Value**
ZYX Corporation security	$400	$1,000	Andy, capital	$ 50	$ 200
Land	100	1,000	Other partners, capital	450	1,800
Total assets	$500	$2,000	Total equity	$500	$2,000

The partnership distributes $200 (value) of the ZYX stock to 10% partner Andy in liquidation of his partnership interest. The amount of the distribution is the $200 fair market value of the stock reduced by Andy's decrease in his share of the inside appreciation in the stock. Before the distribution, Andy's share of appreciation in this stock was $60 [10% × ($1,000 − $400)]. *His share* of appreciation in the stock retained by the partnership is $0, since he no longer owns an interest in the partnership [0% × ($1,000 − $200 value distributed) − ($400 − $80 basis distributed)]. The $200 value of the stock is reduced by $60 ($60 before − $0 after distribution). Andy is treated as if he received a cash distribution of $140.

Andy's outside basis was $50 before the distribution. The $140 deemed cash distribution triggers gain recognition of $90. Andy's basis in the partnership is reduced to $0. ▼

The distributee partner's basis in the security is the sum of (1) the basis in the stock as determined under the regular distribution rules (see the discussion under Ordering Rules above) and (2) the gain recognized on the distribution.

▼ **EXAMPLE 16**

In Example 15, the stock would take a substituted basis of $50 to Andy under the distribution ordering rules. This basis is the lesser of the partnership's inside basis in the stock of $80 (20% × $400) or Andy's outside basis of $50. The recognized gain of $90 increases Andy's basis in the stock to $140.

This basis determination preserves the inherent built-in gain in Andy's partnership interest. Before the distribution, Andy has $150 of appreciation in his interest ($200 − $50). After considering the $90 gain on the stock distribution, he should have $60 of untaxed appreciation. The stock value is $200, and Andy's basis is $140, so the untaxed appreciation is the expected $60 amount. ▼

Unless otherwise indicated, the remaining examples in this chapter assume the partnership is not distributing marketable securities.

Precontribution Gain. Taxable gains may arise on a distribution of property to a partner where precontribution (built-in) gains exist. Specifically, if a partner contributes appreciated property to a partnership, the contributing partner recognizes gain in two situations:

1. If the contributed appreciated property is distributed to another partner within five years of the contribution date, the contributing partner

recognizes the remaining net precontribution gain on the property.[11] The partner's basis in the partnership interest is increased by the amount of gain recognized. Also, the basis of the distributed property is increased by this same amount to prevent double taxation of this precontribution gain when the distributee partner later sells the asset.

EXAMPLE 17

In 1995, Rod contributes nondepreciable property with an adjusted basis of $10,000 and a fair market value of $40,000 to the RTCO Partnership in exchange for a one-fourth interest in profits and capital. In 1997, when the property's fair market value is $50,000, the partnership distributes the property to Tom, another one-fourth partner. Since the property was contributed to the partnership within five years of the date the property was distributed, and precontribution gain was attributable to the property, the built-in gain on the property is taxable to Rod. Therefore, Rod must pay tax on the $30,000 built-in gain in 1997, the year the property was distributed to Tom. Rod increases his basis in his partnership interest by the $30,000 gain recognized. Tom also increases his basis in the property received by $30,000.

Note that if the partnership sold the property to an unrelated third party for $40,000 in 1997, the result is the same for Rod. Under § 704(c)(1)(A), recognized built-in gains must be allocated to the partner who contributed the property, and the partner's outside basis is increased accordingly. ▼

2. The second situation occurs where the partnership distributes *any* property other than cash to a partner within five years after *that* partner contributes appreciated property to the partnership. In this case, the partner recognizes the lesser of (a) the remaining net precontribution (built-in) gain or (b) the excess of the fair market value of the distributed property over the partner's basis in interest before the distribution.[12] The distributee partner's basis in his or her partnership interest is increased by the amount of gain recognized. To maintain a parity between inside and outside basis, the partnership is allowed to increase its basis in the precontribution gain property remaining in the partnership. This rule does not apply if the distributed property was originally contributed by the distributee partner.

EXAMPLE 18

In 1995, Bill contributes land to the BMC Partnership. His basis in the land was $16,000. The fair market value at the contribution date was $40,000. In 1997, the partnership distributes property with an adjusted basis of $16,000 and fair market value of $65,000 to Bill. Bill's basis in his partnership interest was $12,000 before the distribution. Since Bill contributed precontribution gain property within five years of receiving the distribution of other property, he recognizes gain on the distribution. The maximum he must recognize is the net precontribution gain, or $24,000 ($40,000 fair market value – $16,000 adjusted basis of property contributed). He compares this amount to the excess of the fair market value of the distributed property over his basis in his partnership interest, or $53,000 ($65,000 fair market value of property – $12,000 adjusted basis in interest prior to distribution).

Since the $24,000 precontribution gain is less than the $53,000 inherent gain, Bill recognizes gain of $24,000. His basis in his partnership interest increases by the $24,000 gain recognized to $36,000, and the partnership's basis in the "precontribution gain" property Bill originally contributed also increases by $24,000 to $40,000.

If the distribution occurs more than five years after the original contribution, Bill recognizes no gain, and the distribution is handled under the general distribution rules described earlier in this section. ▼

---

[11] § 704(c)(1)(B) and Prop.Reg. § 1.704–4.   [12] § 737 and Prop.Regs. §§ 1.737–1 to –5.

EXAMPLE 19

Assume the same facts as in Example 18, except that Bill's basis in his partnership interest was $60,000 before the distribution. In this case, the excess value of the distributed property is only $5,000 ($65,000 − $60,000), so Bill only recognizes gain of $5,000, with corresponding adjustments to his partnership interest and the partnership's basis in the precontribution gain property.

The remaining precontribution gain of $19,000 ($24,000 − $5,000) is charged to Bill at some point in the future if the partnership sells the precontribution gain property or distributes it to another partner within five years of its contribution. Some or all of the remaining precontribution gain may also be recognized if other appreciated property is distributed to Bill within five years of the original contribution. ▼

DISPROPORTIONATE DISTRIBUTIONS

3 **LEARNING OBJECTIVE**
Describe the general concepts governing tax treatment of disproportionate distributions.

An additional exception to the general gain and loss nonrecognition rule arises when a partnership makes a "disproportionate distribution" of assets. A disproportionate distribution occurs when a partnership makes a distribution of cash or property to a partner and that distribution increases or decreases the distributee partner's proportionate interest in certain of the partnership's ordinary income-producing assets.

These ordinary income-producing assets, called **hot assets,** include substantially appreciated inventory and unrealized receivables. Unrealized receivables are rights to receive future amounts that will result in ordinary income when the income is recognized. Inventory includes all assets that are not cash, capital, or § 1231 assets. Substantially appreciated inventory is inventory that has a fair market value in excess of 120 percent of the partnership's adjusted basis for the inventory. (See additional discussion under Ordering Rules earlier and under Substantially Appreciated Inventory later in the chapter.)

The taxation of disproportionate distributions is based on the aggregate theory of taxation. Under this theory, each partner is deemed to own his or her proportionate share of the underlying assets of the partnership. In line with this concept, each partner is responsible for recognizing and reporting his or her proportionate share of ordinary income potential of the partnership, such as would arise on the sale of substantially appreciated inventory or on the collection of cash basis receivables.

Section 751(b) maintains each partner's proportionate share of ordinary income by recasting any transaction in which a disproportionate distribution of hot assets is made. For example, if the distributee partner receives less than his or her proportionate share of hot assets, the transaction is treated as if two separate events occurred: (1) the partnership made a distribution of some of the hot assets to the distributee partner, and (2) that partner immediately sold these hot assets back to the partnership. The partner recognizes ordinary income on the sale of the hot assets, and the partnership takes a cost basis for the hot assets purchased.

EXAMPLE 20

The balance sheet of the AB Partnership is as follows on December 31, 1997:

	Basis	**Fair Market Value**
Cash	$26,000	$26,000
Unrealized receivables	–0–	26,000
	$26,000	$52,000
Agnes, capital	$13,000	$26,000
Bob, capital	13,000	26,000
	$26,000	$52,000

Agnes and Bob are equal partners in the partnership. The partnership makes a liquidating distribution of the unrealized receivables to Agnes and the cash to Bob. Since the unrealized receivables are a hot asset, Agnes has received more than her proportionate share of the hot asset, and Bob has received less than his proportionate share. As Bob received less than his proportionate share of hot assets, § 751 recasts the transaction into two separate events. First, Bob is deemed to receive a current distribution of his 50% share of hot assets (basis = $0; fair market value = $13,000), which he then immediately sells back to the partnership for $13,000 of the cash. Bob recognizes $13,000 ordinary income on the sale, and the partnership takes a $13,000 basis in the receivables purchased. The remaining $13,000 cash received by Bob reduces his adjusted basis for his partnership interest to $0 ($13,000 cash distributed − $13,000 adjusted basis).

Agnes receives both the $13,000 receivables that the partnership purchased from Bob and her share of the remaining $13,000 unrealized receivables. She takes a substituted basis of $13,000 in the receivables and reduces her adjusted basis for her partnership interest to $0. When she collects all $26,000 of the receivables, she will recognize $13,000 of ordinary income ($26,000 cash collected − $13,000 basis for receivables).

Although the mechanical rules of § 751(b) are complicated, the application of the rules in this example has ensured that each partner eventually recognizes his or her $13,000 share of ordinary income. Bob recognizes his share at the time the partnership is liquidated. Agnes's share is recognized when she collects the unrealized receivables. ▼

Although most of the problems and examples in this text involve proportionate distributions, be aware that disproportionate distributions occur frequently in practice. The calculation of ordinary income in disproportionate distributions can become extremely complex. These more difficult calculations are not discussed in this text.

ETHICAL CONSIDERATIONS

Deferring Partners' Taxes by Delaying Liquidation

Partnerships often use the liabilities included in a partner's basis to shield losses claimed by the partners. By including a share of the partnership's liabilities in basis, the partner may be able to claim ordinary losses greatly in excess of the capital contributions. When the liabilities are repaid or forgiven, the partner is treated as receiving a distribution of cash and recognizes capital gain treatment on the payment or forgiveness of the debt. This is not a bad planning technique—it provides ordinary losses now and capital gains later!

If the capital gain recognition could be deferred, the partners would really be ecstatic. Recently, a large national brokerage firm used such a delaying tactic. Investors originally contributed $200,000 each for an interest in a partnership syndicated by the firm. The partners claimed losses from the partnership far in excess of their original contribution. The property owned by the partnership declined in value, and for various reasons, the partners sued the brokerage firm. In settlement, the firm agreed to loan the partnership up to $20 million and to continue to manage the property for up to 15 years. The partnership used the cash to distribute about $100,000 to each of the partners and to pay off other existing debt.

The partners will continue to hold their partnership interests during the 15 years the general partner manages the property. Debt still exists, so the partners still have basis in their partnership interests, and the partnership still exists, although the partners' interests in the partnership are virtually worthless. Thus, the partners have received losses and then substantial cash distributions and will be able to defer the capital gain on release of liabilities for another 15 years. Example 7 showed that a partner cannot recognize a loss prior to termination. Now it seems a partner cannot be forced to recognize a gain prior to termination. What do you think of this arrangement?

LIQUIDATING DISTRIBUTIONS TO RETIRING OR DECEASED PARTNERS

4 **LEARNING OBJECTIVE**
Determine the tax treatment under § 736 of payments from a partnership to a retiring or deceased partner.

Payments made by an ongoing partnership in complete liquidation of a retiring partner's interest are classified as either *income* or *property* payments by § 736. Payments made to a successor to the interest of a deceased partner are similarly classified by § 736.[13] It is critical to observe that § 736 only classifies the payments. Other Code Sections provide the rules for computing the tax effects of these payments. Although these payments can be made in cash, property, or both cash and property, this discussion assumes that all payments are made in cash.

From a practical standpoint, the partnership and the retiring partner negotiate a total buyout package. The retiring partner expects to be compensated for his or her share of partnership assets—at fair market value. The partner also expects to be compensated for a share of the partnership's going-concern value. *Property* payments [called § 736(b) payments] represent the former type of buyout provision, and *income* payments [§ 736(a) payments] typically represent the latter. Once the total buyout price is determined, § 736 provides rules for determining the allocation between income and property payments, but leaves some room for negotiation between the partner and the partnership over which component of the buyout represents each type of payment.

These paragraphs and Example 21 describe only the general effects of § 736 and do not cover all the nuances of the provision. In general, property payments [§ 736(b) payments] are cash distributions paid by the partnership to the partner in exchange for the partner's interest in partnership assets. The partnership may not deduct these amounts. If the partnership owns no hot assets, the property payment is treated under the normal proportionate distribution rules. If the partnership owns certain hot assets (e.g., depreciation recapture or substantially appreciated inventory), and the retiring partner receives only cash, it is not possible for the distribution to be proportionate. In this case, the property payments to the partner are allocated between (1) cash payments for the partner's share of hot assets (which is treated as a proportionate distribution of hot assets and a sale of those assets back to the partnership, as described in Example 20) and (2) other assets. The income recognized in the hot asset sale is ordinary income, and the gain or loss recognized on the rest of the property payments is capital gain or loss.

Income payments [§ 736(a) payments] are treated as a partner's distributive share of partnership income or, alternatively, as a guaranteed payment to the retiring partner. Recall from Chapter 10 that the partner receiving a guaranteed payment recognizes ordinary income. Depending on whether the amount is a distributive share or a guaranteed payment, either (1) the remaining partners report a lesser share of partnership income (distributive share), or (2) the partnership deducts the guaranteed payment.

---

[13] A successor is typically the estate of the deceased or the party who inherits the decedent's interest.

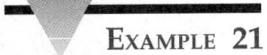

EXAMPLE 21

Pamela receives cash of $15,000 in liquidation of her partnership interest, in which she has a basis of $10,000. The partnership owns no hot assets. After following all the classification requirements of § 736, $12,000 of this amount is classified as a property payment, and $3,000 is classified as a guaranteed payment. The $12,000 property payment is treated as a distribution from the partnership in exchange for her partnership interest, so Pamela recognizes a $2,000 capital gain on this part of her liquidation proceeds ($12,000 property payment – $10,000 basis in interest). She recognizes $3,000 ordinary income for the guaranteed payment, and the partnership deducts the same amount. ▼

PROPERTY PAYMENTS

Cash payments made for the partner's pro rata share of the fair market value of each partnership asset are classified as § 736(b) payments. The following items are not treated as § 736(b) payments, however, if (1) the partnership is primarily a service provider (i.e., "capital is not a material income-producing factor for the partnership") and (2) the retiring or deceased partner was a general partner in the partnership:

- Payments made for the partner's pro rata share of unrealized receivables. For purposes of § 736 only, unrealized receivables do not include potential depreciation recapture.
- Payments made for the partner's pro rata share of the partnership goodwill, unless the partnership agreement states that payments are for goodwill. This exception applies only to payments for goodwill that exceed the partner's pro rata share of the partnership's inside basis for goodwill.
- Certain annuities and lump-sum payments made to retiring partners or deceased partner's successors.

If such payments are made by a service-oriented partnership to a general partner, they are classified as § 736(a) payments.

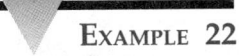

EXAMPLE 22

The ABC Partnership has the following balance sheet on December 31, 1997:

	Adjusted Basis	Fair Market Value
Cash	$36,000	$36,000
Unrealized receivables	–0–	18,000
Land	9,000	27,000
	$45,000	$81,000
Anne, capital	$15,000	$27,000
Bonnie, capital	15,000	27,000
Cindy, capital	15,000	27,000
	$45,000	$81,000

Partner Anne is a general partner retiring from the service-oriented partnership. She receives $36,000 cash, none of which is stated to be for goodwill. Since the fair market value of Anne's share of the three recorded assets is only $27,000 (⅓ × $81,000), the $9,000 excess payment is for unstated goodwill. The payment Anne receives for her interest in the cash and land is a § 736(b) property payment. This payment is $21,000, consisting of $12,000 paid for the cash (⅓ × $36,000) and $9,000 paid for Anne's share of the fair market value of the land (⅓ × $27,000). The remaining cash of $15,000 is for her $6,000 interest in the unrealized receivables and for $9,000 unstated goodwill and is a § 736(a) payment. ▼

Section 736(b) payments for "nonhot" assets are treated first as a return of the partner's outside basis in the partnership.[14] Once the entire basis is returned, any additional amounts are taxed to the partner as capital gain. If the cash distributions are not sufficient to return the partner's entire outside basis, the shortfall is taxed to the partner as a capital loss.[15]

EXAMPLE 23

In Example 22, the property payment of $21,000 cash includes amounts for Anne's share of land and cash only, neither of which is a hot asset. If Anne's outside basis is $15,000, she recognizes capital gain of $6,000 [($12,000 + $9,000) − $15,000] on the distribution. However, if Anne's outside basis is $25,000, she recognizes a $4,000 capital loss on the distribution [($12,000 + $9,000) − $25,000]. The partnership cannot deduct any part of the $21,000 property payment. ▼

If part of the property payment is for the partner's share of hot assets, the § 736(b) payment is allocated between the portion related to hot assets and the portion related to other assets. The portion of the payment *not* related to hot assets is treated as described in Example 23. The portion of the payment related to hot assets is treated as discussed earlier under Disproportionate Distributions. Distributions that are disproportionate to the partner's share of hot assets of the partnership are treated as two separate transactions:

- First, the partner's proportionate share of hot assets is deemed to be distributed. A partner cannot step up the basis in hot assets, so on the distribution, the hot assets take the lesser of the partnership's inside basis for the hot assets or the partner's outside basis in the interest.
- Second, these hot assets are deemed to be sold back to the partnership at fair market value. A portion of the § 736(b) payment is allocated to the partnership's deemed purchase of the hot assets.

EXAMPLE 24

If, in Example 22, Anne was a limited partner or the partnership was capital-intensive, the entire payment of $36,000 is a § 736(b) property payment. The $36,000 payment is allocated between hot assets and other assets. The payment for cash and land is a payment for Anne's other assets, as is the payment for partnership goodwill. The payment for the unrealized receivables, however, is a payment for Anne's share of the partnership's hot assets.[16]

The partnership is treated first as distributing Anne's $6,000 proportionate share of unrealized receivables. Anne's carryover basis in the receivables is $0.

Anne then resells the unrealized receivables to the partnership for their $6,000 fair market value. She reports $6,000 of ordinary income on this sale. The partnership now has a basis of $6,000 in its $18,000 of accounts receivable.

The partnership paid Anne $36,000. Of this amount, $6,000 is to "repurchase" her share of receivables; the remaining $30,000 is in exchange for the partnership's other assets ($12,000 for cash + $9,000 for land + $9,000 for goodwill). Anne calculates and reports a $15,000 capital gain ($30,000 payment − $15,000 basis) in addition to the $6,000 ordinary income. ▼

INCOME PAYMENTS

All payments that are not classified as § 736(b) property payments are categorized as § 736(a) income payments. These income payments are further classified into

---

[14] §§ 736(b) and 731(a)(1).
[15] § 731(a)(2).

[16] See Concept Summary 11−5 for an illustration involving substantially appreciated inventory.

two categories. Payments that are *not* determined by reference to partnership income are treated as guaranteed payments. They are fully taxable as ordinary income to the distributee partner and are fully deductible by the continuing partnership.

Section 736(a) income payments that are determined by reference to partnership income are treated as distributive shares of that income (i.e., an allocation of partnership income for the year). They are taxed to the distributee partner according to their character to the partnership. Thus, for example, they may be taxed as capital gain as well as ordinary income.[17] Since this capital gain and ordinary income are allocated to the liquidated partner, the payments reduce the amount of partnership capital gain and ordinary income allocated to the remaining partners.[18]

EXAMPLE 25   Continue with the same facts as in Example 22 in which the partnership is service oriented. The $6,000 cash payment ($18,000 × ⅓) for Anne's pro rata share of the unrealized receivables is classified as a § 736(a) income payment, as is the $9,000 payment for unstated goodwill.

Because the $15,000 § 736(a) income payment ($6,000 + $9,000) is not determined by reference to partnership income, the payment is classified as a guaranteed payment. It is included as ordinary income on Anne's tax return and is deductible by the partnership. ▼

EXAMPLE 26   The following table summarizes the taxation results of Examples 22 through 25, for a partnership where capital is not a material income-producing factor and where it is. In both cases, Anne's basis in her partnership interest was $15,000 before the distribution.

	Tax Character to Anne	Deduction to ABC
Service-oriented partnership:		
§ 736(b) (Example 23)	$ 6,000 capital gain	None
§ 736(a) (Example 25)	15,000 ordinary income	$15,000
Total gain	$21,000	
Capital-intensive partnership:		
§ 736(b) (Example 24)	$15,000 capital gain	None
§ 736(b) (Example 24)	6,000 ordinary income	None
§ 736(a) (Example 24)	–0– ordinary income	None
Total gain	$21,000	

As this summary illustrates, the characterization under § 736 does not change the overall gain: in both cases Anne recognizes total gain of $21,000. This is appropriate since she receives $36,000 cash against a basis of $15,000.

The character of Anne's income differs solely as a result of the characterization of goodwill: for the service-oriented partnership (with unstated goodwill), the payment for goodwill results in ordinary income to the partner, but for the capital-intensive partnership (or if the partner is a limited partner), goodwill results in capital gain.

---

[17] § 702(b).

[18] Reg. § 1.736–1(a)(4).

From the partnership's point of view, it is entitled to a deduction for goodwill only if it is a service partnership and the retiring partner is a general partner, and then only if the goodwill payment is not stated in the partnership agreement.

The partnership's position also differs as a result of the treatment of unrealized receivables. As a service partnership, it can claim a current deduction for the amount of the distribution related to the receivables. As a capital-intensive partnership, ABC is allocated a basis in the receivables when it is deemed to repurchase them from Anne. When the receivables are collected, the partnership's ordinary income is reduced. ▼

SERIES OF PAYMENTS

Frequently, the partnership and retiring partner agree that the buyout payment may be made over several years in specified installments. This minimizes the negative cash-flow impact on the partnership and allows the retiring partner to maximize the dollar amount of the buyout arrangement. In certain cases, such as where a retiring partner has been instrumental in developing a business relationship with specific clients, the parties can agree that the buyout payments will be determined by reference to the future income generated by those clients or by reference to overall partnership income, rather than being fixed in amount. If the partners deal at arm's length and specifically agree to the §§ 736(a) and (b) allocation and timing of each class of payment, the agreement normally controls. In the absence of an agreement classifying the payments under § 736, Regulations specify classification rules for each payment. In either situation, certain tax planning opportunities arise that are beyond the scope of this text.

Concept Summary 11–3 reviews the rules for liquidating distributions under § 736.

CONCEPT SUMMARY 11–3

Liquidating Distributions of Cash When the Partnership Continues

1. Payments made by an ongoing partnership to a liquidating partner are classified as § 736(a) income payments or as § 736(b) property payments.
2. Section 736(b) property payments are payments made for the liquidated partner's share of partnership assets.
3. Payments made for the liquidated partner's share of unrealized receivables, certain goodwill that is not provided for in the partnership agreement, and certain annuity payments are classified as § 736(a) income payments, if the partnership is a service provider and the partner is a general partner.
4. Section 736(a) income payments are the payments mentioned in Item 3 above and any other payments that are not classified as § 736(b) property payments.
5. To the extent the § 736(b) property payment is for the partner's share of partnership hot assets, the partner is deemed to have received and sold his or her share of such assets to the partnership. The partner reports ordinary income on this transaction, and the partnership will have a cost basis in the hot asset.
6. To the extent the § 736(b) property payments are classified as a payment for the partner's share of the partnership's "nonhot" assets, the payment is taxed as a return of the partner's outside basis. Any excess cash received over the partner's outside basis is taxed as capital gain.
7. Section 736(a) income payments are further classified as either guaranteed payments or distributive shares. Guaranteed payments are taxable as ordinary income to the partner and are deductible by the partnership. Distributive shares retain the same tax character to the partner as they had to the partnership. Distributive shares paid to the liquidated partner are excludible from the continuing partners' tax returns.

SALE OF A PARTNERSHIP INTEREST

5   LEARNING OBJECTIVE
Calculate the selling partner's amount and character of gain or loss on the sale or exchange of a partnership interest.

A partner can sell or exchange a partnership interest, in whole or in part. The transaction can be between the partner and a third party; in this case, it is similar (in concept) to a sale of corporate stock. Or, as the last section described, the transaction can be between the partner and the partnership, in which case it is similar (in concept) to a redemption of corporate stock by the entity. The transfer of a partnership interest produces different results than the transfer of corporate stock, though, because both the entity and aggregate concepts apply to the partnership situation, whereas only the entity concept applies to a sale of stock. The effect of the different rules is that gain or loss resulting from a sale of a partnership interest may be divided into capital gain or loss and ordinary income.

GENERAL RULES

Generally, the sale or exchange of a partnership interest results in gain or loss, measured by the difference between the amount realized and the selling partner's adjusted basis in the partnership interest.[19]

Liabilities.   In computing the amount realized and the adjusted basis of the interest sold, the selling partner's share of partnership liabilities must be determined. Determination of a partner's share of partnership liabilities is discussed in Chapter 10. The purchasing partner includes any assumed indebtedness as a part of the consideration paid for the partnership interest.[20]

EXAMPLE 27

Cole originally contributed $50,000 in cash for a one-third interest in the CDE Partnership. During the time Cole was a partner, his share of partnership income was $90,000, and he withdrew $60,000 cash. Cole's capital account balance is now $80,000, and partnership liabilities are $45,000, of which Cole's share is $15,000. Cole's outside basis is $95,000 ($80,000 capital account + $15,000 share of partnership debts).

Cole sells his partnership interest to Freda for $110,000 cash, with Freda assuming Cole's share of partnership liabilities. The total amount realized by Cole is $125,000 ($110,000 cash received + $15,000 of partnership debts transferred to Freda). Cole's gain on the sale is $30,000 ($125,000 realized − adjusted basis of $95,000).

Freda's adjusted basis for her partnership interest is the purchase price of $125,000 ($110,000 cash paid + $15,000 assumed partnership debt). ▼

Tax Years That Close.   When a partner disposes of an entire investment in the partnership, the partnership's tax year closes for that partner as of the sale date. When a partnership's tax year closes with respect to a partner, the partner's share of income for the period during which he or she was a partner is calculated. This amount is taxed to the partner and increases the selling partner's basis. There are several acceptable methods of determining the partner's share of income.[21] Under one method, the partnership merely prorates annual income and allocates an amount to the buying and selling partners based on the number of days (or months) in the partnership's tax year in which they were partners. Another method is called the *interim closing of the books* method. As the name implies, the partnership determines its actual income through the date the selling partner sold

---

[19] § 741.
[20] § 742.

[21] § 706(d)(1) and Regulations thereunder.

the interest and allocates the proportionate share of income to that partner. If partnership earnings are seasonal, the two methods can produce vastly different results.

▼ EXAMPLE 28

Grace sold her 40% interest in the Owl Partnership to Megan on July 1 of the current tax year. Both Grace and the partnership report on a calendar year basis. The partnership's income was $60,000 through June 30, and its income for the last half of the year was $2,000. Under the annual proration method, the partnership's income for the year is $62,000 of which 40%, or $24,800, is allocated to the 40% interest. Based on the number of months each was a partner, both Grace and Megan report income of $12,400 for the current year.

Under the interim closing method, Grace is allocated 40% of $60,000, or $24,000, and Megan is allocated 40% of $2,000, or $800 of partnership income. ▼

If the partnership uses the cash method for certain items such as interest, taxes, rent, or other amounts that accrue over time, it must allocate these items to each day in the tax year over which they economically accrue and use the interim closing method for these items in determining the amount allocated to a selling partner.[22]

The partnership is not required to issue a Schedule K–1 to the selling partner until the normal filing of its tax return. The partner, though, is required to include the share of partnership income as of the date of sale. Consequently, the partner may have to obtain an extension for filing his or her personal return until the partnership provides a Schedule K–1. If the partnership uses an IRS-approved fiscal year and the partner uses a calendar year, income bunching may occur.

▼ EXAMPLE 29

Assume the same facts as in Example 28, except the Owl Partnership's tax year ended March 31, 1997. Assume Owl earned income of $12,000 as of June 30, 1997, the date Grace's interest was sold. Owl uses the interim closing method. Since the partnership year closes with respect to Grace on the sale date, $4,800 (40%) of partnership income is reported in her 1997 tax year. In addition, Grace also reports her income share from the March 31, 1997, partnership year. ▼

Tax Reporting. Partners who sell or exchange a partnership interest must promptly notify the partnership of the transfers. After notification is received, the partnership may be required to file an information statement with the IRS for the calendar year in which the transfers took place. The statement lists the names and addresses of the transferors and transferees. The partnership provides all parties with a copy of the statement.

EFFECT OF HOT ASSETS

A major exception to capital gain or loss treatment on the sale or exchange of a partnership interest arises when a partnership has hot assets. As noted previously, *hot assets* are certain assets that when collected or disposed of by the partnership would cause it to recognize ordinary income. When a partner sells the interest in a partnership, it is as if he or she sold a proportionate interest in the partnership's hot assets and nonhot assets. The partner's basis in interest must be allocated between "hot" and "nonhot" assets. The selling price of the interest is similarly allocated. The gain on hot assets is taxed as ordinary income. The sale of the nonhot assets can result in capital gain or loss.

---

[22] § 706(d)(2).

Two types of hot assets must be considered: unrealized receivables and substantially appreciated inventory. An amount realized from the sale of a partnership interest that is attributable to *unrealized receivables* or *substantially appreciated inventory* is treated as being from the sale of a noncapital asset.[23] The purpose of this rule is to prevent a partner from converting ordinary income into capital gain through the sale of a partnership interest.

Unrealized Receivables. The term "unrealized receivables" has the same meaning as in the earlier discussion of disproportionate distributions. As previously noted, unrealized receivables include the accounts receivable of a cash basis partnership, the ordinary income portion (if any) of a deferred installment gain, and, for sale or exchange purposes, depreciation recapture potential.[24]

EXAMPLE 30

The cash basis Thrush Partnership owns only a $10,000 receivable for rendering health care advice. Its basis in the receivable is zero because no income has been recognized. This item is a hot asset because ordinary income is generated when Thrush collects on the account.

Harry, a 50% partner, sells his interest to Mark for $5,000. If Harry's basis in his partnership interest is $0, his total gain is $5,000. The entire gain is attributable to the unrealized receivable, so Harry's gain is taxed as ordinary income. ▼

Depreciation recapture represents ordinary income the partnership would recognize if it sold depreciable property. Under the aggregate theory, the selling partner's share of depreciation recapture potential is treated as an unrealized receivable and is taxed to the selling partner as ordinary income, rather than capital gain. (Recall that depreciation recapture is not treated as a hot asset for § 736 purposes, discussed previously.)

EXAMPLE 31

Arthur sells his 40% interest in the accrual basis Wren Partnership. The partnership has a long-term depreciable business asset that it originally purchased for $25,000. The asset now has an adjusted basis of $15,000 and a market value of $30,000. Depreciation recapture potential is $10,000 ($25,000 − $15,000). In this case, Wren holds a $10,000 unrealized receivable with a zero basis and a $20,000 nonhot asset with an adjusted basis of $15,000. If Wren sold the asset for $30,000, it would recognize $10,000 of ordinary income and $5,000 of § 1231 gain. Therefore, Arthur recognizes $4,000 ($10,000 × 40%) of ordinary income when he sells his partnership interest. ▼

The effect of the hot asset rule is that a partner selling an interest in a partnership must treat the sale as two separate events. The partner allocates the selling price of the interest between ordinary income and capital gain (or loss) components based on the fair market values of the underlying partnership assets. The basis in the partnership interest is also allocated; the allocation is by reference to the partnership's bases in the underlying assets. The portion of the selling price related to ordinary income (hot) assets, less the partner's basis related to the ordinary income assets, is taxed to the partner as ordinary income. A similar calculation is made for the capital gain (or loss) component.

Note that the hot asset rule merely reclassifies the gain or loss amount into ordinary income and capital gain (or loss) components—it does not create additional gain.

---

[23] § 751(a).   [24] § 751(a)(1).

EXAMPLE 32

Ahmad sells his interest in the equal ABC Partnership to Dave for $17,000 cash. On the sale date, the partnership's cash basis balance sheet reflects the following:

	Adjusted Basis per Books	Market Value
Assets		
Cash	$10,000	$10,000
Accounts receivable (for services)	–0–	30,000
Nonhot assets	14,000	20,000
Total	$24,000	$60,000
Liabilities and Capital		
Liabilities	$ 9,000	$ 9,000
Capital accounts		
Ahmad	5,000	17,000
Beth	5,000	17,000
Chris	5,000	17,000
Total	$24,000	$60,000

The hot asset rule applies to the sale because the partnership has unrealized receivables. The total amount realized by Ahmad is $20,000 ($17,000 cash price + $3,000 of debt assumed by Dave). Ahmad's one-third interest includes $10,000 of market value in receivables with a $0 basis. Consequently, $10,000 of the $20,000 sales price is considered as received in exchange for Ahmad's interest in the unrealized receivables. The remaining $10,000 is treated as received in exchange for a capital asset.

Ahmad's basis is $8,000 ($5,000 capital account + $3,000 debt share). No portion of this basis can be attributed to the unrealized receivables; they have a $0 basis to the partnership. Thus, the full $10,000 received for the receivables is ordinary income ($10,000 – related $0 basis).

Ahmad's entire basis of $8,000 is treated as being in nonhot assets and is applied against the remaining $10,000 received from the sale ($20,000 amount realized – $10,000 allocated to hot assets). Thus, Ahmad also incurs a $2,000 capital gain ($10,000 – related $8,000 basis).

If Ahmad's gain is calculated ignoring the hot asset rule, he has a selling price of $20,000 for an asset in which he has a basis of $8,000. This results in a $12,000 gain. Under the hot asset rule, Ahmad has ordinary income of $10,000 plus a capital gain of $2,000. Ahmad reports $12,000 of income in both cases; the hot asset rule merely reclassifies part of the gain as ordinary income. The effect of the rule is that the partnership's inherent ordinary income is allocated to the partner who earned it. ▼

EXAMPLE 33

Assume the same facts as in Example 32, except that Ahmad's basis in his partnership interest is $10,000. Under these circumstances, Ahmad's capital gain or loss is zero. Ahmad still has $10,000 of ordinary income because of the unrealized receivables.

If Ahmad's basis in the partnership interest is $11,000 (instead of $10,000), an unusual result occurs. Ahmad has a $9,000 overall gain ($20,000 amount realized – $11,000 basis). The receivables generate $10,000 of ordinary income, and Ahmad's $9,000 overall gain is accounted for with an additional capital *loss* of $1,000. ▼

Substantially Appreciated Inventory. Inventory items are substantially appreciated if, at the time of their sale or distribution, their aggregate fair market value exceeds 120 percent of their total adjusted basis to the partnership. In applying this test, inventory items are evaluated as a group, rather than individually. If substantial appreciation of the entire inventory has occurred, all the inventory items are treated as substantially appreciated, even if a specific item has not appreciated.

For this purpose, the term *inventory* includes all partnership property except money, capital assets, and § 1231 assets. Receivables of an accrual partnership are included in the definition of inventory, since they are neither capital assets nor § 1231 assets.[25]

This definition is broad enough to include all items considered to be unrealized receivables. The disadvantage of their inclusion can be seen in the calculation to determine whether the inventory is substantially appreciated. Since unrealized receivables are included at a zero basis in the substantial appreciation tests, they improve the partner's chances of having substantially appreciated inventory.

EXAMPLE 34

Jan sells her interest in the JKL Partnership to Matt for $20,000 cash. On the sale date, the partnership balance sheet reflects the following:

	Adjusted Basis per Books	Market Value
Cash	$10,000	$10,000
Inventory	21,000	30,000
Nonhot assets	14,000	20,000
Total	$45,000	$60,000
Jan, capital	$15,000	$20,000
Kelly, capital	15,000	20,000
Lynn, capital	15,000	20,000
Total	$45,000	$60,000

The inventory is substantially appreciated. The appreciation is 143% ($30,000 ÷ $21,000), which is above the 120% threshold.

Jan's share of the inside basis of the inventory is $7,000 ($21,000 × ⅓). Jan is deemed to have sold this share of inventory for $10,000 ($30,000 × ⅓), thereby creating ordinary income of $3,000 on the sale of the hot asset. Jan recognizes the $3,000 ordinary income and $2,000 of capital gain from the rest of the sale:

Remaining sales price ($20,000 gross sales price – $10,000 allocated to hot asset sale)	$10,000
Remaining outside basis ($15,000 original outside basis – $7,000 allocated to hot asset sale)	(8,000)
Capital gain	$ 2,000

Concept Summary 11–4 enumerates the rules that apply to sales of partnership interests.

---

[25]§ 751(d)(2).

CONCEPT SUMMARY 11–4

Sale of a Partnership Interest

1. A partnership interest is a capital asset and generally results in capital gain or loss on disposal.
2. The outside bases of the selling and buying partner, as well as the pertinent selling price and purchase price, include an appropriate share of partnership debt.
3. When hot assets are present, the selling partner's overall gain or loss is reclassified into a capital gain or loss portion and an ordinary income amount related to the partnership's underlying hot assets.
4. Hot assets consist of unrealized receivables and substantially appreciated inventory.
5. Unrealized receivables include amounts earned by a cash basis taxpayer from services rendered. They also include depreciation recapture potential that would result if an asset were sold at a gain.
6. Inventory is substantially appreciated when its aggregate fair market value exceeds 120% of its adjusted basis. Inventory includes all partnership property except cash, capital assets, and § 1231 assets. Inventory also includes unrealized receivables.

SALE AND LIQUIDATION OF A PARTNERSHIP INTEREST COMPARED

6   LEARNING OBJECTIVE
Describe the different tax results that might arise on a sale of a partnership interest versus liquidation of the interest under § 736.

The preceding examples in this chapter introduced the concepts involved in liquidating or selling an entire interest in a partnership. The comprehensive examples in Concept Summary 11–5 are designed to compare the various calculations involved in both types of transactions.

In reviewing these examples, note that inventory must be combined with the receivables when calculating the substantial appreciation test. This is necessary because the Code's definition of inventory is expanded to include unrealized receivables. By itself, the supplies inventory is not substantially appreciated, but under the Code definition it is.

Also note that Pat's $3,500 basis for the hot assets includes his one-third share of the $10,500 inside basis for the inventory. Accordingly, Pat's ordinary income is not the $7,000 fair market value of the hot assets deemed sold but $3,500 (the $7,000 fair market value less the $3,500 proportionate basis).

In the liquidating transaction, note that the cash paid for the receivables is a § 736(a) income payment while the cash paid for the inventory is a § 736(b) property payment. Payments for both assets create ordinary income to the recipient.

It is not appropriate to conclude that there are no tax differences between a sale and a liquidation. "Comparing Sales to Liquidations" in the Tax Planning Considerations section of this chapter discusses several of these differences.

OTHER TRANSACTIONS WITH PARTNERSHIP INTERESTS

Partnership property or a partnership interest may be involved in other types of transactions. For example, a partnership may incorporate, or partners in different partnerships may swap interests. As the subsequent Tax in the News indicates, partnerships can also help a community achieve its goals.

Comprehensive Comparison: Sale of an Interest versus Liquidation of Interest under § 736

1. **Sale of an interest**

   Pat sells his one-third interest in TP, a cash basis, calendar year partnership, to Vito for $15,000 cash. The partnership is service oriented and all partners are general partners. The balance sheet of TP immediately before the sale is as follows:

	Adjusted Basis per Books	Market Value
Cash	$18,000	$18,000
Land	3,000	6,000
Receivable	–0–	9,000
Supplies inventory	10,500	12,000
Total	$31,500	$45,000
Capital accounts		
Pat (⅓)	$10,500	$15,000
Terry (⅔)	21,000	30,000
Total	$31,500	$45,000

   The partnership uses the cash method, so revenue from the receivable has not been recognized. Therefore, it is an unrealized receivable. To determine whether *substantially appreciated inventory* exists, the Code requires that all items, excluding cash and capital or § 1231 assets, be considered as inventory. Therefore, the supplies inventory and receivable are combined in the following test, and the inventory is substantially appreciated. Note that if the inventory were tested alone, it would not be considered substantially appreciated.

	Market Value	Adjusted Basis
Receivable	$ 9,000	$ –0–
Supplies inventory	12,000	10,500
Total	$21,000	$ 10,500
		×120%
		$ 12,600

   Inventory is substantially appreciated because
   $21,000 (market value) > $12,600 (120% of basis)

   Now classify TP's property as either hot assets or nonhot assets, and allocate the basis and fair market value to each category.

	Basis in Hot Assets	Basis in Nonhot Assets	Market Value of Hot Assets	Market Value of Nonhot Assets	Pat's One-Third Share of Market Values
Cash		$18,000		$18,000	$ 6,000
Land		3,000		6,000	2,000
Receivable	$ –0–		$ 9,000		3,000
Supplies inventory	10,500		12,000		4,000
Total	$10,500	$21,000	$21,000	$24,000	
Pat's one-third share	$ 3,500	$ 7,000	$ 7,000	$ 8,000	$15,000

Pat allocates the $15,000 amount realized from the sale between the hot assets and nonhot assets and then compares the allocated amounts with his share of the related adjusted basis. As a result, Pat recognizes $3,500 ordinary income and $1,000 capital gain.

Pat's One-Third Share	Hot Assets	Nonhot Assets	Totals
Amount realized	$7,000	$8,000	$15,000
Adjusted basis	3,500	7,000	10,500
Gain/loss recognized	$3,500	$1,000	$ 4,500
	Ordinary income	*Capital gain*	

2. **Liquidation of interest under § 736**
Continue with the same facts, except that now Pat's interest in TP is liquidated with a $15,000 cash payment from the partnership.

Since (1) capital is not a material income-producing factor for the partnership and (2) Pat is a general partner, the cash paid for the unrealized receivable is treated as a § 736(a) income payment and results in ordinary income of $3,000. Since this appears to be a guaranteed payment, the partnership can deduct the $3,000.

The remaining $12,000 portion of the payment ($15,000 – $3,000) is for Pat's interest in partnership property [under § 736(b)]. Since it includes $4,000 for Pat's interest in substantially appreciated inventory, he has additional ordinary income of $500 ($4,000 – $3,500 basis in inventory). The remaining $8,000 portion of the payment ($15,000 – $3,000 – $4,000) is for Pat's interest in the other partnership property. Pat's remaining basis in his partnership interest is $7,000 ($10,500 – $0 for the receivables – $3,500 for the inventory). Therefore, Pat has a capital gain of $1,000 ($8,000 remaining payments – $7,000 basis).

Payments for Income Items	Cash Received	Pat's Basis	Income	Character of Income
Unrealized receivables	$ 3,000	$ –0–	$3,000	
Goodwill	–0–	–0–	–0–	
Total	$ 3,000	$ –0–	$3,000	Ordinary
Payments for Partnership Property				
Substantially appreciated inventory	$ 4,000	$ 3,500	$ 500	Ordinary
Remaining partnership property	8,000	7,000	1,000	Capital gain
Total	$12,000	$10,500	$1,500	
Aggregate amounts	$15,000	$10,500	$4,500	

3. Now compare the results of the two transactions. The effect of a sale of Pat's interest to an unrelated third party produces the same overall $4,500 gain as does a liquidation of the interest by the partnership. In addition, the allocation of the gain between ordinary income ($3,500) and capital gain ($1,000) is the same in both situations. In this particular case, the overall tax effects of the two transactions are the same. In many cases, such as where the partnership has unstated goodwill, the characterization of the gain/income will differ in the two situations.

TRANSFERS TO CONTROLLED CORPORATIONS

The controlled corporation rules of § 351 provide that gain or loss is not recognized on the transfer of property to a corporation solely in exchange for stock in that corporation if, immediately after the exchange, the shareholders are in control of the corporation to which the property was transferred.

TAX IN THE NEWS

A PARTNERSHIP HELPS A LOCAL CAUSE

In the summer of 1995, the IRS issued three rulings, that, when taken together, helped Kansas City to keep its hometown major league baseball team. The Kansas City Royals had experienced at least five years of losses from team operations. The losses were funded by contributions from the team's owner and surrounding city and county governments. In spite of the cash-flow drain, the communities were reluctant to see the team leave because it generated much needed jobs, state tax revenues, and economic growth—not to mention public spirit.

Under the plan approved by the IRS, the ball club now operates as a Subchapter S corporation. Part of its stock is owned by a community foundation created largely by contributions from individuals, private foundations, and local businesses. The foundation is a not-for-profit entity. The IRS allowed the foundation to have exempt status for two reasons. First, without the foundation's contribution, the team would have been forced to move. Second, outside ownership of the team would result in "lessening the [funding] burdens of government."

The remainder of the stock is owned by a for-profit limited partnership. The partnership, foundation, and ball club agreed that for the first three years, partnership interests can only be sold to a party who (1) is acceptable to the Major League Baseball Association, (2) is a resident of Kansas City, and (3) agrees to keep the team in town. After three years, partnership interests can be sold to any party, but "best efforts" must be used to sell the stock to a Kansas City resident. If the ball club can become profitable by 2001, the Royals will probably stay in Kansas City.

The transfer of a partnership interest to a corporation is treated as a nontaxable exchange if the conditions of the controlled corporation rules are met. If the partnership interest transferred represents 50 percent or more of the total interest in capital and profits, the partnership is terminated. Partnership termination is discussed later in the chapter.

Incorporation Methods.   If partners decide to incorporate the entire partnership, at least three alternative methods are available:

- Each partner's interest is transferred to the corporation in exchange for stock under the usual § 351 rules. As a result, the partnership terminates, and the corporation owns all partnership assets. The corporation takes a substituted basis for the assets, and the old partners have a substituted basis for the stock.
- The partnership transfers all of its assets to the corporation in exchange for stock and the assumption of partnership liabilities. The stock then is distributed to the partners (generally in a liquidating distribution) in proportion to their partnership interests. The corporation takes a carryover basis for the assets, and the old partners have a substituted basis for the stock.
- The partnership makes a pro rata distribution of all of its assets and liabilities to its partners in complete liquidation. The partners then transfer their undivided interests in the assets and liabilities to the corporation in exchange for stock under § 351. The corporation's basis for the assets is the substituted basis of those assets to the partners. The partners have a substituted basis for the stock.

Assuming that existing partnership debt does not exceed the basis of transferred assets, none of the three incorporation methods generates a recognized gain or loss. They may, however, result in different inside and outside basis amounts. Moreover, if the resulting corporation intends to elect S status (see Chapter 12), the partners will not want to preclude that election by their own actions (e.g., by allowing the partnership to be a shareholder in the corporation). Thus, selecting the appropriate incorporation method is crucial.

LIKE-KIND EXCHANGES

The nontaxable like-kind exchange rules do not apply to the exchange of interests in different partnerships.[26] However, the nontaxable results obtainable from applying these rules can apply to exchanges of interests in the same partnership.[27]

GIFTS

Generally, the donor of a partnership interest recognizes neither gain nor loss. If the donor's entire interest is transferred, all items of partnership income, loss, deduction, or credit attributable to the interest are prorated between the donor and donee.

However, if the partnership uses the cash method of accounting and has unrealized receivables at the time of transfer, the gift of those unrealized receivables may be considered an anticipatory assignment of income.

DEATH OF A PARTNER

Unless the partners have a buy-sell agreement providing for a deceased partner's interest to be sold immediately to the remaining partners for a formula or fixed price, the partnership's tax year does not close when a partner dies.[28] Furthermore, the transfer of a partnership interest to a deceased partner's estate or other successor is not considered a sale or exchange.

In professional partnerships, local law may prohibit an estate or other successor from continuing as a partner (beyond a certain time period). In most cases, the remaining partners want to buy out or liquidate the deceased partner's interest in the partnership. The previously discussed rules pertaining to sales and liquidations of partnership interests apply to these transactions.

OPTIONAL ADJUSTMENTS TO PROPERTY BASIS

7 **LEARNING OBJECTIVE**
Calculate the optional adjustments to basis under § 754.

When a partner purchases a partnership interest, the purchase price reflects what the acquiring partner believes the interest in the partnership is worth. This price reflects, to a large extent, the value the partner placed on the partnership assets. Because the value of the assets probably differs from their inside bases, a discrepancy exists between the purchasing partner's outside basis and that partner's share of the inside basis of partnership assets.

---

[26] § 1031(a)(2)(D).
[27] Rev.Rul. 84–52, 1984–1 C.B. 157.

[28] § 706(c)(2)(A)(ii).

If the partnership makes a special **optional adjustment election** (§ 754 **election**), the inside basis of the partnership property can be adjusted to reflect the purchase price paid by the partner. If the election is not made, the statute produces some inequitable results.

EXAMPLE 35

A partnership owns a building with an adjusted basis of $450,000 and a fair market value of $900,000. George buys a one-third interest in the partnership for $300,000 (an amount equal to one-third of the value of the building). The partnership does not make an election under § 754. Although the price George paid for the interest was based on fair market value, the building's depreciation continues to be determined on the partnership's related adjusted basis of $450,000, of which George's share is only $150,000. ▼

EXAMPLE 36

In contrast, assume that the building in Example 35 had an adjusted basis of $600,000 and a fair market value of $300,000. Assume also that George purchased the one-third interest for $100,000 (an amount equal to one-third of the value of the building). Although the purchase price was based on fair market value, George obtains the benefit of *double* depreciation deductions since these deductions are calculated on the adjusted basis of the depreciable property ($600,000), which is twice the property's market value. ▼

A result similar to that in Example 35 can take place when a partnership purchases a retiring partner's interest with a cash payment that is greater than that partner's share of the adjusted basis of the partnership assets. Without a § 754 election, the partnership cannot increase the adjusted basis of its assets for the excess share paid to the retiring partner.

To prevent or alleviate the results illustrated above, an optional adjustment election is available. Under this election, the basis of partnership assets may be adjusted following a sale or exchange of an interest, the death of a partner, or a distribution of partnership property.[29]

SALE OR EXCHANGE OF AN INTEREST

If the optional adjustment-to-basis election is in effect and a partner's interest is sold to or exchanged with a third party, or a partner dies, the partnership adjusts the basis of its assets as illustrated in the following calculation:[30]

Transferee's outside basis in the partnership	$ xxx
Less: Transferee's share of the inside basis of all partnership property	(xxx)
Adjustment	$ xxx

If the amount calculated is positive, the partnership increases the adjusted basis of its assets. If the amount is negative, the basis of the assets is decreased. In either case, the adjustment affects the basis of partnership property with respect to the transferee partner only. When the optional adjustment results in a step-up of depreciable property, the transferee partner generally must depreciate the optional adjustment as if it were a newly acquired asset. The transferee partner, therefore, shares in the depreciation taken by the partnership on the original asset and reports all of the depreciation taken on the basis created by the optional adjustment.

---

[29] §§ 743(a) and 734(a), respectively.   [30] § 743(b).

The partner's basis in each property item for which an optional adjustment has been made equals the partner's share of the inside basis for the property item plus or minus the partner's optional basis adjustment that is allocated to that property.

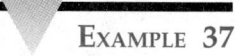

EXAMPLE 37

Keith is a member of the KLM Partnership, and all partners have equal interests in capital and profits. The partnership has made an optional adjustment-to-basis election. Keith's interest is sold to Otis for $76,000. The balance sheet of the partnership immediately before the sale shows the following:

	Adjusted Basis per Books	**Market Value**
Assets		
Cash	$ 15,000	$ 15,000
Depreciable assets	150,000	213,000
Total	$165,000	$228,000
Capital		
Capital accounts		
Keith	$ 55,000	$ 76,000
Leif	55,000	76,000
Marta	55,000	76,000
Total assets	$165,000	$228,000

The adjustment is the difference between the basis of Otis's interest in the partnership and his share of the adjusted basis of partnership property. The basis of Otis's interest is his purchase price, or $76,000. His share of the adjusted basis of partnership property is $55,000 ($165,000 × ⅓). The optional adjustment that is added to the basis of partnership property is $21,000.

Transferee's outside basis in partnership	$ 76,000
Less: Transferee's share of inside basis of all partnership property	(55,000)
Increase	$ 21,000

The $21,000 basis increase is treated as a new depreciable asset. Depreciation on this asset is allocated to Otis. If the partnership later sells all underlying assets, Otis's share of the gain takes into account the remaining (undepreciated) balance of the $21,000 step-up. ▼

PARTNERSHIP DISTRIBUTIONS

Optional adjustments to basis are also available to the partnership when property is distributed to a partner. If an optional adjustment-to-basis election is in effect, the basis of partnership property distributed to a partner is *increased* by the following:[31]

- Any gain recognized by a distributee partner.
- The excess of the partnership's adjusted basis for any distributed property over the adjusted basis of that property in the hands of the distributee partner.

---

[31] § 734(b).

Conversely, the basis of partnership property is *decreased* by the following:

- Any loss recognized by a distributee partner.
- In the case of a liquidating distribution, the excess of the distributee partner's adjusted basis of any distributed property over the basis of that property to the partnership.

EXAMPLE 38

Rena has a basis of $50,000 in her partnership interest and receives a building with an adjusted basis to the partnership of $120,000 in termination of her interest. (The partnership has no hot assets). The building's basis in Rena's hands is $50,000 under the proportionate liquidating distribution rules. If an optional adjustment-to-basis election is in effect, the partnership increases the basis of its remaining property by $70,000.

Partnership's adjusted basis in distributed property	$120,000
Less: Distributee's basis in distributed property	(50,000)
Increase	$ 70,000

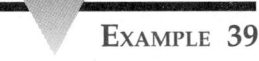

EXAMPLE 39

Assume the same facts as in Example 38, except the partnership's basis in the building was $40,000. Rena's basis in the building is still $50,000, and the partnership reduces the basis of its remaining property by $10,000.

Distributee's basis in distributed property	$ 50,000
Less: Partnership's adjusted basis in distributed property	(40,000)
Decrease	$ 10,000

Although these rules may seem confusing at first reading, understanding the theory on which they are based helps to clarify the situation. Section 734(b) assumes that the inside basis for all partnership assets equals the outside basis for all of the partners' interests immediately before the distribution. When this equality exists both before and after a distribution, no adjustment to the basis of partnership property is necessary. However, when the equality does not exist after the distribution, an adjustment can bring the inside and outside bases back into equality. This is the adjustment that is made by the two increases and the two decreases described above.

EXAMPLE 40

Assume the Cardinal Partnership has an inside basis of $12,000 for its assets, which have a fair market value of $15,000. Aaron, Bill, and Carmen all have outside bases of $4,000 for their partnership interests. If the partnership liquidates partner Aaron's interest with a $5,000 cash distribution, the resulting balance sheet is unbalanced as follows:

	Inside (Assets)		Outside (Capital)
Before	$12,000	=	$12,000
Distribution	(5,000)	≠	(4,000)
After	$ 7,000	≠	$ 8,000

This unbalanced situation can be eliminated by adding $1,000 to the inside basis of the formula. Note that this is the same amount as the gain that Aaron recognizes on the distribution ($5,000 cash − $4,000 outside basis = $1,000 gain). Therefore, by adding the amount of Aaron's gain to the inside basis of the partnership assets, the inside basis = outside basis formula is back in balance.

Inside (Assets)		Outside (Capital)
$ 7,000	≠	$ 8,000
+1,000		
$ 8,000	=	$ 8,000

Note that if the partnership liquidates Aaron's interest with a distribution of land having a $5,000 inside basis, the same unbalanced situation occurs. Although this transaction does not create any recognized gain for Aaron, the $1,000 optional adjustment is the excess of the $5,000 inside basis of the distributed property over the $4,000 substituted basis of that property to Aaron. ▼

The two optional adjustment decreases are also explained by this type of analysis.

The basis adjustments created by distributions affect the bases of all remaining partnership properties. Therefore, any depreciation deductions taken on such basis adjustments are allocated to all partners remaining in the partnership after the distribution. *The partnership* also takes these basis adjustments into account in determining any gains or losses on subsequent sales of partnership properties.

THE BASIS ADJUSTMENT ELECTION

An optional adjustment-to-basis election can be made for any year in which a transfer or distribution occurs by attaching a statement to a timely filed partnership return (including extensions).[32] An election is binding for the year for which it is made and for all subsequent years, unless the IRS consents to its revocation. Permission to revoke is granted for business reasons, such as a substantial change in the nature of the business or a significant increase in the frequency of interest transfers. Permission is not granted if it appears the primary purpose is to avoid downward adjustments to basis otherwise required under the election.

TERMINATION OF A PARTNERSHIP

8 **LEARNING OBJECTIVE**
Outline the methods of terminating a partnership.

When does a partnership's final tax year end? Technically, it ends when the partnership terminates, which occurs on either of the following events:

- No part of the business continues to be carried on by any of the partners in a partnership.
- Within a 12-month period, there is a sale or exchange of 50 percent or more of the partnership's capital and profits.[33]

A partnership's tax year closes when the partnership incorporates or when one partner in a two-party partnership buys out the other partner, thereby creating a sole proprietorship. A termination also occurs when the partnership ceases operations and liquidates.

A partnership tax year usually does not close upon the death of a partner, the entry of a new partner, or the liquidation of a partner in other than a two-party partnership. A partnership tax year also does not close upon the sale or exchange

---

[32] § 754.

[33] § 708(b)(1).

of an existing partnership interest unless the transaction results in 50 percent or more of the interests in partnership capital and profits being sold within a 12-month period.

EXAMPLE 41

Partner Olaf, who held a one-third interest in the Oriole Partnership, died on November 20, 1997. The partnership uses an approved fiscal year ending September 30. Olaf used a calendar year. The partnership agreement does not contain a buy-sell provision that is triggered upon the death of a partner. Thus, the partnership's tax year does not close with Olaf's death. Instead, income from the fiscal year ending September 30, 1998, is taxed to Olaf's estate or other successor. Income from the fiscal year ending September 30, 1997, is reported on Olaf's final income tax return, which covers the period from January 1 to November 20, 1997.

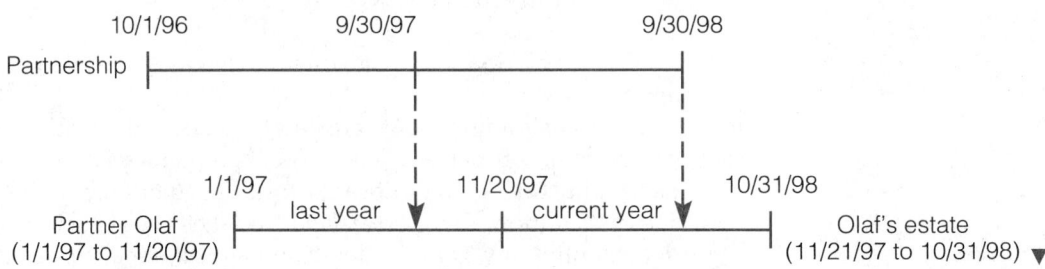

A **technical termination of a partnership** occurs when the partnership business operations continue but the partnership terminates because there has been a sale or exchange of the requisite 50 percent capital and profits interests within 12 months. If the same interest (less than 50 percent) is sold more than once, only one sale is considered in determining whether more than 50 percent has been sold within 12 months. The terminated partnership is deemed to liquidate by transferring its assets and liabilities to a newly formed partnership, which continues its business operations.[34] A technical termination may have numerous consequences, such as changing the taxable year of the new partnership or the cost recovery methods to be used by the new partnership.

OTHER ISSUES

FAMILY PARTNERSHIPS

9 **LEARNING OBJECTIVE**
Describe the special considerations of a family partnership.

Family partnerships are owned and controlled primarily by members of the same family. Such partnerships may be established for a variety of reasons. A daughter may have a particular expertise that, coupled with her parents' abilities, allows them to establish a successful business. Often, however, the primary reason for establishing a family partnership is the desire to save taxes. If the parents are in higher marginal tax brackets than the children, family tax dollars are saved by funneling some of the parents' income to the children.

Nevertheless, valid family partnerships are difficult to establish for tax purposes. A basic tenet of tax law is that income must be taxed to the person who performs the services or owns the capital that generates the income. A parent, therefore, cannot transfer only a profits interest to a child and expect the transfer to be recognized for tax purposes.

---

[34] Prop.Reg. § 1.708–1(b).

TAX IN THE NEWS

FAMILY LIMITED PARTNERSHIPS FOR ESTATE PLANNING

One of the most widely used estate planning tools in recent times has been the family limited partnership. The parents form a partnership with business or other assets and then give a $600,000 interest in the partnership (the unified credit equivalent) to their children or grandchildren. Additional tax-free gifts of $10,000 per donee can also be made annually ($20,000 if the parents elect gift splitting).

The appeal of the family partnership increased considerably in 1993 when the IRS issued Rev.Rul. 93–12 (1993–1 C.B. 202) stating that a minority discount could be applied to gifts made by family members. A minority discount allows the nominal fair market value of a business interest to be reduced to account for the fact that the owner would have difficulty selling it for the cash value of the underlying assets since the purchaser would not have management control over these assets. With a minority discount of 30 percent, for example, a gift with a nominal fair market value of $14,286 could be eligible for the full $10,000 annual exclusion. With such a minority discount, a $1 million interest in a partnership could be transferred to three children in only 12 years, compared to 17 years without the discount. This strategy is particularly useful for assets that are expected to appreciate in value.

Because of the concern that family partnerships are established primarily for tax avoidance purposes, a family member is recognized as a partner only in the following cases:

- Capital is a material income-producing factor in the partnership, and the family member's capital interest is acquired in a bona fide transaction (even if by gift or purchase from another family member) in which ownership and control are received.
- Capital is not a material income-producing factor, but the family member contributes substantial or vital services.[35]

Capital. If a partnership derives a substantial portion of its gross income from the use of capital, such as inventories or investments in plant, machinery, or equipment, the capital is considered to be a material income-producing factor. Ordinarily, capital is not a material income-producing factor if the partnership's income consists principally of fees, commissions, or other compensation for personal services performed by partners or employees.

Children as Partners. When capital is a material income-producing factor and a partnership interest is transferred by gift or sale to a child who is under age 14 and is eligible to be claimed as a dependent by the parent-partner, the kiddie tax may apply. If the child's distributive share of income is in excess of $1,300, it may be taxed at the parent's tax rate, unless the income share constitutes earned income. Regardless of age, if the child provides bona fide services to a partnership and the income share constitutes earned income, the parent-partner's tax rate is

---

[35] § 704(e).

avoided. Consequently, the child's full standard deduction (to the extent of the earned income) can be used.

EXAMPLE 42

Karen operates a first-floor-window-washing business in a summer lakeside resort city. Relatively small amounts of capital are required to operate the sole proprietorship (buckets, sponges, squeegees, etc.). During the summer, Karen normally hires middle and high school students to wash windows. Her 13-year-old daughter and 12-year-old son want to work in the business during the summer to earn money for spending and for college. Each obtains the necessary summer work permit. Karen creates the KDS Partnership and gives each child a 5% interest.

Karen figures that if her children were paid an hourly rate, about 5% of KDS's profits would be distributed to them as wages. Karen believes that an ownership interest will help the children learn what running a profitable business entails and prepare them for an active business life after their education is completed.

Since capital is not a material income-producing factor in the business, and the children's profit percentages approximate what they would earn if they were paid an hourly rate, all of the income is classified as earned income. Thus, the kiddie tax is avoided. ▼

Gift of Capital Interest.   If a family member acquires a capital interest by gift in a family partnership in which capital is a material income-producing factor, only part of the income may be allocated to this interest. First, the donor of the interest is allocated an amount of partnership income that represents reasonable compensation for services to the partnership. Then, the remaining income is divided among the partners in accordance with their capital interests in the partnership. An interest purchased by one family member from another is considered to be created by gift for this purpose.[36]

EXAMPLE 43

A partnership in which a parent transferred a 50% interest by gift to a child generated a profit of $90,000. Capital is a material income-producing factor. The parent performed services valued at $20,000. The child performed no services. Under these circumstances, $20,000 is allocated to the parent as compensation. Of the remaining $70,000 of income attributable to capital, at least 50%, or $35,000, is allocated to the parent. ▼

LIMITED LIABILITY COMPANIES

10 **LEARNING OBJECTIVE**
Describe the application of partnership provisions to limited liability companies (LLCs) and limited liability partnerships (LLPs).

The limited liability company (LLC) is a new form of entity that combines partnership taxation with limited personal liability for all owners of the entity. All of the states and the District of Columbia have passed legislation permitting the establishment of LLCs.

Taxation of LLCs.   A properly structured LLC is taxed as a partnership. Since none of the LLC members is personally liable for any debts of the entity, the LLC is effectively treated as a limited partnership with no general partners. This may result in unusual application of partnership taxation rules. The IRS has not specifically ruled on most aspects of LLC taxation, so several of the following comments are based on speculation about how a partnership with no general partners would be taxed.

- Formation of a new LLC is treated in the same manner as formation of a partnership: generally, no gain or loss is recognized by the LLC member or

---

[36] § 704(e)(3).

TAX IN THE NEWS

ENTITY LINES ARE BLURRING

At one time, selecting the type of entity through which to operate was relatively easy. The owners simply asked themselves: "Do we want (1) flow-through of income and losses or (2) limited liability?" The answer determined whether a partnership or a C corporation was formed.

Many owners wanted both characteristics, however, so gradually, partnerships adopted numerous corporate characteristics while trying to retain flow-through status. The IRS countered these efforts by issuing Regulations (outlined in Chapter 2) providing that an entity is taxed as a corporation if it possesses *more than two* of the following characteristics: (1) continuity of life, (2) free transferability of the ownership interest, (3) limited liability of owners, and (4) centralized management.

In recent years, S corporations and limited partnerships have offered the best of both worlds: flow-through treatment and the above corporate characteristics to the extent possible. But while limited partners have limited liability, general partners are subject to unlimited liability as a price for the flexibility of partnership taxation.

Now LLCs offer limited liability to all the owners. But, by definition, this gives an LLC at least one of the four corporate characteristics. In many cases, too, an LLC is managed by a select (centralized) group of members. To avoid corporate treatment, elaborate LLC charters were developed that set out rigid requirements to ensure that the other two corporate characteristics did *not* exist, while still allowing members some means of transferring their interest and allowing the business to continue uninterrupted for a reasonable period of time (generally 30 years).

Even the best-written charters were subject to interpretation by the IRS, however, and this created uncertainty as to how an LLC would be treated on audit. The IRS conceded that its Regulations could result in unwarranted business practices simply to ensure that certain entity classification requirements were met. In December 1996, Regulations were finalized that will allow LLCs to elect partnership status simply by checking a box on the partnership tax return. This will eliminate the need for an LLC formed in 1997 or later to (1) artificially limit the time frame over which it will conduct business, (2) set arbitrary permission procedures before an interest is transferable, and/or (3) require all managers (rather than a select few) to participate in operating the business.

---

the LLC, the member takes a substituted basis in the LLC interest, and the LLC takes a carryover basis in the assets it receives.

- Contributed property with built-in gains or losses is subject to the allocation rules of § 704(c). Also, an LLC member contributing built-in gain property can be subject to tax on certain distributions within five years of the contribution, as mentioned earlier in the chapter.

- In allocating liabilities to the members for basis purposes, all liabilities are treated as if they are nonrecourse, even when they are nominally recourse in nature. This occurs because under the entity's legal structure, none of the members individually bears the economic risk of loss on a liability.

- An LLC's income and losses are allocated under § 704. Special allocations are permitted, as long as they meet the requirements outlined in Chapter 10.

- Losses are subject to the three deductibility limitations described in Chapter 10: A loss must meet the basis, at-risk, and passive loss limitations to be currently deductible. Since the debt is considered nonrecourse to each of the members, it may not be included in the at-risk limitation unless it qualifies as "qualified nonrecourse financing." Also, the IRS has not issued rulings as to whether a member is treated as a material or active participant of an LLC for passive loss purposes. Presumably, passive or active status will be based on the time the member spends in LLC activities.
- The available taxable years and initial elections discussed in Chapter 10 are applicable to an LLC.
- Transactions between an LLC and its members are treated as described in Chapter 10. Under general partnership taxation rules, however, a limited partner's share of partnership income is not subject to self-employment taxes. The IRS has issued Proposed Regulations that provide that an LLC member is treated as a limited partner for self-employment tax purposes only if the member is not a "manager" of the firm, and if the entity could have been formed as a limited partnership and the member would have been a limited partner in such a partnership.
- The rules described in this chapter for distributions, sales of an interest, and retirement of a member's interest under § 736 all apply to an LLC. An LLC can make an election under § 754 to adjust the inside basis of its assets to reflect changes in the member's outside bases resulting from sales of interests or distributions from the entity. Note that a distribution of appreciated property from a C or S corporation would result in taxable gain to the entity, whereas such property takes a carryover or substituted basis when distributed from an LLC.

Converting to an LLC.   A partnership can convert to an LLC with few, if any, tax ramifications: the old elections of the partnership continue, and the partners retain their bases and ownership interests in the new entity. A C or an S corporation that reorganizes as an LLC is treated as having liquidated prior to forming the new entity. The transaction is taxable to both the corporation and the shareholders.

Advantages of an LLC.   An LLC offers certain advantages over a limited partnership, including the following:

- Generally, none of the owners of an LLC are personally liable for the entity's debts. General partners in a limited partnership have personal liability for partnership recourse debts.
- Limited partners cannot participate in the management of the partnership. All owners of an LLC have the legal right to participate in the entity's management.

An LLC also offers certain advantages over an S corporation, including the following:

- LLCs can have an unlimited number of owners.
- Any taxpayers, including corporations, nonresident aliens, other partnerships, and trusts, can be owners of an LLC. S corporation shareholders are limited.
- The transfer of property to an LLC in exchange for an ownership interest in the entity is governed by partnership tax provisions rather than corporate tax provisions. Thus, the transferors need not satisfy the 80 percent control requirement needed for tax-free treatment under the corporate tax statutes.

- The S corporation taxes on built-in gains and passive income do not apply to LLCs.
- An owner's basis in an LLC includes the owner's share of almost all LLC liabilities under § 752. Only certain S corporation liabilities are included in the S corporation shareholder's basis.
- An LLC may make special allocations under § 704(b), while S corporations must allocate income, loss, etc. on a per share/per day basis.
- The optional adjustments to basis election can be made for the benefit of the LLC and its owners. Such adjustments are not possible in an S corporation.

Disadvantages of an LLC.   The disadvantages of an LLC stem primarily from the entity's relative newness. There is no established body of case law interpreting the various state statutes, so the application of specific provisions is uncertain. An additional uncertainty for LLCs that operate in more than one jurisdiction is which state's law will prevail and how it will be applied.

Among other factors, statutes differ from state to state as to the type of business an LLC can conduct—primarily the extent to which a service-providing firm can operate as an LLC. A service entity may find it cannot operate as an LLC in several jurisdictions where it conducts business.

Despite these uncertainties, LLCs are being formed at increasing rates. Note that S corporation statutes vary from state to state (and do not exist in some states), and the interpretive case law history is relatively limited (10–12 years in many states). Yet many entities have braved this uncertainty and operate as multistate S corporations, and the ranks of multistate LLCs are also rising quickly.

LIMITED LIABILITY PARTNERSHIPS

In 1991, Texas became the first state to allow professionals to organize their practice as a registered limited liability partnership (LLP). Since then, other states have adopted similar legislation. The difference between a general partnership and an LLP is small, but very significant. As you recall, general partners are jointly and severally liable for all partnership debts. In most states, partners in a registered LLP are jointly and severally liable for contractual liability (i.e., they are treated as general partners for commercial debt). They are also personally liable for their own malpractice or other torts. They are not, however, personally liable for the malpractice and torts of their partners. As a result, the exposure of their personal assets to lawsuits filed against other partners and the partnership is considerably reduced.

An LLP must have formal documents of organization and register with the state. Because the LLP is a general partnership in other respects, it does not have to pay any state franchise taxes on its operations—an important difference between LLPs and LLCs in states such as Texas and Florida. LLPs are taxed as partnerships under Federal tax statutes.

The IRS has ruled that the conversion of a general partnership into a registered LLP is a continuation of the old partnership for tax purposes, if all the general partners become LLP partners and hold the same proportionate interests in the LLP that they held in the general partnership. This means that all the old partnership's elections continue in the LLP, including accounting methods, the taxable year-end, and the § 754 election.[37]

---

[37] Ltr.Ruls. 9229016, 9420028, and 9426038.

ANTI-ABUSE REGULATIONS

On January 3, 1995, the IRS finalized Regulations that allow it to disregard the form of a partnership transaction when it believes that the transaction (or series of transactions) is abusive.[38] Under the Regulation, a transaction is abusive if it satisfies two tests. First, it must have a principal purpose of substantially reducing the present value of the partners' aggregate Federal tax liability. In addition, the potential tax reduction must be inconsistent with the intent of Subchapter K. If the IRS disregards the form of a transaction, it will recast the transaction in a manner that reflects the transaction's underlying economic arrangement.

It is often difficult to determine whether a proposed transaction will substantially reduce the present value of the partners' aggregate tax liability. A partner may not know his or her personal tax situation until the transaction occurs and the partner's tax return is completed. Practitioners are concerned that the IRS may try to use "perfect hindsight" to determine if a transaction should be recast. This may make it difficult to anticipate the ultimate tax treatment of many partnership transactions.

The IRS says it will not recast transactions that are bona fide business arrangements and offers several examples in the Regulation. But since the Regulation has not yet been applied by the IRS or evaluated by the courts, in some cases it may not be clear whether a transaction will be recast. One comfort, though, is that the IRS has announced that a field examiner cannot invoke the Regulation without approval. Review by a partnership specialty group within the IRS is required before the IRS will challenge a taxpayer's treatment of a transaction under this Regulation.

**TAX PLANNING
CONSIDERATIONS**

SALES AND EXCHANGES OF PARTNERSHIP INTERESTS

Delaying Ordinary Income. A partner planning to dispose of a partnership interest in a taxable transaction might consider either an installment sale or a pro rata distribution of hot assets, followed by a sale of the remaining interest in the partnership. Although the subsequent disposition of the hot assets usually results in ordinary income, the partner can spread the income over more than one tax year by controlling the disposal dates of the hot assets.

Basis Adjustment for Transferee. If a partnership interest is acquired by purchase, the purchaser may want to condition the acquisition on the partnership's promise to make an election to adjust the basis of partnership assets. Making the election under § 754 results in the basis in the partner's ratable share of partnership assets being adjusted to reflect the purchase price. Failure to do so could result in the loss of future depreciation deductions or could convert ordinary losses into capital losses.

PLANNING PARTNERSHIP DISTRIBUTIONS

General Guidelines. In planning for any partnership distributions, be alert to the following possibilities:

- When gain recognition is undesirable, ascertain that cash distributions from a partnership, including any debt assumptions or repayments, do not exceed the basis of the receiving partner's interest.

---

[38] Reg. § 1.701–2, effective, in general, May 12, 1994.

- Distributions of marketable securities may also result in gain, but the current gain can be minimized if the securities *are* appreciated.
- When a partner is to receive a liquidating distribution and the full basis of the interest will not be recovered, the partner's capital loss can be ensured by providing that the only assets received by the partner are cash, unrealized receivables, and inventory. If a capital loss is undesirable, however, the partnership should also distribute a capital or § 1231 asset that will take the partner's remaining basis in the interest. This may result in a more desirable ordinary deduction or loss in the future.
- Current and liquidating distributions may result in ordinary income recognition for either the receiving partner or the partnership if hot assets are present. When such income is undesirable, consider making a distribution of hot assets pro rata to the receiving partner.
- If precontribution gain property is contributed to a partnership, gain to the contributing partner can be further deferred if the partnership waits five years before (1) distributing the gain property to another partner or (2) distributing property to the gain partner if the value of the property exceeds the gain partner's basis in the partnership.
- When the partnership agreement initially is drafted, consider the importance of the provisions that relate to liquidating distributions of partnership income and property. The specifics of the agreement will be followed by the IRS if these and other relevant points are addressed early in the life of the entity.

Valuation Problems.   Both the IRS and the courts usually consider the value of a partner's interest or any partnership assets agreed upon by all partners to be correct. Thus, when planning the sale or liquidation of a partnership interest, the results of the bargaining process should be documented. To avoid valuation problems on liquidation, include a formula or agreed-upon valuation procedure in the partnership agreement or in a related buy-sell agreement.

COMPARING SALES TO LIQUIDATIONS

When a partner disposes of an entire interest in a partnership for a certain sum, the *before-tax* result of a sale of that interest to another partner or partners is the same as the liquidation of the interest under § 736. In other words, if both transactions result in the same amount of pre-tax dollars, the partner should be ambivalent about which form the transaction takes unless one form offers tax savings that the other does not.

The tax consequences of a sale of a partnership interest and a liquidation of a partner's interest by an ongoing partnership may differ considerably. One difference occurs when the payment for that interest is extended over several years. When a partner sells the partnership interest to another partner, the selling partner can postpone the recognition of income under the installment sale rules. These rules are very restrictive and require that gain and income be recognized at least as quickly as the proportionate share of the receivable is collected. Under § 736, the § 736(b) payments for partnership property can be made before the income payments under § 736(a). Furthermore, the § 736(b) payments can be treated as a return of basis first with gain recognized only after the distributee partner has received amounts equal to the basis. This treatment results in a deferral of gain and income recognition under § 736 that is not available under the installment sale provisions.

The partner who purchases a partnership interest often pays an amount that can be attributed, in part, to partnership goodwill. This purchased goodwill is included in the purchasing partner's outside basis for the partnership interest. The partner cannot amortize the goodwill unless (1) the asset qualifies as a § 197 intangible, amortizable over 15 years, and (2) the partnership makes an election under § 754 to adjust the basis of partnership assets to reflect the purchase price paid. In many cases, the purchasing partner will not obtain a tax benefit from the goodwill until the partnership interest is disposed of. Under § 736, amounts paid by a service partnership for a general partner's share of partnership goodwill can be treated as a § 736(a) payment. If this payment is a guaranteed payment, it is deductible by the partnership. If it is a distributive share, it is excludible from the income stream of the remaining partners. In effect, this is also like a deduction. If (1) capital is a material income-producing factor of the partnership or (2) the distributee partner was a limited partner, payments for goodwill constitute § 736(b) property payments. These payments are not deductible by the partnership and result in increased capital gain (or decreased capital loss) to the retiring partner.

Finally, a partnership terminates if 50 percent or more of the total interest in partnership capital and profits is sold within a 12-month period. A liquidation under § 736, however, is not considered a sale or exchange under this rule. Therefore, a partnership can liquidate a partner's interest without terminating a three-partner partnership, even though that partner is, say, a 98 percent partner in partnership capital and profits immediately before the liquidating distribution.

A sale and a liquidation of a partnership interest also differ in other respects that are beyond the scope of this text. The point to remember is that differences exist that may result in considerable after-tax savings for the partners. Careful planning can result in a properly structured transaction.

OTHER PARTNERSHIP ISSUES

Choice of Entity.   The partnership liquidation rules demonstrate the general superiority of the partnership form to that of the C or S corporation in the final stage of the business's life:

- A service partnership can effectively claim deductions for its payment to a retiring general partner for goodwill.
- The partnership liquidation itself is not a taxable event. Under corporate rules, however, liquidating distributions and sales in preparation for a distribution are fully taxable.
- Tax liability relative to the liquidation is generated at the partner level, but only upon a recognition event (such as receipt of cash in excess of basis, or sale of an asset received in a distribution). The timing of this event is virtually under the control of the (ex-)partner. In this manner, the tax obligations can be optimized (i.e., they can be placed into the most beneficial tax year and rate bracket).

Family Partnerships.   If possible, make certain that very young and elderly members of a family partnership contribute services to the entity, so as to justify their income allocations. These services can comprise the most routine facets of the business, including monitoring and operating copy and fax machines and providing ongoing maintenance of the indoor and outdoor landscaping environments. Although no more than a market level of compensation can be assigned for this purpose, the services themselves constitute evidence of the active role that the partner plays in the operations of the entity.

Since there is no equivalent of the kiddie tax for elderly taxpayers, retention of the founding members of the partnership past the nominal retirement age often facilitates the income-shifting goals of the family.

KEY TERMS

Disproportionate distribution, 11–4

Hot assets, 11–15

Liquidating distribution, 11–3

Nonliquidating distribution, 11–3

Optional adjustment election, 11–32

Proportionate distribution, 11–4

Section 754 election, 11–32

Substantially appreciated inventory, 11–7

Technical termination of partnership, 11–36

Unrealized receivables, 11–6

PROBLEM MATERIALS

DISCUSSION QUESTIONS

1. Discuss the types of proportionate distributions from a partnership and the tax consequences of each.

2. Under what circumstances is a loss recognized by a withdrawing partner whose entire interest is liquidated in a proportionate distribution of assets?

3. How is the basis determined for property received by a partner in a proportionate liquidating or nonliquidating distribution?

4. Distinguish between the tax treatment of § 736 income and property payments. What are the tax consequences of such payments to the retiring partner, the remaining partners, and the partnership?

5. What is the character of a gain or loss recognized on the sale or exchange of a partnership interest, and how is it determined?

6. Discuss the possible collateral effects of a sale or exchange of a partnership interest.

7. Discuss the rationale for allowing a partnership to make a basis adjustment election under § 754. Distinguish between the basis adjustments allowed for sale of a partnership interest by a partner and for distributions of property from the partnership to a partner. When could an unfavorable result occur?

8. Describe the various types of events that can cause a partnership termination. Which of these can cause a "technical" termination?

9. What is a family partnership? Under what circumstances can a family member be a partner in such a partnership? What income allocation is required?

10. Discuss the advantages of a limited liability company over an S corporation. If a limited liability company incurs debt from an independent third-party bank, how do you think that debt should be treated under the liability sharing rules discussed in Chapter 10?

11. To what extent are the personal assets of a general partner, limited partner, or member of an LLC subject to (a) contractual liability (e.g., trade account payable) and (b) tort liability (e.g., malpractice) claims against the entity that party owns? Answer the question for partners or members in a general partnership, LLP, nonprofessional LLC, and limited partnership.

12. A retiring partner often can choose between selling the partnership interest to the other partners or selling it to the partnership. Explain why the method selected may make a difference for tax purposes.

13. Walden is a 40% partner in the WXY Partnership. He became a partner three years ago when he contributed land with a value of $40,000 and a basis of $20,000 (current value is $90,000). Xavier and Yolanda each contributed $30,000 cash for a 30% interest.

Walden's basis in his partnership interest is currently $40,000; the other partners' bases are each $30,000. The partnership has the following assets:

	Basis	Fair Market Value
Cash	$ 60,000	$ 60,000
Accounts receivable	–0–	80,000
Marketable securities	20,000	70,000
Land	20,000	90,000
Total assets	$100,000	$300,000

The partnership will make a distribution of $150,000 (value) to the partners before the end of the current year, but the type of property that will be distributed has not been determined. What issues should the partners consider in each of the following independent distribution alternatives?

a. WXY distributes a $45,000 interest in the land each to Yolanda and Xavier and $60,000 of accounts receivable to Walden.

b. WXY distributes $60,000 cash to Walden, $45,000 of marketable securities to Yolanda, and $45,000 of accounts receivable to Xavier.

c. WXY distributes a $45,000 interest in the land and $15,000 of accounts receivable to Walden and $11,250 of accounts receivable and $18,750 of cash each to Xavier and Yolanda.

 14. Use the assets and partners' bases from Question 13. Assume the partnership distributes all its assets in a liquidating distribution. In deciding the allocation of assets, what issues should the partnership consider to minimize each partner's gains?

PROBLEMS

15. Andrew's outside basis in his interest in the ABC Partnership is $100,000. In a proportionate current distribution, the partnership distributes to him cash of $25,000, inventory (fair market value of $30,000, basis to the partnership of $20,000), and land (fair market value of $60,000, basis to the partnership of $30,000). The partnership continues in existence and owns no hot assets.

a. Does the partnership recognize any gain or loss as a result of this distribution?

b. Does Andrew recognize any gain or loss as a result of this distribution?

c. Calculate Andrew's basis in the land, in the inventory, and in his partnership interest immediately following the distribution.

16. When Peggy's outside basis in the PQR Partnership is $25,000, the partnership distributes to her $10,000 cash, an account receivable (fair market value of $70,000, inside basis to the partnership of $0), and a parcel of land (fair market value of $30,000, inside basis to the partnership of $20,000). Peggy remains a partner in the partnership, and the distribution is proportionate to the partners.

a. Determine the recognized gain or loss to the partnership as a result of this distribution.

b. Determine the recognized gain or loss to Peggy as a result of the distribution.

c. Determine Peggy's basis in the land, account receivable, and PQR Partnership after the distribution.

17. In each of the following independent cases in which the partnership owns no hot assets, indicate:

• Whether the partner recognizes gain or loss.

• Whether the partnership recognizes gain or loss.

• The partner's adjusted basis for the property distributed.

• The partner's outside basis in the partnership after the distribution.

a. Lisa receives $16,000 cash in partial liquidation of her interest in the partnership. Lisa's outside basis for her partnership interest immediately before the distribution is $15,000.

b. Susan receives $6,000 cash and land with an inside basis to the partnership of $12,000 in partial liquidation of her interest. Susan's outside basis for her partnership interest immediately before the distribution is $20,000.

c. Assume the same facts as in (b), except that Susan's outside basis for her partnership interest immediately before the distribution is $15,000.

d. Jim receives $8,000 cash and two tracts of land in partial liquidation of his partnership interest. The two tracts have adjusted bases to the partnership of $5,000 and $15,000, respectively. Each tract has a $25,000 fair market value. Jim's outside basis for his partnership interest immediately before the distribution is $20,000.

 18. Assume the facts of Problem 17. In each independent case, are additional planning opportunities available to the partnership to maximize its inside basis in its assets? If so, by how much can the basis be increased? What is the effect of any basis increase to the distributee partner or the other partners?

 19. Sam Stevens is a 40% partner in the calendar year Oriole Partnership. On January 1, 1997, his basis in his partnership interest is $25,000, including his $13,000 share of partnership liabilities. The partnership has no taxable income or loss for the current year. Oriole repays all liabilities before the end of 1997 from cash on hand. In a nonliquidating distribution, the partnership distributes $15,000 cash on December 15. It also distributes inventory proportionately to all partners. Sam receives inventory with a basis of $8,000 and a fair market value of $6,000. In January 1998, Sam, your client, asks your advice regarding treatment of 1997 operations and distributions. Using the format (1) facts, (2) issues, and (3) conclusion and analysis, draft a letter to Sam at the Oriole Partnership (1622 E. Henry Street, St. Paul, MN 55163) that addresses the following points:

a. How much gain or loss does the partnership recognize as a result of 1997 activities?

b. How much gain or loss must Sam recognize in 1997?

c. What is Sam's basis in his partnership interest at the end of 1997?

d. What is Sam's basis in inventory received?

 20. The basis of Lou's partnership interest is $40,000. Lou receives a pro rata liquidating distribution consisting of $22,500 cash and his proportionate share of inventory with a basis of $24,500 to the partnership and a fair market value of $28,000. Assume the partnership also liquidates.

a. How much gain or loss, if any, must Lou recognize as a result of the distribution?

b. What basis will Lou take in the inventory?

c. If the inventory is sold two years later for $28,000, what are the tax consequences to Lou?

d. What are the tax consequences to the partnership as a result of the liquidating distribution?

e. Is any planning technique available to the partnership to avoid any "lost basis" results?

f. Would your answer to (b) change if this had been a nonliquidating distribution?

 21. Assume the same facts as in Problem 20, except that Lou's basis in the partnership is $70,000 instead of $40,000.

a. How much gain or loss, if any, must Lou recognize on the distribution?

b. What basis will Lou take in the inventory?

c. What are the tax consequences to the partnership?

d. Can you recommend an alternative distribution?

e. Would your answer to (a) or (b) change if this had been a nonliquidating distribution?

22. In each of the following liquidating distributions in which the partnership also liquidates, determine the amount and character of any gain or loss to be recognized by each partner and the basis of each asset (other than cash) received. In each case, assume the partnership has no "hot assets."

a. Rachel has a partnership basis of $9,000 and receives a distribution of $15,000 in cash.

b. Sara has a partnership basis of $20,000 and receives $9,000 cash and a capital asset with a basis to the partnership of $4,000 and a fair market value of $12,000.

c. Tim has a partnership basis of $16,000 and receives $4,000 cash, inventory with a basis to the partnership of $10,000, and a capital asset with a partnership basis of $6,000. The inventory and capital asset have fair market values of $9,000 and $7,000, respectively.

23. Jane's basis in her partnership interest is $60,000. In a proportionate distribution in liquidation of the partnership, Jane receives $35,000 cash and two parcels of land with bases of $10,000 each to the partnership. The partnership holds both parcels of land for investment, and the parcels have fair market values of $10,000 and $20,000, respectively.
   a. How much gain or loss, if any, must Jane recognize on the distribution?
   b. What basis will Jane take in each parcel?
   c. If the land had been held as inventory by the partnership, what effect, if any, would it have on your responses to (a) and (b)?

24. Assume the same facts as in Problem 23, except that Jane receives $35,000 cash and a desk having a basis of $1,200 to the partnership and a fair market value of $2,000.
   a. How much loss, if any, may Jane recognize on the distribution?
   b. What basis will Jane take in the desk?
   c. Suppose Jane's 15-year-old son uses the desk for his personal use for one year before Jane sells it for $100. How much loss may Jane recognize on the sale of the desk? What tax planning procedures could have prevented this result?

25. In 1994, Gabriella contributed land with a basis of $16,000 and a fair market value of $25,000 to the Meadowlark Partnership in exchange for a 25% interest in capital and profits. In 1997, the partnership distributes this property to Juanita, also a 25% partner, in a nonliquidating distribution. The fair market value has increased to $30,000 at the time the property is distributed. Juanita's and Gabriella's bases in their partnership interests are each $30,000 at the time of the distribution.
   a. How much gain or loss, if any, does Gabriella recognize on the distribution to Juanita? What is Gabriella's basis in her partnership interest following the distribution?
   b. What is Juanita's basis in the land she received in the distribution?
   c. How much gain or loss, if any, does Juanita recognize on the distribution? What is Juanita's basis in her partnership interest following the distribution?
   d. How much gain or loss would Juanita recognize if she later sells the land for its $30,000 fair market value? Is this result equitable?
   e. Would your answers to (a) and (b) change if Gabriella originally contributed the property to the partnership in 1984?

26. Winston contributed a tract of undeveloped land to the Nightingale Partnership in 1995. He originally paid $20,000 for the property in 1967, but its value was $70,000 at the date of the contribution. In 1997, the partnership distributes another parcel of land to Winston; the land has a basis to the partnership of $30,000. The fair market value of the distributed property is $100,000 in 1997. Winston's basis in his partnership interest is $60,000 immediately before the distribution.
   a. How much gain or loss, if any, does Winston recognize on the distribution?
   b. What is Winston's basis in his partnership interest following the distribution?
   c. What is Winston's basis in the property he receives in the distribution?
   d. After the distribution, what is the partnership's basis in the property originally contributed by Winston?
   e. Would your answers to (b), (c), and (d) change if Winston originally contributed the property to the partnership in 1986?

27. The FABB Partnership distributes a marketable security to 25% partner Fred in complete liquidation of his interest in the partnership. Use the following facts to answer the questions that follow:

   • The partnership's basis in the security is $10,000, and its value is $20,000. The partnership did not own any of this particular security following the distribution.

- Fred's basis in the partnership interest is $7,500 immediately prior to the distribution.

- Fred is a general partner, and capital is a material income-producing factor to the partnership.

- The partnership owns no hot assets.

a. How is the security classified under § 736?
b. What is the amount of the security distribution that is treated as a cash distribution?
c. How much gain does Fred report on the distribution?
d. What is Fred's basis in the security he receives in the distribution?

28. Maurice is a 10% general partner in the Chartreuse Partnership, which provides consulting services. The partnership distributes $100,000 cash to Maurice in complete liquidation of his partnership interest. Maurice's share of partnership unrealized receivables immediately before the distribution is $40,000. The partnership has no other hot assets. Assume none of the cash payment is for goodwill. Maurice's basis for his partnership interest immediately before the distribution is $30,000.
    a. How is the cash payment treated under § 736?
    b. How much gain or loss must Maurice recognize on the distribution, and what is the character of these amounts?
    c. How does the partnership treat the distribution to Maurice?
    d. What planning opportunities might the partnership wish to consider?
    e. Would your answers to the above questions change if Maurice were a limited partner?

29. Donald sells his interest in the equal DDP Partnership to his partner, Paul, for $47,000 cash and the assumption of Donald's share of partnership liabilities. On the sale date, the partnership's cash basis balance sheet reflects the following (assume capital accounts reflect the partners' bases in their partnership interests, excluding liabilities):

	Basis	**FMV**		**Basis**	**FMV**
Cash	$51,000	$ 51,000	Note payable	$ 9,000	$ 9,000
Accounts receivable	–0–	60,000	Capital accounts		
Capital assets	9,000	39,000	Dale	17,000	47,000
			Donald	17,000	47,000
			Paul	17,000	47,000
Total	$60,000	$150,000		$60,000	$150,000

a. What is the total amount realized by Donald on the sale?
b. How much, if any, ordinary income must Donald recognize on the sale?
c. How much capital gain must Donald report?
d. What is Paul's basis in the partnership interest acquired?
e. If the partnership makes an election to adjust the bases of the partnership assets to reflect the sale, what adjustment is made?

30. Assume in Problem 29 that Donald's partnership interest is not sold to another partner. Instead, the partnership makes a liquidating distribution of $47,000 cash to Donald, and the remaining partners assume his share of the liabilities. How much gain or loss must Donald recognize? Assume Donald is a general partner and capital is not a material income-producing factor to the partnership.

31. Rena, a general partner in the accrual basis RST Partnership, has a 30% interest in partnership profits and losses. The partnership's balance sheet at the end of the current year is as follows (assume the capital account reflects each partner's basis):

	Basis	FMV		Basis	FMV
Cash	$170,000	$170,000	Rena, capital	$ 99,000	$165,000
Inventory	100,000	180,000	Sara, capital	115,500	192,500
Land	60,000	200,000	Ted, capital	115,500	192,500
Totals	$330,000	$550,000	Totals	$330,000	$550,000

Rena sells her interest to Judy at the end of the current year for $165,000 cash.

a. How much, if any, ordinary income must Rena report on the sale?

b. How much capital gain?

c. What is Judy's basis in the partnership interest?

d. What is the effect to Judy if the partnership immediately sells all its inventory for $180,000 and the land for $200,000?

e. What action should Judy request to minimize the effects of the results in (d)?

32. Assume the same facts as in Problem 31, except the partnership makes a distribution of its entire cash balance of $170,000 to Rena in liquidation of her partnership interest. Rena is a general partner, and capital is a material income-producing factor for the partnership. The partnership agreement is silent regarding the treatment of goodwill.

a. How much gain does Rena recognize?

b. How is the $5,000 goodwill payment to Rena treated?

c. What is the character of the gain or loss recognized by Rena?

d. How much of the $170,000 payment to Rena is deductible?

e. What effect does the distribution have on the basis of partnership assets?

f. Are any planning opportunities available to the partnership?

33. Dad is the owner of a 60% general partner interest in the Consulting Services Partnership, in which capital is *not* a material income-producing factor. (Two unrelated partners each own 20% of the remaining partnership interests.) Dad's basis in the partnership interest is $300,000.

Dad's son, Bill, worked for the partnership on a part-time basis while he was in college and has shown a strong aptitude for the business. Dad would like to retire and allow Bill to take over the business, but he needs to cash in his partnership interest for its $600,000 value as soon as possible to do so. The partnership has adequate liquidity to make this distribution.

Dad's share of the partnership's unrealized receivables from services (no depreciation recapture, $0 basis) is $225,000. The partnership has a favorable tax year-end, so the other partners want to make sure the partnership does not terminate. Bill is the beneficiary of a trust fund established by his grandmother. He receives about $60,000 a year and will vest in the $750,000 principal amount in four years, when he reaches age 30.

Dad is considering two courses of action:

- Dad can sell his interest to Bill on an installment basis with a balloon payment of the $600,000 principal balance at the end of four years. Bill would pay Dad adequate interest (for purposes of OID and imputed interest rules) on the deferred balance each year. Under this arrangement, the entire 60% interest is deemed to be sold for tax purposes at the time the installment contract is consummated (although gain is deferred until payments are made).

- Dad can allow the partnership to redeem his partnership interest immediately. To structure a transition to the son, the partnership would enter into an employment arrangement with Bill, whereby Bill vests in a 10% interest in the partnership each year for six years in exchange for services rendered to the partnership.

Draft a letter to Dad Thomas (329 Mesquite Boulevard, Amarillo, TX 79109) addressing the consequences of each proposed alternative. Consider the impact to Dad, the partnership, and Bill.

34. Tiring of the daily grind and uncertainty associated with the home construction industry, Tim is considering selling his partnerhip interest to Una, who is not a current member of the partnership. Both parties, as well as Tim's partners, are concerned about the tax ramifications of the transaction. What potential tax consequences should be called to the attention of all parties involved?

35. At the end of the current year, Kevin, an equal partner in the four-person KLOM Partnership, has an outside basis of $18,000 in the partnership, including a $40,000 share of partnership debt. Kevin's share of the partnership's § 1245 recapture potential is $12,000. The partnership does not have any taxable income or loss in the current year, and all parties use the calendar year. Describe the income tax consequences to Kevin in each of the following situations that take place at the end of the current year:
    a. Kevin sells his partnership interest to Tracy for $25,000 cash and the assumption of the appropriate share of partnership liabilities.
    b. Kevin dies after a lengthy illness on December 31 of the current year. Kevin's widow takes his place in the partnership.

36. Briefly discuss how your responses in Problem 35 would change if the KLOM Partnership had $200,000 of unrealized receivables at the end of the current year, including the § 1245 recapture potential.

37. Sue, a partner in the cash basis SUB Partnership, has a 30% interest in partnership profits and losses. The partnership's balance sheet at the end of the current year is as follows:

	Basis	FMV		Basis	FMV
Cash	$ 25,000	$ 25,000	Sue, capital	$ 45,000	$150,000
Receivables	–0–	325,000	Una, capital	52,500	175,000
Land	125,000	150,000	Bob, capital	52,500	175,000
Totals	$150,000	$500,000	Totals	$150,000	$500,000

Sue sells her interest in the SUB Partnership to Betty at the end of the current year for cash of $150,000.
    a. How much income must Sue report on her tax return for the current year from the sale, and what is its nature?
    b. If the partnership does not make an optional basis adjustment election, what are the type and amount of income that Betty must report in the next year when the receivables are collected?
    c. If the partnership did make an optional basis adjustment election, what are the type and amount of income that Betty must report in the next year when the receivables are collected (assuming no other transactions in the next year)? The land (which is used in the SUB Partnership's business) is sold for $160,000?

38. For each of the following independent fact patterns, indicate whether a termination of the partnership has occurred for tax purposes. Assume no other partnership interests are sold either one year before or one year after the transactions described.
    a. Polly sells her interest in capital and profits of the MPQ Partnership. She owns a 68% interest in capital and a 48% interest in the partnership profits.
    b. Rick and Ron are equal partners in the R & R Partnership. Ron dies on January 15, 1997. Rick purchases Ron's interest from his estate on March 15, 1997. Answer for January 15, 1997.
    c. Answer (b), for March 15, 1997.
    d. Fred, a 58% partner in the profitable F & D Partnership gives his entire interest to his son on July 1, 1997.
    e. Carol, Cora, and Chris are equal partners in the Coot Partnership. On January 22, 1997, Cora sells her entire interest to Ted. On December 29, 1997, Carol sells a 15% interest to Earl. On January 25, 1998, Chris sells his interest to Frank.

39. Sam operates his wholly owned business, SamCo, as a Subchapter S corporation. SamCo has a basis of $600,000 in its assets, and the assets have a fair market value of $625,000. The corporation incurred liabilities of $500,000 from a third-party local bank to purchase real estate. Sam's basis in his stock is $100,000.

    Sam needs capital for expansion and has approached his cousin, Mary, about going into business together. Mary would contribute land valued at $125,000 (basis $50,000) for a 50% ownership interest in the business. The parties expect the expanded business to sustain losses for a year or two as a result of "growing pains."

    Sam and Mary have heard about limited liability companies (LLCs) and ask you about the suitability of such a company for their business.

    Draft a letter to Sam May and Mary Ray at SamCo (1159 Glendale Boulevard, St. Paul, MN 55163). Discuss the advantages SamCo would realize through an LLC structure and any disadvantages that would result from converting to or operating as an LLC. Describe the consequences of admitting Mary as a co-owner of either the S corporation or an LLC, and recommend a procedure for restructuring as an LLC. Use the format (1) facts, (2) issues, and (3) discussion and recommendations in your letter.

40. Peggy and Cindy, parent and child, operate a local apparel shop as a partnership. The PC Partnership earned a profit of $80,000 in the current year. Cindy's equal partnership interest was acquired by purchase from Peggy. Assume that capital is a material income-producing factor and that Peggy manages the day-to-day operations of the shop without any help from Cindy. Reasonable compensation for Peggy's services is $30,000.
    a. How much of the partnership income is allocated to Peggy?
    b. What is the maximum amount of partnership income that can be allocated to Cindy?
    c. Assuming that Cindy is five years old, has no other income, and is claimed as a dependent by Peggy, how is Cindy's income from the partnership taxed?

RESEARCH PROBLEMS

*Note: **West's Federal Taxation on CD-ROM** can be used in preparing solutions to the Research Problems. Alternatively, tax research materials contained in a standard tax library can be used.*

Research Problem 1.   Your client Paul is a one-third general partner in the service-oriented Magpie Partnership. He would like to retire from the partnership at the end of the current year and asks your help in structuring the buyout transaction.

Based on interim financial data and revenue projections for the remainder of the year, the partnership's balance sheet is expected to approximate the following at year-end:

	Basis	FMV
Cash	$ 60,000	$ 60,000
Accounts receivable	–0–	180,000
Land (capital asset)	120,000	210,000
Total assets	$180,000	$450,000
Maggie, capital	$ 60,000	$150,000
Paul, capital	60,000	150,000
Iris, capital	60,000	150,000
Total capital	$180,000	$450,000

Although the partnership has some current cash, the amount is not adequate to purchase Paul's entire interest in the current year. The partnership has proposed to pay Paul, in liquidation of his partnership interest, according to the following schedule:

December 31, 1997	$50,000
December 31, 1998	50,000
December 31, 1999	50,000

Paul has agreed to the above payment schedule, but the parties are not sure of the tax consequences of the buyout and have temporarily halted negotiations to consult with their tax advisers. Paul has come to you to discuss the possible income tax ramifications of the buyout and make sure he negotiates the most advantageous position possible.

   a. If the buyout agreement between Paul and Magpie is silent as to the treatment of each payment, how will each payment be treated by Paul and the partnership?

   b. As Paul's adviser, what payment schedule should Paul negotiate to minimize his current tax liability?

   c. Now assume you are the tax adviser for the partnership. What payment schedule would you propose to ensure the remaining partners receive the earliest possible deductions?

   d. What additional planning opportunity might you recommend to the partnership?

Research Problem 2. The accrual basis KB Partnership had a § 754 election in effect when partner Karen sold her 40% interest to Kristen for $140,000. Kristen's share of the inside basis of partnership assets was $128,000 following the acquisition. The total step-up, then, is $12,000. Complete the following chart, using the basis allocation rules of § 755 and the Regulations thereunder. Indicate the amount of the total adjustment to be allocated to each of the assets of the partnership.

Item	FMV	Basis before § 754 Adjustment	Appreciation	Allocated Adjustment
Capital and § 1231 assets:				
Securities	$ 60,000	$ 42,000	_____	_____
Equipment	110,000	88,000	_____	_____
Land	75,000	100,000	_____	_____
Goodwill	5,000	–0–	_____	_____
Total	$250,000	$230,000	_____	_____
Other assets:				
Cash	$ 15,000	$ 15,000	_____	_____
Receivables	28,000	31,000	_____	_____
Inventory	57,000	44,000	_____	_____
Total	$100,000	$ 90,000	_____	_____
Total assets	$350,000	$320,000	_____	_____

Research Problem 3. The ABC Partnership agreement was drafted in 1984. Though the agreement covered many issues, it did not contain a provision explaining how a retiring partner would be paid for his or her share of partnership goodwill. In 1997, the partnership executed an agreement entitled "Amendment of Limited Partnership Agreement," which provided that Felipe was to receive $100,000 cash from the partnership on July 1, 1998. The payment was to be made to retire Felipe's interest in the partnership. Of that amount, $30,000 is in return for Felipe's one-third interest in the fair market value of the net assets of the partnership. The other $60,000 was referred to as "a guaranteed payment, or a payment for goodwill."

The IRS agent says that the "Amendment of Limited Partnership Agreement" is not clear and, therefore, chooses to treat the payment for goodwill as ordinary income to Felipe and deductible by the partnership. Assume this approach maximizes the tax revenue for the government. Assuming you would prefer return of basis and capital gain treatment for Felipe, what authority can you obtain to support your position?

Use the tax resources of the internet to address the following questions. Do not restrict your search to the World Wide Web, but include a review of newsgroups and general reference materials, practitioner sites and resources, primary sources of the tax law, chat rooms and discussion groups, and other opportunities.

Research Problem 4.   Print an article written by a tax advisor discussing the merits of the family limited partnership. Send an e-mail message to the author, discussing one of the following issues.

   a. The effects of Rev. Rul. 93-12 on the use of the entity.

   b. The effects of § 704(e) on income computations for the entity.

   c. The accuracy of the computations made by the author in the article.

Research Problem 5.   On what form or attachment does a partnership report that it has made a § 754 election? Prepare such a form using the facts of Example 38 in the text.

Research Problem 6.   Download a copy of the legislation with which your state began to allow the formation of limited liability corporations.

12

S CORPORATIONS

LEARNING OBJECTIVES

After completing Chapter 12, you should be able to:

1. Explain the effects of attaining S corporation status.

2. Identify corporations that qualify for the S election.

3. Understand how an S election is made and, once made, how it can be lost.

4. Appreciate the effect of an S election on the corporation and its shareholders.

5. Recognize the situations where S status is desirable or undesirable.

1 LEARNING OBJECTIVE
Explain the effects of attaining S corporation status.

GENERAL CONSIDERATIONS

Subchapter S of the Internal Revenue Code of 1986 allows certain corporations to receive unique treatment for Federal income tax purposes.[1] Although this election essentially results in the S corporation receiving tax treatment that resembles that of a partnership, the entity is still a corporation under state law and for many other tax purposes. Special provisions pertain to the entity, however, under the operational provisions of §§ 1361–1379.

An **S corporation** is largely a tax-reporting, rather than a tax-paying, entity. In this respect, the entity is treated much like a partnership. As in the partnership conduit concept, the taxable income of an S corporation flows through to the shareholders, regardless of whether the income is distributed in the form of actual dividends. There is, in general, no S corporation corporate-level tax, and the income is taxed to the shareholders immediately. The S corporation is not subject to the alternative minimum tax, accumulated earnings tax, or personal holding company tax. Certain S corporations may, however, be subject to an excess passive investment income tax or a built-in gains tax.

Before the Tax Reform Act of 1986, S corporation status had enjoyed steady growth, as indicated by the rising number of S elections. But after TRA of 1986 increased corporate taxes and established a top individual tax rate that was less than the corporate rate, S elections experienced an unprecedented expansion in 1987 and 1988. For example, 52 percent more Form 1120S returns were filed in 1988 than in 1986, while other corporate returns filed dropped by about 11 percent.

This astonishing growth slowed after 1988; nevertheless, 48 percent of all corporate returns filed in 1993 were from S corporations—more than 1.9 million. From TRA of 1986 through 1993, the annual growth rate for S corporation returns averaged 13 percent. The total net income (less deficit) reported by S corporations for 1993 amounted to $66.2 billion, or about 13.3 percent of the adjusted total for all corporations. After 1993, however, some predicted that the growth rate of S corporation elections would slow or reverse due to the increase in the top

---

[1] Under the tax law, a Subchapter S corporation is an "S corporation." A regular corporation that has not elected S status is a "C corporation." C corporations are those governed by Subchapter C of the Code (§§ 301–386).

individual rate to 39.6 percent, making it 4.6 percentage points above the top corporate rate of 35 percent, rather than 3 points below it.

The Small Business Job Protection Act of 1996, however, made comprehensive changes in many of the S corporation rules. Since most of these changes allow for more flexibility in forming, operating, and restructuring S corporations, S elections may see another renaissance. Congress felt that these changes were so significant that any S corporation that terminated its election before 1997 is permitted to reelect without waiting the usual five-year period.

One reason for a possible slowing in the popularity of S corporation elections is that the IRS has ruled that an unincorporated organization formed as a limited liability company (LLC) is taxable as a partnership.[2] Unless legislation is enacted classifying LLCs as taxable corporations, new, closely held businesses may increasingly choose to do business as LLCs. An LLC provides greater flexibility than does S corporation status. For example, LLCs have no restrictions on the number or type of owners, and an LLC may specially allocate income and losses among its owners. The new entity classification procedure, which allows entities merely to check a box on their annual tax return to select treatment as corporations or as pass-through entities, may stimulate a growth in LLCs. Nevertheless, currently LLCs still are few in number and account for only about 0.1 percent of entities, business receipts and net income. In any case, companies facing the decision of selecting the appropriate organizational form must now seriously consider the LLC alternative. This chapter provides the tools for determining when S status is still appropriate.

Despite the increase in the top individual tax rate, the tax structure still creates a preference for the flow-through taxation of a business's income.

EXAMPLE 1

An entity earns $300,000 in 1997. The applicable marginal individual tax rate is 39.6%, the applicable marginal corporate tax rate is 34%, and all after-tax income is distributed currently.

	C Corporation	S Corporation or Limited Liability Company
Earnings	$ 300,000	$ 300,000
Less: Corporate tax	(102,000)	–0–
Available for distribution	$ 198,000	$ 300,000
Less: Tax at owner level	(78,408)	(118,800)
Available after-tax earnings	$ 119,592	$ 181,200

The flow-through business entity generates an extra $61,608 of after-tax earnings, when compared to a C corporation. Moreover, the flow-through business entity avoids the corporate alternative minimum tax (AMT) and the AMT ACE adjustment (refer to Chapter 6). The C corporation might be able to reduce this disadvantage by paying out its earnings as compensation, rents, or interest expense. Tax at the owner level can also be avoided by not distributing after-tax earnings. ▼

The entity's gains and losses are allocated to the shareholders, who report them on their individual tax returns. Other corporate transactions that flow through

---

[2]Rev.Rul. 88–76, 1988–2 C.B. 360, relative to Wyoming law. Another alternative is the limited liability partnership. See Chapter 13.

▼ **FIGURE 12–1**

Flow-Through of Separate Items
of Income and Loss to S
Corporation Shareholders

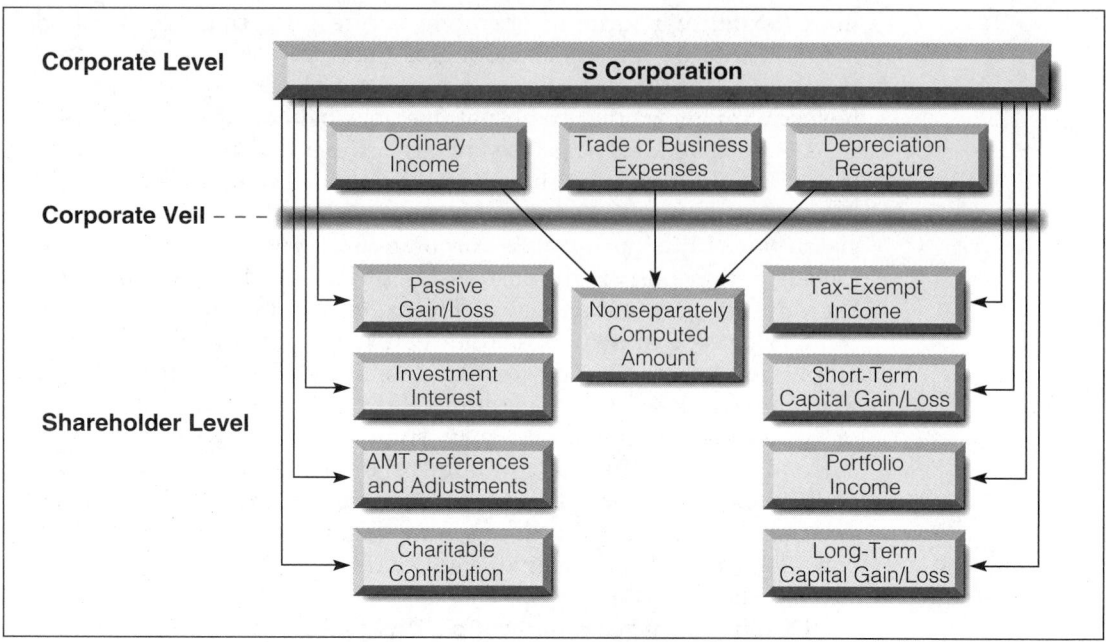

separately under the conduit concept include net long-term capital gains and
losses, charitable contributions, tax-exempt interest, foreign tax credits, and
business credits. Each shareholder of an S corporation separately takes into
account his or her pro rata share of certain items of income, deductions, and
credits (see Figure 12–1). Under § 1366(b), the character of any item of income,
expense, gain, loss, or credit is determined at the corporate level. These tax items
pass through as such to each shareholder, based on the prorated number of days
during the relevant S year that each held stock in the corporation.

SUBCHAPTER S IN PERSPECTIVE

Subchapter S permits certain corporations to avoid the corporate income tax
and enables them to pass through operating losses to their shareholders. It
represents an attempt to achieve a measure of tax neutrality in resolving the issue
of whether a business should be conducted as a sole proprietorship, partnership,
or corporation.

In dealing with Subchapter S, certain observations should be kept in mind.

1. S corporation status is an elective provision. Failure to make the election
will mean that the rules applicable to the taxation of corporations (Subchapter C status) and shareholders will apply (refer to Chapter 2).
2. S corporations are regular corporations in the legal sense. The S election
affects only the Federal income tax consequences of electing corporations.
In fact, a few states, including Michigan and New Jersey, do not recognize
the S election at all and subject such corporations to the state corporate
income tax and any other state corporate taxes that are imposed. See
Chapter 15 for a discussion of multistate income tax effects.

3. Federal income tax law treats S corporations neither as partnerships nor as regular corporations. The tax treatment resembles partnership taxation, but involves a unique set of tax rules. However, Subchapter C controls unless Subchapter S otherwise provides a pertinent tax effect.

4. Because Subchapter S is an elective provision, strict compliance with the applicable Code requirements generally has been demanded by both the IRS and the courts. Any unanticipated deviation from the various governing requirements may therefore lead to an undesirable and often unexpected tax result (e.g., the loss of the S election).

In summary, an S corporation may be subject to the following taxes.

- Preelection built-in gains tax.
- Passive investment income penalty tax.

An S corporation is *not* subject to the following taxes.

- Corporate income tax.
- Accumulated earnings tax.
- Personal holding company tax.
- Alternative minimum tax.
- Environmental excise tax on AMT income.[3]

QUALIFICATION FOR S CORPORATION STATUS

DEFINITION OF A SMALL BUSINESS CORPORATION

2 LEARNING OBJECTIVE
Identify corporations that qualify for the S election.

A **small business corporation** must possess the following characteristics.

- Is a domestic corporation (is incorporated or organized in the United States).
- Is not otherwise ineligible for the election.
- Has no more than 75 (35 before 1997) shareholders.
- Has as its shareholders only individuals, estates, and certain trusts.
- Does not have a nonresident alien shareholder.
- Issues only one class of stock.

No maximum or minimum dollar sales or capitalization restrictions apply to an S corporation.

EXAMPLE 2

Two individuals decide to incorporate their business and make an S election. They note that the definition of "small" in § 1361(b)(1) relates chiefly to the number of shareholders and not to the size of the corporation. With only two shareholders, they clearly meet the definition of a small business corporation with respect to the S election. Once they make the election, the corporation will not be subject to a corporate income tax.

During their shareholders' meeting, the individuals review § 1244(c)(1) to decide whether to issue § 1244 stock. (See Chapter 3 for a discussion of § 1244 stock.) In sharp contrast to § 1361(b)(1), this "small business corporation" definition looks to the extent of the capitalization of the corporation. The individuals agree that the two provisions are not mutually exclusive, because § 1244 stock allows them to receive ordinary *loss* treatment on future stock sales or on bankruptcy. The shareholders vote to issue § 1244 stock. ▼

---

[3] Rev.Rul. 89–82, 1989–1 C.B. 23.

Ineligible Corporation. Certain banks, insurance companies, and Puerto Rico or possessions corporations are not eligible to make an S election. A bank can elect S status after 1996, if it uses the specific charge-off method to account for bad debts (rather than the reserve method). However, the bank's interest income still may be considered passive investment income.

Before 1997, an S corporation was prohibited from being a member of an affiliated group. Now an S corporation may own up to 100 percent of a C corporation or have a wholly owned S corporation subsidiary.[4] The S corporation is *not* allowed a dividends received deduction. The C corporations (but not the parent S corporation) may join in the filing of any consolidated tax return.

EXAMPLE 3

Tops Corporation is formed in Texas to develop and promote a new fast-food franchise system, namely, the "Texas Chicken Delight." If the entity is successful in Texas, the shareholders of Tops will expand the operation to New Mexico, Oklahoma, Arkansas, and Louisiana. With this in mind and with a view toward protecting the name and product identification of the parent corporation, Tops Corporation forms a subsidiary, which in turn establishes subsidiaries in each of these states. Although Tops Corporation and its subsidiaries now constitute an affiliated group, Tops can still qualify as an S corporation. The C subsidiary and its subsidiaries may join in the filing of consolidated tax returns. However, Tops may *not* join in the filing of the consolidated returns and is *not* allowed a dividends received deduction. ▼

Number of Shareholders Limitation. An electing corporation is limited to 75 shareholders (35 before 1997). In testing for the 75-shareholder limitation, a husband and wife are treated as one shareholder as long as they remain married. Furthermore, the estate of a husband or wife and the surviving spouse are treated as one shareholder in § 1361(c)(1).

EXAMPLE 4

Harry and Wilma (husband and wife) jointly own 10 shares in Oriole, Inc., an S corporation, with the remaining 90 shares outstanding owned by 74 other unmarried persons. Harry and Wilma are divorced; pursuant to the property settlement approved by the court, the 10 shares held by Harry and Wilma are divided between them (5 to each). Before the divorce settlement, Oriole had only 75 shareholders. After the settlement, it has 76 shareholders and no longer qualifies as a small business corporation. ▼

Type of Shareholder Limitation. All of an S corporation's shareholders must be either individuals, estates, or certain trusts.[5] Stated differently, none of the shareholders may be partnerships, corporations, or nonqualifying trusts. The justification for this limitation is related to the 75-shareholder restriction. If, for example, a partnership with 80 partners could be a shareholder, could it not be said that the corporation has at least 80 owners? If this interpretation were permitted, the 75-shareholder restriction could easily be circumvented by indirect ownership. Nevertheless, an S corporation can be a partner in a partnership, and it can own stock of another corporation or all the stock of a subsidiary S corporation.

The tax law permits a voting trust arrangement. Moreover, other exceptions mitigate the rule that a trust cannot be a shareholder in an S corporation. Since these exceptions are of limited applicability, they are not discussed in this text.

An S corporation may be a general partner in a partnership. Thus, in such a partnership arrangement, all equity holders (S shareholders and partners) have

---

[4] § 1361(b)(2).

[5] § 1361(b)(1)(B).

both the limited liability of corporate ownership and the pass-through tax treatment of an S corporation. Essentially, the group is free from the 75-shareholder limitation.[6] The 75-shareholder limitation also can be avoided by having two or more S corporations (each with 75 or fewer shareholders) become partners in a partnership or a limited liability company that is conducting the underlying business.

EXAMPLE 5

To obtain more financial capital, Parot Corporation, an S corporation with 75 shareholders, places most of its assets into a limited partnership; Parot is the only general partner. Ten other individuals and two corporations invest as limited partners in the partnership. Parot is to receive 65% of the profits. Now 85 individuals and two corporations effectively own the business. The partnership arrangement avoids double taxation and offers limited liability for its 87 owners. ▼

Nonresident Alien Prohibition. None of an S corporation's shareholders can be nonresident aliens.[7] In a community property jurisdiction where one of the spouses is married to a nonresident alien, this rule can be a trap for the unwary.[8] A resident alien or a nonresident U.S. citizen can be an S corporation shareholder, however.

The probable reason for discrimination against nonresident alien individuals is administrative. It would be difficult to collect the shareholder-level tax from people outside the U.S. taxing jurisdiction. However, as business becomes increasingly international in scope, this prohibition may be subject to criticism.

ETHICAL CONSIDERATIONS

Extortion Payments

Burt is the custodian at Quaker Inn, an S corporation in Grand Isle, Louisiana. Over the years, he has received a total of 276 shares of stock in the corporation through bonus payments.

While listening to a debate on television about a national health care plan, Burt decides that the company's health coverage is unfair. He is concerned about this because his wife is seriously ill.

During the second week in December, Burt informs the president of Quaker that he would like a Christmas bonus of $75,000, or else he will sell 10 shares of his stock to one of his relatives who is a nonresident alien. Burt calculates that the resulting corporate tax on the approximately $400,000 of corporate income would amount to about $136,000.

One Class of Stock Limitation. An S corporation can have only one class of stock issued and outstanding.[9] Congress apparently felt that the capital structure of a small business corporation should be kept relatively simple. Allowing more than one class of stock (e.g., common and preferred) would complicate the pass-through of various corporate tax attributes to the shareholders. Authorized

---

[6]G.C.M. 36966 (December 27, 1976); Ltr.Rul. 8711020 (12/86); Rev.Rul. 94–43, 1994–2 C.B. 199.

[7]§ 1361(b)(1)(C).

[8]See, for example, *Ward v. U.S.*, 81–2 USTC ¶9674, 48 AFTR2d 81–5942, 661 F.2d 226 (Ct.Cls., 1981), where the court found that the stock was owned as community property. Since the taxpayer-shareholder (a U.S. citizen) was married to a citizen and resident of Mexico, the nonresident alien prohibition was violated. If the taxpayer-shareholder had held the stock as separate property, the S election would have been valid.

[9]§ 1361(b)(1)(D).

and unissued stock or treasury stock of another class does *not* disqualify the corporation. Likewise, unexercised stock options, phantom stock, stock appreciation rights, warrants, and convertible debentures often do not constitute a second class of stock, and differences in voting rights among shares of common stock are permitted.[10]

Safe harbor rules provide that "straight debt" is not treated as a second class of stock and does not disqualify an S election.[11] The characteristics of straight debt include the following.

- The debtor is subject to a written, unconditional promise to pay on demand or on a specified date a sum certain in money.
- The interest rate and payment date are not contingent on corporate profit, management discretion, or similar factors.
- The debt is not convertible into stock.
- The creditor is an individual (other than a nonresident alien), an estate, or qualified trust.
- Straight debt can be held by creditors actively and regularly engaged in the business of lending money.

Essentially, an S corporation has one class of stock unless deliberate actions are taken to circumvent the requirement. Facts and circumstances determine the proper tax treatment of business transactions. For example, a second class of stock does not exist where the IRS recharacterizes a payment of excessive compensation as a dividend distribution.

MAKING THE ELECTION

3   **LEARNING OBJECTIVE**
Understand how an S election is made and, once made, how it can be lost.

If the corporation satisfies the definition of a small business corporation, the next step to achieving S status is a valid election. Key factors include who must make the election, and when the election must be made.

Who Must Elect.   The election is made by filing Form 2553, and all shareholders must consent.[12] For this purpose, both husband and wife must file consents if they hold the stock as joint tenants, tenants in common, tenants by the entirety, or community property. Since a husband and wife generally are considered as one shareholder for purposes of the 75-shareholder limitation, this inconsistency in treatment has led to considerable taxpayer grief—particularly in community property states where the spouses may not realize that their stock is jointly owned as a community asset.

EXAMPLE 6

Three shareholders, Ann, Bill, and Cheryl, incorporate in January and file Form 2533. Shareholder Cheryl is married and lives in California. Ann is single and Bill is married; they live in North Carolina. Ann, Bill, and Cheryl all must consent to the S election. Because Cheryl is married and lives in a community property state, her husband must also consent to the election. Since North Carolina is not a community property state, Bill's wife need not consent to the S election. ▼

The consent of a minor shareholder can be made by the minor or a legal or natural guardian (e.g., parent). If the stock is held under a state Uniform Gifts to Minors Act, the custodian of the stock may consent for the minor, but only if the custodian is also the minor's legal or natural guardian. The minor is not required

---

[10] § 1361(c)(4).
[11] § 1361(c)(5)(A).

[12] § 1362(a)(2). But see Example 10 for a situation where a nonshareholder may be required to consent.

to issue a new consent when he or she comes of age and the custodianship terminates.[13]

When the Election Must Be Made. To be effective for the following year, the election can be made at any time during the current year. To be effective for the current year, the election must be made on or before the fifteenth day of the third month of that year. An election can be effective for a short tax year of less than two months and 15 days, even if it is not made until the following tax year.[14]

EXAMPLE 7

In 1997, Xexus Corporation, a calendar year C corporation, decides to become an S corporation beginning January 1, 1998. An election made at any time during 1997 accomplishes this objective. If, however, the election is made in 1998, it must be made on or before March 15, 1998. An election after March 15, 1998, will not make Xexus an S corporation until 1999. ▼

ETHICAL CONSIDERATIONS

A Missing S Election Form

E el Corporation, in Spivey Corners, North Carolina, has filed a Form 1120S for six years, and the local IRS office has sent the company a letter requesting an audit next month. Carrie, who is in charge of tax matters at Eel, cannot find a copy of the original S election, Form 2553.

The original shareholders and officers all agree that a local accountant filed the form, but he passed away last year. Several of the shareholders instruct Carrie to prepare a backdated Form 2553, which they will sign. Carrie could then copy the form and tell the agent that this was a copy of the original Form 2553. What should Carrie do? She estimates that any proposed deficiency would be in the range of $625,000.

Although no statutory authority exists for obtaining an extension of time for filing an S election, a shareholder may obtain an extension of time to file a consent, if a timely election is filed, reasonable cause is given, and the interests of the government are not jeopardized.[15]

EXAMPLE 8

Vern and Yvonne decide to convert their C corporation into a calendar year S corporation for 1997. At the end of February before the election is filed, Yvonne travels to Ukraine and forgets to sign a consent to the election. Yvonne will not return to the United States until June and cannot be reached by fax. Vern files the S election on Form 2553 and also requests an extension of time to file Yvonne's consent to the election. Vern indicates the reasonable cause for the extension (i.e., shareholder out of the country). Since the government's interest is not jeopardized, the IRS probably will grant Yvonne an extension of time to file the consent. Vern must file the election on Form 2553 on or before the fifteenth day of the third month (i.e., March 15) for the election to be effective for January 1, 1997. ▼

An election cannot be made for an entity that does not yet exist.[16] For a newly created corporation, the question may arise as to when the 2½-month election

---

[13] Rev.Rul. 71–287, 1971–2 C.B. 317.
[14] § 1362(b).
[15] Rev.Rul. 60–183, 1960–1 C.B. 625; *William Pestcoe*, 40 T.C. 195 (1963); Temp.Reg. § 18.1362–2(e).

[16] See, for example, *T. H. Campbell & Bros., Inc.*, 34 TCM 695, T.C.Memo. 1975–149; Ltr.Rul. 8807070.

period begins to run. Under the law, the first month begins at the earliest occurrence of any of the following events: (1) when the corporation has shareholders, (2) when it acquires assets, or (3) when it begins doing business.[17]

EXAMPLE 9

Several individuals acquire assets on behalf of Table Corporation on June 29, 1997, and begin doing business on July 3, 1997. They subscribe to shares of stock, file articles of incorporation for Table, and become shareholders on July 7, 1997. The S election must be filed no later than 2½ months from June 29, 1997 (on or before September 12) to be effective for 1997. ▼

Where an S corporation's first taxable year begins after the first day of a month, the first month of the 2½-month period starts with the first day of the tax year and ends after the close of the day *before* the numerically corresponding day of the succeeding month.[18]

Even if the 2½-month rule is met, a current election is not valid until the following year under either of the following conditions.

- The eligibility requirements were not met during any part of the taxable year before the date of election.
- Persons who were shareholders during any part of the taxable year before the election date, but were not shareholders when the election was made, did not consent.

These rules prevent the allocation of income or losses to preelection shareholders who either were ineligible to hold S corporation stock or did not consent to the election.

EXAMPLE 10

As of January 15, 1997, the stock of Robin Corporation (a calendar year C corporation) was held equally by three individual shareholders: Ursula, Vanessa, and Zelda. On that date, Zelda sells her interest to Ursula and Vanessa. On March 14, 1997, Ursula and Vanessa make the S election by filing Form 2553. Robin cannot become an S corporation until 1998. Although the election was timely filed, Zelda did not consent. Had all the shareholders during the year (Ursula, Vanessa, and Zelda) signed Form 2553, S status would have taken effect as of January 1, 1997. ▼

Once an election is made, it need not be renewed. It remains in effect unless otherwise lost.

The IRS can validate an S election that is inadvertently defective from failure to meet a qualification requirement or from a missing shareholder consent. Further, where there is reasonable cause for a late election made for the current year, the IRS may treat the S election as timely.

LOSS OF THE ELECTION

An S election terminates if one of the Code's eligibility rules is violated. In addition, an S election can be lost in any of the following ways.

- A new shareholder owning more than one-half of the stock affirmatively refuses to consent to the election.
- Shareholders owning a majority of shares (voting and nonvoting) voluntarily revoke the election.

---

[17] Reg. § 1.1372–2(b)(1). Also see, for example, *Nick A. Artukovich,* 61 T.C. 100 (1973).

[18] Reg. § 1.1362–(3).

- The number of shareholders exceeds the maximum allowable limitation.
- A class of stock other than voting or nonvoting common stock is created.
- The corporation fails the passive investment income limitation.
- A nonresident alien becomes a shareholder.

Voluntary Revocation. Section 1362(d)(1) permits a voluntary revocation of the election if shareholders owning a majority of shares consent. A revocation filed up to and including the fifteenth day of the third month of the tax year is effective for the entire tax year, unless a prospective effective date is specified. A revocation made after the fifteenth day of the third month of the tax year is effective on the first day of the following tax year. However, if a prospective date is specified, the termination is effective as of the specified date.

EXAMPLE 11

The shareholders of Termite Corporation, a calendar year S corporation, elect to revoke the election on January 5, 1997. Assuming the election is duly executed and timely filed, Termite becomes a regular corporation for calendar year 1997. If the election is not made until June 1997, Termite is not a C corporation until calendar year 1998. ▼

A revocation that designates a prospective effective date results in the splitting of the year into a short S corporation taxable year and a short C corporation taxable year. The day *before* the day on which the revocation occurs is treated as the last day of a short S corporation taxable year, and the day on which the revocation occurs is treated as the first day of the short regular corporate taxable year. The corporation allocates the income or loss for the entire year on a pro rata basis (weighted daily allocation).

EXAMPLE 12

Assume the same facts as in Example 11, except that Termite designates July 1, 1997, as the revocation date. Accordingly, June 30, 1997, is the last day of the S corporation taxable year. The C taxable year runs from July 1, 1997, to December 31, 1997. Any income or loss for the entire year is allocated between the short years on a pro rata basis. ▼

Rather than elect a pro rata allocation, the corporation can elect (with the consent of *all* who were shareholders at any time during the S short year) to report the income or loss on each return on the basis of income or loss as shown on the corporate permanent records. Under this method, items are attributed to the short S and C corporation years according to the time they were incurred (as reflected in the entity's accounting records).[19]

Cessation of Small Business Corporation Status. A corporation not only must be a small business corporation to make the S election but also must continue to qualify as such to keep the election. In other words, meeting the definition of a small business corporation is a continuing requirement for maintaining the S status. In the case of such an involuntary termination, the loss of the election applies as of the date on which the disqualifying event occurs.[20]

EXAMPLE 13

Tamra Corporation has been a calendar year S corporation for three years. On August 13, 1997, one of its 75 unmarried shareholders sells *some* of her stock to an outsider. Tamra now has 76 shareholders, and it ceases to be a small business corporation. For 1997, Tamra is an S corporation through August 12, 1997, and a C corporation from August 13 through December 31, 1997. ▼

---

[19] §§ 1362(e)(1),(2) and (3).   [20] § 1362(d)(2)(B).

Passive Investment Income Limitation. The Code provides a **passive investment income (PII)** limitation for an S corporation that possesses accumulated earnings and profits (E & P) from years in which the entity was a C corporation. If such a corporation has passive income in excess of 25 percent of its gross receipts for three consecutive taxable years, the S election is terminated as of the beginning of the fourth year.[21]

EXAMPLE 14   For 1994, 1995, and 1996, Bacon Corporation, a calendar year S corporation, derived passive income in excess of 25% of its gross receipts. If Bacon holds accumulated E & P from years in which it was a C corporation, its S election is terminated as of January 1, 1997. ▼

Such damaging C corporation E & P could be acquired by an S corporation from a regular corporation where E & P carry over under § 381 (e.g., due to a merger), or they could be earned in years before the S election. S corporations themselves never generate E & P.[22]

Although this definition of passive investment income appears to parallel that of personal holding company income (refer to Chapter 6), the two types of income are not identical. For example, long-term capital gain from the sale of securities would be PII but would not be personal holding company income. Moreover, there are no relief provisions for rent income similar to the personal holding company rules. The inclusion of gains from the sale of securities within the definition of PII generally has made it difficult, if not impossible, for corporations that deal chiefly in security transactions to achieve S status if harmful C corporation E & P exists.

Rents present a unique problem. Although they are classified as passive investment income by the Code, rents do not fall into this category if the corporation (landlord) renders significant services to the occupant (tenant). This exception is similar to the material participation test for passive activity income of § 469.

EXAMPLE 15   Tepee Corporation owns and operates an apartment building. Although the corporation provides utilities for the building, maintains the lobby in the building, and furnishes trash collection for the tenants, this activity does not constitute the rendering of significant services for the occupants.[23] Thus, the rents paid by the tenants of the building are PII to Tepee. ▼

EXAMPLE 16   Assume the facts in Example 15 with one addition—Tepee also furnishes maid services to its tenants. Now the services rendered are significant in that they go beyond what one might normally expect the landlord of an apartment building to provide. Under these circumstances, the rent income no longer constitutes PII. ▼

Reelection after Termination. After the election has been terminated, five years must pass before a new election can be made. The Code does, however, allow the IRS to make exceptions to this rule and permit an earlier reelection by the corporation in two situations.[24]

---

[21] § 1362(d)(3)(A)(ii).

[22] § 1362(d)(3)(B).

[23] Reg. § 1.1372–4(b)(5)(vi). *Bramlette Building Corp., Inc.,* 52 T.C. 200 (1969), *aff'd.* in 70–1 USTC ¶9361, 25 AFTR2d 70–1016, 424 F.2d 751 (CA–5, 1970).

[24] §§ 1362(f) and (g); Reg. § 1.1372–5(a); Rev.Rul. 78–274, 1978–2 C.B. 220.

- There is a more-than-50 percent change in ownership after the first year for which the termination is applicable.
- The event causing the termination was not reasonably within the control of the S corporation or its majority shareholders.

There is a safe harbor for any terminated S election for tax years beginning before 1997. Such corporations may reelect S corporations status without the usual five-year waiting period.

EXAMPLE 17

Kim, the sole owner of an S corporation, voluntarily terminates the S election in February 1997. Unless consent for a new election is given by the Commissioner, the successor corporation cannot make another S election until the year 2002. The Commissioner probably would not allow an early reelection. The same result would occur if the election was involuntarily terminated in 1997 and the precipitating event was within the control of the corporation or shareholder Kim. The corporation does *not* fall under the safe harbor provision for S corporations *before* 1997. ▼

EXAMPLE 18

Suppose, in Example 17, that Kim sells 80% of her stock to Mark in 1998. Since there was a more-than-50% change in ownership, the successor corporation may be able to obtain a consent from the IRS for an early S election. ▼

ETHICAL CONSIDERATIONS

A Voluntary "Involuntary" Termination

Hirschman, Inc., a calendar year S corporation, would like to terminate its S election immediately. However, March 15 has passed, and any voluntary termination would not be effective until the first day of the following tax year. One shareholder, Elena Muñoz, suggests an involuntary termination. She wants to sell several shares of her stock to a nonresident alien.

Elena has come to you, Hirschman's tax adviser. You have briefed her on the tax effects that such a sale would have on the other shareholders. Elena then asks you for some additional advice: Is such a voluntary "involuntary" termination of an S election ethical?

OPERATIONAL RULES

4   LEARNING OBJECTIVE
Appreciate the effect of an S election on the corporation and its shareholders.

Since an S corporation is largely a tax-reporting, rather than a tax-paying, entity, the entity is treated much like a partnership. As in the partnership conduit concept, the taxable income of an S corporation flows through to the shareholders, whether the income is distributed in the form of actual dividends or not. Likewise, losses of the entity are allocated to the shareholders, who deduct them on their individual tax returns. Other corporate transactions that flow through separately under the conduit concept include net long-term capital gains and losses, charitable contributions, tax-exempt interest, foreign tax credits, and business credits.

As under the partnership rules, each shareholder of an S corporation takes into account separately his or her pro rata share of certain items of income, deductions, and credits. Under § 1366(b), the character of any item of income, expense, gain, loss, or credit is determined at the corporate level. These tax items pass through as such to each shareholder, based on the prorated number of days during the relevant S year that each held stock in the corporation.

CHOICE OF TAX YEAR

Since S corporation shareholders report their shares of S items as of the entity's year-end, the selection of a corporate tax year is an important tax decision. An S corporation may use a calendar year or a fiscal year; for tax deferral purposes, a corporate fiscal year ending January 31 and a calendar year shareholder would be ideal.

EXAMPLE 19 An S corporation is organized on October 5, 1997. Its Subchapter S ordinary income for the next 15 months is as follows.

October 5–December 31, 1997	$ 30,000
January 1998	20,000
February–September 30, 1998	180,000
October–December 31, 1998	60,000

If the S corporation elects a calendar year, the shareholders recognize $30,000 of income in 1997. But if a January 31 fiscal year is used, the calendar year shareholders recognize no income for 1997. Furthermore, only $50,000 is taxable to the shareholders in 1998. This deferral of income caused Congress to require most S corporations to use calendar years. If this S corporation could select a September 30 fiscal year, no income is taxable to the shareholders in 1997, and only $230,000 is taxable in 1998. ▼

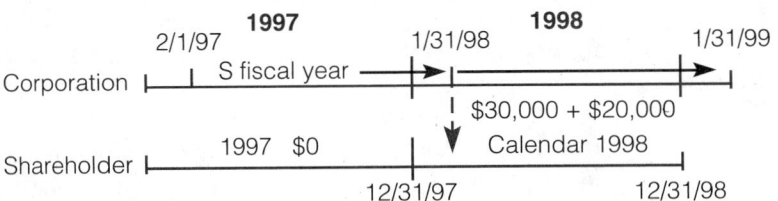

S corporations must conform to the taxable years of their shareholders (the calendar year in most instances). There are two exceptions to this general rule. First, an S corporation may use a taxable year for which it can establish a business purpose.[25] Second, an S corporation may make a one-time election under § 444 on Form 8716 to keep or establish a fiscal year, provided that a corporate-level payment is made on any income deferred by the shareholders.

An S corporation may have valid business reasons to select a fiscal year. For example, a company may have difficulty closing the books, preparing statements, and issuing its Schedules K–1 on a timely basis under a calendar year. An S corporation can establish an acceptable business purpose for a fiscal year in three ways.

- The fiscal year is a natural business year.
- The fiscal year serves an acceptable business purpose.
- An existing S corporation meets certain grandfathering requirements.[26]

Meeting the natural business year exception involves a simple quantitative test. If 25 percent or more of a corporation's gross receipts for the 12-month period is recognized in the last 2 months of that period, and the requirement has been met for three consecutive 12-month periods, the S corporation may adopt, retain, or change to a noncalendar year. If the entity is to establish a natural business year, it must have at least a 47-month gross receipts history.

---

[25] § 1378(a).

[26] Rev.Proc. 87–32, 1987–2 C.B. 396.

EXAMPLE 20

An S corporation's gross receipts total $100,000 for each of the last three calendar years. If the corporation recognizes at least $25,000 of its gross receipts in April and May for three consecutive years, the S corporation may adopt, retain, or change to a May 31 year-end. ▼

Other business purposes may be used to establish a fiscal year that is acceptable to the IRS. However, the fiscal year must be close to the entity's natural business year (e.g., the entity barely fails the 25 percent test). The IRS lists the following factors that do *not* constitute a valid business purpose.[27]

- The use of a particular fiscal year for regulatory or financial accounting purposes.
- Personnel practices of the corporation.
- Tax deferral for the shareholders.
- Use of a fiscal year for administrative purposes (e.g., awarding bonuses or promotions).
- Use of model years, price lists, or other items that change on a noncalendar annual basis.

In general, a taxable year under the § 444 election may not result in a deferral period of more than three months. However, an S corporation in existence before 1987 may elect to retain its previous taxable year for years after 1986, even though such a year results in a deferral period exceeding three months.[28]

The penalty paid for using a fiscal year under § 444 is that the S corporation must make a required payment on April 15 for any tax year for which the election is in effect. This required payment is equal to the base year income times the deferral ratio, times the highest individual income tax rate, plus one percentage point. Thus, the required payment rate is now 40.6 percent (39.6% + 1%). Such payments are not deductible by the S corporation (nor by any other person). They are refundable deposits that do not earn interest and do not pass through to the S shareholders.[29] An electing corporation need not make a required payment until the net § 444 amount for the current and all preceding election years exceeds $500.

In effect, the government collects a deposit from the S corporation based upon any deferred income. The deferral ratio is the number of months in the deferral period of the base year, divided by the number of months in the S corporation's tax year. This required payment is cumulative in nature. Thus, a corporation must pay the deferred amount, less the cumulative amount of the required payments made and refunds received in prior years.

An S corporation claims a refund when the required payments less refunds for all previous election years exceed the current required payment amount before any reductions for prior payments. Upon the termination of a fiscal year election or the liquidation of the S corporation during an election year, the entire net required payment balance is refunded.

EXAMPLE 21

Cohen, Inc., is a C corporation with a September 30 fiscal year. Cohen elects S status for the year ending September 30 and is unable to meet the business purpose exception for maintaining a fiscal year. To maintain its fiscal year, Cohen elects under § 444 on Form 8716 and makes a required payment. Cohen's base period income is $197,020, so the required payment is $19,998 ($197,020 × 3/12 deferral ratio × 40.6% applicable tax rate).

---

[27] Rev.Rul. 87–57, 1987–2 C.B. 117.
[28] Reg. § 1.444–1T(b).

[29] § 7519.

Assuming the required payment in the next year is $17,020, Cohen claims a $2,978 refund ($19,998 − $17,020). ▼

COMPUTATION OF TAXABLE INCOME

Subchapter S taxable income or loss generally is determined in a manner similar to the tax rules that apply to partnerships, except that the S corporation can amortize its organizational expenditures.[30] Furthermore, an S corporation can deduct salaries and payroll taxes. Finally, S corporations must recognize any gains (but not losses) under § 1363(d) on distributions of appreciated property to shareholders.

Certain deductions not allowable for a partnership also are not allowable for an S corporation, including the standard deduction, personal exemption, alimony payments, personal moving expenses, and expenses for the care of certain dependents. Furthermore, special Code provisions affecting only the computation of a C corporation's taxable income, such as the dividends received deduction, are not available.[31]

In general, S corporation items are divided into (1) nonseparately computed income or losses and (2) separately stated income, losses, deductions, and credits that uniquely could affect the tax liability of any shareholders. In essence, nonseparate items are lumped together into an undifferentiated amount that constitutes Subchapter S taxable income or loss. For example, any ordinary gains from the recapture provisions of §§ 1245 and 1250 constitute nonseparately computed income.

Each shareholder is allocated a pro rata portion of this nonseparately computed amount (see Example 23). If a shareholder dies during the year, his or her share of the pro rata items up to the date of death is reported on the final individual income tax return (see Example 24). Tax accounting and other elections are generally made at the corporate level, except for elections that shareholders may make separately (e.g., foreign tax credit election).

The following items, among others, are separately stated on Schedule K of the Form 1120S, and each shareholder takes into account his or her pro rata share (the share is passed through on a Schedule K–1).[32]

- Tax-exempt income.[33]
- Long-term and short-term capital gains and losses.
- Section 1231 gains and losses.
- Charitable contributions.
- Passive gains, losses, and credits.
- Certain portfolio income.
- Section 179 expense deduction.
- Tax preferences.
- Depletion.
- Foreign income or losses.
- Wagering gains or losses.
- Nonbusiness income or loss (§ 212).
- Recoveries of tax benefit items.
- Intangible drilling costs.
- Investment interest, income, and expenses.
- Total property distributions.
- Total dividend distributions from accumulated earnings and profits.

---

[30] §§ 248 and 1363(b).
[31] § 703(a)(2).
[32] §§ 1366(a) and (b).

[33] Tax-exempt income passes through to the shareholders and increases their tax basis in the stock.

This pro rata method assigns an equal amount of each of the S items to each day of the year. If a shareholder's stock holding changes during the year, this per-day method assigns the shareholder a pro rata share of each item for *each* day the stock is owned.

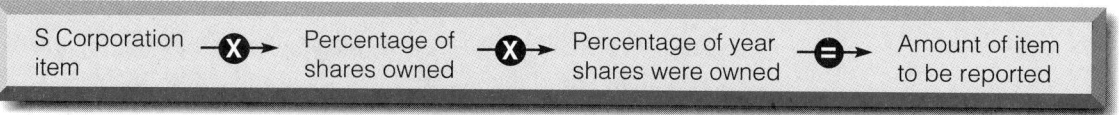

This per-day method must be used, unless the shareholder disposes of his or her entire interest in the entity.[34]

If a shareholder's interest is completely terminated during the tax year, all shareholders affected by the termination and the corporation may elect to treat the S taxable year as two taxable years, with the first year ending on the date of the termination. Under this election, an interim closing of the books is undertaken, and the affected shareholders report their shares of the S corporation items as they occurred during the year.[35] *Affected shareholders* include any whose interest is terminated, as well as all shareholders to whom such a shareholder transferred shares during the year. Where a shareholder transfers shares to the S corporation, affected shareholders include all persons who were shareholders during the year.

EXAMPLE 22

The following is the income statement for Beakon, an S corporation.

Sales		$ 40,000	
Less cost of sales		(23,000)	
Gross profit on sales		$ 17,000	
Less: Interest expense	$1,200		
Charitable contributions	400		
Advertising expenses	1,500		
Other operating expenses	2,000	(5,100)	
		$ 11,900	
Add: Tax-exempt interest		$ 300	
Dividend income		200	
Long-term capital gain		500	
		$1,000	
Less: Short-term capital loss		(150)	850
Net income per books			$12,750

Subchapter S taxable income for Beakon is calculated as follows, using net income for book purposes as a starting point.

Net income per books		$12,750
Separately computed items		
Deduct: Tax-exempt interest	$ 300	
Dividend income	200	
Long-term capital gain	500	
	($1,000)	

---

[34] §§ 1366(a)(1) and 1377(a)(1).   [35] § 1377(a)(2).

Add: Charitable contributions	$400	
Short-term capital loss	150 550	
Net effect of separately computed items		(450)
Subchapter S taxable income		$12,300

The $12,300 of Subchapter S taxable income, as well as the separately computed items, is divided among the shareholders based upon their stock ownership. ▼

EXAMPLE 23

Assume in Example 22 that shareholder Pat owned 10% of the stock for 100 days and 12% for the remaining 265 days. Using the required per-day allocation method, Pat's share of the S corporation items is as follows.

	Schedule K Totals	Pat's Share		Pat's Schedule K–1 Totals
		10%	12%	
Subchapter S taxable income	$12,300	$337	$1,072	$1,409
Tax-exempt interest	300	8	26	34
Dividend income	200	5	17	22
Long-term capital gain	500	14	44	58
Charitable contributions	400	11	35	46
Short-term capital loss	150	4	13	17

Pat's share of the Subchapter S taxable income is the total of $12,300 × [.10 × (100/365)] plus $12,300 × [.12 × (265/365)], or $1,409. Pat's Schedule K–1 totals flow through to Form 1040. ▼

EXAMPLE 24

If Pat in Example 23 dies after owning the stock 100 days, his share of the S corporation items is reported on his final Form 1040. Thus, only the items in the column labeled 10% in Example 23 are reported on Pat's final tax return. S corporation items that occur after a shareholder's death most likely would appear on the Form 1041 (estate's income tax return). ▼

The Code is silent as to the proper allocation of losses among shareholders with limited stock basis. Regulation §§ 1.1367–1(b)(2) and (c)(3) require a workable mix of the share-by-share and aggregate methods of calculating stock basis. In general, each shareholder must maintain records establishing the basis of each share. The Regulations use the separate-share basis calculations for positive adjustments, but losses and distributions are subject to the per-share rule.

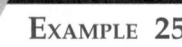

EXAMPLE 25

Ralph is a 50% owner of an S corporation for the entire year. His stock basis is $10,000, and his shares of the various corporate losses are as follows.

Ordinary loss from operations	$8,000
Section 1231 loss	3,000
Capital loss	5,000
Passive loss	2,000

Based upon a pro rata approach, the total $10,000 allocable flow-through would be split among the various losses as follows.

$$\text{Ordinary loss} = \frac{\$8,000}{\$18,000} \times \ 10,000 = \$ \ 4,444.44$$

$$\S \ 1231 \ \text{loss} \ = \frac{\$3,000}{\$18,000} \times \$10,000 = \ 1,666.67$$

$$\text{Capital loss} \ = \frac{\$5,000}{\$18,000} \times \$10,000 = \ 2,777.78$$

$$\text{Passive loss} \ = \frac{\$2,000}{\$18,000} \times \$10,000 = \ \underline{1,111.11}$$

Total allocated loss $\qquad\qquad\qquad$ $\underline{\$10,000.00}$

If Ralph has passive income of his own, he would prefer all of his corporate passive loss to flow through to be offset against his individual passive income. ▼

TAX TREATMENT OF DISTRIBUTIONS TO SHAREHOLDERS

The rules governing distributions to S shareholders blend tax entity and conduit approaches. A distribution to a shareholder of a C corporation is treated as ordinary dividend income to the extent of E & P, as a nontaxable return of capital until the stock basis reaches zero, and as a sale or exchange thereafter. To accommodate both preelection and postelection earnings, effectively a dormant C corporation exists within the distribution framework of an S corporation.

The amount of any distribution to an S corporation shareholder is equal to the cash plus the fair market value of any other property distributed. Either of two sets of distribution rules applies, depending upon whether the electing corporation has accumulated earnings and profits (AEP), e.g., from Subchapter C years.

A distribution by an S corporation having no AEP is not includible in gross income to the extent that it does not exceed the shareholder's adjusted basis in stock. When the amount of the distribution exceeds the adjusted basis of the stock, the excess is treated as a gain from the sale or exchange of property (capital gain in most cases).

EXAMPLE 26

Peacon, Inc., a calendar year S corporation, has no AEP. During 1997, Juan, an individual shareholder, receives a cash dividend of $12,200 from Peacon. Juan's basis in his stock is $9,700. Juan recognizes a capital gain from the cash distribution of $2,500, the excess of the distribution over the stock basis ($12,200 – $9,700). The remaining $9,700 is tax-free, but it reduces Juan's basis in the stock to zero. ▼

An S corporation should maintain an **accumulated adjustments account (AAA)** to help determine the nature of corporate distributions to a shareholder. Essentially, the AAA is a cumulative total of undistributed net income items for S corporation taxable years beginning after 1982. The AAA is adjusted in a similar fashion to the shareholder's stock basis, except there is no adjustment for tax-exempt income and related expenses or for Federal taxes attributable to a C corporation tax year. Further, any decreases in stock basis have no impact on AAA when the AAA balance is negative.

The AAA is a corporate account determined without regard to the circumstances of any shareholders.[36] In contrast, the shareholder basis in the stock investment is calculated at the shareholder level. Therefore, the AAA (unlike the stock basis) can have a negative balance. All losses decrease the AAA balance, even

---

[36] § 1368(e)(1)(A).

those in excess of the shareholder's stock basis. However, distributions may not make AAA negative or increase a negative balance.

The AAA is determined at the end of the year of a distribution rather than at the time the distribution is made. When more than one distribution occurs in the same year, a pro rata portion of each distribution is treated as having been made out of the AAA. This AAA procedure provides the mechanism for taxing the income of an S corporation only once.

In calculating the amount in the AAA for purposes of determining the tax treatment of distributions during a tax year by an S corporation with AEP, the net negative adjustments (e.g., the excess of losses and deductions over income) for that tax year are ignored.

Adjustments to AAA are made in a specified order.

Increase by:

1. Schedule K items other than tax-exempt income.
2. Nonseparately computed income.
3. Depletion in excess of basis in the property.

Decrease by:

4. Adjustments other than distributions (e.g., losses, deductions).
5. Any portion of a distribution that is considered to be tax-free from AAA (not below zero). (Note: 5 and 4 switch when an S corporation has AEP and net negative adjustments.)

Increase or decrease by:

6. Redemption distributions.

A shareholder has a proportionate interest in the AAA regardless of the size of his or her stock basis.[37] However, since the AAA is a corporate account, no connection exists between the prior accumulated S corporation income and any specific shareholder. Thus, the benefits of AAA can be shifted from one shareholder to another. For example, when an S shareholder transfers stock to another shareholder, any AAA on the purchase date is fully available to the purchaser. Similarly, issuing additional stock to a new shareholder in an S corporation having AAA dilutes the account relative to the existing shareholders.

A cash distribution from an S corporation with accumulated E & P is treated as follows.

1. Tax-free up to the amount in the AAA (limited to stock basis).
2. Any previously taxed income (PTI)[38] in the corporation under prior-law rules on a tax-free basis. However, PTI probably cannot be distributed in property other than cash [according to Reg. § 1.1375–4(b), under prior law].
3. The remaining distribution constitutes a dividend to the extent of AEP. With the consent of all of its shareholders, an S corporation may elect to have a distribution treated as made from AEP rather than from the AAA. This mechanism is known as an *AAA bypass election.* Otherwise, no adjustments are made to AEP during S years except for distributions taxed as dividends and adjustments from redemptions, liquidations, reorganizations, and divisions. For example, AEP can be acquired in a reorganization.

---

[37] § 1368(c).

[38] §§ 1368(c)(1) and (e)(1). Before 1983, an account similar to the AAA was in place, namely, previously taxed income (PTI). Any S corporations in existence before 1983 might have PTI, which currently may be distributed tax-free.

4. Any residual amount is applied against the shareholder's remaining basis in the stock.[39] This amount is considered to be a return of capital, which is not taxable. In this context, basis is reduced by the fair market value of the distributed asset.
5. Distributions that exceed the shareholder's tax basis for the stock are taxable as capital gains.

EXAMPLE 27

Tower, a calendar year S corporation, distributes $1,200 cash to its only shareholder, Otis, on December 31, 1997. Otis's basis in the stock is $100 on December 31, 1996, and the corporation has no AEP. For 1997, Tower Corporation had $1,000 of nonseparately computed income from operations, a $500 capital loss, and $400 tax-exempt income.

Otis must report $1,000 of income and $500 of deductions. The tax-exempt income is not taxed to Otis. His stock basis is increased by the $400 tax-exempt income and the $1,000 taxable income, and it is decreased by the $500 of deductions. The results of current operations affect the shareholder's basis before the application of the distribution rule.

Immediately before the distribution, Otis's stock basis is $1,000. Thus, $1,000 of the cash received is tax-free (as recovered AAA and stock basis). Since Otis's stock basis drops to zero, the additional $200 of the distribution is a $200 gain from the sale or exchange of stock ($1,200 – $1,000). Otis's AAA and stock basis are both zero as of December 31, 1997.

	Corporate AAA	Otis's Stock Basis
Balance, 1/1/97	–0–	$ 100
Nonseparately Computed Income	$1,000	1,000
Loss	(500)	(500)
Tax-exempt income	—	400
Subtotal	$ 500	$ 1,000
Distribution	(500)	(1,000)
Balance, 12/31/97	$ –0–	$ –0–

EXAMPLE 28

Assume the same facts as in Example 27, except that Tower had Subchapter C E & P of $750. Tower has an AAA of $500 ($1,000 – $500), which does not include the tax-exempt income. Otis's basis in the stock immediately before the distribution is $1,000 since his basis is increased by the tax-exempt income. Therefore, Otis is not taxed on the first $500, which is a recovery of the AAA. The next $700 is a taxable dividend from the AEP account. (Refer to the first column, step 3, of Concept Summary 12–1.)

Otis's basis in the stock is $500 ($1,000 – $500). Although the taxable portion of the distribution does not reduce Otis's basis in the stock, the nontaxable AAA distribution does. ▼

Where an S corporation has both pre-1983 and post-1982 AEP, for its first tax year beginning after December 31, 1996, the total AEP is reduced by the pre-1983 S corporation AEP, possibly eliminating either or both.

EXAMPLE 29

Collett, a calendar year S corporation, has pre-1983 S corporation AEP of $12,000 and total AEP of $20,000 in 1997. Collett Corporation may offset the $12,000 of pre-1983 S corporation AEP against the $20,000 of AEP, leaving a balance of $8,000 in AEP. ▼

---

[39] § 1368(c).

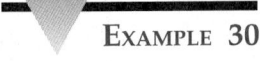

CONCEPT SUMMARY 12–1

Classification Procedures for Distributions from an S Corporation*

Where Earnings and Profits Exist	Where No Earnings and Profits Exist
1. Tax-free to the extent of accumulated adjustments account.**	
2. Any PTI from pre-1983 tax years can be distributed tax-free.	
3. Ordinary dividend from AEP.†	
4. Tax-free reduction in basis of stock.	1. Nontaxable to the extent of adjusted basis in stock.
5. Excess treated as gain from the sale or exchange of stock (capital gain in most cases).	2. Excess treated as gain from the sale or exchange of property (capital gain in most cases).

*A distribution of appreciated property by an electing corporation results in recognized gain that first is allocated to and reported by the shareholders.
**Once stock basis reaches zero, any distribution from AAA is treated as a gain from the sale or exchange of stock. Thus, basis is an upper limit on what a shareholder may receive tax-free.
†An AAA bypass election is available to pay out AEP before reducing the AAA [§ 1368(e)(3)]. For its first taxable year beginning after 1996, an S corporation may reduce the total AEP by any pre-1983 AEP from an S tax year.

The distribution adjustments made by an S corporation during a tax year are taken into account *before* applying the loss limitation for the year. Thus, distributions during a year reduce the adjusted basis for determining the allowable loss for the year, but the loss for the year does *not* reduce the adjusted basis for purposes of determining the tax status of the distributions made during the year.

EXAMPLE 30

Lindstrom, a calendar year S corporation, is partly owned by Doris, who has a beginning stock basis of $10,000. During the year, Doris's share of a long-term capital gain is $2,000, and her share of an ordinary loss is $9,000. If Doris receives a $6,000 distribution, the deductible loss of $6,000 is calculated as follows.

Beginning stock basis	$10,000
Add: LTCG	2,000
Subtotal	$12,000
Less: Distribution	6,000
Basis for loss limitation	$ 6,000
Deductible loss	$ (6,000)
Ending stock basis	$ -0-
Unused loss	($ 3,000)

EXAMPLE 31

Majorie is a shareholder in a calendar year S corporation in 1997. At the beginning of the year, her stock basis is $10,000, her share of AAA is $2,000, and her share of corporate AEP is $5,000. She receives a $6,000 distribution, and her share of S items includes a $2,000 long-term capital gain and a $9,000 ordinary loss. The effects of these events on AAA, stock basis, and AEP are as follows.

	AAA	**Stock Basis**	**AEP**
Beginning balances	$ 2,000	$10,000	$ 5,000
LTCG	2,000	2,000	No Effect
Balance	$ 4,000	$12,000	$ 5,000
Less: Distribution ($6,000)	(4,000)	4,000	(2,000)
Balance	$ –0–	$ 8,000	$ 3,000
Loss ($9,000)	(9,000)	(8,000)	No Effect
Ending balances	($ 9,000)	$ –0–	$ 3,000
Unused loss		$ (1,000)	

Schedule M–2. Schedule M–2 on page 4 of Form 1120S (reproduced below) contains a column labeled "Other adjustments account." Essentially, this account includes items not used in the calculation of the AAA, such as tax-exempt income and any related nondeductible expenses. However, distributions from this account are not taxable. Once the E & P account reaches zero, distributions fall under the two-tier system: (1) nontaxable to the extent of basis, then (2) capital gain. Moreover, there is no need for an "other adjustments account" when a corporation has no AEP.

EXAMPLE 32

During 1997, Sparrow Corporation, a qualifying S corporation, records the following items.

Accumulated adjustments account, beginning of year	$ 8,500
Prior-taxed income, beginning of year	6,250
Ordinary income	25,000
Tax-exempt interest	4,000
Key employee life insurance proceeds received	5,000
Payroll penalty expense	2,000
Charitable contributions	3,000
Unreasonable compensation	5,000
Premiums on key employee life insurance	2,100
Distributions to shareholders	16,000

Sparrow's Schedule M–2 for the current year appears as follows.

Schedule M-2	**Analysis of Accumulated Adjustments Account, Other Adjustments Account, and Shareholders' Undistributed Taxable Income Previously Taxed** (see page 22 of the instructions)		
	(a) Accumulated adjustments account	**(b) Other adjustments account**	**(c) Shareholders' undistributed taxable income previously taxed**
1 Balance at beginning of tax year . . .	8,500		6,250
2 Ordinary income from page 1, line 21 . .	25,000		
3 Other additions		9,000**	
4 Loss from page 1, line 21.	( )		
5 Other reductions	(10,000*)	(2,100)	
6 Combine lines 1 through 5	23,500	6,900	
7 Distributions other than dividend distributions .	16,000		
8 Balance at end of tax year. Subtract line 7 from line 6	7,500	6,900	6,250

*$2,000 (payroll penalty) + $3,000 (charitable contributions) + $5,000 (unreasonable compensation).
**$4,000 (tax-exempt interest) + $5,000 (life insurance proceeds).

Any distribution of *cash* by the corporation with respect to the stock during a post-termination transition period of approximately one year is applied against and reduces the adjusted basis of the stock, to the extent that the amount of the distribution does not exceed the AAA.[40] Thus, a terminated S corporation should make a cash distribution during this post-termination period to the extent of all previously undistributed net income items for all S tax years. Since only cash distributions reduce the AAA during this post-termination period, the C corporation should not make any property distributions. Most likely, the entity should sell any property and distribute the proceeds.

EXAMPLE 33

Quinn, the sole shareholder of Pistol, Inc., a calendar year S corporation during 1996, elects to terminate the S election, effective January 1, 1997. As of the end of 1996, Pistol has an AAA of $1,300. Quinn can receive a nontaxable distribution of cash during a post-termination transition period of approximately one year to the extent of Pistol's AAA. Although a cash distribution of $1,300 during 1997 would be nontaxable to Quinn, it would reduce the adjusted basis of his stock. ▼

Alternative Minimum Tax. An S corporation is not directly subject to the alternative minimum tax (AMT). Under the conduit approach, all tax preference items flow through the S corporation to be included in the shareholders' AMT calculations. The allocation of the tax preference items is based upon the pro rata daily allocation method, unless the corporation has elected the interim closing-of-the-books method. Each shareholder includes the proper portion of each tax preference item in his or her AMT calculations. For a list of tax preference items, see Chapter 6.

An S corporation has the advantage of calculating tax preference items using individual, rather than corporate, rules. Thus, the S corporation has no adjusted current earnings (ACE) amount. For corporations with large ACE adjustments, an S election can be quite attractive. Recall, though, that the 26/28 percent individual AMT rates are higher than the corresponding 20 percent corporate rate.

EXAMPLE 34

During the year, an S corporation has a positive AMT adjustment of $45,000 for mining exploration costs, an excess depletion tax preference of $70,000, and a certified pollution control facility preference of $10,000. The positive ACE adjustment is $80,000. If Donald is a 10% shareholder, he is assigned 10% of $45,000, $70,000, and $10,000 as tax preference items ($4,500 + $7,000 + $1,000), but he generates no ACE adjustment. ▼

An S corporation is allowed to use the amount of any AMT credit carryover arising in a C corporation tax year as an offset against the built-in gains tax.

CORPORATE TREATMENT OF CERTAIN PROPERTY DISTRIBUTIONS

An S corporation recognizes a gain on any distribution of appreciated property (other than in a reorganization) in the same manner as if the asset had been sold to the shareholder at its fair market value.[41] The corporate gain is passed through to the shareholders. There is an important reason for this rule. Without it, property might be distributed tax-free (other than for certain recapture items) and later sold without income recognition to the shareholder because the stepped-up basis

---

[40]§§ 1371(e) and 1377(b).

[41]§ 311(b).

equals the asset's fair market value. The character of the gain—capital gain or ordinary income—depends upon the type of asset being distributed.

The S corporation does not recognize a loss for assets that are worth less than their basis. Furthermore, when such property is distributed, the shareholder's basis in the asset is equal to the asset's fair market value. Thus, the potential loss is postponed until the shareholder sells the stock of the S corporation. Since loss property receives a step-down in basis without any loss recognition by the S corporation, such dividend distributions should be avoided. See Concept Summary 12–2.

▼ **EXAMPLE 35**

Blue, Inc., an S corporation for 10 years, distributes a tract of land held as an investment to its majority shareholder. The land was purchased for $22,000 many years ago and is currently worth $82,000. Blue recognizes a capital gain of $60,000, which increases the AAA by $60,000. Then the property distribution reduces AAA by $82,000 (the fair market value). The tax consequences are the same for appreciated property, whether it is distributed to the shareholders and they dispose of it, or the corporation sells the property and distributes the proceeds to the shareholders.

If the land were purchased for $80,000 many years ago and is currently worth $30,000, the $50,000 realized loss is not recognized at the corporate level, and the shareholder receives a $30,000 basis in the land. The $50,000 realized loss disappears from the corporate level. Since loss is not recognized on the distribution of property that has declined in value, the AAA is not reduced by the unrecognized loss. To recognize the loss on such property, the property must be sold by the S corporation to an unrelated party. ▼

▼ **EXAMPLE 36**

Assume the same facts as in Example 35, except that Blue is a C corporation or a partnership. The partner's basis in the partnership is $25,000.

Appreciated Property			
	S Corporation	**C Corporation**	**Partnership**
Entity gain/loss	$60,000	$60,000	$–0–
Owner's gain/loss/dividend	60,000	82,000*	–0–
Owner's basis	82,000	82,000	22,000

Property That Has Declined in Value			
	S Corporation	**C Corporation**	**Partnership**
Entity gain/loss	$–0–	$–0–	$–0–
Owner's gain/loss/dividend	–0–	30,000*	–0–
Owner's basis	30,000	30,000	25,000 ▼

*Assume sufficient E & P.

SHAREHOLDER'S TAX BASIS

The calculation of the initial tax basis of stock in an S corporation is similar to that for the basis of stock in a C corporation and depends upon the manner in which the shares are acquired (e.g., gift, inheritance, purchase). When a shareholder transfers to an S corporation property that is encumbered by a mortgage, the assumed liability reduces the shareholder's basis in the stock. Once the initial tax basis is determined, various transactions during the life of the corporation affect the shareholder's basis in the stock. Although each shareholder is required to

CONCEPT SUMMARY 12–2

Distribution of Property

	Appreciated Property	Depreciated Property
S corporation	Realized gain is recognized to the corporation, which passes it through to the shareholders. Such gain increases a shareholder's stock basis, generating a basis in the property equal to FMV. On the distribution, the shareholder's stock basis is reduced by the FMV of the property (but not below zero).	Realized loss is not recognized. The shareholder assumes an FMV basis in the property. Loss is postponed indefinitely.
C corporation	Realized gain is recognized under § 311(b) and increases E & P (net of tax). The shareholder assumes an FMV basis and has an FMV taxable dividend.	Realized loss is not recognized.
Partnership	No gain to the partnership or partner. Basis to the partner is limited to the partner's basis in the partnership.	Realized loss is not recognized.

compute his or her own basis in the S shares, neither Form 1120S nor Schedule K–1 provides a place for deriving this amount. See Concept Summary 12–3.

A shareholder's basis is increased by further stock purchases and capital contributions. Operations during the year also cause the following upward adjustments to basis.[42]

- Nonseparately computed income.
- Separately stated income items (e.g., nontaxable income).
- Depletion in excess of basis in the property.

Basis then is reduced by distributions not reported as income by the shareholder (e.g., an AAA or PTI distribution). Next, the following items cause a downward adjustment to basis (but not below zero) in this order.

- Nondeductible expenses of the corporation (e.g., fines, penalties, illegal kickbacks).
- Nonseparately computed loss.
- Separately stated loss and deduction items.

As under the partnership rule, basis is first increased by income items; then it is decreased by distributions and finally by losses. Pass-through items (other than distributions) that reduce stock basis are governed by special ordering rules. Noncapital, nondeductible expenditures reduce stock basis before losses or deductible items. A taxpayer may irrevocably elect under Regulation § 1.1367–1(f) to have deductible items pass through before any noncapital, nondeductible items. In most cases, this election is advantageous.

---

[42] § 1367(a).

CONCEPT SUMMARY 12–3

Adjustments to Stock Basis and AAA

	Stock Basis*	AAA
Original basis (e.g., purchase, inheritance, gift)	Increase	No effect
Stock purchases	Increase	No effect
Taxable income items	Increase	Increase
Nontaxable income	Increase	No effect
Capital gains	Increase	Increase
Deductible expenses	Decrease	Decrease
Expenses related to tax-exempt income	Decrease	No effect
Losses (ordinary and capital)	Decrease	Decrease
LIFO recapture tax at S election	Decrease	No effect
Depletion in excess of basis	Increase	Increase
Depletion (not in excess of basis)	Decrease	Decrease
Corporate distributions (FMV)	Decrease†	Decrease*†

*Can never go below zero.
†Only by tax-free distributions under § 1367(a)(2)(A), and only after the income adjustment.

EXAMPLE 37

In its first year of operations, Pell, Inc., a calendar year S corporation, earns income of $2,000. On February 2 in its second year of operations, Pell distributes $2,000 to Marty, its sole shareholder. During the remainder of the second year, the corporation incurs a $2,000 loss.

Under the S corporation ordering rules, the $2,000 distribution is tax-free AAA to Marty, and the loss is *not* passed through because the stock basis cannot be reduced below zero. ▼

A shareholder's basis in the stock can never be reduced below zero. Any further downward adjustment (losses or deductions) in excess of the stock basis is applied to reduce (but not below zero) the shareholder's basis in any indebtedness from the electing corporation. Any excess of losses or deductions over both bases is *suspended* until there are subsequent bases. Once the basis of any debt is reduced, it is later increased (only up to the original amount) by the subsequent *net* increase resulting from *all* positive and negative basis adjustments. The debt basis is adjusted before any increase is made in the stock basis.[43] A distribution below stock basis does not reduce any debt basis. If a loss and a distribution occur in the same year, the loss reduces the basis after the distribution.[44]

EXAMPLE 38

Stacey, a sole shareholder, has a $7,000 stock basis and a $2,000 basis in a loan that she made to a calendar year S corporation at the beginning of 1997. Subchapter S net income during 1997 is $8,200. The corporation incurred a short-term capital loss of $2,300 and received

---

[43] § 1367(b)(2).

[44] §§ 1366(d)(1)(A) and 1368(d)(1).

$2,000 of tax-exempt interest income. Cash of $15,000 is distributed to Stacey on November 15, 1997. As a result, Stacey's basis in her stock is zero, and her loan basis is still $2,000 at the end of 1997, since only losses and deductions (and not distributions) reduce the debt basis. Stacey recognizes a $100 gain ($15,000 – $14,900). See Concept Summaries 12–2 and 12–3.

	Corporate AAA	Stacey's Stock Basis	Stacey's Loan Basis
Beginning balance	$ –0–	$ 7,000	$2,000
S net income	8,200	8,200	–0–
Tax-exempt income	–0–	2,000	–0–
Short-term capital loss	(2,300)	(2,300)	–0–
Subtotal	$ 5,900	$ 14,900	$2,000
Distribution ($15,000)	(5,900)	(14,900)	–0–
Ending balance	$ –0–	$ –0–	$2,000

Although stock basis cannot be reduced below zero, the $100 excess distribution does not reduce Stacey's loan basis. ▼

The basis rules for an S corporation are somewhat similar to the rules for determining a partner's interest basis in a partnership. However, a partner's basis in the partnership interest includes the partner's direct investment plus a ratable share of any partnership liabilities.[45] Conversely, corporate borrowing has no effect on the stock basis of an S corporation shareholder. If a partnership borrows from a partner, the partner receives a basis increase as if the partnership had borrowed from an unrelated third party.[46] In a similar fashion, an S corporation shareholder has a tax basis in any loan made to the entity, but only by himself or herself. Although S losses may be applied against such loan basis, partnership losses do not reduce a partner's loan basis.

Certain items, such as disallowed accrued salary to an S shareholder or discharge of indebtedness income excluded from gross income, are deferred at the corporate level. They do not affect stock basis until the S corporation takes them into account in computing its taxable income.

TREATMENT OF LOSSES

Net Operating Loss.   One major advantage of an S election is the ability to pass through any net operating loss (NOL) of the corporation directly to the shareholders. A shareholder can deduct such a loss for the year in which the S corporation's tax year ends. The corporation is not entitled to any deduction for the NOL. The individual shareholder's loss is deducted as a deduction *for* AGI. A shareholder's basis in the stock is reduced to the extent of any pass-through of the NOL, and the shareholder's AAA is reduced by the same deductible amount.[47]

EXAMPLE 39

An S corporation incurs a $20,000 NOL for the current year. At all times during the tax year, the stock was owned equally by the same 10 shareholders. Each shareholder is entitled to deduct $2,000 *for* AGI for the tax year in which the corporate tax year ends. ▼

---

[45] § 752(a).
[46] Reg. § 1.752–1(e).

[47] §§ 1368(a)(1)(A) and (e)(1)(A).

Net operating losses are allocated among shareholders in the same manner. NOLs are allocated on a daily basis to all shareholders.[48] Transferred shares are considered to be held by the transferee (not the transferor) on the date of the transfer.[49]

Deductions for an S corporation's NOL pass-through cannot exceed a shareholder's adjusted basis in the stock *plus* the basis of any loans made by the shareholder to the corporation. If a taxpayer is unable to prove the tax basis, the NOL pass-through can be denied.[50] In essence, a shareholder's stock or loan basis cannot go below zero. As noted previously, once a shareholder's adjusted stock basis has been eliminated by an NOL, any excess NOL is used to reduce the shareholder's basis for any loans made to the corporation (but never below zero). The basis for loans is established by the actual advances made to the corporation and not by indirect loans.[51] If the shareholder's basis is insufficient to allow a full flow-through and there is more than one type of loss (e.g., in the same year the taxpayer incurs both a passive loss and a net capital loss), the flow-through amounts are determined on a pro rata basis.

When a shareholder has acquired stock at different times and for varying amounts, a separate-share method is used,[52] rather than a unitary approach.[53] Under the separate-share approach, the basis of each share of stock is increased or decreased by an amount equal to the owner's pro rata portion of an income or loss item, determined on a per-share, per-day basis. Thus, an S corporation maintains a separate basis account for each block of stock. A spillover rule allows a shareholder to apply losses or distributions attributable to one share of stock that are in excess of its basis against the basis of all other stock owned by the shareholder. Where a net basis reduction exceeds a shareholder's total available stock basis for a tax year, any excess (other than distributions) reduces the shareholder's debt basis (but not below zero).

EXAMPLE 40

On December 31, 1997, Erica owns one share of an S corporation's 10 outstanding shares of stock. The basis of Erica's share is $300. On July 3, 1998, Erica purchases 2 shares from another shareholder for $250 each. During 1998, the S corporation has no income or deductions, but incurs a loss of $3,650. Under the separate-share approach, the amount of the loss assigned to each day of the S corporation's tax year is $10 ($3,650 ÷ 365 days). For each day, $1 is allocated to each outstanding share ($10 ÷ 10 shares).

Since Erica owned one share for 365 days, a $365 loss is attributable to that share ($1 × 365 days). Since she owned the other two shares for 182 days, the basis of each of these shares is reduced by $182 ($1 × 182 days). Because the decrease in basis attributable to the first share exceeds its basis by $65 ($365 − $300), the excess is applied proportionately to reduce the remaining bases of the other two shares; thus, each is reduced by $32.50 [$65 × ($68/$136)]. After this reduction, each of the two shares has a $35.50 basis. ▼

Except in the Eleventh Circuit, the fact that a shareholder has guaranteed a loan made to the corporation by a third party has no effect upon the shareholder's loan basis, unless payments have actually been made as a result of the guarantee.[54] If the corporation defaults on an indebtedness and the shareholder makes good on

---

[48] § 1377(a)(1).

[49] Reg. § 1.1374–1(b)(3).

[50] See *Donald J. Sauvigne*, 30 TCM 123, T.C.Memo. 1971–30.

[51] *Ruth M. Prashker*, 59 T.C. 172 (1972); *Frederick G. Brown v. U.S.*, 83–1 USTC ¶9364, 52 AFTR2d 82–5080, 706 F.2d 755 (CA–6, 1983).

[52] Reg. §§ 1.1367–1(b)(2) and (c)(3).

[53] A unitary approach would require that the shareholder's total basis be evenly distributed over all shares owned.

[54] See, for example, *Estate of Leavitt*, 90 T.C. 206 (1988), aff'd. 89–1 USTC ¶9332, 63 AFTR2d 89–1437, 875 F.2d 420 (CA–4, 1989); *Selfe v. U.S.*, 86–1 USTC ¶9115, 57 AFTR2d 86–464, 778 F.2d 769 (CA–11, 1985); *James K. Calcutt*, 91 T.C. 14 (1988).

the guarantee, the shareholder's indebtedness basis is increased to that extent.[55] Such a subsequent increase in basis has no influence on the results of a prior year in which an NOL exceeded a shareholder's adjusted basis. See Concept Summary 12–3 for adjustments to stock basis and AAA.

A shareholder's share of an NOL may be greater than both the basis in the stock and the basis of the indebtedness. A shareholder is entitled to carry forward a loss to the extent that the loss for the year exceeds both the stock basis and the loan basis. Any loss carried forward may be deducted *only* by the same shareholder if and when the basis in the stock of or loans to the corporation is restored.[56]

Any loss carryover remaining at the end of an approximately one-year post-termination transition period is lost forever.[57] The post-termination transition period ends on the later of (1) one year after the effective date of the termination of the S election or the due date for the last S return (whichever is later) or (2) 120 days after the determination that the corporation's S election had terminated for a previous year. The post-termination period includes the 120-day period beginning on the date of any determination pursuant to an audit of a taxpayer that follows the termination of the S corporation's election and that adjusts a Subchapter S item. Further, the period includes a final disposition by the Secretary of the Treasury of a claim for a refund and agreements between the Secretary and any person related to tax liability. Thus, if a shareholder has a loss carryover, he or she should increase the stock or loan basis and flow through the loss before disposing of the stock.

EXAMPLE 41

Dana holds a stock basis of $4,000 in an S corporation. He has loaned $2,000 to the corporation and has guaranteed another $4,000 loan made to the corporation by a local bank. Although his share of the S corporation's NOL for the current year is $9,500, Dana may deduct only $6,000 of the NOL on his individual tax return. Dana may carry forward $3,500 of the NOL, to be deducted when the basis in his stock or loan to the corporation is restored. Dana has a zero basis in both the stock and the loan after the flow-through of the $6,000 NOL. ▼

Net operating losses from C corporation years cannot be utilized at the corporate level (except with respect to built-in gains), nor can they be passed through to the shareholders. Further, the carryforward period continues to run during S status.[58] Consequently, it may not be appropriate for a corporation that has unused NOLs to make the S election. When a corporation is expecting losses in the future, an S election should be made before the loss year.

If a loan's basis has been reduced and is not restored, income is recognized when the loan is repaid. If the corporation issued a note as evidence of the debt, repayment constitutes an amount received in exchange for a capital asset, and the amount that exceeds the shareholder's basis is entitled to capital gain treatment.[59] However, if the loan is made on open account, the repayment constitutes ordinary income to the extent that it exceeds the shareholder's basis in the loan. Each repayment is prorated between the gain portion and the repayment of the debt.[60] Thus, a note should be given to assure capital gain treatment for the income that results from a loan's repayment.

[55] Rev.Rul. 70–50, 1970–1 C.B. 178.
[56] § 1366(d).
[57] § 1377(b).
[58] § 1371(b).

[59] *Joe M. Smith*, 48 T.C. 872 (1967), *aff'd.* and *rev'd.* in 70–1 USTC ¶9327, 25 AFTR2d 70–936, 424 F.2d 219 (CA–9, 1970), and Rev.Rul. 64–162, 1964–1 C.B. 304.
[60] Rev.Rul. 68–537, 1968–2 C.B. 372.

Since the basis rule requires that corporate income be used to restore debt basis before it can be used to restore stock basis, a double tax on current income can result. Any current income distributed, after both debt and stock basis have been reduced to zero, is taxed as capital gain because it is considered a return of capital, but only to the extent of stock basis. To avoid this double tax, shareholders should consider forgiving debt that a solvent S corporation owes them. Such a forgiveness is considered a contribution of capital, with a resulting increase in the shareholder's stock basis. For an insolvent S corporation, discharge of indebtedness income is tax-deferred (not tax-exempt) and does not increase the shareholder's basis.

Passive Losses and Credits.   Section 469 provides that net passive losses and credits are not deductible when incurred and must be carried over to a year when there is passive income. Thus, one must be aware of three major classes of income, losses, and credits—active, portfolio, and passive. S corporations are not directly subject to the limits of § 469, but corporate rental activities are inherently passive, and other activities of an S corporation may be passive unless a shareholder materially participates in operating the business. An S corporation may engage in more than one such activity. If the corporate activity is rental or the shareholder does not materially participate, any passive losses or credits flow through. The shareholders are able to apply them only against income from other passive activities at the shareholder level. A passive activity loss is the amount by which passive deductions exceed any passive gross income. A shareholder's stock basis is reduced by passive losses that flow through to the shareholder, even though the shareholder may not be entitled to a current deduction due to the passive loss limitations. In general, elections involving the aggregation of amounts are made at the entity level, but they affect each of the individual shareholders.

Regular, continuous, and substantial involvement in the S corporation is necessary to meet the material participation requirement. The existence of material participation is determined at the shareholder level. There are seven tests for material participation, including a need to participate in the activity for more than 500 hours during the taxable year.[61]

EXAMPLE 42

Heather is a 50% owner of an S corporation engaged in a passive activity under § 469. Heather, a nonparticipating shareholder, receives a salary of $6,000 for services as a result of the passive activity. This deduction creates a $6,000 passive loss at the corporate level. Heather has $6,000 of earned income as a result of the salary. The $6,000 salary creates a $6,000 deduction/passive loss, which flows through to the shareholders. Heather's $3,000 share of the loss may not be deducted against the $6,000 earned income. Under § 469(e)(3), earned income is not taken into account in computing the income or loss from a passive activity. ▼

At-Risk Rules.   The at-risk rules generally apply to S corporation shareholders. Essentially, an amount at risk is determined separately for each shareholder. The amount of the corporation's losses that are passed through and deductible by the shareholders is not affected by the amount the corporation has at risk. A shareholder usually is considered at risk with respect to an activity to the extent of cash and the adjusted basis of other property contributed to the electing corporation, any amount borrowed for use in the activity for which the taxpayer has personal liability for payment from personal assets, and the net fair market value

---

[61] Reg. § 1.469–5T(a).

CONCEPT SUMMARY 12–4

Treatment of Losses

Step 1.   Allocate total loss to the shareholder on a daily basis, based upon stock ownership.

Step 2.   If the shareholder's loss exceeds his or her stock basis, apply any excess to adjusted basis of indebtedness to the shareholder. Losses from distributions do not reduce debt basis.

Step 3.   Where loss exceeds the debt basis, any excess is suspended and carried over to succeeding tax years.

Step 4.   In succeeding tax years, any net increase (resulting from *all* positive and negative basis adjustments) restores the debt basis first, up to its original amount.

Step 5.   Once debt basis is restored, any net increase remaining is used to increase stock basis.

Step 6.   Any suspended loss from a previous year now reduces stock basis first and debt basis second.

Step 7.   If the S election terminates, any suspended loss carryover may be deducted during the post-termination transition period to the extent of the *stock* basis at the end of this period. Any loss remaining at the end of the period is lost forever.

of personal assets that secure nonrecourse borrowing.[62] Any losses that are suspended under the at-risk rules are carried forward and are available during the post-termination transition period. The S stock basis limitations and at-risk limitations are applied before the passive activity limitations.[63]

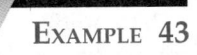

EXAMPLE 43   Shareholder Carl has a basis of $35,000 in his S corporation stock. He takes a $15,000 nonrecourse loan from a local bank and lends the proceeds to the S corporation. Carl now has a stock basis of $35,000 and a debt basis of $15,000. However, due to the at-risk limitation, he can deduct only $35,000 of losses from the S corporation. ▼

TAX ON PREELECTION BUILT-IN GAINS

Because Congress was concerned that certain C corporations would elect S status to avoid the corporate income tax on the sale or exchange of appreciated property (avoid a tax on built-in gains), it completely revamped § 1374. A C corporation converting to S status after 1986 generally incurs a corporate-level tax on any built-in gains when the S corporation disposes of an asset in a taxable disposition within 10 calendar years after the date on which the S election took effect.

General Rules. The **built-in gains tax** is applied to any unrealized gain attributable to appreciation in the value of an asset (e.g., real estate, cash basis receivables, goodwill) or other income items while held by the C corporation. The highest corporate tax rate (applicable to that type of income) is applied to the lesser of (1) the recognized built-in gains of the S corporation for the tax year or (2) the amount that would be the taxable income of the corporation for that tax year if it were a C corporation. Any built-in gain that escapes taxation due to the taxable income limitation is carried forward to future tax years. Then it is treated as recognized built-in gain. Thus, given a low or negative taxable income in any year when built-in gain assets are sold, the taxpayer defers the payment of the

---

[62] The at-risk rules and their significance for income tax purposes are discussed in Chapter 11.

[63] Reg. § 1.469–2T(d)(6).

built-in gains penalty tax liability. The total amount of gain that is ever recognized is limited to the aggregate net built-in gains of the corporation at the time it is converted to S status. Thus, it may be advisable to obtain an independent appraisal when converting a C corporation to an S corporation. Certainly, a memorandum should be prepared listing the fair market values of all assets, along with the methods used to arrive at the values.

EXAMPLE 44

Marble is a former C corporation whose first S corporation year began on January 1, 1997. At that time, Marble had two assets: X, with a value of $1,000 and a basis of $400, and Y, with a value of $400 and a basis of $600. Thus, net unrealized built-in gains as of January 1, 1997, are $400. If asset X is sold for $1,000 during 1997 and asset Y is retained, the recognized built-in gain is limited to $400. ▼

EXAMPLE 45

Assume the same facts as in Example 44, except that Marble's taxable income in 1997 is $300. The built-in gains tax is assessed only on $300. However, the $100 recognized built-in gain that is not taxed in 1997 is carried forward and treated as recognized built-in gain in 1998. There is no statutory limit on the carryforward period, but the gain would effectively expire at the end of the 10-year recognition period applicable to all built-in gains (except for installment sales after March 25, 1990).[64] ▼

ETHICAL CONSIDERATIONS

A Helpful Appraisal

Scuba Unlimited, a diving center in Miami, Florida, is in the process of converting to S corporation status. Some of the assets of the company are highly appreciated.

Jason, the company's accountant, is familiar with the problems of the § 1374 built-in gains tax. His cousin, a qualified appraiser, has agreed to "lowball" the appraisal of the S corporation's assets. How would you react in Jason's situation?

Gains on sales or distributions of all assets by an S corporation are presumed to be built-in gains unless the taxpayer can establish that the appreciation accrued after the conversion. This § 1374 tax is avoided if the S election was made before 1987.[65]

Under § 1366(f)(2), any tax imposed on a built-in gain is treated as a loss that passes through to the shareholder. The character of the loss depends upon the character of the recognized built-in gain giving rise to the built-in gains tax. Postconversion appreciation is subject to the regular S corporation pass-through rules.

EXAMPLE 46

Monkey Corporation elects S status, effective for calendar year 1996. As of January 1, 1996, one of Monkey's capital assets has a basis of $50,000 and a fair market value of $110,000. Early in 1997, the asset is sold for $135,000. Monkey incurs a realized gain of $85,000, of which $60,000 is subject to the § 1374 penalty tax of 35%. The entire $85,000 gain is subject to the corporate pass-through rules (reduced by the built-in gains tax itself), but only $25,000 of the gain fully bypasses the corporate income tax. The built-in gains tax flows through to the shareholders as a capital loss. ▼

---

[64] § 1374(d)(7); Notice 90–27, 1990–1 C.B. 336.   [65] § 1362.

Normally, tax attributes of a C corporation do not carry over to a converted S corporation. For purposes of the tax on built-in gains, however, certain carryovers are allowed. An S corporation can offset these gains by related attributes from prior C corporation years such as unexpired NOLs or capital losses. In a similar manner, AMT credit carryovers (arising in a C corporation tax year) and business credit carryforwards are allowed to offset the built-in gains tax.

EXAMPLE 47

Assume the same facts as in Example 46, except that Monkey also had a $10,000 NOL carryover when it elected S status. The NOL reduces Monkey's built-in gain from $60,000 to $50,000. Thus, only $50,000 is subject to the § 1374 penalty tax. ▼

EXAMPLE 48

An S corporation has a built-in gain of $100,000 and taxable income of $90,000. The built-in gains tax liability is calculated as follows.

Lesser of taxable income or built-in gain	$ 90,000
Less: NOL carryforward from C year	(12,000)
Capital loss carryforward from C year	(8,000)
Tax base	$ 70,000
Highest corporate tax rate	.35
Tentative tax	$ 24,500
Less: Business credit carryforward from C year	(4,000)
AMT credit carryforward from C year	(3,000)
Built-in gains tax liability	$ 17,500

The $10,000 realized (but not taxed) built-in gain in excess of taxable income may be carried forward to the next year, as long as the next year is within the 10-year recognition period. ▼

Concept Summary 12–5 summarizes the calculation of the built-in gains tax.

The § 1374 tax is applied to the net recognized built-in gain of the former C corporation on the date of conversion to S status. Thus, loss assets on the date of conversion reduce the recognized built-in gains and any potential tax under § 1374.[66] However, the IRS indicates that contributions of loss property within two years before the earlier of the date of conversion or the date of filing an S election are presumed to have a tax avoidance motive and will not reduce the corporation's net unrealized built-in gain. Other losses incurred by the electing corporation during the year offset any built-in gains in arriving at net recognized gains.

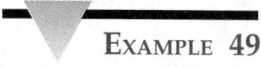

EXAMPLE 49

Donna owns all of the stock of an S corporation, which in turn owns two assets on the S conversion date: asset 1 (basis of $5,000 and FMV of $4,000) and asset 2 (basis of $1,000 and FMV of $5,000). The S corporation has a potential net realized built-in gain of $3,000 (i.e., the built-in gain of $4,000 in asset 2 reduced by the built-in loss of $1,000 in asset 1). If both assets are sold in the same tax year, the loss is netted against the gain before any flow-through to Donna. ▼

Advisably, the taxpayer should maximize built-in losses at the conversion date and minimize the built-in gain assets. For example, a cash basis S corporation can accomplish this by reducing receivables, accelerating payables, and accruing compensation costs. To reduce or defer the penalty tax, the taxpayer might also minimize taxable income in any year when built-in gain assets are sold. Finally,

---

[66] § 1374(c)(2) and (d)(1).

CONCEPT SUMMARY 12–5

Calculation of Built-in Gains Tax Liability

Step 1.   Select the smaller of built-in gains or taxable income.*

Step 2.   Deduct unexpired NOLs and capital losses from a C corporation tax year.

Step 3.   Multiply the tax base obtained in step 2 by the top corporate tax rate.

Step 4.   Deduct any business credit carryforwards and AMT credit carryovers arising in a C corporation tax year from the amount obtained in step 3.

Step 5.   The corporation pays any tax resulting in step 4.

*Any net recognized built-in gain in excess of taxable income may be carried forward to the next year, as long as the next year is within the 10-year recognition period.

realized built-in losses reduce the § 1374 tax liability only if they occur in a year when built-in gains are also realized.

The total amount of built-in gains tax is reduced by the portion of excess net passive income subject to the § 1375 tax that is attributable to the gain.

LIFO Recapture Tax. When a corporation uses the FIFO method for its last year before making the S election, any built-in gain is recognized and taxed as the inventory is sold. A LIFO-basis corporation does not recognize this gain, unless the corporation invades the LIFO layer during the 10-year recognition period. To preclude deferral of gain recognition under LIFO, the law requires a LIFO recapture amount upon making an S election.

A C corporation using LIFO for its last year before making an S election must include in income the excess of the inventory's value under FIFO over the LIFO value. No negative adjustment is allowed if the LIFO value is higher than the FIFO value. The increase in tax liability resulting from LIFO recapture is payable in four equal installments, with the first payment due on or before the due date for the corporate return for the last C corporation year (without regard to any extensions). The remaining three installments must be paid on or before the due dates of the succeeding corporate returns. No interest is due if payments are made by the due dates, and no estimated taxes are due on the four tax installments. The basis of the LIFO inventory is adjusted to take into account this LIFO recapture amount, but AAA is not decreased by payment of the tax.

EXAMPLE 50

Engelage Corporation converts to S corporation status for 1998. Engelage used the LIFO inventory method in 1997 and had an ending LIFO inventory of $110,000 (FIFO value of $190,000). Engelage must add $80,000 of LIFO recapture amount to its 1997 taxable income, resulting in an increased tax liability of $28,000 ($80,000 × 35%). Thus, Engelage must pay one-fourth of the tax ($7,000) with its 1997 corporate tax return. The three succeeding installments of $7,000 each are paid with Engelage's next three tax returns. ▼

PASSIVE INVESTMENT INCOME PENALTY TAX

A tax is imposed on the excess passive income of S corporations that possess accumulated E & P from Subchapter C years. The tax rate is the highest corporate rate for the year. The rate is applied to the portion of the corporation's net passive income that bears the same ratio to the total net passive income for the tax year as excess gross passive income bears to the total gross passive income for the year. However, the amount subject to the tax may not exceed the taxable income of the corporation.[67]

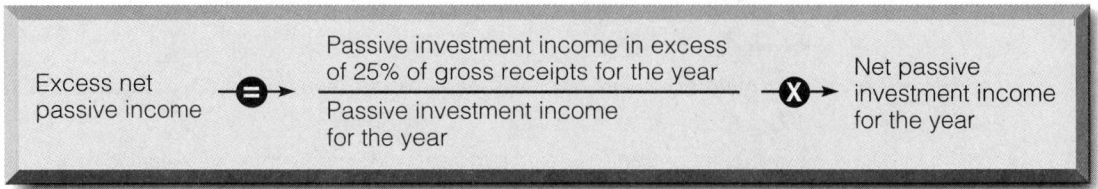

For this purpose, passive investment income (PII) means gross receipts derived from royalties, rents, dividends, interest, annuities, and sales and exchanges of stocks and securities.[68] Only the net gain from the disposition of capital assets (other than stocks and securities) is taken into account in computing gross receipts. Net passive income means passive income reduced by any deductions directly connected with the production of such income. Any passive income tax reduces the amount the shareholders must take into income.

The excess net passive income cannot exceed the corporate taxable income for the year before considering any NOL deduction or the special deductions allowed by §§ 241–250 (except the organization expense deduction of § 248).

EXAMPLE 51

At the end of 1997, Barnhardt Corporation, an electing S corporation, has gross receipts totaling $264,000 (of which $110,000 is PII). Expenditures directly connected to the production of the PII total $30,000. Therefore, Barnhardt has net passive investment income of $80,000 ($110,000 – $30,000), and the amount by which its PII for tax year 1997 exceeds 25% of its gross receipts is $44,000 ($110,000 PII – $66,000). Excess net passive income (ENPI) is $32,000, calculated as follows.

$$\text{ENPI} = \frac{\$44,000}{\$110,000} \times \$80,000 = \$32,000$$

Barnhardt's PII tax for 1997 is $11,200 ($32,000 × 35%). ▼

FRINGE BENEFIT RULES

An S corporation is treated as a partnership with respect to certain fringe benefits made available to a shareholder-employee owning more than 2 percent of the S corporation stock. The constructive ownership rules of § 318 (refer to Chapter 5) are used in applying the 2 percent ownership test.[69] If an S corporation provides a fringe benefit to a more-than-2 percent shareholder and the benefit is not excludible by a partner in a partnership (e.g., health and accident insurance premiums), the S corporation should deduct the amount as compensation, and the employee should report the amount as compensation income. Such treatment occurs upon the receipt of the following benefits, among others.

- Excludible group term life insurance.
- The $5,000 death benefit exclusion.
- An excludible accident and health plan.
- Excludible meals and lodging furnished for the convenience of the employer.[70]

---

[67] §§ 1374(d)(4), and 1375(a) and (b).
[68] § 1362(d)(3)(D)(i).

[69] §§ 1372(a) and (b). See Rev.Rul. 91–26, 1991–1 C.B. 184.
[70] S.Rep. No. 640, 97th Cong., 2d Sess. 22 (1982); Rev.Rul. 91–26, 1991–1 C.B. 184; Ann. 92–16, 1992–5 IRB 5.

EXAMPLE 52

Purple, Inc., an S corporation, pays for the medical care of two shareholder-employees during 1997. Tina, an individual owning 2% of the stock, receives $1,700 for this purpose. Soo, an individual owning 20% of the stock, receives $3,100. Purple deducts the $1,700 as a business expense. The $3,100 paid on behalf of Soo is also deductible by the corporation, but Soo records the amount as compensation income because he owns more than 2% of the stock. Soo can deduct 40% of the $3,100, as allowed by § 162(l). ▼

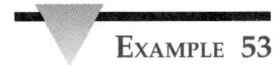

EXAMPLE 53

Assume the same facts as in Example 52, except that Tina is related to another 1% shareholder. Under the constructive ownership rules of § 318, Tina is also a greater-than-2% shareholder and is subject to the same limitations as Soo. ▼

OTHER OPERATIONAL RULES

5 **LEARNING OBJECTIVE**
Recognize the situations where S status is desirable or undesirable.

Oil and Gas Producers.   The repeal of the transferred-proven-property rule by the Revenue Reconciliation Act of 1990 and the issuance of Proposed Regulations on percentage depletion[71] have enhanced the prospects of oil and gas companies operating under S status.

Miscellaneous Rules.   Several other points may be made about the possible effects of various Code provisions on S corporations:

- An S corporation is required to make estimated tax payments with respect to any recognized built-in gain, excess passive investment income, and investment tax credit recapture.
- An S corporation may own stock in another corporation, but an S corporation may not have a C corporation shareholder. An S corporation is *not* eligible for the dividends received deduction and may *not* join in the filing of a consolidated return.
- An S corporation is *not* subject to the 10 percent of taxable income limitation applicable to charitable contributions made by a C corporation.
- Foreign taxes paid by an electing corporation pass through to the shareholders and should be claimed as either a deduction or a credit (subject to the applicable limitations).[72] However, an electing corporation is not eligible for the foreign tax credit with respect to taxes paid by a foreign corporation in which the S corporation is a shareholder.
- After 1996, an S corporation may take advantage of capital gain treatment under § 1237 on the sale of certain subdivided land held for five years. Rules similar to the attribution rules for partnerships apply to S corporations.
- For tax years after 1997, qualified tax-exempt shareholders (e.g., employee stock ownership trusts) may own stock in an S corporation. S corporation income and loss items flow through as unrelated business taxable income (UBTI), and gain or loss on sale of S corporation stock is treated as UBTI. A qualified tax-exempt shareholder counts as one shareholder.
- Any family member who renders services or furnishes capital to an electing corporation must be paid reasonable compensation. Otherwise, the IRS can make adjustments to reflect the value of such services or capital.[73] This rule may make it more difficult for related parties to shift Subchapter S taxable income to children or other family members.

---

[71] Prop.Reg. § 1.613A–3(e).
[72] § 1373(a).

[73] § 1366(e). In addition, beware of an IRS search for the "real owner" of the stock, under Reg. § 1.1373–1(a)(2).

- Although § 1366(a)(1) provides for a flow-through of S corporation items to a shareholder, it does not apply to self-employment income.[74] Thus, a shareholder's portion of S corporation income is not self-employment income and is not subject to the self-employment tax. Compensation for services rendered to an S corporation is, however, subject to FICA taxes.

▼ EXAMPLE 54

Cody and Dana each own one-third of a fast-food restaurant, and their 14-year-old son owns the other shares. Both parents work full-time in the restaurant operations, but the son works infrequently. Neither parent receives a salary this year, when the taxable income of the S corporation is $160,000. The IRS can require that reasonable compensation be paid to the parents to prevent the full one-third of the $160,000 from being taxed to the son. Otherwise, this would be an effective technique to shift earned income to a family member to reduce the total family tax burden. With the § 1(g) "kiddie" tax treatment of the unearned income of children, though, this shifting technique becomes much more valuable. Furthermore, low or zero salaries can reduce FICA taxes due to the Federal government. ▼

- The depletion allowance is computed separately by each shareholder. Each shareholder is treated as having produced his or her pro rata share of the production of the electing corporation, and each is allocated a respective share of the adjusted basis of the electing corporation as to oil or gas property held by the corporation.[75]
- An S corporation is placed on the cash method of accounting for purposes of deducting business expenses and interest owed to a cash basis related party.[76] Thus, the timing of the shareholder's income and the corporate deduction must match.
- The 20 percent basic research credit is *not* available to an S corporation. As a further limitation, this credit may offset only the tax attributable to the S shareholder's interest in the trade or business that generated the credit.
- A few states (namely, Connecticut, Michigan, New Hampshire, New Jersey, Tennessee) and the District of Columbia do *not* recognize the S election.[77] Thus, some or all of the entity's income may be subject to a state-level income tax. Refer to related material in Chapter 15.
- After 1996, the IRS is not required to conduct a deficiency proceeding at the corporate level to assess a tax at the shareholder level for an S corporation–related item. Thus, the tax treatment of items is determined at the corporate level, rather than the individual level.[78]
- An S corporation may *not* be a qualified small business corporation (QSBC) eligible for the 50 percent exclusion of the eligible gain from the sale of QSBC stock held by a taxpayer for more than five years.[79]
- If § 1244 stock is issued to an S corporation, the S corporation and its shareholders may *not* treat losses on such stock as ordinary losses, notwithstanding § 1363, which provides that the taxable income of an S corporation must be computed in the same manner as that of an individual. However, an S corporation may issue § 1244 stock to its shareholders to obtain ordinary loss treatment.

---

[74] Rev.Rul. 59–221, 1959–1 C.B. 225.
[75] § 613A(c)(13).
[76] § 267(b).
[77] Boucher, Raabe, and Taylor, *Multistate S Corporation Tax Guide* (Panel Publishers, 1993).

[78] § 6037(c).
[79] § 1202.

- Losses may be disallowed due to a lack of a profit motive. If the activities at the corporate level are not profit motivated, the losses may be disallowed under the hobby loss rule of § 183.[80]
- When a person inherits S corporation stock after August 19, 1996, the new owner treats as income in respect of a decedent (IRD) his or her pro rata share of any item of income of the corporation that would have been IRD if that item had been acquired directly from the decedent. The person receiving IRD is entitled to a deduction for any estate tax of the decedent with respect to that item, but is *not* entitled to a step-up in basis for the property generating the IRD.

TAX PLANNING CONSIDERATIONS

WHEN THE ELECTION IS ADVISABLE

Effective tax planning with S corporations begins with the determination of whether the election is appropriate. In light of many changes made by the Small Business Job Protection Act of 1996, the taxpayer may wish to reevaluate the desirability of using a C corporation as a means of conducting a trade or business. In this context, one should consider the following factors.

- Are losses from the business anticipated? If so, the S election may be highly attractive because these losses pass through to the shareholders.
- What are the tax brackets of the shareholders? If the shareholders are in high individual income tax brackets, it may be desirable to avoid S corporation status and have profits taxed to the corporation at lower C rates (e.g., 15 percent or 25 percent).
- When the immediate pass-through of Subchapter S taxable income is avoided, profits of the corporation may later be taken out by the shareholders as capital gain income through stock redemptions, some liquidating distributions, or sales of stock to others; received as dividend distributions in low tax bracket years; or negated by a partial or complete step-up in basis upon the death of the shareholder.[81] On the other hand, if the shareholders are in low individual income tax brackets, the pass-through of corporate profits has less effect, and the avoidance of the corporate income tax becomes the paramount consideration. Under these circumstances, the S election could be highly attractive. Although an S corporation usually escapes Federal taxes, it may not be immune from state and local taxes imposed on corporations or from several Federal penalty taxes.
- Does a C corporation have an NOL carryover from a prior year? Such a loss cannot be used in an S year (except for purposes of the built-in gains tax). Even worse, S years count in the 15-year carryover limitation. Thus, even if the S election is made, one might consider terminating the election before the carryover limitation expires. Such a termination would permit the loss to be utilized by what is now a C corporation.
- Both individuals and C corporations are subject to the alternative minimum tax. Many of the tax preference and adjustment items are the same, but some apply only to corporate taxpayers while others are limited to individuals. The alternative minimum tax adjustment relating to accumulated current earnings could create havoc with some C corporations (refer to Chapter 6). S corporations themselves are not subject to this tax.

---

[80] *Michael J. Houston*, T.C.Memo. 1995–159; *Mario G. De Mendoza, III*, T.C.Memo. 1994–314.

[81] See the discussion of § 1014 in Chapter 18.

- Some C corporations must convert from the cash method to the accrual method of accounting (refer to Chapter 2).
- S corporations and partnerships have lost some of the flexibility in the choice of their accounting period (see also Chapter 10).
- By taxing C corporations on nonliquidating and liquidating distributions of appreciated property (refer to Chapter 5), the effect of double taxation is reinforced.
- The modifications made to § 382 (refer to Chapter 7) have imposed severe restrictions on the carryover of NOLs.
- Since the S election may or may not provide the shareholders with tax advantages, one must consider all of the provisions that affect the owners.

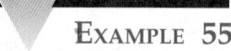

EXAMPLE 55

Tracey has a basis of $500,000 in his business assets, including some land, which is subject to a liability of $700,000. Tracey transfers all of the assets of the business to a newly formed corporation, Red, Inc., in exchange for all of the stock in Red. Red elects to be taxed as an S corporation. Red incurs ordinary losses as follows: Year 1, $50,000; Year 2, $80,000; Year 3, $90,000. Tracey deducts the losses to offset income from other sources. Red is audited in Year 3.

- The IRS asserts that Tracey must recognize a $200,000 gain upon the incorporation of Red under § 357(c), because the liabilities exceed his basis in the assets. Tracey's basis in the Red stock is zero: $500,000 (basis of Tracey's assets) – $700,000 (liabilities assumed by Red) + $200,000 (gain recognized to Tracey).
- Because Tracey's basis in the Red stock is zero, he is not entitled to deduct any of the losses for Year 1, Year 2, or Year 3.
- Because Tracey was actively involved in his business, had he not incorporated, he could have offset total losses of $220,000 against other ordinary income. He would also have eliminated the $200,000 gain upon the incorporation of his business. Thus, the incorporation and S election caused Tracey to generate additional income for tax purposes of $420,000. ▼

The choice of the form of doing business often is dictated by other factors. For example, many businesses cannot qualify for the S election—due to the possibility of a public offering or a need for substantial capital inflow—or would find the partnership or limited liability company forms more practical. Therefore, freedom of action based on tax considerations may not be an attainable goal. Comparative tax attributes of partnerships, S corporations, and C corporations are examined fully in Chapter 13.

MAKING A PROPER ELECTION

Once the parties have decided the election is appropriate, it becomes essential to ensure that the election is made properly.

- Make sure all shareholders consent. If any doubt exists concerning the shareholder status of an individual, it would be wise to have that party issue a consent anyway.[82] Too few consents are fatal to the election; the same cannot be said for too many consents.
- Be sure that the election is timely and properly filed. Either hand carry the election to an IRS office or send it by certified or registered mail. The date used to determine timeliness is the postmark date, not the date the IRS

---

[82] See *William B. Wilson*, 34 TCM 463, T.C.Memo. 1975–92.

receives the election. A copy of the election should become part of the corporation's permanent files.

- Be careful to ascertain when the timely election period begins to run for a newly formed corporation. An election made too soon (before the corporation is in existence) is worse than one made too late. If serious doubts exist as to when this period begins, filing more than one election might be considered a practical means of guaranteeing the desired result.

- It still is beneficial for an S corporation to issue § 1244 stock (refer to Chapter 3). This type of stock allows the original shareholder to obtain an ordinary deduction for a loss on the sale or worthlessness of the stock, rather than long-term capital loss treatment. Shareholders have nothing to lose by complying with § 1244.

ETHICAL CONSIDERATIONS

A Divorce Threatens S Status

Golden Cowrie, Inc., has operated successfully as an S corporation for eight years in Greer, South Carolina. In July 1997, the company had 75 shareholders, but one of the shareholders, Morrie Williams, is considering obtaining a divorce. Both Morrie and his wife Kristy own shares in the corporation.

Morrie discusses the situation with the board of directors, who offer several suggestions.

- Morrie should postpone the divorce until 1998, while the company tries to purchase all of the stock from one of the smaller owners.

- Morrie and Kristy should remain married indefinitely for the good of the S election.

- Two of the unmarried shareholders will be encouraged to marry for the "benefit of the company."

- The company will continue to list Morrie and Kristy as married on Form 1120S after they divorce.

The S election saves the group about $280,000 each year. How would you counsel Morrie to respond to the board's proposals?

PRESERVING THE ELECTION

Recall how an election can be lost and that after 1996 a five-year waiting period generally is imposed before another S election is available. To preserve an S election, the following points should be kept in mind.

- As a starting point, all parties concerned should be made aware of the various transactions that lead to the loss of an election.

- Watch for possible disqualification of a small business corporation. For example, the divorce of a shareholder, accompanied by a property settlement, could violate the 75-shareholder limitation (35 before 1997). The death of a shareholder could result in a nonqualifying trust becoming a shareholder. The latter circumstance might be avoided by utilizing a buy-sell agreement or binding the deceased shareholder's estate to turn in the stock to the corporation for redemption or, as an alternative, to sell it to the surviving shareholders.[83]

---

[83] See Chapter 18 for a discussion of buy-sell agreements. Most such agreements do not create a second class of S stock. Rev.Rul. 85–161, 1985–2 C. B. 191; *Portage Plastics Co. v. U.S.*, 72–2 USTC ¶9567, 30 AFTR2d 72–5229, 470 F.2d 308 (CA–7, 1973).

- Make sure a new majority shareholder (including the estate of a deceased shareholder) does not file a refusal to continue the election.
- Watch for the passive investment income limitation. Avoid a consecutive third year with excess passive income if a corporation has Subchapter C accumulated earnings and profits. In this connection, assets that produce passive investment income (e.g., stocks and bonds, certain rental assets) might be retained by the shareholders in their individual capacities and thereby kept out of the corporation.
- Do not transfer stock to a nonresident alien.
- Do not issue a second class of stock.

PLANNING FOR THE OPERATION OF THE CORPORATION

Operating an S corporation to achieve optimum tax savings for all parties involved requires a great deal of care and, most important, an understanding of the applicable tax rules.

Accumulated Adjustment Account.   Although the corporate-level accumulated adjustments account (AAA) is used primarily by an S corporation with accumulated earnings and profits (AEP) from a Subchapter C year, all S corporations should maintain an accurate record of the AAA. Because there is a grace period for distributing the AAA after termination of the S election, the parties must be in a position to determine the balance of the account.

EXAMPLE 56

Nobles, Inc., an S corporation during 1996, has no AEP from a Subchapter C year. Over the years, Nobles made no attempt to maintain an accurate accounting for the AAA. In 1997, the S election is terminated, and Nobles has a grace period for distributing the AAA tax-free to its shareholders. A great deal of time and expense may be necessary to reconstruct the AAA balance in 1997. ▼

Tax-exempt income is not included in gross income and does not increase AAA. For an S corporation with AEP, tax-exempt income usually is a bad investment. Any subsequent distribution of tax-exempt income exceeds the AAA balance and is treated as dividend income to the extent of any AEP.

When AEP is present, a negative AAA may cause double taxation of S corporation income. With a negative AAA, a distribution of current income restores the negative AAA balance to zero, but is considered to be a distribution in excess of AAA and is taxable as a dividend to the extent of AEP. For tax years beginning after 1996, distributions during the year reduce the stock basis for determining the allowable loss for the year, but the loss does *not* reduce the stock basis for determining the tax status of distributions made during the year. In determining the tax treatment of distributions by an S corporation having AEP, any net adjustments (e.g., excess of losses and deductions over income) for the tax year are ignored.

The AAA bypass election may be used to avoid the accumulated earnings tax or personal holding company tax in the year preceding the first tax year under Subchapter S. This bypass election allows the AEP to be distributed instead.

EXAMPLE 57

Zebra, Inc., an S corporation during 1996, has a significant amount in its AEP account. The shareholders expect to terminate the election in 1997, when they will be subject to low income tax rates. Since the new C corporation may be subject to the accumulated earnings penalty tax in 1997, the shareholders may wish to use the AAA bypass election to distribute some or all of the AEP. Of course, any distributions of the AEP account in 1996 would be taxable to the shareholders. ▼

A net loss allocated to a shareholder reduces the AAA. This required adjustment should encourage an electing corporation to make annual distributions of net income to avoid the reduction of an AAA by a future net loss.

Salary Structure.   The amount of salary paid to a shareholder-employee of an S corporation can have varying tax consequences and should be considered carefully. Larger amounts might be advantageous if the maximum contribution allowed under the retirement plan has not been reached. Smaller amounts may be beneficial if the parties are trying to shift taxable income to lower-bracket shareholders, reduce payroll taxes, curtail a reduction of Social Security benefits, or restrict losses that do not pass through because of the basis limitation.

A strategy of decreasing compensation and correspondingly increasing distributions to shareholder-employees often results in substantial savings in employment taxes. However, a shareholder of an S corporation cannot always perform substantial services and arrange to receive distributions rather than compensation so that the corporation may avoid paying employment taxes. The shareholder may be deemed an employee, with any distributions recharacterized as wages subject to FICA and FUTA taxes.[84] For planning purposes, some level of compensation should be paid to all shareholder-employees to avoid any recharacterization of distributions as deductible salaries—especially in personal service corporations.

The IRS can require that reasonable compensation be paid to family members who render services or provide capital to the S corporation. The IRS, though, can adjust the items taken into account by family-member shareholders to reflect the value of services or capital they provided. Refer to Example 54.

Unreasonable compensation traditionally has not been a problem for S corporations, but deductible compensation under § 162 reduces an S corporation's taxable income, which is relevant to the built-in gains tax. Compensation may be one of the larger items that an electing corporation can use to reduce taxable income to minimize any built-in gains penalty tax. Thus, IRS agents may attempt to classify compensation as unreasonable to increase the § 1374 tax.

Loss Considerations.   A net loss in excess of tax basis may be carried forward and deducted only by the same shareholder in succeeding years. Thus, before disposing of the stock, a shareholder should increase the basis of such stock/loan to flow through the loss. The next shareholder does not obtain the carryover loss.

Any unused carryover loss in existence upon the termination of the S election may be deducted only in the next tax year and is limited to the individual's *stock* basis (not loan basis) in the post-termination year.[85] The shareholder may wish to purchase more stock to increase the tax basis in order to absorb the loss.

The NOL provisions create a need for sound tax planning during the last election year and the post-termination transition period. If it appears that the S corporation is going to sustain an NOL or use up any loss carryover, each shareholder's basis should be analyzed to determine if it can absorb the share of the loss. If basis is insufficient to absorb the loss, further investments should be considered before the end of the post-termination transition year. Such investments can be accomplished through additional stock purchases from the corporation, or from other shareholders, to increase basis. This action ensures the full benefit from the NOL carryover.

---

[84] Rev.Rul. 74–44, 1974–1 C.B. 287; *Spicer Accounting, Inc. v. U.S.,* 91–1 USTC ¶50,103, 66 AFTR 2d 90–5806, 918 F.2d 90 (CA–9, 1990); *Radtke v. U.S.,* 90–1 USTC ¶50,113, 65 AFTR 2d 90–1155, 895 F.2d 1196 (CA–7, 1990).

[85] § 1366(d)(3).

EXAMPLE 58

A calendar year C corporation has an NOL of $20,000 in 1996. The corporation makes a valid S election in 1997 and has another $20,000 NOL in that year. At all times during 1997, the stock of the corporation was owned by the same 10 shareholders, each of whom owned 10% of the stock. Tim, one of the 10 shareholders, has an adjusted basis of $1,800 at the beginning of 1997. None of the 1996 NOL may be carried forward into the S year. Although Tim's share of the 1997 NOL is $2,000, the deduction for the loss is limited to $1,800 in 1997 with a $200 carryover. ▼

Avoiding the Passive Investment Income Tax.   Too much passive investment income (PII) may cause an S corporation to incur a § 1375 penalty tax and/or terminate the S election. Several planning techniques can be used to avoid both of these unfavorable events. Where a small amount of AEP exists, an AAA bypass election may be appropriate to purge the AEP, thereby avoiding the passive income tax altogether. Alternatively, the corporation might reduce taxable income below the excess net passive income; similarly, PII might be accelerated into years in which there is an (offsetting) NOL. In addition, the tax can be avoided if the corporation manufactures needed gross receipts. By increasing gross receipts without increasing PII, the amount of PII in excess of 25 percent of gross receipts is reduced.

EXAMPLE 59

An S corporation has paid a passive income penalty tax for two consecutive years. In the next year, the corporation has a large amount of AAA. If the AEP account is small, a bypass election may be appropriate to purge the corporation of the AEP. Without any AEP, no passive income tax applies, and the S election is not terminated. Any distribution of AEP to the shareholders constitutes taxable dividends, however.

Another alternative is to manufacture a large amount of gross receipts without increasing PII (merge with a grocery store). If the gross receipts from the grocery store are substantial, the amount of the PII in excess of 25% of gross receipts is reduced. ▼

Managing the Built-in Gains Tax.   A taxable income limitation encourages an S corporation to create deductions or accelerate deductions in the years that built-in gains are recognized. Although the postponed built-in gain is carried forward to future years, the time value of money makes the postponement beneficial. For example, payment of compensation, rather than a distribution, creates a deduction that reduces taxable income and postpones the built-in gains tax.

EXAMPLE 60

Mundy, Inc., an S corporation, has built-in gain of $110,000 and taxable income of $120,000 before payment of salaries to its two shareholders. If Mundy pays at least $120,000 in salaries to the shareholders (rather than a distribution), taxable income will drop to zero, and the built-in gain will be postponed. Thus, Mundy needs to keep the salaries as high as possible to postpone the built-in gains tax in future years and reap a benefit from the time value of money. Of course, paying the salaries may increase the payroll tax burden if the salaries are below FICA and FUTA limits. ▼

Giving built-in gain property to a charitable organization does not trigger the built-in gains tax. However, the built-in gain may be a preference item at the shareholder level for purposes of the alternative minimum tax. Built-in *loss* property may be sold in the same year that built-in gain property is sold, to reduce or eliminate the built-in gains tax. Generally, the taxpayer should sell built-in loss property in a year when an equivalent amount of built-in gain property is sold. Otherwise, the built-in loss could be wasted.

▼

EXAMPLE 61

Green Corporation elects S status effective for calendar year 1996. As of January 1, 1996, Green's only asset has a basis of $40,000 and a fair market value of $100,000. If this asset is sold for $120,000 in 1997, Green recognizes an $80,000 gain, of which $60,000 is subject to the corporate built-in gains tax. The other $20,000 of gain is subject to the S corporation pass-through rules and bypasses the corporate income tax.

Unless the taxpayer can show otherwise, any appreciation existing at the sale or exchange is presumed to be preconversion built-in gain. Therefore, Green incurs a built-in gain of $80,000 unless it can prove that the $20,000 gain developed after the effective date of the election. ▼

Controlling Adjustments and Preference Items. The individual alternative minimum tax (AMT) affects more taxpayers than ever before, because the tax base has expanded and the difference between regular tax rates and the individual AMT rate has been narrowed. In an S corporation setting, tax preferences flow through proportionately to the shareholders, who, in computing the individual AMT, treat the preferences as if they were directly realized.

A flow-through of tax preferences can be a tax disaster for a shareholder who is an "almost-AMT taxpayer." Certain steps can be taken to protect such a shareholder from being pushed into the AMT. For example, a large S corporation preference from tax-exempt interest on private activity bonds could adversely affect an "almost-AMT taxpayer." Certain adjustment and preference items are subject to elections that can remove them from a shareholder's AMT computation. Certain positive adjustments can be removed from a shareholder's AMTI base if the S corporation elects to capitalize and amortize certain expenditures over a prescribed period of time. These expenditures include excess intangible drilling and development expenditures, research and experimental costs, mining exploration and development expenditures, and circulation expenses.

Other corporate choices can protect an "almost-AMT shareholder." Using a straight-line method of cost recovery (rather than an accelerated method) can be beneficial to certain shareholders. Many of these decisions and elections may generate conflicts of interest, however, when some shareholders are not so precariously situated and would not suffer from the flow-through of adjustments and tax preference items.

Allocation of Tax Items. If a shareholder dies or stock is transferred during the taxable year, tax items may be allocated under the pro rata approach or the per-books method. Absent the per-books election, a shareholder's pro rata share of tax items is determined by assigning an equal portion of each item to each day of the tax year and then dividing that portion pro rata among the shares outstanding on the transfer day. With the consent of all affected shareholders and the corporation, an S corporation can elect to allocate tax items according to the permanent records using normal tax accounting rules.

The allocation is made as if the taxable year consists of two taxable years. The first portion ends on the date of termination. On the day the shares are transferred, the shares are considered owned by the acquiring shareholder. The selected method may be beneficial to the terminating shareholder and harmful to the acquiring shareholder. An election might result in a higher allocation of losses to a taxpayer who is better able to utilize the losses. In the case of the death of a shareholder, a per-books election prevents the income and loss allocation to a deceased shareholder from being affected by postdeath events.

▼

EXAMPLE 62

Alicia, the owner of all of the shares of an S corporation, transfers all of the stock to Bhaskar at the middle of the tax year. There is a $100,000 NOL for the entire tax year, but $30,000 of the loss occurs during the first half of the year. Without a per-books election, $50,000 of the loss would be allocated to Alicia, with $50,000 allocated to Bhaskar. If the corporation makes the per-books election, Bhaskar will receive $70,000 of the loss. Of course, Bhaskar may have a difficult time convincing Alicia to consent to the election. ▼

EXAMPLE 63

Mountain, a calendar year S corporation, is equally owned by Joey and Karl. Joey dies on June 29 (not a leap year). Mountain has income of $250,000 for January 1 through June 29 and $750,000 for the remainder of the year. Without the per-books election, the income is allocated by assigning an equal portion of the annual income of $1 million to each day (or $2,739.73 per day) and allocating the daily portion between the shareholders. Joey is allocated 50% of the daily income for the 180 days from January 1 to June 29, or $246,575.70 ($2,739.73/2 × 180). Joey's estate would be allocated 50% of the income for the 185 days from June 30 to December 31, or $253,425.02 [($2,739.73/2) × 185].

If the per-books election is made, the income of $250,000 from January 1 to June 29 is divided equally between Joey and Karl, so that each is allocated $125,000. The income of $750,000 from June 30 to December 31 is divided equally between Joey's estate and Karl, or $375,000 to each. ▼

Termination Aspects. It is always advisable to avoid accumulated earnings and profits (AEP) in an S corporation. There is the ever-present danger of terminating the election because of excess passive investment income in three consecutive years. Further, the § 1375 penalty tax is imposed on excess passive net income. Thus, one should try to eliminate such AEP through a dividend distribution or liquidation of the corporation with a subsequent reincorporation. If the AEP account is small, to eliminate the problem, all the shareholders may consent under § 1368(e)(3) to have distributions treated as made first from AEP rather than from the AAA (the AAA bypass election).

One should issue straight debt to avoid creating a second class of stock and establish an instrument with a written unconditional promise to pay on demand or on a specific date a sum certain in money with a fixed interest rate and payment date.

If the shareholders of an S corporation decide to terminate the election other than through voluntary revocation, they should make sure that the disqualifying act possesses substance. When the intent of the parties is obvious and the act represents a technical noncompliance rather than a real change, the IRS may be able to disregard it and keep the parties in S status.[86]

If a trust or estate terminates before the end of an S corporation's tax year, the estate or trust takes in consideration its pro rata share of S corporation items in its final year.

Liquidation of an S Corporation. S corporations are subject to many of the same liquidation rules applicable to C corporations (refer to Chapter 5). In general, the distribution of appreciated property to S shareholders in complete liquidation is treated as if the property were sold to the shareholders in a taxable transaction. Unlike a C corporation, however, the S corporation incurs no incremental tax on the liquidation gains, because such gains flow through to the shareholders subject only to the built-in gains tax of § 1374. Any corporate gain increases the shareholder's stock basis by a like amount and reduces any gain realized by the shareholder when he or she receives the liquidation proceeds. Thus, an S corporation usually avoids the double tax that is imposed on C corporations.

---

[86] See *Clarence L. Hook*, 58 T.C. 267 (1972).

With respect to loss property, a liquidation is more favorable than a nonliquidating distribution. Recall that a loss is not recognized for nonliquidating property distributions. With certain exceptions, an S corporation does recognize a loss on the liquidating distribution of depreciated property.

Until it was changed in 1996, the law itself appeared to preclude an S corporation from making an election under § 338 to have a stock purchase treated as an asset acquisition or from taking advantage of a § 332 liquidation. Section 1371(a)(2) provides that an S corporation in its capacity as a shareholder of another corporation shall be treated as an individual. Since only a corporation can make an election under § 338, before 1997 an S corporation appeared to be unable to make such an election.[87] In one letter ruling, however, the IRS allowed an S corporation to take advantage of §§ 338 and 332.[88]

For tax years beginning after 1996, liquidations of S corporations are governed by the applicable C corporation rules (e.g., §§ 332 and 337), allowing a tax-free liquidation of a corporation into its parent corporation. Any built-in gains of the liquidating corporation may later be subject to the § 1374 penalty tax on disposition. An S corporation is also eligible to make a § 338 election, resulting in the immediate recognition of all of the acquired C corporation's income and losses plus the resulting tax.

KEY TERMS

Accumulated adjustments account (AAA), 12–19	Passive investment income (PII), 12–12	Small business corporation, 12–5
Built-in gains tax, 12–32	S corporation, 12–2	Subchapter S, 12–2

PROBLEM MATERIALS

DISCUSSION QUESTIONS

1. Victoria must decide which type of flow-through entity she will choose for her new service business. Help Victoria decide between a limited liability company and an S corporation vehicle by listing the advantages and disadvantages of an S election.

2. May an S corporation own a subsidiary and obtain a dividends received deduction for any dividends? May an S corporation own an S corporation subsidiary? May an S corporation be a member of a consolidated tax return?

3. On March 2, 1997, the two 50% shareholders of a calendar year corporation decide to elect S status. One of the shareholders, Terry, had purchased her stock from a previous shareholder (a nonresident alien) on January 18, 1997. Identify any potential problems for Terry or the corporation.

4. Elvis Stojko calls you and says that his two-person S corporation was involuntarily terminated in February 1997. He asks you if they can make a new election because of the law changes in 1996. Draft a memo for the file dated September 8, 1997, outlining what you told Elvis.

5. How can an S corporation meet the natural business year exception to qualify for a fiscal year?

---

[87] Doc. 8818049; GCM 39768.

[88] Doc. 9245004. The Regulations are silent on this matter.

6. How are nonseparately computed income or losses and Schedule K items allocated to a shareholder?

7. Collett's S corporation has a small amount of accumulated earnings and profits (AEP), requiring the use of the more complex distribution rules. His accountant tells him that this AEP forces the maintenance of the AAA figure each year. Identify relevant tax issues facing Collett.

8. Caleb Hudson owns 10% of an S corporation. He is confused with respect to his AAA and stock basis. Write a brief memo dated November 1, 1997, to Caleb identifying the key differences between AAA and his stock basis.

9. How do the at-risk rules affect an S corporation?

10. Lynch's share of her S corporation's net operating loss is $37,000, but her stock basis is only $29,000. Point out any tax consequences to Lynch.

11. One of your clients is considering electing S status. Texas, Inc., is a six-year-old company with two equal shareholders, both of whom paid $30,000 for their stock. In 1997, Texas has a $90,000 NOL carryforward. Estimated income is $40,000 for 1998 and $25,000 for each of the next three years. Should Texas make an S election for 1997?

PROBLEMS

12. An S corporation's profit and loss statement for 1997 shows net profits of $90,000 (book income). The corporation has three equal shareholders. From supplemental data, you obtain the following information about the corporation for 1997.

Selling expense	$11,500
Tax-exempt interest	2,000
Dividends received	9,000
Section 1231 gain	6,000
Section 1250 gain	10,000
Recovery of state income taxes	3,400
Capital losses	6,000
Salary to owners (each)	9,000
Cost of goods sold	95,000

   a. Compute Subchapter S taxable income or loss for 1997.
   b. What would be the portion of taxable income or loss for Chang, one of the shareholders?

13. Noon, Inc., a calendar year S corporation in Ruston, Louisiana, is equally owned by Ralph and Thomas. Thomas dies on April 1 (not a leap year), and his estate selects a March 31 fiscal year. Noon has $400,000 of income for January 1 through March 31 and $600,000 for the remainder of the year.
   a. Determine how income is allocated to Ralph and Thomas under the pro rata approach.
   b. Determine how income is allocated to Ralph and Thomas under the per-books method.

14. Polly has been the sole shareholder of a calendar year S corporation since 1981. Polly's stock basis is $15,500, and she receives a distribution of $17,000 in 1997. Corporate-level accounts are as follows (including $100 of pre-1983 AEP).

AAA	$6,000
PTI*	9,000
AEP	500

*PTI = previously taxed income, under old-law provisions.

How is Polly taxed on the distribution?

15. On January 1, 1997, Kinney, Inc., an electing S corporation, has $4,000 AEP and a balance of $10,000 in AAA. Kinney has two shareholders, Erin and Frank, each of whom owns 500 shares of Kinney's stock. Kinney's 1997 taxable income is $5,000. Kinney distributes $6,000 to each shareholder on February 1, 1997, and distributes another $3,000 to each shareholder on September 1. Assuming that Erin and Frank have sufficient stock basis, how are they taxed on the distributions?

16. Goblins, Inc., a calendar year S corporation, has $90,000 of AEP. Tobias, the sole shareholder, has an adjusted basis of $80,000 in his stock with a zero balance in the AAA. Determine the tax aspects if a $90,000 salary is paid to Tobias.

17. Assume the same facts as in Problem 16, except that Tobias receives a dividend of $90,000.

18. Using the categories in the following legend, classify each transaction as a plus (+) or minus (−) on Schedule M–2 of Form 1120S.

Legend	
PTI	= Shareholders' undistributed taxable income previously taxed
AAA	= Accumulated adjustments account
OAA	= Other adjustments account
NA	= No direct effect on Schedule M

   a. Receipt of tax-exempt interest income.
   b. Unreasonable compensation determined.
   c. Section 1250 recapture income.
   d. Distribution of nontaxable income (PTI) from 1981.
   e. Nontaxable life insurance proceeds.
   f. Expenses related to tax-exempt securities.
   g. Charitable contributions.
   h. Business gifts in excess of $25.
   i. Nondeductible fines and penalties.
   j. Organization expenses.

19. During the year, a calendar year S corporation has a positive AMT adjustment of $60,000 for mining exploration costs, an excess depletion tax preference of $96,000, and a certified pollution control facility positive adjustment of $18,000. The firm's positive ACE adjustment is $68,000. If Nancy Epstein is a one-third shareholder, what effect do these items have on her individual tax return?

20. Individuals Adam and Bonnie form an S corporation, with Adam contributing cash of $100,000 for a 50% interest and Bonnie contributing appreciated ordinary income property with an adjusted basis of $20,000 and a FMV of $100,000.
   a. Determine Bonnie's initial basis in her stock, assuming that she receives a 50% interest.
   b. The S corporation sells the property for $120,000. Determine Adam's and Bonnie's stock basis after the sale.
   c. Determine Adam's and Bonnie's gain or loss if the company is liquidated.

21. Money, Inc., a calendar year S corporation, has two unrelated shareholders, each owning 50% of the stock. Both shareholders have a $400,000 stock basis as of January 1, 1997. At the beginning of 1997, Money has AAA of $300,000 and AEP of $600,000. During 1997, Money has operating income of $100,000. At the end of the year, Money distributes securities worth $1 million, with an adjusted basis of $800,000. Determine the tax effects of these transactions.

22. Assume the same facts as in Problem 21, except that the two shareholders consent under § 1368(e)(3) to distribute AEP first.

23. An S corporation's Form 1120S shows taxable income of $88,000 for the year. Matthew owns 40% of the stock throughout the year. The following information is obtained from the corporate records.

Salary paid to Matthew	$52,000
Tax-exempt interest income	3,000
Charitable contributions	6,000
Dividends received from a foreign corporation	5,000
Long-term capital loss	6,000
§ 1250 gain	11,000
Refund of prior state income taxes	5,000
Cost of goods sold	72,000
Short-term capital loss	7,000
Administrative expenses	18,000
Long-term capital gains	14,000
Selling expenses	11,000
Matthew's beginning stock basis	22,000
Matthew's additional stock purchases	7,000
Matthew's beginning AAA	19,000
Matthew's loan to corporation	20,000

   a. Compute book income or loss.
   b. Compute Matthew's ending stock basis.
   c. Calculate ending corporate AAA.

24. At the beginning of the year, Malcolm, a 50% shareholder of a calendar year S corporation, has a stock basis of $22,000. During the year, the corporation has taxable income of $32,000. The following data are obtained from supplemental sources.

Dividends received	$12,000
Tax-exempt interest	18,000
Short-term capital gain	6,000
§ 1245 gain	10,000
§ 1231 gain	7,000
Charitable contributions	5,000
Political contributions	8,000
Short-term capital loss	12,000
Dividends to Malcolm	7,000
Selling expense	14,000
Beginning AAA	44,000

   a. Compute Malcolm's ending stock basis.
   b. Compute ending AAA.

25. For each of the following independent statements, indicate whether the transaction will increase (+), decrease (−), or have no effect (NE) on the adjusted basis of a shareholder's stock in an S corporation.
   a. Expenses related to tax-exempt income.
   b. Short-term capital gain.
   c. Nonseparately computed loss.
   d. Section 1231 gain.
   e. Depletion *not* in excess of basis.
   f. Separately computed income.
   g. Nontaxable return-of-capital distribution by the corporation.

    h. Administrative expenses.
    i. Business gifts in excess of $25.
    j. Section 1245 gain.
    k. Dividends received by the S corporation.
    l. LIFO recapture tax at S election.
   m. Recovery of a bad debt.
    n. Long-term capital loss.
    o. Corporate dividends out of AAA.

26. McHugh, Inc., a calendar year corporation in Grand Isle, Louisiana, has a tax loss of $90,000 and a long-term capital loss of $20,000. Ieyoub, an individual, owns 30% of the corporate stock and has a $25,000 basis in the stock. Calculate the amount of the tax loss and capital loss, if any, that flows through to Ieyoub.

27. Clotile owns 35% of the stock of an S corporation throughout 1997 and lends the corporation $7,000 during the year. Her stock basis in the corporation at the end of the year is $25,000. If the corporation sustains a $110,000 operating loss during the year, what amount, if any, can Clotile deduct with respect to the operating loss?

28. Crew Corporation elects S status effective for tax year 1996. As of January 1, 1996, Crew's assets were appraised as follows.

	Adjusted Basis	**Fair Market Value**
Cash	$ 16,010	$ 16,010
Accounts receivable	–0–	55,400
Inventory (FIFO)	70,000	90,000
Investment in land	110,000	195,000
Building	220,000	275,000
Goodwill	–0–	93,000

In each of the following situations, calculate any § 1374 tax, assuming that the highest corporate rate is 35%.
    a. During 1996, Crew collects $40,000 of the accounts receivable and sells 80% of the inventory for $99,000.
    b. In 1997, Crew sells the land held for investment for $203,000.
    c. In 1998, the building is sold for $270,000.

29. Bryan, a cash basis S corporation, has the following assets and liabilities on January 1, 1997, the date the S election is made.

	Adjusted Basis	**Fair Market Value**
Cash	$ 200,000	$ 200,000
Accounts receivable	–0–	105,000
Equipment	110,000	100,000
Land	1,800,000	2,500,000
Accounts payable	–0–	110,000

During 1997, Bryan collects the accounts receivable and pays the accounts payable. The land is sold for $3 million, and the taxable income for the year is $590,000. Calculate any § 1374 penalty tax.

30. Lejeune, Inc., an S corporation in Boone, North Carolina, has operating revenues of $400,000, taxable interest of $380,000, operating expenses of $250,000, and deductions attributable to the interest income of $140,000. Calculate any § 1375 penalty tax payable by this S corporation or its shareholders.

31. At the end of 1997, Brew, an S corporation, has gross receipts of $190,000 and gross income of $170,000. Brew has accumulated earnings and profits of $22,000 and taxable income of $30,000. It has passive investment income of $100,000, with $40,000 of expenses directly related to the production of passive investment income. Calculate Brew's excess net passive income and any § 1375 penalty tax.

32. At the end of the year, a calendar year S corporation has rent income of $400,000 (significant services are rendered), interest income of $200,000, and royalty income of $150,000 (the trademark was purchased). It incurred operating expenses of $250,000 and deductions attributable to the interest income and trademark of $80,000. Calculate any passive income penalty tax.

33. During the year, Topp Corporation, an electing S corporation, has gross receipts totaling $320,000 ($160,000 of which is passive investment income). Expenditures directly connected to the production of the passive investment income total $30,000. Calculate any passive income penalty tax, assuming taxable income is $68,000.

34. Savoy, Inc., in Auburn, Alabama, is an accrual basis S corporation with three equal shareholders. The three cash basis shareholders have the following stock basis at the beginning of 1997: Andre, $18,000; Crum, $22,000; and Marie, $30,000. Savoy has the following income and expense items during 1997.

Net tax operating loss	$30,000
Short-term capital gain	37,500
§ 1231 loss	9,000
Nondeductible fees and penalties	3,000

The electing corporation distributes $5,000 cash to each of the shareholders during the tax year. Calculate the shareholders' stock bases at the end of 1997.

35. Bonnie and Clyde each own one-third of a fast-food restaurant, and their 13-year-old daughter owns the other shares. Both parents work full-time in the restaurant, but the daughter works infrequently. Neither Bonnie nor Clyde receives a salary during the year, when the taxable income of the S corporation is $180,000. An IRS agent estimates that reasonable salaries for Bonnie, Clyde, and the daughter are $30,000, $35,000, and $10,000, respectively. What adjustments would you expect the IRS to impose upon these taxpayers?

36. An S corporation, C&C Properties, owns two rental real estate undertakings—Carrot and Cantalope. Each property generates an annual $10,000 loss for the year. The S corporation reports the aggregated results of the two ventures on Schedule K–1. The two equal shareholders, Dan and Marta, have a $7,000 stock basis before considering these losses. Marta actively participates in the management of Carrot, but does not actively participate in the Cantalope venture. Dan does not actively participate in either venture. What losses flow through?

37. Friedman, Inc., an S corporation, pays for the medical care of two shareholder-employees during the current year. Yvette, owning 2% of the stock, receives $1,900 for this purpose. Jack, owning 21% of the stock, receives $3,300. Arnold Schwartz, the CFO, calls you, asking how to treat these transactions. Prepare a tax memo dated June 18, 1997, indicating what you told Arnold over the phone.

38. One of your clients is considering electing S status. Dickens, Inc., is a seven-year-old company with two equal shareholders who are in the 39.6% tax bracket. In 1996, Dickens will have an NOL carryforward of approximately $310,000. The difference between LIFO and FIFO inventory is $200,000, and the company will distribute about 50% of taxable income (before any NOL). The company's estimated income, built-in gain recognition, and 8% present value of $1 are as follows.

	Taxable Income	Built-in Gain	Present Value of $1
1997	$210,000	$50,000	0.926
1998	250,000	40,000	0.857
1999	300,000	50,000	0.794
2000	400,000	40,000	0.735
2001	600,000	30,000	0.681

a. Should the corporation elect S corporation status?

b. Would your answer change if most of the taxable income is distributed?

39. Claude Bergeron sold 1,000 shares of Ditta, Inc., an S corporation located in Sour Lake, Texas, for $8,000. He has a stock basis in the shares of $122,000. Assuming that Claude is single and that he is the original owner of these § 1244 stock shares, calculate the appropriate tax treatment of any gain or loss. If he sold the stock for $220,000, could he obtain a 50% exclusion under § 1202 for any gain?

COMPREHENSIVE TAX RETURN PROBLEM

John Martin (Social Security number 234–10–5214) and Stan Mitchell (Social Security number 244–58–8695) are 55% and 45% owners of Ram, Inc. (74–8265910), a textile manufacturing company located at 1011 Wright Avenue, Kannapolis, NC 28083. The company's first S election was on January 1, 1984. The following information was taken from the income statement for 1996.

Other income (active)	$ 380
Interest income	267
Gross sales	1,376,214
Beginning inventory (1996)	7,607
Direct labor	303,102
Direct materials purchased	278,143
Direct other costs	149,356
Ending inventory (1996)	13,467
Taxes	39,235
Contributions to United Fund	445
Contribution to Senator Brown's campaign	5,000
Fines (illegal)	34
Life insurance premiums (the corporation is the beneficiary)	98
Compensation to shareholder/officers (proportionate to ownership)	34,934
Salaries and wages	62,103
Interest	17,222
Repairs	16,106
Depreciation	16,154
Advertising	3,246
Pension plan contributions	6,000
Employee benefit program	2,875
Other deductions	63,784
Net income	384,884

A comparative balance sheet appears below.

	January 1, 1996	December 31, 1996
Cash	$ 47,840	$ 61,242
Accounts receivable	93,100	153,136
Inventories	7,607	13,467
Prepaid expenses	10,333	7,582
Loans to shareholders	313	727
Buildings and trucks	138,203	244,348
Accumulated depreciation	(84,235)	(100,389)
Land	1,809	16,513
Life insurance	11,566	18,344
	$226,536	$ 414,970
Accounts payable	$ 52,404	$ 82,963
Notes payable (less than one year)	5,122	8,989
Loans from shareholders	155,751	191,967
Notes payable (more than one year)	21,821	33,835
Loan on life insurance	5,312	16,206
Capital stock	1,003	1,003
Paid-in capital	9,559	9,559
Retained earnings (unappropriated)	(8,314)	?
Accumulated adjustment account	–0–	?
Other adjustment account	–0–	?
Treasury stock	(16,122)	(16,122)
	$226,536	$ 414,970

The accounting firm provides the following additional information.

Dividends paid to shareholders	$290,000
AMT depreciation adjustment	(1,075)
AMT interest on bonds preference	11,070

From the above information, prepare a complete Form 1120S and Schedule K–1 for John Martin (596 Lane Street, Kannapolis, NC 28083). If any information is missing, make realistic assumptions.

RESEARCH PROBLEMS

Note: **West's Federal Taxation on CD-ROM** *can be used in preparing solutions to the Research Problems. Alternatively, tax research materials contained in a standard tax library can be used.*

Research Problem 1. Mel Bonilla contacts you with respect to the creation of two S corporations, each having approximately 40 shareholders. Most of the assets of the business will be held inside a limited liability company. Both S corporations will be 50% partners in the limited liability company. Draft Mel a letter dated January 14, 1997, indicating whether this business arrangement is appropriate. Mel's address is 10 Newton Avenue, Ocala, FL 34482.

Research Problem 2.   Anita, the accountant for Rockhead, Inc., failed to file a Form 2553 for tax year 1996, even though the four shareholders of the corporation instructed her to qualify the corporation as an S corporation. For 1996 and 1997, Anita did file Forms 1120S, along with Schedule K–1s for all of the shareholders.

When the IRS notified Anita that Rockhead was not a qualified S corporation, she argued that Form 2553 was "nonmandatory." She pointed out that Temp.Reg. § 18.1362–1(a) uses the word "should" rather than "shall" in reference to filing Form 2553.

Anita provided the revenue agent with a copy of *Steve Brody*, 34 TCM 310, T.C.Memo. 1975–47, ¶75,047 P–H Memo T.C. Here, the IRS argued that the taxpayer had elected to be taxed under Subchapter S because the taxpayer filed Form 1120S. The IRS could not provide the court with the necessary Form 2553.

As Rockhead's new tax adviser, prepare a memo dated November 1, 1997, for your file, analyzing Anita's argument.

Research Problem 3.   Tom Lewitske owns an insolvent S corporation. A local bank discharged a debt of $32,500 that the S corporation owed to the bank. This amount was not in excess of the amount by which the S corporation was insolvent. Tom calls you and asks about the tax aspects of this discharge of indebtedness. Prepare a memo for the tax research file dated June 15, 1997, indicating what you told Tom over the phone.

Research Problem 4.   Samuel, the accountant for an S corporation in Thibodeaux, Louisiana, is considering the advantages of establishing an employee stock ownership plan (ESOP). Can an ESOP own S corporation stock? Would all of the tax advantages of using an ESOP still apply to an S corporation owning the ESOP?

Partial list of research aids:
   § 401(a).
   § 401(c)(3).
   § 170(e)(1).
   § 1361(c)(7).

Research Problem 5.   Opal is a major shareholder of Nations, Inc., an electing S corporation. As an incentive to persuade Hugo to work for the corporation, Opal sells Hugo some of her stock at a 20% discount below fair market value. The reason for the discount was to compensate Hugo for accepting a salary from Nations below the market rate. Hugo paid the bargain price for the stock directly to Opal in the form of cash and a promissory note. Hugo is personally liable for the promissory note.

On acquiring the Nations' stock from Opal, Hugo entered into an agreement restricting the transferability of the shares. Does this transaction create a second class of stock, thereby terminating the S election? Write a memo dated November 1, 1997, for the tax research file, analyzing the S election after the agreement is executed. *Solve this problem using just the Code and Income Tax Regulations.*

Partial list of research aids:
   § 1361(b)(1)(D).
   Reg. § 1.1361–1(1)(2)(i).
   Ltr.Rul. 9525035.

Use the tax resources of the internet to address the following questions. Do not restrict your search to the World Wide Web, but include a review of newsgroups and general reference materials, practitioner sites and resources, primary sources of the tax law, chat rooms and discussion groups, and other opportunities.

Research Problem 6.   Search for information about bankruptcy as it affects S corporations. Print material that you have found useful in answering the following questions.

   a. Is a bankruptcy estate a qualified shareholder?
   b. Can an S corporation enter bankruptcy without terminating the S election?
   c. Can an S corporation pass through losses under § 1374, even though it is in bankruptcy?

Partial list of research aids:
    http://www.law.vill.edu/vi
    http://www.dtonline.com/tnv/taxchanges/s-corps.htm

Research Problem 7. The 1996 changes to S corporation tax law did not satisfy everyone. Summarize two more changes to the S provisions that still are being proposed by interested parties.

Research Problem 8. Find a question about S corporation tax planning that has been posted to a news group. Submit to the group your answer to the query. Make a copy of the question and answer.

ADVANCED TAX PRACTICE CONSIDERATIONS

Besides coping with the procedural aspects of tax administration and practice, a specialist in taxation may be confronted with a variety of technical subjects. Some of these include tax considerations in choosing a form for operating a business, the unique rules applicable to tax-exempt entities, and multistate dealings. The following chapters, therefore, reflect a cross section of the myriad problems often encountered in tax practice.

13

COMPARATIVE FORMS OF DOING BUSINESS

LEARNING OBJECTIVES

After completing Chapter 13, you should be able to:

1. Identify the principal legal and tax forms for conducting a business.

2. Appreciate the relative importance of nontax factors in making business decisions.

3. Distinguish between the forms for conducting a business according to whether they are subject to single taxation or double taxation.

4. Identify techniques for avoiding double taxation and for controlling the entity tax.

5. Understand the applicability and the effect of the conduit and entity concepts on contributions to the entity, operations of the entity, entity distributions, passive activity loss and at-risk rules, and special allocations.

6. Analyze the effect of the disposition of a business on the owners and the entity for each of the forms for conducting a business.

OUTLINE

A variety of factors, both tax and nontax, affect the choice of the form of business entity. The form that is appropriate at one point in the life of an entity and its owners may not be appropriate at a different time.

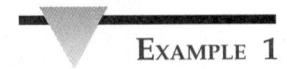

EXAMPLE 1

Eva is a tax practitioner in Kentwood, the Dairy Center of the South. Many of her clients are dairy farmers. She recently had tax planning discussions with two of her clients, Jesse, a Line Creek dairy farmer, and Larry, a Spring Creek dairy farmer.

Jesse recently purchased his dairy farm. He is 52 years old and just retired after 30 years of service as a chemical engineer at an oil refinery in Baton Rouge. Eva recommended that he incorporate his dairy farm and elect S corporation status for Federal income tax purposes.

Larry has owned his dairy farm since 1988. He inherited it from his father. At that time, Larry retired after 20 years of service in the U.S. Air Force. He has a master's degree in Agricultural Economics from LSU. His farm is incorporated, and shortly after the date of incorporation, Eva had advised him to elect S corporation status. She now advises him to revoke the S election. ▼

Example 1 raises a number of interesting questions. Does Eva advise all of her dairy farmer clients to initially elect S corporation status? Why has she advised Larry to revoke his S election? Will she advise Jesse to revoke his S election at some time in the future? Will she advise Larry to make another S election at some time in the future? Why did she not advise Larry to terminate his corporate status? Could Larry and Jesse have achieved the same tax consequences for their dairy farms if they had operated the farms as partnerships instead of incorporating? Does the way the farm is acquired (e.g., purchase versus inheritance) affect the choice of business entity for tax purposes?

This chapter provides the basis for comparatively analyzing the tax consequences of business decisions for four types of tax entities (sole proprietorship, partnership, corporation, and S corporation). Understanding the comparative tax consequences for the different types of entities and being able to apply them effectively to specific fact patterns can lead to effective tax planning, which is exactly what Eva was doing with her two clients. As the following discussion illustrates, a variety of potential answers may exist for each of the questions raised by Eva's advice.

FORMS OF DOING BUSINESS

PRINCIPAL FORMS

1 **LEARNING OBJECTIVE**
Identify the principal legal and tax forms for conducting a business.

The principal *legal* forms for conducting a business entity are a sole proprietorship, partnership, or corporation.[1] From a *Federal income tax* perspective, these same forms are available with the corporate form being divided into two types (S corporation and C or regular corporation). In most instances, the legal form and the tax form are the same. In some cases, however, the IRS may attempt to tax a business entity as a form different from its legal form. This reclassification normally takes one of two possible approaches:

1. The IRS ignores the corporate form and taxes the owners directly (the corporate entity lacks substance).
2. The IRS ignores the partnership form and taxes the partnership as if it were a corporation.

The IRS may try to reclassify a corporation for several reasons. One reason is to prevent taxpayers from taking advantage of the disparity between the corporate and individual tax rates. The Revenue Reconciliation Act (RRA) of 1993 restored the historical norm of the highest corporate statutory rate being lower than the highest individual statutory rate (35 percent versus 39.6 percent). In addition, the specific corporate and individual rates applicable to a particular taxpayer may produce a greater spread than 4.6 percent (39.6% − 35%). For example, an individual may be in the 39.6 percent bracket, and the corporation may be in the 15 percent, 25 percent, or 34 percent bracket. Another reason for taxing the owners directly is to make them ineligible for favorable taxation of certain fringe benefits (see the subsequent discussion in Favorable Treatment of Certain Fringe Benefits).

In the case of a partnership, reclassification of a partnership as if it were a corporation can subject the business entity to double taxation. In addition, the resultant loss of conduit status prevents partnership losses from being passed through to the tax returns of the partners. For example, see the discussion of *associations* in Chapter 2.

The taxpayer generally is bound for tax purposes by the legal form that is selected. The major statutory exception to this is the ability of an S corporation to receive tax treatment similar to that of a partnership.[2] A less important statutory exception allows certain partnerships to elect not to be taxed as a partnership.[3]

An individual conducting a sole proprietorship files Schedule C of Form 1040. If more than one trade or business is conducted, a separate Schedule C is filed for each trade or business. A partnership files Form 1065. A corporation files Form 1120, and an S corporation files Form 1120S.

---

[1] A business entity can also be conducted in the form of a trust or estate. These two forms are not discussed in this chapter. See the discussion of the income taxation of trusts and estates in Chapter 19.

[2] §§ 1361 and 1362.

[3] § 761. In 1996, the Treasury issued Proposed Regulations (referred to as "check-the-box" Regulations) providing a simplified elective procedure that enables certain entities to be classified as partnerships for Federal income tax purposes even though they have corporate characteristics.

LIMITED LIABILITY COMPANY

A **limited liability company (LLC)** is a hybrid business form that combines the corporate characteristic of limited liability for the owners with the tax characteristics of a partnership.[4] All of the states now permit this legal form for conducting a business. At the beginning of 1993, 18 states had passed enabling legislation for LLCs. By the end of 1993, the number had increased to 36, and by the end of 1994, it included all 50 states. Among the early adopters of enabling legislation were Colorado, Florida, Kansas, Texas, Virginia, and Wyoming.

The most frequently cited benefit of an LLC is the limited liability of the owners. Compared to the other forms of ownership, LLCs offer additional benefits, including the following:

S corporation

- Greater flexibility in terms of the number of owners, types of owners, special allocation opportunities, and capital structure.
- Inclusion of entity debt in the owner's basis for an ownership interest.
- More liberal requirements on deferral of recognition of gain on contributions of appreciated property by an owner (determined under § 721 rather than § 351).
- For securities law purposes, an ownership interest in an LLC is not necessarily a security.

C corporation

- Ability to pass tax attributes through to the owners.
- Absence of double taxation.

Limited partnership

- Right of all owners to participate in the management of the business.
- Ability of all owners to have limited liability (no need for a general partner).

---

[4] Depending on state law, an LLC may be organized as a limited liability corporation or a limited liability partnership.

- For securities law purposes, an ownership interest in an LLC is not necessarily a security (the interest of a limited partner normally is classified as a security).

General partnership

- Ability of owners to have limited liability.
- Greater continuity of life.
- Limitation on an owner's ability to withdraw from the business.

Among the disadvantages associated with LLCs are the following:

- Uncertainty as to Federal tax status until the IRS has issued a ruling on an LLC statute in a particular state.
- Absence of a developed body of case law on LLCs.
- Frequent absence of continuity of life (e.g., limited to 30 years by many states) and free transferability of interests.
- Requirement in most states that there be at least two owners.
- Inability to qualify for § 1244 ordinary loss treatment.

ETHICAL CONSIDERATIONS **An Accounting Firm Changes Its Form of Conducting Business**

Ted is the managing partner of a regional accounting firm. Like many accounting firms, Ted's firm has expended considerable resources in defending itself against various liability claims, many of which are spurious.

Ted is meeting with the firm's management committee this afternoon. On the agenda is a continuing discussion of ways to deal with liability issues. Ted has held private discussions with several members of the committee about changing the ownership form from a partnership to a Delaware limited liability company. All of the partners except Albert regard an LLC as a positive option. Albert, a founding partner of the firm who is approaching retirement, has vehemently argued that a professional accounting firm serves the public interest and that operation as an LLC is in conflict with that objective and the related public perception. As a member of the management committee, what position will you take?

As previously discussed, the tax form for a business entity may be different from the legal form. The mere passage of a state law providing for an entity called an LLC does not ensure that the entity will be taxed as a partnership.

The association issue was discussed in Chapter 2. Under § 7701(a)(3) and the related Regulations, a business entity will be considered an association and taxed as a corporation if it possesses a majority of the following characteristics: continuity of life, centralized management, limited liability, and free transferability of interests. But see the effect on associations of the "check-the-box" Proposed Regulations mentioned in Footnote 3.

The tax status of LLCs was uncertain until the IRS issued Revenue Ruling 88–76, which classified a Wyoming LLC as a partnership for tax purposes.[5] The

---

[5] Rev.Rul. 88–76, 1988–2 C.B. 360. See also, for example, Rev.Rul. 93–5, 1993–1 C.B. 227, and Rev.Rul. 93–6, 1993–1 C.B. 229.

TAX IN THE NEWS

BIG 6 PARTNERSHIPS REORGANIZE AS LLPs

All of the Big 6 accounting firms have recently changed their organizational structure from general partnerships to limited liability partnerships (LLPs). These firms include Arthur Andersen, Coopers & Lybrand, Deloitte & Touche, Ernst & Young, KPMG Peat Marwick, and Price Waterhouse. Many other CPA firms are doing likewise.

An LLP helps to provide protection for the purely personal assets of the partners. Under the LLP organizational structure, the only partners whose personal assets are at risk to pay a judgment are those actually involved in the negligence or wrongdoing in question. Note, however, that the accounting firm is still responsible for the full judgment. Thus, the capital of the firm is still at risk.

---

key to this result was the avoidance of association status. Since an LLC will always possess the characteristic of limited liability, it is imperative to avoid at least two of the three remaining characteristics of association status. To avoid classification as an association, an LLC is generally structured to lack continuity of life and free transferability of interests.

NONTAX FACTORS

2   **LEARNING OBJECTIVE**
Appreciate the relative importance of nontax factors in making business decisions.

Taxes are only one of many factors to consider in making any business decision. The substantial reduction in tax rates brought about by TRA of 1986 makes taxation less significant. Although RRA of 1993 restored part of the tax rate reduction of TRA of 1986, nontax factors remain relevant. Above all, any business decision should make economic sense.

EXAMPLE 2

Larry is considering investing $10,000 in a limited partnership. He projects that he will be able to deduct the $10,000 within the next two years (his share of partnership losses). Since Larry's marginal tax rate is 36%, the deductions will produce a positive cash-flow effect of $3,600 ($10,000 × 36%). However, there is a substantial risk that he will not recover any of his original investment. If this occurs, his negative cash flow from the investment in the limited partnership is $6,400 ($10,000 − $3,600). Larry must decide if the investment makes economic sense. ▼

CAPITAL FORMATION

The ability of an entity to raise capital is a factor that must be considered. A sole proprietorship is subject to obvious limitations. Compared to the sole proprietorship, the partnership has a greater opportunity to raise funds through the pooling of owner resources.

EXAMPLE 3

Adam and Beth decide to form a partnership, AB. Adam contributes cash of $200,000, and Beth contributes land with an adjusted basis of $60,000 and a fair market value of $200,000.

The partnership is going to construct an apartment building at a cost of $800,000. AB pledges the land and the building to secure a loan of $700,000. ▼

The limited partnership offers even greater potential than the general partnership form because a limited partnership can secure funds from investors (limited partners).

EXAMPLE 4

Carol and Dave form a limited partnership, CD. Carol contributes cash of $200,000, and Dave contributes land with an adjusted basis of $60,000 and a fair market value of $200,000. The partnership is going to construct a shopping center at a cost of $5 million. Included in this cost is the purchase price of $800,000 for land adjacent to that contributed by Dave. Thirty limited partnership interests are sold for $100,000 each to raise $3 million. CD also pledges the shopping center (including the land) and obtains nonrecourse creditor financing of $2 million. ▼

Both the § 465 at-risk provision and the § 469 passive activity loss provision have reduced the tax attractiveness of investments in real estate, particularly in the limited partnership form. In effect, the tax consequences have a critical effect on the economic consequences.[6]

Of the different forms of business entities, the corporate form offers the greatest ease and potential for obtaining owner financing because it can issue additional shares of stock. The ultimate examples of this form are the large public companies that are listed on the stock exchanges.

LIMITED LIABILITY

Only the corporation has limited liability under state law. This absence of personal liability on the part of the owners is the most frequently cited advantage of the corporate form.

EXAMPLE 5

Ed, Fran, and Gabriella each invest $25,000 for all the shares of stock of Brown Corporation. Brown obtains creditor financing of $100,000. Brown is the defendant in a personal injury suit resulting from an accident involving one of its delivery trucks. The court awards a judgment of $2.5 million to the plaintiff. The award exceeds Brown's insurance coverage by $1.5 million. Even though the judgment will probably result in Brown's bankruptcy, the shareholders will have no personal liability for the unpaid corporate debts. ▼

Limited liability is not available to all corporations. For many years, state laws did not permit professional individuals (e.g., accountants, attorneys, architects, and physicians) to incorporate. Even though professionals are now allowed to incorporate, the statutes do not provide limited liability for the performance of professional services.

Even if state law provides for limited liability, the shareholders of small corporations may have to forgo this benefit. Quite often, such a corporation may be unable to obtain external financing (e.g., a bank loan) unless the shareholders guarantee the loan.

---

[6]See the related discussions in Chapters 10 and 11. For a comprehensive discussion of these provisions, see Chapter 11 in *West's Federal Taxation: Individual Income Taxes.*

▼ FIGURE 13–1
Limited Partnership with a
Corporate General Partner

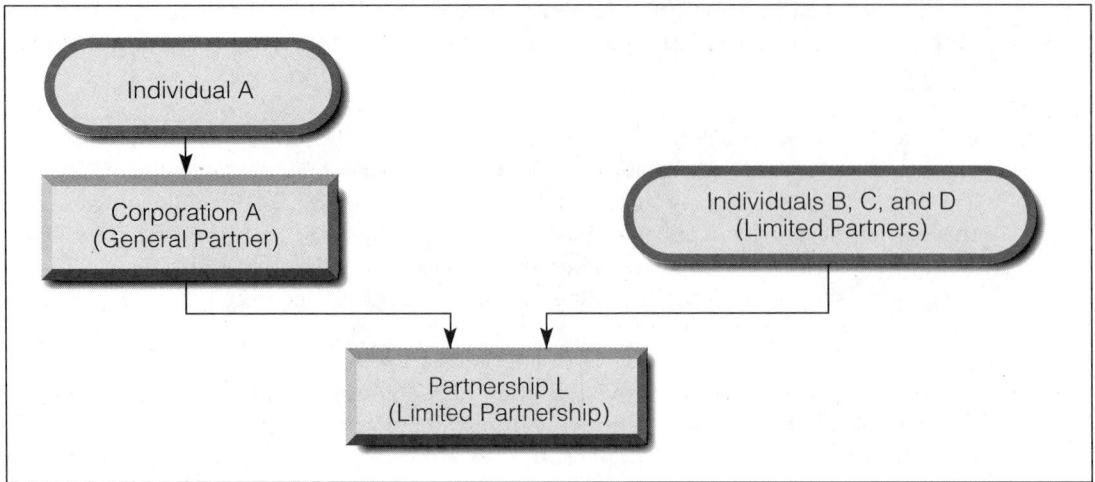

The limited partnership form provides limited liability to the limited partners. Their liability is limited to the amount invested plus any additional amount that they agreed to invest. However, the general partner (or partners) has unlimited liability.

EXAMPLE 6

Hazel, the general partner, invests $250,000 in HIJ, a limited partnership. Iris and Jane, the limited partners, each invest $50,000. While the potential loss for Iris and Jane is limited to $50,000 each, Hazel's liability is unlimited. ▼

Indirectly, it may be possible to provide the general partner with limited liability by having a corporation as the general partner (see Figure 13–1). When the entity is structured this way, the general partner (the corporation) has limited its liability under the corporate statutes. Therefore, individual A is protected from personal liability by being merely the shareholder of Corporation A. Unless the entity is very carefully structured, however, the potential exists that the IRS will treat the limited partnership as an association and therefore taxable as a corporation.[7]

OTHER FACTORS

Other nontax factors may be significant in selecting an organization form including the following: (1) estimated life of the business, (2) number of owners and their roles in the management of the business, (3) freedom of choice in transferring ownership interests, and (4) organizational formality including the related cost and extent of government regulation.

---

[7]See the discussions of associations in Chapter 2 and limited partnerships in Chapter 11. Also see Rev.Proc. 89–12, 1989–1 C.B. 798 and Rev.Rul. 88–76, 1988–2 C.B. 360. But see the effect on associations of the "check-the-box" Proposed Regulations mentioned in Footnote 3.

SINGLE VERSUS DOUBLE TAXATION

OVERALL IMPACT ON ENTITY AND OWNERS

3 LEARNING OBJECTIVE
Distinguish between the forms for conducting a business according to whether they are subject to single taxation or double taxation.

Both the sole proprietorship and the partnership are subject to single taxation. This result occurs because the owner(s) and the entity generally are not considered separate for tax purposes. Thus, the tax liability is levied at the owner level rather than at the entity level.

On the other hand, the corporate form is subject to double taxation. This is frequently cited as the major tax disadvantage of the corporate form. Under double taxation, the entity is taxed on the earnings of the corporation, and the owners are taxed on distributions to the extent they are made from corporate earnings.

The S corporation provides a way to attempt to avoid double taxation and to subject the earnings to a lower tax rate (the actual individual tax rate may be lower than the actual corporate tax rate). However, the ownership structure of an S corporation is restricted in both the number and type of shareholders. In addition, statutory exceptions subject the entity to taxation in certain circumstances. To the extent these exceptions apply, double taxation may result. Finally, the distribution policy of the S corporation may encounter difficulties with the *wherewithal to pay* concept.

EXAMPLE 7

Hawk Corporation has been operating as an S corporation since it began its business two years ago. For both of the prior years, Hawk incurred a tax loss. Hawk has taxable income of $75,000 for 1997 and expects that its earnings will increase each year in the foreseeable future. Part of this earnings increase will result from Hawk's expansion into other communities in the state. Since most of this expansion will be financed internally, no dividend distributions will be made to the shareholders.

Assuming all of Hawk's shareholders are in the 31% tax bracket, their tax liability for 1997 will be $23,250 ($75,000 × 31%). Although the S corporation election will avoid double taxation, the shareholders will have a wherewithal to pay problem. In addition, the actual tax liability for 1997 would have been less if Hawk had not been an S corporation [(15% × $50,000) + (25% × $25,000) = $13,750]. ▼

The data in Example 7 can be used to illustrate two additional tax concepts. First, the current wherewithal to pay problem could be resolved by terminating the S corporation election. The tax liability would then be imposed at the corporate level. Since the corporation does not intend to make any dividend distributions, double taxation at the present time would be avoided. Terminating the election will also reduce the overall shareholder-corporation tax liability by $9,500 ($23,250 − $13,750).[8] Second, tax decisions on the form of business organization should consider more than the current taxable year. If the S election is terminated, another election will not be available for five years. If the earnings exceed the expansion needs, Hawk could encounter an accumulated earnings tax problem (at a 39.6 percent tax rate) if it is a C corporation. Thus, the decision to revoke the election should have at least a five-year time frame. Perhaps a better

---

[8]The absence of distributions to shareholders could create an accumulated earnings tax problem under § 531. However, as long as earnings are used to finance expansion, the "reasonable needs" provision will be satisfied, and the corporation will avoid any accumulated earnings tax.

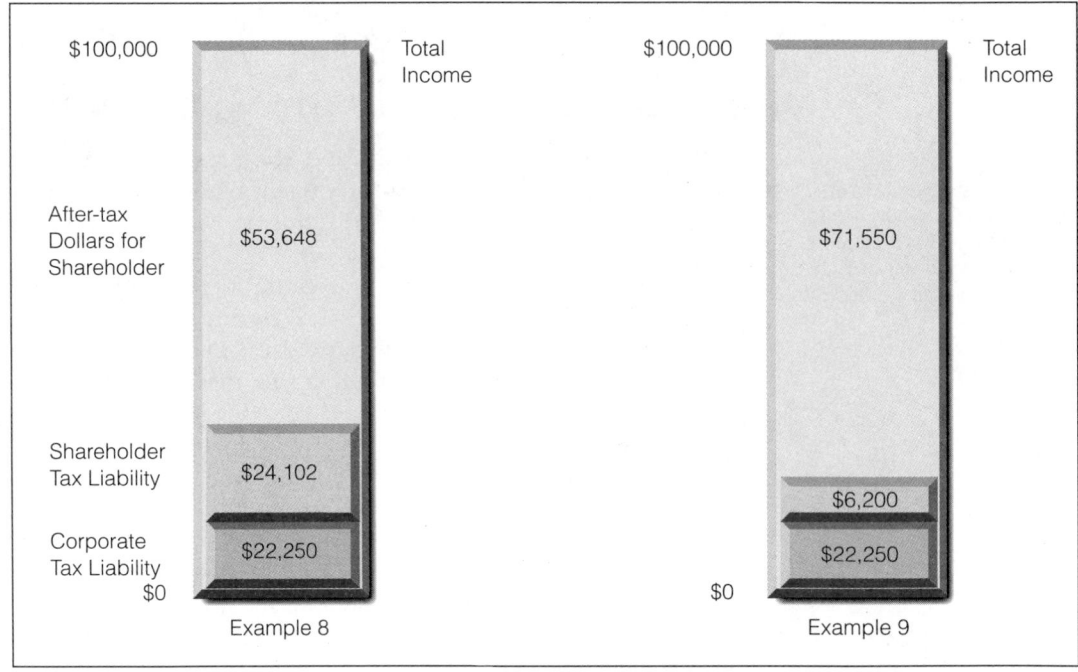

▼ **FIGURE 13–2**
Bar Graph Illustration of
Dividend versus Stock
Redemption

solution would be to retain the election and distribute enough dividends to the S corporation shareholders to enable them to pay the shareholder tax liability.

Two other variables that relate to the adverse effect of double taxation are the timing and form of corporate distributions. If no distributions are made in the short run, then only single taxation occurs in the short run.[9] To the extent that double taxation does occur in the future, the cash-flow effect should be discounted to the present. Second, when the distribution is made, is it in the form of a dividend or a return of capital (a stock redemption or a complete liquidation)?

EXAMPLE 8

Gray Corporation has taxable income of $100,000 for 1997. Gray's tax liability is $22,250. All of Gray's shareholders are in the 31% bracket. If dividends of $77,750 are distributed in 1997, the shareholders will have a tax liability of $24,102 ($77,750 × 31%). The combined corporation-shareholder tax liability is $46,352 ($22,250 + $24,102) for a combined effective tax rate of 46.4%. ▼

EXAMPLE 9

Assume the same facts as in Example 8, except the form of the distribution is a stock redemption and the basis for the redeemed shares is $57,750. The shareholders have a recognized gain of $20,000 and a tax liability of $6,200 ($20,000 × 31%). The combined corporation-shareholder tax liability is $28,450 ($22,250 + $6,200) for a combined effective tax rate of 28.5%. ▼

The differences in the tax consequences in Examples 8 and 9 are even more obvious when illustrated in bar graph form (see Figure 13–2).

[9] This assumes there is no accumulated earnings tax problem. See the subsequent discussion of distributions in Minimizing Double Taxation.

ALTERNATIVE MINIMUM TAX

All of the forms of business are directly or indirectly subject to the alternative minimum tax (AMT).[10] For the sole proprietorship and the corporation, the effect is direct (the AMT liability calculation is attached to the tax form that reports the entity's taxable income—Form 1040 or Form 1120). For the partnership and the S corporation, the effect is indirect (the tax preferences and adjustments are passed through from the entity to the owners, and the AMT liability calculation is not attached to the tax form that reports the entity's taxable income—Form 1065 or Form 1120S).

When compared with the other forms of business, the C corporation appears to have a slight advantage. The corporate AMT rate of 20 percent is less than the individual AMT rates of 26 and 28 percent. An even better perspective is provided by comparing the maximum AMT rate with the maximum regular rate for both the individual and the corporation. For the individual, the AMT rate is 71 percent (28%/39.6%) of the maximum regular rate. The AMT rate for the corporation is 57 percent (20%/35%) of the maximum regular rate. Therefore, on the basis of comparative rates, the C corporation does have an advantage.

The apparent corporate AMT rate advantage may be more than offset by the AMT adjustment that applies only to the C corporation. This is the adjustment for adjusted current earnings (ACE). The amount of the adjustment is 75 percent of the excess of ACE over unadjusted alternative minimum taxable income. If unadjusted alternative minimum taxable income exceeds ACE for the tax year, the adjustment is negative.[11]

If the ACE adjustment is continually going to cause the C corporation to be subject to the AMT, the owners should consider electing S corporation status if the eligibility requirements can be satisfied. Since the S corporation does not have this item as an adjustment, it may be possible to reduce the tax liability.

If the AMT is going to apply for the taxable year, the entity should consider accelerating income into the current taxable year and delaying deductions so that the resultant increased taxable income will be taxed at the lower AMT rate. For the C corporation, the potential rate differential is 15 percent (20 percent AMT rate versus 35 percent regular rate). For the individual taxpayer (i.e., either as a sole proprietor or as a partner), the potential tax rate differential is 11.6 percent (28 percent highest AMT rate versus 39.6 percent regular rate).

STATE TAXATION

In selecting a form for doing business, the determination of the tax consequences should not be limited to Federal income taxes. Consideration should also be given to state income taxes and, if applicable, local income taxes.[12]

The S corporation provides a good illustration of this point. Suppose that the forms of business being considered are a limited partnership or a corporation. An operating loss is projected for the next several years. The owners decide to operate the business in the corporate form. The principal nontax criterion for the decision is the limited liability attribute of the corporation. The owners consent to an

---

[10] § 55.

[11] §§ 56(c)(1) and (f). See the discussion of the corporate AMT in Chapter 6.

[12] See the discussion of multistate corporate taxation in Chapter 15.

TAX IN THE NEWS

WHO PAYS CORPORATE AMT?

One of the issues raised in the debates over tax legislation in 1995 and 1996 was whether the corporate AMT should be repealed. Among the topics discussed were the revenue generated, the related compliance costs, and the number of corporations subject to the AMT.

According to a General Accounting Office (GAO) report, only about 30,000 of the 2.1 million corporations potentially subject to the AMT paid any AMT (i.e., less than 1.5 percent) between 1987 and 1992. Approximately 2,000 corporations accounted for 85 percent of the corporate AMT paid during that period.

Proponents of the corporate AMT argued that these statistics show that the AMT is being paid by the corporations that should pay it (i.e., large corporations). Opponents argued that the same statistics show that the compliance costs borne by the mass of corporations do not justify the continuation of this tax system. Truly, "beauty is in the eye of the beholder."

S corporation election, so the corporate losses can be passed through to the shareholders to deduct on their individual tax returns. However, assume that state law does not permit the S corporation election on the state income tax return. Thus, the owners will not receive the tax benefits of the loss deductions that would have been available on their state income tax returns if they had chosen the limited partnership form. As a result of providing limited liability to the owner who would have been the general partner for the limited partnership, the loss deduction at the state level is forgone.

CONTROLLING THE ENTITY TAX

4   **LEARNING OBJECTIVE**
Identify techniques for avoiding double taxation and for controlling the entity tax.

Of the four forms of business entities, it appears at first glance that only the corporation needs to be concerned with controlling the entity tax. If control is defined in the narrow sense of double taxation, then this issue is restricted to the corporate form. However, from the broader perspective of controlling the tax liability related to the profits of the business entity, whether imposed at the entity or owner level, all four business forms are encompassed.

Techniques that can be used to minimize the current-period tax liability include the following:

1. Distribution policy.
2. Recognizing the interaction between the regular tax liability and the AMT liability.
3. Utilization of special allocations.
4. Favorable treatment of certain fringe benefits.
5. Minimizing double taxation.

Some of the techniques apply to all four forms of business entities. Others apply to only one of the four forms. Even those that apply to all do not minimize taxes equally for all forms. Since the first three techniques are discussed elsewhere in this chapter, only the last two are discussed here.

FAVORABLE TREATMENT OF CERTAIN FRINGE BENEFITS

Ideally, a fringe benefit produces the following tax consequences:

- Deductible by the entity (employer) that provides the fringe benefit.
- Excludible from the gross income of the taxpayer (employee) who receives the fringe benefit.

From the perspective of the owner or owners of an entity, when the entity provides such favorably taxed fringe benefits to an owner, the benefits are paid for with *before-tax* dollars.

EXAMPLE 10

Rocky, the owner of Rocky's Ranch, a C corporation in the 34% tax bracket, is provided with meals and lodging that qualify for exclusion treatment under § 119. The annual cost of the meals and lodging to Rocky's Ranch is $10,000. Since the cost is deductible in calculating the taxable income of Rocky's Ranch on Form 1120, the after-tax cost to the corporation is only $6,600 [$10,000 − (34% × $10,000)]. Since the $10,000 is excluded in calculating Rocky's gross income, there is no additional tax cost at the owner level. If Rocky had paid for the meals and lodging himself, no deduction would have been permitted because these expenditures are nondeductible personal expenditures. Thus, from Rocky's perspective, the receipt of excludible meals and lodging of $10,000 is equivalent to receiving a distribution from the corporation of $15,625 [$10,000/(100% − 36%)], assuming he is in the 36% tax bracket. ▼

Not all favorably taxed fringe benefits receive exclusion treatment. Although not as attractive to the recipient, another approach provided in the Code is deferral treatment (e.g., pension plans and profit sharing plans).

Example 10 illustrates how certain fringe benefits can be used to benefit the owner of an entity and at the same time have a beneficial impact on the combined tax liability of the entity and the owner. In recognition of this, Congress has enacted various nondiscrimination provisions that generally negate favorable tax treatment if the fringe benefit program is discriminatory. In addition, the Code includes several statutory provisions that make the favorably taxed fringe benefit treatment available only to *employees* (e.g., group term life insurance, meal and lodging exclusion).[13]

The IRS defines the term *employee* restrictively. For the owner of a business entity to be treated as an employee, the entity must be a corporation.[14] For this purpose, an S corporation is treated as a partnership, and a greater-than-2 percent shareholder is treated as a partner.[15]

Classification of an owner as a nonemployee produces two negative results. First, the deduction for the cost of the fringe benefit to the entity is disallowed at the entity level. Second, the owner whose fringe benefit has been paid for by the entity must include the cost of the fringe benefit in gross income.

---

[13] §§ 79 and 119.

[14] Reg. § 1.79–0(b). The IRS has not been completely successful with respect to this position.

[15] § 1372(a).

ETHICAL
CONSIDERATIONS

Check-the-Box Tax Benefits

Ernest and Thelma have been operating Copper Partnership for five years. Each owns a 50 percent capital interest and a 50 percent profits interest. They currently receive salaries of $125,000 each and withdraw their shares of partnership profits of $75,000 each.

Thelma is disenchanted with this arrangement because partner-employees are not eligible for the favorable fringe benefit treatment (e.g., group-term life insurance, accident and health insurance) that shareholder-employees receive. She proposes to Ernest that under the check-the-box Regulations they check the box marked "corporation." Then they can avoid double taxation by increasing their salaries to $200,000, which is something she has wanted to do.

Evaluate Thelma's advice from both a tax compliance and an ethical perspective.

MINIMIZING DOUBLE TAXATION

Only the corporate form is potentially subject to double taxation. Several techniques are available for eliminating or at least reducing the second layer of taxation:

1. Making distributions to the shareholders that are deductible to the corporation.
2. Not making distributions to the shareholders.
3. Making distributions that qualify for return of capital treatment at the shareholder level.
4. Making the S corporation election.

Making Deductible Distributions.   Use of the first technique requires careful advance planning. Typical distribution forms that will result in a deduction to the corporation are (1) salary payments to shareholder-employees, (2) lease rental payments to shareholder-lessors, and (3) interest payments to shareholder-creditors. Recognizing the tax benefit of this technique, the IRS scrutinizes these types of transactions carefully. All three types are evaluated in terms of *reasonableness*.[16] In addition, the interest payments may result in the IRS raising the **thin capitalization** issue and reclassifying some or all of the debt as equity.[17] IRS success with either approach will raise the specter of double taxation.

EXAMPLE 11

Donna owns all the stock of Green and is also the chief executive officer. Green's taxable income before salary payments to Donna is as follows:

1995	$ 80,000
1996	50,000
1997	250,000

---

[16] § 162(a)(1). *Mayson Manufacturing Co. v. Comm.*, 49–2 USTC ¶9467, 38 AFTR 1028, 178 F.2d 115 (CA–6, 1949); *Harolds Club v. Comm.*, 65–1 USTC ¶9198, 15 AFTR2d 241, 340 F.2d 861 (CA–9, 1965).

[17] § 385; Rev.Rul. 83–98, 1983–2 C.B. 40; *Bauer v. Comm.*, 84–2 USTC ¶9996, 55 AFTR2d 85–433, 748 F.2d 1365 (CA–9, 1984).

During the year, Donna receives a monthly salary of $3,000. In December of each year, she reviews the operations for the year and determines the year-end bonus to be paid to the key officers (only Donna for bonus purposes). Donna's yearly bonuses are as follows:

1995	$ 44,000
1996	14,000
1997	214,000

The obvious purpose of Green's bonus program is to reduce the corporate taxable income to zero and thereby avoid double taxation. The examination of Green's tax return by the IRS would likely result in a deduction disallowance for unreasonable compensation. ▼

EXAMPLE 12

Tom and Vicki each contribute $20,000 to TV Corporation for all the stock of TV. In addition, they each loan $80,000 to TV. The loan is documented by formal notes, the interest rate is 12%, and the maturity date is 10 years from the date of the loan.

The notes provide the opportunity for the corporation to make payments of $9,600 each year to both Tom and Vicki and for the payments not to be subject to double taxation. That is, the interest payments are includible in the gross income of Tom and Vicki, but are deductible by TV in calculating its taxable income. At the time of repayment in 10 years, neither Tom nor Vicki will have any gross income from the repayment since the $80,000 amount realized is equal to the basis for the note of $80,000 (return of capital concept).

If the IRS succeeded in reclassifying the notes as equity, Tom and Vicki's includible gross income of $9,600 each would remain the same (interest income would be reclassified as dividend income). However, because the dividend payments are not deductible by TV, the corporation's taxable income would increase by $19,200 ($9,600 × 2). To make matters worse, the repayment of the notes in 10 years would not qualify for return of capital treatment and would likely result in dividend income treatment for Tom and Vicki. ▼

Not Making Distributions. Double taxation will not occur unless the corporation makes (actual or deemed) distributions to the shareholders. A closely held corporation that does not make distributions will eventually encounter an accumulated earnings tax problem unless the reasonable needs requirement is satisfied. When making distribution policy decisions each year, the board of directors should be apprised of any potential accumulated earnings tax problem and take the appropriate steps to eliminate it. The accumulated earnings tax rate of 39.6 percent is the same as the maximum tax bracket for individual taxpayers.[18]

EXAMPLE 13

According to an internal calculation made by Dolphin Corporation, its accumulated taxable income is $400,000. The board of directors would prefer not to declare any dividends, but is considering a dividend declaration of $400,000 to avoid the accumulated earnings tax. All of the shareholders are in the 36% bracket.

If a dividend of $400,000 is declared, the tax cost to the shareholders is $144,000 ($400,000 × 36%). If a dividend is not declared and the IRS assesses the accumulated earnings tax, the tax cost to the corporation for the accumulated earnings tax would be $158,400 ($400,000 × 39.6%).

To make matters worse, Dolphin will have incurred the accumulated earnings tax cost without getting any funds out of the corporation to the shareholders. If the unwise decision were now made to distribute the remaining $241,600 ($400,000 − $158,400) to the shareholders, the additional tax cost at the shareholder level would be $86,976 ($241,600 × 36%).

---

[18] § 531. See the discussion of the accumulated earnings tax in Chapter 6.

Therefore, the combined shareholder-corporation tax cost would be $245,376 ($158,400 + $86,976). This is 170% ($245,376/$144,000) of the tax cost that would have resulted from an initial dividend distribution of $400,000. ▼

Assuming that the accumulated earnings tax can be avoided (e.g., a growth company whose reasonable needs justify its no dividend policy), a policy of no distributions to shareholders can avoid the second layer of taxation forever. This will occur if the shares of stock are bequeathed to the taxpayer's beneficiaries. As a result of the step-up in basis rules for inherited property, the basis of the stock for the beneficiaries will be the fair market value at the date of the decedent's death rather than the decedent's basis.

ETHICAL CONSIDERATIONS

Providing Information on the Accumulated Earnings Tax

Heron Corporation has been in operation for 10 years. Since Heron's creation, all of the stock has been owned by Andy, who initially invested $200,000 in the corporation. Heron has been successful far beyond Andy's expectations, and the current fair market value of the stock is $10 million. While he has been paid a salary of $200,000 per year by the corporation, all of Heron's earnings have been reinvested in the growth of the corporation.

Heron is currently being audited by the IRS. One of the issues raised by the revenue agent is the possibility of the assessment of the accumulated earnings tax. Andy is not concerned about this issue because he believes Heron can easily justify the accumulations based on its past rapid expansion by opening new outlets. The expansion program is fully documented in the minutes of Heron's board of directors. Andy has provided this information to the revenue agent.

Two years ago, Andy decided that he would curtail any further expansion into new markets by Heron. In his opinion, further expansion would exceed his ability to manage the corporation effectively. Since the tax year under audit is three years ago, Andy sees no reason to provide the revenue agent with this information.

Heron will continue its policy of no dividend payments into the foreseeable future. Andy believes that if the accumulated earnings issue is satisfactorily resolved on this audit, it probably will not be raised again on any subsequent audits. Thus, double taxation in the form of the tax on dividends at the shareholder level or the accumulated earnings tax at the corporate level can be avoided.

What is Heron's responsibility to disclose to the revenue agent the expected change in its growth strategy? Are Andy's beliefs regarding future accumulated earnings tax issues realistic?

Return of Capital Distributions. The magnitude of the effect of double taxation can be reduced if the corporate distributions to the shareholders can qualify for return of capital rather than dividend treatment. For an ongoing corporation, the stock redemption provisions offer an opportunity to reduce the includible gross income at the shareholder level. The corporate liquidation provisions can be used if the business entity will cease to operate in corporate form.

EXAMPLE 14

Copper Corporation makes a distribution of $400,000 to its shareholders. Mark and Kate, two of the shareholders, each receive $25,000. The form of the distribution permits the shareholders to surrender a certain number of shares of stock. The potential exists that the distribution can qualify for stock redemption treatment at the shareholder level. Mark satisfies the requirements for a substantially disproportionate distribution under § 302. Kate does not because she is in control of the corporation after the distribution (she owns 60% of the stock). Assuming Mark's basis for the shares redeemed is $20,000, he has a capital gain of $5,000 ($25,000 − $20,000). Kate has dividend income of $25,000. She must allocate her stock basis among her remaining shares. ▼

Electing S Corporation Status. Electing S corporation status generally eliminates double taxation by making the corporation a tax reporter rather than a taxpayer. Therefore, the only tax levy is at the shareholder level. Factors to consider in making this election include the following:

- Are all the shareholders willing to consent to the election?
- Can the qualification requirements under § 1361 be satisfied at the time of the election?
- Since the qualification requirements become maintenance requirements, can these requirements continue to be satisfied?
- For what period will the conditions that make the election beneficial continue to prevail?
- Will the corporate distribution policy create wherewithal to pay problems at the shareholder level?

EXAMPLE 15

Emerald Corporation commenced business in January 1997. The two shareholders, Diego and Jaime, are both in the 31% tax bracket. The following operating results are projected for the first five years of operations:

1997	($ 50,000)
1998	400,000
1999	600,000
2000	800,000
2001	1,000,000

The corporation plans to expand rapidly. Therefore, no distributions will be made to shareholders. In addition, beginning in 1998, preferred stock will be offered to a substantial number of investors to help finance the expansion.

If the S corporation election is made for 1997, the $50,000 loss can be passed through to Diego and Jaime's tax returns. Therefore, the cash-flow effect would be $15,500 ($50,000 × 31%). Assume that the election is either revoked or is involuntarily terminated at the beginning of 1998 as a result of the issuance of the preferred stock. The corporate tax liability for 1998 would be $136,000 ($400,000 × 34%).

If the S corporation election is not made for 1997, the $50,000 loss will be a net operating loss. The amount can be carried forward to reduce the 1998 corporate taxable income to $350,000 ($400,000 − $50,000). The resultant tax liability is $119,000 ($350,000 × 34%).

Should the S corporation election be made for just the one-year period? The answer is unclear. With an assumed after-tax rate of return to Diego and Jaime of 10%, the value of the $15,500 one year hence is $17,050 ($15,500 × 110%). Even considering the time value of money, the combined corporation-shareholder negative cash-flow effect of $118,950 ($136,000 − $17,050) in the case of an S election is about the same as the $119,000 corporate tax liability that would result for a regular corporation. The negative cash flow is even greater when related accounting and/or legal fees are considered. ▼

CONDUIT VERSUS ENTITY TREATMENT

Under the **conduit concept,** the entity is viewed as merely an extension of the owners. Under the **entity concept,** the entity is regarded as being separate and distinct from its owners. The effects that these different approaches have are examined for the partnership, C corporation, and S corporation:

- Recognition at time of contribution to the entity.
- Basis of ownership interest.
- Results of operations.
- Recognition at time of distribution.
- Passive activity losses.
- At-risk rules.
- Special allocations.

The sole proprietorship is not analyzed separately because the owner and the business are in essence the same. In one circumstance, however, a tax difference does occur. Recognition does not occur when an owner contributes an asset to a sole proprietorship. Thus, the basis generally is a carryover basis. However, if the asset is a personal use asset, the sole proprietorship's basis is the *lower of* the adjusted basis or the fair market value at the date of contribution. Also note that if a personal use asset is contributed to a partnership or corporation, this *lower of* rule applies.

EFFECT ON RECOGNITION AT TIME OF CONTRIBUTION TO THE ENTITY

Since the conduit approach applies for the partnership, § 721 provides for no recognition on the contribution of property to the partnership in exchange for a partnership interest. Section 721 protects both a contribution associated with the formation of the partnership and later contributions. The partnership has a carryover basis for the contributed property, and the partners have a carryover basis for their partnership interests.[19]

Since the entity approach applies for the corporation, the transfer of property to a corporation in exchange for its stock is a taxable event. However, if the § 351 control requirement is satisfied, no gain or loss is recognized. In this case, both the corporate property and the shareholders' stock will have a carryover basis.[20] This control requirement makes it more likely that shareholders who contribute appreciated property to the corporation *after* the formation of the corporation will recognize gain.

To the extent that the fair market value of property contributed to the entity at the time of formation is not equal to the property's adjusted basis, a special allocation may be desirable. With a special allocation, the owner contributing the property receives the tax benefit or detriment for any recognized gain or loss that subsequently results because of the initial difference between the adjusted basis and the fair market value. For the partnership, this special allocation treatment is

---

[19] See the pertinent discussion in Chapter 10.   [20] See the pertinent discussion in Chapter 3.

mandatory. No such allocation is available for the C corporation form, since the gain or loss is recognized at the corporation level rather than at the shareholder level. For the S corporation, no such allocation is available. The recognized gain or loss will be reported on the shareholders' tax returns based on their stock ownership.

EXAMPLE 16

Khalid contributes land with an adjusted basis of $10,000 and a fair market value of $50,000 for a 50% ownership interest. At the same time, Tracy contributes cash of $50,000 for the remaining 50% ownership interest. Because the entity is unable to obtain the desired zoning, it subsequently sells the land for $50,000.

If the entity is a C corporation, Khalid has a realized gain of $40,000 ($50,000 − $10,000) and a recognized gain of $0 resulting from the contribution. His basis for his stock is $10,000, and the corporation has a basis for the land of $10,000. The corporation has a realized and recognized gain of $40,000 ($50,000 − $10,000) when it sells the land. Thus, what should have been Khalid's recognized gain becomes the corporation's taxable gain. There is no way that the corporation can directly allocate the recognized gain to Khalid. The corporation could distribute the land to Khalid and let him sell the land, but the distribution may be taxable to Khalid as a dividend, and gain may be recognized at the corporate level on the distribution.

If the entity is a partnership, the tax consequences are the same as in the C corporation illustration except for the $40,000 recognized gain on the sale of the land. The partnership has a realized and recognized gain of $40,000 ($50,000 − $10,000). However, even though Khalid's share of profits and losses is only 50%, all of the $40,000 recognized gain is allocated to him. If the entity is an S corporation, the tax consequences are the same as in the C corporation illustration except that Khalid reports $20,000 of the recognized gain on his tax return and Tracy reports $20,000 also. ▼

EFFECT ON BASIS OF OWNERSHIP INTEREST

In a partnership, since the partner is the taxpayer, profits and losses of the partnership affect the partner's basis in the partnership interest. Likewise, the partner's basis is increased by the share of partnership liability increases and is decreased by the share of partnership liability decreases. This liability effect enables the partner to benefit from the leverage concept. Accordingly, the partner's basis changes frequently.[21]

For the C corporation, the corporation is the taxpayer. Therefore, the shareholder's basis for the stock is not affected by corporate profits and losses or corporate liability increases or decreases.

The treatment of an S corporation shareholder falls in between that of the partner and the C corporation shareholder. The S corporation shareholder's stock basis is increased by the share of profits and decreased by the share of losses, but it is not affected by corporate liability increases or decreases. Thus, unlike the partner, the S corporation shareholder does not benefit from the leverage concept.

EXAMPLE 17

Peggy contributes cash of $100,000 to an entity for a 30% ownership interest. The entity borrows $50,000 and repays $20,000 of this amount by the end of the taxable year. The profits for the year are $90,000.

If the entity is a partnership, Peggy's basis at the end of the period is $136,000 ($100,000 investment + $9,000 share of net liability increase + $27,000 share of profits). If

---

[21]§§ 705 and 752.

Peggy is a C corporation shareholder instead, her stock basis is $100,000 ($100,000 original investment). If the corporation is an S corporation, Peggy's stock basis is $127,000 ($100,000 + $27,000). ▼

EFFECT ON RESULTS OF OPERATIONS

The entity concept is responsible for producing potential double taxation for the C corporation form (the corporation is taxed on its earnings, and the shareholders are taxed on the distribution of earnings). Thus, from the perspective of taxing the results of operations, the entity concept appears to be a disadvantage for the corporation. However, whether the entity concept actually produces disadvantageous results depends on the following:

- Whether the corporation generates positive taxable income.
- The tax rates that apply for the corporation and for the shareholders.
- The distribution policy of the corporation.

As discussed previously, techniques exist for getting cash out of the corporation to the shareholders without incurring double taxation (e.g., compensation payments to shareholder-employees, lease rental payments to shareholder-lessors, and interest payments to shareholder-creditors). Since these payments are deductible to the corporation, they reduce corporate taxable income. If the payments can be used to reduce corporate taxable income to zero, the corporation will have no tax liability.

The maximum individual tax bracket (39.6 percent) does exceed the maximum corporate tax bracket (35 percent). However, in a specific situation, the corporate tax rates that apply may be greater than or less than the applicable individual rates. This opportunity for the corporation to be subject to a lower tax rate is less likely to be available for personal service corporations. There, the only rate available is 35 percent.[22]

As previously discussed, double taxation can occur only if distributions are made to the shareholders. Thus, if no distributions are made and if the entity can avoid the accumulated earnings tax (e.g., based on the statutory credit or the reasonable needs adjustment) and the personal holding company tax (e.g., the corporation primarily generates active income), only one current level of taxation will occur. If distributions do occur in the future with respect to current earnings, the resultant tax liability should be discounted for the interim period. If the distribution can qualify for return of capital treatment (stock redemption or liquidation) rather than dividend treatment, the shareholder tax liability will be decreased. Ideally, taxation of the earnings at the shareholder level can be avoided permanently if the stock passes through the decedent shareholder's estate.

The entity concept does result in the earnings components losing their identity when they are passed through to shareholders in the form of dividends. This may produce a negative result for net long-term capital gains, as the potential beneficial capital gain treatment is lost. Since capital gains lose their identity when passed through in the form of dividends, they cannot be used to offset capital losses at the shareholder level. An even more negative result is produced when dividends are paid out of tax-exempt income. Tax-exempt income is excludible in calculating corporate taxable income, but is included in calculating current earnings and profits. Thus, what should not be subject to taxation is taxed because of the entity concept.

---

[22] § 11(b)(2).

Both the partnership and the S corporation use the conduit concept in reporting the results of operations. Any item that is subject to special treatment on the taxpayer-owners' tax return is reported separately to the owners. Other items are netted and reported as taxable income. Thus, taxable income merely represents those income and deduction items that are not subject to special treatment.[23]

Many of the problems that the entity concept may produce for the C corporation form are not present for the partnership or S corporation. Included in this category are double taxation, problems with the reasonableness requirement, and loss of identity of the income or expense item at the owner level.

Only the partnership completely applies the conduit concept in reporting the results of operations. In several circumstances, the S corporation is subject to taxation at the corporate level, including the tax on built-in gains and the tax on certain passive investment income.[24] This limited application of the entity concept necessitates additional planning to attempt to avoid taxation at the corporate level.

EFFECT ON RECOGNITION AT TIME OF DISTRIBUTION

The application of the conduit concept results in distributions not being taxed to the owners. The application of the entity concept produces the opposite result. Therefore, distributions can be made to partners or to S corporation shareholders tax-free, whereas the same distribution would produce dividend income treatment for corporate shareholders.

In this regard, a distinction must be made between distributions of earnings and other distributions for the S corporation. The S corporation generally is treated as a conduit with respect to its operations. However, as previously discussed, in several cases the entity concept is applied, and the S corporation becomes a taxpayer rather than merely a tax reporter. In effect, the conduit concept applies to S corporation operations unless otherwise specified in Subchapter S of the Code. Since distributions of earnings are included in the operations category, they are subject to conduit treatment through the application of the Accumulated Adjustments Account (AAA).[25] Distributions in excess of earnings qualify for return of capital treatment.

A combination entity/conduit concept applies to property distributions to S corporation shareholders. As discussed above, the conduit concept applies with respect to the shareholder. However, if the property distributed is appreciated property, § 311(b) provides that the realized gain is recognized at the corporate level (same treatment as a regular corporation). This gain recognition is an application of the entity concept. Then, however, the conduit concept is applied to the pass-through of the gain to the shareholders.

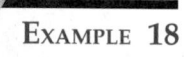

EXAMPLE 18

Tan, an S corporation, is equally owned by Leif and Matt. Tan distributes two parcels of land to Leif and Matt. Tan has a basis of $10,000 for each parcel. Each parcel has a fair market value of $15,000. The distribution results in a $10,000 ($30,000 – $20,000) recognized gain for Tan. Leif and Matt each report $5,000 of the gain on their individual income tax returns. ▼

Stock redemptions and complete liquidations are not covered by the provisions of Subchapter S. Therefore, the tax consequences of an S corporation stock redemption are determined under the regular corporate provisions in § 302, while

---

[23] §§ 701 , 702 , 1363, and 1366.
[24] §§ 1374 and 1375.

[25] § 1368.

those for a complete liquidation are determined under the regular corporate provisions in §§ 331 and 336.

EFFECT ON PASSIVE ACTIVITY LOSSES

The passive activity loss rules apply to the partnership and to the S corporation, but apply to the C corporation only for personal service corporations and closely held corporations. A *closely held corporation* is defined as one that meets the stock ownership requirement under the personal holding company provisions. That is, more than 50 percent of the value of the outstanding stock at any time during the last half of the taxable year is owned by or for not more than five individuals. The definition of a personal service corporation is modified slightly from the standard definition under § 269A. A corporation is classified as a § 469 *personal service corporation* only if the following requirements are satisfied:

- The principal activity of the corporation is the performance of personal services.
- The services are substantially performed by owner-employees.
- Owner-employees own more than 10 percent in value of the stock of the corporation.

The general passive activity loss rules apply to the personal service corporation. Therefore, passive activity losses cannot be offset against either active income or portfolio income. For the closely held corporation, the application of the passive activity rules is less harsh. Although passive activity losses cannot be offset against portfolio income, they can be offset against active income.

The statutory language of § 469(a)(2), which describes the taxpayers subject to the passive activity loss rules, does not mention either the partnership or the S corporation. Instead, it mentions the individual taxpayer. Since the conduit concept applies, the passive activity results are separately stated at the partnership or S corporation level and are passed through to the partners or shareholders with the identity maintained.

EFFECT OF AT-RISK RULES

The at-risk rules of § 465 apply to both the partnership and the S corporation. Although the statutory language of § 465(a) mentions neither, the conduit concept that applies to both entities results in the application of § 465. Section 465 also applies to closely held C corporations (defined the same as under the passive activity loss rules). However, exceptions are available for closely held corporations that are actively engaged in equipment leasing or are defined as qualified C corporations.

The application of the at-risk rules produces a harsher result for the partnership than for the S corporation. This occurs because the partnership, in the absence of § 465, would have a greater opportunity to use the leveraging concept.

EXAMPLE 19

Walt is the general partner, and Ira and Vera are the limited partners in the WIV limited partnership. Walt contributes land with an adjusted basis of $40,000 and a fair market value of $50,000 for his partnership interest, and Ira and Vera each contribute cash of $100,000 for their partnership interests. They agree to share profits and losses equally. To finance construction of an apartment building, the partnership obtains $600,000 of nonrecourse financing [not qualified nonrecourse financing under § 465(b)(6)] using the land and the

TAX IN THE NEWS

IS GOLD AT RISK?

O ver three thousand investors decided that a mining investment plan entitled "Gold for Tax Dollars" was too lucrative to let pass. The investment plan, advertised in a brochure printed to resemble a gold rush broadside, promised investors tax deductions up to four times the amount of their original investment. This promotional material emphasized that each investor's mine was to be operated as a sole proprietorship. There would be no limited partners. The purpose of this structure was "... to avoid the at-risk limitation rules applicable to partnerships." However, when the IRS explained to the Tax Court that each investor's mine consisted of several cubic yards of "auriferous gravel"—the exact amount depended on the dollar amount of the investment—the Court rejected the sole proprietorship spin (*Marion C. and Ruth Gray, et. al.*, 88 T.C. 1306 [1987]). One of the investors in the scheme, who was a pilot, had managed "with substantial difficulty" to actually visit a purported mining site. He testified that he was unable to locate his own particular cubic yards of auriferous gravel and added, "I didn't even know if I was going to get out of there alive."

building as the pledged assets. Each partner's basis for the partnership interest is as follows:

	Walt	**Ira**	**Vera**
Contribution	$ 40,000	$100,000	$100,000
Share of nonrecourse debt	200,000	200,000	200,000
Basis	$240,000	$300,000	$300,000

Without the at-risk rules, Ira and Vera could pass through losses up to $300,000 each even though they invested only $100,000 and have no personal liability for the nonrecourse debt. However, the at-risk rules limit the loss pass-through to the at-risk basis, which is $100,000 for Ira and $100,000 for Vera. Note that the at-risk rules can also affect the general partner. Since Walt is not at risk for the nonrecourse debt, his at-risk basis is $40,000. If the mortgage were recourse debt, his at-risk basis would be $640,000 ($40,000 + $600,000). Thus, as a result of the at-risk rules, leveraging is available only for recourse debt for partners who have potential personal liability. ▼

EXAMPLE 20

Assume the same facts as in Example 19, except that the entity is an S corporation and Walt receives 20% of the stock and Ira and Vera each receive 40%. The basis for their stock is as follows:

Walt	$ 40,000
Ira	100,000
Vera	100,000

The nonrecourse debt does not affect the calculation of stock basis. The stock basis for each shareholder would remain the same even if the debt were recourse debt. Only direct loans by the shareholders increase the ceiling on loss pass-through (basis for stock plus basis for loans by shareholders). ▼

EFFECT OF SPECIAL ALLOCATIONS

An advantage of the conduit concept over the entity concept is the ability to make special allocations. Special allocations are not permitted for the C corporation form. Indirectly, however, the corporate form may be able to achieve results similar to those produced by special allocations through payments to owners (e.g., salary payments, lease rental payments, and interest payments) and through different classes of stock (e.g., preferred, common). However, even in these cases, the breadth of the treatment and the related flexibility are less than that achievable under the conduit concept.

Although the S corporation is a conduit, it is treated more like a C corporation than a partnership with respect to special allocations. This treatment results from the application of the per-share and per-day rule in § 1377(a). Although the S corporation is limited to one class of stock, it can still use the payments to owners procedure. However, the IRS has the authority to reallocate income among members of a family if fair returns are not provided for services rendered or capital invested.[26]

▼

EXAMPLE 21

The stock of an S corporation is owned by Debra (50%), Helen (25%), and Joyce (25%). Helen and Joyce are Debra's adult children. Debra is in the 36% bracket, and Helen and Joyce are in the 15% bracket. Only Debra is an employee of the corporation. She is paid an annual salary of $20,000, whereas employees with similar responsibilities in other corporations earn $100,000. The corporation generates earnings of approximately $200,000 each year.

It appears that the reason Debra is paid a low salary is to enable more of the earnings of the S corporation to be taxed to Helen and Joyce, who are in lower tax brackets. Thus, the IRS could use its statutory authority to allocate a larger salary to Debra. ▼

The partnership has many opportunities to use special allocations, including the following:

- The ability to share profits and losses differently from the share in capital.
- The ability to share profits and losses differently.
- The special allocation required under § 704(c) for the difference between the adjusted basis and the fair market value of contributed property.
- The special allocation of any item permitted under § 704(a) if the substantial economic effect rule of § 704(b) is satisfied.
- The optional adjustment to basis permitted under § 734 that results from partnership distributions.
- The optional adjustment to basis permitted under § 743 that results from an acquisition by purchase, taxable exchange, or inheritance.

DISPOSITION OF A BUSINESS OR AN OWNERSHIP INTEREST

6 ▼ **LEARNING OBJECTIVE**
Analyze the effect of the disposition of a business on the owners and the entity for each of the forms for conducting a business.

A key factor in evaluating the tax consequences of disposing of a business is whether the disposition is viewed as the sale of an ownership interest or as a sale of assets. Generally, the tax consequences are more favorable if the transaction is treated as a sale of the ownership interest.

---

[26] § 1366(e).

SOLE PROPRIETORSHIP

Regardless of the form of the transaction, the sale of a sole proprietorship is treated as the sale of individual assets. Thus, gains and losses must be calculated separately. Classification as capital gain or ordinary income depends on the nature and holding period of the individual assets. Ordinary income property such as inventory will result in ordinary gains and losses. Section 1231 property such as land, buildings, and machinery used in the business will produce § 1231 gains and losses (subject to depreciation recapture under §§ 1245 and 1250). Capital assets such as investment land and stocks qualify for capital gain or loss treatment.

If the amount realized exceeds the fair market value of the identifiable assets, the excess is identified with goodwill, which produces capital gain for the seller. If instead the excess payment were identified with a covenant not to compete, the related gain would be classified as ordinary income rather than capital gain. Prior to RRA of 1993, classification of the excess as goodwill produced negative tax consequences from the purchaser's perspective in that the goodwill could not be amortized. One way to avoid this negative result was to identify the excess with a covenant not to compete. RRA of 1993 neutralized this negative tax consequence for the buyer by providing that both goodwill and covenants are to be amortized over a 15-year statutory period.[27]

▼
EXAMPLE 22

Seth, who is in the 36% tax bracket, sells his sole proprietorship to Wilma for $600,000. The identifiable assets are as follows:

	Adjusted Basis	Fair Market Value
Inventory	$ 20,000	$ 25,000
Accounts receivable	40,000	40,000
Machinery and equipment*	125,000	150,000
Buildings**	175,000	250,000
Land	40,000	100,000
	$400,000	$565,000

*Potential § 1245 recapture of $50,000.
**Potential § 1250 recapture of $20,000.

The sale produces the following results for Seth:

	Gain (Loss)	Ordinary Income	§ 1231 Gain	Capital Gain
Inventory	$ 5,000	$ 5,000		
Accounts receivable	–0–			
Machinery and equipment	25,000	25,000		
Buildings	75,000	20,000	$ 55,000	
Land	60,000		60,000	
Goodwill	35,000			$35,000
	$200,000	$50,000	$115,000	$35,000

If the sale is structured this way, Wilma can deduct the $35,000 paid for goodwill over a 15-year period. If instead Wilma paid the $35,000 to Seth for a covenant not to compete for a period of seven years, she still would amortize the $35,000 over a 15-year period. However, this would result in Seth's $35,000 capital gain being reclassified as ordinary income. If the covenant has no legal relevance to Wilma, in exchange for treating the payment as a goodwill payment, she should negotiate for a price reduction that reflects the benefit of the tax on capital gains to Seth. ▼

PARTNERSHIP

The sale of a partnership can be structured as the sale of assets or as the sale of an ownership interest. If the transaction takes the form of an asset sale, it is treated the same as for a sole proprietorship (described above). The sale of an ownership interest is treated as the sale of a capital asset under § 741 (subject to ordinary income potential under § 751 for unrealized receivables and substantially appreciated inventory). Thus, if capital gain treatment can produce beneficial results for the taxpayer (e.g., has capital losses to offset or has beneficially treated net capital gain), the sale of an ownership interest is preferable.

From the buyers' perspective, the form does not produce different tax consequences. If the transaction is an asset purchase, the basis for the assets is the amount paid for them. Assuming the buyers intend to continue to operate in the partnership form, the assets can be contributed to a partnership under § 721. Therefore, the owners' basis for their partnership interests is equal to the purchase price for the assets. Likewise, if ownership interests are purchased, the owners' basis is the purchase price, and the partnership's basis for the assets is the purchase price since the original partnership will have terminated.[28]

A problem may arise if an individual purchases a partnership interest from another partner and the amount paid exceeds the new partner's pro rata share of the partnership's basis for the assets. If the new partner does not acquire at least a 50 percent capital and profits interest, the old partnership may not terminate.[29]

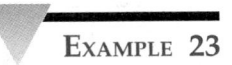

EXAMPLE 23

Paul purchases Sandra's partnership interest for $100,000. He acquires both a 20% capital interest and a 20% interest in profits and losses. At the purchase date, the assets of the partnership are as follows:

	Adjusted Basis	Fair Market Value
Cash	$ 10,000	$ 10,000
Inventory	30,000	35,000
Accounts receivable	15,000	15,000
Machinery and equipment	70,000	90,000
Buildings	100,000	150,000
Land	175,000	200,000
	$400,000	$500,000

In effect, Paul paid $100,000 for his 20% share of partnership assets ($500,000 × 20%). His basis for his partnership interest reflects the purchase price of $100,000. However, Paul's proportionate share of the partnership assets is based on the partnership's adjusted basis

---

[28] § 708(b)(1)(B).

[29] §§ 708(b)(1)(A) and (B).

for the assets of $400,000 (i.e., $400,000 × 20% = $80,000). Since Paul's acquisition of his ownership interest from Sandra did not result in a termination of the partnership, the partnership's adjusted basis for the assets does not change. Therefore, if the partnership were to liquidate all of its assets immediately for $500,000, Paul's share of the recognized gain of $100,000 ($500,000 − $400,000) would be $20,000 ($100,000 × 20%). This result occurs even though Paul paid fair market value for his partnership interest.

The Code does provide an opportunity to rectify this inequity to Paul. If the partnership elects the optional adjustment to basis under § 754, the operational provisions of § 743 will result in Paul having a special additional basis for each of the appreciated partnership assets. The amount is the excess of the amount Paul effectively paid for each of the assets over his pro rata share of the partnership's basis for the assets.

	Amount Paid (20% Share)	Pro Rata Share of Adjusted Basis	Special Basis Adjustment
Cash	$ 2,000	$ 2,000	$ –0–
Inventory	7,000	6,000	1,000
Accounts receivable	3,000	3,000	–0–
Machinery and equipment	18,000	14,000	4,000
Buildings	30,000	20,000	10,000
Land	40,000	35,000	5,000
	$100,000	$80,000	$20,000

Therefore, if the partnership sells the inventory, Paul's share of the ordinary income is $1,000 ($5,000 × 20%). He then reduces this amount by his special additional basis of $1,000. Thus, the net effect, as it equitably should be, is $0 ($1,000 − $1,000). ▼

As Example 23 illustrates, the optional adjustment to basis election under § 754 provides a way to avoid the aforementioned problem. However, four additional factors need to be considered. First, the election must be made by the partnership, not just by the acquiring partner. Therefore, the acquiring partner should obtain a written agreement from the other partners indicating they will consent to the § 754 election. Second, the election is a continuing election. Thus, while the election benefits an acquiring partner if the partnership assets are appreciated at the date of acquisition, it produces detrimental consequences (i.e., a negative special basis adjustment) if the adjusted basis exceeds the fair market value of the assets at the acquisition date. Third, the election not only activates the operational provisions of § 743, it also activates the operational provisions of § 734 with respect to partnership distributions. Fourth, if the members of the partnership change frequently, record keeping can become complex.

C CORPORATION

The sale of the business can be structured as either an asset sale or a stock sale. The stock sale has the dual advantage to the seller of being less complex both as a legal transaction and as a tax transaction. It also has the advantage of providing a way to avoid double taxation. Finally, the gain on the sale of the stock is a capital gain to the shareholder.

EXAMPLE 24 Jane and Zina each own 50% of the stock of Purple Corporation. They have owned the business for 10 years. Jane's basis for her stock is $40,000, and Zina's basis for her stock is $60,000. They agree to sell the stock to Rex for $300,000. Jane has a long-term capital gain of

$110,000 ($150,000 − $40,000), and Zina has a long-term capital gain of $90,000 ($150,000 − $60,000). Rex has a basis for his stock of $300,000. Purple's basis for its assets does not change as a result of the stock sale. ▼

Structuring the sale of the business as a stock sale may produce detrimental tax results for the purchaser. As Example 24 illustrates, the basis of the corporation's assets is not affected by the stock sale. If the fair market value of the stock exceeds the corporation's adjusted basis for its assets, the purchaser is denied the opportunity to step up the basis of the assets to reflect the amount in effect paid for them through the stock acquisition. Note that this is similar to the problem at the partnership level if the § 754 election is not made.

For an asset sale, the seller of the business can be either the corporation or the shareholders. If the seller is the corporation, the corporation sells the business (the assets), pays any debts not transferred, and makes a liquidating distribution to the shareholders. If the sellers are the shareholders, the corporation pays any debts that will not be transferred and makes a liquidating distribution to the shareholders; then the shareholders sell the business.

Regardless of the approach used for an asset sale, double taxation will occur. The corporation is taxed on the actual sale of the assets and is taxed as if it had sold the assets when it makes the liquidating distribution of the assets to the shareholders who then sell the assets. The shareholders are taxed when they receive cash or assets distributed in-kind by the corporation.

The asset sale resolves the purchaser's problem of not being able to step up the basis of the assets to their fair market value. The basis for each asset is the amount paid for it. In order to operate in corporate form (assuming the purchaser is not a corporation), the purchaser needs to transfer the property to a corporation in a § 351 transaction.

From the perspective of the seller, the ideal form of the transaction is a stock sale. Conversely, from the purchaser's perspective, the ideal form is an asset purchase. Prior to TRA of 1986, the corporate liquidation provisions tended to equate the tax consequences of these two forms.

Now neither § 336 nor § 338 permits double taxation to be avoided. Therefore, the bargaining ability of the seller and the purchaser to structure the sale as a stock sale or an asset sale, respectively, has become more critical.

Rather than selling the entire business, an owner may sell his or her ownership interest. Since the form of the transaction is a stock sale, the results for the selling shareholder will be the same as if all the shareholders had sold their stock (i.e., capital gain or capital loss to the shareholder).

S CORPORATION

Since the S corporation is a corporation, it is subject to the provisions for a C corporation discussed previously. Either an asset sale at the corporate level or a liquidating distribution of assets produces recognition at the corporate level. However, under the conduit concept applicable to the S corporation, the recognized amount is taxed at the shareholder level. Therefore, double taxation is avoided directly (only the shareholder is involved) for a stock sale and indirectly (the conduit concept ignores the involvement of the corporation) for an asset sale.

After TRA of 1986 eliminated the corporate liquidation rules that had generally enabled corporations to avoid double taxation, the potential existed for the S corporation election to be made prior to the liquidation of a corporation to avoid double taxation. Recognizing this potential, Congress enacted the built-in gain rules of § 1374 to close this loophole. Thus, if § 1374 applies, taxation occurs at the corporate level, and double taxation results.

See Concept Summary 13–1 for a summary of the tax consequences of the disposition of a business.

OVERALL COMPARISON OF FORMS OF DOING BUSINESS

See Concept Summary 13–2 for a detailed comparison of the tax consequences of the following forms of doing business: sole proprietorship, partnership, S corporation, and C corporation.

TAX PLANNING CONSIDERATIONS

The chapter began with an example that illustrated the relationship between tax planning and the choice of business form; it also raised a variety of questions about the advice given by the tax practitioner. By this time, the student should be able to develop various scenarios supporting the tax advice given. The actual fact situations that produced the tax adviser's recommendations were as follows:

- Jesse's experience in the dairy industry consists of raising a few heifers during the last five years he was employed. Eva anticipates that Jesse will have tax losses for the indeterminate future. In choosing between the partnership and the S corporation forms, Jesse indicated that he and his wife must have limited liability associated with the dairy farm.
- Larry was born and raised on his father's dairy farm. Both his education and his Air Force managerial experience provide him with useful tools for managing his business. However, Larry inherited his farm when milk prices were at a low for the modern era. Since none of her dairy farm clients were generating tax profits at that time, Eva anticipated Larry would operate his dairy farm at a loss. Larry, like Jesse, felt that limited liability was imperative. Thus, he incorporated the dairy farm and made the S corporation election.

  For the first two years, Larry's dairy farm produced tax losses. Since then, the dairy farm has produced tax profits large enough to absorb the losses. Larry anticipates that his profits will remain relatively stable in the $50,000 to $75,000 range. Since he is in the 31 percent marginal tax bracket and anticipates no dividend distributions to him from the corporation, his tax liability associated with the dairy farm will be less if he terminates the S corporation election.

As Jesse and Larry's example illustrates, selection of the proper business form can result in both nontax and tax advantages. Both of these factors should be considered in making the selection decision. Furthermore, this choice should be reviewed periodically, since a proper business form at one point in time may not be the proper form at a different time.

In looking at the tax attributes, consideration should be given to the tax consequences of the following:

- Contribution of assets to the entity by the owners at the time the entity is created and at later dates.
- Taxation of the results of operations.
- Distributions to owners.
- Disposition of an ownership interest.
- Termination of the entity.

CONCEPT SUMMARY 13–1

Tax Treatment of Disposition of a Business

Form of Entity	Form of Transaction	Tax Consequences	
		Seller	**Buyer**
Sole proprietorship	Sale of individual assets.	Gain or loss is calculated separately for the individual assets. Classification as capital or ordinary depends on the nature and holding period of the individual assets. If amount realized exceeds the fair market value of the identifiable assets, the excess is allocated to goodwill (except to the extent identified with a covenant not to compete), which is a capital asset.	Basis for individual assets is the allocated cost. Prefers that any excess of purchase price over the fair market value of identifiable assets be identified with a covenant not to compete if the covenant has legal utility. Otherwise, the buyer is neutral since both goodwill and covenants are amortized over a 15-year statutory period.
	Sale of the business.	Treated as if a sale of the individual assets (as above).	Treated as if a purchase of the individual assets (as above).
Partnership	Sale of individual assets.	Treatment is the same as for the sole proprietorship.	Treatment is the same as for the sole proprietorship. If the intent is to operate in partnership form, the assets can be contributed to a partnership under § 721.
	Sale of ownership interest.	Partnership interest is treated as the sale of a capital asset under § 741 (subject to ordinary income potential under § 751 for unrealized receivables and substantially appreciated inventory).	Basis for new partner's ownership interest is the cost. The new partnership's basis for the assets is also the pertinent cost (i.e., contributed to the partnership under § 721), since the original partnership will have terminated.
C corporation	Sale of corporate assets by corporation (i.e., corporation sells assets, pays debts, and makes liquidating distribution to the shareholders).	Double taxation occurs. Corporation is taxed on the sale of the assets with the gain or loss determination and the classification as capital or ordinary treated the same as for the sole proprietorship. Shareholders calculate gain or loss as the difference between the stock basis and the amount received from the corporation in the liquidating distribution. Capital gain or loss usually results, since stock typically is a capital asset.	Basis for individual assets is the allocated cost. If the intent is to operate in corporate form, the assets can be contributed to a corporation under § 351.
	Sale of corporate assets by the shareholders (i.e., corporation pays debts and makes liquidating distribution to the shareholders).	Double taxation occurs. At the time of the liquidating distribution to the shareholders, the corporation is taxed as if it had sold the assets. Shareholders calculate gain or loss as the difference between the stock basis and the fair market value of the assets received from the corporation in the liquidating distribution. Capital gain or loss usually results, since stock typically is a capital asset.	Same as above.

Form of Entity	Form of Transaction	Tax Consequences	
		Seller	**Buyer**
	Sale of corporate stock.	Enables double taxation to be avoided. Since the corporation is not a party to the transaction, there are no tax consequences at the corporate level. Shareholders calculate gain or loss as the difference between the stock basis and the amount received for the stock. Capital gain or loss usually results, since stock typically is a capital asset.	Basis for the stock is its cost. The basis for the corporate assets is not affected by the stock purchase.
S corporation	Sale of corporate assets by corporation.	Recognition occurs at the corporate level on the sale of the assets with the gain or loss determination and the classification as capital or ordinary treated the same as for the sole proprietorship. Conduit concept applicable to the S corporation results in the recognized amount being taxed at the shareholder level. Double taxation associated with the asset sale is avoided, because the shareholder's stock basis is increased by the amount of gain recognition and decreased by the amount of loss recognition. Shareholders calculate gain or loss as the difference between the stock basis and the amount received from the corporation in the liquidating distribution. Capital gain or loss usually results, since stock typically is a capital asset.	Basis for individual assets is the allocated cost. If the intent is to operate in corporate form (i.e., as an S corporation), the assets can be contributed to a corporation under § 351.
	Sale of corporate assets by the shareholders.	At the time of the liquidating distribution to the shareholders, recognition occurs at the corporation level as if the corporation had sold the assets. The resultant tax consequences for the shareholders and the corporation are the same as for the sale of corporate assets by the S corporation.	Same as above.
	Sale of corporate stock.	Same as the treatment for the sale of stock of a C corporation.	Same as the treatment for the purchase of stock of a C corporation.

CONCEPT SUMMARY 13–2

Tax Attributes of Different Forms of Business
(Assume Partners and Shareholders Are All Individuals)

	Sole Proprietorship	Partnership*	S Corporation**	Regular Corporation***
Restrictions on type or number of owners	One owner. The owner must be an individual.	Must have at least 2 owners.	Only individuals, estates, and certain trusts can be owners. Maximum number of shareholders limited to 75.	None, except some states require a minimum of 2 shareholders.
Incidence of tax	Sole proprietorship's income and deductions are reported on Schedule C of the individual's Form 1040. A separate Schedule C is prepared for each business.	Entity not subject to tax. Partners in their separate capacity subject to tax on their distributive share of income. Partnership files Form 1065.	Except for certain built-in gains and passive investment income when earnings and profits are present from C corporation tax years, entity not subject to Federal income tax. S corporation files Form 1120S. Shareholders are subject to tax on income attributable to their stock ownership.	Income subject to double taxation. Entity subject to tax, and shareholder subject to tax on any corporate dividends received. Corporation files Form 1120.
Highest tax rate	39.6% at individual level.	39.6% at partner level.	39.6% at shareholder level.	35% at corporate level plus 39.6% on any corporate dividends at shareholder level.
Choice of tax year	Same tax year as owner.	Selection generally restricted to coincide with tax year of majority partners or principal partners, or to tax year determined under the least aggregate deferral method.	Restricted to a calendar year unless IRS approves a different year for business purposes or other exceptions apply.	Unrestricted selection allowed at time of filing first tax return.
Timing of taxation	Based on owner's tax year.	Partners report their share of income in their tax year with or within which the partnership's tax year ends. Partners in their separate capacities are subject to payment of estimated taxes.	Shareholders report their shares of income in their tax year with or within which the corporation's tax year ends. Generally, the corporation uses a calendar year, but see "Choice of tax year" above. Shareholders may be subject to payment of estimated taxes. Corporation may be subject to payment of estimated taxes for the taxes imposed at the corporate level.	Corporation subject to tax at close of its tax year. May be subject to payment of estimated taxes. Dividends will be subject to tax at the shareholder level in the tax year received.

	Sole Proprietorship	Partnership*	S Corporation**	Regular Corporation***
Basis for allocating income to owners	Not applicable (only one owner).	Profit and loss sharing agreement. Cash basis items of cash basis partnerships are allocated on a daily basis. Other partnership items are allocated after considering varying interests of partners.	Pro rata share based on stock ownership. Shareholder's pro rata share is determined on a daily basis, according to the number of shares of stock held on each day of the corporation's tax year.	Not applicable.
Contribution of property to the entity	Not a taxable transaction.	Generally not a taxable transaction.	Is a taxable transaction unless the § 351 requirements are satisfied.	Is a taxable transaction unless the § 351 requirements are satisfied.
Character of income taxed to owners	Retains source characteristics.	Conduit—retains source characteristics.	Conduit—retains source characteristics.	All source characteristics are lost when income is distributed to owners.
Basis for allocating a net operating loss to owners	Not applicable (only one owner).	Profit and loss sharing agreement. Cash basis items of cash basis partnerships are allocated on a daily basis. Other partnership items are allocated after considering varying interests of partners.	Prorated among shareholders on a daily basis.	Not applicable.
Limitation on losses deductible by owners	Investment plus liabilities.	Partner's investment plus share of liabilities.	Shareholder's investment plus loans made by shareholder to corporation.	Not applicable.
Subject to at-risk rules	Yes, at the owner level. Indefinite carryover of excess loss.	Yes, at the partner level. Indefinite carryover of excess loss.	Yes, at the shareholder level. Indefinite carryover of excess loss.	Yes, for closely held corporations. Indefinite carryover of excess loss.
Subject to passive activity loss rules	Yes, at the owner level. Indefinite carryover of excess loss.	Yes, at the partner level. Indefinite carryover of excess loss.	Yes, at the shareholder level. Indefinite carryover of excess loss.	Yes, for closely held corporations and personal service corporations. Indefinite carryover of excess loss.
Tax consequences of earnings retained by entity	Taxed to owner when earned and increases his or her investment in the sole proprietorship.	Taxed to partners when earned and increases their respective interests in the partnership.	Taxed to shareholders when earned and increases their respective bases in stock.	Taxed to corporation as earned and may be subject to penalty tax if accumulated unreasonably.
Nonliquidating distributions to owners	Not taxable.	Not taxable unless money received exceeds recipient partner's basis in partnership interest. Existence of § 751 assets may cause recognition of ordinary income.	Generally not taxable unless the distribution exceeds the shareholder's AAA or stock basis. Existence of accumulated earnings and profits could cause some distributions to be dividends.	Taxable in year of receipt to extent of earnings and profits or if exceeds basis in stock.

	Sole Proprietorship	Partnership*	S Corporation**	Regular Corporation***
Capital gains	Taxed at owner level using maximum 28% rate.	Conduit—partners must account for their respective shares.	Conduit, with certain exceptions (a possible penalty tax)—shareholders must account for their respective shares.	Taxed at corporate level with a maximum 35% rate. No other benefits.
Capital losses	Only $3,000 of capital losses can be offset each tax year against ordinary income. Indefinite carryover.	Conduit—partners must account for their respective shares.	Conduit—shareholders must account for their respective shares.	Carried back three years and carried forward five years. Deductible only to the extent of capital gains.
§ 1231 gains and losses	Taxable or deductible at owner level. Five-year lookback rule for § 1231 losses.	Conduit—partners must account for their respective shares.	Conduit—shareholders must account for their respective shares.	Taxable or deductible at corporate level only. Five-year lookback rule for § 1231 losses.
Foreign tax credits	Available at owner level.	Conduit—passed through to partners.	Generally conduit—passed through to shareholders.	Available at corporate level only.
§ 1244 treatment of loss on sale of interest	Not applicable.	Not applicable.	Available.	Available.
Basis treatment of entity liabilities	Includible in interest basis.	Includible in interest basis.	Not includible in stock basis.	Not includible in stock basis.
Built-in gains	Not applicable.	Not applicable.	Possible corporate tax.	Not applicable.
Special allocations to owners	Not applicable (only one owner).	Available if supported by substantial economic effect.	Not available.	Not applicable.
Availability of fringe benefits to owners	None.	None.	None unless a 2% or less shareholder.	Available within antidiscrimination rules.
Effect of liquidation/ redemption reorganization on basis of entity assets	Not applicable.	Usually carried over from entity to partner unless a § 754 election is made, excessive cash is distributed, or more than 50% of the capital interests are transferred within 12 months.	Taxable step-up to fair market value.	Taxable step-up to fair market value.
Sale of ownership interest	Treated as the sale of individual assets. Classification of recognized gain or loss depends on the nature of the individual assets.	Treated as the sale of a partnership interest. Recognized gain or loss is classified as capital under § 741, subject to ordinary income treatment under § 751.	Treated as the sale of corporate stock. Recognized gain is classified as capital gain. Recognized loss is classified as capital loss, subject to ordinary loss treatment under § 1244.	Treated as the sale of corporate stock. Recognized gain is classified as capital gain. Recognized loss is classified as capital loss, subject to ordinary loss treatment under § 1244.

	Sole Proprietorship	**Partnership***	**S Corporation****	**Regular Corporation*****
Distribution of appreciated property	Not taxable.	No recognition at the partnership level.	Recognition at the corporate level to the extent of the appreciation. Conduit—amount of recognized gain is passed through to shareholders.	Taxable at the corporate level to the extent of the appreciation.
Splitting of income among family members	Not applicable (only one owner).	Difficult—IRS will not recognize a family member as a partner unless certain requirements are met.	Rather easy—gift of stock will transfer tax on a pro rata share of income to the donee. However, IRS can make adjustments to reflect adequate compensation for services.	Same as an S corporation, except that donees will be subject to tax only on earnings actually or constructively distributed to them. Other than unreasonable compensation, IRS generally cannot make adjustments to reflect adequate compensation for services and capital.
Organizational costs	Start-up expenditures are amortizable over 60 months.	Amortizable over 60 months.	Same as partnership.	Same as partnership.
Charitable contributions	Limitations apply at owner level.	Conduit—partners are subject to deduction limitations in their own capacities.	Conduit—shareholders are subject to deduction limitations in their own capacities.	Limited to 10% of taxable income before certain deductions.
Alternative minimum tax	Applies at owner level. AMT rates are 26% and 28%.	Applies at the partner level rather than at the partnership level. AMT preferences and adjustments are passed through from the partnership to the partners.	Applies at the shareholder level rather than at the corporate level. AMT preferences and adjustments are passed through from the S corporation to the shareholders.	Applies at the corporate level. AMT rate is 20%.
ACE adjustment	Does not apply.	Does not apply.	Does not apply.	The adjustment is made in calculating AMTI. The adjustment is 75% of the excess of adjusted current earnings over unadjusted AMTI. If the unadjusted AMTI exceeds adjusted current earnings, the adjustment is negative.
Tax preference items	Apply at owner level in determining AMT.	Conduit—passed through to partners who must account for such items in their separate capacities.	Conduit—passed through to shareholders who must account for such items in their separate capacities.	Subject to AMT at corporate level.

*Refer to Chapters 10 and 11 for additional details on partnerships.
**Refer to Chapter 12 for additional details on S corporations.
***Refer to Chapters 2 through 9 for additional details on regular corporations.

KEY TERMS

Conduit concept,
13–18

Entity concept,
13–18

Limited liability
company (LLC),
13–4

Thin capitalization,
13–14

**PROBLEM
MATERIALS**

DISCUSSION QUESTIONS

1. What are the principal legal forms for conducting a business entity? What are the principal Federal income tax forms for doing so?

2. The legal form of conducting a business entity is not always the same as the tax form. Discuss two instances in which the IRS may attempt to tax an entity in a form different from its legal form.

3. A corporation is one of the legal forms that can be used to conduct a business. Discuss why the corporate form is divided into S corporations and C corporations for Federal income tax purposes.

4. The maximum statutory corporate tax rate of 35% is less than the maximum statutory individual tax rate of 39.6%. Therefore, for any given amount of taxable income, the corporate tax liability is less than the individual tax liability. Comment on this statement.

5. The maximum individual tax rate is greater than the maximum corporate tax rate. Why would the IRS attempt to tax an entity that legally is a partnership as a corporation?

6. What are the advantages of a limited liability company compared with an S corporation?

7. What are the advantages of a limited liability company compared with a general partnership?

8. All of the Big 6 accounting firms recently changed their ownership form from a general partnership to a limited liability partnership. Discuss the legal and tax ramifications of this modification of ownership form.

9. Compare the partnership and corporate business forms in terms of each of the following nontax factors:
   a. Capital formation.
   b. Limited liability.
   c. Estimated life of the business.
   d. Number of owners and their roles in the management of the business.

10. Several taxpayers would like to conduct a business in partnership form with all of the owners having limited liability. Can a partnership, other than a limited liability partnership, be structured in such a way that this objective is accomplished? If so, are there any related tax pitfalls?

11. Gary is an entrepreneur who likes to be actively involved in his business ventures. He is going to invest $400,000 in a business that he projects will produce a tax loss of approximately $75,000 per year in the short run. However, once consumers become aware of the new product being sold by the business and the quality of the service it provides, he is confident the business will generate a profit of at least $100,000 per year. Gary has substantial other income (from both business ventures and investment activities) each year. Advise Gary on the business form he should select for the short run. He will be the sole owner.

12. Sam is trying to decide whether he should operate his business as a C corporation or as an S corporation. Due to potential environmental hazard problems, it is imperative that the business have limited liability. Sam is leaning toward the S corporation form because it avoids double taxation. However, he is concerned that he may encounter difficulty several years in the future when he may want to issue some preferred stock to his son as a way of motivating him to remain active in the business. Sue, a friend of his, says that he can maintain maximum flexibility by operating as a C corporation. According to her, Sam can avoid double taxation by paying himself a salary equal to the before-tax earnings. As Sam's tax adviser, what is your advice to him?

13. Philip, who is in the 31% tax bracket, is the sole shareholder of a corporation. He receives a salary of $40,000 each year. To avoid double taxation, he makes an S election for the corporation. The corporation currently is earning $100,000, and he expects earnings to grow at a rate between 15% and 20%. The earnings are reinvested in the growth of the corporation. No plans exist for distributions to Philip. What problem may Philip have created by making the S election?

14. Which of the following either directly or indirectly are subject to the AMT?

    • Sole proprietorship.

    • Partnership.

    • C corporation.

    • S corporation.

15. What AMT adjustment applies only to the corporate taxpayer? Does it apply to both C corporations and S corporations?

16. Nell is going to operate her business entity as a partnership or as a corporation. If she decides to operate it as a corporation, she will elect S corporation status so that she can deduct the tax losses projected for the first two years on her individual tax returns. Assuming she is going to operate the business in three states, what question is relevant if she chooses the corporate form but is not relevant if she chooses the partnership form? Assume that Nell satisfies the qualification requirements for the S corporation election.

17. Are different types of favorably taxed fringe benefits taxed similarly? Explain.

18. Otto created Teal Corporation five years ago. The C corporation has paid Otto as president a salary of $100,000 each year. Annual earnings after taxes have been about $500,000 each year. Teal has not paid any dividends nor does it intend to do so in the future. Instead, Otto wants his beneficiaries to receive the step-up in stock basis when he dies. Identify the relevant tax issues.

19. Tara is considering contributing $100,000 to Swallow, a C corporation. However, a business acquaintance suggests that she invest only $60,000 and lend $40,000 to the corporation. Are there any tax benefits to following this advice? Are there any tax pitfalls?

20. Liane owns land and a building that she has been using in her sole proprietorship. She is going to incorporate her sole proprietorship as a C corporation. Liane is trying to decide whether to contribute the land and building to the corporation or to lease them to the corporation. The net income of the sole proprietorship for the past five years has averaged $200,000. Advise Liane on the tax consequences.

21. Minnow Corporation has been operating for 10 years. Minnow's taxable income each year has been approximately $100,000. Minnow has not made any dividend distributions during this period and does not intend to do so in the near future. What negative result may occur because of this policy? Describe a set of circumstances for Minnow under which this negative result would not occur.

22. Orange and Rust have both been in business for approximately eight years. Each corporation has five shareholders. The taxable income for each corporation has been

about $200,000 per year. Neither corporation has made any dividend distributions, and neither intends to do so in the near future. Explain why Orange may encounter an accumulated earnings tax problem and Rust will definitely not do so.

23. Arnold is going to conduct his business in corporate form. What factors should he consider in deciding between operating as a C corporation or as an S corporation?

24. Tammy and Arnold own 40% of the stock of Roadrunner, an S corporation. The other 60% is owned by 74 other family members. Tammy and Arnold have agreed to a divorce and are in the process of negotiating a property settlement. Identify the relevant tax issues for Tammy and Arnold.

25. Susan is going to contribute a computer to her business. She purchased the computer five years ago and used it exclusively for personal purposes during this period. Are the tax consequences different if she contributes it to a C corporation in which she is a shareholder rather than a partnership in which she is a partner?

26. Tab and Nora are considering organizing their business either as a partnership or as a corporation. Distinguish between the effects of the conduit concept and the entity concept with respect to the recognition of gain or loss at the time of the transfer of assets to the entity. Is it possible to organize the business as a corporation and not have the entity concept apply?

27. Why are special allocations either permitted or required for the partners in a partnership, yet are not permitted for the shareholders in a corporation?

28. Entity liabilities have an effect on the calculation of a partner's basis for his or her partnership interest. Yet entity liabilities do not have any effect on a corporate shareholder's calculation of his or her stock basis. What is the reason for this difference in tax treatment?

29. In calculating the basis of a partner's interest in the partnership, the partner's basis is increased by the share of the partnership liabilities. Since an S corporation is taxed similarly to a partnership, is the same adjustment made in calculating an S corporation shareholder's basis for the stock?

30. The conduit concept applies to the S corporation. Are there any circumstances in which the S corporation is a taxpayer rather than merely a tax reporter?

31. Darren, a partner in Pelican Partnership, uses the cash method of accounting. Why are distributions of earnings by the partnership not taxed to Darren?

32. Distributions of earnings of a C corporation are taxed at the shareholder level as dividend income. Why are the earnings of an S corporation that are distributed to shareholders not treated as dividend income by the shareholders?

33. A partner's ability to pass through and deduct the share of the partnership loss is limited by the partnership interest basis. Why does the Code further limit the loss pass-through and deduction with the at-risk basis? What effect do the passive activity loss rules have on this area?

34. Sandra and Renee each own 50% of the stock of Olive, a C corporation. They have decided to dispose of their ownership interests in the corporation, and a substantial gain will result. Sandra thinks they should sell their stock whereas Renee thinks they should first liquidate the corporation and then sell the assets to the buyers. Advise them on the preferred form of the transaction.

35. Vladimir owns all the stock of Ruby. The fair market value of the stock (and Ruby's assets) is about four times his adjusted basis for the stock. Vladimir is negotiating with an investor group for the sale of the corporation. Identify the relevant tax issues for Vladimir.

36. Using the legend provided, indicate which form of business entity each of the following characteristics describes. Some of the characteristics may apply to more than one form of business entity.

Legend

SP = Applies to sole proprietorship

P = Applies to partnership

S = Applies to S corporation

C = Applies to C corporation

---

  a. Has limited liability.

  b. Greatest ability to raise capital.

  c. Subject to double taxation.

  d. Not subject to double taxation.

  e. Subject to accumulated earnings tax.

  f. Limit on types and number of shareholders.

  g. Has unlimited liability.

  h. Sale of the business can be subject to double taxation.

37. Using the legend provided, indicate which form of business entity each of the following characteristics describes. Some of the characteristics may apply to more than one form of business entity.

Legend

P = Applies to partnership

S = Applies to S corporation

C = Applies to C corporation

---

  a. Basis for an ownership interest is increased by an investment by the owner.

  b. Basis for an ownership interest is decreased by a distribution to the owner.

  c. Basis for an ownership interest is increased by entity profits.

  d. Basis for an ownership interest is decreased by entity losses.

  e. Basis for an ownership interest is increased as the entity's liabilities increase.

  f. Basis for an ownership interest is decreased as the entity's liabilities decrease.

PROBLEMS

38. A business entity has the following assets and liabilities on its balance sheet:

	Net Book Value	Fair Market Value
Assets	$675,000	$950,000
Liabilities	100,000	100,000

The business entity has just lost a product liability suit with damages of $5 million being awarded to the plaintiff. Although the business entity will appeal the judgment, legal counsel indicates the judgment is highly unlikely to be overturned by the appellate court. The product liability insurance carried by the business has a policy ceiling of $3 million. What is the amount of liability of the entity and its owners if the form of the business entity is a:

  a. Sole partnership?

  b. Partnership?

  c. C corporation?

  d. S corporation?

39. Red, White, Blue, and Orange, have taxable income as follows:

Corporation	Taxable Income
Red	$ 80,000
White	260,000
Blue	500,000
Orange	20,000,000

   a. Calculate the marginal tax rate and the effective tax rate for each of the C corporations.
   b. Explain why the marginal tax rate for a C corporation can exceed 35%, but the effective tax rate cannot do so.

40. Amy and Jeff are going to operate their florist shop as a partnership or as an S corporation. After paying salaries of $40,000 to each of the owners, the shop's earnings are projected to be about $50,000. The earnings are to be invested in the growth of the business. Advise Amy and Jeff as to which of the two entity forms they should select.

41. Jack, an unmarried taxpayer, is going to establish a manufacturing business. He anticipates that the business will be profitable immediately due to a patent that he holds. He anticipates that profits for the first year will be about $200,000 and will increase at a rate of about 20% per year for the foreseeable future. He will be the sole owner of the business. Advise Jack on the form of business entity he should select. Assume Jack will be in the 36% tax bracket.

42. Silver Corporation will begin operations on January 1. Earnings for the next five years are projected to be relatively stable at about $100,000 per year. The shareholders of Silver are in the 31% tax bracket.
   a. Assume that Silver will reinvest its after-tax earnings in the growth of the company. Should Silver operate as a C corporation or as an S corporation?
   b. Assume that Silver will distribute its after-tax earnings each year to its shareholders. Should Silver operate as a C corporation or as an S corporation?

43. Mabel and Alan, who are in the 31% tax bracket, recently acquired a fast-food franchise. Each of them will work in the business and receive a salary of $80,000. They anticipate that the annual profits of the business, after deducting salaries, will be approximately $300,000. The entity will distribute enough cash each year to Mabel and Alan to cover their Federal income taxes associated with the franchise.
   a. What amount will the entity distribute if the franchise operates as a C corporation?
   b. What amount will the entity distribute if the franchise operates as an S corporation?
   c. What will be the amount of the combined entity/owner tax liability in (a) and (b)?

44. Parrott is a closely held corporation owned by 10 shareholders (each has 10% of the stock). Selected financial information provided by Parrott follows:

Taxable income	$200,000
Positive AMT adjustments (excluding ACE adjustment)	30,000
Negative AMT adjustments	(20,000)
Tax preferences	50,000
Retained earnings	500,000
Accumulated E & P	525,000
ACE adjustment	90,000

   a. Calculate Parrott's tax liability if Parrott is a C corporation.
   b. Calculate Parrott's tax liability if Parrott is an S corporation.
   c. How would your answers in (a) and (b) change if Parrott is not closely held (e.g., 5,000 shareholders with no shareholder owning more than 2% of the stock)?

45. Pelican Corporation, an offshore drilling company, is going to sell drilling equipment that it no longer needs; currently, the equipment is warehoused in Grand Isle, Louisiana. The adjusted basis for the drilling equipment is $400,000 ($700,000 – $300,000 MACRS accumulated depreciation), and the fair market value is $500,000. ADS 150% declining-balance depreciation would have been $275,000. The buyer of the drilling equipment would like to close the transaction prior to the end of the calendar year. Pelican is uncertain whether the tax consequences would be better if it sold the equipment this year or next year and is considering the following options:

    • $500,000 in cash payable on December 31, 1997.

    • The sale will be closed on December 31, 1997, with the consideration being a $500,000 note issued by the buyer. The maturity date of the note is January 2, 1998, with the drilling equipment being pledged as security.

    Pelican projects its taxable income for 1997 and 1998 to be $600,000 without the sale of the drilling equipment. Pelican's accounting period is the calendar year. Determine the tax consequences to Pelican under either option and recommend which option Pelican should select.

46. Two unmarried brothers own and operate a farm. They live on the farm and take their meals on the farm for the "convenience of the employer." The fair market value of their lodging is $14,000, and the fair market value of their meals is $10,000. The meals are prepared for them by the farm cook who prepares their meals along with those of the three other farm employees.
    a. Determine the tax consequences of the meals and lodging to the brothers if the farm is incorporated.
    b. Determine the tax consequences of the meals and lodging to the brothers if the farm is not incorporated.

47. A business entity's taxable income before the cost of certain fringe benefits paid to owners and other employees is $400,000. The amounts paid for these fringe benefits are as follows:

	Owners	**Other Employees**
Group term life insurance	$20,000	$40,000
Meals and lodging incurred for the convenience of the employer	50,000	75,000
Pension plan	30,000*	90,000

*H.R. 10 (Keogh) plan for partnership and S corporation.

    The business entity is equally owned by four owners.
    a. Calculate the taxable income of the business entity if the entity is a partnership, a C corporation, or an S corporation.
    b. Determine the effect on the owners for each of the three business forms.

48. Fawn, a C corporation, has taxable income of $200,000 before paying salaries to the two shareholder-employees, Gus and Janet. Fawn follows a policy of distributing all after-tax earnings to the shareholders.
    a. Determine the tax consequences for Fawn, Gus, and Janet if the corporation pays salaries to Gus and Janet as follows:

Option 1		**Option 2**	
Gus	$120,000	Gus	$45,000
Janet	80,000	Janet	30,000

    b. Is Fawn likely to encounter any tax problems associated with either option?

49. Swallow, a C corporation, is owned by Sandra (50%) and Fran (50%). Sandra is the president, and Fran is the vice president for sales. Late in 1996, Swallow encounters working capital difficulties. Thus, Sandra and Fran each loan the corporation $100,000 on an 8% note that is due in five years with interest payable annually.
    a. Determine the tax consequences to Swallow, Sandra, and Fran for 1997 if the notes are classified as debt.
    b. Determine the tax consequences to Swallow, Sandra, and Fran for 1997 if the notes are classified as equity.

50. Marci and Jennifer each own 50% of the stock of Lavender, a C corporation. After paying each of them a "reasonable" salary of $125,000, the taxable income of Lavender is normally around $600,000. The corporation is about to purchase a $2,000,000 shopping mall ($1,500,000 allocated to the building and $500,000 allocated to the land). The mall will be rented to tenants at a net rental income (i.e., includes rental commissions, depreciation, etc.) of $500,000 annually. Marci and Jennifer will contribute $1 million each to the corporation to provide the cash required for the acquisition. Their CPA has suggested that Marci and Jennifer purchase the shopping mall as individuals and lease it to Lavender for a fair rental of $300,000. Both Marci and Jennifer are in the 39.6% tax bracket. The acquisition will occur on January 2, 1997. Determine whether the shopping mall should be acquired by Lavender or by Marci and Jennifer in accordance with their CPA's recommendation. Assume the depreciation on the shopping mall in 1997 is $37,000.

51. Frank owns 600 shares of the stock of Autumn Corporation, and Grace owns the remaining 400 shares. Frank's stock basis is $120,000, and Grace's is $80,000. As part of a stock redemption, Frank redeems 100 of his shares for $50,000, and Grace redeems 250 of her shares for $125,000. Determine the tax consequences of the stock redemption to Frank and Grace.

52. Eagle Corporation has been an electing S corporation since its incorporation 10 years ago. During the first three years of operations, it incurred total losses of $250,000. Since then Eagle has generated earnings of approximately $150,000 each year. None of the earnings have been distributed to the three equal shareholders, Claire, Lynn, and Todd, because the corporation has been in an expansion mode. At the beginning of 1997, Claire sells her stock to Nell for $400,000. Nell has reservations about the utility of the S election. Therefore, Lynn, Todd, and Nell are discussing whether the election should be continued. They expect the earnings to remain at approximately $150,000 each year. However, since they perceive that the expansion period is over and Eagle has adequate working capital, they may start distributing the earnings to the shareholders. All of the shareholders are in the 31% tax bracket. Advise the three shareholders on whether the S election should be maintained.

53. Bob and Carl each own 50% of the stock of Deer, a C corporation. When the corporation was organized, Bob contributed cash of $90,000, and Carl contributed land with an adjusted basis of $60,000 and a fair market value of $115,000. Deer assumed Carl's $25,000 mortgage on the land. In addition to the capital contributions, Bob and Carl each loaned the corporation $50,000. The maturity date of the loan is in 10 years, and the interest rate is 12%, the same as the Federal rate.
    a. Determine the tax consequences to Bob, Carl, and Deer of the initial contribution of assets, the shareholder loans, and the annual interest payments if the loans are classified as debt.
    b. If the loans are reclassified as equity.

54. Agnes, Becky, and Carol form a business entity with each contributing the following:

	Adjusted Basis	Fair Market Value
Agnes: Cash	$100,000	$100,000
Becky: Land	60,000	120,000
Carol: Services		50,000

Their ownership percentages will be as follows:

Agnes   40%
Becky   40%
Carol   20%

Becky's land has a $20,000 mortgage that is assumed by the entity. Carol is an attorney who receives her ownership interest in exchange for legal services. Determine the recognized gain to the owners, the basis for their ownership interests, and the entity's basis for its assets if:
a. The entity is a partnership.
b. The entity is a C corporation.
c. The entity is an S corporation.

55. Alicia contributes $25,000 to a business entity in exchange for a 20% ownership interest. During the first year of operations, the entity earns a profit of $150,000. At the end of that year, the entity has liabilities of $60,000.
a. Calculate Alicia's basis for her stock if the entity is a C corporation.
b. Calculate Alicia's basis for her stock if the entity is an S corporation.
c. Calculate Alicia's basis for her partnership interest if the entity is a partnership.

56. An entity engages in the following transactions during the taxable year:

- Sells stock held for three years as an investment for $30,000. The adjusted basis of the stock is $20,000.

- Sells land used in the business for $65,000. The land had been used as a parking lot and originally cost $40,000.

- Receives tax-exempt interest on municipal bonds of $5,000.

- Receives dividends on IBM stock of $8,000.

Describe the effect of these transactions on the entity and the owners of the entity if the entity is:
a. A partnership.
b. A C corporation.
c. An S corporation.

57. An entity has the following income for the current year:

Operations	$80,000
Tax-exempt interest income	15,000
Long-term capital gain	45,000

The entity has earnings and profits of $200,000 at the beginning of the year. A distribution of $90,000 is made to the owners.
a. Calculate the taxable income if the entity is (1) a C corporation and (2) an S corporation.
b. Determine the effect of the distribution on the shareholders if the entity is (1) a C corporation and (2) an S corporation.

58. JK is a partnership that is owned by James and Karen. James's basis for his partnership interest is $60,000, and Karen's basis is $80,000. JK distributes $50,000 to James and $60,000 to Karen.
a. Determine the tax consequences of the distribution to James, Karen, and JK.
b. Assume that JK is a C corporation rather than a partnership. JK's earnings and profits are $200,000. James's basis for his stock is $60,000, and Karen's stock basis is $80,000. Determine the tax consequences of the distribution to James, Karen, and JK.

59. Spring Corporation distributes land to Sam in a transaction that qualifies as a stock redemption. Spring's basis for the land is $15,000, and the fair market value is $40,000.

Sam surrenders shares of stock that have a basis of $16,000. After the redemption, Sam owns 10% of the Spring stock. At the same time, Spring distributes $100,000 cash to Allison. Allison surrenders shares of stock that have a basis to her of $25,000. Because Allison owns 60% of the Spring stock after the redemption, she does not qualify for stock redemption treatment.

    a. Determine the tax consequences to Spring, Sam, and Allison if Spring is a C corporation.

    b. Determine the tax consequences to Spring, Sam, and Allison if Spring is an S corporation.

60. Yellow, a personal service corporation, has the following types of income and losses for 1997:

Active income	$90,000
Portfolio income	20,000
Passive activity losses	50,000

    a. Calculate Yellow's taxable income for 1997.

    b. Assume that instead of being a personal service corporation, Yellow is a closely held corporation. Calculate Yellow's taxable income for 1997.

61. Rosa contributes $50,000 to a business entity in exchange for a 10% ownership interest. The business entity incurs a loss of $900,000 for 1997. The entity liabilities at the end of 1997 are $700,000. Of this amount, $150,000 is for recourse debt, and $550,000 is for nonrecourse debt.

    a. Assume the business entity is a partnership. How much of Rosa's share of the loss can be deducted on her 1997 individual tax return? What is Rosa's basis for her partnership interest at the end of 1997?

    b. Assume the business entity is a C corporation. How much of Rosa's share of the loss can be deducted on her 1997 individual tax return? What is Rosa's basis for her stock at the end of 1997?

62. Megan owns 60% of a business entity, and Vern owns 40%. For 1997, the entity has a tax loss of $100,000. The owners would like to share profits with 60% for Megan and 40% for Vern and to share losses with 90% for Vern and 10% for Megan.

    a. Determine the tax consequences for 1997 if the entity is a partnership.

    b. Determine the tax consequences for 1997 if the entity is a C corporation.

    c. Determine the tax consequences for 1997 if the entity is an S corporation.

63. Sanjay contributes land to a business entity in January 1997 for a 30% ownership interest. Sanjay's basis for the land is $60,000, and the fair market value is $100,000. The business entity was formed three years ago by Polly and Rita, who have equal ownership. The entity is unsuccessful in getting the land rezoned from agricultural to residential. In October 1997, the land is sold for $110,000.

    a. Determine the tax consequences of the sale of the land for the business entity and the three owners if the organization form is a C corporation.

    b. Determine the tax consequences of the sale of the land for the business entity and the three owners if the organization form is an S corporation.

    c. Determine the tax consequences of the sale of the land for the business entity and the three owners if the organization form is a partnership.

64. Emily and Freda are negotiating with George to purchase the business that he operates in corporate form (George, Inc.). The assets of George, Inc., a C corporation, are as follows:

Asset	Basis	FMV
Cash	$ 20,000	$ 20,000
Accounts receivable	50,000	50,000
Inventory	100,000	110,000
Furniture and fixtures	150,000	170,000*
Building	200,000	250,000**
Land	40,000	150,000

*Potential depreciation recapture under § 1245 is $45,000.
**The straight-line method was used to depreciate the
 building. The balance in the accumulated depreciation
 account is $340,000.

George's basis for the stock of George, Inc., is $560,000. George is in the 31% tax bracket, and George, Inc., is in the 34% tax bracket.

a. Assume that Emily and Freda purchase the stock of George, Inc., from George and that the purchase price is $900,000. Determine the tax consequences to Emily and Freda, George, Inc., and George.

b. Assume that Emily and Freda purchase the assets from George, Inc., and that the purchase price is $900,000. Determine the tax consequences to Emily and Freda, George, Inc., and George.

c. Assume that the purchase price is $550,000 because the fair market value of the building is $150,000, and the fair market value of the land is $50,000. Also, assume that no amount is assigned to goodwill. Emily and Freda purchase the stock of George, Inc., from George. Determine the tax consequences to Emily and Freda, George, Inc., and George.

65. Linda is the owner of a sole proprietorship. The entity has assets as follows:

Asset	Basis	FMV
Cash	$10,000	$10,000
Accounts receivable	–0–	25,000
Office furniture and fixtures*	15,000	17,000
Building**	75,000	90,000
Land	60,000	80,000

*Potential depreciation recapture under § 1245 of $5,000.
**The straight-line method of depreciation has been used to
 depreciate the building.

Linda sells the business for $260,000 to Juan.

a. Determine the tax consequences to Linda, including the classification of any recognized gain or loss.

b. Determine the tax consequences to Juan.

c. Advise Juan on how the purchase agreement could be modified to produce more beneficial tax consequences for him.

66. Gail and Harry own the GH Partnership. They have conducted the business in partnership form for 10 years. The bases for their partnership interests are as follows:

Gail	$100,000
Harry	150,000

GH Partnership has the following assets:

Asset	Basis	FMV
Cash	$ 10,000	$ 10,000
Accounts receivable	30,000	28,000
Inventory	25,000	26,000
Building*	100,000	150,000
Land	250,000	400,000

*The straight-line method has been used to depreciate the
building. Accumulated depreciation is $70,000.

Gail and Harry sell their partnership interests to Keith and Liz for $307,000 each.
a. Determine the tax consequences of the sale to Gail, Harry, and GH Partnership.
b. From a tax perspective, should it matter to Keith and Liz whether they purchase Gail and Harry's partnership interests or the partnership assets from GH Partnership?

67. Bill Evans is going to purchase either the stock or the assets of Dane Corporation. All of the Dane stock is owned by Chuck. Bill and Chuck agree that Dane is worth $500,000. The tax basis for Dane's assets is $350,000. Write a letter to Bill advising him on whether he should negotiate to purchase the stock or the assets. Also, prepare a memo for the files. Bill's address is 100 Village Green, Chattanooga, TN 37403.

RESEARCH PROBLEMS

Use the tax resources of the internet to address the following questions. Do not restrict your search to the World Wide Web, but include a review of newsgroups and general reference materials, practitioner sites and resources, primary sources of the tax law, chat rooms and discussion groups, and other opportunities.

Research Problem 1.   Find an anecdote about a professional consulting firm that recently converted to LLP status. Is the firm and its competition and clients agreeable to the conversion of operating status?

Research Problem 2.   When did your state adopt LLC legislation? When did it receive IRS approval to apply partnership tax law to the entities?

Research Problem 3.   Find an article describing how a specific business put together its employee fringe benefit package in light of the limitations presented by the tax law and its form of operation.

14

EXEMPT ENTITIES

LEARNING OBJECTIVES

After completing Chapter 14, you should be able to:

1. Identify the different types of exempt organizations.

2. Enumerate the requirements for exempt status.

3. Know the tax consequences of exempt status, including the different consequences for public charities and private foundations.

4. Determine which exempt organizations are classified as private foundations.

5. Recognize the taxes imposed on private foundations and calculate the related initial tax and additional tax amounts.

6. Determine when an exempt organization is subject to the unrelated business income tax and calculate the amount of the tax.

7. List the reports exempt organizations must file with the IRS and the related due dates.

8. Identify tax planning opportunities for exempt organizations.

Ideally, any entity that generates profit would prefer not to be subject to the Federal income tax. All of the types of entities discussed in Chapter 13 are subject to the Federal income tax at one (e.g., sole proprietorships, partnerships, and S corporations generally are only subject to single taxation) or more (e.g., C corporations are subject to double taxation) levels. However, entities classified as **exempt organizations** may be able to escape Federal income taxation altogether.

Churches are among the types of organizations that are exempt from Federal income tax. Nevertheless, one must be careful not to conclude that anything labeled a church will qualify for exempt status.

During the 1970s and 1980s, a popular technique for attempting to avoid Federal income tax was the establishment of so-called mail-order churches. For example, in one scheme, a nurse obtained a certificate of ordination and a church charter from an organization that sold such documents.[1] The articles of incorporation stated that the church was organized exclusively for religious and charitable purposes, including a religious mission of healing the spirit, mind, emotions, and body. The nurse was the church's minister, director, and principal officer. Taking a vow of poverty, she transferred all her assets, including a house and car, to the church. The church assumed all of the nurse's liabilities, including the mortgage on her house and her credit card bills. The nurse continued to work at a hospital and deposited her salary in the church's bank account. The church provided her with a living allowance sufficient to maintain or improve her previous standard of living. She was also permitted to use the house and car for personal purposes.

The IRS declared that such organizations were shams and not bona fide churches. For a church to be tax-exempt under § 501(c)(3), none of its net earnings may be used to the benefit of any private shareholder or individual. In essence, the organization should serve a public rather than a private interest. While the courts have consistently upheld the IRS position, numerous avoidance schemes such as this have been attempted.

As discussed in Chapter 1, the major objective of the Federal tax law is to raise revenue. If revenue raising were the only objective, however, the Code would not contain provisions that permit certain organizations to be either partially or completely exempt from Federal income tax. Social considerations may also affect

---

[1] Rev.Rul. 81-94, 1981-1 C.B. 330.

TAX IN THE NEWS

GIVING UP TAX-EXEMPT STATUS

Trigon Blue Cross/Blue Shield of Virginia is in the process of giving up its tax-exempt status to become a taxable entity. The organization concluded that this step was necessary for it to compete effectively in the changing medical insurance business, which is undergoing massive restructuring and consolidation.

The organization will become a public company whose shares can be traded on Wall Street. Access to the financial marketplace for public stock offerings will provide the new entity with the resources it needs to compete with large insurance companies moving into Virginia and help it improve the services it provides.

The conversion does not come without costs, though. Trigon has agreed to pay the state about $175 million as compensation for past tax benefits Trigon received as a result of its exempt status.

the tax law. This objective bears directly on the decision by Congress to provide for exempt organization tax status. The House Report on the Revenue Act of 1938 explains:

> The exemption from taxation of money or property devoted to charitable and other purposes is based upon the theory that the Government is compensated for the loss of revenue by its relief from the financial burden which would otherwise have to be met by appropriations from public funds, and by the benefits resulting from the promotion of the general welfare.[2]

Recognizing this social consideration objective, Subchapter F (Exempt Organizations) of the Code (§§ 501–529) provides the authority under which certain organizations are exempt from Federal income tax. Exempt status is not open-ended in that two general limitations exist. First, the nature or scope of the organization may result in it being only partially exempt from tax.[3] Second, the organization may engage in activities that are subject to special taxation.[4]

TYPES OF EXEMPT ORGANIZATIONS

1   **LEARNING OBJECTIVE**
Identify the different types of exempt organizations.

An organization qualifies for exempt status *only* if it fits into one of the categories provided in the Code. Examples of qualifying exempt organizations and the specific statutory authority for their exempt status are listed in Exhibit 14–1.[5]

---

[2] See 1939–1 (Part 2) C.B. 742 for reprint of H.R. No. 1860, 75th Congress, 3rd Session.

[3] See the subsequent discussion of Unrelated Business Income Tax.

[4] See the subsequent discussions of Prohibited Transactions and Taxes Imposed on Private Foundations.

[5] Section § 501(a) provides for exempt status for organizations described in §§ 401 and 501. The orientation of this chapter is

toward organizations that conduct business activities. Therefore, the exempt organizations described in § 401 (qualified pension, profit sharing, and stock bonus trusts) are outside the scope of the chapter and are not discussed.

▼ **EXHIBIT 14–1**
Types of Exempt Organizations

Statutory Authority	Brief Description	Examples or Comments
§ 501(c)(1)	Federal and related agencies.	Commodity Credit Corporation, Federal Deposit Insurance Corporation, Federal Land Bank.
§ 501(c)(2)	Corporations holding title to property for and paying income to exempt organizations.	Corporation holding title to college fraternity house.
§ 501(c)(3)	Religious, charitable, educational, scientific, literary, etc., organizations.	Boy Scouts of America, Red Cross, Salvation Army, Episcopal Church, United Fund, University of Richmond.
§ 501(c)(4)	Civic leagues and employee unions.	Garden club, tenants' association promoting tenants' legal rights in entire community, League of Women Voters.
§ 501(c)(5)	Labor, agricultural, and horticultural organizations.	Teachers' association, organization formed to promote effective agricultural pest control, organization formed to test soil and to educate community members in soil treatment, garden club.
§ 501(c)(6)	Business leagues, chambers of commerce, real estate boards, etc.	Chambers of Commerce, American Plywood Association, NFL, medical association peer review board, organization promoting acceptance of women in business and professions.
§ 501(c)(7)	Social clubs.	Country club, rodeo and riding club, press club, bowling club, college fraternities.
§ 501(c)(8)	Fraternal beneficiary societies.	Lodges. Must provide for the payment of life, sickness, accident, or other benefits to members or their dependents.
§ 501(c)(9)	Voluntary employees' beneficiary associations.	Provide for the payment of life, sickness, accident, or other benefits to members, their dependents, or their designated beneficiaries.
§ 501(c)(10)	Domestic fraternal societies.	Lodges. Must not provide for the payment of life, sickness, accident, or other benefits; and must devote the net earnings exclusively to religious, charitable, scientific, literary, educational, and fraternal purposes.
§ 501(c)(11)	Local teachers' retirement fund associations.	Only permitted sources of income are amounts received from (1) public taxation, (2) assessments on teaching salaries of members, and (3) income from investments.
§ 501(c)(12)	Local benevolent life insurance associations, mutual or cooperative telephone companies, etc.	Local cooperative telephone company, local mutual water company, local mutual electric company.
§ 501(c)(13)	Cemetery companies.	Must be operated exclusively for the benefit of lot owners who hold the lots for burial purposes.
§ 501(c)(14)	Credit unions.	Other than credit unions exempt under § 501(c)(1).
§ 501(c)(15)	Mutual insurance companies.	Mutual fire insurance company, mutual automobile insurance company.
§ 501(c)(16)	Corporations organized by farmers' cooperatives for financing crop operations.	Related farmers' cooperative must be exempt from tax under § 521.
§ 501(c)(19)	Armed forces members' posts or organizations.	Veterans of Foreign Wars (VFW), Reserve Officers Association.
§ 501(c)(20)	Group legal service plans.	Provided by a corporation for its employees.
§ 501(d)	Religious and apostolic organizations.	Communal organization. Members must include pro rata share of the net income of the organization in their gross income as dividends.
§ 501(e)	Cooperative hospital service organizations.	Centralized purchasing organization for exempt hospitals.
§ 501(f)	Cooperative service organization of educational institutions.	Organization formed to manage universities' endowment funds.
§ 529	Qualified state tuition program.	State-sponsored prepaid tuition and educational savings program.

REQUIREMENTS FOR EXEMPT STATUS

2   LEARNING OBJECTIVE
Enumerate the requirements for exempt status.

Exempt status frequently requires more than mere classification in one of the categories of exempt organizations. Many of the organizations that qualify for exempt status share the following characteristics.

- The organization serves some type of *common good*.[6]
- The organization is *not a for-profit* entity.[7]
- *Net earnings* do not benefit the members of the organization.[8]
- The organization does not exert *political influence*.[9]

SERVING THE COMMON GOOD

The underlying rationale for all exempt organizations is that they serve some type of *common good*. However, depending on the type of the exempt organization, the term *common good* may be interpreted broadly or narrowly. If the test is interpreted broadly, the group being served is the general public or some large subgroup thereof. If it is interpreted narrowly, the group is the specific group referred to in the statutory language. One of the factors in classifying an exempt organization as a private foundation is the size of the group it serves.

NOT-FOR-PROFIT ENTITY

The organization may not be organized or operated for the purpose of making a profit. For some types of exempt organizations, the *for-profit prohibition* appears in the statutory language. For other types, the prohibition is implied.

NET EARNINGS AND MEMBERS OF THE ORGANIZATION

What uses are appropriate for the net earnings of a tax-exempt organization? The logical answer would seem to be that the earnings should be used for the exempt purpose of the organization. However, where the organization exists for the good of a specific group of members, such an open-ended interpretation could permit net earnings to benefit specific group members. Therefore, the Code specifically prohibits certain types of exempt organizations from using their earnings in this way.

> . . . no part of the net earnings . . . inures to the benefit of any private shareholder or individual. . .[10]

In other instances, a statutory prohibition is unnecessary because the definition of the exempt organization in the Code effectively prevents such use.

> . . . the net earnings of which are devoted exclusively to religious, charitable, scientific, literary, educational, and fraternal purposes . . .[11]

POLITICAL INFLUENCE

Religious, charitable, educational, etc., organizations are generally prohibited from attempting to influence legislation or participate in political campaigns. Participation in political campaigns includes participation both *on behalf of* a candidate and *in opposition to* a candidate.

---

[6] See, for example, §§ 501(c)(3) and (4).
[7] See, for example, §§ 501(c)(3), (4), (6), (13), and (14).
[8] See, for example, §§ 501(c)(3), (6), (7), (9), (10), (11), and (19).

[9] See, for example, § 501(c)(3).
[10] § 501(c)(6).
[11] § 501(c)(10).

Only in limited circumstances are such exempt organizations permitted to attempt to influence legislation. See the subsequent discussion under Prohibited Transactions.

ETHICAL CONSIDERATIONS

A Church Attempts to Change Society

Amos Heck is the founder, and the man behind the throne, of the Church of the Future television ministry. Ministry broadcasts originate from church services in California and New York and are broadcast via cable throughout the United States. While the membership of the Church of the Future is small (approximately 1,500 members), the typical member is quite wealthy. In addition to contributions to the church by its members, donations are solicited and received from viewers of the TV broadcasts. The church is tax-exempt under § 501(c)(3).

The stated mission of the church is religious in nature. However, Amos firmly believes, as do the members of the board of deacons of the church, that certain societal goals must be accomplished for the prophecies of the church to come true (i.e., their divine being expects them to be active missionaries). Among its basic beliefs, the church advocates government control and possession of all guns, the legalization of drugs, abortion on demand once approved by the appropriate government agency, the withdrawal of all U.S. troops from foreign soil and the termination of all military alliances, the abolition of capital punishment, and the availability of tuition-free university education to all U.S. citizens.

The ministers of the Church of the Future are expected to include these basic beliefs, at the subliminal level, in their sermons. Some do so more effectively and more frequently than others, but all are required to do so. Amos and the board of deacons are dismayed that more of their beliefs have not been incorporated into American society.

Amos proposes to the board of deacons that the church take a more proactive role. The employment contract of the ministers will now require them to include the basic beliefs in their sermons in an active manner. No longer can the beliefs just be incorporated subliminally. All the beliefs must be covered quarterly, and every sermon must present at least one of the basic beliefs. The ministers will encourage the church members and TV viewers to actively support these positions at both the state and Federal level.

As a new member of the board of deacons, you wholeheartedly support Amos's position. However, you are concerned about the effect of this open advocacy of positions on the tax-exempt status of the church. Amos responds that the "church has friends in high places" and assures you that the tax-exempt status will not be endangered.

TAX CONSEQUENCES OF EXEMPT STATUS: GENERAL

3   LEARNING OBJECTIVE
Know the tax consequences of exempt status, including the different consequences for public charities and private foundations.

An organization that is appropriately classified as one of the types of exempt organizations is generally exempt from Federal income tax. Four exceptions to this general statement exist, however. An exempt organization that engages in a *prohibited transaction* or is a so-called *feeder organization* is subject to tax. If the organization is classified as a *private foundation*, it may be partially subject to tax. Finally, an exempt organization is subject to tax on its *unrelated business taxable income*.

In addition to being exempt from Federal income tax, an exempt organization may be eligible for other benefits, including the following.

- The organization may be exempt from state income tax, state franchise tax, sales tax, or property tax.
- The organization may receive discounts on postage rates.
- Donors of property to the exempt organization may qualify for charitable contribution deductions on their Federal and state income tax returns. However, *not* all exempt organizations are qualified charitable contribution recipients (e.g., gifts to the National Football League, PGA Tour, and Underwriters Laboratories are not deductible).

PROHIBITED TRANSACTIONS

Engaging in a § 503 prohibited transaction can produce two negative results. First, part or all of the organization's income may be subject to Federal income tax. Even worse, the organization may forfeit its exempt status.

Failure to Continue to Qualify. Organizations initially qualify for exempt status only if they are organized as indicated in Exhibit 14–1. The initial qualification requirements then effectively become maintenance requirements. Failure to continue to meet the qualification requirements results in the loss of the entity's exempt status.

New Faith, Inc., is an excellent example of an exempt organization that failed to continue to qualify for tax exemption.[12] The stated purposes of the organization were to feed and shelter the poor. In its application for exempt status, New Faith indicated that it would derive its financial support from donations, bingo games, and raffles. The IRS approved the exempt status.

New Faith's only source of income was the operation of several lunch trucks, which provided food to the general public in exchange for scheduled "donations." Evidence provided by the organization to the Tax Court did not show that the food from the lunch trucks was provided free of charge or at reduced prices. In addition, no evidence was presented to show that the people who received food for free or at below-cost prices were impoverished or needy. The court concluded that the primary purpose of the activity was the conduct of a trade or business. It upheld the IRS's revocation of New Faith's exempt status.

Election Not to Forfeit Exempt Status for Lobbying. Organizations exempt under § 501(c)(3) (religious, charitable, educational, etc., organizations) generally are prohibited from attempting to influence legislation (lobbying activities) or from participating in political campaigns.[13] Any violation can result in the forfeiture of exempt status.

Certain § 501(c)(3) exempt organizations are permitted to engage in lobbying activities on a limited basis.[14] Eligible for such treatment are most § 501(c)(3) exempt organizations (educational institutions, hospitals, and medical research organizations; organizations supporting government schools; organizations publicly supported by charitable contributions; certain organizations that are publicly supported by various sources including admissions, sales, gifts, grants, contributions, or membership fees; and certain organizations that support certain types of public charities). Churches, their integrated auxiliaries, and *private foundations* are not permitted to engage in lobbying activities, however.

---

[12] *New Faith, Inc.,* 64 TCM 1050, T.C.Memo. 1992–601.
[13] § 501(c)(3).

[14] § 501(h). An affirmative election to lobby must be made.

PARTICIPATION IN THE POLITICAL PROCESS

Section 501(c)(3) tax-exempt groups are prohibited from participating in political campaigns. The prohibition includes either being "for a candidate" or being "against a candidate." A technical advice memorandum issued by the IRS points out that the prohibition also includes activities such as rating political candidates and organizing forums where members of the public rate political candidates. Any such participation can result in the loss of tax-exempt status.

The IRS has warned tax-exempts that it is stepping up scrutiny in this area. At the date of its warning, the IRS was aware of at least 50 organizations that were being examined or had requests for tax-exempt status pending in which political activity was an issue.

An eligible § 501(c)(3) organization must make an affirmative election to participate in lobbying activities on a limited basis. The lobbying expenditures of electing § 501(c)(3) organizations are subject to a ceiling. Exceeding the ceiling can lead to the forfeiture of exempt status. Even when the ceiling is not exceeded, a tax may be imposed on some of the lobbying expenditures (discussed subsequently).

Two terms are key to the calculation of the ceiling amount: **lobbying expenditures** and **grass roots expenditures.** Lobbying expenditures are made for the purpose of influencing legislation through either of the following.

- Attempting to affect the opinions of the general public or any segment thereof.
- Communicating with any legislator or staff member or with any government official or staff member who may participate in the formulation of legislation.

Grass roots expenditures are made for the purpose of influencing legislation by attempting to affect the opinions of the general public or any segment thereof.

The statutory ceiling is imposed on both lobbying expenditures and grass roots expenditures and is computed as follows.

- 150% × Lobbying nontaxable amount = Lobbying expenditures ceiling.
- 150% × Grass roots nontaxable amount = Grass roots expenditures ceiling.

The *lobbying nontaxable amount* is the lesser of (1) $1 million or (2) the amount determined in Figure 14–1.[15] The *grass roots nontaxable amount* is 25 percent of the lobbying nontaxable amount.[16]

An electing exempt organization is assessed a tax on **excess lobbying expenditures** as follows.[17]

- 25% × Excess lobbying expenditures = Tax liability.

Excess lobbying expenditures are the greater of the following.[18]

---

[15] § 4911(c)(2).
[16] § 4911(c)(4).

[17] § 4911(a)(1).
[18] § 4911(b).

▼ **FIGURE 14–1**
Calculation of Lobbying
Nontaxable Amount

Exempt Purpose Expenditures	Lobbying Nontaxable Amount Is
Not over $500,000	20% of exempt purpose expenditures*
Over $500,000 but not over $1 million	$100,000 + 15% of the excess of exempt purpose expenditures over $500,000
Over $1 million but not over $1.5 million	$175,000 + 10% of the excess of exempt purpose expenditures over $1 million
Over $1.5 million	$225,000 + 5% of the excess of exempt purpose expenditures over $1.5 million

*Exempt purpose expenditures generally are the amounts paid or incurred for the taxable year to accomplish the following purposes: religious, charitable, scientific, literary, educational, fostering national or international amateur sports competition, or the prevention of cruelty to children or animals.

- Excess of the lobbying expenditures for the taxable year over the lobbying nontaxable amount.
- Excess of the grass roots expenditures for the taxable year over the grass roots nontaxable amount.

EXAMPLE 1

Tan, Inc., a qualifying § 501(c)(3) organization, incurs lobbying expenditures of $500,000 for the taxable year and grass roots expenditures of $0. Exempt purpose expenditures for the taxable year are $5,000,000. Tan elects to be eligible to make lobbying expenditures on a limited basis.

Applying the data in Figure 14–1, the lobbying nontaxable amount is $400,000 [$225,000 + 5% ($5,000,000 − $1,500,000)]. The ceiling on lobbying expenditures is $600,000 (150% × $400,000). Therefore, the $500,000 of lobbying expenditures are under the permitted $600,000. However, the election results in the imposition of tax on the excess lobbying expenditures of $100,000 ($500,000 lobbying expenditures − $400,000 lobbying nontaxable amount). The resulting tax liability is $25,000 ($100,000 × 25%). ▼

A § 501(c)(3) organization that makes disqualifying lobbying expenditures is subject to a 5 percent tax on the lobbying expenditures for the taxable year. A 5 percent tax may also be levied on the organization's management. The tax is imposed on management only if the managers knew that making the expenditures was likely to result in the organization no longer qualifying under § 501(c)(3), and if the managers' actions were willful and not due to reasonable cause. The tax does not apply to private foundations (see the subsequent discussion).[19] Concept Summary 14–1 capsulizes the rules on influencing legislation.

FEEDER ORGANIZATIONS

A **feeder organization** carries on a trade or business for the benefit of an exempt organization and remits its profits to the exempt organization. Such organizations are not exempt from Federal income tax. This provision is intended to prevent an entity whose primary purpose is to conduct a trade or business for profit from escaping taxation merely because all of its profits are payable to one or more exempt organizations.[20]

---

[19] § 4912.

[20] § 502(a).

CONCEPT SUMMARY 14–1

Exempt Organizations and Influencing Legislation

Factor	Tax Result
Entity subject to rule	§ 501(c)(3) organization.
Effect of influencing legislation	Subject to tax on lobbying expenditures under § 4912.
	Forfeit exempt status under § 501(c)(3).
	Not eligible for exempt status under § 501(c)(4).
Effect of electing to make lobbying expenditures	Permitted to make limited lobbying expenditures.
	Subject to tax under § 4911.

Some income and activities are *not* subject to the feeder organization rules.[21]

- Rent income that would be excluded from the definition of the term *rent* for purposes of the unrelated business income tax (discussed subsequently).
- A trade or business where substantially all the work is performed by volunteers.
- The trade or business of selling merchandise where substantially all the merchandise has been received as contributions or gifts.

Concept Summary 14–2 highlights the consequences of exempt status.

PRIVATE FOUNDATIONS

TAX CONSEQUENCES OF PRIVATE FOUNDATION STATUS

4 LEARNING OBJECTIVE
Determine which exempt organizations are classified as private foundations.

Certain exempt organizations are classified as **private foundations.** This classification produces two negative consequences. First, the classification may have an adverse impact on the contributions received by the donee exempt organization. Contributions may decline because the tax consequences for donors may not be as favorable as if the entity were not a private foundation.[22] Second, the classification may result in taxation at the exempt organization level. The reason for this less beneficial tax treatment is that private foundations define common good more narrowly and therefore are seen as not being supported by, and operated for the good of, the public.

Definition of a Private Foundation. The following § 501(c)(3) organizations are *not* private foundations.[23]

1. Churches; educational institutions; hospitals and medical research organizations; charitable organizations receiving a major portion of their support from the general public or the United States, a state, or a political

---

[21] § 502(b).
[22] § 170(e)(1)(B)(ii).

[23] § 509(a).

CONCEPT SUMMARY 14–2

Consequences of Exempt Status

General	Exempt from Federal income tax.
	Exempt from most state and local income, franchise, sales, and property taxes.
	Qualify for reductions in postage rates.
	Gifts to the organization often can be deducted by donor.
Exceptions	May be subject to Federal income tax associated with the following.
	• Engaging in a prohibited transaction.
	• Being a feeder organization.
	• Being a private foundation.
	• Generating unrelated business taxable income.

subdivision thereof that is operated for the benefit of a college or university; and governmental units (favored activities category).

2. Organizations that are broadly supported by the general public (excluding disqualified persons), by governmental units, or by organizations described in (1) above.
3. Entities organized and operated exclusively for the benefit of organizations described in (1) or (2) [a supporting organization].
4. Entities organized and operated exclusively for testing for public safety.

To meet the broadly supported requirement in (2) above, both the following tests must be satisfied.

• External support test.
• Internal support test.

Under the *external support test*, more than one-third of the organization's support each taxable year *normally* must come from the three groups listed in (2) above, in the following forms.

• Gifts, grants, contributions, and membership fees.
• Gross receipts from admissions, sales of merchandise, performance of services, or the furnishing of facilities in an activity that is not an unrelated trade or business for purposes of the unrelated business income tax (discussed subsequently). However, such gross receipts from any person or governmental agency in excess of the greater of $5,000 or 1 percent of the organization's support for the taxable year are not counted.

The *internal support test* limits the amount of support *normally* received from the following sources to one-third of the organization's support for the taxable year.[24]

• Gross investment income (gross income from interest, dividends, rents, and royalties).
• Unrelated business taxable income (discussed subsequently) minus the related tax.

---

[24] Reg. § 1.509(a)–3(c) generally requires that the external and internal support tests be met in each of the four preceding tax years.

EXAMPLE 2

Lion, Inc., a § 501(c)(3) organization, received the following support during the taxable year.

Governmental unit A for services rendered	$30,000
Governmental unit B for services rendered	20,000
General public for services rendered	20,000
Gross investment income	15,000
Contributions from individual substantial contributors (disqualified persons)	15,000

For purposes of the *external support test,* the support from A is counted only to the extent of $5,000 (greater of $5,000 or 1% of $100,000 support). Likewise, for B, only $5,000 is counted as support. Thus, the total countable support is $30,000 ($20,000 from the general public + $5,000 + $5,000), and Lion fails the test for the taxable year ($30,000/$100,000 = 30%; need >33.3%). The $15,000 received from disqualified persons is excluded from the numerator but is included in the denominator.

In calculating the *internal support test,* only the gross investment income of $15,000 is included in the numerator. Thus, the test is satisfied ($15,000/$100,000 = 15%; cannot >33%) for the taxable year.

Since Lion did not satisfy both tests, it does not qualify as an organization that is broadly supported. ▼

The intent of the two tests is to exclude from private foundation status those § 501(c)(3) organizations that are responsive to the general public rather than to the private interests of a limited number of donors or other persons.

Examples of § 501(c)(3) organizations that are properly classified as private foundations receiving broad public support include the United Fund, the Girl Scouts, university alumni associations, symphony orchestras, and the PTA.

TAXES IMPOSED ON PRIVATE FOUNDATIONS

5 **LEARNING OBJECTIVE**
Recognize the taxes imposed on private foundations and calculate the related initial tax and additional tax amounts.

In general, a private foundation is exempt from Federal income tax. However, because a private foundation is usually not a broadly, publicly supported organization, it may be subject to the following taxes.[25]

- Tax based on investment income.
- Tax on self-dealing.
- Tax on failure to distribute income.
- Tax on excess business holdings.
- Tax on investments that jeopardize charitable purposes.
- Tax on taxable expenditures.

These taxes restrict the permitted activities of private foundations. Two levels of tax may be imposed on the private foundation and the foundation manager: an initial tax and an additional tax. The initial taxes (first-level), with the exception of the tax based on investment income, are imposed because the private foundation engages in so-called *prohibited transactions.* The additional taxes (second-level) are imposed only if the prohibited transactions are not corrected within a statutory time period.[26] See Concept Summary 14–3 for additional details.

The tax on a failure to distribute income will be used to illustrate how expensive these taxes can be and the related importance of avoiding their

---

[25] §§ 4940–4945.

[26] § 4961.

CONCEPT SUMMARY 14–3

Taxes Imposed on Private Foundations

Type of Tax	Code Section	Purpose	Private Foundation		Foundation Manager	
			Initial Tax	Additional Tax	Initial Tax	Additional Tax
On investment income	§ 4940	Audit fee to defray IRS expenses.	2%*			
On self-dealing	§ 4941	Engaging in transactions with disqualified persons.	5%**	200%**	2.5%†	50%†
On failure to distribute income	§ 4942	Failing to distribute adequate amount of income for exempt purposes.	15%	100%		
On excess business holdings	§ 4943	Investments that enable the private foundation to control unrelated businesses.	5%	200%		
On jeopardizing investments	§ 4944	Speculative investments that put the private foundation's assets at risk.	5%	25%	5%††	5%†
On taxable expenditures	§ 4945	Expenditures that should not be made by private foundations.	10%	100%	2.5%††	50%†

*May be possible to reduce the tax rate to 1%. In addition, an exempt operating foundation [see §§ 4940(d)(2) and 4942(j)(3)] is not subject to the tax.
**Imposed on the disqualified person rather than the foundation.
†Subject to a statutory ceiling of $10,000.
††Subject to a statutory ceiling of $5,000.

imposition. Both an initial (first-level) tax and an additional (second-level) tax may be imposed on a private nonoperating foundation for failure to distribute a sufficient portion of its income. The initial tax is imposed at a rate of 15 percent on the undistributed income for the taxable year that is not distributed by the end of the following taxable year. The initial tax is imposed on such undistributed income for each year until the IRS assesses the tax.

The additional tax is imposed at a rate of 100 percent on the amount of the inadequate distribution that is not distributed by the assessment date. The additional tax is effectively waived if the undistributed income is distributed within 90 days after the mailing of the deficiency notice for the additional tax. Extensions of this period may be obtained.

Undistributed income is the excess of the distributable amount (in effect, the amount that should have been distributed) over qualifying distributions made by the entity. The distributable amount is the excess of the minimum investment return over the sum of the (1) unrelated business income tax and (2) the excise tax based on net investment income.[27] The minimum investment return is 5 percent of the excess of the fair market value of the foundation's assets over the unpaid debt associated with acquiring or improving these assets. The foundation's assets employed directly in carrying on the foundation's exempt purpose are not used in making this calculation.

▼ **EXAMPLE 3**

Gold, Inc., a private foundation, has undistributed income of $80,000 for its taxable year 1994. It distributes $15,000 of this amount during 1995 and an additional $45,000 during 1996. An IRS deficiency notice is mailed to Gold on August 5, 1997. The initial tax is $12,750 [($65,000 × 15%) + ($20,000 × 15%)].

At the date of the deficiency notice, no additional distributions have been made from the 1994 undistributed income. Therefore, since the remaining undistributed income of $20,000 has not been distributed by August 5, 1997, an additional tax of $20,000 ($20,000 × 100%) is imposed.

If Gold distributes the $20,000 of undistributed income for 1994 within 90 days of the deficiency notice, the additional tax is waived. Without this distribution, however, the foundation will owe $32,750 in taxes. ▼

UNRELATED BUSINESS INCOME TAX

6   LEARNING OBJECTIVE
Determine when an exempt organization is subject to the unrelated business income tax and calculate the amount of the tax.

As explained in the previous section, private foundations are subject to excise taxes for certain actions. One of these excise taxes penalizes the private foundation for using the foundation to gain control of unrelated businesses (tax on excess business holdings). However, *unrelated business* has different meanings for purposes of that excise tax and for the unrelated business income tax.

The **unrelated business income tax (UBIT)** is designed to treat the entity as if it were subject to the corporate income tax. Thus, the rates that are used are those applicable to a corporate taxpayer.[28] In general, **unrelated business income** is derived from activities not related to the exempt purpose of the exempt organization. The tax is levied because the organization is engaging in substantial commercial activities.[29] Without such a tax, nonexempt organizations (regular taxable business entities) would be at a substantial disadvantage when trying to compete with the exempt organization. Thus, the UBIT is intended to neutralize the exempt entity's tax advantage.[30]

▼ **EXAMPLE 4**

Historic, Inc., is an exempt private foundation. Its exempt activity is to maintain a restoration of eighteenth-century colonial life (houses, public buildings, taverns, businesses, and craft demonstrations) that is visited by over a million people each year. A fee is charged for admission to the "restored area." In addition to this "museum" activity, Historic operates two hotels and three restaurants that are available to the general public. The earnings from the hotel and restaurant business are used to defray the costs of operating the "museum" activity.

The "museum" activity is not subject to the Federal income tax, except to the extent of any tax liability for any of the aforementioned excise taxes that are levied on private foundations. However, even though the income from the hotel and restaurant business is used for exempt purposes, that income is unrelated business income and is subject to the UBIT. ▼

---

[27] § 4940.
[28] § 511(a)(1).

[29] § 512(a)(1).
[30] Reg. § 1.513–1(b).

The UBIT applies to all organizations that are exempt from Federal income tax under § 501(c), except Federal agencies. In addition, the tax applies to state colleges and universities.[31]

A materiality exception generally exempts an entity from being subject to the UBIT if such income is insignificant. See the later discussion of the $1,000 statutory deduction generally available to all exempt organizations.

UNRELATED TRADE OR BUSINESS

An exempt organization may be subject to the UBIT in the following circumstances.[32]

- The organization conducts a trade or business.
- The trade or business is not substantially related to the exempt purpose of the organization.
- The trade or business is regularly carried on by the organization.

The Code specifically exempts the following activities from classification as an unrelated trade or business. Thus, even if all of the above factors are present, the activity is not classified as an unrelated trade or business.[33]

- The individuals performing substantially all the work of the trade or business do so without compensation (e.g., an orphanage operates a retail store for sales to the general public, and all the work is done by volunteers).
- The trade or business of selling merchandise, and substantially all of the merchandise has been received as gifts or contributions (e.g., thrift shops).
- For § 501(c)(3) organizations and for state colleges or universities, the trade or business is conducted primarily for the convenience of the organization's members, students, patients, officers, or employees (e.g., a laundry operated by the college for laundering dormitory linens and students' clothing, a college bookstore).
- For most employee unions, the trade or business consists of selling to members, at their usual place of employment, work-related clothing and equipment and items normally sold through vending machines, snack bars, or food-dispensing facilities.

Definition of Trade or Business. Trade or business, for this purpose, is broadly defined. It includes any activity conducted for the production of income through the sale of merchandise or the performance of services. An activity need not generate a profit to be treated as a trade or business. The activity may be part of a larger set of activities conducted by the organization, some of which may be related to the exempt purpose. Being included in a larger set does not cause the activity to lose its identity as an unrelated trade or business.[34]

EXAMPLE 5

Health, Inc., is an exempt hospital that operates a pharmacy. The pharmacy provides medicines and supplies to the patients in the hospital (i.e., it contributes to the conduct of the hospital's exempt purpose). In addition, the pharmacy sells medicines and supplies to the general public. The activity of selling to the general public constitutes a trade or business for purposes of the UBIT. ▼

---

[31] § 511(a)(2) and Reg. § 1.511–2(a)(2).
[32] § 513(a) and Reg. § 1.513–2(a).

[33] § 513(a).
[34] Reg. § 1.513–1(b).

Not Substantially Related to the Exempt Purpose.   Exempt organizations frequently conduct unrelated trades or businesses to provide income to help defray the costs of conducting the exempt purpose (like the hotel and restaurant business in Example 4). Providing financial support for the exempt purpose will not prevent an activity from being classified as an unrelated trade or business and thereby being subject to the UBIT.

To be related to the accomplishment of the exempt purpose, the conduct of the business activities must be causally related and contribute importantly to the exempt purpose. Whether a causal relationship exists and the degree of its importance are determined by examining the facts and circumstances. One must consider the size and extent of the activities in relation to the nature and extent of the exempt function that the activities serve.[35]

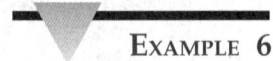
EXAMPLE 6

Art, Inc., an exempt organization, operates a school for training children in the performing arts. As an essential part of that training, the children perform for the general public. The children are paid at the minimum wage for the performances, and Art derives gross income by charging admission to the performances.

The income from admissions is not income from an unrelated trade or business, because the performances by the children contribute importantly to the accomplishment of the exempt purpose of providing training in the performing arts. ▼

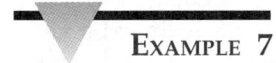
EXAMPLE 7

Assume the facts are the same as in Example 6, except that four performances are conducted each weekend of the year. Assume that this number of performances far exceeds that required for training the children. Thus, the part of the income derived from admissions for these excess performances is income from an unrelated trade or business. ▼

The trade or business may sell merchandise that has been produced as part of the accomplishment of the exempt purpose. The sale of such merchandise is normally treated as related to the exempt purpose. However, if the merchandise is not sold in substantially the same state it was in at the completion of the exempt purpose, the gross income subsequently derived from the sale of the merchandise is income from an unrelated trade or business.[36]

EXAMPLE 8

Help, Inc., an exempt organization, conducts programs for the rehabilitation of the handicapped. One of the programs includes training in radio and television repair. Help derives gross income by selling the repaired items. The income is substantially related to the accomplishment of the exempt purpose. ▼

An asset or facility used in the exempt purpose may also be used in a nonexempt purpose. Income derived from use for a nonexempt purpose is income from an unrelated trade or business.[37]

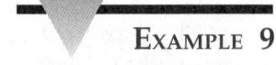
EXAMPLE 9

Civil, Inc., an exempt organization, operates a museum. As part of the exempt purpose of the museum, educational lectures are given in the museum's theater during the operating hours of the museum. In the evening, when the museum is closed, the theater is leased to an individual who operates a movie theater. The lease income received from the individual who operates the movie theater is income from an unrelated trade or business. ▼

---

[35] Reg. § 1.513–1(d).
[36] Reg. § 1.513–1(d)(4)(ii).

[37] Reg. § 1.513–1(d)(4)(iii) addresses the allocation of expenses to exempt and nonexempt activities.

TAX IN THE NEWS

BINGO BENEFITS CHARITIES?

Bingo games are legal in Virginia only if they are conducted by a charity. Such games do not necessarily constitute small business, in that bingo is a $200 million industry in the state.

One of the alleged problems of the state's bingo industry is that the return to charities is not large enough. Currently, according to bingo auditors, in many cases as little as 2 percent of bingo game revenues goes to the charities.

In response to frequent criticism of the way the games are run and questions about who is benefiting from them, the state is proposing new rules to regulate the bingo industry. The new rules establish strict financial reporting requirements, require criminal background checks for bingo managers, and require that between 6 percent and 16 percent of gross revenues go to charity, depending on the size of the bingo game.

Opponents of the new rules contend that the rules will have a chilling effect on people wanting to play bingo. No longer are bingo players "little old ladies in tennis shoes." Instead, they are described as educated, sophisticated, and demanding. Since the new rules are projected to reduce the payout to winners (primarily because of the increased amount going to charity), opponents believe fewer people will come to play.

Special Rule for Bingo Games. A special provision applies in determining whether income from bingo games is from an unrelated trade or business. Under this provision, a *qualified bingo game* is not an unrelated trade or business if both of the following requirements are satisfied.[38]

- The bingo game is legal under both state and local law.
- Commercial bingo games (conducted for a profit motive) ordinarily are not permitted in the jurisdiction.

 **EXAMPLE 10**

Play, Inc., an exempt organization, conducts weekly bingo games. The laws of the state and municipality in which Play conducts the games expressly provide that exempt organizations may conduct bingo games, but do not permit profit-oriented entities to do so. Since both of the requirements for bingo games are satisfied, the bingo games conducted by Play are not an unrelated trade or business. ▼

 **EXAMPLE 11**

Game, Inc., an exempt organization, conducts weekly bingo games in City X and City Y. State law expressly permits exempt organizations to conduct bingo games. State law also provides that profit-oriented entities may conduct bingo games in X, which is a resort community. Several businesses regularly conduct bingo games there.

The bingo games conducted by Game in Y are not an unrelated trade or business. However, the bingo games that Game conducts in X are an unrelated trade or business, because commercial bingo games are regularly permitted to be conducted there. ▼

---

[38]§ 513(f).

ETHICAL CONSIDERATIONS

Tax-Exempt Bingo

Assist, Inc., is a § 501(c)(3) exempt organization. Its mission is to help feed and clothe the homeless. Assist does this through providing a shelter, clothes closet, and soup kitchen for the homeless in the inner city.

Donations (i.e., both cash and property) are the principal source of Assist's revenue. Contributions result from mailings and from help kettles located outside area supermarkets. In addition, Assist sponsors bingo games on Friday and Saturday evenings. Approximately 30 percent of Assist's revenues come from the bingo games.

You are a new member of Assist's board of directors. You are an employee (recently promoted to manager) of an accounting firm, and you specialize in the financial services industry. Over lunch with one of your firm's tax partners (your unofficial mentor), you mention your service on Assist's board of directors. She provides you with information on the normal Federal income tax reporting requirements of exempt organizations [i.e., Form 1023: Application for Recognition of Exemption under Section 501(a); Form 990: Return of Organization Exempt from Income Tax, or Form 990–PF: Return of Private Foundation; and Form 990–T: Exempt Organization Business Income Tax Return].

You later ask Al Martin, Assist's foundation manager, who was the driving force behind the creation of Assist 15 years ago, for copies of these forms. He provides you with a copy of Form 1023 and a copy of Form 990–PF for the past three years. He says the CPA who served on the board prior to you told him that it was not necessary for Assist to file any Federal tax returns associated with the bingo games because Assist is tax-exempt.

You are aware that bingo games are illegal in your state. You also are aware that many tax-exempt organizations in your city and in other locales in the state conduct bingo games. The police "look the other way" as long as the sponsor is a tax-exempt organization. In fact, several local churches are Assist's biggest bingo game competitors. How should you respond?

Special Rule for Distribution of Low-Cost Articles.   If an exempt organization distributes low-cost items as an incidental part of its solicitation for charitable contributions, the distributions may not be considered an unrelated trade or business. A low-cost article is one that costs $6.90 for 1997 (indexed annually) or less. Examples of such items are pens, stamps, stickers, stationery, and address labels. If more than one item is distributed to a person during the calendar year, the costs of the items are combined.[39]

Special Rule for Rental or Exchange of Membership Lists.   If an exempt organization conducts a trade or business that consists of either exchanging with or renting to other exempt organizations the organization's donor or membership list (mailing lists), the activity is not an unrelated trade or business.[40]

Other Special Rules.   Other special rules are used in determining whether each of the following activities is an unrelated trade or business.[41]

---

[39] § 513(h)(1)(A).
[40] § 513(h)(1)(B).

[41] §§ 513(d), (e), and (g).

- Qualified public entertainment activities (e.g., a state fair).
- Qualified convention and trade show activities.
- Certain services provided at cost or less by a hospital to other small hospitals.
- Certain pole rentals by telephone or electric companies.

UNRELATED BUSINESS INCOME

Even when an exempt organization conducts an unrelated trade or business, a tax is assessed only if the exempt organization regularly conducts the activity and the business produces unrelated business income.

Regularly Carried on by the Organization. An activity is classified as unrelated business income only if it is regularly carried on by the exempt organization. This provision assures that only activities that are actually competing with taxable organizations are subject to the unrelated business income tax. Accordingly, factors to be considered in applying the *regularly carried on* test include the frequency of the activity, the continuity of the activity, and the manner in which the activity is pursued.[42]

EXAMPLE 12

Silver, Inc., an exempt organization, owns land that is located next to the state fairgrounds. During the 10 days of the state fair, Silver uses the land as a parking lot and charges individuals attending the state fair for parking there. The activity is not regularly carried on. ▼

EXAMPLE 13

Black, Inc., an exempt organization, has its offices in the downtown area. It owns a parking lot adjacent to its offices on which its employees park during the week. On Saturdays, it rents the spaces in the parking lot to individuals shopping or working in the downtown area. Black is conducting a business activity on a year-round basis, even though it is only for one day per week. Thus, an activity is regularly being carried on. ▼

Unrelated Business Income Defined. Unrelated business income is generally that derived from the unrelated trade or business, reduced by the deductions directly connected with the conduct of the unrelated trade or business.[43]

UNRELATED BUSINESS TAXABLE INCOME

General Tax Model. The model for unrelated business taxable income (UBTI) appears in Figure 14–2.

Positive adjustments[44]

1. A charitable contribution deduction is permitted without regard to whether the charitable contributions are associated with the unrelated trade or business. However, to the extent the charitable contributions deducted in calculating net unrelated business income (see Figure 14–2) exceed 10 percent of UBTI (without regard to the charitable contribution deduction), the excess is treated as a positive adjustment.

---

[42] § 512(a)(1) and Reg. § 1.513–1(c).
[43] § 512(a)(1).

[44] §§ 512(a)(1) and (b) and Reg. § 1.512(b)–1.

▼ **FIGURE 14–2**
Tax Formula for Unrelated
Business Taxable Income

> Gross unrelated business income
>
> − Deductions
>
> = Net unrelated business income
>
> ± Modifications
>
> = Unrelated business taxable income

EXAMPLE 14

Brown, Inc., an exempt organization, has UBTI of $100,000 (excluding any modifications associated with charitable contributions). Total charitable contributions (all associated with the unrelated trade or business) are $13,000. Assuming that the $13,000 is deducted in calculating net unrelated business income, the excess of $3,000 [$13,000 − 10%($100,000)] is a positive adjustment in calculating UBTI. ▼

2. Unrelated debt-financed income net of the unrelated debt-financed deductions (see the subsequent discussion of Unrelated Debt-Financed Income).
3. Certain interest, annuity, royalty, and rent income received by the exempt organization from an organization it controls (80 percent test). This provision overrides the modifications for these types of income (negative adjustment 3).

Negative adjustments

1. Income from dividends, interest, and annuities net of all deductions directly related to producing such income.
2. Royalty income, regardless of whether it is measured by production, gross income, or taxable income from the property, net of all deductions directly related to producing such income.
3. Rent income from real property and from certain personal property net of all deductions directly related to producing such income. Personal property rents are included in the negative adjustment only if the personal property is leased with the real property. In addition, the personal property rent income must be incidental (does not exceed 10 percent of the total rent income under the lease) to be used in computing the negative adjustment. In both of the following cases, however, none of the rent income is treated as a negative adjustment.

   • More than 50 percent of the rent income under the lease is from personal property.
   • Rent income is calculated using the tenant's profits.

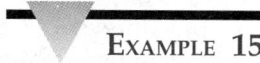

EXAMPLE 15

Beaver, Inc., an exempt organization, leases land and a building (realty) and computers (personalty) housed in the building. Under the lease, $46,000 of the rent is for the land and building, and $4,000 is for the computers. Expenses incurred for the land and building are $10,000. The net rent income from the land and building of $36,000 ($46,000 − $10,000) and the income from the computers of $4,000 are negative adjustments. ▼

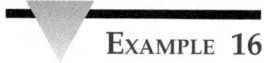

EXAMPLE 16

Assume the same facts as in Example 15, except that the rent income is $35,000 from the land and building and $15,000 from the computers. Since the rent income from the computers exceeds $5,000 (10% × $50,000) and is not incidental, it is not a negative adjustment. ▼

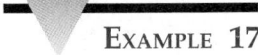

EXAMPLE 17

Assume the same facts as in Example 15, except that the rent income is $20,000 from the land and building and $30,000 from the computers. Since over 50% of the rent income under the lease is from the computers, neither the rent income from the land and building nor that from the computers is a negative adjustment. ▼

If the lessor of real property provides significant services to the lessee, such income, for this purpose, is not rent income.

4. Gains and losses from the sale, exchange, or other disposition of property *except for* inventory.

EXAMPLE 18

Beaver, the owner of the land, building, and computers in Example 15 sells these assets for $450,000. Their adjusted basis is $300,000. Beaver's recognized gain of $150,000 is a negative adjustment. ▼

5. Certain research income net of all deductions directly related to producing that income.

6. The charitable contribution deduction is permitted without regard to whether the charitable contributions are associated with the unrelated trade or business. Therefore, to the extent that the charitable contributions exceed those deducted in calculating net unrelated business income (see Figure 14–2), the excess is a negative adjustment in calculating UBTI. In making this calculation, be aware that the 10 percent of UBTI (without regard to the charitable contribution deduction) limit still applies (see positive adjustment 1).

EXAMPLE 19

Canine, Inc., an exempt organization, has unrelated business taxable income of $100,000 (excluding any modifications associated with charitable contributions). The total charitable contributions are $9,000, of which $7,000 (those associated with the unrelated trade or business) have been deducted in calculating net unrelated business income. Therefore, the remaining $2,000 of charitable contributions is a negative adjustment in calculating UBTI. ▼

7. A specific deduction of $1,000 is permitted.

EXAMPLE 20

Petit Care, Inc., an exempt organization, has net unrelated business income of $800. Since Petit will receive a specific deduction of $1,000, its UBTI is $0. Therefore, its income tax liability is $0. ▼

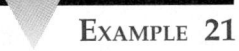

EXAMPLE 21

Patient, Inc., an exempt organization, has UBTI of $500,000. Patient's income tax liability is $170,000 ($500,000 UBTI × 34% corporate tax rate). ▼

UNRELATED DEBT-FINANCED INCOME

In the formula for calculating the tax on unrelated business income (see Figure 14–2), unrelated debt-financed income is one of the positive adjustments. Examples of income from debt-financed property include the rental of real estate, rental of tangible personal property, and investments in corporate stock, including gains from the disposition of such property. Gains from unrelated business income property are also included to the extent the gains are not otherwise treated as unrelated business income.

In terms of the UBIT, the positive adjustment for unrelated debt-financed income is a significant one. Without this provision, a tax-exempt organization could use borrowed funds to acquire unrelated business or investment property and use the untaxed (i.e., exempt) earnings from the acquisition to pay for the property.

Definition of Debt-Financed Income.   **Debt-financed income** is the gross income generated from debt-financed property. *Debt-financed property* is all property of the exempt organization that is held to produce income and on which there is acquisition indebtedness, *except* for the following.[45]

- Property where substantially all (at least 85 percent) of the use is for the achievement of the exempt purpose of the exempt organization.[46]
- Property whose gross income is otherwise treated as unrelated business income.
- Property whose gross income is from the following sources and is not otherwise treated as unrelated business income.

  - Income from research performed for the United States or a Federal governmental agency, or a state or a political subdivision thereof.
  - For a college, university, or hospital, income from research.
  - For an organization that performs fundamental (i.e., not applied) research for the benefit of the general public, income from research.

- Property used in an activity that is not an unrelated trade or business.

If the 85 percent test is not satisfied, only the portion of the property that is *not* used for the exempt purpose is debt-financed property.

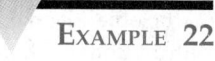

EXAMPLE 22

Deer, Inc., an exempt organization, owns a five-story office building on which there is acquisition indebtedness. Three of the floors are used for Deer's exempt purpose. The two other floors are leased to Purple Corporation. In this case, the *substantially all* test is not satisfied. Therefore, 40% of the office building is debt-financed property, and 60% is not. ▼

Certain land that is acquired by an exempt organization for later exempt use is excluded from debt-financed property if the following requirements are satisfied.[47]

- The principal purpose of acquiring the land is for (substantially all its) use in achieving the organization's exempt purpose.
- This use will begin within 10 years of the acquisition date.
- At the date when the land is acquired, it is located in the *neighborhood* of other property of the organization for which substantially all the use is for achieving the organization's exempt purpose.

Even if the third requirement is not satisfied, the land still is excluded from debt-financed property if it is converted to use for achieving the organization's exempt purpose within the 10-year period. Qualification under this provision will result in a refund of taxes previously paid. If the exempt organization is a church, the 10-year period becomes a 15-year period, and the neighborhood requirement is waived.

Definition of Acquisition Indebtedness.   Acquisition indebtedness is debt sustained by the exempt organization in association with the acquisition of

---

[45] § 514(b).
[46] Reg. § 1.514(b)–1(b)(1)(ii).

[47] § 514(b)(3).

property. More precisely, *acquisition indebtedness* consists of the unpaid amounts of the following for debt-financed property.[48]

- Debt incurred in acquiring or improving the property.
- Debt incurred before the property was acquired or improved, but which would not have been incurred without the acquisition or improvement.
- Debt incurred after the property was acquired or improved, but which would not have been incurred without the acquisition or improvement.

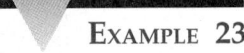

EXAMPLE 23

Red, Inc., an exempt organization, acquires land for $100,000. To finance the acquisition, Red mortgages the land and receives loan proceeds of $80,000. Red leases the land to Duck Corporation. The mortgage is acquisition indebtedness. ▼

EXAMPLE 24

Rose, Inc., an exempt organization, makes improvements to an office building that it rents to Bird Corporation. Excess working capital funds are used to finance the improvements. Rose is later required to mortgage its laboratory building, which it uses for its exempt purpose, to replenish working capital. The mortgage is acquisition indebtedness. ▼

Portion of Debt-Financed Income and Deductions Treated as Unrelated Business Taxable Income. Once the amount of the debt-financed income and deductions is determined, one must ascertain what portion thereof constitutes unrelated debt-financed income and deductions. Unrelated debt-financed income increases unrelated business taxable income, and unrelated debt-financed deductions decrease unrelated business taxable income.

The calculation is made for each debt-financed asset. The gross income from the property is multiplied by the following percentage.[49]

$$\frac{\text{Average acquisition indebtedness for the property}}{\text{Average adjusted basis of the property}} = \text{Debt/basis percentage}$$

This percentage cannot exceed 100. If debt-financed property is disposed of during the taxable year at a gain, average acquisition indebtedness in the formula is replaced with highest acquisition indebtedness. *Highest acquisition indebtedness* is the largest amount of acquisition indebtedness for the property during the 12-month period preceding the date of disposition.[50]

Deductions are allowed for expenses directly related to the debt-financed property and the income from it. Cost recovery deductions must apply the straight-line method. Once allowable deductions are determined, this amount is multiplied by the debt/basis percentage.[51]

EXAMPLE 25

White, Inc., an exempt organization, owns an office building that it leases to Squirrel Corporation for $120,000 per year. The average acquisition indebtedness is $300,000, and the average adjusted basis is $500,000. Since the office building is debt-financed property, the unrelated debt-financed income is

$$\frac{\$300,000}{\$500,000} \times \$120,000 = \$72,000 \qquad ▼$$

Average Acquisition Indebtedness. The *average acquisition indebtedness* for debt-financed property is the average amount of the outstanding debt for the

---

[48]§ 514(c)(1). Educational organizations can exclude certain debt incurred for real property acquisitions from classification as acquisition indebtedness.

[49]§ 514(a)(1).
[50]§ 514(c)(7).
[51]§ 514(a)(3).

taxable year (ignoring interest) during the portion of the year the property is held by the exempt organization. This amount is calculated by summing the outstanding debt on the first day of each calendar month the property is held by the exempt organization. Then this total is divided by the number of months the property is held by the organization.[52]

EXAMPLE 26

On August 12, Yellow, Inc., an exempt organization, acquires an office building that is debt-financed property for $500,000. The initial mortgage on the property is $400,000. The principal amount of the debt on the first of each month is as follows.

Month	Principal Amount
August	$ 400,000
September	380,000
October	360,000
November	340,000
December	320,000
Total	$1,800,000

Average acquisition indebtedness is $360,000 ($1,800,000 ÷ 5 months). August is treated as a full month. ▼

Average Adjusted Basis. The *average adjusted basis* of debt-financed property is calculated by summing the adjusted bases of the property on the first and last days during the taxable year the property is held by the exempt organization and then dividing by two.[53]

EXAMPLE 27

Assume the facts are the same as in Example 26. In addition, during the taxable year, depreciation of $5,900 is deducted. The average adjusted basis is $497,050 [($500,000 + $494,100) ÷ 2]. ▼

Concept Summary 14–4 presents the rules concerning the UBIT.

REPORTING REQUIREMENTS

OBTAINING EXEMPT ORGANIZATION STATUS

7   **LEARNING OBJECTIVE**
List the reports exempt organizations must file with the IRS and the related due dates.

Not all exempt organizations are required to obtain IRS approval for their exempt status. Among those required by statute to do so are organizations exempt under §§ 501(c)(3), 501(c)(9), and 501(c)(20).[54] Even in these cases, exceptions are provided (e.g., churches).

Even when not required to obtain IRS approval, most exempt organizations do apply for exempt status. Typically, an organization does not want to assume that it qualifies for exempt status and describe itself in that way to the public, only to have the IRS rule later that it does not qualify. Organizations exempt under § 501(c)(3) use Form 1023 [Application for Recognition of Exemption under

---

[52] § 514(c)(7) and Reg. § 1.514(a)–1(a)(3). A partial month is treated as a full month.

[53] § 514(a)(1) and Reg. § 1.514(a)–1(a)(2).
[54] §§ 505(c), 508(a) and 508(c).

CONCEPT SUMMARY 14–4

Unrelated Business Income Tax

Purpose	To tax the entity on unrelated business income as if it were subject to the corporate income tax.
Applicable tax rates	Corporate tax rates.
Exempt organizations to which applicable	All organizations exempt under § 501(c), except Federal agencies.
Entities subject to the tax	The organization conducts a trade or business; the trade or business is not substantially related to the exempt purpose of the organization; and the trade or business is regularly carried on by the organization.
Exceptions to the tax	• All the work is performed by volunteers. • Substantially all of the merchandise being sold has been received by gift. • For § 501(c)(3) organizations, the business is conducted primarily for the benefit of the organization's members, students, patients, officers, or employees. • For most employee unions, the trade or business consists of selling to members work-related clothing and equipment and items normally sold through vending machines, snack bars, or food-dispensing facilities.
$1,000 provision	If the gross income from an unrelated trade or business is less than $1,000, it is not necessary to file a return associated with the unrelated business income tax.

Section 501(c)(3)]. Form 1024 [Application for Recognition of Exemption under Section 501(a)] is used by most other types of exempt organizations.

If an organization is required to obtain IRS approval for its exempt status and does not do so, it does not qualify as an exempt organization.

ETHICAL CONSIDERATIONS

Filing for Exempt Status: A CPA's Dilemma

Waldo is the treasurer of the Alpine Sky Divers Club. In his opinion, the club satisfies all the requirements for exempt status as a social club under § 501(c)(7). When Annette, the club president and an assistant DA, asks him if he has completed all the paperwork with the IRS relating to the club's tax-exempt status, Waldo assures her that he has taken care of everything.

If this were another client, Waldo would have filed a Form 1024 [Application for Recognition of Exemption under Section 501(a)]. He has not done so for Alpine because he has been very busy at work and feels fairly certain that the IRS will never raise the issue of whether the club qualifies for tax-exempt status. He told Annette he had filed the papers with the IRS because she is a stickler for detail and does everything by the book. He also has had several dates with her and does not want to take a chance on spoiling their relationship.

Evaluate Waldo's behavior.

ANNUAL FILING REQUIREMENTS

Most exempt organizations are required to file an annual information return.[55] The return is filed on Form 990 (Return of Organization Exempt from Income Tax). The following exempt organizations need not file Form 990.[56]

- Federal agencies.
- Churches.
- Organizations whose annual gross receipts do not exceed $25,000.
- Private foundations.

Private foundations are required to file Form 990–PF (Return of Private Foundation). Form 990–PF requires more information than Form 990.

The due date for Form 990 or Form 990–PF is the fifteenth day of the fifth month after the end of the taxable year. These returns are filed with the appropriate IRS Service Center based on the location of the exempt organization's principal office. Requests for extensions on filing are made by filing Form 2758 (Applications for Extension of Time).

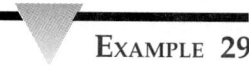

EXAMPLE 28

Green, Inc., a § 501(c)(3) organization, has a fiscal year that ends June 30, 1997. The due date for the annual return is November 15, 1997. If Green were a calendar year entity, the due date for the 1997 annual return would be May 15, 1998. ▼

Exempt organizations that are subject to the UBIT may be required to file Form 990–T (Exempt Organization Business Income Tax Return). The return must be filed if the organization has gross income of at least $1,000 from an unrelated trade or business. The due date for the return is the fifteenth day of the fifth month after the end of the taxable year.

If an exempt organization is subject to any of the excise taxes imposed on private foundations, Form 4720 (Return of Certain Excise Taxes on Charities and Other Persons) must be filed. The return is filed with the private foundation's Form 990–PF.

EXAMPLE 29

During the year, the First Church of Kentwood receives parishioner contributions of $450,000. Of this amount, $125,000 is designated for the church building fund. First Church is not required to file an annual return (Form 990) because churches are exempt from doing so. In addition, it is not required to file Form 990–T because it has no unrelated business income.

Colonial, Inc., is an exempt private foundation. Gross receipts for the year total $800,000, of which 60% is from admission fees paid by members of the general public who visit Colonial's museum of eighteenth-century life. The balance is endowment income. Because Colonial is a private foundation, it must file Form 990–PF.

Orange, Inc., is an exempt organization and is not a private foundation. Gross receipts for the year are $20,000. None of this amount is unrelated business income. Orange is not required to file Form 990 because its annual gross receipts do not exceed $25,000.

Restoration, Inc., is an exempt private foundation. Gross receipts for the year are $20,000. None of this amount is unrelated business income. Restoration must file Form 990–PF because private foundations are not eligible for the $25,000 filing exception.

During the year, the Second Church of Port Allen receives parishioner contributions of $300,000. In addition, the church has unrelated business income of $5,000. Second Church is not required to file Form 990 because churches are exempt from doing so. Form 990–T must be filed, however, because churches are not exempt from the UBIT and Second Church has exceeded the $1,000 floor. ▼

---

[55] § 6033(a)(1).

[56] § 6033(a)(2).

TAX PLANNING CONSIDERATIONS

8   **LEARNING OBJECTIVE**
Identify tax planning opportunities for exempt organizations.

GENERAL

Exempt organizations provide at least two potential tax benefits. First, the entity may be exempt from Federal income tax. Second, contributions to the entity may be deductible by the donor.

An organization that qualifies as an exempt organization may still be subject to certain types of Federal income tax, including the following.

- Tax on prohibited transactions.
- Tax on feeder organizations.
- Tax on private foundations.
- Tax on unrelated business income.

Therefore, classification as an exempt organization should not be interpreted to mean that the organization need not be concerned with any Federal income tax. Such a belief can result in the organization engaging in transactions that produce a substantial tax liability.

An organization is exempt from taxation only if it fits into one of the categories enumerated in the Code. Thus, particular attention must be given to the qualification requirements. These requirements must continue to be satisfied to avoid termination of exempt status (in effect they are now maintenance requirements).

MAINTAINING EXEMPT STATUS

To maintain exempt status, the organization must satisfy both an organizational test and an operational test. The organizational test requires that the entity satisfy the statutory requirements for exempt status on paper. The operational test ensures that the entity does, in fact, satisfy the statutory requirements for exempt status.

King Shipping Consum., Inc. (Zion Coptic Church, Inc.) indicates that it is usually much easier to satisfy the organizational test than the operational test.[57] Zion's stated purpose was to engage in activities usually and normally associated with churches. Based on this, the IRS approved Zion's exempt status as a § 501(c)(3) organization.

Zion's real intent, however, was to smuggle illegal drugs into the country and to distribute them for profit. The church's justification for the drugs was that it used marijuana in its sacrament. During a four-month period, however, the police confiscated 33 tons of marijuana from church members. The IRS calculated that, even assuming the maximum alleged church membership of several thousand, each member would have had to smoke over 33 pounds of marijuana during the four-month confiscation period.

The court concluded that Zion's real purpose was to cloak a large commercial drug smuggling operation. Since this activity was inconsistent with the religious purpose for exempt status, the court upheld the IRS's revocation of Zion's exempt status and the deficiency assessment of approximately $1.6 million.

PRIVATE FOUNDATION STATUS

Exempt organizations that can qualify as public charities receive more beneficial tax treatment than do those that qualify as private foundations. Thus, if possible, the organization should be structured to qualify as a public charity. The following can result when an exempt organization is classified as a private foundation.

---

[57] 58 TCM 574, T.C.Memo. 1989–593.

- Taxes may be imposed on the private foundation.
  - Tax based on investment income.
  - Tax on self-dealing.
  - Tax on failure to distribute income.
  - Tax on excess business holdings.
  - Tax on investments that jeopardize charitable purposes.
  - Tax on taxable expenditures.
- Donors may receive less favorable tax deduction treatment under § 170 than they would if the exempt organization were not a private foundation.

EXAMPLE 30

David has IBM stock ($25,000 adjusted basis, $100,000 fair market value) that he is going to contribute to one of the following exempt organizations: Blue, Inc., a public charity, or Teal, Inc., a private nonoperating foundation. David has owned the stock for five years.

David asks the manager of each organization to describe the tax benefits of contributing to that organization. He tells them he is in the 31% tax bracket.

Based on the data provided by the managers, David decides to contribute the stock to Blue, Inc. He calculates the amount of the charitable contribution under each option as follows.[58]

Donee	Contribution Deduction	Tax Rate	Contribution Borne by U.S. Government
Blue	$100,000	31%	$31,000
Teal	25,000 ($100,000 − $75,000)	31%	7,750

One method of avoiding private foundation status is to have a tax-exempt purpose that results in the organization not being classified as a private foundation (the *organization* approach). If this is not feasible, it may be possible to operate the organization so that it receives broad public support and thereby avoids private foundation status (the *operational* approach).

If the organization is a private foundation, care must be exercised to avoid the assessment of tax liability on prohibited transactions. This objective can best be achieved by establishing controls that prevent the private foundation from engaging in transactions that trigger the imposition of the taxes. If an initial tax is assessed, corrective actions should be implemented to avoid the assessment of an additional tax. See Concept Summary 14–5.

UNRELATED BUSINESS INCOME TAX

If the exempt organization conducts an unrelated trade or business, it may be subject to tax on the unrelated business income. Worse yet, the unrelated trade or business could result in the loss of exempt status if the IRS determines that the activity is the primary purpose of the organization. Thus, caution and planning should be used to eliminate the latter possibility and to minimize the former.

One approach that can be used to avoid the imposition of the UBIT is to establish a taxable subsidiary to conduct the unrelated trade or business. With a subsidiary, the revenues and expenses of the exempt organization can be separated from those of the unrelated trade or business. When the subsidiary remits its

---

[58]See Chapter 2 of this text and Chapter 10 in *West's Federal Taxation: Individual Income Taxes.*

CONCEPT SUMMARY 14–5

Private Foundation Status

	Exempt Organization Is	
	A Private Foundation	**Not a Private Foundation**
Reason for classification	Does not serve the common good because it lacks an approved exempt purpose or does not receive broad public financial support.	Serves the common good.
Eligible for exempt status?	Yes	Yes
Most beneficial charitable contribution deduction treatment available to donors?	Depends. No, if the private foundation is classified as a private *nonoperating* foundation.	Yes
Subject to excise taxes levied on prohibited transactions?	Yes	No
Subject to tax on unrelated business income?	Yes	Yes

after-tax profits to the exempt organization in the form of dividends, the dividends will not be taxable to the exempt organization. In addition, having a taxable subsidiary conduct the unrelated trade or business avoids the possibility that the IRS will consider the unrelated business income to be an excessive percentage of the total revenues of the exempt organization. Such a view can lead to the IRS questioning the exempt organization's right to retain its exempt status.

Another approach to avoiding the UBIT is to fail the definition of an unrelated trade or business. This is accomplished by *not* satisfying at least one of the following requirements.

- The organization conducts a trade or business.
- The trade or business is not substantially related to the exempt purpose of the organization.
- The trade or business is regularly carried on by the organization.

Even if the definitional requirements for an unrelated trade or business appear to be satisfied, the negative adjustments in calculating unrelated business taxable income (see Figure 14–2) can be used to minimize the tax liability.

Rental activities best illustrate the necessity of careful planning to avoid including the income from the activity in calculating unrelated business taxable income. The income from the rental of real property by an exempt organization is not part of unrelated business taxable income. However, leases must be drafted so as to preserve the negative adjustment and avoid the UBIT prevalent in the following circumstances.

- If personal property is leased with real property and more than 50 percent of the rent income under the lease is from personal property, all the rent income is included in calculating unrelated business taxable income.

- If rent income from real property is calculated completely, or in part, based on the profits of the lessee (unless the calculation is based on a fixed percentage of sales or receipts), the rent income is included in calculating unrelated business taxable income.
- If the lessor of real property provides significant services to the lessee, the income is not treated as rent income and thus is included in the computation of unrelated business taxable income.
- If the rent income is received from an organization that the exempt organization controls (80 percent), the income is included in calculating unrelated business taxable income.
- To the extent the rent income is classified as unrelated debt-financed income, it is included in calculating unrelated business taxable income.

KEY TERMS

Debt-financed income, 14–22	Feeder organization, 14–9	Private foundation, 14–10
Excess lobbying expenditure, 14–8	Grass roots lobbying expenditure, 14–8	Unrelated business income, 14–14
Exempt organization, 14–2	Lobbying expenditure, 14–8	Unrelated business income tax (UBIT), 14–14

PROBLEM MATERIALS

DISCUSSION QUESTIONS

1. Are all churches exempt from Federal income tax?

2. Why are certain organizations either partially or completely exempt from Federal income tax?

3. Which of the following organizations qualify for exempt status?
   a. Tulane University.
   b. Virginia Qualified Tuition Program.
   c. Red Cross.
   d. Disneyland.
   e. PTA.
   f. Jacksonville Chamber of Commerce.
   g. Colonial Williamsburg Foundation.
   h. National Football League (NFL).

4. Identify the statutory authority under which each of the following is exempt from Federal income tax.
   a. Kingsmill Country Club.
   b. Shady Lawn Cemetery.
   c. Amber Credit Union.
   d. Veterans of Foreign Wars.
   e. Boy Scouts of America.
   f. United Fund.
   g. Federal Deposit Insurance Corporation.
   h. Bruton Parish Episcopal Church.
   i. PTA.
   j. National Press Club.

5. Adrenna is the treasurer for two exempt organizations. One exempt organization pays no Federal income taxes for 1997, and the other pays Federal income taxes of $100,000 for 1997. Discuss potential reasons for this difference in tax results.

6. Roy contributes $1,000 to an exempt organization. Abby contributes $1,000 to a different exempt organization. Why is Abby permitted a $1,000 charitable contribution deduction in calculating her itemized deductions and Roy is not?

7. Can a church make an election that will enable it to engage in lobbying on a limited basis?

8. Cashmier, Inc., a § 501(c)(3) organization, loses its exempt status in 1997 for attempting to influence legislation. Golden, Inc., another § 501(c)(3) organization, also attempts to influence legislation and is in no danger of losing its exempt status. Explain.

9. Rex is the chief executive officer of Helping People, Inc., a § 501(c)(3) exempt organization located in Mobile, Alabama. He and the organization's board of directors are concerned about the effect that proposed legislation would have on the organization's budget and its ability to carry out its mission. They are discussing a proposal to have a law firm in Washington, D.C., aid in opposing the legislation. What tax issues are relevant to Helping People, Inc., as it makes this decision?

10. The Living Museum is a tax-exempt organization. Dolphin Corporation, a wholly owned subsidiary of the Living Museum, sells boats. Dolphin remits all of its earnings each year to its parent. Is Dolphin exempt from Federal income tax because it is a subsidiary of a tax-exempt organization and remits all of its earnings to a tax-exempt organization?

11. Which of the following activities are not subject to the tax imposed on feeder organizations?
    a. Substantially all of the work is performed by volunteers.
    b. Substantially all of the services are performed by paid employees of the exempt organization.
    c. Substantially all of the merchandise being sold is used property.
    d. Substantially all of the merchandise being sold was received as contributions or gifts.
    e. Rental of building to a tenant who uses the building as a warehouse for her business.

12. What is a private foundation, and what are the disadvantages of an exempt organization being classified as a private foundation?

13. Describe the external support test and the internal support test for a private foundation.

14. What types of taxes may be levied on a private foundation? Why are the taxes levied?

15. What is the purpose of the tax on the investment income of a private foundation? Discuss the applicable tax rates.

16. A private foundation engages in a transaction with a disqualified person. What are the tax consequences to the private foundation and to the disqualified person?

17. At the end of the tax year, a private foundation has excess business holdings of $100,000. This is the first year that the private foundation has had any excess business holdings. What are the tax consequences to the private foundation?

18. During the tax year, a private foundation makes speculative investments of $500,000 that are classified as jeopardizing investments. What are the tax consequences to the private foundation?

19. A private foundation has taxable expenditures of $50,000. What are the tax consequences to the private foundation?

20. Welcome, Inc., a tax-exempt organization, receives 25% of its support from disqualified persons. Another disqualified person has agreed to match this support if Welcome will appoint him to the organization's board of directors. What tax issues are relevant to Welcome as it makes this decision?

21. An exempt organization has unrelated business taxable income of $400,000 and total earnings of $1 million. Why is only the $400,000 subject to the Federal income tax?

22. First Church has been selling cards and small books in the church tower. A contribution box was provided for payments to be deposited. To increase church revenues, a task force is evaluating setting up a gift shop in the church parish house. What tax issues are relevant to the task force as it makes its decision?

23. An exempt hospital operates a pharmacy that is staffed by a pharmacist 24 hours per day. The pharmacy serves only hospital patients. Is the pharmacy an unrelated trade or business?

24. An exempt hospital receives as a gift from a wealthy donor all the shares of stock of Compute, Inc., a retail computer chain. Because the chain is very profitable and its CEO has offered to continue to manage it, the hospital has decided to operate the chain rather than sell the stock. All of the profits of the chain will be used in carrying out the exempt mission of the hospital. Advise the hospital on whether better tax consequences can be achieved by operating the chain as a subsidiary or as a division of the hospital corporation.

25. An exempt organization is considering conducting bingo games on Thursday nights as a way of generating additional revenue to support its exempt purpose. Before doing so, however, the president of the organization has come to you for advice regarding the effect on the organization's exempt status and whether the net income from the bingo games will be taxable. Identify the relevant tax issues.

26. Discuss the significance of the "regularly carried on" test as it relates to the unrelated business income tax.

27. Define each of the following with respect to unrelated debt-financed property:
    a. Debt-financed income.
    b. Debt-financed property.
    c. Acquisition indebtedness.
    d. Average acquisition indebtedness.
    e. Average adjusted basis.

28. Tom is the treasurer of the City Garden Club, a new garden club. A friend, who is the treasurer of the garden club in a neighboring community, tells Tom that it is not necessary for the garden club to file a request for exempt status with the IRS. Has Tom received correct advice?

29. The People's Church, a § 501(c)(3) organization, generates $55,000 of gross receipts this year. Is the church required to file an annual information return? If so, what form should be used and what is the filing due date?

30. Sparrow, Inc., a § 501(c)(3) organization, generated $900,000 gross receipts this year. Must Sparrow file an annual information return? If so, what form should be used?

PROBLEMS

31. Match the following exempt organizations with the statutory authority under which exempt status is granted. The statutory authority may apply to more than one exempt organization.

Exempt Organizations	Statutory Authority
Boy Scouts	§ 501(c)(1)
Episcopal Church	§ 501(c)(2)
National Football League (NFL)	§ 501(c)(3)
American Red Cross	§ 501(c)(4)
Salvation Army	§ 501(c)(5)
United Fund	§ 501(c)(6)

Colonial Williamsburg Foundation	§ 501(c)(7)
Wake Forest University	§ 501(c)(8)
Underwriters Laboratory (UL)	§ 501(c)(9)
PGA Tour	§ 501(c)(10)
Veterans of Foreign Wars (VFW)	§ 501(c)(11)
Dallas Rodeo Club	§ 501(c)(12)
PTA	§ 501(c)(13)
Toano Cemetery Association	§ 501(c)(14)
Alpha Chi Omega Sorority	§ 501(c)(15)
Green, Inc., Legal Services Plan	§ 501(c)(16)
National Press Club	§ 501(c)(19)
Federal Deposit Insurance Corporation (FDIC)	§ 501(c)(20)
League of Women Voters	§ 501(d)

32. Teach, Inc., a § 501(c)(3) educational institution, makes lobbying expenditures of $290,000. Teach incurs exempt purpose expenditures of $1.6 million in carrying out its educational mission.
    a. Determine the tax consequences to Teach if it does not elect to be eligible to participate in lobbying activities on a limited basis.
    b. Determine the tax consequences to Teach if it does elect to be eligible to participate in lobbying activities on a limited basis.

33. Research, Inc., a § 501(c)(3) medical research organization, makes lobbying expenditures of $1.2 million. Research incurs exempt purpose expenditures of $20 million in carrying out its medical research mission.
    a. Determine the tax consequences to Research if it does not elect to be eligible to participate in lobbying activities on a limited basis.
    b. Determine the tax consequences to Research if it does elect to be eligible to participate in lobbying activities on a limited basis.
    c. In light of pending health care legislation, Research is considering increasing its lobbying expenditures by 50% annually. Advise Research whether this is a wise thing to do from a tax perspective.

34. Roadrunner, Inc., is an exempt medical organization. Quail, Inc., a sporting goods retailer, is a wholly owned subsidiary of Roadrunner. Roadrunner inherited the Quail stock last year from a major benefactor of the medical organization. Quail's taxable income is $400,000. Quail will remit all of its earnings, net of any taxes, to Roadrunner to support the exempt purpose of the parent.
    a. Is Quail subject to Federal income tax? If so, calculate the liability.
    b. Arthur Morgan, the treasurer of Roadrunner, has contacted you regarding minimizing or eliminating Quail's tax liability. He would like to know if the tax consequences would be better if Quail were liquidated into Roadrunner. Write a letter to Morgan that contains your advice. Roadrunner's address is 500 Rouse Tower, Rochester, NY 14627.

35. Determine which of the following organizations are *not* private foundations.
    a. Baptist church.
    b. Girl Scouts.
    c. League of Women Voters.
    d. PGA Tour.
    e. American Institute of CPAs.
    f. PTA.
    g. American Red Cross.
    h. Salvation Army.
    i. Veterans of Foreign Wars.

36. Cardinal, Inc., a § 501(c)(3) organization, received support from the following sources.

Governmental unit A for services rendered	$ 6,000
General public for services rendered	80,000
Gross investment income	40,000
Contributions from disqualified persons	20,000
Contributions from other than disqualified persons	95,000

     a. Does Cardinal satisfy the test for receiving broad public support?
     b. Is Cardinal a private foundation?

37. Gray, Inc., a private foundation, has the following items of income and deductions.

Interest income	$18,000
Rent income	60,000
Dividend income	15,000
Royalty income	5,000
Unrelated business income	50,000
Rent expenses	12,000
Unrelated business expenses	10,000

     Gray is not an exempt operating foundation and is not eligible for the 1% tax rate.
     a. Calculate the net investment income.
     b. Calculate the tax on net investment income.
     c. What is the purpose of the tax on net investment income?

38. Eagle, Inc., a private foundation, has been in existence for 10 years. During this period, Eagle has been unable to satisfy the requirements for classification as a private operating foundation. At the end of 1996, it had undistributed income of $100,000. Of this amount, $40,000 was distributed in 1997, and $60,000 was distributed during the first quarter of 1998. The IRS deficiency notice was mailed on August 1, 1999.
     a. Calculate the initial tax for 1996, 1997, and 1998.
     b. Calculate the additional tax for 1999.

39. Otis is the CEO of Rectify, Inc., a private foundation. Otis invests $500,000 (80%) of the foundation's investment portfolio in derivatives. Previously, the $500,000 had been invested in corporate bonds with an AA rating that earned 7% per annum. If the derivatives investment works as Otis's investment adviser claims, the annual earnings could be as high as 20%.
     a. Determine if Rectify is subject to any of the taxes imposed on private foundations.
     b. If so, calculate the amount of the initial tax.
     c. If so, calculate the amount of the additional tax if the act causing the imposition of the tax is not addressed within the correction period.
     d. Are Otis and the foundation better off financially if the prohibited transaction, if any, is addressed within the correction period?

40. The board of directors of Pearl, Inc., a private foundation, consists of Alice, Beth, and Carlos. They vote unanimously to provide a $100,000 grant to Doug, their business associate. The grant is to be used for travel and education and does not qualify as a permitted grant to individuals (i.e., it is a taxable expenditure under § 4945). Each director knows that Doug was selected for the grant because he is a friend of the organization and that the grant is a taxable expenditure.
     a. Calculate the initial tax imposed on the private foundation.
     b. Calculate the initial tax imposed on the foundation manager (i.e., board of directors).

41. The Open Museum is an exempt organization that operates a gift shop. The museum's annual operations budget is $2.5 million. Gift shop sales generate a profit of $750,000. Another $500,000 of endowment income is generated. Both the income from the gift shop and the endowment income are used to support the exempt purpose of the

museum. The balance of $1.25 million required for annual operations is provided through admission fees. Wayne Davis, a new board member, does not understand why the museum is subject to tax at all, particularly since the profits are used in carrying out the mission of the museum.

a. Calculate the amount of unrelated business income.

b. Assume that the endowment income is reinvested rather than being used to support annual operations. Calculate the amount of unrelated business income.

c. As the museum treasurer, write a letter to Wayne explaining the reason for the tax consequences. Mr. Davis's address is 45 Pine Avenue, Peoria, IL 61625.

42. Salmon, Inc., an exempt organization, has unrelated business taxable income of $20 million.

a. Calculate Salmon's unrelated business income tax.

b. Prepare an outline of a presentation you are going to give to the new members of Salmon's board on why Salmon is subject to the UBIT even though it is an exempt organization.

43. For each of the following organizations, determine the amount of the UBIT.

a. AIDS, Inc., an exempt charitable organization that provides support for individuals with AIDS, operates a retail medical supply store open to the general public. The net income of the store, before any Federal income taxes, is $325,000.

b. The local Episcopal church operates a retail gift shop. The inventory consists of the typical items sold by commercial gift shops in the city. The director of the gift shop estimates that 80% of the gift shop sales are to tourists and 20% are to church members. The net income of the gift shop, before the salaries of the three gift shop employees and any Federal income taxes, is $300,000. The salaries of the employees total $80,000.

c. Education, Inc., a private university, has vending machines in the student dormitories and academic buildings on campus. In recognition of recent tuition increases, the university has adopted a policy of merely trying to recover its costs associated with the vending machine activity. For the current year, however, the net income of the activity, before any Federal income taxes, is $75,000.

d. Worn, Inc., an exempt organization, provides food for the homeless. It operates a thrift store that sells used clothing to the general public. The thrift shop is staffed by four salaried employees. All of the clothes it sells are received as contributions. The $100,000 profit generated for the year by the thrift shop is used in Worn's mission of providing food to the homeless.

e. Small, Inc., an exempt organization, has unrelated business income of $900 and unrelated business expenses of $400.

44. Medium, Inc., an exempt organization, has unrelated business income of $2,300 and unrelated business expenses of $1,200. Calculate the amount of the UBIT.

45. Falcon Basketball League, an exempt organization, is a youth basketball league for children ages 12 through 14. The league has been in existence for 30 years. In the past, revenue for operations has been provided through community fund-raising and the sale of snacks at the games by the parents. Due to a projected revenue shortfall of approximately $5,000, the governing board has decided to charge admission to the basketball games of $1.00 for adults and $.50 for children.

a. Will the admission charge affect Falcon's exempt status?

b. What are the tax consequences to Falcon of the net income from snack sales and the new admission fee?

c. As the volunteer treasurer of the Falcon League, prepare a memo for the board in which you explain the effect, if any, of the admission fee policy on Falcon's exempt status.

46. Help, Inc., is an exempt organization that assists disabled individuals by training them in computer repair. Used computers are donated to Help, Inc., by both organizations and individuals. Some of the donated computers are operational, but others are not. After being used in the training program, the computers, all of which are now

operational, are sold to the general public. Help's revenues and expenses for the current period are as follows.

Contributions	$ 800,000
Revenues from computer sales	2,600,000
Administrative expenses	600,000
Material and supplies for computer repairs	800,000
Utilities	20,000
Wages paid to disabled individuals in the training program (at minimum wage rate)	1,400,000
Rent for building and equipment	200,000

Any revenues not expended during the current period are deposited in a reserve fund to finance future activities.

a. Is the computer repair and sales activity an unrelated trade or business?

b. Calculate the net income of Help, Inc., and the related Federal income tax liability, if any.

47. Faith Church is exempt from Federal income taxation under § 501(c)(3). To supplement its contribution revenue, it holds bingo games on Saturday night. It has the licenses and permits required to do so. The net income from the bingo games is $75,000. These funds are used to support the ministry of the church. Faith Church is located in a city where bingo games can only be conducted by churches and charities.

a. Will conducting the bingo games affect the exempt status of Faith Church?

b. Calculate the Federal tax liability, if any, associated with the bingo games.

48. Bluebird, Inc., an exempt organization, has unrelated business taxable income (before any modifications associated with charitable contributions) of $200,000. Charitable contributions made by Bluebird that are associated with the unrelated trade or business are $15,000, and those made that are not associated with the unrelated trade or business are $10,000. Calculate the effect of the charitable contributions on Bluebird's unrelated business taxable income.

49. Comfort, Inc., an exempt hospital, is going to operate a pharmacy that will be classified as an unrelated trade or business. Comfort establishes the pharmacy as a wholly owned subsidiary. During the current year, the subsidiary generates taxable income of $100,000 and pays dividends of $100,000 to Comfort.

a. What are the tax consequences to the subsidiary?

b. What are the tax consequences to Comfort?

50. Rabbit, Inc., an exempt organization, has net unrelated business income of $75,000 excluding any rent income received. Rabbit owns two buildings that are leased to tenants. The net rent income on the first building is $20,000, and that on the second building is $15,000. The lessee of the first building is unrelated to Rabbit whereas the lessee of the second building is a 100% owned for-profit subsidiary. Calculate Rabbit's unrelated business taxable income.

51. Kind, Inc., an exempt organization, leases land, a building, and factory equipment to Shirts', Inc. Shirts' is a taxable entity that manufactures shirts for distribution through its factory outlet stores. The rent income and the related expenses for Kind are as follows.

	Rent Income	Rent Expenses
Land and building	$100,000	$40,000
Factory equipment	125,000	25,000

a. Calculate the amount of Kind's unrelated business taxable income.

b. Assume instead that Kind's rent income and expenses are as follows.

	Rent Income	Rent Expenses
Land and building	$100,000	$20,000
Factory equipment	125,000	50,000

Calculate the amount of Kind's unrelated business taxable income.

52. Tranquility, Inc., an exempt organization, leases factory equipment to Blouses, Inc. Blouses is a taxable entity that manufactures blouses for distribution through up-scale department stores. Blouses owns the land and building in which it conducts its manufacturing operations. The original cost of the building to Blouses was $800,000, and the cost recovery deduction for the current year is $20,512. Rent income to Tranquility for the factory equipment is $300,000, and the related expenses are $170,000. Calculate Tranquility's unrelated business taxable income.

53. Assistance, Inc., an exempt organization, sells the following assets during the taxable year:

Asset	Gain (Loss)	Use
Land and building	$ 80,000	In exempt purpose
Land	50,000	Leased to a taxable entity
Equipment	(20,000)	Leased to a taxable entity
Automobile	(5,000)	In exempt purpose

Determine the effect of these transactions on Assistance's unrelated business taxable income.

54. Medical, Inc., an exempt organization, has unrelated business taxable income of $400,000 (excluding any modifications associated with charitable contributions). Of total charitable contributions of $38,000 made by Medical, $31,000 are associated with its unrelated trade or business. Determine the effect of the charitable contributions on Medical's unrelated business taxable income.

55. Benevolent, Inc., an exempt organization, owns the following properties.

Property	Basis	Acquisition Indebtedness	% Used in Exempt Purpose
Building A	$400,000	$300,000	100%
Building B	500,000	–0–	60%
Building C	600,000	200,000	90%
Building D	700,000	500,000	70%

Calculate the adjusted basis to Benevolent of its debt-financed property.

56. Fix, Inc., an exempt organization, owns a one-story building. Fix's adjusted basis for the building is $900,000. Of the building's total area of 10,000 square feet, the front portion (approximately 3,000 square feet) is used in carrying out Fix's exempt purpose. The remainder of the building is leased for $300,000 each year to Belts, Inc., a taxable entity, to use for storing its inventory. The unamortized balance of a mortgage relating to the original acquisition of the building is $600,000. Determine the portion of the adjusted basis that is treated as debt-financed property and the amount of the mortgage that is acquisition indebtedness.

57. Rust, Inc., an exempt organization, acquires a building for $900,000 on August 1, 1997. The principal amount of the related mortgage on the first day of the following months is as follows.

August	$505,000
September	500,000
October	495,000
November	490,000
December	485,000

Depreciation deducted during 1997 was $8,667. Rust leases the building to Build Corporation.
a. Calculate the average acquisition indebtedness for the building.
b. Calculate the average adjusted basis for the building.
c. Calculate the debt/basis percentage.

58. Rodeo, Inc., is a social club that is exempt under § 501(c)(7). Its annual gross receipts are $250,000. Of this amount, $20,000 is from an unrelated trade or business. Rodeo's fiscal year ends on April 30.
   a. Is Rodeo required to file an annual information return? If so, what form should be used?
   b. Is Rodeo subject to the UBIT? If so, what form should be used?
   c. If tax returns must be filed, what is the due date?

59. Education, Inc., a § 501(c)(3) organization, is a private foundation with a tax year that ends on June 30, 1997. Gross receipts for the fiscal year are $180,000, and the related expenses are $160,000.
   a. Is Education required to file an annual information return?
   b. If so, what form is used?
   c. If so, what is the due date?
   d. How would your answers in (a), (b), and (c) change if Education is an exempt organization that is not a private foundation?

60. Historic Burg is an exempt organization that operates a museum depicting eighteenth-century life. Sally gives the museum an eighteenth-century chest that she has owned for 10 years. Her adjusted basis is $55,000, and the chest's appraised value is $100,000. Sally's adjusted gross income is $300,000.
   a. Calculate Sally's charitable contribution deduction if Historic Burg is a private operating foundation.
   b. Calculate Sally's charitable contribution deduction if Historic Burg is a private nonoperating foundation.

RESEARCH PROBLEMS

*Note: **West's Federal Taxation on CD-ROM** can be used in preparing solutions to the Research Problems. Alternatively, tax research materials contained in a standard tax library can be used.*

Research Problem 1. Allied Fund, a charitable organization exempt under § 501(c)(3), has branches located in each of the 50 states. Allied is not a private foundation. Rather than having each of the state units file an annual return with the IRS, Allied would like to file a single return that reports the activities of all of its branches. Is this permissible? What is the due date of the return?

Partial list of research aids:
§ 6033.
§ 6072.
Reg. § 1.6033–2(d).

Research Problem 2. State University has operated a television station since 1950. The station operates under a commercial license and is an affiliate of ABC. In addition to the regular network programming, the television station broadcasts educational programming in the form of in-school classroom instruction, educational extension programming, and closed circuit educational programming. The station is also used in the training of students who are enrolled in degree programs as preparation for careers in the television industry.

State University maintains that the television station is substantially related to the purpose for which the university was granted exempt status under § 501(c)(3). The only purpose for operating the television station is to contribute to the achievement of the educational goals of the university.

Determine if the television station is subject to the tax on unrelated business income.

Research Problem 3. The Shark Club, an exempt organization, conducts bingo games on the weekends. Profit entities are prohibited from conducting bingo games in the state, but tax-exempt organizations are permitted to do so. Shark uses the net profits from the bingo games in carrying out its tax-exempt mission.

The bingo games are conducted by volunteers. However, the volunteers are permitted to accept tips from the players. Tipping by players is a frequent occurrence.

Determine whether Shark is subject to the unrelated business income tax on its bingo activities.

Research Problem 4. Great Outdoors, Inc., is a tax-exempt organization. Its mission is to explore, enjoy, and protect the wild places of the earth; to practice and promote the responsible use of the earth's ecosystems and resources; to educate and enlist humanity to protect and restore the quality of the natural and human environment; and to use all lawful means to carry out these objectives.

William Johnson, the chief financial officer, presents you with the following information. Great Outdoors raises funds to support its mission in a variety of ways including contributions and membership fees. As part of this effort, Great Outdoors develops and maintains mailing lists of its members, donors, catalog purchasers, and other supporters.

Great Outdoors has exclusive ownership rights in its mailing lists. To acquire the names of prospective members and supporters, Great Outdoors occasionally exchanges membership lists with other organizations. In addition, Great Outdoors permits other tax-exempt organizations and commercial entities to pay a fee, as set forth in a fee schedule, to use its mailing lists on a one-time basis per transaction.

Johnson is aware of the UBIT. He also is aware of the § 512(b)(2) provision that excludes royalties from the UBIT. A Revenue Agent has raised the issue that the revenue from the use of the mailing lists by other entities may be taxable as unrelated business income. Johnson would like for you to research this issue for him.

Write a letter to Johnson that contains your findings, and prepare a memo for the tax files. Great Outdoors's address is 100 Central Avenue, Pocatello, ID 83209.

Research Problem 5. The American Accounting Association holds its regional meetings at seven locations in the spring and its national meeting in August of each year. The meetings include the formal presentation of papers, panel discussions, business sessions, and various committee meetings. In addition, textbook publishers are permitted to display their wares in a publisher's exhibit hall. The book exhibitors must pay a fee to the AAA for the right to do so. Are these fees unrelated business income?

Use the tax resources of the internet to address the following questions. Do not restrict your search to the World Wide Web, but include a review of newsgroups and general reference materials, practitioner sites and resources, primary sources of the tax law, chat rooms and discussion groups, and other opportunities.

Research Problem 6. Download an application for tax exempt status that would be filed with the IRS. Write a one-page letter to an organization that is contemplating the filing of such an application, walking through the application and highlighting the information that must be provided and the estimated time required to comply with the directives of the form.

Research Problem 7. Summarize a recent newspaper or magazine story that relates a perceived abuse of the § 501(c)(3) provisions by a business owner or politician.

Research Problem 8. Find an account of IRS plans to step up its audits of universities, with respect to both maintenance of exempt status and computations of the UBIT. In a two-page outline, summarize these plans and comment on whether this is an appropriate use of the agency's audit resources.

MULTISTATE CORPORATE TAXATION

LEARNING OBJECTIVES

After completing Chapter 15, you should be able to:

1. Illustrate the computation of a multistate corporation's state tax liability.

2. Define nexus and its role in state income taxation.

3. Distinguish between allocation and apportionment of a multistate corporation's taxable income.

4. Describe the nature and treatment of business and nonbusiness income.

5. Discuss the sales, payroll, and property apportionment factors.

6. Apply the unitary method of state taxation.

7. Discuss the states' income tax treatment of S corporations.

8. Describe other commonly encountered state and local taxes on businesses.

9. Recognize tax planning opportunities available to minimize a corporation's state and local tax liability.

OUTLINE

Although most of this text concentrates on the effects of the Federal income tax law upon the computation of a taxpayer's annual tax liability, a variety of tax bases apply to most business taxpayers. For instance, a multinational corporation may be subject to tax in a number of different countries (see Chapter 9). Similarly, the taxpayer may be subject to a county-level wheel tax on its business vehicles, a state sales or use tax on many of its asset purchases, and state and local income or franchise taxes on its net income or on the privilege of doing business in the taxing jurisdiction. Indeed, estimates are that nearly 50 percent of the tax dollars paid by business taxpayers go to state and local authorities.

Businesses operate in a multistate environment for a variety of reasons. For the most part, nontax motivations drive such location decisions as where to build new plants or distribution centers or whether to move communications and data processing facilities and corporate headquarters. For instance, a business typically wants to be close to its largest markets and to operate in a positive private- and public-sector business climate, where it has access to well-trained and reasonably priced labor, suppliers and support operations, sources of natural resources and well-educated personnel, and highway and airport facilities.

Many location decisions, though, are motivated by multistate tax considerations.

- The taxpayer's manufacturing, wholesaling, sales, retailing, and credit operations each may be centered in a different state to take advantage of various economic development incentives created by politicians.
- Mail-order and other catalog operations blur the traditional jurisdictional boundaries for buyer and seller alike. Often advertising campaigns boast "no sales tax payable."
- Similarly, the ability to transfer sales and purchase orders, pricing information, and other data via telephone lines, computer networks, and satellite

TAX IN THE NEWS

SEARCHING FOR NEW TAXPAYERS

In recent years, state and local taxes have grown to constitute nearly 50 percent of most businesses' tax liabilities. Likewise, as revenue pressures continue to increase, the jurisdictions have become more aggressive in identifying new taxpayers and new taxable transactions.

For instance, current taxpayers in some states receive questionnaires from the department of revenue, asking them to identify their three most important competitors in the state. The governments use these data to make certain that all taxpayers present in the state are subject to applicable income and sales/use taxes.

Similarly, registrants at large conventions or trade shows are likely to receive information packets from the state, describing just how the sales and use tax laws apply to an organized one-time sales event.

transmissions may tempt the taxpayer to overlook traditional applications of the property and sales tax base. For instance, is computer software tangible (and subject to property tax) or intangible property? Is canned software, transferred via telephone lines and modems, rather than by disk, subject to sales tax? Which jurisdiction's property tax should apply to a communications satellite?

- In addition to flying over virtually the entire country, the major airlines depart from and land in the majority of the states. Which state's income tax should apply to the ticket income? Should sales or income tax apply to sales of liquor while the plane is airborne?

- Local political concerns lead to a multiplicity of tax rules as politicians attempt to serve their constituents by introducing a variety of special tax incentives. This variety can be confusing, however. Taxpayers may have difficulty determining whether they qualify for energy or investment tax credits, S corporation status, exemptions from sales tax liability or income tax withholding, or passive loss relief at the local level.

- Politicians have a strong incentive to impose new tax burdens on visitors and others who have no direct say in their reelection. Thus, it is increasingly common to see tourist and hotel-bed taxes on convention delegates, city payroll taxes on commuters, and the use of obscure tax formulas that otherwise discriminate against those with limited contact in the area.

- Each jurisdiction in which the entity is subject to tax represents a geometrical increase in compliance responsibilities. For instance, how many tax returns must be filed by a three-shareholder S corporation operating in 15 states?

- Various states and localities have adopted revenue-raising statutes that vary in sophistication and operate on different time schedules. For instance, although fewer than half the states have adopted an alternative minimum tax, more jurisdictions are likely to adopt these taxes in the near future. Thus far, states that have imposed the tax have tended to select different bases. In addition, the aggressiveness with which departments of revenue enforce their tax statutes varies from state to state, even in a context of universal pressure to enhance revenues. Accordingly, the taxpayer must deal with a patchwork of germane taxing provisions in an environment that is often uncertain.

This chapter reviews the basic tax concepts that are predominant among most states that impose a tax based on net income and discusses the major areas in which tax planning can reduce a corporation's overall state tax burden.

Most of this chapter is devoted to a discussion of state taxes that are based on income. Each state is free to identify its corporate tax by a different term. Not all of the states that impose a tax on corporate income call the tax an "income tax." Rather, some states refer to their tax on corporate income as a franchise tax,[1] a business tax, a license tax, or a business profits tax.

ETHICAL CONSIDERATIONS

Encouraging Economic Development through Tax Concessions

The tax professional occasionally is in a position to negotiate with a state or city taxing jurisdiction to garner tax relief for a client as an incentive to locate a plant or distribution center in that geographic area. In times when unemployment rates are high and interstate competition is fierce, such tax concessions can be significant.

For instance, to encourage a business to build a large distribution center in the area, community leaders might be agreeable to (1) paying for roads, sewer, water, and other improvements through taxpayer bonds; (2) reducing property taxes by 50 percent for the first 10 years of the center's operations; and (3) permanently excluding any distribution-related vehicles and equipment from the personal property tax.

The community would grant the concessions even though the influx of new workers would place a great strain on public school facilities and likely necessitate improvements in traffic patterns and other infrastructure. Local residents, even those who obtain jobs at the new facility, and the tax adviser may wonder whether the tax concessions are supportable in light of these changes in the community's quality of life.

Take the position of a large employer that has been located in the area for more than 50 years. By how much should it be willing to absorb the tax increases that result when economic development concessions are used to attract new, perhaps temporary, businesses to the area? Does your analysis change if the new business competes with the long-time resident for sales? For employees? For political power?

OVERVIEW OF CORPORATE STATE INCOME TAXATION

Forty-six states and the District of Columbia impose a tax based on a corporation's taxable income. Since each state is free to create its own tax provisions, the tax

---

[1] Although a franchise tax in some states is a business privilege tax based on a corporation's capital stock or net worth, several states use that term for the tax that they impose on a corporation's net income.

practitioner could be faced with 47 entirely different state tax provisions.[2] Fortunately, however, to simplify the filing of tax returns and increase compliance with state tax laws, the majority of states "piggyback" onto the Federal income tax base. This means they have adopted *en masse* part or all of the Federal provisions governing the definition of income and the allowance of various exemptions, exclusions, and deductions. None of the states, however, has piggybacked its tax collections with the IRS.

COMPUTING STATE TAXABLE INCOME

1 LEARNING OBJECTIVE
Illustrate the computation of a multistate corporation's state tax liability.

In more than 40 of the states that impose a corporate income tax, the starting point in computing state taxable income is taxable income as reflected on the Federal corporate income tax return (Form 1120). These states typically use either taxable income before the net operating loss and special deductions (line 28) or taxable income itself (line 30). Those states whose computation of state taxable income is not coupled to the Federal tax return have their own state-specific definitions of gross and taxable income. Nonetheless, even these states typically adopt most Federal income and deduction provisions.

Although Federal tax law plays a significant role in the computation of state taxable income, there is a wide disparity in both the methods used to determine a state's taxable income and the tax rates imposed on that income. Accordingly, increasing the number of states in which a corporation is subject to tax causes the complexity of determining the corporation's state income tax liability to rise exponentially.

The formula used by a multistate corporation to determine its tax liability in a typical state is illustrated in Figure 15–1.

▼ **FIGURE 15–1**
Computing Corporate State
Income Tax Liability

	Starting point in computing taxable income**
±	State modification items
	State tax base
±	Total net allocable (loss)/income (nonbusiness income)
	Total apportionable income/(loss) (business income)
×	State's apportionment percentage
	Income apportioned to the state
±	Income/(loss) allocated to the state
	State taxable income/(loss)
×	State tax rate
	Gross income tax liability for state
−	State's tax credits
	Net income tax liability for the state

**Most states use either line 28 or line 30 of the Federal corporate income tax return (Form 1120). In other states, the corporation is required to identify and report each element of income and deduction on the state return.

---

[2] Although the District of Columbia is not a state, it operates in much the same manner as a state and imposes a tax based on income. Four states impose no corporate income tax at all: Nevada, South Dakota, Washington, and Wyoming. Corporations, however, are subject to a business and occupation tax in Washington.

OPERATIONAL IMPLICATIONS

Generally, the accounting period and methods used by a corporation for state tax purposes must be the same as those used on the Federal return. States often apply different rules, however, in identifying the members of a group filing a consolidated return and the income of each group member that is subject to tax.

As the starting point for computing state taxable income often is directly related to the Federal taxable income amount, most states also piggyback onto the IRS's audit process. Consequently, virtually all of the states require notification,

▼ **EXHIBIT 15–1**
Common State Modifications

Addition Modifications

- Interest income received on state and municipal obligations and any other interest income that is exempt from Federal income tax. For this purpose, some states exempt interest earned on their own obligations.

- Expenses deducted in computing Federal taxable income that are directly or indirectly related to U.S. obligations.

- Income-based franchise and income taxes imposed by any state and the District of Columbia that were deducted in computing Federal taxable income.

- The amount by which the Federal deductions for depreciation, amortization, or depletion exceed those permitted by the state. This adjustment is not necessary in states that have continuously conformed to the Federal depreciation, amortization, and depletion provisions.

- The amount by which the state gain or loss from the disposal of assets differs from the Federal gain or loss. Due to the difference in permitted depreciation methods and other adjustments, a corporation's assets may have different Federal and state tax bases. This adjustment is not necessary if the state and Federal basis provisions are identical.

Adjustments required as a result of different elections being made for state and Federal purposes. Examples of such elections include the methods under which income from installment sales or long-term contracts are determined.

Federal net operating loss deduction. This modification is not required by states in which the starting point in the computation of taxable income is Federal income before special deductions.

Subtraction Modifications

- Interest on U.S. obligations or obligations of Federal agencies to the extent included in Federal taxable income but exempt from state income taxes under U.S. law. Although a state is prohibited from imposing an income tax on U.S. government obligations, a state may impose an income-based franchise tax on that interest income.

- Expenses that are directly or indirectly related to the state and municipal interest that is taxable for state purposes.

- Refunds of franchise and income taxes imposed by any state and the District of Columbia, to the extent included in Federal taxable income.

- The amount by which the state deductions for depreciation, amortization, or depletion exceed the deductions permitted for Federal tax purposes.

Adjustments required as a result of different elections being made for state and Federal purposes. Examples of such elections include the methods under which income from installment sales or long-term contracts is determined.

Dividends received from certain out-of-state corporations, to the extent included in Federal taxable income.

Net operating loss deduction as determined for state tax purposes.

Deduction for Federal income tax paid.

usually within 90 days, of the final settlement of a Federal income tax audit. State authorities then adjust the originally calculated state tax liability appropriately.

STATE MODIFICATIONS

Federal taxable income generally is used as the starting point in computing the state's income tax base, but numerous state adjustments or modifications are often necessary to:

- Reflect differences between state and Federal tax statutes.
- Remove income that a state is constitutionally prohibited from taxing.
- Eliminate the recovery of income for which the state did not permit a deduction on an earlier tax return.

The required modifications to Federal taxable income vary significantly among the states. Accordingly, this section discusses the most common additions and subtractions that the states require. Exhibit 15–1 lists the most frequently encountered modifications; those denoted by a bullet are required by a majority of the states. In computing the taxable income for a given state, only a selected number of these modifications may be applicable.

EXAMPLE 1

Blue Corporation is subject to tax only in State A. The starting point in computing A taxable income is Federal taxable income. Modifications then are made to reflect, among other provisions, the exempt status of interest on A obligations, all dividends received from in-state corporations, and the disallowance of a deduction for state income taxes. Blue generated the following income and deductions.

Sales	$1,500,000
Interest on Federal obligations	50,000
Interest on municipal obligations of State B	100,000
Dividends received from 50%-owned State A corporations	200,000
Total income	$1,850,000
Expenses related to Federal obligations	$ 1,000
Expenses related to municipal obligations	5,000
State income tax expense	50,000
Depreciation allowed for Federal tax purposes (the deduction allowed for state purposes is $300,000)	400,000
Other allowable deductions	1,000,000
Total deductions	$1,456,000

Blue's taxable income for Federal and state purposes is $139,000 and $295,000, respectively.

Federal Taxable Income	
Sales	$1,500,000
Interest on Federal obligations	50,000
Dividends received from domestic corporations	200,000
Total income	$1,750,000
Expenses related to Federal obligations	$ 1,000
State income tax expense	50,000
Depreciation	400,000
Other allowable deductions	1,000,000
Total deductions	$1,451,000

Taxable income before special deductions	$299,000
Less: Dividends received deduction (80% × $200,000)	160,000
Federal taxable income	$139,000

State A Taxable Income

Federal taxable income	$139,000

Addition Modifications

Interest on State B obligations	100,000
State income tax expense	50,000
Excess depreciation deduction allowed for Federal purposes ($400,000 – $300,000)	100,000
Expenses related to Federal obligations	1,000

Subtraction Modifications

Expenses related to B obligations	(5,000)
Dividends from in-state corporations included in Federal taxable income ($200,000 – $160,000)	(40,000)
Interest on Federal obligations	(50,000)
State A taxable income	$295,000

EXAMPLE 2

Continue with the facts of Example 1, except that the $100,000 of municipal interest was generated from State A obligations. The computation of Federal taxable income is unaffected by this change. Since A exempts interest on its own obligations from taxation, Blue's A taxable income is $200,000.

State A Taxable Income

Federal taxable income	$139,000

Addition Modifications

State income tax expense	50,000
Excess depreciation deduction allowed for Federal purposes ($400,000 – $300,000)	100,000
Expenses related to Federal obligations	1,000

Subtraction Modifications

Dividends from in-state corporations included in Federal taxable income ($200,000 – $160,000)	(40,000)
Interest on Federal obligations	(50,000)
State A taxable income	$200,000

UDITPA AND THE MULTISTATE TAX COMMISSION

The Uniform Division of Income for Tax Purposes Act (**UDITPA**) is a model law relating to the assignment of income among the states for corporations that maintain operations in more than one state (multistate corporations). Many states have adopted the provisions of UDITPA, either by joining the Multistate Tax Compact or by modeling their laws after the provisions of UDITPA.

The **Multistate Tax Commission (MTC)**, which is appointed by the member states of the Multistate Tax Compact, writes regulations and other rules that interpret UDITPA. When a new MTC rule or regulation is created, the member states propose its adoption to their respective legislatures. The majority of member states adopt the regulations with no exceptions or only minor changes.[3]

JURISDICTION TO IMPOSE TAX: PUBLIC LAW 86–272

2 **LEARNING OBJECTIVE**
Define nexus and its role in state income taxation.

The state in which a business is incorporated has the jurisdiction to tax the corporation, regardless of the volume of its business activity within the state. Whether a state can tax the income of a business that is incorporated in another state usually depends on the relationship between the state and the corporation. If a corporation is to be subject to a tax in a state other than its state of incorporation, sufficient nexus must be established with that state.

Nexus describes the degree of business activity that must be present before a taxing jurisdiction has the right to impose a tax on an entity's income. The measure of the relationship that is necessary to create nexus is defined by state statute. Typically, sufficient nexus is present when a corporation derives income from sources within the state, owns or leases property in the state, employs personnel in the state, or has physical or financial capital there. **Public Law 86–272** limits the states' right to impose an income tax on interstate activities.[4] This Federal law prohibits a state from taxing a business whose only connection with the state is to solicit orders for sales of tangible personal property that is sent outside the state for approval or rejection. If approved, the orders must be filled and shipped by the business from a point outside the state.

Only the sale of tangible personal property is immune from taxation under the law, however. Leases, rentals, and other dispositions of tangible personal property are not protected activities. Moreover, dispositions of real property and intangible property, as well as sales of services, do not receive immunity under Public Law 86–272. In this regard, each state constructs its own definition of tangible and intangible property. In addition, since property ownership is not a protected activity, providing company-owned fax, copy, or computer equipment to an out-of-state salesperson may create nexus with a state, even though the salesperson merely solicits sales orders.

An activity that consists merely of solicitation is immune from taxation. The statute does not define the term *solicitation*, but the Supreme Court has held that *solicitation of orders* includes any explicit verbal request for orders and any speech or conduct that implicitly invites an order.[5] The Court also created a *de minimis* rule, allowing immunity from nexus where a limited amount of solicitation occurs.

Carrying out any of the following (common but substantively) minimal activities within a state, in addition to the traditional sales-solicitation tasks of the taxpayer's sales force, could establish nexus.

- Conducting training seminars or classes for persons other than sales personnel.
- Repairing or maintaining the company's products (even if performed at no charge to the customer).
- Setting up promotional items or approving credit requests by sales personnel.

Exhibit 15–2 summarizes the activities that the MTC has identified as being directly related to solicitation (protected activities) and activities unrelated to solicitation (which establish income tax nexus for the entity).

---

[3] Many of the states that are not members of the Multistate Tax Compact also model their laws after UDITPA and the MTC regulations.

[4] 15 U.S.C. 381–385.
[5] *Wisconsin Department of Revenue v. William Wrigley, Jr., Co.,* 112 S.Ct. 2447 (1992).

General rule: P.L. 86–272 immunity applies where the sales representative's activities are ancillary to the order-solicitation process.

Activities That Usually Do Not Create Nexus under P.L. 86–272

- Advertising campaigns.
- Carrying free samples only for display or distribution.
- Owning or furnishing automobiles to salespersons.
- Passing inquiries or complaints on to the home office.
- Checking customers' inventories for reorder.
- Maintaining a sample or display room for two weeks or less during the year.
- Soliciting sales by an in-state resident employee, provided that the employee does not maintain a place of business in the state, including an office in the home.

Activities Usually Sufficient to Establish Nexus

- Making repairs or providing maintenance.
- Collecting delinquent accounts; investigating creditworthiness.
- Installation or supervision of installation.
- Conducting training classes, seminars, or lectures for persons other than sales personnel.
- Providing engineering services.
- Approving or accepting orders.
- Repossessing property.
- Picking up or replacing damaged or returned property.
- Hiring, training, or supervising personnel other than sales employees.
- Providing shipping information and coordinating deliveries.
- Maintaining a sample or display room in excess of two weeks.
- Carrying samples for sale, exchange, or distribution in any manner for consideration or other value.
- Owning, leasing, maintaining, or otherwise using any of the following facilities or property in the state: real estate; repair shop; parts department; employment office; purchasing office; warehouse; meeting place for directors, officers, or employees; stock of goods; telephone answering service; or mobile stores (i.e., trucks with driver-salespersons).
- Consigning tangible personal property to any person, including an independent contractor.
- Maintaining an office for an employee, including an office in the home.

SOURCE: "Information Concerning Practices of MTC States under P.L. 86–272," MTC 1993.

Independent Contractors. Public Law 86–272 extends immunity to certain in-state activities conducted by an independent contractor that would not be permitted if performed directly by the taxpayer. Generally, an independent contractor may engage in the following limited activities without establishing nexus: (1) soliciting sales, (2) making sales, and (3) maintaining a sales office. Maintenance of inventory by an independent contractor under consignment or any other type of arrangement with the principal normally results in the loss of immunity.

ALLOCATION AND APPORTIONMENT OF INCOME

3 **LEARNING OBJECTIVE**
Distinguish between allocation and apportionment of a multistate corporation's taxable income.

A corporation that conducts business activities in more than one state must determine the portion of its net income that is subject to tax by each state. A corporation that has established sufficient nexus with another state generally must both **allocate** and **apportion** its income.

Apportionment is a means by which a corporation's business income is divided among the states in which it conducts business. Under an apportionment procedure, a corporation determines allowable income and deductions for the company as a whole and then apportions some of its net income to a given state, according to an approved formula.

Allocation is a method under which specific components of a corporation's income, net of related expenses, are directly assigned to a certain state. Allocation differs from apportionment in that allocable income is assigned to one state, whereas apportionable income is divided among several states. Nonapportionable (nonbusiness) income generally includes

- Income or losses derived from the sale of nonbusiness real or tangible property, or
- Income or losses derived from rentals and royalties from nonbusiness real or tangible personal property.

This income normally is assigned to the state where the property that generated the income or loss is located.

As Figure 15–1 indicated, total allocable (nonapportionable) income or loss typically is removed from corporate net income before the state's apportionment percentage is applied. The nonapportionable income or loss assigned to a state then is combined with the income apportionable to that state to arrive at total income subject to tax in the state.

EXAMPLE 3

Green Corporation conducts business in States N, O, P, and Q. Green's $900,000 taxable income is comprised of $800,000 of apportionable income and $100,000 of allocable income generated from transactions conducted in State Q. Green's sales, property, and payroll are evenly divided among the four states, and all of the states employ the identical apportionment formula. Accordingly, $200,000 of Green's income is taxable in each of States N, O, and P. Green is subject to income tax on $300,000 of income in State Q.

Apportionable income	$ 800,000
Apportionment percentage (apportionable income is divided equally among the four states)	× 25%
Income apportioned to each state	$ 200,000

	State N	State O	State P	State Q
Income apportioned	$200,000	$200,000	$200,000	$200,000
Income allocated	–0–	–0–	–0–	100,000
Taxable income	$200,000	$200,000	$200,000	$300,000

THE APPORTIONMENT PROCEDURE

Apportionment assumes that the production of business income is linked to business activity, and the laws of each state define a number of factors believed to indicate the amount of corporate activity conducted within the state. However, apportionment often does not provide a uniform division of an organization's income based on its business activity, because each state is free to choose the type and number of factors that it believes are indicative of the business activity conducted within its borders. Therefore, a corporation may be subject to state income tax on more or less than 100 percent of its income.

An equally incongruous consequence of apportionment may occur when the operations in a state result in a loss.

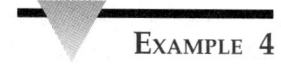

EXAMPLE 4

Red Corporation's operations include two manufacturing facilities, located in States A and B, respectively. The plant located in A generated $500,000 of income, and the plant located in B generated a loss of $200,000. Therefore, Red's total taxable income is $300,000.

By applying the statutes of each state, Red determines that its apportionment factors for A and B are .65 and .35, respectively. Accordingly, Red's income is apportioned to the states as follows.

Income apportioned to State A: .65 × $300,000 = $195,000

Income apportioned to State B: .35 × $300,000 = $105,000

Red is subject to tax in B on $105,000 of income, even though the operations conducted in that state resulted in a loss. ▼

BUSINESS AND NONBUSINESS INCOME

4 LEARNING OBJECTIVE
Describe the nature and treatment of business and nonbusiness income.

Business income is assigned among the states by using an apportionment formula. In contrast, *nonbusiness income* may either be apportioned or allocated to the state in which the income-producing asset is located. For instance, income derived from the rental of nonbusiness real property generally is allocated to the state in which the property is located. If the corporation is not taxed in the state in which the income-producing asset is located, most states allocate the income to the state in which the corporation's trade or business is directed or managed.[6]

----

[6] UDITPA § 1(b).

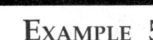

EXAMPLE 5

TNT Corporation, a manufacturer of explosive devices, is a multistate taxpayer that has nexus with States P and Q. During the taxable year, TNT's net sales of explosive devices were $900,000; $600,000 were made in P and $300,000 were made in Q. The corporation also received $90,000 from the rental of nonbusiness real property located in P.

Both states employ a three-factor apportionment formula under which sales, property, and payroll are equally weighted. However, the states do not agree on the definition of apportionable income. Under P's tax provisions, nonbusiness rent income is allocable and business income is apportionable, while Q requires a corporation to apportion all of its (business and nonbusiness) income. The sales factor (the ratio of in-state sales to total sales) for each of the states is computed as follows.

$$\text{State P:} \quad \frac{\$600,000 \text{ (sales in State P)}}{\$900,000 \text{ (total sales)}} = 66.67\%$$

$$\text{State Q:} \quad \frac{\$300,000 \text{ (sales in State Q)}}{\$990,000 \text{ (total sales)}^*} = 30.30\%$$

*Since rent income is treated as business income, rents are included in the denominator of the sales factor. ▼

EXAMPLE 6

Continue with the facts of Example 5, except that the rent income was generated from property located in Q, rather than from property located in P. Although the sales factor for P remains the same, the sales factor for Q changes.

$$\text{State P:} \quad \frac{\$600,000 \text{ (sales in State P)}}{\$900,000 \text{ (total sales)}} = 66.67\%$$

$$\text{State Q:} \quad \frac{\$390,000 \text{ (sales in State Q)}}{\$990,000 \text{ (total sales)}} = 39.39\%$$

Due to the composition of the sales factor in the two states, TNT's income never is perfectly apportioned: the aggregate of the sales factors is either more or less than 100%. ▼

DEFINING BUSINESS INCOME

Business income arises from the taxpayer's regular course of business or constitutes an integral part of the taxpayer's regular business.[7] In determining whether an item of income is (apportionable) business income, state courts have developed a variety of approaches to determine what constitutes a taxpayer's "regular course of business."[8]

A few states, including Connecticut and New Jersey, fail to distinguish between business and nonbusiness income. In these states, all of a corporation's income is deemed to be business income and subject to apportionment.

EXAMPLE 7

Scarlet Corporation is subject to income tax in several states. Scarlet earned $2,500,000 from the sales of its products and $1,000,000 from the sale of assets that were unrelated to its regular business operations.

In the states that distinguish between business and nonbusiness income, $2,500,000 of Scarlet's income is apportioned to the state according to the state's apportionment formula. The gain on the sale of the nonbusiness assets is allocated to the state in which the assets

[7] MTC Reg. IV.1.(a).
[8] *Atlantic Richfield Co. v. State of Colorado and Joseph F. Dolan*, 601 P.2d 628 (Colo.S.Ct., 1979); *Appeal of A. Epstein and Sons, Inc.*, (Cal.State Bd. of Equalization, 1984).

were located. In the states that subject a corporation's entire income to apportionment, $3,500,000 ($2,500,000 + $1,000,000) is apportioned to the states in which the taxpayer conducts business. ▼

NONBUSINESS INCOME

Nonbusiness income is defined as "all income other than business income."[9] Thus, nonbusiness income is the corporation's income that is unrelated to its regular business operations. Usually, nonbusiness income comprises passive and portfolio income, such as dividends, interest, rents, royalties, and certain capital gains. However, passive or portfolio income may be classified as business income when the acquisition, management, and disposition of the underlying property constitute an integral part of the taxpayer's regular business operation.

EXAMPLE 8

Gray Corporation owns and operates two manufacturing facilities, one in State A and the other in State B. Due to a temporary decline in sales, Gray has rented 10% of its A facility to an unaffiliated corporation. Gray generated $100,000 net rent income and $900,000 income from manufacturing.

Both A and B classify such rent income as allocable nonbusiness income. By applying the statutes of each state, as discussed in the next section, Gray determines that its apportionment factors are .40 for A and .60 for B. Gray's income attributable to each state is determined as shown below.

Income Subject to Tax in State A	
Taxable income	$1,000,000
Less: Allocable income	(100,000)
Apportionable income	$ 900,000
Times: Apportionment factor	40%
Income apportioned to State A	$ 360,000
Plus: Income allocated to State A	100,000
Income subject to tax in State A	$ 460,000

Income Subject to Tax in State B	
Taxable income	$1,000,000
Less: Allocable income	(100,000)
Apportionable income	$ 900,000
Times: Apportionment factor	60%
Income apportioned to State B	$ 540,000
Plus: Income allocated to State B	–0–
Income subject to tax in State B	$ 540,000

▼

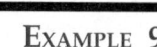

EXAMPLE 9

Continue with the facts of Example 8, but assume that B does not distinguish between business and nonbusiness income. Thus, all of Gray's income is apportionable.

Gray properly determines that its apportionment factors are .40 for A and .58 for B. Since the apportionment factors used by the two states are derived differently, Gray's income that is subject to tax does not equal 100%.

[9] UDITPA § 1(e).

Income Subject to Tax in State A	$ 460,000
Income Subject to Tax in State B	
Apportionable income	$1,000,000
Times: Apportionment factor	58%
Income apportioned to State B	$ 580,000

Due to differences in the states' definitions of apportionable and allocable income, $1,040,000 of Gray's $1,000,000 Federal taxable income is subject to state income taxation. ▼

APPORTIONMENT FACTORS: ELEMENTS AND PLANNING

5 **LEARNING OBJECTIVE**
Discuss the sales, payroll, and property apportionment factors.

Business income is apportioned among the states by determining the appropriate apportionment percentage for each state that has a right to tax the entity. To determine the apportionment percentage for each state, a ratio is established for each of the factors included in the state's apportionment formula. Each ratio is calculated by comparing the level of a specific business activity within a state to the total corporate activity of that type. The ratios then are summed, averaged, and appropriately weighted (if required) to determine the corporation's apportionment percentage for a specific state.

Although apportionment formulas vary among jurisdictions, most states use a three-factor formula that equally weights sales, property, and payroll. However, approximately 25 states use a modified three-factor formula, where the sales factor is assigned a double weight. The use of a double-weighted sales factor tends to pull a larger percentage of an out-of-state corporation's income into the taxing jurisdiction of the state, because the corporation's major activity within the state—the sales of its products—is weighted more heavily than are its payroll and property activities. Double weighting the sales factor, however, provides tax relief for corporations that are domiciled in the state. Those corporations generally own significantly more property and incur more payroll costs (factors that are given less weight in the apportionment formula) within the state than do out-of-state corporations.

This discussion applies generally to manufacturing entities. Certain industries, such as financial institutions, insurance companies, air and motor carriers, pipeline companies, and public utilities, typically are required to use special apportionment formulas.

EXAMPLE 10

Musk Corporation realized $500,000 of taxable income from the sales of its products in States A and B. Musk's activities in both states establish nexus for income tax purposes. Musk's sales, payroll, and property in the states include the following.

	State A	State B	Total
Sales	$1,250,000	$750,000	$2,000,000
Property	2,500,000	–0–	2,500,000
Payroll	1,500,000	–0–	1,500,000

If State B uses an equally weighted three-factor apportionment formula, $62,500 of Musk's taxable income is apportioned to B.

Sales ($750,000/$2,000,000)	=	37.5%
Property ($0/$2,500,000)	=	–0–
Payroll ($0/$1,500,000)	=	–0–
Sum of apportionment factors		37.5%
Average	÷	3
Apportionment factor for State B		12.5%
Taxable income	×	$500,000
Income apportioned to State B		$ 62,500

If State B uses a double-weighted sales factor in its three-factor apportionment formula, $93,750 of Musk's taxable income is apportioned to B.

Sales ($750,000/$2,000,000)	= 37.5% × 2 =		75%
Property ($0/$2,500,000)	=		–0–
Payroll ($0/$1,500,000)	=		–0–
Sum of apportionment factors			75%
Average		÷	4
Apportionment factor for State B			18.75%
Taxable income		×	$500,000
Income apportioned to State B			$ 93,750

When a state uses a double-weighted sales factor, typically a larger percentage of an out-of-state corporation's income is subject to tax in the state. Here, an additional $31,250 ($93,750 – $62,500) of Musk's income is subject to tax in B. ▼

A single-factor apportionment formula consisting solely of a sales factor is even more detrimental to an out-of-state corporation than an apportionment factor that double weights the sales factor. Currently, only Iowa, Nebraska, and Texas require the use of a single-factor apportionment formula. Figure 15–2 shows the variety of apportionment formulas that are applied by the states.[10]

EXAMPLE 11

PPR Corporation, a retailer of paper products, owns retail stores in States A, B, and C. A uses a three-factor apportionment formula under which the sales, property, and payroll factors are equally weighted. B uses a three-factor apportionment formula under which sales are double weighted. C employs a single-factor apportionment factor, based solely on sales.

PPR's operations generated $800,000 of apportionable income, and its sales and payroll activity and average property owned in each of the three states are as follows.

	State A	**State B**	**State C**	**Total**
Sales	$500,000	$400,000	$300,000	$1,200,000
Payroll	100,000	125,000	75,000	300,000
Property	150,000	250,000	100,000	500,000

---

[10] Data for Figures 15–2 and 15–3 are from Raabe and Boucher, *1996 Multistate Corporate Tax Guide* (Greenvale, N.Y.: Panel Publishers).

▼ **FIGURE 15–2**
Apportionment Factor
Weights—Manufacturing
Enterprises

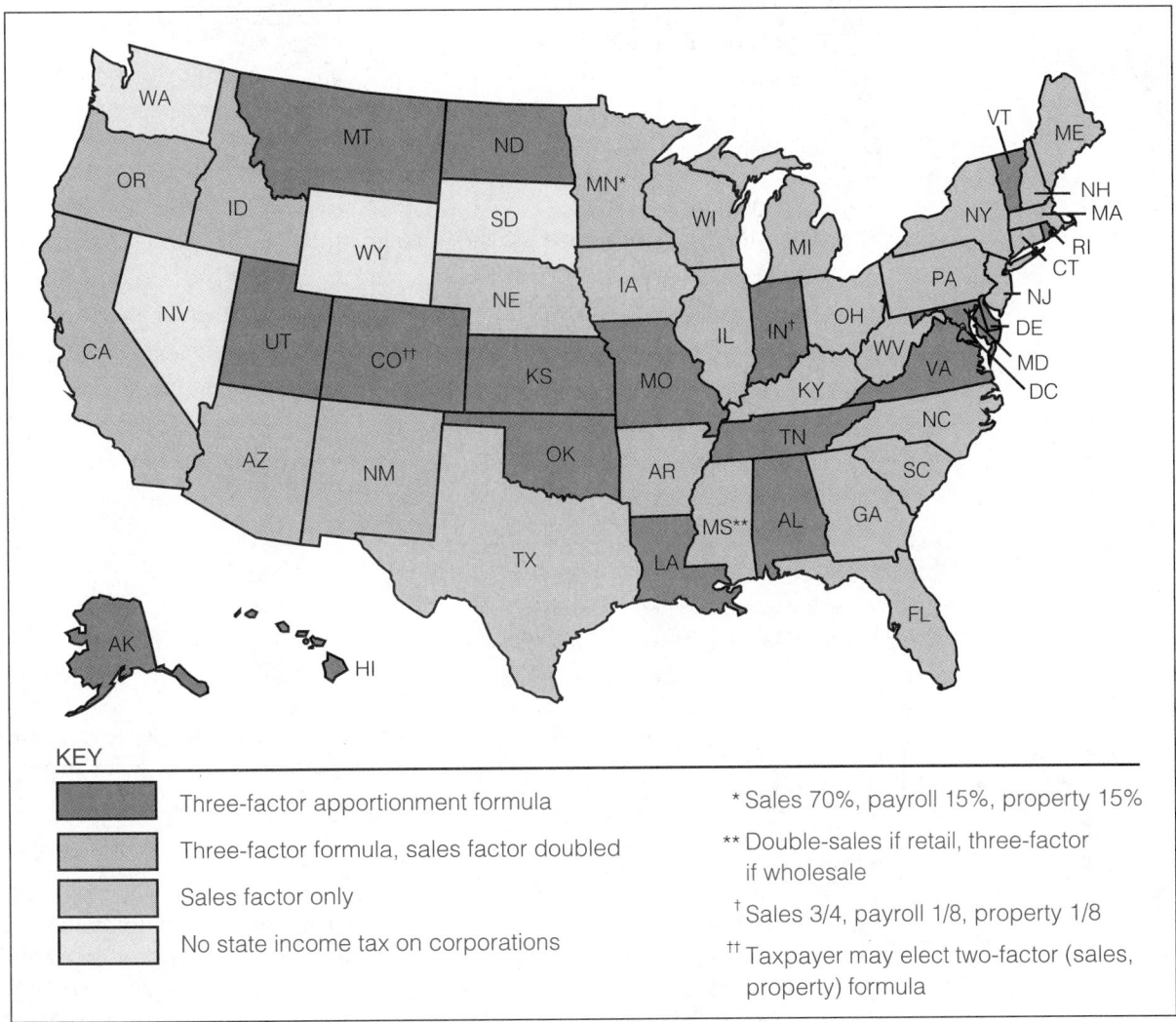

KEY

▮ (dark)	Three-factor apportionment formula
▮ (medium)	Three-factor formula, sales factor doubled
▮ (light)	Sales factor only
▯ (white)	No state income tax on corporations

* Sales 70%, payroll 15%, property 15%

** Double-sales if retail, three-factor
if wholesale

† Sales 3/4, payroll 1/8, property 1/8

†† Taxpayer may elect two-factor (sales,
property) formula

$280,000 of PPR's apportionable income is assigned to A.

Sales ($500,000/$1,200,000)	=	41.67%
Payroll ($100,000/$300,000)	=	33.33%
Property ($150,000/$500,000)	=	30.00%
Sum of apportionment factors		105.00%
Average	÷	3
Apportionment factor for State A		35.00%
Apportionable income	×	$800,000
Income apportioned to State A		$280,000

$316,640 of PPR's apportionable income is assigned to B.

Sales ($400,000/$1,200,000) = 33.33% × 2	=	66.66%
Payroll ($125,000/$300,000)	=	41.67%
Property ($250,000/$500,000)	=	50.00%
Sum of apportionment factors		158.33%
Average	÷	4
Apportionment factor for State B		39.58%
Apportionable income	×	$800,000
Income apportioned to State B		$316,640

$200,000 of PPR's apportionable income is assigned to C.

Sales ($300,000/$1,200,000)	=	25.00%
Sum of apportionment factors		25.00%
Average	÷	1
Apportionment factor for State C		25.00%
Apportionable income	×	$800,000
Income apportioned to State C		$200,000

Summary

Income apportioned to State A	$280,000
Income apportioned to State B	316,640
Income apportioned to State C	200,000
Total income apportioned	$796,640

Due to the variations in the apportionment formulas employed by the various states, only 99.58% ($796,640/$800,000) of PPR's income is apportioned to the states in which it is subject to tax. ▼

THE SALES FACTOR

The **sales factor** is a fraction, whose numerator is the corporation's total sales in the state during the tax period. The denominator is the corporation's total sales everywhere during the tax period. Gross sales for this purpose generally are net of returns, allowances, and discounts. Moreover, interest income, service charges, carrying charges, and time-price differential charges incidental to the sales are included in the sales factor. Federal and state excise taxes and state sales taxes are included in the factor, if these taxes are either passed on to the buyer or included in the selling price of the goods.

Since the sales factor is a component in the formula used to apportion a corporation's business income to a state, only sales that generate business income are includible in the fraction. The "sales" factor actually resembles a "receipts" factor since it also generally includes business income from the sale of inventory or services, interest, dividends, rentals, royalties, sales of assets, and other business income. Income on Federal obligations, however, is not included in the sales factor. When the sale involves capital assets, some states require that the gross proceeds, rather than the net gain or loss, be included in the fraction.

Most of the states have adopted the MTC Regulations, which provide exceptions to UDITPA's general rule under which all business gross receipts are included in the sales factor.[11] For instance, incidental or occasional asset sales and sales of certain intangible assets are excluded from gross receipts under these regulations.

In determining the numerator of the sales factor, most states follow UDITPA's "ultimate destination concept," under which tangible asset sales are assumed to take place at the point of delivery, not at the location at which the shipment originates.

EXAMPLE 12

Olive Corporation, whose only manufacturing plant is located in State A, sells its products to residents of A through its local retail store. Olive also ships its products to customers in States B and C. The products that are sold to residents of A are assigned to A, while the products that are delivered to B and C are assigned to B and C, respectively. ▼

Dock Sales. **Dock sales** occur where a purchaser uses its owned or rented vehicles, or a common carrier with whom it has made arrangements, to take delivery of the product at the seller's shipping dock. Most states apply the destination test to dock sales in the same manner as it is applied to other sales. Thus, if the seller makes dock sales to a purchaser that has an out-of-state location to which it returns with the product, the sale is assigned to the purchaser's state.

Throwback Rule. Out-of-state sales that are not subject to tax in the destination state are pulled back into the origination state if that state has adopted a **throwback rule**. This rule is an exception to the destination test. The rule provides that, when a corporation is not subject to tax in the destination state or the purchaser is the U.S. government, the sales are treated as in-state sales of the origination state, and the actual destination of the product is disregarded. Consequently, when the seller is immune from tax in the destination state under Public Law 86–272, the sales are considered to be in-state sales of the origination state if that state has a throwback provision.

The throwback rule seems inappropriate when the sale is made to a purchaser in a foreign country, where the transaction is subject to a gross-receipts tax (but no income tax). In these cases, the taxpayer truly is subject to double taxation, as state taxes increase but no Federal foreign tax credit is available. Nonetheless, most of the throwback states fail to distinguish between U.S. and foreign throwback sales. Figure 15–3 indicates which states currently apply some form of throwback rule.

EXAMPLE 13

Braun Corporation's entire operations are located in State A. Seventy percent ($700,000) of Braun's sales are made in A, and the remaining 30% ($300,000) are made in State B. Braun's solicitation of sales in B is limited to mailing a monthly catalog to its customers in that state. However, Braun employees do pick up and replace damaged merchandise in State B.

The pickup and replacement of damaged goods establishes nexus with A. Braun's activities in B are sufficient (as determined by A's law) to subject Braun to a positive tax, based on its income. Therefore, Braun is permitted to apportion its income between A and B. However, B's interpretation of activities necessary to create nexus is less strict than that imposed by A; in B, the mere pickup and replacement of damaged goods does not subject a corporation's income to tax.

---

[11] MTC Reg. IV.18.(c).

▼ **FIGURE 15–3**
Throwback Rule for Sales

KEY

	Applies a throwback rule, but only to sales within U.S.
	Applies a throwback rule for sales
	No throwback rule for sales
	No state income tax on corporations

Braun's taxable income is $900,000. Both A and B impose a 10% corporate income tax and include only the sales factor in their apportionment formulas. If A has not adopted a throwback rule, Braun's effective state income tax rate is 7%.

	Apportionment Factors	Net Income	Tax Rate	Tax
State A	70%	$900,000	10%	$63,000
State B	*	900,000	10%	–0–
Total tax liability				$63,000
Effective state income tax rate: $63,000/$900,000 =				7%

*As determined under B's laws, Braun's income is not apportionable to State B, because insufficient nexus is present.

If A has adopted a throwback rule, Braun will not benefit from its lack of nexus with B, because the sales in B are considered to be in-state sales of A. Thus, Braun's effective tax rate is 10%.

	Apportionment Factors	Net Income	Tax Rate	Tax
State A	100%	$900,000	10%	$90,000
State B	–0–	900,000	10%	–0–
Total tax liability				$90,000
Effective state income tax rate: $90,000/$900,000 =				10%
Tax increase due to throwback provision ($90,000 – $63,000)				$27,000

▼

THE PAYROLL FACTOR

The **payroll factor** is determined by comparing the compensation paid for services rendered within a state to the total compensation paid by the corporation. Generally, the payroll factor is a fraction, whose numerator is the total amount that a corporation paid or accrued for compensation in a state during the tax period. The denominator is the total amount paid or accrued by the corporation for compensation during the tax period. For purposes of the payroll factor, compensation includes wages, salaries, commissions, and any other form of remuneration paid or accrued to employees for personal services. Compensation may also include the value of board, rent, housing, lodging, and other benefits or services furnished to employees by the taxpayer in return for personal services, if these amounts constitute Federal gross income.

Payments made to an independent contractor or any other person who is not properly classifiable as an employee generally are excluded from the numerator and denominator of the payroll factor. Some states exclude from the payroll factor any compensation paid to corporate officers.

Several states provide that earnings paid to a cash or deferred compensation plan, excluded from Federal gross income under § 401(k), are to be included in the numerator and the denominator of the payroll factor. Accordingly, the total compensation that is included in the denominator of a corporation's payroll factor may vary among the states in which the corporation's income is apportioned.

▼
EXAMPLE 14

Mice Corporation's sales office and manufacturing plant are located in State A. Mice also maintains a manufacturing plant and sales office in State C. For purposes of apportionment, A defines payroll as all compensation paid to employees, including contributions to § 401(k) deferred compensation plans. Under the statutes of C, neither compensation paid to officers nor contributions to § 401(k) plans are included in the payroll factor. Mice incurred the following personnel costs.

	State A	State C	Total
Wages and salaries for employees other than officers	$350,000	$250,000	$600,000
Salaries for officers	150,000	100,000	250,000
Contributions to § 401(k) plans	30,000	20,000	50,000
Total	$530,000	$370,000	$900,000

The payroll factor for State A is computed as follows.

$$\frac{\$530,000}{\$900,000} = 58.89\%$$

Since C defines payroll as excluding compensation paid to officers and contributions to § 401(k) plans, the payroll factor for C is computed as follows.

$$\frac{\$250,000}{\$600,000} = 41.67\%$$

The aggregate of Mice's payroll factors is 100.56% (58.89% + 41.67%). In certain cases, the sum of a corporation's payroll factors may be significantly more or less than 100%. ▼

The compensation of an employee normally is not split between two or more states during the year, unless he or she is transferred or changes positions during the year. Instead, each employee's compensation is allocated to only one state. Under UDITPA, compensation is treated as paid in the state (it is included in the numerator of the payroll factor) in which the services are primarily performed.

When an employee's services are performed in more than one state, his or her compensation is attributed to the employee's base of operations or, if there is no base of operations in any state in which some part of the service is performed, to the place from which the services are directed or controlled. When no services are performed in the state that serves as the base of operations or the place from which the services are directed, the employee's compensation is attributed to his or her state of residency.[12]

EXAMPLE 15   Geese Corporation has its headquarters and a manufacturing plant in State A. Reggie, a resident of State Y, works at the A manufacturing plant. His compensation is included in the numerator of the payroll factor of A, as the service is performed entirely in A. ▼

Only compensation that is related to the production of apportionable income is included in the payroll factor. Accordingly, in those states that distinguish between business and nonbusiness income, compensation related to the operation, maintenance, protection, or supervision of nonbusiness income is not includible in the payroll factor.

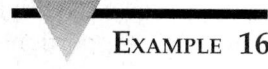

EXAMPLE 16   Dog Corporation, a manufacturer of automobile parts, is subject to tax in States X and Y. Dog incurred the following payroll costs.

	State X	State Y	Total
Wages and salaries for officers and personnel of manufacturing facilities	$450,000	$350,000	$800,000
Wages and salaries for personnel involved in nonbusiness rental activities	50,000	–0–	50,000

If both states distinguish between business and nonbusiness income in determining apportionable income and include officers' compensation in the payroll factor, Dog's payroll factors are computed as follows.

---

[12] UDITPA § 14.

Payroll factor for State X: $450,000/$800,000 = 56.25%

Payroll factor for State Y: $350,000/$800,000 = 43.75% ▼

▬▼
EXAMPLE 17

Continue with the facts of Example 16, but assume that Y defines apportionable income as the corporation's total income (business and nonbusiness income). Dog's payroll factor for X remains unchanged, but its payroll factor for Y is reduced.

Payroll factor for State X: $450,000/$800,000 = 56.25%

Payroll factor for State Y: $350,000/$850,000* = 41.18%

*$800,000 (compensation related to business income) + $50,000 (compensation related to nonbusiness income). ▼

Compensation related to the operation, maintenance, protection, or supervision of property used in the production of both apportionable and nonapportionable income or losses generally is prorated between business and nonbusiness sources.

▬▼
EXAMPLE 18

Tall Corporation, a manufacturer of paper products, operates paper mills in States A and B. In addition, the corporation owns nonbusiness rental real property in A. Tall incurred the following compensation expenses.

	State A	**State B**	**Total**
Wages and salaries for mill employees	$1,200,000	$1,500,000	$2,700,000
Wages and salaries for administrative staff	600,000	500,000	1,100,000
Compensation of officers	800,000	400,000	1,200,000

Ten percent of the time spent by the administrative staff located in A and 5% of the time spent by officers located in A are devoted to the operation, maintenance, and supervision of the nonbusiness rental property. Both states exclude such rent income from the definition of apportionable income.

Payroll factor for State A

$$\frac{\$2,500,000\ [\$1,200,000 + 90\%(\$600,000) + 95\%(\$800,000)]}{\$4,900,000\ [\$2,700,000 + 90\%(\$600,000) + \$500,000 + 95\%(\$800,000) + \$400,000]} = 51.02\%$$

Payroll factor for State B

$$\frac{\$2,400,000\ (\$1,500,000 + \$500,000 + \$400,000)}{\$4,900,000\ [\$2,700,000 + 90\%(\$600,000) + \$500,000 + 95\%(\$800,000) + \$400,000]} = 48.98\%$$ ▼

THE PROPERTY FACTOR

The **property factor** generally is a fraction, whose numerator is the average value of the corporation's real and tangible personal property owned and used or rented and used in the state during the taxable year. The denominator is the average value of all of the corporation's real and tangible property owned or rented and used during the taxable year, wherever it is located. In this manner, a state's property factor reflects the extent of total property usage by the taxpayer in the state.

For this purpose, real and tangible property includes land, buildings, machinery, inventory, equipment, and other real and tangible personal property, other than coins or currency.[13] Other types of property that may be included in the factor are construction in progress (even though it does not yet contribute to the production of income), offshore property, outer space property (satellites), and partnership property.

In the case of property that is in transit between locations of the taxpayer or between a buyer and seller, the assets are included in the numerator of the destination state. With respect to mobile or movable property, such as construction equipment, trucks, and leased equipment, which is both in- and outside the state during the tax period, the numerator of a state's property factor generally is determined on the basis of the total time that the property was within the state. However, automobiles assigned to a traveling employee are included in the numerator of the property factor of the state to which the employee's compensation is assigned under the payroll factor or the state in which the automobile is licensed.[14]

Space satellites used in the communication industry generally are included in the numerator of the property factor based on the ratio of earth stations serviced. For example, if a satellite is being serviced by earth stations located in San Francisco, Chicago, New York, and Houston, 25 percent of the cost of the satellite is included in the numerator of the property factor for each of the four corresponding states.

Property owned by the corporation typically is valued at its average original or historical cost plus the cost of additions and improvements, but without adjusting for depreciation. Some states allow property to be included at net book value or adjusted tax basis. The value of the property usually is determined by averaging the values at the beginning and end of the tax period. Alternatively, some states allow or require the amount to be calculated on a monthly basis if annual computation results in or require substantial distortions.

EXAMPLE 19

Blond Corporation, a calendar year taxpayer, owns property in States A and B. Both A and B require that the average value of assets be included in the property factor. A requires that the property be valued at its historical cost, and B requires that the property be included in the property factor at its net book value.

	State A	State B	Total
	Account Balances at January 1		
Inventories	$150,000	$100,000	$250,000
Building and machinery (cost)	200,000	400,000	600,000
Accumulated depreciation for building and machinery	(150,000)	(50,000)	(200,000)
Land	50,000	100,000	150,000
Total	$250,000	$550,000	$800,000

---

[13] MTC Reg. IV.10.(a).   [14] MTC Reg. IV.10.(d).

Account Balances at December 31			
	State A	**State B**	**Total**
Inventories	$ 250,000	$ 200,000	$ 450,000
Building and machinery (cost)	200,000	400,000	600,000
Accumulated depreciation for building and machinery	(175,000)	(100,000)	(275,000)
Land	50,000	100,000	150,000
Total	$ 325,000	$ 600,000	$ 925,000

	State A Property Factor		
Historical Cost	**January 1**	**December 31**	**Average**
Property in State A	$ 400,000*	$500,000**	$ 450,000
Total property	1,000,000†	1,200,000††	1,100,000

*$150,000 + $200,000 + $50,000.
**$250,000 + $200,000 + $50,000.
†$250,000 + $600,000 + $150,000.
††$450,000 + $600,000 + $150,000.

$$\text{Property factor for State A: } \frac{\$450,000}{\$1,100,000} = 40.91\%$$

	State B Property Factor		
Net Book Value	**January 1**	**December 31**	**Average**
Property in State B	$550,000	$600,000	$575,000
Total property	800,000	925,000	862,500

$$\text{Property factor for State B: } \frac{\$575,000}{\$862,500} = 66.67\%$$

Due to the variations in the property factors, the aggregate of Blond's property factors equals 107.58%. ▼

Under MTC rules, leased property, when included in the property factor, is valued at eight times its annual rental, less any nonbusiness subrentals. For this purpose, annual rentals may include payments, such as real estate taxes and insurance, made by the lessee in lieu of rent.

▼
EXAMPLE 20

Jasper Corporation is subject to tax in States D and G. Both states require that leased or rented property be included in the property factor at eight times the annual rental costs, and that the average historical cost be used for other assets. Information regarding Jasper's property and rental expenses follows.

Average Historical Cost	
Property located in State D	$ 750,000
Property located in State G	450,000
Total property	$1,200,000

Lease and Rental Expenses	
State D	$ 50,000
State G	150,000
Total	$200,000

Property factor for State D

$$\frac{\$1,150,000\ [\$750,000 + 8(\$50,000)]}{\$2,800,000\ [\$1,200,000 + 8(\$200,000)]} = 41.07\%$$

Property factor for State G

$$\frac{\$1,650,000\ [\$450,000 + 8(\$150,000)]}{\$2,800,000\ [\$1,200,000 + 8(\$200,000)]} = 58.93\%$$ ▼

Only property that is used in the production of apportionable income is includible in the numerator and denominator of the property factor. In this regard, idle property and property that is used in producing nonapportionable income generally are excluded. However, property that is temporarily idle or unused generally remains in the property factor.

A corporation may benefit by storing inventory in a low- or no-tax state because the average property value in the state in which the manufacturing operation is located is reduced significantly. When the manufacturing operation is located in a high-tax state, the establishment of a distribution center in a low- or no-tax state may reduce the overall state tax liability.

▼

EXAMPLE 21

Trill Corporation realized $200,000 of taxable income from selling its product in States A and B. Trill's manufacturing plant, product distribution center, and warehouses are located in A. The corporation's activities within the two states are as follows:

	State A	State B	Total
Sales	$500,000	$200,000	$700,000
Property	300,000	50,000	350,000
Payroll	100,000	10,000	110,000

Trill is subject to tax in A and B. Both states utilize a three-factor apportionment formula that equally weights sales, property, and payroll; however, A imposes a 10% corporate income tax, while B levies a 3% tax. Trill incurs a total income tax liability of $17,575.

	Apportionment Formulas			
	State A		State B	
Sales	$500,000/$700,000 =	71.43%	$200,000/$700,000 =	28.57%
Property	$300,000/$350,000 =	85.71%	$50,000/$350,000 =	14.29%
Payroll	$100,000/$110,000 =	90.91%	$10,000/$110,000 =	9.09%
Total		248.05%		51.95%
Apportionment factor (totals/3)		82.68%		17.32%

Income apportioned to the state ($200,000 × apportionment factor)	$165,360	$34,640
Tax rate	10%	3%
Tax liability	$ 16,536	$ 1,039
Total tax liability	$17,575	

EXAMPLE 22

Continue with the facts of Example 21, and further assume that Trill's product distribution center and warehouse operations were acquired for $200,000 and the payroll of these operations is $20,000. Ignoring all nontax considerations, Trill could reduce its tax liability by $3,514 (a 20% reduction) by moving its distribution center, warehouses, and applicable personnel to B.

	State A	State B	Total
Sales	$500,000	$200,000	$700,000
Property	100,000	250,000	350,000
Payroll	80,000	30,000	110,000

	Apportionment Formulas				
	State A		**State B**		
Sales	$500,000/$700,000 =	71.43%	$200,000/$700,000 =	28.57%	
Property	$100,000/$350,000 =	28.57%	$250,000/$350,000 =	71.43%	
Payroll	$80,000/$110,000 =	72.73%	$30,000/$110,000 =	27.27%	
Total		172.73%		127.27%	

Apportionment factor (totals/3)	57.58%		42.42%
Income apportioned to the state ($200,000 × apportionment factor)	$115,160		$84,840
Tax rate	10%		3%
Tax liability	$ 11,516		$ 2,545
Total tax liability		$14,061	
Tax imposed before move to State B		17,575	
Tax reduction due to move		$ 3,514	

EFFECTS OF THE UNITARY THEORY

6 LEARNING OBJECTIVE
Apply the unitary method of state taxation.

The **unitary theory** developed in response to the early problems that the states faced in attributing the income of a multistate business among the states in which the business was conducted. Originally, this theory was applied to justify apportionment of the income of multiple operating divisions within a single company. Over the years, however, the concept has been extended to require the combined reporting of certain affiliated corporations, including those outside the United States.

When two affiliated corporations are subject to tax in different states, each entity must file a return and report its income in the state in which it conducts business. Each entity reports its income separately from that of its affiliated corporations. In an effort to minimize overall state income tax, multistate entities have attempted to legally separate the parts of the business that are carried on in the various states.

EXAMPLE 23   Arts Corporation owns a chain of retail stores located in several states. To enable each store to file and report the income earned only in that state, each store was organized as a separate subsidiary in the state in which it did business. In this manner, each store is separately subject to tax only in the state in which it is located. ▼

Since most states attempt to allocate as much income to in-state sources as possible, several states have adopted the *unitary* approach to computing state taxable income. Under this method, a corporation is required to file a combined or consolidated return that includes the results from all of the operations of the related corporations, not just from those that transacted business in the state. In this manner, the unitary method allows a state to apply formula apportionment to a firm's nationwide or worldwide unitary income. To include the activities of the corporation's subsidiaries in the apportionment formula, the state must determine that the subsidiaries' activities are an integral part of a unitary business and, as a result, are subject to apportionment.

WHAT IS A UNITARY BUSINESS?

A unitary business operates as a unit and cannot be segregated into independently operating divisions. The operations are integrated, and each division depends on or contributes to the operation of the business as a whole. It is not necessary that each unit operating within a state contribute to the activities of all divisions outside the state. The unitary theory ignores the separate legal existence of the entities and focuses instead on practical business realities. Accordingly, the separate entities are treated as a single business for state income tax purposes, and the apportionment formula is applied to the combined income of the unitary business.

EXAMPLE 24   Continue with the facts of Example 23. Arts manufactured no goods, but conducted central management, purchasing, distributing, advertising, and administrative departments. The subsidiaries carried on a purely intrastate business, and they paid for the goods and services received at the parent company's cost, plus overhead. Arts and the subsidiaries constitute a unitary business, due to their unitary operations (purchasing, distributing, advertising, and administrative functions). Accordingly, in states that have adopted the unitary method, the income and apportionment factors of the entire unitary group are combined and apportioned to the states in which at least one member of the group has nexus. ▼

EXAMPLE 25   Crafts Corporation organized its departments as separate corporations on the basis of function: mining copper ore, refining the ore, and fabricating the refined copper into consumer products. Regardless of the fact that the various steps in the process are operated substantially independently of each other with only general supervision from Crafts's executive offices, Crafts is engaged in a single unitary business. Its various divisions are part of a large, vertically structured enterprise, in which each business segment needs the products or raw materials provided by another. Thus, each division contributes to or depends on the operations as a whole. The flow of products between the affiliates also provides evidence of functional integration, which generally requires some form of central decision or policy making, another characteristic of a unitary business. ▼

Notice that the application of the unitary theory is based on a series of subjective observations about the organization and operation of the taxpayer's businesses, whereas the availability of Federal controlled and affiliated group status is based on objective, mechanical ownership tests. About half of the states require or allow unitary reporting, a somewhat smaller number than in the early 1980s.

TAX EFFECTS OF THE UNITARY THEORY

Use of the unitary approach by a state eliminates several of the planning techniques that could be used to shift income between corporate segments to avoid or minimize state taxes. In addition, the unitary approach usually results in a larger portion of the corporation's income being taxable in states where the compensation, property values, and sales prices are high relative to other states. This occurs because the larger in-state costs (numerators in the apportionment formula) include in the tax base a larger portion of the taxable income within the state's taxing jurisdiction. This has an adverse effect upon the corporation's overall state tax burden if the states in which the larger portions are allocated impose a high tax rate relative to the other states in which the business is conducted.

The presence of a unitary business is favorable when losses of unprofitable affiliates may be offset against the earnings of profitable affiliates. It also is favorable when income earned in a high-tax state may be shifted to low-tax states due to the use of combined apportionment factors.

EXAMPLE 26

Rita Corporation owns two subsidiaries, A and B. A, located in State K, generated taxable income of $700,000. During this same period, B, located in State M, generated a loss of $400,000. If A and B are independent corporations, A is required to pay K tax on $700,000 of income. However, if the corporations constitute a unitary business, the incomes, as well as the apportionment factors, of the two entities are combined. As a result, the combined income of $300,000 ($700,000 – $400,000) is apportioned to unitary states K and M. ▼

EXAMPLE 27

Everett Corporation, a wholly owned subsidiary of Dan Corporation, generated $1,000,000 taxable income. Everett's activities and sales are restricted to State P, which imposes a 10% income tax. Dan's income for the taxable period is $1,500,000. Dan's activities and sales are restricted to State Q, which imposes a 5% income tax. Both states use a three-factor apportionment formula that equally weights sales, payroll, and property. Sales, payroll, and average property for each of the corporations are as follows.

	Everett Corporation	**Dan Corporation**	**Total**
Sales	$3,000,000	$7,000,000	$10,000,000
Payroll	2,000,000	3,500,000	5,500,000
Property	2,500,000	4,500,000	7,000,000

If the corporations are independent entities, the overall state income tax liability is $175,000.

State P (10% × $1,000,000)	=	$100,000
State Q (5% × $1,500,000)	=	75,000
Total state income tax		$175,000

If the corporations are members of a unitary business, the income and apportionment factors are combined in determining the income tax liability in unitary states P and Q. As a result of the combined reporting, the overall state income tax liability is reduced.

State P Income Tax

Total apportionable income			$2,500,000
Apportionment formula			
Sales ($3,000,000/$10,000,000)	=	30.00%	
Payroll ($2,000,000/$5,500,000)	=	36.36%	
Property ($2,500,000/$7,000,000)	=	35.71%	
Total		102.07%	
Average (102.07% ÷ 3)			× 34.02%
State P taxable income			$ 850,500
Tax rate			× 10%
State P tax liability			$ 85,050

State Q Income Tax

Total apportionable income			$2,500,000
Apportionment formula			
Sales ($7,000,000/$10,000,000)	=	70.00%	
Payroll ($3,500,000/$5,500,000)	=	63.64%	
Property ($4,500,000/$7,000,000)	=	64.29%	
Total		197.93%	
Average (197.93% ÷ 3)			× 65.98%
State Q taxable income			$1,649,500
Tax rate			× 5%
State Q tax liability			$ 82,475
Total state income tax, if unitary ($85,050 + $82,475)			$ 167,525
Total state income tax, if nonunitary			175,000
Tax reduction from combined reporting			$ 7,475

The results of unitary reporting would have been detrimental if Q had imposed a higher rate of tax than P, because a larger percentage of the corporation's income is attributable to Q when the apportionment factors are combined. ▼

By identifying the states that have adopted the unitary method and the criteria under which a particular state defines a unitary business, a taxpayer may reduce its overall state tax by restructuring its corporate relationships to create or guard against a unitary relationship. For instance, an independent business enterprise can be made unitary by exercising day-to-day operational control and by centralizing functions, such as marketing, financing, accounting, and legal services.

WATER'S EDGE ELECTION

The Supreme Court has affirmed the constitutionality of a state's authority to require worldwide combined reporting of a U.S. parent company with the income of its foreign subsidiaries.[15] Nevertheless, as a result of pressure from the business community, the Federal government, and foreign countries, most of the states that

---

[15] *Container Corporation of America v. Franchise Tax Board*, 103 S.Ct. 2933 (1983).

impose an income tax on a unitary business's worldwide operations permit a multinational business to elect **water's edge** unitary reporting as an alternative to worldwide unitary filing.

The water's edge provision permits a multinational corporation to elect to limit the reach of the state's taxing jurisdiction over out-of-state affiliates to activities occurring within the boundaries of the United States. The decision to make a water's edge election may have a substantial effect on the tax liability of a multinational corporation. For instance, a water's edge election usually cannot be revoked for a number of years without permission from the appropriate tax authority. Moreover, corporations making this election may be assessed an additional tax for the privilege of excluding out-of-state entities from the combined report.

CONSOLIDATED AND COMBINED RETURNS

As discussed in Chapter 8, an affiliated group of corporations may file a consolidated return if all members of the group consent. Once such a return has been filed, the group must continue to file on a consolidated basis as long as it remains in existence, or until permission to file separate returns has been obtained. The consolidated return essentially treats the controlled corporations as a single taxable entity. Thus, the affiliated group pays only one tax, based upon the combined income of its members after certain adjustments (e.g., net operating losses) and eliminations (e.g., intercompany dividends and inventory profits).

Several states permit affiliated corporations to file a consolidated return if such a return has been filed for Federal purposes. The filing of a consolidated return is mandatory in only a few states.

Usually, only corporations that are subject to tax in the state can be included in a consolidated return, unless specific requirements are met or the state permits the inclusion of corporations without nexus.

In contrast, several states, including Illinois and Montana, allow or require the filing of a *combined* return, which eases the compliance burdens associated with a multistate unitary taxpayer. A combined return is filed in every unitary state in which one or more unitary members have nexus. The computations reflect apportioned and allocated income of the unitary members, resulting in a summary of the taxable income of the entities in each state. The combined method chiefly permits the unitary taxpayer to develop the summary of assigned taxable incomes, which is accepted by (and disclosed to) all of the states.

TAXATION OF S CORPORATIONS

7   LEARNING OBJECTIVE
Discuss the states' income tax treatment of S corporations.

The majority of the 46 states that impose a corporate income tax have special provisions, similar to the Federal law, that govern the taxation of S corporations. As of 1997, only a few states—Connecticut, Michigan, New Hampshire, Tennessee, and Texas—and the District of Columbia do not provide special (no corporate-level tax) treatment for Federal S corporations. In addition, Massachusetts imposes a corporate-level tax on S corporations that have gross receipts in excess of $6 million; several states require additional S consent forms for the entity to be recognized; and California assesses a 1.5 percent tax on the Federal taxable income of an S corporation. In the non-S election states, a Federal S corporation generally is subject to tax in the same manner as a regular C corporation. Accordingly, if a multistate S corporation operates in any of these states, it is subject to state income tax and does not realize one of the primary benefits of S status—the avoidance of

---

CONCEPT SUMMARY 15–1

Principles of Multistate Corporate Taxation

1. Taxability of an organization's income in a state other than the one in which it is incorporated depends on the laws, regulations, and judicial interpretations of the other state; the nature and level of the corporation's activity in, or contacts with, that state; and, to a limited extent, the application of P.L. 86–272.

2. Each state has adopted its own multistate income tax laws, regulations, methods, and judicial interpretations; consequently, the nonuniformity of state income taxing provisions provides a multitude of planning techniques that allow a multistate corporation to reduce its overall state tax liability legally.

3. The apportionment procedure is used to assign the income of a multistate taxpayer to the various states in which business is conducted. Generally, nonbusiness income is allocated, rather than apportioned, directly to the state in which the nonbusiness income-generating assets are located.

4. The various state apportionment formulas offer planning opportunities in that more or less than 100% of the taxpayer's income may be subjected to state income tax. When a loss is generated in one of the states, an unexpected assignment of income may result.

5. Most states employ an equally weighted three-factor apportionment formula. In some states, the sales factor is doubled, and occasionally only the sales factor is used in apportioning multistate taxable income. Generally, the greater the relative weight assigned to the sales factor, the greater the tax burden on out-of-state taxpayers.

6. The sales factor is based upon the destination concept except where a throwback rule applies. The payroll factor generally includes compensation that is included in Federal gross income, but some states include excludible fringe benefits. An employee's compensation usually is not divided among states. The property factor is derived using the average undepreciated historical costs for the assets and eight times the rental value of the asset.

7. The unitary theory may require the taxpayer to include worldwide activities and holdings in the apportionment factors. A water's edge election can limit these amounts to U.S. transactions.

---

double taxation. Other potential tax-related benefits of the S election, including the pass-through of net operating losses and the reduction in the rate of tax imposed on individual and corporate taxpayers, may be curtailed.

EXAMPLE 28

Bryan, an S corporation, has established nexus in States A and B. A recognizes S status, while B does not. Bryan generated $600,000 of ordinary business income and $100,000 of dividends that were received from corporations in which Bryan owns 50% of the stock. Bryan's State B apportionment percentage is 50%.

For B tax purposes, Bryan must first compute its income as though it were a regular corporation and then apportion the resulting income to B. Assuming that B has adopted the Federal provisions governing the dividends received deduction, Bryan's income, determined as though it were a C corporation, is $620,000 [$600,000 + (100% − 80%) × $100,000]. Accordingly, Bryan is subject to corporate income tax in B on $310,000 ($620,000 × 50% apportionment percentage) of taxable income. ▼

Most states impose a different tax rate for corporate and individual taxpayers. Assuming that the state recognizes the entity's S status, if the corporation is generating income and the state corporate tax rate is higher than the rate imposed on individuals, an S election reduces the overall state tax liability. Where the state has a graduated tax rate structure, the difference between the corporate and individual tax rates must be analyzed in light of the amount of the corporation's income and the marginal tax rate under which the shareholders fall.

ELIGIBILITY

All of the states that recognize S status permit a corporation to be treated as an S corporation for state purposes only if the corporation has a valid Federal S election in place. Generally, the filing of a Federal S election is sufficient to render the corporation an S corporation for state tax purposes. In most states, an entity that is an S corporation for Federal tax purposes automatically is treated as an S corporation for state tax purposes. However, where an entity is an S corporation for Federal tax purposes, only a few states permit the entity to *elect out* of its S status for state purposes.

Some states impose other eligibility requirements that must be satisfied before the corporation's S status will be recognized. Several states require that a copy of the Federal election be filed with the state. A few states require the corporation to make a special state S election. A number of states, including Alabama and Georgia, require that all nonresident shareholders consent to the S election for state purposes.

CORPORATE-LEVEL TAX

Although S corporations generally are not taxable entities, Federal income tax liability may arise if the corporation has excess passive investment income or built-in gains. Several states have adopted similar provisions, and, therefore, an S corporation is exempt from the related state income tax only to the extent that it is exempt from corresponding Federal income taxes. In the majority of these states, the imposition of Federal income taxes generates a corporate-level tax for state purposes to the extent that corporate income is allocated or apportioned to the state.

EXAMPLE 29

Amp, an S corporation, has nexus with States X and Y, both of which recognize S status. X imposes a corporate-level tax on S corporations to the extent that the corporation is subject to Federal income tax. Amp's Federal excessive passive income is $60,000. The amount of income subject to tax in X depends on whether the passive income is classified as business or nonbusiness income and on Amp's apportionment percentage for X.

If the passive income is business income and Amp's State X apportionment percentage is 50%, Amp is subject to a corporate-level tax in X on $30,000 of passive income ($60,000 × 50%).

If the passive income is nonbusiness income that is allocated to Y, Amp is not subject to a corporate-level tax in X because none of the corporation's passive income is assigned to that state. ▼

A few states deviate from the Federal S corporation provisions and provide that an S corporation is entirely exempt from state income tax only if all of its shareholders are residents of the state. In these states, an S corporation is taxed on the portion of its income that is attributable to nonresident shareholders. Some of these states permit the S corporation to escape corporate-level tax on this income if its nonresident shareholders sign a form, agreeing to pay state tax on their share of the corporation's income. Moreover, a few states require the corporation to withhold taxes on the nonresident shareholders' portions of the entity's income.

EXAMPLE 30

ARGO, an S corporation, is subject to income tax only in Vermont. On the last day of its taxable year, 40% of ARGO's stock is held by nonresident shareholders. To the extent that ARGO's stock is held by resident shareholders, the corporation is not subject to income tax. Accordingly, ARGO is not subject to tax on 60% of its income.

The corporation *is* subject to tax on the remaining 40% of its income. Thus, ARGO computes the corporate income tax that it would be required to pay if it were a C corporation; the resulting tax then is multiplied by the percentage of stock held by nonresident shareholders. Consequently, ARGO pays 40% of the tax that it would be required to pay had it been a C corporation. ▼

TREATMENT OF MULTISTATE S CORPORATION SHAREHOLDERS

An S corporation is required to apportion and allocate its income in the same manner as a regular corporation. Similarly, an S corporation generally is required to file a state income tax return in each state in which it has established nexus. To enable its shareholders to determine their income that is subject to state income tax, the corporation must report the amount of state income that is passed through to its shareholders.

In most of the jurisdictions that do not recognize S status, shareholders of S corporations are not subject to state income tax on their pro rata share of the corporation's undistributed income. However, the shareholders may be subject to tax on actual distributions from the corporation. In this manner, the distributions received are treated in the same manner as dividends received from a C corporation.

COMPOSITE TAX RETURN

In an effort to decrease compliance burdens and simplify the filing process for nonresident shareholders of S corporations, several states allow an S corporation to file a single income tax return and pay the resulting tax on behalf of some or all of its nonresident shareholders. State requirements for the filing of a composite or "block" return vary substantially.

▼ OTHER STATE AND LOCAL TAXES

STATE AND LOCAL SALES AND USE TAXES

8 **LEARNING OBJECTIVE**
Describe other commonly encountered state and local taxes on businesses.

Forty-five states and the District of Columbia impose a consumers' sales tax on retail sales of tangible personal property for use or consumption. For most states, the sales and use tax is the chief source of revenue, surpassing even the individual income tax.

In many of these states, in-state localities, including cities, towns, school districts, or counties, also have the power to levy a sales tax. A consumers' sales tax is a tax imposed directly on the purchaser who acquires the asset at retail; the tax is measured by the price of the sale. The vendor or retailer merely acts as a collection agent for the state.

The use tax, which may be imposed either as a separate tax or as an extension of the sales tax, is designed to complement the sales tax. The purpose of the use tax is to prevent consumers from evading sales tax by purchasing goods outside the state for in-state use and to provide an equitable sales environment between in-state and out-of-state retailers.

All of the states exempt certain items, such as prescriptions and medical devices, from the tax. Several states provide that selected services are subject to tax.

Sales and use taxes are imposed on the final consumer of the taxable item. Sales by manufacturers, producers, and processors usually are exempt from the tax because these transactions are made in anticipation of a resale. Hence, sales to retailers who will resell the item to the ultimate consumer generally are exempt from the sales tax.

TAX-EXEMPT GOODS AND SERVICES—DO BOTTLED WATER AND PET SITTING QUALIFY?

Sales tax exemptions can strain the usual definitions of terms. Most states offset the perceived regressivity of the sales tax by exempting food, medicine, newspapers, and other staples. California exempts bottled water yet assesses a sales tax on carbonated beverages, thereby forcing its tax administrators to issue regulations distinguishing, perhaps, among Pepsi, Snapple, and Evian. Similarly, in Connecticut, pumpkins are exempt from the sales tax as food, but taxable when they are carved into a jack-o-lantern, painted, or otherwise turned into a decorative item.

As the nation's economy shifts away from agriculture and manufacturing, many states are broadening their sales tax to apply to certain services, but current statutes force some unusual distinctions into the tax system. Typically, for instance, an accountant's services are exempt from sales tax, but the tax must be collected with respect to document copies that the accountant makes for the client. In the same vein, sales tax often is assessed on the home contractor's material purchases, but not on the value of the contractor's construction activities, and the landscape engineer might collect sales tax for fertilizers purchased and applied to the client's property, but not for time spent spreading the fertilizer on the lawn. In Wisconsin, pet-sitting services still are exempt from sales tax, although the state argues that the service represents the "taxable maintenance of personal property."

Certain sales to manufacturers, producers, and processors also are exempt in the majority of states. The exemptions applicable to such taxpayers usually include one or more of the following.

- Containers and other packing, packaging, and shipping materials actually used to transfer merchandise to customers of the purchaser.
- Tangible personal property that becomes an ingredient or component part of an article of tangible personal property destined for sale.
- Tangible personal property (other than fuel or electricity) that is consumed or destroyed or loses its identity in the manufacture of tangible personal property destined for sale.
- Machines and specific processing equipment and repair parts or replacements exclusively and directly used in manufacturing tangible personal property.

The states apply a separate set of nexus rules that generally subject *more* taxpayers to the sales/use tax than are caught by income tax nexus rules. The Supreme Court has held that the regular solicitation of sales by independent brokers establishes sufficient nexus to require a nonresident seller to register and collect the use tax, even though the seller does not have regular employees, agents, and an office or other place of business in the state.[16] As a result, a corporation may be required to collect sales and use taxes in a state where it is immune from the imposition of an income tax.

---

[16] *Scripto, Inc. v. Carson*, 80 S.Ct. 619 (1960).

When conducting income tax planning, the tax adviser must be aware of the impact that sales and use taxes may have on a transaction that might otherwise be tax-free. For example, although the transfer of property to a controlled corporation in exchange for its stock generally is not subject to corporate income taxes, several states provide that such transfers constitute taxable sales for sales and use tax purposes. Similarly, a corporate reorganization may be structured to avoid the imposition of income taxes, but under the statutes of several states, such transfers are considered to be taxable sales and, accordingly, will be subject to sales and use taxes.

LOCAL PROPERTY TAXES

Property taxes, a major source of revenue at the city and county level, are referred to as *ad valorem* taxes because they are based on the value of property that is located in the state on a specific date. Generally, that date fixes taxable ownership, situs (location), and the valuation of the property. Nonetheless, to avoid tax evasion, personal property that is temporarily outside the state may be taxed at the domicile of the owner.

Property taxes can take the form of either real property taxes or personal property taxes. States apply different tax rates and means of assessment to the two classes of property. The methods of assessing the value of the real and tangible property also vary in different taxing jurisdictions.

Although a personal property tax may be imposed on both intangible and tangible property, most states limit the tax to tangible property. The distinction between the various items of personal property is important because special rates or exemptions apply to certain types of property. For instance, inventory constitutes tangible personal property, but is exempt from taxation in most states. Moreover, in the states that do include inventory in the personal property tax base, the amount included in the tax base usually is measured by the average inventory on hand during the preceding year, rather than the inventory on hand on a specific date.

OTHER TAXES

States may impose a variety of other state and local taxes on corporations, including incorporation or entrance fees or taxes; gross receipt taxes; stock transfer taxes; realty transfer and mortgage recording taxes; license taxes; and franchise taxes based on net worth or capital stock outstanding.

An incorporation or entrance fee or tax is an excise tax for the corporate privilege conferred on the business. At the time the business is incorporated, the state generally imposes a fee or tax for the privilege of conducting business within the state as a corporation. Similarly, an out-of-state corporation usually must pay an entrance fee or tax before it can transact business in a state other than its state of incorporation.

Some states base the incorporation or entrance tax on the par value of the authorized stock. To prevent tax evasion, a few of these states impose a similar fee or tax on subsequent increases in the corporation's authorized stock. Where the incorporation fee or tax is based on the amount of authorized stock, the tax may be based on the total amount of the stock, even though the corporation conducts business in several states.

A license tax is an excise tax on the privilege of engaging in a certain business, occupation, or profession. A state may impose business, occupational, or professional license taxes as a means of generating revenue or regulating the activities of the business, occupation, or profession for the public welfare.

Stock and realty transfer and mortgage recording taxes are nonrecurring taxes that are imposed at the time of recording or transfer. Stock transfer taxes are imposed on the transfer of shares or certificates of stock of domestic and foreign corporations. The tax typically is based on the number of shares transferred and the par or market value of the stock. Generally, the following stock transfers are exempt from the transfer tax: original issues, surrenders for reissue in smaller denominations, surrenders for reissuance to executor or administrator, deposits of stock as security for a loan, and transfers to a broker for sale or purchase.

The basis of the realty transfer tax usually is measured by the consideration paid or to be paid for the realty. The mortgage recording tax may be based on the actual consideration given, the value of the property, or the debt to be secured by the instrument.

Typically, a capital stock tax is an excise tax imposed on a domestic corporation for the privilege of existing as a corporation or imposed on an out-of-state corporation, either for the privilege of doing business or for the actual transaction of business within the state. This annual tax usually is based on the book value of the corporation's net worth, including capital, surplus, and retained earnings. In a few states, a corporation is subject to a franchise tax only to the extent that the tax exceeds the corporate income tax, but in the majority of states, the entity is subject to both taxes.

The majority of capital stock taxes are apportioned if the corporation does business or maintains an office in another state. In some states, however, the tax is levied on the entire authorized or issued capital stock of a domestic corporation, even though the corporation may be engaged in business in other states. For corporations based in other states, the tax is imposed only on the capital that is employed in the state as determined by an apportionment formula.

EXAMPLE 31

The balance sheet of Bull, a domestic corporation of State A, at the end of its taxable year is as follows.

Cash	$100,000
Equipment (net of $50,000 accumulated depreciation)	150,000
Building (net of $75,000 accumulated depreciation)	225,000
Land	125,000
Total assets	$600,000
Accounts payable and other short-term liabilities	$100,000
Long-term liabilities	200,000
Capital stock	50,000
Paid-in capital in excess of par value	50,000
Retained earnings	200,000
Total liabilities and equity	$600,000

A imposes a 2% franchise tax based on the entire net worth of a domestic corporation. Bull is subject to a franchise tax in A of $6,000 ($600,000 assets − $300,000 liabilities = $300,000 net worth × 2% rate). ▼

EXAMPLE 32

Continue with the facts of Example 31, except that A subjects a domestic corporation to tax only on the capital that is employed in the state. Bull properly determines its A apportionment percentage as 20%. In this case, Bull's A franchise tax liability is $1,200 ($300,000 net worth × 20% apportionment percentage = $60,000 capital employed in A × 2% rate). ▼

Capital stock tax liabilities can be significant for capital-intensive taxpayers to the extent that they reinvest a large portion of retained earnings (the tax base) in productive assets. If all nontax factors are equal, a taxpayer with sizable exposure to a capital stock tax should consider (1) funding expansion with debt, rather than retained earnings; (2) funding subsidiary operations with debt, rather than direct capital contributions; and (3) regularly paying dividends to parent companies that are domiciled in tax-favored states, such as Delaware. See the discussion of Passive Investment Companies later in the chapter.

TAX PLANNING CONSIDERATIONS

The inconsistencies in the tax laws and rates among the states not only complicate state tax planning, but also provide the nucleus of pertinent planning opportunities. Although several tax planning devices are available to a corporation that does business in only one state, most planning techniques are directed toward corporations that do business or maintain property in more than one state. All suggested tax planning strategies should be reviewed in light of practical business considerations and the additional administrative and other costs that may be incurred, because simply minimizing state taxes may not be prudent from a business perspective.

REDIRECTION OF CORPORATE ACTIVITIES

9   LEARNING OBJECTIVE
Recognize tax planning opportunities available to minimize a corporation's state and local tax liability.

Traditional state tax planning involves a review of a corporation's activities within the various states to identify activities that can be redirected so as to reduce the organization's overall state tax liability. These planning techniques include legally manipulating the percentage of income that is apportioned among the states by minimizing the apportionment factors in certain states. However, the potential tax reductions generated under this approach may not be cost-effective for a corporation whose income is widely distributed among a large number of states that impose a tax on income.

Typically, the techniques applied in state income taxation are intertwined, so altering an organization's activities or entities may have a significant impact on several aspects of its overall tax liability. In determining which activities should be altered, carefully analyze the effects each change will have upon the corporation's total tax liability to ensure that the tax saved in one state is not offset or exceeded by an increase in the tax incurred in another state.

SELECTING THE OPTIMAL STATE IN WHICH TO OPERATE

Because the states employ different definitions of the amount and type of activity necessary to establish nexus, a company has some latitude in selecting the states with which it desires to be taxed. When a corporation has only a limited connection with a high-tax state, it may abandon that activity by electing an alternative means of accomplishing the same result. For example, if providing a sales representative with a company-owned computer constitutes nexus in an undesired state, the company could eliminate its connection with that state by reimbursing sales personnel for equipment expenses, instead of providing a company computer. Similarly, when nexus is caused by conducting customer training sessions or seminars in the state, the corporation could bypass this connection. This can be done by sending the personnel to a nearby state in which nexus clearly has been established, or in which the activity would not constitute nexus.

In addition, when sufficient activity originates from the repair and maintenance of the corporation's products or the activities performed by the sales

---

TAX IN THE NEWS

NEXUS APPLIES TO PROFESSIONAL ATHLETES AND OTHER PERFORMERS

States apply nexus rules to individuals as well as to corporations. For instance, California, New York, Illinois, Maryland, Louisiana, Pennsylvania, and Wisconsin, among others, assess individual income taxes on visiting professional athletes and entertainers, often forcing the respective host teams and promoters to withhold state tax directly from the gate receipts and other payments to the performers on "game day." Six games played by a major league baseball team in a host stadium can net the state over $1 million in taxable income [$28 million average major league payroll × (6 games in-state/162 games in a season) = $1,037,036] from the visitors. Where nexus is so clearly verified by box scores or concert reviews, the performers often have no recourse against the taxes.

Planning techniques employed by many individuals, such as those living in low- or no-tax states like Texas, have limited applicability to public figures, most obviously for stars such as Troy Aikman, Hakeem Olajuwon, Juan Gonzalez, and Emmitt Smith, but also for support personnel and benchwarmers. Almost half of the state liabilities of such taxpayers are payable to states they visit during the year on road trips. Because each city and state compute taxable income and nonresident deductions and exemptions differently, complying with these rules can be a nightmare for the performers' managers and a windfall for the host states' treasuries. And what about other high-income professionals such as golfers, attorneys, writers, and television reporters? How should their incomes be allocated among the states?

Furthermore, how should nexus rules be applied in an age of electronic presence? Montana does not have any major league team, but Montana residents view hundreds of professional games broadcast to them over the air waves or by satellite. For that matter, should part of Michael Jackson's *Dangerous* tour receipts be subject to Montana income tax, since one performance was presented on HBO pay-per-view? To Wyoming income tax?

---

representatives within the state, the organization could incorporate the service or sales divisions. This would invalidate a nonunitary state's right to tax the parent corporation's income; only the income of the service or sales divisions would be subject to tax. However, this technique will be successful only if the incorporated division is a *bona fide* business operation. Therefore, the pricing of any sales or services between the new subsidiary and the parent corporation must be at arm's length, and the operations of the new corporation preferably should result in a profit.

Although most planning techniques are employed to disconnect a corporation's activities from an undesirable state, they can also be utilized to create nexus in a desirable state. For example, when the presence of a company-owned computer creates nexus in a desirable state, the corporation could provide its sales representatives in that state with company-owned equipment, rather than reimbursing or providing increased compensation for equipment costs.

Establishing nexus in a state is advantageous, for instance, when that state has a lower tax rate than the state in which the income currently is taxed.

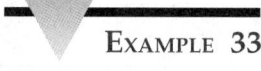

EXAMPLE 33

Bird Corporation generates $500,000 of taxable income from selling goods; specifically, 40% of its product is sold in State A and 60% in State B. Both states levy a corporate income tax and include only the sales factor in their apportionment formulas. The tax rate in A is 10%; B's rate is only 3%. Bird's manufacturing operation is located in A; therefore, the corporation's income is subject to tax in that state. Currently, Bird is immune from tax under Public Law 86–272 in B. Since A has adopted a throwback provision, Bird incurs $50,000 of state income taxes.

	Apportionment Formula	Net Income	Tax Rate	Tax
State A	100/100	$500,000	10%	$50,000
State B	0/100	500,000	3%	–0–
Total tax liability				$50,000

Because B imposes a lower tax rate than A, Bird substantially reduces its state tax liability if sufficient nexus is created with B.

	Apportionment Formula	Net Income	Tax Rate	Tax
State A	40/100	$500,000	10%	$20,000
State B	60/100	500,000	3%	9,000
Total tax liability				$29,000

RESTRUCTURING CORPORATE ENTITIES

One of the major objectives of state tax planning is to design the proper mix of corporate entities. An optimal mix of entities often generates the lowest combined state income tax for the corporation. Ideally, the income from all of the entities will be subject to a low tax rate or no tax at all. However, this generally is not possible. Consequently, the goal of designing a good corporate combination often is to situate the highly profitable entities in states that impose a low (or no) income tax.

Matching Tax Rates and Corporate Income.   When the corporation must operate in a high-tax state, divisions that generate losses also should be located there. Alternatively, unprofitable or less profitable operations can be merged into profitable operations to reduce the overall income subject to tax in the state. An ideal candidate for this type of merger may be a research and development subsidiary that is only marginally profitable, but is vital to the parent corporation's strategic goals. By using computer simulation models, a variety of different combinations can be tested to determine the optimal corporate structure.

Passive Investment Companies.   The creation of a **passive investment company** is another restructuring technique utilized to minimize a corporation's state tax burden. Nonbusiness or passive income generally is allocated to the state in which the income-producing asset is located, rather than apportioned among the states in which the corporation does business. Therefore, significant tax savings may be realized when nonbusiness assets are located in a state that either does not levy an income tax or provides favorable tax treatment for passive income. The corporation need not be domiciled in the state to benefit from these favorable provisions. Instead, the tax savings can be realized by forming a passive investment subsidiary to hold the intangible assets and handle the corporation's investment activities. The passive investment subsidiary technique usually produces the desired result in any no-tax state. Delaware, however, often is selected for this purpose due to its other corporate statutory provisions and favorable political, business, and legal climate.

Delaware does not impose an income tax upon a corporation whose only activity within the state is the maintenance and management of intangible investments and the collection and distribution of income from such investments or from tangible property physically located in another state. Consequently, trademarks, patents, stock, and other intangible property can be transferred to a Delaware corporation whose activity is limited to collecting passive income. The assets can be transferred to the subsidiary without incurring a Federal income tax under § 351 (see Chapter 3).

However, to receive the desired preferential state tax treatment, the holding company's activities within the state must be sufficient to establish nexus in the state. The passive investment company should avoid performing any activity outside the state that may result in establishing nexus with another state. In addition, the formation of the subsidiary must be properly implemented to assure the legal substance of the operation. The passive investment company must have a physical office, and it must function as an independent operation. Ensuring nexus and proper formation is not difficult since numerous consulting organizations are available to furnish new passive investment companies with all of the elements necessary to fulfill these requirements.

Because the subsidiary's activities are confined to Delaware (or some other no- or low-tax state), and its operations generate only passive income, its income will not be taxed in any nonunitary state. Moreover, most states exclude dividends from taxation or otherwise treat them favorably; therefore, the earnings of a passive investment subsidiary can be distributed as a dividend to the parent at a minimal tax cost. If the state in which the parent is located does not levy the full income tax on dividends received, the entire measure of passive income may escape taxation. Formation of a passive investment subsidiary also may favorably affect the parent corporation's apportionment formula in nonunitary states because the passive income earned by the subsidiary is excluded from the numerator of its sales factor.

▼ **EXAMPLE 34**

Purple Corporation generates $800,000 of taxable income; $600,000 is income from its manufacturing operations, and $200,000 is dividend income from passive investments. All of Purple's sales are made, and assets are kept, in State A, which imposes a 10% corporate income tax and permits a 100% deduction for dividends received from subsidiaries. The corporation is not subject to tax in any other state. Consequently, Purple incurs $80,000 of income tax (tax base $800,000 × tax rate 10%).

If Purple creates a passive investment subsidiary in State B, which does not impose an income tax upon a corporation whose only activity within the state is the maintenance and management of passive investments, Purple's tax liability is reduced by $20,000 (a 25% decrease). Since passive income is nonbusiness income (which is allocated for state tax purposes to the state in which it is located), the income earned from its passive investments is not subject to tax in A.

	State A (Purple Corporation)	State B (Passive Investment Company)
Taxable income	$600,000	$200,000
Tax rate	10%	–0–*
Tax liability	$ 60,000	$ –0–
Total tax liability		$ 60,000
Tax imposed without restructuring		80,000
Tax reduction due to use of subsidiary		$ 20,000

*B does not impose an income tax on a passive investment corporation.

The income earned by the subsidiary from its passive investments can be distributed to Purple as a dividend without incurring a tax liability because A allows a 100% deduction for dividends that are received from subsidiary corporations. ▼

These desired results, however, will not be fully available in states that view the entire corporate operation as being unitary. Since those states require combined reporting, the income earned by the passive investment subsidiary is included in the corporation's apportionable or allocable income.

Other Parent-Subsidiary Techniques.   By using *bona fide* intercompany financing and allocations among subsidiaries, the income of out-of-state subsidiaries may be minimized or maximized, depending upon the tax rates imposed by the states. When the parent is located in a high-tax state, increasing the income of a subsidiary that is located in a low- or no-tax state reduces the corporation's overall state tax liability. When the parent is located in a low- or no-tax state, the overall state tax is reduced by decreasing the income of a subsidiary located in a high-tax state. This planning technique is not successful in unitary states because the income of the entire affiliated group is subject to apportionment by the state.

SUBJECTING THE CORPORATION'S INCOME TO APPORTIONMENT

When a multistate organization is domiciled in a high-tax state, some of its apportionable income is eliminated from the tax base in that state. In light of the high tax rate, this may result in significant tax savings. Apportioning income will be especially effective where the income that is attributed to the other states is not subject to income tax. The income removed from the taxing jurisdiction of the domicile state entirely escapes state income taxation when the state to which the income is attributed (1) does not levy a corporate income tax; (2) requires a higher level of activity necessary to subject an out-of-state company to taxation than that adopted by the state of domicile; or (3) is prohibited under Public Law 86–272 from taxing the income (assuming that the domicile state has not adopted a throwback provision). Thus, the right to apportion income may provide substantial benefits because the out-of-state sales are excluded from the numerator of the sales factor and may not be taxed in another state.

However, to acquire the right to apportion its income, the organization must have sufficient activities in, or contacts with, one or more other states. Whether the type and amount of activities and/or contacts are considered adequate is determined by the domicile state's nexus rules. When the company's activities in or contacts with another state would, if carried on by an out-of-state corporation within the domicile state, subject the out-of-state corporation to tax, the company typically is entitled to apportion its income. The corporation's right to apportion its income is based entirely upon this criterion; the fact that the corporation actually is or is not paying tax, or whether the corporation is even taxable in another state, generally is disregarded. Therefore, a corporation should analyze its current activities in, and contacts with, other states to determine which, if any, activities or contacts could be redirected so that the corporation gains the right to apportion its income.

PLANNING WITH APPORTIONMENT FACTORS

Sales Factor. The sales factor often yields the greatest planning opportunities for a multistate corporation. In-state sales include those to purchasers with a destination point in that state; sales delivered to out-of-state purchasers are included in the numerator of the sales factor of the destination state. However, to be permitted to exclude out-of-state sales from the sales factor of the origination state, the seller generally must substantiate the shipment of goods to an out-of-state location. Therefore, the destinations of sales that a corporation makes and the means by which the goods are shipped must be carefully reviewed. The corporation's overall state tax possibly can be reduced by establishing a better record-keeping system or by manipulating the numerator of the sales factor by changing the delivery location or method.

For example, a corporation may substantially reduce its state tax if the delivery location of its sales is changed from a state in which the company is taxed to one in which it is not. This technique may not benefit the corporation if the state in which the sales originate has adopted the throwback rule.

Property Factor. Because most fixed assets are physically stationary in nature, the property factor is not so easily manipulated. Nonetheless, significant tax savings can be realized by establishing a leasing subsidiary in a low- or no-tax state. If the property is located in a state that does not include leased assets in the property factor, the establishment of a subsidiary from which to lease the property eliminates the assets from the property factor in the parent's state. This technique allows the corporation to change the character of the property from "owned" (which increases the tax base) to merely "used" (which is excluded from the property factor).

Permanently idle property generally is excluded from the property factor. Accordingly, a corporation should identify and remove such assets from the property factor to ensure that the factor is not distorted. It is equally important to identify and remove nonbusiness assets from the property factor in states that distinguish between business and nonbusiness income.

EXAMPLE 35

Quake Corporation's property holdings were as follows.

	State A	Total
Equipment (average historical cost)	$1,200,000	$2,000,000
Accumulated depreciation (average)	800,000	1,000,000

Twenty percent of the equipment in State A is fully depreciated and is idle. Assuming that A includes property in the factor at historical cost, Quake's property factor is 54.55%

[($1,200,000 − $240,000 idle property)/($2,000,000 − $240,000)]. If the idle property is not removed from the property factor, Quake's property factor in A is incorrectly computed as 60% ($1,200,000/$2,000,000). ▼

Although the value of a taxpayer's property generally is determined by averaging the values at the beginning and end of the tax period, some states permit or require the average value to be calculated on a monthly basis if annual computation results in a substantial distortion. When the taxpayer experiences substantial variations in the property that is owned during the tax period, a monthly computation (where permitted) may be appropriate.

EXAMPLE 36

Stretch Corporation, a calendar year taxpayer, is a manufacturer of swimwear with facilities in several states. Since the swimwear usually is shipped to customers in mid-January, the inventory value is at its peak at the beginning and the end of the tax period. If the state permits, Stretch may benefit from determining its average property value on a monthly basis. ▼

Payroll Factor. The payroll factor provides limited planning potential, unless several corporate employees spend substantial periods of time outside their state of employment or the corporation is able to relocate highly paid employees to low- or no-tax states. Use of an independent contractor who works for more than one principal, however, can be beneficial under certain circumstances. Since the commissions paid to independent contractors are excluded from the payroll factor, the taxpayer may reduce its payroll factor in a high-tax state.

EXAMPLE 37

Yellow Corporation's total payroll costs are $1,400,000. Of this amount, $1,000,000 was attributable to State A, a high-tax state. Yellow's payroll factor in A is 71.43% ($1,000,000/$1,400,000).

Assuming that $200,000 of the A compensation had been paid to sales representatives and that Yellow replaced its sales force with independent contractors, Yellow's payroll factor in A would be reduced to 66.67% [($1,000,000 − $200,000)/($1,400,000 − $200,000)].
▼

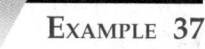

ETHICAL CONSIDERATIONS

Replacing Salaried and Wage-Based Workers with Independent Contractors

A greater use of independent contractors can bring payroll factor relief, as illustrated in Example 37. This is also a means of reducing fringe benefit costs and making the employer's workforce more flexible to changes in workload needs.

At the same time, eliminating salaried and wage-based positions creates difficulties for the families of the affected workers. Typically, health care becomes more expensive, and the workers are tempted to reduce or eliminate their overall contributions to qualified retirement plans for the benefit of themselves and their families.

Employer personnel policies must be consulted before the tax adviser suggests the somewhat drastic steps illustrated in Example 37. What obligation does an employer have to provide noncash benefits to its employees? Does productivity suffer when employees are fully responsible for their own health care, child care, and retirement planning? How does the reduction of employer-provided benefits affect morale, productivity, employee turnover, and other factors that may contribute more to the "bottom line" than the narrow tax provisions that prompted the change in policy?

KEY TERMS

Allocate,   15–11

Apportion,   15–11

Dock sales,   15–19

Multistate Tax
Commission (MTC),
15–8

Nexus,   15–9

Passive investment
company,   15–40

Payroll factor,
15–21

Property factor,
15–23

Public Law 86–272,
15–9

Sales factor,   15–18

Throwback rule,
15–19

UDITPA,   15–8

Unitary theory,
15–27

Water's edge election,
15–31

**PROBLEM
MATERIALS**

DISCUSSION QUESTIONS

1. Identify some of the state and local tax incentives that might be considered by a business that is contemplating a relocation in order to improve the cost-effectiveness of its workforce.

2. How does the term *piggyback* relate to multistate taxation?

3. Define UDITPA and explain its role in multistate taxation.

4. Define the Multistate Tax Commission and explain its role in multistate taxation.

5. Why does *nexus* play such an important role in a business's decision to stay or relocate in a different state?

6. What are "immune sales" under P.L. 86–272?

7. Define *solicitation* for purposes of identifying immune activities under P.L. 86–272.

8. Distinguish between an *allocation* and an *apportionment* of income for state income tax purposes.

9. Give several examples of nonbusiness income, as defined for apportionment purposes.

10. If you were a state legislator, would you push for your state to adopt a double-weighted sales or sales-factor-only apportionment formula? Why?

11. Discuss the general rule for including tangible-property sales in the numerator of the sales factor.

12. How does the use of a double-weighted sales factor affect a taxpayer that does not have any physical facilities in the state?

13. What is the throwback rule? When is it applicable? Why was such a rule adopted?

14. Discuss the general rule for including compensation in the numerator of the payroll factor.

15. How are rental or lease payments generally treated for purposes of determining a state's property factor?

16. Discuss the unitary approach to state taxation.

17. Discuss each of the following statements relative to multistate S corporations.
    a. Tennessee does not recognize the S election.
    b. Massachusetts income tax law limits the benefits available under its S election.
    c. Generally, the securing of a Federal S election is effective in establishing S status in a state.
    d. The S corporation may be required to withhold income tax with respect to the pass-through of in-state income to its nonresident shareholders.
    e. States are assisting the nonresident shareholders of multistate S corporations in meeting compliance requirements.

18. Parent Corporation wants to acquire Junior, Inc., in a merger transaction. Parent's advisers are consulting statutory and judicial law under § 368 to make certain that the transaction is classified as a reorganization. What advice can you offer the parties to the deal?

19. Your client, Ecru Limited, is considering an expansion of its sales operations, but it fears adverse resulting tax consequences. Write a memo for the tax research file identifying the planning opportunities presented by the ability of a corporation to terminate or create nexus. Be certain to discuss the *Wrigley* case in your analysis.

20. Your client, Royal Corporation, generates significant interest income from its working capital liquid investments. Write a memo for the tax research file discussing the planning opportunities presented by establishing a passive investment company. Support your memo with a diagram of the resulting flow of assets and income.

PROBLEMS

21. For each of the following independent cases, indicate whether the circumstances call for an addition modification (*A*), a subtraction modification (*S*), or no modification (*N*) in computing state taxable income. Also, indicate the amount of any modification. The starting point in computing State Q taxable income is the year's Federal taxable income.
    a. Q income taxes, deducted on the Federal return as a business expense = $10,000.
    b. State R income taxes, deducted on the Federal return as a business expense = $10,000.
    c. Federal income taxes paid = $30,000.
    d. Refund received from last year's Q income taxes = $3,000.
    e. Local property taxes, deducted on the Federal return as a business expense = $7,000.
    f. Federal cost recovery = $10,000, and Q cost recovery = $15,000.
    g. Federal cost recovery = $15,000, and Q cost recovery = $10,000.
    h. An asset was sold for $18,000; its purchase price was $20,000. Accumulated Federal cost recovery = $11,000, and accumulated Q cost recovery = $8,000.
    i. Federal investment tax credit = $0, and Q investment tax credit = $5,000.
    j. Dividend income received from State R corporation = $10,000, subject to a Federal dividends received deduction of 70%.

22. Perk Corporation is subject to tax only in State A. Perk generated the following income and deductions.

Federal taxable income	$500,000
State A income tax expense	50,000
Refund of State A income tax	5,000
Depreciation allowed for Federal tax purposes	100,000
Depreciation allowed for state tax purposes	75,000

Federal taxable income is the starting point in computing A taxable income. In addition, state income taxes are not deductible for A tax purposes. Determine Perk's A taxable income.

23. Flip Corporation is subject to tax only in State X. Flip generated the following income and deductions. State income taxes are not deductible for X income tax purposes.

Sales	$7,000,000
Cost of sales	4,250,000
State X income tax expense	70,000
Depreciation allowed for Federal tax purposes	300,000
Depreciation allowed for state tax purposes	400,000
Interest on Federal obligations	50,000
Interest on X obligations	150,000
Expenses related to X obligations	12,000

a. The starting point in computing the X income tax base is Federal taxable income. Derive this amount.

b. Determine Flip's X taxable income, assuming that interest on X obligations is exempt from X income tax.

c. Determine Flip's taxable income, assuming that interest on X obligations is subject to X income tax.

24. Jest Corporation owns and operates two facilities that manufacture paper products. One of the facilities is located in State D, and the other is located in State E. Jest generated $2,500,000 of taxable income, comprised of $1,800,000 of income from its manufacturing facilities and a $700,000 gain from the sale of nonbusiness property, located in E. E does not distinguish between business and nonbusiness income, but D only apportions business income. Jest's activities within the two states are outlined below.

	State D	State E	Total
Sales of paper products	$4,500,000	$5,800,000	$10,300,000
Property	3,600,000	4,500,000	8,100,000
Payroll	1,200,000	900,000	2,100,000

Both D and E utilize a three-factor apportionment formula, under which sales, property, and payroll are equally weighted. Determine the amount of Jest's income that is subject to income tax by each state.

25. Assume the same facts as Problem 24, except that, under the statutes of both D and E, only business income is subject to apportionment.

26. Condor Corporation generated $350,000 of state taxable income from selling its product in States A and B. For the taxable year, the corporation's activities within the two states were as follows.

	State A	State B	Total
Sales	$700,000	$200,000	$900,000
Property	300,000	150,000	450,000
Payroll	100,000	10,000	110,000

Condor has determined that it is subject to tax in both A and B. Both states utilize a three-factor apportionment formula that equally weights sales, property, and payroll. The rates of corporate income tax imposed in A and B are 10% and 6%, respectively. Determine Condor's state income tax liability.

27. Millie Corporation has nexus in States A and B. Millie's activities for the year are summarized below.

	State A	State B	Total
Sales	$1,200,000	$ 800,000	$2,000,000
Property			
Average cost	500,000	300,000	800,000
Average accumulated depreciation	(300,000)	(100,000)	(400,000)
Payroll	450,000	150,000	600,000
Rent expense	10,000	25,000	35,000

Determine the apportionment factors for A and B, assuming that A uses a three-factor apportionment formula under which sales, property (net depreciated basis), and payroll are equally weighted, and B employs a single-factor formula that consists solely of sales. State A has adopted UDITPA with respect to the inclusion of rent payments in the property factor.

28. Assume the facts of Problem 27, except that A uses a single-factor apportionment formula that consists solely of sales, and B uses a three-factor apportionment formula that equally weights sales, property (at historical cost), and payroll. State B does not include rent payments in the property factor.

29. Assume the facts of Problem 27, except that both states employ a three-factor formula, under which sales are double weighted. The basis of the property factor in A is historical cost, while the basis of this factor in B is the net depreciated basis. Neither A nor B includes rent payments in the property factor.

30. CARE Co., a calendar year taxpayer, was incorporated this year. CARE's entire first-year operations consisted of renovating two old manufacturing facilities that it had acquired, obtaining raw materials, ordering and installing equipment, hiring personnel, and producing several of CARE's products. However, the corporation sold no products during the year.

    CARE's operations generated a net operating loss of $1,500,000. The corporation has income tax nexus in the two states (K and B) in which its manufacturing facilities are located. Determine the amount of CARE's net operating loss that is apportioned to each state, assuming that K employs a three-factor apportionment formula that equally weights sales, property, and payroll. B uses a three-factor formula under which sales are double weighted.

	State K	State B	Total
Average property (historical cost)	$1,100,000	$900,000	$2,000,000
Payroll	800,000	600,000	1,400,000

31. Falcon Corporation operates in two states, as indicated below. This year's operations generated $100,000 of apportionable income.

	State A	State B	Total
Sales	$500,000	$200,000	$700,000
Property	300,000	50,000	350,000
Payroll	100,000	10,000	110,000

Compute Falcon's State A taxable income, assuming that State A is:
   a. Alabama.
   b. Arizona.
   c. Iowa.
   d. Minnesota.
   e. Indiana.

32. Tootie Corporation operates in two states, as indicated below. All goods are manufactured in State A. Determine the sales to be assigned to both states to be used in computing Tootie's sales factor for the year. Both states follow UDITPA and the MTC regulations in this regard.

Sales shipped to A locations	$200,000
Sales shipped to B locations	150,000
Sales picked up by B purchasers in A under a dock sale contract	40,000
Interest income from Tootie checking accounts	3,000
Rental income from excess space in A warehouse	12,000
Interest income from Treasury bills in Tootie brokerage account, holding only idle cash from operations	15,000
One-time sale of display equipment to B purchaser	45,000
Royalty received from holding patent, licensed to B user	60,000

33. Shaker Corporation operates in two states, as indicated below. All goods are manufactured in State A. Determine the sales to be assigned to both states to be used in computing Shaker's sales factor for the year. Both states follow UDITPA and the MTC regulations in this regard.

	State A	State B
Gross sales to purchasers in state	$200,000	$150,000
Sales returns	3,000	12,000
Discounts allowed	11,000	7,000
Carrying charges collected	5,000	6,500
Sales taxes passed on to purchaser	10,000	9,000
Rental income	20,000*	11,000**

*Excess warehouse space.
**Land held for speculation.

34. Although Bowl Corporation's manufacturing facility, distribution center, and retail store are located in State K, Bowl sells its products to residents located in States K, M, and N. Sales to residents of K are conducted through a retail store. Sales to residents of M are obtained by Bowl's sales representative who has the authority to accept and approve sales orders. Residents of N are able to purchase Bowl's product only if they arrange to take delivery of the product at Bowl's shipping dock. Bowl's sales were as follows.

Sales to residents of State K	$1,300,000
Sales to residents of State M	800,000
Sales to residents of State N	300,000

Bowl's activities within the three states are limited to those described above. All of the states have adopted a throwback provision and utilize a three-factor apportionment formula under which sales, property, and payroll are equally weighted. K sources dock sales to the destination state. Determine Bowl's sales factors for K, M, and N.

35. State E applies a throwback rule to sales, while State F does not. State G has not adopted an income tax to date. Orange Corporation, headquartered in F, reported the following sales for the year. All of the goods were shipped from Orange's F manufacturing facilities. Orange's degree of operations is sufficient to establish nexus only in E and F. Determine its sales factor in those states.

Customer	Customer's Location	This Year's Sales
NorCo	E	$ 64,000,000
Tools, Inc.	F	71,000,000
UniBell	G	30,000,000
U.S. Department of Education	All 50 U.S. states	18,000,000
Total		$183,000,000

36. Aqua Corporation is subject to tax in States G, H, and I. Aqua's compensation expense includes the following.

	State G	State H	State I	Total
Salaries and wages for nonofficers	$200,000	$400,000	$100,000	$700,000
Officers' salaries	–0–	–0–	250,000	250,000
Total				$950,000

Officers' salaries are included in the payroll factor for G and H, but not for I. Compute Aqua's payroll factors for G, H, and I.

37. Judy, a regional sales manager, has her office in State X. Her region includes several states, as indicated in the sales report below. Judy is compensated through straight commissions on the sales in her region and a fully excludible cafeteria plan conveying various fringe benefits to her. Determine how much of Judy's $100,000 commissions and $40,000 fringe benefit package is assigned to the payroll factor of State X.

State	Sales Generated	Judy's Time Spent There
U	$3,000,000	20%
V	4,000,000	55%
X	5,000,000	25%

38. Justine Corporation operates manufacturing facilities in State G and State H. In addition, the corporation owns nonbusiness rental property in H. Justine incurred the following compensation expenses.

	State G	State H	Total
Manufacturing wages	$375,000	$200,000	$575,000
Administrative wages	95,000	65,000	160,000
Officers' salaries	180,000	80,000	260,000

Twenty percent of the time spent by the administrative staff located in H and 10% of the time spent by officers located in H are devoted to the operation, maintenance, and supervision of the rental property. G includes all income in the definition of apportionable income, while H excludes nonbusiness income from apportionable income. Both states include officers' compensation in the payroll factor. Determine Justine's payroll factors for G and H.

39. Kim Corporation, a calendar year taxpayer, has manufacturing facilities in States A and B. A summary of Kim's property holdings follows.

	Beginning of Year		
	State A	State B	Total
Inventory	$ 300,000	$ 200,000	$ 500,000
Plant and equipment	2,200,000	1,500,000	3,700,000
Accumulated depreciation: plant and equipment	(1,200,000)	(500,000)	(1,700,000)
Land	500,000	600,000	1,100,000
Rental property*	900,000	300,000	1,200,000
Accumulated depreciation: rental property	(200,000)	(50,000)	(250,000)

	End of Year		
	State A	State B	Total
Inventory	$ 400,000	$ 100,000	$ 500,000
Plant and equipment	2,500,000	1,200,000	3,700,000
Accumulated depreciation: plant and equipment	(1,500,000)	(450,000)	(1,950,000)
Land	600,000	400,000	1,000,000
Rental property*	900,000	300,000	1,200,000
Accumulated depreciation: rental property	(300,000)	(100,000)	(400,000)

*Unrelated to Kim's regular business operations.

Determine Kim's property factors, assuming that the statutes of both A and B provide that average historical cost of business property is to be included in the property factor.

40. Assume the facts of Problem 39, except that A's statutes provide that the average historical cost of business property is to be included in the property factor, while B's statutes provide that the average depreciated basis of business property is included in the property factor.

41. a. Assume the facts of Problem 39, except that nonbusiness income is apportionable in B.
    b. Assume the facts of Problem 40, except that nonbusiness income is apportionable in A and in B.

42. Crate Corporation, a calendar year taxpayer, has established nexus with numerous states. On January 2, Crate sold one of its two facilities in State X. The cost of this facility was $800,000.

   On January 1, Crate owned property with a cost of $3 million, $1.5 million of which was located in X. On December 31, Crate owned property with a cost of $2.2 million, $700,000 of which was located in X.

   X law allows the use of average annual or monthly amounts in determining the property factor. If Crate wants to minimize the property factor in X, which method should be used to determine the property factor there?

43. True Corporation, a wholly owned subsidiary of Trumaine Corporation, generated a $500,000 taxable loss in its first year of operations. True's activities and sales are restricted to State A, which imposes an 8% income tax. Trumaine's income for the taxable period is $1 million. Trumaine's activities and sales are restricted to State B, which imposes an 11% income tax. Both states use a three-factor apportionment formula that equally weights sales, payroll, and property, and both require a unitary group to file on a combined basis. Sales, payroll, and average property for each corporation are as follows.

	True Corporation	Trumaine Corporation	Total
Sales	$2,500,000	$4,000,000	$6,500,000
Property	1,000,000	2,500,000	3,500,000
Payroll	800,000	1,200,000	2,000,000

True and Trumaine have been found to be members of a unitary business.
a. Determine the overall state income tax for the unitary group.
b. Determine aggregate state income tax for the entities if they were nonunitary.
c. Incorporate this analysis in a letter to Trumaine's board of directors. Corporate offices are located at 1234 Mulberry Lane, Chartown AL, 35298.

44. Gerald Corporation is part of a three-corporation unitary business. The group has a water's edge election in effect with respect to unitary State Q. State B does not apply the unitary concept with respect to its corporate income tax laws. Nor does Despina, a European country to which Geraldine paid a $4 million value added tax this year.

    Geraldine was organized in Despina and conducts all of its business there. Given the summary of operations that follows, determine Gerald's and Elena's sales factors in B and Q.

Corporation	Customer's Location	Sales
Gerald	B	$10,000,000
	Q	11,000,000
Elena	Q	20,000,000
Geraldine	Despina	25,000,000

45. Troy, an S corporation, is subject to tax only in State A. On Schedule K of its Federal Form 1120S, Troy reported ordinary income of $600,000 from its business, taxable interest of $200,000, and charitable contributions of $100,000. A does not recognize S status, but it does follow the Federal provisions with respect to the determination of taxable income for a corporation. Determine Troy's A taxable income.

46. Hernandez, which has been an S corporation since inception, is subject to tax in States Y and Z. On Schedule K of its Federal Form 1120S, Hernandez reported ordinary income of $500,000 from its business, taxable interest income of $10,000, capital loss of $30,000, and $40,000 of dividend income from a corporation in which it owns 30%.

    Both states apportion income by use of a three-factor formula that equally weights sales, payroll, and the average cost of property; both states treat interest and dividends as business income. In addition, both Y and Z follow Federal provisions with respect to the determination of taxable income for a corporation. Y recognizes S status, but Z does not. Based on the following information, write a memo to the shareholders of Hernandez, detailing the amount of taxable income on which Hernandez will pay tax in Y and Z. Hernandez corporate offices are located at 5678 Alabaster Circle, Koopville, KY, 47697.

	State Y	State Z
Sales	$1,000,000	$800,000
Property (average cost)	500,000	200,000
Payroll	800,000	300,000

47. Using the following information from the books and records of Grande Corporation, determine Grande's total sales that are subject to State C's sales tax. Grande operates a retail hardware store.

Sales to C consumers, general merchandise	$100,000
Sales to C consumers, crutches and other medical supplies	11,000
Sales to consumers in State D, via mail order	24,000
Purchases from suppliers	35,000

48. As a retailer, Granite Corporation sells software programs manufactured and packaged by other parties. Granite also purchases computer parts, assembles them as specified by a customer in a purchase order, and sells them as operating stand-alone computers. All of Granite's operations take place in State F, which levies a 6% sales tax. Results for the current year are as follows:

Sales of software	$100,000
Purchases of computer parts	500,000
Sales of computer systems	800,000
Purchases of office supplies	10,000
Purchases of packaging materials for the computer systems	7,500
Purchases of tools used by computer assemblers	2,000

a. What is Granite's own sales tax expense for the year?

b. How much F sales tax must Granite collect and pay over to the state on behalf of other taxpayers subject to the tax?

49. Wayne Corporation is subject to State A's franchise tax. The tax is imposed at a rate of 3% of the corporation's net worth that is apportioned to the state by use of a two-factor (sales and property equally weighted) formula. The property factor includes real and tangible personal property, valued at historical cost as of the end of the taxable year.

Forty percent of Wayne's sales are attributable to A, and $300,000 of the cost of Wayne's tangible personal property is located in A.

Determine the A franchise tax payable by Wayne this year, given the following end-of-the-year balance sheet.

Cash		$ 500,000
Equipment	$1,000,000	
Accumulated depreciation	(300,000)	700,000
Furniture and fixtures	$ 200,000	
Accumulated depreciation	(50,000)	150,000
Intangible assets		350,000
Total assets		$1,700,000
Accounts and taxes payable		$ 600,000
Long-term debt		350,000
Common stock		1,000
Additional paid-in capital		249,000
Retained earnings		500,000
Total liabilities and equity		$1,700,000

50. Perfect Corporation generates $1 million taxable income per year, all in State F, where its marginal state tax rate is 8%. The taxable income includes $200,000 in interest income from Treasury bills. How might Perfect reduce its state tax liability? Suggest three alternatives Perfect should consider. Ignore any nontax considerations.

RESEARCH PROBLEMS

Use the tax resources of the internet to address the following questions. Do not restrict your search to the World Wide Web, but include a review of newsgroups and general reference materials, practitioner sites and resources, primary sources of the tax law, chat rooms and discussion groups, and other opportunities.

Research Problem 1. Key Supreme Court decisions in the last decade have addressed the authority of the states to tax interstate businesses. Focus on the *Wrigley* and *Quill* cases and summarize how the state and local tax laws are affected by provisions of the U.S. Constitution. Quote the language of the Constitution and these landmark cases in your memo.

Research Problem 2. In general, are the treasuries of the states currently in good shape, or are they facing net revenue shortfalls? Be specific in your comments.

Research Problem 3. Summarize a key change in the tax laws of your home state that (a) is presently under debate or (b) was adopted in the last year. Be specific as to citations to bill language and numbering. Diagram how a tax law change is adopted in your state, i.e., illustrate the legislative process with respect to new tax law.

TAX ADMINISTRATION AND PRACTICE

LEARNING OBJECTIVES

After completing Chapter 16, you should be able to:

1. Describe the organization and structure of the IRS.

2. Identify the various administrative pronouncements issued by the IRS and explain how they can be used in tax practice.

3. Describe the audit process, including how returns are selected for audit and the various types of audits.

4. Explain the taxpayer appeal process, including various settlement options available.

5. Determine the amount of interest on a deficiency or a refund and when it is due.

6. Discuss the various penalties that can be imposed on acts of noncompliance by taxpayers and return preparers.

7. Understand the rules governing the statute of limitations on assessments and on refunds.

8. Summarize the legal and ethical guidelines that apply to those engaged in tax practice.

Few events arouse so much fear in the typical individual or corporation as the receipt of a letter from the Internal Revenue Service (IRS), notifying the taxpayer that prior years' tax returns are to be the subject of an audit. Almost immediately, calls are made to the tax adviser. Advice is sought as to what to reveal (or not reveal) in the course of the audit, how to delay or avoid the audit, and how friendly one should be with the auditor when he or she ultimately does arrive.

Indeed, many tax practitioners' reputations with their clients have been made or broken by the way they are observed to behave under the pressure of an audit situation. The strategy and tactics of audits—including such seemingly unimportant issues as whether the tax adviser brings donuts or other refreshments to the audit session, the color of his or her suit and tie, and the most effective negotiation techniques—are the subject of both cocktail party banter and scholarly review.

In actuality, the practitioner can render valuable services to the taxpayer in an audit context, thereby assuring that tax payments for the disputed years are neither under- nor overreported, as part of an ongoing tax practice. In this regard, the adviser must appreciate the following.

- The elements of the Treasury's tax administration process and opportunities for appeal within the structure of the IRS.
- The extent of the negative sanctions that can be brought to bear against taxpayers whose returns are found to have been inaccurate.
- The ethical and professional constraints on the advice tax advisers can give and the actions they can take on behalf of their clients, within the context of an adversarial relationship with the IRS.

TAX ADMINISTRATION

The Treasury has delegated the administration and enforcement of the tax laws to its subsidiary agency, the IRS. In this process, the Service is responsible for providing adequate information, in the form of publications and forms with instructions, to taxpayers so that they can comply with the laws in an appropriate manner. The IRS also identifies delinquent tax payments and carries out assessment and collection procedures under the restrictions of due process and other constitutional guarantees.

TAX IN THE NEWS

SHOULD THE IRS BE LARGER?

What is the optimal size of the IRS? The IRS maintains that it can produce three to four dollars of revenue for every dollar spent on its ongoing operations. Actually, the rate of return might be higher, especially for special projects that the Service itself devises and undertakes. As the agency becomes more proficient with computers and more aggressive in finding and treating nonfilers, the temptation to enlarge the Service increases as well.

Given the Federal budget deficits and an underground economy measured in the hundreds of billions of dollars, one might expect the IRS personnel count to keep increasing, even though it is one of the largest Federal agencies, with a staff averaging between 100,000 and 115,000 throughout the year. Yet, the last few presidents have found that (1) pledges to cut back the size of government also apply to the IRS (i.e., the public does not apply such a rate of return test itself), and (2) the image of the Service as the taxpayer's friend and educator becomes tainted as more returns are subjected to audit. The public seems to support an IRS that aggressively finds unreported income from foreign corporations or drug dealers, but not from targets closer to home.

In 1996, some candidates found enthusiastic public support for pledges to close down the IRS altogether. Congress has made major cuts in the agency's computerization and modernization programs. Thus, more than an economic cost/benefit analysis seems to be going on when it comes to the IRS.

In meeting these responsibilities, the Service conducts audits of selected tax returns. Less than 1 percent of all individual tax returns are subjected to audit in a given tax year. However, certain types of both taxpayers and income—including, for instance high-income individuals (5 percent), cash-oriented businesses, real estate transactions, and estate- and gift-taxable transfers (18 percent)—are subject to much higher probabilities of audit. One's state of residence also affects the chances of audit, ranging from 2 percent in Nevada to 0.25 percent in Wisconsin.

Recently, however, much of the IRS's effort has been devoted to developing statutory and administrative requirements relative to information reporting and document matching. For instance, when a taxpayer engages in a like-kind exchange or sells a personal residence, various parties to the transaction are required to report the nature and magnitude of the transaction to the IRS. Later the Treasury's computers determine whether the transaction has been reported properly by comparing the information reported by the third parties with the events included on the relevant taxpayers' returns for the year.

In addition, the IRS has been placing increasing pressure on the community of tax advisers. Severe penalties may be assessed on those who have prepared the appropriate return when the Service's interpretation of applicable law conflicts with that of the preparer.

The IRS processes over 100 million tax returns every year, about 10 million of which are filed electronically. It collects over $1 trillion in tax revenues and pays refunds to about 90 million taxpayers every year. The Mission Statement of the IRS reads as follows.

The purpose of the Internal Revenue Service is to collect the proper amount of tax revenue at the least cost; serve the public by continually improving the quality of our

▼ **FIGURE 16–1**
IRS National Office Organization

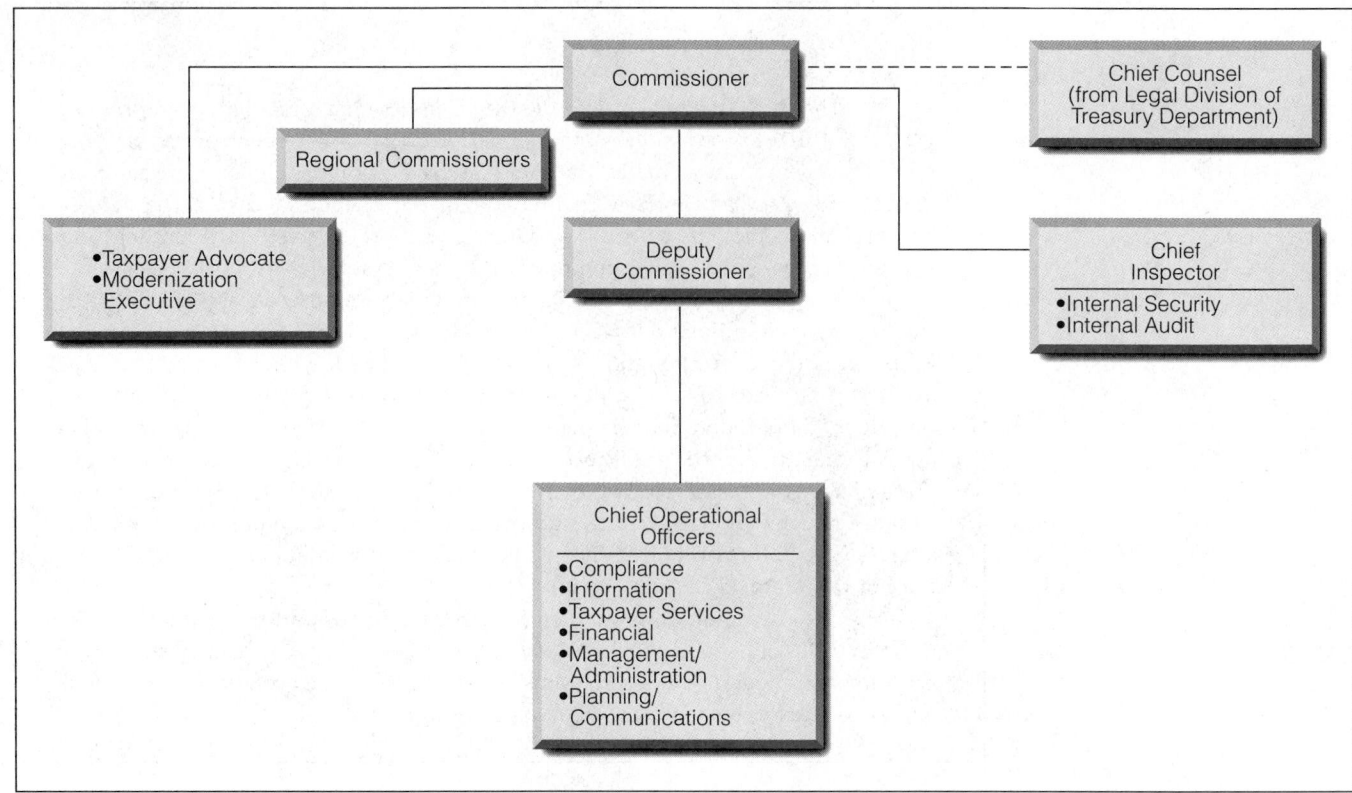

products and services; and perform in a manner warranting the highest degree of public confidence in our integrity, efficiency and fairness.

Current operational strategies of the IRS include the following.

• A focus on taxpayer education.
• Emphasis on dealing with nonfilers.
• Adaptation to the changing cultural and linguistic needs of the public.
• Accelerating the modernization of equipment and operating methods.
• Making the regulations and tax procedures as simple and fair as possible.

The IRS believes that, under these principles, the taxpayer will benefit in a number of ways.

• Taxpayers will spend significantly less time dealing with the IRS.
• Taxpayers will pay less interest.
• Taxpayers will have more filing and payment choices.
• The IRS will issue refunds more rapidly.

ORGANIZATIONAL STRUCTURE OF THE IRS

1 ▼ **LEARNING OBJECTIVE**
Describe the organization and structure of the IRS.

The structure of the National Office of the IRS, as simplified late in 1994, is illustrated in Figure 16–1. The IRS Commissioner, a presidential appointee, has organized the functions of the agency into three broad categories: (1) operations, under which the day-to-day activities of the Service are conducted on a regional basis, augmented by assistant commissioners in support and specialty areas, such as those relating to international and retirement-plan transactions; (2) internal and

▼ **FIGURE 16–2**
Organization of the IRS Field
Organization

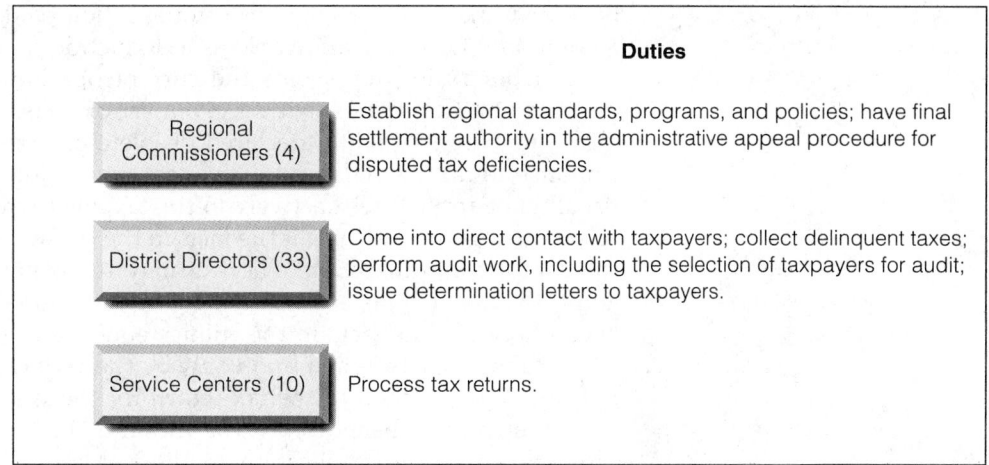

FIGURE 16–2
Organization of the IRS Field Organization

	Duties
Regional Commissioners (4)	Establish regional standards, programs, and policies; have final settlement authority in the administrative appeal procedure for disputed tax deficiencies.
District Directors (33)	Come into direct contact with taxpayers; collect delinquent taxes; perform audit work, including the selection of taxpayers for audit; issue determination letters to taxpayers.
Service Centers (10)	Process tax returns.

external affairs (i.e., dealing with Congress and the public), and internal quality control; and (3) management and planning, including matters of internal personnel and finance.

The Chief Counsel, another presidential appointee, is the head legal officer of the IRS. The Chief Counsel's office provides legal advice to the IRS and guidance to the public on matters pertaining to the administration and enforcement of the tax laws. For instance, the Chief Counsel's duties include establishing uniform nationwide interpretative positions on the law, drafting tax guide material for taxpayers and IRS personnel, issuing technical rulings to taxpayers, and providing advice and technical assistance to IRS personnel. The Chief Counsel represents the IRS in all litigation before the Tax Court.

Operational duties are carried out by the offices shown in Figure 16–2. Geographically, these functions are divided among more than 30 districts, where face-to-face informational and audit work is carried out. Functionally, these duties are distributed among 10 Service Centers, where returns are received and processed by IRS clerical personnel.

IRS PROCEDURE—LETTER RULINGS

2 **LEARNING OBJECTIVE**
Identify the various administrative pronouncements issued by the IRS and explain how they can be used in tax practice.

When a tax issue is controversial or a transaction involves considerable tax dollars, the taxpayer often wishes to obtain either assurance or direction from the IRS as to the treatment of the event. The **letter ruling** process is an effective means of dealing directly with the IRS while in the planning stages of a large or otherwise important transaction.

Rulings issued by the National Office provide a written statement of the position of the IRS concerning the tax consequences of a course of action contemplated by the taxpayer. Letter (individual) rulings do not have the force and effect of law, but they do provide guidance and support for taxpayers in similar transactions. The IRS will issue rulings only on uncompleted, actual (rather than hypothetical) transactions or on transactions that have been completed before the filing of the tax return for the year in question.

In certain circumstances, the IRS will not issue a ruling. It ordinarily will not rule in cases that essentially involve a question of fact.[1] For example, no ruling will

---

[1] Rev.Proc. 97–1, I.R.B. No. 1, 11.

be issued to determine whether compensation paid to employees is reasonable in amount and therefore allowable as a deduction.[2]

A letter ruling represents the current opinion of the IRS on the tax consequences of a transaction with a given set of facts. IRS rulings are not unchangeable. They are frequently declared obsolete or are superseded by new rulings in response to tax law changes. However, revocation or modification of a ruling is usually not applied retroactively to the taxpayer who received the ruling, if it was relied on in good faith and if the facts in the ruling request were in agreement with the completed transaction. The IRS may revoke any ruling if, upon subsequent audit, the agent finds a misstatement or omission of facts or substantial discrepancies between the facts in the ruling request and the actual situation.

A ruling may be relied upon only by the taxpayer who requested and received it. It must be attached to the tax return for the year in question.

Letter rulings benefit both the IRS and the taxpayer. Not only do they help promote a uniform application of the tax laws, but they may also reduce the potential for litigation or disputes with revenue agents. In addition, they make the IRS aware of significant transactions being consummated by taxpayers. A fee is charged for processing a ruling request.

IRS PROCEDURE—OTHER ISSUANCES

In addition to issuing unpublished letter rulings and published rulings and procedures, the IRS issues determination letters and technical advice memoranda.

The District Director orders a **determination letter** for a completed transaction when the issue involved is covered by judicial or statutory authority, Regulations, or rulings. Determination letters are issued for various death, gift, income, excise, and employment tax matters.

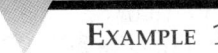

EXAMPLE 1   True Corporation recently opened a car clinic and has employed numerous mechanics. The corporation is not certain if the mechanics are to be treated as employees or as independent contractors for withholding and payroll tax purposes. True may request a determination letter from the appropriate District Director. ▼

EXAMPLE 2   Assume the same facts as in Example 1. True would like to establish a pension plan that qualifies for the tax advantages of § 401(k). To determine whether the plan qualifies, True should request and obtain a determination letter from the IRS. ▼

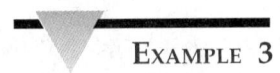

EXAMPLE 3   A group of physicians plans to form an association to construct and operate a hospital. The determination letter procedure is appropriate to ascertain the group's status—either subject to the Federal income tax or tax-exempt. ▼

A **technical advice memorandum** is issued by the National Office to the District Director and/or Regional Commissioner in response to a specific request by an agent, Appellate Conferee, or District Director. The taxpayer may request a technical advice memorandum if an issue in dispute is not treated by the law or precedent and/or published rulings or Regulations. Technical advice memoranda are also appropriate when there is reason to believe that the IRS is not administering the tax law consistently. For example, a taxpayer may inquire why an agent

---

[2] Rev.Proc. 97–3, I.R.B. No. 1, 84.

proposes to disallow a certain expenditure when agents in other districts permit the deduction. Technical advice requests arise from the audit process, whereas ruling requests are issued before any IRS audit.

ADMINISTRATIVE POWERS OF THE IRS

Examination of Records. The Code authorizes the IRS to examine the taxpayer's books and records as part of the process of determining the correct amount of tax due. The IRS can also require the persons responsible for the return to appear and to produce any necessary books and records.[3] Taxpayers are required to maintain certain record-keeping procedures and retain the records necessary to facilitate the audit. Therefore, the taxpayer and not the IRS has the burden of substantiating any item on the tax return that is under examination. The files, workpapers, and other memoranda of a tax practitioner may be subpoenaed, since communications between CPAs and their clients generally are not privileged.

Assessment and Demand. The Code permits the IRS to assess a deficiency and to demand payment for the tax.[4] However, no assessment or effort to collect the tax may be made until 90 days after a statutory notice of a deficiency (a *90-day letter*) is issued. The taxpayer therefore has 90 days to file a petition to the U.S. Tax Court, effectively preventing the deficiency from being assessed or collected pending the outcome of the case.[5]

Following assessment of the tax, the IRS issues a notice and demand for payment. The taxpayer is usually given 30 days after the notice and demand for payment to pay the tax. This assessment procedure has certain exceptions.

- The IRS may issue a deficiency assessment without waiting 90 days if mathematical errors on the return incorrectly state the tax at less than the true liability.
- If the IRS believes the assessment or collection of a deficiency is in jeopardy, it may assess the deficiency and demand immediate payment.[6] The taxpayer can avoid (*stay*) the collection of the jeopardy assessment by filing a bond for the amount of the tax and interest. This action prevents the IRS from selling any property it has seized.

IRS Collection Procedures. If the taxpayer neglects or refuses to pay the tax after receiving the demand for payment, a lien in favor of the IRS is placed on all property (realty and personalty, tangible and intangible) belonging to the taxpayer.

The levy power of the IRS is very broad. It allows the IRS to garnish (*attach*) wages and salary and to seize and sell all nonexempt property by any means. The IRS can make successive seizures on any property owned by the taxpayer until the levy is satisfied.[7] In exceptional cases, the IRS grants an extension for payment of a deficiency to prevent undue hardship.[8]

If property is transferred and any related tax is not paid, the subsequent owners of the property may be liable for the tax. For example, if an estate is

---

[3] § 7602.
[4] § 6212.
[5] § 6213.
[6] § 6861. A jeopardy assessment is appropriate, for instance, where the IRS fears that the taxpayer will flee the country or destroy valuable property.

[7] The taxpayer can keep certain personal and business property and a minimal amount of his or her income as a subsistence allowance, even if a lien is outstanding. § 6334.
[8] § 6161(b).

insolvent and unable to pay the estate tax, the executor or the beneficiaries may be liable for the payment.[9]

THE AUDIT PROCESS

3 **LEARNING OBJECTIVE**
Describe the audit process, including how returns are selected for audit and the various types of audits.

Selection of Returns for Audit. The IRS utilizes mathematical formulas to select tax returns that are most likely to contain errors and yield substantial amounts of additional tax revenues upon audit. The IRS does not openly disclose all of its audit selection techniques. However, some observations can be made regarding the probability of a return's selection for audit.

- Certain groups of taxpayers are subject to audit more frequently than others. These groups include individuals with gross income in excess of $100,000, self-employed individuals with substantial business income and deductions, and cash businesses where the potential for tax evasion is high.

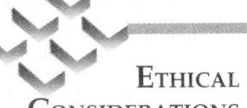
EXAMPLE 4

Tracey owns and operates a liquor store. As nearly all of her sales are for cash, Tracey might be a prime candidate for an audit by the IRS. Cash transactions are easier to conceal than those made on credit. ▼

ETHICAL CONSIDERATIONS

Do You Live in an Audit-Friendly Part of the Country?

Tax advisers have long suspected that the area of the country in which taxpayers live is one of the most important factors determining their susceptibility to audit. Theoretically, why should taxpayers living in Las Vegas be more likely to be audited than those living in Baltimore? Aren't all tax returns created equal?

Not according to confidential IRS documents and policies reviewed by a team from *Money* magazine (see the August 1994 issue). For the roughly one million individual income tax returns that are audited every year, the taxpayer's zip code partly determines not only the probability of being audited, but also the chances of success in reaching compromises with the IRS as the audit is settled.

The magazine analyzed confidential audit and collection data for all the IRS districts. Then it derived a "toughness" measure for each district, taking into account such factors as high audit rates, high collection rates, and a low probability of the IRS accepting a taxpayer's offer in compromise.

The "toughest" districts were found to be Las Vegas and San Francisco, both with overall audit rates of about 1.7 percent. At the other end was the Milwaukee district, which was found to be the least tough of all, auditing only about 0.25 percent of its returns and agreeing in full to the taxpayer's compromise offer about two-thirds of the time.

Don't use these statistics thoughtlessly. When a tax return is audited and the tax liability is not changed, has the government's money been wasted? Are auditors in the low-audit-rate areas lazier or less productive than those who produce more dollars for the government? Should the government set minimums for collections made under compromise offers accepted from taxpayers? Should the IRS collect at least 10 cents on the dollar? Twenty-five cents?

The official IRS answer to these inquiries is that "[a]ny perceived 'geographic' variations result from (other factors, such as) differences in compliance levels, taxpayer behavior, and economic and business trends." But are Las Vegas taxpayers seven times more likely to cheat than those in Milwaukee? An accounting firm partner sums it up this way: "Some IRS offices come on like sheriffs with both guns blazing, while other offices act like kindly crossing guards shepherding taxpayers through the system."

Can these facts affect tax filing strategies? What if a Las Vegas client of yours wants to file this year using your firm's Milwaukee address?

- If a taxpayer has been audited in a past year and the audit led to the assessment of a substantial deficiency, the IRS often makes a return visit.
- An audit might materialize if information returns (e.g., Form W–2, Form 1099) are not in substantial agreement with the income reported on the taxpayer's return. Obvious discrepancies do not necessitate formal audits and usually can be handled by correspondence with the taxpayer.
- If an individual's itemized deductions are in excess of norms established for various income levels, the probability of an audit increases. Certain deductions (e.g., casualty and theft losses, business use of the home, tax-sheltered investments) are sensitive areas, since the IRS realizes that many taxpayers determine the amount of the deduction incorrectly or may not be entitled to the deduction at all.
- The filing of a refund claim by the taxpayer may prompt an audit of the return.
- Certain returns are chosen on a random basis (known as the Taxpayer Compliance Measurement Program [TCMP]) to develop, update, and improve the mathematical formulas used in selecting returns. TCMP is a long-term research project designed to measure and evaluate taxpayer compliance characteristics. TCMP audits are tedious and time-consuming, as the taxpayer generally is asked to verify most or all items on the tax return. The last TCMP audits took place almost a decade ago.
- Information is often obtained from other sources (e.g., other government agencies, news items, informants). The IRS then applies an "economic reality" check and may audit the return to address questions such as, Why did dividend income increase so much this year? Why did mortgage interest payments decrease? How did the taxpayer pay for such a large vacation home, sold this year?

    Sometimes, the IRS sends a questionnaire to the taxpayer on Form 4448, asking how he or she spends income, where the children go to school, and so on. Funding for economic reality audits is under review by Congress.
- The IRS can pay rewards to persons who provide information that leads to the detection and punishment of those who violate the tax laws. The rewards are paid at the discretion of a District Director and cannot exceed 10 percent of the taxes, fines, and penalties recovered as a result of such information.[10]

EXAMPLE 5

Phil reports to the police that burglars broke into his home while he was out of town and took a shoe box containing $25,000 in cash, among other things. A representative of the IRS reading the newspaper account of the burglary might wonder why Phil kept such a large amount of cash in a shoe box at home. ▼

---

[10] § 7623 and Reg. § 301.7623–1.

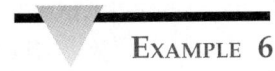

EXAMPLE 6

After 15 years, Betty is discharged by her employer, Dr. Franklin. Shortly thereafter, the IRS receives a letter from Betty informing it that Franklin keeps two sets of books, one of which substantially understates his cash receipts. ▼

Many individual taxpayers mistakenly assume that if they do not hear from the IRS within a few weeks after filing their return or if they have received a refund check, no audit will be forthcoming. As a practical matter, most individual returns are examined about two years from the date of filing. If not, they generally remain unaudited. All large corporations, however, are subject to annual audits.

Verification and Audit Procedures.   The tax return is immediately reviewed for mathematical accuracy. A check is also made for deductions, exclusions, etc., that are clearly erroneous. An example of obvious error would be the failure to comply with the 7.5 percent limitation on the deduction for medical expenses. In such cases, the Service Center merely sends the taxpayer revised computations and a bill or refund as appropriate. Taxpayers usually are able to settle such matters through direct correspondence with the IRS without the necessity of a formal audit.

Office audits are conducted by a representative of the District Director's Office, either in the office of the IRS or through correspondence. Individual returns with few or no items of business income are usually handled through the office audit procedure. In most instances, the taxpayer is required merely to substantiate a deduction, credit, or item of income that appears on the return. The taxpayer presents documentation in the form of canceled checks, invoices, etc., for the items in question.

The *field audit* procedure is commonly used for corporate returns and for returns of individuals engaged in business or professional activities. This type of audit generally involves a more complete examination of a taxpayer's transactions.

A field audit is conducted by IRS agents at the office or home of the taxpayer or at the office of the taxpayer's representative. The agent's work may be facilitated by a review of certain tax workpapers and discussions with the taxpayer's representative about items appearing on the tax return.

Prior to or at the initial interview, the IRS must provide the taxpayer with an explanation of the audit process that is the subject of the interview and describe the taxpayer's rights under that process. If the taxpayer clearly states at any time during the interview the desire to consult with an attorney, CPA, or enrolled agent or any other person permitted to represent the taxpayer before the IRS, then the IRS representative must suspend the interview.[11]

Any officer or employee of the IRS must, upon advance request, allow a taxpayer to make an audio recording of any in-person interview with the officer or employee concerning the determination and collection of any tax. The recording of IRS audit conferences may have significant legal implications. For example, if an IRS employee recklessly or intentionally disregards pertinent rules in the collection of Federal tax, the taxpayer can bring a civil action for damages in a Federal District Court.[12]

Settlement with the Revenue Agent.   Following an audit, the IRS agent may either accept the return as filed or recommend certain adjustments. The **Revenue Agent's Report (RAR)** is reviewed by the agent's group supervisor and the Review Staff within the IRS. In most instances, the agent's proposed adjustments

---

[11] § 7521(b).   [12] § 7433.

are approved. However, the Review Staff or group supervisor may request additional information or raise new issues.

Agents must adhere strictly to IRS policy as reflected in published rulings, Regulations, and other releases. The agent cannot settle an unresolved issue based upon the probability of winning the case in court. Usually, issues involving factual questions can be settled at the agent level, and it may be advantageous for both the taxpayer and the IRS to reach agreement at the earliest point in the settlement process. For example, it may be to the taxpayer's advantage to reach agreement at the agent level and avoid any further opportunity for the IRS to raise new issues.

A deficiency (an amount in excess of tax shown on the return or tax previously assessed) may be proposed at the agent level. The taxpayer may wish to pursue to a higher level the disputed issues upon which this deficiency is based. The taxpayer's progress through the appeal process is discussed in subsequent sections of this chapter.

If agreement is reached upon the proposed deficiency, the taxpayer signs Form 870 (Waiver of Restrictions on Assessment and Collection of Deficiency in Tax). One advantage to the taxpayer of signing Form 870 at this point is that interest stops accumulating on the deficiency 30 days after the form is filed.[13] When this form is signed, the taxpayer effectively waives the right to receive a statutory notice of deficiency (90-day letter) and to subsequently petition the Tax Court. In addition, it is no longer possible for the taxpayer to go to the IRS Appeals Division. The signing of Form 870 at the agent level generally closes the case. However, the IRS is not restricted by Form 870 and may assess additional deficiencies if deemed necessary.

THE TAXPAYER APPEAL PROCESS

4   **LEARNING OBJECTIVE**
Explain the taxpayer appeal process, including various settlement options available.

If agreement cannot be reached at the agent level, the taxpayer receives a copy of the Revenue Agent's Report and a **30-day letter.** The taxpayer has 30 days to request an administrative appeal. If an appeal is not requested, a **90-day letter** is issued. Figure 16–3 illustrates the taxpayer's alternatives when a disagreement with the IRS persists.

A taxpayer who wishes to appeal must make an appropriate request to the Appeals Division. The request must be accompanied by a written protest, except in the following cases.

- The proposed tax deficiency does not exceed $10,000 for any of the tax periods involved in the audit.
- The deficiency resulted from a correspondence or office audit (i.e., not as a result of a field audit).

The Appeals Division is authorized to settle all tax disputes based on the hazards of litigation (the chances of winning in court). Since the Appeals Division has final settlement authority until a 90-day letter has been issued, the taxpayer may be able to negotiate a settlement. In addition, an overall favorable settlement may be reached by "trading" disputed issues. The Appeals Division occasionally may raise new issues if the grounds are substantial and of significant tax impact.

Both the Appeals Division and the taxpayer have the right to request technical advice memoranda from the National Office of the IRS. A technical advice memorandum that is favorable to the taxpayer is binding on the Appeals Division. Even if the technical advice memorandum is favorable to the IRS, the Appeals Division may nevertheless settle the case based on the hazards of litigation.

---

[13] § 6601(c). A specimen Form 870 is included in Appendix B.

▼ FIGURE 16–3
Income Tax Appeal Procedure

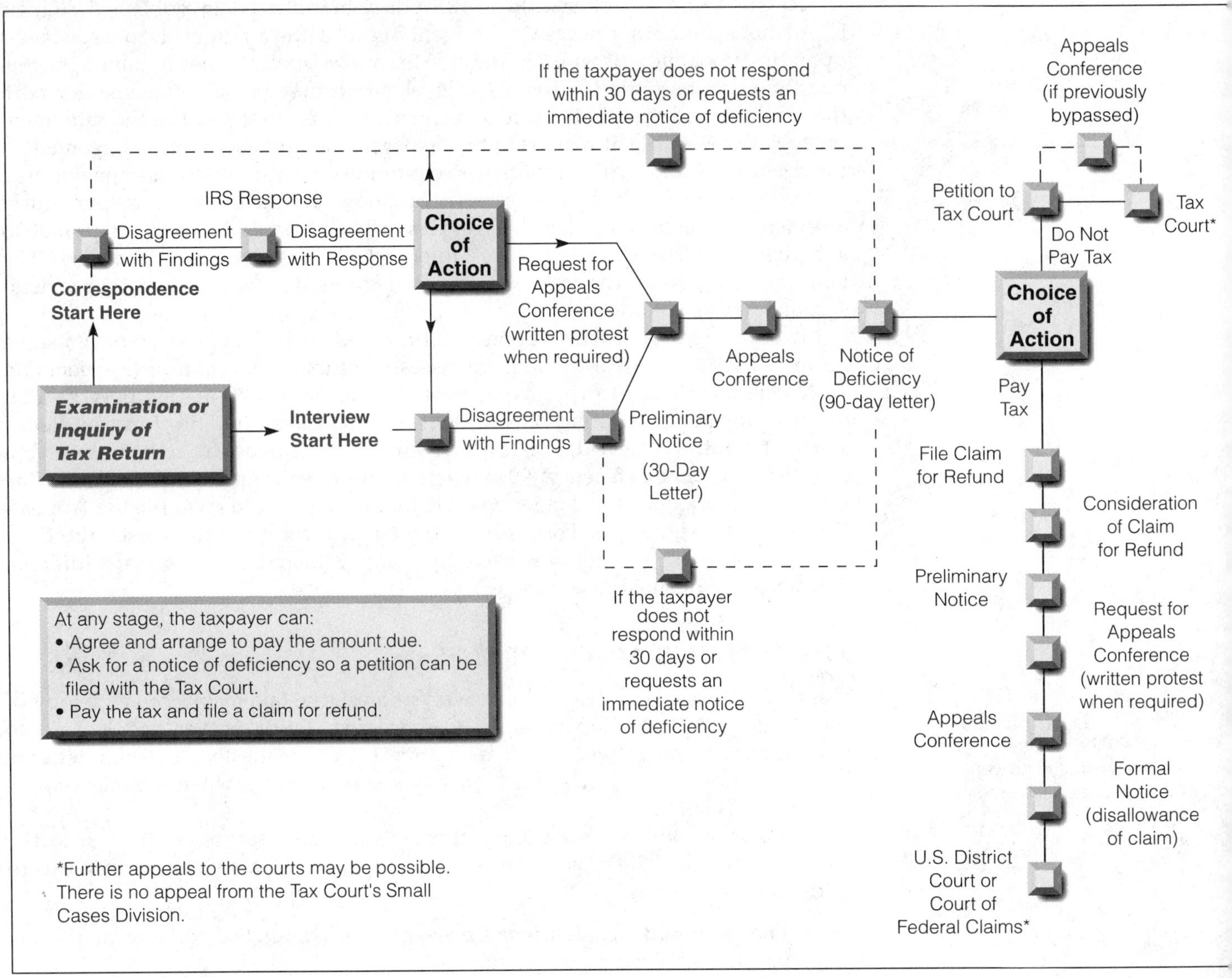

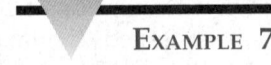

If the taxpayer does not respond within 30 days or requests an immediate notice of deficiency

Appeals Conference (if previously bypassed)

IRS Response

Disagreement with Findings — Disagreement with Response — **Choice of Action**

Correspondence Start Here

Request for Appeals Conference (written protest when required)

Petition to Tax Court

Do Not Pay Tax

Tax Court*

Appeals Conference

Notice of Deficiency (90-day letter)

Choice of Action

Pay Tax

Examination or Inquiry of Tax Return

Interview Start Here

Disagreement with Findings

Preliminary Notice (30-Day Letter)

File Claim for Refund

Consideration of Claim for Refund

If the taxpayer does not respond within 30 days or requests an immediate notice of deficiency

Preliminary Notice

Request for Appeals Conference (written protest when required)

Appeals Conference

Formal Notice (disallowance of claim)

At any stage, the taxpayer can:
• Agree and arrange to pay the amount due.
• Ask for a notice of deficiency so a petition can be filed with the Tax Court.
• Pay the tax and file a claim for refund.

U.S. District Court or Court of Federal Claims*

*Further appeals to the courts may be possible. There is no appeal from the Tax Court's Small Cases Division.

EXAMPLE 7

At the time Terri is audited, the corporation that she controls had advances outstanding to her in the amount of $80,000. The IRS field agent held that these advances were constructive dividends to her (refer to the discussion in Chapter 4). Some facts point toward this result (e.g., the corporation is closely held, Terri has made no repayments, and the loan balance has increased over several years). Other facts, however, appear to indicate that these advances are bona fide loans (e.g., a written instrument provides for interest, Terri has the independent means of repayment, and the corporation has a good dividend-paying record).

The Appeals Division and Terri's representative assess the hazards of litigation as being 50% for each side. Thus, if Terri chooses to take the issue to court, she would have an even chance of winning or losing her case. Based on this assessment, both sides agree to treat $40,000 of the advance as a dividend and $40,000 as a bona fide loan. The agreement enables Terri to avoid $40,000 of dividend income (the loan portion) and saves her the cost of litigating the issue.

Thus, by going to the Appeals Division, Terri obtained a satisfactory settlement otherwise unobtainable from the agent. ▼

Taxpayers who file a petition with the U.S. Tax Court have the option of having the case heard before the informal Small Cases Division if the amount of tax in dispute does not exceed $10,000.[14] If the Small Cases Division is used, neither party may appeal the case. The decisions of the Small Cases Division are not published or otherwise available as precedents for other cases.

The economic costs of a settlement offer from the Appeals Division should be weighed against the costs of litigation and the probability of winning the case. The taxpayer should also consider the impact of the settlement upon the tax liability for future periods in addition to the years under audit.

If a settlement is reached with the Appeals Division, the taxpayer is required to sign Form 870AD. Interest stops running on the deficiency when the Appeals Division accepts the Form 870AD. According to the IRS, this settlement is binding upon both parties unless fraud, malfeasance, concealment, or misrepresentation of material fact has occurred. Nevertheless, the question of whether this settlement form prevents the taxpayer from filing a subsequent refund claim and suit for refund has been litigated with conflicting results.[15]

OFFERS IN COMPROMISE AND CLOSING AGREEMENTS

The IRS can negotiate a compromise if the taxpayer's ability to pay the tax is doubtful.[16] If the taxpayer is financially unable to pay the total amount of the tax, a Form 656 (**Offer in Compromise**) can be filed with the District Director or the IRS Service Center.

The IRS investigates the claim by evaluating the taxpayer's financial ability to pay the tax. In some instances, the compromise settlement includes an agreement for final settlement of the tax through payments of a specified percentage of the taxpayer's future earnings. This settlement procedure usually entails lengthy periods of negotiation with the IRS.

The IRS has statutory authority to enter into a written agreement allowing taxes to be paid on an installment basis if that arrangement facilitates the tax collection. The agreement may later be modified or terminated because of (1) inadequate information, (2) subsequent change in financial condition, or (3) failure to pay an installment when due or to provide requested information.[17]

A **closing agreement** is binding on both the taxpayer and the IRS, except upon a subsequent showing of fraud, malfeasance, or misrepresentation of a material fact.[18] The closing agreement may be used when disputed issues carry over to future years. It may also be employed to dispose of a dispute involving a specific issue for a prior year or a proposed transaction involving future years. If, for example, the IRS is willing to make substantial concessions in the valuation of assets for death tax purposes, it may require a closing agreement from the recipient of the property to establish the income tax basis of the assets.

---

[14] § 7463(a).

[15] Compare *Stair v. U.S.*, 75–1 USTC ¶9463, 35 AFTR2d 75–1515, 516 F.2d 560 (CA–2, 1975), with *Unita Livestock Corp. v. U.S.*, 66–1 USTC ¶9193, 17 AFTR2d 254, 355 F.2d 761 (CA–10, 1966).

[16] § 7122.

[17] § 6159. A specimen Form 656 is included in Appendix B.

[18] § 7121(b).

INTEREST

5   **LEARNING OBJECTIVE**
Determine the amount of interest on a deficiency or a refund and when it is due.

Determination of the Interest Rate. Several years ago, Congress recognized that the interest rates applicable to Federal tax underpayments (deficiencies) and overpayments (refunds) should be closer to the rates available in financial markets. The Code provides for the rates to be determined quarterly.[19] Thus, the rates that are determined during January are effective for the following April through June.

IRS interest is based on the Federal short-term rates published periodically by the IRS in Revenue Rulings. They are based on the average market yield on outstanding marketable obligations of the United States with remaining maturity of three years or less.

Underpayments are subject to the Federal short-term rates plus three percentage points, and overpayments carry the Federal short-term rates plus two percentage points. Consequently, the rate for tax deficiencies is one percentage point higher than the rate for tax refunds. For the first quarter of 1997, interest on tax deficiencies was set at 9 percent, and interest on refunds was 8 percent. In previous years, interest rates have ranged from 6 percent to 20 percent.

Computation of the Amount of Interest. Interest is compounded daily.[20] Depending on the applicable interest rate, daily compounding doubles the payable amount over a period of five to eight years.

Tables for determining the daily compounded amount are available from the IRS. The tables ease the burden of those who prepare late returns where additional taxes are due.[21]

IRS Deficiency Assessments. Interest usually accrues from the unextended due date of the return until 30 days after the taxpayer agrees to the deficiency by signing Form 870. If the taxpayer does not pay the amount shown on the IRS's "notice and demand" (tax bill) within 30 days, interest again accrues on the deficiency.

Refund of Taxpayer's Overpayments. If an overpayment is refunded to the taxpayer within 45 days after the date the return is filed or is due, no interest is allowed. When the taxpayer files an amended return or makes a claim for refund of a prior year's tax (e.g., when net operating loss carrybacks result in refunds of a prior year's tax payments), however, interest is authorized from the original due date of the return through the date when the amended return is filed.

In the past, when interest rates were sometimes as high as 20 percent, many taxpayers found it advantageous to delay filing various tax returns that led to refunds. Thus, the IRS was placed in the unplanned role of providing taxpayers with a high-yield savings account. Under current law, however, taxpayers applying for refunds receive interest as follows.

- When a return is filed after the due date, interest on any overpayment accrues from the date of filing. However, no interest is due if the IRS makes the refund within 45 days of the date of filing.

---

[19] § 6621.
[20] § 6622.

[21] Rev.Proc. 95–17, 1995–1 C.B. 556.

TAX IN THE NEWS

THE IRS STRIVES TO BECOME CONSUMER-FRIENDLY

When country singer Willie Nelson was found guilty of underreporting his Federal income taxes, chiefly due to his involvement in real estate tax shelters, the total deficiency, including taxes, interest, and penalties, came to $16.7 million. The IRS intended to collect the full amount by forcing auctions of Nelson's most valuable possessions, placing claims on royalties from his recordings, encouraging him to make television commercials for fast-food outlets, and prompting him to sue his prior tax advisers for offsetting damages (to be paid directly to the IRS). Three years of such collections totaled only about $4 million.

As part of a nationwide effort to expand the use of the offer in compromise program, the IRS then settled with Nelson for total collections of $9 million, to be paid over a five-year period, with no future liens or collection activities. An IRS spokesperson asserted that the broader use of the compromise powers indicated the agency was "willing to settle for something less than the entire amount . . . to be more reasonable with taxpayers" having difficulty finding the full deficiency amount. Given the slow economy, more taxpayers are having such difficulties, and the IRS seems willing to collect what it can, rather than haggle in court for years to collect the "last penny" due.

Nelson's new adviser stated that the IRS was "taking a much more pragmatic and realistic approach to tax collection," as indicated by the change in the offer in compromise policy. In previous years, the IRS accepted only 25 percent of taxpayers' offers, covering about $40 million in deficiencies. Acceptance rates now average about 60 percent, for more than $100 million in collections.

In fact, the taxpayer can now initiate an installment payment plan on the original return. Form 9465, Installment Agreement Request (see Appendix B), lays out the taxpayer's plan for payment, which incurs only a 0.5 percent penalty in addition to the late-payment interest charge. The standard arrangement is a three-year payment plan where the amount due is less than $10,000; subsequent-year tax liabilities must be satisfied in full.

Reportedly, the IRS is also considering accepting tax payments through major credit cards and other "consumer-friendly" efforts to collect revenues.

EXAMPLE 8 Naomi, a calendar year taxpayer, files her 1996 return on December 1, 1997. The return reflects an overwithholding of $2,500. On June 8, 1998, Naomi receives a refund of her 1996 overpayment. Interest on the refund began to accrue on December 1, 1997 (not April 15, 1997). ▼

EXAMPLE 9 Assume the same facts as in Example 8, except that the refund is paid to Naomi on January 5, 1998 (rather than June 8, 1998). No interest is payable by the IRS, since the refund was made within 45 days of the filing of the return. ▼

- In no event will interest accrue on an overpayment unless the return that is filed is in "processible form." Generally, this means that the return must contain enough information in a readable format to enable the IRS to identify the taxpayer and to determine the tax (and overpayment) involved.

- In the case of a carryback (e.g., net operating loss, capital loss, tax credit), interest on any refund begins to accrue on the due date of the return (disregarding extensions) for the year in which the carryback arises. Even then, however, no interest accrues until a return is filed or, if the return has been filed, the IRS pays the refund within 45 days.

EXAMPLE 10

Top Corporation, a calendar year taxpayer, incurs a net operating loss during 1997 that it can carry back to tax year 1994 and obtain a refund. On December 27, 1998, Top files a claim for refund. The earliest that interest can begin to accrue in this situation is March 15, 1998, but since the return was not filed until December 27, 1998, the later date controls. If, however, the IRS pays the refund within 45 days of December 27, 1998, no interest need be paid. ▼

TAXPAYER PENALTIES

6　LEARNING OBJECTIVE
Discuss the various penalties that can be imposed on acts of noncompliance by taxpayers and return preparers.

To promote and enforce taxpayer compliance with the U.S. voluntary self-assessment system of taxation, Congress has enacted a comprehensive array of penalties.

Tax penalties may involve both criminal and civil offenses. Criminal tax penalties are imposed only after the usual criminal process, in which the taxpayer is entitled to the same constitutional guarantees as nontax criminal defendants. Normally, a criminal penalty provides for imprisonment. Civil tax penalties are collected in the same manner as other taxes and usually provide only for monetary fines. Criminal and civil penalties are not mutually exclusive; therefore, both types of sanctions may be imposed on a taxpayer.

The Code characterizes tax penalties as additions to tax; thus, they cannot subsequently be deducted by the taxpayer.

Ad valorem penalties are additions to tax that are based upon a percentage of the owed tax. *Assessable penalties*, on the other hand, typically include a flat dollar amount. Assessable penalties are not subject to review by the Tax Court, but ad valorem penalties are subject to the same deficiency procedures that apply to the underlying tax.

Failure to File and Failure to Pay.　For a failure to file a tax return by the due date (including extensions), a penalty of 5 percent per month (up to a maximum of 25 percent) is imposed on the amount of tax shown as due on the return, with a minimum penalty amount of $100.[22] If the failure to file is attributable to fraud, the penalty becomes 15 percent per month, to a minimum of 75 percent of the tax.[23]

For a failure to pay the tax due as shown on the return, a penalty of 0.5 percent per month (up to a maximum of 25 percent) is imposed on the amount of the tax. The penalty is doubled if the taxpayer fails to pay the tax after receiving a deficiency assessment.

In all of these cases, a fraction of a month counts as a full month. These penalties relate to the net amount of the tax due.

EXAMPLE 11

Conchita, a calendar year self-employed taxpayer, prepays $18,000 for income taxes during 1997. Her total tax liability for 1997 proves to be $20,000. Without obtaining an extension from the IRS, she files her Form 1040 in early August 1998 and encloses a check for the balance due of $2,000. The failure to file and the failure to pay penalties apply to $2,000 (not $20,000). ▼

---

[22] § 6651(a).　　　　　　[23] § 6651(f).

During any month in which both the failure to file penalty and the failure to pay penalty apply, the failure to file penalty is reduced by the amount of the failure to pay penalty.

EXAMPLE 12

Jason files his tax return 10 days after the due date. Along with the return, he remits a check for $3,000, which is the balance of the tax he owes. Disregarding any interest liabilities, Jason's total penalties are as follows.

Failure to pay penalty (½% × $3,000)		$ 15
Failure to file penalty (5% × $3,000)	$150	
Less failure to pay penalty for the same period	15	
Failure to file penalty		135
Total penalties		$150

The penalties for one full month are imposed even though Jason was delinquent by only 10 days. Unlike the method used to compute interest, any part of a month is treated as a whole month. ▼

These penalties can be avoided if the taxpayer shows that the failure to file and/or failure to pay was due to reasonable cause and not due to willful neglect. The Code is silent on what constitutes reasonable cause, and the Regulations do little to clarify this important concept.[24] Reasonable cause for failure to pay is presumed under the automatic four-month extension (Form 4868) when the additional tax due is not more than 10 percent of the tax liability shown on the return. In addition, the courts have ruled on some aspects of **reasonable cause.**

- Reasonable cause was found where the taxpayer relied on the advice of a competent tax adviser given in good faith, the facts were fully disclosed to the adviser, and he or she considered that the specific question represented reasonable cause.[25] No reasonable cause was found, however, where the taxpayer delegated the filing task to another, even when that person was an accountant or an attorney.[26]
- Among the reasons not qualifying as reasonable cause were lack of information on the due date of the return,[27] illness that did not incapacitate a taxpayer from completing a return,[28] refusal of the taxpayer's spouse to cooperate for a joint return,[29] and ignorance or misunderstanding of the tax law.[30]

Accuracy-Related Penalties. Major civil penalties relating to the accuracy of tax return data, including misstatements stemming from taxpayer negligence and improper valuation of income and deductions, are coordinated under the umbrella term **accuracy-related penalties.**[31] This consolidation of related penalties into a single levy eliminates the possibility that multiple penalties will be stacked (i.e., when more than one type of penalty applies to a single understatement of tax).

---

[24] Reg. § 301.6651–1(c)(1) likens reasonable cause to the exercise of "ordinary business care and prudence" on the part of the taxpayer.

[25] *Estate of Norma S. Bradley,* 33 TCM 70, T.C.Memo. 1974–17.

[26] *U.S. v. Boyle,* 85–1 USTC ¶13,602, 55 AFTR2d 85–1535, 105 S.Ct. 687 (USSC, 1985).

[27] *Beck Chemical Equipment Co.,* 27 T.C. 840 (1957).

[28] *Jacob Gassman,* 26 TCM 213, T.C.Memo. 1967–42, and *Babetta Schmidt,* 28 T.C. 367 (1957). Compare *Estate of Kirchner,* 46 B.T.A. 578 (1942).

[29] *Electric and Neon, Inc.,* 56 T.C. 1324 (1971).

[30] *Stevens Brothers Foundation, Inc.,* 39 T.C. 93 (1965).

[31] § 6662.

The accuracy-related penalties each amount to 20 percent of the portion of the tax underpayment that is attributable to one or more of the following infractions.

- Negligence or disregard of rules and regulations.
- Substantial understatement of tax liability.
- Substantial valuation overstatement.
- Substantial valuation understatement.

The penalties apply only where the taxpayer fails to show a reasonable basis for the position taken on the return.[32]

Negligence.   For purposes of this accuracy-related penalty, **negligence** includes any failure to make a reasonable attempt to comply with the provisions of the tax law. The penalty also applies to any disregard (whether careless, reckless, or intentional) of rules and regulations.[33] The penalty can be avoided upon a showing of reasonable cause and that the taxpayer acted in good faith.[34]

The negligence penalty applies to *all* taxes, except when fraud is involved. A negligence penalty may be assessed when the taxpayer fails to report gross income, overstates deductions, or fails to keep adequate records. When the taxpayer takes a nonnegligent position on the return that is contrary to a judicial precedent or published pronouncement of the IRS, the penalty is waived if the taxpayer has a reasonable basis for the interpretation and has disclosed the disputed position on Form 8275.

Substantial Understatement of Tax Liability.   The understatement penalty is designed to strike at middle- and high-income taxpayers who are tempted to play the so-called audit lottery.[35] Some taxpayers take questionable and undisclosed positions on their tax returns in the hope that the return will not be selected for audit. Disclosing the positions would have called attention to the return and increased the probability of audit.

A substantial understatement of a tax liability transpires when the understatement exceeds the larger of 10 percent of the tax due or $5,000 ($10,000 for a C corporation). The understatement to which the penalty applies is the difference between the amount of tax required to be shown on the return and the amount of tax actually shown on the return.

The penalty is avoided under any of the following circumstances.

- The taxpayer has **substantial authority** for the treatment.[36]
- The relevant facts affecting the treatment are adequately disclosed in the return by attaching Form 8275 (see Appendix B).
- The taxpayer has a reasonable basis for taking the disputed position.

Penalty for Overvaluation.   The objective of the overvaluation penalty is to deter taxpayers from inflating values (or basis), usually of charitable contributions of property, to reduce income taxes.[37]

- The penalty is 20 percent of the additional tax that would have been paid had the correct valuation (or basis) been used.[38]
- The penalty applies only when the valuation (or basis) used is 200 percent or more of the correct valuation (or basis).

---

[32] Temporary Regulations issued as TD 8533, 1994–1 C.B. 307. Most tax professionals measure this standard as a one-fourth probability of prevailing in court.

[33] § 6662(c).

[34] § 6664(c)(1).

[35] § 6662(b)(2).

[36] Review the discussion related to Footnote 52 in Chapter 1.

[37] § 6662(b)(3).

[38] For gross valuation misstatements (i.e., 400% or more), the penalty increases to 40%. § 6662(h).

• The penalty applies only to the extent that the resulting income tax underpayment exceeds $5,000 ($10,000 for C corporations).

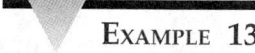

EXAMPLE 13

Gretchen (a calendar year taxpayer) purchased a painting for $10,000. Years later, when the painting is worth $18,000 (as later determined by the IRS), Gretchen donates the painting to an art museum. Based on the appraisal of a cousin who is an amateur artist, she deducts $40,000 for the donation. Since Gretchen was in the 31% tax bracket, overstating the deduction by $22,000 results in a tax underpayment of $6,820.

Gretchen's penalty for overvaluation is $1,364 [20% × $6,820 (the underpayment that resulted from using $40,000 instead of $18,000)]. ▼

The substantial valuation overstatement penalty is avoided if the taxpayer can show reasonable cause and good faith. However, when the overvaluation involves *charitable deduction property*, the taxpayer must show two *additional* facts.

• The claimed value of the property is based on a qualified appraisal made by a qualified appraiser.
• The taxpayer made a good faith investigation of the value of the contributed property.[39]

Based on these criteria, Gretchen in Example 13 would find it difficult to avoid the penalty. A cousin who is an amateur artist does not meet the definition of a qualified appraiser. Likewise, she apparently has not made a good faith investigation of the value of the contributed property.

Penalty for Undervaluation. When attempting to minimize the income tax, it is to the benefit of taxpayers to *overvalue* deductions. When attempting to minimize transfer taxes (estate and gift taxes), however, executors and donors may be inclined to *undervalue* the assets transferred. A lower valuation reduces estate and gift taxes. An accuracy-related penalty is imposed for substantial estate or gift tax valuation understatements.[40] As with other accuracy-related penalties, reasonable cause and good faith on the part of the taxpayer are a defense.

The penalty is 20 percent of the additional transfer tax that would have been due had the correct valuation been used on Form 706 (estate tax return) or Form 709 (gift and generation-skipping tax return). The penalty only applies if the value of the property claimed on the return is 50 percent or less than the amount determined to be correct. The penalty applies only to an additional transfer tax liability in excess of $5,000. The penalty is doubled if the reported valuation was 25 percent or less than the correct determination.

ETHICAL CONSIDERATIONS

Good Faith Valuations

The undervaluation penalty pushes the tax adviser from a position of adversarial alliance with the taxpayer to one of mediator for the court. Good faith value estimates, especially for family-owned businesses, can easily vary by as much as the 50 percentage points specified for the penalty. Even a gross undervaluation can occur when someone in the business other than the donor or decedent is a particularly talented entrepreneur, an effective sales representative, and/or the founder of the company; similarly, a business may be substantially undervalued when a minority equity interest is

[39] § 6664(c)(2).

[40] § 6662(b)(5).

involved, or an intangible asset conveys a sizable nominal amount of goodwill to the valuation.

Because most taxpayers are highly averse to incurring any nondeductible penalties, the client may be tempted to compromise on the business valuation "too soon" (i.e., when the return is filed), eliminating any possibility of a more favorable valuation being presented before the Appeals Division or a court. Keeping in mind all of the potential taxpayer and preparer penalties that might apply, the tax professional should stick with a good faith appraisal of the business value, no matter what its nominal amount.

How would you react if your client, a musical composer, wanted to deduct $100,000 for the contribution of an obscure manuscript to the Symphony Society? What if your (first) appraiser placed the value of the manuscript at $15,000? What course of action would you propose to the client concerning the deduction? Any consequent penalties?

Civil Fraud Penalty.   A 75 percent civil penalty is imposed on any underpayment resulting from **fraud** by the taxpayer who has filed a return.[41] For this penalty, the burden of proof *is on the IRS* to show by a preponderance of the evidence that the taxpayer had a specific intent to evade a tax.

Once the IRS has initially established that fraud has occurred, the taxpayer then bears the burden of proof to show by a preponderance of the evidence the portion of the underpayment that is not attributable to fraud.

Although the Code and Regulations do not provide any assistance in ascertaining what constitutes civil fraud, it is clear that mere negligence on the part of the taxpayer (however great) will not suffice. Fraud has been found in cases of manipulation of the books,[42] substantial omissions from income,[43] and erroneous deductions.[44]

EXAMPLE 14

Frank underpaid his income tax by $90,000. The IRS can prove that $60,000 of the underpayment was due to fraud. Frank responds by a preponderance of the evidence that $30,000 of the underpayment was not due to fraud. The civil fraud penalty is $45,000 (75% × $60,000). ▼

If the underpayment of tax is partially attributable to negligence and partially attributable to fraud, the fraud penalty is applied first.

Criminal Penalties.   In addition to civil fraud penalties, the Code contains numerous criminal sanctions that carry various monetary fines and/or imprisonment. The difference between civil and criminal fraud often is one of degree. A characteristic of criminal fraud is the presence of willfulness on the part of the taxpayer. Thus, § 7201, dealing with attempts to evade or defeat a tax, contains the following language.

> Any person who *willfully* attempts in any manner to evade or defeat any tax imposed by this title or the payment thereof shall, in addition to other penalties provided by law, be guilty of a felony and, upon conviction thereof, shall be fined not more than $100,000 ($500,000 in the case of a corporation), or imprisoned not more than five years, or both, together with the costs of prosecution. [Emphasis added.]

[41] § 6663. As noted later in the chapter, fraudulent acts are not subject to a statute of limitations.

[42] *Dogget v. Comm.*, 60–1 USTC ¶9342, 5 AFTR2d 1034, 275 F.2d 823 (CA–4, 1960).

[43] *Harvey Brodsky*, 21 TCM 578, T.C.Memo. 1962–105.

[44] *Lash v. Comm.*, 57–2 USTC ¶9725, 51 AFTR 492, 245 F.2d 20 (CA–1, 1957).

TAX IN THE NEWS

BLAMING THE TAX PRACTITIONER

In the last few years, courts have been amenable to taxpayers who defend against criminal charges by asserting that their dependence upon competent tax counsel led to the understatement of tax. Taxpayers who have used this defense successfully have usually shown that they relied on the practitioner's advice because of his or her professional expertise. Other successful defenses have included the argument that it was the practitioner's idea to willfully evade the tax, or that the adviser was not current with the controlling law and therefore issued bad advice that led to the error.

For instance, taxpayers have succeeded with this defense where they could show that the practitioner initiated and implemented the practice of keeping two sets of books or manipulating the cash receipts. Similarly, where the adviser facilitated the underpayment of tax estimates or payroll tax deposits, the IRS's charges against the taxpayer were severely weakened.

Often, taxpayers have submitted videotapes or written materials prepared by the practitioner as evidence in such cases. Severe preparer penalties compound the IRS's retribution against the practitioner when such a defense by the taxpayer prevails in court.

As to the burden of proof, the IRS must show that the taxpayer was guilty of willful evasion "beyond the shadow of any reasonable doubt." Recall that for civil fraud, the standard applied to measure culpability is "by a preponderance of the evidence."

Failure to Pay Estimated Taxes.   A penalty is imposed for a failure to pay estimated income taxes. The penalty applies to individuals and corporations and is based on the rate of interest in effect for deficiency assessments.[45] The penalty also applies to trusts and certain estates that are required to make estimated tax payments. The penalty is not imposed if the tax due for the year (less amounts withheld and credits) is less than $500. For employees, an equal part of withholding is deemed paid on each due date.

Quarterly payments are to be made on or before the fifteenth day of the fourth month (April 15 for a calendar year taxpayer), sixth month, ninth month, and the first month of the following year. Corporations must make the last quarterly payment by the twelfth month of the same year.

An individual's underpayment of estimated tax is the difference between the estimates that were paid and the least of (1) 90 percent of the current-year tax, (2) 100 percent of the prior-year tax (the tax year must have been a full 12 months, and a return must have been filed), and (3) 90 percent of the tax that would be due on an annualized income computation for the period running through the end of the quarter. When the taxpayer's prior-year adjusted gross income (AGI) exceeds

---

[45] §§ 6655 (corporations) and 6654 (other taxpayers). Other computations can avoid the penalty. See §§ 6654(d)(2) and (k), 6655(e) and (i)

$150,000, the required payment percentage for the prior-year alternative is 110 percent.

A corporation's underpayment of estimated tax is the difference between the estimates that were paid and the least of (1) the current-year tax, (2) the prior-year tax, and (3) the tax on an annualized income computation using one of three methods of computation sanctioned by the Code. For the prior-year alternative, (1) the prior-tax year must have been a full 12 months, (2) a nonzero tax amount must have been generated for that year, and (3) large corporations (taxable income of $1 million or more in any of the three immediately preceding tax years) can use the alternative only for the first installment of a year.

In computing the penalty, Form 2210 (Underpayment of Estimated Tax by Individuals) or Form 2220 (Underpayment of Estimated Tax by Corporations) is used (see Appendix B).

False Information with Respect to Withholding.   Withholding from wages is an important element of the Federal income tax system, which is based on a pay-as-you-go approach. One way employees might hope to avoid this withholding would be to falsify the information provided to the employer on Form W–4 (Employee Withholding Allowance Certificate). For example, by overstating the number of exemptions, income tax withholdings could be cut or completely eliminated.

To encourage compliance, a civil penalty of $500 applies when a taxpayer claims withholding allowances based on false information. The criminal penalty for willfully failing to supply information or for willfully supplying false or fraudulent information in connection with wage withholding is an additional fine of up to $1,000 and/or up to one year of imprisonment.[46]

Failure to Make Deposits of Taxes and Overstatements of Deposits. When business is not doing well or cash-flow problems develop, employers have a great temptation to "borrow" from Uncle Sam. One way this can be done is to fail to pay to the IRS the amounts that have been withheld from the wages of employees for FICA and income tax purposes. The IRS does not appreciate being denied the use of these funds and has a number of weapons at its disposal to discourage the practice.

- A penalty of up to 15 percent of any underdeposited amount not paid, unless the employer can show that the failure is due to reasonable cause and not to willful neglect.[47]
- Various criminal penalties.[48]
- A 100 percent penalty if the employer's actions are willful.[49] The penalty is based on the amount of the tax evaded, not collected, or not accounted for or paid over. Since the penalty is assessable against the "responsible person" of the business, more than one party may be vulnerable (e.g., the president and treasurer of a corporation). Although the IRS may assess the penalty against several persons, it cannot collect more than the 100 percent due.
- In addition to these penalties, the actual tax due must be remitted. An employer remains liable for the amount that should have been paid, even if the withholdings have not been taken out of the wages of its employees.[50]

---

[46] §§ 6682 and 7205.
[47] § 6656.
[48] See, for example, § 7202 (willful failure to collect or pay over a tax).
[49] § 6672.
[50] § 3403.

STATUTES OF LIMITATIONS

7 ▸ **LEARNING OBJECTIVE**
Understand the rules governing the statute of limitations on assessments and on refunds.

A **statute of limitations** defines the period of time during which one party may pursue against another party a cause of action or other suit allowed under the governing law. Failure to satisfy any requirement provides the other party with an absolute defense should the statute be invoked. Inequity would result if no limits were placed on such suits. Permitting an extended period of time to elapse between the initiation of a claim and its pursuit could place the defense at a serious disadvantage. Witnesses may have died or disappeared; records or other evidence may have been discarded or destroyed.

Assessment and the Statute of Limitations.   In general, any tax that is imposed must be assessed within three years of the filing of the return (or, if later, the due date of the return).[51] Some exceptions to this three-year limitation exist.

- If no return is filed or a fraudulent return is filed, assessments can be made at any time. There is, in effect, no statute of limitations in these cases.
- If a taxpayer omits an amount of gross income in excess of 25 percent of the gross income stated on the return, the statute of limitations is increased to six years. The courts have interpreted this rule as including only items affecting income and not the omission of items affecting cost of sales.[52] In addition, gross income includes capital gains in the *gross* income amount (not reduced by capital losses).

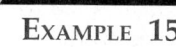

EXAMPLE 15

During 1992, Jerry had the following income transactions (all of which were duly reported on his timely filed return).

Gross receipts		$ 480,000
Cost of sales		(400,000)
Net business income		$ 80,000
Capital gains and losses		
Capital gain	$36,000	
Capital loss	12,000	24,000
Total income		$ 104,000

Jerry retains your services in 1997 as a tax consultant. It seems that he inadvertently omitted some income on his 1992 return and he wishes to know if he is "safe" under the statute of limitations. The six-year statute of limitations would apply, putting Jerry in a vulnerable position only if he omitted more than $129,000 on his 1992 return [($480,000 + $36,000) × 25%]. ▼

- The statute of limitations may be extended by mutual consent of the District Director and the taxpayer.[53] This extension covers a definite period and is made by signing Form 872 (Consent to Extend the Time to Assess Tax). The extension is frequently requested by the IRS when the lapse of the statutory period is imminent and the audit has not been completed. This practice is

---

[51] §§ 6501(a) and (b)(1).
[52] *The Colony, Inc. v. Comm.*, 58–2 USTC ¶9593, 1 AFTR2d 1894, 78 S.Ct. 1033 (USSC, 1958).

[53] § 6501(c)(4).

often applied to audits of corporate taxpayers and explains why many corporations have more than three "open years."

Special rules relating to assessment are applicable in the following situations.

- Taxpayers (corporations, estates, etc.) may request a prompt assessment of the tax.
- The period for assessment of the personal holding company tax is extended to six years after the return is filed only if certain filing requirements are met.
- If a partnership or trust files a tax return (a partnership or trust return) in good faith and a later determination renders the entity taxable as a corporation, the return is deemed to be the corporate return for purposes of the statute of limitations.
- The assessment period for capital loss, net operating loss, and investment credit carrybacks is generally related to the determination of tax in the year of the loss or unused credit rather than in the carryback years.

If the tax is assessed within the period of limitations, the IRS has 10 years from the date of assessment to collect the tax. However, if the IRS issues a statutory notice of deficiency to the taxpayer, who then files a Tax Court petition, the statute is suspended on both the deficiency assessment and the period of collection until 60 days after the decision of the Tax Court becomes final.

Refund Claims and the Statute of Limitations. To receive a tax refund, the taxpayer is required to file a valid refund claim. The official form for filing a claim is Form 1040X for individuals and Form 1120X for corporations. If the refund claim does not meet certain procedural requirements, the IRS may reject the claim with no consideration of its merit.

- A separate claim must be filed for each taxable period.
- The grounds for the claim must be stated in sufficient detail.
- The statement of facts must be sufficient to permit the IRS to evaluate the merits of the claim.

The refund claim must be filed within three years of the filing of the tax return or within two years following the payment of the tax if this period expires on a later date.[54]

▼
EXAMPLE 16

On March 10, 1994, Louise filed her 1993 income tax return reflecting a tax of $10,500. On July 10, 1995, she filed an amended 1993 return showing an additional $3,000 of tax that was then paid. On May 18, 1997, she filed a claim for refund of $4,500.

Assuming that Louise is correct in claiming a refund, how much tax can she recover? The answer is only $3,000. Because the claim was not filed within the three-year period, Louise is limited to the amount she actually paid during the last two years. ▼

Special rules are available for claims relating to bad debts and worthless securities. A seven-year period of limitations applies in lieu of the normal three-year rule.[55] The extended period is provided in recognition of the inherent difficulty of identifying the exact year in which a bad debt or security becomes worthless.

---

[54] §§ 6511(a) and 6513(a).   [55] § 6511(d)(1).

Tax Practice

THE TAX PRACTITIONER

Definition. Who is a tax practitioner? What service does the practitioner perform? To begin defining the term *tax practitioner*, one should consider whether the individual is qualified to practice before the IRS. Generally, practice before the IRS is limited to CPAs, attorneys, and persons who have been enrolled to practice before the IRS (called **enrolled agents [EAs]).** In most cases, EAs are admitted to practice only if they pass an examination administered by the IRS. CPAs and attorneys are not required to take this examination and are automatically admitted to practice if they are in good standing with the appropriate licensing board regulating their profession.

Persons other than CPAs, attorneys, and EAs may be allowed to practice before the IRS in limited situations. Circular 230 (entitled "Rules Governing the Practice of Attorneys and Agents Before the Internal Revenue Service,") issued by the Treasury Department permits certain notable exceptions.

- A taxpayer may always represent him- or herself. A person may also represent a member of the immediate family if no compensation is received for such services.
- Regular full-time employees may represent their employers.
- Corporations may be represented by any of their bona fide officers.
- Partnerships may be represented by any of the partners.
- Trusts, receiverships, guardianships, or estates may be represented by their trustees, receivers, guardians, or administrators or executors.
- A taxpayer may be represented by whoever prepared the return for the year in question. However, such representation cannot proceed beyond the agent level.

Example 17

Joel is currently undergoing audit by the IRS for tax years 1996 and 1997. He prepared the 1996 return himself but paid AddCo, a bookkeeping service, to prepare the 1997 return. AddCo may represent Joel only in matters concerning 1997. However, even for 1997, AddCo would be unable to represent Joel at an Appeals Division proceeding. Joel could, of course, represent himself, or he could retain a CPA, attorney, or EA to represent him in matters concerning both years under examination. ▼

Rules Governing Tax Practice. Circular 230 further prescribes the rules governing practice before the IRS. The following are some of the most important rules imposed on CPAs, attorneys, and EAs.

- A prohibition against taking a position on a tax return unless there is a *realistic possibility* of the position being sustained on its merits. Generally, the realistic possibility standard is met when a person knowledgeable in the tax law would conclude that the position has at least a one-in-three probability of prevailing in court.
- A prohibition against taking frivolous tax return positions.
- A requirement that nonfrivolous tax return positions that fail the realistic possibility standard be disclosed in the return (i.e., using Form 8275).
- A requirement to inform clients of penalties likely to apply to return positions and of ways such penalties can be avoided.
- A requirement to make known to a client any error or omission the client may have made on any return or other document submitted to the IRS.

- A duty to submit records or information lawfully requested by the IRS.
- An obligation to exercise due diligence in preparing and filing tax returns accurately.
- A restriction against unreasonably delaying the prompt disposition of any matter before the IRS.
- A restriction against charging the client "an unconscionable fee" for representation before the IRS.
- A restriction against representing clients with conflicting interests.

Anyone can prepare a tax return or render tax advice, regardless of his or her educational background or level of competence. Likewise, nothing prevents the "unlicensed" tax practitioner from advertising his or her specialty, directly soliciting clients, or otherwise violating any of the standards of conduct controlling CPAs, attorneys, and EAs. Nevertheless, some restraints do govern all parties engaged in rendering tax returns for the general public.

- If the party holds him- or herself out to the general public as possessing tax expertise, he or she could be liable to the client if services are performed in a negligent manner. At a minimum, the practitioner is liable for any interest and penalties the client incurs because of the practitioner's failure to exercise due care.
- If one agrees to perform a service (e.g., prepare a tax return) and subsequently fails to do so, the aggrieved party may be in a position to obtain damages for breach of contract.
- The IRS requires all persons who prepare tax returns for a fee to sign as preparer of the return.[56] Failure to comply with this requirement could result in penalty assessment against the preparer.
- The Code prescribes various penalties for the deliberate filing of false or fraudulent returns. These penalties apply to a tax practitioner who either was aware of the situation or actually perpetrated the false information or the fraud.[57]
- Penalties are prescribed for tax practitioners who disclose to third parties information they have received from clients in connection with the preparation of tax returns or the rendering of tax advice.[58]

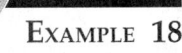

EXAMPLE 18

Sarah operates a tax return preparation service. Her brother-in-law, Butch, has just taken a job as a life insurance salesman. To help Butch find contacts, Sarah furnishes him with a list of the names and addresses of all of her clients who report AGI of $10,000 or more. Sarah is subject to penalties. ▼

- All nonattorney tax practitioners should avoid becoming engaged in activities that constitute the unauthorized practice of law. If they engage in this practice, action could be instituted against them in the appropriate state court by the local or state bar association. What actions constitute the unauthorized practice of law is largely undefined, though, and such charges are filed only rarely today.

Preparer Penalties.   The Code also provides for penalties to discourage improper actions by tax practitioners.

---

[56] Reg. § 1.6065–1(b)(1). Rev.Rul. 84–3, 1984–1 C.B. 264, contains a series of examples illustrating when a person is deemed to be a preparer of the return.

[57] § 7206.
[58] § 7216.

1. A $250 penalty for understatements due to taking unrealistic positions.[59] Unless adequate tax return disclosure of the position is made, the penalty is imposed if two conditions are satisfied.

   - Any part of any understatement of tax liability on any return or claim for refund is due to a position that did not have a realistic possibility of being sustained on its merits.
   - Any person who was an income tax return preparer for that return or claim knew (or should have known) of this position.

   The penalty can be avoided by showing reasonable cause and by showing that the preparer acted in good faith.

2. A $1,000 penalty for willful and reckless conduct.[60] The penalty applies if any part of the understatement of a taxpayer's liability on a return or claim for refund is due to:

   - The preparer's willful attempt to understate the taxpayer's tax liability in any manner.
   - Any reckless or intentional disregard of IRS rules or regulations by the preparer.

   Adequate disclosure can avoid the penalty. If both this penalty and the unrealistic position penalty (see item 1 above) apply to the same return, the total penalty cannot exceed $1,000.

3. A $1,000 ($10,000 for corporations) penalty per return or document is imposed against persons who aid in the preparation of returns or other documents that they know (or have reason to believe) would result in an understatement of the tax liability of another person.[61] Clerical assistance in the preparation process does not incur the penalty.

   If this penalty applies, neither the unrealistic position penalty (item 1) nor the willful and reckless conduct penalty (item 2) is assessed.

4. A $50 penalty is assessed against the preparer for failure to sign a return or furnish the preparer's identifying number.[62]

5. A $50 penalty is assessed if the preparer fails to furnish a copy of the return or claim for refund to the taxpayer.

6. A $500 penalty may be assessed if a preparer endorses or otherwise negotiates a check for refund of tax issued to the taxpayer.

ETHICAL CONSIDERATIONS—"STATEMENTS ON RESPONSIBILITIES IN TAX PRACTICE"

Tax practitioners who are CPAs, attorneys, or EAs must abide by the codes or canons of professional ethics applicable to their respective professions. The various codes and canons have much in common with and parallel the standards of conduct set forth in Circular 230.[63]

In the belief that CPAs engaged in tax practice required further guidance in the resolution of ethical problems, the Tax Committee of the AICPA began issuing periodic statements on selected topics. The first of these "Statements on Responsibilities in Tax Practice" was released in 1964. All of the Statements were revised

---

[59] § 6694(a).
[60] § 6694(b).
[61] § 6701.
[62] § 6695.

[63] For an additional discussion of tax ethics, see Raabe, Whittenburg, and Bost, *West's Federal Tax Research,* 4th ed. (St. Paul: West Publishing Co., 1997), especially Chapters 1 and 13.

in August 1988. The most important Statements that have been issued to date are discussed below.[64]

The Statements merely represent guides to action and are not part of the AICPA's Code of Professional Ethics. But because the Statements are representative of standards followed by members of the profession, a violation might indicate a deviation from the standard of due care exercised by most CPAs. The standard of due care is at the heart of any suit charging negligence that is brought against a CPA.

Statement No. 1: Positions Contrary to IRS Interpretations.   Under certain circumstances, a CPA may take a position that is contrary to that taken by the IRS. In order to do so, however, the CPA must have a good faith belief that the position has a realistic possibility of being sustained administratively or judicially on its merits if challenged.

The client should be fully advised of the risks involved and the penalties that may result if the position taken by the CPA is not successful. The client should also be informed that disclosure on the return may avoid some or all of these penalties.

In no case, though, should the CPA exploit the audit lottery. That is, the CPA should not take a questionable position based on the probabilities that the client's return will not be chosen by the IRS for audit. Furthermore, the CPA should not "load" the return with questionable items in the hope that they might aid the client in a later settlement negotiation with the IRS.

Statement No. 2: Questions on Returns.   A CPA should make a reasonable effort to obtain from the client, and provide, appropriate answers to all questions on a tax return before signing as preparer. Reasonable grounds may exist for omitting an answer.

- The information is not readily available, and the answer is not significant in computing the tax.
- The meaning of the question as it applies to a particular situation is genuinely uncertain.
- The answer to the question is voluminous.

The fact that an answer to a question could prove disadvantageous to the client does not justify omitting the answer.

Statement No. 3: Procedural Aspects of Preparing Returns.   In preparing a return, a CPA may in good faith rely without verification on information furnished by the client or by third parties. However, the CPA should make reasonable inquiries if the information appears to be incorrect, incomplete, or inconsistent. In this regard, the CPA should refer to the client's returns for prior years whenever appropriate.

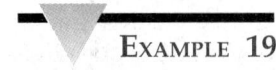

EXAMPLE 19

A CPA normally can take a client's word for the validity of dependency exemptions. But suppose a recently divorced client wants to claim his three children as dependents (when he does not have custody). You must act in accordance with § 152(e)(2) in preparing the return, and this will require evidence of a waiver by the custodial parent. Without this waiver, you should not claim the dependency exemptions on your client's tax return. ▼

---

[64] Other, less frequently encountered statements are omitted from this discussion.

EXAMPLE 20

While preparing a client's income tax return for 1997, you review her income tax return for 1996. In comparing the dividend income reported on the 1996 Schedule B with that received in 1997, you note a significant decrease. Further investigation reveals the variation is due to a stock sale in 1997 that was unknown to you until now. Thus, the review of the 1996 return has unearthed a transaction that should be reported on the 1997 return. ▼

If the Code or Regulations require certain types of verification (as is the case with travel and entertainment expenditures), the CPA must advise the client of these rules. Further, inquiry must be made to ascertain whether the client has complied with the verification requirements.

Statement No. 4: Estimates.   A CPA may prepare a tax return using estimates received from a taxpayer if it is impracticable to obtain exact data. The estimates must be reasonable under the facts and circumstances as known to the CPA. When estimates are used, they should be presented in such a manner as to avoid the implication of greater accuracy than exists.

Statement No. 5: Recognition of Administrative Proceeding.   As facts may vary from year to year, so may the position taken by a CPA. In these types of situations, the CPA is not bound by an administrative or judicial proceeding involving a prior year.

EXAMPLE 21

Upon audit of Ramon Corporation's income tax return for 1996, the IRS disallowed $18,000 of the $400,000 salary paid to its president and sole shareholder on the grounds that it is unreasonable [§ 162(a)(1)]. You are the CPA who has been engaged to prepare Ramon's income tax return for 1997. Again the corporation paid its president a salary of $400,000 and chose to deduct this amount. Because you are not bound in 1997 by what the IRS deemed reasonable for 1996, the full $400,000 can be claimed as a salary deduction. ▼

Other problems that require a CPA's use of judgment include reclassification of corporate debt as equity (thin capitalization) and corporate accumulations beyond the reasonable needs of the business (for the penalty tax under § 531).

Statement No. 6: Knowledge of Error.   A CPA should promptly advise a client upon learning of an error in a previously filed return or upon learning of a client's failure to file a required return. The advice can be oral or written and should include a recommendation of the corrective measures, if any, to be taken. The error or other omission should not be disclosed to the IRS without the client's consent.

If the past error is material and is not corrected by the client, the CPA may be unable to prepare the current year's tax return. This situation might occur if the error has a carryover effect that prevents the CPA from determining the correct tax liability for the current year.

EXAMPLE 22

In preparing a client's 1997 income tax return, you discover that final inventory for 1996 was materially understated. First, you should advise the client to file an amended return for 1996 reflecting the correct amount in final inventory. Second, if the client refuses to make this adjustment, you should consider whether the error will preclude you from preparing a substantially correct return for 1997. Because this will probably be the case (the final inventory for 1996 becomes the beginning inventory for 1997), you should withdraw from the engagement.

If the client corrects the error, you may proceed with the preparation of the tax return for 1997. You must assure yourself that the error is not repeated. ▼

CONCEPT SUMMARY 16–1

Tax Administration and Practice

1. The Internal Revenue Service (IRS) enforces the tax laws of the United States. Its size and form of organization reflect its various responsibilities relative to taxpayer interaction, litigation and collection, as well as its internal functions.
2. The IRS issues various pronouncements, communicating its position on certain tax issues. These pronouncements promote the uniform enforcement of the tax law among taxpayers and among the internal divisions of the IRS. Taxpayers should seek such rulings and memoranda when the nature or magnitude of a pending transaction requires a high degree of certainty in the planning process.
3. IRS audits can take several forms. Taxpayers are selected for audit based on the probable net dollar return to the Treasury from the process. Offers in compromise and closing agreements can be a useful means of completing an audit without resorting to litigation.
4. Certain IRS personnel are empowered to consider the hazards of litigation in developing a settlement with the taxpayer during the audit process.
5. The IRS pays interest to taxpayers on overpaid taxes, starting essentially 45 days after the due date of the return, at two percentage points over the Federal short-term rate. Interest paid to the IRS on underpayments is computed at three points over this Federal rate, starting essentially on the due date of the return. Interest for both purposes is compounded daily.
6. The Treasury assesses penalties when the taxpayer fails to file a required tax return or pay a tax. Penalties also are assessed when an inaccurate return is filed due to negligence or other disregard of IRS rules. Tax preparers are subject to penalties for assisting a taxpayer in filing an inaccurate return, failing to follow IRS rules in an appropriate manner, or mishandling taxpayer data or funds.
7. Statutes of limitations place outer boundaries on the timing and amounts of proposed amendments to completed tax returns that can be made by the taxpayer or the IRS.
8. Tax practitioners must operate under constraints imposed on them by codes of ethics or pertinent professional societies and by Treasury Circular 230. These rules also define the parties who can represent others in an IRS proceeding.

Statement No. 8: Advice to Clients. In providing tax advice to a client, the CPA must use judgment to assure that the advice reflects professional competence and appropriately serves the client's needs. No standard format or guidelines can be established to cover all situations and circumstances involving written or oral advice by the CPA.

The CPA may communicate with the client when subsequent developments affect previous advice on significant matters. However, the CPA cannot be expected to assume responsibility for initiating the communication, unless he or she is assisting a client in implementing procedures or plans associated with the advice. The CPA may undertake this obligation by specific agreement with the client.

TAX PLANNING CONSIDERATIONS

STRATEGIES IN SEEKING AN ADMINISTRATIVE RULING

Determination Letters. In many instances, the request for an advance ruling or a determination letter from the IRS is a necessary or desirable planning strategy. The receipt of a favorable ruling or determination reduces the risk associated with a transaction when the tax results are in doubt. For example, the initiation or amendment of a qualified pension or profit sharing plan should be accompanied by a determination letter from the District Director. Otherwise, on subsequent IRS review, the plan may not qualify, and the tax deductibility of contributions to the plan will be disallowed. In some instances, the potential tax effects of a transaction are so numerous and of such consequence that proceeding without a ruling is unwise.

Letter Rulings.   In some cases, it may not be necessary or desirable to request an advance ruling. For example, it is generally not desirable to request a ruling if the tax results are doubtful and the company is committed to complete the transaction in any event. If a ruling is requested and negotiations with the IRS indicate that an adverse determination will be forthcoming, it is usually possible to have the ruling request withdrawn. However, the National Office of the IRS may forward its findings, along with a copy of the ruling request, to the District Director. In determining the advisability of a ruling request, the taxpayer should consider the potential exposure of other items in the tax returns of all "open years."

A ruling request may delay the consummation of a transaction if the issues are novel or complex. Frequently, a ruling can be processed within six months, although in some instances a delay of a year or more may be encountered.

Technical Advice Memoranda.   A taxpayer in the process of contesting a proposed deficiency with the Appeals Division should consider requesting a technical advice memorandum from the National Office of the IRS. If the memorandum is favorable to the taxpayer, it is binding on the Appeals Division. The request may be particularly appropriate when the practitioner feels that the agent or Appeals Division has been too literal in interpreting an IRS ruling.

CONSIDERATIONS IN HANDLING AN IRS AUDIT

As a general rule, a taxpayer should attempt to settle disputes at the earliest possible stage of the administrative appeal process. It is usually possible to limit the scope of the examination by furnishing pertinent information requested by the agent. Extraneous information or fortuitous comments may result in the opening of new issues and should be avoided. Agents usually appreciate prompt and efficient responses to inquiries, since their performance may in part be judged by their ability to close or settle assigned cases.

To the extent possible, it is advisable to conduct the investigation of field audits in the practitioner's office, rather than the client's office. This procedure permits greater control over the audit investigation and facilitates the agent's review and prompt closure of the case.

Many practitioners feel that it is generally not advisable to have clients present at the scheduled conferences with the agent, since the client may give emotional or gratuitous comments that impair prompt settlement. If the client is not present, however, he or she should be advised of the status of negotiations. The client makes the final decision on any proposed settlement.

ETHICAL CONSIDERATIONS

Should the Client Attend an Audit?

Whether the client should be present during an audit is a matter of some debate. Certainly, the client's absence tends to slow down the negotiating process because the taxpayer must make all final decisions on settlement terms and is the best source of information for open questions of fact. Nevertheless, most practitioners discourage their clients from attending audits or conferences with the Appeals Division involving an income tax dispute. Ignorance of the law and of the conventions of the audit process can make the taxpayer a "loose cannon" that can do more harm than good if unchecked. All too often, a client will "say too much" in the presence of a government official.

In reality, though, by discouraging clients from attending the audit, practitioners may be interfering with the IRS's function of gathering evidence, depending on what precisely the taxpayer is being prevented from saying. To many practitioners, a "wrong" answer is one that increases taxes, not one that misrepresents the truth. A popular saying among tax advisers is "Don't tell me more than I want to know." Although this philosophy is supportable under various professional codes of conduct, it is hardly defensible in the larger scheme of things.

In your opinion, under what circumstances should the client attend such a session? To what degree should the tax professional "coach" the client as to how to behave in that setting? Or do a taxpayer's rights include the right to increase his or her own tax liability?

Preparing for the Audit. The tax professional must prepare thoroughly for the audit or Appeals proceeding. Practitioners often cite the following steps as critical to such preparations. Carrying out a level of due diligence in preparing for the proceeding is part of the tax professional's responsibility in representing the client.

- Make certain that both sides agree on the issues to be resolved in the audit. The goal here is to limit the agent's list of open issues.
- Identify all of the facts underlying the issues in dispute, including those favorable to the IRS. Gather evidence to support the taxpayer's position, and evaluate the evidence supporting the other side.
- Research current tax law authorities as they bear on the facts and open issues. Remember that the IRS agent is bound only by Supreme Court cases and IRS pronouncements. Determine the degree of discretion that the IRS is likely to have in disposing of the case.
- Prepare a list of points supporting and contradicting the taxpayer's case. Include both minor points bearing little weight and core principles. Short research memos will also be useful in the discussion with the agent. Points favoring the taxpayer should be mentioned during the discussion and "entered into the record."
- Prepare tax and interest computations showing the effects of points that are in dispute, so that the consequences of closing or compromising an issue can be readily determined.
- Determine a "litigation point" (i.e., at which the taxpayer will withdraw from further audit negotiation and pursue the case in the courts). This position should be based on the dollars of tax, interest, and penalty involved, the chances of prevailing in various trial-level courts, and other strategies discussed with the taxpayer. One must have an "end game" strategy for the audit, and thorough tax research is critical in developing that position in this context.

Offers in Compromise. The IRS is encouraging the use of offers in compromise to a greater degree than ever before as part of its "consumer-friendly" approach to its enforcement obligations and its efforts to bring more nonfilers into compliance with the tax system.

Both parties to a tax dispute may find a compromise offer useful because it conclusively settles all of the issues covered by the agreement and may include a favorable payment schedule for the taxpayer.

On the other hand, several attributes of an offer in compromise may work to the detriment of the taxpayer. Just as the IRS no longer can raise new issues as part of the audit proceedings against the taxpayer, he or she cannot contest or appeal any such agreement. As part of the offer process, the taxpayer must disclose all relevant finances and resources, including details he or she might not want the government to know. Furthermore, both parties are bound to the filing positions established by the compromise for five tax years, a level of inflexibility that may work against a taxpayer whose circumstances change over time.

Documentation Issues. The tax practitioner's workpapers should include all research memoranda, and a list of resolved and unresolved issues should be continually updated during the course of the IRS audit. Occasionally, agents request access to excessive amounts of accounting data in order to engage in a so-called fishing expedition. Providing blanket access to working papers should be avoided. Workpapers should be carefully reviewed to minimize opportunities for the agent to raise new issues not otherwise apparent. It is generally advisable to provide the agent with copies of specific workpapers upon request. An accountant's workpapers generally are not privileged and may be subpoenaed by the IRS.

In unusual situations, a Special Agent may appear to gather evidence in the investigation of possible criminal fraud. When this occurs, the taxpayer should be advised to seek legal counsel to determine the extent of his or her cooperation in providing information to the agent. Further, it is frequently desirable for the tax adviser to consult personal legal counsel in such situations. If the taxpayer receives a Revenue Agent's Report (RAR), it generally indicates that the IRS has decided not to initiate criminal prosecution proceedings. The IRS usually does not take any action upon a tax deficiency until the criminal matter has been resolved. If, for whatever reasons, the criminal action is dropped, the 75 percent civil fraud penalty normally is assessed.

LITIGATION CONSIDERATIONS

During the process of settlement with the IRS, the taxpayer must assess the economic consequences of possible litigation. Specifically, the probability of winning in court should be weighed against the costs of settlement (legal, support, and court costs). In some instances, taxpayers become overly emotional and do not adequately consider the economic and psychological costs of litigation.

Signing Form 870 or Form 870–AD precludes the use of the Tax Court as a forum for future litigation. In that event, the taxpayer's only recourse is to pay the taxes and sue for a refund upon denial of a claim for refund. The Tax Court was established to provide taxpayers an opportunity to litigate issues without first paying the tax on the deficiency. Some taxpayers, however, prefer to litigate the case in a Federal District Court or the Court of Federal Claims, since the payment of tax effectively stops the running of interest on the deficiency.

In selecting a proper tax forum, consideration should be given to the decisions of the various courts in related cases. The Tax Court follows the decisions of Courts of Appeals if the court is one to which the taxpayer may appeal.[65] For example, if an individual is in the jurisdiction of the Fifth Court of Appeals and that court has issued a favorable opinion on the same issue that currently confronts the taxpayer, the Tax Court will follow this opinion in deciding the taxpayer's case, even if previous Tax Court decisions have been adverse.

If the issue involves a question in which equity is needed, strategy may dictate the choice of a Federal District Court (where a jury trial is obtainable) or the Court of Federal Claims, which has frequently given greater weight to equity considerations than to strict legal precedent.

---

[65] *Jack E. Golsen*, 54 T.C. 742 (1970).

PENALTIES

Penalties are imposed upon a taxpayer's failure to file a return or pay a tax when due. These penalties can be avoided if the failure is due to reasonable cause and not due to willful neglect. Reasonable cause, however, has not been liberally interpreted by the courts and should not be relied upon in the routine situation.[66] A safer way to avoid the failure to file penalty is to obtain from the IRS an extension of time for filing the return.

The penalty for failure to pay estimated taxes can become quite severe. Often trapped by the provision are employed taxpayers with outside income. They may forget about the outside income and assume the amount withheld from wages and salaries is adequate to cover their liability. Not only does April 15 provide a real shock (in terms of the additional tax owed) for these persons, but a penalty situation may have evolved. One way for an employee to mitigate this problem (presuming the employer is willing to cooperate) is described in the following example.

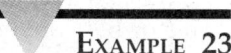

EXAMPLE 23

Patty, a calendar year taxpayer, is employed by Finn Corporation and earns (after withholding) a monthly salary of $4,000 payable at the end of each month. Patty also receives income from outside sources (interest, dividends, and consulting fees). After some quick calculations in early October, Patty determines that she has underestimated her tax liability by $7,500 and will be subject to the penalty for the first two quarters of the year and part of the third quarter. Patty, therefore, completes a new Form W–4 in which she arbitrarily raises her income tax withholding by $2,500 a month. Finn accepts the Form W–4, and as a result, an extra $7,500 is paid to the IRS on Patty's account for the payroll period from October through December.

Patty avoids penalties for the underpayment for the first three quarters because withholding of taxes is allocated pro rata over the year involved. Thus, a portion of the additional $7,500 withheld in October–December is assigned to the January 1–April 15 period, the April 16–June 15 period, etc. Had Patty merely paid the IRS an additional $7,500 in October, the penalty would still have been assessed for the earlier quarters. ▼

KEY TERMS

Accuracy-related penalty,   16–17

Closing agreement,   16–13

Determination letter,   16–6

Enrolled agent (EA),   16–25

Fraud,   16–20

Letter ruling,   16–5

Negligence,   16–18

Ninety-day letter,   16–11

Offer in compromise,   16–13

Reasonable cause,   16–17

Revenue Agent's Report (RAR),   16–10

Statute of limitations,   16–23

Substantial authority,   16–18

Technical advice memorandum,   16–6

Thirty-day letter,   16–11

---

[66] *Dustin v. Comm.*, 72–2 USTC ¶9610, 30 AFTR2d 72–5313, 467 F.2d 47 (CA–9, 1972), *aff'g.* 53 T.C. 491 (1969).

PROBLEM MATERIALS

DISCUSSION QUESTIONS

1. Why must the tax professional be cognizant of how tax law administration works?

2. Name the three major functions of the National Office of the IRS.

3. What is the role of the IRS in the revenue process?

4. What are the chances of having a tax return audited this year?

5. What techniques other than the random selection of returns for audit does the IRS use in its enforcement function?

6. Should the IRS audit more or fewer returns every year?

7. Your tax supervisor has informed you that the firm has received an unfavorable answer to a ruling request. In a memo to the supervisor, describe the appropriate weight that she should assign to the holding in the ruling.

8. Who bears the burden of proof when the IRS challenges items reported on a tax return?

9. Describe the powers of the IRS to seize taxpayer assets when a tax is due.

10. Sarah tells you, "I was worried about getting audited on the tax return I filed two months ago, but I received my refund check today, so the IRS must agree with my figures." Comment.

11. Why may it be desirable to settle with an agent rather than to continue by appealing to a higher level within the IRS?

12. When should a taxpayer take a matter to the Tax Court's Small Cases Division?

13. When can the taxpayer use an "installment plan" to pay his or her delinquent taxes and associated interest and penalties?

14. What bearing should the interest rate currently in effect have on each of the following situations?
    a. Whether a taxpayer litigates in the U.S. Tax Court or the Court of Federal Claims.
    b. The penalty for underpayment of estimated taxes.

15. On February 9, 1997, Quon, a calendar year taxpayer, files her 1996 income tax return on which she claims a $1,200 refund. If Quon receives her refund check on May 2, 1997, will it include any interest? Explain.

16. For the completion and filing of his 1996 income tax return, Ron retains the services of a CPA. Because of a particularly hectic tax season, the CPA does not complete and file the return until June 1997. Would Ron be excused from the failure to file and pay penalties under the reasonable cause exception? Would it make any difference if Ron were entitled to a refund?

17. Indicate whether each of the following statements is true or false.
    a. The government never pays a taxpayer interest on an overpayment of tax.
    b. Penalties may be included as an itemized deduction on an individual's tax return, but net of the 2%-of-AGI floor.
    c. An extension of time for filing a return results in an automatic extension of the time in which the tax may be paid.
    d. The IRS can compromise on the amount of tax liability if there is doubt as to the taxpayer's ability to pay.
    e. The statute of limitations for assessing a tax never extends beyond three years from the filing of a return.
    f. A taxpayer's claim for a refund is not subject to a statute of limitations.

18. What is the role of the statute of limitations in the Federal income tax system? How do such statutes protect the taxpayer? The government?

19. In each of the following cases, distinguish between the terms.
    a. Offer in compromise and closing agreement.
    b. Failure to file and failure to pay.

    c. Ninety-day letter and thirty-day letter.

    d. Negligence and fraud.

    e. Criminal and civil penalties.

20. Certain individuals have stated that the preparation of a tax return by a qualified professional lends credibility to the return. Therefore, CPAs and attorneys should act impartially in preparing tax returns and should serve society's overall needs for the administration and enforcement of tax justice. Should a tax professional be an "umpire" or an "advocate"?

21. Lorraine, a vice president of Scott Corporation, prepared and filed the corporate Form 1120 for 1996. This return is being audited by the IRS in 1998.

    a. May Lorraine represent Scott during the audit?

    b. Can Lorraine's representation continue beyond the agent level (e.g., before the Appeals Division)?

22. Indicate which codes, canons, and other bodies of ethical statements apply to each of the following tax practitioners.

    a. CPAs who are members of the AICPA.

    b. CPAs who are not members of the AICPA.

    c. Attorneys.

    d. Enrolled agents.

    e. Tax preparers who are not CPAs, EAs, or attorneys.

PROBLEMS

23. Compute the failure to pay and failure to file penalties for John, who filed his 1997 income tax return on December 20, 1998, paying the $4,000 amount due. On April 1, 1998, John had received a four-month extension of time in which to file his return. He has no reasonable cause for failing to file his return by August 15 or for failing to pay the tax that was due on April 15, 1998. John's failure to comply with the tax laws was not fraudulent.

24. Orville, a cash basis, calendar year taxpayer, filed his income tax return 75 days after the due date. Orville never extended his return, and he paid the taxes that were due. What penalty will Orville incur, and how much will he have to pay if his additional tax is $900? Disregard any interest he must pay.

25. Rhoda, a calendar year individual taxpayer, files her 1996 return on March 11, 1998. She did not obtain an extension for filing her return, and the return reflects additional income tax due of $5,000.

    a. What are Rhoda's penalties for failure to file and to pay?

    b. Would your answer to (a) change if Rhoda, before the due date of the return, had retained a CPA to prepare the return and it was the CPA's negligence that caused the delay?

26. Kim underpaid her taxes by $15,000. Of this amount, $9,500 was due to negligence on her part, as her record-keeping system is highly inadequate. Determine the amount of any negligence penalty.

27. Dana underpaid his taxes by $250,000. A portion of the underpayment was shown to be attributable to Dana's negligence ($40,000). Another portion of the deficiency was found to constitute civil fraud ($100,000). Compute the total penalties incurred.

28. Olivia, a calendar year taxpayer, does not file her 1997 return until June 4, 1998. At this point, she pays the $3,000 balance due on her 1997 tax liability of $30,000. Olivia did not apply for and obtain any extension of time for filing the 1997 return. When questioned by the IRS on her delinquency, Olivia asserts: "If I was too busy to file my regular tax return, I was too busy to request an extension."

    a. Is Olivia liable for any penalties for failure to file and for failure to pay?

    b. If so, compute the penalty amounts.

29. Compute the overvaluation penalty for each of the following independent cases involving the taxpayer's reporting of the fair market value of charitable contribution property. In each case, assume a marginal income tax rate of 30%.

	Taxpayer	Corrected IRS Value	Reported Valuation
a.	Individual	$ 10,000	$ 20,000
b.	C corporation	10,000	30,000
c.	S corporation	10,000	30,000
d.	Individual	100,000	150,000
e.	Individual	100,000	300,000
f.	C corporation	100,000	500,000

30. Compute the undervaluation penalty for each of the following independent cases involving the executor's reporting of the value of a closely held business in the decedent's gross estate. In each case, assume a marginal estate tax rate of 50%.

	Reported Value	Corrected IRS Valuation
a.	$12,000	$ 15,000
b.	50,000	90,000
c.	50,000	150,000
d.	50,000	200,000

31. Arnold made a charitable contribution of property that he valued at $20,000. He deducted this amount as an itemized deduction on his tax return. The IRS can prove that the real value of the property is $8,000. Arnold is in the 31% income tax bracket. Determine Arnold's overvaluation penalty.

32. Marla owns and operates a tavern. Because she had been keeping "two sets of books," one for herself and one for the benefit of the IRS, she has been charged with civil fraud in the District Court. The IRS assesses an additional $75,000 in taxes, but Marla shows by a preponderence of the evidence that half of that amount was due to her negligence, not to her fraudulent actions. Compute Marla's civil fraud tax penalty in this matter.

33. Moose, a former professional athlete, now supplements his income by signing autographs at collectors' shows. Unfortunately, Moose has not been conscientious about reporting all of this income on his tax return. Now the IRS has charged him with additional taxes of $50,000 due to negligence in his record keeping and $80,000 due to an intent to defraud the U.S. of income taxes. No criminal fraud charges are brought against Moose. The District Court finds by a preponderance of the evidence that only half of the $80,000 underpayment was due to Moose's fraudulent action; the remainder was due to his negligence. Compute the accuracy-related and civil fraud penalties in this matter.

34. Trudy's AGI last year was $50,000. Her Federal income tax came to $16,000, which she paid through a combination of withholding and estimated payments. This year, her AGI will be $170,000, with a projected tax liability of $46,000, all to be paid through estimates. Ignore the annualized income method. Compute Trudy's quarterly estimated payment schedule for this year.

35. Kold Corporation estimates that its 1998 taxable income will be $900,000. Thus, it is subject to a flat 34% income tax rate and incurs a $306,000 liability. For each of the following independent cases, compute Kold's minimum quarterly estimated tax payments that will avoid an underpayment penalty.
    a. For 1997, taxable income was ($100,000). Kold carried back all of this loss to prior years and exhausted the entire net operating loss in creating a zero 1997 liability.
    b. For 1997, taxable income was $200,000, and tax liability was $68,000.
    c. For 1996, taxable income was $2 million, and tax liability was $680,000. For 1997, taxable income was $200,000, and tax liability was $68,000.

36. When Maggie accepted employment with Martin Corporation, she completed a Form W–4 listing 14 exemptions. Since Maggie was single and had no dependents, she

misrepresented the situation on Form W–4. What penalties, if any, might the IRS impose upon Maggie?

37. The Scooter Company, owned equally by Julie (chair of the board of directors) and Jeff (company president), is in very difficult financial straits. Last month, Jeff used the $100,000 withheld from employee paychecks for Federal payroll and income taxes to pay off a creditor who threatened to cut off all supplies. To keep the company afloat, Jeff used these government funds willfully for the operations of the business, but even that effort was not enough. The company missed the next two payrolls, and today other creditors took action to shut down Scooter altogether. How much will the IRS assess in taxes and penalties in this matter, and from whom? How can you as a tax professional best offer service to Julie, Jeff, and Scooter? Address these matters in a memo for the tax research file.

38. What is the applicable statute of limitations in each of the following independent situations?
    a. No return was filed by the taxpayer.
    b. In 1992, the taxpayer incurred a bad debt loss that she failed to claim.
    c. On his 1992 return, a taxpayer inadvertently omitted a large amount of gross income.
    d. Same as (c), except that the omission was deliberate.
    e. For 1992, a taxpayer innocently overstated her deductions by a large amount.

39. Suzanne (a calendar year taxpayer) had the following transactions, all of which were properly reported on a timely filed return.

Gross receipts		$ 960,000
Cost of sales		(800,000)
Gross profit		$ 160,000
Capital gain	$ 72,000	
Capital loss	(24,000)	48,000
Total income		$ 208,000

   a. Presuming the absence of fraud, how much of an omission from gross income is required before the six-year statute of limitations applies?
   b. Would it matter if cost of sales had been inadvertently overstated by $100,000?
   c. How does the situation change in the context of fraud by Suzanne?

40. On April 2, 1994, Mark filed his 1993 income tax return, which showed a tax due of $40,000. On June 1, 1996, he filed an amended return for 1993 that showed an additional tax of $12,000. Mark paid the additional amount. On May 18, 1997, Mark filed a claim for a refund of $18,000.
    a. If Mark's claim for a refund is correct in amount, how much tax will he recover?
    b. What is the period that interest runs with respect to Mark's claim for a refund?
    c. How would you have advised him differently?

41. Mimi had $40,000 withheld in 1993. Due to a sizable amount of itemized deductions, she figured that she had no further tax to pay for the year. For this reason and because of personal problems, and without securing an extension, she did not file her 1993 return until July 1, 1994. Actually, the return showed a refund of $2,400, which Mimi ultimately received. On May 10, 1997, Mimi filed a $16,000 claim for refund of her 1993 taxes.
    a. How much, if any, of the $16,000 may Mimi recover?
    b. Would it have made any difference if Mimi had requested and secured from the IRS an extension of time for filing her 1993 tax return?

42. Rod's Federal income tax returns (Form 1040) for the past three years were prepared by the following persons.

Year	Preparer
1995	Rod
1996	Ann
1997	Cheryl

Ann is Rod's next-door neighbor and owns and operates a pharmacy. Cheryl is a licensed CPA and is engaged in private practice. In the event Rod is audited and all three returns are examined, who may represent him before the IRS at the agent level? Who may represent Rod before the Appeals Division?

43. Discuss which penalties, if any, might be imposed on the tax adviser in each of the following independent circumstances. In this regard, assume that the tax adviser:
    a. suggested to the client various means by which to acquire excludible income.
    b. suggested to the client various means by which to conceal cash receipts from gross income.
    c. suggested to the client means by which to improve her cash flow by delaying for six months or more the deposit of the employee's share of Federal employment taxes.
    d. kept in his own safe deposit box the concealed income of item (c).
    e. failed, because of pressing time conflicts, to conduct the usual review of the client's tax return. The IRS later discovered that the return included fraudulent data.
    f. failed, because of pressing time conflicts, to conduct the usual review of the client's tax return. The IRS later discovered a mathematical error in the computation of the personal exemption.

44. Compute the preparer penalty that the IRS could assess on Gerry in each of the following independent cases.
    a. On March 21, the copy machine was not working, so Gerry gave original returns to her thirty clients that day without providing any duplicates for them. Copies for Gerry's files and for use in preparing state tax returns had been made on March 20.
    b. Because Gerry extended her vacation a few days, she missed the Annual Tax Update seminar that she usually attends. As a result, she was unaware that Congress had changed a law affecting limited partnerships. The change affected the transactions of 20 of Gerry's clients, all of whom understated their tax as a result.
    c. Gerry heard that the IRS was increasing its audits of corporations that hold assets in a foreign trust. As a result, Gerry instructed the intern who prepared the initial drafts of the returns for three corporate clients to leave blank the question about such trusts. Not wanting to lose his position, the intern, a senior accounting major at State University, complied with Gerry's instructions.

45. You are the chair of the Ethics Committee of your state's CPA Licensing Commission. Interpret controlling AICPA authority in addressing the following assertions by your membership.
    a. When a CPA has reasonable grounds for not answering an applicable question on a client's return, a brief explanation of the reason for the omission should not be provided, because it would flag the return for audit by the IRS.
    b. If a CPA discovers during an IRS audit that the client has a material error in the return under examination, he should immediately withdraw from the engagement.
    c. If the client tells you that she had contributions of $500 for unsubstantiated cash donations to her church, you should deduct an odd amount on her return (e.g., $499), because an even amount ($500) would indicate to the IRS that her deduction was based on an estimate.
    d. Basing an expense deduction on the client's estimates is not acceptable.
    e. If a CPA knows that the client has a material error in a prior year's return, he should not, without the client's consent, disclose the error to the IRS.
    f. If a CPA's client will not correct a material error in a prior year's return, the CPA should not prepare the current year's return for the client.

RESEARCH PROBLEMS

*Note: **West's Federal Taxation on CD-ROM** can be used in preparing solutions to the Research Problems. Alternatively, tax research materials contained in a standard tax library can be used.*

Research Problem 1. Leigh Van Camp was convicted of underpayment of Federal income tax. He had set up several branches of the "Church of America's Salvation" in Arizona, and he was found to have used church donations to support an extravagant lifestyle for himself and his family, rather than to advance the goals of the church. In the Tax Court proceedings, Leigh bargained down the charges from criminal fraud to mere underpayment of tax. Nevertheless, the settlement did not end the bad feelings between Leigh and personnel in the local IRS office.

Leigh owed $250,000 in interest, penalty, and tax after the Tax Court issued its verdict. He placed $200,000 in escrow with respect to this tax. IRS agents then received a tip that Leigh had sold his largest remaining asset, the family home, and was "moving to Niagara Falls in two days." Fearing that Leigh would leave the country without paying the tax from the court settlement or the tax on the gain from the sale of the residence, the agents placed a jeopardy assessment on the $500,000 cash proceeds of the sale.

Angry at the way the IRS is intruding into his life, Leigh calls you from New York and hires you to "get the IRS off my back" and obtain the return of his funds in full. Assess the IRS's position in a memo to the research file.

Partial list of research aids:
Reg. §§1.6851–1(a)(1)(i) through (iii).
Robert Lee McWilliams, 103 T.C. 320 (1994).

Research Problem 2. Fast Track, Inc., has put together a highly successful five-year operation renovating old housing units in the Lincoln Park area of Chicago. The company acquires properties at very low prices, uses nonunion and retired employees and contractors to revive the residential and common areas, and enjoys various state and Federal tax credits, local rehabilitation grants, and low-interest bank loans in a manner that produces a very impressive tax and accounting profit.

Cash flow is another story. For the nine months a unit is under renovation, Fast Track generates no revenues, so it must meet expenses with income, loan, or grant monies from other sources. For the operation's first five years, that was no problem, but this winter was particularly harsh, and Fast Track found itself in tough straits several times. Once, on the day of a deadline for remitting withheld Federal income and payroll taxes, Fast Track used those funds to cover operating expenses instead.

Fast Track carried out this misappropriation through instructions to the Lincoln Park Bank, with which it had built a successful relationship. The bank virtually ran Fast Track's checking account and operating loans, applying rules that the two parties had developed for the timing and amount of payments to be made. This arrangement allowed the bank to maintain significant control and monitoring over Fast Track's funds; in exchange, the bank did not charge Fast Track service fees for any of its accounts.

Six months later, the IRS discovered the company's failure to pay the withholdings. With respect to your client, Barbara Williams, a Fast Track construction employee, the IRS has determined that $1,000 of income tax and $1,500 of Social Security taxes are due before penalties and interest are computed. Write a memo to the tax research file discussing from whom the IRS can assess the $2,500 in taxes due—Williams, Fast Track, or the bank.

Research Problem 3. Blanche Creek (111 Elm Avenue, Patriotville, IN 40123) has engaged you because she feels that she has been subjected to double jeopardy with respect to her 1995 tax return. Last year, revenue agent Brad Johnson completed a review of Blanche's itemized deductions and alternative minimum tax computations. Both sides agreed to a small settlement, and Blanche assumed that the matter was closed. Now she has received a letter requesting a field audit, to be conducted by revenue agent Gloria Perez, to examine the deductions claimed by Blanche's S corporation, which accounts for about 70% of Blanche's adjusted gross income every year. Blanche's nephew, a tax attorney, found Code § 7605(b), which states:

> No taxpayer shall be subjected to unnecessary examination or investigations, and only one inspection of a taxpayer's books of account shall be made for each taxable year unless the taxpayer requests otherwise. . . .

Write a letter to Blanche, addressing only the application of § 7605(b) to her situation. She has not hired you to do the work for the S corporation audit, nor is Blanche currently a client of yours.

Partial list of research aids:
Donald R. Digby, 103 T.C. 441 (1994).

Use the tax resources of the internet to address the following questions. Do not restrict your search to the World Wide Web, but include a review of newsgroups and general reference materials, practitioner sites and resources, primary sources of the tax law, chat rooms and discussion groups, and other opportunities.

Research Problem 4.   Find an article in which a tax professional describes the audit process and offers suggestions to taxpayers as to how to interact with IRS audit personnel.

Research Problem 5.   Who is your IRS District Director? What is his or her address and phone number? Who is your state's Secretary of Revenue? What is his or her address and phone number?

Research Problem 6.   How much money did the Treasury collect last year in income tax penalties? Interest? Fees for ruling requests? You might need to send an e-mail request to answer these queries.

FAMILY TAX PLANNING

Family tax planning has as its objective the minimization of *all* taxes imposed on the family unit. Carrying out this objective requires familiarity with the rules applicable to transfers by gift and by death. These rules must then be applied to reduce the transfer tax burden. Also to be considered are the income tax consequences of the transfers made. Finally, entities created as a result of these transfers (trusts and estates) are subject to unique income tax rules.

17

THE FEDERAL GIFT AND ESTATE TAXES

LEARNING OBJECTIVES

After completing Chapter 17, you should be able to:

1. Understand the nature of the Federal gift and estate taxes.

2. Work with the Federal gift tax formula.

3. Work with the Federal estate tax formula.

4. Explain the operation of the Federal gift tax.

5. Explain the computation of the Federal gift tax.

6. Describe the components of the gross estate.

7. Describe the components of the taxable estate.

8. Determine the Federal estate tax liability.

9. Appreciate the role of the generation skipping transfer tax.

TRANSFER TAXES—IN GENERAL

Until now, this text has dealt primarily with the various applications of the Federal income tax. Also important in the Federal tax structure are various excise taxes that cover transfers of property. Sometimes called transaction taxes, excise taxes are based on the value of the property transferred, not on the income derived from the property. Two such taxes—the Federal gift tax and the Federal estate tax—are the central focus of Chapters 17 and 18.

The importance of being familiar with rules governing transfer taxes can be shown with a simple illustration.

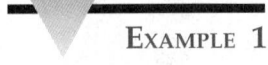

EXAMPLE 1

After 20 years of marriage to George, Helen decides to elope with Mark, a bachelor and long-time friend. Helen and Mark travel to a country in the Caribbean where Helen obtains a divorce, and she and Mark are married. Fifteen years later, Helen dies. Her will leaves all of her property (estimated value of $2,600,000) to Mark. Under the unlimited marital deduction (discussed later in the chapter), Helen's estate has no tax to pay. ▼

But the marital deduction applies only to transfers between husband and wife. Suppose the jurisdiction where Helen and Mark live does not recognize the validity of divorces granted by the Caribbean country involved. If this is the case, Helen and Mark are not married because Helen was never legally divorced from George. If Mark is not Helen's spouse, no marital deduction is available. Helen's estate must pay an estate tax of $780,800.

NATURE OF THE TAXES

1 LEARNING OBJECTIVE
Understand the nature of the Federal gift and estate taxes.

Before the enactment of the Tax Reform Act of 1976, Federal law imposed a tax on the gratuitous transfer of property in one of two ways. If the transfer occurred during the owner's life, it was subject to the Federal gift tax. If the property passed by virtue of the death of the owner, the Federal estate tax applied. The two taxes were governed by different rules including separate sets of tax rates. As Congress felt that lifetime transfers of wealth should be encouraged, the gift tax rates were lower than the estate tax rates.

The Tax Reform Act of 1976 significantly changed the approach taken by the Federal gift and estate taxes. Much of the distinction between life and death transfers was eliminated. Instead of subjecting these transfers to two separate tax rate schedules, the Act substituted a **unified transfer tax** that covers all gratuitous

---

TAX IN THE NEWS

DO TRANSFER TAXES ADVERSELY AFFECT THE ECONOMY?

A recent study found that transfer taxes (i.e., estate and gift taxes) impose especially high economic costs in terms of lost savings and capital formation. This burden is particularly high on small family-owned businesses.

As another layer of tax on savings, transfer taxes increase the cost of wealth accumulation as compared to the cost of consumption. According to an econometric simulation of what would have happened to the U.S. economy between 1971 and 1991 without Federal transfer taxes, 262,000 more jobs would have been created, the stock of capital would have been $398.6 billion higher, and the gross domestic product would have been $46.3 billion higher in 1991.

The study concludes that repeal of the Federal estate and gift taxes would strengthen the incentive people have to create capital and would lead to higher wages, greater employment, and larger overall tax collections over the long run.

SOURCE: Richard E. Wagner, *Federal Transfer Taxation: A Study in Social Cost* (Washington, D.C.: Institute for Research on the Economics of Taxation, The Center for the Study of Taxation, 1993).

---

transfers. Thus, gifts are subject to a gift tax at the same rates as those applicable to transfers at death. In addition, current law eliminates the prior exemptions allowed under each tax and replaces them with a unified tax credit.

The Federal estate tax dates from 1916 and, like many taxes, was originally enacted to generate additional revenue in anticipation of this country's entry into World War I. The tax is designed to tax transfers at death. It may also have some application to lifetime transfers that become complete upon the death of the donor or to certain gifts made within three years of death.

The estate tax differs in several respects from the typical **inheritance tax** imposed by many states and some local jurisdictions. First, the Federal estate tax is imposed on the decedent's entire estate. It is a tax on the right to pass property at death. Inheritance taxes are taxes on the right to receive property at death and are therefore levied on the heirs. Second, the relationship of the heirs to the decedent usually has a direct bearing on the inheritance tax. In general, the more closely related the parties, the larger the exemption and the lower the applicable rates.[1] Except for transfers to a surviving spouse that may result in a marital deduction, the relationship of the heirs to the decedent has no effect on the Federal estate tax.

The Federal gift tax, enacted later, was designed to make the income and estate taxes more effective. Congress felt that individuals should not be able to give away property—thereby shifting the income tax consequences to others and avoiding estate taxes—without incurring some tax liability. The result is the Federal gift tax, which covers inter vivos (lifetime) transfers.

---

[1] For example, one state's inheritance tax provides an exemption of $50,000 for surviving spouses, with rates ranging from 5% to 10% on the taxable portion. In contrast, an exemption of only $1,000 is provided for strangers (persons unrelated to the deceased), with rates ranging from 14% to 18% on the taxable portion. Other exemptions and rates between these extremes cover beneficiaries variously related to the decedent.

The Federal gift tax is imposed on the right to transfer property by one person (the donor) to another (the donee) for less than full and adequate consideration. The tax is payable by the donor.[2] If the donor fails to pay the tax when due, the donee may be held liable for the tax to the extent of the value of the property received.[3]

Persons Subject to the Tax.   To determine whether a transfer is subject to the Federal gift tax, first ascertain if the donor is a citizen or resident of the United States. If the donor is not a citizen or a resident, it is important to determine whether the property involved in the gift was situated within the United States.

The Federal gift tax is applied to all transfers by gift of property wherever located by individuals who, at the time of the gift, were *citizens* or *residents* of the United States. The term "United States" includes only the 50 states and the District of Columbia; it does not include U.S. possessions or territories.[4] For a U.S. citizen, the place of residence at the time of the gift is irrelevant.

For individuals who are neither citizens nor residents of the United States, the Federal gift tax is applied only to gifts of property situated within the United States.[5] A gift of intangible personal property (stocks and bonds) by a nonresident alien usually is not subject to the Federal gift tax.[6]

A gift by a corporation is considered a gift by the individual shareholders. A gift to a corporation is generally considered a gift to the individual shareholders. In certain cases, however, a gift to a charitable, public, political, or similar organization may be regarded as a gift to the organization as a single entity.[7]

The Federal estate tax is applied to the entire estate of a decedent who, at the time of death, was a resident or citizen of the United States. If the decedent was a U.S. citizen, the residence at death makes no difference.[8]

If the decedent was neither a resident nor a citizen of the United States at the time of death, the Federal estate tax is imposed on the value of any property located within the United States. In that case, the tax determination is controlled by a separate subchapter of the Internal Revenue Code.[9] In certain instances, the tax consequences outlined in the Code may have been modified by death tax conventions (treaties) between the United States and various foreign countries.[10] Further coverage of this area is beyond the scope of this text. The following discussion is limited to the tax treatment of decedents who were residents or citizens of the United States at the time of death.[11]

2   LEARNING OBJECTIVE
Work with the Federal gift tax formula.

Formula for the Gift Tax.   Like the income tax, which uses taxable income (not gross income) as a tax base, the gift tax usually does not apply to the full amount

---

[2] § 2502(c).

[3] § 6324(b). Known as the doctrine of transferee liability, this rule also operates to enable the IRS to enforce the collection of other taxes (e.g., income tax, estate tax).

[4] § 7701(a)(9).

[5] § 2511(a).

[6] §§ 2501(a)(2) and (3). But see § 2511(b) and Reg. §§ 25.2511–3(b)(2), (3), and (4) for exceptions.

[7] Reg. §§ 25.0–1(b) and 25.2511–1(h)(1). But note the exemption from the Federal gift tax for certain transfers to political organizations discussed later.

[8] § 2001(a). If a person renounces U.S. citizenship so as to avoid estate taxes, § 2107 imposes a 10-year waiting period before the loss of citizenship is effective.

[9] Subchapter B (§§ 2101 through 2108) covers the estate tax treatment of decedents who are neither residents nor citizens. Sub-

chapter A (§§ 2001 through 2056A) covers the estate tax treatment of those who are either residents or citizens.

[10] At present, the United States has death tax conventions with the following countries: Australia, Austria, Denmark, Finland, France, Germany, Greece, Ireland, Italy, Japan, Netherlands, Norway, Republic of South Africa, Sweden, Switzerland, and the United Kingdom. The United States has gift tax conventions with Australia, France, Germany, Japan, and the United Kingdom.

[11] Further information concerning Subchapter B (§§ 2101 through 2108) can be obtained from the relevant Code Sections (and the related Treasury Regulations). See also the Instructions to Form 706NA (U.S. Estate Tax Return of Nonresident Not a Citizen of the U.S.).

▼ **FIGURE 17–1**
Formula for the Federal Gift Tax

Determine whether the transfers are considered gifts by referring to §§ 2511 through 2519; list the fair market value of only the covered transfers		$xxx,xxx
Determine the deductions allowed by § 2522 (charitable) and § 2523 (marital)	$ xx,xxx	
Claim the annual exclusion (per donee) under § 2503(b), if available	10,000	xx,xxx
Taxable gifts [as defined by § 2503(a)] for the current period		$ xx,xxx
Add: Taxable gifts from prior years		xx,xxx
Total of current and past taxable gifts		$ xx,xxx
Compute the gift tax on the total of current and past taxable gifts by using the rates in Appendix A		$ x,xxx
Subtract: Gift tax paid or deemed paid on past taxable gifts and the unified tax credit		xxx
Gift tax due on transfers during the current period		$ xxx

of the gift. Deductions and the annual exclusion may be allowed to arrive at an amount called the **taxable gift.** However, unlike the income tax, which does not consider taxable income from prior years, *prior taxable gifts* must be added in arriving at the tax base to which the unified transfer tax rate is applied. Otherwise, the donor could start over again each year with a new set of progressive rates.

EXAMPLE 2

Don makes taxable gifts of $500,000 in 1985 and $500,000 in 1997. Presuming no other taxable gifts and *disregarding the effect of the unified tax credit,* Don must pay a tax of $155,800 (see Appendix A, page A–7) on the 1985 transfer and a tax of $345,800 on the 1997 transfer (using a tax base of $1 million). If the 1985 taxable gift had not been included in the tax base for the 1997 gift, the tax would have been $155,800. The correct tax liability of $345,800 is more than twice $155,800! ▼

Because the gift tax is cumulative in effect, a credit is allowed against the gift taxes paid (or deemed paid) on prior taxable gifts included in the tax base. The deemed paid credit is explained later in the chapter.

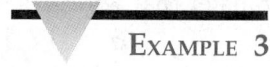

EXAMPLE 3

Assume the same facts as in Example 2. Don will be allowed a credit of $155,800 against the gift tax of $345,800. Thus, his gift tax liability for 1997 becomes $190,000 ($345,800 – $155,800). ▼

In 1982, the annual exclusion was increased from $3,000 to $10,000. By allowing larger amounts to be exempt from the gift tax, taxpayer compliance may improve, as the tax will apply only to larger, planned gifts and not to day-to-day transfers. As noted in Chapter 1, the result is to ease the audit function of the IRS.

The formula for the gift tax is summarized in Figure 17–1. (Note: Section [§] references are to the portion of the Internal Revenue Code involved.)

3 **LEARNING OBJECTIVE**
Work with the Federal estate tax formula.

Formula for the Federal Estate Tax. The Federal unified transfer tax at death, commonly known as the Federal estate tax, is summarized in Figure 17–2. (Note: Section [§] references are to the portion of the Internal Revenue Code involved.)

The reason post-1976 taxable gifts are added to the taxable estate to arrive at the tax base goes back to the scheme of the unified transfer tax. Starting in 1977, all

▼ **FIGURE 17–2**
Formula for the Federal Estate Tax

Gross estate (§§ 2031–2046)		$xxx,xxx
Subtract:		
Expenses, indebtedness, and taxes (§ 2053)	$xx	
Losses (§ 2054)	xx	
Charitable bequests (§ 2055)	xx	
Marital deduction (§§ 2056 and 2056A)	xx	x,xxx
Taxable estate (§ 2051)		$ xx,xxx
Add: Post-1976 taxable gifts [§ 2001(b)]		x,xxx
Tax base		$xxx,xxx
Tentative tax on total transfers [§ 2001(c)]		$ xx,xxx
Subtract:		
Unified transfer tax on post-1976 taxable gifts (gift taxes paid or deemed paid)	$xx	
Tax credits (including the unified tax credit) (§§ 2010–2016)	xx	x,xxx
Estate tax due		$ xxx

transfers, whether lifetime or by death, are treated the same. Consequently, taxable gifts made after 1976 must be accounted for upon the death of the donor. Note that the double tax effect of including these gifts is mitigated by allowing a credit against the estate tax for the gift taxes previously paid or deemed paid.

Role of the Unified Tax Credit. Before the unified transfer tax, the gift tax allowed a $30,000 specific exemption for the lifetime of the donor. A comparable $60,000 exemption was allowed for estate tax purposes. The purpose of these exemptions was to allow donors and decedents to transfer modest amounts of wealth without being subject to the gift and estate taxes. Unfortunately, inflation took its toll, and more taxpayers became subject to these transfer taxes than Congress believed was appropriate. The congressional solution was to rescind the exemptions and replace them with the **unified tax credit.**[12]

To curtail revenue loss, the credit was phased in as shown in Table 17–1.

The **exemption equivalent** is the amount of the transfer that will pass free of the gift or estate tax by virtue of the credit.

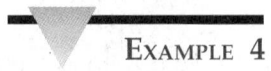

EXAMPLE 4

In 1997, Janet makes a taxable gift of $600,000. Presuming she has made no prior taxable gifts, Janet will not owe any gift tax. Under the tax rate schedules (see Appendix A, page A–7), the tax on $600,000 is $192,800, which is the exact amount of the credit allowed.[13] ▼

The Tax Reform Act of 1976 allowed donors one last chance to use the $30,000 specific exemption on lifetime gifts. If, however, the exemption was used on gifts made after September 8, 1976 (and before January 1, 1977), the unified tax credit must be reduced by 20 percent of the exemption utilized.[14] The credit must be adjusted whether the gift tax or the estate tax is involved. No adjustment is

---

[12] §§ 2010 and 2505.
[13] The rate schedules are contained in § 2001(c).

[14] §§ 2010(c) and 2505(c).

▼ **TABLE 17–1**
Phase-in of Unified Tax Credit

Year of Death	Amount of Credit	Amount of Exemption Equivalent
1977	$ 30,000	$120,667
1978	34,000	134,000
1979	38,000	147,333
1980	42,500	161,563
1981	47,000	175,625
1982	62,800	225,000
1983	79,300	275,000
1984	96,300	325,000
1985	121,800	400,000
1986	155,800	500,000
1987 & thereafter	192,800	600,000

necessary for post-1976 gifts since the specific exemption was no longer available for such transfers.

EXAMPLE 5

Net of the annual exclusion, Myrtle, a widow, made gifts of $10,000 in June 1976 and $20,000 in December 1976. Assume Myrtle has never used any of her specific exemption and chooses to use the full $30,000 to cover the 1976 gifts. Under these circumstances, the unified tax credit will be reduced by $4,000 (20% × $20,000). The use of the specific exemption on transfers made before September 9, 1976, has no effect on the credit. ▼

VALUATION FOR ESTATE AND GIFT TAX PURPOSES

The value of the property on the date of its transfer generally determines the amount that is subject to the gift tax or the estate tax. Under certain conditions, however, an executor can elect to value estate assets on the **alternate valuation date** (§ 2032).

The alternate valuation date election was designed as a relief provision to ease the economic hardship that could result when estate assets decline in value over the six months after the date of death. If the election is made, all assets of the estate are valued six months after death *or* on the date of disposition if this occurs earlier.[15] The election covers *all* assets in the gross estate and cannot be applied to only a portion of the property.

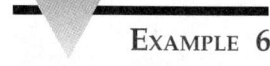

EXAMPLE 6

Robert's gross estate consists of the following property:

	Value on Date of Death	Value Six Months Later
Land	$ 800,000	$ 840,000
Stock in Brown Corporation	900,000	700,000
Stock in Green Corporation	500,000	460,000
Total	$2,200,000	$2,000,000

[15] § 2032(a).

If Robert's executor elects the alternate valuation date, the estate must be valued at $2,000,000. It is not permissible to value the land at its date of death value ($800,000) and choose the alternate valuation date for the rest of the gross estate. ▼

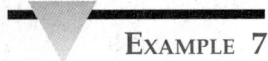

EXAMPLE 7

Assume the same facts as in Example 6 except that the executor sells the stock in Green Corporation for $480,000 four months after Robert's death. If the alternate valuation date is elected, the estate must be valued at $2,020,000 ($840,000 + $700,000 + $480,000). As to the Green stock, the value on its date of disposition controls because that date occurred prior to the six months' alternate valuation date. ▼

The alternate valuation date election is not available unless the estate must file a Form 706 (Estate Tax Return). When an estate is required to file a Form 706 is discussed later in this chapter.

The election of the alternate valuation date must decrease the value of the gross estate *and* decrease the estate tax liability.[16] The reason for this last requirement is that the income tax basis of property acquired from a decedent will be the value used for estate tax purposes (discussed further in Chapter 18).[17] Without a special limitation, the alternate valuation date could be elected solely to add to income tax basis.

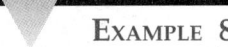

EXAMPLE 8

Al's gross estate is comprised of assets with a date of death value of $1,000,000 and an alternate valuation date value of $1,100,000. Under Al's will, all of his property passes outright to Jean (Al's wife). Because of the marital deduction, no estate tax results regardless of which value is used. But if the alternate valuation date could be elected, Jean would have an income tax basis of $1,100,000 in the property acquired from Al. ▼

The alternate valuation date cannot be elected in Example 8 for two reasons, either of which would suffice. First, the alternate valuation date will not decrease Al's gross estate. Second, the election will not decrease Al's estate tax liability. Thus, his estate must use the date of death valuation of $1,000,000. As a result, Jean's income tax basis in the property received from Al is $1,000,000.

Another valuation option available for estate tax purposes is the special use valuation method. Election of this method is limited to certain situations involving interests in closely held businesses (usually farms). Special use valuation is discussed in Chapter 18.

KEY PROPERTY CONCEPTS

When property is transferred either by gift or by death, the form of ownership can have a direct bearing on any transfer tax consequences. Understanding the different forms of ownership is necessary for working with Federal gift and estate taxes.

Undivided Ownership.   Assume Dan and Vicky own an undivided but equal interest in a tract of land. Such ownership can fall into any of four categories: joint tenancy, tenancy by the entirety, tenancy in common, or community property.

If Dan and Vicky hold ownership as **joint tenants** or **tenants by the entirety,** the right of survivorship exists. This means that the last tenant to survive receives full ownership of the property. Thus, if Dan predeceases Vicky, the land belongs entirely to Vicky. None of the land will pass to Dan's heirs or will be subject to

---

[16] § 2032(c).   [17] § 1014(a).

administration by Dan's executor. A tenancy by the entirety is a joint tenancy between husband and wife.

If Dan and Vicky hold ownership as **tenants in common** or as community property, death does not defeat an owner's interest. Thus, if Dan predeceases Vicky, Dan's one-half interest in the land will pass to his estate or heirs.

Community property interests arise from the marital relationship. Normally, all property acquired after marriage, except by gift or inheritance, by husband and wife residing in a community property state becomes part of the community. The following states have the community property system in effect: Louisiana, Texas, New Mexico, Arizona, California, Washington, Idaho, Nevada, and Wisconsin. All other states follow the common law system of ascertaining a spouse's rights to property acquired after marriage.

Partial Interests. Interests in assets can be divided in terms of rights to income and principal. Particularly when property is placed in trust, it is not uncommon to carve out various income interests that must be accounted for separately from the ultimate disposition of the property itself.

EXAMPLE 9

Under Bill's will, a ranch is to be placed in trust, life estate to Sam, Bill's son, with remainder to Sam's children (Bill's grandchildren). Under this arrangement, Sam is the life tenant and, as such, is entitled to the use of the ranch (including any income) during his life. Upon Sam's death, the trust terminates, and its principal passes to his children. Thus, Sam's children receive outright ownership in the ranch when Sam dies. ▼

THE FEDERAL GIFT TAX

GENERAL CONSIDERATIONS

4 **LEARNING OBJECTIVE**
Explain the operation of the Federal gift tax.

Requirements for a Gift. For a gift to be complete under state law, the following elements must be present:

- A donor competent to make the gift.
- A donee capable of receiving and possessing the property.
- Donative intent on behalf of the donor.
- Actual or constructive delivery of the property to the donee or the donee's representative.
- Acceptance of the gift by the donee.

Incomplete Transfers. The Federal gift tax does not apply to transfers that are incomplete. Thus, if the transferor retains the right to reclaim the property or has not really parted with the possession of the property, a taxable event has not taken place.

EXAMPLE 10

Lesly creates a trust, income payable to Mary for life, remainder to Paul. Under the terms of the trust instrument, Lesly can revoke the trust at any time and repossess the trust principal and the income earned. No gift takes place on the creation of the trust; Lesly has not ceased to have dominion and control over the property. ▼

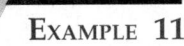

EXAMPLE 11

Assume the same facts as in Example 10, except that one year after the transfer, Lesly relinquishes his right to terminate the trust. At this point, the transfer becomes complete, and the Federal gift tax applies. ▼

> ### TAX IN THE NEWS
>
> #### IS AN ANNUITY TO SETTLE A PALIMONY CLAIM A GIFT?
>
> A wealthy banker entered into a "close and exclusive" relationship with a woman not his wife. To devote more time to the banker, the banker's friend closed an interior decorating business she was operating. After nine years, the banker ended the relationship. To keep the matter from becoming public and to secure his friend's release from any support claim (i.e., palimony), the banker purchased a 20-year annuity for her. The relationship and its settlement remained secret until the banker died a decade later.
>
> The IRS is pursuing the banker's estate for the gift tax that should have been paid as a result of the annuity settlement. The estate maintains that the settlement was not a gift but was in "exchange for a good and valuable consideration." According to the estate, the consideration was the "general release" from any support claim signed by the former companion and her agreement not to disclose the relationship.
>
> At this time, the controversy is still pending before the U.S. Tax Court.

Business versus Personal Setting. In a business setting, full and adequate consideration is apt to exist. Regulation § 25.2512–8 provides that "a sale, exchange, or other transfer of property made in the ordinary course of business (a transaction that is bona fide, at arm's length, and free of any donative intent) will be considered as made for an adequate and full consideration in money or money's worth." If the parties are acting in a personal setting, however, a gift usually is the result.

EXAMPLE 12   Grace loans money to Debby in connection with a business venture. About a year later, Grace forgives part of the loan. Grace probably has not made a gift to Debby if she and Debby are unrelated parties.[18] ▼

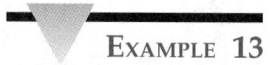

EXAMPLE 13   Assume the same facts as in Example 12, except that Grace and Debby are mother and daughter and no business venture is involved. If the loan itself was not actually a disguised gift, the later forgiveness is probably a gift. ▼

Regulation § 25.2512–8 also holds that valuable consideration (such as would preclude a gift result) does not include a payment or transfer based on "love and affection . . . promise of marriage, etc." Consequently, property settlements in consideration of marriage (i.e., pre- or antenuptial agreements) are regarded as gifts.

Do not conclude that the presence of *some* consideration is enough to preclude Federal gift tax consequences. Again, the answer may rest on whether the transfer occurred in a business setting.

EXAMPLE 14   Peter sells Bob some real estate for $40,000. Unknown to Peter, the property contains valuable mineral deposits and is really worth $100,000. Peter may have made a bad business deal, but he has not made a gift of $60,000 to Bob. ▼

---

[18] The forgiveness could result in taxable income to Debby under § 61(a)(12).

EXAMPLE 15

Assume the same facts as in Example 14, except that Peter and Bob are father and son. In addition, Peter is very much aware that the property is worth $100,000. Peter has made a gift of $60,000 to Bob. ▼

Certain Excluded Transfers. Transfers to political organizations are exempt from the application of the Federal gift tax.[19] This provision in the Code made unnecessary the previous practice whereby candidates for public office established multiple campaign committees to maximize the number of annual exclusions available to their contributors. As noted later, an annual exclusion of $10,000 (previously $3,000) for each donee passes free of the Federal gift tax.

The Federal gift tax does not apply to tuition payments made to an educational organization (e.g., a college) on another's behalf. Nor does it apply to amounts paid on another's behalf for medical care.[20] In this regard, the law is realistic since it is unlikely that most donors would recognize these items as transfers subject to the gift tax.

Satisfying an obligation of support is not subject to the gift tax. Thus, no gift takes place when parents pay for their children's education because one of the obligations of parents is to educate their children. What constitutes an obligation of support is determined by applicable state law.

Lifetime versus Death Transfers. Be careful to distinguish between lifetime (inter vivos) and death (testamentary) transfers.

EXAMPLE 16

Wilber buys a U.S. savings bond, which he registers as follows: "Wilber, payable to Alice upon Wilber's death." No gift is made when Wilber buys the bond; Alice has received only a mere expectancy (i.e., to obtain ownership of the bond at Wilber's death). Anytime before his death, Wilber may redeem or otherwise dispose of the bond and cut off Alice's interest. On Wilber's death, no gift is made because the bond passes to Alice by testamentary disposition. As noted later, the bond will be included in Wilber's gross estate as property in which the decedent had an interest (§ 2033). ▼

TRANSFERS SUBJECT TO THE GIFT TAX

Whether a transfer is subject to the Federal gift tax depends upon the application of §§ 2511 through 2519 and the applicable Regulations.

Gift Loans. To understand the tax ramifications of gift loans, an illustration is helpful.

EXAMPLE 17

Before his daughter (Denise) leaves for college, Victor lends her $300,000. Denise signs a note that provides for repayment in five years. The loan contains no interest element, and neither Victor nor Denise expects any interest to be paid. Following Victor's advice, Denise invests the loan proceeds in income-producing securities. During her five years in college, she uses the income from the investments to pay for college costs and other living expenses. On the maturity date of the note, Denise repays the $300,000 she owes Victor. ▼

In a gift loan arrangement, the following consequences ensue:

- Victor has made a gift to Denise of the interest element. The amount of the gift is determined by the difference between the amount of interest charged

---

[19] § 2501(a)(5).   [20] § 2503(e).

(in this case, none) and the market rate (as determined by the yield on certain U.S. government securities).

- The interest element is included in Victor's gross income and is subject to the Federal income tax.
- Denise may be allowed an income tax deduction for the interest element, but may benefit from this result only if she is in a position to itemize her deductions *from* adjusted gross income.

The Code defines a gift loan as "any below-market loan where the foregoing [sic] of interest is in the nature of a gift."[21] Unless tax avoidance was one of the principal purposes of the loan, special limitations apply if the gift loan does not exceed $100,000. In such a case, the interest element may not exceed the borrower's net investment income.[22] Furthermore, if the net investment income does not exceed $1,000, it is treated as zero. Under a $1,000 *de minimis rule,* the interest element is disregarded.

Certain Property Settlements (§ 2516). Normally, the settlement of certain marital rights is not regarded as being for consideration and is subject to the Federal gift tax.[23] As a special exception to this general approach, Congress enacted § 2516. By this provision, transfers of property interests made under the terms of a written agreement between spouses in settlement of their marital or property rights are deemed to be for adequate consideration. These transfers are exempt from the Federal gift tax if a final decree of divorce is obtained within the three-year period beginning on the date one year before the parties entered into the agreement. Likewise excluded are transfers to provide a reasonable allowance for the support of minor children (including legally adopted children) of a marriage. The agreement need not be approved by the divorce decree.

Disclaimers (§ 2518). A **disclaimer** is a refusal by a person to accept property that is designated to pass to him or her. The effect of the disclaimer is to pass the property to someone else.

EXAMPLE 18

Earl dies without a will and is survived by a son, Andy, and a grandson, Jay. At the time of his death, Earl owned real estate that, under the applicable state law, passes to the closest lineal descendant, Andy in this case. If, however, Andy disclaims his interest in the real estate, state law provides that the property passes to Jay. At the time of Earl's death, Andy has considerable property of his own, and Jay has none. ▼

Why might Andy want to consider disclaiming his inheritance and have the property pass directly from Earl to Jay? By doing so, an extra transfer tax may be avoided. If the disclaimer does not take place (i.e., Andy accepts the inheritance) and the property eventually passes to Jay (either by gift or by death), the later transfer is subject to the application of either the gift tax or the estate tax.

For many years, whether a disclaimer was effective in avoiding a Federal transfer tax depended on the application of state law. To illustrate by using the facts of Example 18, if state law determined that the real estate was deemed to have passed through Andy despite his disclaimer after Earl's death, the Federal gift tax applied. In essence, Andy was treated as if he had inherited the property

---

[21] § 7872(f)(3).

[22] Net investment income has the same meaning given to the term by § 163(d). Generally, net investment income is investment income (e.g., interest, dividends) less related expenses.

[23] Reg. § 25.2512–8.

from Earl and then given it to Jay. As state law was not always consistent in this regard and sometimes was not even known, the application or nonapplication of Federal transfer taxes depended on where the parties lived. To remedy this situation and provide some measure of uniformity, §§ 2046 (relating to disclaimers for estate tax purposes) and 2518 were added to the Code.

In the case of the gift tax, when the requirements of § 2518 are met and Andy issues a timely lifetime disclaimer (refer to Example 18), the property is treated as if it goes directly from Earl to Jay. Since the property is not treated as passing through Andy (regardless of what state law holds), it is not subject to the Federal gift tax.

The tax law also permits the Federal gift tax to be avoided in cases of a partial disclaimer of an undivided interest.

EXAMPLE 19

Assume the same facts as in Example 18, except that Andy wishes to retain half of the real estate for himself. If Andy makes a timely disclaimer of an undivided one-half interest in the property, the Federal gift tax does not apply to the portion passing to Jay. ▼

Other Transfers Subject to Gift Tax. Other transfers that may carry gift tax consequences (e.g., the exercise of a power of appointment, the creation of joint ownership) are discussed and illustrated in connection with the Federal estate tax.

ANNUAL EXCLUSION

In General. The first $10,000 of gifts made to any one person during any calendar year (except gifts of future interests in property) is excluded in determining the total amount of gifts for the year.[24] The **annual exclusion** applies to all gifts of a present interest made during the calendar year in the order in which they are made until the $10,000 exclusion per donee is exhausted. For a gift in trust, each beneficiary of the trust is treated as a separate person for purposes of the exclusion.

A **future interest** is defined as one that will come into being (as to use, possession, or enjoyment) at some future date. Examples of future interests include such rights as remainder interests that are commonly encountered when property is transferred to a trust. A *present interest* is an unrestricted right to the immediate use, possession, or enjoyment of property or of the income.

EXAMPLE 20

During the current year, Laura makes the following cash gifts: $8,000 to Rita and $12,000 to Maureen. Laura may claim an annual exclusion of $8,000 with respect to Rita and $10,000 with respect to Maureen. ▼

EXAMPLE 21

By a lifetime gift, Ron transfers property to a trust with a life estate (with income payable annually) to June and remainder upon June's death to Albert. Ron has made two gifts: one to June of a life estate and one to Albert of a remainder interest. (The valuation of each of these gifts is discussed in Chapter 18.) The life estate is a present interest and qualifies for the annual exclusion. The remainder interest granted to Albert is a future interest and does not qualify for the exclusion. Note that Albert's interest does not come into being until some future date (on the death of June). ▼

Although Example 21 indicates that the gift of an income interest is a present interest, this is not always the case. If a possibility exists that the income

---

[24] § 2503(b).

beneficiary may not receive the immediate enjoyment of the property, the transfer is of a future interest.

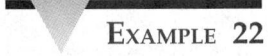

EXAMPLE 22

Assume the same facts as in Example 21, except that the income from the trust need not be payable annually to June. It may, at the trustee's discretion, be accumulated and added to the principal. Since June's right to receive the income from the trust is conditioned on the trustee's discretion, it is not a present interest. No annual exclusion is allowed. The mere possibility of diversion is enough. It would not matter if the trustee never exercised the discretion to accumulate and did, in fact, distribute the trust income to June annually. ▼

Trust for Minors.   Section 2503(c) offers an important exception to the future interest rules just discussed. Under this provision, a transfer for the benefit of a person who has not attained the age of 21 years on the date of the gift may be considered a gift of a present interest. This is true even though the minor is not given the unrestricted right to the immediate use, possession, or enjoyment of the property. For the exception to apply, the following conditions must be satisfied:

- Both the property and its income may be expended by or for the benefit of the minor before the minor attains the age of 21.
- Any portion of the property or its income not expended by the time the minor reaches the age of 21 shall pass to the minor at that time.
- If the minor dies before attaining the age of 21, the property and its income will be payable either to the minor's estate or as the minor may designate under a general power of appointment (discussed later in the chapter).

The exception allows a trustee to accumulate income on behalf of a minor beneficiary without converting the income interest to a future interest.

EXAMPLE 23

Bret places property in trust, income payable to Billy until he reaches 21, remainder to Billy or Billy's estate. Under the terms of the trust instrument, the trustee is empowered to accumulate the trust income or apply it toward Billy's benefit. In either event, the accumulated income and principal must be paid to Billy whenever he reaches 21 years of age or to whomever Billy designates in his will if he dies before reaching that age. The conditions of § 2503(c) are satisfied, and Bret's transfer qualifies for the annual exclusion. Billy's interest is a present interest. ▼

DEDUCTIONS

In arriving at taxable gifts, a deduction is allowed for transfers to certain qualified charitable organizations. On transfers between spouses, a marital deduction may be available. Since both the charitable and marital deductions apply in determining the Federal estate tax, these deductions are discussed later in the chapter.

COMPUTING THE FEDERAL GIFT TAX

5   LEARNING OBJECTIVE
Explain the computation of the Federal gift tax.

The Unified Transfer Tax Rate Schedule.   The top rates of the unified transfer tax rate schedule originally reached as high as 70 percent (see Appendix A, page A–4). Over the years, these top rates have been reduced to 55 percent. As noted later in the chapter, the benefits of the graduated rates are phased out for larger gifts beginning after 1987. Keep in mind that the unified transfer tax rate schedule applies to all transfers (by gift or death) after 1976. Different rate schedules apply for pre-1977 gifts (see Appendix A, page A–9) and pre-1977 deaths (see Appendix A, page A–8).

The Deemed Paid Adjustment. Review the formula for the gift tax in Figure 17–1, and note that the tax base for a current gift includes *all* past taxable gifts. The effect of the inclusion is to force the current taxable gift into a higher bracket due to the progressive nature of the unified transfer tax rates (refer to Example 2). To mitigate such double taxation, the donor is allowed a credit for any gift tax previously paid or deemed paid (refer to Example 3).

Limiting the donor to a credit for the gift tax *actually paid* on pre-1977 taxable gifts would be unfair. Pre-1977 taxable gifts were subject to a lower set of rates (see Appendix A, page A–9) than those in the unified transfer tax rate schedule. As a consequence, the donor is allowed a *deemed paid* credit on pre-1977 taxable gifts. This is the amount that would have been due under the unified transfer tax rate schedule had it been applicable. *Post-1976* taxable gifts *also* are subject to the deemed paid adjustment since the same rate schedule may not be involved in all gifts. Compare the variation in rates in Appendix A, pages A–4, A–5, A–6, and A–7. For post-1976 taxable gifts, it is entirely possible that the deemed paid credit allowed could be *less* than the gift tax that was actually paid.

EXAMPLE 24

In early 1976, Lisa made taxable gifts of $500,000, upon which a Federal gift tax of $109,275 (see Appendix A, page A–9) was paid. Assume Lisa makes further taxable gifts of $700,000 in 1997. The unified transfer tax on the 1997 gifts is determined as follows:

Taxable gifts made in 1997		$ 700,000
Add: Taxable gifts made in 1976		500,000
Total of current and past taxable gifts		$1,200,000
Unified transfer tax on total taxable gifts per Appendix A, page A–7 [$345,800 + (41% × $200,000)]		$ 427,800
Subtract:		
Deemed paid tax on pre-1977 taxable gifts per Appendix A, page A–7 [$70,800 + (34% × $250,000)]	$155,800	
Unified tax credit for 1997	192,800	(348,600)
Gift tax due on the 1997 taxable gift		$ 79,200

Note that the gift tax actually paid on the 1976 transfer was $109,275. Nevertheless, Lisa is allowed a deemed paid credit on the gift of $155,800, considerably different from what was paid. ▼

The Election to Split Gifts by Married Persons. To understand the reason for the gift-splitting election of § 2513, consider the following situations:

EXAMPLE 25

Dick and Margaret are husband and wife and reside in Michigan, a common law state. Dick has been the only breadwinner in the family, and Margaret has no significant property of her own. Neither has made any prior taxable gifts or has used the $30,000 specific exemption previously available for pre-1977 gifts. In 1997, Dick makes a gift to Leslie of $1,220,000. Presuming the election to split gifts did not exist, Dick's gift tax is as follows:

Amount of gift	$1,220,000
Subtract: Annual exclusion	(10,000)
Taxable gift	$1,210,000
Gift tax on $1,210,000 per Appendix A, page A–7 [$345,800 + (41% × $210,000)]	$ 431,900
Subtract: Unified tax credit for 1997	(192,800)
Gift tax due on the 1997 taxable gift	$ 239,100

▼

EXAMPLE 26

Assume the same facts as in Example 25, except that Dick and Margaret always have resided in California (a community property state). Even though Dick is the sole breadwinner, income from personal services generally is community property. Consequently, the gift to Leslie probably involves community property. If this is the case, the gift tax is as follows:

	Dick	Margaret
Amount of the gift (50% × $1,220,000)	$ 610,000	$ 610,000
Subtract: Annual exclusion	(10,000)	(10,000)
Taxable gifts	$ 600,000	$ 600,000
Gift tax on $600,000 per Appendix A, page A–7	$ 192,800	$ 192,800
Subtract: Unified tax credit for 1997	(192,800)	(192,800)
Gift tax due on the 1997 taxable gifts	$ –0–	$ –0–

As the results of Examples 25 and 26 indicate, married donors residing in community property jurisdictions possessed a significant gift tax advantage over those residing in common law states. To rectify this inequity, the Revenue Act of 1948 incorporated into the Code the predecessor to § 2513. Under this provision, a gift made by a person to someone other than his or her spouse may be considered, for Federal gift tax purposes, as having been made one-half by each spouse. Returning to Example 25, Dick and Margaret could treat the gift passing to Leslie as being made one-half by each of them. They may do this even though the cash belonged to Dick. As a result, the parties are able to achieve the same tax consequence as in Example 26.

To split gifts, the spouses must be legally married to each other at the time of the gift. If they are divorced later in the calendar year, they may still split the gift if neither marries anyone else during that year. They both must indicate on their separate gift tax returns their consent to have all gifts made in that calendar year split between them. In addition, both must be citizens or residents of the United States on the date of the gift. A gift from one spouse to the other spouse cannot be split. Such a gift might, however, be eligible for the marital deduction.

The election to split gifts is not necessary when husband and wife transfer community property to a third party. It is available, however, if the gift consists of the separate property of one of the spouses. Generally, separate property is property acquired before marriage and property acquired after marriage by gift or inheritance. The election, then, is not limited to residents of common law states.

PROCEDURAL MATTERS

Having determined which transfers are subject to the Federal gift tax and the various deductions and exclusions available to the donor, the procedural aspects of the tax should be considered. The following sections discuss the return itself, the due dates for filing and paying the tax, and other related matters.

The Federal Gift Tax Return.   For transfers by gift, a Form 709 (U.S. Gift Tax Return) must be filed whenever the gifts for any one calendar year exceed the annual exclusion or involve a gift of a future interest. A Form 709 need not be filed, however, for transfers between spouses that are offset by the unlimited marital deduction regardless of the amount of the transfer.[25]

---

[25] § 6019(a)(2).

CONCEPT SUMMARY 17–1

Federal Gift Tax Provisions

1. The Federal gift tax applies to all gratuitous transfers of property made by U.S. citizens or residents. In this regard, it does not matter where the property is located.
2. In the eyes of the IRS, a gratuitous transfer is one not supported by full and adequate consideration. If the parties are acting in a business setting, such consideration usually exists. If, however, purported sales are between family members, a gift element may be suspected.
3. If one party lends money to another and intends some or all of the interest element to be a gift, the arrangement is categorized as a gift loan. To the extent that the interest provided for is less than the market rate, three tax consequences result. First, a gift has taken place between the lender and the borrower as to the interest element. Second, income may result to the lender. Third, an income tax deduction may be available to the borrower.
4. Property settlements can escape the gift tax if a divorce occurs within a prescribed period of time.
5. A disclaimer is a refusal by a person to accept property designated to pass to that person. The effect of a disclaimer is to pass the property to someone else. If certain conditions are satisfied, the issuance of a disclaimer will not be subject to the Federal gift tax.
6. Except for gifts of future interests, a donor is allowed an annual exclusion of $10,000. The future interest limitation does not apply to certain trusts created for minors.
7. The election to split a gift enables a married couple to be treated as two donors. The election doubles the annual exclusion and makes the unified tax credit available to the nonowner spouse.
8. The election to split gifts is not necessary if the property is jointly owned by the spouses. That is the case when the property is part of the couple's community.
9. In determining the tax base for computing the gift tax, all prior taxable gifts must be added to current taxable gifts. Thus, the gift tax is cumulative in nature.
10. Gifts are reported on Form 709 or Form 709–A. The return is due on April 15 following the year of the gift.

EXAMPLE 27

In 1997, Larry makes five gifts, each in the amount of $10,000, to his five children. If the gifts do not involve future interests, a Form 709 need not be filed to report the transfers. ▼

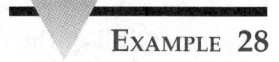

EXAMPLE 28

During 1997, Esther makes a gift of $20,000 cash of her separate property to her daughter. To double the amount of the annual exclusion allowed, Jerry (Esther's husband) is willing to split the gift. Since the § 2513 election can be made only on a gift tax return, a form must be filed even though no gift tax will be due as a result of the transfer. Useful for this purpose is Form 709–A (U.S. Short Form Gift Tax Return). This form is available to simplify the gift-splitting procedure. ▼

Presuming a gift tax return is due, it must be filed on or before the fifteenth day of April following the year of the gift.[26] As is the case with other Federal taxes, when the due date falls on Saturday, Sunday, or a legal holiday, the date for filing the return is the next business day. Note that the filing requirements for Form 709 have no correlation to the accounting year used by a donor for Federal income tax purposes. Thus, a fiscal year taxpayer must follow the April 15 rule for any reportable gifts. If sufficient reason is shown, the IRS is authorized to grant reasonable extensions of time for filing the return.[27]

---

[26] § 6075(b)(1).

[27] § 6081. Under § 6075(b)(2), an extension of time granted to a calendar year taxpayer for filing an income tax return automatically extends the due date of a gift tax return.

THE FEDERAL ESTATE TAX

The following discussion of the estate tax coincides with the formula that appeared earlier in the chapter in Figure 17–2. The key components in the formula are the gross estate, the taxable estate, the tax base, and the credits allowed against the tentative tax. This formula can be summarized as follows:

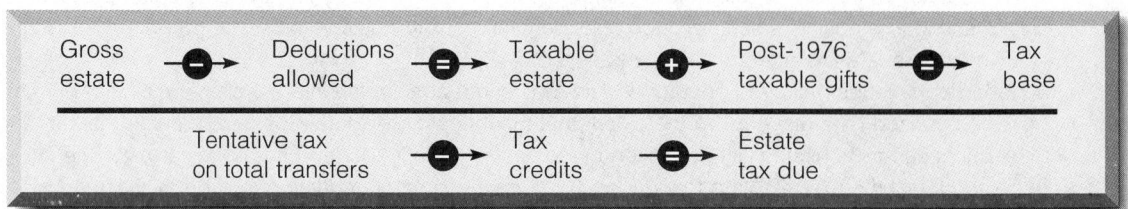

GROSS ESTATE

6   LEARNING OBJECTIVE
Describe the components of the gross estate.

Simply stated, the **gross estate** includes all property subject to the Federal estate tax. This depends on the provisions of the Internal Revenue Code as supplemented by IRS pronouncements and the judicial interpretations of Federal courts.

In contrast to the gross estate, the **probate estate** is controlled by state (rather than Federal) law. The probate estate consists of all of a decedent's property subject to administration by the executor or administrator of the estate. The administration is supervised by a local court of appropriate jurisdiction (usually designated as a probate court). An executor (or executrix) is the decedent's personal representative appointed under the decedent's will. When a decedent dies without a will or fails to name an executor in the will (or that person refuses to serve), the local probate court appoints an administrator (or administratrix).

The probate estate is frequently smaller than the gross estate. It contains only property owned by the decedent at the time of death and passing to heirs under a will or under the law of intestacy (the order of distribution for those dying without a will). As noted later, such items as the proceeds of many life insurance policies become part of the gross estate but are not included in the probate estate.

All states provide for an order of distribution in the event someone dies without a will. After the surviving spouse, who receives some or all of the estate, the preference is usually in the following order: down to lineal descendants (e.g., children, grandchildren), up to lineal ascendants (e.g., parents, grandparents), and out to collateral relations (e.g., brothers, sisters, aunts, and uncles).

Property Owned by the Decedent (§ 2033).   Property owned by the decedent at the time of death is included in the gross estate. The nature of the property or the use to which it was put during the decedent-owner's lifetime has no significance as far as the estate tax is concerned. Thus, personal effects (such as clothing), stocks, bonds, furniture, jewelry, works of art, bank accounts, and interests in businesses conducted as sole proprietorships and partnerships are all included in the deceased owner's gross estate. No distinction is made between tangible and intangible, depreciable and nondepreciable, business and personal assets. However, a deceased spouse's gross estate does not include the surviving spouse's share of the community property.

The application of § 2033 is illustrated as follows:

EXAMPLE 29

Irma dies owning some City of Denver bonds. The fair market value of the bonds plus any interest accrued to the date of Irma's death is included in her gross estate. Although interest on municipals is normally not taxable under the Federal income tax, it is property owned by Irma at the time of death. However, any interest accrued after death is not part of Irma's gross estate. ▼

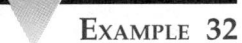

EXAMPLE 30

Sharon dies on April 8, 1997, at a time when she owns stock in Robin Corporation and Wren Corporation. On March 3 of this year, both corporations authorized a cash dividend payable on May 2. Robin's dividend is payable to shareholders of record as of April 1. Wren's date of record is April 11. Sharon's gross estate includes the following: the stock in Robin Corporation, the stock in Wren Corporation, and the dividend on the Robin stock. It does not include the dividend on the Wren stock. ▼

EXAMPLE 31

Ray dies holding some promissory notes issued to him by his son. In his will, Ray forgives these notes, relieving the son of the obligation to make any payments. The fair market value of these notes is included in Ray's gross estate. ▼

EXAMPLE 32

Jonathan died while employed by Eagle Corporation. Under an informal but non-binding company policy, Eagle awards half of Jonathan's annual salary to Jonathan's widow as a death benefit. Presuming that Jonathan had no vested interest in and that the widow had no enforceable right to the payment, none of it is included in his gross estate.[28] ▼

Dower and Curtesy Interests (§ 2034). In its common law (nonstatutory) form, dower generally gave a surviving widow a life estate in a portion of her husband's estate (usually the real estate he owned) with the remainder passing to their children. Most states have modified and codified these common law rules, and the resulting statutes often vary between jurisdictions. In some states, for example, by statute, a widow is entitled to outright ownership of a percentage of her deceased husband's real estate and personal property. Curtesy is a similar right held by the husband in his wife's property that takes effect in the event he survives her. Most states have abolished the common law curtesy concept and have, in some cases, substituted a modified statutory version.

Dower and curtesy rights are incomplete interests and may never materialize. Thus, if a wife predeceases her husband, the dower interest in her husband's property is lost.

EXAMPLE 33

Martin dies without a will, leaving an estate of $900,000. Under state law, Belinda (Martin's widow) is entitled to one-third of his property. The $300,000 Belinda receives is included in Martin's gross estate. Depending on the nature of the interest Belinda receives in the $300,000, this amount could qualify Martin's estate for a marital deduction. (This possibility is discussed at greater length later in the chapter. For the time being, however, the focus is on what is or is not included as part of the decedent's gross estate.) ▼

Adjustments for Gifts Made within Three Years of Death (§ 2035). At one time, all taxable gifts made within three years of death were included in the donor's gross estate unless it could be shown that the gifts were not made in contemplation of death. The prior rule was intended to preclude tax avoidance since the gift tax and estate tax rates were separate and the former was lower than the latter. When the gift and estate tax rates were combined into the unified transfer tax, the reason for the rule for gifts in contemplation of death largely disappeared. The three-year rule has, however, been retained for the following items:

---

[28] *Barr's Estate*, 40 T.C. 227 (1963).

- Inclusion in the gross estate of any gift tax paid on gifts made within three years of death. Called the *gross-up* procedure, it prevents the gift tax amount from escaping the estate tax.
- Any property interests transferred by gift within three years of death that would have been included in the gross estate by virtue of the application of § 2036 (transfers with a retained life estate), § 2037 (transfers taking effect at death), § 2038 (revocable transfers), and § 2042 (proceeds of life insurance). All except § 2037 are discussed later in the chapter.

EXAMPLE 34

Before her death in 1997, Jennifer made the following taxable gifts:

Year of Gift	Nature of the Asset	Fair Market Value		Gift Tax Paid
		Date of Gift	Date of Death	
1989	Hawk Corporation stock	$100,000	$150,000	$ –0–
1995	Policy on Jennifer's life	40,000 (cash value)	200,000 (face value)	–0–
1996	Land	400,000	410,000	8,200

Jennifer's *gross estate* includes $208,200 [$200,000 (life insurance proceeds) + $8,200 (gross-up for the gift tax on the 1996 taxable gift)] as to these transfers. Referring to the formula for the estate tax (see Figure 17–2), the other post-1976 taxable gifts are added to the *taxable estate* (at the fair market value on the date of the gift) in arriving at the tax base. Jennifer's estate is allowed a credit for the gift tax paid (or deemed paid) on the 1996 transfer. ▼

The three-year rule also applies in testing for qualification under § 303 (stock redemptions to pay death taxes and administration expenses), § 2032A (special valuation procedures), and § 6166 (extensions of time to pay death taxes). All these provisions are discussed in Chapter 18.

Transfers with a Retained Life Estate (§ 2036).   Code §§ 2036 through 2038 were enacted on the premise that the estate tax can be avoided on lifetime transfers only if the decedent does not retain control over the property. The logic of this approach is somewhat difficult to dispute. One should not be able to escape the tax consequences of property transfers at death while remaining in a position to enjoy some or all of the fruits of ownership during life.

Under § 2036, the value of any property transferred by the deceased during lifetime for less than adequate consideration must be included if either of the following was retained:

- The possession or enjoyment of, or the right to the income from, the property.
- The right, either alone or in conjunction with any person, to designate the persons who shall possess or enjoy the property or the income.

"The possession or enjoyment of, or the right to the income from, the property," as it appears in § 2036(a)(1), is considered to have been retained by the decedent to the extent that such income, etc., is to be applied toward the discharge of a legal obligation of the decedent. The term "legal obligation" includes a legal obligation of the decedent to support a dependent during the decedent's lifetime.[29]

The following examples illustrate the practical application of § 2036.

---

[29] Reg. § 20.2036–1(b)(2).

EXAMPLE 35

Carl's will passes all of his property to a trust, income to Alan for his life (Alan is given a life estate). Upon Alan's death, the principal goes to Melissa (Melissa is granted a remainder interest). On Alan's death, none of the trust property is included in his gross estate. Although Alan held a life estate, § 2036 is inapplicable because he was not the transferor (Carl was) of the property. Section 2033 (property owned by the decedent) causes any income distributions Alan was entitled to receive at the time of his death to be included in his gross estate. ▼

EXAMPLE 36

By deed, Nora transfers the remainder interest in her ranch to Marcia, retaining for herself the right to continue occupying the property until death. Upon Nora's death, the fair market value of the ranch is included in her gross estate. Furthermore, Nora is subject to the gift tax. The amount of the gift is the fair market value of the ranch on the date of the gift less the portion applicable to Nora's retained life estate. (See Chapter 18 for the way this gift is determined.) ▼

Revocable Transfers (§ 2038). Another type of lifetime transfer that is drawn into a decedent's gross estate is covered by § 2038. The gross estate includes the value of property interests transferred by the decedent (except to the extent that the transfer was made for full consideration) if the enjoyment of the property transferred was subject, at the date of the decedent's death, to any power of the decedent to *alter, amend, revoke, or terminate* the transfer. This includes the power to change the beneficiaries or the power to accelerate or increase any beneficiary's enjoyment of the property.

The capacity in which the decedent could exercise the power is immaterial. If the decedent gave property in trust, making him- or herself the trustee with the power to revoke the trust, the property is included in his or her gross estate. If the decedent named another person as trustee with the power to revoke, but reserved the power to later appoint him- or herself trustee, the property is also included in his or her gross estate. If, however, the power to alter, amend, revoke, or terminate was held at all times solely by a person other than the decedent and the decedent did not reserve a right to assume these powers, the property is not included in the decedent's gross estate.

The Code and the Regulations make it clear that one cannot avoid inclusion in the gross estate under § 2038 by relinquishing a power within three years of death.[30] Recall that § 2038 is one of several types of situations listed as exceptions to the usual rule excluding gifts made within three years of death from the gross estate.

In the event § 2038 applies, the amount includible in the gross estate is the portion of the property transferred that is subject, at the decedent's death, to the decedent's power to alter, amend, revoke, or terminate.

The classic § 2038 situation results from the use of a revocable trust.

EXAMPLE 37

Maria creates a trust, life estate to her children, remainder to her grandchildren. Under the terms of the trust, Maria reserves the right to revoke the trust and revest the trust principal and income in herself. As noted in Example 10, the creation of the trust does not result in a gift because the transfer is not complete. However, if Maria dies still retaining the power to revoke, the trust is included in her gross estate under § 2038. ▼

In application, the provisions related to incomplete transfers (§§ 2036 and 2038) tend to overlap. It is not unusual to find that either or both of these Sections apply to a particular transfer.

---

[30] § 2038(a)(1) and Reg. § 20.2038–1(e)(1).

Annuities (§ 2039). Annuities can be divided by their origin into commercial and noncommercial contracts. Noncommercial annuities are issued by private parties and, in some cases, charitable organizations that do not regularly issue annuities. The two varieties have much in common, but noncommercial annuities present special income tax problems and are not treated further in this discussion.

Regulation § 20.2039–1(b)(1) defines an annuity as representing "one or more payments extending over any period of time." According to the Regulation, the payments may be equal or unequal, conditional or unconditional, periodic or sporadic. Annuity contracts that terminate upon the death of the person covered (i.e., annuitant) are designated as straight-life annuities. Other contracts provide for a survivorship feature (e.g., reduced payments to a surviving spouse).

In the case of a straight-life annuity, nothing is included in the gross estate of the annuitant at death. Section 2033 (property in which the decedent had an interest) does not apply because the annuitant's interest in the contract is terminated by death. Section 2036 (transfers with a retained life estate) does not cover the situation; a transfer made for full consideration is specifically excluded from § 2036 treatment. A commercial annuity is presumed to have been purchased for full consideration unless some evidence exists to indicate that the parties were not acting at arm's length.

EXAMPLE 38

Arnold purchases a straight-life annuity that will pay him $6,000 a month when he reaches age 65. Arnold dies at age 70. Except for the payments he received before his death, nothing relating to this annuity affects Arnold's gross estate. ▼

In the case of a survivorship annuity, the estate tax consequences under § 2039(a) are usually triggered by the death of the first annuitant. The amount included in the gross estate is the cost from the same company of a comparable annuity covering the survivor at his or her attained age on the date of the deceased annuitant's death.

EXAMPLE 39

Assume the same facts as in Example 38, except that the annuity contract provides for Veronica to be paid $3,000 a month for life as a survivorship feature. Veronica is 62 years of age when Arnold dies. Under these circumstances, Arnold's gross estate includes the cost of a comparable contract that provides an annuity of $3,000 per month for the life of a female, age 62. ▼

Full inclusion of the survivorship element in the gross estate is subject to an exception under § 2039(b). The amount includible is to be based on the proportion of the deceased annuitant's contribution to the total cost of the contract. This is expressed by the following formula:

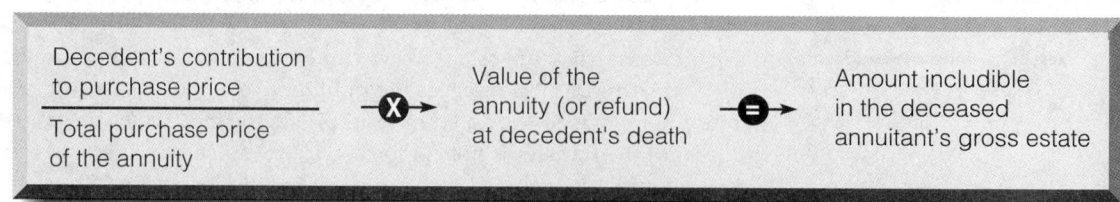

$$\frac{\text{Decedent's contribution to purchase price}}{\text{Total purchase price of the annuity}} \times \text{Value of the annuity (or refund) at decedent's death} = \text{Amount includible in the deceased annuitant's gross estate}$$

EXAMPLE 40

Assume the same facts as in Example 39, except that Arnold and Veronica are husband and wife and have always lived in a community property state. The premiums on the contract were paid with community funds. Since Veronica contributed half of the cost of the contract, only half of the amount determined under Example 39 is included in Arnold's gross estate. ▼

The result reached in Example 40 is not unique to community property jurisdictions. The outcome would have been the same in a noncommunity property state if Veronica had furnished half of the consideration from her own funds.

Joint Interests (§§ 2040 and 2511).   Recall that joint tenancies and tenancies by the entirety are characterized by the right of survivorship. Thus, upon the death of a joint tenant, title to the property passes to the surviving tenant. None of the property is included in the *probate* estate of the deceased tenant. In the case of tenancies in common and community property, death does not defeat an ownership interest. Further, the deceased owner's interest is part of the probate estate.

The Federal *estate tax treatment* of tenancies in common or of community property follows the logical approach of taxing only the portion of the property included in the deceased owner's probate estate. Thus, if Homer, Wilma, and Thelma are tenants in common in a tract of land, each owning an equal interest, and Homer dies, only one-third of the value of the property is included in the gross estate. This one-third interest is also the same amount that passes to Homer's heirs.

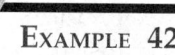

EXAMPLE 41

Homer, Wilma, and Thelma acquire a tract of land, ownership listed as tenants in common, each party furnishing $20,000 of the $60,000 purchase price. When the property is worth $90,000, Homer dies. If Homer's undivided interest in the property is 33⅓%, the gross estate *and* probate estate each include $30,000. ▼

Unless the parties have provided otherwise, each tenant is deemed to own an interest equal to the portion of the original consideration he or she furnished. The parties in Example 41 could have provided that Homer would receive an undivided half interest in the property although he contributed only one-third of the purchase price. In that case, Wilma and Thelma have made a gift to Homer when the tenancy was created, and Homer's gross estate and probate estate each include $45,000.

For certain joint tenancies, the tax consequences are different. All of the property is included in the deceased co-owner's gross estate unless it can be proven that the surviving co-owners contributed to the cost of the property.[31] If a contribution can be shown, the amount to be *excluded* is calculated by the following formula:

$$\frac{\text{Surviving co-owner's contribution}}{\text{Total cost of the property}} \times \text{Fair market value of the property}$$

In computing a survivor's contribution, any funds received as a gift *from the deceased co-owner* and applied to the cost of the property cannot be counted. However, income or gain from gift assets can be counted.

If the co-owners receive the property as a gift *from another,* each co-owner is deemed to have contributed to the cost of his or her own interest.

The preceding rules can be illustrated as follows.

EXAMPLE 42

Keith and Steve (father and son) acquire a tract of land, ownership listed as joint tenancy with right of survivorship. Keith furnished $40,000 and Steve $20,000 of the $60,000

---

[31] § 2040(a).

purchase price. Of the $20,000 provided by Steve, $10,000 had previously been received as a gift from Keith. When the property is worth $90,000, Keith dies. Because only $10,000 of Steve's contribution can be counted (the other $10,000 was received as a gift from Keith), Steve has furnished only one-sixth ($10,000/$60,000) of the cost. Thus, Keith's gross estate must include five-sixths of $90,000, or $75,000. This presumes Steve can prove that he did in fact make the $10,000 contribution. In the absence of such proof, the full value of the property is included in Keith's gross estate. Keith's death makes Steve the immediate owner of the property by virtue of the right of survivorship. None of the property is part of Keith's probate estate. ▼

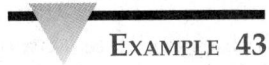

EXAMPLE 43

Francis transfers property to Irene and Martin as a gift, listing ownership as joint tenancy with the right of survivorship. Upon Irene's death, one-half of the value of the property is included in the gross estate. Since the property was received as a gift and the donees are equal owners, each is considered to have furnished half of the consideration. ▼

To simplify the joint ownership rules for *married persons*, § 2040(b) provides for an automatic inclusion rule upon the death of the first joint-owner spouse to die. Regardless of the amount contributed by each spouse, one-half of the value of the property is included in the gross estate of the spouse who dies first. The special rule eliminates the need to trace the source of contributions and recognizes that any inclusion in the gross estate is neutralized by the marital deduction.

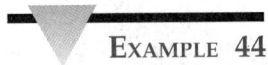

EXAMPLE 44

In 1986, Hank purchases real estate for $100,000 using his separate funds and listing title as "Hank and Louise, joint tenants with the right of survivorship." Hank predeceases Louise ten years later when the property is worth $300,000. If Hank and Louise are husband and wife, Hank's gross estate includes $150,000 (½ of $300,000) as to the property. ▼

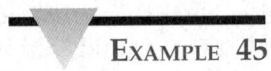

EXAMPLE 45

Assume the same facts as in Example 44, except that Louise (instead of Hank) dies first. Presuming the value at the date of death to be $300,000, Louise's gross estate includes $150,000 as to the property. In this regard, it is of no consequence that Louise did not contribute to the cost of the real estate. ▼

In both Examples 44 and 45, inclusion in the gross estate of the first spouse to die is neutralized by the unlimited marital deduction allowed for estate tax purposes (see the discussion of § 2056 later in the chapter). Under the right of survivorship, the surviving joint tenant obtains full ownership of the property. The marital deduction generally is allowed for property passing from one spouse to another.

Whether a *gift* results when property is transferred into some form of joint ownership depends on the consideration furnished by each of the contributing parties for the ownership interest acquired.

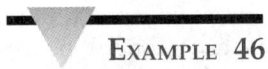

EXAMPLE 46

Brenda and Sarah purchase real estate as tenants in common, each furnishing $40,000 of the $80,000 cost. If each is an equal owner in the property, no gift has occurred. ▼

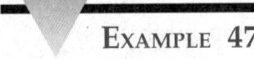

EXAMPLE 47

Assume the same facts as in Example 46, except that of the $80,000 purchase price, Brenda furnishes $60,000 and Sarah furnishes only $20,000. If each is an equal owner in the property, Brenda has made a gift to Sarah of $20,000. ▼

EXAMPLE 48

Martha purchases real estate for $240,000, the title to the property being listed as follows: "Martha, Sylvia, and Dan as joint tenants with the right of survivorship." If under state law the mother (Martha), the daughter (Sylvia), and the son (Dan) are deemed to be equal owners in the property, Martha is treated as having made gifts of $80,000 to Sylvia and $80,000 to Dan. ▼

Several important *exceptions* exist to the general rule that gift treatment is triggered by the creation of a joint ownership with disproportionate interests resulting from unequal consideration. First, if the transfer involves a joint bank account, there is no gift at the time of the contribution.[32] If a gift occurs, it is when the noncontributing party withdraws the funds provided by the other joint tenant. Second, the same rule applies to the purchase of U.S. savings bonds. Again, any gift tax consequences are postponed until the noncontributing party appropriates some or all of the proceeds for his or her individual use.

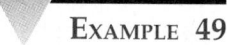

EXAMPLE 49

Cynthia deposits $200,000 in a bank account under the names of Cynthia and Carla as joint tenants. Both Cynthia and Carla have the right to withdraw funds from the account without the other's consent. Cynthia has not made a gift to Carla when the account is established. ▼

EXAMPLE 50

Assume the same facts as in Example 49. At some later date, Carla withdraws $50,000 from the account for her own use. At this point, Cynthia has made a gift to Carla of $50,000. ▼

EXAMPLE 51

Wesley purchases a U.S. savings bond that he registers in the names of Wesley and Harriet. After Wesley dies, Harriet redeems the bond. No gift takes place when Wesley buys the bond. In addition, Harriet's redemption is not treated as a gift since the bond passed to her by testamentary disposition (Harriet acquired the bond by virtue of surviving Wesley) and not through a lifetime transfer. However, the fair market value of the bond is included in Wesley's gross estate under § 2040. ▼

ETHICAL CONSIDERATIONS

A Joint Bank Account and a Subsequent Marriage

Horace, a well-to-do widower, wants to marry Fran, his much younger secretary. Fran is agreeable to marriage but would like to achieve some degree of financial independence. Upon advice of his attorney, Horace uses $900,000 to establish a bank account listing himself and Fran as joint tenants. Horace and Fran are married, and shortly thereafter she withdraws the $900,000 and places the funds in a new account in her name only.

If the transfer from Horace to Fran took place before their marriage, it generates a Federal gift tax. The position of the IRS is that premarital settlements are gifts because they are not supported by adequate consideration. If the transfer from Horace to Fran took place after marriage, a gift tax is avoided due to the application of the marital deduction.

Has Horace successfully avoided the Federal gift tax?

Powers of Appointment (§§ 2041 and 2514). A **power of appointment** is a power to determine who shall own or enjoy, presently or in the future, the property subject to the power. It must be created by another and does not include a power created or retained by the decedent when he or she transferred his or her own property.

Powers of appointment fall into one of two classifications: *general* and *special.* A general power of appointment is one in which the decedent could have

---

[32] Reg. § 25.2511–1(h)(4).

appointed himself, his creditors, his estate, or the creditors of his estate. In contrast, a special power enables the holder to appoint to others but *not* to herself, her creditors, her estate, or the creditors of her estate. Assume, for example, that D has the power to designate how the principal of the trust will be distributed among X, Y, and Z. At this point, D's power is only a special power of appointment. If D is given the further right to appoint the principal to himself, what was a special power of appointment becomes a general power.

Three things can happen to a power of appointment: exercise, lapse, and release. Exercising the power involves appointing the property to one or all of the parties designated. A lapse occurs upon failure to exercise a power. Thus, if a holder, D, fails to indicate how the principal of a trust will be distributed among X, Y, and Z, D's power of appointment will lapse, and the principal will pass in accordance with the terms of the trust instrument. A release occurs if the holder relinquishes a power of appointment.

Powers of appointment have the following transfer tax consequences:

1. No tax implications result from the exercise, lapse, or release of a special power of appointment.
2. The exercise, lapse, or release of a general power of appointment created after October 21, 1942, during life or upon the death of the holder causes the fair market value of the property (or income interest) subject to the power to be a gift or to be included in the holder's gross estate.
3. In connection with (2), a lapse of a general power is subject to gift or estate taxation only to the extent that the value of the property that could have been appointed exceeds the greater of either $5,000 or 5 percent of the aggregate value of the property out of which the appointment could have been satisfied.
4. In connection with (2), a holder is not considered to have had a general power of appointment if he or she had a right to consume or invade for his or her own benefit, as long as that right is limited by an ascertainable standard. The standard must relate to the holder's health, education, support, or maintenance. A power to use the property for the "comfort, welfare, or happiness" of the holder is not an ascertainable standard and therefore is a general power of appointment.

The following examples illustrate these rules.

EXAMPLE 52   Justin, Monica's father, leaves his property in trust, life estate to Monica and remainder to whichever of Monica's children she decides to appoint in her will. Monica's power is not a general power of appointment because she cannot exercise it in favor of herself. Thus, regardless of whether Monica exercises the power or not, none of the trust property subject to the power is included in her gross estate. ▼

EXAMPLE 53   Assume the same facts as in Example 52. In addition to having the testamentary power to designate the beneficiary of the remainder interest, Monica is given a power to direct the trustee to pay to her from time to time as much of the principal as she might request "for her support." Although Monica now has a power that she can exercise in favor of herself, it is not a general power of appointment. The power is limited to an ascertainable standard. Thus, none of the property subject to these powers is subject to the gift tax or is included in Monica's gross estate at her death. ▼

Life Insurance (§ 2042). Under § 2042, the gross estate includes the proceeds of life insurance on the decedent's life if (1) they are receivable by the estate, (2) they are receivable by another for the benefit of the estate, or (3) the decedent possessed an incident of ownership in the policy.

Life insurance on the life of another owned by a decedent at the time of death is included in the gross estate under § 2033 (property in which the decedent had an interest) and not under § 2042. The amount includible is the replacement value of the policy.[33] Under these circumstances, inclusion of the face amount of the policy is inappropriate as the policy has not yet matured.

EXAMPLE 54

At the time of his death, Luigi owned a life insurance policy on the life of Benito, face amount of $100,000 and replacement value of $25,000, with Sofia as the designated beneficiary. Since the policy has not matured at Luigi's death, § 2042 is inapplicable. However, § 2033 (property in which the decedent had an interest) compels the inclusion of $25,000 (the replacement value) in Luigi's gross estate. If Luigi and Sofia owned the policy as community property, only $12,500 is included in Luigi's gross estate. ▼

The term *life insurance* includes whole life policies, term insurance, group life insurance, travel and accident insurance, endowment contracts (before being paid up), and death benefits paid by fraternal societies operating under the lodge system.[34]

As just noted, proceeds of insurance on the life of the decedent receivable by the executor or administrator or payable to the decedent's estate are included in the gross estate. The estate need not be specifically named as the beneficiary. Assume, for example, the proceeds of the policy are receivable by an individual beneficiary and are subject to an obligation, legally binding upon the beneficiary, to pay taxes, debts, and other charges enforceable against the estate. The proceeds are included in the decedent's gross estate to the extent of the beneficiary's obligation. If the proceeds of an insurance policy made payable to a decedent's estate are community assets and, under state law, one-half belongs to the surviving spouse, only one-half of the proceeds will be considered as receivable by or for the benefit of the decedent's estate.

Proceeds of insurance on the life of the decedent not receivable by or for the benefit of the estate are includible if the decedent at death possessed any of the incidents of ownership in the policy. In this connection, the term *incidents of ownership* not only means the ownership of the policy in a technical legal sense but also, generally speaking, the right of the insured or his or her estate to the economic benefits of the policy. Thus, it also includes the power to change beneficiaries, revoke an assignment, pledge the policy for a loan, or surrender or cancel the policy.[35]

EXAMPLE 55

At the time of death, Broderick was the insured under a policy (face amount of $100,000) owned by Gregory with Demi as the designated beneficiary. Broderick took out the policy five years ago and immediately transferred it as a gift to Gregory. Under the assignment, Broderick transferred all rights in the policy except the right to change beneficiaries. Broderick died without having exercised this right, and the policy proceeds are paid to Demi. Under § 2042(2), Broderick's retention of an incident of ownership in the policy (i.e., the right to change beneficiaries) causes $100,000 to be included in his gross estate. ▼

Assuming that the deceased-insured holds the incidents of ownership in a policy, how much is included in the gross estate if the insurance policy is a

---

[33] Reg. § 20.2031–8(a)(1).
[34] Reg. § 20.2042–1(a)(1). As to travel and accident insurance, see *Comm. v. Estate of Noel*, 65–1 USTC ¶12,311, 15 AFTR2d 1397, 85 S.Ct. 1238 (USSC, 1965).

[35] Reg. § 20.2042–1(c)(2).

community asset? Only one-half of the proceeds becomes part of the deceased spouse's gross estate.

In determining whether a policy is *community property* or what portion of it might be so classified, state law controls. The states appear to follow one of two general approaches. Under the inception of title approach, the classification depends on when the policy was originally purchased. If purchased before marriage, the policy is separate property regardless of how many premiums were paid after marriage with community funds. However, if the noninsured spouse is not the beneficiary of the policy, he or she may be entitled to reimbursement from the deceased-insured spouse's estate for half of the premiums paid with community funds. The inception of title approach is followed in at least three states: Louisiana, Texas, and New Mexico.

Some community property jurisdictions classify a policy using the tracing approach: the nature of the funds used to pay premiums controls. Thus, a policy paid for 20 percent with separate funds and 80 percent with community funds is 20 percent separate property and 80 percent community property. The point in time when the policy was purchased makes no difference. Conceivably, a policy purchased after marriage with the premiums paid exclusively from separate funds is classified entirely as separate property. The tracing approach appears to be the rule in California and Washington.

Merely purchasing a life insurance contract with someone else designated as the beneficiary does not constitute a *gift*. As long as the purchaser still owns the policy, nothing has really passed to the beneficiary. Even on the death of the insured-owner, no gift takes place. The proceeds paid to the beneficiary constitute a testamentary and not a lifetime transfer. But consider the following possibility:

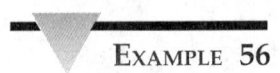
EXAMPLE 56

Kurt purchases an insurance policy on his own life that he transfers to Olga. Kurt retains no interest in the policy (such as the power to change beneficiaries). In these circumstances, Kurt has made a gift to Olga. Furthermore, if Kurt continues to pay the premiums on the transferred policy, each payment constitutes a separate gift. ▼

Under certain conditions, the death of the insured may constitute a gift to the beneficiary of part or all of the proceeds. This occurs when the owner of the policy is not the insured.

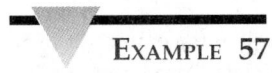
EXAMPLE 57

Randolph owns an insurance policy on the life of Frank, with Tracy as the designated beneficiary. Up until the time of Frank's death, Randolph retained the right to change the beneficiary of the policy. The proceeds paid to Tracy by the insurance company by reason of Frank's death constitute a gift from Randolph to Tracy.[36] ▼

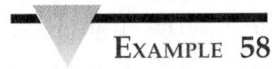
EXAMPLE 58

Hubert and Carrie live in a community property state. With community funds, Hubert purchases an insurance policy with a face amount of $100,000 on his own life and designates Ann as the revocable beneficiary. On Hubert's death, the proceeds of the policy are paid to Ann. If under state law Hubert's death makes the transfer by Carrie complete, Carrie has made a gift to Ann of $50,000. Since the policy is community property, Carrie is the owner of only one-half of the policy. Furthermore, one-half of the proceeds of the policy ($50,000) is included in Hubert's gross estate under § 2042. ▼

---

[36] *Goodman v. Comm.*, 46–1 USTC ¶10,275, 34 AFTR 1534, 156 F.2d 218 (CA–2, 1946).

7   LEARNING OBJECTIVE
Describe the components of the taxable estate.

TAXABLE ESTATE

After the gross estate has been determined, the next step is to determine the taxable estate. By virtue of § 2051, the **taxable estate** is the gross estate less the following: expenses, indebtedness, and taxes (§ 2053); losses (§ 2054); charitable transfers (§ 2055); and the marital deduction (§§ 2056 and 2056A). As previously noted, the charitable and marital deductions also have gift tax ramifications (§§ 2522 and 2523).

Expenses, Indebtedness, and Taxes (§ 2053). A deduction is allowed for funeral expenses; expenses incurred in administering property; claims against the estate; and unpaid mortgages and other charges against property, whose value is included in the gross estate (without reduction for the mortgage or other indebtedness).

Expenses incurred in administering community property are deductible only in proportion to the deceased spouse's interest in the community.[37]

Administration expenses include commissions of the executor or administrator, attorney's fees of the estate, accountant's fees, court costs, and certain selling expenses for disposition of estate property.

Claims against the estate include property taxes accrued before the decedent's death, unpaid income taxes on income received by the decedent before he or she died, and unpaid gift taxes on gifts made by the decedent before death.

Amounts that may be deducted as claims against the estate are only for enforceable personal obligations of the decedent at the time of death. Deductions for claims founded on promises or agreements are limited to the extent that the liabilities were contracted in good faith and for adequate and full consideration. However, a pledge or subscription in favor of a public, charitable, religious, or educational organization is deductible to the extent that it would have constituted an allowable deduction had it been a bequest.[38]

ETHICAL CONSIDERATIONS

Claims against the Estate

Ten years before her death, Irene (a wealthy widow) started the following annual ritual:

- Each year she makes a gift of $10,000 to each of her five married children and their spouses (for a total of $100,000).
- Shortly after each gift, each donee loans the money back to Irene.
- In connection with the loan, Irene signs a note (interest provided for) payable on demand.

After Irene's death, each of her children and their spouses file a claim against her estate for $100,000 plus accrued interest. The executor of Irene's estate pays off the notes and accrued interest. The amount paid out is deducted on Form 706 (estate tax return) as a § 2053 item.

Is the estate tax deduction proper?

---

[37] *U.S. v. Stapf*, 63–2 USTC ¶12,192, 12 AFTR2d 6326, 84 S.Ct. 248 (USSC, 1963).

[38] § 2053(c)(1)(A) and Reg. § 20.2053–5.

Deductible funeral expenses include the cost of interment, the burial plot or vault, a gravestone, perpetual care of the grave site, and the transportation expense of the person bringing the body to the place of burial. If the decedent had, before death, acquired cemetery lots for him- or herself and family, no deduction is allowed, but the lots are not included in the decedent's gross estate under § 2033 (property in which the decedent had an interest).

Losses (§ 2054).   Section 2054 permits an estate tax deduction for losses from casualty or theft incurred during the period when the estate is being settled. As is true with casualty or theft losses for income tax purposes, any anticipated insurance recovery must be taken into account in arriving at the amount of the deductible loss. Unlike the income tax, however, the deduction is not limited by a floor ($100) or a percentage amount (the excess of 10 percent of adjusted gross income). If the casualty occurs to property after it has been distributed to an heir, the loss belongs to the heir and not to the estate. If the casualty occurs before the decedent's death, it should be claimed on the appropriate Form 1040. The fair market value of the property (if any) on the date of death plus any insurance recovery is included in the gross estate.

As is true of certain administration expenses, a casualty or theft loss of estate property can be claimed as an income tax deduction on the fiduciary return of the estate (Form 1041). But a double deduction prohibition applies, and claiming the income tax deduction requires a waiver of the estate tax deduction.[39]

Transfers to Charity (§§ 2055 and 2522).   A deduction is allowed for the value of property in the decedent's gross estate that is transferred by the decedent through testamentary disposition to (or for the use of) any of the following:

1. The United States or any of its political subdivisions.
2. Any corporation or association organized and operated exclusively for religious, charitable, scientific, literary, or educational purposes.
3. Various veterans' organizations.

The organizations just described are identical to those that qualify for the Federal gift tax deduction under § 2522. With the following exceptions, they are also the same organizations that qualify a donee for an income tax deduction under § 170:

- Certain nonprofit cemetery associations qualify for income tax but not estate and gift tax purposes.
- Foreign charities may qualify under the estate and gift tax but not under the income tax.

No deduction is allowed unless the charitable bequest is specified by a provision in the decedent's will or the transfer was made before death and the property is subsequently included in the gross estate. Generally speaking, a deduction does not materialize when an individual dies intestate (without a will). The amount of the bequest to charity must be mandatory and cannot be left to someone else's discretion. It is, however, permissible to allow another person— such as the executor of the estate—to choose which charity will receive the specified donation. Likewise, a bequest may be expressed as an alternative and still be effective if the noncharitable beneficiary disclaims (refuses) the intervening interest before the due date for the filing of the estate tax return (nine months after the decedent's death plus any extensions of time granted for filing).

---

[39] § 642(g).

Marital Deduction (§§ 2056, 2056A, and 2523). The **marital deduction** originated with the Revenue Act of 1948 as part of the same legislation that permitted married persons to secure the income-splitting advantages of filing joint income tax returns. The purpose of these statutory changes was to eliminate the major tax variations that existed between taxpayers residing in community property and common law states. The marital deduction was designed to provide equity in the estate and gift tax areas.

In a community property state, for example, no marital deduction generally was allowed, since the surviving spouse already owned one-half of the community and that portion was not included in the deceased spouse's gross estate. In a common law state, however, most if not all of the assets often belonged to the breadwinner of the family. When that spouse died first, all of these assets were included in the gross estate. Recall that a dower or curtesy interest (regarding a surviving spouse's right to some of the deceased spouse's property) does not reduce the gross estate. To equalize the situation, therefore, a marital deduction, usually equal to one-half of all separate assets, was allowed upon the death of the first spouse.

Ultimately, Congress decided to dispense with these historical justifications and recognize husband and wife as a single economic unit. Consistent with the approach taken under the income tax, spouses are considered as one for transfer tax purposes. By making the marital deduction unlimited in amount, neither the gift tax nor the estate tax is imposed on outright interspousal transfers of property. The unlimited marital deduction even includes one spouse's share of the community property transferred to the other spouse.

Under § 2056, the marital deduction is allowed only for property that is included in the deceased spouse's gross estate *and* that passes or has passed to the surviving spouse. In determining whether the parties are legally married, look to state law (see Example 1 earlier). Property that *passes* from the decedent to the surviving spouse includes any interest received as (1) the decedent's heir or donee; (2) the decedent's surviving tenant by the entirety or joint tenant; (3) the appointee under the decedent's exercise (or lapse or release) of a general power of appointment; or (4) the beneficiary of insurance on the life of the decedent.

EXAMPLE 59

At the time of his death in the current year, Matthew owned an insurance policy on his own life (face amount of $100,000) with Minerva (his wife) as the designated beneficiary. Matthew and Minerva also owned real estate (worth $250,000) as tenants by the entirety (Matthew had furnished all of the purchase price). As to these transfers, $225,000 ($100,000 + $125,000) is included in Matthew's gross estate, and this amount represents the property that passes to Minerva for purposes of the marital deduction.[40] ▼

Disclaimers can affect the amount passing to the surviving spouse. If, for example, the surviving spouse is the remainderperson under the will of the deceased spouse, a disclaimer by another heir increases the amount passing to the surviving spouse. This, in turn, will increase the amount of the marital deduction allowed to the estate of the deceased spouse.

A problem arises when a property interest passing to the surviving spouse is subject to a mortgage or other encumbrance. In this case, only the net value of the interest after reduction by the amount of the mortgage or other encumbrance

---

[40] Inclusion in the gross estate falls under § 2042 (proceeds of life insurance) and § 2040 (joint interests). Although Matthew provided the full purchase price for the real estate, § 2040(b) requires inclusion of only one-half of the value of the property when one spouse predeceases the other.

qualifies for the marital deduction. To allow otherwise results in a double deduction since a decedent's liabilities are separately deductible under § 2053.

EXAMPLE 60

In his will, Oscar leaves real estate (fair market value of $200,000) to his wife. If the real estate is subject to a mortgage of $40,000 (upon which Oscar was personally liable), the marital deduction is limited to $160,000 ($200,000 – $40,000). The $40,000 mortgage is deductible under § 2053 as an obligation of the decedent (Oscar). ▼

However, if the executor is required under the terms of the decedent's will or under local law to discharge the mortgage out of other assets of the estate or to reimburse the surviving spouse, the payment or reimbursement is an additional interest passing to the surviving spouse.

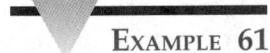

EXAMPLE 61

Assume the same facts as in Example 60, except that Oscar's will directs that the real estate is to pass to his wife free of any liabilities. Accordingly, Oscar's executor pays off the mortgage by using other estate assets and distributes the real estate to Oscar's wife. The marital deduction now becomes $200,000. ▼

Federal estate taxes or other death taxes paid out of the surviving spouse's share of the gross estate are not included in the value of property passing to the surviving spouse. Therefore, it is usually preferable for the deceased spouse's will to provide that death taxes be paid out of the portion of the estate that does not qualify for the marital deduction.

Certain interests in property passing from the deceased spouse to the surviving spouse are referred to as **terminable interests.** Such an interest will terminate or fail after the passage of time, upon the happening of some contingency, or upon the failure of some event to occur. Examples are life estates, annuities, estates for terms of years, and patents. A terminable interest will not qualify for the marital deduction if another interest in the same property passed from the deceased spouse to some other person. By reason of the passing, that other person or his or her heirs may enjoy part of the property after the termination of the surviving spouse's interest.[41]

EXAMPLE 62

Vicky's will places her property in trust, life estate to her husband, Brett, remainder to Andrew or his heirs. The interest passing from Vicky to Brett does not qualify for the marital deduction. It will terminate on Brett's death, and Andrew or his heirs will then possess or enjoy the property. ▼

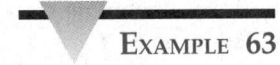

EXAMPLE 63

Assume the same facts as in Example 62, except that Vicky created the trust during her life. No marital deduction is available for gift tax purposes for the same reason as in Example 62.[42] ▼

The justification for the terminable interest rule can be illustrated by examining the possible results of Examples 62 and 63. Without the rule, Vicky could have passed property to Brett at no cost because of the marital deduction. Yet, on Brett's death, none of the property would have been included in his gross estate. Section 2036 (transfers with a retained life estate) would not apply to Brett since he was

---

[41] §§ 2056(b)(1) and 2523(b)(1).

[42] Both Examples 62 and 63 contain the potential for a qualified terminable interest property (QTIP) election discussed later in this section.

not the original transferor of the property. The marital deduction should not be available in situations where the surviving spouse can enjoy the property and still pass it to another without tax consequences. The marital deduction merely postpones the transfer tax on the death of the first spouse and operates to shift any such tax to the surviving spouse.

The terminable interest rule can be avoided under a *power of appointment exception.*[43] Under the exception, a property interest passing from the deceased spouse to the surviving spouse qualifies for the marital deduction (and is not considered a terminable interest) if the surviving spouse is granted a general power of appointment over the property. Thus, the exercise, release, or lapse of the power during the survivor's life or at death will be subject to either the gift or the death tax.[44] If Examples 62 and 63 are modified to satisfy this condition, the life estate passing from Vicky to Brett is not a terminable interest and will qualify for the marital deduction.

As previously noted, the purpose of the terminable interest rule is to ensure that property not taxed to the transferor-spouse (due to the marital deduction) will be subject to the gift or estate tax upon disposition by the transferee-spouse.

Consistent with the objective of the terminable interest rule, another exception offers an alternative means for obtaining the marital deduction. Under this provision, the marital deduction is allowed for transfers of **qualified terminable interest property** (commonly referred to as QTIP). This is defined as property that passes from one spouse to another by gift or at death and for which the transferee-spouse has a qualifying income interest for life.

For a donee or a surviving spouse, a qualifying income interest for life exists under the following conditions:

- The person is entitled for life to all of the income from the property (or a specific portion of it), payable at annual or more frequent intervals.
- No person (including the spouse) has a power to appoint any part of the property to any person other than the surviving spouse during his or her life.[45]

If these conditions are met, an election can be made to claim a marital deduction as to the QTIP. For estate tax purposes, the executor of the estate makes the election on Form 706 (the Federal estate tax return). For gift tax purposes, the donor spouse makes the election on Form 709 (the Federal gift tax return). The election is irrevocable.

If the election is made, a transfer tax is imposed upon the QTIP when the transferee-spouse disposes of it by gift or upon death. If the disposition occurs during life, the gift tax applies, measured by the fair market value of the property as of that time.[46] If no lifetime disposition takes place, the fair market value of the property on the date of death (or alternate valuation date if applicable) is included in the gross estate of the transferee-spouse.[47]

EXAMPLE 64

In 1997, Clyde dies and provides in his will that certain assets (fair market value of $400,000) are to be transferred to a trust under which Gertrude (Clyde's wife) is granted a life estate with the remainder passing to their children upon Gertrude's death. Presuming all of the preceding requirements are satisfied and Clyde's executor so elects, his estate receives a marital deduction of $400,000. ▼

---

[43] For the estate tax, see § 2056(b)(5). The gift tax counterpart is in § 2523(e).

[44] §§ 2514 and 2041.

[45] §§ 2523(f) and 2056(b)(7).

[46] § 2519.

[47] § 2044.

EXAMPLE 65

Assume the same facts as in Example 64, with the further stipulation that Gertrude dies in 1999 when the trust assets are worth $900,000. This amount is included in her gross estate. ▼

Because the estate tax is imposed on assets not physically included in the probate estate, the law allows the liability for those assets to be shifted to the heirs. The amount to be shifted is determined by comparing the estate tax liability both with and without the inclusion of the QTIP. This right of recovery can be canceled by a provision in the deceased spouse's will.[48]

The major difference between the power of appointment and the QTIP exceptions to the terminable interest rules relates to the control the surviving spouse has over the principal of the trust. In the power of appointment situation, the surviving spouse can appoint the principal to him- or herself (or to his or her estate). Only if this power is not exercised will the property pass as specified in the deceased spouse's will. In the QTIP situation, however, the surviving spouse has no such control. If the QTIP election is made, the principal must pass as prescribed by the transferor (the donor in the case of a lifetime transfer or the decedent in the case of a death transfer).

In the case of a nonresident alien whose spouse is a U.S. citizen, the marital deduction is allowed for estate and gift tax purposes. Property passing to a surviving spouse who is not a U.S. citizen is not eligible for the estate tax marital deduction.[49] Similarly, no gift tax marital deduction is allowed where the spouse is not a U.S. citizen. However, the annual exclusion for these gift transfers is increased from $10,000 to $100,000.[50]

For the estate tax, an exception exists for certain transfers to a surviving spouse who is not a U.S. citizen.[51] If the transfer is to a *qualified domestic trust*, the marital deduction is allowed. A qualified domestic trust must meet the following conditions:[52]

- The trust instrument provides that all trustees must be U.S. citizens or domestic corporations.
- The surviving spouse is entitled to all income from the trust payable at least annually.
- The trust must be subject to the estate tax upon the death of the surviving spouse.
- The executor makes an irrevocable election for the trust on the deceased spouse's estate tax return.

The reason for the qualified domestic trust exception is to guarantee that the marital deduction property will not escape estate taxes on the death of the surviving spouse. This would be possible if the property and spouse are outside the jurisdiction of the U.S. tax laws.

COMPUTING THE FEDERAL ESTATE TAX

8 ▼ **LEARNING OBJECTIVE**
Determine the Federal estate tax liability.

Once the taxable estate has been determined, post-1976 taxable gifts are added to arrive at the tax base. Note that pre-1977 taxable gifts do not enter into the computation of the tax base.

---

[48] § 2207A(a).
[49] § 2056(d)(1).
[50] § 2523(i).

[51] § 2056(d)(2).
[52] § 2056A.

EXAMPLE 66

Joyce dies in 1997, leaving a taxable estate of $800,000. During her life, Joyce made taxable gifts as follows: $50,000 in 1975 and $100,000 in 1982. For estate tax purposes, the Federal estate tax base becomes $900,000 determined as follows: $800,000 (taxable estate) + $100,000 (taxable gift made in 1982). ▼

With the unified transfer tax rate schedule contained in § 2001(c), the tentative tax on the tax base is computed. Using the facts in Example 66, the tentative tax on $900,000 is $306,800 [$248,300 + (39% × $150,000)]—see Appendix A, page A–7.

See the discussion below for the phase-out of the unified tax credit and the graduated tax rates for certain large estates.

All available estate tax credits are subtracted from the tentative estate tax to arrive at the estate tax (if any) that is due.

ESTATE TAX CREDITS

Unified Tax Credit (§ 2010).   Recall from previous discussion of this credit that the amount of the credit allowed depends upon the year of the transfer. Returning to Example 66, the credit allowed on the gift in 1982 was $62,800. Since the exemption equivalent of this amount is $225,000 (refer to Table 17–1), no gift tax was due on the transfer. On Joyce's death in 1997, however, the unified tax credit is $192,800, which is less than the tentative tax of $306,800 (refer to the discussion following Example 66). Disregarding the effect of any other estate tax credits, Joyce's estate owes a tax of $114,000 [$306,800 (tentative tax on a tax base of $900,000) – $192,800 (unified tax credit for 1997)].

An adjustment to the unified tax credit is necessary if any portion of the specific exemption was utilized on gifts made after September 8, 1976, and before January 1, 1977. In this regard, refer to Example 5.

Under the Revenue Act of 1987, the benefit of the unified tax credit and the graduated unified tax rates is phased out for taxable transfers exceeding a certain amount. The gift and estate tax liability for taxable transfers in excess of $10 million is increased by 5 percent of the excess until the benefit of the credit and graduated brackets is recaptured.

Credit for State Death Taxes (§ 2011).   The Code allows a limited credit for the amount of any death tax actually paid to any state (or to the District of Columbia) attributable to any property included in the gross estate. Like the credit for foreign death taxes paid, this provision mitigates the harshness of subjecting the same property to multiple death taxes.

The credit allowed is limited to the lesser of the amount of tax actually paid or the amount provided for in a table contained in § 2011(b). (See Appendix A, page A–10.) The table amount is based on the adjusted taxable estate, which for this purpose is the taxable estate less $60,000. No credit is allowed if the adjusted taxable estate is $40,000 or less.

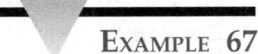

EXAMPLE 67

Butch's taxable estate is $98,000, and the state of appropriate jurisdiction imposes a death tax of $1,500 on this amount. Since the adjusted taxable estate is $38,000 ($98,000 − $60,000), none of the $1,500 paid qualifies for the state death tax credit. ▼

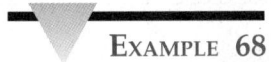

EXAMPLE 68

Butch's taxable estate is $200,000, and the state of appropriate jurisdiction imposes a death tax of $3,000 on this amount. Because the adjusted taxable estate is $140,000 ($200,000 − $60,000), the table amount limits the death tax credit to $1,200. ▼

As Examples 67 and 68 illustrate, the credit allowed by § 2011 may be less than the amount of state death taxes paid. The reverse is possible but usually is not the case. Most states make sure that the minimum tax payable to the jurisdiction is at least equal to the credit allowed by the table. Sometimes this result is accomplished by a soak-up or sponge tax superimposed on the regular inheritance tax. Thus, if the regular inheritance tax yields $2,500, but the maximum credit allowed by the table is $3,200, a soak-up tax would impose an additional $700 in state death taxes. In other states, the state death tax liability depends entirely upon the amount allowed for Federal death tax purposes under the table. In the previous illustration, the state death tax would be an automatic $3,200.

Credit for Tax on Prior Transfers (§ 2013).   Suppose Nancy owns some property that she passes at death to Lisa. Shortly thereafter, Lisa dies and passes the property to Rita. Assuming both estates are subject to the Federal estate tax, the successive deaths result in a multiple effect. To mitigate the possible multiple taxation that might result, § 2013 provides relief in the form of a credit for a death tax on prior transfers. In the preceding hypothetical case, Lisa's estate may be able to claim as an estate tax credit some of the taxes paid by Nancy's estate.

The credit is limited to the lesser of the following amounts:

1. The amount of the Federal estate tax attributable to the transferred property in the transferor's estate.
2. The amount of the Federal estate tax attributable to the transferred property in the decedent's estate.

To apply the limitations, certain adjustments must be made that are not covered in this text.[53] However, it is not necessary for the transferred property to be identified in the present decedent's estate or for it to be in existence at the time of the present decedent's death. It is sufficient that the transfer of property was subjected to the Federal estate tax in the estate of the transferor and that the transferor died within the prescribed period of time.

---

[53] See the instructions to Form 706 and Reg. §§ 20.2013–2 and –3.

If the transferor dies within two years after or before the present decedent's death, the credit is allowed in full (subject to the preceding limitations). If the transferor died more than two years before the decedent, the credit is a certain percentage: 80 percent if the transferor died within the third or fourth year preceding the decedent's death, 60 percent if within the fifth or sixth year, 40 percent if within the seventh or eighth year, and 20 percent if within the ninth or tenth year.

EXAMPLE 69

Under Nancy's will, Lisa inherits property. One year later Lisa dies. Assume the estate tax attributable to the inclusion of the property in Nancy's gross estate was $15,000 and the estate tax attributable to the inclusion of the property in Lisa's gross estate is $12,000. Under these circumstances, Lisa's estate claims a credit against the estate tax of $12,000 (refer to limitation 2). ▼

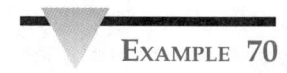

EXAMPLE 70

Assume the same facts as in Example 69, except that Lisa dies three years after Nancy. The applicable credit is now 80% of $12,000, or $9,600. ▼

Credit for Foreign Death Taxes (§ 2014). A credit is allowed against the estate tax for any estate, inheritance, legacy, or succession tax actually paid to a foreign country. For purposes of this provision, the term *foreign country* means not only states in the international sense but also possessions or political subdivisions of foreign states and possessions of the United States.

The credit is allowed for death taxes paid with respect to (1) property situated within the foreign country to which the tax is paid, (2) property included in the decedent's gross estate, and (3) the decedent's estate. No credit is allowed for interest or penalties paid in connection with foreign death taxes.

The credit is limited to the lesser of the following amounts:

1. The amount of the foreign death tax attributable to the property situated in the country imposing the tax and included in the decedent's gross estate for Federal estate tax purposes.
2. The amount of the Federal estate tax attributable to particular property situated in a foreign country, subject to death tax in that country, and included in the decedent's gross estate for Federal estate tax purposes.

Both of these limitations may require certain adjustments to arrive at the amount of the allowable credit. These adjustments are illustrated in the Regulations and are not discussed in this text.[54] In addition to the credit for foreign death taxes under the provisions of Federal estate tax law, similar credits are allowable under death tax conventions with a number of foreign countries.[55] If a credit is allowed under either the provisions of law or the provisions of a convention, the credit that is most beneficial to the estate should be claimed.

PROCEDURAL MATTERS

A Federal estate tax return, if required, is due nine months after the date of the decedent's death.[56] The time limit applies to all estates regardless of the nationality or residence of the decedent. Not infrequently, an executor will request and obtain from the IRS an extension of time for filing Form 706 (estate tax return).[57]

---

[54] Reg. §§ 20.20–2 and –3.
[55] For the list of countries with which the United States has death tax conventions, refer to Footnote 10.

[56] § 6075(a).
[57] § 6081.

CONCEPT SUMMARY 17–2

Federal Estate Tax Provisions

1. The Federal gift and estate taxes are both excise taxes on the transfer of wealth.
2. The starting point for applying the Federal estate tax is to determine which assets are subject to tax. Such assets comprise a decedent's gross estate.
3. The gross estate generally will not include any gifts made by the decedent within three years of death. It does include any gift tax paid on these transfers.
4. Based on the premise that one should not continue to enjoy or control property and not have it subject to the estate tax, certain incomplete transfers are included in the gross estate.
5. Upon the death of a joint tenant, the full value of the property is included in the gross estate unless the survivor(s) made a contribution toward the cost of the property. Spouses are subject to a special rule that calls for automatic inclusion of half of the value of the property in the gross estate of the first tenant to die. The creation of joint ownership is subject to the gift tax when a tenant receives a lesser interest in the property than is warranted by the consideration furnished.
6. A power of appointment is the right to determine who shall own or enjoy, presently or in the future, the property subject to the power. The exercise, lapse, or release of a general power of appointment during the life of the holder is subject to the gift tax. If the exercise, lapse, or release occurs at death, the property subject to the power is included in the holder's gross estate. If, however, a special power of appointment is involved, no gift or estate tax consequences result.
7. If the decedent is the insured, life insurance proceeds are included in the gross estate if either of two conditions is satisfied. First, the proceeds are paid to the estate or for the benefit of the estate. Second, the decedent possessed incidents of ownership (e.g., the right to change beneficiaries) over the policy.
8. In moving from the gross estate to the taxable estate, certain deductions are allowed. Under § 2053, deductions are permitted for various administration expenses (e.g., executor's commissions, funeral costs), debts of the decedent, and certain unpaid taxes. Casualty and theft losses incurred during the administration of an estate can be deducted in arriving at the taxable estate.
9. Charitable transfers are deductible if the designated organization holds qualified status with the IRS at the time of the gift or upon death.
10. Transfers to a spouse qualify for the gift or estate tax marital deduction. Except as noted in (11), such transfers are subject to the terminable interest limitation.
11. The terminable interest limitation will not apply if the transferee-spouse is given a general power of appointment over the property or the QTIP election is made. In the case of a lifetime transfer, the donor-spouse makes the QTIP election. In the case of a testamentary transfer, the executor of the estate of the deceased spouse has the election responsibility.
12. The tax base for determining the estate tax is the taxable estate plus all post-1976 taxable gifts. All available credits are subtracted from the tax.
13. Of prime importance in the tax credit area is the unified tax credit. Except for large taxable transfers, the unified tax credit is $192,800 (exemption equivalent of $600,000).
14. Other Federal estate tax credits include credits for state death taxes, tax on prior transfers, and foreign death taxes.
15. If due, a Federal estate tax return (Form 706) must be filed within nine months of the date of the decedent's death.

The filing requirements parallel the exemption equivalent amounts of the unified tax credit available for each year (refer to Table 17–1). The filing requirements may be lower when the decedent has made taxable gifts after 1976 or has utilized any of the $30,000 specific gift tax exemption after September 8, 1976.

EXAMPLE 71

Carlos dies in 1997, leaving a gross estate of $595,000. If Carlos did not make any post-1976 taxable gifts or use the specific gift tax exemption after September 8, 1976, his estate need not file Form 706. ▼

EXAMPLE 72

Assume the same facts as in Example 71, except that Carlos made a taxable gift of $20,000 in 1980. Since the filing requirement now becomes $580,000 [$600,000 (the regular filing requirement for 1997) – $20,000 (the post-1976 taxable gift)], Carlos's estate must file Form 706. ▼

THE GENERATION SKIPPING TRANSFER TAX

9   LEARNING OBJECTIVE
Appreciate the role of the generation skipping transfer tax.

In order to prevent partial avoidance of Federal gift and estate taxes on large transfers, the tax law imposes an additional generation skipping transfer tax.

THE PROBLEM

Previously, by structuring the transaction carefully, it was possible to bypass a generation of transfer taxes.

EXAMPLE 73

Under his will, Edward creates a trust, life estate to Stephen (Edward's son) and remainder to Ava (Edward's granddaughter) upon Stephen's death. Edward is subject to the Federal estate tax, but no tax results on Stephen's death. Stephen held a life estate, but § 2036 does not apply because he was not the grantor of the trust. Nor does § 2033 (property owned by the decedent) come into play because Stephen's interest disappeared upon his death. The ultimate result is that the property in trust skips a generation of transfer taxes. ▼

EXAMPLE 74

Amy gives assets to Eric (her grandson). Called a direct skip, the gift would circumvent any transfer taxes that would have resulted had the assets been channeled through Eric's parents. ▼

THE SOLUTION

The generation skipping transfer tax (GSTT) is imposed when a younger generation is bypassed in favor of a later generation.[58] The GSTT applies to lifetime transfers by gift and to transfers by death. The tax rate imposed is the highest rate under the gift and estate tax schedule, or 55 percent. Consequently, the GSTT does not permit the use of the graduated rate structure.

The application of the GSTT depends upon the type of arrangement involved. In Example 73, the GSTT would be imposed upon the death of Stephen (the life

---

[58] The generation skipping transfer tax provisions are contained in §§ 2601–2663 of the Code.

tenant). The tax, however, is levied against the trust. In effect, it reduces the amount that is distributed to Ava (the remainderperson).

In Example 74, the GSTT is imposed upon Amy when the gift is made to Eric. In this situation, not only will Amy be subject to the GSTT but the amount of the tax represents an additional gift to Eric.[59] Thus, if a gift is a direct skip (such as Example 74), the total transfer tax (the GSTT plus the gift tax) may exceed what the donee receives.

Though the GSTT seemingly yields a confiscatory result, every grantor is entitled to a $1 million exemption. The exemption can be applied to whichever transfers the grantor (or personal representative of the grantor) chooses. Any appreciation attributable to the exempted portion of the transfer is not subject to the GSTT.

EXAMPLE 75

Assume the same facts as in Example 73 except that the trust created by Edward contained assets valued at $1 million. Ten years later when Stephen dies, the trust is now worth $3 million. If the exemption of $1 million is used upon the creation of the trust, no GSTT results upon Stephen's death. ▼

ETHICAL CONSIDERATIONS

A Gift That Keeps Giving!

Should a tax cheat be treated less harshly than a rich person under the tax system? First, consider Joe who is in the 39.6 percent income tax bracket. Joe deliberately omits $100,000 of income from his Form 1040. He is caught and forced to pay a tax of $39,600 and a civil fraud penalty of $75,000 (75% × $100,000) for a total outlay of $114,600.

Second, consider Jack who makes a gift of $100,000 to his grandson. Assuming Jack has exhausted the $1 million generation skipping transfer tax (GSST) exemption and is in the top gift tax bracket, his tax is computed as follows.

Gift tax (55% × $100,000)	$ 55,000
GSST (55% × $100,000)	55,000
Gift tax on GSST (55% × $55,000)	30,250
Total tax	$140,250

Compare $114,600 (Joe, the tax cheat) with $140,250 (Jack, the rich person), and see who is better off. Keep in mind that in each case the same amount (i.e., $100,000) is involved. Needless to say, the GSTT is a gift that keeps giving!

TAX PLANNING CONSIDERATIONS

Tax planning for the Federal gift and estate tax is discussed in Chapter 18 in connection with family tax planning.

---

[59] § 2515.

KEY TERMS

Alternate valuation date,   17–7

Annual exclusion, 17–13

Disclaimers,   17–12

Exemption equivalent, 17–6

Future interest, 17–13

Gross estate,   17–18

Inheritance tax, 17–3

Joint tenants,   17–8

Marital deduction, 17–31

Power of appointment, 17–25

Probate estate, 17–18

Qualified terminable interest property (QTIP),   17–33

Taxable estate, 17–29

Taxable gift,   17–5

Tenants by the entirety,   17–8

Tenants in common, 17–9

Terminable interests, 17–32

Unified tax credit, 17–6

Unified transfer tax, 17–2

PROBLEM MATERIALS

DISCUSSION QUESTIONS

1. Why can the unified transfer tax be categorized as an excise tax? In this regard, how does it differ from an income tax?

2. Do Federal transfer taxes carry negative economic implications? Explain.

3. What are the major differences between the Federal estate tax and the typical inheritance tax levied by some states?

4. What was the intended purpose of the Federal gift tax?

5. Omar is a wealthy citizen and resident of Yemen. His family physician has recommended that Omar go to the Mayo Clinic in Minnesota for an operation to remove a malignant growth. Omar is hesitant to do so because he fears the imposition of the U.S. Federal estate tax if the operation is unsuccessful. Does place of death control the application of the Federal estate tax? Explain.

6. Onishi Yamato is a resident and citizen of Japan. Because real estate is so expensive and scarce in Japan, he is intrigued by the investment opportunities in such locales as Arizona and New Mexico. As a result, he has invested heavily in unimproved land that has development potential. Discuss what could happen for estate tax purposes in the event of Onishi's death.

7. Pearl comes to you regarding the making of gifts to family members in the current year. When you ask her about prior gifts, she responds, "What difference does it make what I did in the past?" Please clarify matters for Pearl.

8. In determining the *tax base* for computing the *tentative estate tax*, all prior taxable gifts must be added to the taxable estate. Do you agree or disagree? Why?

9. At your recent college reunion, a former classmate was probably trying to impress you when she remarked: "I have made a lot of gifts to my grandchildren, but I still have my estate tax exemption equivalent." Interpret this remark under the following assumptions:
   a. That your classmate correctly understands the tax law.
   b. That your classmate does not understand the tax law.

10. What is the justification for the alternate valuation date election?

11. What conditions must be satisfied before the alternate valuation date can be used?

12. What are the similarities between each of the following?
    a. Joint tenancy and tenancy by the entirety.
    b. Tenancy in common and community property.
    c. Tenancy by the entirety and community property.

13. Although Rick, age 35, has two degrees in chemistry, he has decided to quit his job and attend medical school full-time. Andrea, Rick's widowed mother, has agreed to pay all of his related expenses. Are there any gift tax ramifications? Why or why not?

14. Carla purchases a U.S. savings bond and registers ownership as follows: "Carla, payable to George on Carla's death." Four years later, Carla dies and George redeems the bond. When has a gift taken place? Explain.

15. In connection with gift loans, comment on the following points:
    a. Since any interest element recognized by the lender as income can be deducted by the borrower, the income tax effect is neutralized for the family unit.
    b. The borrower's net investment income for the year is less than $1,000.
    c. The gift loan involved $95,000.
    d. The lender charged the borrower interest of 2%.

16. What purpose does § 2516 serve?

17. Under Leon's will, all of his property is to pass to his son, Jody. Jody is a widower, and his only survivor is a daughter, Brenda. Jody has considerable wealth of his own and is in poor health. Do you recognize an attractive estate tax option for the parties?

18. What is the justification for the annual exclusion?

19. Mike creates an irrevocable trust. Under the terms of the trust, his daughter Jean is granted a life estate, and her children receive the remainder interest. Has Mike made a gift of a future interest? What difference does it make?

20. In connection with the gift-splitting provision of § 2513, comment on the following:
    a. What it was designed to accomplish.
    b. How the election is made.
    c. Its utility in a community property jurisdiction.

21. In connection with the filing of a Federal gift tax return, comment on the following:
    a. No Federal gift tax is due.
    b. The § 2513 election to split gifts is to be used.
    c. A gift of a future interest is involved.
    d. The donor uses a fiscal year for Federal income tax purposes.
    e. The donor obtained from the IRS an extension of time for filing his or her Federal income tax return.

22. Distinguish between the following:
    a. The gross estate and the taxable estate.
    b. The gross estate and the probate estate.

23. What is the estate tax treatment of a surviving spouse's dower interest that is claimed from the estate of the deceased spouse? Does this differ from the treatment of the surviving spouse's share of the community property? Explain.

24. What was the original justification for § 2035? Does this justification still exist? Explain.

25. At the time of Emile's death, he was a joint tenant with Colette in a parcel of real estate. With regard to the inclusion in Emile's gross estate under § 2040, comment on the following independent assumptions:
    a. Emile and Colette received the property as a gift from Douglas.
    b. Colette provided all of the purchase price of the property.
    c. Colette's contribution was received as a gift from Emile.
    d. Emile's contribution was derived from income generated by property he received as a gift from Colette.

26. If the holder can use the power to appoint some of the property for his or her benefit, it is a general power of appointment. Do you agree? Why or why not?

27. Warren owns an insurance policy on the life of Sylvia with Eric as the designated beneficiary. Of the three persons involved, Sylvia is the eldest and in poor health. What potential tax problems are involved?

28. Zane and Kara are husband and wife when Zane dies. Which of the following *independent* situations satisfies the "passing" requirement for marital deduction purposes?
    a. Kara elects her dower interest. Under state law, this gives her one-third outright ownership in Zane's property.
    b. Zane and Kara held real estate as tenants by the entirety.
    c. Kara owned an insurance policy on Zane's life, with Kim (their son) as the designated beneficiary.

29. In terms of the QTIP (qualified terminable interest property) election, comment on the following:
    a. Who makes the election.
    b. What the election accomplishes.
    c. The tax effect of the election upon the death of the surviving spouse.

30. Property passing to a surviving spouse who is not a U.S. citizen is not eligible for the estate tax marital deduction. Is this statement always valid? Explain.

31. Does the credit for state death taxes (§ 2011) eliminate the double taxation of an estate? Explain.

32. Would the credit for tax on prior transfers (§ 2013) ever apply in the husband and wife–type of situation? Explain.

33. On a gift that is a "direct skip," it is possible that the total transfer taxes might exceed what the donee receives. Explain.

PROBLEMS

34. An estate holds the following assets:

	Value on Date of Death	Value Six Months Later
Land	$890,000	$900,000
Stock in Cardinal Corporation	790,000	680,000
Stock in Flamingo Corporation	700,000	710,000

The stock in Cardinal Corporation is sold by the estate for $690,000 eight months after the owner's death, while the stock in Flamingo Corporation is sold for $705,000 four months after death.
    a. Is the § 2032 election available to the estate?
    b. If so and the election is made, what value results?
    c. What value results if the § 2032 election is not available or is not made?

35. In which, if any, of the following *independent* situations, could the alternate valuation date *not be* elected? In all cases, Rudy and Ashley are husband and wife, and Rudy dies first.
    a. Rudy's will passes all of his property to Ashley.
    b. Rudy's will passes one-half of his property to Ashley and the other half to the city of Boise, Idaho.
    c. The election would decrease the estate tax liability but increase the value of the gross estate.
    d. Rudy's gross estate is $590,000.
    e. Rudy's gross estate is $550,000. Rudy made a taxable gift of $60,000 four years ago.

36. In each of the following independent situations, indicate whether the transfer by Phillip is, or could be, subject to the Federal gift tax:
    a. Phillip makes a contribution to an influential political figure.
    b. Phillip makes a contribution to Crow Corporation, of which he is not a shareholder.
    c. In consideration of his upcoming marriage to Teri, Phillip establishes a savings account in Teri's name.
    d. Same as (c). After their marriage, Phillip establishes a joint checking account in the names of "Phillip and Teri."
    e. Same as (d). One year after the checking account is established, Teri withdraws all of the funds.
    f. Phillip exercises a special power of appointment in favor of Teri.
    g. Phillip enters into an agreement with Teri where he will transfer property to her in full satisfaction of her marital rights. One month after the agreement, the transfer occurs. Later Phillip and Teri are divorced.
    h. Phillip purchases U.S. savings bonds, listing ownership as "Phillip and Teri." Several years later, and after Phillip's death, Teri redeems the bonds.

37. In each of the following independent situations, indicate whether the transfer by Jeff is, or could be, subject to the Federal gift tax:
    a. Jeff purchases real estate and lists title as "Jeff and Chris as joint tenants." Jeff and Chris are brothers.
    b. Same as (a), except that Jeff and Chris are husband and wife.
    c. Jeff creates a revocable trust with Chris as the designated beneficiary.
    d. Same as (c). One year after creating the trust, Jeff releases all power to revoke the trust.
    e. Jeff takes out an insurance policy on his life, designating Chris as the beneficiary.
    f. Same as (e). Two years later, Jeff dies and the policy proceeds are paid to Chris.
    g. Jeff takes out an insurance policy on the life of Gretchen and designates Chris as the beneficiary. Shortly thereafter, Gretchen dies and the policy proceeds are paid to Chris.
    h. Jeff pays for Chris's college tuition.

38. In January 1997, Roger and Jean enter into a property settlement under which Roger agrees to pay $500,000 to Jean in return for the release of her marital rights. At the time the agreement is signed, Roger pays Jean $100,000 as a first installment. Although the parties intended to obtain a divorce, Roger dies in July 1997 before legal proceedings have been instituted. After Roger's death, the executor of his estate pays to Jean the $400,000 remaining balance due under the property settlement.
    a. What are the gift tax consequences of the $100,000 payment made upon the signing of the agreement? Why?
    b. What are the estate tax consequences of the $400,000 paid to Jean from estate assets after Roger's death? Why?

39. In 1997, Alice made gifts of stock (fair market value of $800,000) to her adult son. Alice has never made any prior taxable gifts. Alice's husband, Bill, previously made a taxable gift of $750,000 in early 1976 upon which he paid a gift tax of $174,900. At the time of the gift, Bill was not married to Alice.
    a. Determine the amount of the gift tax on the 1997 transfer if the § 2513 election is not made.
    b. If the § 2513 election is made.

40. On the date of her death on May 7, 1997, Geraldine owned the following property:

	Fair Market Value
Stock in Falcon Corporation	$300,000
Stock in Harrier Corporation	410,000
City of Richmond bonds	505,000

Falcon Corporation declared a dividend on March 27, 1997, payable on May 15, 1997, to shareholders of record as of April 30, 1997. Harrier Corporation declared a dividend on April 4, 1997, payable on May 23, 1997, to shareholders of record as of May 8, 1997.

In the month of May 1997, Geraldine's executor receives the following amounts: $5,000 dividend from Falcon; $7,000 dividend from Harrier; and $12,500 interest ($12,200 accrued to date of death) from the City of Richmond.

How much of these amounts is included in Geraldine's gross estate?

41. Will, a widower, dies in 1997. Previously, he made the following transfers:

    • Land, fair market value of $400,000, given to his son in 1995. A gift tax of $20,000 was paid as a result of the gift. The land has a date of death value of $450,000.

    • Insurance policy on Will's life given to his daughter (the designated beneficiary) in 1995. Because it was term insurance, the policy had a value of less than the annual exclusion. Consequently, no taxable gift resulted. The policy has a maturity value of $70,000.

    • Stock worth $80,000 given to Will's grandson in 1981. The transfer resulted in no gift tax and had a date of death value of $200,000.

    As to these transfers, how much is included in Will's gross estate?

42. In 1976, Irma created a revocable trust with securities worth $300,000. National Trust Company was designated as the trustee. Under the terms of the trust, Irma retained a life estate with remainder to her children. In 1995, Irma releases her right to revoke the trust. Irma dies in 1997 when the trust assets have a fair market value of $1,200,000.
    a. What, if any, are Irma's gift tax consequences in 1976?
    b. What, if any, is included in Irma's gross estate in 1997?
    c. Would your answer to (b) change if Irma *also* released her life estate in 1995? Explain.

43. In 1980, Jim and Maude purchase a commercial annuity. Jim furnishes 75% of the cost, and Maude provides the balance. Under the terms of the contract, Jim is to receive $48,000 per year for his life. If Jim predeceases Maude, she is to receive $36,000 per year for her life.
    a. If Jim dies first when the value of the survivorship feature is $400,000, how much, if any, is included in his gross estate?
    b. Would anything regarding the annuity be included in Maude's gross estate when she dies five years after Jim? Explain.

44. In 1974, John purchased real estate for $400,000, listing ownership as follows: "John and Mary, equal tenants in common." John predeceases Mary in 1997 when the property is worth $900,000. Before 1974, John had not made any taxable gifts or utilized the $30,000 specific exemption. Assume John and Mary are father and daughter.
    a. Determine John's gift tax consequences, if any, in 1974.
    b. How much, if any, of the property should be included in John's gross estate?

45. In 1966, Myrna transfers by gift a personal residence to Louise and Leon, her daughter and son-in-law. The gift is a wedding present, and title to the property is listed as "Louise and Leon, tenants in common."
    a. Did Myrna have gift tax consequences in 1966? Explain.
    b. If the value of the residence is $400,000 when Louise predeceases Leon in 1997, how much, if any, is included in her gross estate?

46. In 1985, Dana purchased real estate for $600,000, listing title to the property as follows: "Dana and June, joint tenants with the right of survivorship." June predeceases Dana in 1997 when the real estate is worth $950,000. Assume Dana and June are sisters and that neither has made any other taxable gifts or utilized her $30,000 specific exemption.
    a. Determine Dana's gift tax consequences, if any, in 1985.
    b. How much, if any, of the property should be included in June's gross estate?

47. Assume the same facts as in Problem 46, except that Dana and June are husband and wife (rather than sisters).

a. Determine Dana's gift tax consequences, if any, in 1985.

b. How much, if any, of the property should be included in June's gross estate? Will any such inclusion generate an estate tax liability? Explain.

48. Mike Edwards would like to make a lifetime transfer in trust of $300,000 to his son, Keith, and accomplish the following objectives:

• Avoid any death tax on the deaths of Mike, Keith, and Bette (Keith's wife).

• Give Keith the right to determine what portion of the remainder should be allocated between Bette and their children.

• Give Keith some additional security by allowing him to reach the principal should the need materialize.

• Prevent Keith from squandering all of the principal to the detriment of Bette or her children.

Write a letter to Mike recommending a course of action. Mike's address is 4320 Richmond Avenue, Syracuse, NY 13244.

49. In each of the following independent situations, determine how much should be included in Burton's gross estate under § 2042 as to the various life insurance policies involved. Assume that none of the policies are community property.

a. At the time of his death, Burton owned a paid-up policy on the life of Suzana, with Penny as the designated beneficiary. The policy had a replacement cost of $80,000 and a maturity value of $300,000.

b. Nancy owns a policy on the life of Burton ($300,000 maturity value) with Burton's estate as the designated beneficiary. Upon Burton's death, the insurance company pays $300,000 to his estate.

c. Four years before his death, Burton transferred a policy on his life ($300,000 maturity value) to Ann as a gift. Burton retained the power to change beneficiaries. At the time of the transfer, the designated beneficiary was Ann. Because Burton had never exercised his right to change beneficiaries, the insurance company pays Ann $300,000 upon Burton's death.

d. Same as (c), except that Burton releases the power to change beneficiaries one year before his death.

50. In each of the following independent situations, determine the amount of the decedent's *gross estate*. All deaths occur in 1997.

	Decedent			
	Carol	Grace	Herb	Don
Real estate	$500,000	$400,000	$800,000	$900,000
Dower interest claimed by Herb's surviving spouse (outright ownership of 50% of the real estate)	—	—	400,000	—
Pre-1976 taxable gifts	200,000	—	—	—
Post-1976 taxable gifts	—	—	—	300,000
Marketable securities	400,000	300,000	400,000	800,000
Fair market value of a note due from Grace's son that is forgiven in her will	—	200,000	—	—

51. Comment on how each of the following independent situations should be handled for estate tax purposes:

a. Before her death, Linda issued a note payable to her daughter in the amount of $100,000. Linda never received any consideration for the note. After Linda's death, the daughter files a claim against the estate and collects $100,000 on the note.

b. At the time of her death, Saleha (a widow) owned 10 cemetery lots (each worth $5,000), which she had purchased many years before for herself and her family.

c. At the time of his death, Stanley was delinquent in the payment of back Federal income taxes. Stanley's executor pays the taxes from assets of the estate.

52. At the time of his death in the current year, Jerome owned the following real estate:

Tract A	$1,000,000
Mortgage on tract A	(200,000)
Tract B	700,000
Mortgage on tract B	(100,000)

Under Jerome's will, both tracts of land pass to Janice (Jerome's surviving spouse). However, Jerome's will directs the executor to pay off the mortgage on tract B from the remainder interest passing to the children.
   a. How much marital deduction will Jerome's estate be allowed?
   b. What is the deduction for indebtedness under § 2053?

53. In 1997, Brad places in trust $500,000 worth of securities. Under the terms of the trust instrument, Wanda (Brad's wife) is granted a life estate, and on Wanda's death, the remainder interest passes to Brad and Wanda's children (as Wanda determines in her will). Upon Wanda's death 18 years later, the trust assets are valued at $2 million.
   a. How much, if any, marital deduction will be allowed on the gift made in 1997?
   b. How much, if any, of the trust will be included in Wanda's gross estate upon her death?

54. Assume the same facts as in Problem 53, except that Brad made the QTIP election when the trust was created. Further assume that Wanda has no choice as to which of her children will receive the remainder interest upon her death.
   a. How much, if any, marital deduction will be allowed on the gift made in 1997?
   b. How much, if any, of the trust will be subject to the Federal estate tax upon Wanda's later death?

55. Determine the credit for state death taxes in each of the following independent situations:
   a. The adjusted taxable estate is $124,000. The amount of state death tax paid is $1,200.
   b. The adjusted taxable estate is $450,000. The amount of state death tax paid is $9,500.
   c. The adjusted taxable estate is $900,000. The state death tax is a soak-up tax that was paid.

56. Under Ira's will, Jill (Ira's sister) inherits property. Three years later, Jill dies. Determine Jill's credit for tax on prior transfers based on the following assumptions:
   a. The estate tax attributable to the inclusion of the property in Ira's gross estate is $70,000, and the estate tax attributable to the inclusion of the property in Jill's gross estate is $50,000.
   b. The estate tax attributable to the inclusion of the property in Ira's gross estate is $60,000, and the estate tax attributable to the inclusion of the property in Jill's gross estate is $80,000.

57. In each of the following independent situations, determine the decedent's final estate tax liability (net of any unified tax credit):

	Decedent		
	Lucinda	**Roland**	**Warren**
Year of death	1984	1986	1997
Taxable estate	$400,000	$600,000	$900,000
Post-1976 taxable gift			
Made in 1982	300,000	—	—
Made in 1984	—	350,000	—
Made in 1989	—	—	500,000

58. Dena, a wealthy widow, has exhausted her $1 million generation skipping transfer tax (GSTT) exemption. Past gifts have also placed her in the 55% gift tax bracket. In 1997, Dena gives stock worth $110,000 to *each* of her three grandchildren. Determine Dena's total tax liability.

COMPREHENSIVE TAX RETURN PROBLEM

During 1996, William and Margaret Rusk (Social Security numbers 010–56–0603 and 165–52–3929) resided at 432 Sunken Court, Funston, UT 84602. In their 26 years of marriage, the Rusks have always lived in common law states. William Rusk is a major partner in a local stock brokerage firm, and Margaret Rusk is a well-known plastic surgeon. Both practices have been highly successful. Over the years, the Rusks have received gifts and inheritances from various sources and have invested the funds wisely.

In 1996, the Rusks made the following transfers (without adjustment for the annual exclusion or the marital deduction):

	William Rusk	**Margaret Rusk**
Cash donation to the building fund of Brigham Young University.	$ 50,000	$ 50,000
Birthday gift (Jaguar auto) from Margaret to William.	—	68,000
Payments made as a result of Joan Canby's retina operation. Joan is Margaret's aunt but does not qualify as her dependent. The payments were made directly to the care providers (e.g., hospital, surgeons).	—	19,000
Donation to the political campaign of a candidate who ran unsuccessfully for the U.S. Congress.	11,000	11,000
Cash Christmas gift to Ida Gambel who has been the Rusks' housekeeper for 10 years.	12,000	—
Using stock in Wren Corporation, William creates the Rusk Family Trust.	850,000*	—
After the creation of the Rusk Family Trust, Margaret transfers stock in Eagle Corporation.	—	550,000**

*The stock in Wren Corporation is publicly traded and was inherited by William from his mother in 1972 when it had a value of $290,000. The Rusk Family Trust designates the Trust Department of Funston National Bank as the trustee. Under the terms of the trust, income is payable annually to the Rusks' three children (Angela, age 24; Arthur, age 23; and Helen, age 21) for life, remainder to their children.

**The stock in Eagle Corporation is publicly traded and was received by Margaret from her mother in 1982. At that time it had a value of $200,000 and a basis to Margaret's mother of $120,000.

In 1981, the Rusks made taxable gifts of $300,000 (i.e., $150,000 each) when they set up educational trusts for their three children. No gift tax was paid on these gifts, and the election to split gifts was made.

Required:
Complete Form 709 (U.S. Federal Gift Tax Return) for gifts made by the Rusks in 1996. The § 2513 election to split gifts is to be made.

RESEARCH PROBLEMS

Note: **West's Federal Taxation on CD-ROM** *can be used in preparing solutions to the Research Problems. Alternatively, tax research materials contained in a standard tax library can be used.*

Research Problem 1. In 1992, Marge Hurt creates an irrevocable trust using income-producing real estate worth $70,000. The trust arrangement is as follows:

- Frank and Lillian (Marge's adult children) are designated as co-trustees.

- The income from the trust is to be distributed to Frank and Lillian during Marge's life and for 120 days thereafter.

- If Frank and Lillian survive Marge by 120 days, each is to receive an equal share of the corpus.

- If either Frank or Lillian does not survive Marge by 120 days, income from the trust is payable to his or her children. If Marge dies and either Frank or Lillian does not survive her by 120 days, corpus is to pass to his or her children (Marge's grandchildren). Frank has two children; Lillian has three.

- As to every annual gift to the trust by Marge, all present (Frank and Lillian) and potential (the children of Frank and Lillian) beneficiaries have the right to withdraw the amount of the § 2503(b) gift tax exclusion. The right of withdrawal exists for 15 days after the gift in trust.

In 1993, Marge contributes additional real estate (worth $70,000) to the trust. Marge dies in 1994 before any further gifts can be made. One hundred and twenty days after Marge's death, the trust corpus and accumulated income are divided between Frank and Lillian, and the trust is dissolved. Following the gifts made by Marge, none of the beneficiaries (neither Frank nor Lillian nor their children) exercise the right of withdrawal.

No gift tax return is filed reflecting either the 1992 or 1993 gifts by Marge. Nor are these gifts noted on the estate tax return filed by the executors of Marge's estate.

Upon audit of the estate tax return, the IRS determines that Marge made taxable gifts of $50,000 in both 1992 and 1993.

a. Why did the IRS choose $50,000 as the amount of each taxable gift?

b. On an audit of Marge's estate tax return, why should the IRS care about the possibility of prior taxable gifts?

c. Is the IRS correct or not about the existence of prior taxable gifts? Explain.

Partial list of research aids:

Crummey v. Comm., 68–1 USTC ¶12,541, 22 AFTR2d 6023, 397 F.2d 82 (CA–9, 1968).

Research Problem 2. At the time of his death, Henry Horton left an estate of approximately $30 million. Under his will, large portions of the estate were to pass to certain qualified charities and to Virginia Horton, Henry's surviving spouse. Under the terms of the will, Henry's executor was granted the option to pay administration expenses from either income or principal. Unless the will dictates otherwise, applicable state law requires that such expenses be charged to principal.

Due to litigation regarding the validity of the will, the administration of Henry's estate was prolonged. During the period of administration, estate assets generated approximately $4.5 million of income. Of the $2 million of administration expenses that resulted, the executor charged $500,000 to principal and the remainder (i.e., $1.5 million) to income.

When filing the Form 706 for the estate, the executor reduced the charitable and marital deductions only by the administration expenses charged to principal. Upon audit, the IRS contends that all of the administration expenses must reduce the charitable and marital deductions. Who is correct and why?

Partial list of research aids:

Code §§ 642, 2053, 2055, and 2056.

Estate of Otis C. Hubert, 101 T.C. 314 (1993).

Estate of Street v. Comm., 92–2 USTC ¶60,112, 70 AFTR2d 92–6220, 974 F.2d 723 (CA–6, 1992).

Burke v. U.S., 93–2 USTC ¶60, 146, 72 AFTR2d 93–6705, 994 F.2d 1576 (CA–Fed.Cir., 1992).

Research Problem 3. Sarah created a trust by transferring income-producing assets to a trust company. Specifics regarding the trust agreement are summarized as follows.

- Income of the trust inures to the benefit of Sarah's five minor granddaughters. The trustee is accorded the right to accumulate or distribute current income.

- The trust company is a corporation chartered under state law. Sarah owns none of the stock.

- Sarah retains the right to replace the trustee with another independent corporate trust company. This right is never exercised by Sarah during her lifetime.

- At the discretion of the trustee, both income and corpus may be expended on behalf of the beneficiaries before they attain the age of 21.

- At age 21, each beneficiary has the right to withdraw her share of corpus and accumulated income (if any) from the trust. If the right to distribution is not exercised, the trust is to continue until the beneficiary reaches age 35 or dies, whichever occurs first. At this point, a final liquidating distribution will be made to the beneficiary (or her estate) of her interest.

- If a beneficiary dies before attaining the age of 21, her interest in the trust is payable to her estate or as she designates under a general power of appointment.

In the year the trust was created, Sarah filed a Form 709 reflecting the gift. In computing the gift tax liability, Sarah claimed five annual exclusions.

Five years after the gift in trust was made, Sarah died. Sarah's executor includes none of the value of the trust in the gross estate. When the estate's Form 706 is audited, the IRS determines that the trust must be included. Because of the retained right to replace trustees, Sarah's transfer was incomplete. Consequently, the IRS maintains that Code §§ 2036(a)(2) and 2038(a)(1) are applicable.

a. Is Sarah correct in claiming five annual exclusions for the gift in trust? Why or why not?
b. Is the IRS correct in including the trust in Sarah's gross estate? Why or why not?

Research Problem 4.   Hector dies on April 24, 1989, and under his will a major portion of the estate passes to a trust. The provisions of the trust grant a life estate to Ellen (Hector's surviving spouse), remainder to their adult children. The income is payable to Ellen quarter-annually or at more frequent intervals. Income accrued or held undistributed by the trust at the time of Ellen's death shall pass to the remainder interest.

On January 24, 1990, Hector's estate filed a Federal estate tax return and made the QTIP election. On July 3, 1990, Hector's estate filed an amended return based on the premise that the QTIP election was improper. As a result of the loss of the marital deduction, the amended return was accompanied by a payment of additional estate taxes.

On February 11, 1990, Ellen dies. All of her assets, including those in Hector's trust, pass to the children.

a. Why did Hector's estate file an amended return revoking the QTIP election?
b. Is the revocation of the election proper procedure?
c. Did Hector's estate ever qualify for the election?

Partial list of research aids:
Code §§ 2056(b)(7) and 2013.
Estate of Rose D. Howard, 91 T.C. 329 (1988), *rev'd* in 90–2 USTC ¶60,033, 66 AFTR2d 90–5994, 910 F.2d 633 (CA–9, 1990).

Use the tax resources of the internet to address the following questions. Do not restrict your search to the World Wide Web, but include a review of newsgroups and general reference materials, practitioner sites and resources, primary sources of the tax law, chat rooms and discussion groups, and other opportunities.

Research Problem 5.   Find a calculator on the World Wide Web that will estimate the Federal estate or gift tax liability. Use this device to check your answer to one of the Problems that you have completed in this chapter.

Research Problem 6.   How have Federal estate taxes affected the ownership structure of National Football League franchises? Summarize one such scenario.

Research Problem 7.   Find an estate and gift planning article posted by a tax professional. Reply via e-mail to this posting, offering an additional planning suggestion.

FAMILY TAX PLANNING

LEARNING OBJECTIVES

After completing Chapter 18, you should be able to:

1. Use various established concepts in carrying out the valuation process.

2. Apply the special use valuation method in appropriate situations.

3. Identify problems involved in valuing an interest in a closely held business.

4. Compare the income tax basis rules applying to property received by gift and by death.

5. Plan gifts so as to minimize gift taxes and avoid estate taxes.

6. Make gifts so as to avoid income taxes for the donor.

7. Reduce probate costs in the administration of an estate.

8. Apply procedures that reduce estate tax consequences.

9. Obtain liquidity for an estate.

Broadly speaking, *family tax planning* involves the use of various procedures that minimize the effect of taxation on transfers within the family unit. As such, planning involves a consideration not only of transfer taxes (i.e., gift and estate) but also of the income tax ramifications to both the transferor (i.e., donor or decedent) and the transferees (i.e., donees or heirs).

The valuation of the transferred property also is an essential element of family tax planning. The gift tax is based on the fair market value of the property on the date of the transfer. For the Federal estate tax, the fair market value on the date of the owner's death or the alternate valuation date (if available and elected) controls.

VALUATION CONCEPTS

1 **LEARNING OBJECTIVE**
Use various established concepts in carrying out the valuation process.

The central focus of this chapter concerns the valuation of property involved in transfers by gift and by death. The expansive nature of the assets that possess value for these purposes is illustrated by the Tax in the News feature on the next page.

VALUATION IN GENERAL

The Internal Revenue Code refers to "value" and "fair market value," but does not discuss these terms at length.[1] Section 2031(b) comes closest to a definition when it treats the problem of stocks and securities for which no sales price information (the usual case with closely held corporations) is available. In such situations, "the value thereof shall be determined by taking into consideration, in addition to all other factors, the value of stock or securities of corporations engaged in the same or similar line of business which are listed on an exchange."

Regulation § 20.2031–1(b) is more specific in defining fair market value as "the price at which property would change hands between a willing buyer and a willing seller, neither being under any compulsion to buy or to sell and both having reasonable knowledge of relevant facts." The same Regulation makes clear that the fair market value of an item of property is not determined by a forced sale price. Nor is the fair market value determined by the sale price of the item in a

---

[1]See, for example, §§ 1001(b), 2031(a), and 2512(a). Sections 2032A(e)(7) and (8) set forth certain procedures for valuing farms and interests in closely held businesses.

TAX IN THE NEWS

IS THERE LIFE AFTER DEATH FOR A NOVELIST?

At the time of her death, Virginia Andrews was a highly successful novelist. Her novels fit into the "children in jeopardy" genre and typically involved a child overcoming the adversities caused by adults (usually family members). As she enjoyed a very loyal readership among teenage girls and young women, every new title became an instant hit.

After Andrews's death, her publisher (Pocket Books, a division of Simon & Schuster, Inc.) contacted the estate and heirs about the possibility of sequels to existing novels. Under the proposal, several novels would be written by a ghostwriter and published under Andrews's name. An agreement was reached, and the novels were written and published. As the sequels were successful, substantial royalties were paid to the estate.

When the estate tax return was filed, it included no value for the postdeath sequels. The executor contended that the postdeath ventures were too speculative to possess any value to the estate. Sales would depend on the expertise of the ghostwriter and whether prospective buyers would accept that the novels were the work of Virginia Andrews. In fact, if the sequels were failures, sales of earlier books would suffer.

The IRS disagreed and assigned a value of approximately $1,200,000 to the potential use of the Andrews name. In *Estate of Virginia Andrews v. U.S.* [94–2 USTC ¶60,170, 73 AFTR2d 94–2395, 850 F.Supp. 1279 (D.Ct.Va., 1994)], a court agreed with the IRS. Because of the uncertainty, however, the gross estate value was discounted to approximately $900,000.

This shows that there is value in a dead author's name!

---

market other than that in which the item is most commonly sold to the public. Sentiment should not play a part in the determination of value. Suppose, for example, the decedent's daughter is willing to pay $500 for a portrait of her mother. If the painting is really worth $200 (i.e., what the general public would pay), then that should be its value.

The item's location must also be considered. Thus, the fair market value of property that generally is obtained by the public in a retail market is the price at which the property (or comparable items) would be sold at retail.

▼

EXAMPLE 1

At the time of his death, Don owned three automobiles. The automobiles are included in Don's gross estate at their fair market value on the date of his death or on the alternate valuation date (if elected). The fair market value of the automobiles is determined by looking to the price a member of the general public would pay for automobiles of approximately the same description, make, model, age, condition, etc. The price a dealer in used cars would pay for these automobiles is inappropriate, because an automobile is an item obtainable by the public in a retail market. ▼

If tangible personalty is sold as a result of an advertisement in the classified section of a newspaper and the property is of a type often sold in this manner, or if the property is sold at a public auction, the price for which it is sold is presumed to be the retail sales price of the item at the time of the sale. The retail sales price also is used if the sale is made within a reasonable period following the valuation date, and market conditions affecting the value of similar items have not changed substantially.[2] Tangible personalty includes all property except real estate and intangible property.

VALUATION OF SPECIFIC ASSETS

Stocks and Bonds. If there is a market for stocks and bonds on a stock exchange, in an over-the-counter market, or otherwise, the mean between the highest and lowest quoted selling prices on the valuation date is the fair market value per unit. A special rule applies if no sales occurred on the valuation date but did occur on dates within a reasonable period before and after the valuation date. The fair market value is the weighted average of the means between the highest and the lowest sales prices on the nearest date before and the nearest date after the valuation date. The average is weighted *inversely* by the respective number of trading days between the selling dates and the valuation date.[3]

EXAMPLE 2

Carla makes a gift to Antonio of shares of stock in Green Corporation. The transactions involving this stock that occurred closest to the date of the gift took place two trading days before the date of the gift at a mean selling price of $10 and three trading days after the gift at a mean selling price of $15. The $12 fair market value of each share of Green stock is determined as follows.

$$\frac{(3 \times \$10) + (2 \times \$15)}{5} = \$12$$

▼

If no transactions occurred within a reasonable period before and after the valuation date, the fair market value is determined by taking a weighted average of the means between the bona fide bid and asked prices on the nearest trading dates before and after the valuation date. However, both dates must be within a reasonable period of time.

If no actual sales prices or bona fide bid and asked prices are available for dates within a reasonable period relative to the valuation date, the mean between the highest and lowest available sales prices or bid and asked prices on that date may be taken as the value.

In many instances, there are no established market prices for securities. This lack of information is typically the case with stock in closely held corporations. Problems unique to valuing interests in closely held businesses are discussed later in this chapter.

Notes Receivable. The fair market value of notes, secured or unsecured, is the amount of unpaid principal plus interest accrued to the valuation date, unless the parties (e.g., executor, donor) establish a lower value or prove the notes are worthless. Factors such as a low interest rate and a distant maturity date are relevant in showing that a note is worth less than its face amount. Crucial elements in proving that a note is entirely or partially worthless are the financial condition of the borrower and the absence of any value for the property pledged or mortgaged as security for the obligation.[4]

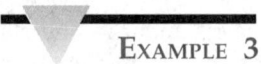

EXAMPLE 3

At the time of his death, Ira held a note (face amount of $50,000) issued by his son, Kevin. Although Kevin is solvent, he is relieved of the obligation because Ira forgives the note in

---

[2] Rev.Proc. 65–19, 1965–2 C.B. 1002.
[3] Reg. §§ 20.2031–2(b) and 25.2512–2(b).

[4] Reg. §§ 20.2031–4 and 25.2512–4.

his will. Presuming the note is payable on demand, it is included in Ira's gross estate at $50,000 plus accrued interest. If the note is not due immediately and/or the interest provided for is under the current rate, a discount may be in order, and the fair market value of the note would be less than $50,000. The burden of proof in supporting a discount for the note is on the executor. ▼

Insurance Policies and Annuity Contracts. The value of a life insurance policy on the life of a person other than the decedent, or the value of an annuity contract issued by a company regularly engaged in selling annuities, is the cost of a comparable contract.[5]

EXAMPLE 4

Paul purchased a joint and survivor annuity contract from an insurance company. Under the contract's terms, Paul is to receive payments of $60,000 per year for his life. Upon Paul's death, his wife (Kate) is to receive $45,000 annually for her life. Ten years after purchasing the annuity, when Kate is 40 years old, Paul dies. The value of the annuity contract on the date of Paul's death [and the amount includible in Paul's gross estate under § 2039(a)] is the amount the insurance company would charge in the year of Paul's death for an annuity that would pay $45,000 annually for the life of a female 40 years of age. ▼

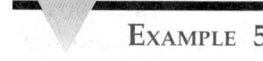

EXAMPLE 5

At the time of her death, Lana owns an insurance policy (face amount of $200,000) on the life of her son, Sam. No further payments need be made on the policy (e.g., it is a single premium policy or a paid-up policy). The value of the policy on the date of Lana's death (and the amount includible in her gross estate under § 2033 as property owned by the decedent) is the amount the insurance company would charge in the year of her death for a single premium contract (face amount of $200,000) on the life of someone Sam's age. ▼

Determining the value of an insurance policy by using the amount charged for a comparable policy is more difficult when, on the date of valuation, the contract has been in force for some time and further premium payments are to be made. In such a case, the value may be approximated by adding to the interpolated terminal reserve the proportionate part of the gross premium last paid before the valuation date that covers the period extending beyond that date.[6]

The valuation of annuities issued by parties *not regularly engaged in the sale of annuities* (i.e., noncommercial contracts) requires the use of special tables issued by the IRS.

Life Estates, Terms for Years, Reversions, and Remainders. As with noncommercial annuities, the valuation of life estates, income interests for a term of years, reversions, and remainders involves the use of tables.

Because interest rates fluctuate constantly, the IRS is required to issue new tables periodically to reflect the current rate.[7] These tables contain 50 different possibilities (ranging from 4.2 percent to 14 percent), but *only a portion of the tables is reproduced* in Appendix A.[8]

The tables provide only the remainder factor. If the income interest (life estate) also has been transferred, the factor to be used is one minus the remainder factor.

---

[5] Reg. §§ 20.2031–8(a)(1) and 25.2512–6(a).
[6] The terminal reserve value of a life insurance policy generally approximates the policy's cash surrender value. For an illustration on how to arrive at the interpolated terminal reserve value, see Reg. § 20.2031–8(a)(3) (Ex. 3).

[7] § 7520.
[8] Notice 89–60, 1989–1 C.B. 700. The valuation factors in the tables represent 120% of whatever the Federal mid-term rate is for the month of the valuation date.

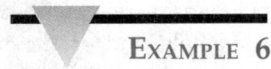

EXAMPLE 6

Matt transfers $100,000 in trust, specifying a life estate to Rita, remainder to Rick on Rita's death. The gift took place on May 3, 1997, when Rita was age 35. Assume that the appropriate rate is 8.8%. Using the table extract in Appendix A (Table S) for a person age 35 under the 8.8% column, the value of the remainder interest is $6,439 (.06439 × $100,000). The life estate factor is .93561 (1.00000 − .06439). Thus, Matt has made a gift to Rita of $93,561 and a gift to Rick of $6,439. ▼

In computing the value of an income interest for a term of years, a different table is used. Again, the table furnishes the remainder factor. The income interest factor is the difference between one and the remainder factor. *Only a portion of the tables is reproduced* in Appendix A.

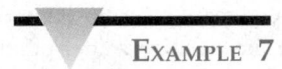

EXAMPLE 7

On April 30, 1997, Julia transfers $200,000 by gift to a trust. Under the terms of the trust, income is payable to Paul for eight years. After the eight-year period, the trust terminates, and the trust principal passes to Sara. For the month in which the trust was created, the appropriate rate was 8.8%. The present worth of $1 due at the end of eight years is $0.509294. Thus, Julia has made a gift to Sara of $101,858.80 (.509294 × $200,000) and a gift to Paul of $98,141.20 (.490706 × $200,000). ▼

What is the significance of dividing a gift into several distinct parts? This is important in determining the applicability of the annual exclusion and the marital deduction. Under the facts of Example 6, an annual exclusion probably would be allowed for the gift to Rita but not for the interest passing to Rick (because of the future interest limitation). If Rita is Matt's wife, no marital deduction is allowed because the life estate is a terminable interest. As noted in Chapter 17, however, this problem could be cured with a qualified terminable interest property (QTIP) election.

REAL ESTATE AND THE SPECIAL USE VALUATION METHOD

2 LEARNING OBJECTIVE
Apply the special use valuation method in appropriate situations.

Proper valuation principles usually require that real estate be valued at its most suitable (i.e., "best" or "highest") use. Section 2032A, however, permits an executor to elect to value certain classes of real estate used in farming or in connection with a closely held business at its "current" use, rather than the most suitable use. The major objective of the **special use value** election is to provide a form of limited relief to protect the heirs against the possibility of having to sell a portion of the family farm to pay estate taxes.

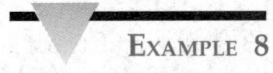

EXAMPLE 8

At the time of his death, Rex owned a dairy farm on the outskirts of a large city. For farming purposes, the property's value is $300,000 (the current use value).[9] As a potential site for a shopping center, however, the property is worth $800,000 (the most suitable use value). The executor of Rex's estate can elect to include only $300,000 in the gross estate. ▼

The special use valuation procedure permits a reduction of no more than $750,000 in estate tax valuation.

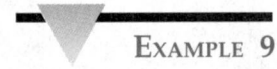

EXAMPLE 9

At the time of her death, Wanda owned a farm with a most suitable use value of $2 million but a current use value of $1 million. Assuming the property qualifies under § 2032A and

---

[9]Sections 2032A(e)(7) and (8) set forth various methods of valuation to be applied in arriving at current use value.

the special use valuation election is made, Wanda's gross estate must include $1,250,000. Only $750,000 can be excluded under § 2032A. ▼

The special use valuation election is available if *all* of the following conditions are satisfied.

- At least 50 percent of the adjusted value of the gross estate consists of *real* or *personal* property devoted to a qualifying use (used for farming or in a closely held business) at the time of the owner's death.[10]
- The *real* property devoted to a qualifying use comprises at least 25 percent of the adjusted value of the gross estate.

   For purposes of satisfying both the 50 percent test (above) and the 25 percent test, the qualifying property is considered at its most suitable use value. Thus, in Example 8, the property would be treated as if it had a value of $800,000 (not $300,000). The adjusted value of the gross estate is the gross estate less certain unpaid mortgages and other indebtedness.

- The qualifying property passes to a qualifying heir of the decedent. Qualifying heirs are certain family members as set forth in § 2032A(e)(2).
- The *real* property has been owned by the decedent or the decedent's family for five out of the eight years ending on the date of the decedent's death and was devoted to a qualifying use during that period.
- The decedent or a member of the decedent's family participated materially in the operation of the farm or business during the five-year period specified above.[11]

Section 2032A(c) provides that the estate tax savings derived from the special use valuation method are recaptured from the heir, if he or she disposes of the property or ceases to use it as qualifying use property within a period of 10 years from the date of the decedent's death.

EXAMPLE 10

Assume the same facts as in Example 9. Further assume that by electing § 2032A, Wanda's estate tax liability was reduced by $245,000. Three years after Wanda's death, Otis (the qualifying heir) leases the farm to an unrelated party. At this point, Otis must pay the $245,000 additional estate tax liability that would have been imposed had § 2032A not been utilized. ▼

In the event recapture occurs, the qualifying heir may *elect* to increase the income tax basis of the property by the amount of the recapture. If the election is made, however, interest on the additional estate tax due must be paid.[12]

In this regard, the Code gives the IRS security for compliance with the terms of § 2032A by placing a special lien on the qualifying property.[13]

ETHICAL CONSIDERATIONS

A Temporary Special Use Value Election?

George is executor and sole heir of his father's estate. The major asset in the estate is a pecan grove located on the outskirts of a large metropolitan area. Because of suburban expansion, the grove has substantially appreciated in value over like

---

[10] §§ 2032A(b)(1)(A) and (b)(2). For a definition of "farm" and "farming," see §§ 2032A(e)(4) and (5).

[11] § 2032A(b)(1)(C)(ii). "Material participation" is defined in § 2032A(e)(6).

[12] § 1016(c).

[13] § 6324B.

agricultural use property. Several of George's friends who are knowledgeable in real estate matters tell him that in five or six years the land may be worth several times its present value. George owns his own grove and will have no difficulty satisfying the qualified use requirement of § 2032A.

George makes the special use valuation election for his father's property. Although he has no intention of keeping the property as a grove for 10 years, he reasons "why pay estate taxes today that you can put off until tomorrow." Has George acted wisely?

VALUATION PROBLEMS WITH A CLOSELY HELD BUSINESS

3 LEARNING OBJECTIVE
Identify problems involved in valuing an interest in a closely held business.

General Guidelines.   Revenue Ruling 59–60 sets forth the approach, methods, and factors to be considered in valuing the shares of closely held corporations for gift and estate tax purposes.[14] The following factors, although not all-inclusive, are fundamental and require careful analysis in each case.

- The nature of the business and the history of the enterprise from its inception.
- The economic outlook in general and the condition and outlook of the specific industry in particular.
- The book value of the stock and the financial condition of the business.
- The earning capacity of the company.
- The company's dividend-paying capacity.
- Whether the enterprise has goodwill or other intangible value.
- The prices and number of shares of the stock sold previously and the size of the block of stock to be valued.
- The market price of stocks issued by corporations in the same or a similar line of business and actively traded in a free and open market, either on an exchange or over-the-counter.

Some of these factors are discussed in depth in the pages to follow.

Goodwill Aspects.   If a closely held corporation's record of past earnings is higher than is usual for the industry, the IRS is apt to claim the presence of goodwill as a corporate asset.

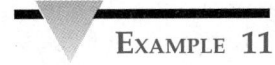

EXAMPLE 11

Adam owned 70% of the stock of White Corporation, with the remaining 30% held by various family members. Over the past five years, White Corporation has generated average net profits of $100,000, and on the date of Adam's death, the book value of the corporation's stock was $250,000. If the IRS identifies 8% as an appropriate rate of return, one approach to the valuation of White stock would yield the following result.

Average net profit for the past five years	$100,000
8% of the $250,000 book value	20,000
Excess earnings over 8%	$ 80,000
Value of goodwill (5 × $80,000)	$400,000
Book value	250,000
Total value of the White stock	$650,000

Thus, the IRS might contend that the stock should be included in Adam's gross estate at 70 percent of $650,000, or $455,000. If the estate wishes to argue for a lower valuation, relevant factors might include any of the following.

---

[14] 1959–1 C.B. 237. See also Reg. § 20.2031–2(f).

- The average net profit figure for the past five years ($100,000) may not be representative. Perhaps it includes some extraordinary gains that normally do not occur or are extraneous to the business conducted by the corporation. An example might be a windfall profit for a specific year because of an unusual market situation. The corporation may have recognized a large gain from an appreciated investment held for many years. The figure may fail to take into account certain expenses that normally would be incurred but for some justifiable reason have been deferred. In a family business during periods of expansion and development, it is not uncommon to find an unusually low salary structure. Profits might be considerably less if the owner-employees of the business were being paid the true worth of their services.
- The appropriate rate of return for this type of business may not be 8 percent. If it is higher, there would be less goodwill because the business is not as profitable as it seems.
- If Adam was a key person in the operation of White Corporation, could some or all of any goodwill developed by the business be attributed to his efforts? If so, is it not reasonable to assume that the goodwill might be seriously impaired by Adam's death?

Other Factors. Aside from the issue of goodwill, the valuation of closely held stock must take other factors into account. For example, consider the percentage of ownership involved. If the percentage represents a *minority interest* and the corporation has a poor dividend-paying record, a substantial discount is in order.[15] The justification for the discount is the general inability of the holder of the minority interest to affect corporate policy, particularly with respect to the distribution of dividends. At the other extreme is an interest large enough to represent control, either actual or effective. Considered alone, a controlling interest calls for valuation at a premium.[16]

A controlling interest may be so large, however, that the disposition of the stock within a reasonable period of time after the valuation date could have a negative effect on the market for such shares. The **blockage rule** recognizes what may happen to per-unit value when a large block of shares is marketed at one time.[17] Most often, the rule is applied to stock that has a recognized market. The rule permits a discount from the amount at which smaller lots are selling on or about the valuation date.[18] Although the blockage rule may have a bearing on the valuation of other assets, it is more frequently applied to stocks and securities.[19]

Because most stock in closely held corporations does not trade in a recognized market, a discount for *lack of marketability* may be in order. The discount recognizes the costs that would be incurred in creating a market for such shares to effect their orderly disposition.[20] The discount could be significant considering typical underwriting expenses and other costs involved in going public.

Resolving the Valuation Problem for Stock in Closely Held Corporations. Since the valuation of closely held stock is subject to so many variables, planning should be directed toward bringing about some measure of certainty.

---

[15] See, for example, *Jack D. Carr*, 49 TCM 507, T.C.Memo. 1985-19.

[16] *Helvering v. Safe Deposit and Trust Co. of Baltimore, Exr. (Estate of H. Walters)*, 38-1 USTC ¶9240, 21 AFTR 12, 95 F.2d 806 (CA-4, 1938), *aff'g*. 35 B.T.A. 259 (1937).

[17] Reg. § 20.2031-2(e).

[18] See, for example, *Estate of Robert Damon*, 49 T.C. 108 (1967).

[19] In *Estate of David Smith*, 57 T.C. 650 (1972), the estate of a now-famous sculptor successfully argued for the application of the blockage rule to 425 sculptures included in the gross estate.

[20] See, for example, *Estate of Mark S. Gallo*, 50 TCM 470, T.C.Memo. 1985-363. In this case, the taxpayer also argued that a bad product image (i.e., the Thunderbird, Ripple, and Boone's Farm brands) would depress the value of the stock. Since the trend was toward better wines, association with cheaper products had a negative consumer impact.

TAX IN THE NEWS

BLOCKAGE RULE APPLIED TO ART WORKS

When the well-known artist Georgia O'Keeffe died in 1986 at the age of 98, her gross estate included approximately 400 works or groups of works she had created during her lifetime. Both the executor of O'Keeffe's estate and the IRS agreed that the *total* of the *individual* fair market values of *each* of the works exceeded $72,759,000. But since it would be ridiculous to expect the estate to receive this amount if it sold all of the art works at once, both sides agreed that a discount for *blockage* should be allowed.

The estate introduced expert appraisal testimony in an effort to establish a discount factor of 75 percent. A 75 percent blockage discount would have reduced the value of the estate from $72,759,000 to approximately $18 million. At the other extreme, the valuation experts of the IRS argued for a discount of 10 to 37 percent. The difference between the two positions amounted to about $6 million in estate taxes.

With so much at stake, the issue went to court. In a decision not uncommon in valuation controversies, the court settled on a valuation of $36,400,000, or roughly midway between the valuations proposed by the estate and the IRS (*Estate of Georgia T. O'Keeffe*, 63 TCM 2699, T.C.Memo. 1992–210).

▼

EXAMPLE 12

Polly wants to transfer some of her stock in Brown Corporation to a trust formed for her children. She would also like to make a substantial contribution to her alma mater, State University. At present, the Brown stock is owned entirely by Polly and has never been traded on any market or otherwise sold or exchanged. Brown's past operations have proved profitable, and Brown has established a respectable record of dividend distributions. Based on the best available information and taking into account various adjustments (e.g., discount for lack of marketability), Polly feels each share of Brown stock possesses a fair market value of $120. ▼

If Polly makes a gift of some of the stock to the trust set up for the children and uses the $120 per share valuation, what assurance is there that the IRS will accept this figure? If the IRS is successful in increasing the fair market value per share, Polly could end up with additional gift tax liability.

Polly could hedge against any further gift tax liability. Concurrently with the gift of stock to the trust formed for the children, Polly could make an outright transfer of some of the shares to State University, thereby generating an income tax deduction. Polly would base the income tax deduction on the value used for gift tax purposes.[21] If the IRS later raises the value and assesses more gift tax, Polly can file an amended income tax return, claim a larger charitable contribution deduction, and obtain an offsetting income tax refund. To carry out this hedge, Polly would derive the amount of her gift of Brown stock by comparing her prevailing gift tax and income tax brackets for the year of the transfers. By virtue of the charitable deduction allowed for gift tax purposes by § 2522 (discussed in

---

[21] The use of fair market value as the measure of the charitable contribution deduction presumes the Brown stock would yield long-term capital gain if sold by Polly. See § 170(e).

Chapter 17), no gift tax liability is incurred for the stock transferred to State University.

The Buy-Sell Agreement and Valuation.   The main objective of a **buy-sell agreement** is to effect the orderly disposition of a business interest without the risk of the interest falling into the hands of outsiders. Moreover, a buy-sell agreement can ease the problems of estate liquidity and valuation.

Two types of buy-sell agreements exist: **entity** and **cross-purchase** arrangements. Under the entity type, the business itself (partnership or corporation) agrees to buy out the interest of the withdrawing owner (partner or shareholder). For a corporation, this normally takes the form of a stock redemption plan set up to qualify for income tax purposes under either § 302(b) or § 303. By making use of these provisions, corporate distributions can qualify for sale or exchange treatment rather than being treated as dividends (see Chapter 5). Under a cross-purchase agreement, the surviving owners (partners or shareholders) agree to buy out the withdrawing owner. The structures of the most typical buy-sell agreements are illustrated in Figure 18–1.

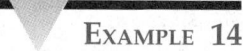

EXAMPLE 13   Iris, Ned, and Hal are equal and unrelated shareholders in Blue Corporation, and all three share in Blue's management. All agree to turn in their stock to the corporation for redemption at $100 per share if any one of them withdraws (by death or otherwise) from the business. Shortly thereafter, Hal dies, and the estate redeems the Blue stock at the agreed-upon price of $100 per share. ▼

EXAMPLE 14   Assume the same facts as in Example 13, except the agreement is the cross-purchase type under which each shareholder promises to buy a share of the withdrawing shareholder's interest. When Hal dies, the estate sells the Blue stock to Iris and Ned for $100 per share. ▼

Will the $100 per share paid to Hal's estate determine the amount to be included in his gross estate? The answer is *yes*, subject to the following conditions.

- The price is the result of a bona fide business agreement.
- The agreement is not a device to transfer property to family members.
- The agreement is comparable to other arrangements entered into by persons dealing at arm's length.[22]

ETHICAL CONSIDERATIONS   ## Income Tax Consequences from a Botched Buy-Sell Agreement

Rohm, Turner, and Walker are equal shareholders in Crane Corporation. They agree that if any one of them withdraws from the business, by death or otherwise, the remaining shareholders will purchase the departing partner's interest.

When Rohm dies, Turner and Walker lack the funds to buy his interest from the estate. Consequently, they have Crane Corporation redeem the stock. Since Turner and Walker have received nothing from this transaction, they feel it has no income tax consequences for them.

Do you agree with Turner and Walker? Why or why not?

---

[22] § 2703.

▼ **FIGURE 18–1**
Structures of Typical Buy-Sell
Agreements

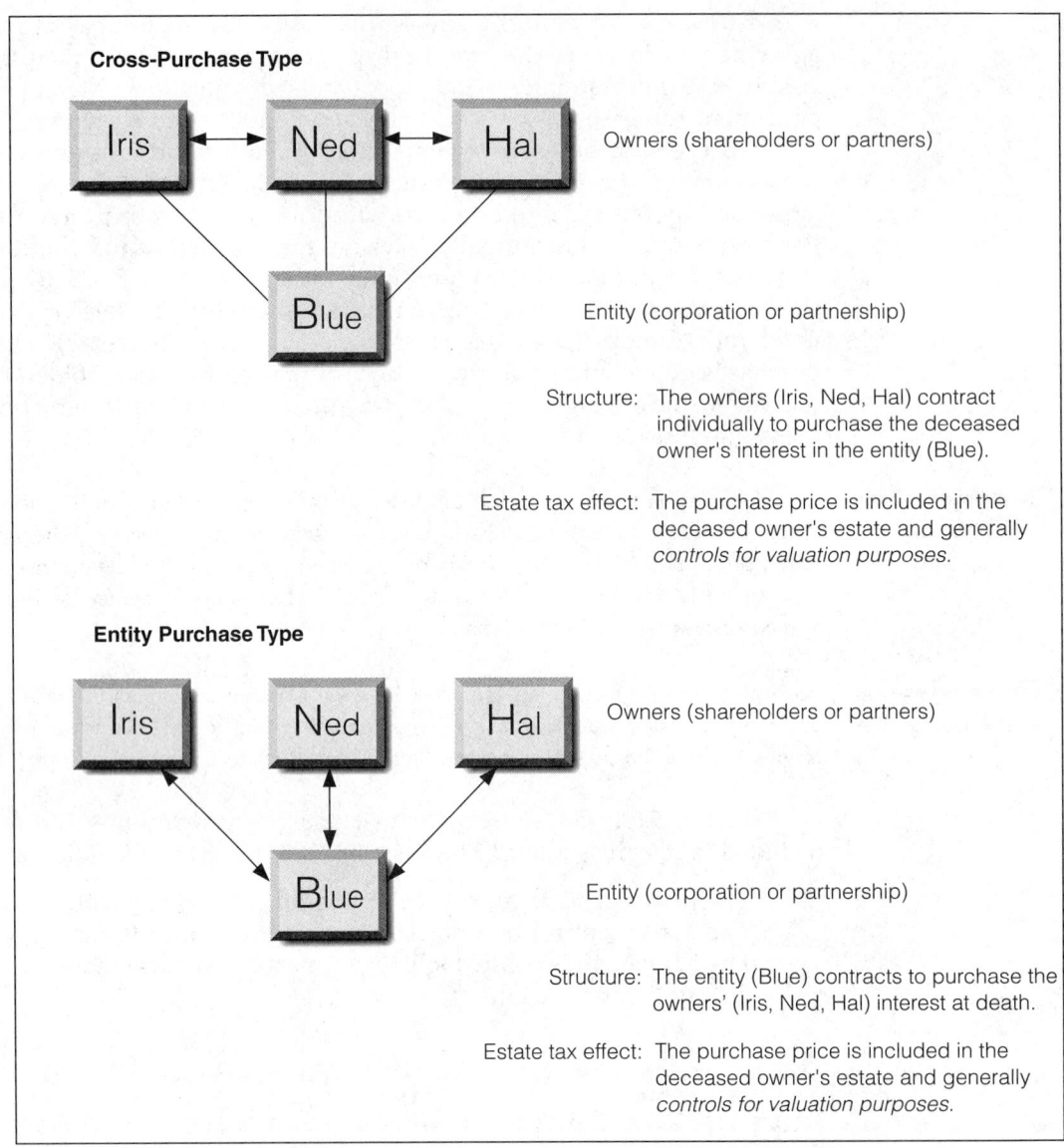

Cross-Purchase Type

Iris ⟷ Ned ⟷ Hal   Owners (shareholders or partners)

Blue   Entity (corporation or partnership)

Structure: The owners (Iris, Ned, Hal) contract individually to purchase the deceased owner's interest in the entity (Blue).

Estate tax effect: The purchase price is included in the deceased owner's estate and generally *controls for valuation purposes.*

Entity Purchase Type

Iris   Ned   Hal   Owners (shareholders or partners)

Blue   Entity (corporation or partnership)

Structure: The entity (Blue) contracts to purchase the owners' (Iris, Ned, Hal) interest at death.

Estate tax effect: The purchase price is included in the deceased owner's estate and generally *controls for valuation purposes.*

Estate Freezes—Corporations.   Over the years, owners of closely held businesses have searched for ways to transfer the major value of the business to their heirs while retaining some security interest. The typical approach with corporations has been for the owner to retain preferred stock and make gifts of common stock to the family. The approach freezes the amount that will be included in the owner's gross estate to the value of the preferred stock. Any post-gift appreciation in the business is attributed to the common stock and is *not* part of the owner's gross estate.

Under recent legislation, some degree of the **estate freeze** is permitted.[23] Unfortunately, current law is designed to maximize the amount of the gift made

---

[23] § 2701.

by the donor upon the creation of the freeze. Generally, the retained interest is valued at zero, thereby resulting in the transfer of the *full* value of the business.

EXAMPLE 15

Quinn owns all of the stock in Robin Corporation valued as follows: $2 million common stock and $500,000 preferred stock. The preferred stock is noncumulative, does not have a redemption date, and possesses no liquidation preference. Quinn gives the common stock to his adult children and retains the preferred stock. Quinn has made a gift to the children of $2,500,000. The $500,000 worth of preferred stock Quinn retained is treated as having no value. ▼

Special rules apply if the preferred stock is cumulative, has a redemption date, or carries certain other preferential rights. These rules allow some value to be assigned to the preferred stock, thereby reducing the amount of the gift. The adjustments can become complex and are not discussed further in the text.

The estate freeze rules *do not apply* to transfers of the following assets.

- Retained interests for which market quotations are readily available.
- Retained interests that are the same as those transferred (e.g., common stock, a partnership interest in which all partners share equally).

The response of the business community to the current estate freeze rules has not been positive. Consider some of the inherent disadvantages.

- Although the retained interest is deemed to be a gift, it is also included in the donor's gross estate upon death. In Example 15, therefore, the preferred stock is included in Quinn's gross estate upon his subsequent death.
- The donor loses the use of any gift tax paid on the retained interest.

The estate freeze does, however, escape later estate taxation on any post-transfer appreciation that develops.

EXAMPLE 16

Assume the same facts as in Example 15. Quinn dies 10 years after the gift when the Robin Corporation common and preferred stock are worth $5 million and $500,000, respectively. Quinn's estate includes only $500,000 for the preferred stock. The $3 million appreciation on the common stock ($5 million – $2 million) has escaped a transfer tax. ▼

Estate Freezes—Partnerships. Due to the statutory limitations imposed on estate freezes using corporations, the adoption of a family limited partnership (FLP) to carry out an estate freeze has become popular. A common scenario is for grandparents to form an FLP to hold a closely held business or other assets that can be expected to appreciate (e.g., real estate). The grandparents make themselves general partners (GP) and over a period of years make gifts of limited partnership interests to their children and grandchildren.

In valuing gifts of limited partnership interests, generous discounts (from 25 percent to 60 percent) are made for lack of marketability and minority interest. As the grandparents are the general partners, they remain in control of the business (i.e., the FLP).

At one point, the IRS contended that a discount for a minority interest was not available as long as the business was held fully within the family unit (e.g., grandparents, children, grandchildren). After losing on the issue in several court cases, the IRS conceded that the valuation discount is available.[24]

---

[24] Rev.Rul. 93–12, 1993–1 C.B. 202, rescinding Rev.Rul. 81–253, 1981–1 C.B. 187.

CONCEPT SUMMARY 18–1

Valuation Concepts

1. Fair market value is "the price at which property would change hands between a willing buyer and a willing seller, neither being under any compulsion to buy or to sell and both having reasonable knowledge of relevant facts."
2. Special rules govern the valuation of life insurance policies and annuity contracts. In the case of unmatured life insurance policies, value depends on whether the policies are paid up or not. Use of the IRS valuation tables is necessary when the annuities are issued by parties not regularly engaged in selling annuities.
3. The IRS valuation tables must be used to value multiple interests in property. Such interests include income for a term of years, life estates, and remainders.
4. Section 2032A provides valuation relief for the estates of persons who hold real estate used in farming or in connection with a closely held business. If the requirements of the provision are met and if the executor elects, the property can be valued at its *current use* rather than its *most suitable use.*
5. Determining the value of the stock in a closely held corporation presents unique problems. The presence or absence of *goodwill* at the corporate level has a direct bearing on the stock being valued. A discount may be in order for any of the following: a minority interest, lack of marketability, and the application of the blockage rule. The IRS will contend that a premium attaches to an interest that represents control of the corporation.
6. A properly structured buy-sell agreement will control the value to be assigned a deceased owner's interest in a partnership or a corporation.
7. An estate tax freeze is useful in avoiding post-transfer appreciation that develops on the partnership or corporate interest involved. However, the donor must consider the gift tax consequences that result when the freeze is created.

The overall expectation underlying the FLP approach is that a lesser value of the business can be transferred by gift than would be the case if everything is passed by death. The key to success, however, is the acceptability of the discounts used to value the gifts. Overly generous discount percentages could result in vulnerability to the penalty for undervaluation.[25]

In light of what happened to the estate freeze of corporate stock previously discussed, it is not unlikely that Congress might enact statutory limitations on the use of FLPs.

Valuation concepts are reviewed in Concept Summary 18–1.

INCOME TAX CONCEPTS

Family tax planning also involves an assessment of the income tax positions of the transferor (the donor or decedent) and the transferee (the donee or heir).

BASIS OF PROPERTY ACQUIRED BY GIFT

4   **LEARNING OBJECTIVE**
Compare the income tax basis rules applying to property received by gift and by death.

The income tax basis of property acquired by gift depends on whether the donee sells the property for a gain or for a loss and, in certain cases, on when the gift occurred.

- If the gift took place after 1920 and before 1977, the donee's basis for gain is the donor's adjusted basis plus any gift tax paid on the transfer (but not to

---

[25] § 6662(b)(5). See the discussion of accuracy-related penalties in Chapter 16.

exceed the fair market value on the date of the gift). The basis for loss is the lower of the basis for gain or the fair market value of the property on the date of the gift.

- If the gift took place after 1976, the donee's basis for gain is the donor's adjusted basis plus only the gift tax attributable to the appreciation of the property to the point of the gift. The basis for loss is the lesser of the basis for gain or the fair market value of the property on the date of the gift.[26]

EXAMPLE 17

In 1975, Norm receives stock as a gift from Lana. The stock cost Lana $10,000 and was worth $50,000 on the date of the gift. As a result of the transfer, Lana paid a gift tax of $5,000. Norm's income tax basis for gain or loss is $15,000 [$10,000 (Lana's basis) + $5,000 (gift tax paid by Lana)]. Norm does not have a different basis for loss; the fair market value of the property on the date of the gift ($50,000) is not less than the basis for gain ($15,000). ▼

EXAMPLE 18

Assume the same facts as in Example 17, except that the gift took place in 1997.

Lana's adjusted basis on the date of the gift	$10,000
Gift tax attributable to the $40,000 appreciation [($40,000/$50,000) × $5,000]	4,000
Norm's income tax basis for gain	$14,000

Norm's basis for loss also is $14,000, based on the same reasoning as in Example 17. ▼

The effect of the rule illustrated in Example 18 is to deny a donee any increase in basis for the gift tax attributable to the donor's adjusted basis.

Because the donee usually assumes the donor's basis in the property, transfers by gifts are considered carryover situations. Consistent with this approach, the donee's holding period includes that of the donor.[27]

BASIS OF PROPERTY ACQUIRED BY DEATH

General Rule. Except as otherwise noted in the following sections, the income tax basis of property acquired from a decedent is the fair market value on the date of death or, if elected, on the alternate valuation date. When property has appreciated in value between acquisition and date of death, a **step-up in** income tax **basis** occurs for the estate or heir of the deceased owner. A step-up in basis means that appreciation existing at death escapes the application of the Federal income tax.

EXAMPLE 19

Upon her death in 1997, Nancy owned real estate (adjusted basis of $100,000) worth $400,000 that she leaves to Jack. Assuming that the alternate valuation date is not elected, Jack's income tax basis in the property becomes $400,000. Thus, a subsequent sale of the real estate by Jack for $400,000 results in no gain or loss to him. ▼

EXAMPLE 20

Assume the same facts as in Example 19, except that, shortly before her death, Nancy sells the real estate for $400,000. Nancy has a taxable gain of $300,000 for income tax purposes. ▼

By contrasting Examples 19 and 20, one can see that the rules place a premium on holding appreciated property until death, to take advantage of the step-up in basis rule. The same cannot be said for property that has declined in value. Here,

---

[26]§§ 1015(a) and (d).

[27]§ 1223(2).

death causes a **step-down in basis.** This result should be avoided if selling the property would generate a deductible income tax loss.

EXAMPLE 21

Upon his death in 1997, Wes held stock as an investment with an adjusted basis of $50,000 and a fair market value of $30,000. Because only $30,000 is included in the gross estate, the basis of the stock to the estate or heir is this amount. Had Wes sold the stock before his death, a deduction for some or all of the $20,000 loss might have been available. ▼

The holding period to the estate or heir of property acquired from a decedent is automatically treated as long term.[28]

Community Property. Although there is usually no change in basis for property that is not part of a decedent's gross estate, a special exception applies to community property. In such situations, the surviving spouse's half of the community takes the same basis as the half included in the deceased spouse's gross estate.[29] The following examples illustrate the reason for and the effect of this special rule.

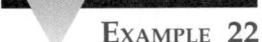

EXAMPLE 22

Leif and Rosa were husband and wife and lived in a common law state. At the time of Leif's death, he owned assets (worth $800,000 with a basis to him of $100,000), which he bequeathed to Rosa. Presuming the transfer qualifies under § 2056, Leif's estate is allowed a marital deduction of approximately $800,000. As the property passes through Leif's estate, Rosa receives a step-up in basis to $800,000. ▼

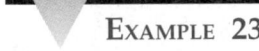

EXAMPLE 23

Assume the same facts as in Example 22, except that Leif and Rosa had always lived in California (a community property state). If the $800,000 of assets are community property, only one-half of this value is included in Leif's gross estate. Because the other half does not pass through Leif's estate (it already belongs to Rosa), is it fair to deny Rosa a new basis in it? Therefore, allowing the surviving spouse's share of the community to take on a basis equal to the half included in the deceased spouse's gross estate equalizes the income tax result generally achieved in common law states through the use of the marital deduction. By giving Rosa an income tax basis of $800,000 ($400,000 for Leif's half passing to her plus $400,000 for her half) and including only $400,000 in Leif's gross estate, the tax outcome is the same as in Example 22. ▼

Step-Up in Basis and the One-Year Rule. To understand the need for § 1014(e), consider the following situation.

EXAMPLE 24

Gary and Hazel are husband and wife and reside in a common law state. When the couple learns that Hazel has a terminal illness, Gary transfers property (basis of $50,000 and fair market value of $200,000) to her as a gift. Hazel dies shortly thereafter, and under the provisions of her will, the property returns to Gary. ▼

If it were not for § 1014(e), what have the parties accomplished? No gift tax occurs on the transfer from Gary to Hazel because of the application of the marital deduction. Upon Hazel's death, her bequest to Gary does not generate any estate tax because the inclusion of the property in her gross estate is offset by the marital deduction. Through the application of the general rule of § 1014, Gary ends up with the same property, with its basis stepped up to $200,000. Thus, the procedure enables Gary to get a "free" increase in income tax basis of $150,000.

---

[28] § 1223(11).   [29] § 1014(b)(6).

When applicable, § 1014(e) forces Gary (the original donor) to assume the property with the same basis it had to Hazel immediately before her death. Hazel's basis would have been determined under § 1015 (basis of property acquired by gift). The basis would have been $50,000 (donor's adjusted basis) plus any gift tax adjustment (none in this case) and any capital additions made by the donee (none in this case), or $50,000. If § 1014(e) applies to Example 24, Gary ends up where he started (with $50,000) in terms of income tax basis.

For § 1014(e) to be operative, the following conditions must be satisfied.

- The decedent must have received appreciated property as a gift during the one-year period ending with his or her death.
- The property is acquired from the decedent by the donor (or the donor's spouse).

Example 24 concerns a transfer between spouses, but the application of § 1014(e) is not so limited. The provision applies with equal effect if, for example, the donor-heir were a daughter of the donee-decedent. In such cases, moreover, the technique used in Example 24 might be susceptible to the imposition of gift or estate taxes, because of the unavailability of the marital deduction.

Income in Respect of a Decedent.   Income in respect of a decedent (IRD) is income earned by a decedent to the point of his or her death but not reportable on the final income tax return under the method of accounting used. IRD is most frequently applicable to decedents using the cash basis of accounting. IRD also occurs, for example, when a taxpayer at the time of death held installment notes receivable on which the gain has been deferred.

IRD is included in the gross estate at its fair market value on the appropriate valuation date. However, the income tax basis of the decedent transfers to the estate or heirs. Neither a basis step-up nor a step-down is possible as is true of property received by death.[30] Furthermore, the recipient of IRD must classify it in the same manner (e.g., ordinary income, capital gain) as the decedent would have.[31]

How Conclusive Is the Value Used for Estate Tax Purposes? Suppose a value is used for estate tax purposes and reflected on the estate tax return. At some future date, an heir to the property included in the gross estate believes the value used for estate tax purposes was incorrect. An heir might desire a change in value for countless reasons, including the following.

- The property is sold. Higher value leads to higher basis and less income tax gain.
- The property is depreciable. More basis means larger depreciation deductions.
- A home equity loan is obtained. With a higher value, a larger loan is allowed.
- If the heir is a charitable organization, higher value could improve its fund-raising potential.

Is there any chance of success in arguing for a different value and thereby changing the income tax basis? The answer is yes, but with definite reservations.

If the statute of limitations has not lapsed for the estate tax return, the heir may try for a higher income tax basis by having the estate tax valuation raised. Any new valuation, however, requires both cooperation from the decedent's executor and acceptance by the IRS.

---

[30] § 1014(c).

[31] § 691(a)(3). See Chapter 19 for a further discussion of IRD.

CONCEPT SUMMARY 18–2

Income Tax Concepts

1. The income tax basis of property acquired by gift is the donor's basis with appropriate adjustment for any gift tax paid. With built-in loss situations, the income tax basis is the fair market value of the property on the date of the gift.
2. The income tax basis of property acquired through the death of the owner is its fair market value on the appropriate estate tax valuation date.
3. No step-up in basis is allowed if the property returns to the donor or donor's spouse within one year.
4. Items of income in respect of a decedent do not undergo a step-up or step-down in basis.
5. The value used for estate tax purposes is presumed to establish basis for income tax purposes. This presumption can be rebutted, but only with great difficulty.

If the statute of limitations has lapsed for the estate tax return, the success of the heir's challenge depends on the following factors.

- The value reflected on the estate tax return and accepted by the IRS is presumed to be correct.[32] The heir must rebut the presumption.
- To rebut the presumption of correctness, it is important to determine by what means the property was originally valued. Did the valuation result from a unilateral determination by the IRS, or was it the result of carefully considered compromise between the estate and the IRS? The presumption is more difficult for the heir to overcome in the latter instance.
- Did the heir have a hand in setting the original value? If so, allowing the value to be changed now would seem to give the heir an unfair advantage. The heir used or influenced the use of a lower value for estate tax purposes (thereby eliminating estate taxes) and now wants a higher value for income tax purposes (thereby reducing a recognized gain).[33]
- Even if the concept of fairness is not applicable because the heir was not involved in setting the original value, justification for a new value must be produced.

GIFT PLANNING

5 LEARNING OBJECTIVE
Plan gifts so as to minimize gift taxes and avoid estate taxes.

One of the ways to carry out family tax planning is to start a program of lifetime giving. The objectives of such a program are to minimize transfer taxes while keeping income tax consequences in mind.

MINIMIZING GIFT TAXES

The Federal gift tax can be avoided through proper use of the annual exclusion. Because a new annual exclusion is available each year, spacing gifts over multiple years increases the amount that can be transferred free of gift tax.

---

[32] Rev.Rul. 54–97, 1954–1 C.B. 113; *H. B. Levy,* 17 T.C. 728 (1951); and *Malcolm C. Davenport,* 6 T.C. 62 (1946).

[33] In *William A. Beltzer,* 74–1 USTC ¶9373, 33 AFTR2d 74–1173, 495 F.2d 211 (CA–8, 1974), *aff'g.* 73–2 USTC ¶9512, 32 AFTR2d

73–5250 (D.Ct.Neb., 1973), the concept of fairness was *invoked against the taxpayer* since, as the executor of the estate, he had been instrumental in setting the original value reported on the death tax return.

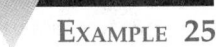

EXAMPLE 25

Starting in 1992, Cora makes annual gifts of $10,000 to each of her five grandchildren. Through 1997, Cora will have transferred $300,000 [$10,000 (annual exclusion) × 5 (number of donees) × 6 (number of years)] with no gift tax consequences. ▼

For married donors, the § 2513 election to split gifts can double the amount of a tax-free transfer.

EXAMPLE 26

Assume the same facts as in Example 25, except that Cora is married to Leon. If Leon consents to the § 2513 elections, Cora can transfer $600,000 [$20,000 (annual exclusion for two donors) × 5 (number of donees) × 6 (number of years)] with no gift tax consequences. ▼

From a practical standpoint, many donors who want to take advantage of the annual exclusion do not wish to give cash or near-cash assets (e.g., marketable securities). Where the value of the gift property substantially exceeds the amount of the annual exclusion, as is often the case with real estate, gifts of a partial interest are an attractive option.

EXAMPLE 27

Seth and Kate want to give a parcel of unimproved land to their three adult children and five grandchildren as equal owners. The land has an adjusted basis of $100,000, is held by Seth and Kate as community property, and has an appraised value of $320,000 as of December 21, 1996. On December 22, 1996, Seth and Kate convey a one-half undivided interest in the land to their children and grandchildren as tenants in common. This is followed by a transfer of the remaining one-half interest on January 2, 1997. Neither transfer causes gift tax, because each is fully offset by annual exclusions of $160,000 [$20,000 (annual exclusion for two donors) × 8 (number of donees)]. Thus, in a period of less than two weeks, Seth and Kate transfer $320,000 in value free of any Federal tax consequences. ▼

Further examination of Example 27 leads to the following observations.

- No income tax consequences ensue from the gift. However, had Seth and Kate first sold the land and made a gift of the cash proceeds, recognized gain of $220,000 [$320,000 (selling price) – $100,000 (adjusted basis)] would have resulted.
- The § 2513 election to split gifts is not necessary, because the land was community property. If the land had been held by one of the spouses as separate property, the election would have been necessary to generate the same $320,000 of exclusions.
- Good tax planning generally dictates that sizable gifts of property be supported by reliable appraisals. In the case of successive gifts of partial interests in the same property, multiple appraisals should be obtained to cover each gift. This advice was not followed in Example 27 due to the short interval between gifts. Barring exceptional circumstances, the value of real estate will not change within a period of less than two weeks.

MINIMIZING ESTATE TAXES

Aside from the annual exclusion, do lifetime gifts offer any tax advantages over transfers at death? Someone familiar with the tax law applicable to asset transfers would answer "no" to this question. Under the unified transfer tax scheme, the tax rates and credit are the same. Consequently, there seems to be no transfer tax difference between transfer by gift and at death. However, as the following discussion shows, lifetime transfers may be preferable to those at death.

Avoiding a Transfer Tax on Future Appreciation.   If property is expected to appreciate in value, a gift removes the appreciation from the donor's gross estate.

EXAMPLE 28

In 1986, Wilma transfers an insurance policy on her life to Karen, the designated beneficiary. At the time of the transfer, the policy had a fair market value of $50,000 and a face amount of $250,000. Wilma dies in 1997, and the insurance company pays the $250,000 proceeds to Karen. By making the gift, Wilma has kept $200,000 in value from being subject to a transfer tax. ▼

ETHICAL
CONSIDERATIONS

How Not to Avoid Appreciation at Death

A t the time of his death in 1997, Walter was thought to be the owner of the family vacation home in Colorado. When Walter's executor obtained access to his safe deposit box, however, a deed to the property was found. The deed indicated that Walter had transferred ownership to his adult children in 1980.

The records of the county where the vacation home is located reflect the transfer and list the children as the owners of record. They also reveal that Walter continued to pay the property tax assessments up to the date of his death. Although the value of the home in 1980 was estimated to be $110,000, no Federal gift tax return was ever filed.

As of the date of Walter's death, the property is estimated to be worth around $400,000. The executor of Walter's estate files a Form 709 for 1980 listing a gift of $110,000, but includes none of the property on Form 706. What do you think?

Besides life insurance, other assets that often appreciate in value include real estate, art objects, and special collections (e.g., rare books, coins, and stamps).

Preparing for the Special Use Valuation Method.   The § 2032A election is not available for valuing transfers by gift. Yet, if its use is planned in estate tax situations, gifts of nonqualifying property may aid in meeting the requirements of § 2032A. Recall that one of the requirements of § 2032A is that qualified use property must constitute at least 50 percent of the adjusted value of the gross estate.

EXAMPLE 29

In 1993, Floyd's estate includes the following.

	Fair Market Value
Farm operated by Floyd with current use value of $250,000	$1,000,000
Stock in a local bank	700,000
Marketable securities and cash	400,000

At this point, Floyd's estate does not qualify for the § 2032A election. The qualifying property [$1,000,000 (farm)] does not equal or exceed 50% of the adjusted gross estate [$1,000,000 (farm) + $700,000 (bank stock) + $400,000 (marketable securities and cash)]. ▼

EXAMPLE 30

Continuing with the facts of Example 29, Floyd makes a gift of one-half of the bank stock in 1993. He dies in 1997 with no change in asset values. Floyd's estate now qualifies for § 2032A treatment since $1,000,000 (farm) is 50% or more of $1,750,000 [$1,000,000 (farm) + $350,000 (bank stock) + $400,000 (marketable securities and cash)]. The election enables the estate to value the farm at $250,000 (current use). As a result, the estate tax on $500,000 in value is saved. ▼

Care must be taken to avoid gifts of property within three years of death. Though such gifts usually are not included in the gross estate of the donor for estate tax purposes, they are counted when testing for the percentage requirements of § 303 (stock redemptions to pay death taxes and administration expenses—refer to Chapter 5), § 2032A, and § 6166 (extension of time to pay estate taxes in installments—discussed below).[34]

EXAMPLE 31   Assume the same facts as in Example 30, except that the gift occurs in 1995 (not 1993). Although only $350,000 of the bank stock is included in Floyd's gross estate for estate tax purposes, $700,000 is used for the percentage requirements of the special use valuation provisions. As a result, the estate fails to qualify for the election. ▼

Avoiding State Transfer Taxes.   Another element that may favor lifetime over death transfers is the state's transfer tax system. All states impose some type of death tax, but only a few impose a gift tax. Thus, a gift may completely avoid a state transfer tax.

The states currently imposing a state gift tax include Connecticut, Delaware, Louisiana, New York, North Carolina, and Tennessee. Unfortunately, this could lead to multiple taxation of the same transfer. Unlike the *state death* tax credit (see the discussion of § 2011 in Chapter 17), the Code does not allow a credit for state gift taxes paid. In fact, the only credit allowed against the Federal gift tax is the unified transfer tax credit.

Effect of Gift Taxes Paid.   As to taxable gifts that generate a tax, consider the time value of the gift taxes paid. Since the donor loses the use of these funds, the predicted interval between the gift (and the imposition of the gift tax) and death (the imposition of the estate tax) may make the gift less attractive.

EXAMPLE 32   In 1992, Gail makes a gift that results in a gift tax of $50,000. She dies five years later. Presuming a 10% rate of return, the gift tax paid would have been worth $80,550 at Gail's death. Therefore, Gail has lost $30,550 by making the gift. ▼

The analysis used in Example 32 requires refinement to yield a meaningful result. Variables that need to be questioned or interjected include the following.

- The life expectancy of the donor at the time of the gift. Actuarial tables can provide a start, but this kind of information must be adjusted for the general health and lifestyle of the donor. In any event, accurately predicting when a specific person will die is more chance than science.
- The interest factor used. Anticipating even short-rate changes, erratic at best, becomes mere guesswork as the time interval increases.
- Any change in the value of the property from the point of gift to the date of death. Appreciation in value during this interval makes the gift look like a wise choice. The opposite is true if value declines.
- The income tax ramifications of the gift. A donor escapes any post-transfer income yielded by the property. Thus, the income tax burden is shifted away from the donor to the donee.

---

[34] §§ 2035(d)(3) and (4).

Finally, a present value analysis must consider the estate tax effect of any gift tax paid. Except for gifts within three years of death (see Chapter 17), the gift tax paid itself is not subject to estate tax. Referring to Example 32, the $50,000 in gift taxes paid escapes inclusion in Gail's gross estate.

INCOME TAX CONSIDERATIONS

6 **LEARNING OBJECTIVE**
Make gifts so as to avoid income taxes for the donor.

Income Shifting. One way to lower the overall tax burden on the family unit is to shift income from high-bracket taxpayers to lower-bracket family members. To accomplish this shifting, however, income-producing property must be transferred.

If a gift of property is to shift income to the donee, the transfer must be *complete*. Continued control over the property by the donor may lead the IRS to question the finality of the gift.

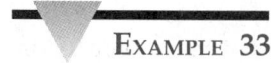

EXAMPLE 33   Vera, subject to a 39.6% marginal income tax rate, owns all of the stock in Orange, an S corporation. Vera transfers by gift 60% of the Orange stock to her four children. The children range in age from 14 to 19 years and are all in the 15% income tax bracket. After the transfer, Vera continues to operate the business. No shareholder meetings are held. Except for reporting 60% of the pass-through of Orange's profits, Vera's children have no contact with the business. Aside from the salary paid to Vera, Orange makes no cash distributions to its shareholders. ▼

The situation posed in Example 33 occurs frequently and is fraught with danger. If the purported gift by Vera lacks economic reality and Vera is the true economic owner of all of Orange's stock, the pass-through to the children is disregarded.[35] The profits are taxed to Vera at her 39.6 percent rate rather than to the children at their 15 percent rates. Consequently, the transfer has not accomplished the intended shifting of income.

What can be done to make the transfer in Example 33 tax-effective? First, a distribution of dividends would provide some economic benefit to the children. As the transfer is currently constituted, all that the children have received as a result of the gift is an economic detriment, because they must pay income taxes on their share of Orange's pass-through of profits. Second, some steps should be taken to recognize and protect the interests of the children as donees. One way to do this is to make use of the state's Uniform Gifts to Minors Act.[36] Vera could designate a family member as the custodian of the stock. The custodian would have a fiduciary responsibility to safeguard the interests of the children. Once the children reach age 21 and the custodianship relationship ends, shareholder meetings should be encouraged. That the children do not actively participate in the business of Orange is of no consequence, as long as they are given the opportunity to do so.

As was true in Example 33, income shifting techniques assume that the donee is in a lower tax bracket than the donor. When the donee is under age 14, however, kiddie tax treatment can neutralize the income tax effect of a gift. Under this provision, certain unearned income (e.g., interest, dividends) of a child is taxed at the marginal rate applicable to the parent.[37] In Example 33, suppose one of Vera's children was not yet 14 years old. Giving Orange stock to the child would not serve any purpose. Even if the transfer was complete and the child recognized the profit pass-through, the applicable rate would be 39.6 percent, not 15 percent. Once the child reaches age 14, however, kiddie tax treatment no longer applies.

---

[35] *Michael F. Beirne*, 52 T.C. 210 (1969) and 61 T.C. 268 (1973).   [37] § 1(g).
[36] *Donald O. Kirkpatrick*, 36 TCM 1122, T.C.Memo. 1977–281.

Income Tax Consequences to the Donor. Generally, a gift of property results in no income tax consequences to the donor. Two important exceptions, however, involve installment notes receivable and U.S. savings bonds.

A gift of an installment note receivable is a taxable disposition, and the donor is treated as if the note had been sold for its fair market value.[38] As a result, the donor recognizes the deferred profit.

EXAMPLE 34

In 1995, Adam sells real estate (basis of $100,000) to Norm (an unrelated party) for $400,000. Norm (the obligor) issues two notes of $200,000 each, one due in 1996 and one due in 1997. Adam (the obligee) does not elect out of the installment method. In 1996 and before the first note becomes due, Adam gives both notes to his son, Sam. On this date, the notes have a fair market value of $380,000. As a result of the gift to Sam, Adam recognizes a gain of $280,000 [$380,000 (fair market value of the notes) – $100,000 (Adam's unrecovered basis)]. ▼

A gift of U.S. savings bonds is not effective unless the bonds are re-registered in the donee's name. This forces the donor to recognize any deferred income accrued on the bonds. The result may surprise donors who expect to postpone the recognition of interest income until the bonds are redeemed. Thus, the donor who desires to avoid income tax consequences should avoid gifts of installment notes receivable and U.S. savings bonds.

For purposes of contrasting tax results, what happens if these properties are passed by death?

- Installment notes receivable are taxed to whoever collects the notes (the estate or heirs).[39] If the notes are forgiven or canceled by the decedent's will, the income is taxed to the estate.
- Deferred interest income on U.S. savings bonds is taxed to whoever redeems the bonds (the estate or heirs).
- Recapture potential disappears at death.[40] The estate or heirs take the property free of any recapture potential existing at the time of the owner's death.

Carryover Basis Situations. When considering the income tax effect of a transfer on the donee or heir, the basis rules of §§ 1014 and 1015 warrant close examination. When appreciated property is involved, receiving the property from a decedent is preferred to a lifetime transfer.

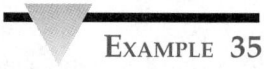

EXAMPLE 35

Keith plans to transfer unimproved real estate (basis of $100,000 and fair market value of $400,000) to his daughter, Esther. If the property passes by death, Esther's basis is $400,000. If the property passes by gift, her income tax basis (presuming no gift tax adjustment) is $100,000. The step-up effect of § 1014 provides Esther with an additional basis of $300,000. ▼

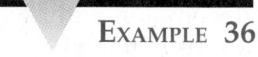

EXAMPLE 36

Keith plans to transfer unimproved real estate (basis of $150,000 and fair market value of $100,000) to his daughter, Esther. If the property passes by death, Esther's basis is $100,000. If the property passes by gift, her income tax basis is $100,000 for losses and $150,000 for gains. Receiving the property as a gift, therefore, might be more advantageous to Esther than the complete step-down in basis under § 1014. ▼

---

[38] § 453B(a).
[39] § 453B(c).
[40] §§ 1245(b)(1) and 1250(d)(1). Contrast this result with what happens when § 1245 or § 1250 property is transferred by gift. Here, the recapture potential carries over to the donee.

For Keith, the options posed by Example 36 are not attractive. By making a gift or passing the property by death, Keith sacrifices the potential loss deduction of $50,000. Presuming he holds the land as an investment, he can use the capital loss to offset capital gains or apply it against ordinary income to the extent of $3,000 per year. Unused capital losses can be carried over indefinitely but will not survive Keith's death.

ESTATE PLANNING

Estate planning considers the nontax and tax aspects of death. In the nontax area are the various steps that can be taken to reduce the costs of probating an estate. In the tax area, the focus is on controlling the amount of the gross estate and maximizing estate tax deductions.

PROBATE COSTS

7 LEARNING OBJECTIVE
Reduce probate costs in the administration of an estate.

The probate estate consists of all properties subject to administration by an executor. The administration is conducted under the supervision of a local court, usually called a probate court. In certain states, probate functions are performed by county courts, surrogate courts, or orphan's courts.

Probate costs include attorney fees, accountant fees, appraisal and inventory fees, court costs, expenses incident to the disposition of assets and satisfaction of liabilities, litigation costs needed to resolve will contests, and charges for the preparation of tax returns. The total amount of probate costs cannot be accurately predicted because so many variables are involved. A conservative range might be from 5 to 15 percent of the amount of the probate estate.

Many procedures can be used to reduce the probate estate and thereby save probate costs, including the following.

- Owning property as joint tenants (or tenants by the entirety) with right of survivorship. Upon death, the property passes to the surviving tenant and generally is not subject to probate.
- Making life insurance payable to a beneficiary other than the estate.
- Utilizing a revocable trust. Upon the death of the creator, the trust becomes irrevocable and is not subject to probate. The revocable trust is often popularly referred to as a **living trust.**

Another advantage of bypassing the probate estate is that the beneficiary can obtain immediate possession and enjoyment of the property. The probate process can become prolonged, and the heir may have to await the final settlement of the estate before getting the property.

In terms of probate costs, the ownership of out-of-state real estate can cause horrendous problems. Out-of-state ownership is not uncommon with decedents who have relocated after retirement or who maintain vacation homes.

EXAMPLE 37

After retirement and five years before his death, Ted moved from Nebraska to Arizona. At death, Ted still owns a rental house in Nebraska and a vacation home in Idaho. To clear title to these properties, Ted's executor must institute ancillary probate proceedings in Nebraska and Idaho. This will result in additional attorney fees and court costs. ▼

The solution to the dilemma posed in Example 37 is to dispose of these properties before death. Although this may generate some legal fees, they will be far less than the cost of ancillary probate proceedings.

CONTROLLING THE AMOUNT OF THE GROSS ESTATE

8 **LEARNING OBJECTIVE**
Apply procedures that reduce estate tax consequences.

Unlike the probate estate, the gross estate determines what property is subject to the Federal estate tax. In fact, many of the steps taken to reduce the probate estate will not have a similar effect on the gross estate—see the discussion of §§ 2036 and 2038 in Chapter 17.

Valuation procedures sometimes can be applied to control the amount of the gross estate. The special use valuation method of § 2032A can be elected when the estate consists of real estate used in farming or in connection with a closely held business. When the estate comprises assets that have declined in value shortly after death, the use of the alternate valuation date of § 2032 (see Chapter 17) is advised.

PROPER HANDLING OF ESTATE TAX DEDUCTIONS

Estate taxes can be reduced either by decreasing the size of the gross estate or by increasing the total allowable deductions. The lower the taxable estate, the less estate tax is generated. Planning with deductions involves the following considerations.

* Making proper use of the marital deduction.
* Working effectively with the charitable deduction.
* Optimizing other deductions and losses allowed under §§ 2053 and 2054.

Approaches to the Marital Deduction. When planning for the estate tax marital deduction, both tax and nontax factors are taken into account. Two major tax goals guide the planning. They are the *equalization* and *deferral* approaches.

* Attempt to equalize the estates of both spouses. Clearly, for example, the estate tax on $2 million is more than double the estate tax on $1 million [compare $780,800 with $691,600 ($345,800 × 2)].
* Try to postpone estate taxation as long as possible. On a $1 million amount, for example, what is the time value of $345,800 in estate taxes deferred for a period of, say, 10 years?

Barring certain circumstances, the deferral approach generally is preferable. By maximizing the marital deduction on the death of the first spouse to die, taxes are saved, and the surviving spouse can trim his or her future estate by entering into a program of lifetime giving. By making optimum use of the annual exclusion, considerable amounts can be shifted without incurring *any* transfer tax.

Tax planning must remain flexible and be tailored to the individual circumstances of the parties involved. The equalization approach may be most attractive in the following situations.

* Both spouses are of advanced age and/or in poor health, and neither is expected to survive the other for a prolonged period of time.
* The spouse who is expected to survive has considerable assets of his or her own. To illustrate, a spouse who passes a $250,000 estate to the survivor who already has assets of $1 million is trading a 32 percent bracket for a later 43 percent bracket.
* Because of appreciation, property worth $250,000 today when it passes to the surviving spouse may be worth $1 million five years later when the survivor dies.

The Marital Deduction—Sophistication of the Deferral Approach. When saving estate taxes for the family unit is the sole consideration, the equalization and deferral approaches can be combined with maximum effect.

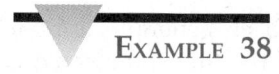

EXAMPLE 38

At the time of his death in 1997, Vito had never made any taxable gifts. Under Vito's will, his *disposable estate* of $1,100,000 passes to his wife, Zina.[41] ▼

EXAMPLE 39

Assume the same facts as in Example 38, except that Vito's will provides as follows: $600,000 to the children and the remainder ($500,000) to Zina. ▼

From a tax standpoint, which is the better plan? Although no estate tax results from either arrangement, Example 38 represents an overfunding in terms of the marital deduction. Why place an additional $600,000 in Zina's potential estate when it can pass free of tax to the children through the application of the $192,800 unified tax credit available for 1997? (The exemption equivalent of $192,800 is $600,000.) The exemption equivalent is known as the *bypass amount*. The arrangement in Example 39 is preferred because it avoids unnecessary concentration of wealth in Zina's estate.

On occasion, disclaimers can be used to effect the deferral approach.

EXAMPLE 40

Upon his death in 1997, Pete had never made any taxable gifts. Under Pete's will, his disposable estate of $1,500,000 passes as follows: $700,000 to Jim (Pete's adult son) and the

---

[41] For this purpose, the *disposable estate* includes the gross estate less all deductions (e.g., debts, administration and funeral expenses) except the marital deduction. The term is not in the Code but is useful in evaluating tax options.

remainder ($800,000) to Clare (Pete's surviving spouse). Shortly after Pete's death, Jim issues a disclaimer as to $100,000 of his $700,000 bequest. This amount, therefore, passes to Clare as the remainderperson under Pete's will. ▼

Jim's disclaimer avoids an estate tax on $100,000. The result is an increase of $100,000 in the marital deduction and the elimination of *any* estate tax upon Pete's death.

Effectively Working with the Charitable Deduction. As a general guide to obtaining overall tax savings, lifetime charitable transfers are preferred over testamentary dispositions. For example, an individual who gives $10,000 to a qualified charity during his or her life secures an income tax deduction, avoids any gift tax, and reduces the gross estate by the amount of the gift. By way of contrast, if the $10,000 is willed to charity, no income tax deduction is available, and the amount of the gift is includible in the decedent's gross estate (though later deducted for estate tax purposes). In short, the lifetime transfer provides a double tax benefit (income tax deduction plus reduced estate taxes) at no gift tax cost. The testamentary transfer merely neutralizes the effect of the inclusion of the property in the gross estate (inclusion under § 2033 and then deduction under § 2055).

To ensure that an estate tax deduction is allowed for a charitable contribution, the designated recipient must fall within the classifications set forth in § 2055. The status of the organization on the date the transfer becomes effective controls, and not the date the will authorizing the transfer was executed.

EXAMPLE 41

In 1982, Lisa drew up and executed a will in which she provided for $100,000 to pass to the Rose Academy, a nonprofit educational organization described in § 2055(a)(2) and, at that time, approved by the IRS as a qualified recipient. In 1984, the qualified status of the academy was revoked for practicing racial discrimination in the enrollment of its student body.[42] Lisa dies in 1997, and the executor of her estate, being compelled to satisfy the provisions of the will, transfers $100,000 to the academy. ▼

Even though Lisa may have been unaware of the action taken by the IRS in 1984, her estate is not allowed a charitable deduction. The recipient was no longer qualified on the date of Lisa's death. It may be that Lisa, even if she had known about the probable loss of the charitable deduction, would still have wished the bequest carried out as originally conceived. If not, it is easy to see that the error was of Lisa's own making because of her failure to review her estate planning situation.

One way to circumvent the quandary posed by Example 41 (other than changing Lisa's will before her death) is to express the charitable bequest in more flexible terms. The transfer to the academy could have been conditioned on the organization's continued status as a qualified recipient at the time of Lisa's death. Alternatively, Lisa's will may grant her executor the authority to substitute a different, but comparable, charitable organization *that is qualified* in the event of the disqualification of the named group.

On occasion, a charitable bequest depends on the issuance of a disclaimer by a noncharitable heir. Such a situation frequently arises with special types of property or collections, which the decedent may feel a noncharitable heir should have a choice of receiving.

---

[42] Most of the organizations that are qualified recipients (which will permit the donor a charitable deduction) are listed in IRS Publication 78. This compilation, revised and supplemented from time to time, addresses § 170 (income tax deduction) transfers. Publication 78, with the exceptions noted in Chapter 17, also applies to § 2055 (estate tax deduction) and § 2522 (gift tax deduction) transfers.

EXAMPLE 42

Megan specified in her will that her valuable art collection is to pass to her son or, if the son refuses, to a designated and qualified art museum. At the time the will was drawn, Megan knew that her son was not interested in owning the collection. If, after Megan's death, the son issues a timely disclaimer, the collection passes to the museum, and Megan's estate takes a charitable deduction for its death tax value. ▼

EXAMPLE 43

Dick's will specifies that one-half of his disposable estate is to pass to his wife and the remainder of his property to a specified qualified charitable organization. If the wife issues a timely disclaimer after Dick's death, all of the property passes to the charity and qualifies for the § 2055 charitable deduction. ▼

Has the son in Example 42 acted wisely if he issues the disclaimer in favor of the museum? Although such a disclaimer will provide Megan's estate with a deduction for the value of the art collection, consider the income tax deduction alternative. If the son accepts the bequest, he can still dispose of the collection (and fulfill his mother's philanthropic objectives) through a lifetime donation to the museum. At the same time, he obtains an income tax deduction under § 170. Whether this saves taxes for the family depends on a comparison of the mother's estate tax bracket with the estimated income tax bracket of the son. If the value of the collection runs afoul of the percentage limitations of § 170(b)(1), the donations could be spread over more than one year. If this is done, and to protect against the contingency of the son's dying before the entire collection is donated, the son can neutralize any potential death tax consequences by providing in his will for the undonated balance to pass to the museum.

The use of a disclaimer in Example 43 would be sheer folly. It would not reduce Dick's estate tax; it would merely substitute a charitable deduction for the marital deduction. Whether the wife issues a disclaimer or not, no estate taxes will be due. The wife should accept her bequest and, if she is so inclined, make lifetime gifts of it to a qualified charity. In so doing, she generates an income tax deduction for herself.

Proper Handling of Other Deductions and Losses under §§ 2053 and 2054. Many § 2053 and § 2054 deductions and losses may be claimed either as estate tax deductions or as income tax deductions by the estate on the fiduciary return (Form 1041), but not both.[43] The income tax deduction is not allowed unless the estate tax deduction is waived. It is possible for these deductions to be apportioned between the two returns.

PROVIDING ESTATE LIQUIDITY

9 ▼ **LEARNING OBJECTIVE**
Obtain liquidity for an estate.

Recognizing the Problem. Even with effective predeath family tax planning directed toward a minimization of transfer taxes, the smooth administration of an estate necessitates a certain degree of liquidity. After all, probate costs will be incurred, and most important of all, death taxes must be satisfied. In the meantime, the surviving spouse and dependent beneficiaries may need financial support. Without funds to satisfy these claims, estate assets may have to be sold at sacrifice prices, and most likely, the decedent's scheme of testamentary disposition will be defeated.

EXAMPLE 44

At the time of Myrtle's death, her estate was made up almost entirely of a large ranch currently being operated by Jim, one of Myrtle's two sons. Because the ranch had been in

---

[43] § 642(g) and Reg. § 20.2053–1(d).

the family for several generations and was a successful economic unit, Myrtle hoped that Jim would continue its operation and share the profits with Bob, her other son. Unfortunately, Bob, on learning that his mother had died without a will, demanded and obtained a partition and sale of his share of the property. Additional land was sold to pay for administration expenses and death taxes. After all of the sales had taken place, the portion remaining for Jim could not be operated profitably, and he was forced to give up the family ranch activity. ▼

What type of predeath planning might have avoided the result reached in Example 44? Certainly, Myrtle should have recognized and provided for the cash needs of the estate. Life insurance payable to her estate, although it adds to the estate tax liability, could have eased or solved the problem. This presumes that Myrtle was insurable or that the cost of the insurance would not be prohibitive. Furthermore, Myrtle made a serious error in dying without a will. A carefully drawn will could have precluded Bob's later course of action and perhaps kept much more of the ranch property intact. The ranch could have been placed in trust, life estate to Jim and Bob, remainder to their children. With such an arrangement, Bob would have been unable to sell the principal (the ranch).

Being able to defer the payment of death taxes may be an invaluable option for an estate that lacks cash or near-cash assets (e.g., marketable securities). In this connection, two major possibilities exist.

- The discretionary extension of time (§ 6161).
- The extension of time when the estate consists largely of an interest in a closely held business (§ 6166).

Discretionary Extension of Time to Pay Estate Taxes—§ 6161.

Currently, an executor or administrator may request an extension of time for paying the death tax for a period not to exceed 10 years from the date fixed for the payment. The IRS grants such requests whenever there is "reasonable cause." Reasonable cause is not limited to a showing of undue hardship. It includes cases in which the executor or administrator is unable to marshal liquid assets readily because they are located in several jurisdictions. It also includes situations where the estate is largely made up of assets in the form of payments to be received in the future (e.g., annuities, copyright royalties, contingent fees, or accounts receivable), or where the assets that must be liquidated to pay the estate tax must be sold at a sacrifice or in a depressed market.

Extension of Time When the Estate Consists Largely of an Interest in a Closely Held Business—§ 6166.

Congress always has been sympathetic to the plight of an estate that consists of an interest in a closely held business. The immediate imposition of the estate tax in such a situation may force the liquidation of the business at distress prices or cause the interest to be sold to outside parties.

A possible resolution of the problem is to use § 6166, which requires the IRS to accept a 15-payment procedure (5 interest-only payments, followed by 10 installment payments of the estate tax). This delay can enable the business to generate enough income to buy out the deceased owner's interest without disruption of operations or other financial sacrifice.

To meet the requirements of § 6166, the decedent's interest in a farm or other closely held business must exceed 35 percent of the decedent's adjusted gross estate.[44] The adjusted gross estate is the gross estate less the sum allowable as

---

[44] § 6166(a)(1).

deductions under § 2053 (expenses, indebtedness, and taxes) and § 2054 (casualty and theft losses during the administration of an estate).

An interest in a closely held business includes the following.[45]

- Any sole proprietorship.
- An interest in a partnership carrying on a trade or business, if 20 percent of the capital interest in the partnership is included in the gross estate *or* the partnership has 15 or fewer partners.
- Stock in a corporation carrying on a trade or business, if 20 percent or more of the value of the voting stock of the corporation is included in the gross estate *or* the corporation has 15 or fewer shareholders.

In meeting the preceding requirements, a decedent and his or her surviving spouse are treated as one owner (shareholder or partner) if the interest is held as community property, tenants in common, joint tenants, or tenants by the entirety. Attribution from family members is allowed.[46]

EXAMPLE 45

Decedent Bonnie held a 15% capital interest in the Wren Partnership. Her son holds another 10%. Wren had 16 partners including Bonnie and her son. Since the son's interest is attributed to Bonnie, the estate is deemed to hold a 25% interest, and Wren (for purposes of § 6166) has only 15 partners. ▼

In satisfying the more-than-35 percent test for qualification under § 6166, interests in more than one closely held business are aggregated when the decedent's gross estate includes 20 percent or more of the value of each such business.[47]

EXAMPLE 46

Henry's estate includes stock in Green Corporation and Brown Corporation, each of which qualifies as a closely held business. If the stock held in each entity represents 20% or more of the total value outstanding, the stocks can be combined for purposes of the more-than-35% test. ▼

If the conditions of § 6166 are satisfied and the provision is elected, the following results transpire.

- No payments on the estate tax attributable to the inclusion of the interest in a closely held business in the gross estate need be made with the first 5 payments. Then, annual installments are made over a period not longer than 10 years.
- From the outset, interest at the rate of 4 percent is paid.[48] This low rate is limited to the first $1 million of estate tax value for the business.
- Acceleration of deferred payments may be triggered upon the disposition of the interest or failure to make scheduled principal or interest payments.[49]

In qualifying for § 6166, prune the potential estate of assets that may cause the 35 percent test to be failed. In this regard, lifetime gifts of such assets as marketable securities and life insurance should be considered.[50]

Some of the estate planning procedures covered in the last part of this chapter appear in Concept Summary 18–3.

---

[45] § 6166(b)(1).
[46] As described in § 267(c)(4).
[47] § 6166(c).
[48] § 6601(j)(1).

[49] § 6166(g).
[50] A gift within three years of death is not effective for this purpose. § 2035(d)(4).

▼

Concept Summary 18–3

Estate and Gift Planning

1. In reducing (or eliminating) gift taxes, one can take advantage of the annual exclusion and the election to split gifts. In the case of a single asset with high value (e.g., land), annual gifts of partial interests should be considered.
2. Gifts can reduce later estate taxes. This is accomplished by giving away assets that will appreciate in value (e.g., life insurance policies, art works, rare collections).
3. Timely gifts can help an estate qualify for § 2032A (special use valuation method), § 6166 (15-year payout of estate taxes), and § 303 (stock redemptions to pay death taxes). To be effective, the gift must avoid the three-year rule of § 2035.
4. Gifts can relieve the income tax burden on the family unit. This objective is accomplished by shifting the income from the gift property to family members who are in a lower income tax bracket. In this regard, make sure the gift is *complete* and circumvents kiddie tax treatment.
5. Avoid gifts of property that result in income tax consequences to the donor.
6. Potential *probate costs* can be an important consideration in meaningful estate planning. Some procedures that reduce these costs include joint tenancies with the right of survivorship, living trusts, and predeath dispositions of out-of-state real estate. Keep in mind that most of these procedures *do not reduce estate taxes.*
7. A program of lifetime gifts and proper use of valuation techniques will reduce a decedent's *gross estate.* Further planning can reduce the *taxable estate* by proper handling of estate tax deductions.
8. For a married decedent, the most important deduction is the *marital deduction.* The two major approaches to the marital deduction are the *equalization* and *deferral* approaches.
9. Whether the equalization approach or the deferral approach is emphasized, make use of the *by-pass amount.*
10. Lifetime charitable contributions are preferable to transfers by death. The lifetime contributions provide the donor with an income tax deduction, and the amount donated is not included in the gross estate.
11. The *disclaimer* procedure can be used to control (either lower or raise) the amount of the marital deduction. It also can be used to increase the amount of the charitable deduction.
12. Gift planning can help ease potential *estate liquidity* problems (see item 3 above). After death, § 6166 can be useful if the estate qualifies. The provision allows installment payments of deferred estate taxes over an extended period of time.

KEY TERMS

Blockage rule, 18–9	Entity buy-sell agreement, 18–11	Special use value, 18–6
Buy-sell agreement, 18–11	Estate freeze, 18–12	Step-down in basis, 18–16
Cross-purchase buy-sell agreement, 18–11	Living trust, 18–24	Step-up in basis, 18–15
	Probate costs, 18–24	

▼

Problem Materials

DISCUSSION QUESTIONS

1. Discuss the relevance of the following in defining "fair market value" for Federal gift and estate tax purposes.

    a. § 2031(b).

    b. The definition contained in Reg. § 20.2031–1(b).

    c. A forced sale price.

    d. The location of the property being valued.

    e. The sentimental value of the property being valued.

    f. The wholesale price of the property.

    g. Tangible personalty sold as a result of an advertisement in the classified section of a newspaper.

2. Marvin's daughter is a student at an exclusive private women's college. Each year that she attends, Marvin has her sign a note for $20,000 to cover books, tuition, and room and board. Fifteen years after the daughter graduates, Marvin dies without a will. The notes are found in his safe deposit box. Although the daughter has become a successful business executive, Marvin never discussed the notes with her or made any attempts at collection. What are the pertinent tax issues? [Note: In answering this question, a review of the earlier part of Chapter 17 might prove useful.]

3. In valuing life insurance, what difference does it make whether the policy is paid up or not paid up?

4. In valuing annuity contracts, when should the tables issued by the IRS be used?

5. Jerry creates a trust, specifying a life estate to Jennifer, remainder to Tom upon Jennifer's death. Why is it necessary to value the life estate and the remainder interest separately?

6. Contrast current use value with most suitable use value. Why might the two values differ?

7. Comment on the special use valuation method in connection with the following.

    a. The 50% test and the 25% test.

    b. Qualifying property.

    c. The five-out-of-eight-years requirement.

    d. The qualifying heir.

    e. The $750,000 limitation.

8. At the time of her death, Sally owned and operated the family farm located on the fringes of a large metropolitan area. Brad, Sally's son and sole heir, is a practicing orthopedic surgeon in the city. Brad recognizes the potential of the farm for commercial development (e.g., housing subdivision, shopping center). Further, he feels that the property may double in value over the next few years. To defer estate taxes, Brad plans to continue using the property as a farm. Since he knows nothing about farming, Brad hopes to lease the property to Sally's neighbor, who is a family friend. What, if any, are the tax issues involved?

9. In filing his mother's estate tax return, Shawn (her sole heir) properly elects the special use valuation provision of § 2032A. Five years later, Shawn sells the property to a real estate developer. What are the tax issues confronting Shawn regarding the income tax basis of the property sold?

10. A program of lifetime gifts aids in planning for the election of the special use valuation method. Explain.

11. In valuing the stock of a closely held corporation, the IRS attributes a large amount to the goodwill of the business. What arguments can the taxpayers make to dispute this finding?

12. What effect, if any, will each of the following factors have on the valuation of stock in a closely held corporation?

    a. The "blockage rule."

    b. A minority interest is involved.

    c. A majority interest is involved.

    d. The cost the corporation would incur in going public.

13. Can the "blockage rule" apply to assets other than stock? Explain.

14. During the same year, a donor gives stock in a closely held corporation to family members and to a qualified charitable organization. In terms of tax planning, what might such a procedure accomplish?

15. Regarding buy-sell agreements, comment on the following.
    a. The difference between the entity and cross-purchase varieties.
    b. The purpose served.

16. What conditions must be satisfied in order for a buy-sell agreement price to control value?

17. Under current law, what are some of the advantages and disadvantages of an estate freeze as to corporations?

18. Are there any pitfalls in using a family limited partnership to carry out an estate freeze? Explain.

19. Can any gift tax paid always be added to the donee's income tax basis in the property received as a gift? Explain.

20. Prior to his death, Orson was negotiating for the sale of a tract of land he owned. The land has a cost basis of $110,000 and had been held as an investment for nine years. A sale price of $450,000 had been agreed to, but the down payment, payout period, and interest to be charged on the installment notes were still undetermined. After Orson's death, his executor consummates the sale. What income tax issues, if any, are involved?

21. Jonathan Rand is distressed with the basis of some land he inherited five years ago and recently sold for a large gain. He feels that the value placed on the property is too low. Consequently, he requests your advice as to whether he is bound by this value.
    a. Write a letter to Jonathan regarding this matter. Jonathan's address is 326 Wisteria Avenue, Charlotte, NC 28223.
    b. Include in the letter a list of further information you will need before you can assess the probability of success in challenging the value used by the estate.

22. In terms of saving future estate taxes, give some examples of assets that should be transferred by gift.

23. Rita and Larry Owen own all of the stock in Crow Company, an S corporation. In order to shift income, they are proposing making gifts of some of the stock to their children: Lisa (age 17), Mike (age 16), Lori (age 15), and Donald (age 13). They request your advice on how to make these gifts effective for tax purposes.
    a. Write a letter to Rita and Larry on this matter. The Owens' address is 408 Commerce Street, Kingston, RI 02881.
    b. Prepare a memo for your firm's files.

24. In considering the income tax ramifications of lifetime gifts, discuss each of the following factors.
    a. The transferred property is an installment note receivable.
    b. The transferred property is a U.S. savings bond.
    c. The transferred property is depreciable with recapture potential under § 1245 or § 1250.

25. Charles Horn wants his daughter Sharon to get stock that he owns in Crimson Corporation. He acquired the stock two years ago at a cost of $800,000, and it currently has a fair market value of $650,000. Charles has made prior taxable gifts and is in poor health. He seeks your advice as to whether he should gift the stock to Sharon or pass it to her under his will. Charles has a large capital loss carryover and has no prospect for any capital gains.
    a. Write a letter to Charles regarding the tax implications of the alternatives he has suggested. His address is 648 Scenic Drive, Chattanooga, TN 37403.
    b. Prepare a memo for your firm's files on this matter.

26. What are the advantages of bypassing the probate estate? How can this be accomplished?

27. Juan sold his business in New Jersey and moved to Florida to retire. He still owns rental property in New Jersey and a vacation cottage in Wisconsin. Comment on Juan's potential probate cost problems.

28. For married persons, the real danger of an estate tax burden materializes upon the death of the surviving spouse. Do you agree? Why or why not?

29. Elena, a naturalized U.S. citizen who immigrated from Spain, has accumulated considerable wealth during her lifetime. She is in poor health and probably will not live for more than a few years. For some time, she has wanted to make a large donation to her church but has feared that she might need the funds to live on. Suggest means by which Elena might carry out her wish with a significant tax saving.

30. Jim's will leaves his valuable antique gun collection to his wife, Doreen. If Doreen does not want the collection, it is to pass to a designated museum (a qualified charity). Doreen abhors firearms. What course of action do you suggest?

31. In connection with § 6166, comment on each of the following.
    a. The more-than-35% test.
    b. The definition of a closely held business.
    c. The family attribution rules.
    d. The business-aggregation rules.

32. The estate of Janet, currently still alive, almost qualifies for an election under § 6166. Janet is not concerned, however, because she plans on giving away her life insurance policy before her death. This, she believes, will allow her estate to meet the requirements of § 6166. Any comment?

PROBLEMS

33. When Polly died, she owned 9,000 shares of Falcon Corporation. The stock is traded in an over-the-counter market. The nearest trades before and after Polly's death are as follows.

	Per Share Mean Selling Price
Six days before Polly's death	$75
Four days after Polly's death	79

Assuming the alternate valuation date is not elected, at what value should the Falcon stock be included in Polly's gross estate?

34. Paul creates a trust with property valued at $800,000. Under the terms of the trust, Anne (age 44) receives a life estate, and Billy (age 15) receives the remainder interest. Determine the value of the gifts. In the month the trust was created, the appropriate interest rate was 7.8%.

35. Ronald transfers $500,000 in trust. Under the terms of the trust instrument, income is payable to Bart (age 16) for 12 years, remainder to Elvira (age 40). Determine the taxable gifts. In the month the trust was created, the appropriate interest rate was 7.4%.

36. Mona (age 65) creates a trust with property worth $800,000. Under the terms of the trust, Mona retains a life estate with the remainder interest passing to Debby (Mona's daughter) upon Mona's death. Mona dies in 1997 when the value of the trust is $1,100,000 and Debby is age 44. Determine the taxable gift, if any, if the trust was created in 1995. In the month the trust was created, the appropriate rate was 8.6%.

37. Assume the same facts as in Problem 36. How much, if any, of the trust is included in Mona's gross estate? Refer to Chapter 17 if necessary.

38. Comment on each of the following statements relating to § 2032A.
    a. Section 2032A applies even if the qualifying property is willed by the decedent to a nonfamily member.
    b. If § 2032A applies, current use value (as opposed to most suitable use value) can be used for the qualifying property, but not to exceed a limit on the adjustment of $1 million.
    c. The special use valuation method cannot be used in setting the valuation of a lifetime gift.
    d. Full recapture of the benefit of the special use valuation method will not occur if the qualifying heir sells the property 10 years after the decedent's death.
    e. Recapture occurs only if the qualifying property is sold.
    f. Lifetime gifts of nonqualifying assets may help in satisfying the 50% and 25% requirements of § 2032A.
    g. In satisfying the 50% and 25% requirements, the qualifying property is valued at most suitable use value.
    h. In the event recapture occurs, the amount of additional value used must be added to the existing income tax basis of the property.

39. At the time of his death, Peter owns 60% of the stock in Drake Corporation, with the remaining 40% held by family members. Over the past five years, Drake has generated average net profits of $200,000. On the date of Peter's death, the book value (corporate net worth) of the corporation's stock is $500,000. An appropriate rate of return for the type of business Drake conducts is 7%.
    a. Presuming that some goodwill exists, what value should be included in Peter's gross estate for the Drake Corporation stock?
    b. What arguments could Peter's executor make in maintaining that the value arrived at under (a) is too high?

40. Noretta owns all of the stock in Gull Corporation, valued as follows: $2 million common stock and $300,000 preferred stock. The preferred is noncumulative, does not have a redemption date, and possesses no liquidation preference. Noretta gives the common stock to her adult children and retains the preferred stock. Comment on Noretta's gift tax consequences.

41. Assume the same facts as in Problem 40. Ten years after the gift, Noretta dies. At this time, the Gull Corporation stock is worth $3 million (common) and $400,000 (preferred). What amount is included in Noretta's gross estate?

42. June gives stock to Emily when the shares have a fair market value of $100,000. June acquired the stock 10 years before the gift at a cost of $20,000. Determine Emily's income tax basis for gain or loss under each of the following assumptions.
    a. The gift occurred in 1960. June paid a gift tax of $5,000 on the transfer.
    b. The gift occurred in 1997. June paid a gift tax of $5,000 on the transfer.

43. In the current year, Ross gives stock to Susan when the shares have a fair market value of $90,000. Ross acquired the stock four years ago at a cost of $100,000. As a result of the transfer, Ross incurred and paid a gift tax of $5,000. Determine Susan's gain or loss if the stock is sold later for:
    a. $75,000.
    b. $95,000.
    c. $105,000.

44. Virginia and Kim Andrews are married and have always lived in a community property state. Kim (age 76) is terminally ill, while Virginia (age 63) is in good health. Among the assets they own as part of their community are the following investments.

	Adjusted Basis	Fair Market Value
Stock in Mallard Corporation	$150,000	$100,000
Stock in Dove Corporation	50,000	100,000

Virginia and Kim need $100,000 to meet current needs and pay Kim's medical expenses.

a. Do you have any suggestions as to which stock Virginia and Kim might sell?

b. Write a letter to them explaining your recommendations. The Andrews' live at 1420 Burro Lane, Reno, NV 89557.

c. Prepare a memo on this matter for your firm's client files.

45. In April 1996, George gives Beverly a house (basis of $50,000 and fair market value of $150,000) to be used as her personal residence. As a result of the transfer, George incurs and pays a gift tax of $9,000. Before her death in March 1997, Beverly installs a swimming pool in the backyard at a cost of $10,000. The residence is worth $170,000 on the date of Beverly's death, and her estate does not elect the alternate valuation date. Determine the income tax basis of the property to the heir, based on the following independent assumptions.

a. Under Beverly's will, the residence passes to George.

b. Under Beverly's will, the residence passes to Junior (Beverly's son).

46. Boyd and Belle are husband and wife and have five married children. Starting in December 1997, they would like to transfer a tract of land (worth $400,000) equally to their children (including spouses) as quickly as possible and without making a taxable gift. What do you suggest?

47. At the time of her death, Hortense has an adjusted gross estate of $3,100,000. Her estate includes the family farm, with a most suitable use value of $1,600,000 and a current use value of $800,000. The farm is inherited by Phil, Hortense's son, who has worked it for her since 1985. Phil plans to continue farming indefinitely.

a. Based on the information given, is the § 2032A election available to Hortense's estate?

b. If so, what value must be used for the farm?

c. Suppose Hortense had made a gift of securities (fair market value of $150,000) to her cousin six months before her death. Does this fact affect your analysis? Explain.

48. Last year, Dean sold real estate (basis of $80,000) to Paul (an unrelated party) for $200,000, receiving $40,000 in cash and Paul's notes for the balance. The notes carry a 10% rate of interest and mature annually at $16,000 each year over a period of 10 years. Dean did not elect out of the installment method for reporting the gain of the sale. Before any of the notes mature and when the notes have a total fair market value of $150,000, Dean gives them to Shelley. Disregarding the interest element, what are Dean's income tax consequences as a result of the gift?

49. At the time of her death in the current year, Julia held the following assets.

	Fair Market Value
Checking account at City National Bank (Julia listed as owner)	$ 40,000
Certificate of deposit at State Savings Association (listed as "Julia and Susan as joint tenants with right of survivorship")	200,000
Insurance policy on Julia's life, issued by White Company (Julia's estate is the designated beneficiary)	100,000
Insurance policy on Julia's life, issued by Brown Company (George is the designated beneficiary)	300,000
Living trust created by Julia four years ago (life estate to Susan, remainder to Susan's children)	800,000
Personal residence (title listed as "Julia and Sam, tenants by the entirety with right of survivorship")	400,000

Presuming Susan, George, and Sam survive Julia, how much is included in Julia's *probate* estate?

50. During their marriage, Brenda and Victor have operated a business together. Each has managed to accumulate approximately $600,000 of income-producing property. Because she is 10 years younger and in better health, Brenda is expected to survive Victor. Upon the death of the survivor, they want their property to pass to their adult children.

     Outline an estate plan for Victor that would accomplish the following objectives.

     • Give Brenda maximum income protection.

     • Avoid a concentration of wealth in Brenda's estate that would cause an estate tax liability on her later death.

     • Avoid estate taxes on Victor's prior death.

     Neither Brenda nor Victor has made any prior taxable gifts. Victor has a niece, Julia, who is a practicing attorney and is familiar with the state's trust laws. Victor has close ties with Julia as he financed her education.

     In this connection, consider Code §§ 2036 and 2041 (discussed in Chapter 17).

51. In the following independent situations, describe the effect of a disclaimer on the estate tax position of the parties.
     a. Jean's will passes $700,000 to Michael (her son) and the remainder of her assets to William (Jean's husband). Michael disclaims $200,000.
     b. Jean's will passes $900,000 to William (Jean's husband) and the $400,000 remainder to Michael (her son). William disclaims $200,000.
     c. Andrea (a widow) provides in her will that $800,000 passes to George (her son, a priest) and the remainder to George's church. George disclaims $200,000.

52. At the time of his death, Clint had an adjusted gross estate of $2,100,000. Included in the estate is a 15 percent capital interest in a partnership valued at $800,000. Except for Clint's daughter Phoebe, none of the other 28 partners are related to him. Phoebe holds a 10 percent capital interest.
     a. Does Clint's estate qualify for the § 6166 election?
     b. Suppose that one year prior to his death, Clint gave $200,000 cash to Phoebe. Does this change your analysis?

53. At the time of his death, Stacey had an adjusted gross estate of $1,200,000. Included in the estate were the following business interests.

	Fair Market Value
Stock in Teal Corporation (a 24% interest in the outstanding shares)	$150,000
A 25% capital interest in the THG Partnership	200,000
A plumbing supply company, operated as a sole proprietorship	230,000

Teal Corporation has 30 shareholders, none of whom are related to Stacey. THG has 17 partners, but 2 of them are Stacey's surviving spouse and son.
     a. Does Stacey's estate qualify for the § 6166 election?
     b. If so, which businesses are affected?

RESEARCH PROBLEMS

Note: West's Federal Taxation on CD-ROM can be used in preparing solutions to the Research Problems. Alternatively, tax research materials contained in a standard tax library can be used.

Research Problem 1. In 1986, Mortimer made a gift of a mineral interest to his son. Mortimer had never made any prior taxable gifts. The property given was valued at $37,000. Due to the operation of the annual exclusion and the unified transfer tax credit, no gift tax was due on the transfer. However, because the gift exceeded the annual exclusion, Mortimer properly filed a Form 709 (Federal Gift Tax Return) in a timely manner.

Mortimer dies in 1997 leaving a taxable estate of $2,100,000. In arriving at the tax base (see Figure 17–2), the executor adds in the 1987 taxable gift at the amount reported on Form 709. Upon audit of the estate's Form 706 (Estate Tax Return), the IRS redetermines the value of the 1987 taxable gift to be $190,000 (not $37,000). This change increases the amount of estate tax due. Mortimer's executor thinks that such an adjustment is precluded by the statute of limitations. What do you think?

Partial list of research aids:
Code §§ 2001(c) and 2504(c).
Evanson v. U.S., 94–2 USTC ¶60,174, 74 AFTR2d 94–5326, 30 F.3d 960 (CA–8, 1994).

Research Problem 2.   At the time of her death, Leona (a widow) owned a considerable amount of farmland. The executor of Leona's estate duly elected to use the special use valuation of § 2032A. The heirs of the estate, Leona's daughter and son-in-law, consented to the election. Through use of § 2032A, the amount of the taxable estate was reduced by approximately $600,000. The IRS accepted the estate tax return (i.e., Form 706) as filed and allowed the use of § 2032A without audit.

Several years after the regular statute of limitations has expired on the Form 706 filed by Leona's estate, the IRS makes a follow-up inquiry as to the use of the farmland. When it discovers that the qualified heirs have cash-leased the property to others, the IRS levies a tax assessment under the recapture provisions of § 2032A(c).

The heirs dispute the assessment because it is barred by the regular statute of limitations [§§ 6501(a) and 6901(c)]. The IRS contends that the special 10-year statute of § 2032A(c)(1) applies. The heirs deny the applicability of § 2032A, in that the qualified use requirements were never met due to the cash-rental arrangements.

In the event the IRS is correct on the statute of limitations issue, the heirs wish to increase the estate's § 2053 deduction for the cost of litigating the § 2032A matter. How should the controversy be resolved and why?

Research Problem 3.   Dana Kerr owns all of the single-class outstanding stock of Crane Corporation. Dana transfers a 20% interest to each of her five adult children. For purposes of § 2512, is each gift to be valued as one of a minority interest? Would it not be appropriate to treat this as a gift of a controlling interest, since the ownership of Crane Corporation remains within the family group? Summarize your position in a letter to Dana. Dana's address is 1402 Milsap Avenue, Kearney, NE 68849.

Research Problem 4.   Al and Melissa are husband and wife, and each has considerable wealth. Under Al's will, all of his property is to pass to Melissa if she survives him. If not, the property is to go to their children. Under Melissa's will, all of her property is to pass to Al if he survives her. If not, the property is to go to their children. Al dies first and Melissa dies four months later. Melissa's executor issues a disclaimer as to the inheritance from Al. The disclaimer is issued within nine months of the date Al's will was admitted to probate but not within nine months of Al's death.
a. Which date controls (i.e., date of probate or date of death)?
b. What difference does it make whether the disclaimer is effective?

Use the tax resources of the internet to address the following questions. Do not restrict your search to the World Wide Web, but include a review of newsgroups and general reference materials, practitioner sites and resources, primary sources of the tax law, chat rooms and discussion groups, and other opportunities.

Research Problem 5.   Find newspaper and magazine reports of a recent occurrence of one of the following, and summarize the potential tax effects that may arise.
a. The development of a new suburban office complex.
b. An auction of valuable art and collectibles.
c. The transfer of business assets subsequent to a divorce.
d. The operation of a professional sports franchise.

Research Problem 6. Locate a professional firm or association that regularly does asset appraisals. Under which codes of behavioral conduct does that entity operate?

Research Problem 7. Write a one-page outline applying the rules of § 2032A to farmland. Post your outline to an appropriate newsgroup.

19

INCOME TAXATION OF TRUSTS AND ESTATES

LEARNING OBJECTIVES

After completing Chapter 19, you should be able to:

1. Use working definitions with respect to trusts, estates, beneficiaries, and other parties.

2. Identify the steps in determining the accounting and taxable income of a trust or estate and the related taxable income of the beneficiaries.

3. Illustrate the uses and implications of distributable net income.

4. Apply the effects of statutory restrictions on the taxation of distributions from accumulation trusts.

5. Use the special rules that apply to trusts where the creator (grantor) of the trust retains certain rights.

An Overview of Subchapter J

Taxpayers create trusts for a variety of reasons. Some trusts are established primarily for tax purposes while others are designed to accomplish a specific financial goal or to provide for the orderly management of assets in case of emergency. Table 19–1 lists some of the more common reasons for creating a trust.

▼ **TABLE 19–1**
Motivations for Creating a Trust

Type of Trust	Financial and Other Goals
Life insurance trust	Holds life insurance policies on the insured, removes the proceeds of the policies from the gross estate (if an irrevocable trust), and safeguards against receipt of the proceeds by a young or inexperienced beneficiary.
"Living" (revocable) trust	Manages assets, reduces probate costs, provides privacy for asset disposition, protects against medical or other emergencies, and provides relief from the necessity of day-to-day management of the underlying assets.
Trust for minors	Provides funds for a college education, shifts income to lower-bracket taxpayers, and transfers accumulated income without permanently parting with the underlying assets.
"Blind" trust	Holds and manages the assets of the grantor without his/her input or influence (e.g., while the grantor holds political office or some other sensitive position).
Retirement trust	Manages asset contributions under a qualified retirement plan.
Alimony trust	Manages the assets of an ex-spouse and assures they will be distributed in a timely fashion to specified beneficiaries.
Liquidation trust	Collects and distributes the last assets of a corporation that is undergoing a complete liquidation.

Because a trust is a separate tax entity, its gross income and deductions must be measured, and an annual tax return must be filed. Similarly, when an individual dies, a legal entity is created in the form of his or her estate. This chapter examines the rules related to the income taxation of trusts and estates.

Figure 19–1 illustrates the structure of a typical trust and estate.

The income taxation of trusts and estates is governed by Subchapter J of the Internal Revenue Code, §§ 641 through 692. Certain similarities are apparent between Subchapter J and the income taxation of individuals (e.g., the definitions of gross income and deductible expenditures), partnerships (e.g., the conduit

▼ **FIGURE 19–1**
Structure of a Typical Trust and Estate

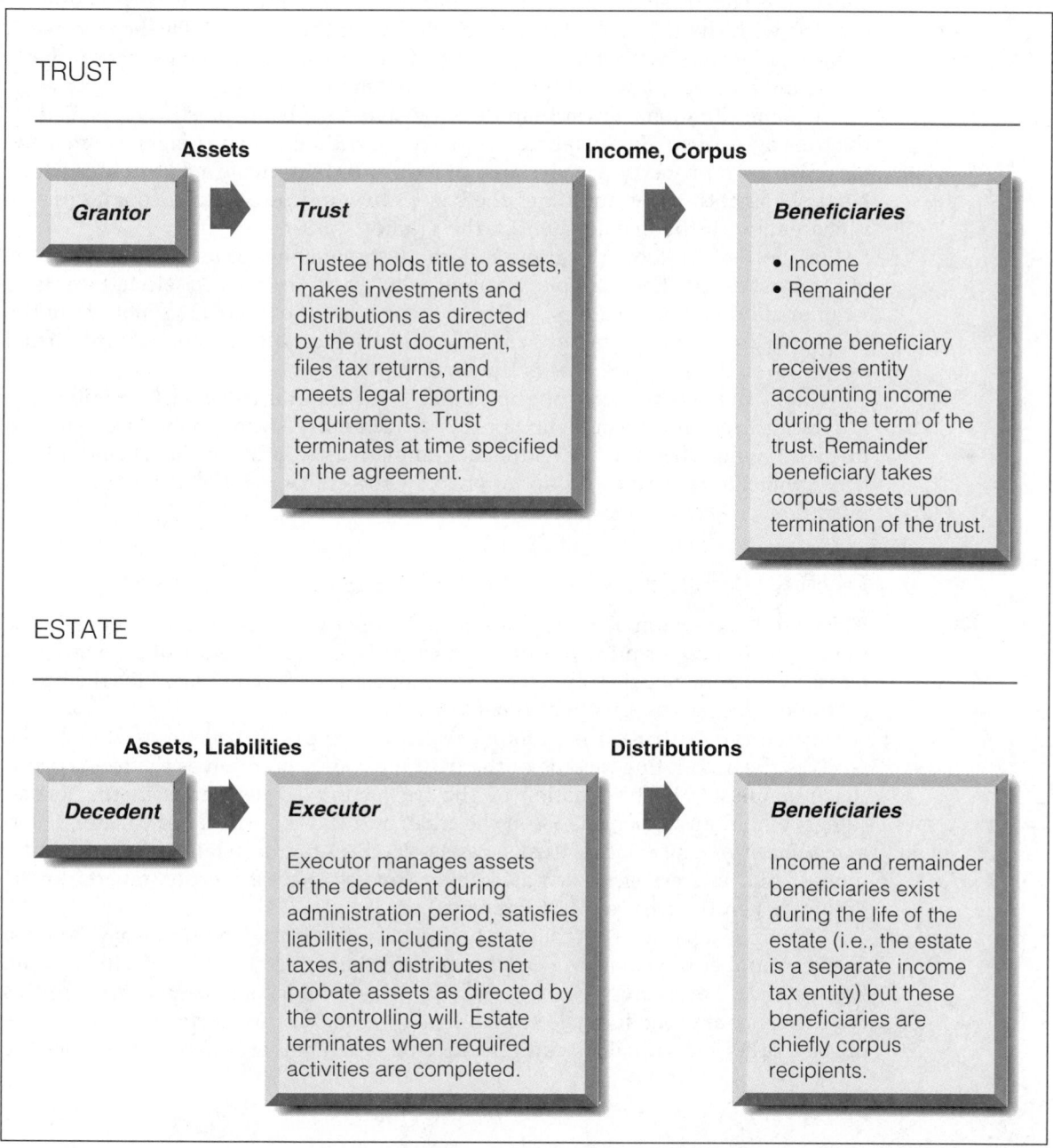

TRUST

Assets → **Income, Corpus** →

Grantor → **Trust**

Trustee holds title to assets, makes investments and distributions as directed by the trust document, files tax returns, and meets legal reporting requirements. Trust terminates at time specified in the agreement.

Beneficiaries

• Income
• Remainder

Income beneficiary receives entity accounting income during the term of the trust. Remainder beneficiary takes corpus assets upon termination of the trust.

ESTATE

Assets, Liabilities → **Distributions** →

Decedent → **Executor**

Executor manages assets of the decedent during administration period, satisfies liabilities, including estate taxes, and distributes net probate assets as directed by the controlling will. Estate terminates when required activities are completed.

Beneficiaries

Income and remainder beneficiaries exist during the life of the estate (i.e., the estate is a separate income tax entity) but these beneficiaries are chiefly corpus recipients.

principle), and S corporations (e.g., the conduit principle and the trust as a separate taxable entity). Trusts also involve several important new concepts, however, including the determination of distributable net income and the tier system of distributions to beneficiaries.

WHAT IS A TRUST?

1 LEARNING OBJECTIVE
Use working definitions with respect to trusts, estates, beneficiaries, and other parties.

The Code does not contain a definition of a trust. However, the term usually refers to an arrangement created by a will or by an *inter vivos* (lifetime) declaration, through which trustees take title to property for the purpose of protecting or conserving it for the beneficiaries.[1]

Typically, the creation of a trust involves at least three parties: (1) The **grantor** (sometimes referred to as the settler or donor) transfers selected assets to the trust entity. (2) The trustee, who may be either an individual or a corporation, is charged with the fiduciary duties associated with the trust. (3) The beneficiary is designated to receive income or property from the trust; the beneficiary's rights are defined by state law and by the trust document.

In some situations, fewer than three persons may be involved, as specified by the trust agreement. For instance, an elderly individual who no longer can manage his or her own property (e.g., because of ill health) may create a trust under which he or she is both the grantor and the beneficiary. In this case, a corporate trustee is charged with the management of the grantor's assets.

In another situation, the grantor might designate him- or herself as the trustee of the trust assets. For example, a parent who wants to transfer selected assets to a minor child could use a trust entity to assure that the minor does not waste the property. By naming him- or herself as the trustee, the parent retains virtual control over the property that is transferred.

Under the general rules of Subchapter J, the **grantor trusts** just described are not recognized for income tax purposes. Similarly, when only one party is involved (when the same individual is grantor, trustee, and sole beneficiary of the trust), Subchapter J rules do not apply, and the entity is ignored for income tax purposes.

OTHER DEFINITIONS

When the grantor transfers title of selected assets to a trust, those assets become the **corpus** (body), or principal, of the trust. Trust corpus, in most situations, earns *income*, which may be distributed to the beneficiaries or accumulated for the future by the trustee, as the trust instrument directs.

In the typical trust, the grantor creates two types of beneficiaries: one who receives the accounting income of the trust and one who receives the trust corpus that remains at the termination of the trust entity. Beneficiaries in the former category hold an *income interest* in the trust, and those in the latter category hold a *remainder interest* in the trust's assets. If the grantor retains the remainder interest, the interest is known as a **reversionary interest** (corpus reverts to the grantor when the trust entity terminates).

The trust document establishes the term of the trust. The term may be for a specific number of years (*term certain*) or until the occurrence of a specified event. For instance, a trust might exist (1) for the life of the income beneficiary—in this case, the income beneficiary is known as a *life tenant* in trust corpus; (2) for the life of some other individual; (3) until the income or remainder beneficiary reaches the

---

[1] Reg. § 301.7701–4(a).

age of majority; or (4) until the beneficiary, or another individual, marries, receives a promotion, or reaches some specified age.

The trustee may be required to distribute the accounting income of the entity according to a distribution schedule specified in the agreement. Sometimes, however, the trustee is given more discretion with respect to the timing and nature of the distributions. If the trustee can determine, within guidelines that may be included in the trust document, either the timing of the income or corpus distributions or the specific beneficiaries who will receive them (from among those identified in the agreement), the trust is called a **sprinkling trust.** Here, the trustee can "sprinkle" the distributions among the various beneficiaries. As discussed in Chapters 17 and 18, family-wide income taxes can be reduced by directing income to those who are subject to lower marginal tax rates. Thus, by giving the trustee a sprinkling power, the income tax liability of the family unit can be manipulated via the trust agreement.

For purposes of certain provisions of Subchapter J, a trust must be classified as either a **simple trust** or a **complex trust.** A simple trust (1) is required to distribute its entire accounting income to designated beneficiaries every year, (2) has no beneficiaries that are qualifying charitable organizations, and (3) makes no distributions of trust corpus during the year. A complex trust is any trust that is not a simple trust.[2] These criteria are applied to the trust every year. Thus, every trust is classified as a complex trust in the year in which it terminates (because it will be distributing all of its corpus during that year).

WHAT IS AN ESTATE?

An estate is created upon the death of every individual. The entity is charged with collecting and conserving all of the individual's assets, satisfying all liabilities, and distributing the remaining assets to the heirs identified by state law or the will.

Typically, the creation of an estate involves at least three parties: the decedent, all of whose probate assets are transferred to the estate for disposition; the executor, who is appointed under the decedent's valid will (or the administrator, if no valid will exists); and the beneficiaries of the estate, who are to receive assets or income from the entity, as the decedent has indicated in the will. The executor or administrator holds the fiduciary responsibility to operate the estate as directed by the will, applicable state law, and the probate court.

Recall that the assets that make up the probate estate are not identical to those that constitute the gross estate for transfer tax purposes (refer to Chapter 18). Many of the gross estate assets are not a part of the probate estate and thus are not subject to disposition by the executor or administrator. For instance, property held by the decedent as a joint tenant passes to the survivor(s) by operation of the applicable state's property law rather than through the probate estate. Proceeds of insurance policies on the life of the decedent, over which the decedent held the incidents of ownership, are not under the control of the executor or administrator. The designated beneficiaries of the policy receive the proceeds outright under the insurance contract.

An estate is a separate taxable entity. Under certain circumstances, taxpayers may find it profitable to prolong an estate's existence. This situation is likely to arise when the heirs are already in a high income tax bracket and would, therefore, prefer to have the income generated by the estate assets taxed at the estate's lower marginal income tax rates. If an estate's existence is unduly prolonged, however,

---

[2] Reg. § 1.651(a)–1.

DOING ESTATE PLANNING ON TELEVISION

The chief technique offered by those who sell books and seminars on "How to Avoid Probate" is the living or revocable trust. Materials supporting these media productions often consist of no more than "fill-in-the-blank" templates that enable an individual to draft and adopt such a trust document, assuming no special rules apply in the state of residence or asset location.

Revocable trusts are especially attractive where the probate process might be especially long or costly because of the nature of the assets held by the decedent (perhaps a family business or important art collection) or a need for privacy (say, where a celebrity is involved).

Yet executing such an arrangement is costly in itself. Titles to assets must all be recast to show the trustee as owner of the property. An attorney should be consulted, at least to determine the extent to which the standard forms being used will be accepted by local probate courts. And when the grantor dies and the document is used to distribute assets, legal fees often are incurred to address challenges from beneficiaries who feel that they have received too little from the dearly departed.

Moreover, in view of the more competitive legal community and statutory "simple probate" procedures in many states, most estate planners believe these sales pitches overstate the cost and difficulty associated with probate today.

the IRS can terminate it for Federal income tax purposes after the expiration of a reasonable period for completing the duties of administration.[3]

NATURE OF TRUST AND ESTATE TAXATION

In general, the taxable income of a trust or estate is taxed to the entity or to its beneficiaries to the extent that each has received the accounting income of the entity. Thus, Subchapter J creates a modified conduit principle relative to the income taxation of trusts, estates, and their beneficiaries. Whoever receives the accounting income of the entity, or some portion of it, is liable for the income tax that results.

EXAMPLE 1

Adam receives 80% of the accounting income of the Zero Trust. The trustee accumulated the other 20% of the income at her discretion under the trust agreement and added it to trust corpus. Adam is liable for income tax only on the amount of the distribution, while Zero is liable for the income tax on the accumulated portion of the income. ▼

FILING REQUIREMENTS

The fiduciary is required to file a Form 1041 (U.S. Fiduciary Income Tax Return) in the following situations.[4]

- For an estate that has gross income of $600 or more for the year.
- For a trust that either has any taxable income or, if there is no taxable income, has gross income of $600 or more.

---

[3] Reg. § 1.641(b)–3(a).   [4] § 6012(a).

The fiduciary return (and any related tax liability) is due no later than the fifteenth day of the fourth month following the close of the entity's taxable year. The return is filed with the Internal Revenue Service Center for the region in which the fiduciary resides or has his or her principal place of business.

TAX ACCOUNTING PERIODS, METHODS, AND PAYMENTS

An estate or trust may use many of the tax accounting methods available to individuals. The method of accounting used by the grantor of a trust or the decedent of an estate need not carry over to the entity.

An estate has the same options for choosing a tax year as any new taxpayer. Thus, the estate of a calendar year decedent dying on March 3 can select any fiscal year or report on a calendar year basis. If the latter is selected, the estate's first taxable year will include the period from March 3 to December 31. If the first or last tax years are short years (less than one calendar year), income for those years need not be annualized.

To eliminate the possibility of deferring the taxation of fiduciary-source income simply by using a fiscal tax year, all trusts (other than tax-exempt trusts) must use a calendar tax year.[5]

Trusts and estates are required to make estimated Federal income tax payments using the same quarterly schedule that applies to individual taxpayers. This requirement applies to estates and grantor trusts only for tax years that end two or more years after the date of the decedent's death. Charitable trusts and private foundations are exempt from estimated payment requirements altogether.[6]

The two-year estimated tax exception for estates recognizes the liquidity problems that an executor often faces during the early months of administering the estate. The exception does not assure, however, that an estate in existence less than 24 months will never be required to make an estimated tax payment.

EXAMPLE 2

Juanita died on March 15, 1996. Her executor elected a fiscal year ending on July 31 for the estate. Estimated tax payments will be required from the estate starting with the tax year that begins on August 1, 1997. ▼

TAX RATES AND PERSONAL EXEMPTION

Congress's desire to stop trusts from being used as income-shifting devices has made the fiduciary entity the highest-taxed taxpayer in the Code. The entity reaches a 39.6 percent marginal rate with only $7,900 of 1996 taxable income, so the grantor's ability to shift income in a tax-effective manner is nearly eliminated. The following table, which lists the 1996 taxes paid by various entities on taxable income of $30,000, shows how expensive the accumulation of income within an estate or trust can be today. Proper income shifting now would move assets *out of* the estate or trust and into the hands of the grantor or beneficiary.

Filing Status/Entity	Taxable Income	1996 Tax Liability
Single	$30,000	$ 5,280
Married, filing jointly	30,000	4,500
C corporation	30,000	4,500
Trust or estate	30,000	10,984

---

[5] § 645.   [6] § 6654(l).

TAX IN THE NEWS

EVERYONE GETS WET WHEN YOU SOAK THE RICH

Fiduciary taxation has fallen prey to the "soak the rich" approach to tax reform of the last five years. In an environment of taxes on millionaires and luxury vehicles, the tax rates that apply to trusts and estates have also increased, and the width of the lower brackets has become so narrow that these entities now are subject to the highest marginal rate structure in U.S. income tax law. Higher tax rates for trusts and estates affect all fiduciary arrangements, however, even those designed for reasons other than tax avoidance.

Perhaps by design, these rate changes have dampened the planning potential of fiduciary entities as a means of shifting income among generations (e.g., from parent to child) or over time (i.e., from the taxpayer's present tax return to a future one). But they have also deepened the tax burden on fixed-income retirees, handicapped individuals, children of divorced parents, and other commonly encountered fiduciary beneficiaries.

Most trust beneficiaries are passive recipients of investment income generated by a stock portfolio managed by a corporate trustee or by the distant managers of the mutual funds in which the funds are invested. In those cases, the beneficiaries exercise little decision-making authority over the yield or timing of the entity's distributions, which are fixed by the controlling instrument. Under such circumstances, tax rate increases seem to punish the powerless as well as to soak the rich.

A fiduciary's net long-term capital gains can be taxed at a nominal rate of no more than 28 percent. In addition to the regular income tax, an estate or trust may be subject to the alternative minimum tax.[7] Trusts may also be subject to a special tax imposed by § 644 on built-in gains from the sale or exchange of certain appreciated property.

Both trusts and estates are allowed a personal exemption in computing the fiduciary tax liability. All estates are allowed a personal exemption of $600. The exemption available to a trust depends upon the type of trust involved. A trust that is required to distribute all of its income currently is allowed an exemption of $300. All other trusts are allowed an exemption of $100 per year.[8]

The classification of trusts as to the appropriate personal exemption is similar but not identical to the distinction between simple and complex trusts. The classification as a simple trust is more stringent.

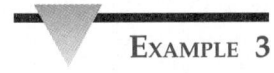

EXAMPLE 3

Three trusts appear to operate in a similar fashion, but they are subject to different Subchapter J classifications and exemptions.

Trust Alpha is required to distribute all of its current accounting income to Susan. Thus, it is allowed a $300 personal exemption. No corpus distributions or charitable contributions are made during the year. Accordingly, Alpha is a simple trust.

Trust Beta is required to distribute all of its current accounting income; it is allowed a $300 personal exemption. The beneficiaries of these distributions are specified in the trust instrument: one-half of accounting income is to be distributed to Tyrone, and one-half is to

---

[7] § 55.   [8] § 642(b).

be distributed to State University, a qualifying charitable organization. Since Beta has made a charitable distribution for the tax year, it is a complex trust.

The trustee of Trust Gamma can, at her discretion, distribute the current-year accounting income or corpus of the trust to Dr. Chapman. As the trustee is not required to distribute current accounting income, only a $100 personal exemption is allowed. During the current year, the trustee distributed all of the accounting income of the entity to Dr. Chapman, but made no corpus or charitable distributions. Nonetheless, because it lacks the current-year income distribution requirement, Gamma is a complex trust. ▼

ALTERNATIVE MINIMUM TAX

The alternative minimum tax (AMT) may apply to a trust or estate in any tax year. Given the nature and magnitude of the tax preferences, adjustments, and exemptions that determine alternative minimum taxable income (AMTI), however, most trusts and estates are unlikely to incur the tax. Nevertheless, they could be vulnerable if they are actively engaged in a business that uses accelerated cost recovery provisions. Similarly, an estate may be liable for the AMT if it receives a sizable portfolio of stock options shortly after the decedent's death under a deferred compensation plan.

In general, derivation of AMTI for the entity follows the rules that apply to individual taxpayers. Thus, the corporate ACE adjustment does not apply to fiduciary entities, but AMTI may be created through the application of most of the other AMT preference and adjustment items discussed in Chapter 6.

The entity has a $22,500 annual exemption, similar to that available to a married individual who files a separate return. The exemption phases out at a rate of one-fourth of the amount by which AMTI exceeds $75,000.

A 26 percent alternative minimum tax rate is applied to AMTI, increasing to 28 percent when AMTI in excess of the exemption reaches $175,000. In addition, estimated tax payments for the entity must include any applicable AMT liability.

TAXABLE INCOME OF TRUSTS AND ESTATES

2   **LEARNING OBJECTIVE**
Identify the steps in determining the accounting and taxable income of a trust or estate and the related taxable income of the beneficiaries.

Generally, the taxable income of an estate or trust is computed similarly to that for an individual. Subchapter J does, however, include several important exceptions and provisions that make it necessary to use a systematic approach to calculating the taxable income of these entities. Figure 19–2 illustrates the procedure implied by the Code, and Figure 19–3 presents a systematic computation method to be followed in this chapter.

ENTITY ACCOUNTING INCOME

The first step in determining the taxable income of a trust or estate is to compute the entity's accounting income for the period. Although this prerequisite is not apparent from a cursory reading of Subchapter J, a closer look at the Code reveals a number of references to the *income* of the entity.[9] Wherever the term *income* is used in Subchapter J without some modifier (e.g., *gross* income or *taxable* income), the statute is referring to the accounting income of the trust or estate for the tax year.

---

[9]For example, see §§ 651(a)(1), 652(a), and 661(a)(1).

▼ **FIGURE 19–2**
Accounting Income,
Distributable Net Income, and
Taxable Income of the Entity
and Its Beneficiaries (5 Steps)

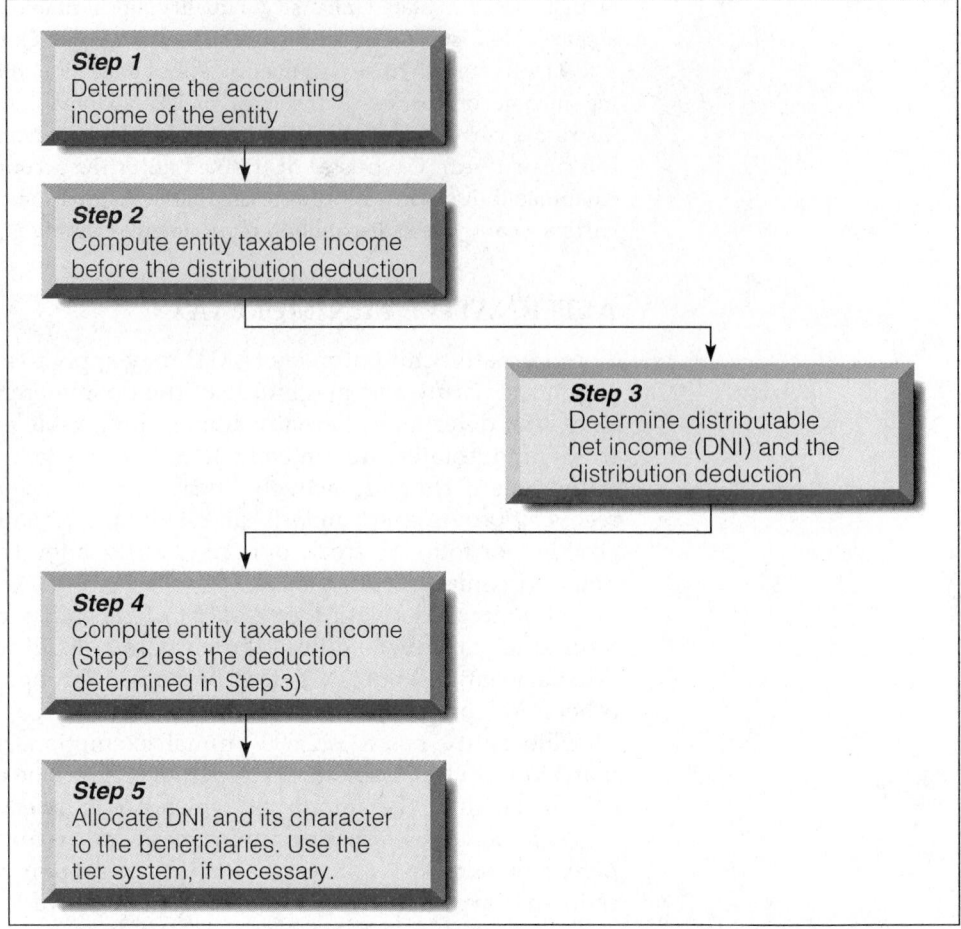

Step 1
Determine the accounting
income of the entity

Step 2
Compute entity taxable income
before the distribution deduction

Step 3
Determine distributable
net income (DNI) and the
distribution deduction

Step 4
Compute entity taxable income
(Step 2 less the deduction
determined in Step 3)

Step 5
Allocate DNI and its character
to the beneficiaries. Use the
tier system, if necessary.

▼ **FIGURE 19–3**
Computational Template
Applying the Five-Step
Procedure

Item	Totals	Accounting Income	Taxable Income	Distributable Net Income/Distribution Deduction
Income	‾‾‾	‾‾‾	‾‾‾	
Income	‾‾‾	‾‾‾	‾‾‾	
Expense	‾‾‾	‾‾‾	‾‾‾	
Expense	‾‾‾	‾‾‾	‾‾‾	
Personal exemption			‾‾‾	
Accounting income/taxable income before the distributions deduction		‾‾‾ *Step 1*	‾‾‾ *Step 2*	
Exemption				‾‾‾
Corpus capital gain/loss				‾‾‾
Net exempt income				‾‾‾
Distributable net income				‾‾‾
Distribution deduction			‾‾‾ *Step 3*	
Entity taxable income			‾‾‾ *Step 4*	

Note: Beneficiary taxable income is addressed in **Step 5.**

▼ **TABLE 19–2**
Common Allocations of Items to
Income or Corpus

Allocable to Income	Allocable to Corpus
• Ordinary and operating net income from trust assets.	• Depreciation on business assets.
• Interest, dividend, rent, and royalty income.	• Casualty gain/loss on income-producing assets.
• Stock dividends.	• Insurance recoveries on income-producing assets.
• One-half of fiduciary fees/commissions.	• Capital gain/loss on investment assets.
	• Stock splits.
	• One-half of fiduciary fees/commissions.

A definition of entity accounting income is critical to understanding the Subchapter J computation of fiduciary taxable income. Under state law, entity accounting income is the amount that the income beneficiary of the simple trust or estate is eligible to receive from the entity. More importantly, the calculation of accounting income is virtually under the control of the grantor or decedent (through a properly drafted trust agreement or will). If the document has been drafted at arm's length, a court will enforce a fiduciary's good faith efforts to carry out the specified computation of accounting income.

Entity accounting income generally is defined by state laws that are derived from the Uniform Principal and Income Act. Most states have adopted some form of the Uniform Act, which essentially constitutes generally accepted accounting principles (GAAP) in the fiduciary tax setting.

By allocating specific items of income and expenditure either to the income beneficiaries or to corpus, the desires of the grantor or decedent are put into effect. Table 19–2 shows typical assignments of revenue and expenditure items to fiduciary income or corpus.

Where the controlling document is silent as to whether an item should be assigned to income or corpus, state law prevails. These allocations are an important determinant of the benefits received from the entity by its beneficiaries and the timing of those benefits.

EXAMPLE 4

The Arnold Trust is a simple trust. Mrs. Bennett is its sole beneficiary. In the current year, the trust earns $20,000 in taxable interest and $15,000 in tax-exempt interest. In addition, the trust recognizes an $8,000 long-term capital gain. The trustee assesses a fee of $11,000 for the year. If the trust agreement allocates fees and capital gains to corpus, trust accounting income is $35,000, and Mrs. Bennett receives that amount. Thus, the income beneficiary receives no immediate benefit from the trust's capital gain, and she bears none of the financial burden of the fiduciary's fees.

Interest income	$35,000
Long-term capital gain	± –0–*
Fiduciary's fees	± –0–*
Trust accounting income	$35,000

*Allocable to corpus. ▼

EXAMPLE 5

Assume the same facts as in Example 4, except that the trust agreement allocates the fiduciary's fees to income. The trust accounting income is $24,000, and Mrs. Bennett receives that amount.

Interest income	$ 35,000
Long-term capital gain	± –0–*
Fiduciary's fees	–11,000
Trust accounting income	$ 24,000

*Allocable to corpus.

EXAMPLE 6

Assume the same facts as in Example 4, except that the trust agreement allocates to income all capital gains and losses and one-half of the trustee's commissions. The trust accounting income is $37,500, and Mrs. Bennett receives that amount.

Interest income	$35,000
Long-term capital gain	+8,000
Fiduciary's fees	–5,500*
Trust accounting income	$37,500

*One-half allocable to corpus.

GROSS INCOME

The gross income of an estate or trust is similar to that of an individual. In determining the gain or loss to be recognized by an estate or trust upon the sale or other taxable disposition of assets, the rules for basis determination are similar to those applicable to other taxpayers. Thus, an estate's basis for property received from a decedent is stepped up or stepped down to gross estate value (refer to Chapter 18 for a more detailed discussion). Property received as a gift (the usual case in trust arrangements) usually takes the donor's basis. Property purchased by the trust from a third party is assigned a basis equal to the purchase price.

Property Distributions. In general, the entity does not recognize gain or loss upon its distribution of property to a beneficiary under the provisions of the will or trust document. The distributed property has the same basis to the beneficiary of the distribution as it did to the estate or trust. Moreover, the distribution absorbs distributable net income (DNI) and qualifies for a distribution deduction (both of which are explained later in this chapter) to the extent of the lesser of the distributed asset's basis to the beneficiary or the asset's fair market value as of the distribution date.[10]

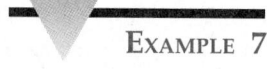

EXAMPLE 7

The Howard Trust distributes a painting, basis of $40,000 and fair market value of $90,000, to beneficiary Kate. Kate's basis in the painting is $40,000. The distribution absorbs $40,000 of Howard's DNI, and Howard claims a $40,000 distribution deduction relative to the transaction. ▼

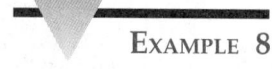

EXAMPLE 8

Assume the same facts as in Example 7, except that Howard's basis in the painting is $100,000. Kate's basis in the painting is $100,000. The distribution absorbs $90,000 of Howard's DNI, and Howard claims a $90,000 distribution deduction. ▼

A trustee or executor can elect to recognize gain or loss with respect to all of its in-kind property distributions for the year. If the election is made, the beneficiary's basis in the asset is equal to the asset's fair market value as of the distribution date. The distribution absorbs DNI and qualifies for a distribution deduction to

---

[10] § 643(e).

the extent of the asset's fair market value. However, § 267 can restrict a trust's deduction for such losses.

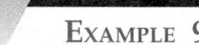

EXAMPLE 9

The Green Estate distributes an antique piano, basis to Green of $10,000 and fair market value of $15,000, to beneficiary Kyle. The executor elects that Green recognize the related $5,000 gain on the distribution. Accordingly, Kyle's basis in the piano is $15,000 ($10,000 basis to Green + $5,000 gain recognized). Without the election, Green would not recognize any gain, and Kyle's basis in the piano would be $10,000. ▼

EXAMPLE 10

Assume the same facts as in Example 9, except that Green's basis in the piano is $18,000. The executor elects that Green recognize the related $3,000 loss on the distribution. Accordingly, Kyle's basis in the piano is $15,000 ($18,000 − $3,000). Without the election, Green would not recognize any loss, and Kyle's basis in the piano would be $18,000. ▼

Income in Respect of a Decedent.   The gross income of a trust or estate includes **income in respect of a decedent (IRD)** that the entity received.[11] For a cash basis decedent, IRD includes accrued salary, interest, rent, and other income items that were not constructively received before death. For both cash and accrual basis decedents, IRD includes, for instance, death benefits from qualified retirement plans and deferred compensation contracts.

The tax consequences of IRD are as follows.

- The fair market value of the right to IRD on the appropriate valuation date is included in the decedent's gross estate.[12] Thus, it is subject to the Federal estate tax.[13]
- The decedent's basis in the property carries over to the recipient (the estate or heirs). There is no step-up or step-down in the basis of IRD items.
- The recipient of the income recognizes gain or loss, measured by the difference between the amount realized and the adjusted basis of the IRD in the hands of the decedent. The character of the gain or loss depends upon the treatment that it would have received had it been realized by the decedent before death. Thus, if the decedent would have realized capital gain, the recipient must do likewise.
- Expenses related to the IRD (such as interest, taxes, and depletion) that properly were not reported on the final income tax return of the decedent may be claimed by the recipient. These items are known as **expenses in respect of a decedent.** Typically, such expenses also include fiduciary fees, commissions paid to dispose of estate assets, and state gift taxes payable. They are deductible for both Federal estate and income tax purposes, for or from adjusted gross income (AGI) as would have been the case for the decedent.
- If the IRD item would have created an AMT preference or adjustment for the decedent (e.g., with respect to the collection of certain tax-exempt interest by the entity), an identical AMT item is created for the recipient.

EXAMPLE 11

Amanda died on July 13 of the current year. On August 2, the estate received a check (before deductions) for $1,200 from Amanda's former employer; this was Amanda's compensation for the last pay period of her life. On November 23, the estate received a $45,000 distribution from the qualified profit sharing plan of Amanda's employer, the full

---

[11] § 691 and the Regulations thereunder. The concept of IRD was introduced in Chapter 18.

[12] § 2033.

[13] To mitigate the effect of double taxation (imposition of both the estate tax and the income tax), § 691(c) allows the recipient an income tax deduction for the incremental estate tax attributable to the net IRD. For individual recipients, this is an itemized deduction, not subject to the 2%-of-AGI floor.

amount to which Amanda was entitled under the plan. Both Amanda and the estate are calendar year, cash basis taxpayers.

The last salary payment and the profit sharing plan distribution constitute IRD to the estate. Amanda had earned these items during her lifetime, and the estate had an enforceable right to receive each of them after Amanda's death. Consequently, the gross estate includes $46,200 with respect to these two items. However, the income tax basis to the estate for these items is not stepped up (from zero to $1,200 and $45,000, respectively) upon distribution to the estate.

The estate must report gross income of $46,200 for the current tax year with respect to the IRD items. The gain recognized upon the receipt of the IRD is $46,200 [$1,200 + $45,000 (amounts realized) – $0 (adjusted bases)]. ▼

Including the IRD in both the taxpayer's gross estate and the gross income of the estate may seem harsh. Nevertheless, the tax consequences of IRD are similar to the treatment that applies to all of a taxpayer's earned income. The item is subject to income tax upon receipt, and to the extent that it is not consumed by the taxpayer before death, it is included in the gross estate.

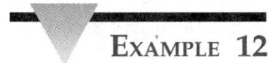

EXAMPLE 12

Assume the same facts as in Example 11, except that Amanda is an accrual basis taxpayer. IRD now includes only the $45,000 distribution from the qualified retirement plan. Amanda's last paycheck is included in the gross income of her own last return (January 1 through date of death). The $1,200 salary is already properly recognized under Amanda's usual method of tax accounting. It does not constitute IRD and is not gross income when received by the executor. ▼

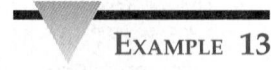

EXAMPLE 13

Assume the same facts as in Example 11. Amanda's last paycheck was reduced by $165 for state income taxes that were withheld by the employer. The $165 tax payment is an expense in respect of a decedent and is allowed as a deduction on *both* Amanda's estate tax return *and* the estate's income tax return. ▼

ORDINARY DEDUCTIONS

As a general rule, the taxable income of an estate or trust is similar to that of an individual. Deductions are allowed for ordinary and necessary expenses paid or incurred in carrying on a trade or business; for the production or collection of income; for the management, conservation, or maintenance of property; and in connection with the determination, collection, or refund of any tax.[14] Reasonable administration expenses, including fiduciary fees and litigation costs in connection with the duties of administration, also are deductible.

The trust or estate must apply the 2 percent-of-AGI floor to many of the § 212 expenses that it incurs. For this purpose, AGI appears to be the greater of (1) the pertinent-year AGI of the grantor of the trust or (2) the AGI of the trust or estate, computed as though the entity were an individual. The floor does not apply, however, to items like fiduciary fees or the personal exemption (i.e., items that would not be incurred by an individual).[15]

Expenses attributable to the production or collection of tax-exempt income are not deductible.[16] The amount of the disallowed deduction is found by using a formula based upon the composition of the income elements of entity accounting

---

[14] §§ 162 and 212.

[15] §§ 67(b) and (e). *O'Neill Trust v. Comm.*, 93–1 USTC ¶50,332, 71 AFTR2d 93–2052, 994 F.2d 302 (CA–6, 1993), *rev'g* 98 T.C. 227 (1992).

[16] § 265.

income for the year of the deduction. The § 212 deduction is apportioned without regard to the accounting income allocation of such expenses to income or to corpus. The deductibility of the fees is determined strictly by the Code (under §§ 212 and 265), and the allocation of expenditures to income and to corpus is controlled by the trust agreement or will or by state law.

▼

EXAMPLE 14

The Silver Trust operates a business and invests idle cash in marketable securities. Its sales proceeds for the current year are $180,000. Expenses for wages, cost of sales, and office administration are $80,000. Interest income recognized is $20,000 from taxable bonds and $50,000 from tax-exempt bonds. The trustee claims a $35,000 fee for its activities. According to the trust agreement, $30,000 of this amount is allocated to the income beneficiaries and $5,000 is allocated to corpus.

Sales income	$180,000
Cost of sales	−80,000
Interest income ($50,000 is exempt)	+70,000
Fiduciary's fees, as allocated	−30,000
Trust accounting income	$140,000

The sales proceeds are included in the gross income of the trust under § 61. The costs associated with the business are deductible in full under § 162. The taxable income is included in Silver's gross income under § 61, but the tax-exempt income is excluded under § 103. The fiduciary's fees are deductible by Silver under § 212, but a portion of the deduction is lost because § 265 prohibits deductions for expenses incurred in the generation of tax-exempt income.

Specifically, 50/250 of the fees of $35,000 can be traced to tax-exempt income, and $7,000 of the fees is nondeductible. For purposes of the computation, only the income elements of the year's trust accounting income are included in the denominator. Moreover, the allocation of portions of the fees to income and to corpus is irrelevant in the calculation. The disallowed deduction for fiduciary's fees is computed in a certain manner.

$$\$35,000^{*} \text{ (total fees paid)} \times \frac{\$50,000^{**} \ (\textit{exempt} \text{ income elements of trust accounting income})}{\$250,000^{**} \ (\textit{all} \text{ income elements of trust accounting income})}$$

$$= \$7,000 \text{ (amount disallowed)}$$

*All of the fees, and not just those that are allocated to income, are deductible by the trust under § 212.

**The numerator and denominator of this fraction are *not* reduced by expense items allocable to income (e.g., cost of sales).   ▼

Under § 642(g), amounts deductible as administration expenses or losses for death tax purposes (under §§ 2053 and 2054) cannot be claimed by the estate for income tax purposes, unless the estate files a waiver of the death tax deduction. Although these expenses cannot be deducted twice, they may be allocated as the fiduciary sees fit between Forms 706 and 1041; they need not be claimed in their entirety on either return.[17] As discussed earlier, the prohibition against double deductions does not extend to expenses in respect of a decedent.

Trusts and estates are allowed cost recovery deductions. However, such deductions are assigned proportionately among the recipients of the entity accounting income.[18]

---

[17] Reg. § 1.642(g)–2.   [18] §§ 167(h) and 611(b)(3) and (4).

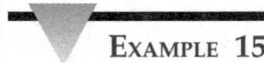

EXAMPLE 15

Lisa and Martin are the equal income beneficiaries of the Needle Trust. Under the terms of the trust agreement, the trustee has complete discretion as to the timing of the distributions from Needle's current accounting income. The trust agreement allocates all depreciation expense to income. In the current year, the trustee distributes 40% of the current trust accounting income to Lisa and 40% to Martin; thus, 20% of the income is accumulated. The depreciation deduction allowable to Needle is $100,000. This deduction is allocated among the trust and its beneficiaries on the basis of the distribution of current accounting income: Lisa and Martin can each claim a $40,000 deduction, and the trust can deduct $20,000. ▼

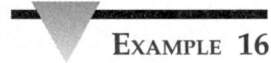

EXAMPLE 16

Assume the same facts as in Example 15, except that the trust agreement allocates all depreciation expense to corpus. Lisa and Martin both still claim a $40,000 depreciation deduction, and Needle retains its $20,000 deduction. The Code assigns the depreciation deduction proportionately to the recipients of entity accounting income. Allocation of depreciation to income or to corpus is irrelevant in determining which party can properly claim the deduction. ▼

When a trust sells property received by transfer from the grantor, the amount of depreciation subject to recapture includes the depreciation claimed by the grantor before the transfer of the property to the trust. However, depreciation recapture potential disappears at death.

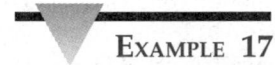

EXAMPLE 17

Jaime transferred an asset to the Shoulder Trust via a lifetime gift. The asset's total depreciation recapture potential was $40,000. If Shoulder sells the asset at a gain, ordinary income not to exceed $40,000 is recognized by the trust. Had Jaime transferred the asset after his death to his estate through a bequest, the $40,000 recapture potential would have disappeared. ▼

DEDUCTIONS FOR LOSSES

An estate or trust is allowed a deduction for casualty or theft losses that are not covered by insurance or other arrangement. Such losses may also be deductible by an estate for Federal death tax purposes under § 2054. As a result, an estate is not allowed an income tax deduction unless the death tax deduction is waived.[19]

The net operating loss (NOL) deduction is available for estates and trusts (i.e., where trade or business income is generated). The carryback of an NOL may reduce the distributable net income of the trust or estate for the carryback year and therefore affect the amount taxed to the beneficiaries for that year.

Certain losses realized by an estate or trust also may be disallowed, as they are for all taxpayers. Thus, the wash sales provisions of § 1091 disallow losses on the sale or other disposition of stock or securities when substantially identical stock or securities are acquired by the estate or trust within the prescribed 30-day period. Likewise, § 267 disallows certain losses, expenses, and interest with respect to transactions between related taxpayers (including certain parties involved in a trust arrangement).

Except for the possibility of unused losses in the year of termination, the net capital losses of an estate or trust are used only on the fiduciary income tax return.[20] The tax treatment of these losses is the same as for individual taxpayers.

---

[19] See Reg. § 1.642(g)–1 for the required statement waiving the estate tax deduction. In addition, see Reg. §§ 1.165–7(c) and 1.165–8(b), requiring that a statement be filed to allow an income tax deduction for such losses.

[20] § 642(h).

CHARITABLE CONTRIBUTIONS

An estate or complex trust is allowed a deduction for contributions to charitable organizations under certain conditions.

- The contribution is made pursuant to the will or trust instrument, and its amount is determinable using the language of that document.
- The recipient is a qualified organization. For this purpose, qualified organizations include the same charities for which individual and corporate donors are allowed deductions, except that estates and trusts are permitted a deduction for contributions to certain foreign charitable organizations.
- Generally, the contribution is claimed in the tax year it is paid, but a fiduciary can treat amounts paid in the year immediately following as a deduction for the preceding year.[21] Under this rule, estates and complex trusts receive more liberal treatment than individuals or corporations.

Unlike the charitable contribution deductions of individuals and corporations, the deductions of estates and complex trusts are not limited (e.g., to a percentage of taxable or adjusted gross income). Nonetheless, an entity's charitable contribution may not be fully deductible.[22] Specifically, the deduction is limited to amounts included in the gross income of the entity in the year of the contribution. A contribution is deemed to have been made proportionately from each of the income elements of entity accounting income. Thus, if the entity has tax-exempt income, the contribution is deductible only to the extent that the income elements of entity accounting income for the year of the deduction are included in the entity's gross income.

This rule is similar to that used to limit the § 212 deduction for fiduciary fees and other expenses incurred to generate tax-exempt income. However, if the will or trust agreement requires that the contribution be made from a specific type of income or from the current income from a specified asset, the allocation of the contribution to taxable and tax-exempt income will not be required.

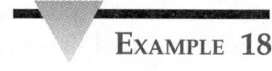

EXAMPLE 18

The Capper Trust has 1996 gross rent income of $80,000, expenses attributable to the rents of $60,000, and tax-exempt interest from state bonds of $20,000. Under the trust agreement, the trustee is to pay 30% of the annual trust accounting income to the United Way, a qualifying organization. Accordingly, the trustee pays $12,000 to the charity in 1997 (i.e., 30% × $40,000). The charitable contribution deduction allowed for 1996 is $9,600 [($80,000/$100,000) × $12,000]. ▼

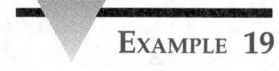

EXAMPLE 19

Assume the same facts as in Example 18, except that the trust instrument also requires that the contribution be paid from the net rent income. The agreement controls, and the allocation formula need not be applied. The entire $12,000 is allowed as a charitable deduction. ▼

DEDUCTION FOR DISTRIBUTIONS TO BENEFICIARIES

The modified conduit approach of Subchapter J is embodied in the deduction allowed to trusts and estates for the distributions made to beneficiaries during the year. Some portion of any distribution that a beneficiary receives from a trust may be subject to income tax on the beneficiary's own return. At the same time, the distributing entity is allowed a deduction for some or all of the distribution.

---

[21] § 642(c)(1) and Reg. § 1.642(c)–1(b).

[22] Reg. §§ 1.642(c)–3(b) and (c).

Consequently, the modified conduit principle of Subchapter J is implemented. A good analogy is to the taxability of corporate profits distributed to employees as taxable wages. The corporation is allowed a deduction for the payment, but the employee receives gross income in the form of compensation.

3 LEARNING OBJECTIVE
Illustrate the uses and implications of distributable net income.

A critical value that is used in computing the amount of the entity's distribution deduction is **distributable net income (DNI).** As it is defined in Subchapter J, DNI serves several functions.

- DNI is the maximum amount of the distribution on which the beneficiaries can be taxed.[23]
- DNI is the maximum amount that the entity can use as a distribution deduction for the year.[24]
- The makeup of DNI carries over to the beneficiaries (the items of income and expenses retain their DNI character in the hands of the distributees).[25]

Subchapter J defines DNI in a circular manner, however. The DNI value is necessary to determine the entity's distribution deduction and therefore its taxable income for the year. Nonetheless, the Code defines DNI as a modification of the entity's taxable income itself. Using the systematic approach to determining the taxable income of the entity and its beneficiaries, as shown earlier in Figure 19–2, first compute *taxable income before the distribution deduction,* modify that amount to determine DNI and the distribution deduction, return to the calculation of *taxable income,* and apply the deduction that has resulted.

Taxable income before the distribution deduction includes all of the entity's items of gross income, deductions, gains, losses, and exemptions for the year. Therefore, to compute this amount, (1) determine the appropriate personal exemption for the year and (2) account for all of the other gross income and deductions of the entity.

The next step in Figure 19–2 is the determination of *distributable net income,* computed by making the following adjustments to the entity's *taxable income before the distribution deduction.*[26]

- Add back the personal exemption.
- Add back *net* tax-exempt interest. To arrive at this amount, reduce the total tax-exempt interest by charitable contributions and by related expenses not deductible under § 265.
- Add back the entity's *net* capital losses.
- Subtract any net capital gains allocable to corpus. In other words, the only net capital gains included in DNI are those attributable to income beneficiaries or to charitable contributions.

Since taxable income before the distribution deduction is computed by deducting all of the expenses of the entity (whether they were allocated to income or to corpus), DNI is reduced by expenses that are allocated to corpus. The effect is to reduce the taxable income of the income beneficiaries. The actual distributions to the beneficiaries exceed DNI because the distributions are not reduced by expenses allocated to corpus. Aside from this shortcoming of Subchapter J, DNI offers a good approximation of the current-year economic income available for distribution to the entity's income beneficiaries.

DNI includes the net tax-exempt interest income of the entity, so that amount must be removed from DNI in computing the distribution deduction. Moreover,

---

[23] §§ 652(a) and 662(a).
[24] §§ 651(b) and 661(c).

[25] §§ 652(b) and 662(b).
[26] These and other (less common) adjustments are detailed in § 643.

for estates and complex trusts, the amount actually distributed during the year may include discretionary distributions of income and distributions of corpus permissible under the will or trust instrument. Thus, the distribution deduction for estates and complex trusts is computed as the lesser of (1) the deductible portion of DNI or (2) the taxable amount actually distributed to the beneficiaries during the year. For a simple trust, however, full distribution is always assumed, relative to both the entity and its beneficiaries, in a manner similar to the partnership and S corporation conduit entities.

EXAMPLE 20
The Zinc Trust is a simple trust. Because of severe liquidity problems, its 1996 accounting income is not distributed to its sole beneficiary, Mark, until early in 1997. Zinc still is allowed a full distribution deduction for, and Mark still is taxable upon, the entity's 1996 income in 1996. ▼

EXAMPLE 21
The Pork Trust is required to distribute its current accounting income annually to its sole income beneficiary, Barbara. Capital gains and losses and all other expenses are allocable to corpus. In the current year, Pork incurs the following items.

Dividend income	$25,000
Taxable interest income	15,000
Tax-exempt interest income	20,000
Net long-term capital gains	10,000
Fiduciary's fees	6,000

Item	Totals	Accounting Income	Taxable Income	Distributable Net Income/ Distribution Deduction
Dividend income	$25,000	$25,000	$ 25,000	
Taxable interest income	15,000	15,000	15,000	
Exempt interest income	20,000	20,000		
Net long-term capital gain	10,000		10,000	
Fiduciary fees	6,000		(4,000)	
Personal exemption			(300)	
Accounting income/taxable income before the distributions deduction		$60,000	$45,700	$ 45,700
		Step 1	*Step 2*	

Exemption	300
Corpus capital gain/loss	(10,000)
Net exempt income	18,000
Distributable net income	$ 54,000

Distribution deduction	*Step 3*	(36,000)
Entity taxable income	*Step 4*	($ 9,700)

Step 1. Trust accounting income is $60,000; this includes the tax-exempt interest income, but not the fees or the capital gains, pursuant to the trust document. Barbara receives $60,000 from the trust for the current year.

Step 2. Taxable income before the distribution deduction is computed as directed by the Code. The tax-exempt interest is excluded under § 103. Only a portion of the fees is deductible because some of the fees are traceable to the tax-exempt income. The trust claims a $300 personal exemption as it is required to distribute its annual trust accounting income.

Step 3. DNI and the distribution deduction reflect the required adjustments. The distribution deduction is the lesser of the distributed amount ($60,000) or the deductible portion of DNI ($54,000 – $18,000 net exempt income).

Step 4. Finally, return to the computation of the taxable income of the Pork Trust. A simple test should be applied at this point to assure that the proper figure for the trust's taxable income has been determined. On what is Pork to be taxed? Pork has distributed to Barbara all of its gross income except the $10,000 net long-term capital gains. The $300 personal exemption reduces taxable income to $9,700. ▼

EXAMPLE 22

The Quick Trust is required to distribute all of its current accounting income equally to its two beneficiaries, Faith and the Universal Church, a qualifying charitable organization. Capital gains and losses and depreciation expenses are allocable to income. Fiduciary fees are allocable to corpus. In the current year, Quick incurs various items as indicated.

Item	Totals	Accounting Income	Taxable Income	Distributable Net Income/ Distribution Deduction
Rent income	$100,000	$100,000	$100,000	
Expenses—rent income	30,000	(30,000)	(30,000)	
Depreciation—rent income	15,000	(15,000)		
Net long-term capital gain	20,000	20,000	20,000	
Charitable contribution			(37,500)	
Fiduciary fees	18,000		(18,000)	
Personal exemption		——	(300)	
Accounting income/taxable income before the distributions deduction		$ 75,000	$34,200	$34,200
		Step 1	**Step 2**	
Exemption				300
Corpus capital gain/loss				
Net exempt income				
Distributable net income				$34,500
Distribution deduction			**Step 3** (34,500)	
Entity taxable income			**Step 4** ($ 300)	

TAX IN THE NEWS

IS IT A CHARITY OR A BENEFICIARY?

The general prohibition against "double deductions" is unclear when the beneficiary of a distribution from the fiduciary is a charity. Does the entity claim a charitable deduction or a distribution deduction for the payment?

Neither the Code nor the Regulations under Subchapter J address this question. Most practitioners apply a "volume" test, as was done in Example 22, using the charitable deduction for small payments from the estate's gross income and the distribution deduction for larger (especially recurring) contributions.

In *U.S. Trust Co. v. Comm.*, 86–2 USTC ¶9777, 58 AFTR2d 86–6152, 803 F.2d 1363 (CA–5, 1986), though, the taxpayer boldly claimed two deductions for a $2.5 million payment by the decedent to a qualifying charity, one as a charitable deduction on the estate tax return and the other as a distribution deduction on the estate's income tax return. The trustee explained that the distribution deduction was used because the will did not specify that the payment be made from the gross income of the estate.

The taxpayer's approach is not strictly prohibited by the Code. In fact, the Federal Appeals Court noted that multiple tax benefits accrue when an estate makes a payment to charity. The double deduction would have survived had the will specified the amount and source of the charitable gift as some type of gross income recognized by the estate.

But that was not the case here, and the distribution deduction was denied. In essence, the Appeals Court viewed the gift as a bequest specified by the will, not a distribution of postdeath income. Bequests are not deductible for income tax purposes, and neither was this payment.

Step 1. Trust accounting income of $75,000 reflects the indicated allocations of items to income and to corpus. Each income beneficiary receives $37,500.

Step 2. In the absence of tax-exempt income, a deduction is allowed for the full amount of the fiduciary's fees. Quick is a complex trust, but since it is required to distribute its full accounting income annually, a $300 exemption is allowed. The trust properly does not deduct any depreciation for the rental property. The depreciation deduction is available only to the recipients of the entity's accounting income for the period. Thus, the deduction is split equally between Faith and the church. The deduction probably is of no direct value to the church, as the church is not subject to the income tax. The trust's charitable contribution deduction is based upon the $37,500 that the charity actually received (one-half of trust accounting income).

Step 3. As there is no tax-exempt income, the only adjustment needed to compute DNI is to add back the trust's personal exemption. Subchapter J requires no adjustment for the charitable contribution. DNI is computed only from the perspective of Faith, who also received $37,500 from the trust.

Step 4. Perform the simple test (referred to above) to assure that the proper taxable income for the Quick Trust has been computed. All of the trust's gross income has been distributed to Faith and the charity. As is the case with most trusts that distribute all of their annual income, the Quick Trust "wastes" the personal exemption. ▼

In a year in which the AMT applies to the estate or trust, an AMT distribution deduction is also applied against alternative minimum taxable income in deriving the amount that is subject to the § 55 tax.

TAX CREDITS

An estate or trust may claim the foreign tax credit to the extent that it is not passed through to the beneficiaries.[27] Similarly, other credits are apportioned between the estate or trust and the beneficiaries on the basis of the entity accounting income allocable to each.

TAXATION OF BENEFICIARIES

The beneficiaries of an estate or trust receive taxable income from the entity under the modified conduit principle of Subchapter J. Distributable net income determines the maximum amount that can be taxed to the beneficiaries for any tax year. The constitution of DNI also carries over to the beneficiaries (e.g., net long-term capital gains retain their character when they are distributed from the entity to the beneficiary).

The timing of any tax consequences to the beneficiary of a trust or estate presents a problem only when the parties involved use different tax years. A beneficiary includes in gross income an amount based upon the DNI of the trust for any taxable year or years of the entity ending with or within his or her taxable year.[28]

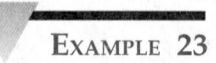

EXAMPLE 23

An estate uses a fiscal year ending on March 31 for tax purposes. Its sole income beneficiary is a calendar year taxpayer. For calendar year 1997, the beneficiary reports the income assignable to her for the entity's fiscal year April 1, 1996, to March 31, 1997. If the estate is terminated by December 31, 1997, the beneficiary also includes any trust income assignable to her for the short year. This could result in a bunching of income in 1997. ▼

DISTRIBUTIONS BY SIMPLE TRUSTS

The amount taxable to the beneficiaries of a simple trust is limited by the trust's DNI. However, since DNI includes net tax-exempt income, the amount included in the gross income of the beneficiaries could be less than DNI. When there is more than one income beneficiary, the elements of DNI are apportioned ratably according to the amount required to be distributed currently to each.

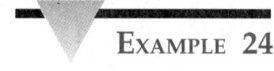

EXAMPLE 24

A simple trust has ordinary income of $40,000, a long-term capital gain of $15,000 (allocable to corpus), and a trustee commission expense of $4,000 (payable from corpus). The two income beneficiaries, Allie and Bart, are entitled to the trust's annual accounting income, based on shares of 75% and 25%, respectively. Although Allie receives $30,000 as her share (75% × trust accounting income of $40,000), she is allocated DNI of only $27,000 (75% × $36,000). Likewise, Bart is entitled to receive $10,000 (25% × $40,000), but he is allocated DNI of only $9,000 (25% × $36,000). The $15,000 capital gain is taxed to the trust. ▼

---

[27] §§ 642(a)(1) and 901.

[28] §§ 652(c) and 662(c).

DISTRIBUTIONS BY ESTATES AND COMPLEX TRUSTS

A problem arises with estates and complex trusts when more than one beneficiary receives a distribution from the entity and the controlling document does not require a distribution of the entire accounting income of the entity.

▼

EXAMPLE 25

The trustee of the Wilson Trust has the discretion to distribute the income or corpus of the trust in any proportion between the two beneficiaries of the trust, Wong and Washington. Under the trust instrument, Wong must receive $15,000 from the trust every year. In the current year, the trust's accounting income is $50,000, and its DNI is $40,000. The trustee pays $15,000 to Wong and $25,000 to Washington. ▼

How is Wilson's DNI to be divided between Wong and Washington? Several arbitrary methods of allocating DNI between the beneficiaries could be devised. Subchapter J resolves the problem by creating a two-tier system to govern the taxation of beneficiaries in such situations.[29] The tier system determines which distributions will be included in the gross income of the beneficiaries in full, which will be included in part, and which will not be included at all.

Income that is required to be distributed currently, whether or not it is distributed, is categorized as a *first-tier distribution*. All other amounts properly paid, credited, or required to be distributed are *second-tier distributions*.[30] A formula is used to allocate DNI among the appropriate beneficiaries when only first-tier distributions are made and those amounts exceed DNI.

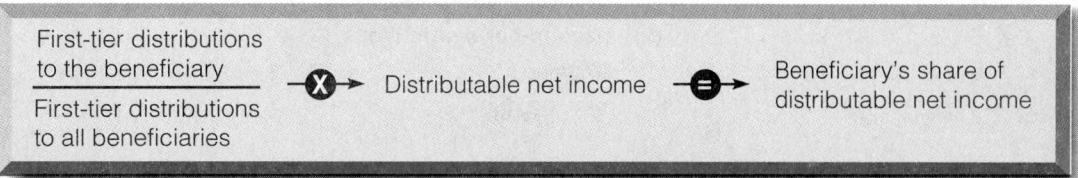

When both first-tier and second-tier distributions are made and the first-tier distributions exceed DNI, the above formula is applied to the first-tier distributions. In this case, none of the second-tier distributions are taxed, because all of the DNI has been allocated to the first-tier beneficiaries.

If both first-tier and second-tier distributions are made and the first-tier distributions do not exceed DNI, but the total of both first-tier and second-tier distributions does exceed DNI, the second-tier beneficiaries recognize income as shown below.

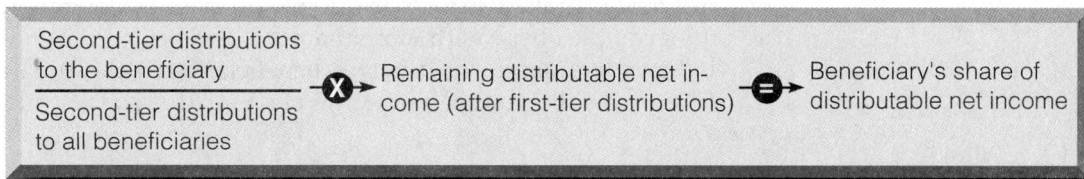

---

[29] §§ 662(a)(1) and (2).

[30] Reg. §§ 1.662(a)–2 and –3.

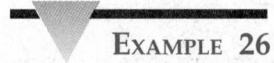

EXAMPLE 26

The trustee of the Gray Trust is required to distribute $10,000 per year to both Harriet and Wally, the two beneficiaries of the entity. In addition, he is empowered to distribute other amounts of trust income or corpus at his sole discretion. In the current year, the trust has accounting income of $60,000 and DNI of $50,000. However, the trustee distributes only the required $10,000 each to Harriet and to Wally. The balance of the income is accumulated and added to trust corpus.

In this case, only first-tier distributions have been made, but the total amount of the distributions does not exceed DNI for the year. Although DNI is the maximum amount that is included by the beneficiaries for the year, they can include no more in gross income than is distributed by the entity. Thus, both Harriet and Wally may be subject to tax on $10,000 as their proportionate shares of DNI. ▼

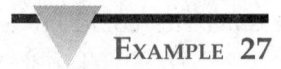

EXAMPLE 27

Assume the same facts as in Example 26, except that DNI is $12,000. Harriet and Wally each receive $10,000, but they cannot be taxed in total on more than DNI. Each is taxed on $6,000 [DNI of $12,000 × ($10,000/$20,000 of the first-tier distributions)]. ▼

EXAMPLE 28

Return to the facts in Example 25. Wong receives a first-tier distribution of $15,000. Second-tier distributions include $20,000 to Wong and $25,000 to Washington. Wilson's DNI is $40,000. The DNI is allocated between Wong and Washington as follows.

(1) First-tier distributions

To Wong	$15,000 DNI
To Washington	–0–
Remaining DNI = $25,000	

(2) Second-tier distributions

To Wong	$11,111 DNI [(20/45) × $25,000]
To Washington	$13,889 DNI [(25/45) × $25,000] ▼

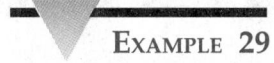

EXAMPLE 29

Assume the same facts as in Example 28, except that accounting income is $80,000 and DNI is $70,000. DNI is allocated between Wong and Washington as follows.

(1) First-tier distributions

To Wong	$15,000 DNI
To Washington	–0–
Remaining DNI = $55,000	

(2) Second-tier distributions

To Wong	$20,000 DNI
To Washington	$25,000 DNI ▼

Separate Share Rule.   For the sole purpose of determining the amount of DNI for a complex trust with more than one beneficiary, the substantially separate and independent shares of different beneficiaries in the trust are treated as *separate trusts*.[31] An illustration shows the need for this special rule.

EXAMPLE 30

A trustee has the discretion to distribute or accumulate income on behalf of Greg and Hannah (in equal shares). The trustee also has the power to invade corpus for the benefit of either beneficiary to the extent of that beneficiary's one-half interest in the trust. For the

---

[31] Reg. § 1.663(c)–1(a).

current year, DNI is $10,000. Of this amount, $5,000 is distributed to Greg, and $5,000 is accumulated on behalf of Hannah. In addition, the trustee pays $20,000 from corpus to Greg. Without the separate share rule, Greg is taxed on $10,000 (the full amount of the DNI). With the separate share rule, Greg is taxed on only $5,000 (his share of the DNI) and receives the $20,000 corpus distribution tax-free. The trust is taxed on Hannah's $5,000 share of the DNI that is accumulated. ▼

The separate share rule is designed to prevent the inequity that results if the corpus payments are treated under the regular rules applicable to second-tier beneficiaries. In Example 30, the effect of the separate share rule is to produce a two-trust result: one trust for Greg and one trust for Hannah, each with DNI of $5,000.

CHARACTER OF INCOME

Consistent with the modified conduit principle of Subchapter J, various classes of income (e.g., dividends, passive or portfolio gain and loss, AMT preferences, and tax-exempt interest) retain the same character for the beneficiaries that they had when they were received by the entity. If there are multiple beneficiaries *and* if all of the DNI is distributed, a problem arises in allocating the various classes of income among the beneficiaries.

Distributions are treated as consisting of the same proportion as the items that enter into the computation of DNI. This allocation does not apply, however, if local law or the governing instrument specifically allocates different classes of income to different beneficiaries.[32]

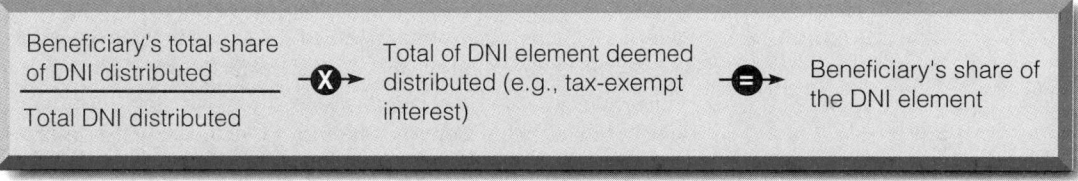

If the entity distributes only a part of its DNI, the amount of a specific class of DNI that is deemed distributed must first be determined.

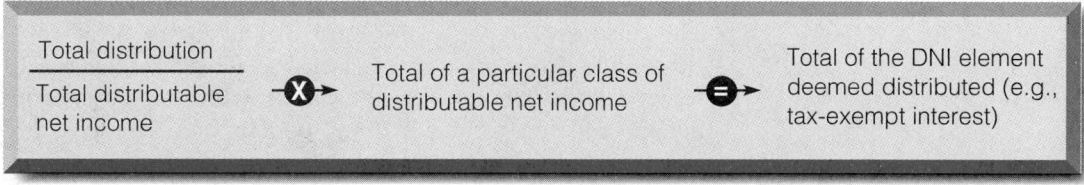

EXAMPLE 31

The Baron Trust has DNI of $40,000, including the following: $10,000 of taxable interest, $10,000 of tax-exempt interest, and $20,000 of passive activity income. The trustee distributes, at her discretion, $8,000 to Mike and $12,000 to Nancy.

---

[32] Reg. § 1.662(b)–1 seems to allow special allocations, but see *Harkness v. U.S.*, 72–2 USTC ¶9740, 30 AFTR2d 72–5754, 469 F.2d 310 (Ct.Cls., 1972).

Beneficiary	Amount Received	Income Type		
		Taxable Interest	Exempt Interest	Passive Income
Mike	$ 8,000	$2,000*	$2,000	$4,000
Nancy	12,000	3,000	3,000	6,000

*$8,000 distribution/$40,000 total DNI × $10,000 taxable interest in DNI.   ▼

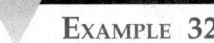

EXAMPLE 32

Continue with the facts of Example 31. The character of the income that flows through to Mike and Nancy is effective for all other tax purposes. For instance, the $2,000 exempt interest allocated to Mike is used in computing the taxable portion of any Social Security benefits Mike receives. If this exempt interest relates to nonessential activities of the issuing agency, Mike includes a $2,000 AMT preference on his current-year return.

The $4,000 passive activity income that is allocated to Mike is available for offset against passive losses that he has incurred from limited partnerships and rental activities for the year. Similarly, the $3,000 taxable interest income allocated to Nancy can be used to increase the amount of investment interest expense deductible by her in the year of the flow-through. The interest is treated as portfolio income to the same extent as that received directly by the taxpayer. ▼

Special Allocations.   Under certain circumstances, the parties may modify the character-of-income allocation method set forth above. A modification is permitted only to the extent that the allocation is required in the trust instrument and only to the extent that it has an economic effect independent of the cash-flow and income tax consequences of the allocation.[33]

EXAMPLE 33

Return to the facts in Example 31. Assume that the beneficiaries are elderly individuals who have pooled their investment portfolios to avail themselves of the trustee's professional asset management skills. Suppose the trustee has the discretion to allocate different classes of income to different beneficiaries and that she designates all of Nancy's $12,000 distribution as being from the tax-exempt income. Such a designation *would not be recognized* for tax purposes, and the allocation method of Example 31 must be used.

Suppose, however, that the trust instrument stipulated that Nancy was to receive all of the income from tax-exempt securities because she alone contributed the exempt securities to trust corpus. Under this provision, the $10,000 of the nontaxable interest is paid to Nancy. This allocation *is recognized*, and $10,000 of Nancy's distribution is tax-exempt. ▼

LOSSES IN THE TERMINATION YEAR

The ordinary net operating and capital losses of a trust or estate do not flow through to the entity's beneficiaries, as would such losses from a partnership or an S corporation. However, in the year in which an entity terminates its existence, the beneficiaries do receive a direct benefit from the loss carryovers of the trust or estate.[34]

Net operating losses and net capital losses are subject to the same carryover rules that otherwise apply to an individual. Consequently, NOLs can be carried back 3 years and then carried forward 15 years while net capital losses can be carried forward only, and for an indefinite period of time. However, if the entity incurs a negative taxable income in the last year of its existence, the excess of deductions over the entity's gross income is allowed to the beneficiaries (it will

---

[33] Reg. § 1.652(b)–2(b). This is similar to the § 704(b) requirement for partnerships.

[34] Reg. §§ 1.642(h)–1 and –2.

flow through to them directly). The net loss is available as a deduction *from* AGI in the beneficiary's tax year with or within which the entity's tax year ends. The amount allowed is in proportion to the relative amount of corpus assets that each beneficiary receives upon the termination of the entity, and it is subject to the 2-percent-of-AGI floor.

Any carryovers of the entity's other losses flow through to the beneficiaries in the year of termination in proportion to the relative amount of corpus assets that each beneficiary receives. The character of the loss carryover is retained by the beneficiary, except that a carryover of a net capital loss to a corporate beneficiary is always treated as short term. Beneficiaries who are individuals use these carryovers as deductions *for* AGI.

▼
EXAMPLE 34

The Edgar Estate terminates on December 31, 1998. It had used a fiscal year ending July 31. For the termination year, the estate incurred a $15,000 negative taxable income. In addition, the estate had an unused NOL carryover of $23,000 from the year ending July 31, 1995, and an unused net long-term capital loss carryover of $10,000 from the year ending July 31, 1997. Dawn receives $60,000 of corpus upon termination, and Blue Corporation receives the remaining $40,000. Dawn and Blue are calendar year taxpayers.

Dawn can claim an itemized deduction of $9,000 [($60,000/$100,000) × $15,000] for the entity's negative taxable income in the year of termination. This deduction is subject to the 2%-of-AGI floor on miscellaneous itemized deductions. In addition, Dawn can claim a $13,800 deduction *for* AGI in 1998 (60% × $23,000) for Edgar's NOL carryover, and she can use $6,000 of the estate's net long-term capital loss carryover with her other 1998 capital transactions.

Blue receives ordinary business deductions in 1998 for Edgar's NOLs: $6,000 for the loss in the year of termination and $9,200 for the carryover from fiscal 1995. Moreover, Blue can use the $4,000 carryover of Edgar's net capital losses to offset against its other 1998 capital transactions, although the loss must be treated as short term. ▼

BUILT-IN GAINS TAX COMPUTATION FOR TRUSTS

Congress enacted § 644 to discourage taxpayers from transferring appreciated property to a trust, which would then sell the property. The purpose of the transfer was to shift the gain on the appreciation of the asset to the trust's lower tax rates. This provision, which can be described as the original "built-in gains tax," imposes a special liability on trusts that sell or exchange property at a gain within two years after it is transferred to the trust. The special tax applies only if the fair market value of the property at the time of the initial transfer exceeded the adjusted basis of the property immediately after the transfer (after any applicable adjustment for gift taxes paid).

The tax imposed by § 644 is equal to the amount of additional income tax that the transferor would have been required to pay (including any AMT) had the gain been included in his or her gross income for the tax year of the sale. The tax applies only to the *includible gain*, which is the lesser of the following.

- The gain recognized by the trust on the sale or exchange of any property.
- The unrealized gain on the property at the time of the initial transfer to the trust.[35]

---

[35] §§ 644(b) and (d)(2).

In several situations, the tax will not be imposed. For instance, the tax does not apply to the sale or exchange of property (1) acquired by the trust from a decedent or (2) that occurs after the death of the transferor.

EXAMPLE 35

On July 1, 1997, Grandma created an irrevocable trust with a transfer of 200 shares of Zeta Corporation stock. At the time of the transfer, the stock was a capital asset to her. It had a fair market value of $30,000; its basis to the trust was $20,000. On October 1, 1997, the trust sold the stock for $35,000. Section 644 applies because the stock was sold at a gain within two years after its transfer to the trust *and* its fair market value at the time of the initial transfer exceeded its adjusted basis to the trust immediately after the transfer. The trust must report a § 644 gain of $10,000 [the lesser of its gain recognized on the sale ($15,000) or the appreciation in the hands of Grandma]. The $10,000 is taxed to the trust at Grandma's 1997 income tax rates on a net capital gain. The remaining $5,000 of the gain is taxed to the trust under the usual Subchapter J rules. ▼

THE THROWBACK RULE

4 **LEARNING OBJECTIVE**
Apply the effects of statutory restrictions on the taxation of distributions from accumulation trusts.

Generally, a trust's beneficiary is not taxed on any distributions in excess of the trust's DNI. Thus, trustees of complex trusts might be tempted to arrange distributions in a way that results in minimal income tax consequences to all of the parties involved. For instance, if the trust is subject to a lower marginal income tax rate than are its beneficiaries, income could be accumulated at the trust level for several years before being distributed to the beneficiaries. Thus, the income taxed to the beneficiaries in the year of distribution is limited by the trust's DNI for that year. Further tax savings could be achieved by using multiple trusts. This device spreads the income during the accumulation period over more than one taxpaying entity and avoids the graduated tax rates.

To discourage the use of these tax minimization schemes, a throwback rule was added to the Code. Under the rule, a beneficiary's tax on a distribution of income accumulated by a trust in a prior year will approximate the increased tax that the beneficiary would have owed for that prior year if the income had been distributed in the year that it was earned by the trust. The tax as computed, however, is levied for the actual year of the distribution. The purpose of the throwback rule is to place the beneficiaries of complex trusts in the same nominal tax position they would have been in if they had received the distributions during the years in which the trust was accumulating the income.

BASIC TERMS

The definitions of two terms are important in understanding the throwback rule: (1) **undistributed net income** and (2) **accumulation distribution.** Undistributed net income is the distributable net income of the trust reduced by first-tier and second-tier distributions and the income tax paid by the trust on any remaining undistributed DNI.[36] An accumulation distribution is any distribution from a trust for a tax year in excess of the trust's DNI for the year.[37]

The throwback rule applies only to complex trusts that do not distribute all current accounting income. The rule does not apply to estates or simple trusts. Moreover, the rule applies only in years when the complex trust makes an

---

[36] § 665(a).

[37] § 665(b).

accumulation distribution. When this occurs, the distribution is "thrown back" to the earliest year in which the trust had any undistributed net income. The accumulation is thrown back to succeeding years sequentially until it is used up.

Accumulation distributions may not be thrown back to years before 1969. Distributions of accounting income, capital gains that are allocable to corpus, and income accumulated before the beneficiary attained age 21 are not subject to the throwback procedure.[38]

Under the throwback rule, the beneficiary may be required to pay an additional income tax in the year of the accumulation distribution. The trust may not claim a refund (i.e., if the tax that it paid exceeded that which would have been paid by the beneficiary).[39]

EXAMPLE 36

In 1983, the Taylor Trust was subject to a marginal Federal income tax rate of 19%, while its sole income beneficiary, Karen, was subject to a 33% marginal rate. Karen encouraged the trustee to accumulate $7,500 of the trust's DNI, which totaled $10,000. The balance of the DNI was distributed to Karen. If Taylor's tax on this accumulation, after credits, is $1,200, its undistributed net income for 1983 is $6,300 [$10,000 (DNI) − $2,500 (distribution of income) − $1,200 (taxes paid)].

By 1997, Karen's marginal rate had fallen to 15%, and she encouraged the trustee to distribute to her, in that year, an amount equal to the 1997 DNI of $12,000 plus the $6,300 that had been accumulated, after taxes, in 1983. When the trustee complied with Karen's wish, he made an accumulation distribution of $6,300.

The tax on the accumulation distribution is levied upon Karen in 1997. Her additional tax will approximate what she would have paid in 1983 had the trust distributed its full DNI in that year (the $6,300 accumulation distribution is subject to a tax rate of approximately 33% and not to Karen's prevailing 15% rate). ▼

Although no interest or penalty is due with the tax on the accumulation distribution, the additional tax discourages the manipulation of trust distributions for tax avoidance purposes.[40]

THE SIXTY-FIVE-DAY RULE

Amounts paid or credited to the beneficiaries in the first 65 days of the trust's tax year may be treated as paid on the last day of the preceding taxable year.[41] This provision offers the trustee some flexibility in timing distributions so that trust accumulations, and the resulting throwback procedures, can be avoided.

GRANTOR TRUSTS

5　LEARNING OBJECTIVE
Use the special rules that apply to trusts where the creator (grantor) of the trust retains certain rights.

A series of special provisions contained in §§ 671 through 679 applies when the grantor of the trust retains beneficial enjoyment or substantial control over the trust property or income. In that event, the grantor is taxed on the trust income, and the trust is disregarded for income tax purposes. The person who is taxed on the income is allowed to claim, on his or her own return, any deductions or credits

---

[38] § 668(e).
[39] § 666(e).
[40] For further details on calculating the tax, see § 667(b) and the instructions to Schedule J (Form 1041).

[41] See Reg. § 1.663(b)–2 for the manner and timing of the election.

attributable to the income. Such taxes restrict the grantor's ability to redirect the income recognized from trust corpus to the trust or its beneficiaries.

REVERSIONARY TRUSTS

Creation of virtually any new reversionary trust is subject to the Federal gift tax. If the grantor dies before the income interest expires, the present value of the reversionary interest is included in his or her gross estate under § 2033; thus, a Federal estate tax could also result.

POWERS RETAINED BY THE GRANTOR

Sections 674 through 677 contain other restrictions on the extent of the powers over the trust that the grantor can retain without incurring grantor trust status. If any of these provisions is violated, the income of the trust is taxed to the grantor, and the usual Subchapter J rules do not apply to the trust.

The grantor is taxed on the income if he or she retains (1) the beneficial enjoyment of corpus or (2) the power to dispose of the trust income without the approval or consent of any adverse party. An adverse party is any person having a substantial beneficial interest in the trust who could be affected adversely by the power the grantor possesses over the trust assets.[42]

A number of important powers, including the following, will *not* cause such income to be taxed to the grantor:[43]

- To apply the income toward the support of the grantor's dependents (except to the extent that it actually is applied for this purpose).[44]
- To allocate trust income or corpus among charitable beneficiaries.
- To invade corpus on behalf of a designated beneficiary.
- To withhold income from a beneficiary during his or her minority or disability.
- To allocate receipts and disbursements between income and corpus.

The retention by the grantor or a nonadverse party of certain administrative powers over the trust causes the income to be taxed to the grantor. Such powers include those to deal with trust income or corpus for less than full and adequate consideration and to borrow from the trust without providing adequate interest or security.[45]

The grantor of a trust is taxed on the trust's income if he or she (or a nonadverse party) possesses the power to revoke the trust.[46] In addition, a grantor is taxed on all or part of the income of a trust when, without the consent of any adverse party, the income is or, at the discretion of the grantor or a nonadverse party (or both), may be:

- Distributed to the grantor or the grantor's spouse.
- Held or accumulated for future distribution to the grantor or the grantor's spouse.
- Applied to the payment of premiums on insurance policies on the life of the grantor or the grantor's spouse.[47]

---

[42] §§ 672(a), (b), and 674. See Reg. § 1.672(a)–1 for examples of adverse party situations.

[43] § 674(b).

[44] § 677(b).

[45] See Reg. § 1.675–1(b) for a further discussion of this matter.

[46] § 676.

[47] § 677(a).

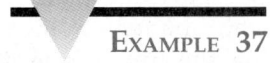

CONCEPT SUMMARY 19–1

Principles of Fiduciary Taxation

1. Estates and trusts are temporary entities created to locate, maintain, and distribute assets and to satisfy liabilities according to the wishes of the decedent or grantor as expressed in the will or trust document.
2. Generally, the estate or trust acts as a conduit of the taxable income that it receives. To the extent that the income is distributed by the entity, it is taxed to the beneficiary. Taxable income retained by the entity is taxed to the entity itself.
3. The entity's accounting income must first be determined. Accounting conventions that are stated in the controlling document or, lacking such provisions, in state law allocate specific items of receipt and expenditure either to income or to corpus. Income beneficiaries typically receive payments from the entity that are equal to the accounting income.
4. The taxable income of the entity is computed using the scheme in Figure 19–2. The entity usually recognizes income in respect of a decedent. Deductions for fiduciary's fees and for charitable contributions may be reduced if the entity received any tax-exempt income during the year. Cost recovery deductions are assigned proportionately to the recipients of accounting income. Upon election, realized gain or loss on assets that properly are distributed in kind can be recognized by the entity.
5. A distribution deduction, computationally derived from distributable net income (DNI), is allowed to the entity. DNI is the maximum amount on which entity beneficiaries can be taxed. Moreover, the constitution of DNI is preserved for the recipients of the distributions.
6. Additional taxes are levied under Subchapter J to discourage (1) the transfer of appreciated assets to a lower-bracket estate or trust that quickly disposes of the assets in a taxable exchange, (2) the accumulation of trust income at the lower marginal tax rates of the entity followed by a subsequent distribution of the accumulation to beneficiaries, and (3) the retention of excessive administrative powers by the grantor of a trust when the gross income is taxed to a lower-bracket beneficiary.

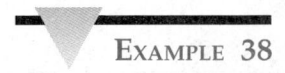

EXAMPLE 37 Frank creates an irrevocable trust for his children with a transfer of income-producing property and an insurance policy on the life of Marion, his wife. During the year, the trustee uses $3,000 of the trust income to pay the premiums on the policy covering Marion's life. Frank is taxed on $3,000 of the trust's income. ▼

Moreover, trust income accumulated for the benefit of someone whom the grantor is *legally obligated* to support is taxed to the grantor but only to the extent that it is actually applied for that purpose.[48]

EXAMPLE 38 Melanie creates an irrevocable accumulation trust. Her son, Sean, is the life beneficiary, and the remainder goes to any grandchildren. During the year, the trust income of $8,000 is applied as follows: $5,000 toward Sean's college tuition and other related educational expenses and $3,000 accumulated on Sean's behalf. If, under state law, Melanie has an obligation to support Sean and this obligation includes providing a college education, Melanie is taxed on the $5,000 that is so applied. ▼

TAX PLANNING CONSIDERATIONS Many of the tax planning possibilities for estates and trusts were discussed in Chapter 18. However, several specific tax planning possibilities are available to help minimize the income tax effects on estates and trusts and their beneficiaries.

---

[48] § 677(b). The taxpayer's legal obligations vary according to state law, financial resources, and family expectations. See *Frederick C. Braun, Jr.,* 48 TCM 210, T.C.Memo. 1984–285, and *Cristopher Stone,* 54 TCM 462, T.C.Memo. 1987–454.

A TRUST OR ESTATE AS AN INCOME-SHIFTING DEVICE

The compressed tax rate schedule applicable to Subchapter J entities may have reversed the traditional techniques by which families set aside funds for long-term activities, such as business start-ups, college education, and home purchases. When the tax rate schedules for trusts and estates were more accommodating, high-income individuals would shift income-producing assets to trusts to take advantage of the lower effective tax rate that would fall on the income accumulated within the trust. The target of the plan, usually a child, would receive the accumulated income (and, perhaps, trust corpus) at a designated age, and more funds would be available because a lower tax rate had been applied over the life of the investment in the trust.

Today, such an income shift would *deplete,* rather than shelter, the family's assets, as the rates falling on individuals are much more graduated than are those applicable to fiduciaries, and the kiddie tax also penalizes attempts to shift taxable income to children. Assuming that the objectives of the plan remain unchanged, possible strategies in view of these rate changes include the following.

- Trust corpus should be invested in growth assets that are low on yield but high on appreciation, so that the trustee can determine the timing of the gain and somewhat control the effective tax rate that applies.
- Trust corpus should be invested in tax-exempt securities, such as municipal bonds and mutual funds that invest in them, to eliminate the tax costs associated with the investment. If this approach is taken, a trust might be unnecessary—the parent should simply retain full control over the assets and invest in the exempt securities in his or her own account.
- The grantor should retain high-yield assets, so that control over the assets is not surrendered when the tax cost is too high.
- Use of trust vehicles should be reserved for cases where professional management of the assets is necessary for portfolio growth and the additional tax costs can be justified.
- An income-shifting strategy may require several steps to achieve the desired result. For instance, the grantor might increase contributions to his or her own qualified retirement plan, thereby sheltering the funds from all tax liabilities. Then the grantor could use the tax dollars saved from these contributions to purchase tax-deferred annuity contracts, savings bonds, exempt securities, or other assets where the tax liabilities are reduced or deferred. The grantor could then either retain these exempt securities as discussed above or transfer them to the trust at a later date.

INCOME TAX PLANNING FOR ESTATES

As a separate taxable entity, an estate can select its own tax year and accounting methods. The executor of an estate should consider selecting a fiscal year because this will determine when beneficiaries must include income distributions from the estate in their own tax returns. Beneficiaries must include the income for their tax year with or within which the estate's tax year ends. Proper selection of the estate's tax year can result in a smoothing out of income and a reduction of the income taxes for all parties involved.

Caution should be taken in determining when the estate is to be terminated. Selecting a fiscal year for the estate can result in a bunching of income to the beneficiaries in the year in which the estate is closed. Prolonging the termination of an estate can be effective income tax planning, but the IRS carefully examines the purpose of keeping the estate open. Since the unused losses of an estate pass through to the beneficiaries only in the termination year, the estate should be closed when the beneficiaries can enjoy the maximum tax benefit of the losses.

The timing and amounts of income distributions to the beneficiaries also present important tax planning opportunities. If the executor can make discretionary income distributions, he or she should evaluate the relative marginal income tax rates of the estate and its beneficiaries. By timing the distributions properly, the overall income tax liability can be minimized. Care should be taken, however, to time the distributions in light of the estate's DNI.

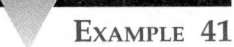

EXAMPLE 39

For several years before his death on March 7, Don had entered into annual deferred compensation agreements with his employer. These agreements collectively called for the payment of $200,000 six months after Don's retirement or death. To provide a maximum 12-month period within which to generate deductions to offset this large item of income in respect of a decedent, the executor or administrator of the estate should elect a fiscal year ending August 31. The election is made simply by filing the estate's first tax return for the short period of March 7 to August 31. ▼

EXAMPLE 40

Carol, the sole beneficiary of an estate, is a calendar year, cash basis taxpayer. If the estate elects a fiscal year ending January 31, all distributions during the period of February 1 to December 31, 1997, will be reported on Carol's tax return for calendar year 1998 (due April 15, 1999). Thus, assuming estimated tax requirements have otherwise been met, any income taxes that result from a $50,000 distribution made by the estate on February 20, 1997, are deferred until April 15, 1999. ▼

EXAMPLE 41

Assume the same facts as in Example 40. If the estate is closed on December 15, 1998, the DNI for both the fiscal year ending January 31, 1998, and the final tax year ending December 15, 1998, is included in Carol's tax return for the calendar year 1998. To avoid the effect of this bunching of income, the estate should not be closed until calendar year 1999. ▼

EXAMPLE 42

Assume the same facts as in Example 41, except that the estate has a substantial NOL for the period February 1 to December 15, 1998. If Carol is subject to a high income tax rate for calendar year 1998, the estate should be closed in that year so that the excess deductions are passed through to its beneficiary. However, if Carol anticipates being in a higher tax bracket in 1999, the termination of the estate should be postponed. ▼

EXAMPLE 43

Review Examples 28 and 29 carefully. Note, for instance, the flexibility that is available to the executor or administrator in timing the second-tier distributions of income and corpus of the estate. To illustrate, if Washington is subject to a high tax rate, distributions to him should be minimized except in years when DNI is low. In this manner, Washington's exposure to gross income from the distributions can be controlled so that most of the distributions he receives will be free of income tax. ▼

In general, those beneficiaries who are subject to high income tax rates should be made beneficiaries of second-tier (but not IRD) distributions of the estate. Most likely, these individuals will have less need for an additional steady stream of (taxable) income while their income tax savings can be relatively large. Moreover, a special allocation of tax-favored types of income and expenses should be considered. For example, tax-exempt income can be directed more easily to beneficiaries in higher income tax brackets.

Should a Tax Adviser Also Be a Trustee?

Tax clients need to be counseled on the best use of the trust entity and the proper choice of beneficiary of the trust income. The objectives of the grantor typically will best be served by transferring more power to the trustee; sprinkling powers, in particular, enable the trustee to be sensitive to the short-term and ongoing needs of the various beneficiaries. The client, however, may not appreciate this suggestion when the trust document is drafted. Especially if the tax adviser is the trustee or a co-trustee, the client may balk at the professional's well-intended suggestion that future developments might favor one beneficiary over another in a manner that cannot be anticipated at the time.

Should the source of the estate plan—the tax adviser—also then be designated as the trustee by the grantor? When the adviser serves in that capacity, who is "the client"? Merely the grantor? How about the beneficiaries? And the trust itself? To avoid any potential for conflict with their clients, some professional firms have adopted a policy of refusing to serve as trustee of a client's trust (or executor of his or her estate). Certainly, surrendering a sprinkling power to a fiduciary who is less sensitive to the tax ramifications of Subchapter J may be costly to all of the parties, but these firms see the preservation of the client relationship as more valuable in the long term.

Recall, also, that, although both of her children are attorneys, Jacqueline Kennedy Onassis was careful to make other parties the executor of her estate and the trustees of her fiduciary entities. In more typical estates, though, the grantor must address critical issues: How much power and control over assets and income should be surrendered to "outsiders" through the trust? Which items lend themselves to such transfers of control?

INCOME TAX PLANNING WITH TRUSTS

The great variety of trusts provides the grantor, trustee, and beneficiaries with excellent opportunities for tax planning. Many of the same tax planning opportunities available to the executor of an estate are available to the trustee. For instance, the distributions from a trust are taxable to the trust's beneficiaries to the extent of the trust's DNI. If income distributions are discretionary, the trustee can time the distributions to minimize the income tax consequences to all parties.

Remember that the throwback rule applies to complex trusts. Consequently, the benefit from the timing of distributions may be more limited than it is for estates. Indeed, improper timing could result in a greater nominal tax than if the distributions had been made annually. The trustee of a complex trust should thus consider the *65-day rule*. The rule permits the trust to treat distributions made within 65 days of the end of its tax year as if they were made on the last day of that year. Proper use of this provision can help the trustee in both minimizing the overall income tax consequences and avoiding the throwback rule for the beneficiaries.

DISTRIBUTIONS OF IN-KIND PROPERTY

The ability of the trustee or executor to elect to recognize the realized gain or loss relative to a distributed noncash asset allows the gain or loss to be allocated to the optimal taxpayer.

EXAMPLE 44

The Yorba Linda Estate distributed some stock, basis of $40,000 and fair market value of $41,500, to beneficiary Larry. Yorba Linda is subject to a 15% marginal income tax rate, and Larry is subject to a 31% marginal rate. The executor of Yorba Linda should elect that the entity recognize the related $1,500 realized gain, thereby subjecting the gain to the estate's lower marginal tax rate and reducing Larry's future capital gain income. ▼

DEDUCTIBILITY OF FIDUCIARY EXPENSES

Many § 2053 and § 2054 estate tax deductions and losses may be claimed either as estate tax deductions or as income tax deductions of the estate on the fiduciary return (Form 1041), at the taxpayer's choice.[49] In such a case, the deduction for income tax purposes is not allowed unless the estate tax deduction is waived. These deductions can be apportioned between the two returns.

An expense deductible for estate tax purposes may not qualify as an income tax deduction. Interest expense incurred to carry tax-exempt bonds is disallowed for income tax purposes. If this expense is not claimed under § 2053 for estate tax purposes, it is completely lost.

Medical expenses incurred by the decedent but unpaid at the time of the decedent's death are covered by a special rule. If paid by the estate during a one-year period beginning with the day after death, the expenses may be claimed as an income tax deduction in the year incurred or as an estate tax deduction, but not both.[50] The choice is between the decedent's appropriate Form 1040 and his or her estate tax return. The expenses may be divided in any way between Form 1040 and the estate tax return.

EXAMPLE 45

The executor of Dane's estate pays $5,000 in burial expenses (authorized under local law and approved by the probate court) from estate assets. The $5,000 expense should be claimed on the estate tax return, as it is not deductible at all for income tax purposes. ▼

KEY TERMS

---

[49] § 642(g) and Reg. § 20.2053–1(d).

[50] § 213(c).

PROBLEM
MATERIALS

DISCUSSION QUESTIONS

1. When should a client be counseled to create a trust? What tax motivations might lead to the use of a fiduciary? List important tax and nontax objectives that might be satisfied by the use of a trust created during the taxpayer's lifetime.

2. Identify the parties involved in the creation of a trust. Do the same for an estate.

3. When is the trustee required to file a Form 1041?

4. Why has Congress subjected trusts and estates to such a compressed tax rate schedule? Demonstrate this compression numerically.

5. What is the personal exemption allowed an estate? A trust?

6. Is the fiduciary entity subject to the alternative minimum tax? What tax rates and exemptions apply?

7. Outline the five-step process of determining the taxable income amounts for the parties to a trust arrangement.

8. What happens when a trust distributes an asset to a beneficiary and the asset's basis is less than its fair market value?

9. How does Subchapter J assign the cost recovery deductions attributable to the operations of a trust?

10. How does a trust or estate treat charitable contribution deductions?

11. The Flan Trust is scheduled to terminate in two years, when Amy Flan reaches age 30. The trust operated a business several years ago, and it generated a sizable NOL carryforward that the trust has not been able to use. In addition, due to poor investment advice, the value of the entity's investment portfolio has declined 15% from its purchase price. What issues must you consider in giving Amy and the corporate trustee tax planning advice?

12. Willie holds an asset that has appreciated from its $100,000 basis to a current value of $250,000. He wants to transfer the asset to his daughter Gloria when she reaches the age of majority in five years, but he does not want tax payments to reduce the value of his gift. Willie and Gloria are in good health, but she is not ready to take on the responsibilities of managing such a sizable asset. How should Willie approach this situation?

13. Draft an outline for a speech to your university's accounting club, addressing the use of the throwback rule in fiduciary taxation.

14. Kramer and Benes are the income beneficiaries of the Costello Trust. This year, the trust's distributable net income is $100,000, and income distributions total $40,000. Identify tax issues that may be important in future years for Costello, Kramer, and Benes.

15. Harriet wants to transfer some assets to a trust this year; the income beneficiaries will be her two grandchildren. The trust will be used to pay the grandchildren's tuition to private high schools and universities. Upon the younger grandchild's graduation, the trust assets will return to Harriet's ownership. Identify tax issues related to Harriet's plan to use a temporary fiduciary entity.

16. Write a memo for the tax research file discussing the tax planning opportunities presented by an estate's ability to select a noncalendar tax year. Your clients seek advice as to the estate of a decedent who died on May 3. Large payments of IRD will be received in the first three months after the date of death.

PROBLEMS

17. Illustrate the nature and operations of each of the following trusts by creating a fact pattern to match each result.

   a. A simple trust.

   b. A complex trust with a $300 personal exemption.

   c. A complex trust with a $100 personal exemption.

18. The Purple Trust incurred the following items this year.

Taxable interest income	$50,000
Tax-exempt interest income, not on private activity bonds	60,000
Tax-exempt interest income, on private activity bonds	70,000

Compute Purple's tentative minimum tax for the year. Purple does not have any credits available to reduce the AMT liability.

19. The Grouper Trust will incur the following items next year, its first year of existence.

Interest income	$50,000
Rent income	12,000
Cost recovery expense	9,500
Capital gain income	20,000
Fiduciary and tax preparation fees	5,000

Betty, the grantor of the trust, is working with you on the language in the trust instrument relative to the derivation of annual accounting income for the entity. She will name Shirley as the sole income beneficiary and Benny as the remainder beneficiary.

   a. Suggest language to Betty that will maximize the annual income distribution to Shirley.

   b. Suggest language to Betty that will minimize the annual distribution to Shirley and maximize the accumulation on Benny's behalf.

20. Complete the following chart, indicating the comparative attributes of the typical trust and estate by answering yes/no or explaining the differences between the entities where appropriate.

Attribute	Estate	Trust
Separate income tax entity		
Controlling document		
Termination date is determinable from controlling document		
Legal owner of assets under fiduciary's control		
Document identifies both income and remainder beneficiaries		
Throwback rules apply		
Separate share rules apply		
Generally must use calendar tax year		

21. Complete the chart below, indicating trust accounting income for each of the alternatives. For this purpose, use the following information.

Interest income, taxable	$40,000
Interest income, tax-exempt	10,000
Interest income, tax-exempt but AMT preference	20,000
Long-term capital gain	15,000
Trustee fee	8,000

Trust Agreement Provisions	Trust Accounting Income
Fees and capital gains allocable to corpus	_____
Capital gains allocable to corpus, one-half of fees allocable to income	_____
Capital gains allocable to income, silent concerning allocation of fees	_____
Fees and exempt income allocable to corpus, silent concerning allocation of capital gain/loss	_____

22. Bob is one of the income beneficiaries of the LeMans Estate, which is subject to a 40% marginal Federal estate tax rate, a 30% marginal Federal income tax rate, and a 5% marginal state income tax rate. This year, Bob received $20,000 of sales commissions that were earned and payable to LeMans (cash basis) at her death. Compute Bob's § 691(c) deduction for the current year, given the following financial data.

Sales commissions receivable	$30,000
Deferred gain on installment sale, three payments remaining	70,000

23. In its first tax year, the Wittmann Estate generated $50,000 of taxable interest income and $25,000 of tax-exempt interest income. It paid fiduciary fees of $4,000. The estate is subject to a 37% marginal estate tax rate and a 31% marginal income tax rate.
   a. How should the executor assign the deductions for the payment of the fees?
   b. How does the 2%-of-AGI floor apply to the fees assigned to the estate's income tax return?

24. Brown incurred the following items in 1997.

Business income	$20,000
Tax-exempt interest income	5,000
Payment to charity from 1997 income, paid 3/1/98	3,000

Complete the following chart, indicating how the Code treats charitable contributions under the various assumptions.

Assumption	1997 Deduction for Contribution
Brown is a cash basis individual.	_____
Brown is an accrual basis corporation.	_____
Brown is a trust.	_____

25. The Prasad Trust operates a welding business. Its current-year cost recovery deductions properly amounted to $35,000. Prasad's accounting income was $150,000, of which $80,000 was distributed to first-tier beneficiary Chuck, $60,000 was distributed to second-tier beneficiary Ruby, and $10,000 was accumulated by the trustee. Ruby also received a $15,000 corpus distribution. Prasad's DNI was $52,000. Identify the treatment of Prasad's cost recovery deductions.

26. The Oliver Trust has generated $40,000 in depreciation deductions for the year. Its accounting income is $21,000. In computing this amount, pursuant to the trust document, depreciation was allocated to corpus. Accounting income was distributed at the trustee's discretion: $15,000 to Hernandez and $6,000 to Jackson.
   a. Compute the depreciation deductions that Hernandez, Jackson, and Oliver may claim.
   b. Same as (a), except that depreciation was allocated to income.

c. Same as (a), except that the trustee distributed $6,000 each to Hernandez and to Jackson and retained the remaining accounting income.

d. Same as (a), except that Oliver is an estate (and not a trust).

27. The Ricardo Trust is a simple trust that correctly uses the calendar year for tax purposes. Its three income beneficiaries (Lucy, Mark, and Ethel) are entitled to the trust's annual accounting income in shares of one-third each. For the current calendar year, the trust generates ordinary income of $75,000, a long-term capital gain of $15,000 (allocable to corpus), and a trustee commission expense of $9,000 (allocable to corpus). Use the format of Figure 19–3 to address the following items.

a. How much income is each beneficiary entitled to receive?

b. What is the trust's DNI?

c. What is the trust's taxable income?

d. How much is taxed to each of the beneficiaries?

28. Assume the same facts as in Problem 27, except that the trust instrument allocates the capital gain to income.

a. How much income is each beneficiary entitled to receive?

b. What is the trust's DNI?

c. What is the trust's taxable income?

d. How much is taxed to each of the beneficiaries?

29. Under the terms of the trust instrument, the trustee has discretion to distribute or accumulate income on behalf of Willie, Sylvia, and Drahman in equal shares. The trustee also can invade corpus for the benefit of any of the beneficiaries to the extent of each person's respective one-third interest in the trust. In the current year, the trust has DNI of $48,000. Of this amount, $16,000 is distributed to Willie and $10,000 is distributed to Sylvia. The remaining $6,000 of Sylvia's share of DNI and Drahman's entire $16,000 share are accumulated by the trust. Additionally, the trustee distributes $20,000 from corpus to Willie.

a. How much income is taxed to Willie?

b. To Sylvia?

c. To Drahman?

d. To the trust?

30. A trust is required to distribute $40,000 annually to its two income beneficiaries, Clare and David, in shares of 75% and 25%, respectively. If trust income is not sufficient to pay these amounts, the trustee can invade corpus to the extent necessary. During the current year, the trust generates only taxable interest income and has DNI of $90,000; the trustee distributes $60,000 to Clare and $40,000 to David.

a. How much of the $60,000 distributed to Clare is included in her gross income?

b. How much of the $40,000 distributed to David is included in his gross income?

c. Are these distributions first-tier or second-tier distributions?

31. An estate has $75,000 of DNI, composed of $30,000 in dividends, $20,000 in taxable interest, $15,000 passive activity income, and $10,000 in tax-exempt interest. The trust's two noncharitable income beneficiaries, Brenda and Del, receive $30,000 each. How much of each class of income is deemed to have been distributed to Brenda? To Del?

32. The trustee of the Purple Trust can distribute any amount of accounting income and corpus to the trust's beneficiaries, Lydia and Kent. This year, the trust incurred the following.

Taxable interest income	$40,000
Tax-exempt interest income	60,000
Long-term capital gains—allocable to corpus	35,000
Fiduciary's fees—allocable to corpus	12,000

The trustee distributed $40,000 to Lydia and $30,000 to Kent.

a. What is Purple's trust accounting income?

b. What is Purple's DNI?

c. What is Purple's taxable income?

d. How much is taxed to each of the beneficiaries?

33. Donna contributes 100 shares of Ying Corporation stock to an irrevocable trust on July 1, 1995, income to her son, remainder to her grandson in 12 years. Donna's basis in the stock is $40,000; the fair market value of the stock at the date of the transfer is $300,000. On June 20, 1997, the trust sells the stock on the open market for $175,000. What is the amount of gain or loss recognized by the trust on the sale? How is the tax computed, and who is liable for it? How would the recognized gain have been treated had the stock been sold for $415,000?

34. Each of the following items was incurred by José, the cash basis, calendar year decedent. Applying the rules for income and deductions in respect of a decedent, indicate on which return each item should be reported: the recipient/heir's last Form 1040 income tax (*Form 1040*); José's estate's first Form 1041 income tax (*Form 1041*); or José's estate's Form 706 estate tax (*Form 706*). More than one alternative may apply in some cases.

Item Incurred	**Form(s) Reported on**
a. Wages, last paycheck	_____
b. State income tax withheld on last paycheck	_____
c. Capital gain portion of installment payment received	_____
d. Ordinary income portion of installment payment received	_____
e. Dividend income, record date was two days prior to José's death	_____
f. Unrealized appreciation on a mutual fund investment	_____
g. Depreciation recapture accrued as of date of death	_____
h. Medical expenses of last illness	_____
i. Apartment building, rents accrued but not collected as of death	_____
j. Apartment building, property tax accrued and assessed but not paid as of death	_____

35. In each of the following independent cases, write a memo for the tax research file in preparation for a meeting with Gary. In each memo, explain whether the proposed plan meets his objective of shifting income and avoiding the grantor trust rules.

a. Gary transfers property in trust, income payable to Winnie (his wife) for life, remainder to his grandson. Gary's son is designated as the trustee.

b. Gary transfers income-producing assets and a life insurance policy to a trust, life estate to his children, remainder to his grandchildren. The policy is on Winnie's life, and the trustee (an independent trust company) is instructed to pay the premiums with income from the income-producing assets. The trust is designated as the beneficiary of the policy.

c. Gary transfers property in trust. The trust income is payable to Gary's grandchildren, as Winnie sees fit. Winnie and an independent trust company are designated as trustees.

d. Gary transfers property in trust, income payable to Winnie (Gary's ex-wife), remainder to Gary or his estate upon Winnie's death. The transfer was made in satisfaction of Gary's alimony obligation to Winnie. An independent trust company is designated as the trustee.

36. Determine the tax effects of the indicated losses for the Yellow Estate for both tax years. The estate holds a variety of investment assets, which it received from the decedent, Mrs. Yellow. The estate's sole income and remainder beneficiary is Yellow, Jr.

Tax Year	Loss Generated
1997 (first tax year)	Taxable income ($300)
	Capital loss ($15,000)
1998 (final tax year)	Taxable income ($1,000)

37. Woody wishes to transfer some of the income from his investment portfolio to his daughter, age 6. Woody wants the trust to be able to accumulate income on his daughter's behalf and to meet any excessive expenses associated with the daughter's prep school and private college education. Furthermore, Woody wants the trust to protect his daughter against his own premature death without increasing his Federal gross estate. Thus, Woody provides the trustee with the powers to purchase insurance on his life and to meet tuition, fee, and book expenses of his daughter's education. The trust is created in 1987. A whole life insurance policy with five annual premium payments is purchased during that year. The trustee spends $10,000 for the daughter's college expenses in 1999 (but in no other year). Woody dies in 2005. Has the trust been tax-effective?

38. Complete the following chart, indicating the comparative attributes of the typical simple and complex trust by answering yes/no or explaining the differences between the entities where appropriate.

Attribute	Simple Trust	Complex Trust
Separate share rules apply	_____	_____
Throwback rules apply	_____	_____
Trust could incur its own tax liability for the year	_____	_____
Trust generally distributes all of DNI	_____	_____
Trust can deduct its charitable contributions in the year of, or the year after, payment	_____	_____
Trust could claim a foreign tax credit	_____	_____
Maximum tax rate on net long-term capital gains = 28%	_____	_____
AMT preferences and adjustments flow through to beneficiaries ratably	_____	_____
Amount of personal exemption	_____	_____

39. Selena is the sole income beneficiary of a well-endowed trust. She believes that the trustee should be accumulating the trust accounting income that is being earned so that she can receive it after she retires and, presumably, when she will be subject to a lower income tax rate. Selena currently is subject to a 40% combined state and Federal rate.

Given Selena's desire to reduce the present value of her tax liabilities, in each of the following independent cases discuss the feasibility of her objective, explaining how the throwback rule inhibits the trustee from manipulating the timing of income distributions in this manner.

a. Selena is age 45.
b. Selena is age 15.
c. The trust allocates capital gains to income.
d. The entity is the estate of Selena's father.

COMPREHENSIVE TAX RETURN PROBLEM

Prepare the 1996 fiduciary income tax return (Form 1041) for the Rodriguez Trust. In addition, determine the amount and character of the income and expense items that each beneficiary must report for 1996 and prepare a Schedule K–1 for Maria Lopez.

The 1996 activities of the trust include the following.

Business operating loss	$200,000
Dividend income, all U.S. stocks	250,000
Taxable interest income	100,000
Tax-exempt interest income	50,000
Net long-term capital gain	125,000
Fiduciary's fees	20,000

Under the terms of the trust instrument, depreciation, net capital gains and losses, and one-half of the fiduciary's fees are allocable to corpus. The trustee is required to distribute $100,000 to Maria every year. For 1996, the trustee distributed $150,000 to Maria and $100,000 to her sister, Elena Rodriguez. No other distributions were made.

In computing DNI, the trustee properly assigned all of the deductible fiduciary fees to the dividend income. The trustee paid $25,000 in estimated taxes for the year on behalf of the trust. Any 1996 refund is to be credited to 1997 estimates. The exempt income was not derived from private activity bonds.

The trust was created on December 14, 1953. It is not subject to any recapture taxes, nor does it have any tax credits. None of its income was derived under a personal services contract. The trust has no economic interest in any foreign trust. Its Federal identification number is 89–7842067.

The trustee, Wisconsin State National Bank, is located at 3100 East Wisconsin Avenue, Milwaukee, WI 53201. Its employer identification number is 84–7602487.

Maria lives at 9880 East North Avenue, Shorewood, WI 53211. Her identification number is 498–01–8058.

Elena lives at 6772 East Oklahoma Avenue, St. Cecilia, WI 53204. Her identification number is 499–02–6531.

RESEARCH PROBLEMS

*Note: **West's Federal Taxation on CD-ROM** can be used in preparing solutions to the Research Problems. Alternatively, tax research materials contained in a standard tax library can be used.*

Research Problem 1. Your client, Chuck Konkol, is a self-employed investment adviser who provides services to individuals and small investment clubs for an hourly fee. He is aware of the difficulty that his clients have in deducting payments to him due to the 2%-of-AGI floor on miscellaneous itemized deductions, such as advisory fees.

His new client, the Ferguson Trust, wants to be certain that it can deduct such fees in computing entity taxable income. Konkol asks you to make a presentation to the trust's officers on this subject. Provide a speaker's outline for this purpose, with citations only to the most important statutory and judicial law.

Research Problem 2. Your client, Annie O'Toole (22 Beneficiary Lane, Bowling Green, KY 42101), has come to you for some advice regarding gifts of property. She has just learned that she must undergo major surgery, and she would like to make certain gifts before entering the hospital. On your earlier advice, she had established a plan of lifetime giving for four prior years.

Build a spreadsheet, supplemented by a list of your assumptions, and write a cover letter to Annie, discussing each of the following assets that she is considering using as gifts to family and friends. In doing so, evaluate the income tax consequences of having such property pass through her estate to the designated legatee. *For this purpose, you need consult only the Code and pertinent Regulations.*

a. Annie plans to give a cottage to her son to fulfill a promise made many years ago. She has owned the cottage for the past 15 years and has a basis in it of $30,000 (fair market value of $20,000).

b. Annie has $100,000 of long-term capital losses that she has been carrying forward for the past few years. Now, she is considering making a gift of $200,000 in installment notes to her daughter. Her basis in the notes is $100,000, and the notes' current fair market value is $190,000.

c. Annie has promised to make a special cash bequest of $25,000 to her grandson in her will. However, she does not anticipate having that much cash immediately available after her death. Annie requests your advice concerning the income tax consequences to the estate if the cash bequest is settled with some other property.

Research Problem 3.   Your client, Celia van Sustern, wants to send her daughter Muffy to private grade school to avoid the problems of crime, drugs, and other roadblocks to Muffy's personal growth. Celia, a resident of Beverly Hills, is fully supported by a trust she set up to manage her investment funds, chiefly given to her 10 years ago by her father. She receives monthly distributions of various amounts, each made only after approval by the trustee.

    If Celia convinces the trustee to pay for Muffy's tuition, directly by a check from the trust to the school, are there any income tax consequences to Celia?

Partial list of research aids:
§ 677(b).
Frederick C. Braun, Jr., 48 TCM 210, T.C.Memo. 1984–285.

Research Problem 4.   Laura is the executor of her mother's estate. She is collecting assets and paying off liabilities as she finds them, as she is required to do under the terms of the will. Three months after her mother died, Laura received for the estate a check from her father for back alimony payments that were due her mother at the date of death. The alimony payment was sizable, and Laura had sufficient cash with which to meet the rest of the obligations of the estate, so she distributed $100,000 of the total $300,000 check to herself this year, as the estate's sole beneficiary.

    Laura has come to you to help her determine the proper income tax treatment for the alimony. She maintains it is a tax-free inheritance from the estate. Summarize your analysis in a memorandum to the tax research file.

Partial list of research aids:
§§682(b), 691.
Holloway v. U.S., 70–2 USTC ¶9548, 26 AFTR2d 70–5034, 428 F.2d 140 (CA–9, 1970).

Use the tax resources of the internet to address the following questions. Do not restrict your search to the World Wide Web, but include a review of newsgroups and general reference materials, practitioner sites and resources, primary sources of the tax law, chat rooms and discussion groups, and other opportunities.

Research Problem 5.   Summarize tax planning opportunities allowed under current law with respect to grantors and beneficiaries of foreign trusts. Provide full citations for the sources of your advice.

Research Problem 6.   What are the relative advantages and shortcomings of the traditional will, the living will, and the revocable trust? Do not limit your comments to tax consequences, but be certain to mention some pertinent tax effects.

Research Problem 7.   List some of the most important steps to be followed when an individual selects a trustee to manage his or her assets.

Appendix A
Tax Rate Schedules and Tables

1996 Tax Rate Schedules

Single—Schedule X

If taxable income is: Over—	But not over—	The tax is:		of the amount over—
$0	$ 24,000	...............15%		$0
24,000	58,150	$3,600.00 +	28%	24,000
58,150	121,300	13,162.00 +	31%	58,150
121,300	263,750	32,738.50 +	36%	121,300
263,750	....	84,020.50 +	39.6%	263,750

Head of household—Schedule Z

If taxable income is: Over—	But not over—	The tax is:		of the amount over—
$0	$ 32,150	...............15%		$0
32,150	83,050	$4,822.50 +	28%	32,150
83,050	134,500	19,074.50 +	31%	83,050
134,500	263,750	35,024.00 +	36%	134,500
263,750	....	81,554.00 +	39.6%	263,750

Married filing jointly or Qualifying widow(er)—Schedule Y-1

If taxable income is: Over—	But not over—	The tax is:		of the amount over—
$0	$ 40,100	...............15%		$0
40,100	96,900	$6,015.00 +	28%	40,100
96,900	147,700	21,919.00 +	31%	96,900
147,700	263,750	37,667.00 +	36%	147,700
263,750	....	79,445.00 +	39.6%	263,750

Married filing separately—Schedule Y-2

If taxable income is: Over—	But not over—	The tax is:		of the amount over—
$0	$ 20,050	...............15%		$0
20,050	48,450	$3,007.50 +	28%	20,050
48,450	73,850	10,959.50 +	31%	48,450
73,850	131,875	18,833.50 +	36%	73,850
131,875	....	39,722.50 +	39.6%	131,875

1997 Tax Rate Schedules

Single—Schedule X

If taxable income is: Over—	But not over—	The tax is:		of the amount over—
$0	$ 24,650	...............15%		$0
24,650	59,750	$3,697.50 +	28%	24,650
59,750	124,650	13,525.50 +	31%	59,750
124,650	271,050	33,644.50 +	36%	124,650
271,050	....	86,348.50 +	39.6%	271,050

Head of household—Schedule Z

If taxable income is: Over—	But not over—	The tax is:		of the amount over—
$0	$ 33,050	...............15%		$0
33,050	85,350	$4,957.50 +	28%	33,050
85,350	138,200	19,601.50 +	31%	85,350
138,200	271,050	35,985.00 +	36%	138,200
271,050	....	83,811.00 +	39.6%	271,050

Married filing jointly or Qualifying widow(er)—Schedule Y-1

If taxable income is: Over—	But not over—	The tax is:		of the amount over—
$0	$ 41,200	...............15%		$0
41,200	99,600	$6,180.00 +	28%	41,200
99,600	151,750	22,532.00 +	31%	99,600
151,750	271,050	38,698.50 +	36%	151,750
271,050	....	81,646.50 +	39.6%	271,050

Married filing separately—Schedule Y-2

If taxable income is: Over—	But not over—	The tax is:		of the amount over—
$0	$ 20,600	...............15%		$0
20,600	49,800	$3,090.00 +	28%	20,600
49,800	75,875	11,266.00 +	31%	49,800
75,875	135,525	19,349.25 +	36%	75,875
135,525	....	40,823.25 +	39.6%	135,525

INCOME TAX RATES—ESTATES AND TRUSTS

TAX YEAR 1996

Taxable Income		The Tax Is:	Of the Amount
Over—	But not Over—		Over—
$ 0	$1,600	15%	$ 0
1,600	3,800	$ 240 + 28%	1,600
3,800	5,800	856 + 31%	3,800
5,800	7,900	1,476 + 36%	5,800
7,900	—	2,232 + 39.6%	7,900

TAX YEAR 1997

Taxable Income		The Tax Is:	Of the Amount
Over—	But not Over—		Over—
$ 0	$1,650	15%	$ 0
1,650	3,900	$ 247.50 + 28%	1,650
3,900	5,950	877.50 + 31%	3,900
5,950	8,100	1,513.00 + 36%	5,950
8,100	—	2,287.00 + 39.6%	8,100

INCOME TAX RATES—CORPORATIONS

Taxable Income			Of the Amount
Over—	But not Over—	Tax Is:	Over—
$ 0	$ 50,000	15%	$ 0
50,000	75,000	$ 7,500 + 25%	50,000
75,000	100,000	13,750 + 34%	75,000
100,000	335,000	22,250 + 39%	100,000
335,000	10,000,000	113,900 + 34%	335,000
10,000,000	15,000,000	3,400,000 + 35%	10,000,000
15,000,000	18,333,333	5,150,000 + 38%	15,000,000
18,333,333	—	35%	0

UNIFIED TRANSFER TAX RATES

FOR GIFTS MADE AND FOR DEATHS AFTER 1976 AND BEFORE 1982

If the Amount with Respect to Which the Tentative Tax to Be Computed Is:	The Tentative Tax Is:
Not over $10,000	18 percent of such amount.
Over $10,000 but not over $20,000	$1,800, plus 20 percent of the excess of such amount over $10,000.
Over $20,000 but not over $40,000	$3,800, plus 22 percent of the excess of such amount over $20,000.
Over $40,000 but not over $60,000	$8,200, plus 24 percent of the excess of such amount over $40,000.
Over $60,000 but not over $80,000	$13,000, plus 26 percent of the excess of such amount over $60,000.
Over $80,000 but not over $100,000	$18,200, plus 28 percent of the excess of such amount over $80,000.
Over $100,000 but not over $150,000	$23,800, plus 30 percent of the excess of such amount over $100,000.
Over $150,000 but not over $250,000	$38,800, plus 32 percent of the excess of such amount over $150,000.
Over $250,000 but not over $500,000	$70,800, plus 34 percent of the excess of such amount over $250,000.
Over $500,000 but not over $750,000	$155,800, plus 37 percent of the excess of such amount over $500,000.
Over $750,000 but not over $1,000,000	$248,300, plus 39 percent of the excess of such amount over $750,000.
Over $1,000,000 but not over $1,250,000	$345,800, plus 41 percent of the excess of such amount over $1,000,000.
Over $1,250,000 but not over $1,500,000	$448,300, plus 43 percent of the excess of such amount over $1,250,000.
Over $1,500,000 but not over $2,000,000	$555,800, plus 45 percent of the excess of such amount over $1,500,000.
Over $2,000,000 but not over $2,500,000	$780,800, plus 49 percent of the excess of such amount over $2,000,000.
Over $2,500,000 but not over $3,000,000	$1,025,800, plus 53 percent of the excess of such amount over $2,500,000.
Over $3,000,000 but not over $3,500,000	$1,290,800, plus 57 percent of the excess of such amount over $3,000,000.
Over $3,500,000 but not over $4,000,000	$1,575,800, plus 61 percent of the excess of such amount over $3,500,000.
Over $4,000,000 but not over $4,500,000	$1,880,800, plus 65 percent of the excess of such amount over $4,000,000.
Over $4,500,000 but not over $5,000,000	$2,205,800, plus 69 percent of the excess of such amount over $4,500,000.
Over $5,000,000	$2,550,800, plus 70 percent of the excess of such amount over $5,000,000.

UNIFIED TRANSFER TAX RATES

FOR GIFTS MADE AND FOR DEATHS IN 1982

If the Amount with Respect to Which the Tentative Tax to Be Computed Is:	The Tentative Tax Is:
Not over $10,000	18 percent of such amount.
Over $10,000 but not over $20,000	$1,800, plus 20 percent of the excess of such amount over $10,000.
Over $20,000 but not over $40,000	$3,800, plus 22 percent of the excess of such amount over $20,000.
Over $40,000 but not over $60,000	$8,200, plus 24 percent of the excess of such amount over $40,000.
Over $60,000 but not over $80,000	$13,000, plus 26 percent of the excess of such amount over $60,000.
Over $80,000 but not over $100,000	$18,200, plus 28 percent of the excess of such amount over $80,000.
Over $100,000 but not over $150,000	$23,800, plus 30 percent of the excess of such amount over $100,000.
Over $150,000 but not over $250,000	$38,800, plus 32 percent of the excess of such amount over $150,000.
Over $250,000 but not over $500,000	$70,800, plus 34 percent of the excess of such amount over $250,000.
Over $500,000 but not over $750,000	$155,800, plus 37 percent of the excess of such amount over $500,000.
Over $750,000 but not over $1,000,000	$248,300, plus 39 percent of the excess of such amount over $750,000.
Over $1,000,000 but not over $1,250,000	$345,800, plus 41 percent of the excess of such amount over $1,000,000.
Over $1,250,000 but not over $1,500,000	$448,300, plus 43 percent of the excess of such amount over $1,250,000.
Over $1,500,000 but not over $2,000,000	$555,800, plus 45 percent of the excess of such amount over $1,500,000.
Over $2,000,000 but not over $2,500,000	$780,800, plus 49 percent of the excess of such amount over $2,000,000.
Over $2,500,000 but not over $3,000,000	$1,025,800, plus 53 percent of the excess of such amount over $2,500,000.
Over $3,000,000 but not over $3,500,000	$1,290,800, plus 57 percent of the excess of such amount over $3,000,000.
Over $3,500,000 but not over $4,000,000	$1,575,800, plus 61 percent of the excess of such amount over $3,500,000.
Over $4,000,000.	$1,880,800, plus 65 percent of the excess of such amount over $4,000,000.

UNIFIED TRANSFER TAX RATES

FOR GIFTS MADE AND FOR DEATHS IN 1983

If the Amount with Respect to Which the Tentative Tax to Be Computed Is:	The Tentative Tax Is:
Not over $10,000	18 percent of such amount.
Over $10,000 but not over $20,000	$1,800, plus 20 percent of the excess of such amount over $10,000.
Over $20,000 but not over $40,000	$3,800, plus 22 percent of the excess of such amount over $20,000.
Over $40,000 but not over $60,000	$8,200, plus 24 percent of the excess of such amount over $40,000.
Over $60,000 but not over $80,000	$13,000, plus 26 percent of the excess of such amount over $60,000.
Over $80,000 but not over $100,000	$18,200, plus 28 percent of the excess of such amount over $80,000.
Over $100,000 but not over $150,000	$23,800, plus 30 percent of the excess of such amount over $100,000.
Over $150,000 but not over $250,000	$38,800, plus 32 percent of the excess of such amount over $150,000.
Over $250,000 but not over $500,000	$70,800, plus 34 percent of the excess of such amount over $250,000.
Over $500,000 but not over $750,000	$155,800, plus 37 percent of the excess of such amount over $500,000.
Over $750,000 but not over $1,000,000	$248,300, plus 39 percent of the excess of such amount over $750,000.
Over $1,000,000 but not over $1,250,000	$345,800, plus 41 percent of the excess of such amount over $1,000,000.
Over $1,250,000 but not over $1,500,000	$448,300, plus 43 percent of the excess of such amount over $1,250,000.
Over $1,500,000 but not over $2,000,000	$555,800, plus 45 percent of the excess of such amount over $1,500,000.
Over $2,000,000 but not over $2,500,000	$780,800, plus 49 percent of the excess of such amount over $2,000,000.
Over $2,500,000 but not over $3,000,000	$1,025,800, plus 53 percent of the excess of such amount over $2,500,000.
Over $3,000,000 but not over $3,500,000	$1,290,800, plus 57 percent of the excess of such amount over $3,000,000.
Over $3,500,000	$1,575,800, plus 60 percent of the excess of such amount over $3,500,000.

Unified Transfer Tax Rates

FOR GIFTS MADE AND FOR DEATHS AFTER 1983

If the Amount with Respect to Which the Tentative Tax to Be Computed Is:	The Tentative Tax Is:
Not over $10,000	18 percent of such amount.
Over $10,000 but not over $20,000	$1,800, plus 20 percent of the excess of such amount over $10,000.
Over $20,000 but not over $40,000	$3,800, plus 22 percent of the excess of such amount over $20,000.
Over $40,000 but not over $60,000	$8,200, plus 24 percent of the excess of such amount over $40,000.
Over $60,000 but not over $80,000	$13,000, plus 26 percent of the excess of such amount over $60,000.
Over $80,000 but not over $100,000	$18,200, plus 28 percent of the excess of such amount over $80,000.
Over $100,000 but not over $150,000	$23,800, plus 30 percent of the excess of such amount over $100,000.
Over $150,000 but not over $250,000	$38,800, plus 32 percent of the excess of such amount over $150,000.
Over $250,000 but not over $500,000	$70,800, plus 34 percent of the excess of such amount over $250,000.
Over $500,000 but not over $750,000	$155,800, plus 37 percent of the excess of such amount over $500,000.
Over $750,000 but not over $1,000,000	$248,300, plus 39 percent of the excess of such amount over $750,000.
Over $1,000,000 but not over $1,250,000	$345,800, plus 41 percent of the excess of such amount over $1,000,000.
Over $1,250,000 but not over $1,500,000	$448,300, plus 43 percent of the excess of such amount over $1,250,000.
Over $1,500,000 but not over $2,000,000	$555,800, plus 45 percent of the excess of such amount over $1,500,000.
Over $2,000,000 but not over $2,500,000	$780,800, plus 49 percent of the excess of such amount over $2,000,000.
Over $2,500,000 but not over $3,000,000	$1,025,800, plus 53 percent of the excess of such amount over $2,500,000.
Over $3,000,000*	$1,290,800, plus 55 percent of the excess of such amount over $3,000,000.

*For large taxable transfers (generally in excess of $10 million) there is a phase-out of the graduated rates and the unified tax credit.

ESTATE TAX RATES (BEFORE 1977)

(A)	(B)	(C)	(D)
Taxable Estate Equal to or More Than	Taxable Estate Less Than	Tax on Amount in Column (A)	Rate of Tax on Excess Over Amount in Column (A) (Percentage)
0	$ 5,000	0	3
$ 5,000	10,000	$ 150	7
10,000	20,000	500	11
20,000	30,000	1,600	14
30,000	40,000	3,000	18
40,000	50,000	4,800	22
50,000	60,000	7,000	25
60,000	100,000	9,500	28
100,000	250,000	20,700	30
250,000	500,000	65,700	32
500,000	750,000	145,700	35
750,000	1,000,000	233,200	37
1,000,000	1,250,000	325,700	39
1,250,000	1,500,000	423,200	42
1,500,000	2,000,000	528,200	45
2,000,000	2,500,000	753,200	49
2,500,000	3,000,000	998,200	53
3,000,000	3,500,000	1,263,200	56
3,500,000	4,000,000	1,543,200	59
4,000,000	5,000,000	1,838,200	63
5,000,000	6,000,000	2,468,200	67
6,000,000	7,000,000	3,138,200	70
7,000,000	8,000,000	3,838,200	73
8,000,000	10,000,000	4,568,200	76
10,000,000		6,088,200	77

GIFT TAX RATES (BEFORE 1977)

(A) Amount of Taxable Gifts Equal to or More Than	(B) Amount of Taxable Gifts Less Than	(C) Tax on Amount in Column (A)	(D) Rate of Tax on Excess Over Amount in Column (A) (Percentage)
0	$ 5,000	0	2¼
$ 5,000	10,000	$ 112.50	5¼
10,000	20,000	375.00	8¼
20,000	30,000	1,200.00	10½
30,000	40,000	2,250.00	13½
40,000	50,000	3,600.00	16½
50,000	60,000	5,250.00	18¾
60,000	100,000	7,125.00	21
100,000	250,000	15,525.00	22½
250,000	500,000	49,275.00	24
500,000	750,000	109,275.00	26¼
750,000	1,000,000	174,900.00	27¾
1,000,000	1,250,000	244,275.00	29¼
1,250,000	1,500,000	317,400.00	31½
1,500,000	2,000,000	396,150.00	33¾
2,000,000	2,500,000	564,900.00	36¾
2,500,000	3,000,000	748,650.00	39¾
3,000,000	3,500,000	947,400.00	42
3,500,000	4,000,000	1,157,400.00	44¼
4,000,000	5,000,000	1,378,650.00	47¼
5,000,000	6,000,000	1,851,150.00	50¼
6,000,000	7,000,000	2,353,650.00	52½
7,000,000	8,000,000	2,878,650.00	54¾
8,000,000	10,000,000	3,426,150.00	57
10,000,000		4,566,150.00	57¾

TABLE FOR COMPUTATION OF MAXIMUM CREDIT FOR STATE DEATH TAXES

(A) Adjusted Taxable Estate* Equal to or More Than	(B) Adjusted Taxable Estate* Less Than	(C) Credit on Amount in Column (A)	(D) Rate of Credit on Excess Over Amount in Column (A) (Percentage)
0	$ 40,000	0	None
$ 40,000	90,000	0	0.8
90,000	140,000	$ 400	1.6
140,000	240,000	1,200	2.4
240,000	440,000	3,600	3.2
440,000	640,000	10,000	4.0
640,000	840,000	18,000	4.8
840,000	1,040,000	27,600	5.6
1,040,000	1,540,000	38,800	6.4
1,540,000	2,040,000	70,800	7.2
2,040,000	2,540,000	106,800	8.0
2,540,000	3,040,000	146,800	8.8
3,040,000	3,540,000	190,800	9.6
3,540,000	4,040,000	238,800	10.4
4,040,000	5,040,000	290,800	11.2
5,040,000	6,040,000	402,800	12.0
6,040,000	7,040,000	522,800	12.8
7,040,000	8,040,000	650,800	13.6
8,040,000	9,040,000	786,800	14.4
9,040,000	10,040,000	930,800	15.2
10,040,000		1,082,800	16.0

*Adjusted Taxable Estate = Taxable Estate − $60,000

Valuation Tables (After April 30, 1989)

Table S   Single Life Remainder Factors Interest Rate

Age	7.4%	7.6%	7.8%	8.0%	8.2%	8.4%	8.6%	8.8%
0	.02676	.02579	.02492	.02413	.02341	.02276	.02217	.02163
1	.01587	.01486	.01395	.01312	.01237	.01170	.01108	.01052
2	.01609	.01504	.01408	.01321	.01243	.01172	.01107	.01048
3	.01662	.01552	.01451	.01361	.01278	.01203	.01135	.01073
4	.01735	.01619	.01514	.01418	.01332	.01253	.01182	.01116
5	.01822	.01700	.01590	.01490	.01400	.01317	.01241	.01172
6	.01919	.01792	.01677	.01572	.01477	.01390	.01310	.01238
7	.02027	.01894	.01773	.01664	.01563	.01472	.01389	.01312
8	.02146	.02007	.01881	.01766	.01660	.01564	.01477	.01396
9	.02278	.02133	.02000	.01880	.01770	.01669	.01577	.01492
10	.02423	.02271	.02133	.02006	.01891	.01785	.01688	.01599
11	.02583	.02424	.02279	.02147	.02026	.01915	.01814	.01720
12	.02755	.02589	.02438	.02299	.02173	.02056	.01950	.01852
13	.02934	.02761	.02603	.02458	.02326	.02204	.02092	.01989
14	.03113	.02933	.02768	.02617	.02478	.02351	.02234	.02126
15	.03290	.03103	.02930	.02773	.02628	.02495	.02372	.02259
16	.03466	.03270	.03090	.02926	.02774	.02635	.02507	.02388
17	.03638	.03434	.03247	.03075	.02917	.02772	.02637	.02513
18	.03812	.03599	.03404	.03225	.03059	.02907	.02767	.02637
19	.03990	.03769	.03565	.03378	.03205	.03046	.02899	.02763
20	.04173	.03943	.03731	.03535	.03355	.03188	.03035	.02892
21	.04362	.04122	.03901	.03697	.03509	.03334	.03173	.03024
22	.04559	.04309	.04078	.03865	.03669	.03487	.03318	.03162
23	.04766	.04505	.04265	.04042	.03837	.03646	.03470	.03306
24	.04987	.04715	.04465	.04233	.04018	.03819	.03634	.03463
25	.05224	.04941	.04680	.04438	.04214	.04006	.03812	.03633
26	.05481	.05187	.04915	.04662	.04428	.04210	.04008	.03820
27	.05759	.05454	.05170	.04906	.04662	.04434	.04223	.04025
28	.06059	.05740	.05445	.05170	.04915	.04677	.04456	.04249
29	.06380	.06049	.05742	.05456	.05189	.04941	.04709	.04493
30	.06725	.06381	.06061	.05763	.05485	.05226	.04984	.04757
31	.07095	.06738	.06405	.06095	.05805	.05535	.05282	.05045
32	.07491	.07120	.06774	.06451	.06149	.05867	.05603	.05356
33	.07913	.07529	.07170	.06834	.06520	.06226	.05950	.05692
34	.08363	.07964	.07592	.07243	.06916	.06609	.06322	.06052

Valuation Tables
(After April 30, 1989, *continued*)

TABLE S   SINGLE LIFE REMAINDER FACTORS INTEREST RATE

Age	7.4%	7.6%	7.8%	8.0%	8.2%	8.4%	8.6%	8.8%
35	.08841	.08428	.08041	.07679	.07339	.07020	.06720	.06439
36	.09344	.08917	.08516	.08140	.07787	.07455	.07143	.06850
37	.09876	.09433	.09018	.08628	.08262	.07917	.07593	.07287
38	.10436	.09978	.09549	.09145	.08765	.08407	.08069	.07751
39	.11025	.10553	.10109	.09690	.09296	.08925	.08574	.08243
40	.11644	.11157	.10698	.10266	.09858	.09472	.09109	.08765
41	.12294	.11792	.11318	.10871	.10449	.10050	.09673	.09316
42	.12973	.12456	.11967	.11505	.11069	.10656	.10265	.09895
43	.13682	.13149	.12645	.12169	.11718	.11291	.10887	.10503
44	.14421	.13873	.13355	.12864	.12399	.11958	.11540	.11143
45	.15192	.14630	.14096	.13591	.13111	.12656	.12224	.11814
46	.15995	.15418	.14870	.14350	.13856	.13387	.12941	.12516
47	.16830	.16238	.15676	.15141	.14633	.14150	.13690	.13252
48	.17696	.17090	.16513	.15964	.15442	.14945	.14471	.14020
49	.18591	.17970	.17379	.16816	.16280	.15769	.15281	.14816
50	.19514	.18879	.18274	.17697	.17147	.16622	.16121	.15643
51	.20466	.19818	.19199	.18609	.18045	.17507	.16993	.16501
52	.21453	.20791	.20159	.19556	.18979	.18427	.17899	.17394
53	.22474	.21799	.21154	.20537	.19947	.19383	.18842	.18324
54	.23526	.22839	.22181	.21552	.20950	.20372	.19819	.19288
55	.24611	.23912	.23243	.22601	.21986	.21397	.20831	.20288
56	.25728	.25019	.24338	.23685	.23058	.22457	.21879	.21324
57	.26881	.26161	.25469	.24805	.24167	.23554	.22965	.22399
58	.28069	.27339	.26637	.25962	.25314	.24690	.24090	.23512
59	.29290	.28550	.27839	.27155	.26497	.25863	.25252	.24664
60	.30540	.29792	.29073	.28379	.27712	.27068	.26448	.25849
61	.31817	.31062	.30334	.29633	.28956	.28304	.27674	.27067
62	.33117	.32356	.31621	.30912	.30228	.29567	.28929	.28312
63	.34441	.33674	.32933	.32217	.31525	.30857	.30211	.29586
64	.35789	.35016	.34270	.33548	.32851	.32176	.31522	.30890
65	.37166	.36390	.35639	.34912	.34209	.33528	.32868	.32229
66	.38576	.37797	.37043	.36312	.35604	.34918	.34253	.33609
67	.40019	.39238	.38482	.37749	.37037	.36347	.35678	.35028
68	.41494	.40713	.39956	.39221	.38508	.37815	.37142	.36489
69	.42995	.42215	.41458	.40722	.40008	.39313	.38638	.37982

VALUATION TABLES
(AFTER APRIL 30, 1989, *continued*)

TABLE S   SINGLE LIFE REMAINDER FACTORS INTEREST RATE

Age	7.4%	7.6%	7.8%	8.0%	8.2%	8.4%	8.6%	8.8%
70	.44516	.43738	.42983	.42248	.41533	.40838	.40162	.39504
71	.46051	.45276	.44523	.43790	.43076	.42382	.41705	.41047
72	.47599	.46829	.46079	.45349	.44638	.43945	.43269	.42611
73	.49161	.48397	.47652	.46926	.46218	.45527	.44854	.44197
74	.50744	.49986	.49247	.48527	.47823	.47137	.46466	.45812
75	.52351	.51601	.50870	.50156	.49459	.48777	.48112	.47462
76	.53984	.53245	.52522	.51817	.51127	.50452	.49793	.49148
77	.55639	.54912	.54200	.53504	.52823	.52157	.51505	.50867
78	.57310	.56596	.55896	.55212	.54541	.53885	.53242	.52613
79	.58983	.58283	.57597	.56925	.56267	.55621	.54989	.54369
80	.60646	.59961	.59290	.58632	.57987	.57354	.56733	.56125
81	.62283	.61615	.60959	.60316	.59685	.59065	.58457	.57860
82	.63886	.63235	.62595	.61968	.61351	.60746	.60151	.59567
83	.65447	.64813	.64191	.63579	.62978	.62387	.61806	.61236
84	.66969	.66353	.65748	.65153	.64567	.63992	.63426	.62869
85	.68456	.67859	.67271	.66693	.66125	.65565	.65014	.64472
86	.69896	.69318	.68748	.68188	.67636	.67092	.66557	.66030
87	.71271	.70711	.70159	.69616	.69081	.68554	.68034	.67522
88	.72588	.72046	.71512	.70986	.70468	.69957	.69453	.68956
89	.73870	.73347	.72831	.72323	.71821	.71326	.70838	.70357
90	.75129	.74625	.74128	.73638	.73153	.72676	.72204	.71739
91	.76349	.75864	.75385	.74913	.74447	.73986	.73532	.73083
92	.77499	.77033	.76572	.76118	.75669	.75225	.74787	.74354
93	.78568	.78120	.77677	.77239	.76807	.76379	.75957	.75540
94	.79547	.79115	.78688	.78266	.77849	.77437	.77030	.76627
95	.80431	.80014	.79602	.79195	.78792	.78394	.78001	.77611
96	.81215	.80812	.80414	.80019	.79630	.79244	.78863	.78485
97	.81927	.81537	.81151	.80769	.80391	.80016	.79646	.79280
98	.82569	.82190	.81815	.81443	.81076	.80712	.80352	.79996
99	.83161	.82792	.82427	.82066	.81709	.81354	.81004	.80657
100	.83711	.83352	.82997	.82644	.82296	.81950	.81609	.81270
101	.84236	.83886	.83539	.83196	.82855	.82518	.82185	.81854
102	.84782	.84442	.84104	.83770	.83438	.83110	.82785	.82462
103	.85362	.85031	.84703	.84378	.84056	.83737	.83420	.83106
104	.86005	.85686	.85369	.85054	.84743	.84433	.84127	.83822

VALUATION TABLES
(AFTER APRIL 30, 1989, *continued*)

TABLE S   SINGLE LIFE REMAINDER FACTORS INTEREST RATE

Age	7.4%	7.6%	7.8%	8.0%	8.2%	8.4%	8.6%	8.8%
105	.86800	.86494	.86191	.85890	.85591	.85295	.85001	.84709
106	.87940	.87656	.87374	.87094	.86816	.86540	.86266	.85993
107	.89584	.89334	.89085	.88838	.88592	.88348	.88105	.87863
108	.92250	.92060	.91870	.91681	.91493	.91306	.91119	.90934
109	.96555	.96468	.96382	.96296	.96211	.96125	.96041	.95956

VALUATION TABLES
(AFTER APRIL 30, 1989, *continued*)

TABLE B   TERM CERTAIN REMAINDER FACTORS
INTEREST RATE

Years	7.4%	7.6%	7.8%	8.0%	8.2%	8.4%	8.6%	8.8%
1	.931099	.929368	.927644	.925926	.924214	.922509	.920810	.919118
2	.866945	.863725	.860523	.857339	.854172	.851023	.847892	.844777
3	.807211	.802718	.798259	.793832	.789438	.785077	.780747	.776450
4	.751593	.746021	.740500	.735030	.729610	.724241	.718920	.713649
5	.699808	.693328	.686920	.680583	.674316	.668119	.661989	.655927
6	.651590	.644357	.637217	.630170	.623213	.616346	.609566	.602874
7	.606694	.598845	.591111	.583490	.575982	.568585	.561295	.554112
8	.564892	.556547	.548340	.540269	.532331	.524524	.516846	.509294
9	.525971	.517237	.508664	.500249	.491988	.483879	.475917	.468101
10	.489731	.480704	.471859	.463193	.454703	.446383	.438230	.430240
11	.455987	.446750	.437717	.428883	.420243	.411792	.403526	.395441
12	.424569	.415196	.406046	.397114	.388394	.379882	.371571	.363457
13	.395316	.385870	.376666	.367698	.358960	.350445	.342147	.334060
14	.368078	.358615	.349412	.340461	.331756	.323288	.315052	.307040
15	.342717	.333285	.324130	.315242	.306613	.298236	.290103	.282206
16	.319103	.309745	.300677	.291890	.283376	.275126	.267130	.259381
17	.297117	.287867	.278921	.270269	.261901	.253806	.245976	.238401
18	.276645	.267534	.258739	.250249	.242052	.234139	.226497	.219119
19	.257584	.248638	.240018	.231712	.223708	.215995	.208561	.201396
20	.239836	.231076	.222651	.214548	.206754	.199257	.192045	.185107
21	.223311	.214755	.206541	.198656	.191085	.183817	.176837	.170135
22	.207925	.199586	.191596	.183941	.176604	.169573	.162834	.156374
23	.193598	.185489	.177733	.170315	.163220	.156432	.149939	.143726
24	.180259	:172387	.164873	.157699	.150850	.144310	.138065	.132101
25	.167839	.160211	.152943	.146018	.139418	.133128	.127132	.121416
26	.156275	.148895	.141877	.135202	.128852	.122811	.117064	.111596
27	.145507	.138379	.131611	.125187	.119087	.113295	.107794	.102570
28	.135482	.128605	.122088	.115914	.110062	.104515	.099258	.094274
29	.126147	.119521	.113255	.107328	.101721	.096416	.091398	.086649
30	.117455	.111079	.105060	.099377	.094012	.088945	.084160	.079640
31	.109362	.103233	.097458	.092016	.086887	.082053	.077495	.073199
32	.101827	.095942	.090406	.085200	.080302	.075694	.071358	.067278
33	.094811	.089165	.083865	.078889	.074216	.069829	.065708	.061837
34	.088278	.082867	.077797	.073045	.068592	.064418	.060504	.056835
35	.082196	.077014	.072168	.067635	.063394	.059426	.055713	.052238

VALUATION TABLES
(AFTER APRIL 30, 1989, *continued*)

TABLE B   TERM CERTAIN REMAINDER FACTORS
INTEREST RATE

Years	7.4%	7.6%	7.8%	8.0%	8.2%	8.4%	8.6%	8.8%
36	.076532	.071574	.066946	.062625	.058589	.054821	.051301	.048013
37	.071259	.066519	.062102	.057986	.054149	.050573	.047239	.044130
38	.066349	.061821	.057609	.053690	.050045	.046654	.043498	.040560
39	.061778	.057454	.053440	.049713	.046253	.043039	.040053	.037280
40	.057521	.053396	.049573	.046031	.042747	.039703	.036881	.034264
41	.053558	.049625	.045987	.042621	.039508	.036627	.033961	.031493
42	.049868	.046120	.042659	.039464	.036514	.033789	.031271	.028946
43	.046432	.042862	.039572	.036541	.033746	.031170	.028795	.026605
44	.043233	.039835	.036709	.033834	.031189	.028755	.026515	.024453
45	.040254	.037021	.034053	.031328	.028825	.026527	.024415	.022475
46	.037480	.034406	.031589	.029007	.026641	.024471	.022482	.020657
47	.034898	.031976	.029303	.026859	.024622	.022575	.020701	.018986
48	.032493	.029717	.027183	.024869	.022756	.020825	.019062	.017451
49	.030255	.027618	.025216	.023027	.021031	.019212	.017552	.016039
50	.028170	.025668	.023392	.021321	.019437	.017723	.016163	.014742
51	.026229	.023855	.021699	.019742	.017964	.016350	.014833	.013550
52	.024422	.022170	.020129	.018280	.016603	.015083	.013704	.012454
53	.022739	.020604	.018673	.016925	.015345	.013914	.012619	.011446
54	.021172	.019149	.017322	.015672	.014182	.012836	.011620	.010521
55	.019714	.017796	.016068	.014511	.013107	.011841	.010699	.009670
56	.018355	.016539	.014906	.013436	.012114	.010923	.009852	.008888
57	.017091	.015371	.013827	.012441	.011196	.010077	.009072	.008169
58	.015913	.014285	.012827	.011519	.010347	.009296	.008354	.007508
59	.014817	.013276	.011899	.010666	.009563	.008576	.007692	.006901
60	.013796	.012339	.011038	.009876	.008838	.007911	.007083	.006343

APPENDIX B
Tax Forms

Form **656**
(Rev. Sept. 1993)

Department of the Treasury—Internal Revenue Service
Offer in Compromise

► See Instructions
Page 5

(1) Name and Address of Taxpayers	For Official Use Only	
	Offer is (*Check applicable box*) ☐ Cash (*Paid in full*) ☐ Deferred payment	Serial Number
		(*Cashier's stamp*)

(2) Social Security Number	(3) Employer Identification Number	Alpha CSED Incl. _____
To: **Commissioner of Internal Revenue Service**		Amount Paid $

(4) **I/we** (includes all types of taxpayers) **submit this offer to compromise the tax liabilities plus any interest, penalties, additions to tax, and additional amounts required by law (tax liability)** for the tax type and period checked below: (Please mark "X" for the correct description and fill in the correct tax period(s), adding additional periods if needed.)

☐ Income tax for the year(s) 19 _____ , 19 _____ , and 19 _____

☐ Trust fund recovery penalty (formerly called the 100-percent penalty) as a responsible person of _____
_____ (enter business name) for failure to pay withholding and Federal Insurance Contribution Act taxes (Social Security taxes), for the period(s) ended _____ /_____ /_____ , _____ /_____ /_____ , _____ /_____ /_____ , _____ /_____ /_____ (for example - 06/30/92)

☐ Withholding and Federal Insurance Contributions Act taxes (Social Secuirty taxes) for the period(s) ended _____ /_____ /_____ , _____ /_____ , _____ /_____ /_____ , _____ /_____ /_____ (for example - 06/30/92)

☐ Federal Unemployment Tax Act taxes for the year(s) 19 _____ , 19 _____ , and 19 _____

☐ Other (Be specific.) _____

(5) **I/we offer to pay $**_____

If you aren't making full payment with your offer, describe below when you will make full payment (for example–within ten (10) days from the date the offer is accepted). See the instructions for Item 5.

_____

_____

_____

As required by section 6621 of the Internal Revenue Code, the Internal Revenue Service (IRS) will add interest to the offered amount from the date IRS accepts the offer until the date you can completely pay the amount offered. IRS compounds interest daily, as required by section 6622 of the Internal Revenue Code.

(6) **I/we submit this offer for the reason(s) checked below.**

☐ Doubt as to collectibility ("I can't pay.") You must include a completed financial statement (Form 433-A and/or Form 433-B).

☐ Doubt as to liability ("I don't believe I owe this tax.") You must include a detailed explanation of the reason(s) why you believe you don't owe the tax.

IMPORTANT: SEE REVERSE FOR TERMS AND CONDITIONS

I accept waiver of the statutory period of limitations for the Internal Revenue Service.	Under penalties of perjury, I declare that I have examined this offer. Including accompanying schedules and statements, and to the best of my knowledge and belief, it is true, correct and complete.	
Signature of authorized Internal Revenue Service Officer	(8a) Signature of Taxpayer proponent	Date
Title Date	(8b) Signature of Taxpayer proponent	Date

Dispose of prior issues.   **Part 1 IRS Copy**   Cat. No. 16728N   Form **656** (Rev. 9-93)

Form **709**	**United States Gift (and Generation-Skipping Transfer) Tax Return**	
(Rev. December 1996)	(Section 6019 of the Internal Revenue Code) (For gifts made after December 31, 1991)	OMB No. 1545-0020

Department of the Treasury
Internal Revenue Service

Calendar year 19 ....

▶ **See separate instructions. For Privacy Act Notice, see the Instructions for Form 1040.**

Part 1—General Information

1 Donor's first name and middle initial	2 Donor's last name	3 **Donor's social security number**
4 Address (number, street, and apartment number)		5 Legal residence (domicile) (county and state)
6 City, state, and ZIP code		7 Citizenship

		Yes	No
8	If the donor died during the year, check here ▶ ☐ and enter date of death................ , ...		
9	If you received an extension of time to file this Form 709, check here ▶ ☐ and attach the Form 4868, 2688, 2350, or extension letter		
10	Enter the total number of separate donees listed on Schedule A—count each person only once. ▶		
11a	Have you (the donor) previously filed a Form 709 (or 709-A) for any other year? If the answer is "No," do not complete line 11b .		
11b	If the answer to line 11a is "Yes," has your address changed since you last filed Form 709 (or 709-A)?		
12	Gifts by husband or wife to third parties.—Do you consent to have the gifts (including generation-skipping transfers) made by you and by your spouse to third parties during the calendar year considered as made one-half by each of you? (See instructions.) (If the answer is "Yes," the following information must be furnished and your spouse must sign the consent shown below. **If the answer is "No," skip lines 13–18 and go to Schedule A.**)		
13	Name of consenting spouse 14 SSN		
15	Were you married to one another during the entire calendar year? (see instructions)		
16	If the answer to 15 is "No," check whether ☐ married ☐ divorced or ☐ widowed, and give date (see instructions) ▶		
17	Will a gift tax return for this calendar year be filed by your spouse?		
18	Consent of Spouse—I consent to have the gifts (and generation-skipping transfers) made by me and by my spouse to third parties during the calendar year considered as made one-half by each of us. We are both aware of the joint and several liability for tax created by the execution of this consent.		

Consenting spouse's signature ▶   Date ▶

Part 2—Tax Computation

1	Enter the amount from Schedule A, Part 3, line 15	1	
2	Enter the amount from Schedule B, line 3	2	
3	Total taxable gifts (add lines 1 and 2)	3	
4	Tax computed on amount on line 3 (see Table for Computing Tax in separate instructions). . .	4	
5	Tax computed on amount on line 2 (see Table for Computing Tax in separate instructions). . .	5	
6	Balance (subtract line 5 from line 4)	6	
7	Maximum unified credit (nonresident aliens, see instructions)	7	192,800 00
8	Enter the unified credit against tax allowable for all prior periods (from Sch. B, line 1, col. C) . .	8	
9	Balance (subtract line 8 from line 7)	9	
10	Enter 20% (.20) of the amount allowed as a specific exemption for gifts made after September 8, 1976, and before January 1, 1977 (see instructions)	10	
11	Balance (subtract line 10 from line 9)	11	
12	Unified credit (enter the smaller of line 6 or line 11)	12	
13	Credit for foreign gift taxes (see instructions)	13	
14	Total credits (add lines 12 and 13)	14	
15	Balance (subtract line 14 from line 6) (do not enter less than zero)	15	
16	Generation-skipping transfer taxes (from Schedule C, Part 3, col. H, Total)	16	
17	Total tax (add lines 15 and 16)	17	
18	Gift and generation-skipping transfer taxes prepaid with extension of time to file	18	
19	If line 18 is less than line 17, enter BALANCE DUE (see instructions)	19	
20	If line 18 is greater than line 17, enter AMOUNT TO BE REFUNDED	20	

Under penalties of perjury, I declare that I have examined this return, including any accompanying schedules and statements, and to the best of my knowledge and belief it is true, correct, and complete. Declaration of preparer (other than donor) is based on all information of which preparer has any knowledge.

Donor's signature ▶ _____   Date ▶ _____

Preparer's signature
(other than donor) ▶ _____   Date ▶ _____

Preparer's address
(other than donor) ▶ _____

(left margin: Attach check or money order here.)

For Paperwork Reduction Act Notice, see page 1 of the separate instructions for this form.   Cat. No. 16783M   Form **709** (Rev. 12-96)

Form 709 (Rev. 12-96)

Page **2**

SCHEDULE A	Computation of Taxable Gifts

Does the value of any item listed on Schedule A reflect any valuation discount? If the answer is "Yes," see instructions . . . . Yes ☐ No ☐

Part 1—Gifts Subject Only to Gift Tax. *Gifts less political organization, medical, and educational exclusions—see instructions*

A Item number	B • Donee's name and address • Relationship to donor (if any) • Description of gift • If the gift was made by means of a trust, enter trust's identifying number and attach a copy of the trust instrument • If the gift was of securities, give CUSIP number	C Donor's adjusted basis of gift	D Date of gift	E Value at date of gift
1				

Total of Part 1 (add amounts from Part 1, column E) . . . . ▶

Part 2—Gifts That are Direct Skips and are Subject to Both Gift Tax and Generation-Skipping Transfer Tax. You must list the gifts in chronological order. *Gifts less political organization, medical, and educational exclusions—see instructions. (Also list here direct skips that are subject only to the GST tax at this time as the result of the termination of an "estate tax inclusion period." See instructions.)*

A Item number	B • Donee's name and address • Relationship to donor (if any) • Description of gift • If the gift was made by means of a trust, enter trust's identifying number and attach a copy of the trust instrument • If the gift was of securities, give CUSIP number	C Donor's adjusted basis of gift	D Date of gift	E Value at date of gift
1				

Total of Part 2 (add amounts from Part 2, column E) . . . . ▶

Part 3—Taxable Gift Reconciliation

1	Total value of gifts of donor (add totals from column E of Parts 1 and 2)	1	
2	One-half of items _____ attributable to spouse (see instructions)	2	
3	Balance (subtract line 2 from line 1)	3	
4	Gifts of spouse to be included (from Schedule A, Part 3, line 2 of spouse's return—see instructions) .	4	
	If any of the gifts included on this line are also subject to the generation-skipping transfer tax, check here ▶ ☐ and enter those gifts also on Schedule C, Part 1.		
5	Total gifts (add lines 3 and 4)	5	
6	Total annual exclusions for gifts listed on Schedule A (including line 4, above) (see instructions) . . .	6	
7	Total included amount of gifts (subtract line 6 from line 5)	7	

Deductions (see instructions)

8	Gifts of interests to spouse for which a marital deduction will be claimed, based on items _____ of Schedule A	8		
9	Exclusions attributable to gifts on line 8	9		
10	Marital deduction—subtract line 9 from line 8	10		
11	Charitable deduction, based on items _____ less exclusions . .	11		
12	Total deductions—add lines 10 and 11		12	
13	Subtract line 12 from line 7		13	
14	Generation-skipping transfer taxes payable with this Form 709 (from Schedule C, Part 3, col. H, Total)		14	
15	Taxable gifts (add lines 13 and 14). Enter here and on line 1 of the Tax Computation on page 1 . . .		15	

(If more space is needed, attach additional sheets of same size.)

Form 709 (Rev. 12-96)   Page **3**

SCHEDULE A	**Computation of Taxable Gifts** *(continued)*

16 Terminable Interest (QTIP) Marital Deduction. (See instructions for line 8 of Schedule A.)

If a trust (or other property) meets the requirements of qualified terminable interest property under section 2523(f), and

   a. The trust (or other property) is listed on Schedule A, and

   b. The value of the trust (or other property) is entered in whole or in part as a deduction on line 8, Part 3 of Schedule A,

then the donor shall be deemed to have made an election to have such trust (or other property) treated as qualified terminable interest property under section 2523(f).

If less than the entire value of the trust (or other property) that the donor has included in Part 1 of Schedule A is entered as a deduction on line 8, the donor shall be considered to have made an election only as to a fraction of the trust (or other property). The numerator of this fraction is equal to the amount of the trust (or other property) deducted on line 10 of Part 3, Schedule A. The denominator is equal to the total value of the trust (or other property) listed in Part 1 of Schedule A.

If you make the QTIP election (see instructions for line 8 of Schedule A), the terminable interest property involved will be included in your spouse's gross estate upon his or her death (section 2044). If your spouse disposes (by gift or otherwise) of all or part of the qualifying life income interest, he or she will be considered to have made a transfer of the entire property that is subject to the gift tax (see Transfer of Certain Life Estates on page 3 of the instructions).

17 Election Out of QTIP Treatment of Annuities

☐ ◀ Check here if you elect under section 2523(f)(6) **NOT** to treat as qualified terminable interest property any joint and survivor annuities that are reported on Schedule A and would otherwise be treated as qualified terminable interest property under section 2523(f). (See instructions.)
Enter the item numbers (from Schedule A) for the annuities for which you are making this election ▶

SCHEDULE B	**Gifts From Prior Periods**

If you answered "Yes" on line 11a of page 1, Part 1, see the instructions for completing Schedule B. If you answered "No," skip to the Tax Computation on page 1 (or Schedule C, if applicable).

A Calendar year or calendar quarter (see instructions)	**B** Internal Revenue office where prior return was filed	**C** Amount of unified credit against gift tax for periods after December 31, 1976	**D** Amount of specific exemption for prior periods ending before January 1, 1977	**E** Amount of taxable gifts

1 Totals for prior periods (without adjustment for reduced specific exemption) **1**

2 Amount, if any, by which total specific exemption, line 1, column D, is more than $30,000 . . . . . . **2**

3 Total amount of taxable gifts for prior periods (add amount, column E, line 1, and amount, if any, on line 2). (Enter here and on line 2 of the Tax Computation on page 1.) **3**

(If more space is needed, attach additional sheets of same size.)

Form 709 (Rev. 12-96)

SCHEDULE C	**Computation of Generation-Skipping Transfer Tax**

Note: *Inter vivos direct skips that are completely excluded by the GST exemption must still be fully reported (including value and exemptions claimed) on Schedule C.*

Part 1—Generation-Skipping Transfers

A Item No. (from Schedule A, Part 2, col. A)	B Value (from Schedule A, Part 2, col. E)	C Split Gifts (enter ½ of col. B) (see instructions)	D Subtract col. C from col. B	E Nontaxable portion of transfer	F Net Transfer (subtract col. E from col. D)
1					
2					
3					
4					
5					
6					

If you elected gift splitting and your spouse was required to file a separate Form 709 (see the instructions for "Split Gifts"), you must enter all of the gifts shown on Schedule A, Part 2, of your spouse's Form 709 here. In column C, enter the item number of each gift in the order it appears in column A of your spouse's Schedule A, Part 2. We have preprinted the prefix "S-" to distinguish your spouse's item numbers from your own when you complete column A of Schedule C, Part 3. In column D, for each gift, enter the amount reported in column C, Schedule C, Part 1, of your spouse's Form 709.	Split gifts from spouse's Form 709 (enter item number)	Value included from spouse's Form 709	Nontaxable portion of transfer	Net transfer (subtract col. E from col. D)
	S-			
	S-			
	S-			
	S-			
	S-			
	S-			
	S-			
	S-			

Part 2—GST Exemption Reconciliation (Section 2631) and Section 2652(a)(3) Election

Check box ▶ ☐ if you are making a section 2652(a)(3) (special QTIP) election (see instructions)

Enter the item numbers (from Schedule A) of the gifts for which you are making this election ▶ ....

1	Maximum allowable exemption	1	$1,000,000
2	Total exemption used for periods before filing this return	2	
3	Exemption available for this return (subtract line 2 from line 1)	3	
4	Exemption claimed on this return (from Part 3, col. C total, below)	4	
5	Exemption allocated to transfers not shown on Part 3, below. **You must attach a Notice of Allocation.** (See instructions.)	5	
6	Add lines 4 and 5	6	
7	Exemption available for future transfers (subtract line 6 from line 3)	7	

Part 3—Tax Computation

A Item No. (from Schedule C, Part 1)	B Net transfer (from Schedule C, Part 1, col. F)	C GST Exemption Allocated	D Divide col. C by col. B	E Inclusion Ratio (subtract col. D from 1.000)	F Maximum Estate Tax Rate	G Applicable Rate (multiply col. E by col. F)	H Generation-Skipping Transfer Tax (multiply col. B by col. G)
1					55% (.55)		
2					55% (.55)		
3					55% (.55)		
4					55% (.55)		
5					55% (.55)		
6					55% (.55)		
					55% (.55)		
					55% (.55)		
					55% (.55)		
Total exemption claimed. Enter here and on line 4, Part 2, above. May not exceed line 3, Part 2, above		**Total generation-skipping transfer tax.** Enter here, on line 14 of Schedule A, Part 3, and on line 16 of the Tax Computation on page 1					

(If more needed, attach additional sheets of same size.) ✪

Form **851**
(Rev. September 1994)
Department of the Treasury
Internal Revenue Service

Affiliations Schedule

▶ **File with each consolidated income tax return**

Tax year ending _____ , 19 _____

OMB No. 1545-0025

Common parent corporation	Employer identification number

Number, street, and room or suite no. (If a P.O. box, see instructions.)

City or town, state, and ZIP code

Part I   Prepayment Credits

No.	Name and address of corporation	Employer identification number	Prepayment Credits	
			Portion of Form 7004 tax deposits	Portion of estimated tax credits and deposits
1	Common parent corporation			
	Subsidiary corporations:			
2				
3				
4				
5				
6				
7				
8				
9				
10				

Totals (Must equal amounts shown on the consolidated tax return) . . . . ▶

Part II   Voting Stock Information, Principal Business Activity, Etc. (See instructions.)

No.	Principal business activity (PBA)	PBA Code No.	Did the subsidiary make any nondividend distributions? (See instructions.)		Stock holdings at beginning of year			
			Yes	No	Number of shares	Percent of voting power	Percent of value	Owned by corporation no.
1	Common parent corporation							
	Subsidiary corporations:							
2						%	%	
3						%	%	
4						%	%	
5						%	%	
6						%	%	
7						%	%	
8						%	%	
9						%	%	
10						%	%	

For Paperwork Reduction Act Notice, see instructions.   Cat. No. 16880G   Form **851** (Rev. 9-94)

Form 851 (Rev. 9-94)

Part III Changes in Stock Holdings During the Year (See instructions.)

	Corporation	Stock-holder (Corpora-tion No.)	Change in stock holdings during the year				
No.	Name		Date	(a) Changes		(b) Shares held after changes described in column (a)	
				Shares acquired	Shares disposed of	Percent of voting power	Percent of value
						%	%
						%	%
						%	%
						%	%
						%	%
						%	%
						%	%
						%	%
						%	%

Note: *If additional stock was issued, or if any stock was retired during the year, show the dates and amounts for these transactions.*

If the equitable owners of any capital stock shown above were other than the holders of record, give full details.

Form 851 (Rev. 9-94)   Page **3**

Part IV	Additional Information (See instructions.)

1   During the tax year, did the corporation have more than one class of stock outstanding?

No.	Name	Answer to Question 1		If yes, list and describe each class of stock.
		Yes	No	

2   During the tax year, was there any member of the consolidated group that reaffiliated within 60 months of disaffiliation, or was there any member of the affiliated group that was deconsolidated under Rev. Proc. 91-11, 1991-1 C.B. 470 (as modified by Rev. Proc. 91-39, 1991-2 C.B. 694)?

No.	Name	Answer to Question 2		If yes for any part of question 2, list and explain the circumstances.
		Yes	No	

3a   During the tax year, was there any arrangement in existence by which one or more persons that were not members of the affiliated group could acquire any stock, or acquire any voting power without acquiring stock, in the corporation, other than a de minimis amount, from the corporation or another member of the affiliated group?

No.	Name	Answer to Question 3a		Item 3b (see instructions)	Item 3c (see instructions)	Item 3d (see instructions)
		Yes	No			
				%	%	%
				%	%	%
				%	%	%
				%	%	%

No.	Item 3e—Description of arrangements.

Please Sign Here

Under penalties of perjury, I declare that I have examined this form, including accompanying statements, and to the best of my knowledge and belief, it is true, correct, and complete for the tax year as stated.

▶ _____ | _____ ▶ _____
     Signature of officer   Date   Title

Instructions

Section references are to the Internal Revenue Code.

Paperwork Reduction Act Notice

We ask for the information on this form to carry out the Internal Revenue laws of the United States. You are required to give us the information. We need it to ensure that you are complying with these laws and to allow us to figure and collect the right amount of tax.

The time needed to complete and file this form will vary depending on individual circumstances. The estimated average time is:

Recordkeeping . . . . 8 hr., 51 min.
**Learning about the
law or the form** . . . . . . 35 min.
**Preparing and sending
the form to the IRS** . . . . 46 min.

If you have comments concerning the accuracy of these time estimates or suggestions for making this form more simple, we would be happy to hear from you. You can write to both the IRS and the Office of Management and Budget at the addresses listed in the instructions for the tax return with which this form is filed.

Purpose of Form

Form 851 is filed by the parent corporation for itself and for corporations in the affiliated group. File Form 851 by attaching it to the consolidated tax return for the group.

Affiliated Group

The term "affiliated group" means one or more chains of includible corporations connected through stock ownership with a common parent corporation. See sections 1504(a) and (b). The common parent must be an includible corporation and the following requirements must be met:

1. The common parent must own directly stock that represents at least 80% of the total voting power and at least 80% of the total value of the stock of at least one of the other includible corporations.

2. Stock that represents at least 80% of the total voting power, and at least 80% of the total value of the stock of each of the other corporations (except for the common parent) must be owned directly by one or more of the other includible corporations.

For this purpose, the term "stock" generally does not include any stock that (1) is nonvoting, (2) is nonconvertible, (3) is limited and preferred as to dividends and does not participate significantly in corporate growth, and (4) has redemption and liquidation rights that do not exceed the issue price of the stock (except for a reasonable redemption or liquidation premium).

Address

Include the suite, room, or other unit number after the street address. If the Post Office does not deliver mail to the street address and the corporation has a P.O. box, show the box number instead of the street address.

Corporation Numbers

When listing information in Parts II, III, and IV, be sure to use the same number for each corporation as you used in Part I, page 1.

Part II

PBA (Principal Business Activity) code number.—Enter in Part II the PBA code number for the parent corporation and each subsidiary. A list of the PBA code numbers can be found in the Instructions for Forms 1120 and 1120-A. Use the code number for the specific industry group from which the largest percentage of each corporation's total receipts is derived.

Also list for each subsidiary the corresponding principal business activity on which the code is based.

Nondividend distributions.—For purposes of Part II, nondividend distributions are any distributions (other than stock dividends and distributions in exchange for stock) paid during the tax year for which the consolidated tax return is filed that were in excess of the corporation's current and accumulated earnings and profits. See sections 301 and 316.

Part IV

Question 1.—For purposes of Question 1 only, disregard section 1504(a)(4).

Question 3a.—The term "arrangement" includes, but is not limited to, phantom stock, stock appreciation rights, an option, warrant, conversion feature, or similar arrangement. If you answer "Yes" to question 3a, complete items 3b through 3e.

Item 3b.—If you answer "Yes" to question 3a, show the percentage of the value of the outstanding stock that the person(s) could acquire.

Item 3c.—If you answer "Yes" to question 3a, and the arrangement was associated with voting stock, show the percentage of outstanding voting stock that the person(s) could acquire.

Item 3d.—If you answer "Yes" to question 3a, and the arrangement was associated with the acquisition of voting power without the acquisition of the related stock, show the percentage of voting power that the person(s) could acquire.

Item 3e.—If you answer "Yes" to question 3a, give a brief description of any arrangement (defined above) by which a person that is not a member of the affiliated group could acquire any stock, or acquire any voting power without acquiring stock, in the corporation.

Form **870** (Rev. February 1986)	Department of the Treasury—Internal Revenue Service **Waiver of Restrictions on Assessment and Collection of Deficiency in Tax and Acceptance of Overassessment**	Date Received by Internal Revenue Service

Names and address of taxpayers (*Number, street, city or town, State, ZIP code*)	Social security or employer identification number

Increase (Decrease) in Tax and Penalties

Tax year ended	Tax	Penalties			
	$	$	$	$	$
	$	$	$	$	$
	$	$	$	$	$
	$	$	$	$	$
	$	$	$	$	$
	$	$	$	$	$
	$	$	$	$	$

(For instructions, see back of form)

Consent to Assessment and Collection

I consent to the immediate assessment and collection of any deficiencies (*increase in tax and penalties*) and accept any overassessment (*decrease in tax and penalties*) shown above, plus any interest provided by law. I understand that by signing this waiver, I will not be able to contest these years in the United States Tax Court, unless additional deficiencies are determined for these years.

Signatures			Date
			Date
	By	Title	Date

Form **870** (Rev. 2-86)

Form **990**

Department of the Treasury
Internal Revenue Service

Return of Organization Exempt From Income Tax

Under section 501(c) of the Internal Revenue Code (except black lung benefit trust or private foundation) or section 4947(a)(1) nonexempt charitable trust

Note: *The organization may have to use a copy of this return to satisfy state reporting requirements.*

OMB No. 1545-0047

19**96**

This Form is
Open to Public
Inspection

A For the 1996 calendar year, OR tax year period beginning _____ , 1996, and ending _____ , 19 ___

B Check if:
☐ Change of address
☐ Initial return
☐ Final return
☐ Amended return (required also for State reporting)

Please use IRS label or print or type. See Specific Instructions.

C Name of organization

Number and street (or P.O. box if mail is not delivered to street address) | Room/suite

City, town, or post office, state, and ZIP+4

D Employer identification number

E State registration number

F Check ▶ ☐ if exemption application is pending

G Type of organization ▶ ☐ Exempt under section 501(c)( ) ◀ (insert number) OR ▶ ☐ section 4947(a)(1) nonexempt charitable trust

Note: *Section 501(c)(3) exempt organizations and 4947(a)(1) nonexempt charitable trusts MUST attach a completed Schedule A (Form 990).*

H(a) Is this a group return filed for affiliates? . . . . ☐ Yes ☐ No

(b) If "Yes," enter the number of affiliates for which this return is filed: . ▶ _____

(c) Is this a separate return filed by an organization covered by a group ruling? ☐ Yes ☐ No

I If either box in H is checked "Yes," enter four-digit group exemption number (GEN) ▶ _____

J Accounting method: ☐ Cash ☐ Accrual
☐ Other (specify) ▶

K Check here ▶ ☐ if the organization's gross receipts are normally not more than $25,000. The organization need not file a return with the IRS; but if it received a Form 990 Package in the mail, it should file a return without financial data. **Some states require a complete return.**

Note: *Form 990-EZ may be used by organizations with gross receipts less than $100,000 and total assets less than $250,000 at end of year.*

Part I | **Revenue, Expenses, and Changes in Net Assets or Fund Balances** (See Specific Instructions on page 9.)

1	Contributions, gifts, grants, and similar amounts received:		
a	Direct public support	1a	
b	Indirect public support	1b	
c	Government contributions (grants)	1c	
d	**Total** (add lines 1a through 1c) (attach schedule of contributors) (cash $ _____ noncash $ _____)	1d	
2	Program service revenue including government fees and contracts (from Part VII, line 93)	2	
3	Membership dues and assessments	3	
4	Interest on savings and temporary cash investments	4	
5	Dividends and interest from securities	5	
6a	Gross rents	6a	
b	Less: rental expenses	6b	
c	Net rental income or (loss) (subtract line 6b from line 6a)	6c	
7	Other investment income (describe ▶)	7	
8a	Gross amount from sale of assets other than inventory	(A) Securities / 8a	(B) Other
b	Less: cost or other basis and sales expenses.	8b	
c	Gain or (loss) (attach schedule)	8c	
d	Net gain or (loss) (combine line 8c, columns (A) and (B))	8d	
9	Special events and activities (attach schedule)		
a	Gross revenue (not including $ _____ of contributions reported on line 1a)	9a	
b	Less: direct expenses other than fundraising expenses .	9b	
c	Net income or (loss) from special events (subtract line 9b from line 9a)	9c	
10a	Gross sales of inventory, less returns and allowances . .	10a	
b	Less: cost of goods sold	10b	
c	Gross profit or (loss) from sales of inventory (attach schedule) (subtract line 10b from line 10a) .	10c	
11	Other revenue (from Part VII, line 103)	11	
12	**Total revenue** (add lines 1d, 2, 3, 4, 5, 6c, 7, 8d, 9c, 10c, and 11)	12	
13	Program services (from line 44, column (B))	13	
14	Management and general (from line 44, column (C))	14	
15	Fundraising (from line 44, column (D))	15	
16	Payments to affiliates (attach schedule)	16	
17	**Total expenses** (add lines 16 and 44, column (A))	17	
18	Excess or (deficit) for the year (subtract line 17 from line 12)	18	
19	Net assets or fund balances at beginning of year (from line 73, column (A))	19	
20	Other changes in net assets or fund balances (attach explanation)	20	
21	Net assets or fund balances at end of year (combine lines 18, 19, and 20)	21	

(left margin labels: Revenue / Expenses / Net Assets)

For Paperwork Reduction Act Notice, see page 1 of the separate instructions.   Cat. No. 11282Y   Form **990** (1996)

Form 990 (1996)   Page **2**

Part II	**Statement of Functional Expenses**	All organizations must complete column (A). Columns (B), (C), and (D) are required for section 501(c)(3) and (4) organizations and section 4947(a)(1) nonexempt charitable trusts but optional for others. (See Specific Instructions on page 13.)

Do not include amounts reported on line 6b, 8b, 9b, 10b, or 16 of Part I.		**(A)** Total	**(B)** Program services	**(C)** Management and general	**(D)** Fundraising
22	Grants and allocations (attach schedule) . . (cash $ _____ noncash $ _____)	**22**			
23	Specific assistance to individuals (attach schedule)	**23**			
24	Benefits paid to or for members (attach schedule).	**24**			
25	Compensation of officers, directors, etc. . .	**25**			
26	Other salaries and wages	**26**			
27	Pension plan contributions	**27**			
28	Other employee benefits	**28**			
29	Payroll taxes	**29**			
30	Professional fundraising fees	**30**			
31	Accounting fees	**31**			
32	Legal fees	**32**			
33	Supplies	**33**			
34	Telephone	**34**			
35	Postage and shipping	**35**			
36	Occupancy	**36**			
37	Equipment rental and maintenance . . .	**37**			
38	Printing and publications	**38**			
39	Travel	**39**			
40	Conferences, conventions, and meetings . .	**40**			
41	Interest	**41**			
42	Depreciation, depletion, etc. (attach schedule)	**42**			
43	Other expenses (itemize): **a** _____	**43a**			
b	_____	**43b**			
c	_____	**43c**			
d	_____	**43d**			
e	_____	**43e**			
44	**Total functional expenses** (add lines 22 through 43) **Organizations completing columns (B)-(D), carry these totals to lines 13-15**	**44**			

Reporting of Joint Costs.—Did you report in column (B) (Program services) any joint costs from a combined educational campaign and fundraising solicitation? . . . . ▶ ☐ Yes ☐ No

If "Yes," enter **(i)** the aggregate amount of these joint costs $_____ ; **(ii)** the amount allocated to Program services $_____ ; **(iii)** the amount allocated to Management and general $_____ ; and **(iv)** the amount allocated to Fundraising $_____

Part III	**Statement of Program Service Accomplishments** (See Specific Instructions on page 16.)

What is the organization's primary exempt purpose? ▶ _____

	Program Service Expenses (Required for 501(c)(3) and (4) orgs., and 4947(a)(1) trusts; but optional for others.)

All organizations must describe their exempt purpose achievements. State the number of clients served, publications issued, etc. Discuss achievements that are not measurable. (Section 501(c)(3) and (4) organizations and 4947(a)(1) nonexempt charitable trusts must also enter the amount of grants and allocations to others.)

a _____
_____
_____ (Grants and allocations $ _____)

b _____
_____
_____ (Grants and allocations $ _____)

c _____
_____
_____ (Grants and allocations $ _____)

d _____
_____
_____ (Grants and allocations $ _____)

e Other program services (attach schedule)   (Grants and allocations $ _____)

f **Total of Program Service Expenses** (should equal line 44, column (B), Program services) . . . . . ▶

Form 990 (1996)

Part IV Balance Sheets (See Specific Instructions on page 16.)

			(A) Beginning of year		(B) End of year
Note:	*Where required, attached schedules and amounts within the description column should be for end-of-year amounts only.*				
	45 Cash—non-interest-bearing			**45**	
	46 Savings and temporary cash investments			**46**	
	47a Accounts receivable	**47a**			
	b Less: allowance for doubtful accounts	**47b**		**47c**	
	48a Pledges receivable	**48a**			
	b Less: allowance for doubtful accounts	**48b**		**48c**	
	49 Grants receivable			**49**	
	50 Receivables from officers, directors, trustees, and key employees (attach schedule)			**50**	
	51a Other notes and loans receivable (attach schedule)	**51a**			
	b Less: allowance for doubtful accounts	**51b**		**51c**	
	52 Inventories for sale or use			**52**	
	53 Prepaid expenses and deferred charges			**53**	
	54 Investments—securities (attach schedule)			**54**	
	55a Investments—land, buildings, and equipment: basis	**55a**			
	b Less: accumulated depreciation (attach schedule)	**55b**		**55c**	
	56 Investments—other (attach schedule)			**56**	
	57a Land, buildings, and equipment: basis	**57a**			
	b Less: accumulated depreciation (attach schedule)	**57b**		**57c**	
	58 Other assets (describe ▶ _____)			**58**	
	59 **Total assets** (add lines 45 through 58) (must equal line 74)			**59**	
	60 Accounts payable and accrued expenses			**60**	
	61 Grants payable			**61**	
	62 Deferred revenue			**62**	
	63 Loans from officers, directors, trustees, and key employees (attach schedule)			**63**	
	64a Tax-exempt bond liabilities (attach schedule)			**64a**	
	b Mortgages and other notes payable (attach schedule)			**64b**	
	65 Other liabilities (describe ▶ _____)			**65**	
	66 **Total liabilities** (add lines 60 through 65)			**66**	
	Organizations that follow SFAS 117, check here ▶ ☐ and complete lines 67 through 69 and lines 73 and 74.				
	67 Unrestricted			**67**	
	68 Temporarily restricted			**68**	
	69 Permanently restricted			**69**	
	Organizations that do not follow SFAS 117, check here ▶ ☐ and complete lines 70 through 74.				
	70 Capital stock, trust principal, or current funds			**70**	
	71 Paid-in or capital surplus, or land, building, and equipment fund			**71**	
	72 Retained earnings, endowment, accumulated income, or other funds			**72**	
	73 **Total net assets or fund balances** (add lines 67 through 69 OR lines 70 through 72; column (A) must equal line 19 and column (B) must equal line 21)			**73**	
	74 **Total liabilities and net assets / fund balances** (add lines 66 and 73)			**74**	

Assets — lines 45–59
Liabilities — lines 60–66
Net Assets or Fund Balances — lines 67–74

Part IV-A	Reconciliation of Revenue per Audited Financial Statements with Revenue per Return (See Specific Instructions, page 18.)		Part IV-B	Reconciliation of Expenses per Audited Financial Statements with Expenses per Return	

a Total revenue, gains, and other support per audited financial statements . ▶ **a**

b Amounts included on line **a** but not on line 12, Form 990:

(1) Net unrealized gains on investments . . $

(2) Donated services and use of facilities $

(3) Recoveries of prior year grants . . . $

(4) Other (specify):

------------------------ $

Add amounts on lines **(1)** through **(4)** ▶ **b**

c Line **a** minus line **b**. . . . . . ▶ **c**

d Amounts included on line 12, Form 990 but not on line **a:**

(1) Investment expenses not included on line 6b, Form 990 . . . $

(2) Other (specify):

------------------------ $

Add amounts on lines **(1)** and **(2)** ▶ **d**

e Total revenue per line 12, Form 990 (line **c** plus line **d**) . . . . . . ▶ **e**

a Total expenses and losses per audited financial statements . . ▶ **a**

b Amounts included on line **a** but not on line 17, Form 990:

(1) Donated services and use of facilities $

(2) Prior year adjustments reported on line 20, Form 990 . . . . $

(3) Losses reported on line 20, Form 990 . $

(4) Other (specify):

------------------------ $

Add amounts on lines **(1)** through **(4)** ▶ **b**

c Line **a** minus line **b** . . . . . ▶ **c**

d Amounts included on line 17, Form 990 but not on line **a:**

(1) Investment expenses not included on line 6b, Form 990. . . $

(2) Other (specify):

------------------------ $

Add amounts on lines **(1)** and **(2)** ▶ **d**

e Total expenses per line 17, Form 990 (line **c** plus line **d**) . . . . . ▶ **e**

Part V	List of Officers, Directors, Trustees, and Key Employees (List each one even if not compensated; see Specific Instructions on page 18.)

(A) Name and address	(B) Title and average hours per week devoted to position	(C) Compensation (If not paid, enter -0-.)	(D) Contributions to employee benefit plans & deferred compensation	(E) Expense account and other allowances

75 Did any officer, director, trustee, or key employee receive aggregate compensation of more than $100,000 from your organization and all related organizations, of which more than $10,000 was provided by the related organizations? ▶ ☐ **Yes** ☐ **No**
If "Yes," attach schedule—see Specific Instructions on page 18.

Part VI	**Other Information** (See Specific Instructions on page 19.)		Yes	No

76 Did the organization engage in any activity not previously reported to the IRS? If "Yes," attach a detailed description of each activity . | **76** | | |

77 Were any changes made in the organizing or governing documents but not reported to the IRS? . . . | **77** | | |
If "Yes," attach a conformed copy of the changes.

78a Did the organization have unrelated business gross income of $1,000 or more during the year covered by this return?. | **78a** | | |
  b If "Yes," has it filed a tax return on **Form 990-T** for this year? . . . . | **78b** | | |

79 Was there a liquidation, dissolution, termination, or substantial contraction during the year? If "Yes," attach a statement | **79** | | |

80a Is the organization related (other than by association with a statewide or nationwide organization) through common membership, governing bodies, trustees, officers, etc., to any other exempt or nonexempt organization? . . . | **80a** | | |
  b If "Yes," enter the name of the organization ▶ ....
.... and check whether it is ☐ exempt **OR** ☐ nonexempt.

81a Enter the amount of political expenditures, direct or indirect, as described in the instructions for line 81. . . . . |81a|
  b Did the organization file **Form 1120-POL** for this year? . . . . | **81b** | | |

82a Did the organization receive donated services or the use of materials, equipment, or facilities at no charge or at substantially less than fair rental value? . . . . | **82a** | | |
  b If "Yes," you may indicate the value of these items here. Do not include this amount as revenue in Part I or as an expense in Part II. (See instructions for reporting in Part III.). . . . . |82b|

83a Did the organization comply with the public inspection requirements for returns and exemption applications? | **83a** | | |
  b Did the organization comply with the disclosure requirements relating to quid pro quo contributions? . . | **83b** | | |

84a Did the organization solicit any contributions or gifts that were not tax deductible? . . . . | **84a** | | |
  b If "Yes," did the organization include with every solicitation an express statement that such contributions or gifts were not tax deductible? . . . . | **84b** | | |

85 501(c)(4), (5), or (6) organizations.—**a** Were substantially all dues nondeductible by members? . . . . . | **85a** | | |
  b Did the organization make only in-house lobbying expenditures of $2,000 or less? . . . . | **85b** | | |
If "Yes" was answered to either 85a or 85b, **do not** complete 85c through 85h below unless the organization received a waiver for proxy tax owed for the prior year.
  c Dues, assessments, and similar amounts from members . . . . . |85c|
  d Section 162(e) lobbying and political expenditures . . . . . |85d|
  e Aggregate nondeductible amount of section 6033(e)(1)(A) dues notices . . . |85e|
  f Taxable amount of lobbying and political expenditures (line 85d less 85e) . . |85f|
  g Does the organization elect to pay the section 6033(e) tax on the amount in 85f?. . . . . | **85g** | | |
  h If section 6033(e)(1)(A) dues notices were sent, does the organization agree to add the amount in 85f to its reasonable estimate of dues allocable to nondeductible lobbying and political expenditures for the following tax year?. . . | **85h** | | |

86 501(c)(7) organizations.—Enter: **a** Initiation fees and capital contributions included on line 12 . . . . |86a|
  b Gross receipts, included on line 12, for public use of club facilities . . . . . |86b|

87 501(c)(12) organizations.—Enter: **a** Gross income from members or shareholders |87a|
  b Gross income from other sources. (Do not net amounts due or paid to other sources against amounts due or received from them.) . . . . |87b|

88 At any time during the year, did the organization own a 50% or greater interest in a taxable corporation or partnership? If "Yes," complete Part IX . . . . | **88** | | |

89a 501(c)(3) organizations.—Enter: Amount of tax paid during the year under:
section 4911 ▶............... ; section 4912 ▶............... ; section 4955 ▶...............
  b 501(c)(3) and 501(c)(4) organizations.—Did the organization engage in any section 4958 excess benefit transaction during the year? If "Yes," attach a statement explaining each transaction . . . . | **89b** | | |
  c Enter: Amount of tax paid by the organization managers or disqualified persons during the year under section 4958 . . . . ▶ ....
  d Enter: Amount of tax in **89c,** above, reimbursed by the organization . . . . ▶ ....

90 List the states with which a copy of this return is filed ▶ ....

91 The books are in care of ▶ .... Telephone no. ▶ (...........)...........
Located at ▶ .... ZIP + 4 ▶ ....

92 Section 4947(a)(1) nonexempt charitable trusts filing Form 990 in lieu of **Form 1041**—Check here . . . . ▶ ☐
and enter the amount of tax-exempt interest received or accrued during the tax year . . ▶ | **92** |

Form 990 (1996)   Page **6**

Part VII	**Analysis of Income-Producing Activities** (See Specific Instructions on page 22.)					

Enter gross amounts unless otherwise indicated.

		Unrelated business income		Excluded by section 512, 513, or 514		**(E)** Related or exempt function income
		(A) Business code	**(B)** Amount	**(C)** Exclusion code	**(D)** Amount	
93	Program service revenue:					
a						
b						
c						
d						
e						
f						
g	Fees and contracts from government agencies					
94	Membership dues and assessments					
95	Interest on savings and temporary cash investments					
96	Dividends and interest from securities					
97	Net rental income or (loss) from real estate:					
a	debt-financed property					
b	not debt-financed property					
98	Net rental income or (loss) from personal property					
99	Other investment income					
100	Gain or (loss) from sales of assets other than inventory					
101	Net income or (loss) from special events					
102	Gross profit or (loss) from sales of inventory					
103	Other revenue: a					
b						
c						
d						
e						
104	Subtotal (add columns (B), (D), and (E))					

105 Total (add line 104, columns (B), (D), and (E)) . . . . ▶ _____

Note: *(Line 105 plus line 1d, Part I, should equal the amount on line 12, Part I.)*

Part VIII	**Relationship of Activities to the Accomplishment of Exempt Purposes** (See Specific Instructions on page 23.)

Line No. ▼	Explain how each activity for which income is reported in column (E) of Part VII contributed importantly to the accomplishment of the organization's exempt purposes (other than by providing funds for such purposes).

Part IX	**Information Regarding Taxable Subsidiaries (Complete this Part if the "Yes" box on line 88 is checked.)**				

Name, address, and employer identification number of corporation or partnership	Percentage of ownership interest	Nature of business activities	Total income	End-of-year assets
	%			
	%			
	%			
	%			

Please Sign Here

Under penalties of perjury, I declare that I have examined this return, including accompanying schedules and statements, and to the best of my knowledge and belief, it is true, correct, and complete. Declaration of preparer (other than officer) is based on all information of which preparer has any knowledge. (See General Instructions on page 8.)

▶ _____   _____   ▶ _____
Signature of officer   Date   Type or print name and title.

Paid Preparer's Use Only

Preparer's signature ▶		Date	Check if self-employed ▶ ☐	Preparer's SSN
Firm's name (or yours if self-employed) and address ▶			EIN ▶	
			ZIP + 4 ▶	

✪

Form **990-T**

Exempt Organization Business Income Tax Return
(and proxy tax under section 6033(e))

OMB No. 1545-0687

Department of the Treasury
Internal Revenue Service

For calendar year 1996 or other tax year beginning .... , 1996, and ending .... , 19 ....
▶ **See separate instructions.**

19**96**

A ☐ Check box if address changed

B Exempt under section
☐ 501( )( ) or
☐ 408(e)

C Book value of all assets at end of year

Please Print or Type

Name of organization

Number, street, and room or suite no. (If a P.O. box, see page 5 of instructions.)

City or town, state, and ZIP code

D Employer identification number
(Employees' trust, see instructions for Block D on page 5.)

E Unrelated business activity codes
(see instructions for Block E on page 5.)

F Group exemption number (see instructions for Block F on page 5) ▶

G Check type of organization . ▶ ☐ 501(c) Corporation ☐ 501(c) Trust ☐ Section 401(a) trust ☐ Section 408(a) trust

H Describe the organization's primary unrelated business activity. ▶

I During the tax year, was the corporation a subsidiary in an affiliated group or a parent-subsidiary controlled group? . . ▶ ☐ Yes ☐ No
If "Yes," enter the name and identifying number of the parent corporation. ▶

J The books are in care of ▶   Telephone number ▶ (   )

Part I	**Unrelated Trade or Business Income**		**(A) Income**	**(B) Expenses**	**(C) Net**
1a	Gross receipts or sales				
b	Less returns and allowances _____ **c** Balance ▶	**1c**			
2	Cost of goods sold (Schedule A, line 7)	**2**			
3	Gross profit (subtract line 2 from line 1c)	**3**			
4a	Capital gain net income (attach Schedule D)	**4a**			
b	Net gain (loss) (Form 4797, Part II, line 20) (attach Form 4797)	**4b**			
c	Capital loss deduction for trusts	**4c**			
5	Income (loss) from partnerships (attach statement) . . .	**5**			
6	Rent income (Schedule C)	**6**			
7	Unrelated debt-financed income (Schedule E).	**7**			
8	Interest, annuities, royalties, and rents from controlled organizations (Schedule F)	**8**			
9	Investment income of a section 501(c)(7), (9), or (17) organization (Schedule G)	**9**			
10	Exploited exempt activity income (Schedule I).	**10**			
11	Advertising income (Schedule J)	**11**			
12	Other income (see page 6 of the instructions—attach schedule)	**12**			
13	TOTAL (combine lines 3 through 12)	**13**			

Part II	**Deductions Not Taken Elsewhere** (See page 7 of the instructions for limitations on deductions.)		
	(Except for contributions, deductions must be directly connected with the unrelated business income.)		
14	Compensation of officers, directors, and trustees (Schedule K)	**14**	
15	Salaries and wages	**15**	
16	Repairs and maintenance	**16**	
17	Bad debts	**17**	
18	Interest (attach schedule)	**18**	
19	Taxes and licenses	**19**	
20	Charitable contributions (see page 8 of the instructions for limitation rules)	**20**	
21	Depreciation (attach Form 4562) **21**		
22	Less depreciation claimed on Schedule A and elsewhere on return . **22a**	**22b**	
23	Depletion	**23**	
24	Contributions to deferred compensation plans	**24**	
25	Employee benefit programs	**25**	
26	Excess exempt expenses (Schedule I)	**26**	
27	Excess readership costs (Schedule J)	**27**	
28	Other deductions (attach schedule)	**28**	
29	TOTAL DEDUCTIONS (add lines 14 through 28)	**29**	
30	Unrelated business taxable income before net operating loss deduction (subtract line 29 from line 13) .	**30**	
31	Net operating loss deduction	**31**	
32	Unrelated business taxable income before specific deduction (subtract line 31 from line 30) . .	**32**	
33	Specific deduction	**33**	
34	Unrelated business taxable income (subtract line 33 from line 32). If line 33 is greater than line 32, enter the smaller of zero or line 32	**34**	

For Paperwork Reduction Act Notice, see page 1 of separate instructions.   Cat. No. 11291J   Form **990-T** (1996)

Form 990-T (1996)   Page **2**

Part III	**Tax Computation**		

35 **Organizations Taxable as Corporations** (see instructions for tax computation on page 9). Controlled group members (sections 1561 and 1563)—check here ☐ . **See instructions** and:

a Enter your share of the $50,000, $25,000, and $9,925,000 taxable income brackets (in that order):

(1) |$ | | **(2)** |$ | | **(3)** |$ | |

b Enter organization's share of: **(1)** additional 5% tax (not more than $11,750) |$ | |

    (2) additional 3% tax (not more than $100,000) . . . . |$ | |

c Income tax on the amount on line 34 . . . . ▶ | **35c** | |

36 **Trusts Taxable at Trust Rates** (see instructions for tax computation on page 10) Income tax on the amount on line 34 from: ☐ Tax rate schedule or ☐ Schedule D (Form 1041) . . . . ▶ | **36** | |

37 **Proxy tax** (see page 10 of the instructions). . . . . ▶ | **37** | |

38 **Total** (add line 37 to line 35c or 36, whichever applies). . . . . | **38** | |

Part IV	**Tax and Payments**		

39a Foreign tax credit (corporations attach Form 1118; trusts attach Form 1116) . | **39a** | |

  b Other credits. (see page 10 of the instructions) . . . . | **39b** | |

  c General business credit—Check if from:

    ☐ Form 3800 or ☐ Form (specify) ▶................................... | **39c** | |

  d Credit for prior year minimum tax (attach Form 8801 or 8827) . . . | **39d** | |

  e Total (add lines 39a through 39d) . . . . | **39e** | |

40 Subtract line 39e from line 38 . . . . | **40** | |

41 Recapture taxes. Check if from: ☐ Form 4255 ☐ Form 8611 . . . . | **41** | |

42 Alternative minimum tax . . . . | **42** | |

43 **Total tax** (add lines 40, 41, and 42) . . . . | **43** | |

44 **Payments: a** 1995 overpayment credited to 1996 . . . . | **44a** | |

  b 1996 estimated tax payments . . . . | **44b** | |

  c Tax deposited with Form 7004 or Form 2758 . . . . | **44c** | |

  d Foreign organizations—Tax paid or withheld at source (see instructions) | **44d** | |

  e Backup withholding (see instructions) . . . . | **44e** | |

  f Other credits and payments (see instructions). . . . . | **44f** | |

45 Total payments (add lines 44a through 44f). . . . . | **45** | |

46 Estimated tax penalty (see page 3 of the instructions). Check ▶ ☐ if Form 2220 is attached . | **46** | |

47 **Tax due**—If line 45 is less than the total of lines 43 and 46, enter amount owed . . . . . ▶ | **47** | |

48 **Overpayment**—If line 45 is larger than the total of lines 43 and 46, enter amount overpaid . . ▶ | **48** | |

49 Enter the amount of line 48 you want: **Credited to 1997 estimated tax** ▶ | **Refunded** ▶ | **49** | |

Part V	**Statements Regarding Certain Activities and Other Information** (See instructions on page 11.)	Yes	No

1 At any time during the 1996 calendar year, did the organization have an interest in or a signature or other authority over a financial account in a foreign country (such as a bank account, securities account, or other financial account)?

If "Yes," the organization may have to file Form TD F 90-22.1. If "Yes," enter the name of the foreign country here ▶ ....

2 During the tax year, did the organization receive a distribution from, or was it the grantor of, or transferor to, a foreign trust? . . . .

If "Yes," see page 12 of the instructions for other forms the organization may have to file.

3 Enter the amount of tax-exempt interest received or accrued during the tax year ▶ $

SCHEDULE A—COST OF GOODS SOLD (See instructions on page 12.)

Method of inventory valuation (specify) ▶

1 Inventory at beginning of year	**1**			**6** Inventory at end of year. . . .	**6**		
2 Purchases.	**2**			**7** Cost of goods sold. Subtract line 6 from line 5. (Enter here and on line 2, Part I.)			
3 Cost of labor	**3**						
4a Additional section 263A costs (attach schedule)	**4a**				**7**		
b Other costs (attach schedule)	**4b**			**8** Do the rules of section 263A (with respect to property produced or acquired for resale) apply to the organization?		Yes	No
5 TOTAL—Add lines 1 through 4b	**5**						

Please Sign Here

Under penalties of perjury, I declare that I have examined this return, including accompanying schedules and statements, and to the best of my knowledge and belief, it is true, correct, and complete. Declaration of preparer (other than taxpayer) is based on all information of which preparer has any knowledge.

▶ _____ | _____ | ▶ _____
Signature of officer or fiduciary | Date | Title

Paid Preparer's Use Only

Preparer's signature ▶		Date	Check if self-employed ▶ ☐	Preparer's social security number
Firm's name (or yours, if self-employed) and address ▶			EIN ▶	
			ZIP code ▶	

SCHEDULE C—RENT INCOME (FROM REAL PROPERTY AND PERSONAL PROPERTY LEASED WITH REAL PROPERTY)
(See instructions on page 12.)

1 Description of property

(1)

(2)

(3)

(4)

2 Rent received or accrued		**3** Deductions directly connected with the income in columns 2(a) and 2(b) (attach schedule)
(a) From personal property (if the percentage of rent for personal property is more than 10% but not more than 50%)	**(b)** From real and personal property (if the percentage of rent for personal property exceeds 50% or if the rent is based on profit or income)	
(1)		
(2)		
(3)		
(4)		
Total	Total	

Total Income (Add totals of columns 2(a) and 2(b). Enter here and on line 6, column (A), Part I, page 1.) . . ▶

Total deductions. Enter here and on line 6, column (B), Part I, page 1 . . ▶

SCHEDULE E—UNRELATED DEBT-FINANCED INCOME (See instructions on page 13.)

1 Description of debt-financed property	**2** Gross income from or allocable to debt-financed property	**3** Deductions directly connected with or allocable to debt-financed property	
		(a) Straight line depreciation (attach schedule)	**(b)** Other deductions (attach schedule)
(1)			
(2)			
(3)			
(4)			

4 Amount of average acquisition debt on or allocable to debt-financed property (attach schedule)	**5** Average adjusted basis of or allocable to debt-financed property (attach schedule)	**6** Column 4 divided by column 5	**7** Gross income reportable (column 2 × column 6)	**8** Allocable deductions (column 6 × total of columns 3(a) and 3(b))
(1)		%		
(2)		%		
(3)		%		
(4)		%		
			Enter here and on line 7, column (A), Part I, page 1.	Enter here and on line 7, column (B), Part I, page 1.

Totals . . . . ▶

Total dividends-received deductions included in column 8 . . . . ▶

SCHEDULE F—INTEREST, ANNUITIES, ROYALTIES, AND RENTS FROM CONTROLLED ORGANIZATIONS
(See instructions on page 14.)

1 Name and address of controlled organization(s)	**2** Gross income from controlled organization(s)	**3** Deductions of controlling organization directly connected with column 2 income (attach schedule)	**4** Exempt controlled organizations		
			(a) Unrelated business taxable income	**(b)** Taxable income computed as though not exempt under sec. 501(a), or the amount in col. (a), whichever is larger	**(c)** column (a) divided by column (b)
(1)					%
(2)					%
(3)					%
(4)					%

5 Nonexempt controlled organizations			**6** Gross income reportable (column 2 × column 4(c) or column 5(c))	**7** Allowable deductions (column 3 × column 4(c) or column 5(c))
(a) Excess taxable income	**(b)** Taxable income, or amount in column (a), whichever is larger	**(c)** Column (a) divided by Column (b)		
(1)		%		
(2)		%		
(3)		%		
(4)		%		
			Enter here and on line 8, column (A), Part I, page 1.	Enter here and on line 8, column (B), Part I, page 1.

Totals. . . . . ▶

Form 990-T (1996)   Page **4**

SCHEDULE G—INVESTMENT INCOME OF A SECTION 501(c)(7), (9), OR (17) ORGANIZATION
(See instructions on page 14.)

1 Description of income	**2** Amount of income	**3** Deductions directly connected (attach schedule)	**4** Set-asides (attach schedule)	**5** Total deductions and set-asides (col. 3 plus col. 4)
(1)				
(2)				
(3)				
(4)				
Totals ▶	Enter here and on line 9, column (A), Part I, page 1.			Enter here and on line 9, column (B), Part I, page 1.

SCHEDULE I—EXPLOITED EXEMPT ACTIVITY INCOME, OTHER THAN ADVERTISING INCOME
(See instructions on page 14.)

1 Description of exploited activity	**2** Gross unrelated business income from trade or business	**3** Expenses directly connected with production of unrelated business income	**4** Net income (loss) from unrelated trade or business (column 2 minus column 3). If a gain, compute cols. 5 through 7.	**5** Gross income from activity that is not unrelated business income	**6** Expenses attributable to column 5	**7** Excess exempt expenses (column 6 minus column 5, but not more than column 4).
(1)						
(2)						
(3)						
(4)						
Column totals ▶	Enter here and on line 10, col. (A), Part I, page 1.	Enter here and on line 10, col. (B), Part I, page 1.				Enter here and on line 26, Part II, page 1.

SCHEDULE J—ADVERTISING INCOME (See instructions on page 15.)

Part I Income From Periodicals Reported on a Consolidated Basis

1 Name of periodical	**2** Gross advertising income	**3** Direct advertising costs	**4** Advertising gain or (loss) (col. 2 minus col. 3). If a gain, compute cols. 5 through 7.	**5** Circulation income	**6** Readership costs	**7** Excess readership costs (column 6 minus column 5, but not more than column 4).
(1)						
(2)						
(3)						
(4)						
Column totals (carry to Part II, line (5)) ▶						

Part II Income From Periodicals Reported on a Separate Basis (For each periodical listed in Part II, fill in columns 2 through 7 on a line-by-line basis.)

(1)						
(2)						
(3)						
(4)						
(5) Totals from Part I						
Column totals, Part II ▶	Enter here and on line 11, col. (A), Part I, page 1.	Enter here and on line 11, col. (B), Part I, page 1.				Enter here and on line 27, Part II, page 1.

SCHEDULE K—COMPENSATION OF OFFICERS, DIRECTORS, AND TRUSTEES (See instructions on page 15.)

1 Name	**2** Title	**3** Percent of time devoted to business	**4** Compensation attributable to unrelated business
		%	
		%	
		%	
		%	
Total—Enter here and on line 14, Part II, page 1 ▶			

Form **1041** Department of the Treasury—Internal Revenue Service
U.S. Income Tax Return for Estates and Trusts   19**96**

For calendar year 1996 or fiscal year beginning _____ , 1996, and ending _____ , 19 ___   OMB No. 1545-0092

A Type of entity:	Name of estate or trust (If a grantor type trust, see page 7 of the instructions.)	**C** Employer identification number
☐ Decedent's estate		
☐ Simple trust		**D** Date entity created
☐ Complex trust	Name and title of fiduciary	
☐ Grantor type trust		**E** Nonexempt charitable and split-interest trusts, check applicable boxes (see page 8 of the instructions):
☐ Bankruptcy estate–Ch. 7		
☐ Bankruptcy estate–Ch. 11	Number, street, and room or suite no. (If a P.O. box, see page 7 of the instructions.)	☐ Described in section 4947(a)(1)
☐ Pooled income fund		☐ Not a private foundation
B Number of Schedules K-1 attached (see instructions) ▶	City or town, state, and ZIP code	☐ Described in section 4947(a)(2)

F Check applicable boxes: ☐ Initial return ☐ Final return ☐ Amended return   **G** Pooled mortgage account (see page 9 of the instructions):
☐ Change in fiduciary's name ☐ Change in fiduciary's address   ☐ Bought   ☐ Sold   Date: _____

Income

1	Interest income	1
2	Dividends	2
3	Business income or (loss) (attach Schedule C or C-EZ (Form 1040))	3
4	Capital gain or (loss) (attach Schedule D (Form 1041))	4
5	Rents, royalties, partnerships, other estates and trusts, etc. (attach Schedule E (Form 1040))	5
6	Farm income or (loss) (attach Schedule F (Form 1040))	6
7	Ordinary gain or (loss) (attach Form 4797)	7
8	Other income. List type and amount	8
9	**Total income.** Combine lines 1 through 8 ▶	9

Deductions

10	Interest. Check if Form 4952 is attached ▶ ☐	10
11	Taxes	11
12	Fiduciary fees	12
13	Charitable deduction (from Schedule A, line 7)	13
14	Attorney, accountant, and return preparer fees	14
15a	Other deductions NOT subject to the 2% floor (attach schedule)	15a
b	Allowable miscellaneous itemized deductions subject to the 2% floor	15b
16	**Total.** Add lines 10 through 15b	16
17	Adjusted total income or (loss). Subtract line 16 from line 9. Enter here and on Schedule B, line 1 ▶	17
18	Income distribution deduction (from Schedule B, line 17) (attach Schedules K-1 (Form 1041))	18
19	Estate tax deduction (including certain generation-skipping taxes) (attach computation)	19
20	Exemption	20
21	**Total deductions.** Add lines 18 through 20 ▶	21

Tax and Payments

22	Taxable income. Subtract line 21 from line 17. If a loss, see page 13 of the instructions	22
23	**Total tax** (from Schedule G, line 8)	23
24	**Payments: a** 1996 estimated tax payments and amount applied from 1995 return	24a
b	Estimated tax payments allocated to beneficiaries (from Form 1041-T)	24b
c	Subtract line 24b from line 24a	24c
d	Tax paid with extension of time to file: ☐ Form 2758 ☐ Form 8736 ☐ Form 8800	24d
e	Federal income tax withheld. If any is from Form(s) 1099, check ▶ ☐	24e
	Other payments: **f** Form 2439 _____ ; **g** Form 4136 _____ ; Total ▶	24h
25	**Total payments.** Add lines 24c through 24e, and 24h ▶	25
26	Estimated tax penalty (see page 13 of the instructions)	26
27	**Tax due.** If line 25 is smaller than the total of lines 23 and 26, enter amount owed	27
28	**Overpayment.** If line 25 is larger than the total of lines 23 and 26, enter amount overpaid	28
29	Amount of line 28 to be: **a** Credited to 1997 estimated tax ▶ _____ ; **b** Refunded ▶	29

Please Sign Here

Under penalties of perjury, I declare that I have examined this return, including accompanying schedules and statements, and to the best of my knowledge and belief, it is true, correct, and complete. Declaration of preparer (other than fiduciary) is based on all information of which preparer has any knowledge.

▶ _____ ▶ _____

Signature of fiduciary or officer representing fiduciary   Date   EIN of fiduciary if a financial institution (see page 4 of the instructions)

Paid Preparer's Use Only

Preparer's signature ▶	Date	Check if self-employed ▶ ☐	Preparer's social security no.
Firm's name (or yours if self-employed) and address ▶		EIN ▶	
		ZIP code ▶	

For Paperwork Reduction Act Notice, see page 1 of the separate instructions.   Cat. No. 11370H   Form **1041** (1996)

Form 1041 (1996)   Page **2**

Schedule A — Charitable Deduction. Do not complete for a simple trust or a pooled income fund.

1	Amounts paid for charitable purposes from gross income	**1**
2	Amounts permanently set aside for charitable purposes from gross income	**2**
3	Add lines 1 and 2	**3**
4	Tax-exempt income allocable to charitable contributions (see page 14 of the instructions)	**4**
5	Subtract line 4 from line 3	**5**
6	Capital gains for the tax year allocated to corpus and paid or permanently set aside for charitable purposes	**6**
7	**Charitable deduction.** Add lines 5 and 6. Enter here and on page 1, line 13	**7**

Schedule B — Income Distribution Deduction

1	Adjusted total income (from page 1, line 17) (see page 14 of the instructions)	**1**
2	Adjusted tax-exempt interest	**2**
3	Total net gain from Schedule D (Form 1041), line 17, column (a) (see page 15 of the instructions)	**3**
4	Enter amount from Schedule A, line 6	**4**
5	Long-term capital gain for the tax year included on Schedule A, line 3	**5**
6	Short-term capital gain for the tax year included on Schedule A, line 3	**6**
7	If the amount on page 1, line 4, is a capital loss, enter here as a positive figure	**7**
8	If the amount on page 1, line 4, is a capital gain, enter here as a negative figure	**8**
9	**Distributable net income (DNI).** Combine lines 1 through 8. If zero or less, enter -0-	**9**
10	If a complex trust, enter accounting income for the tax year as determined under the governing instrument and applicable local law **10**	
11	Income required to be distributed currently	**11**
12	Other amounts paid, credited, or otherwise required to be distributed	**12**
13	Total distributions. Add lines 11 and 12. If greater than line 10, see page 15 of the instructions	**13**
14	Enter the amount of tax-exempt income included on line 13	**14**
15	Tentative income distribution deduction. Subtract line 14 from line 13	**15**
16	Tentative income distribution deduction. Subtract line 2 from line 9. If zero or less, enter -0-	**16**
17	**Income distribution deduction.** Enter the smaller of line 15 or line 16 here and on page 1, line 18	**17**

Schedule G — Tax Computation (see page 16 of the instructions)

1	**Tax: a** ☐ Tax rate schedule or ☐ Schedule D (Form 1041)	**1a**
	b Other taxes	**1b**
	c Total. Add lines 1a and 1b	▶ **1c**
2a	Foreign tax credit (attach Form 1116)	**2a**
b	Check: ☐ Nonconventional source fuel credit ☐ Form 8834	**2b**
c	General business credit. Enter here and check which forms are attached: ☐ Form 3800 or ☐ Forms (specify) ▶............	**2c**
d	Credit for prior year minimum tax (attach Form 8801)	**2d**
3	**Total credits.** Add lines 2a through 2d	▶ **3**
4	Subtract line 3 from line 1c	**4**
5	Recapture taxes. Check if from: ☐ Form 4255 ☐ Form 8611	**5**
6	Alternative minimum tax (from Schedule I, line 41)	**6**
7	Household employment taxes. Attach Schedule H (Form 1040)	**7**
8	**Total tax.** Add lines 4 through 7. Enter here and on page 1, line 23	▶ **8**

Other Information

		Yes	No
1	Did the estate or trust receive tax-exempt income? If "Yes," attach a computation of the allocation of expenses. Enter the amount of tax-exempt interest income and exempt-interest dividends ▶ $		
2	Did the estate or trust receive all or any part of the earnings (salary, wages, and other compensation) of any individual by reason of a contract assignment or similar arrangement?		
3	At any time during calendar year 1996, did the estate or trust have an interest in or a signature or other authority over a bank, securities, or other financial account in a foreign country? See page 17 of the instructions for exceptions and filing requirements for Form TD F 90-22.1. If "Yes," enter the name of the foreign country ▶		
4	During the tax year, did the estate or trust receive a distribution from, or was it the grantor of, or transferor to, a foreign trust? If "Yes," see page 17 of the instructions for other forms the estate or trust may have to file		
5	Did the estate or trust receive, or pay, any seller-financed mortgage interest? If "Yes," see page 17 of the instructions for required attachment		
6	If this is a complex trust making the section 663(b) election, check here (see page 17 of the instructions) ▶ ☐		
7	To make a section 643(e)(3) election, attach Schedule D (Form 1041), and check here (see page 17). ▶ ☐		
8	If the decedent's estate has been open for more than 2 years, check here ▶ ☐		

| Schedule I | **Alternative Minimum Tax** (see pages 18 through 22 of the instructions) |

Part I—Estate's or Trust's Share of Alternative Minimum Taxable Income

1	Adjusted total income or (loss) (from page 1, line 17)	1	
2	Net operating loss deduction. Enter as a positive amount	2	
3	Add lines 1 and 2	3	
4	**Adjustments and tax preference items:**		
a	Interest	4a	
b	Taxes	4b	
c	Miscellaneous itemized deductions (from page 1, line 15b)	4c	
d	Refund of taxes	4d ( )	
e	Depreciation of property placed in service after 1986	4e	
f	Circulation and research and experimental expenditures	4f	
g	Mining exploration and development costs	4g	
h	Long-term contracts entered into after February 28, 1986	4h	
i	Amortization of pollution control facilities	4i	
j	Installment sales of certain property	4j	
k	Adjusted gain or loss (including incentive stock options).	4k	
l	Certain loss limitations	4l	
m	Tax shelter farm activities	4m	
n	Passive activities	4n	
o	Beneficiaries of other trusts or decedent's estates	4o	
p	Tax-exempt interest from specified private activity bonds	4p	
q	Depletion	4q	
r	Accelerated depreciation of real property placed in service before 1987	4r	
s	Accelerated depreciation of leased personal property placed in service before 1987	4s	
t	Intangible drilling costs	4t	
u	Other adjustments	4u	
5	Combine lines 4a through 4u	5	
6	Add lines 3 and 5	6	
7	Alternative tax net operating loss deduction (see page 21 of the instructions for limitations). .	7	
8	Adjusted alternative minimum taxable income. Subtract line 7 from line 6. Enter here and on line 13	8	
	Note: *Complete Part II before going to line 9.*		
9	Income distribution deduction from line 27	9	
10	Estate tax deduction (from page 1, line 19)	10	
11	Add lines 9 and 10	11	
12	Estate's or trust's share of alternative minimum taxable income. Subtract line 11 from line 8 .	12	

12   If line 12 is:

    ● $22,500 or less, stop here and enter -0- on Schedule G, line 6. The estate or trust is not liable for the alternative minimum tax.

    ● Over $22,500, but less than $165,000, go to line 28.

    ● $165,000 or more, enter the amount from line 12 on line 34 and go to line 35.

(continued on page 4)

Part II—Income Distribution Deduction on a Minimum Tax Basis

13	Adjusted alternative minimum taxable income (from line 8)	**13**
14	Adjusted tax-exempt interest (other than amounts included on line 4p)	**14**
15	Total net gain from Schedule D (Form 1041), line 17, column (a). If a loss, enter -0-	**15**
16	Capital gains for the tax year allocated to corpus and paid or permanently set aside for charitable purposes (from Schedule A, line 6)	**16**
17	Capital gains paid or permanently set aside for charitable purposes from current year's income (see page 21 of the instructions).	**17**
18	Capital gains computed on a minimum tax basis included on line 8	**18** ( )
19	Capital losses computed on a minimum tax basis included on line 8. Enter as a positive amount	**19**
20	Distributable net alternative minimum taxable income (DNAMTI). Combine lines 13 through 19 .	**20**
21	Income required to be distributed currently (from Schedule B, line 11)	**21**
22	Other amounts paid, credited, or otherwise required to be distributed (from Schedule B, line 12)	**22**
23	Total distributions. Add lines 21 and 22	**23**
24	Tax-exempt income included on line 23 (other than amounts included on line 4p)	**24**
25	Tentative income distribution deduction on a minimum tax basis. Subtract line 24 from line 23 .	**25**
26	Tentative income distribution deduction on a minimum tax basis. Subtract line 14 from line 20 .	**26**
27	**Income distribution deduction on a minimum tax basis.** Enter the smaller of line 25 or line 26. Enter here and on line 9	**27**

Part III—Alternative Minimum Tax

28	Exemption amount		**28** $22,500
29	Enter the amount from line 12	**29**	
30	Phase-out of exemption amount	**30** $75,000	
31	Subtract line 30 from line 29. If zero or less, enter -0-	**31**	
32	Multiply line 31 by 25% (.25)		**32**
33	Subtract line 32 from line 28. If zero or less, enter -0-		**33**
34	Subtract line 33 from line 29		**34**
35	If line 34 is:		
	• $175,000 or less, multiply line 34 by 26% (.26).		
	• Over $175,000, multiply line 34 by 28% (.28) and subtract $3,500 from the result		**35**
36	Alternative minimum foreign tax credit (see page 21 of instructions).		**36**
37	Tentative minimum tax. Subtract line 36 from line 35		**37**
38	Regular tax before credits (see page 22 of instructions)	**38**	
39	Section 644 tax included on Schedule G, line 1b	**39**	
40	Add lines 38 and 39		**40**
41	**Alternative minimum tax.** Subtract line 40 from line 37. If zero or less, enter -0-. Enter here and on Schedule G, line 6		**41**

| SCHEDULE J
(Form 1041)

Department of the Treasury
Internal Revenue Service | **Accumulation Distribution for a Complex Trust**

▶ File with Form 1041.
▶ See the separate Form 1041 instructions. | OMB No. 1545-0092

19**96** |

| Name of trust | Employer identification number |

Part I — Accumulation Distribution in 1996

Note: *See the Form 4970 instructions for certain income that minors may exclude and special rules for multiple trusts.*

1 Other amounts paid, credited, or otherwise required to be distributed for 1996 (from Schedule B of Form 1041, line 12) **1**

2 Distributable net income for 1996 (from Schedule B of Form 1041, line 9) . . . **2**

3 Income required to be distributed currently for 1996 (from Schedule B of Form 1041, line 11) **3**

4 Subtract line 3 from line 2. If zero or less, enter -0- **4**

5 Accumulation distribution for 1996. Subtract line 4 from line 1 . . . . **5**

Part II — Ordinary Income Accumulation Distribution (Enter the applicable throwback years below.)

Note: *If the distribution is thrown back to more than five years (starting with the earliest applicable tax year beginning after 1968), attach additional schedules. (If the trust was a simple trust, see Regulations section 1.665(e)-1A(b).)*		Throwback year ending 19	Throwback year ending 19	Throwback year ending 19	Throwback year ending 19	Throwback year ending 19 ....
6 Distributable net income (see page 24 of the instructions) .	**6**					
7 Distributions (see page 24 of the instructions)	**7**					
8 Subtract line 7 from line 6 .	**8**					
9 Enter amount from page 2, line 25 or line 31, as applicable	**9**					
10 Undistributed net income Subtract line 9 from line 8 .	**10**					
11 Enter amount of prior accumulation distributions thrown back to any of these years	**11**					
12 Subtract line 11 from line 10	**12**					
13 Allocate the amount on line 5 to the earliest applicable year first. Do not allocate an amount greater than line 12 for the same year (see page 24 of the instructions). . .	**13**					
14 Divide line 13 by line 10 and multiply result by amount on line 9	**14**					
15 Add lines 13 and 14 . . .	**15**					
16 Tax-exempt interest included on line 13 (see page 24 of the instructions)	**16**					
17 Subtract line 16 from line 15	**17**					

For Paperwork Reduction Act Notice, see page 1 of the Instructions for Form 1041.   Cat. No. 11382Z   **Schedule J (Form 1041) 1996**

Part III **Taxes Imposed on Undistributed Net Income** (Enter the applicable throwback years below.) (see page 24 of the instructions)

Note: *If more than five throwback years are involved, attach additional schedules. If the trust received an accumulation distribution from another trust, see Regulations section 1.665(d)-1A.*

If the trust elected the alternative tax on capital gains (repealed for tax years beginning after 1978), **SKIP** lines 18 through 25 and **COMPLETE** lines 26 through 31.		Throwback year ending 19	Throwback year ending 19	Throwback year ending 19	Throwback year ending 19	Throwback year ending 19 ....
18 Regular tax	18					
19 Trust's share of net short-term gain	19					
20 Trust's share of net long-term gain.	20					
21 Add lines 19 and 20. . . .	21					
22 Taxable income	22					
23 Enter percent. Divide line 21 by line 22, but do not enter more than 100%	23	%	%	%	%	%
24 Multiply line 18 by the percentage on line 23. . .	24					
25 Tax on undistributed net income. Subtract line 24 from line 18. Enter here and on page 1, line 9.	25					
Do not complete lines 26 through 31 unless the trust elected the alternative tax on long-term capital gain.						
26 Tax on income other than long-term capital gain . .	26					
27 Trust's share of net short-term gain	27					
28 Trust's share of taxable income less section 1202 deduction	28					
29 Enter percent. Divide line 27 by line 28, but do not enter more than 100%	29	%	%	%	%	%
30 Multiply line 26 by the percentage on line 29. . .	30					
31 Tax on undistributed net income. Subtract line 30 from line 26. Enter here and on page 1, line 9	31					

Part IV **Allocation to Beneficiary**

Note: *Be sure to complete **Form 4970,** Tax on Accumulation Distribution of Trusts.*

Beneficiary's name

Identifying number

Beneficiary's address (number and street including apartment number or P.O. box)		(a) This beneficiary's share of line 13	(b) This beneficiary's share of line 14	(c) This beneficiary's share of line 16
City, state, and ZIP code				
32 Throwback year 19	32			
33 Throwback year 19	33			
34 Throwback year 19	34			
35 Throwback year 19	35			
36 Throwback year 19	36			
37 Total. Add lines 32 through 36. Enter here and on the appropriate lines of Form 4970.	37			

SCHEDULE K-1 (Form 1041)	**Beneficiary's Share of Income, Deductions, Credits, etc.**	OMB No. 1545-0092
Department of the Treasury Internal Revenue Service	for the calendar year 1996, or fiscal year beginning .... , 1996, ending .... , 19 .... ▶ **Complete a separate Schedule K-1 for each beneficiary.**	19**96**

Name of trust or decedent's estate

☐ Amended K-1
☐ Final K-1

Beneficiary's identifying number ▶	**Estate's or trust's EIN** ▶
Beneficiary's name, address, and ZIP code	Fiduciary's name, address, and ZIP code

(a) Allocable share item		**(b)** Amount	**(c)** Calendar year 1996 Form 1040 filers enter the amounts in column (b) on:
1	Interest.	**1**		Schedule B, Part I, line 1
2	Dividends	**2**		Schedule B, Part II, line 5
3a	Net short-term capital gain	**3a**		Schedule D, line 5, column (g)
b	Net long-term capital gain	**3b**		Schedule D, line 13, column (g)
4a	Annuities, royalties, and other nonpassive income before directly apportioned deductions	**4a**		Schedule E, Part III, column (f)
b	Depreciation	**4b**		Include on the applicable line of the appropriate tax form
c	Depletion	**4c**		
d	Amortization	**4d**		
5a	Trade or business, rental real estate, and other rental income before directly apportioned deductions (see instructions) .	**5a**		Schedule E, Part III
b	Depreciation	**5b**		Include on the applicable line of the appropriate tax form
c	Depletion	**5c**		
d	Amortization	**5d**		
6	Income for minimum tax purposes	**6**		
7	Income for regular tax purposes (add lines 1 through 3b, 4a, and 5a)	**7**		
8	Adjustment for minimum tax purposes (subtract line 7 from line 6).	**8**		Form 6251, line 12
9	Estate tax deduction (including certain generation-skipping transfer taxes)	**9**		Schedule A, line 27
10	Foreign taxes.	**10**		Form 1116 or Schedule A (Form 1040), line 8
11	Adjustments and tax preference items (itemize):			
a	Accelerated depreciation	**11a**		Include on the applicable line of Form 6251
b	Depletion	**11b**		
c	Amortization	**11c**		
d	Exclusion items	**11d**		1997 Form 8801
12	Deductions in the final year of trust or decedent's estate:			
a	Excess deductions on termination (see instructions)	**12a**		Schedule A, line 22
b	Short-term capital loss carryover	**12b**		Schedule D, line 5, column (f)
c	Long-term capital loss carryover	**12c**		Schedule D, line 13, column (f)
d	Net operating loss (NOL) carryover for regular tax purposes	**12d**		Form 1040, line 21
e	NOL carryover for minimum tax purposes	**12e**		See the instructions for Form 6251, line 20
f	....	**12f**		Include on the applicable line of the appropriate tax form
g	....	**12g**		
13	Other (itemize):			
a	Payments of estimated taxes credited to you . .	**13a**		Form 1040, line 53
b	Tax-exempt interest	**13b**		Form 1040, line 8b
c	....	**13c**		Include on the applicable line of the appropriate tax form
d	....	**13d**		
e	....	**13e**		
f	....	**13f**		
g	....	**13g**		
h		**13h**		

For Paperwork Reduction Act Notice, see page 1 of the Instructions for Form 1041.   Cat. No. 11380D   **Schedule K-1 (Form 1041) 1996**

Instructions for Beneficiary Filing Form 1040

Note: *The fiduciary's instructions for completing Schedule K-1 are in the Instructions for Form 1041.*

General Instructions

Purpose of Form

The fiduciary of a trust or decedent's estate uses Schedule K-1 to report your share of the trust's or estate's income, credits, deductions, etc. **Keep it for your records. Do not file it with your tax return.** A copy has been filed with the IRS.

Tax Shelters

If you receive a copy of **Form 8271,** Investor Reporting of Tax Shelter Registration Number, see the instructions for Form 8271 to determine your reporting requirements.

Errors

If you think the fiduciary has made an error on your Schedule K-1, notify the fiduciary and ask for an amended or a corrected Schedule K-1. Do not change any items on your copy. Be sure that the fiduciary sends a copy of the amended Schedule K-1 to the IRS.

Beneficiaries of Generation-Skipping Trusts

If you received **Form 706-GS(D-1),** Notification of Distribution From a Generation-Skipping Trust, and paid a generation-skipping transfer (GST) tax on **Form 706-GS(D),** Generation-Skipping Transfer Tax Return for Distributions, you can deduct the GST tax paid on income distributions on Schedule A (Form 1040), line 8. To figure the deduction, see the instructions for Form 706-GS(D).

Specific Instructions

Lines 3a and 3b

If there is an attachment to this Schedule K-1 reporting a disposition of a passive activity, see the instructions for **Form 8582,** Passive Activity Loss Limitations, for information on the treatment of dispositions of interests in a passive activity.

Lines 5b through 5d

The deductions on lines 5b through 5d may be subject to the passive loss limitations of Internal Revenue Code section 469, which generally limits deductions from passive activities to the income from those activities. The rules for applying these limitations to beneficiaries have not yet been issued. For more details, see **Pub. 925,** Passive Activity and At-Risk Rules.

Line 11d

If you pay alternative minimum tax in 1996, the amount on line 11d will help you figure any minimum tax credit for 1997. See the 1997 **Form 8801,** Credit for Prior Year Minimum Tax—Individuals, Estates, and Trusts, for more information.

Line 13a

To figure any underpayment and penalty on **Form 2210,** Underpayment of Estimated Tax by Individuals, Estates, and Trusts, treat the amount entered on line 13a as an estimated tax payment made on January 15, 1997.

Lines 13c through 13h

The amount of gross farming and fishing income is included on line 5a. This income is also separately stated on line 13 to help you determine if you are subject to a penalty for underpayment of estimated tax. Report the amount of gross farming and fishing income on Schedule E (Form 1040), line 41.

Form 1065

Department of the Treasury
Internal Revenue Service

U.S. Partnership Return of Income

For calendar year 1996, or tax year beginning ...., 1996, and ending ...., 19 .....
▶ **See separate instructions.**

OMB No. 1545-0099

1996

A Principal business activity	Use the IRS label. Other-wise, please print or type.	Name of partnership	**D** Employer identification number
B Principal product or service		Number, street, and room or suite no. If a P.O. box, see page 10 of the instructions.	**E** Date business started
C Business code number		City or town, state, and ZIP code	**F** Total assets (see page 10 of the instructions) $

G Check applicable boxes: **(1)** ☐ Initial return **(2)** ☐ Final return **(3)** ☐ Change in address **(4)** ☐ Amended return

H Check accounting method: **(1)** ☐ Cash **(2)** ☐ Accrual **(3)** ☐ Other (specify) ▶ ....

I Number of Schedules K-1. Attach one for each person who was a partner at any time during the tax year ▶ ....

Caution: *Include **only** trade or business income and expenses on lines 1a through 22 below. See the instructions for more information.*

Income

1a Gross receipts or sales	**1a**	
b Less returns and allowances	**1b**	**1c**
2 Cost of goods sold (Schedule A, line 8)		**2**
3 Gross profit. Subtract line 2 from line 1c		**3**
4 Ordinary income (loss) from other partnerships, estates, and trusts *(attach schedule)* . . .		**4**
5 Net farm profit (loss) *(attach Schedule F (Form 1040))*		**5**
6 Net gain (loss) from Form 4797, Part II, line 20.		**6**
7 Other income (loss) *(attach schedule)*		**7**
8 **Total income (loss).** Combine lines 3 through 7		**8**

Deductions (see page 11 of the instructions for limitations)

9 Salaries and wages (other than to partners) (less employment credits) .		**9**
10 Guaranteed payments to partners		**10**
11 Repairs and maintenance		**11**
12 Bad debts		**12**
13 Rent		**13**
14 Taxes and licenses		**14**
15 Interest		**15**
16a Depreciation (if required, attach Form 4562)	**16a**	
b Less depreciation reported on Schedule A and elsewhere on return	**16b**	**16c**
17 Depletion **(Do not deduct oil and gas depletion.)**		**17**
18 Retirement plans, etc.		**18**
19 Employee benefit programs		**19**
20 Other deductions *(attach schedule)*		**20**
21 **Total deductions.** Add the amounts shown in the far right column for lines 9 through 20 .		**21**
22 **Ordinary income (loss)** from trade or business activities. Subtract line 21 from line 8 . .		**22**

Please Sign Here

Under penalties of perjury, I declare that I have examined this return, including accompanying schedules and statements, and to the best of my knowledge and belief, it is true, correct, and complete. Declaration of preparer (other than general partner or limited liability company member) is based on all information of which preparer has any knowledge.

▶ _____ ▶ _____
Signature of general partner or limited liability company member   Date

Paid Preparer's Use Only	Preparer's signature ▶	Date	Check if self-employed ▶ ☐	Preparer's social security no.
	Firm's name (or yours if self-employed) and address ▶		EIN ▶	
			ZIP code ▶	

For Paperwork Reduction Act Notice, see page 1 of separate instructions.   Cat. No. 11390Z   Form **1065** (1996)

Schedule A   **Cost of Goods Sold** (see page 13 of the instructions)

1 Inventory at beginning of year	**1**	
2 Purchases less cost of items withdrawn for personal use	**2**	
3 Cost of labor.	**3**	
4 Additional section 263A costs *(attach schedule)*	**4**	
5 Other costs *(attach schedule)*	**5**	
6 **Total.** Add lines 1 through 5	**6**	
7 Inventory at end of year	**7**	
8 **Cost of goods sold.** Subtract line 7 from line 6. Enter here and on page 1, line 2	**8**	

9a Check all methods used for valuing closing inventory:
    (i) ☐ Cost as described in Regulations section 1.471-3
    (ii) ☐ Lower of cost or market as described in Regulations section 1.471-4
    (iii) ☐ Other (specify method used and attach explanation) ▶ _____
    b Check this box if there was a writedown of "subnormal" goods as described in Regulations section 1.471-2(c). . . . ▶ ☐
    c Check this box if the LIFO inventory method was adopted this tax year for any goods *(if checked, attach Form 970)* . . ▶ ☐
    d Do the rules of section 263A (for property produced or acquired for resale) apply to the partnership? . . ☐ **Yes** ☐ **No**
    e Was there any change in determining quantities, cost, or valuations between opening and closing inventory? ☐ **Yes** ☐ **No**
    If "Yes," attach explanation.

Schedule B   **Other Information**

	Yes	No
1 What type of entity is filing this return? Check the applicable box:		
a ☐ General partnership **b** ☐ Limited partnership **c** ☐ Limited liability company		
d ☐ Other (see page 14 of the instructions) ▶ _____		
2 Are any partners in this partnership also partnerships?		
3 Is this partnership a partner in another partnership?		
4 Is this partnership subject to the consolidated audit procedures of sections 6221 through 6233? If "Yes," see **Designation of Tax Matters Partner** below		
5 Does this partnership meet **ALL THREE** of the following requirements?		
a The partnership's total receipts for the tax year were less than $250,000;		
b The partnership's total assets at the end of the tax year were less than $600,000; **AND**		
c Schedules K-1 are filed with the return and furnished to the partners on or before the due date (including extensions) for the partnership return.		
If "Yes," the partnership is not required to complete Schedules L, M-1, and M-2; Item F on page 1 of Form 1065; or Item J on Schedule K-1		
6 Does this partnership have any foreign partners?		
7 Is this partnership a publicly traded partnership as defined in section 469(k)(2)?		
8 Has this partnership filed, or is it required to file, **Form 8264,** Application for Registration of a Tax Shelter? . .		
9 At any time during calendar year 1996, did the partnership have an interest in or a signature or other authority over a financial account in a foreign country (such as a bank account, securities account, or other financial account)? See page 14 of the instructions for exceptions and filing requirements for Form TD F 90-22.1. If "Yes," enter the name of the foreign country. ▶ _____		
10 During the tax year, did the partnership receive a distribution from, or was it the grantor of, or transferor to, a foreign trust? If "Yes," see page 14 of the instructions for other forms the partnership may have to file . . .		
11 Was there a distribution of property or a transfer (e.g., by sale or death) of a partnership interest during the tax year? If "Yes," you may elect to adjust the basis of the partnership's assets under section 754 by attaching the statement described under **Elections Made By the Partnership** on page 5 of the instructions		

Designation of Tax Matters Partner (see page 15 of the instructions)
Enter below the general partner designated as the tax matters partner (TMP) for the tax year of this return:

Name of designated TMP ▶ _____   Identifying number of TMP ▶ _____

Address of designated TMP ▶ _____

Form 1065 (1996)   Page **3**

Schedule K	Partners' Shares of Income, Credits, Deductions, etc.		

	(a) Distributive share items		**(b) Total amount**	
Income (Loss)	**1** Ordinary income (loss) from trade or business activities (page 1, line 22)	**1**		
	2 Net income (loss) from rental real estate activities *(attach Form 8825)*	**2**		
	3a Gross income from other rental activities	**3a**		
	b Expenses from other rental activities *(attach schedule)*	**3b**		
	c Net income (loss) from other rental activities. Subtract line 3b from line 3a	**3c**		
	4 Portfolio income (loss): **a** Interest income	**4a**		
	b Dividend income	**4b**		
	c Royalty income	**4c**		
	d Net short-term capital gain (loss) *(attach Schedule D (Form 1065))*	**4d**		
	e Net long-term capital gain (loss) *(attach Schedule D (Form 1065))*	**4e**		
	f Other portfolio income (loss) *(attach schedule)*	**4f**		
	5 Guaranteed payments to partners	**5**		
	6 Net gain (loss) under section 1231 (other than due to casualty or theft) *(attach Form 4797)*	**6**		
	7 Other income (loss) *(attach schedule)*	**7**		
Deductions	**8** Charitable contributions *(attach schedule)*	**8**		
	9 Section 179 expense deduction *(attach Form 4562)*	**9**		
	10 Deductions related to portfolio income (itemize)	**10**		
	11 Other deductions *(attach schedule)*	**11**		
Investment Interest	**12a** Interest expense on investment debts	**12a**		
	b (1) Investment income included on lines 4a, 4b, 4c, and 4f above	**12b(1)**		
	(2) Investment expenses included on line 10 above	**12b(2)**		
Credits	**13a** Low-income housing credit:			
	(1) From partnerships to which section 42(j)(5) applies for property placed in service before 1990	**13a(1)**		
	(2) Other than on line 13a(1) for property placed in service before 1990	**13a(2)**		
	(3) From partnerships to which section 42(j)(5) applies for property placed in service after 1989	**13a(3)**		
	(4) Other than on line 13a(3) for property placed in service after 1989	**13a(4)**		
	b Qualified rehabilitation expenditures related to rental real estate activities *(attach Form 3468)*	**13b**		
	c Credits (other than credits shown on lines 13a and 13b) related to rental real estate activities	**13c**		
	d Credits related to other rental activities	**13d**		
	14 Other credits	**14**		
Self-Employment	**15a** Net earnings (loss) from self-employment	**15a**		
	b Gross farming or fishing income	**15b**		
	c Gross nonfarm income	**15c**		
Adjustments and Tax Preference Items	**16a** Depreciation adjustment on property placed in service after 1986	**16a**		
	b Adjusted gain or loss	**16b**		
	c Depletion (other than oil and gas)	**16c**		
	d (1) Gross income from oil, gas, and geothermal properties	**16d(1)**		
	(2) Deductions allocable to oil, gas, and geothermal properties	**16d(2)**		
	e Other adjustments and tax preference items *(attach schedule)*	**16e**		
Foreign Taxes	**17a** Type of income ▶ .... **b** Foreign country or U.S. possession ▶			
	c Total gross income from sources outside the United States *(attach schedule)*	**17c**		
	d Total applicable deductions and losses *(attach schedule)*	**17d**		
	e Total foreign taxes (check one): ▶ ☐ Paid ☐ Accrued	**17e**		
	f Reduction in taxes available for credit *(attach schedule)*	**17f**		
	g Other foreign tax information *(attach schedule)*	**17g**		
Other	**18** Section 59(e)(2) expenditures: **a** Type ▶ .... **b** Amount ▶	**18b**		
	19 Tax-exempt interest income	**19**		
	20 Other tax-exempt income	**20**		
	21 Nondeductible expenses	**21**		
	22 Distributions of money (cash and marketable securities)	**22**		
	23 Distributions of property other than money	**23**		
	24 Other items and amounts required to be reported separately to partners *(attach schedule)*			
Analysis	**25a** Income (loss). Combine lines 1 through 7 in column (b). From the result, subtract the sum of lines 8 through 12a, 17e, and 18b	**25a**		

		(b) Individual		**(c) Partnership**	**(d) Exempt organization**	**(e) Nominee/Other**
b Analysis by type of partner:	**(a) Corporate**	**i. Active**	**ii. Passive**			
(1) General partners						
(2) Limited partners						

Form 1065 (1996)   Page **4**

Note: *If Question 5 of Schedule B is answered "Yes," the partnership is not required to complete Schedules L, M-1, and M-2.*

Schedule L   Balance Sheets per Books

Assets	Beginning of tax year		End of tax year	
	(a)	(b)	(c)	(d)
1 Cash				
2a Trade notes and accounts receivable				
b Less allowance for bad debts				
3 Inventories				
4 U.S. government obligations				
5 Tax-exempt securities				
6 Other current assets *(attach schedule)* . . .				
7 Mortgage and real estate loans				
8 Other investments *(attach schedule)* . . .				
9a Buildings and other depreciable assets . .				
b Less accumulated depreciation				
10a Depletable assets				
b Less accumulated depletion				
11 Land (net of any amortization)				
12a Intangible assets (amortizable only). . . .				
b Less accumulated amortization				
13 Other assets *(attach schedule)*				
14 **Total** assets				
Liabilities and Capital				
15 Accounts payable				
16 Mortgages, notes, bonds payable in less than 1 year.				
17 Other current liabilities *(attach schedule)* . . .				
18 All nonrecourse loans				
19 Mortgages, notes, bonds payable in 1 year or more .				
20 Other liabilities *(attach schedule)*				
21 Partners' capital accounts				
22 **Total** liabilities and capital				

Schedule M-1   Reconciliation of Income (Loss) per Books With Income (Loss) per Return
(see page 23 of the instructions)

1 Net income (loss) per books	6 Income recorded on books this year not included on Schedule K, lines 1 through 7 (itemize):	
2 Income included on Schedule K, lines 1 through 4, 6, and 7, not recorded on books this year (itemize):	a Tax-exempt interest $	
....		
3 Guaranteed payments (other than health insurance)	7 Deductions included on Schedule K, lines 1 through 12a, 17e, and 18b, not charged against book income this year (itemize):	
4 Expenses recorded on books this year not included on Schedule K, lines 1 through 12a, 17e, and 18b (itemize):	a Depreciation $	
a Depreciation $	....	
b Travel and entertainment $		
....	8 Add lines 6 and 7	
5 Add lines 1 through 4	9 Income (loss) (Schedule K, line 25a). Subtract line 8 from line 5	

Schedule M-2   Analysis of Partners' Capital Accounts

1 Balance at beginning of year	6 Distributions: a Cash	
2 Capital contributed during year	b Property	
3 Net income (loss) per books	7 Other decreases (itemize):	
4 Other increases (itemize):	....	
....		
....	8 Add lines 6 and 7	
5 Add lines 1 through 4	9 Balance at end of year. Subtract line 8 from line 5	

SCHEDULE K-1
(Form 1065)
Department of the Treasury
Internal Revenue Service

Partner's Share of Income, Credits, Deductions, etc.

▶ **See separate instructions.**

For calendar year 1996 or tax year beginning _____ , 1996, and ending _____ , 19 ___

OMB No. 1545-0099

1996

Partner's identifying number ▶

Partnership's identifying number ▶

Partner's name, address, and ZIP code

Partnership's name, address, and ZIP code

A This partner is a ☐ general partner ☐ limited partner
☐ limited liability company member

B What type of entity is this partner? ▶ ....

C Is this partner a ☐ domestic or a ☐ foreign partner?

D Enter partner's percentage of:

	(i) Before change or termination	**(ii)** End of year
Profit sharing	.... %	.... %
Loss sharing	.... %	.... %
Ownership of capital	.... %	.... %

E IRS Center where partnership filed return:

F Partner's share of liabilities (see instructions):

Nonrecourse . . . . $ ....

Qualified nonrecourse financing . $ ....

Other . . . . $ ....

G Tax shelter registration number . ▶ ....

H Check here if this partnership is a publicly traded partnership as defined in section 469(k)(2) . . . . ☐

I Check applicable boxes: **(1)** ☐ Final K-1 **(2)** ☐ Amended K-1

J Analysis of partner's capital account:

(a) Capital account at beginning of year	**(b)** Capital contributed during year	**(c)** Partner's share of lines 3, 4, and 7, Form 1065, Schedule M-2	**(d)** Withdrawals and distributions	**(e)** Capital account at end of year (combine columns (a) through (d))
			( )	

	(a) Distributive share item		**(b)** Amount	**(c)** 1040 filers enter the amount in column (b) on:
Income (Loss)	**1**	Ordinary income (loss) from trade or business activities . . .	**1**	⎫ See pages 5 and 6 of Partner's Instructions for Schedule K-1 (Form 1065).
	2	Net income (loss) from rental real estate activities	**2**	
	3	Net income (loss) from other rental activities	**3**	⎭
	4	Portfolio income (loss):		
	a	Interest	**4a**	Sch. B, Part I, line 1
	b	Dividends	**4b**	Sch. B, Part II, line 5
	c	Royalties	**4c**	Sch. E, Part I, line 4
	d	Net short-term capital gain (loss)	**4d**	Sch. D, line 5, col. (f) or (g)
	e	Net long-term capital gain (loss).	**4e**	Sch. D, line 13, col. (f) or (g)
	f	Other portfolio income (loss) (attach schedule)	**4f**	Enter on applicable line of your return.
	5	Guaranteed payments to partner	**5**	⎫ See page 6 of Partner's Instructions for Schedule K-1 (Form 1065).
	6	Net gain (loss) under section 1231 (other than due to casualty or theft)	**6**	⎭
	7	Other income (loss) (attach schedule)	**7**	Enter on applicable line of your return.
Deductions	**8**	Charitable contributions (see instructions) (attach schedule) . .	**8**	Sch. A, line 15 or 16
	9	Section 179 expense deduction	**9**	⎫ See page 7 of Partner's Instructions for Schedule K-1 (Form 1065).
	10	Deductions related to portfolio income (attach schedule) . . .	**10**	
	11	Other deductions (attach schedule)	**11**	⎭
Investment Interest	**12a**	Interest expense on investment debts	**12a**	Form 4952, line 1
	b	**(1)** Investment income included on lines 4a, 4b, 4c, and 4f above	**b(1)**	⎫ See page 7 of Partner's Instructions for Schedule K-1 (Form 1065).
		(2) Investment expenses included on line 10 above	**b(2)**	⎭
Credits	**13a**	Low-income housing credit:		
		(1) From section 42(j)(5) partnerships for property placed in service before 1990	**a(1)**	⎫
		(2) Other than on line 13a(1) for property placed in service before 1990	**a(2)**	
		(3) From section 42(j)(5) partnerships for property placed in service after 1989	**a(3)**	⎬ Form 8586, line 5
		(4) Other than on line 13a(3) for property placed in service after 1989	**a(4)**	⎭
	b	Qualified rehabilitation expenditures related to rental real estate activities	**13b**	⎫
	c	Credits (other than credits shown on lines 13a and 13b) related to rental real estate activities	**13c**	⎬ See page 8 of Partner's Instructions for Schedule K-1 (Form 1065).
	d	Credits related to other rental activities	**13d**	
	14	Other credits	**14**	⎭

For Paperwork Reduction Act Notice, see Instructions for Form 1065.

Cat. No. 11394R

Schedule K-1 (Form 1065) 1996

Schedule K-1 (Form 1065) 1996   Page **2**

	(a) Distributive share item		(b) Amount	(c) 1040 filers enter the amount in column (b) on:
Self-employment	**15a**	Net earnings (loss) from self-employment	15a	Sch. SE, Section A or B
	b	Gross farming or fishing income.	15b	See page 8 of Partner's Instructions for Schedule K-1 (Form 1065).
	c	Gross nonfarm income.	15c	
Adjustments and Tax Preference Items	**16a**	Depreciation adjustment on property placed in service after 1986	16a	
	b	Adjusted gain or loss	16b	See pages 8 and 9 of Partner's Instructions for Schedule K-1 (Form 1065) and Instructions for Form 6251.
	c	Depletion (other than oil and gas)	16c	
	d	**(1)** Gross income from oil, gas, and geothermal properties . .	d(1)	
		(2) Deductions allocable to oil, gas, and geothermal properties	d(2)	
	e	Other adjustments and tax preference items *(attach schedule)*	16e	
Foreign Taxes	**17a**	Type of income ▶		Form 1116, check boxes
	b	Name of foreign country or U.S. possession ▶		
	c	Total gross income from sources outside the United States *(attach schedule)*	17c	Form 1116, Part I
	d	Total applicable deductions and losses *(attach schedule)* . .	17d	
	e	Total foreign taxes (check one): ▶ ☐ Paid ☐ Accrued . . .	17e	Form 1116, Part II
	f	Reduction in taxes available for credit *(attach schedule)* . . .	17f	Form 1116, Part III
	g	Other foreign tax information *(attach schedule)*	17g	See Instructions for Form 1116.
Other	**18**	Section 59(e)(2) expenditures: **a** Type ▶		See page 9 of Partner's Instructions for Schedule K-1 (Form 1065).
	b	Amount	18b	
	19	Tax-exempt interest income	19	Form 1040, line 8b
	20	Other tax-exempt income.	20	See page 9 of Partner's Instructions for Schedule K-1 (Form 1065).
	21	Nondeductible expenses	21	
	22	Distributions of money (cash and marketable securities) . . .	22	
	23	Distributions of property other than money	23	
	24	Recapture of low-income housing credit:		
	a	From section 42(j)(5) partnerships	24a	Form 8611, line 8
	b	Other than on line 24a.	24b	

Supplemental Information

25 Supplemental information required to be reported separately to each partner *(attach additional schedules if more space is needed):*

Form 1120-A

Department of the Treasury
Internal Revenue Service

U.S. Corporation Short-Form Income Tax Return

See separate instructions to make sure the corporation qualifies to file Form 1120-A.
For calendar year 1996 or tax year beginning .... , 1996, ending .... , 19 ....

OMB No. 1545-0890

1996

A Check this box if the corp. is a personal service corp. (as defined in Temporary Regs. section 1.441-4T—see instructions) ▶ ☐

Use IRS label. Other-wise, print or type.

Name

Number, street, and room or suite no. (If a P.O. box, see page 6 of instructions.)

City or town, state, and ZIP code

B Employer identification number

C Date incorporated

D Total assets (see page 6 of instructions)

$

E Check applicable boxes: **(1)** ☐ Initial return **(2)** ☐ Change of address
F Check method of accounting: **(1)** ☐ Cash **(2)** ☐ Accrual **(3)** ☐ Other (specify) . . ▶

Income

1a	Gross receipts or sales [____] **b** Less returns and allowances [____] **c** Balance ▶	1c
2	Cost of goods sold (see page 11 of instructions).	2
3	Gross profit. Subtract line 2 from line 1c	3
4	Domestic corporation dividends subject to the 70% deduction	4
5	Interest	5
6	Gross rents	6
7	Gross royalties	7
8	Capital gain net income (attach Schedule D (Form 1120))	8
9	Net gain or (loss) from Form 4797, Part II, line 20 (attach Form 4797)	9
10	Other income (see page 7 of instructions)	10
11	**Total income.** Add lines 3 through 10 ▶	11

Deductions

(See instructions for limitations on deductions.)

12	Compensation of officers (see page 7 of instructions)	12
13	Salaries and wages (less employment credits)	13
14	Repairs and maintenance	14
15	Bad debts	15
16	Rents	16
17	Taxes and licenses	17
18	Interest	18
19	Charitable contributions (see page 8 of instructions for 10% limitation)	19
20	Depreciation (attach Form 4562) 20	
21	Less depreciation claimed elsewhere on return 21a	21b
22	Other deductions (attach schedule)	22
23	**Total deductions.** Add lines 12 through 22 ▶	23
24	Taxable income before net operating loss deduction and special deductions. Subtract line 23 from line 11	24
25	**Less: a** Net operating loss deduction (see page 10 of instructions) 25a	
	b Special deductions (see page 10 of instructions) 25b	25c

Tax and Payments

26	**Taxable income.** Subtract line 25c from line 24	26
27	**Total tax** (from page 2, Part I, line 7)	27
28	**Payments:**	
a	1995 overpayment credited to 1996 28a	
b	1996 estimated tax payments 28b	
c	Less 1996 refund applied for on Form 4466 28c ( ) Bal ▶ 28d	
e	Tax deposited with Form 7004 28e	
f	Credit from regulated investment companies (attach Form 2439) 28f	
g	Credit for Federal tax on fuels (attach Form 4136). See instructions 28g	
h	Total payments. Add lines 28d through 28g	28h
29	Estimated tax penalty (see page 11 of instructions). Check if Form 2220 is attached ▶ ☐	29
30	**Tax due.** If line 28h is smaller than the total of lines 27 and 29, enter amount owed	30
31	**Overpayment.** If line 28h is larger than the total of lines 27 and 29, enter amount overpaid	31
32	Enter amount of line 31 you want: **Credited to 1997 estimated tax** ▶ Refunded ▶	32

Sign Here

Under penalties of perjury, I declare that I have examined this return, including accompanying schedules and statements, and to the best of my knowledge and belief, it is true, correct, and complete. Declaration of preparer (other than taxpayer) is based on all information of which preparer has any knowledge.

▶ _____   _____   ▶ _____
Signature of officer   Date   Title

Paid Preparer's Use Only

Preparer's signature ▶	Date	Check if self-employed ▶ ☐	Preparer's social security number
Firm's name (or yours if self-employed) and address ▶		EIN ▶	
		ZIP code ▶	

For Paperwork Reduction Act Notice, see page 1 of the instructions.   Cat. No. 11456E   Form **1120-A** (1996)

Form 1120-A (1996)   Page **2**

Part I Tax Computation (See page 13 of instructions.)

1	Income tax. If the corporation is a qualified personal service corporation (see page 13), check here ▶ ☐	**1**	
2a	General business credit. Check if from Form(s): ☐ 3800 ☐ 3468 ☐ 5884 ☐ 6478 ☐ 6765 ☐ 8586 ☐ 8830 ☐ 8826 ☐ 8835 ☐ 8844 ☐ 8845 ☐ 8846 ☐ 8820 ☐ 8847	**2a**	
b	Credit for prior year minimum tax (attach Form 8827)	**2b**	
3	**Total credits.** Add lines 2a and 2b	**3**	
4	Subtract line 3 from line 1	**4**	
5	Recapture taxes. Check if from: ☐ Form 4255 ☐ Form 8611	**5**	
6	Alternative minimum tax (attach Form 4626)	**6**	
7	**Total tax.** Add lines 4 through 6. Enter here and on line 27, page 1	**7**	

Part II Other Information (See page 15 of instructions.)

1 See page 17 of the instructions and state the principal:

a Business activity code no. ▶ ....

b Business activity ▶ ....

c Product or service ▶ ....

2 Did any individual, partnership, estate, or trust at the end of the tax year own, directly or indirectly, 50% or more of the corporation's voting stock? (For rules of attribution, see section 267(c).) . . . . ☐ Yes ☐ No

If "Yes," attach a schedule showing name and identifying number.

3 Enter the amount of tax-exempt interest received or accrued during the tax year . . . ▶ |$ |

4 Enter amount of cash distributions and the book value of property (other than cash) distributions made in this tax year . . . . ▶ |$ |

5a If an amount is entered on line 2, page 1, see the worksheet on page 11 for amounts to enter below:

(1) Purchases

(2) Additional sec. 263A costs (attach schedule) . . . .

(3) Other costs (attach schedule) .

b If property is produced or acquired for resale, do the rules of section 263A apply to the corporation? . . . . ☐ Yes ☐ No

6 At any time during the 1996 calendar year, did the corporation have an interest in or a signature or other authority over a financial account (such as a bank account, securities account, or other financial account) in a foreign country? . . . . . ☐ Yes ☐ No
If "Yes," the corporation may have to file Form TD F 90-22.1
If "Yes," enter the name of the foreign country ▶ ....

Part III Balance Sheets per Books

Assets		(a) Beginning of tax year		(b) End of tax year	
1	Cash				
2a	Trade notes and accounts receivable				
b	Less allowance for bad debts	(	)	(	)
3	Inventories				
4	U.S. government obligations				
5	Tax-exempt securities (see instructions)				
6	Other current assets (attach schedule)				
7	Loans to stockholders				
8	Mortgage and real estate loans				
9a	Depreciable, depletable, and intangible assets				
b	Less accumulated depreciation, depletion, and amortization	(	)	(	)
10	Land (net of any amortization)				
11	Other assets (attach schedule)				
12	Total assets				

Liabilities and Stockholders' Equity					
13	Accounts payable				
14	Other current liabilities (attach schedule)				
15	Loans from stockholders				
16	Mortgages, notes, bonds payable				
17	Other liabilities (attach schedule)				
18	Capital stock (preferred and common stock)				
19	Paid-in or capital surplus				
20	Retained earnings				
21	Less cost of treasury stock	(	)	(	)
22	Total liabilities and stockholders' equity				

Part IV Reconciliation of Income (Loss) per Books With Income per Return (You are not required to complete Part IV if the total assets on line 12, column (b), Part III are less than $25,000.)

1	Net income (loss) per books		6 Income recorded on books this year not included on this return (itemize)............	
2	Federal income tax			
3	Excess of capital losses over capital gains		7 Deductions on this return not charged against book income this year (itemize)............	
4	Income subject to tax not recorded on books this year (itemize)			
5	Expenses recorded on books this year not deducted on this return (itemize)		8 Income (line 24, page 1). Enter the sum of lines 1 through 5 less the sum of lines 6 and 7 . . .	

Form **1120**	**U.S. Corporation Income Tax Return**	OMB No. 1545-0123
Department of the Treasury Internal Revenue Service	For calendar year 1996 or tax year beginning .... , 1996, ending .... , 19 ... ► Instructions are separate. See page 1 for Paperwork Reduction Act Notice.	19**96**

A Check if a:
1 Consolidated return (attach Form 851) ☐
2 Personal holding co. (attach Sch. PH) ☐
3 Personal service corp. (as defined in Temporary Regs. sec. 1.441-4T— see instructions) ☐

Use IRS label. Otherwise, print or type.

Name

Number, street, and room or suite no. (If a P.O. box, see page 6 of instructions.)

City or town, state, and ZIP code

B Employer identification number

C Date incorporated

D Total assets (see page 6 of instructions) $

E Check applicable boxes: (1) ☐ Initial return (2) ☐ Final return (3) ☐ Change of address

Income

1a	Gross receipts or sales [____] **b** Less returns and allowances [____] **c** Bal ►	1c
2	Cost of goods sold (Schedule A, line 8)	2
3	Gross profit. Subtract line 2 from line 1c	3
4	Dividends (Schedule C, line 19)	4
5	Interest	5
6	Gross rents	6
7	Gross royalties	7
8	Capital gain net income (attach Schedule D (Form 1120)) . . .	8
9	Net gain or (loss) from Form 4797, Part II, line 20 (attach Form 4797) .	9
10	Other income (see page 7 of instructions—attach schedule) . . .	10
11	**Total income.** Add lines 3 through 10 . . . . ►	11

Deductions (See instructions for limitations on deductions.)

12	Compensation of officers (Schedule E, line 4)		12
13	Salaries and wages (less employment credits)		13
14	Repairs and maintenance		14
15	Bad debts		15
16	Rents		16
17	Taxes and licenses		17
18	Interest		18
19	Charitable contributions (see page 8 of instructions for 10% limitation) .		19
20	Depreciation (attach Form 4562)	20	
21	Less depreciation claimed on Schedule A and elsewhere on return . .	21a	21b
22	Depletion		22
23	Advertising		23
24	Pension, profit-sharing, etc., plans		24
25	Employee benefit programs		25
26	Other deductions (attach schedule)		26
27	**Total deductions.** Add lines 12 through 26 . . . . . . ►		27
28	Taxable income before net operating loss deduction and special deductions. Subtract line 27 from line 11		28
29	**Less:** a Net operating loss deduction (see page 10 of instructions) . .	29a	
	b Special deductions (Schedule C, line 20)	29b	29c

Tax and Payments

30	**Taxable income.** Subtract line 29c from line 28		30
31	**Total tax** (Schedule J, line 10)		31
32	**Payments: a** 1995 overpayment credited to 1996	32a	
b	1996 estimated tax payments . .	32b	
c	Less 1996 refund applied for on Form 4466	32c (___) **d** Bal ►	32d
e	Tax deposited with Form 7004	32e	
f	Credit from regulated investment companies (attach Form 2439) . . .	32f	
g	Credit for Federal tax on fuels (attach Form 4136). See instructions . .	32g	32h
33	Estimated tax penalty (see page 11 of instructions). Check if Form 2220 is attached . . . ► ☐		33
34	**Tax due.** If line 32h is smaller than the total of lines 31 and 33, enter amount owed . . .		34
35	**Overpayment.** If line 32h is larger than the total of lines 31 and 33, enter amount overpaid . .		35
36	Enter amount of line 35 you want: **Credited to 1997 estimated tax** ► [____] **Refunded** ►		36

Sign Here

Under penalties of perjury, I declare that I have examined this return, including accompanying schedules and statements, and to the best of my knowledge and belief, it is true, correct, and complete. Declaration of preparer (other than taxpayer) is based on all information of which preparer has any knowledge.

► _____ Signature of officer   Date

► _____ Title

Paid Preparer's Use Only

Preparer's signature ►	Date	Check if self-employed ☐	Preparer's social security number
Firm's name (or yours if self-employed) and address ►		EIN ►	
		ZIP code ►	

Cat. No. 11450Q

Form 1120 (1996)

Schedule A   Cost of Goods Sold (See page 11 of instructions.)

1	Inventory at beginning of year	1
2	Purchases	2
3	Cost of labor	3
4	Additional section 263A costs (attach schedule)	4
5	Other costs (attach schedule)	5
6	**Total.** Add lines 1 through 5	6
7	Inventory at end of year	7
8	**Cost of goods sold.** Subtract line 7 from line 6. Enter here and on page 1, line 2	8

9a   Check all methods used for valuing closing inventory:

     (i) ☐ Cost as described in Regulations section 1.471-3

     (ii) ☐ Lower of cost or market as described in Regulations section 1.471-4

     (iii) ☐ Other (Specify method used and attach explanation.) ▶ ....

   b   Check if there was a writedown of subnormal goods as described in Regulations section 1.471-2(c) ▶ ☐

   c   Check if the LIFO inventory method was adopted this tax year for any goods (if checked, attach Form 970) ▶ ☐

   d   If the LIFO inventory method was used for this tax year, enter percentage (or amounts) of closing inventory computed under LIFO   **9d**

   e   If property is produced or acquired for resale, do the rules of section 263A apply to the corporation? ☐ Yes ☐ No

   f   Was there any change in determining quantities, cost, or valuations between opening and closing inventory? If "Yes," attach explanation   ☐ Yes ☐ No

Schedule C   Dividends and Special Deductions (See page 12 of instructions.)

		(a) Dividends received	(b) %	(c) Special deductions (a) × (b)
1	Dividends from less-than-20%-owned domestic corporations that are subject to the 70% deduction (other than debt-financed stock)		70	
2	Dividends from 20%-or-more-owned domestic corporations that are subject to the 80% deduction (other than debt-financed stock)		80	
3	Dividends on debt-financed stock of domestic and foreign corporations (section 246A)		see instructions	
4	Dividends on certain preferred stock of less-than-20%-owned public utilities		42	
5	Dividends on certain preferred stock of 20%-or-more-owned public utilities		48	
6	Dividends from less-than-20%-owned foreign corporations and certain FSCs that are subject to the 70% deduction		70	
7	Dividends from 20%-or-more-owned foreign corporations and certain FSCs that are subject to the 80% deduction		80	
8	Dividends from wholly owned foreign subsidiaries subject to the 100% deduction (section 245(b))		100	
9	**Total.** Add lines 1 through 8. See page 12 of instructions for limitation			
10	Dividends from domestic corporations received by a small business investment company operating under the Small Business Investment Act of 1958		100	
11	Dividends from certain FSCs that are subject to the 100% deduction (section 245(c)(1))		100	
12	Dividends from affiliated group members subject to the 100% deduction (section 243(a)(3))		100	
13	Other dividends from foreign corporations not included on lines 3, 6, 7, 8, or 11			
14	Income from controlled foreign corporations under subpart F (attach Form(s) 5471)			
15	Foreign dividend gross-up (section 78)			
16	IC-DISC and former DISC dividends not included on lines 1, 2, or 3 (section 246(d))			
17	Other dividends			
18	Deduction for dividends paid on certain preferred stock of public utilities			
19	**Total dividends.** Add lines 1 through 17. Enter here and on line 4, page 1 ▶			
20	**Total special deductions.** Add lines 9, 10, 11, 12, and 18. Enter here and on line 29b, page 1 ▶			

Schedule E   Compensation of Officers (See instructions for line 12, page 1.)

Complete Schedule E only if total receipts (line 1a plus lines 4 through 10 on page 1, Form 1120) are $500,000 or more.

(a) Name of officer	(b) Social security number	(c) Percent of time devoted to business	Percent of corporation stock owned (d) Common	(e) Preferred	(f) Amount of compensation
1		%	%	%	
		%	%	%	
		%	%	%	
		%	%	%	
		%	%	%	

2	Total compensation of officers	
3	Compensation of officers claimed on Schedule A and elsewhere on return	
4	Subtract line 3 from line 2. Enter the result here and on line 12, page 1	

Schedule J Tax Computation (See page 13 of instructions.)

1 Check if the corporation is a member of a controlled group (see sections 1561 and 1563) . . . . . ▶ ☐

   Important: Members of a controlled group, see instructions on page 13.

2a If the box on line 1 is checked, enter the corporation's share of the $50,000, $25,000, and $9,925,000 taxable income brackets (in that order):

   (1) $ _____   **(2)** $ _____   **(3)** $ _____

b Enter the corporation's share of:

   (1) Additional 5% tax (not more than $11,750) $ _____

   (2) Additional 3% tax (not more than $100,000) $ _____

3 Income tax. Check this box if the corporation is a qualified personal service corporation as defined in section 448(d)(2) (see instructions on page 13). . . . . ▶ ☐ | **3** |

4a Foreign tax credit (attach Form 1118) . . . . | **4a** |

b Possessions tax credit (attach Form 5735) . . . . | **4b** |

c Check: ☐ Nonconventional source fuel credit ☐ QEV credit (attach Form 8834) | **4c** |

d General business credit. Enter here and check which forms are attached:

   ☐ 3800 ☐ 3468 ☐ 5884 ☐ 6478 ☐ 6765 ☐ 8586 ☐ 8830

   ☐ 8826 ☐ 8835 ☐ 8844 ☐ 8845 ☐ 8846 ☐ 8820 ☐ 8847 | **4d** |

e Credit for prior year minimum tax (attach Form 8827) . . . . | **4e** |

5 **Total credits.** Add lines 4a through 4e . . . . | **5** |

6 Subtract line 5 from line 3 . . . . | **6** |

7 Personal holding company tax (attach Schedule PH (Form 1120)) . . . . | **7** |

8 Recapture taxes. Check if from: ☐ Form 4255 ☐ Form 8611 . . . . . | **8** |

9 Alternative minimum tax (attach Form 4626) . . . . | **9** |

10 **Total tax.** Add lines 6 through 9. Enter here and on line 31, page 1 . . . . | **10** |

Schedule K Other Information (See page 15 of instructions.)

	Yes	No

1 Check method of accounting: **a** ☐ Cash

   b ☐ Accrual **c** ☐ Other (specify) ▶ _____

2 See page 17 of the instructions and state the principal:

a Business activity code no. ▶ _____

b Business activity ▶ _____

c Product or service ▶ _____

3 Did the corporation at the end of the tax year own, directly or indirectly, 50% or more of the voting stock of a domestic corporation? (For rules of attribution, see section 267(c).) . . . .

   If "Yes," attach a schedule showing: (a) name and identifying number, (b) percentage owned, and (c) taxable income or (loss) before NOL and special deductions of such corporation for the tax year ending with or within your tax year.

4 Is the corporation a subsidiary in an affiliated group or a parent-subsidiary controlled group? . . . . . .

   If "Yes," enter employer identification number and name of the parent corporation ▶ _____

5 Did any individual, partnership, corporation, estate or trust at the end of the tax year own, directly or indirectly, 50% or more of the corporation's voting stock? (For rules of attribution, see section 267(c).) . . . . . .

   If "Yes," attach a schedule showing name and identifying number. (Do not include any information already entered in **4** above.) Enter percentage owned ▶ _____

6 During this tax year, did the corporation pay dividends (other than stock dividends and distributions in exchange for stock) in excess of the corporation's current and accumulated earnings and profits? (See secs. 301 and 316.) . . . .

   If "Yes," file Form 5452. If this is a consolidated return, answer here for the parent corporation and on **Form 851,** Affiliations Schedule, for each subsidiary.

	Yes	No

7 Was the corporation a U.S. shareholder of any controlled foreign corporation? (See sections 951 and 957.) . . .

   If "Yes," attach Form 5471 for each such corporation. Enter number of Forms 5471 attached ▶ _____

8 At any time during the 1996 calendar year, did the corporation have an interest in or a signature or other authority over a financial account (such as a bank account, securities account, or other financial account) in a foreign country?

   If "Yes," the corporation may have to file Form TD F 90-22.1.

   If "Yes," enter name of foreign country ▶ _____

9 During the tax year, did the corporation receive a distribution from, or was it the grantor of, or transferor to, a foreign trust? If "Yes," see page 16 of the instructions for other forms the corporation may have to file . . . .

10 Did one foreign person at any time during the tax year own, directly or indirectly, at least 25% of: **(a)** the total voting power of all classes of stock of the corporation entitled to vote, or **(b)** the total value of all classes of stock of the corporation? If "Yes,"

a Enter percentage owned ▶ _____

b Enter owner's country ▶ _____

c The corporation may have to file Form 5472. Enter number of Forms 5472 attached ▶ _____

11 Check this box if the corporation issued publicly offered debt instruments with original issue discount . ▶ ☐

   If so, the corporation may have to file Form 8281.

12 Enter the amount of tax-exempt interest received or accrued during the tax year ▶ $ _____

13 If there were 35 or fewer shareholders at the end of the tax year, enter the number ▶ _____

14 If the corporation has an NOL for the tax year and is electing to forego the carryback period, check here ▶ ☐

15 Enter the available NOL carryover from prior tax years (Do not reduce it by any deduction on line 29a.) ▶ $ _____

Form 1120 (1996)　　　　　　　　　　　　　　　　　　　　　　　　　　　　　Page **4**

Schedule L	Balance Sheets per Books	Beginning of tax year		End of tax year	
	Assets	**(a)**	**(b)**	**(c)**	**(d)**
1	Cash				
2a	Trade notes and accounts receivable . . .				
b	Less allowance for bad debts	( )		( )	
3	Inventories				
4	U.S. government obligations				
5	Tax-exempt securities (see instructions) . .				
6	Other current assets (attach schedule) . .				
7	Loans to stockholders				
8	Mortgage and real estate loans . . .				
9	Other investments (attach schedule) . .				
10a	Buildings and other depreciable assets . .				
b	Less accumulated depreciation	( )		( )	
11a	Depletable assets				
b	Less accumulated depletion	( )		( )	
12	Land (net of any amortization)				
13a	Intangible assets (amortizable only) . . .				
b	Less accumulated amortization	( )		( )	
14	Other assets (attach schedule)				
15	Total assets				
	Liabilities and Stockholders' Equity				
16	Accounts payable				
17	Mortgages, notes, bonds payable in less than 1 year				
18	Other current liabilities (attach schedule) . .				
19	Loans from stockholders				
20	Mortgages, notes, bonds payable in 1 year or more				
21	Other liabilities (attach schedule)				
22	Capital stock:　**a** Preferred stock . . .				
	b Common stock . . .				
23	Paid-in or capital surplus				
24	Retained earnings—Appropriated (attach schedule)				
25	Retained earnings—Unappropriated . . .				
26	Less cost of treasury stock		( )		( )
27	Total liabilities and stockholders' equity . .				

Note: *You are not required to complete Schedules M-1 and M-2 below if the total assets on line 15, column (d) of Schedule L are less than $25,000.*

Schedule M-1	Reconciliation of Income (Loss) per Books With Income per Return (See page 16 of instructions.)

1	Net income (loss) per books		**7** Income recorded on books this year not included on this return (itemize):	
2	Federal income tax		Tax-exempt interest $	
3	Excess of capital losses over capital gains .		....	
4	Income subject to tax not recorded on books this year (itemize):		**8** Deductions on this return not charged against book income this year (itemize):	
	....		**a** Depreciation . . . . $	
5	Expenses recorded on books this year not deducted on this return (itemize):		**b** Contributions carryover　$	
a	Depreciation . . . . $		....	
b	Contributions carryover　$			
c	Travel and entertainment　$			
	....		**9** Add lines 7 and 8	
6	Add lines 1 through 5		**10** Income (line 28, page 1)—line 6 less line 9	

Schedule M-2	Analysis of Unappropriated Retained Earnings per Books (Line 25, Schedule L)

1	Balance at beginning of year		**5** Distributions:　**a** Cash	
2	Net income (loss) per books		**b** Stock	
3	Other increases (itemize):		**c** Property	
	....		**6** Other decreases (itemize):	
	....		....	
	....		**7** Add lines 5 and 6	
4	Add lines 1, 2, and 3		**8** Balance at end of year (line 4 less line 7)	

| SCHEDULE PH
(Form 1120)

Department of the Treasury
Internal Revenue Service | U.S. Personal Holding Company (PHC) Tax
► See separate instructions. Attach to tax return.
For Paperwork Reduction Act Notice, see page 1 of the Instructions for Forms 1120 and 1120-A. | OMB No. 1545-0123

1996 |

| Name | | Employer identification number |

Part I — Undistributed Personal Holding Company Income (See instructions.)

Additions

1	Taxable income before net operating loss deduction and special deductions. Enter amount from Form 1120, line 28	1
2	Contributions deducted in figuring line 1. Enter amount from Form 1120, line 19	2
3	Excess expenses and depreciation under section 545(b)(6). Enter amount from Part V, line 2	3
4	Total. Add lines 1 through 3	4

Deductions

5	Federal and foreign income, war profits, and excess profits taxes not deducted in figuring line 1 (attach schedule)	5
6	Contributions deductible under section 545(b)(2). See instructions for limitation	6
7	Net operating loss for the preceding tax year deductible under section 545(b)(4)	7
8a	Net capital gain. Enter amount from Schedule D (Form 1120), line 12. Foreign corporations, see instructions	8a		
b	Less: Income tax on this net capital gain (see section 545(b)(5)). Attach computation	8b	8c
9	Deduction for dividends paid (other than dividends paid after the end of the tax year). Enter amount from Part VI, line 5	9
10	Total. Add lines 5 through 9	10
11	Subtract line 10 from line 4	11
12	Dividends paid after the end of the tax year (other than deficiency dividends defined in section 547(d)), but not more than the smaller of line 11 or 20% of line 1, Part VI . . .	12
13	**Undistributed PHC income.** Subtract line 12 from line 11. Foreign corporations, see instructions	13

Note: *If the information in Part II and Part IV is not submitted with the return, the limitation period for assessment and collection of the PHC tax is 6 years. See section 6501(f).*

Part II — Personal Holding Company Income (See instructions.)

14	Dividends		14
15a	Interest	15a	
b	Less: Amounts excluded under section 543(a)(1)(A), 543(a)(1)(B), 543(a)(1)(D), or 543(b)(2)(C) (attach schedule)	15b	15c
16	Royalties (other than mineral, oil, gas, or copyright royalties)		16
17	Annuities		17
18a	Rents	18a	
b	Less: Adjustments described in section 543(b)(2)(A) (attach schedule)	18b	18c
19a	Mineral, oil, and gas royalties	19a	
b	Less: Adjustments described in section 543(b)(2)(B) (attach schedule)	19b	19c
20	Copyright royalties		20
21	Produced film rents		21
22	Compensation received for use of corporation property by 25% or more shareholder . . .		22
23	Amounts received under personal service contracts and from their sale		23
24	Amounts includible in taxable income from estates and trusts		24
25	**PHC income.** Add lines 14 through 24		25

Part III — Tax on Undistributed Personal Holding Company Income

26	**PHC tax.** Enter 39.6% of line 13 here and on Schedule J (Form 1120), line 7, or on the proper line of the appropriate tax return	26

Cat. No. 11465P   Schedule PH (Form 1120) 1996

Part IV   Stock Ownership

Enter the names and addresses of the individuals who together owned directly or indirectly at any time during the last half of the tax year more than 50% in value of the outstanding stock of the corporation.

(a) Name	(b) Address	Highest percentage of shares owned during last half of tax year	
		(c) Preferred	(d) Common
1		%	%
		%	%
		%	%
		%	%
		%	%
2 Add the amounts in columns (c) and (d) and enter the totals here . . . . ▶		%	%

Part V   Excess of Expenses and Depreciation Over Income From Property Not Allowable Under Section 545(b)(6) (See instructions for Part I, line 3.)

(a) Kind of property	(b) Date acquired	(c) Cost or other basis	(d) Depreciation	(e) Repairs, insurance, and other expenses (section 162) (attach schedule)	(f) Total of columns (d) and (e)	(g) Income from rent or other compensation	(h) Excess (col. (f) less col. (g))
1							

2 Total excess of expenses and depreciation over rent or other compensation. Add the amounts in column (h) and enter the total here and on Part I, line 3 . . . .

Note: *Attach a statement showing the names and addresses of persons from whom rent or other compensation was received for the use of, or the right to use, each property.*

Part VI   Deduction for Dividends Paid (Determined Under Section 562)

1	Taxable dividends paid. Do not include dividends considered as paid in the preceding tax year under section 563 or deficiency dividends as defined in section 547	**1**	
2	Consent dividends. Attach Forms 972 and 973	**2**	
3	Taxable distributions. Add lines 1 and 2	**3**	
4	Dividend carryover from first and second preceding tax years. Attach computation	**4**	
5	Deduction for dividends paid. Add lines 3 and 4 and enter the result here and on Part I, line 9	**5**	

Form 1120-F

Department of the Treasury
Internal Revenue Service

U.S. Income Tax Return of a Foreign Corporation

For calendar year 1996, or tax year beginning .... , 1996, and ending .... , 19 .....
▶ See separate instructions.

OMB No. 1545-0126

1996

Please type or print

Name

Employer identification number

Number, street, and room or suite no. (see page 5 of instructions)

City or town, state and ZIP code, or country

Check applicable boxes:
☐ Initial return ☐ Amended return
☐ Final return ☐ Change of address

A Country of incorporation ....

B Foreign country under whose laws the income reported on this return is subject to tax ....

C Date incorporated ....

D Location of corporation's primary books and records:

City, state and country ....

Principal location of business ....

E If the corporation had an agent in the United States at any time during the tax year, enter:

Kind of agent ....

Name ....

Address ....

F Refer to the list on page 17 of the instructions and state the corporation's principal:

(1) Business activity code number ▶ ....

(2) Business activity ▶ ....

(3) Product or service ▶ ....

G Check method of accounting: **(1)** ☐ Cash **(2)** ☐ Accrual
(3) ☐ Other (specify) ▶ ....

	Yes	No
H Did the corporation file a U.S. income tax return for the preceding tax year?		
I Was the corporation at any time during the tax year engaged in a trade or business in the United States?		
J Did the corporation at any time during the tax year have a permanent establishment in the United States for purposes of applying section 894(b) and any applicable tax treaty between the United States and a foreign country?		

If "Yes," enter the name of the foreign country:

....

K Is the corporation a foreign personal holding company? (See section 552 for definition.) . .

If "Yes," have you filed Form 5471? (Sec. 6035). See page 4 of the instructions

L Did the corporation have any transactions with related parties? . . . .

If "Yes," you may have to file Form 5472 (section 6038A and section 6038C). See page 4 of the instructions.

Enter number of Forms 5472 attached ▶ ....

Note: *Additional information is required at the bottom of pages 2 and 5.*

Computation of Tax Due or Overpayment

1	Tax from Section I, line 11, page 2	**1**
2	Tax from Section II, Schedule J, line 9, page 4	**2**
3	Tax from Section III (add lines 6 and 10 on page 5)	**3**
4	Personal holding company tax (attach Schedule PH (Form 1120))—see page 6 of instructions	**4**
5	**Total tax.** Add lines 1 through 4	**5**
6	**Payments:**	
a	1995 overpayment credited to 1996 **6a**	
b	1996 estimated tax payments . . **6b**	
c	Less 1996 refund applied for on Form 4466 **6c** ( ) Bal ▶ **6d**	
e	Tax deposited with Form 7004 . . . **6e**	
f	Credit from regulated investment companies (attach Form 2439) **6f**	
g	Credit for Federal tax on fuels (attach Form 4136). See instructions . . **6g**	
h	U.S. income tax paid or withheld at source (add line 12, page 2, and amounts from Forms 8288-A and 8805 (attach Forms 8288-A and 8805)) **6h**	
i	Total payments. Add lines 6d through 6h	**6i**
7	Estimated tax penalty (see page 6 of instructions). Check if Form 2220 is attached . . . . . ▶ ☐	**7**
8	**Tax due.** If line 6i is smaller than the total of lines 5 and 7, enter amount owed	**8**
9	**Overpayment.** If line 6i is larger than the total of lines 5 and 7, enter amount overpaid . .	**9**
10	Enter amount of line 9 you want: **Credited to 1997 estimated tax** ▶ Refunded ▶	**10**

Please Sign Here

Under penalties of perjury, I declare that I have examined this return, including accompanying schedules and statements, and to the best of my knowledge and belief, it is true, correct, and complete. Declaration of preparer (other than taxpayer) is based on all information of which preparer has any knowledge.

▶ Signature of officer   Date   ▶ Title

Paid Preparer's Use Only

Preparer's signature ▶		Date	Check if self-employed ▶ ☐	Preparer's social security number
Firm's name (or yours if self-employed) and address ▶			EIN ▶	
			ZIP code ▶	

For Paperwork Reduction Act Notice, see page 1 of separate instructions.   Cat. No. 11470I   Form **1120-F** (1996)

SECTION I.—Certain Gains, Profits, and Income From U.S. Sources That Are NOT Effectively Connected With the Conduct of a Trade or Business in the United States (See page 6 of instructions.)

If you are required to complete Section II or are using Form 1120-F as a claim for refund of tax withheld at source, include below **ALL** income from U.S. sources that is **NOT** effectively connected with the conduct of a trade or business in the United States. Otherwise, include only those items of income on which the U.S. income tax was not fully paid at the source. The rate of tax on each item of **gross** income listed below is 30% (4% for the gross transportation tax) or such lower rate specified by tax treaty. No deductions are allowed against these types of income. Fill in treaty rates where applicable. **If the corporation claimed a lower treaty rate, also complete Item W, page 5.**

Name of treaty country, if any ▶

(a) Nature of income	(b) Gross income	(c) Rate of tax (%)	(d) Amount of tax	(e) Amount of U.S. income tax paid or withheld at the source
1 Interest				
2 Dividends				
3 Rents				
4 Royalties				
5 Annuities				
6 Gains from disposal of timber, coal, or domestic iron ore with a retained economic interest (attach supporting schedule)				
7 Gains from sale or exchange of patents, copyrights, etc.				
8 Fiduciary distributions (attach supporting schedule)				
9 Gross transportation income (see page 6 of instructions).		4		
10 Other fixed or determinable annual or periodic gains, profits, and income .				
11 Total. Enter here and on line 1, page 1 . . . . ▶				
12 Total. Enter here and include on line 6h, page 1. . . . . ▶				

Additional Information Required (continued from page 1)

		Yes	No
M	Is the corporation a personal holding company? (See section 542 for definition.).		
N	Is the corporation a controlled foreign corporation? (See section 957 for definition.)		
O	Is the corporation a personal service corporation? (See page 6 of instructions for definition.).		
P	Enter tax-exempt interest received or accrued during the tax year (see instructions) ▶ $ _____		
Q	Did the corporation at the end of the tax year own, directly or indirectly, 50% or more of the voting stock of a U.S. corporation? (See section 267(c) for rules of attribution.)		

If "Yes," attach a schedule showing (1) name and identifying number of such U.S. corporation; (2) percentage owned; and (3) taxable income or (loss) before NOL and special deductions of such U.S. corporation for the tax year ending with or within your tax year.

R If the corporation has a net operating loss (NOL) for the tax year and is electing to forego the carryback period, check here . . . . ▶ ☐

		Yes	No
S	Enter the available NOL carryover from prior tax years. (Do not reduce it by any deduction on line 30a, page 3.) ▶ $ _____		
T	Is the corporation a subsidiary in a parent-subsidiary controlled group?		

If "Yes," enter the name and employer identification number of the parent corporation ▶ _____

U Did any individual, partnership, corporation, estate, or trust at the end of the tax year own, directly or indirectly, 50% or more of the corporation's voting stock? (See section 267(c) for attribution rules.) . .

If "Yes," attach a schedule showing the name and identifying number. (Do not include any information already entered in **T** above).

Enter percentage owned ▶ _____

Note: Additional information is required at the bottom of page 5.

SECTION II.—Income Effectively Connected With the Conduct of a Trade or Business in the United States
(See page 7 of instructions.)

IMPORTANT—Fill in all applicable lines and schedules. If you need more space, see **Attachments** on page 5 of instructions.

Income

1a Gross receipts or sales ⌐_____⌐ **b** Less returns and allowances ⌐_____⌐ **c** Bal ▶	1c	
2 Cost of goods sold (Schedule A, line 8)	2	
3 Gross profit (subtract line 2 from line 1c)	3	
4 Dividends (Schedule C, line 14)	4	
5 Interest	5	
6 Gross rents	6	
7 Gross royalties	7	
8 Capital gain net income (attach Schedule D (Form 1120))	8	
9 Net gain or (loss) from Form 4797, Part II, line 20 (attach Form 4797) . .	9	
10 Other income (see page 8 of instructions—attach schedule).	10	
11 **Total income.** Add lines 3 through 10 . . . . ▶	11	

Deductions (See instructions for limitations on deductions.)

12 Compensation of officers (Schedule E, line 4). Deduct only amounts connected with a U.S. business	12	
13 Salaries and wages (less employment credits)	13	
14 Repairs and maintenance	14	
15 Bad debts	15	
16 Rents	16	
17 Taxes and licenses	17	
18 Interest deduction allowable under Regulations section 1.882-5 . . .	18	
19 Charitable contributions (see page 10 of instructions for 10% limitation) .	19	
20 Depreciation (attach Form 4562) **20**		
21 Less depreciation claimed on Schedule A and elsewhere on return **21**		
22 Balance (subtract line 21 from line 20)	22	
23 Depletion	23	
24 Advertising	24	
25 Pension, profit-sharing, etc., plans	25	
26 Employee benefit programs	26	
27 Other deductions (see page 10 of instructions—attach schedule) . . .	27	
28 **Total deductions.** Add lines 12 through 27 . . . . ▶	28	
29 Taxable income before NOL deduction and special deductions (subtract line 28 from line 11) .	29	
30 **Less: a** Net operating loss deduction (see page 11 of instructions) **30a**		
b Special deductions (Schedule C, line 15). **30b**	30c	
31 Taxable income or (loss). Subtract line 30c from line 29	31	

Schedule A   Cost of Goods Sold (See instructions beginning on page 11.)

1 Inventory at beginning of year	1	
2 Purchases	2	
3 Cost of labor	3	
4 Additional section 263A costs (see page 12 of instructions—attach schedule)	4	
5 Other costs (attach schedule)	5	
6 Add lines 1 through 5	6	
7 Inventory at end of year	7	
8 **Cost of goods sold.** Subtract line 7 from line 6. Enter here and on Section II, line 2	8	

9a Check all methods used for valuing closing inventory:

(1) ☐ Cost as described in Regulations section 1.471-3

(2) ☐ Lower of cost or market as described in Regulations section 1.471-4

(3) ☐ Other (Specify method used and attach explanation.) ▶ ------------------------------

b Check if there was a writedown of subnormal goods as described in Regulations section 1.471-2(c) . . . . . ▶ ☐

c Check if the LIFO inventory method was adopted this tax year for any goods . . . . ▶ ☐

If checked, attach Form 970.

d If the LIFO inventory method was used for this tax year, enter percentage (or amounts) of closing inventory computed under LIFO **9d**

e Do the rules of section 263A (for property produced or acquired for resale) apply to the corporation? . . ☐ **Yes** ☐ **No**

f Was there any change in determining quantities, cost, or valuations between opening and closing inventory? . ☐ **Yes** ☐ **No**

If "Yes," attach explanation.

Form 1120-F (1996)   Page **4**

Schedule C	Dividends and Special Deductions (See instructions.)	(a) Dividends received	(b) %	(c) Special deductions: (a) × (b)
1	Dividends from less-than-20%-owned domestic corporations that are subject to the 70% deduction (other than debt-financed stock) . . .		70	
2	Dividends from 20%-or-more-owned domestic corporations that are subject to the 80% deduction (other than debt-financed stock) . . .		80	
3	Dividends on debt-financed stock of domestic and foreign corporations (section 246A)		see instructions	
4	Dividends on certain preferred stock of less-than-20%-owned public utilities		42	
5	Dividends on certain preferred stock of 20%-or-more-owned public utilities		48	
6	Dividends from less-than-20%-owned foreign corporations that are subject to the 70% deduction		70	
7	Dividends from 20%-or-more-owned foreign corporations that are subject to the 80% deduction		80	
8	**Total.** Add lines 1 through 7. See page 12 of instructions for limitation .			
9	Other dividends from foreign corporations not included on lines 3, 6, and 7			
10	Foreign dividend gross-up (section 78)			
11	IC-DISC and former DISC dividends not included on lines 1, 2, or 3 (section 246(d))			
12	Other dividends			
13	Deduction for dividends paid on certain preferred stock of a public utility			
14	Total dividends. Add lines 1 through 12. Enter here and on line 4, page 3			
15	Total deductions. Add lines 8 and 13. Enter here and on line 30b, page 3			

Schedule E	Compensation of Officers (Complete Schedule E only if total receipts (line 1a plus lines 4 through 10 of Section II) are $500,000 or more. See **Line 12. Compensation of officers** on page 9 of instructions.)

(a) Name of officer	(b) Social security number	(c) Percent of time devoted to business	Percent of corporation stock owned		(f) Amount of compensation
			(d) Common	(e) Preferred	
1		%	%	%	
		%	%	%	
		%	%	%	
		%	%	%	
		%	%	%	
		%	%	%	
		%	%	%	

2 Total compensation of officers . . . .

3 Compensation of officers claimed on Schedule A and elsewhere on this return . . . . .

4 Subtract line 3 from line 2. Enter the result here and on line 12, page 3 . . . .

Schedule J	Tax Computation (See page 13 of instructions.)

1 Check if the corporation is a member of a controlled group (see sections 1561 and 1563) ▶ ☐
Important: Members of a controlled group, see instructions on page 13.

2a If the box on line 1 is checked, enter the corporation's share of the $50,000, $25,000, and $9,925,000 taxable income bracket amounts (in that order):
(1) $ _____ **(2)** $ _____ **(3)** $ _____

b Enter the corporation's share of:
(1) Additional 5% tax (not more than $11,750) $ _____
(2) Additional 3% tax (not more than $100,000) $ _____

3 Income tax. Check this box if the corporation is a qualified personal service corporation (see page 14 of the instructions) ▶ ☐ **3**

4a Foreign tax credit (attach Form 1118) **4a**

b Check: ☐ Nonconventional source fuel credit
☐ QEV credit (attach Form 8834)   **4b**

c General business credit. Enter here and check which **forms** are attached:
☐ 3800   ☐ 3468   ☐ 5884   ☐ 6478   ☐ 6765
☐ 8586   ☐ 8830   ☐ 8826   ☐ 8835   ☐ 8844
☐ 8845   ☐ 8846   ☐ 8820   ☐ 8847   **4c**

d Credit for prior year minimum tax (attach Form 8827) **4d**

5 **Total credits.** Add lines 4a through 4d **5**

6 Subtract line 5 from line 3 . . . .   **6**

7 Recapture taxes. Check if from: ☐ Form 4255 ☐ Form 8611 . . . .   **7**

8 Alternative minimum tax (attach Form 4626) **8**

9 **Total tax under section 882(a).** Add lines 6 through 8. Enter here and on line 2, page 1 . .   **9**

SECTION III.—Branch Profits Tax and Tax on Excess Interest (See page 15 of the instructions.)

Part I—Branch Profits Tax

1 Enter the amount from Section II, line 29 . . . . | **1** | | |

2 Enter total adjustments made to get effectively connected earnings and profits. (Attach a schedule showing the nature and amount of adjustments.) (See instructions.) . . . . . | **2** | | |

3 Effectively connected earnings and profits. Combine line 1 and line 2. Enter the result here . . | **3** | | |

4a Enter U.S. net equity at the end of the current tax year. (Attach schedule.) . . . . . . | **4a** | | |

b Enter U.S. net equity at the end of the prior tax year. (Attach schedule.) . . . . | **4b** | | |

c Increase in U.S. net equity. If line 4a is greater than or equal to line 4b, subtract line 4b from line 4a. Enter the result here and skip to line 4e . . . . | **4c** | | |

d Decrease in U.S. net equity. If line 4b is greater than line 4a, subtract line 4a from line 4b. Enter the result here . . . . | **4d** | | |

e Non-previously taxed accumulated effectively connected earnings and profits. Enter excess, if any, of effectively connected earnings and profits for preceding tax years beginning after 1986 over any dividend equivalent amounts for those tax years . . . . | **4e** | | |

5 Dividend equivalent amount. Subtract line 4c from line 3. Enter the result here. If zero or less, enter -0-. If no amount is entered on line 4c, add the lesser of line 4d or line 4e to line 3 and enter the total here . . . . | **5** | | |

6 **Branch profits tax.** Multiply line 5 by 30% (or lower treaty rate if the corporation is a qualified resident or otherwise qualifies for treaty benefits). Enter here and include on line 3, page 1. (See instructions.) **Also complete Items W and X below** . . . . | **6** | | |

Part II—Tax on Excess Interest

7a Enter the interest from Section II, line 18 . . . . | **7a** | | |

b Enter the interest apportioned to the effectively connected income of the foreign corporation that is capitalized or otherwise nondeductible. . . . . | **7b** | | |

c Add lines 7a and 7b . . . . | **7c** | | |

8 Enter the branch interest (including capitalized and other nondeductible interest). (See instructions for definition.) If the interest paid by the foreign corporation's U.S. trade or business was increased because 80% or more of the foreign corporation's assets are U.S. assets, check this box . . . . ▶ ☐ | **8** | | |

9a Excess interest. Subtract line 8 from line 7c. If zero or less, enter -0-. . . . . | **9a** | | |

b If the foreign corporation is a bank, enter the excess interest treated as interest on deposits. Otherwise, enter -0-. (See page 16 of instructions.). . . . . | **9b** | | |

c Subtract line 9b from line 9a . . . . | **9c** | | |

10 **Tax on excess interest.** Multiply line 9c by 30% or lower treaty rate (if the corporation is a qualified resident or otherwise qualifies for treaty benefits). (See page 16 of instructions.) Enter here and include on line 3, page 1. **Also complete Items W and X below** . . . . | **10** | | |

Additional Information Required (continued from page 2)

	Yes	No
V Is the corporation claiming a reduction in, or exemption from, the branch profits tax due to:		
(1) A complete termination of all U.S. trades or businesses?		
(2) The tax-free liquidation or reorganization of a foreign corporation?.		
(3) The tax-free incorporation of a U.S. trade or business?		

If **(1)** applies or **(2)** applies and the transferee is domestic, attach Form 8848.

If **(3)** applies, attach the statement required by Regulations section 1.884-2T(d)(5).

	Yes	No
W Is the corporation taking a position on this return that a U.S. tax treaty overrules or modifies an Internal Revenue law of the United States thereby causing a reduction of tax?		

If "Yes," complete and attach Form 8833.

Note: *Failure to disclose a treaty-based return position may result in a $10,000 penalty (see section 6712).*

X If the corporation is claiming it is a qualified resident of its country of residence for purposes of computing its branch profits tax and excess interest tax, check the basis for that claim:

Stock ownership and base erosion test . . . . ☐
Publicly traded test . . . . ☐
Active trade or business test . . . . ☐
Private letter ruling . . . . ☐

Form 1120-F (1996)   Page **6**

Additional schedules to be completed for Section II or Section III (See page 16 of instructions.)

Schedule L Balance Sheets per Books	Beginning of tax year		End of tax year	
ASSETS	(a)	(b)	(c)	(d)
1 Cash				
2a Trade notes and accounts receivable				
b Less allowance for bad debts . . .	( )		( )	
3 Inventories				
4 U.S. government obligations . . .				
5 Tax-exempt securities (see instructions)				
6 Other current assets (attach schedule)				
7 Loans to stockholders				
8 Mortgage and real estate loans . .				
9 Other investments (attach schedule) .				
10a Buildings and other fixed depreciable assets				
b Less accumulated depreciation . .	( )		( )	
11a Depletable assets				
b Less accumulated depletion . . .	( )		( )	
12 Land (net of any amortization) . . .				
13a Intangible assets (amortizable only) .				
b Less accumulated amortization . .	( )		( )	
14 Other assets (attach schedule). . .				
15 Total assets				
LIABILITIES AND STOCKHOLDERS' EQUITY				
16 Accounts payable				
17 Mtges., notes, bonds payable in less than 1 year				
18 Other current liabilities (attach schedule)				
19 Loans from stockholders				
20 Mtges., notes, bonds payable in 1 year or more				
21 Other liabilities (attach schedule) . .				
22 Capital stock: **a** Preferred stock . .				
b Common stock . .				
23 Paid-in or capital surplus				
24 Retained earnings—Appropriated (attach schedule)				
25 Retained earnings—Unappropriated .				
26 Less cost of treasury stock		( )		( )
27 Total liabilities and stockholders' equity				

Note: *The corporation is not required to complete Schedules M-1 and M-2 below if the total assets on Schedule L, line 15, column (d) are less than $25,000.*

Schedule M-1   Reconciliation of Income (Loss) per Books With Income per Return

1 Net income (loss) per books . . .		**7** Income recorded on books this year not included on this return (itemize):
2 Federal income tax		**a** Tax-exempt interest . $ ....
3 Excess of capital losses over capital gains		
4 Income subject to tax not recorded on books this year (itemize):		**8** Deductions on this return not charged against book income this year (itemize):
		a Depreciation . . . $ ....
5 Expenses recorded on books this year not deducted on this return (itemize):		**b** Contributions carryover $ ....
a Depreciation . . . $		**9** Add lines 7 and 8 . . . . . .
b Contributions carryover $		**10** Income (line 29, page 3)—line 6 less line 9 . . . .
c Travel and entertainment $		
6 Add lines 1 through 5		

Schedule M-2   Analysis of Unappropriated Retained Earnings per Books (Schedule L, line 25)

1 Balance at beginning of year . . .		**5** Distributions: **a** Cash . . . . . .
2 Net income (loss) per books . . .		**b** Stock . . . . .
3 Other increases (itemize):		**c** Property . . . .
		6 Other decreases (itemize): ....
		7 Add lines 5a through 6 . . . . .
4 Add lines 1, 2, and 3		**8** Balance at end of year (line 4 less line 7)

Form 1120S

Department of the Treasury
Internal Revenue Service

U.S. Income Tax Return for an S Corporation

▶ **Do not file this form unless the corporation has timely filed
Form 2553 to elect to be an S corporation.**
▶ **See separate instructions.**

OMB No. 1545-0130

1996

For calendar year 1996, or tax year beginning _____ , 1996, and ending _____ , 19 ____

A Date of election as an S corporation	**Use IRS label. Otherwise, please print or type.**	Name	**C** Employer identification number
B Business code no. (see Specific Instructions)		Number, street, and room or suite no. (If a P.O. box, see page 9 of the instructions.)	**D** Date incorporated
		City or town, state, and ZIP code	**E** Total assets (see Specific Instructions) $

F Check applicable boxes: **(1)** ☐ Initial return **(2)** ☐ Final return **(3)** ☐ Change in address **(4)** ☐ Amended return

G Check this box if this S corporation is subject to the consolidated audit procedures of sections 6241 through 6245 (see instructions before checking this box) ▶ ☐

H Enter number of shareholders in the corporation at end of the tax year . . . . ▶ ____

Caution: *Include **only** trade or business income and expenses on lines 1a through 21. See the instructions for more information.*

Income

1a Gross receipts or sales _____ **b** Less returns and allowances _____ **c** Bal ▶	**1c**	
2 Cost of goods sold (Schedule A, line 8)	**2**	
3 Gross profit. Subtract line 2 from line 1c	**3**	
4 Net gain (loss) from Form 4797, Part II, line 20 *(attach Form 4797)*	**4**	
5 Other income (loss) *(attach schedule)*	**5**	
6 **Total income (loss).** Combine lines 3 through 5 . . . . ▶	**6**	

Deductions (see page 10 of the instructions for limitations)

7 Compensation of officers	**7**	
8 Salaries and wages (less employment credits)	**8**	
9 Repairs and maintenance.	**9**	
10 Bad debts	**10**	
11 Rents	**11**	
12 Taxes and licenses.	**12**	
13 Interest	**13**	
14a Depreciation *(if required, attach Form 4562)* **14a**		
b Depreciation claimed on Schedule A and elsewhere on return . . **14b**		
c Subtract line 14b from line 14a	**14c**	
15 Depletion **(Do not deduct oil and gas depletion.)**	**15**	
16 Advertising	**16**	
17 Pension, profit-sharing, etc., plans	**17**	
18 Employee benefit programs	**18**	
19 Other deductions *(attach schedule)*	**19**	
20 **Total deductions.** Add the amounts shown in the far right column for lines 7 through 19 . ▶	**20**	
21 Ordinary income (loss) from trade or business activities. Subtract line 20 from line 6 . . .	**21**	

Tax and Payments

22 Tax: a Excess net passive income tax *(attach schedule)*. . . **22a**		
b Tax from Schedule D (Form 1120S) **22b**		
c Add lines 22a and 22b (see page 13 of the instructions for additional taxes)	**22c**	
23 Payments: a 1996 estimated tax payments and amount applied from 1995 return **23a**		
b Tax deposited with Form 7004 . . . . **23b**		
c Credit for Federal tax paid on fuels *(attach Form 4136)* . . . **23c**		
d Add lines 23a through 23c	**23d**	
24 Estimated tax penalty. Check if Form 2220 is attached . . . . ▶ ☐	**24**	
25 **Tax due.** If the total of lines 22c and 24 is larger than line 23d, enter amount owed. See page 3 of the instructions for depository method of payment . . . . ▶	**25**	
26 **Overpayment.** If line 23d is larger than the total of lines 22c and 24, enter amount overpaid ▶	**26**	
27 Enter amount of line 26 you want: **Credited to 1997 estimated tax** ▶ _____	**Refunded** ▶	**27**	

Please Sign Here

Under penalties of perjury, I declare that I have examined this return, including accompanying schedules and statements, and to the best of my knowledge and belief, it is true, correct, and complete. Declaration of preparer (other than taxpayer) is based on all information of which preparer has any knowledge.

▶ _____   _____   ▶ _____
Signature of officer   Date   Title

Paid Preparer's Use Only

Preparer's signature ▶	Date	Check if self-employed ▶ ☐	Preparer's social security number
Firm's name (or yours if self-employed) and address ▶		EIN ▶	
		ZIP code ▶	

For Paperwork Reduction Act Notice, see page 1 of separate instructions.   Cat. No. 11510H   Form **1120S** (1996)

Schedule A   Cost of Goods Sold (see page 14 of the instructions)

1 Inventory at beginning of year	**1**	
2 Purchases	**2**	
3 Cost of labor	**3**	
4 Additional section 263A costs *(attach schedule)*	**4**	
5 Other costs *(attach schedule)*	**5**	
6 **Total.** Add lines 1 through 5	**6**	
7 Inventory at end of year	**7**	
8 **Cost of goods sold.** Subtract line 7 from line 6. Enter here and on page 1, line 2	**8**	

9a Check all methods used for valuing closing inventory:

   (i) ☐ Cost as described in Regulations section 1.471-3

   (ii) ☐ Lower of cost or market as described in Regulations section 1.471-4

   (iii) ☐ Other (specify method used and attach explanation) ▶ _____

 b Check if there was a writedown of ™subnormal∫ goods as described in Regulations section 1.471-2(c) . . . . . ▶ ☐

 c Check if the LIFO inventory method was adopted this tax year for any goods *(if checked, attach Form 970)* . . . . . ▶ ☐

 d If the LIFO inventory method was used for this tax year, enter percentage (or amounts) of closing inventory computed under LIFO . . . . **9d** | |

 e Do the rules of section 263A (for property produced or acquired for resale) apply to the corporation? . . . ☐ Yes ☐ No

 f Was there any change in determining quantities, cost, or valuations between opening and closing inventory? . ☐ Yes ☐ No
   If ™Yes,∫ attach explanation.

Schedule B   Other Information

	Yes	No
1 Check method of accounting: **(a)** ☐ Cash **(b)** ☐ Accrual **(c)** ☐ Other (specify) ▶ _____		
2 Refer to the list on page 24 of the instructions and state the corporation's principal:		
(a) Business activity ▶ _____ **(b)** Product or service ▶ _____		
3 Did the corporation at the end of the tax year own, directly or indirectly, 50% or more of the voting stock of a domestic corporation? (For rules of attribution, see section 267(c).) If ™Yes,∫ attach a schedule showing:**(a)** name, address, and employer identification number and **(b)** percentage owned.		
4 Was the corporation a member of a controlled group subject to the provisions of section 1561?		
5 At any time during calendar year 1996, did the corporation have an interest in or a signature or other authority over a financial account in a foreign country (such as a bank account, securities account, or other financial account)? (See page 14 of the instructions for exceptions and filing requirements for Form TD F 90-22.1.)		
If ™Yes,∫ enter the name of the foreign country▶ _____		
6 During the tax year, did the corporation receive a distribution from, or was it the grantor of, or transferor to, a foreign trust? If ™Yes,∫ see page 14 of the instructions for other forms the corporation may have to file		
7 Check this box if the corporation has filed or is required to file **Form 8264,** Application for Registration of a Tax Shelter . . . . ▶ ☐		
8 Check this box if the corporation issued publicly offered debt instruments with original issue discount . . ▶ ☐		
If so, the corporation may have to file **Form 8281,** Information Return for Publicly Offered Original Issue Discount Instruments.		
9 If the corporation: **(a)** filed its election to be an S corporation after 1986, **(b)** was a C corporation before it elected to be an S corporation **or** the corporation acquired an asset with a basis determined by reference to its basis (or the basis of any other property) in the hands of a C corporation, and **(c)** has net unrealized built-in gain (defined in section 1374(d)(1)) in excess of the net recognized built-in gain from prior years, enter the net unrealized built-in gain reduced by net recognized built-in gain from prior years (see page 14 of the instructions) . . . . ▶ $ _____		
10 Check this box if the corporation had subchapter C earnings and profits at the close of the tax year (see page 15 of the instructions) . . . . ▶ ☐		

Designation of Tax Matters Person (see page 15 of the instructions)

Enter below the shareholder designated as the tax matters person (TMP) for the tax year of this return:

Name of designated TMP ▶ _____	Identifying number of TMP ▶ _____

Address of designated TMP ▶ _____

Schedule K — Shareholders' Shares of Income, Credits, Deductions, etc.

	(a) Pro rata share items		(b) Total amount	
Income (Loss)	1 Ordinary income (loss) from trade or business activities (page 1, line 21)	**1**		
	2 Net income (loss) from rental real estate activities *(attach Form 8825)*	**2**		
	3a Gross income from other rental activities	**3a**		
	b Expenses from other rental activities *(attach schedule)*	**3b**		
	c Net income (loss) from other rental activities. Subtract line 3b from line 3a	**3c**		
	4 Portfolio income (loss):			
	a Interest income	**4a**		
	b Dividend income	**4b**		
	c Royalty income	**4c**		
	d Net short-term capital gain (loss) *(attach Schedule D (Form 1120S))*	**4d**		
	e Net long-term capital gain (loss) *(attach Schedule D (Form 1120S))*	**4e**		
	f Other portfolio income (loss) *(attach schedule)*	**4f**		
	5 Net gain (loss) under section 1231 (other than due to casualty or theft) *(attach Form 4797)*	**5**		
	6 Other income (loss) *(attach schedule)*	**6**		
Deductions	7 Charitable contributions *(attach schedule)*	**7**		
	8 Section 179 expense deduction *(attach Form 4562)*	**8**		
	9 Deductions related to portfolio income (loss) (itemize)	**9**		
	10 Other deductions *(attach schedule)*	**10**		
Investment Interest	11a Interest expense on investment debts	**11a**		
	b (1) Investment income included on lines 4a, 4b, 4c, and 4f above	**11b(1)**		
	(2) Investment expenses included on line 9 above	**11b(2)**		
Credits	12a Credit for alcohol used as a fuel *(attach Form 6478)*	**12a**		
	b Low-income housing credit:			
	(1) From partnerships to which section 42(j)(5) applies for property placed in service before 1990	**12b(1)**		
	(2) Other than on line 12b(1) for property placed in service before 1990	**12b(2)**		
	(3) From partnerships to which section 42(j)(5) applies for property placed in service after 1989	**12b(3)**		
	(4) Other than on line 12b(3) for property placed in service after 1989	**12b(4)**		
	c Qualified rehabilitation expenditures related to rental real estate activities *(attach Form 3468)*	**12c**		
	d Credits (other than credits shown on lines 12b and 12c) related to rental real estate activities	**12d**		
	e Credits related to other rental activities	**12e**		
	13 Other credits	**13**		
Adjustments and Tax Preference Items	14a Depreciation adjustment on property placed in service after 1986	**14a**		
	b Adjusted gain or loss	**14b**		
	c Depletion (other than oil and gas)	**14c**		
	d (1) Gross income from oil, gas, or geothermal properties	**14d(1)**		
	(2) Deductions allocable to oil, gas, or geothermal properties	**14d(2)**		
	e Other adjustments and tax preference items *(attach schedule)*	**14e**		
Foreign Taxes	15a Type of income ▶			
	b Name of foreign country or U.S. possession ▶			
	c Total gross income from sources outside the United States *(attach schedule)*	**15c**		
	d Total applicable deductions and losses *(attach schedule)*	**15d**		
	e Total foreign taxes (check one): ▶ ☐ Paid ☐ Accrued	**15e**		
	f Reduction in taxes available for credit *(attach schedule)*	**15f**		
	g Other foreign tax information *(attach schedule)*	**15g**		
Other	16 Section 59(e)(2) expenditures: a Type ▶			
	b Amount	**16b**		
	17 Tax-exempt interest income	**17**		
	18 Other tax-exempt income	**18**		
	19 Nondeductible expenses	**19**		
	20 Total property distributions (including cash) other than dividends reported on line 22 below	**20**		
	21 Other items and amounts required to be reported separately to shareholders *(attach schedule)*			
	22 Total dividend distributions paid from accumulated earnings and profits	**22**		
	23 **Income (loss).** (Required only if Schedule M-1 must be completed.) Combine lines 1 through 6 in column (b). From the result, subtract the sum of lines 7 through 11a, 15e, and 16b	**23**		

Form 1120S (1996)   Page **4**

Schedule L	Balance Sheets per Books	Beginning of tax year		End of tax year	
	Assets	**(a)**	**(b)**	**(c)**	**(d)**
1	Cash				
2a	Trade notes and accounts receivable . .				
b	Less allowance for bad debts				
3	Inventories				
4	U.S. Government obligations				
5	Tax-exempt securities				
6	Other current assets (attach schedule) . .				
7	Loans to shareholders				
8	Mortgage and real estate loans				
9	Other investments (attach schedule) . .				
10a	Buildings and other depreciable assets .				
b	Less accumulated depreciation				
11a	Depletable assets				
b	Less accumulated depletion				
12	Land (net of any amortization)				
13a	Intangible assets (amortizable only) . . .				
b	Less accumulated amortization				
14	Other assets (attach schedule)				
15	Total assets				
	Liabilities and Shareholders' Equity				
16	Accounts payable				
17	Mortgages, notes, bonds payable in less than 1 year				
18	Other current liabilities (attach schedule)				
19	Loans from shareholders				
20	Mortgages, notes, bonds payable in 1 year or more				
21	Other liabilities (attach schedule) . . .				
22	Capital stock				
23	Paid-in or capital surplus				
24	Retained earnings				
25	Less cost of treasury stock		( )		( )
26	Total liabilities and shareholders' equity . .				

Schedule M-1   **Reconciliation of Income (Loss) per Books With Income (Loss) per Return** (You are not required to complete this schedule if the total assets on line 15, column (d), of Schedule L are less than $25,000.)

1	Net income (loss) per books	5	Income recorded on books this year not included on Schedule K, lines 1 through 6 (itemize):
2	Income included on Schedule K, lines 1 through 6, not recorded on books this year (itemize): _____	a	Tax-exempt interest $ _____
	_____		_____
3	Expenses recorded on books this year not included on Schedule K, lines 1 through 11a, 15e, and 16b (itemize):	6	Deductions included on Schedule K, lines 1 through 11a, 15e, and 16b, not charged against book income this year (itemize):
a	Depreciation $ _____	a	Depreciation $ _____
b	Travel and entertainment $ _____		_____
	_____	7	Add lines 5 and 6 . . . .
4	Add lines 1 through 3	8	Income (loss) (Schedule K, line 23). Line 4 less line 7

Schedule M-2   **Analysis of Accumulated Adjustments Account, Other Adjustments Account, and Shareholders' Undistributed Taxable Income Previously Taxed** (see page 22 of the instructions)

		(a) Accumulated adjustments account	**(b)** Other adjustments account	**(c)** Shareholders' undistributed taxable income previously taxed
1	Balance at beginning of tax year . . .			
2	Ordinary income from page 1, line 21 . .			
3	Other additions			
4	Loss from page 1, line 21	( )		
5	Other reductions	( )	( )	
6	Combine lines 1 through 5			
7	Distributions other than dividend distributions .			
8	Balance at end of tax year. Subtract line 7 from line 6			

SCHEDULE K-1
(Form 1120S)

Department of the Treasury
Internal Revenue Service

Shareholder's Share of Income, Credits, Deductions, etc.
▶ See separate instructions.

For calendar year 1996 or tax year
beginning   , 1996, and ending   , 19

OMB No. 1545-0130

1996

Shareholder's identifying number ▶ | **Corporation's identifying number ▶**

Shareholder's name, address, and ZIP code | Corporation's name, address, and ZIP code

A Shareholder's percentage of stock ownership for tax year (see instructions for Schedule K-1) . . . . . . ▶ _____ %

B Internal Revenue Service Center where corporation filed its return ▶ -----------------------------------

C Tax shelter registration number (see instructions for Schedule K-1) . . . . . . ▶ ------------------------

D Check applicable boxes: **(1)** ☐ Final K-1   **(2)** ☐ Amended K-1

	(a) Pro rata share items		(b) Amount	(c) Form 1040 filers enter the amount in column (b) on:
Income (Loss)	**1** Ordinary income (loss) from trade or business activities . . .	1		See pages 4 and 5 of the Shareholder's Instructions for Schedule K-1 (Form 1120S).
	2 Net income (loss) from rental real estate activities	2		
	3 Net income (loss) from other rental activities	3		
	4 Portfolio income (loss):			
	a Interest	4a		Sch. B, Part I, line 1
	b Dividends	4b		Sch. B, Part II, line 5
	c Royalties	4c		Sch. E, Part I, line 4
	d Net short-term capital gain (loss)	4d		Sch. D, line 5, col. (f) or (g)
	e Net long-term capital gain (loss)	4e		Sch. D, line 13, col. (f) or (g)
	f Other portfolio income (loss) (attach schedule)	4f		(Enter on applicable line of your return.)
	5 Net gain (loss) under section 1231 (other than due to casualty or theft)	5		See Shareholder's Instructions for Schedule K-1 (Form 1120S).
	6 Other income (loss) (attach schedule)	6		(Enter on applicable line of your return.)
Deductions	**7** Charitable contributions (attach schedule)	7		Sch. A, line 15 or 16
	8 Section 179 expense deduction	8		See page 6 of the Shareholder's Instructions for Schedule K-1 (Form 1120S).
	9 Deductions related to portfolio income (loss) (attach schedule) .	9		
	10 Other deductions (attach schedule)	10		
Investment Interest	**11a** Interest expense on investment debts	11a		Form 4952, line 1
	b **(1)** Investment income included on lines 4a, 4b, 4c, and 4f above	b(1)		See Shareholder's Instructions for Schedule K-1 (Form 1120S).
	(2) Investment expenses included on line 9 above	b(2)		
Credits	**12a** Credit for alcohol used as fuel	12a		Form 6478, line 10
	b Low-income housing credit:			
	(1) From section 42(j)(5) partnerships for property placed in service before 1990 .	b(1)		Form 8586, line 5
	(2) Other than on line 12b(1) for property placed in service before 1990	b(2)		
	(3) From section 42(j)(5) partnerships for property placed in service after 1989	b(3)		
	(4) Other than on line 12b(3) for property placed in service after 1989	b(4)		
	c Qualified rehabilitation expenditures related to rental real estate activities	12c		See page 7 of the Shareholder's Instructions for Schedule K-1 (Form 1120S).
	d Credits (other than credits shown on lines 12b and 12c) related to rental real estate activities	12d		
	e Credits related to other rental activities	12e		
	13 Other credits	13		
Adjustments and Tax Preference Items	**14a** Depreciation adjustment on property placed in service after 1986	14a		See page 7 of the Shareholder's Instructions for Schedule K-1 (Form 1120S) and Instructions for Form 6251
	b Adjusted gain or loss	14b		
	c Depletion (other than oil and gas)	14c		
	d **(1)** Gross income from oil, gas, or geothermal properties . . .	d(1)		
	(2) Deductions allocable to oil, gas, or geothermal properties .	d(2)		
	e Other adjustments and tax preference items (attach schedule) .	14e		

For Paperwork Reduction Act Notice, see page 1 of Instructions for Form 1120S.   Cat. No. 11520D   **Schedule K-1 (Form 1120S) 1996**

	(a) Pro rata share items		(b) Amount	(c) Form 1040 filers enter the amount in column (b) on:
Foreign Taxes	**15a** Type of income ▶			Form 1116, Check boxes
	b Name of foreign country or U.S. possession ▶			
	c Total gross income from sources outside the United States *(attach schedule)*	**15c**		Form 1116, Part I
	d Total applicable deductions and losses *(attach schedule)*	**15d**		
	e Total foreign taxes (check one): ▶ ☐ Paid ☐ Accrued	**15e**		Form 1116, Part II
	f Reduction in taxes available for credit *(attach schedule)*	**15f**		Form 1116, Part III
	g Other foreign tax information *(attach schedule)*	**15g**		See Instructions for Form 1116
Other	**16** Section 59(e)(2) expenditures: **a** Type ▶			See Shareholder's Instructions for Schedule K-1 (Form 1120S).
	b Amount	**16b**		
	17 Tax-exempt interest income	**17**		Form 1040, line 8b
	18 Other tax-exempt income	**18**		
	19 Nondeductible expenses	**19**		See pages 7 and 8 of the Shareholder's Instructions for Schedule K-1 (Form 1120S).
	20 Property distributions (including cash) other than dividend distributions reported to you on Form 1099-DIV	**20**		
	21 Amount of loan repayments for "Loans From Shareholders"	**21**		
	22 Recapture of low-income housing credit:			
	a From section 42(j)(5) partnerships	**22a**		Form 8611, line 8
	b Other than on line 22a	**22b**		

23 Supplemental information required to be reported separately to each shareholder *(attach additional schedules if more space is needed)*:

(Supplemental Information)

⊛

Form **1122**
(Rev. December 1983)
Department of the Treasury
Internal Revenue Service

Authorization and Consent of Subsidiary Corporation to be Included in a Consolidated Income Tax Return
(Please type or print)

▶ For the first year a consolidated return is filed, this form must be attached for each subsidiary.

For the calendar year 19_____, or other tax year beginning _____, 19____ and ending _____, 19____

Name	Employer identification number
Number and street	
City or town, State, and ZIP code	

Name of common parent corporation	Employer identification number

The subsidiary corporation named above authorizes its common parent corporation to include it in a consolidated return for the tax year indicated and for each later year the group must make a consolidated return under the regulations. If the parent corporation does not make a consolidated return on behalf of the subsidiary, the subsidiary authorizes the Commissioner or District Director of Internal Revenue to do so.

The subsidiary consents to be bound by the provisions of the consolidated return regulations.

Signature

Under penalties of perjury, I declare that the subsidiary named above has authorized me to sign this form on its behalf, that I have examined this form, and the information contained herein, and to the best of my knowledge and belief, it is true, correct, and complete.

▶ _____   ▶ _____
Signature of officer   Date   Title

Form **1122** (Rev. 12-83)

Form **2210**

Department of the Treasury
Internal Revenue Service

Underpayment of
Estimated Tax by Individuals, Estates, and Trusts
▶ See separate instructions.
▶ Attach to Form 1040, 1040A, 1040NR, 1040NR-EZ, or 1041.

OMB No. 1545-0140

19**96**

Attachment
Sequence No. **06**

Name(s) shown on tax return	Identifying number

Note: *In most cases, you **do not** need to file Form 2210. The IRS will figure any penalty you owe and send you a bill. File Form 2210 **only** if one or more boxes in Part I apply to you. If you do not need to file Form 2210, you still may use it to figure your penalty. Enter the amount from line 20 or line 36 on the penalty line of your return, but **do not** attach Form 2210.*

Part I   **Reasons for Filing**—If 1a, b, or c below applies to you, you may be able to lower or eliminate your penalty. But you MUST check the boxes that apply and file Form 2210 with your tax return. If 1d below applies to you, check that box and file Form 2210 with your tax return.

1   Check whichever boxes apply (if none apply, see the **Note** above):

a ☐ You request a **waiver.** In certain circumstances, the IRS will waive all or part of the penalty. See **Waiver of Penalty** on page 2 of the instructions.

b ☐ You use the **annualized income installment method.** If your income varied during the year, this method may reduce the amount of one or more required installments. See page 4 of the instructions.

c ☐ You had Federal income tax withheld from wages and, for estimated tax purposes, you treat the withheld tax as paid on the dates it was actually withheld, instead of in equal amounts on the payment due dates. See the instructions for line 22 on page 3.

d ☐ Your required annual payment (line 13 below) is based on your 1995 tax and you filed or are filing a joint return for either 1995 or 1996 but not for both years.

Part II   **Required Annual Payment**

2	Enter your 1996 tax after credits (see page 2 of the instructions)	**2**	
3	Other taxes (see page 2 of the instructions)	**3**	
4	Add lines 2 and 3	**4**	
5	Earned income credit **5**		
6	Credit for Federal tax paid on fuels **6**		
7	Add lines 5 and 6	**7**	
8	Current year tax. Subtract line 7 from line 4	**8**	
9	Multiply line 8 by 90% (.90) **9**		
10	Withholding taxes. **Do not** include any estimated tax payments on this line (see page 2 of the instructions)	**10**	
11	Subtract line 10 from line 8. If less than $500, **stop here; do not** complete or file this form. You do not owe the penalty	**11**	
12	Enter the tax shown on your 1995 tax return (110% of that amount if the adjusted gross income shown on that return is more than $150,000, or if married filing separately for 1996, more than $75,000). **Caution:** *See page 2 of the instructions*	**12**	
13	**Required annual payment.** Enter the **smaller** of line 9 or line 12	**13**	

     Note: *If line 10 is equal to or more than line 13, stop here; you do not owe the penalty. Do not file Form 2210 unless you checked box 1d above.*

Part III   **Short Method** (**Caution:** *See page 2 of the instructions to find out if you can use the short method. If you checked box **1b** or **c** in Part I, skip this part and go to Part IV.*)

14	Enter the amount, if any, from line 10 above **14**		
15	Enter the total amount, if any, of estimated tax payments you made **15**		
16	Add lines 14 and 15	**16**	
17	**Total underpayment for year.** Subtract line 16 from line 13. If zero or less, stop here; you do not owe the penalty. Do not file Form 2210 unless you checked box 1d above	**17**	
18	Multiply line 17 by .05914	**18**	
19	● If the amount on line 17 was paid **on or after** 4/15/97, enter -0-.		
	● If the amount on line 17 was paid **before** 4/15/97, make the following computation to find the amount to enter on line 19. Amount on line 17 × Number of days paid before 4/15/97 × .00025	**19**	
20	**PENALTY.** Subtract line 19 from line 18. Enter the result here and on Form 1040, line 63; Form 1040A, line 34; Form 1040NR, line 63; Form 1040NR-EZ, line 26; or Form 1041, line 26 . . ▶	**20**	

For Paperwork Reduction Act Notice, see page 1 of separate instructions.   Cat. No. 11744P   Form **2210** (1996)

Part IV **Regular Method** (See page 2 of the instructions if you are filing Form 1040NR or 1040NR-EZ.)

		Payment Due Dates			
		(a) 4/15/96	**(b)** 6/15/96	**(c)** 9/15/96	**(d)** 1/15/97

Section A—Figure Your Underpayment

21	**Required installments.** If box 1b applies, enter the amounts from Schedule AI, line 26. Otherwise, enter ¼ of line 13, Form 2210, in each column	21				
22	Estimated tax paid and tax withheld (see page 3 of the instructions). For column (a) only, also enter the amount from line 22 on line 26. If line 22 is equal to or more than line 21 for all payment periods, stop here; you do not owe the penalty. Do not file Form 2210 unless you checked a box in Part I . . . . **Complete lines 23 through 29 of one column before going to the next column.**	22				
23	Enter amount, if any, from line 29 of previous column	23				
24	Add lines 22 and 23	24				
25	Add amounts on lines 27 and 28 of the previous column	25				
26	Subtract line 25 from line 24. If zero or less, enter -0-. For column (a) only, enter the amount from line 22 .	26				
27	If the amount on line 26 is zero, subtract line 24 from line 25. Otherwise, enter -0-	27				
28	**Underpayment.** If line 21 is equal to or more than line 26, subtract line 26 from line 21. Then go to line 23 of next column. Otherwise, go to line 29 . . ▶	28				
29	**Overpayment.** If line 26 is more than line 21, subtract line 21 from line 26. Then go to line 23 of next column	29				

Section B—Figure the Penalty (Complete lines 30 through 35 of one column before going to the next column.)

			(a)	(b)	(c)	(d)
Rate Period 1		**April 16, 1996—June 30, 1996**	4/15/96	6/15/96		
	30	Number of days FROM the date shown above line 30 TO the date the amount on line 28 was paid **or** 6/30/96, whichever is earlier	Days:	Days:		
			30				
	31	Underpayment on line 28 (see page 4 of the instructions) × Number of days on line 30 / 366 × .08 ▶	31 $	$		
Rate Period 2		**July 1, 1996—December 31, 1996**	6/30/96	6/30/96	9/15/96	
	32	Number of days FROM the date shown above line 32 TO the date the amount on line 28 was paid **or** 12/31/96, whichever is earlier	Days:	Days:	Days:	
			32				
	33	Underpayment on line 28 (see page 4 of the instructions) × Number of days on line 32 / 366 × .09 ▶	33 $	$	$	
Rate Period 3		**January 1, 1997—April 15, 1997**	12/31/96	12/31/96	12/31/96	1/15/97
	34	Number of days FROM the date shown above line 34 TO the date the amount on line 28 was paid **or** 4/15/97, whichever is earlier	Days:	Days:	Days:	Days:
			34				
	35	Underpayment on line 28 (see page 4 of the instructions) × Number of days on line 34 / 365 × .09 ▶	35 $	$	$	$

36	**PENALTY.** Add all amounts on lines 31, 33, and 35 in all columns. Enter the total here and on Form 1040, line 63; Form 1040A, line 34; Form 1040NR, line 63; Form 1040NR-EZ, line 26; or Form 1041, line 26 . . . . ▶	36 $

Form 2210 (1996)   Page **3**

Schedule AI—Annualized Income Installment Method (see pages 4 and 5 of the instructions)

Estates and trusts, **do not** use the period ending dates shown to the right.
Instead, use the following: 2/29/96, 4/30/96, 7/31/96, and 11/30/96.

		(a) 1/1/96–3/31/96	(b) 1/1/96–5/31/96	(c) 1/1/96–8/31/96	(d) 1/1/96–12/31/96

Part I   Annualized Income Installments   **Caution:** *Complete lines 20–26 of one column **before** going to the next column.*

#	Description		(a)	(b)	(c)	(d)
1	Enter your adjusted gross income for each period (see instructions). (Estates and trusts, enter your taxable income without your exemption for each period.)	1				
2	Annualization amounts. (Estates and trusts, see instructions.)	2	4	2.4	1.5	1
3	Annualized income. Multiply line 1 by line 2	3				
4	Enter your itemized deductions for the period shown in each column. If you do not itemize, enter -0- and skip to line 7. (Estates and trusts, enter -0-, skip to line 9, and enter the amount from line 3 on line 9.)	4				
5	Annualization amounts	5	4	2.4	1.5	1
6	Multiply line 4 by line 5 (see instructions if line 3 is more than $58,975)	6				
7	In each column, enter the full amount of your standard deduction from Form 1040, line 34, or Form 1040A, line 19 (Form 1040NR or 1040NR-EZ filers, enter -0-. **Exception:** Indian students and business apprentices, enter standard deduction from Form 1040NR, line 33 or Form 1040NR-EZ line 10.)	7				
8	Enter the **larger** of line 6 or line 7.	8				
9	Subtract line 8 from line 3	9				
10	In each column, multiply $2,550 by the total number of exemptions claimed (see instructions if line 3 is more than $88,475). (Estates and trusts and Form 1040NR or 1040NR-EZ filers, enter the exemption amount shown on your tax return.)	10				
11	Subtract line 10 from line 9	11				
12	Figure your tax on the amount on line 11 (see instructions)	12				
13	Form 1040 filers only, enter your self-employment tax from line 35 below	13				
14	Enter other taxes for each payment period (see instructions)	14				
15	Total tax. Add lines 12, 13, and 14	15				
16	For each period, enter the same type of credits as allowed on Form 2210, lines 2, 5, and 6 (see instructions)	16				
17	Subtract line 16 from line 15. If zero or less, enter -0-	17				
18	Applicable percentage	18	22.5%	45%	67.5%	90%
19	Multiply line 17 by line 18	19				
20	Add the amounts in all preceding columns of line 26	20				
21	Subtract line 20 from line 19. If zero or less, enter -0-	21				
22	Enter ¼ of line 13 on page 1 of Form 2210 in each column	22				
23	Enter amount from line 25 of the preceding column of this schedule	23				
24	Add lines 22 and 23 and enter the total	24				
25	Subtract line 21 from line 24. If zero or less, enter -0-	25				
26	Enter the **smaller** of line 21 or line 24 here and on Form 2210, line 21 ▶	26				

Part II   Annualized Self-Employment Tax

#	Description		(a)	(b)	(c)	(d)
27a	Net earnings from self-employment for the period (see instructions)	27a				
b	Annualization amounts	27b	4	2.4	1.5	1
c	Multiply line 27a by line 27b	27c				
28	Social security tax limit	28	$62,700	$62,700	$62,700	$62,700
29	Enter actual wages subject to social security tax or the 6.2% portion of the 7.65% railroad retirement (tier 1) tax	29				
30	Annualization amounts	30	4	2.4	1.5	1
31	Multiply line 29 by line 30	31				
32	Subtract line 31 from line 28. If zero or less, enter -0-	32				
33	Multiply the smaller of line 27c or line 32 by .124	33				
34	Multiply line 27c by .029	34				
35	Add lines 33 and 34. Enter the result here and on line 13 above ▶	35				

Form **2220**

Department of the Treasury
Internal Revenue Service

Underpayment of Estimated Tax by Corporations

▶ See separate instructions.

▶ Attach to the corporation's tax return.

OMB No. 1545-0142

1996

Name	Employer identification number

Note: *In most cases, the corporation **does not** need to file Form 2220. The IRS will figure any penalty owed and bill the corporation. File Form 2220 **only** if any of the boxes or the **Note** in Part I applies to the corporation. If the corporation does not need to file Form 2220, it may still use it to figure the penalty. Enter the amount from line 36 on the penalty line of the corporation's income tax return, but do not attach Form 2220.*

Part I **Reasons For Filing**—Check the boxes below that apply to the corporation. If any box is checked or the **Note** below applies, the corporation must file Form 2220 with the corporation's tax return, even if it does not owe the penalty. If the box on line 1 or line 2 applies, the corporation may be able to lower or eliminate the penalty. See page 2 of the instructions.

1 ☐ The corporation is using the annualized income installment method.

2 ☐ The corporation is using the adjusted seasonal installment method.

3 ☐ The corporation is a "large corporation" figuring its first required installment based on the prior year's tax.

Note: *The corporation must also file Form 2220 if it is claiming a waiver of the penalty. See **Waiver of penalty** on page 3 of the instructions.*

Part II **Figuring the Underpayment**

4	Total tax (see page 2 of the instructions)	**4**
5a	Personal holding company tax included on line 4 (Schedule PH (Form 1120), line 26) .	**5a**
b	Interest due under the look-back method of section 460(b)(2) for completed long-term contracts included on line 4	**5b**
c	Credit for Federal tax paid on fuels (see page 2 of the instructions)	**5c**
d	**Total.** Add lines 5a through 5c	**5d**
6	Subtract line 5d from line 4. If the result is less than $500, **do not** complete or file this form. The corporation does not owe the penalty	**6**
7	Enter the tax shown on the corporation's 1995 income tax return. **(CAUTION: See page 2 of the instructions before completing this line.)**	**7**
8	Enter the **smaller** of line 6 or line 7. If the corporation must skip line 7, enter the amount from line 6 on line 8 .	**8**

		(a)	(b)	(c)	(d)
9	**Installment due dates.** Enter in columns (a) through (d) the 15th day of the 4th, 6th, 9th, and 12th months of the corporation's tax year . . . . ▶				
10	**Required installments.** If the box on line 1 or line 2 above is checked, enter the amounts from Schedule A, line 41. If the box on line 3 (but not 1 or 2) is checked, see page 2 of the instructions for the amounts to enter. If none of these boxes are checked, enter 25% of line 8 above in each column				
11	Estimated tax paid or credited for each period (see page 2 of the instructions). For column (a) only, enter the amount from line 11 on line 15				
	Complete lines 12 through 18 of one column before going to the next column.				
12	Enter amount, if any, from line 18 of the preceding column				
13	Add lines 11 and 12 .				
14	Add amounts on lines 16 and 17 of the preceding column .				
15	Subtract line 14 from line 13. If zero or less, enter -0-				
16	If the amount on line 15 is zero, subtract line 13 from line 14. Otherwise, enter -0-				
17	**Underpayment.** If line 15 is less than or equal to line 10, subtract line 15 from line 10. Then go to line 12 of the next column. Otherwise, go to line 18 (see page 3 of the instructions)				
18	**Overpayment.** If line 10 is less than line 15, subtract line 10 from line 15. Then go to line 12 of the next column . .				

Complete Part III on page 2 to figure the penalty. If there are no entries on line 17, no penalty is owed.

For Paperwork Reduction Act Notice, see page 1 of the instructions.

Cat. No. 11746L

Form **2220** (1996)

Part III   Figuring the Penalty

		(a)	(b)	(c)	(d)
19	Enter the date of payment or the 15th day of the 3rd month after the close of the tax year, whichever is earlier (see page 3 of the instructions). *(Form 990-PF and Form 990-T filers:* Use 5th month instead of 3rd month.)				
20	Number of days from due date of installment on line 9 to the date shown on line 19				
21	Number of days on line 20 after 4/15/96 and before 7/1/96 .				
22	Underpayment on line 17 $\times \dfrac{\text{Number of days on line 21}}{366} \times 8\%$ . .	\$	\$	\$	\$
23	Number of days on line 20 after 6/30/96 and before 1/1/97 .				
24	Underpayment on line 17 $\times \dfrac{\text{Number of days on line 23}}{366} \times 9\%$ . .	\$	\$	\$	\$
25	Number of days on line 20 after 12/31/96 and before 4/1/97.				
26	Underpayment on line 17 $\times \dfrac{\text{Number of days on line 25}}{365} \times 9\%$ . .	\$	\$	\$	\$
27	Number of days on line 20 after 3/31/97 and before 7/1/97 .				
28	Underpayment on line 17 $\times \dfrac{\text{Number of days on line 27}}{365} \times {}^*\%$ . .	\$	\$	\$	\$
29	Number of days on line 20 after 6/30/97 and before 10/1/97.				
30	Underpayment on line 17 $\times \dfrac{\text{Number of days on line 29}}{365} \times {}^*\%$ . .	\$	\$	\$	\$
31	Number of days on line 20 after 9/30/97 and before 1/1/98 .				
32	Underpayment on line 17 $\times \dfrac{\text{Number of days on line 31}}{365} \times {}^*\%$ . .	\$	\$	\$	\$
33	Number of days on line 20 after 12/31/97 and before 2/16/98				
34	Underpayment on line 17 $\times \dfrac{\text{Number of days on line 33}}{365} \times {}^*\%$ . .	\$	\$	\$	\$
35	Add lines 22, 24, 26, 28, 30, 32, and 34.	\$	\$	\$	\$

36 **Penalty.** Add columns (a) through (d), of line 35. Enter the total here and on Form 1120, line 33; Form 1120-A, line 29; or the comparable line for other income tax returns . . . . **36** | \$

*If the corporation's tax year ends after December 31, 1996, see **Lines 28, 30, 32,** and **34** on page 3 of the instructions.

Form 2220 (1996)

Schedule A	Required Installments Using the Annualized Income Installment Method and/or the Adjusted Seasonal Installment Method Under Section 6655(e) (see pages 3 and 4 of the instructions)

Form 1120S filers: *For lines 2, 14, 15, and 16, below, "taxable income" refers to excess net passive income or the amount on which tax is imposed under section 1374(a) (or the corresponding provisions of prior law), whichever applies.*

Part I—Annualized Income Installment Method

			(a) First ____ months	(b) First ____ months	(c) First ____ months	(d) First ____ months
1	Annualization period (see page 3 of the instructions).	1				
2	Enter taxable income for each annualization period.	2				
3	Annualization amount (see page 3 of the instructions).	3				
4	Annualized taxable income. Multiply line 2 by line 3.	4				
5	Figure the tax on the amount in each column on line 4 using the instructions for Form 1120, Schedule J, line 3 (or the comparable line of the tax return).	5				
6	Enter other taxes for each payment period (see page 3 of the instructions).	6				
7	Total tax. Add lines 5 and 6.	7				
8	For each period, enter the same type of credits as allowed on Form 2220, lines 4 and 5c (see page 3 of the instructions).	8				
9	Total tax after credits. Subtract line 8 from line 7. If zero or less, enter -0-.	9				
10	Applicable percentage.	10	25%	50%	75%	100%
11	Multiply line 9 by line 10.	11				
12	Add the amounts in all preceding columns of line 41 (see page 3 of the instructions).	12				
13	**Annualized income installments.** Subtract line 12 from line 11. If zero or less, enter -0-.	13				

Part II—Adjusted Seasonal Installment Method (Caution: *Use this method only if the base period percentage for any 6 consecutive months is at least 70%. See pages 3 and 4 of the instructions for more information.***)**

			(a) First 3 months	(b) First 5 months	(c) First 8 months	(d) First 11 months
14	Enter taxable income for the following periods:					
a	Tax year beginning in 1993	14a				
b	Tax year beginning in 1994	14b				
c	Tax year beginning in 1995	14c				
15	Enter taxable income for each period for the tax year beginning in 1996.	15				

			First 4 months	First 6 months	First 9 months	Entire year
16	Enter taxable income for the following periods:					
a	Tax year beginning in 1993	16a				
b	Tax year beginning in 1994	16b				
c	Tax year beginning in 1995	16c				
17	Divide the amount in each column on line 14a by the amount in column (d) on line 16a.	17				
18	Divide the amount in each column on line 14b by the amount in column (d) on line 16b.	18				
19	Divide the amount in each column on line 14c by the amount in column (d) on line 16c.	19				

		(a) First 4 months	(b) First 6 months	(c) First 9 months	(d) Entire year
20	Add lines 17 through 19. **20**				
21	Divide line 20 by 3. **21**				
22	Divide line 15 by line 21. **22**				
23	Figure the tax on the amount on line 22 using the instructions for Form 1120, Schedule J, line 3 (or the comparable line of the return). **23**				
24	Divide the amount in columns (a) through (c) on line 16a by the amount in column (d) on line 16a. **24**				
25	Divide the amount in columns (a) through (c) on line 16b by the amount in column (d) on line 16b. **25**				
26	Divide the amount in columns (a) through (c) on line 16c by the amount in column (d) on line 16c. **26**				
27	Add lines 24 through 26. **27**				
28	Divide line 27 by 3. **28**				
29	Multiply the amount in columns (a) through (c) of line 23 by columns (a) through (c) of line 28. In column (d), enter the amount from line 23, column (d). **29**				
30	Enter other taxes for each payment period (see page 4 of the instructions). **30**				
31	Total tax. Add lines 29 and 30. **31**				
32	For each period, enter the same type of credits as allowed on Form 2220, lines 4 and 5c (see page 4 of the instructions). **32**				
33	Total tax after credits. Subtract line 32 from line 31. If zero or less, enter -0-. **33**				
34	Add the amounts in all preceding columns of line 41 (see page 4 of the instructions). **34**				
35	**Adjusted seasonal installments.** Subtract line 34 from line 33. If zero or less, enter -0-. **35**				

Part III—Required Installments

		1st installment	2nd installment	3rd installment	4th installment
36	If only one of the above parts is completed, enter the amount in each column from line 13 or line 35. If both parts are completed, enter the smaller of the amounts in each column from line 13 or line 35. **36**				
37	Enter 25% of line 8 on page 1 of Form 2220 in each column. **(Note:** *"Large corporations"* see the instructions for Form 2220, line 10, on page 2 for the amounts to enter.**)** **37**				
38	Enter the amount from line 40 of the preceding column. **38**				
39	Add lines 37 and 38. **39**				
40	If line 39 is more than line 36, subtract line 36 from line 39. Otherwise, enter -0-. **40**				
41	**Required installments.** Enter the **smaller** of line 36 or line 39 here and on page 1 of Form 2220, line 10. **41**				

✪

Form **4626**	**Alternative Minimum Tax—Corporations**	OMB No. 1545-0175

▶ **See separate instructions.**
▶ **Attach to the corporation's tax return.**

1996

Department of the Treasury
Internal Revenue Service

Name	Employer identification number

1	Taxable income or (loss) before net operating loss deduction.	1	

2 **Adjustments and preferences:**

a	Depreciation of post-1986 property	2a	
b	Amortization of certified pollution control facilities	2b	
c	Amortization of mining exploration and development costs	2c	
d	Amortization of circulation expenditures (personal holding companies only) . .	2d	
e	Adjusted gain or loss	2e	
f	Long-term contracts	2f	
g	Installment sales	2g	
h	Merchant marine capital construction funds	2h	
i	Section 833(b) deduction (Blue Cross, Blue Shield, and similar type organizations only)	2i	
j	Tax shelter farm activities (personal service corporations only)	2j	
k	Passive activities (closely held corporations and personal service corporations only)	2k	
l	Loss limitations	2l	
m	Depletion	2m	
n	Tax-exempt interest from specified private activity bonds	2n	
o	Charitable contributions	2o	
p	Intangible drilling costs	2p	
q	Accelerated depreciation of real property (pre-1987)	2q	
r	Accelerated depreciation of leased personal property (pre-1987) (personal holding companies only)	2r	
s	Other adjustments	2s	
t	Combine lines 2a through 2s	2t	

3	Preadjustment alternative minimum taxable income (AMTI). Combine lines 1 and 2t	3	

4 **Adjusted current earnings (ACE) adjustment:**

a	Enter the corporation's ACE from line 10 of the worksheet on page 8 of the instructions	4a	
b	Subtract line 3 from line 4a. If line 3 exceeds line 4a, enter the difference as a negative amount (see examples beginning on page 4 of the instructions) . .	4b	
c	Multiply line 4b by 75% (.75). Enter the result as a positive amount	4c	
d	Enter the excess, if any, of the corporation's total increases in AMTI from prior year ACE adjustments over its total reductions in AMTI from prior year ACE adjustments (see page 5 of the instructions). **Note:** *You* **must** *enter an amount on line 4d (even if line 4b is positive)*	4d	
e	ACE adjustment: ● If you entered a positive number or zero on line 4b, enter the amount from line 4c here as a positive amount. ● If you entered a negative number on line 4b, enter the smaller of line 4c or line 4d here as a negative amount.	4e	

5	Combine lines 3 and 4e. If zero or less, stop here; the corporation does not owe alternative minimum tax	5	
6	Alternative tax net operating loss deduction (see page 5 of the instructions)	6	
7	**Alternative minimum taxable income.** Subtract line 6 from line 5.	7	

For Paperwork Reduction Act Notice, see separate instructions.   Cat. No. 12955I   Form **4626** (1996)

8   Enter the amount from line 7 (alternative minimum taxable income) . . . . | **8** |

9   **Exemption phase-out computation** (if line 8 is $310,000 or more, skip lines 9a and 9b and enter -0- on line 9c):

   a   Subtract $150,000 from line 8 (if you are completing this line for a member of a controlled group, see page 5 of the instructions). If zero or less, enter -0- . . | **9a** |

   b   Multiply line 9a by 25% (.25). . . . . | **9b** |

   c   Exemption. Subtract line 9b from $40,000 (if you are completing this line for a member of a controlled group, see page 5 of the instructions). If zero or less, enter -0- . . . . | **9c** |

10   Subtract line 9c from line 8. If zero or less, enter -0- . . . . | **10** |

11   Multiply line 10 by 20% (.20). . . . . | **11** |

12   Alternative minimum tax foreign tax credit. See page 5 of the instructions for limitations. . . . . | **12** |

13   Tentative minimum tax. Subtract line 12 from line 11. . . . . | **13** |

14   Regular tax liability before all credits except the foreign tax credit and possessions tax credit . . . | **14** |

15   **Alternative minimum tax.** Subtract line 14 from line 13. Enter the result on the appropriate line of the corporation's income tax return (e.g., Form 1120, Schedule J, line 9). If zero or less, enter -0- . | **15** |

Form **8275**
(Rev. April 1995)
Department of the Treasury Internal Revenue Service

Disclosure Statement

Do not use this form to disclose items or positions that are contrary to Treasury regulations. Instead, use Form 8275-R, Regulation Disclosure Statement. See separate instructions.

▶ **Attach to your tax return.**

OMB No. 1545-0889

Attachment
Sequence No. **92**

Name(s) shown on return	Identifying number shown on return

Part I   **General Information** (See instructions.)

	(a) Rev. Rul., Rev. Proc., etc.	(b) Item or Group of Items	(c) Detailed Description of Items	(d) Form or Schedule	(e) Line No.	(f) Amount
1						
2						
3						

Part II   **Detailed Explanation** (See instructions.)

1

2

3

Part III   **Information About Pass-Through Entity.** To be completed by partners, shareholders, beneficiaries, or residual interest holders.

Complete this part only if you are making adequate disclosure with respect to a pass-through item.

Note: *A pass-through entity is a partnership, S corporation, estate, trust, regulated investment company, real estate investment trust, or real estate mortgage investment conduit (REMIC).*

1 Name, address, and ZIP code of pass-through entity	**2** Identifying number of pass-through entity
	3 Tax year of pass-through entity / / to / /
	4 Internal Revenue Service Center where the pass-through entity filed its return

For Paperwork Reduction Act Notice, see separate instructions.   Cat. No. 61935M   Form **8275** (Rev. 4-95)

Form 8275 (Rev. 4-95)   Page **2**

Part IV	**Explanations** *(continued from Parts I and/or II)*

Form 8832

(December 1996)

Department of the Treasury
Internal Revenue Service

Entity Classification Election

OMB No. 1545-1516

Please Type or Print

| Name of entity | Employer identification number (EIN) |

Number, street, and room or suite no. If a P.O. box, see instructions.

City or town, state, and ZIP code. If a foreign address, enter city, province or state, postal code and country.

1 Type of election (see instructions):

a ☐ Initial classification by a newly-formed entity (or change in current classification of an existing entity to take effect on January 1, 1997)

b ☐ Change in current classification (to take effect later than January 1, 1997)

2 Form of entity (see instructions):

a ☐ A domestic eligible entity electing to be classified as an association taxable as a corporation.

b ☐ A domestic eligible entity electing to be classified as a partnership.

c ☐ A domestic eligible entity with a single owner electing to be disregarded as a separate entity.

d ☐ A foreign eligible entity electing to be classified as an association taxable as a corporation.

e ☐ A foreign eligible entity electing to be classified as a partnership.

f ☐ A foreign eligible entity with a single owner electing to be disregarded as a separate entity.

3 Election is to be effective beginning (month, day, year) (see instructions) . . . . ▶ ___ / ___ / ___

4 Name and title of person whom the IRS may call for more information

5 That person's telephone number

Consent Statement and Signature(s) (see instructions)

Under penalties of perjury, I (we) declare that I (we) consent to the election of the above-named entity to be classified as indicated above, and that I (we) have examined this consent statement, and to the best of my (our) knowledge and belief, it is true, correct, and complete. If I am an officer, manager, or member signing for all members of the entity, I further declare that I am authorized to execute this consent statement on their behalf.

Signature(s)	Date	Title

For Paperwork Reduction Act Notice, see page 2.　　　　Cat. No. 22598R　　　　Form **8832** (12-96)

General Instructions

Section references are to the Internal Revenue Code unless otherwise noted.

Paperwork Reduction Act Notice

We ask for the information on this form to carry out the Internal Revenue laws of the United States. You are required to give us the information. We need it to ensure that you are complying with these laws and to allow us to figure and collect the right amount of tax.

You are not required to provide the information requested on a form that is subject to the Paperwork Reduction Act unless the form displays a valid OMB control number. Books or records relating to a form or its instructions must be retained as long as their contents may become material in the administration of any Internal Revenue law. Generally, tax returns and return information are confidential, as required by section 6103.

The time needed to complete and file this form will vary depending on individual circumstances. The estimated average time is:

Recordkeeping . . .1 hr., 20 min.
Learning about the law or the form . . .1 hr., 41 min.
Preparing and sending the form to the IRS . . . .17 min.

If you have comments concerning the accuracy of these time estimates or suggestions for making this form simpler, we would be happy to hear from you. You can write to the Tax Forms Committee, Western Area Distribution Center, Rancho Cordova, CA 95743-0001. **DO NOT** send the form to this address. Instead, see **Where To File** on page 3.

Purpose of Form

For Federal tax purposes, certain business entities automatically are classified as corporations. See items **1** and **3** through **8** under the definition of corporation on this page. Other business entities may choose how they are classified for Federal tax purposes. Except for a business entity automatically classified as a corporation, a business entity with at least two members can choose to be classified as either an association taxable as a corporation or a partnership, and a business entity with a single member can choose to be classified as either an association taxable as a corporation or disregarded as an entity separate from its owner.

Generally, an eligible entity that does not file this form will be classified under the default rules described below. An eligible entity that chooses not to be classified under the default rules or that wishes to change its current classification must file Form 8832 to elect a classification. The IRS will use the information entered on this form to establish the entity's filing and reporting requirements for Federal tax purposes.

Default Rules

Existing entity default rule.— Certain domestic and foreign entities that are already in existence before January 1, 1997, and have an established Federal tax classification, generally do not need to make an election to continue that classification. However, for an eligible entity with a single owner that claimed to be a partnership under the law in effect before January 1, 1997, that entity will now be disregarded as an entity separate from its owner. If an existing entity decides to change its classification, it may do so subject to the rules in Regulations section 301.7701-3(c)(1)(iv). A foreign eligible entity is treated as being in existence prior to the effective date of this section only if the entity's classification is relevant at any time during the 60 months prior to January 1, 1997.

Domestic default rule.—Unless an election is made on Form 8832, a domestic eligible entity is:

1. A partnership if it has two or more members.

2. Disregarded as an entity separate from its owner if it has a single owner.

Foreign default rule.—Unless an election is made on Form 8832, a foreign eligible entity is:

1. A partnership if it has two or more members and at least one member does not have limited liability.

2. An association if all members have limited liability.

3. Disregarded as an entity separate from its owner if it has a single owner that does not have limited liability.

Definitions

Business entity.—A business entity is any entity recognized for Federal tax purposes that is not properly classified as a trust under Regulations section 301.7701-4 or otherwise subject to special treatment under the Code. See Regulations section 301.7701-2(a).

Corporation.—For Federal tax purposes, a corporation is any of the following:

1. A business entity organized under a Federal or state statute, or under a statute of a federally recognized Indian tribe, if the statute describes or refers to the entity as incorporated or as a corporation, body corporate, or body politic.

2. An association (as determined under Regulations section 301.7701-3).

3. A business entity organized under a state statute, if the statute describes or refers to the entity as a joint-stock company or joint-stock association.

4. An insurance company.

5. A state-chartered business entity conducting banking activities, if any of its deposits are insured under the Federal Deposit Insurance Act, as amended, 12 U.S.C. 1811 et seq., or a similar Federal statute.

6. A business entity wholly owned by a state or any political subdivision thereof.

7. A business entity that is taxable as a corporation under a provision of the Code other than section 7701(a)(3).

8. A foreign business entity listed in Regulations section 301.7701-2(b)(8). However, a foreign business entity listed in those regulations generally will not be treated as a corporation if all of the following apply:

a. The entity was in existence on May 8, 1996.

b. The entity's classification was relevant (as defined below) on May 8, 1996.

c. No person (including the entity) for whom the entity's classification was relevant on May 8, 1996, treats the entity as a corporation for purposes of filing that person's Federal income tax returns, information returns, and withholding documents for the tax year including May 8, 1996.

d. Any change in the entity's claimed classification within the 60 months prior to May 8, 1996, was a result of a change in the organizational documents of the entity, and the entity and all members of the entity recognized the Federal tax consequences of any change in the entity's classification within the 60 months prior to May 8, 1996.

e. The entity had a reasonable basis (within the meaning of section 6662) for treating the entity as other than a corporation on May 8, 1996.

f. Neither the entity nor any member was notified in writing on or before May 8, 1996, that the classification of the entity was under examination (in which case the entity's classification will be determined in the examination).

Binding contract rule.—If a foreign business entity described in Regulations section 301.7701-2(b)(8)(i) is formed after May 8, 1996, under a written binding contract (including an accepted bid to develop a project) in effect on May 8, 1996, and all times thereafter, in which the parties agreed to engage (directly or indirectly) in an active and substantial business operation in the jurisdiction in which the entity is formed, **8** on page 2 is applied by substituting the date of the entity's formation for May 8, 1996.

Eligible entity.—An eligible entity is a business entity that is not included in items **1** or **3** through **8** under the definition of corporation on page 2.

Limited liability.—A member of a foreign eligible entity has limited liability if the member has no personal liability for any debts of or claims against the entity by reason of being a member. This determination is based solely on the statute or law under which the entity is organized (and, if relevant, the entity's organizational documents). A member has personal liability if the creditors of the entity may seek satisfaction of all or any part of the debts or claims against the entity from the member as such. A member has personal liability even if the member makes an agreement under which another person (whether or not a member of the entity) assumes that liability or agrees to indemnify that member for that liability.

Partnership.—A partnership is a business entity that has **at least** two members and is not a corporation as defined on page 2.

Relevant.—A foreign eligible entity's classification is relevant when its classification affects the liability of any person for Federal tax or information purposes. The date the classification of a foreign eligible entity is relevant is the date an event occurs that creates an obligation to file a Federal tax return, information return, or statement for which the classification of the entity must be determined.

Effect of Election

The resulting tax consequences of a change in classification remain the same no matter how a change in entity classification is achieved. For example, if an organization classified as an association elects to be classified as a partnership, the organization and its owners must recognize gain, if any, under the rules applicable to liquidations of corporations.

Who Must File

File this form for an **eligible entity** that is one of the following:

● A domestic entity electing to be classified as an association taxable as a corporation.

● A domestic entity electing to change its current classification (even if it is currently classified under the default rule).

● A foreign entity that has more than one owner, all owners have limited liability, and it elects to be classified as a partnership.

● A foreign entity that has at least one owner without limited liability, and it elects to be classified as an association taxable as a corporation.

● A foreign entity with a single owner having limited liability, and it elects to have the entity disregarded as an entity separate from its owner.

● A foreign entity electing to change its current classification (even if it is currently classified under the default rule).

Do not file this form for an eligible entity that is:

● Tax-exempt under section 501(a), or

● A real estate investment trust (REIT), as defined in section 856.

When To File

See the instructions for line 3.

Where To File

File Form 8832 with the Internal Revenue Service Center, Philadelphia, PA 19255. Also attach a copy of Form 8832 to the entity's Federal income tax or information return for the tax year of the election. If the entity is not required to file a return for that year, a copy of its Form 8832 must be attached to the Federal income tax or information returns of all direct or indirect owners of the entity for the tax year of the owner that includes the date on which the election took effect. Although failure to attach a copy will not invalidate an otherwise valid election, each member of the entity is required to file returns that are consistent with the entity's election. In addition, penalties may be assessed against persons who are required to, but who do not, attach Form 8832 to their returns. Other penalties may apply for filing Federal income tax or information returns inconsistent with the entity's election.

Specific Instructions

Employer Identification Number (EIN)

Show the correct EIN on Form 8832. If the entity does not have an EIN, it generally must apply for one on **Form SS-4,** Application for Employer Identification Number. If the filing of Form 8832 is the only reason the entity is applying for an EIN, check the "Other" box on line 9 of Form SS-4 and write "Form 8832" to the right of that box. If the entity has not received an EIN by the time Form 8832 is due, write "Applied for" in the space for the EIN. **Do not** apply for a new EIN for an existing entity that is changing its classification. If you are electing to disregard an entity as separate from its owner, enter the owner's EIN.

Address

Include the suite, room, or other unit number after the street address. If the Post Office does not deliver mail to the street address and the entity has a P.O. box, show the box number instead of the street address.

Line 1

Check box 1a if the entity is choosing a classification for the first time **and** the entity does not want to be classified under the applicable default classification. **Do not** file this form if the entity wants to be classified under the default rules.

Check box 1b if the entity is changing its current classification to take effect later than January 1, 1997, whether or not the entity's current classification is the default classification. However, once an eligible entity makes an election to change its classification (other than an election made by an existing entity to change its classification as of January 1, 1997), the entity cannot change its classification by election again during the 60 months after the effective date of the election. However, the IRS may permit (by private letter ruling) the entity to change its classification by election within the 60-month period if more than 50% of the ownership interests in the entity as of the effective date of the election are owned by persons that did not own any interests in the entity on the effective date of the entity's prior election.

Line 2

Check the appropriate box if you are changing a current classification (no matter how achieved), or are electing out of a default classification. **Do not** file this form if you fall within a default classification that is the desired classification for the new entity.

Line 3

Generally, the election will take effect on the date you enter on line 3 of this form or on the date filed if no date is entered on line 3. However, an election specifying an entity's classification for Federal tax purposes can take effect no more than 75 days prior to the date the election is filed, nor can it take effect later than 12 months after the date on which the election is filed. If line 3 shows a date more than 75 days prior to the date on which the election is filed, the election will take effect 75 days before the date it is filed. If line 3 shows an effective date more than 12 months from the filing date, the election will take effect 12 months after the date the election was filed.

Regardless of the date filed, an election will in no event take effect before January 1, 1997.

Consent Statement and Signatures

Form 8832 must be signed by:

1. Each member of the electing entity who is an owner at the time the election is filed; or

2. Any officer, manager, or member of the electing entity who is authorized (under local law or the organizational documents) to make the election and who represents to having such authorization under penalties of perjury.

If an election is to be effective for any period prior to the time it is filed, each person who was an owner between the date the election is to be effective and the date the election is filed, and who is not an owner at the time the election is filed, must also sign.

If you need a continuation sheet or use a separate consent statement, attach it to Form 8832. The separate consent statement must contain the same information as shown on Form 8832.

Form **9465**	**Installment Agreement Request**	OMB No. 1545-1350
(Rev. January 1996)	▶ See instructions below and on back.	
Department of the Treasury Internal Revenue Service		

Note: *Do not file this form if you are currently making payments on an installment agreement. You must pay your other Federal tax liabilities in full or you will be in default on your agreement.*

If you can't pay the full amount you owe, you can ask to make monthly installment payments. If we approve your request, you will be charged a $43 fee. **Do not include the fee with this form.** We will deduct the fee from your first payment after we approve your request, unless you choose **Direct Debit** (see the line 13 instructions). We will usually let you know within 30 days after we receive your request whether it is approved or denied. But if this request is for tax due on a return you filed after March 31, it may take us longer than 30 days to reply.

To ask for an installment agreement, complete this form. Attach it to the front of your return when you file. If you have already filed your return or you are filing this form in response to a notice, see **How Do I File Form 9465?** on page 2. If you have any questions about this request, call 1-800-829-1040.

Caution: *A Notice of Federal Tax Lien may be filed to protect the government's interest until you pay in full.*

1 Your first name and initial   Last name   Your social security number

If a joint return, spouse's first name and initial   Last name   Spouse's social security number

Your current address (number and street). If you have a P.O. box and no home delivery, show box number.   Apt. number

City, town or post office, state, and ZIP code. If a foreign address, show city, state or province, postal code, and full name of country.

2 If this address is new since you filed your last tax return, check here . . . . ▶ ☐

3 ( ) _____ _____   **4** ( ) _____ _____ _____
     Your home phone number   Best time for us to call   Your work phone number   Ext.   Best time for us to call

5 Name of your bank or other financial institution: **6** Your employer's name:

Address   Address

City, state, and ZIP code   City, state, and ZIP code

7 Enter the tax return for which you are making this request (for example, Form 1040). But if you are filing this form in response to a notice, don't complete lines 7 through 9. Instead, attach the bottom section of the notice to this form and go to line 10 . . . . ▶ _____

8 Enter the tax year for which you are making this request (for example, 1995) . . . . ▶ _____

9 Enter the total amount you owe as shown on your tax return . . . . ▶ $ _____

10 Enter the amount of any payment you are making with your tax return (or notice). See instructions . ▶ $ _____

11 Enter the amount you can paym each month. **Make your payments as large as possible to limit interest and penalty charges.** The charges will continue until you pay in full . . . . ▶ $ _____

12 Enter the date you want to make your payment each month. Do not enter a date later than the 28th ▶ _____

13 If you would like to make your monthly payments using **Direct Debit** (automatic withdrawals from your bank account), check here. . . . . ▶ ☐

Your signature	Date	Spouse's signature. If a joint return, BOTH must sign.	Date

Cat. No. 14842Y   Form **9465** (Rev. 1-96)

The time needed to complete and file this form will vary depending on individual circumstances. The estimated average time is: **Learning about the law or the form,** 2 min.; **Preparing the form,** 24 min.; and **Copying, assembling, and sending the form to the IRS,** 20 min.

If you have comments concerning the accuracy of this time estimate or suggestions for making this form simpler, we would be happy to hear from you. You can write to the Tax Forms Committee, Western Area Distribution Center, Rancho Cordova, CA 95743-0001. **DO NOT** send the form to this address. Instead, see **How Do I File Form 9465?** on this page.

General Instructions

If you cannot pay the full amount you owe shown on your tax return (or on a notice we sent you), you can ask to make monthly installment payments. But before requesting an installment agreement, you should consider other less costly alternatives, such as a bank loan.

You will be charged interest and may be charged a late payment penalty on any tax not paid by its due date, even if your request to pay in installments is granted. To limit interest and penalty charges, file your return on time and pay as much of the tax as possible with your return (or notice).

You will be charged a $43 fee if your request is approved. **Do not include the fee with this form.** We will send you a letter telling you your request has been approved, how to pay the fee, and how to make your first installment payment. After we receive each payment, we will send you a letter showing the remaining amount you owe, and the due date and amount of your next payment.

By approving your request, we agree to let you pay the tax you owe in monthly installments instead of immediately paying the amount in full. In return, you agree to make your monthly payments on time. **You also agree to meet all your future tax liabilities.** This means that you must have adequate withholding or estimated tax payments so that your tax liability for future years is paid in full when you timely file your return. If you do not make your payments on time or have an outstanding past-due amount in a future year, you will be in default on your agreement and we may take enforcement actions to collect the entire amount you owe.

Bankruptcy—Offer-in-Compromise.—If you are in bankruptcy or we have accepted your offer-in-compromise, **do not** file this form. Instead, call your local IRS District Office Special Procedures function. You can get the number by calling 1-800-829-1040.

Specific Instructions

Line 1

If you are making this request for a joint tax return, show the names and SSNs in the same order as on your tax return.

Line 10

Even if you can't pay the full amount you owe now, you should pay as much of it as possible to limit penalty and interest charges. If you are filing this form with your tax return, make the payment with your return. If you are filing this form by itself, for example, in response to a notice, include a check or money order payable to the Internal Revenue Service with this form. **Do not** send cash. On your payment, write your name, address, social security number, daytime phone number, and the tax year and tax return for which you are making this request (for example, "1995 Form 1040").

Line 11

You should try to make your payments large enough so that your balance due will be paid off by the due date of your next tax return.

Line 12

You can choose the date your monthly payment is due. For example, if your rent or mortgage payment is due on the first of the month, you may want to make your installment payments on the 15th. When we approve your request, we will tell you the month and date that your first payment is due. If we have not replied by the date you choose for your first payment, you may send the first payment to the Internal Revenue Service Center at the address shown on this page for the place where you live. Make your check or money order payable to the Internal Revenue Service. See the instructions for line 10 for what to write on your payment.

Line 13

Check the box on line 13 if you want your monthly payments automatically deducted **(Direct Debit)** from your bank account. If your installment agreement request is approved, we will send you the required Direct Debit enrollment form and you must include the $43 fee when you return it.

How Do I File Form 9465?

● If you haven't filed your return, attach Form 9465 to the front of your return.

● If you have already filed your return, you are filing your return electronically, or you are filing this form in response to a notice, mail it to the **Internal Revenue Service Center** at the address shown below for the place where you live. No street address is needed.

If you live in:	Use this address:
Florida, Georgia, South Carolina	Atlanta, GA 39901
New Jersey, New York (New York City and counties of Nassau, Rockland, Suffolk, and Westchester)	Holtsville, NY 00501
New York (all other counties), Connecticut, Maine, Massachusetts, New Hampshire, Rhode Island, Vermont	Andover, MA 05501
Illinois, Iowa, Minnesota, Missouri, Wisconsin	Kansas City, MO 64999
Delaware, District of Columbia, Maryland, Pennsylvania, Virginia	Philadelphia, PA 19255
Indiana, Kentucky, Michigan, Ohio, West Virginia	Cincinnati, OH 45999
Kansas, New Mexico, Oklahoma, Texas	Austin, TX 73301
Alaska, Arizona, California (counties of Alpine, Amador, Butte, Calaveras, Colusa, Contra Costa, Del Norte, El Dorado, Glenn, Humboldt, Lake, Lassen, Marin, Mendocino, Modoc, Napa, Nevada, Placer, Plumas, Sacramento, San Joaquin, Shasta, Sierra, Siskiyou, Solano, Sonoma, Sutter, Tehama, Trinity, Yolo, and Yuba), Colorado, Idaho, Montana, Nebraska, Nevada, North Dakota, Oregon, South Dakota, Utah, Washington, Wyoming	Ogden, UT 84201
California (all other counties), Hawaii	Fresno, CA 93888
Alabama, Arkansas, Louisiana, Mississippi, North Carolina, Tennessee	Memphis, TN 37501
American Samoa Guam: Nonpermanent residents only* Puerto Rico (or if excluding income under section 933) Virgin Islands: Nonpermanent residents only* Foreign country (or if a dual-status alien): U.S. citizens and those filing Form 2555, 2555-EZ, or 4563 All APO and FPO addresses	Philadelphia, PA 19255

*Permanent residents of Guam and the Virgin Islands cannot use Form 9465.

Printed on recycled paper

APPENDIX C
Glossary of Tax Terms

The words and phrases in this glossary have been defined to reflect their conventional use in the field of taxation. The definitions may therefore be incomplete for other purposes.

A

Accelerated cost recovery system (ACRS). A method in which the cost of tangible property is recovered over a prescribed period of time. Enacted by the Economic Recovery Tax Act (ERTA) of 1981 and substantially modified by the Tax Reform Act (TRA) of 1986, the approach disregards salvage value, imposes a period of cost recovery that depends upon the classification of the asset into one of various recovery periods, and prescribes the applicable percentage of cost that can be deducted each year. The modified system is referred to as MACRS. § 168.

Accelerated depreciation. Various methods of depreciation that yield larger deductions in the earlier years of the life of an asset than the straight-line method. Examples include the double declining-balance and the sum-of-the-years' digits methods of depreciation.

Accounting method. The method under which income and expenses are determined for tax purposes. Important accounting methods include the cash basis and the accrual basis. Special methods are available for the reporting of gain on installment sales, recognition of income on construction projects (the completed contract and percentage of completion methods), and the valuation of inventories (last-in, first-out and first-in, first-out). §§ 446–474. See also *accrual basis, cash basis, completed contract method,* and *percentage of completion method.*

Accounting period. The period of time, usually a year, used by a taxpayer for the determination of tax liability. Unless a fiscal year is chosen, taxpayers must determine and pay their income tax liability by using the calendar year (January 1 through December 31) as the period of measurement. An example of a fiscal year is July 1 through June 30. A change in accounting periods (e.g., from a calendar year to a fiscal year) generally requires the consent of the IRS. Some new taxpayers, such as a newly formed corporation, are free to select either an initial calendar or a fiscal year without the consent of the IRS. §§ 441–443. See also *annual accounting period concept.*

Accrual basis. A method of accounting that reflects expenses incurred and income earned for any one tax year. In contrast to the cash basis of accounting, expenses do not have to be paid to be deductible, nor does income have to be received to be taxable. Unearned income (e.g., prepaid interest and rent) generally is taxed in the year of receipt regardless of the method of accounting used by the taxpayer. § 446(c)(2). See also *accounting method, cash basis,* and *unearned income.*

Accumulated adjustments account (AAA). An account that aggregates an S corporation's post-1982 income, loss, and deductions for the tax year (including nontaxable income and nondeductible losses and expenses). After the year-end income and expense adjustments are made, the account is reduced by distributions made during the tax year.

Accumulated earnings and profits. Net undistributed tax-basis earnings of the corporation aggregated from March 1, 1913, to the end of the prior tax year. Used to determine the amount of dividend income associated with a distribution to shareholders. See *current earnings and profits* and *earnings and profits.* § 316 and Reg. § 1.316-2.

Accumulated earnings credit. A reduction allowed in arriving at accumulated taxable income, in determining the accumulated earnings tax. See also *accumulated earnings tax* and *accumulated taxable income.*

Accumulated earnings tax (AET). A special tax imposed on corporations that accumulate (rather than distribute) their earnings beyond the reasonable needs of the business. The accumulated earnings tax and related interest are imposed on accumulated taxable income in addition to the corporate income tax. §§ 531–537.

Accumulated taxable income. The base upon which the accumulated earnings tax is imposed. Generally, it is the taxable income of the corporation as adjusted for certain items (e.g., the Federal income tax, excess charitable contributions, the dividends received deduction) less the dividends paid deduction and the accumulated earnings credit. § 535.

Accumulating trust. See *discretionary trust.*

Accumulation distribution. The amount by which total distributions for the tax year exceed a complex trust's

C–1

distributable net income. This amount is thrown back to previous years, and any excess tax that would have been due at the beneficiary level is collectible under a short-cut computation. The purpose of the tax is to discourage trustees from delaying distributions until the beneficiary's marginal rate is less than that of the trust. Accumulations prior to a beneficiary's reaching age 21, by an estate, or of corpus capital gains are not subject to this tax.

Accuracy-related penalty. Major civil taxpayer penalties relating to the accuracy of tax return data, including misstatements stemming from taxpayer negligence and improper valuation of income and deductions, are coordinated under this umbrella term. The penalty usually equals 20 percent of the understated tax liability.

Acquiescence. Agreement by the IRS on the results reached in most of the Regular decisions of the U.S. Tax Court; sometimes abbreviated *Acq.* or *A.* See also *nonacquiescence.*

Acquisition. See *corporate acquisition.*

ACRS. See *accelerated cost recovery system.*

Ad valorem tax. A tax imposed on the value of property. The most common ad valorem tax is that imposed by states, counties, and cities on real estate. Ad valorem taxes can be imposed on personal property as well. See also *personalty.*

Adjusted basis. The cost or other basis of property reduced by depreciation allowed or allowable and increased by capital improvements. Other special adjustments are provided in § 1016 and the related Regulations. See also *basis.*

Adjusted current earnings (ACE). An adjustment in computing corporate alternative minimum taxable income (AMTI), computed at 75 percent of the excess of adjusted current earnings and profits over AMTI. ACE computations reflect restrictions on the timing of certain recognition events. Exempt interest, life insurance proceeds, and other receipts that are included in earnings and profits but not in taxable income also increase the ACE adjustment. See also *alternative minimum tax* and *earnings and profits.*

Adjusted gross estate. The gross estate of a *decedent* reduced by § 2053 expenses (e.g., administration, funeral) and § 2054 losses (e.g., casualty). Necessary in testing for the extension of time for installment payment of estate taxes under § 6166. See also *gross estate.*

Adjusted gross income (AGI). A tax determination peculiar to individual taxpayers. Generally, it represents the gross income of an individual, less business expenses and less any appropriate capital gain or loss adjustment. See also *gross income.*

Adjusted ordinary gross income. A determination peculiar to the *personal holding company tax.* In ascertaining whether a corporation is a personal holding company, personal holding company income divided by adjusted ordinary gross income must equal 60 percent or more.

Adjusted ordinary gross income is the corporation's gross income less capital gains, § 1231 gains, and certain expenses. §§ 541 and 543(b)(2). See also *personal holding company income.*

Adjusted taxable estate. The taxable estate reduced by $60,000. The adjusted taxable estate is utilized only in applying § 2011 for determining the limit on the credit for state death taxes paid that will be allowed against the Federal estate tax. See also *taxable estate.*

Administration. The supervision and winding up of an estate. The administration of an estate runs from the date of an individual's death until all assets have been distributed and liabilities paid.

Administrator. A person appointed by the court to administer (manage or take charge of) the assets and liabilities of a decedent (the deceased). See also *executor.*

Affiliated group. A parent-subsidiary group of corporations that is eligible to elect to file on a consolidated basis. Eighty percent ownership of the voting power and value of all of the corporations must be achieved on every day of the tax year, and an identifiable parent corporation must exist, i.e., it must own at least 80 percent of another group member without applying attribution rules.

AFTR. *American Federal Tax Reports* contain all of the Federal tax decisions issued by the U.S. District Courts, U.S. Court of Federal Claims, U.S. Courts of Appeals, and the U.S. Supreme Court.

AFTR2d. The second series of the *American Federal Tax Reports,* dealing with 1954 and 1986 Code case law.

Aggregate concept. The theory of partnership taxation under which, in certain cases, a partnership is treated as a mere extension of each partner.

Alimony. Alimony deductions result from the payment of a legal obligation arising from the termination of a marital relationship. Payments designated as alimony generally are included in the gross income of the recipient and are deductible *for* AGI by the payer.

Allocable share of income. Certain entities receive conduit treatment under the Federal income tax law. This means the earned income or loss is not taxed to the entity, but is allocated to the owners or beneficiaries, regardless of the magnitude or timing of corresponding distributions. The portion of the entity's income that is taxed to the owner or beneficiary is the allocable share of the entity's income or loss for the period. The allocations are determined by (1) the partnership agreement for partners, (2) a weighted-average stock ownership computation for shareholders of an S corporation, and (3) the controlling will or trust instrument for the beneficiaries of an estate or trust.

Allocate. The assignment of income for various tax purposes. A *multistate corporation*'s nonbusiness income usually is allocated to the state where the nonbusiness assets are located; it is not *apportioned* with the rest of the entity's income. The income and expense items of an estate or trust are allocated between income and corpus components. Specific items of income, expense, gain, loss, and credit can be allocated to specific partners or shareholders in an S corporation, if a substantial economic nontax purpose for the allocation is established. See also *apportion* and *substantial economic effect*.

Alternate valuation date. Property passing from a *decedent* by death may be valued for death tax purposes as of the date of death or the alternate valuation date. The alternate valuation date is six months from the date of death or the date the property is disposed of by the estate, whichever comes first. To use the alternate valuation date, the *executor* or *administrator* of the estate must make an affirmative election. The election of the alternate valuation date is not available unless it decreases the amount of the gross estate *and* reduces the estate tax liability.

Alternative minimum tax (AMT). AMT is a fixed percentage of alternative minimum taxable income (AMTI). AMTI generally starts with the taxpayer's adjusted gross income (for individuals) or taxable income (for other taxpayers). To this amount, the taxpayer (1) adds designated preference items (e.g., interest income on private activity bonds), (2) makes other specified adjustments (e.g., to reflect a longer, straight-line cost recovery deduction), (3) subtracts certain AMT itemized deductions for individuals (e.g., interest incurred on housing but not taxes paid), and (4) subtracts an exemption amount (e.g., $40,000 on an individual joint return). The taxpayer must pay the greater of the resulting AMT (reduced by only the foreign tax credit) or the regular income tax (reduced by all allowable tax credits).

Alternative minimum taxable income (AMTI). The base for computing a taxpayer's *alternative minimum tax*. Generally, the taxable income for the year, modified for AMT adjustments, preferences, and exemptions.

Amortization. The tax deduction for the cost or other basis of an intangible asset over the asset's estimated useful life. Examples of amortizable intangibles include patents, copyrights, and leasehold interests. Most intangible assets are amortized over 15 years. § 195. For tangible assets, see *depreciation*. For natural resources, see *depletion*. See also *estimated useful life* and *goodwill*.

Amount realized. The amount received by a taxpayer upon the sale or exchange of property. Amount realized is the sum of the cash and the fair market value of any property or services received by the taxpayer, plus any related debt assumed by the buyer. Determining the amount realized is the starting point for arriving at realized gain or loss. § 1001(b). See also *realized gain or loss* and *recognized gain or loss*.

Annual accounting period concept. In determining a taxpayer's income tax liability, only transactions taking place during a specified tax year are taken into consideration. For reporting and payment purposes, therefore, the tax life of taxpayers is divided into equal annual accounting periods.

See also *accounting period* and *mitigation of the annual accounting period concept*.

Annual exclusion. In computing the taxable gifts for the year, each donor excludes the first $10,000 of a gift to each donee. Usually, the annual exclusion is not available for gifts of future interests. § 2503(b). See also *future interest* and *gift splitting*.

Annuitant. The party entitled to receive payments from an annuity contract. See also *annuity*.

Annuity. A fixed sum of money payable to a person at specified times for a specified period of time or for life. If the party making the payment (i.e., the obligor) is regularly engaged in this type of business (e.g., an insurance company), the arrangement is classified as a commercial annuity. A so-called private annuity involves an obligor that is not regularly engaged in selling annuities (e.g., a charity or family member).

Anticipatory assignment of income. See *assignment of income*.

Appellate court. For Federal tax purposes, appellate courts include the Courts of Appeals and the Supreme Court. If the party losing in the trial (or lower) court is dissatisfied with the result, the dispute may be carried to the appropriate appellate court. See also *Court of Appeals* and *trial court*.

Apportion. The assignment of the business income of a multistate corporation to specific states for income taxation. Usually, the apportionment procedure accounts for the property, payroll, and sales activity levels of the various states, and a proportionate assignment of the entity's total income is made, using a three-factor apportionment formula. These activities indicate the commercial domicile of the corporation, relative to that income. Some states exclude nonbusiness income from the apportionment procedure; they *allocate* nonbusiness income to the states where the nonbusiness assets are located. See also *allocate, domicile, nonbusiness income, payroll factor, property factor,* and *sales factor*.

Arm's length concept. The standard under which unrelated parties would carry out a transaction. Suppose Bint Corporation sells property to its sole shareholder for $10,000. In determining whether $10,000 is an arm's length price, one would ascertain the amount for which the corporation could have sold the property to a disinterested third party.

Articles of incorporation. The legal document specifying a corporation's name, period of existence, purpose and powers, authorized number of shares, classes of stock, and other conditions for operation. The organizers of the corporation file the articles with the state of incorporation. If the articles are satisfactory and other conditions of the law are satisfied, the state will issue a charter recognizing the organization's status as a corporation.

Assessment. The process whereby the IRS imposes an additional tax liability. If, for example, the IRS audits a taxpayer's income tax return and finds gross income understated or deductions overstated, it will assess a deficiency in the amount of the tax that should have been paid in light of the adjustments made. See also *deficiency*.

Assignment of income.   A procedure whereby a taxpayer attempts to avoid the recognition of income by assigning to another the property that generates the income. Such a procedure will not avoid the recognition of income by the taxpayer making the assignment if it can be said that the income was earned at the point of the transfer. In this case, usually referred to as an *anticipatory assignment of income*, the income will be taxed to the person who earns it.

Association.   An organization treated as a corporation for Federal tax purposes even though it may not qualify as such under applicable state law. An entity designated as a trust or a partnership, for example, may be classified as an association if it clearly possesses corporate attributes. Corporate attributes include centralized management, continuity of life, free transferability of interests, and limited liability. § 7701(a)(3).

Assumption of liabilities.   In a corporate takeover or asset purchase, the buyer often takes assets subject to preexisting debt. Such actions do not create *boot* received on the transaction for the new shareholder, unless there is no *bona fide* business purpose for the exchange, or the principal purpose of the debt assumption is the avoidance of tax liabilities. § 357.

At-risk amount.   The taxpayer has an amount at risk in a business or investment venture to the extent that personal assets have been subjected to the risks of the business. Typically, the taxpayer's at-risk amount includes (1) the amount of money or other property that the investor contributed to the venture for the investment, (2) the amount of any of the entity's liabilities for which the taxpayer personally is liable and that relate to the investment, and (3) an allocable share of nonrecourse debts incurred by the venture from third parties in arm's length transactions for real estate investments.

At-risk limitation.   Generally, a taxpayer can deduct losses related to a trade or business, S corporation, partnership, or investment asset only to the extent of the at-risk amount.

Attribution.   Under certain circumstances, the tax law applies attribution rules to assign to one taxpayer the ownership interest of another taxpayer. If, for example, the stock of Tree Corporation is held 60 percent by Mary and 40 percent by Sam, Mary may be deemed to own 100 percent of Tree if Sam is her son. In that case, the stock owned by Sam is attributed to Mary. Stated differently, Mary has a 60 percent direct and a 40 percent indirect interest in Tree. It can also be said that Mary is the constructive owner of Sam's interest.

Audit.   Inspection and verification of a taxpayer's return or other transactions possessing tax consequences. See also *correspondence audit, field audit,* and *office audit*.

Automobile expenses.   Automobile expenses generally are deductible only to the extent the automobile is used in business or for the production of income. Personal commuting expenses are not deductible. The taxpayer may deduct actual expenses (including depreciation and insurance), or the standard (automatic) mileage rate may be used (31.5 cents per mile for 1997) during any one year. Automobile expenses incurred for medical purposes or in connection with job-related moving expenses are deductible to the extent of actual out-of-pocket expenses or at the rate of 9 cents per mile (12 cents for charitable activities).

B

Bailout.   Various procedures whereby the owners of an entity can obtain the entity's profits with favorable tax consequences. With corporations, for example, the bailout of corporate profits without dividend consequences might be the desired objective. The alternative of distributing the profits to the shareholders as dividends generally is less attractive since dividend payments are not deductible. See also *preferred stock bailout*.

Bargain sale or purchase.   A sale or purchase of property for less than fair market value. The difference between the sale or purchase price and the fair market value of the property may have tax consequences. If, for example, a corporation sells property worth $1,000 to one of its shareholders for $700, the $300 difference probably represents a constructive dividend to the shareholder. Suppose, instead, the shareholder sells the property (worth $1,000) to his or her corporation for $700. The $300 difference probably represents a contribution by the shareholder to the corporation's capital. Bargain sales and purchases among members of the same family may lead to gift tax consequences. See also *constructive dividend*.

Basis.   The acquisition cost assigned to an asset for income tax purposes. For assets acquired by purchase, basis is cost (§ 1012). Special rules govern the basis of property received by virtue of another's death (§ 1014) or by gift (§ 1015), the basis of stock received on a transfer of property to a controlled corporation (§ 358), the basis of the property transferred to the corporation (§ 362), and the basis of property received upon the liquidation of a corporation (§ 334). See also *adjusted basis*.

Basis in partnership interest.   The acquisition cost of the partner's ownership interest in the *partnership*. Includes purchase price and associated debt acquired from other partners and in the course of the entity's trade or business.

Beneficiary.   A party who will benefit from a transfer of property or other arrangement. Examples include the beneficiary of a trust, the beneficiary of a life insurance policy, and the beneficiary of an estate.

Bequest.   A transfer of personal property by will. To bequeath is to leave such property by will. See also *devise* and *personal property*.

Blockage rule.   A factor to be considered in valuing a large block of stock. Application of this rule generally justifies a discount in the fair market value since the disposition of a large amount of stock at any one time may depress the value of the shares in the marketplace.

Bona fide. In good faith, or real. In tax law, this term is often used in connection with a business purpose for carrying out a transaction. Thus, was there a bona fide business purpose for a shareholder's transfer of a liability to a controlled corporation? § 357(b)(1)(B). See also *business purpose*.

Book value. The net amount of an asset after reduction by a related reserve. The book value of machinery, for example, is the amount of the machinery less the reserve for depreciation.

Boot. Cash or property of a type not included in the definition of a nontaxable exchange. The receipt of boot will cause an otherwise nontaxable transfer to become taxable to the extent of the lesser of the fair market value of the boot or the realized gain on the transfer. For example, see transfers to controlled corporations under § 351(b) and like-kind exchanges under § 1031(b). See also *like-kind exchange* and *realized gain or loss*.

Branch profits tax. A tax on the effectively connected earnings and profits of the U.S. branch of a foreign corporation. The tax is levied in addition to the usual § 11 tax, in an amount equal to 30 percent of the dividend equivalent amount. Treaties can override the tax or reduce the withholding percentage. Earnings reinvested in the U.S. operations of the entity are not subject to the tax until repatriation. See *dividend equivalent amount*.

Bribes and illegal payments. Section 162 denies a deduction for bribes or kickbacks, fines and penalties paid to a government official or employee for violation of law, and two-thirds of the treble damage payments made to claimants for violation of the antitrust law. Denial of a deduction for bribes and illegal payments is based upon the judicially established principle that allowing such payments would be contrary to public policy.

Brother-sister controlled group. More than one corporation owned by the same shareholders. If, for example, Clara and Dan each own one-half of the stock in Top Corporation and Bottom Corporation, then Top and Bottom form a brother-sister controlled group.

B.T.A. The Board of Tax Appeals was a trial court that considered Federal tax matters. This Court is now the U.S. Tax Court.

Built-in gains tax. A penalty tax designed to discourage a shift of the incidence of taxation on unrealized gains from a C corporation to its shareholders, via an S election. Under this provision, any recognized gain during the first 10 years of S status generates a corporate-level tax on a base not to exceed the aggregate untaxed built-in gains brought into the S corporation upon its election from C corporation taxable years.

Burden of proof. The requirement in a lawsuit to show the weight of evidence and thereby gain a favorable decision. Except in cases of tax fraud, the burden of proof in a tax case generally is on the taxpayer. See also *fraud*.

Business bad debts. A tax deduction allowed for obligations obtained in connection with a trade or business that have become either partially or completely worthless. In contrast to nonbusiness bad debts, business bad debts are deductible as business expenses. § 166. See also *nonbusiness bad debts*.

Business purpose. A justifiable business reason for carrying out a transaction. Mere tax avoidance is not an acceptable business purpose. The presence of a business purpose is crucial in the area of corporate reorganizations and certain liquidations. See also *bona fide*.

Buy-sell agreement. An arrangement, particularly appropriate in the case of a closely held corporation or a partnership, whereby the surviving owners (shareholders or partners) or the entity agrees to purchase the interest of a withdrawing owner. The buy-sell agreement provides for an orderly disposition of an interest in a business and may aid in setting the value of the interest for death tax purposes. See also *cross-purchase buy-sell agreement* and *entity buy-sell agreement*.

By-pass amount. The amount that can be transferred by gift or death free of any unified transfer tax. Currently, the by-pass amount is $600,000. See also *exemption equivalent amount*.

C

Calendar year. See *accounting period*.

Capital account. The financial accounting analog of a partner's tax basis in the entity.

Capital asset. Broadly speaking, all assets are capital except those specifically excluded by the Code. Major categories of noncapital assets include property held for resale in the normal course of business (inventory), trade accounts and notes receivable, and depreciable property and real estate used in a trade or business (§ 1231 assets). § 1221. See also *capital gain* and *capital loss*.

Capital contribution. Various means by which a shareholder makes additional funds available to the corporation (placed at the risk of the business), sometimes without the receipt of additional stock. If no stock is received, the contributions are added to the basis of the shareholder's existing stock investment and do not generate gross income to the corporation. § 118.

Capital expenditure. An expenditure that should be added to the basis of the property improved. For income tax purposes, this generally precludes a full deduction for the expenditure in the year paid or incurred. Any cost recovery in the form of a tax deduction comes in the form of depreciation, depletion, or amortization. § 263.

Capital gain. The gain from the sale or exchange of a capital asset. See also *capital asset*.

Capital interest. Usually, the percentage of the entity's net assets that a partner would receive on liquidation. Typically determined by the partner's capital sharing ratio.

Capital loss. The loss from the sale or exchange of a capital asset. See also *capital asset.*

Capital sharing ratio. A partner's percentage ownership of the entity's capital.

Capital stock tax. A state-level tax, usually imposed on out-of-state corporations for the privilege of doing business in the state. The tax may be based on the entity's apportionable income or payroll, or on its apportioned net worth as of a specified date.

Carryover basis. When a taxpayer exchanges one asset for another, many provisions in the tax law allow the basis assigned to the received asset to be precisely that of the traded asset. Thus, no step-up or -down of basis occurs as a result of the exchange. For instance, when an investor contributes an asset to a corporation or partnership, the entity generally takes a carryover basis in the property. § 723.

Cash basis. A method of accounting that reflects deductions as paid and income as received in any one tax year. However, deductions for prepaid expenses that benefit more than one tax year (e.g., prepaid rent and prepaid interest) usually must be spread over the period benefited rather than deducted in the year paid. § 446(c)(1). See also *constructive receipt of income.*

Cash surrender value. The amount of money that an insurance policy would yield if cashed in with the insurance company that issued the policy.

CCH. Commerce Clearing House (CCH) is the publisher of a tax service and of Federal tax decisions (USTC series).

C corporation. A separate taxable entity, subject to the rules of Subchapter C of the Code. This business form may create a double taxation effect relative to its shareholders. The entity is subject to the regular corporate tax and a number of penalty taxes at the Federal level. §§ 301ff.

Centralized management. A concentration of authority among certain persons who may make independent business decisions on behalf of the entity without the need for continuing approval by the owners of the entity. It is a characteristic of a corporation since day-to-day business operations are handled by appointed officers and not by the shareholders. Reg. § 301.7701–2(c). See also *association.*

Cert. den. By denying the Writ of Certiorari, the U.S. Supreme Court refuses to accept an appeal from a U.S. Court of Appeals. The denial of *certiorari* does not, however, mean that the U.S. Supreme Court agrees with the result reached by the lower court.

Certiorari. Appeal from a U.S. Court of Appeals to the U.S. Supreme Court is by Writ of Certiorari. The Supreme Court need not accept the appeal, and it usually does not

(*cert. den.*) unless a conflict exists among the lower courts that must be resolved or a constitutional issue is involved. See also *cert. den.*

Cf. Compare.

Charitable contributions. Contributions are deductible (subject to various restrictions and ceiling limitations) if made to qualified nonprofit charitable organizations. A cash basis taxpayer is entitled to a deduction solely in the year of payment. Accrual basis corporations may accrue contributions at year-end if payment is properly authorized before the end of the year and payment is made within two and one-half months after the end of the year. § 170.

Civil fraud. See *fraud.*

Closely held corporation. A corporation where stock ownership is not widely dispersed. Rather, a few shareholders are in control of corporate policy and are in a position to benefit personally from that policy.

Closing agreement. In a tax dispute, the parties sign a closing agreement to spell out the terms under which the matters are settled. The agreement is binding on both the IRS and the taxpayer for the disputed year and for all future years.

Collapsing. To disregard a transaction or one of a series of steps leading to a result. See also *step transaction, substance vs. form concept,* and *telescoping.*

Commissioner of the IRS. The head of IRS operations, a presidential appointee.

Common law state. See *community property.*

Community property. Louisiana, Texas, New Mexico, Arizona, California, Washington, Idaho, Nevada, and Wisconsin have community property systems. The rest of the states are common law property jurisdictions. The difference between common law and community property systems centers around the property rights possessed by married persons. In a common law system, each spouse owns whatever he or she earns. Under a community property system, one-half of the earnings of each spouse is considered owned by the other spouse. Assume, for example, Hal and Wanda are husband and wife and their only income is the $50,000 annual salary Hal receives. If they live in New York (a common law state), the $50,000 salary belongs to Hal. If, however, they live in Texas (a community property state), the $50,000 salary is owned one-half each by Hal and Wanda. See also *separate property.*

Complete termination redemption. See *redemption (complete termination).*

Completed contract method. A method of reporting gain or loss on certain long-term contracts. Under this method of accounting, gross income and expenses are recognized in the tax year in which the contract is completed. Reg. § 1.451–3. See also *percentage of completion method.*

Complex trust. Not a *simple trust.* Such trusts may have charitable beneficiaries, accumulate income, and distribute corpus. §§ 661–663.

Component depreciation. The process of dividing an asset (e.g., a building) into separate components or parts for the purpose of calculating depreciation. The advantage of dividing an asset into components is to use shorter depreciation lives for selected components under § 167. Generally, the same cost recovery period must be used for all the components of an asset under § 168.

Concur. To agree with the result reached by another, but not necessarily with the reasoning or the logic used in reaching the result. For example, Judge Ross agrees with Judges Smith and Tanaka (all being members of the same court) that the income is taxable but for a different reason. Judge Ross would issue a concurring opinion to the majority opinion issued by Judges Smith and Tanaka.

Condemnation. The taking of property by a public authority. The taking is by legal action, and the owner of the property is compensated by the public authority.

Conduit concept. An approach assumed by the tax law in the treatment of certain entities and their owners. Permits specified tax characteristics to pass through the entity without losing their identity. For example, long-term capital losses realized by a limited liability company are passed through as such to the individual members of the entity. Varying forms of the conduit concept apply for partnerships, trusts, estates, and S corporations. See also *aggregate concept.*

Consent dividend. For purposes of avoiding or reducing the penalty tax on the unreasonable accumulation of earnings or the personal holding company tax, a corporation may declare a consent dividend. No cash or property is distributed to the shareholders, although the corporation obtains a dividends paid deduction. The consent dividend is taxed to the shareholders and increases the basis in their stock investment. § 565.

Consolidated return. A procedure whereby certain affiliated corporations may file a single return, combine the tax transactions of each corporation, and arrive at a single income tax liability for the group. The election to file a consolidated return usually is binding on future years. §§ 1501–1505 and related Regulations.

Consolidation. The combination of two or more corporations into a newly created corporation. Thus, Apt Corporation and Bye Corporation combine to form Cart Corporation. A consolidation may qualify as a nontaxable *reorganization* if certain conditions are satisfied. §§ 354 and 368(a)(1)(A).

Constructive dividend. A taxable benefit derived by a shareholder from his or her corporation that is not actually called a dividend. Examples include unreasonable compensation, excessive rent payments, bargain purchases of corporate property, and shareholder use of corporate property. Constructive dividends generally are found in closely held corporations. See also *bargain sale or purchase, closely held corporation,* and *unreasonable compensation.*

Constructive liquidation scenario. The means by which recourse debt is shared among partners in basis determination.

Constructive ownership. See *attribution.*

Constructive receipt of income. If income is unqualifiedly available although not physically in the taxpayer's possession, it is subject to the income tax. An example is accrued interest on a savings account. Under the constructive receipt of income concept, the interest is taxed to a depositor in the year available, rather than the year actually withdrawn. The fact that the depositor uses the cash basis of accounting for tax purposes is irrelevant. See Reg. § 1.451–2. See also *cash basis.*

Continuity of business enterprise. In a tax-free *reorganization,* a shareholder or corporation that has substantially the same investment after an exchange as before should not be taxed on the transaction. Specifically, the transferee corporation must continue the historic business of the transferor or use a significant portion of the transferor's assets in the new business.

Continuity of interest test. In a tax-free *reorganization,* a shareholder or corporation that has substantially the same investment after an exchange as before should not be taxed on the transaction. Specifically, the seller must acquire an equity interest in the purchasing corporation equal in value to at least 50 percent of all formerly outstanding stock of the acquired entity.

Continuity of life or existence. The death or other withdrawal of an owner of an entity does not terminate the existence of the entity. This is a characteristic of a corporation since the death or withdrawal of a shareholder does not affect the corporation's existence. Reg. § 301.7701–2(b). See also *association.*

Contributions to the capital of a corporation. See *capital contribution.*

Contributory qualified pension or profit sharing plan. A plan funded with both employer and employee contributions. Since the employee's contributions to the plan are subject to income tax, a later distribution of the contributions to the employee generally is tax-free. See also *qualified pension or profit sharing plan.*

Control. Holding a specified level of stock ownership in a corporation. For § 351, the new shareholder(s) must hold at least 80 percent of the total combined voting power of all voting classes of stock, and at least 80 percent of the shares of all nonvoting classes. Other tax provisions require different levels of control to bring about desired effects, such as 50 or 100 percent.

Controlled foreign corporation (CFC). A non-U.S. corporation in which more than 50 percent of the total combined voting power of all classes of stock entitled to vote or the total value of the stock of the corporation is owned by "U.S. shareholders" on any day during the taxable year of the foreign corporation. For purposes of this definition, a U.S.

shareholder is any U.S. person who owns, or is considered as owning, 10 percent or more of the total combined voting power of all classes of voting stock of the foreign corporation. Stock owned directly, indirectly, and constructively is used in this measure.

Controlled group.   A controlled group of corporations is required to share the lower-level corporate tax rates and various other tax benefits among the members of the group. A controlled group may be either a brother-sister or a parent-subsidiary group.

Corporate acquisition.   The takeover of one corporation by another if both parties retain their legal existence after the transaction. An acquisition can be effected via a stock purchase or through a tax-free exchange of stock. See also *corporate reorganization* and *merger.*

Corporate liquidation.   Occurs when a corporation distributes its net assets to its shareholders and ceases its legal existence. Generally, a shareholder recognizes capital gain or loss upon the liquidation of the entity, regardless of the corporation's balance in its earnings and profits account. However, the distributing corporation recognizes gain and loss on assets that it distributes to shareholders in kind.

Corporate reorganization.   Occurs, among other instances, when one corporation acquires another in a merger or acquisition, a single corporation divides into two or more entities, a corporation makes a substantial change in its capital structure, or a corporation undertakes a change in its legal name or domicile. The exchange of stock and other securities in a corporate reorganization can be effected favorably for tax purposes if certain statutory requirements are followed strictly. Tax consequences include the nonrecognition of any gain that is realized by the shareholders except to the extent of boot received. See also *corporate acquisition* and *merger.*

Corpus.   The body or principal of a trust. Suppose, for example, George transfers an apartment building into a trust, income payable to Wanda for life, remainder to Sam upon Wanda's death. Corpus of the trust is the apartment building.

Correspondence audit.   An audit conducted by the IRS by mail. Typically, the IRS writes to the taxpayer requesting the verification of a particular deduction or exemption. The completion of a special form or the remittance of copies of records or other support is all that is requested of the taxpayer. See also *audit, field audit,* and *office audit.*

Court of Appeals.   Any of 13 Federal courts that consider tax matters appealed from the U.S. Tax Court, a U.S. District Court, or the U.S. Court of Federal Claims. Appeal from a U.S. Court of Appeals is to the U.S. Supreme Court by *Writ of Certiorari.* See also *appellate court, Court of Federal Claims,* and *trial court.*

Court of Federal Claims.   A trial court (court of original jurisdiction) that decides litigation involving Federal tax matters. Appeal is to the Court of Appeals for the Federal Circuit.

Credit for prior transfers.   The death tax credit for prior transfers applies when property is taxed in the estates of different decedents within a 10-year period. The credit is determined using a decreasing statutory percentage, with the magnitude of the credit decreasing as the length of time between the multiple deaths increases. § 2013.

Criminal fraud.   See *fraud.*

Cross-purchase buy-sell agreement.   Under this type of arrangement, the surviving owners of the business agree to buy out the withdrawing owner. Assume, for example, Ron and Sara are equal shareholders in Tip Corporation. Under a cross-purchase buy-sell agreement, Ron and Sara would contract to purchase the other's interest should that person decide to withdraw from the business. See also *buy-sell agreement* and *entity buy-sell agreement.*

Current earnings and profits.   Net tax-basis earnings of the corporation aggregated during the current tax year. A corporate distribution is deemed to be first from the entity's current earnings and profits and then from accumulated earnings and profits. Shareholders recognize dividend income to the extent of the earnings and profits of the corporation. A dividend results to the extent of current earnings and profits, even if there is a larger negative balance in accumulated earnings and profits. § 316 and Reg. § 1.316-2.

Current use valuation.   See *special use value.*

Curtesy.   A husband's right under state law to all or part of his wife's property upon her death. See also *dower.*

D

Death benefit.   A payment made by an employer to the beneficiary or beneficiaries of a deceased employee on account of the death of the employee. Under certain conditions, the first $5,000 of the payment is exempt from the income tax. § 101(b)(1).

Death tax.   A tax imposed on property transferred by the death of the owner. See also *estate tax* and *inheritance tax.*

Debt-financed income.   Included in computations of the *unrelated business income* of an *exempt organization,* the gross income generated from debt-financed property.

Decedent.   An individual who has died.

Deduction.   The Federal income tax is not imposed upon gross income. Rather, it is imposed upon taxable income. Congressionally identified deductions are subtracted from gross income to arrive at the tax base, taxable income.

Deductions in respect of a decedent.   Deductions accrued at the moment of death but not recognizable on the final income tax return of a decedent because of the method of accounting used. Such items are allowed as deductions on the estate tax return and on the income tax return of the estate (Form 1041) or the heir (Form 1040). An example of a deduction in respect of a decedent is interest expense accrued to the date of death by a cash basis debtor.

Deferred compensation. Compensation that will be taxed when received and not when earned. An example is contributions by an employer to a qualified pension or profit sharing plan on behalf of an employee. The contributions will not be taxed to the employee until they are distributed (e.g., upon retirement). See also *qualified pension or profit sharing plan*.

Deficiency. Additional tax liability owed by a taxpayer and assessed by the IRS. See also *assessment* and *statutory notice of deficiency*.

Deficiency dividend. Once the IRS has established a corporation's liability for the personal holding company tax in a prior year, the tax may be reduced or avoided by the issuance of a deficiency dividend under § 547. The deficiency dividend procedure is not available in cases where the deficiency was due to fraud with intent to evade tax or to a willful failure to file the appropriate tax return [§ 547(g)]. Nor does the deficiency dividend procedure avoid the usual penalties and interest applicable for failure to file a return or pay a tax.

Deficit. A negative balance in the earnings and profits account.

Demand loan. A loan payable upon request by the creditor, rather than on a specific date.

Depletion. The process by which the cost or other basis of a natural resource (e.g., an oil or gas interest) is recovered upon extraction and sale of the resource. The two ways to determine the depletion allowance are the cost and percentage (or statutory) methods. Under the cost method, each unit of production sold is assigned a portion of the cost or other basis of the interest. This is determined by dividing the cost or other basis by the total units expected to be recovered. Under the percentage (or statutory) method, the tax law provides a special percentage factor for different types of minerals and other natural resources. This percentage is multiplied by the gross income from the interest to arrive at the depletion allowance. §§ 613 and 613A.

Depreciation. The deduction for the cost or other basis of a tangible asset over the asset's estimated useful life. For intangible assets, see *amortization*. For natural resources, see *depletion*. See also *estimated useful life*.

Depreciation recapture. Upon the disposition of depreciable property used in a trade or business, gain or loss is measured by the difference between the consideration received (the amount realized) and the adjusted basis of the property. The gain recognized could be § 1231 gain and qualify for long-term capital gain treatment. The recapture provisions of the Code (e.g., §§ 219, 1245, and 1250) may operate to convert some or all of the previous § 1231 gain into ordinary income. The justification for depreciation recapture is that it prevents a taxpayer from converting a dollar of ordinary deduction (in the form of depreciation) into deferred tax-favored income (§ 1231 or long-term capital gain). The depreciation recapture rules do not apply when the property is disposed of at a loss or via a gift. See also *Section 1231 gains and losses*.

Determination letter. Upon the request of a taxpayer, an IRS District Director will comment on the tax status of a completed transaction. Determination letters frequently are used to clarify employee status, determine whether a retirement or profit sharing plan qualifies under the Code, and determine the tax-exempt status of certain nonprofit organizations.

Devise. A transfer of real estate by will. See also *bequest*.

Disclaimers. Rejections, refusals, or renunciations of claims, powers, or property. Section 2518 sets forth the conditions required to avoid gift tax consequences as the result of a disclaimer.

Discretionary trust. Trusts under which the trustee or another party has the right to accumulate (rather than distribute) the income for each year. Depending on the terms of the trust instrument, the income may be accumulated for future distributions to the income beneficiaries or added to corpus for the benefit of the remainderperson. See also *corpus* and *income beneficiary*.

Disguised sale. When a partner contributes property to the entity and soon thereafter receives a distribution from the partnership, the transactions are collapsed, and the distribution is seen as a purchase of the asset by the partnership. § 707(a)(2)(B).

Disproportionate. Not pro rata or ratable. Suppose, for example, Fin Corporation has two shareholders, Cal and Dot, each of whom owns 50 percent of its stock. If Fin distributes a cash dividend of $2,000 to Cal and only $1,000 to Dot, the distribution is disproportionate. The distribution would have been proportionate if Cal and Dot had received $1,500 each.

Disproportionate distribution. A distribution from a partnership to one or more of its partners in which at least one partner's interest in partnership hot assets is increased or decreased. For example, a distribution of cash to one partner and hot assets to another changes both partners' interest in hot assets and is disproportionate. The intent of rules for taxation of disproportionate distributions is to ensure each partner eventually recognizes his or her proportionate share of partnership ordinary income.

Disproportionate redemption. See *redemption (disproportionate)*.

Disregard of corporate entity. To treat a corporation as if it did not exist for tax purposes. In that event, each shareholder accounts for an allocable share of all corporate transactions possessing tax consequences. See also *entity*.

Dissent. To disagree with the majority. If, for example, Judge Bird disagrees with the result reached by Judges Crown and Dove (all of whom are members of the same court), Judge Bird could issue a dissenting opinion.

Distributable net income (DNI). The measure that determines the nature and amount of the distributions from estates and trusts that the beneficiaries must include in income. DNI also limits the amount that estates and trusts can claim as a deduction for such distributions. § 643(a).

Distribution deduction. Used to compute an estate or trust's taxable income for the year. The lesser of the amount distributed to beneficiaries from income, or the deductible portion of distributable net income for the period.

Distributions in kind. A transfer of property "as is." If, for example, a corporation distributes land to its shareholders, a distribution in kind has taken place. A sale of land followed by a distribution of the cash proceeds would not be a distribution in kind of the land.

District Court. A Federal District Court is a trial court for purposes of litigating Federal tax matters. It is the only trial court in which a jury trial can be obtained. See also *trial court.*

District Director. The head of an IRS district's operations.

Dividend. A nondeductible distribution to the shareholders of a corporation. A dividend constitutes gross income to the recipient if it is from the current or accumulated earnings and profits of the corporation.

Dividend equivalent amount (DEA). The amount subject to the branch profits tax, it is equal to the effectively connected earnings and profits of the U.S. branch of a foreign corporation, reduced/(increased) by an increase/(reduction) in U.S. net equity.

Dividends paid deduction. Relative to the accumulated earnings and personal holding company taxes, reductions in the tax base are allowed to the extent that the corporation made dividends payments during the year. Thus, this adjustment reduces *accumulated taxable income* and *personal holding company income.*

Dividends received deduction. A deduction allowed a corporate shareholder for dividends received from a domestic corporation. The deduction usually is 70 percent of the dividends received, but it could be 80 or 100 percent depending upon the ownership percentage held by the payee corporation. §§ 243–246.

Divisive reorganization. A corporate division: some of the assets of one corporation are transferred to another corporation in exchange for control of the transferee. Then, in a spin-off or split-off, stock of the transferee is distributed to the transferor's shareholders.

Dock sale. A purchaser uses its owned or rented vehicles to take possession of the product at the seller's shipping dock. In most states, the sale is apportioned to the operating state of the purchaser, rather than the seller. See also *apportion* and *sales factor.*

Domestic corporation. A corporation created or organized in the United States or under the law of the United States or any state. § 7701(a)(4). Only dividends received from domestic corporations qualify for the dividends received deduction (§ 243). See also *foreign corporation.*

Domicile. A person's legal home.

Donee. The recipient of a gift.

Donor. The maker of a gift.

Double-weighted apportionment formula. A means by which the total taxable income of a *multistate corporation* is assigned to a specific state. Usually, the payroll, property, and sales factors are equally treated, and the weighted average of these factors is used in the *apportionment* procedure. In some states, however, the sales factor may receive a double weight, or it may be the only factor considered. These latter formulas place a greater tax burden on the income of out-of-state corporations. See also *apportion, payroll factor, property factor, sales factor,* and *UDITPA.*

Dower. A wife's right to all or part of her deceased husband's property, unique to common law states as opposed to community property jurisdictions. See also *curtesy.*

E

Earned income. Income from personal services. Distinguished from passive, portfolio, and other unearned income (sometimes referred to as "active" income). See §§ 469, 911, and the related Regulations.

Earnings and profits (E & P). Measures the economic capacity of a corporation to make a distribution to shareholders that is not a return of capital. Such a distribution results in dividend income to the shareholders to the extent of the corporation's current and accumulated earnings and profits.

Economic effect test. Requirements that must be met before a special allocation may be used by a partnership. The premise behind the test is that each partner who receives an allocation of income or loss from a partnership bears the economic benefit or burden of the allocation.

Effectively connected income. Income of a nonresident alien or foreign corporation that is attributable to the operations of a U.S. trade or business under either the asset-use or the business-activities test.

Employee stock ownership plan (ESOP). A type of qualified profit sharing plan that invests in securities of the employer. In a noncontributory ESOP, the employer usually contributes its shares to a trust and receives a deduction for the fair market value of the stock. Generally, the employee does not recognize income until the stock is sold after its distribution to him or her upon retirement or other separation from service. See also *qualified pension or profit sharing plan.*

En banc. The case was considered by the whole court. Typically, for example, only one of the judges of the U.S. Tax Court will hear and decide on a tax controversy. However, when the issues involved are unusually novel or of wide impact, the case will be heard and decided by the full Court sitting *en banc.*

Energy tax credit—business property. A 10 percent tax credit is available to businesses that invest in certain energy property. The purpose of the credit is to create incentives for conservation and to develop alternative energy sources. The credit is available on the acquisition of solar and geothermal property. §§ 46 and 48.

Enrolled agent (EA). A tax practitioner who has gained admission to practice before the IRS by passing an IRS examination.

Entity. An organization or being that possesses separate existence for tax purposes. Examples are corporations, partnerships, estates, and trusts. See also *disregard of corporate entity.*

Entity accounting income. Entity accounting income is not identical to the taxable income of a trust or estate, nor is it determined in the same manner as the entity's financial accounting income would be. The trust document or will determines whether certain income, expenses, gains, or losses are allocated to the corpus of the entity or to the entity's income beneficiaries. Only the items that are allocated to the income beneficiaries are included in entity accounting income.

Entity buy-sell agreement. The entity is to purchase a withdrawing owner's interest. When the entity is a corporation, the agreement generally involves a stock redemption on the part of the withdrawing shareholder. See also *buy-sell agreement* and *cross-purchase buy-sell agreement.*

Entity concept. Even in so-called flow-through entities, tax accounting elections are made (e.g., a tax year is adopted) and conventions are adopted (e.g., with respect to cost recovery methods) at the entity level. This may seem to violate the *conduit concept,* but such exceptions tend to ease the administration of such conduit taxpayers, especially in the context of a large number of shareholders/partners/members/beneficiaries.

Equity structure shift. A tax-free *reorganization* other than a *divisive reorganization* or *recapitalization.* If there is a more than 50 percent change in the ownership of a loss corporation in an equity structure shift, § 382 limits the use of net operating loss carryovers of the loss corporation. Specifically, the annual net operating loss carryover deduction is limited to the value of the loss corporation immediately before the equity structure shift times the *long-term tax-exempt rate.*

Escrow. Money or other property placed with a third party as security for an existing or proposed obligation. Cyd, for example, agrees to purchase Don's stock in Rip Corporation but needs time to raise the necessary funds. Don places the stock with Ernie (the escrow agent), with instructions to deliver it to Cyd when the purchase price is paid.

Estate. An entity that locates, collects, distributes, and discharges the assets and liabilities of a decedent.

Estate freeze. Procedures directed toward fixing and stabilizing the value of an interest retained in a business, while transferring the growth portion to family members. In the case of a closely held corporation, the estate freeze usually involves keeping the preferred stock and giving away the common stock. The ultimate objective is to reduce estate value when the original owner-donor dies.

Estate tax. A tax imposed on the right to transfer property by death. Thus, an estate tax is levied on the decedent's estate and not on the heir receiving the property. See also *death tax* and *inheritance tax.*

Estimated useful life. The period over which an asset will be used by the taxpayer. Assets such as collectible artwork do not have an estimated useful life. The estimated useful life of an asset is essential to measuring the annual tax deduction for depreciation and amortization.

Estoppel. The process of being stopped from proving something (even if true) in court due to a prior inconsistent action. It is usually invoked as a matter of fairness to prevent one party (either the taxpayer or the IRS) from taking advantage of a prior error.

Excess lobbying expenditure. An excise tax is applied on otherwise tax-exempt organizations with respect to the excess of total lobbying expenditure over *grass roots lobbying expenditure* for the year.

Excess loss account. When a subsidiary has generated more historical losses than its parent has invested in the entity, the parent's basis in the subsidiary is zero, and the parent records additional losses in an excess loss account. This treatment allows the parent to continue to deduct losses of the subsidiary, even where no basis reduction is possible, while avoiding the need to show a negative stock basis on various financial records. If the subsidiary stock is sold while an excess loss account exists, capital gain income usually is recognized to the extent of the balance in the account.

Excise tax. A tax on the manufacture, sale, or use of goods; on the carrying on of an occupation or activity; or on the transfer of property. Thus, the Federal estate and gift taxes are, theoretically, excise taxes.

Executor. A person designated by a will to administer (manage or take charge of) the assets and liabilities of a decedent. See also *administrator.*

Exemption. An amount by which the tax base is reduced for all qualifying taxpayers. Individuals can receive personal and dependency exemptions, and taxpayers apply an exemption in computing their alternative minimum taxable income. Often, the exemption amount is phased out as the tax base becomes sizable.

Exemption equivalent. The maximum value of assets that can be transferred to another party without incurring any Federal gift or death tax because of the application of the unified tax credit.

Exemption equivalent amount. The amount of value (currently $600,000) that is the equivalent of the unified transfer tax credit allowed (currently $192,800). See also *by-pass amount*.

Exempt organization. An organization that is either partially or completely exempt from Federal income taxation. § 501.

Expenses in respect of a decedent. See *deductions in respect of a decedent*.

F

Fair market value. The amount at which property would change hands between a willing buyer and a willing seller, neither being under any compulsion to buy or to sell, and both having reasonable knowledge of the relevant facts. Reg. § 20.2031–1(b).

Federal Register. The first place that the rules and regulations of U.S. administrative agencies (e.g., the U.S. Treasury Department) are published.

F.3d. An abbreviation for the third series of the *Federal Reporter*, the official series in which decisions of the U.S. Court of Federal Claims and the U.S. Court of Appeals are published. The second series is denoted F.2d.

F.Supp. The abbreviation for *Federal Supplement*, the official series in which the reported decisions of the U.S. Federal District Courts are published.

Feeder organization. An entity that carries on a trade or business for the benefit of an *exempt organization*. However, such a relationship does not result in the feeder organization itself being tax-exempt. § 502.

Fiduciary. A person who manages money or property for another and who must exercise a standard of care in the management activity imposed by law or contract. A trustee, for example, possesses a fiduciary responsibility to the beneficiaries of the trust to follow the terms of the trust and the requirements of applicable state law. A breach of fiduciary responsibility would make the trustee liable to the beneficiaries for any damage caused by the breach.

Field audit. An audit conducted by the IRS on the business premises of the taxpayer or in the office of the tax practitioner representing the taxpayer. See also *audit, correspondence audit*, and *office audit*.

FIRPTA. Under the Foreign Investment in Real Property Tax Act, gains or losses realized by nonresident aliens and non-U.S. corporations on the disposition of U.S. real estate create U.S.-source income and are subject to U.S. income tax.

First-in, first-out (FIFO). An accounting method for determining the cost of inventories. Under this method, the inventory on hand is deemed to be the sum of the cost of the most recently acquired units. See also *last-in, first-out (LIFO)*.

Fiscal year. See *accounting period*.

Flat tax. In its pure form, a flat tax would eliminate all exclusions, deductions, and credits and impose a one-rate tax on gross income.

Foreign corporation. A corporation that is not created in the United States or organized under the laws of one of the states of the United States. § 7701(a)(5). See also *domestic corporation*.

Foreign currency transaction. An exchange that could generate a foreign currency gain or loss for a U.S. taxpayer. For instance, if A contracts to purchase foreign goods, payable in a currency other than U.S. dollars, at a specified date in the future, any change in the exchange rate between the dollar and that currency will generate a foreign currency gain or loss upon completion of the contract. This gain or loss is treated as separate from the underlying transaction; it may create ordinary or capital gain or loss.

Foreign earned income exclusion. The Code allows exclusions for earned income generated outside the United States to alleviate any tax base and rate disparities among countries. In addition, the exclusion is allowed for housing expenditures incurred by the taxpayer's employer with respect to the non-U.S. assignment, and self-employed individuals can deduct foreign housing expenses incurred in a trade or business.

Foreign personal holding company (FPHC). A foreign corporation in which (1) 60 percent or more of the gross income for the taxable year is FPHC income and (2) more than 50 percent of the total combined voting power or the total value of the stock is owned, directly or indirectly, by five or fewer individuals who are U.S. persons (the U.S. group) at any time during the taxable year. The 60 percent of gross income test drops to 50 percent or more after the 60 percent requirement has been met for one tax year, until the foreign corporation does not meet the 50 percent test for three consecutive years or the stock ownership requirement is not met for an entire tax year.

Foreign sales corporation (FSC). An entity qualifying for a partial exemption of its gross export receipts from U.S. tax. Most FSCs must maintain a presence in a foreign country. In addition, an FSC cannot issue preferred stock, nor can it have more than 25 shareholders.

Foreign-source income. Income that is not sourced within the United States. Examples include earnings from the performance of a personal services contract outside the United States, interest received from a non-U.S. corporation, and income from the use of property outside the United States.

Foreign tax credit or deduction. A U.S. citizen or resident who incurs or pays income taxes to a foreign country on income subject to U.S. tax may be able to claim some of these taxes as a deduction or a credit against the U.S. income tax. §§ 27, 164, and 901–905.

Form 706. The U.S. Estate Tax Return. In certain cases, this form must be filed for a decedent who was a resident or citizen of the United States.

Form 709. The U.S. Gift Tax Return.

Form 709–A. The U.S. Short Form Gift Tax Return.

Form 870. The signing of Form 870 (Waiver of Restriction on Assessment and Collection of Deficiency in Tax and Acceptance of Overassessments) by a taxpayer permits the IRS to assess a proposed deficiency without issuing a statutory notice of deficiency (90-day letter). This means the taxpayer must pay the deficiency and cannot file a petition to the U.S. Tax Court. § 6213(d).

Form 872. The signing of this form by a taxpayer extends the period during which the IRS can make an assessment or collection of a tax. In other words, Form 872 extends the applicable statute of limitations. § 6501(c)(4).

Form 1041. The U.S. Fiduciary Income Tax Return, required to be filed by estates and trusts. See Appendix B for a specimen form.

Form 1065. The U.S. Partnership Return of Income. See Appendix B for a specimen form.

Form 1120. The U.S. Corporation Income Tax Return. See Appendix B for a specimen form.

Form 1120–A. The U.S. Short-Form Corporation Income Tax Return. See Appendix B for a specimen form.

Form 1120S. The U.S. Small Business Corporation Income Tax Return, required to be filed by S corporations. See Appendix B for a specimen form.

Fraud. Tax fraud falls into two categories: civil and criminal. Under civil fraud, the IRS may impose as a penalty an amount equal to as much as 75 percent of the underpayment [§ 6651(f)]. Fines and/or imprisonment are prescribed for conviction of various types of criminal tax fraud (§§ 7201–7207). Both civil and criminal fraud involve a specific intent on the part of the taxpayer to evade the tax; mere negligence is not enough. Criminal fraud requires the additional element of willfulness (i.e., done deliberately and with evil purpose). In practice, it becomes difficult to distinguish between the degree of intent necessary to support criminal, rather than civil, fraud. In either situation, the IRS has the burden of proving fraud. See also *burden of proof.*

Free transferability of interests. The capability of the owner of an entity to transfer his or her ownership interest to another without the consent of the other owners. It is a characteristic of a corporation since a shareholder usually can freely transfer the stock to others without the approval of the existing shareholders. Reg. § 301.7701–2(e). See also *association.*

Fringe benefits. Compensation or other benefits received by an employee that are not in the form of cash. Some fringe benefits (e.g., accident and health plans, group term life insurance) may be excluded from the employee's gross income and thus are not subject to the Federal income tax.

Functional currency. The currency of the economic environment in which the taxpayer carries on most of its activities and transacts most of its business.

Future interest. An interest that will come into being at some future time. Distinguished from a present interest, which already exists. Assume that Dora transfers securities to a newly created trust. Under the terms of the trust instrument, income from the securities is to be paid each year to Nan for her life, with the securities passing to Steve upon Nan's death. Nan has a present interest in the trust since she is currently entitled to receive the income from the securities. Steve has a future interest since he must wait for Nan's death to benefit from the trust. The *annual exclusion* of $10,000 is not allowed for a gift of a future interest. § 2503(b). See also *annual exclusion* and *gift splitting.*

G

General business credit. The summation of various nonrefundable business credits, including the jobs credit, alcohol fuels credit, and research activities credit. The amount of general business credit that can be used to reduce the tax liability is limited to the taxpayer's net income tax reduced by the greater of (1) the tentative minimum tax or (2) 25 percent of the net regular tax liability that exceeds $25,000. Unused general business credits can be carried back 3 years and forward 15 years. § 38.

General partner. A partner who is fully liable in an individual capacity for the debts of the partnership to third parties. A general partner's liability is not limited to the investment in the partnership. See also *limited partner.*

General partnership. A partnership that is owned by one or more *general partners.* Creditors of a general partnership can collect amounts owed them from both the partnership assets and the assets of the partners individually.

General power of appointment. See *power of appointment.*

Gift. A transfer of property for less than adequate consideration. Gifts usually occur in a personal setting (such as between members of the same family). They are excluded from the income tax base but may be subject to a transfer tax.

Gift splitting. A special election for Federal gift tax purposes under which husband and wife can treat a gift by one of them to a third party as being made one-half by each. If, for example, Hal (the husband) makes a gift of $20,000 to Sharon, Winnie (the wife) may elect to treat $10,000 of the gift as coming from her. The major advantage of the election is that it enables the parties to take advantage of the nonowner spouse's (Winnie in this case) annual exclusion and unified credit. § 2513. See also *annual exclusion.*

Gift tax. A tax imposed on the transfer of property by gift. The tax is imposed upon the donor of a gift and is based on the fair market value of the property on the date of the gift.

Gifts within three years of death. Some taxable gifts automatically are included in the gross estate of the donor if death occurs within three years of the gift. § 2035.

Goodwill. The reputation and built-up business of a company. For accounting purposes, goodwill has no basis unless it is purchased. In the purchase of a business, goodwill generally is the difference between the purchase price and the value of the assets acquired. The intangible asset goodwill is amortized over 15 years. § 195. See also *amortization.*

Grantor.   A transferor of property. The creator of a trust is usually referred to as the grantor of the trust.

Grantor trust.   A trust under which the grantor retains control over the income or corpus (or both) to such an extent that he or she is treated as the owner of the property and its income for income tax purposes. Income from a grantor trust is taxable to the grantor, and not to the beneficiary who receives it. §§ 671–679. See also *reversionary interest.*

Grass roots lobbying expenditure.   Exempt organizations are prohibited from engaging in political activities, but spending incurred to influence the opinions of the general public relative to specific legislation is permitted by the law. See also *excess lobbying expenditure.*

Green card test.   Form I–551, received from a U.S. consul as a receipt showing that the holder has immigration status in the United States, and used to refute alien status for tax purposes.

Gross estate.   The property owned or previously transferred by a *decedent* that is subject to the Federal estate tax. Distinguished from the *probate estate,* which is property actually subject to administration by the *administrator* or *executor* of an estate. §§ 2031–2046. See also *adjusted gross estate* and *taxable estate.*

Gross income.   Income subject to the Federal income tax. Gross income does not include all economic income. That is, certain exclusions are allowed (e.g., interest on municipal bonds). For a manufacturing or merchandising business, gross income usually means gross profit (gross sales or gross receipts less cost of goods sold). § 61 and Reg. § 1.61–3(a). See also *adjusted gross income* and *taxable income.*

Gross up.   To add back to the value of the property or income received the amount of the tax that has been paid. For gifts made within three years of death, any gift tax paid on the transfer is added to the gross estate. § 2035.

Group term life insurance.   Life insurance coverage provided by an employer for a group of employees. Such insurance is renewable on a year-to-year basis, and typically no cash surrender value is built up. The premiums paid by the employer on the insurance are not taxed to the employees on coverage of up to $50,000 per person. § 79 and Reg. § 1.79–1(b).

Guaranteed payment.   Made by a partnership to a partner for services rendered or for the use of capital, to the extent that the payments are determined without regard to the income of the partnership. The payments are treated as though they were made to a nonpartner and thus are usually deductible by the entity.

Guardianship.   A legal arrangement under which one person (a guardian) has the legal right and duty to care for another (the ward) and his or her property. A guardianship is established because the ward is unable to act legally on his or her own behalf (e.g., because of minority [he or she is not of age] or mental or physical incapacity).

H

Head of household.   An unmarried individual who maintains a household for another and satisfies certain conditions set forth in § 2(b). This status enables the taxpayer to use a set of income tax rates that are lower than those applicable to other unmarried individuals but higher than those applicable to surviving spouses and married persons filing a joint return.

Heir.   A person who inherits property from a decedent.

Hobby.   An activity not engaged in for profit. The Code restricts the amount of losses that an individual can deduct for hobby activities so that these transactions cannot be used to offset income from other sources. § 183.

Holding period.   The period of time during which property has been held for income tax purposes. The holding period is significant in determining whether gain or loss from the sale or exchange of a capital asset is long term or short term. § 1223.

Hot assets.   Unrealized receivables and substantially appreciated inventory under § 751. When hot assets are present, the sale of a partnership interest or the disproportionate distribution of the assets can cause ordinary income to be recognized.

H.R. 10 plans.   See *Keogh plans.*

I

Imputed interest.   For certain long-term sales of property, the IRS can convert some of the gain from the sale into interest income if the contract does not provide for a minimum rate of interest to be paid by the purchaser. The application of this procedure has the effect of forcing the seller to recognize less long-term capital gain and more ordinary income (interest income). § 483 and the related Regulations.

Incident of ownership.   An element of ownership or degree of control over a life insurance policy. The retention by an insured of an incident of ownership in a life insurance policy will cause the policy proceeds to be included in the insured's gross estate upon death. § 2042(2) and Reg. § 20.2042–1(c). See also *gross estate* and *insured.*

Includible gain.   Section 644 imposes a built-in gains tax on trusts that sell or exchange property at a gain within two years after the date of its transfer in trust by the transferor. The provision applies only if the fair market value of the property at the time of the initial transfer exceeds the adjusted basis of the property immediately after the transfer. The tax imposed by § 644 is the amount of additional tax the transferor would pay (including any minimum tax) had the gain been included in the transferor's gross income for the tax year of the sale. However, the tax applies only to an amount known as *includible gain*. This is the lesser of the following: the gain recognized by the trust on the sale or exchange of any property, or the excess of the fair market value of the property at the time of the initial transfer in trust by the transferor over the adjusted basis of the property immediately after the transfer.

Income beneficiary. The party entitled to income from property. In a typical trust situation, Art is to receive the income for life with corpus or principal passing to Bev upon Art's death. In this case, Art is the income beneficiary of the trust.

Income in respect of a decedent (IRD). Income earned by a decedent at the time of death but not reportable on the final income tax return because of the method of accounting that appropriately is utilized. Such income is included in the gross estate and is taxed to the eventual recipient (either the estate or heirs). The recipient is, however, allowed an income tax deduction for the estate tax attributable to the income. § 691.

Income interest. The right of a beneficiary to receive distributions from the fiduciary income of a trust or estate.

Income shifting. Occurs when an individual transfers some of his or her gross income to a taxpayer who is subject to a lower tax rate, thereby reducing the total income tax liability of the group. Income shifting produces a successful assignment of income. It can be accomplished by transferring income-producing property to the lower-bracket taxpayer or to an effective trust for his or her benefit, or by transferring ownership interests in a family partnership or in a closely held corporation.

Incomplete transfer. A transfer made by a decedent during lifetime that, because of certain control or enjoyment retained by the transferor, is not considered complete for Federal estate tax purposes. Thus, some or all of the fair market value of the property transferred is included in the transferor's gross estate. §§ 2036–2038. See also *gross estate* and *revocable transfer.*

Indexation. Various components of the tax formula are adjusted periodically for the effects of inflation, so that the effects of the formula are not eroded by price level changes. Tax rate schedules, exemption amounts, and the standard deduction, among other items, are indexed in this manner.

Individual retirement account (IRA). Individuals with earned income are permitted to set aside up to 100 percent of that income per year (not to exceed $2,000) for a retirement account. The amount so set aside can be deducted by the taxpayer and is subject to income tax only upon withdrawal. The Code limits the amount of this contribution that can be deducted *for* AGI depending upon (1) whether the taxpayer or spouse is an active participant in an employer-provided qualified retirement plan, and (2) the magnitude of the taxpayer's AGI before the IRA contribution is considered. § 219.

Inheritance tax. A tax imposed on the right to receive property from a *decedent*. Thus, theoretically, an inheritance tax is imposed on the heir. The Federal estate tax is imposed on the estate. See also *death tax* and *estate tax.*

In kind. See *distributions in kind.*

Inside basis. A partnership's basis in each of the assets it owns.

Installment method. A method of accounting enabling certain taxpayers to spread the recognition of gain on the sale of property over the collection period. Under this procedure, the seller arrives at the gain to be recognized by computing the gross profit percentage from the sale (the gain divided by the contract price) and applying it to each payment received. § 453.

Insured. A person whose life is the subject of an insurance policy. Upon the death of the insured, the life insurance policy matures, and the proceeds become payable to the designated beneficiary. See also *life insurance.*

Intangible asset. Property that is a "right" rather than a physical object. Examples are patents, stocks and bonds, goodwill, trademarks, franchises, and copyrights. See also *amortization* and *tangible property.*

Inter vivos transfer. A transfer of property during the life of the owner. Distinguished from testamentary transfers, where the property passes at death.

Interest-free loans. Bona fide loans that carry no interest (or a below-market rate). If made in a nonbusiness setting, the imputed interest element is treated as a gift from the lender to the borrower. If made by a corporation to a shareholder, a constructive dividend could result. In either event, the lender may recognize interest income. § 7872.

Internal Revenue Code. The collected statutes that govern the taxation of income, property transfers, and other transactions in the United States and the enforcement of those provisions. Enacted by Congress, the Code is amended frequently, but it has not been reorganized since 1954. However, because of the extensive revisions to the statutes that occurred with the Tax Reform Act of 1986, Title 26 of the U.S. Code is now known as the Internal Revenue Code of 1986.

Internal Revenue Service (IRS). The Federal agency, a division of the Department of the Treasury, charged with administering the U.S. revenue enforcement and collection provisions.

Interpolated terminal reserve. The measure used in valuing insurance policies for gift and estate tax purposes when the policies are not paid up at the time of their transfer. Reg. § 20.2031–8(a)(3), Ex. (3).

Intestate. No will exists at the time of death. In such cases, state law prescribes who will receive the decedent's property. The laws of intestate succession generally favor the surviving spouse, children, and grandchildren, and then parents and grandparents and brothers and sisters.

Investment income. Consisting of virtually the same elements as portfolio income, a measure by which to justify a deduction for interest on investment indebtedness. See also *investment indebtedness* and *portfolio income.*

Investment indebtedness. Debt incurred to carry or incur investments by the taxpayer in assets that will produce portfolio income. Limitations are placed upon interest deductions that are incurred in connection with the debt (generally to the corresponding amount of investment income).

Investment tax credit. A tax credit that usually was equal to 10 percent (unless a reduced credit was elected) of the qualified investment in tangible personalty used in a trade or business. If the tangible personalty had a recovery period of five years or more, the full cost of the property qualified for the credit. Only 60 percent qualified for property with a recovery period of three years. However, the regular investment tax credit was repealed by TRA of 1986 for property placed in service after December 31, 1985. § 46. See also *general business credit.*

Investor losses. Losses on stock and securities. If stocks and bonds are capital assets in the hands of the holder, a capital loss materializes as of the last day of the taxable year in which the stocks or bonds become worthless. Under certain circumstances involving stocks and bonds of affiliated corporations, an ordinary loss is permitted upon worthlessness.

Involuntary conversion. The loss or destruction of property through theft, casualty, or condemnation. Any gain realized on an involuntary conversion can, at the taxpayer's election, be deferred for Federal income tax purposes if the owner reinvests the proceeds within a prescribed period of time in property that is similar or related in service or use. § 1033.

IRA. See *individual retirement account.*

Itemized deductions. Personal and employee expenditures allowed by the Code as deductions from adjusted gross income. Examples include certain medical expenses, interest on home mortgages, and charitable contributions. Itemized deductions are reported on Schedule A of Form 1040. Certain miscellaneous itemized deductions are reduced by 2 percent of the taxpayer's adjusted gross income. In addition, a taxpayer whose adjusted gross income exceeds a certain level (indexed annually) must reduce the itemized deductions by 3 percent of the excess of adjusted gross income over that level. Medical, casualty and theft, and investment interest deductions are not subject to the 3 percent reduction. The 3 percent reduction may not reduce itemized deductions that are subject to the reduction to below 20 percent of their initial amount.

J

Jeopardy assessment. If the collection of a tax appears in question, the IRS may assess and collect the tax immediately without the usual formalities. The IRS can terminate a taxpayer's taxable year before the usual date if it feels that the collection of the tax may be in peril because the taxpayer plans to leave the country. §§ 6851 and 6861–6864.

Joint and several liability. Permits the IRS to collect a tax from one or all of several taxpayers. A husband and wife who file a joint income tax return usually are collectively or individually liable for the full amount of the tax liability. § 6013(d)(3).

Joint tenants. Two or more persons having undivided ownership of property with the right of survivorship. Right of survivorship gives the surviving owner full ownership of the property. Suppose Betty and Cheryl are joint tenants of a tract of land. Upon Betty's death, Cheryl becomes the sole owner of the property. For the estate tax consequences upon the death of a joint tenant, see § 2040. See also *tenancy by the entirety* and *tenancy in common.*

Joint venture. A one-time grouping of two or more persons in a business undertaking. Unlike a partnership, a joint venture does not entail a continuing relationship among the parties. A joint venture is treated like a partnership for Federal income tax purposes. § 7701(a)(2).

K

Keogh plans. Retirement plans available to self-employed taxpayers. They are also referred to as H.R. 10 plans. Under such plans, a taxpayer may deduct each year up to either 20 percent of net earnings from self-employment or $30,000, whichever is less.

Kiddie tax. See *tax on unearned income of a child under age 14.*

L

Lapse. The expiration of a right either by the death of the holder or upon the expiration of a period of time. Thus, a power of appointment lapses upon the death of the holder if he or she has not exercised the power during life or at death (through a will).

Last-in, first-out (LIFO). An accounting method for valuing inventories for tax purposes. Under this method, it is assumed that the inventory on hand is valued at the cost of the earliest acquired units. § 472. See also *first-in, first-out (FIFO).*

Leaseback. The transferor of property later leases it back. In a sale-leaseback situation, for example, Ron sells property to Sal and subsequently leases the property from Sal. Thus, Ron becomes the lessee and Sal the lessor.

Least aggregate deferral rule. A test applied to determine the allowable fiscal year of a *partnership* or *S corporation.* Possible year-ends are tested, and the fiscal year allowed by the IRS is the one that offers the least amount of income deferral to the owners on an individual basis.

Legacy. A transfer of cash or other property by will.

Legal age. The age at which a person may enter into binding contracts or commit other legal acts. In most states, a minor reaches legal age or majority (comes of age) at age 18.

Legal representative. A person who oversees the legal affairs of another; for example, the executor or administrator of an estate or a court-appointed guardian of a minor or incompetent person.

Legatee. The recipient of property under a will and transferred by the death of the owner.

Lessee. One who rents property from another. In the case of real estate, the lessee is also known as the tenant.

Lessor. One who rents property to another. In the case of real estate, the lessor is also known as the landlord.

Letter ruling. The written response of the IRS to a taxpayer's request for interpretation of the revenue laws with respect to a proposed transaction, e.g., concerning the tax-free status of a reorganization. Not to be relied on as precedent by other than the party who requested the ruling.

LEXIS. An on-line database system by which the tax researcher can obtain access to the Internal Revenue Code, Regulations, administrative rulings, and court case opinions.

Liabilities in excess of basis. On the contribution of capital to a corporation or partnership, an investor recognizes gain on the exchange to the extent that contributed assets carry liabilities with a face amount in excess of the tax basis of the contributed assets. This rule keeps the investor from holding the investment asset received with a negative basis. § 357(c).

Life estate. A legal arrangement under which the beneficiary (the life tenant) is entitled to the income from the property for his or her life. Upon the death of the life tenant, the property is transferred to the holder of the remainder interest. See also *income beneficiary* and *remainder interest*.

Life insurance. A contract between the holder of a policy and an insurance company (the carrier) under which the company agrees, in return for premium payments, to pay a specified sum (the face value or maturity value of the policy) to the designated beneficiary upon the death of the insured. See also *insured*.

Like-kind exchange. An exchange of property held for productive use in a trade or business or for investment (except inventory and stocks and bonds) for other investment or trade or business property. Unless non-like-kind property (*boot*) is received, the exchange is nontaxable. § 1031.

Limited liability. The liability of an entity and its owners to third parties is limited to the investment in the entity. This is a characteristic of a corporation, as shareholders generally are not responsible for the debts of the corporation and, at most, may lose the amount paid in for the stock issued. Reg. § 301.7701–2(d). See also *association*.

Limited liability company (LLC). A form of entity allowed by virtually all of the states. The entity is taxed as a partnership in which all owners of the LLC are treated much like limited partners. There are no restrictions on ownership, all partners may participate in management, and none of the owners has personal liability for the entity's debts.

Limited liability partnership (LLP). A form of entity allowed by many of the states, where a general partnership registers with the state as an LLP. Owners are general partners, but a partner is not liable for any malpractice committed by other partners. The personal assets of the partners are at risk for the entity's contractual liabilities, such as accounts payable. The personal assets of a specific partner are at risk for his or her own professional malpractice and tort liability, and for malpractice and torts committed by those whom he or she supervises.

Limited partner. A partner whose liability to third-party creditors of the partnership is limited to the amount he or she has invested in the partnership. See also *general partner* and *limited partnership*.

Limited partnership. A partnership in which some of the partners are *limited partners*. At least one of the partners in a limited partnership must be a *general partner*.

Liquidating distribution. A distribution by a partnership or corporation that is in complete liquidation of the entity's trade or business activities. Typically, such distributions generate capital gain or loss to the investors without regard, for instance, to the earnings and profits of the corporation or to the partnership's basis in the distributed property. They can, however, lead to recognized gain or loss at the corporate level.

Liquidation. See *corporate liquidation*.

Living trust. A revocable trust. Often touted as a means of avoiding some probate costs.

Lobbying expenditure. An expenditure made for the purpose of influencing legislation. Such payments can result in the loss of the exempt status of, and the imposition of Federal income tax on, an exempt organization.

Long-term capital gain or loss. Results from the sale or other taxable exchange of a capital asset that had been held by the seller for more than one year or from other transactions involving statutorily designated assets, including § 1231 property and patents.

Long-term tax-exempt rate. Used in deriving net operating loss limitations in the context of an equity structure shift. The highest of the Federal long-term interest rates in effect for any of the last three months. § 382.

Low-income housing credit. Beneficial treatment to owners of low-income housing is provided in the form of a tax credit. The calculated credit is claimed in the year the building is placed in service and in the following nine years. § 42. See also *general business credit*.

Lump-sum distribution. Payment of the entire amount due at one time rather than in installments. Such distributions often occur from qualified pension or profit sharing plans upon the retirement or death of a covered employee.

M

MACRS. See *accelerated cost recovery system (ACRS)*.

Majority. See *legal age*.

Malpractice. Professional misconduct; an unreasonable lack of skill.

Marital deduction. A deduction allowed against the taxable estate or taxable gifts upon the transfer of property from one spouse to another. § 2056.

Market value. See *fair market value*.

Meaningful reduction test. A decrease in the shareholder's voting control. Used to determine whether a redemption qualifies for sale or exchange treatment.

Merger. The absorption of one corporation by another with the corporation being absorbed losing its legal identity. Flow Corporation is merged into Jobs Corporation, and the shareholders of Flow receive stock in Jobs in exchange for their stock in Flow. After the merger, Flow ceases to exist as a separate legal entity. If a merger meets certain conditions, it is nontaxable to the parties involved. § 368(a)(1)(A). See also *corporate acquisition* and *corporate reorganization*.

Minimum credit (AET). A fixed amount, $150,000 for personal service firms and $250,000 for all others, below which the *accumulated earnings credit* cannot be derived. Assures that small and start-up corporations can generate a minimum amount of earnings before being subject to the AET.

Minimum tax. See *alternative minimum tax*.

Minimum tax credit (AMT). When a corporation pays an alternative minimum tax, a minimum tax credit is created on a dollar-for-dollar basis, to be applied against regular tax liabilities incurred in future years. The credit is carried forward indefinitely, but it is not carried back. The effect of the credit for corporate taxpayers alternating between the AMT and regular tax models is to make the AMT liabilities a prepayment of regular taxes. Noncorporate AMT taxpayers are allowed the credit only with respect to the elements of the AMT that reflect timing differences between the two tax models.

Minority. See *legal age*.

Mitigate. To make less severe. See also *mitigation of the annual accounting period concept* and *mitigation of the statute of limitations*.

Mitigation of the annual accounting period concept. Various tax provisions that provide relief from the effect of the finality of the annual accounting period concept. For example, the net operating loss carryover provisions allow the taxpayer to apply the negative taxable income of one year against a corresponding positive amount in another tax accounting period. See also *annual accounting period concept*.

Mitigation of the statute of limitations. A series of tax provisions that prevents either the IRS or a taxpayer from obtaining a double benefit from the application of the statute of limitations. It would be unfair, for example, to permit a taxpayer to depreciate an asset that was previously expensed, but that should have been capitalized, if the statute of limitations prevents the IRS from adjusting the tax liability for the year the asset was purchased. §§ 1311–1315. See also *statute of limitations*.

Mortgagee. The party who holds the mortgage; the creditor.

Mortgagor. The party who mortgages the property; the debtor.

Most suitable use value. For gift and estate tax purposes, property that is transferred normally is valued in accordance with its most suitable or optimal use. Thus, if a farm is worth more as a potential shopping center, the value as a shopping center is used, even though the transferee (the donee or heir) continues to use the property as a farm. For an exception to this rule concerning the valuation of certain kinds of real estate transferred by death, see *special use value*.

Multistate corporation. A corporation that has operations in more than one of the states of the United States. Issues arise relative to the assignment of appropriate amounts of the entity's taxable income to the states in which it has a presence. See also *allocate, apportion, nexus,* and *UDITPA*.

Multistate Tax Commission (MTC). A regulatory body of the states that develops operating rules and regulations for the implementation of *UDITPA* and other provisions that assign the total taxable income of a *multistate corporation* to specific states.

Multitiered partnerships. See *tiered partnerships*.

N

Necessary. Appropriate and helpful in furthering the taxpayer's business or income-producing activity. §§ 162(a) and 212. See also *ordinary*.

Negligence. Failure to exercise the reasonable or ordinary degree of care of a prudent person in a situation that results in harm or damage to another. Code § 6651 imposes a penalty on taxpayers who show negligence or intentional disregard of rules and Regulations with respect to the underpayment of certain taxes. See also *accuracy-related penalty*.

Net operating loss. To mitigate the effect of the annual accounting period concept, § 172 allows taxpayers to use an excess loss of one year as a deduction for certain past or future years. In this regard, a carryback period of 3 years and a carryforward period of 15 years currently are allowed. See also *mitigation of the annual accounting period concept*.

Net worth method. An approach used by the IRS to reconstruct the income of a taxpayer who fails to maintain adequate records. Under this method, the gross income for the year is estimated as the increase in net worth of the taxpayer (assets in excess of liabilities), with appropriate adjustment for nontaxable receipts and nondeductible expenditures. The net worth method often is used when tax fraud is suspected.

Nexus. A *multistate corporation*'s taxable income can be apportioned to a specific state only if the entity has established a sufficient presence, or nexus, with that state. State law, which often follows *UDITPA*, specifies various activities that lead to nexus in various states.

Ninety-day letter. See *statutory notice of deficiency*.

Nonacquiescence. Disagreement by the IRS on the result reached by the U.S. Tax Court in a Regular decision. Sometimes abbreviated *Nonacq.* or *NA*. See also *acquiescence*.

Nonbusiness bad debt. A bad debt loss that is not incurred in connection with a creditor's trade or business. The loss is classified as a short-term capital loss and is allowed only in the year the debt becomes entirely worthless. In addition to family loans, many investor losses are nonbusiness bad debts. § 166(d). See also *business bad debts*.

Nonbusiness income. Income generated from investment assets or from the taxable disposition thereof. In some states, the nonbusiness income of a *multistate corporation* is held out of the apportionment procedure and allocated to the state in which the nonbusiness asset is located. See also *allocate* and *apportion*.

Noncontributory qualified pension or profit sharing plan. A plan funded entirely by the employer with no contributions being made by the covered employees. See also *qualified pension or profit sharing plan*.

Nonliquidating distribution. A payment made by a partnership or corporation to the entity's owner is a nonliquidating distribution when the entity's legal existence does not cease thereafter. If the payor is a corporation, such a distribution can result in dividend income to the shareholders. If the payor is a partnership, the partner usually assigns a basis in the distributed property that is equal to the lesser of the partner's basis in the partnership interest or the basis of the distributed asset to the partnership. In this regard, the partner first assigns basis to any cash that he or she receives in the distribution. The partner's remaining basis, if any, is assigned to the noncash assets according to their relative bases to the partnership.

Nonrecourse debt. Debt secured by the property that it is used to purchase. The purchaser of the property is not personally liable for the debt upon default. Rather, the creditor's recourse is to repossess the related property. Nonrecourse debt generally does not increase the purchaser's at-risk amount.

Nonresident alien. An individual who is neither a citizen nor a resident of the United States. Citizenship is determined under the immigration and naturalization laws of the United States. Residency is determined under § 7701(b) of the Internal Revenue Code.

Nonseparately stated income. The net income of an S corporation that is combined and allocated to the shareholders. Other items, such as capital gains and charitable contributions, that could be treated differently on the individual tax returns of the shareholders are not included in this amount but are allocated to the shareholders separately.

Not essentially equivalent redemption. See *redemption (not equivalent to a dividend)*.

O

Obligee. The party to whom someone else is obligated under a contract. Thus, if Coop loans money to Dawn, Coop is the obligee and Dawn is the obligor under the loan.

Obligor. See *obligee*.

Offer in compromise. A settlement agreement offered by the IRS in a tax dispute, especially where there is doubt as to the collectibility of the full deficiency. Offers in compromise can include installment payment schedules, as well as reductions in the tax and penalties owed by the taxpayer.

Office audit. An audit conducted by the IRS in the agent's office. See also *audit, correspondence audit*, and *field audit*.

On all fours. A judicial decision exactly in point with another as to result, facts, or both.

Optimal use value. Synonym for most suitable use value.

Optional adjustment election. See *Section 754 election*.

Ordinary. Common and accepted in the general industry or type of activity in which the taxpayer is engaged. It comprises one of the tests for the deductibility of expenses incurred or paid in connection with a trade or business; for the production or collection of income; for the management, conservation, or maintenance of property held for the production of income; or in connection with the determination, collection, or refund of any tax. §§ 162(a) and 212. See also *necessary*.

Ordinary and necessary. See *necessary* and *ordinary*.

Ordinary gross income. A concept peculiar to personal holding companies and defined in § 543(b)(1). See also *adjusted ordinary gross income*.

Organizational expenditures. Items incurred early in the life of a corporate entity, qualifying for a 60-month amortization under Federal tax law. Amortizable expenditures exclude those incurred to obtain capital (underwriting fees) or assets (subject to cost recovery). Typically, amortizable expenditures include legal and accounting fees, and state incorporation payments. Such items must be incurred by the end of the entity's first tax year. § 248.

Outside basis. A partner's basis in his or her partnership interest.

Owner shift. Any change in the respective ownership of stock by a 5 percent-or-more shareholder. Change is determined relative to a testing period of the prior three years. If there is a more-than-50 percent change in the ownership of a loss corporation, § 382 limitations apply to the use of net operating loss carryovers of the loss corporation.

P

Parent-subsidiary controlled group. A *controlled* or *affiliated group* of corporations, where at least one corporation is at least 80 percent owned by one or more of the others. The affiliated group definition is more difficult to meet.

Partial liquidation. A stock redemption where noncorporate shareholders are permitted sale or exchange treatment. In certain cases, an active business must have existed for at least five years. Only a portion of the outstanding stock in the entity is retired.

Partner. See *general partner* and *limited partner*.

Partnership. For income tax purposes, a partnership includes a syndicate, group, pool, or joint venture, as well as ordinary partnerships. In an ordinary partnership, two or more parties combine capital and/or services to carry on a business for profit as co-owners. § 7701(a)(2). See also *limited partnership* and *tiered partnerships*.

Passive foreign investment company (PFIC). A non-U.S. corporation that generates a substantial amount of personal holding company income. Upon receipt of an excess distribution from the entity or the sale of its shares, its U.S. shareholders are taxable on their pro rata shares of the tax that has been deferred with respect to the corporation's taxable income, plus an applicable interest charge.

Passive investment company. A means by which a *multistate corporation* can reduce the overall effective tax rate by isolating investment income in a low- or no-tax state.

Passive investment income (PII). Gross receipts from royalties, certain rents, dividends, interest, annuities, and gains from the sale or exchange of stock and securities. With certain exceptions, if the passive investment income of an *S corporation* exceeds 25 percent of the corporation's gross receipts for three consecutive years, S status is lost.

Passive loss rules. Any loss from (1) activities in which the taxpayer does not materially participate and (2) rental activities. Net passive losses cannot be used to offset income from nonpassive sources. Rather, they are suspended until the taxpayer either generates net passive income (and a deduction of such losses is allowed) or disposes of the underlying property (at which time the loss deductions are allowed in full). Landlords who actively participate in the rental activities can deduct up to $25,000 of passive losses annually. However, this amount is phased out when the landlord's AGI exceeds $100,000. See also *portfolio income*.

Payroll factor. The proportion of a *multistate corporation's* total payroll that is traceable to a specific state. Used in determining the taxable income that is to be apportioned to that state. See also *apportion*.

Pecuniary bequest. A bequest of money to an heir by a decedent. See also *bequest*.

Percentage depletion. See *depletion*.

Percentage of completion method. A method of reporting gain or loss on certain long-term contracts. Under this method of accounting, the gross contract price is included in income as the contract is completed. Reg. § 1.451–3. See also *completed contract method*.

Personal and household effects. Items owned by a decedent at the time of death. Examples include clothing, furniture, sporting goods, jewelry, stamp and coin collections, silverware, china, crystal, cooking utensils, books, cars, televisions, radios, stereo equipment, etc.

Personal holding company (PHC). A corporation that satisfies the requirements of § 542. Qualification as a personal holding company means a penalty tax may be imposed on the corporation's undistributed personal holding company income for the year.

Personal holding company income. Income as defined by § 543. It includes interest, dividends, certain rents and royalties, income from the use of corporate property by certain shareholders, income from certain personal service contracts, and distributions from estates and trusts. Such income is relevant in determining whether a corporation is a personal holding company and is therefore subject to the penalty tax on personal holding companies. See also *adjusted ordinary gross income*.

Personal holding company tax. A penalty tax imposed on certain closely held corporations with excessive investment income. Assessed at the top individual tax rate on *personal holding company income*, reduced by dividends paid and other adjustments. § 541.

Personal property. Generally, all property other than real estate. It is sometimes referred to as personalty when real estate is termed realty. Personal property can also refer to property not used in a taxpayer's trade or business or held for the production or collection of income. When used in this sense, personal property can include both realty (e.g., a personal residence) and personalty (e.g., personal effects such as clothing and furniture). See also *bequest*.

Personal service corporation (PSC). An entity whose principal activity is the providing of services by owner-employees. Subject to a flat 35 percent tax rate and limited to a calendar tax year.

Personalty. Personalty is all property that is not attached to real estate (realty) and is movable. Examples of personalty are machinery, automobiles, clothing, household furnishings, inventory, and personal effects. See also *ad valorem tax* and *realty*.

Portfolio income. Income from interest, dividends, rentals, royalties, capital gains, or other investment sources. Net passive losses cannot be used to offset net portfolio income. See also *passive loss rules* and *investment income*.

Power of appointment. A legal right granted to someone by will or other document that gives the holder the power to dispose of property or the income from property. When the holder may appoint the property to his or her own benefit, the power usually is called a general power of appointment. If the holder cannot benefit himself or herself but may only appoint to certain other persons, the power is a special power of appointment. Assume Gary places $500,000 worth of securities in trust granting Donna the right to determine each year how the trustee is to divide the income between Ann and Babs. Under these circumstances, Donna has a special power of appointment. If Donna had the further right to appoint the income to herself, she probably possesses a general power of appointment. For the estate tax and gift tax effects of powers of appointment, see §§ 2041 and 2514. See also *testamentary power of appointment*.

Precontribution gain. Partnerships allow for a variety of *special allocations* of gain or loss among the partners, but gain or loss that is "built-in" on an asset contributed to the partnership is assigned specifically to the contributing partner. § 704(c)(1)(A).

Preferences (AMT). See *alternative minimum tax (AMT)* and *tax preference items*.

Preferred stock bailout. A process where a shareholder used the issuance and sale, or later redemption of a preferred stock dividend to obtain long-term capital gains, without any loss of voting control over the corporation. In effect, the shareholder receives corporate profits without suffering the consequences of dividend income treatment. This procedure led Congress to enact § 306, which, if applicable, converts the prior long-term capital gain on the sale or redemption of the stock to ordinary income. See also *bailout*.

Present interest. See *future interest*.

Presumption. An inference in favor of a particular fact. If, for example, the IRS issues a notice of deficiency against a taxpayer, a presumption of correctness attaches to the assessment. Thus, the taxpayer has the burden of proof of showing that he or she does not owe the tax listed in the deficiency notice. See also *rebuttable presumption*.

Previously taxed income (PTI). Before the Subchapter S Revision Act of 1982, the undistributed taxable income of an S corporation was taxed to the shareholders as of the last day of the corporation's tax year and usually could be withdrawn by the shareholders without tax consequences at some later point in time. The role of PTI has been taken over by the accumulated adjustments account. See also *accumulated adjustments account*.

Principal. Property as opposed to income. The term is often used as a synonym for the corpus of a trust. If, for example, Gil places real estate in trust with income payable to Ann for life and the remainder to Barb upon Ann's death, the real estate is the principal, or corpus, of the trust.

Private foundation. An *exempt organization* subject to additional statutory restrictions on its activities and on contributions made to it. Excise taxes may be levied on certain prohibited transactions, and the Code places more stringent restrictions on the deductibility of contributions to private foundations. § 509.

Pro rata. Proportionately. Assume, for example, a corporation has 10 shareholders, each of whom owns 10 percent of the stock. A pro rata dividend distribution of $1,000 would mean that each shareholder would receive $100.

Pro se. The taxpayer represents himself or herself before the court without the benefit of counsel.

Probate. The legal process by which the estate of a decedent is administered. Generally, the probate process involves collecting a decedent's assets, liquidating liabilities, paying necessary taxes, and distributing property to heirs.

Probate costs. The costs incurred in administering a decedent's estate. See also *probate estate*.

Probate court. The usual designation for the state or local court that supervises the administration (probate) of a decedent's estate.

Probate estate. The property of a decedent that is subject to administration by the executor or administrator of an estate. See also *administration*.

Profit and loss sharing ratios. Specified in the partnership agreement and used to determine each partner's allocation of ordinary taxable income and separately stated items. Profits and losses can be shared in different ratios. The ratios can be changed by amending the partnership agreement. § 704(a).

Profits interest. A partner's percentage allocation of partnership operating results, determined by the *profits and loss sharing ratio*.

Property. Assets defined in the broadest legal sense. Property includes the *unrealized receivables* of a cash basis taxpayer, but not services rendered. § 351.

Property dividend. A dividend consisting of in-kind (non-cash) assets of the payor, measured by the FMV of the property on the date of distribution. The portion of the distribution representing E & P is a dividend; any excess is treated as a return of capital. Distribution of in-kind property causes the distributing corporation to recognize any underlying realized gain, but not loss.

Property factor. The proportion of a *multistate corporation*'s total property that is traceable to a specific state. Used in determining the taxable income that is to be apportioned to that state. See also *apportion*.

Property tax. An *ad valorem tax*, usually levied by a city or county government, on the value of real or personal property that the taxpayer owns on a specified date. Most states exclude intangible property and assets owned by exempt organizations from the tax base, and some exclude inventory, pollution control or manufacturing equipment, and other items to provide relocation or retention incentives for the taxpayer.

Proportionate distribution.   A distribution in which each partner in a partnership receives a pro rata share of hot assets being distributed. For example, a distribution of $10,000 of hot assets equally to two 50 percent partners is a proportionate distribution.

Prop.Reg.   An abbreviation for Proposed Regulation. A Regulation may first be issued in proposed form to give interested parties the opportunity for comment. When and if a Proposed Regulation is finalized, it is known as a Regulation (abbreviated Reg.).

PTI.   See *previously taxed income.*

Public Law 86–272.   A congressional limit on the ability of the state to force a multistate corporation to assign income to that state. Under P.L. 86–272, where orders for tangible personal property are both filled and delivered outside the state, the entity must establish more than the mere solicitation of such orders before any income can be *apportioned* to the state.

Public policy limitation.   A concept developed by the courts precluding an income tax deduction for certain expenses related to activities deemed to be contrary to the public welfare. In this connection, Congress has incorporated into the Code specific disallowance provisions covering such items as illegal bribes, kickbacks, and fines and penalties. §§ 162(c) and (f).

Q

Qualified nonrecourse debt.   Issued on realty by a bank, retirement plan, or governmental agency. Included in the *at-risk amount* by the investor. § 465(b)(6).

Qualified pension or profit sharing plan.   An employer-sponsored plan that meets the requirements of § 401. If these requirements are met, none of the employer's contributions to the plan will be taxed to the employee until distributed to him or her (§ 402). The employer is allowed a deduction in the year the contributions are made (§ 404). See also *contributory qualified pension or profit sharing plan, deferred compensation,* and *noncontributory pension or profit sharing plan.*

Qualified small business corporation.   A C corporation that has aggregate gross assets not exceeding $50 million and that is conducting an active trade or business. § 1202.

Qualified small business stock.   Stock in a qualified small business corporation, purchased as part of an original issue after August 10, 1993. The shareholder may exclude from gross income 50 percent of the realized gain on the sale of the stock, if he or she held the stock for more than five years. § 1202.

Qualified terminable interest property (QTIP).   Generally, the *marital deduction* (for gift and estate tax purposes) is not available if the interest transferred will terminate upon the death of the transferee spouse and pass to someone else. Thus, if Hannah places property in trust, life estate to Will, and remainder to their children upon Will's death, this is a terminable interest that will not provide Hannah (or her estate) with a marital deduction. If, however, the transfer in trust is treated as qualified terminable interest property (the QTIP election is made), the terminable interest restriction is waived and the marital deduction becomes available. In exchange for this deduction, the surviving spouse's gross estate must include the value of the QTIP election assets, even though he or she has no control over the ultimate disposition of the asset. Terminable interest property qualifies for this election if the donee (or heir) is the only beneficiary of the asset during his or her lifetime and receives income distributions relative to the property at least annually. For gifts, the donor spouse is the one who makes the QTIP election. As to property transferred by death, the *executor* of the estate of the deceased spouse has the right to make the election. §§ 2056(b)(7) and 2523(f).

R

RAR.   A *Revenue Agent's Report,* which reflects any adjustments made by the agent as a result of an audit of the taxpayer. The RAR is mailed to the taxpayer along with the *30-day letter,* which outlines the appellate procedures available to the taxpayer.

Realistic possibility.   A preparer penalty is assessed where a tax return includes a position that has no realistic possibility of being sustained by a court.

Realized gain or loss.   The difference between the amount realized upon the sale or other disposition of property and the adjusted basis of such property. § 1001. See also *adjusted basis, amount realized, basis,* and *recognized gain or loss.*

Realty.   Real estate. See also *personalty.*

Reasonable cause.   Relief from taxpayer and preparer penalties often is allowed where there is a reasonable cause for the taxpayer's actions. For instance, a reasonable cause for the late filing of a tax return might be a flood that damaged the taxpayer's record-keeping systems and made a timely completion of the return difficult.

Reasonable needs of the business.   A means of avoiding the penalty tax on unreasonable accumulation of earnings. In determining base for this tax (*accumulated taxable income*), § 535 allows a deduction for "such part of earnings and profits for the taxable year as are retained for the reasonable needs of the business." § 537.

Rebuttable presumption.   A presumption that can be overturned upon the showing of sufficient proof. See also *presumption.*

Recapitalization.   An E reorganization, constituting a major change in the character and amount of outstanding equity of a corporation. For instance, common stock exchanged for preferred stock can qualify for tax-free E reorganization treatment.

Recapture. To recover the tax benefit of a deduction or a credit previously taken. See also *depreciation recapture.*

Recapture potential. A measure with respect to property that, if disposed of in a taxable transaction, would result in the recapture of depreciation (§§ 1245 or 1250), deferred LIFO gain, or deferred installment method gain.

Recognized gain or loss. The portion of realized gain or loss subject to income taxation. See also *realized gain or loss.*

Recourse debt. Debt for which the lender may both foreclose on the property and assess a guarantor for any payments due under the loan, even from personal assets. A lender also may make a claim against the assets of any general partner in a partnership to which debt is issued, without regard to whether that partner has guaranteed the debt.

Redemption. See *stock redemption.*

Redemption (complete termination). Sale or exchange treatment is available relative to this type of redemption. The shareholder must retire all of his or her outstanding shares in the corporation (ignoring family attribution rules) and cannot hold an interest, other than that of a creditor, for the 10 years following the redemption. § 302(b)(3).

Redemption (disproportionate). Sale or exchange treatment is available relative to this type of redemption. After the exchange, the shareholder owns less than 80 percent of his or her pre-redemption interest in the corporation and only a minority interest in the entity. § 302(b)(2).

Redemption (not equivalent to a dividend). Sale or exchange treatment is given to this type of redemption. Although various safe harbor tests are failed, the nature of the redemption is such that dividend treatment is avoided, because it represents a meaningful reduction in the shareholder's interest in the corporation. § 302(b)(1).

Redemption to pay death taxes. Sale or exchange treatment is available relative to this type of redemption, to the extent of the proceeds up to the total amount paid by the estate or heir for death taxes and administration expenses. The stock value must exceed 35 percent of the value of the decedent's adjusted gross estate. In meeting this test, one can combine shareholdings in corporations where the decedent held at least 20 percent of the outstanding shares.

Regular corporation. See *C corporation.*

Regulations. The U.S. Treasury Department Regulations (abbreviated Reg.) represent the position of the IRS as to how the Internal Revenue Code is to be interpreted. Their purpose is to provide taxpayers and IRS personnel with rules of general and specific application to the various provisions of the tax law. Regulations are published in the *Federal Register* and in all tax services.

Related corporations. See *controlled group.*

Related parties. Various Code sections define related parties and often include a variety of persons within this (usually detrimental) category. Generally, related parties are accorded different tax treatment from that applicable to other taxpayers who enter into similar transactions. For instance, realized losses that are generated between related parties are not recognized in the year of the loss. However, these deferred losses can be used to offset recognized gains that occur upon the subsequent sale of the asset to a nonrelated party. Other uses of a related-party definition include the conversion of gain upon the sale of a depreciable asset into all ordinary income (§ 1239) and the identification of constructive ownership of stock relative to corporate distributions, redemptions, liquidations, reorganizations, and compensation.

Remainder interest. The property that passes to a beneficiary after the expiration of an intervening income interest. If, for example, Greg places real estate in trust with income to Ann for life and remainder to Bill upon Ann's death, Bill has a remainder interest. See also *life estate* and *reversionary interest.*

Remand. To send back. An appellate court may remand a case to a lower court, usually for additional fact finding. In other words, the appellate court is not in a position to decide the appeal based on the facts determined by the lower court. Remanding is abbreviated "rem'g."

Reorganization. See *corporate reorganization.*

Research activities credit. A tax credit whose purpose is to encourage research and development. It consists of two components: the incremental research activities credit and the basic research credit. The incremental research activities credit is equal to 20 percent of the excess qualified research expenditures over the base amount. The basic research credit is equal to 20 percent of the excess of basic research payments over the base amount. § 41. See also *general business credit.*

Residential rental property. Buildings for which at least 80 percent of the gross rents are from dwelling units (e.g., an apartment building). This type of building is distinguished from nonresidential (commercial or industrial) buildings in applying the recapture of depreciation provisions. The term also is relevant in distinguishing between buildings that are eligible for a 27.5-year life versus a 31.5- or 39-year life for MACRS purposes.

Residual method. Used to allocate the new stepped-up basis of a subsidiary's assets among its property when a § 338 election is in effect. The purchase price that exceeds the aggregate fair market values of the tangible and identifiable intangible assets is allocated to goodwill or going-concern value. § 1060.

Restoration event. Sales between members of a *consolidated return,* and other intragroup transactions, are subject to special recognition deferral rules, so that the members cannot artificially create taxable gains or losses solely when tax conditions call for them. Rather, when a restoration event occurs, e.g., when the asset ultimately is sold outside the group, the recognition of all intragroup gains and losses is restored.

Return of capital.   When a taxpayer reacquires financial resources that he or she previously had invested in an entity or venture, the return of his or her capital investment itself does not increase gross income for the recovery year. A return of capital may result from an annuity or insurance contract, the sale or exchange of any asset, or a distribution from a partnership or corporation.

Revenue Agent's Report.   See *RAR*.

Revenue neutral.   A change in the tax system that results in the same amount of revenue. Revenue neutral, however, does not mean that any one taxpayer will pay the same amount of tax as before. Thus, as a result of a tax law change, corporations could pay more taxes, but the excess revenue will be offset by lower taxes on individuals.

Revenue Procedure.   A matter of procedural importance to both taxpayers and the IRS concerning the administration of the tax laws is issued as a Revenue Procedure (abbreviated Rev.Proc.). A Revenue Procedure is first published in an *Internal Revenue Bulletin* (I.R.B.) and later transferred to the appropriate *Cumulative Bulletin* (C.B.). Both the *Internal Revenue Bulletins* and the *Cumulative Bulletins* are published by the U.S. Government Printing Office.

Revenue Ruling.   A Revenue Ruling (abbreviated Rev.Rul.) is issued by the National Office of the IRS to express an official interpretation of the tax law as applied to specific transactions. It is more limited in application than a Regulation. A Revenue Ruling is first published in an *Internal Revenue Bulletin* (I.R.B.) and later transferred to the appropriate *Cumulative Bulletin* (C.B.). Both the *Internal Revenue Bulletins* and the *Cumulative Bulletins* are published by the U.S. Government Printing Office.

Reversed (Rev'd.).   An indication that a decision of one court has been reversed by a higher court in the same case.

Reversing (Rev'g.).   An indication that the decision of a higher court is reversing the result reached by a lower court in the same case.

Reversionary interest.   The property that reverts to the grantor after the expiration of an intervening income interest. Assume Gail places real estate in trust with income to Art for 11 years, and upon the expiration of this term, the property returns to Gail. Under these circumstances, she holds a reversionary interest in the property. A reversionary interest is the same as a remainder interest, except that, in the latter case, the property passes to someone other than the original owner (e.g., the grantor of a trust) upon the expiration of the intervening interest. See also *grantor trust* and *remainder interest*.

Revocable transfer.   A transfer of property where the transferor retains the right to recover the property. The

creation of a revocable trust is an example of a revocable transfer. § 2038. See also *incomplete transfer*.

Rev.Proc.   Abbreviation for an IRS Revenue Procedure. See *Revenue Procedure*.

Rev.Rul.   Abbreviation for an IRS Revenue Ruling. See *Revenue Ruling*.

Right of survivorship.   See *joint tenants*.

S

Sales factor.   The proportion of a *multistate corporation*'s total sales that is traceable to a specific state. Used in determining the taxable income that is to be apportioned to that state. See also *apportion*.

Sales tax.   A state- or local-level tax on the retail sale of specified property. Generally, the purchaser pays the tax, but the seller collects it, as an agent for the government. Various taxing jurisdictions allow exemptions for purchases of specific items, including certain food, services, and manufacturing equipment. If the purchaser and seller are in different states, a *use tax* usually applies.

Schedule M-1.   On the Form 1120, a reconciliation of book net income with Federal taxable income. Accounts for timing and permanent differences in the two computations, such as depreciation differences, exempt income, and nondeductible items.

Schedule PH.   A tax form required to be filed by corporations that are personal holding companies. The form must be filed in addition to Form 1120 (U.S. Corporation Income Tax Return).

S corporation.   The designation for a small business corporation. See also *Subchapter S*.

Section 306 stock.   Preferred stock issued as a nontaxable stock dividend that, if sold or redeemed, would result in ordinary income recognition. § 306(c). See also *preferred stock bailout*.

Section 306 taint.   The ordinary income that would result upon the sale or other taxable disposition of § 306 stock.

Section 338 election.   When a corporation acquires at least 80 percent of a subsidiary in a 12-month period, it can elect to treat the acquisition of such stock as an asset purchase. The acquiring corporation's basis in the subsidiary's assets then is the cost of the stock. The subsidiary is deemed to have sold its assets for an amount equal to the grossed-up basis in its stock.

Section 754 election.   An election that may be made by a partnership to adjust the basis of partnership assets to reflect a purchasing partner's outside basis in interest or to reflect a gain, loss, or basis adjustment of a partner receiving a distribution from a partnership. The intent of the election is to maintain the equivalence between outside and inside basis. Once the election is made, the partnership must make basis adjustments for all future transactions, unless the IRS consents to revoke the election.

Section 1231 assets. Depreciable assets and real estate used in a trade or business and held for the appropriate holding period. Under certain circumstances, the classification also includes timber, coal, domestic iron ore, livestock (held for draft, breeding, dairy, or sporting purposes), and unharvested crops. § 1231(b). See also *Section 1231 gains and losses.*

Section 1231 gains and losses. If the combined gains and losses from the taxable dispositions of § 1231 assets plus the net gain from business involuntary conversions (of both § 1231 assets and long-term capital assets) is a gain, such gains and losses are treated as long-term capital gains and losses. In arriving at § 1231 gains, however, the depreciation recapture provisions (e.g., §§ 1245 and 1250) are first applied to produce ordinary income. If the net result of the combination is a loss, the gains and losses from § 1231 assets are treated as ordinary gains and losses. § 1231(a). See also *depreciation recapture* and *Section 1231 assets.*

Section 1244 stock. Stock issued under § 1244 by qualifying small business corporations. If § 1244 stock becomes worthless, the shareholders may claim an ordinary loss rather than the usual capital loss, within statutory limitations.

Section 1245 recapture. Upon a taxable disposition of § 1245 property, all depreciation claimed on such property is recaptured as ordinary income (but not to exceed recognized gain from the disposition).

Section 1250 recapture. Upon a taxable disposition of § 1250 property, some of the depreciation or cost recovery claimed on the property may be recaptured as ordinary income.

Securities. Generally, stock, debt, and other financial assets. To the extent securities other than the stock of the transferee corporation are received in a § 351 exchange, the new shareholder recognizes gross income.

Separate property. In a community property jurisdiction, property that belongs entirely to one of the spouses is separate property. Generally, it is property acquired before marriage or acquired after marriage by gift or inheritance. See also *community property.*

Separate return limitation year (SRLY). A series of rules limits the amount of an acquired corporation's net operating loss carryforwards that can be used by the acquiror. Generally, a *consolidated return* can include the acquiree's NOL carryforward only to the extent of the lesser of the subsidiary's (1) current-year or (2) cumulative positive contribution to consolidated taxable income. Prop.Reg. § 1.1502-21(c).

Separately stated item. Any item of a partnership or S corporation that might be taxed differently to any two owners of the entity. These amounts are not included in ordinary income of the entity, but instead are reported separately to the owners; tax consequences are determined at the owner level.

Sham. A transaction without substance that will be disregarded for tax purposes.

Short-term capital gain or loss. Results from the sale or other taxable exchange of a capital asset that had been held by the seller for one year or less or from other transactions involving statutorily designated assets, including nonbusiness bad debts.

Simple trust. Simple trusts are those that are not complex trusts. Such trusts may not have a charitable beneficiary, accumulate income, or distribute corpus. See also *complex trust.*

Small business corporation. A corporation that satisfies the definition of § 1361(b), § 1244(c), or both. Satisfaction of § 1361(b) permits an S election, and satisfaction of § 1244 enables the shareholders of the corporation to claim an ordinary loss on the worthlessness of stock.

Small Cases Division of the U.S. Tax Court. Jurisdiction is limited to claims of $10,000 or less. There is no appeal from this court.

Special allocation. Any amount for which an agreement exists among the partners of a partnership outlining the method used for assigning the item among the partners.

Special power of appointment. See *power of appointment.*

Special use value. Permits the executor of an estate to value, for death tax purposes, real estate used in a farming activity or in connection with a closely held business at its current use value rather than at its most suitable or optimal use value. Under this option, a farm is valued for farming purposes even though, for example, the property might have a higher potential value as a shopping center. For the executor of an estate to elect special use valuation, the conditions of § 2032A must be satisfied. See also *most suitable use value.*

Spin-off. A type of reorganization where, for example, Ace Corporation transfers some assets to Bow Corporation in exchange for enough Bow stock to represent control. Ace then distributes the Bow stock to its shareholders.

Split-off. A type of reorganization where, for example, Arc Corporation transfers some assets to Bond Corporation in exchange for enough Bond stock to represent control. Arc then distributes the Bond stock to its shareholders in exchange for some of their Arc stock.

Split-up. A type of reorganization where, for example, Ally Corporation transfers some assets to Bar Corporation and the remainder to Zip Corporation. In return, Ally receives enough Bar and Zip stock to represent control of each corporation. Ally then distributes the Bar and Zip stock to its shareholders in return for all of their Ally stock. The result of the split-up is that Ally is liquidated, and its shareholders now have control of Bar and Zip.

Sprinkling trust. When a trustee has the discretion to either distribute or accumulate the entity accounting income of the trust and to distribute it among the trust's income beneficiaries in varying magnitudes, a sprinkling trust exists. The trustee can "sprinkle" the income of the trust.

Statute of limitations. Provisions of the law that specify the maximum period of time in which action may be taken on a past event. Code §§ 6501–6504 contain the limitation periods applicable to the IRS for additional assessments, and §§ 6511–6515 relate to refund claims by taxpayers.

Statutory depletion. See *depletion.*

Statutory notice of deficiency. Commonly referred to as the *90-day letter,* this notice is sent to a taxpayer upon request, upon the expiration of the *30-day letter,* or upon exhaustion by the taxpayer of his or her administrative remedies before the IRS. The notice gives the taxpayer 90 days in which to file a petition with the U.S. Tax Court. If such a petition is not filed, the IRS will demand payment of the assessed deficiency. §§ 6211–6216. See also *deficiency.*

Step-down in basis. A reduction in the tax basis of property. See *step-up in basis.*

Step transaction. Disregarding one or more transactions to arrive at the final result. Assume, for example, that the shareholders of Clue Corporation liquidate the corporation and receive cash and operating assets. Immediately after the liquidation, the shareholders transfer the operating assets to newly formed Blue Corporation. Under these circumstances, the IRS may contend that the liquidation of Clue should be disregarded (thereby depriving the shareholders of capital gain treatment). What may really have happened is a *reorganization* of Clue with a distribution of boot (ordinary income) to Clue's shareholders. If so, there will be a carryover of basis in the assets transferred from Clue to Blue.

Step-up in basis. An increase in the income tax basis of property. The classic step-up in basis occurs when a decedent dies owning appreciated property. Since the estate or heir acquires a basis in the property equal to the property's fair market value on the date of death (or alternate valuation date if available and elected), any appreciation is not subject to the income tax. Thus, a step-up in basis is the result, with no income tax consequences.

Stock attribution. See *attribution.*

Stock dividend. A dividend consisting of stock of the payor. Not taxable if a pro rata distribution of stock or stock rights on common stock. However, some stock dividends are taxable. § 305.

Stock redemption. A corporation buys back its own stock from a specified shareholder. Typically, the corporation recognizes any realized gain on the noncash assets that it uses to effect a redemption, and the shareholder obtains a capital gain or loss upon receipt of the purchase price.

Stock rights. An asset that conveys to the holder the power to purchase corporate stock at a specified price, often for a limited period of time. Stock rights received may be taxed as a distribution of earnings and profits. After the right is exercised, the basis of the acquired share includes the investor's purchase price or gross income, if any, to obtain the right. Disposition of the right also is a taxable event, with basis often assigned from the shares held prior to the issuance of the right.

Subchapter S. Sections 1361–1379 of the Internal Revenue Code. An elective provision permitting certain small business corporations (§ 1361) and their shareholders (§ 1362) to elect to be treated for income tax purposes in accordance with the operating rules of §§ 1363–1379. S corporations usually avoid the corporate income tax and corporate losses can be claimed by the shareholders.

Subpart F. The subpart of the Code that identifies the current tax treatment of income earned by a controlled foreign corporation. Certain types of income are included in U.S. gross income by U.S. shareholders of such an entity as the income is generated, not when it is repatriated.

Substance vs. form concept. A standard used when one must ascertain the true reality of what has occurred. Suppose, for example, a father sells stock to his daughter for $1,000. If the stock is really worth $50,000 at the time of the transfer, the substance of the transaction is probably a gift to her of $49,000.

Substantial authority. Taxpayer understatement penalties are waived where substantial authority existed for the disputed position taken on the return.

Substantial economic effect. Partnerships are allowed to *allocate* items of income, expense, gain, loss, and credit in any manner that is authorized in the partnership agreement, provided that the allocation has an economic effect aside from the corresponding tax results. The necessary substantial economic effect is present, for instance, if the post-contribution appreciation in the value of an asset that was contributed to the partnership by a partner was allocated to that partner for cost recovery purposes.

Substantially appreciated inventory. "Inventory" (as defined for this purpose) for which the fair market value exceeds 120 percent of the partnership's basis in the asset. This definition is relevant for purposes of determining the character of income, gain, or loss from (1) the sale of a partnership interest, (2) the liquidation of a partner's interest under § 736, and (3) disproportionate distributions. Inventory is broadly defined as any partnership asset other than cash, capital assets, or § 1231 assets. This definition is broad enough to include any accounts receivable, including unrealized receivables.

Substituted basis. When a taxpayer exchanges one asset for another, many provisions in the tax law allow an assignment of basis in the received asset to be that of the traded asset(s) in the hands of its former owner. Thus, no step-up or -down of basis occurs as a result of the exchange. For instance, when an investor contributes an asset to a corporation or partnership, the partner generally takes a substituted basis in the partnership interest, i.e., the investment asset (partnership interest) has a basis equal to the aggregated bases of the assets contributed by that partner. § 723.

Surviving spouse. When a husband or wife predeceases the other spouse, the survivor is known as a surviving spouse. Under certain conditions, a surviving spouse may be entitled to use the income tax rates in § 1(a) (those applicable to married persons filing a joint return) for the two years after the year of death of his or her spouse.

Survivorship. See *joint tenants.*

Syndication costs. Incurred in promoting and marketing partnership interests for sale to investors. Examples include legal and accounting fees, printing costs for prospectus and placement documents, and state registration fees. These items are capitalized by the partnership as incurred, with no amortization thereof allowed.

T

Tangible property. All property that has form or substance and is not intangible. See also *intangible asset.*

Tax benefit rule. Limits the recognition of income from the recovery of an expense or loss properly deducted in a prior tax year to the amount of the deduction that generated a tax saving. Assume that last year Tom had medical expenses of $3,000 and adjusted gross income of $30,000. Because of the 7.5 percent limitation, he could deduct only $750 of these expenses [$3,000 − (7.5% × $30,000)]. If, this year, Tom is reimbursed by his insurance company for $900 of these expenses, the tax benefit rule limits the amount of income from the reimbursement to $750 (the amount previously deducted with a tax saving).

Tax Court. The U.S. Tax Court is one of four trial courts of original jurisdiction that decide litigation involving Federal income, death, or gift taxes. It is the only trial court where the taxpayer must not first pay the deficiency assessed by the IRS. The Tax Court will not have jurisdiction over a case unless a statutory notice of deficiency (90-day letter) has been issued by the IRS and the taxpayer files the petition for hearing within the time prescribed.

Tax haven. A country in which either locally sourced income or residents of the country are subject to a low rate of taxation.

Tax on unearned income of a child under age 14. Passive income, such as interest and dividends, that is recognized by such a child is taxed *to him or her* at the rates that would have applied had the income been incurred by the child's parents, generally to the extent that the income exceeds $1,200. The additional tax is assessed regardless of the source of the income or the income's underlying property. If the child's parents are divorced, the custodial parent's rates are used. The parents' rates reflect any applicable alternative minimum tax and the phase-outs of lower tax brackets and other deductions. § 1(g).

Tax preference items. Various items that may result in the imposition of the *alternative minimum tax.* §§ 55–58.

Tax treaty. An agreement between the U.S. State Department and another country, designed to alleviate double taxation of income and asset transfers and to share administrative information useful to tax agencies in both countries. The United States has income tax treaties with over 40 countries and transfer tax treaties with about 20.

Tax year. See *accounting period.*

Taxable estate. The *gross estate* of a *decedent* reduced by the deductions allowed by §§ 2053–2057 (e.g., administration expenses and marital and charitable deductions). The taxable estate is subject to the unified transfer tax at death. See also *adjusted taxable estate* and *gross estate.* § 2051.

Taxable gift. Amount of a gift that is subject to the unified transfer tax. Thus, a taxable gift has been adjusted by the annual exclusion and other appropriate deductions (e.g., marital and charitable). § 2503.

Taxable income. The tax base with respect to the prevailing Federal income tax. Taxable income is defined by the Internal Revenue Code, Treasury Regulations, and pertinent court cases. Currently, taxable income includes gross income from all sources except those specifically excluded by the statute. In addition, taxable income is reduced for certain allowable deductions. Deductions for business taxpayers must be related to a trade or business. Individuals can also deduct certain personal expenses in determining their taxable incomes. See also *gross income.*

Tax-free exchange. Transfers of property specifically exempted from income tax consequences by the tax law. Examples are a transfer of property to a controlled corporation under § 351(a) and a like-kind exchange under § 1031(a).

T.C. An abbreviation for the U.S. Tax Court used in citing a Regular Decision of the U.S. Tax Court.

T.C.Memo. An abbreviation used to refer to a Memorandum Decision of the U.S. Tax Court.

Technical advice memorandum. An interpretation of the tax law with respect to a disputed item, issued by the National Office of the IRS or a Regional Commissioner, in response to a request from an agent, appellate conferee, or District Director. Often used to reconcile perceived differences in the application of the law among taxpayers or to identify an IRS position where no pertinent regulations or rulings exist.

Technical termination of partnership. The entity is treated for tax purposes as though it has terminated, even though it continues in its activities. When there has been a sale or exchange of more than 50 percent of the capital interests of the partnership within 12 months, the partnership is deemed to have terminated when the 50 percent threshold is crossed. A new partnership immediately is formed through asset contributions by the partners. These activities can affect the entity's tax year and its bases in the assets it holds.

Telescoping.　To look through one or more transactions to arrive at the final result. It is also referred to as the *step transaction* approach or the *substance vs. form concept.*

Tenancy by the entirety.　Essentially, a joint tenancy between husband and wife. See also *joint tenants* and *tenancy in common.*

Tenancy in common.　A form of ownership where each tenant (owner) holds an undivided interest in property. Unlike a joint tenancy or a tenancy by the entirety, the interest of a tenant in common does not terminate upon that individual's death (there is no right of survivorship). Assume Brad and Connie acquire real estate as equal tenants in common, each having furnished one-half of the purchase price. Upon Brad's death, his one-half interest in the property passes to his estate or heirs, not to Connie. For a comparison of results, see *joint tenants* and *tenancy by the entirety.*

Term certain.　A fixed period of years used to determine the length of an income interest, i.e., prior to the termination of a trust or estate.

Terminable interest rule.　An interest in property that terminates upon the death of the holder or upon the occurrence of some other specified event. The transfer of a terminable interest by one spouse to the other may not qualify for the marital deduction. §§ 2056(b) and 2523(b). See also *marital deduction.*

Testamentary disposition.　The passing of property to another upon the death of the owner.

Testamentary power of appointment.　A power of appointment that can be exercised only through the will (upon the death) of the holder. See also *power of appointment.*

Thin capitalization.　When debt owed by a corporation to the shareholders becomes too large in relation to the corporation's capital structure (i.e., stock and shareholder equity), the IRS may contend that the corporation is thinly capitalized. In effect, this means that some or all of the debt is reclassified as equity. The immediate result is to disallow any interest deduction to the corporation on the reclassified debt. To the extent of the corporation's earnings and profits, interest payments and loan repayments are treated as dividends to the shareholders.

Thirty-day letter.　A letter that accompanies a *Revenue Agent's Report* issued as a result of an IRS audit of a taxpayer (or the rejection of a taxpayer's claim for refund). The letter outlines the taxpayer's appeal procedure before the IRS. If the taxpayer does not request any such procedures within the 30-day period, the IRS will issue a statutory notice of deficiency (the 90-day letter). See also *statutory notice of deficiency.*

Three-factor apportionment formula.　A means by which the total taxable income of a *multistate corporation* is assigned to a specific state. Usually, the payroll, property, and sales factors are treated equally, and the average of these factors is used in the apportionment procedure. In some states, however, the sales factor may receive a double weight, or it may be the only factor considered. These latter formulas place greater tax burden on the income of out-of-state corporations. See also *apportion, payroll factor, property factor, sales factor,* and *UDITPA.*

Throwback rule.　If there is no income tax in the state to which a sale otherwise would be *apportioned,* the sale essentially is exempt from state income tax, even though the seller is *domiciled* in a state that levies an income tax. Nonetheless, if the seller's state has adopted a throwback rule, the sale is attributed to the *seller's* state, and the transaction is subjected to a state-level tax.

Tiered partnerships.　An ownership arrangement wherein one partnership (the parent or first tier) is a partner in one or more partnerships (the subsidiary/subsidiaries or second tier). Frequently, the first tier is a holding partnership, and the second tier is an operating partnership.

Trade or business.　Any business or professional activity conducted by a taxpayer. The mere ownership of rental or other investment assets does not constitute a trade or business. Generally, a trade or business generates relatively little passive investment income.

Transfer tax.　A tax imposed upon the transfer of property. See also *unified transfer tax.*

Transferee liability.　Under certain conditions, if the IRS is unable to collect taxes owed by a transferor of property, it may pursue its claim against the transferee of the property. The transferee's liability for taxes is limited to the extent of the value of the assets transferred. For example, the IRS can force a donee to pay the gift tax when such tax cannot be paid by the donor making the transfer. §§ 6901–6905.

Treasury Regulations.　See *Regulations.*

Treaty shopping.　An international investor attempts to use the favorable aspects of a tax treaty to his or her advantage, often elevating the form of the transaction over its substance, e.g., by establishing only a nominal presence in the country offering the favorable treaty terms.

Trial court.　The court of original jurisdiction; the first court to consider litigation. In Federal tax controversies, trial courts include U.S. District Courts, the U.S. Tax Court, the U.S. Court of Federal Claims, and the Small Cases Division of the U.S. Tax Court. See also *appellate court, Court of Federal Claims, District Court, Small Cases Division of the U.S. Tax Court,* and *Tax Court.*

Trust.　A legal entity created by a grantor for the benefit of designated beneficiaries under the laws of the state and the valid trust instrument. The trustee holds a fiduciary responsibility to manage the trust's corpus assets and income for the economic benefit of all of the beneficiaries.

Trustee. An individual or corporation that takes the fiduciary responsibilities under a trust agreement.

U

UDITPA. The Uniform Division of Income for Tax Purposes Act has been adopted in some form by many of the states. The Act develops criteria by which the total taxable income of a *multistate corporation* can be assigned to specific states. See also *allocate, apportion, Multistate Tax Commission (MTC)*, and *nexus*.

Undistributed net income. The excess of a complex trust's distributable net income over its distributions for the year. This accumulation may be subject to the throwback procedures in later years.

Undistributed personal holding company income. The penalty tax on personal holding companies is imposed on the corporation's undistributed personal holding company income for the year. The adjustments necessary to convert taxable income to undistributed personal holding company income are set forth in § 545.

Unearned income. Income received but not yet earned. Normally, such income is taxed when received, even for accrual basis taxpayers.

Unified tax credit. A credit allowed against any unified transfer tax. §§ 2010 and 2505.

Unified transfer tax. Rates applicable to transfers by gift and death made after 1976. § 2001(c).

Uniform Gift to Minors Act. A means of transferring property (usually stocks and bonds) to a minor. The designated custodian of the property has the legal right to act on behalf of the minor without requiring a guardianship. Generally, the custodian possesses the right to change investments (e.g., sell one type of stock and buy another), apply the income from the custodial property to the minor's support, and even terminate the custodianship. In this regard, however, the custodian is acting in a fiduciary capacity on behalf of the minor. The custodian could not, for example, appropriate the property for his or her own use because it belongs to the minor. During the period of the custodianship, the income from the property is taxed to the minor. The custodianship terminates when the minor reaches legal age. See also *guardianship* and *legal age*.

Unitary state. A state that has adopted the unitary theory in its apportionment of the total taxable income of a multistate corporation to the state.

Unitary theory. Sales, property, and payroll of related corporations are combined for *nexus* and *apportionment* purposes, and the worldwide income of the unitary entity is apportioned to the state. Subsidiaries and other affiliated corporations found to be part of the corporation's unitary business (because they are subject to overlapping ownership, operation, or management) are included in the apportionment procedure. This approach can be limited if a *water's edge election* is in effect.

Unrealized receivables. Amounts earned by a cash basis taxpayer but not yet received. Because of the method of accounting used by the taxpayer, these amounts have no income tax basis. When unrealized receivables are distributed to a partner, they generally convert a transaction from nontaxable to taxable or convert otherwise capital gain to ordinary income.

Unreasonable compensation. A deduction is allowed for "reasonable" salaries or other compensation for personal services actually rendered. To the extent compensation is "excessive" ("unreasonable"), no deduction is allowed. Unreasonable compensation usually is found in closely held corporations, where the motivation is to pay out profits in some form that is deductible to the corporation. Deductible compensation therefore becomes an attractive substitute for nondeductible dividends when the shareholders also are employed by the corporation.

Unrelated business income. Income recognized by an exempt organization that is generated from activities not related to the exempt purpose of the entity. For instance, the pharmacy located in a hospital often generates unrelated business income. § 511.

Unrelated business income tax. Levied on the *unrelated business income* of an *exempt organization*.

Use tax. A sales tax that is collectible by the seller where the purchaser is domiciled in a different state.

U.S.-owned foreign corporation. A foreign corporation in which 50 percent or more of the total combined voting power or total value of the stock of the corporation is held directly or indirectly by U.S. persons. A U.S. corporation is treated as a U.S.-owned foreign corporation if the dividend or interest income it pays is classified as foreign source under § 861.

U.S. real property interest. Any direct interest in real property situated in the United States and any interest in a domestic corporation (other than solely as a creditor) unless the taxpayer can establish that a domestic corporation was not a U.S. real property holding corporation during the five-year period ending on the date of disposition of such interest (the base period). See *FIRPTA*.

USSC. An abbreviation for the U.S. Supreme Court, used in citing court opinions.

U.S. shareholder. For purposes of classification of an entity as a *controlled foreign corporation*, a U.S. person who owns, or is considered to own, 10 percent or more of the total combined voting power of all classes of voting stock of a foreign corporation. Stock owned directly, indirectly, and constructively is counted for this purpose.

U.S.-source income. Generally, income taxed by the United States, regardless of the citizenship or residence of its creator. Examples include income from sales of U.S. real estate and dividends from U.S. corporations.

U.S. Tax Court. See *Tax Court*.

USTC. Published by Commerce Clearing House, *U.S. Tax Cases* contain all of the Federal tax decisions issued by the U.S. District Courts, U.S. Court of Federal Claims, U.S. Courts of Appeals, and the U.S. Supreme Court.

V

Value. See *fair market value*.

Vested. Absolute and complete. If, for example, a person holds a vested interest in property, such interest cannot be taken away or otherwise defeated.

Voting trust. A trust that holds the voting rights to stock in a corporation. It is a useful device when a majority of the shareholders in a corporation cannot agree on corporate policy.

W

Wash sale. A loss from the sale of stock or securities that is disallowed because the taxpayer has, within 30 days before or after the sale, acquired stock or securities substantially identical to those sold. § 1091.

Water's edge election. A limitation on the worldwide scope of the *unitary theory*. If a corporate water's edge election is in effect, the state can consider only the activities that occur within the boundaries of the United States in the *apportionment* procedure.

WESTLAW. An on-line database system, produced by West Publishing Company, by which the tax researcher can obtain access to the Internal Revenue Code, Regulations, administrative rulings, and court case opinions.

Wherewithal to pay. A construct of tax equity that delays the recognition of gain on a transaction until the taxpayer has received means by which to pay the tax. The *installment method*, whereunder gain is taxed proportionately as installment proceeds are received, embodies the wherewithal to pay concept. See also *involuntary conversion* and *like-kind exchange*.

Writ of Certiorari. See *certiorari*.

APPENDIX D-1
Table of Code Sections Cited

[See Title 26 U.S.C.A.]

APPENDIX D-2
Table of Regulations Cited

Appendix D-3
Table of Revenue Procedures and Revenue Rulings Cited

APPENDIX E
Table of Cases Cited

INDEX

UNIFIED TRANSFER TAX RATES

FOR GIFTS MADE AND FOR DEATHS AFTER 1983

If the Amount with Respect to Which the Tentative Tax to Be Computed Is:	The Tentative Tax Is:
Not over $10,000	18 percent of such amount.
Over $10,000 but not over $20,000	$1,800, plus 20 percent of the excess of such amount over $10,000.
Over $20,000 but not over $40,000	$3,800, plus 22 percent of the excess of such amount over $20,000.
Over $40,000 but not over $60,000	$8,200, plus 24 percent of the excess of such amount over $40,000.
Over $60,000 but not over $80,000	$13,000, plus 26 percent of the excess of such amount over $60,000.
Over $80,000 but not over $100,000	$18,200, plus 28 percent of the excess of such amount over $80,000.
Over $100,000 but not over $150,000	$23,800, plus 30 percent of the excess of such amount over $100,000.
Over $150,000 but not over $250,000	$38,800, plus 32 percent of the excess of such amount over $150,000.
Over $250,000 but not over $500,000	$70,800, plus 34 percent of the excess of such amount over $250,000.
Over $500,000 but not over $750,000	$155,800, plus 37 percent of the excess of such amount over $500,000.
Over $750,000 but not over $1,000,000	$248,300, plus 39 percent of the excess of such amount over $750,000.
Over $1,000,000 but not over $1,250,000	$345,800, plus 41 percent of the excess of such amount over $1,000,000.
Over $1,250,000 but not over $1,500,000	$448,300, plus 43 percent of the excess of such amount over $1,250,000.
Over $1,500,000 but not over $2,000,000	$555,800, plus 45 percent of the excess of such amount over $1,500,000.
Over $2,000,000 but not over $2,500,000	$780,800, plus 49 percent of the excess of such amount over $2,000,000.
Over $2,500,000 but not over $3,000,000	$1,025,800, plus 53 percent of the excess of such amount over $2,500,000.
Over $3,000,000*	$1,290,800, plus 55 percent of the excess of such amount over $3,000,000.

*For large taxable transfers (generally in excess of $10 million) there is a phase-out of the graduated rates and the unified tax credit.